1000 VEGETARIAN

RECIPES FROM AROUND THE WORLD

1000
VEGETARIAN

RECIPES FROM AROUND THE WORLD

p

This is a Parragon Publishing Book
This edition published in 2003

Parragon Publishing
Queen Street House
4 Queen Street
Bath BA1 1HE, UK

ISBN: 0-75258-427-8

Printed in China

Produced by Haldane Mason, London

Acknowledgements
Art Director: Ron Samuel
Publishing Director: Sydney Francis
Project Editor: Jo-Anne Cox & Elizabeth Towers
Design: clap ltd
Nutritional information: Jill Scott & Sue Baic

Material in this book has previously appeared in
Ultimate Chinese Recipes, Ultimate Low Fat Recipes,
Ultimate Italian Recipes, Ultimate Vegetarian Recipes

Note
Use all metric or all imperial quantities, as the two are not interchangeable.
Cup measurements in this book are for American cups. Tablespoons are assumed to
be 15 ml. Unless otherwise stated, milk is assumed to be full fat, eggs are medium
and pepper is freshly ground black pepper.

The nutritional information provided for each recipe is per serving or per portion.
Optional ingredients, variations or serving suggestions have not been included in the
calculations. The times given for each recipe are an approximate guide only as the
preparation times may differ according to the techniques used by different people and
the cooking times may vary as a result of the type of oven used.

contents

INTRODUCTION

This book contains 1,000 vegetarian recipes that have been carefully selected to provide an almost unlimited variety of healthy and delicious meals. Each recipe contains the following information: nutritional calculations, preparation and cooking times, and level of difficulty (one chef's hat for an easy recipe, rising to five chef's hats for a difficult recipe).

basic recipes

Fresh Vegetable Bouillon

Keep this bouillon refrigerated for up to 3 days, or frozen for up to 3 months.

makes 6 cups

9 oz/250 g shallots

1 large carrot, diced

1 celery stalk, chopped

½ fennel bulb

1 garlic clove

1 bay leaf

4–6 sprigs of fresh parsley and tarragon

8 cups water

pepper

1 Put all the ingredients in a large pan and bring to a boil.

2 Skim off the surface scum with a flat spoon and reduce to a gentle simmer. Partially cover and cook for 45 minutes. Let cool.

3 Line a sieve with clean cheesecloth and put it over a large pitcher or bowl. Pour the bouillon through the sieve. Discard the herbs and vegetables.

4 Cover with plastic wrap and store in the refrigerator or freezer until ready to use.

Béchamel Sauce

generous 1 cup skimmed milk

4 cloves

1 bay leaf

pinch of freshly grated nutmeg

2 tbsp polyunsaturated margarine

2 tbsp all-purpose flour

pepper and lowsodium salt

1 Put the milk in a pan and add the cloves, bay leaf, and nutmeg. Gradually bring to a boil. Remove from the heat and leave for 15 minutes.

2 Melt the margarine in another pan and stir in the flour to make a roux. Cook gently, stirring, for 1 minute. Remove the pan from the heat.

3 Strain the milk and gradually blend into the roux. Return the pan to the heat and gently bring to a boil, stirring, until the sauce thickens. Season to taste.

VARIATIONS

All sorts of ingredients can be added to the basic Béchamel recipe to make interesting, low-fat sauces which go particularly well with vegetables.

Watercress Sauce

Add 1 small bunch of watercress, finely chopped, to the basic sauce.

Green Herb Sauce

Add 1–2 tablespoons chopped fresh mixed herbs to the sauce just before serving.

Parsley Sauce

Add 2 tablespoons finely chopped fresh parsley to the basic sauce.

Mushroom Sauce

Wash and finely slice 4 oz/125 g white mushrooms, and add them to the basic sauce with 1 tablespoon of finely chopped fresh tarragon.

Lemon Sauce

Add some finely grated lemon zest and juice to the basic sauce.

Mustard Sauce

Add 1 tablespoon French mustard and a squeeze of lemon juice to the basic sauce.

Basic Tomato Sauce

1 tbsp olive oil

1 small onion, chopped

1 garlic clove, chopped

14 oz/400 g canned chopped tomatoes

2 tbsp chopped fresh parsley

1 tsp dried oregano

2 bay leaves

2 tbsp tomato paste

1 tsp sugar

pepper and lowsodium salt

1 Heat the oil in a pan over a medium heat and fry the onion for 2–3 minutes or until translucent. Add the garlic and fry for 1 minute. Stir in the chopped tomatoes, parsley, oregano, bay leaves, tomato paste, and sugar, and season with pepper and a pinch of salt.

2 Bring the sauce to a boil, then lower the heat and simmer, uncovered, for 15–20 minutes, or until the sauce has reduced by half. Discard the bay leaves just before serving.

Red Wine Sauce

2 cups Vegetable Bouillon (see page 6)

2 cups red wine

small piece of onion, peeled

1 garlic clove, peeled and sliced

1 bay leaf

1 sprig fresh thyme

2–3 sprigs fresh parsley

½ tsp black peppercorns

1 tbsp redcurrant jelly

3 tbsp polyunsaturated margarine

1½ tbsp all-purpose flour

pepper and lowsodium salt

1 Put the bouillon and wine in a pan with the onion, garlic, bay leaf, thyme, parsley, and peppercorns. Bring to a boil and boil for 10–15 minutes to reduce the liquid by half.

2 Strain the liquid into a clean pan and mix in the redcurrant jelly, some pepper and a pinch of salt.

3 Mix half the margarine with the flour to make a paste and add to the warm sauce in small pieces. Mix well after each addition.

4 Return the sauce to the heat and stir gently until it thickens slightly. Simmer gently for a few minutes to cook the flour. Beat in the remaining margarine just before serving.

Honey and Yogurt Dressing

makes about ½ cup

1 tbsp clear honey

6 tbsp low-fat plain yogurt

salt and pepper

1 Put the honey and yogurt in a glass bowl and beat with a fork until thoroughly combined. Season to taste with salt and pepper.

Mild Mustard Sauce

2 egg yolks

2 tbsp lemon juice

2 garlic cloves, chopped

⅔ cup olive oil

1 tbsp Dijon mustard

salt and pepper

Put the egg yolks, lemon juice, and garlic in a blender or food processor and process until combined and smooth. With the motor running, gradually add the olive oil through the feeder tube until thick and creamy. Transfer to a bowl, stir in the Dijon mustard, and season to taste with salt and pepper.

Mayonnaise

makes 1¼ cups

2 egg yolks

⅔ cup sunflower oil

⅔ cup olive oil

1 tbsp white wine vinegar

2 tsp Dijon mustard

salt and pepper

1 Beat the egg yolks with a pinch of salt. Combine the oils in a pitcher. Gradually add the oil, a drop at a time, beating constantly with a whisk or electric mixer.

2 When a quarter of the oil has been incorporated, beat in the vinegar. Continue adding the oil, in a steady stream, beating constantly.

3 Stir in the mustard and season to taste with salt and pepper.

Chili Flowers

To make chili flowers, hold the stem of the chili and cut down its length several times with a sharp knife. Place in a bowl of chilled water and chill so that the "petals" turn out. Remove the chili seeds when the "petals" have opened.

Homemade Crème Fraîche

1 cup whipping cream

2 tbsp buttermilk

1 Combine the two ingredients well in a glass container.

2 Cover and let stand at room temperature from 8 to 24 hours or until very thick. Use as required.

Rich Shortcrust Pastry Dough

makes 1 x 9 in/23 cm flan

generous 1 cup all-purpose flour

3 oz/85 g butter, plus extra for greasing

1 egg yolk

3 tbsp iced water

salt

1 Sift the flour with a pinch of salt into a bowl. Add the butter, cut it into the flour, and then rub in with your fingertips until the mixture resembles fine breadcrumbs.

2 Beat the egg yolk with the water in a small bowl. Sprinkle the liquid over the flour mixture and combine with a round-bladed knife or your fingertips.

3 Form the dough into a ball, cover, and chill for 30 minutes.

Crêpe Batter

makes 12 crêpes

4 oz/115 g all-purpose flour

1 egg, lightly beaten

1⅓ cups milk

1 tsp sunflower oil

salt

1 Sift the flour with a pinch of salt into a bowl. Using a wooden spoon, beat in the egg and half the milk. Continue beating until the mixture is smooth and lump free.

2 Stir in the remaining milk and the sunflower oil.

3 Pour the batter into a jug and, if you have time, set aside to rest for 30–60 minutes. Stir the batter before cooking.

4 Remove the pan from the heat and stir in the remaining butter and Parmesan. Season to taste with salt and a little pepper. Cover and stand for about 1 minute, then sprinkle with extra Parmesan.

Cheese Sauce

2 tbsp polyunsaturated margarine

5 tsp all-purpose flour

1 bay leaf

scant 2 cups skim milk

¾ cup grated sharp half-fat colby cheese

1 tsp English mustard powder

pinch of cayenne pepper

black pepper

1 Melt the margarine in a pan and stir in the flour. Cook, stirring, over a low heat until the roux is light in color and crumbly in texture. Add the bay leaf. Stir in one-third of the milk, beat until the sauce is thick, then repeat twice to use all the milk.

2 Remove the sauce from the heat, remove the bay leaf, and beat in the grated colby cheese, English mustard powder, a tiny pinch of cayenne pepper, and the black pepper. There is no need to add extra salt because the cheese will be salty.

Basic Cheesy Rice

2–2¾ oz/60–75 g unsalted butter

1 onion, finely chopped

1½ cups risotto or carnaroli rice

½ cup dry white vermouth or white wine

5 cups Vegetable Bouillon, simmering (see page 6)

1 cup freshly grated Parmesan cheese, plus extra for sprinkling

salt and pepper

1 Heat 1 oz/25 g of the butter in a large heavy-based pan over a medium heat. Add the onion and cook for about 2 minutes until just beginning to soften. Add the rice and cook for about 2 minutes, stirring frequently, until the mixture is translucent and well coated with the butter.

2 Pour in the vermouth: it will bubble and steam rapidly and evaporate almost immediately. Add a ladleful (about 1 cup) of the simmering bouillon and cook, stirring constantly, until the bouillon is absorbed.

3 Continue adding the bouillon, about half a ladleful at a time, allowing each addition to be absorbed before adding the next—never allow the rice to cook "dry." This should take 20–25 minutes. The mix should have a creamy consistency and the rice grains should be tender, but still firm to the bite.

Soups, Appetizers & Snacks

The fabulous recipes in this chapter, gathered

from around the world, can be used for many

purposes—as appetizers before a formal dinner

party, as light lunch or supper dishes served

with bread and salad greens, or as buffet or

picnic food. You can choose your recipe to

suit your mood, the occasion, and even the weather—try

chilled Avocado & Mint Soup on a hot summer day, or

comforting Sausages & Mash when there's a chill in the air.

All the recipes include a healthy range of ingredients, from

fresh vegetables to nuts, grains, legumes, and cheese, all of

which are very important in the vegetarian diet.

Asparagus Soup

Fresh asparagus is now available for most of the year, so this soup can be made at any time. It can also be made using canned asparagus.

NUTRITIONAL INFORMATION

Calories 196	Sugars 7g
Protein 7g	Fat 12g
Carbohydrate ...15g	Saturates 4g

 5-10 mins   55 mins

SERVES 6

I N G R E D I E N T S

1 bunch asparagus, about 12 oz/350 g, or 2 packs mini asparagus, about 5½ oz/150 g each

3 cups vegetable bouillon

¼ cup butter or margarine

1 onion, chopped

3 tbsp all-purpose flour

¼ tsp ground coriander

1 tbsp lemon juice

2 cups milk

4–6 tbsp heavy or light cream

salt and pepper

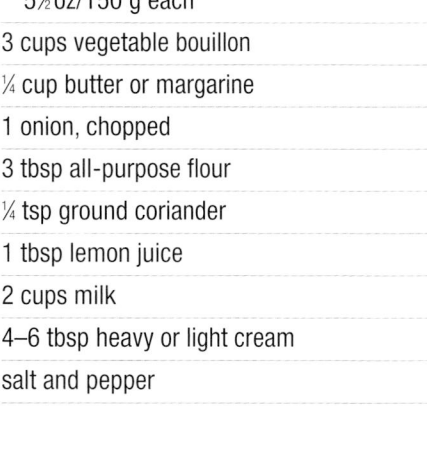

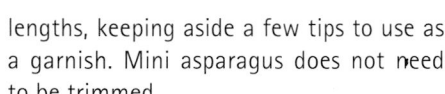

COOK'S TIP

If using canned asparagus, drain off the liquid and use as part of the measured bouillon. Remove a few small asparagus tips for garnish and chop the remainder. Continue as above.

1 Wash and trim the asparagus, discarding the lower, woody part of the stem. Cut the remainder into short lengths, keeping aside a few tips to use as a garnish. Mini asparagus does not need to be trimmed.

2 Cook the tips in the minimum of boiling salted water for 5–10 minutes. Drain and set aside.

3 Put the asparagus in a pan with the bouillon, bring to a boil, cover, and simmer for about 20 minutes, until soft. Drain and reserve the bouillon.

4 Melt the butter or margarine in a pan. Add the onion and cook over low heat until soft, but only barely colored. Stir in the flour and cook for 1 minute, then gradually whisk in the reserved bouillon, and bring to a boil.

5 Simmer for 2–3 minutes, until thickened, then stir in the cooked asparagus, seasoning, coriander, and lemon juice. Simmer for 10 minutes, then cool a little, and either press through a strainer with the back of a spoon or process in a blender or food processor until smooth.

6 Pour into a clean pan, add the milk and reserved asparagus tips, and bring to a boil. Simmer for 2 minutes. Stir in the cream, reheat gently, and serve.

Exotic Mushroom Soup

The Calabrian mountains in southern Italy provide large amounts of exotic mushrooms. Rich in flavor and color, they make a wonderful soup.

NUTRITIONAL INFORMATION

Calories 452   Sugars 5g
Protein ....15g   Fat 26g
Carbohydrate ...42g   Saturates 12g

 5 mins   25–30 mins

SERVES 4

INGREDIENTS

2 tbsp olive oil

1 onion, chopped

1 lb/450 g mixed mushrooms, such as porcini, oyster, and white

1¼ cups milk

3¾ cups hot vegetable bouillon

8 slices of French stick

3 tbsp butter, melted

2 garlic cloves, minced

¾ cup finely grated Swiss cheese

salt and pepper

1 Heat the oil in a large skillet and cook the onion for 3–4 minutes, or until soft and golden.

2 Wipe each mushroom with a damp cloth and cut any large mushrooms into smaller, bite-size pieces.

3 Add the mushrooms to the skillet, stirring quickly to coat them in the oil.

4 Add the milk to the skillet, bring to a boil, cover, and leave to simmer for about 5 minutes. Gradually stir in the hot vegetable bouillon.

5 Under a preheated broiler, toast the bread on both sides until golden.

6 Mix together the butter and garlic and then spoon generously over the toast.

7 Place the toast in the bottom of a large tureen or 4 individual serving bowls and pour over the hot soup.

8 Top with the grated Swiss cheese and serve at once.

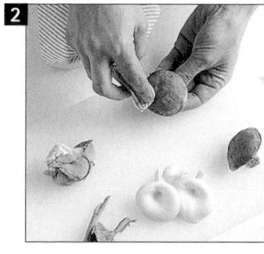  

Bell Pepper & Chili Soup

This soup has a real Mediterranean flavor, using sweet red bell peppers, tomato, chili and basil. It is great served with olive bread.

NUTRITIONAL INFORMATION

Calories 55	Sugars 10g
Protein 2g	Fat 0.5g
Carbohydrate 11g	Saturates 0.1g

 10 mins   25 mins

SERVES 4

INGREDIENTS

½ lb/225 g red bell peppers, seeded and sliced

1 onion, sliced

2 garlic cloves, crushed

1 green chili, chopped

1¼ cups strained tomatoes

2½ cups vegetable bouillon

2 tbsp chopped basil

basil sprigs, to garnish

VARIATION
This soup is also delicious served cold with ⅔ cup unsweetened yogurt swirled into it.

1 Put the red bell peppers in a large pan with the onion, garlic, and chili. Add the strained tomatoes and the vegetable bouillon and bring to a boil, stirring well.

2 Reduce the heat to a simmer and continue to cook the vegetables for 20 minutes, or until the bell peppers are soft. Drain, reserving the liquid and vegetables separately.

3 Using the back of a spoon, press the vegetables through a strainer. Alternatively, process in a food processor until smooth.

4 Return the vegetable purée to a clean pan with the reserved cooking liquid. Add the basil and heat through until hot. Garnish the soup with fresh basil sprigs and serve immediately.

Sweet Potato & Onion Soup

This simple recipe uses the sweet potato with its distinctive flavor and color, combined with a hint of orange and cilantro.

NUTRITIONAL INFORMATION

Calories 320   Sugars 26g
Protein . . . . .7g   Fat 7g
Carbohydrate . . .62g   Saturates 1g

 15 mins   30 mins

SERVES 4

I N G R E D I E N T S

2 tbsp vegetable oil

2 lb/900 g sweet potatoes, diced

1 carrot, diced

2 onions, sliced

2 garlic cloves, crushed

2½ cups vegetable bouillon

1¼ cups unsweetened orange juice

1 cup low-fat unsweetened yogurt

2 tbsp chopped fresh cilantro

salt and pepper

TO GARNISH

fresh cilantro sprigs

orange rind

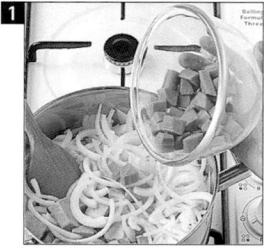  

1 Heat the vegetable oil in a large, heavy pan and add the sweet potatoes, carrot, onions, and garlic. Sauté the vegetables over low heat, stirring constantly for 5 minutes until soft.

2 Pour in the vegetable bouillon and orange juice and bring to a boil.

3 Reduce the heat to a simmer, cover the pan, and cook the vegetables for 20 minutes or until the sweet potatoes and carrot are tender.

4 Transfer the mixture to a food processor or blender, in batches, and process for 1 minute until puréed. Return the purée to the rinsed-out pan.

5 Stir in the yogurt and chopped cilantro and season to taste with salt and pepper.

6 Serve the soup in warm bowls and garnish with cilantro sprigs and orange rind.

VARIATION
This soup can be chilled before serving, if preferred. If chilling, stir the yogurt into the dish just before serving. Serve in chilled bowls.

Carrot, Apple & Celery Soup

For this fresh-tasting soup, use your favorite variety of eating apple rather than a cooking variety, which will give too tart a flavor.

NUTRITIONAL INFORMATION

Calories 153	Sugars 34g	
Protein 2g	Fat 1g	
Carbohydrate ...36g	Saturates 0.2g	

30 mins   40 mins

SERVES 4

INGREDIENTS

2 lb/900 g carrots, finely diced

1 medium onion, chopped

3 celery stalks, diced

4 cups vegetable bouillon

3 medium-size eating apples

2 tbsp tomato paste

1 bay leaf

2 tsp superfine sugar

¼ large lemon

salt and pepper

celery leaves, shredded, to garnish

1 Place the carrots, onion, and celery in a large, heavy pan and add the bouillon. Bring to a boil, lower the heat, cover, and simmer for 10 minutes.

2 Meanwhile, peel, core, and dice 2 of the apples. Add the pieces of apple, the tomato paste, bay leaf, and sugar to the pan and bring to a boil over medium heat. Reduce the heat, half cover, and simmer for 20 minutes. Remove and discard the bay leaf.

3 Meanwhile, wash, core, and cut the remaining apple into thin slices, without peeling.

4 Place the apple slices in a small pan and squeeze over the lemon juice. Heat the apple slices gently and simmer for 1–2 minutes until tender.

5 Drain the apple slices and set aside until required.

6 Place the carrot and apple mixture in a blender or food processor and process until smooth. Alternatively, press the mixture through a strainer with the back of a wooden spoon.

7 Gently reheat the soup if necessary and season with salt and pepper to taste. Ladle the soup into warmed bowls and serve topped with the reserved apple slices and shredded celery leaves.

Parisian Pea Soup

This is one occasion when cooking with just a little butter is worthwhile because of its rich flavor.

NUTRITIONAL INFORMATION

Calories	114	Sugars	........3g
Protein	.........5g	Fat	..........6g
Carbohydrate	...10g	Saturates	.......4g

 10 mins   15 mins

SERVES 4

INGREDIENTS

2 tbsp butter

2 shallots, finely chopped

1 lb shelled peas

1 small romaine or Boston lettuce, shredded

5 cups vegetable bouillon

pinch of freshly grated nutmeg

salt and ground black pepper

1 Melt the butter in a large pan. Add the shallots and cook over medium heat, stirring occasionally, for 5 minutes, until softened.

2 Add the peas, shredded lettuce, and bouillon to the pan and season to taste with nutmeg, salt, and pepper. Bring to a boil, cover, and simmer for 10–15 minutes until the peas are tender.

3 Remove the pan from the heat and let cool slightly. Pour into a blender or food processor and process to a purée.

4 Return the soup to the clean pan and heat through gently before serving.

VARIATION
For a classic side dish, cook as for soup, but add only ½ cup of bouillon and serve without processing.

Spinach & Ginger Soup

This mildly spiced, rich green soup is delicately scented with ginger and lemon grass. It makes a good light appetizer or summer lunch dish.

NUTRITIONAL INFORMATION

Calories	38	Sugars	.......0.8g
Protein	........3.2g	Fat	..........1.8g
Carbohydrate	...2.4g	Saturates	.....0.2g

5–10 mins   25 mins

SERVES 4

INGREDIENTS

2 tbsp sunflower oil

1 onion, chopped

2 garlic cloves, finely chopped

2 tsp chopped fresh ginger root

½ lb/225 g young spinach leaves

1 small lemon grass stalk, finely chopped

4 cups vegetable bouillon

1½ cups potatoes, chopped

1 tbsp rice wine or dry sherry

1 tsp sesame oil

salt and pepper

1 Heat the oil in a large pan. Add the onion, garlic, and ginger and cook over low heat, stirring occasionally, for 3–4 minutes until softened.

2 Reserve 2–3 small spinach leaves. Add the remaining leaves and lemon grass to the pan, stirring until the spinach is wilted. Add the bouillon and potatoes to the pan and bring to a boil. Lower the heat, cover, and simmer for about 10 minutes.

3 Remove the pan from the heat and let cool slightly. Then tip the soup into a blender or food processor and process until completely smooth.

4 Return the soup to the pan and add the rice wine, then adjust the seasoning to taste with salt and pepper. Heat until just about to boil.

5 Finely shred the reserved spinach leaves and sprinkle some over the top. Drizzle a few drops of sesame oil into the soup. Ladle into warmed soup bowls, garnish each bowl with a sprinkling of the remaining shredded spinach, and serve the soup immediately.

COOK'S TIP

To make a creamy-textured spinach and coconut soup, stir in about 4 tablespoons creamed coconut or replace about 1¼ cups of the bouillon with coconut milk. Serve the soup with shavings of fresh coconut scattered over the surface.

Celery & Stilton Soup

This is a classic combination of ingredients all brought together in a delicious, creamy soup. Serve with whole-wheat bread for a light lunch.

NUTRITIONAL INFORMATION

Calories	...392	Sugars	...8g
Protein	...15g	Fat	...30g
Carbohydrate	...15g	Saturates	...16g

 10 mins   30 mins

SERVES 4

INGREDIENTS

4 tbsp butter

2 shallots, chopped

3 celery stalks, chopped

1 garlic clove, finely chopped

2 tbsp all-purpose flour

2½ cups vegetable bouillon

1¼ cups milk

1½ cups crumbled blue Stilton cheese, plus extra to garnish

2 tbsp walnut halves, roughly chopped

⅔ cup unsweetened yogurt

salt and pepper

chopped celery leaves, to garnish

1 Melt the butter in a large, heavy pan and sauté the shallots, celery, and garlic for 2–3 minutes, stirring, until soft.

2 Lower the heat, add the flour and cook, stirring, for 30 seconds.

3 Gradually stir in the vegetable bouillon and milk and bring to a boil.

4 Reduce the heat to a simmer and add the crumbled blue Stilton cheese and walnut halves. Cover and simmer for 20 minutes.

5 Stir the unsweetened yogurt into the soup and heat for a further 2 minutes without boiling.

6 Season the soup, then transfer to a warm soup tureen or individual serving bowls,

7 Garnish the soup with the chopped celery leaves and extra crumbled blue Stilton cheese, and serve immediately.

COOK'S TIP
As well as adding protein, vitamins, and useful fats to the diet, nuts add important flavor and texture to vegetarian meals.

Indian Potato & Pea Soup

A slightly hot and spicy Indian flavor is given to this soup with the use of garam masala, chile, cumin, and cilantro.

NUTRITIONAL INFORMATION

Calories 160   Sugars 8g
Protein ....6g   Fat 7g
Carbohydrate ...21g   Saturates 1g

 5 mins   35 mins

SERVES 4

INGREDIENTS

2 tbsp vegetable oil

1¼ cups diced mealy potatoes

1 large onion, chopped

2 garlic cloves, crushed

1 tsp garam masala

1 tsp ground coriander

1 tsp ground cumin

3¾ cups vegetable bouillon

1 red chile, chopped

¾ cup frozen peas

4 tbsp unsweetened yogurt

salt and pepper

chopped cilantro, to garnish

warm bread, to serve

COOK'S TIP

For slightly less heat, seed the chile before adding it to the soup. Always wash your hands after handling chiles because they contain volatile oils that can irritate the skin and make your eyes burn if you touch your face.

1 Heat the vegetable oil in a large pan and add the diced potatoes, onion, and garlic. Sauté gently for about 5 minutes, stirring constantly.

2 Add the garam masala, ground coriander, and ground cumin, and cook for 1 minute, stirring all the time.

3 Stir in the vegetable bouillon and chopped red chile and bring the mixture to a boil. Reduce the heat, then cover the pan and simmer for 20 minutes, until the potatoes begin to break down.

4 Add the peas and cook for a further 5 minutes. Stir in the yogurt and season to taste.

5 Pour into warmed soup bowls. Garnish with chopped fresh cilantro and serve hot with warm bread.

Spicy Dhal & Carrot Soup

This nutritious soup uses split red lentils and carrots as the two main ingredients and includes a selection of spices to give it a kick.

NUTRITIONAL INFORMATION

Calories	173	Sugars	........11g
Protein	.........9g	Fat	...........5g
Carbohydrate	...24g	Saturates	.......1g

🍳 15 mins   🕐 45 mins

SERVES 6

I N G R E D I E N T S

¾ cup split red lentils

5 cups vegetable bouillon

3 cups carrots, sliced

2 onions, chopped

1 cup canned chopped tomatoes

2 garlic cloves, chopped

2 tbsp vegetable ghee or oil

1 tsp ground cumin

1 tsp ground coriander

1 fresh green chili, seeded and chopped, or 1 tsp minced chili

½ tsp ground turmeric

1 tbsp lemon juice

salt

1¼ cups milk

2 tbsp chopped cilantro

unsweetened yogurt, to serve

2 Meanwhile, heat the ghee or oil in a small pan. Add the cumin, ground coriander, chili, and turmeric and cook over low heat for 1 minute. Remove from the heat and stir in the lemon juice. Season with salt to taste.

3 Process the soup in batches in a blender or food processor. Return the soup to the pan, add the spice mixture and the remaining 2½ cups of bouillon, and simmer over low heat for 10 minutes.

4 Add the milk, taste, and adjust the seasoning, if necessary. Stir in the chopped cilantro and reheat gently. Serve the soup hot in warmed bowls, garnished with a swirl of yogurt.

1 Place the lentils in a strainer and rinse well under cold running water. Drain and place in a large pan, together with 2½ cups of the bouillon, the carrots, onions, tomatoes, and garlic. Bring the mixture to a boil, reduce the heat, cover, and simmer for 30 minutes. or until the vegetables and lentils are tender.

Parsnip Soup with Ginger

The exotic flavors give this simple soup a lift. If you wish, use bought ginger purée instead of grating it; add to taste as the strength varies.

NUTRITIONAL INFORMATION

Calories 151   Sugars 19g
Protein . . . . .4g   Fat 3g
Carbohydrate . . .29g   Saturates 0g

 10 mins   55 mins

SERVES 6

INGREDIENTS

2 tsp olive oil

1 large onion, chopped

1 large leek, sliced

1¾ lb /800 g parsnips, sliced

2 carrots, thinly sliced

4 tbsp grated fresh ginger root

2–3 garlic cloves, finely chopped

grated zest of ½ orange

6¼ cups water

1 cup orange juice

salt and pepper

chopped chives or slivers of scallion,
  to garnish

1 Heat the olive oil in a large pan over medium heat. Add the onion and leek and cook, stirring occasionally, for about 5 minutes until soft.

2 Add the parsnips, carrots, ginger, garlic, grated orange zest, water, and a pinch of salt. Reduce the heat, cover, and simmer, stirring occasionally, for about 40 minutes until the vegetables are soft.

3 Remove from the heat and let cool slightly, then transfer to a blender or food processor, and process to a smooth purée, in batches if necessary.

4 Return the soup to the pan and stir in the orange juice. Add a little water or more orange juice, if you prefer a thinner consistency. Taste and adjust the seasoning with salt and pepper.

5 Simmer for about 10 minutes to heat through. Ladle the soup into warmed bowls, garnish with chives or slivers of scallion, and serve immediately.

VARIATION

You could make the soup using equal amounts (1 lb each) of carrots and parsnips.

Greek Bean Soup

This is based on a simple soup typical of Greek home cooking.
The artichoke hearts make it fancier, but they are not essential.

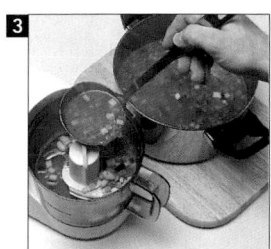

NUTRITIONAL INFORMATION

Calories	109	Sugars	.........7g
Protein	.........6g	Fat	...........3g
Carbohydrate	...16g	Saturates	.......0g

 10 mins   1¼ hrs

SERVES 6

INGREDIENTS

1 tbsp olive oil

1 large onion, finely chopped

1 large carrot, finely diced

2 celery stalks, finely chopped

4 tomatoes, peeled, seeded, and chopped,
    or 1¼ cups drained canned tomatoes

2 garlic cloves, finely chopped

3 cups canned cannellini or navy beans,
    drained and rinsed

5 cups water

1 zucchini, finely diced

grated zest of ½ lemon

1 tbsp chopped fresh mint or ¼ tsp
    dried mint

1 tsp chopped fresh thyme or ⅛ tsp
    dried thyme

1 bay leaf

14 oz/400 g canned artichoke hearts,
    drained

salt and pepper

1 Heat 1 teaspoon of the olive oil in a large pan over medium heat. Add the onion and cook, stirring occasionally, for 3–4 minutes until soft. Add the carrot, celery, tomatoes, and garlic to the pan and continue cooking for a further 5 minutes, stirring frequently.

2 Add the beans and water. Bring to a boil, reduce the heat, cover, and cook gently for about 10 minutes.

3 Add the zucchini, lemon zest, mint, thyme, and bay leaf and season to taste with salt and pepper. Cover and simmer for about 40 minutes until all the vegetables are tender. Remove the pan from the heat and let cool slightly. Remove and discard the bay leaf and transfer 2 cups of the soup to a blender or food processor, process to a smooth purée, and recombine.

4 Meanwhile, heat the remaining oil in a skillet over medium heat. Cook the artichokes, cut side down, until lightly browned. Turn over and cook long enough to heat through. Ladle the soup into warmed bowls and top each with an artichoke heart. Serve immediately.

Celery Root & Potato Soup

It is hard to imagine that celery root, a coarse, knobby vegetable, can taste so sweet. It makes a wonderfully flavorful soup.

NUTRITIONAL INFORMATION

Calories . . . . .20 Sugars 1.3g
Protein . . . . .0.8g Fat 0.7g
Carbohydrate . . .2.7g Saturates 0.4g

 10 mins   35 mins

SERVES 4

INGREDIENTS

1 tbsp butter

1 onion, chopped

2 large leeks, halved lengthwise and sliced

1½ lb/750 g celery root, peeled
   and cubed

1½ cups potatoes, cubed

1 carrot, quartered and thinly sliced

5 cups water

pinch of dried marjoram

1 bay leaf

freshly grated nutmeg

salt and pepper

celery leaves, to garnish

3 Let the soup cool slightly. Transfer to a blender or food processor and process until smooth. (If using a food processor, strain off the cooking liquid and reserve. Purée the soup solids with enough cooking liquid to moisten them, then combine with the remaining liquid.)

4 Return the puréed soup to the pan and stir well. Season with nutmeg, salt, and pepper to taste, then simmer over medium–low heat until it is reheated.

5 Ladle the soup into warm bowls, garnish with celery leaves, and serve.

1 Melt the butter in a large pan over medium–low heat. Add the onion and leeks and cook, stirring frequently, until just soft; do not let color.

2 Add the celery root, potatoes, carrot, water, marjoram, and bay leaf with a pinch of salt. Bring to a boil, reduce the heat, cover, and simmer for about 25 minutes until the vegetables are tender. Remove and discard the bay leaf.

Plum Tomato Soup

Homemade tomato soup is easy to make and always tastes better than bought varieties. Try this version with its Mediterranean influences.

NUTRITIONAL INFORMATION

Calories ....402 Sugars 14g
Protein ....7g Fat 32g
Carbohydrate ...16g Saturates 3g

20 mins

30-35 mins

SERVES 4

I N G R E D I E N T S

2 tbsp olive oil

2 red onions, chopped

2 celery stalks, chopped

1 carrot, chopped

1 lb/450 g plum tomatoes, halved

3 cups vegetable bouillon

1 tbsp chopped oregano

1 tbsp chopped basil

⅔ cups dry white wine

2 tsp superfine sugar

1 cup hazelnuts (filberts), toasted

1 cup black or green olives

handful of basil leaves

1 tbsp olive oil

1 loaf ciabatta bread

salt and pepper

basil sprigs to garnish

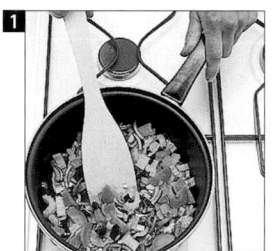

1 Heat the oil in a large pan. Add the onions, celery, and carrot and cook over low heat, stirring frequently, until soft, but not colored.

2 Add the tomatoes, bouillon, chopped herbs, wine, and sugar. Bring to a boil, cover, and simmer for 20 minutes.

3 Place the toasted hazelnuts in a blender or food processor, together with the olives and basil leaves, and process until thoroughly combined, but not too smooth. Alternatively, finely chop the nuts, olives, and basil leaves, and pound them together in a mortar with a pestle, then turn into a small bowl. Add the olive oil and process or beat thoroughly for a few seconds to combine. Turn the mixture into a serving bowl.

4 Meanwhile, warm the ciabatta bread in a preheated oven, 375°F/190°C, for 3-4 minutes.

5 Process the soup in a blender or a food processor, or press through a strainer, until smooth, Check the seasoning. Ladle into warmed soup bowls and garnish with sprigs of basil. Slice the warm bread and spread with the olive and hazelnut paste. Serve with the soup.

Pumpkin Soup

This American classic has now become popular worldwide.
When pumpkin is out of season, use butternut squash in its place.

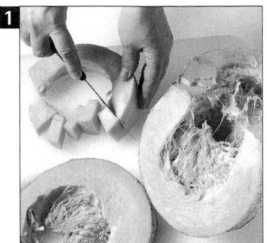

NUTRITIONAL INFORMATION

Calories 112	Sugars 7g
Protein 4g	Fat 7g
Carbohydrate 8g	Saturates 2g

 10 mins   30 mins

SERVES 6

INGREDIENTS

about 2 lb/900 g pumpkin

3 tbsp butter or margarine

1 onion, sliced thinly

1 garlic clove, crushed

3½ cups vegetable bouillon

½ tsp ground ginger

1 tbsp lemon juice

3–4 thinly pared strips of orange zest (optional)

1–2 bay leaves or 1 bouquet garni

1¼ cups milk

salt and pepper

TO GARNISH

4–6 tbsp light or heavy cream or unsweetened yogurt

snipped chives

1 Peel the pumpkin, remove the seeds, and then cut the flesh into 1 inch/ 2.5 cm cubes.

2 Melt the butter or margarine in a large, heavy pan. Add the onion and garlic and cook over low heat until soft, but not colored.

3 Add the pumpkin and toss with the onion for 2–3 minutes.

4 Add the bouillon and bring to a boil over medium heat. Season to taste with salt and pepper and add the ground ginger and lemon juice, the strips of orange zest, if using, and the bay leaves or bouquet garni.

5 Cover the pan and gently simmer the soup over low heat for about 20 minutes, stirring occasionally, until the pumpkin is tender.

6 Discard the orange zest, if using, and the bay leaves or bouquet garni. Cool the soup slightly, then press through a strainer with the back of a spoon, or process in a food processor until smooth. Pour into a clean pan.

7 Add the milk and reheat gently. Adjust the seasoning. Garnish with a swirl of cream or unsweetened yogurt and snipped chives, and serve.

Pistou

This hearty soup of beans and vegetables is from Nice and gets its name from the fresh basil sauce stirred in at the last minute.

NUTRITIONAL INFORMATION

Calories ....55 Sugars 1.2g
Protein ....3.8g Fat 2.6g
Carbohydrate ...4.2g Saturates 0.6g

 10 mins   25 mins

SERVES 6

INGREDIENTS

2 young carrots

1 lb/450 g potatoes

½ cup fresh or frozen peas in their pods

1½ cups thin green beans

1 cup young zucchini

2 tbsp olive oil

1 garlic clove, crushed

1 large onion, finely chopped

11¼ cups vegetable bouillon or water

1 bouquet garni of 2 fresh parsley sprigs and 1 bay leaf tied in a 3 inch/7.5 cm piece of celery

¾ cup dried small soup pasta

1 large tomato, peeled, seeded, and chopped or diced

Parmesan cheese shavings, to serve

PISTOU SAUCE

3 cups fresh basil leaves

1 garlic clove

5 tbsp extra virgin olive oil

salt and pepper

1 To make the pistou sauce, put the basil leaves, garlic, and olive oil in a food processor and process until thoroughly blended. Season with salt and pepper to taste. Scrape the sauce into a bowl, cover with plastic wrap, and store in the refrigerator until required.

2 Cut the carrots in half lengthwise, then slice. Cut the potatoes into quarters lengthwise, then slice. Let stand in a bowl of water until ready to use to prevent them from discoloring.

3 Trim the beans and cut them into 1 inch/2.5 cm pieces. Cut the zucchini in half lengthwise, then slice.

4 Heat the oil in a large pan or flameproof casserole. Add the garlic and cook for 2 minutes, stirring. Add the onion and cook for a further 2 minutes until soft. Add the carrots and potatoes and stir for about 30 seconds.

5 Pour in the bouillon and bring to a boil. Lower the heat, partially cover, and simmer for 8 minutes until the vegetables are starting to become tender.

6 Stir in the peas, beans, zucchini, bouquet garni, and pasta. Season and cook for 4 minutes until the vegetables and pasta are tender. Stir in the pistou sauce and serve with Parmesan shavings.

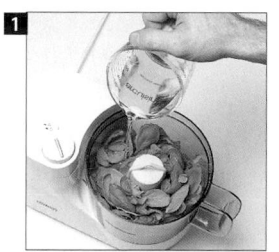  

Minted Pea & Yogurt Soup

A deliciously refreshing, summery soup that is full of goodness.
It is also extremely tasty served chilled.

NUTRITIONAL INFORMATION

Calories ....208 Sugars 9g
Protein ....10g Fat 7g
Carbohydrate ...26g Saturates 2g

15 mins

25 mins

SERVES 6

INGREDIENTS

2 tbsp vegetable ghee or sunflower oil

2 onions, coarsely chopped

2 cups potato, coarsely chopped

2 garlic cloves

1 inch/2.5 cm root ginger, chopped

1 tsp ground coriander

1 tsp ground cumin

1 tbsp all-purpose flour

3½ cups vegetable bouillon

1 lb frozen peas

2–3 tbsp chopped mint

salt and pepper

⅔ cup strained Greek yogurt, plus extra to serve

½ tsp cornstarch

1¼ cups pint milk

mint sprigs, to garnish

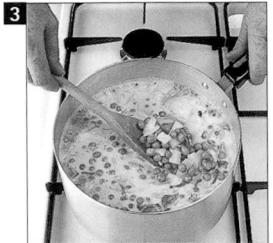

1 Heat the vegetable ghee or sunflower oil in a pan, add the onions and potato, and cook over low heat, stirring occasionally, for about 3 minutes, until the onion is soft and translucent.

2 Stir in the garlic, ginger, coriander, cumin, and flour and cook, stirring constantly, for 1 minute.

3 Add the vegetable bouillon, peas, and half the mint and bring to a boil, stirring. Reduce the heat, cover, and simmer gently for 15 minutes, or until the vegetables are tender.

4 Process the soup, in batches, in a blender or food processor. Return the mixture to the pan and season with salt and pepper to taste. Blend the yogurt with the cornstarch to a smooth paste and stir into the soup.

5 Add the milk and bring almost to a boil, stirring constantly. Cook very gently for 2 minutes. Serve hot, sprinkled with the remaining mint, a swirl of extra yogurt, and topped with mint sprigs.

Garlic & Potato Soup

The combination of potato, garlic, and onion works marvelously in soup. In this recipe the garlic is roasted to give it added dimension and depth.

NUTRITIONAL INFORMATION

Calories 240   Sugars 7g
Protein ....8g   Fat 10g
Carbohydrate ...33g   Saturates 5g

 10 mins   1 hr

SERVES 4

I N G R E D I E N T S

1 large bulb garlic with large cloves, peeled (about ¼ lb/100 g)

2 tsp olive oil

2 large leeks, thinly sliced

1 large onion, finely chopped

2¾ cups diced potatoes

5 cups vegetable bouillon

1 bay leaf

⅔ cup light cream

freshly grated nutmeg

fresh lemon juice (optional)

salt and pepper

snipped fresh chives, to garnish

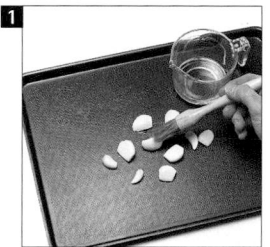  

1 Put the garlic cloves in a baking dish. Lightly brush with oil and bake in a preheated oven at 350°F/180°C for about 20 minutes until golden.

2 Heat the oil in a large pan over medium heat. Add the leeks and onion, then cover and cook for about 3 minutes, stirring frequently, until they begin to soften.

3 Add the potatoes, roasted garlic, bouillon, and bay leaf. Season with salt (unless the bouillon is salty) and pepper. Bring to a boil, then reduce the heat, cover, and cook gently for about 30 minutes until the vegetables are tender. Remove the bay leaf.

4 Let the soup cool slightly, then transfer to a blender or food processor and purée until smooth, working in batches if necessary. (If using a food processor, strain off the cooking liquid and reserve. Purée the soup solids with enough cooking liquid to moisten them, then combine with the remaining liquid.)

5 Return the soup to the pan and stir in the cream and a generous grating of nutmeg. Taste and adjust the seasoning, if necessary, adding a few drops of lemon juice, if wished. Reheat over low heat. Ladle into warm soup bowls, then garnish with chives or parsley and serve.

Thick Onion Soup

A delicious creamy soup with grated carrot and parsley for texture and color. Serve with crusty cheese biscuits for a hearty lunch.

NUTRITIONAL INFORMATION

Calories	277	Sugars	........12g
Protein	.........6g	Fat	..........20g
Carbohydrate	...19g	Saturates	.......8g

🥔 20 mins   🕐 1hr 10 mins

SERVES 4

I N G R E D I E N T S

⅓ cup butter

1 lb/450 g onions, finely chopped

1 garlic clove, crushed

⅓ cup all-purpose flour

2½ cups vegetable bouillon

2½ cups milk

2–3 tsp lemon or lime juice

good pinch of ground allspice

1 bay leaf

1 carrot, coarsely grated

4–6 tbsp heavy cream

2 tbsp chopped parsley

salt and pepper

CHEESE BISCUITS

1⅓ cups malted wheat or whole-wheat flour

2 tsp baking powder

¼ cup butter

4 tbsp grated Parmesan cheese

1 egg, beaten

about ⅓ cup milk

1 Melt the butter in a pan and cook the onions and garlic over low heat, stirring frequently, for 10–15 minutes, until soft, but not colored. Stir in the flour and cook, stirring, for 1 minute, then gradually stir in the bouillon and bring to a boil, stirring frequently. Add the milk, then bring back to a boil.

2 Season to taste with salt and pepper and add 2 teaspoons of the lemon or lime juice, the allspice, and the bay leaf. Cover and simmer for about 25 minutes until the vegetables are tender. Discard the bay leaf.

3 Meanwhile, make the biscuits. Combine the flour, baking powder, and seasoning and rub in the butter until the mixture resembles fine bread crumbs. Stir in 3 tablespoons of the cheese, the egg, and enough milk to mix to a soft dough.

4 Shape into a bar about 2 cm/¾ inch thick. Place on a floured cookie sheet and mark into slices. Sprinkle with the remaining cheese and bake in a preheated oven, 220°C/425°F, for about 20 minutes, until risen and a golden brown color.

5 Stir the carrot into the soup and simmer for 2–3 minutes. Add more lemon or lime juice, if necessary. Stir in the cream and reheat. Garnish and serve with the warm biscuits.

Chinese Cabbage Soup

This is a piquant soup, which is slightly sweet-and-sour in flavor.
It can be served as a hearty meal or appetizer.

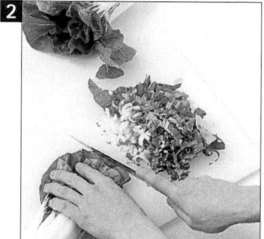

NUTRITIONAL INFORMATION

Calories 65   Sugars 7g
Protein . . . . .3g   Fat 0.5g
Carbohydrate . . . .11g   Saturates 0.1g

 5 mins   30 mins

SERVES 4

I N G R E D I E N T S

1 lb/450 g bok choi

2½ cups vegetable bouillon

1 tbsp rice wine vinegar

1 tbsp light soy sauce

1 tbsp superfine sugar

1 tbsp dry sherry

1 fresh red chili, thinly sliced

1 tbsp cornstarch

2 tbsp water

1 Wash the bok choi thoroughly under cold running water, rinse, and drain. Pat dry on paper towels.

2 Trim the stems of the bok choi and shred the leaves.

3 Heat the vegetable bouillon in a large pan. Add the bok choi and cook for 10–15 minutes.

4 Mix together the rice wine vinegar, soy sauce, sugar, and sherry in a small bowl. Add this mixture to the bouillon, together with the sliced chili.

5 Bring to a boil, lower the heat, and cook for 2–3 minutes.

6 Blend the cornstarch with the water to form a smooth paste.

7 Gradually stir the cornstarch mixture into the soup and cook, stirring constantly, until it thickens. Cook for a further 4–5 minutes.

8 Ladle the Chinese cabbage soup into individual warm serving bowls and serve immediately.

COOKS TIP
Bok choi, also known as pak choi or spoon cabbage, has long, white leaf stalks and fleshy, spoon-shaped, shiny green leaves. There are a number of varieties available, which differ mainly in size rather than flavor.

Broccoli Soup

Adding soft cheese to this soup just before serving makes it very special, while the rice and croûtons provide an excellent contrast of textures.

NUTRITIONAL INFORMATION

Calories 384	Sugars 7g
Protein 8g	Fat 30g
Carbohydrate ...21g	Saturates 18g

 5 mins   40 mins

SERVES 4

I N G R E D I E N T S

1 lb broccoli (from 1 large head)

2 tsp butter

1 tsp oil

1 onion, finely chopped

1 leek, thinly sliced

1 small carrot, finely chopped

3 tbsp white rice

3¾ cups water

1 bay leaf

4 tbsp heavy cream

½ cup cream cheese

freshly grated nutmeg

salt and pepper

croûtons, to serve (see Cook's Tip)

COOK'S TIP
To make croûtons, remove the crusts from thick slices of bread, then cut the bread into dice. Fry in vegetable oil, stirring constantly, until evenly browned, then drain on paper towels.

1 Divide the broccoli into small florets and cut off the stems. Peel the large stems and then chop all the stems into small pieces.

2 Heat the butter and oil in a large pan over medium heat and add the onion, leek, and carrot. Cook for 3–4 minutes, stirring frequently, until the onion is soft.

3 Add the broccoli stems, rice, water, bay leaf, and a pinch of salt. Bring just to a boil and reduce the heat to low. Cover and simmer for 15 minutes. Add the broccoli florets to the pan and continue cooking, covered, for 15–20 minutes until the rice and vegetables are tender. Remove the bay leaf.

4 Stir in the cream and soft cheese. Season the soup with nutmeg, pepper, and, if needed, more salt. Simmer over low heat for a few minutes until heated through, stirring occasionally. Taste and adjust the seasoning, if needed.

5 Ladle into warm bowls and serve sprinkled with croûtons.

Carrot & Almond Soup

Ground almonds add valuable protein and a rich, luxurious depth to this delicately colored soup.

NUTRITIONAL INFORMATION

Calories ....275 Sugars 10g
Protein ....9g Fat 20g
Carbohydrate ...16g Saturates 2g

 10 mins   50 mins

SERVES 4–6

INGREDIENTS

2 tsp olive oil

1 onion, finely chopped

1 leek, thinly sliced

4 cups carrots, thinly sliced

6¼ cups water

1 loosely packed cup soft white bread crumbs

1½ cups ground almonds

1 tbsp fresh lemon juice, or to taste

salt and pepper

snipped fresh chives, to garnish

1 Heat the oil in a large pan over medium heat and add the onion and leek. Cover and cook for about 3 minutes, stirring occasionally, until just soft; do not let them brown.

2 Add the carrots and water and season with a little salt and pepper. Bring to a boil, reduce the heat and simmer gently, partially covered, for about 45 minutes until the vegetables are tender.

3 Soak the bread crumbs in cold water to cover for 2–3 minutes, then strain them and press out the remaining water.

4 Put the almonds and bread crumbs in a blender or food processor with a ladleful of the carrot cooking water and purée until smooth and paste-like.

5 Transfer the soup vegetables and remaining cooking liquid to the blender or food processor and purée until smooth, working in batches if necessary. (If using a food processor, strain off the cooking liquid and reserve. Purée the soup solids with enough cooking liquid to moisten them, then combine with the remaining liquid.)

6 Return the soup to the pan and simmer over low heat, stirring occasionally, until heated through. Add lemon juice, salt, and pepper to taste.

7 Ladle the soup into warm bowls, garnish with chives, and serve.

Fresh Mushroom Soup

A creamy, fresh mushroom soup always makes an elegant start
to a dinner party. Sherry has a particular affinity with mushrooms.

NUTRITIONAL INFORMATION

Calories 229   Sugars 5g
Protein . . . . .6g   Fat 17g
Carbohydrate . . . .11g   Saturates 10g

10 mins   40 mins

SERVES 4

INGREDIENTS

3 tbsp butter

1½ lb/675 g mushrooms, sliced

1 onion, finely chopped

1 shallot, finely chopped

3 tbsp all-purpose flour

2–3 tbsp sherry or dry white wine

6 cups vegetable bouillon

⅔ cup light cream

2 tbsp chopped fresh parsley

fresh lemon juice (optional)

salt and pepper

4 tbsp sour cream or crème fraîche, to
garnish

1 Melt half the butter in a large skillet
over medium heat. Add the mushrooms
and season with salt and pepper. Cook for
about 8 minutes until they are golden
brown, stirring occasionally at first, then
more often after they start to color.
Remove the mushrooms from the heat.

2 Melt the remaining butter in a pan
over medium heat, add the onion and
shallot, and cook for 2–3 minutes until just
soft. Stir the flour into the pan and
continue cooking for 2 minutes. Add the
wine and bouillon and stir well.

3 Set aside about one quarter of the
mushrooms. Add the remainder to the
pan. Reduce the heat, cover, and cook
gently for 20 minutes, stirring occasionally.

4 Let the soup cool slightly, then
transfer to a blender or food
processor and purée until smooth, working
in batches, if necessary. (If using a food
processor, strain off the cooking liquid and
reserve. Purée the soup solids with enough
cooking liquid to moisten them, then
combine with the remaining liquid.)

5 Return the soup to the pan and stir in
the reserved mushrooms, the cream,
and the parsley. Cook for about 5 minutes
to heat through. Taste and adjust the
seasoning, adding a few drops of lemon
juice if wished. Ladle into warm bowls and
decorate with sour cream.

Cauliflower & Cider Soup

Cauliflower can taste rather bland, but using hard cider in this creamy soup gives it an unusual kick.

NUTRITIONAL INFORMATION

Calories 312	Sugars 13g
Protein 7g	Fat 21g
Carbohydrate . . .15g	Saturates 13g

 10 mins   55 mins

SERVES 4

I N G R E D I E N T S

2 tbsp butter

1 onion, finely chopped

1 garlic clove, crushed

1 carrot, thinly sliced

5 cups cauliflower florets

2½ cups hard cider

freshly grated nutmeg

½ cup milk

½ cup heavy cream

salt and pepper

snipped chives, to garnish

1 Melt the butter in a pan over medium heat. Add the onion and garlic and cook for about 5 minutes, stirring occasionally, until just soft.

2 Add the carrot and cauliflower to the pan and pour over the cider. Season with salt, pepper, and a generous grating of nutmeg. Bring to a boil, then reduce the heat to low. Cover and cook gently for about 50 minutes until the vegetables are very soft.

3 Let the soup cool slightly, then transfer to a blender or food processor and purée until smooth, working in batches if necessary. (If using a food processor, strain off the cooking liquid and reserve. Purée the soup solids with enough cooking liquid to moisten them, then combine with the remaining liquid.)

4 Return the soup to the pan and stir in the milk and cream. Taste and adjust the seasoning, if necessary. Simmer the soup over low heat, stirring occasionally, until heated through.

5 Ladle the soup into warm bowls, garnish with chives, and serve.

COOK'S TIP
If you don't have hard cider, substitute ½ cup each white wine, apple juice, and water.

Vegetable & Corn Chowder

This is a really filling soup, which should be served before a light entrée. It is easy to prepare and filled with flavor.

NUTRITIONAL INFORMATION

Calories	378	Sugars	........20g
Protein	........16g	Fat	..........13g
Carbohydrate	...52g	Saturates	.......6g

 15 mins   30 mins

SERVES 4

INGREDIENTS

1 tbsp vegetable oil

1 red onion, diced

1 red bell pepper, seeded and diced

3 garlic cloves, crushed

1¾ cups diced potatoes

2 tbsp all-purpose flour

2½ cups milk

1¼ cups vegetable bouillon

½ cup broccoli florets

3 cups canned corn kernels, drained

¾ cup grated Cheddar cheese

salt and pepper

1 tbsp chopped cilantro, to garnish

COOK'S TIP

Vegetarian cheeses are made with rennets of non-animal origin, using microbial or fungal enzymes.

1 Heat the oil in a large pan. Add the onion, bell pepper, garlic, and potato and sauté over low heat, stirring frequently, for 2–3 minutes.

2 Stir in the flour and cook, stirring for 30 seconds. Gradually stir in the milk and bouillon.

3 Add the broccoli and corn kernels. Bring the mixture to a boil, stirring constantly, then reduce the heat and simmer for about 20 minutes, or until all the vegetables are tender.

4 Add ½ cup of the cheese and stir until it melts.

5 Season and spoon the chowder into a warm soup tureen. Garnish with the remaining cheese and the chopped cilantro and serve.

Garbanzo & Tomato Soup

A thick vegetable soup which is a delicious meal in itself.
Serve with Parmesan cheese and warm sun-dried tomato bread.

NUTRITIONAL INFORMATION

Calories 285   Sugar 11g
Protein ....16g   Fats 12g
Carbohydrates ...29g   Saturates 3g

 5 mins   15 mins

SERVES 4

I N G R E D I E N T S

2 tbsp olive oil

2 leeks, sliced

2 zucchini, diced

2 garlic cloves, crushed

4 cup canned chopped tomatoes

1 tbsp tomato paste

1 fresh bay leaf

3½ cups vegetable bouillon

14 oz/400 g can garbanzo beans
  (chickpeas), drained and rinsed

8 oz/225 g spinach

TO SERVE

freshly-grated Parmesan cheese

sun-dried tomato bread

1 Heat the oil in a large pan, then add the leeks and zucchini and cook them briskly for 5 minutes, stirring constantly.

2 Add the garlic, tomatoes, tomato paste, bay leaf, vegetable bouillon, and garbanzo beans.

3 Bring the soup to a boil and simmer for 5 minutes.

4 Shred the spinach finely, add to the soup, and cook for 2 minutes. Season to taste.

5 Discard the bay leaf. Serve the soup immediately with freshly grated Parmesan cheese and warm sun-dried tomato bread.

COOK'S TIP
Garbanzo beans (chickpeas) are used extensively in North African cuisine and are also found in Spanish, Middle Eastern, and Indian cooking. They have a nutty flavor with a firm texture and are excellent canned.

Lentil & Pasta Soup

Packed with the flavor of garlic, this soup is a filling supper dish when it is served with crusty bread and a crisp salad.

NUTRITIONAL INFORMATION

Calories	390	Sugars	........12g
Protein	........20g	Fat	...........5g
Carbohydrate	....71g	Saturates	......1g

 10 mins   55 mins

SERVES 4

I N G R E D I E N T S

1 tbsp olive oil

1 medium onion, chopped

4 garlic cloves, finely chopped

1½ cups carrot, sliced

1 stick celery, sliced

1½ cups red lentils

2½ cups vegetable bouillon

3 cups boiling water

1½ cups pasta shapes

⅔ cups low-fat unsweetened
   yogurt, plus extra to serve

salt and pepper

2 tbsp fresh parsley, chopped, to garnish

COOK'S TIP

Avoid boiling the soup once
the yogurt has been added.
Otherwise it will separate and
become watery, spoiling the
appearance of the soup.

1 Heat the olive oil in a large pan and sauté the prepared onion, garlic, carrot, and celery, stirring gently, for about 5 minutes or until the vegetables begin to soften.

2 Add the lentils, bouillon, and boiling water. Season well, stir, and bring back to a boil. Simmer, uncovered, for 15 minutes until the lentils are completely tender. Let cool for 10 minutes.

3 Meanwhile, bring another pan of water to a boil and cook the pasta according to the instructions on the package. Drain well and set aside.

4 Place the soup in a blender and process until smooth. Return to a pan and add the pasta. Bring back to a simmer and heat for 2–3 minutes until piping hot. Remove from the heat and stir in the unsweetened yogurt. Adjust the seasoning if necessary.

5 Serve sprinkled with freshly ground black pepper and chopped parsley and with extra yogurt if wished.

Sweet Potato & Apple Soup

This soup makes a marvelous late-fall or winter appetizer. It has a delicious texture and cheerful golden color.

NUTRITIONAL INFORMATION

Calories 57   Sugars 3.8g
Protein . . . . .0.7g   Fat 2.9g
Carbohydrate . . .7.4g   Saturates 1.8g

 10 mins   45 mins

SERVES 6

INGREDIENTS

1 tbsp butter

3 leeks, thinly sliced

1 large carrot, thinly sliced

1¼ lbs/560 g sweet potatoes, peeled and cubed

2 large tart eating apples, peeled and cubed

5 cups water

freshly grated nutmeg

1 cup apple juice

1 cup whipping or light cream

salt and pepper

snipped fresh chives or cilantro, to garnish

1 Melt the butter in a large pan over medium-low heat. Add the leeks, then cover and cook for 6–8 minutes, or until soft, stirring frequently.

2 Add the carrot, sweet potatoes, apples, and water to the pan and season lightly with salt, pepper, and nutmeg. Bring to a boil, then reduce the heat and simmer, covered, for about 20 minutes, stirring occasionally, until the vegetables are very tender.

3 Let the soup cool slightly, then transfer to a blender or food processor and purée until smooth, working in batches if necessary. (If using a food processor, strain off the cooking liquid and reserve. Purée the soup solids with enough cooking liquid to moisten them, then combine with the remaining liquid.)

4 Return the puréed soup to the pan and stir in the apple juice. Place over low heat and simmer for about 10 minutes until heated through.

5 Stir in the cream and continue simmering for about 5 minutes, stirring frequently, until heated through. Taste and adjust the seasoning, adding more salt, pepper, and nutmeg, if necessary. Ladle the soup into warm bowls, then garnish with chives or cilantro and serve.

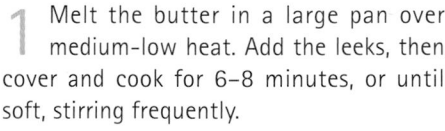

Potato & Garbanzo Soup

This spicy and substantial soup uses ingredients you are likely to have to hand and makes a delicious meal-in-a-bowl.

NUTRITIONAL INFORMATION

Calories ....40 Sugars 1.6g
Protein ....1.8g Fat 1g
Carbohydrate ...6.5g Saturates 0.1g

5 mins   50 mins

SERVES 4

I N G R E D I E N T S

1 tbsp olive oil

1 large onion, finely chopped

2–3 garlic cloves, finely chopped or crushed

1 carrot, quartered and thinly sliced

3 medium potatoes, diced

¼ tsp ground turmeric

¼ tsp garam masala

¼ tsp mild curry powder

14 oz canned chopped tomatoes

3¾ cups water

¼ tsp chili paste or to taste

14 oz/400 g canned garbanzo beans (chickpeas), rinsed and drained

¾ cup fresh or frozen peas

salt and pepper

chopped fresh cilantro, to garnish

3 Add the tomatoes, water, and chili paste with a pinch of salt. Reduce the heat, cover, and simmer for 30 minutes, stirring occasionally.

4 Add the garbanzo beans and peas to the pan, then simmer for a further 15 minutes or until all the vegetables are tender.

5 Taste the soup and adjust the seasoning, if necessary, adding a little more chili if desired. Ladle into warm soup bowls and sprinkle with cilantro.

1 Heat the olive oil in a large pan over medium heat. Add the onion and garlic and cook for 3–4 minutes, stirring occasionally, until the onion is beginning to soften.

2 Add the carrot, potatoes, turmeric, garam masala, and curry powder and continue cooking for 1–2 minutes.

Minestrone

This version of the classic Italian soup has chunks of colorful pumpkin as well as all the traditional ingredients.

NUTRITIONAL INFORMATION

Calories 143   Sugars 6g
Protein ....7g   Fat 2g
Carbohydrate ...25g   Saturates 0.5g

30 mins   1¼ hrs

SERVES 6–8

INGREDIENTS

1 tbsp olive oil

1 onion, finely chopped

1 leek, halved lengthwise and thinly sliced

2 garlic cloves, finely chopped

14 oz can chopped tomatoes in juice

1 carrot, finely diced

1 small turnip, finely diced

1 small potato, finely diced

1 cup peeled celery root, finely diced

½ lb peeled pumpkin or winter squash flesh, finely diced

3 cups water

4 cups vegetable bouillon

14 oz can cannellini or borlotti beans, drained and rinsed

¼ lb leafy cabbage, such as cavolo nero

¾ cup small pasta shapes or broken spaghetti

salt and pepper

freshly grated Parmesan cheese, to serve

1 Heat the olive oil in a large pan over medium heat. Add the onion, leek, and garlic to the pan and cook for 3–4 minutes, stirring occasionally, until slightly softened.

2 Add the tomatoes, carrot, turnip, potato, celery root, pumpkin, water, and bouillon. Bring the soup to a boil, stirring occasionally.

3 Stir in the beans and cabbage and season lightly with salt and pepper.

4 Reduce the heat and simmer, partially covered, for about 50 minutes or until all the vegetables are tender.

5 Toward the end of the cooking time, bring salted water to a boil in a pan. Add the pasta and cook until it is just tender. Drain and add to the soup.

6 Taste the soup and adjust the seasoning if necessary. Ladle into warm bowls and serve with freshly grated Parmesan cheese to sprinkle on top.

Pear & Watercress Soup

This unusual combination of ingredients makes a creamy and sophisticated soup, which may be served hot or chilled.

NUTRITIONAL INFORMATION

Calories 136	Sugars 11g
Protein 1g	Fat 10g
Carbohydrate 11g	Saturates 6g

15 mins, plus chilling (optional) 20 mins

SERVES 6

INGREDIENTS

1 bunch of watercress

4 pears, cored and sliced

3½ cups vegetable bouillon

juice of ½ lemon

½ cup heavy cream

salt and ground black pepper

CROUTONS (OPTIONAL)

2-3 slices day-old bread

2 tbsp olive oil

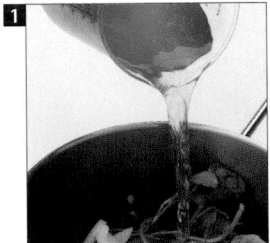
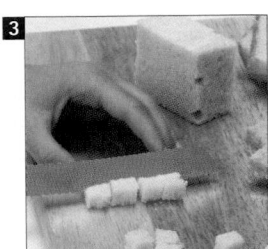

1 Core the pears and slice them lengthways. Set aside about one-third of the watercress leaves. Place the remaining leaves with the stalks in a heavy pan and add the pears and bouillon. Bring to a boil, lower the heat, and simmer for 15 minutes.

2 Remove the pan from the heat, let cool slightly, then add the reserved watercress leaves. Pour into a blender or food processor and process until smooth. Pour the soup through a fine-mesh strainer into a bowl, stir in the lemon juice, and season with salt and pepper to taste.

3 To make the croûtons, cut the bread cut into ¼ inch/5 mm squares. Heat the olive oil in a heavy skillet and add the bread cubes. Cook, tossing and stirring constantly until evenly colored. Drain on paper towels.

4 If serving hot, stir in the cream and return the soup to the clean pan. Heat gently until warmed through, then serve immediately, garnished with the croûtons. If serving cold, let the soup cool before you stir in the cream, then cover and chill in the refrigerator.

Gardener's Broth

This hearty soup uses a variety of green vegetables with a flavoring of ground coriander. A finishing touch of thinly sliced leeks adds texture.

NUTRITIONAL INFORMATION

Calories 169   Sugars 5g
Protein ....4g   Fat 13g
Carbohydrate ....8g   Saturates 5g

 10 mins   45 mins

SERVES 6

INGREDIENTS

3 tbsp butter

1 onion, chopped

1–2 garlic cloves, crushed

1 large leek

½ lb/225 g Brussels sprouts

¾ cup green beans

5 cups vegetable bouillon

1 cup frozen peas

1 tbsp lemon juice

½ tsp ground coriander

4 tbsp heavy cream

salt and pepper

MELBA TOAST

4–6 slices white bread

1 Melt the butter in a pan. Add the onion and garlic and cook over low heat, stirring occasionally, until they begin to soften, but not color.

2 Slice the white part of the leek very thinly and reserve; slice the remaining leek. Slice the Brussels sprouts and thinly slice the beans.

3 Add the green part of the leeks, the Brussels sprouts, and the beans to the pan. Add the bouillon and bring to a boil. Simmer for 10 minutes.

4 Add the frozen peas, seasoning, lemon juice, and coriander and continue to simmer for 10–15 minutes, until the vegetables are tender.

5 Cool the soup a little, then press through a strainer or process in a food processor or blender until smooth. Pour into a clean pan.

6 Add the reserved slices of leek to the soup, bring back to a boil, and simmer for about 5 minutes, until the leek is tender. Adjust the seasoning, stir in the cream, and reheat gently.

7 To make the melba toast, toast the bread on both sides under a preheated broiler. Cut horizontally through the slices, then toast the uncooked sides until they curl up. Serve the melba toast immediately with the soup.

Tarragon Pea Soup

This soup is simple and quick to make using frozen peas and a bouillon cube, ingredients you are likely to have to hand.

NUTRITIONAL INFORMATION

Calories 160   Sugars 7g
Protein . . . . .9g   Fat 4g
Carbohydrate . . .23g   Saturates 2g

 10 mins   55 mins

SERVES 4

INGREDIENTS

2 tsp butter

1 onion, finely chopped

2 leeks, finely chopped

1½ tbsp white rice

4½ cups frozen peas

4 cups water

1 vegetable bouillon cube

½ tsp dried tarragon

salt and pepper

chopped hard-cooked egg or croûtons
(see page 32), to garnish

1 Melt the butter in a large pan over medium-low heat. Add the onion, leeks, and rice. Cover and cook, stirring occasionally, for about 10 minutes until the vegetables are softened.

2 Add the peas, water, bouillon cube, and tarragon and bring just to a boil. Season with a little pepper. Cover and simmer gently, stirring occasionally, for about 35 minutes until the vegetables are very tender.

3 Let the soup cool slightly, then transfer to a blender or food processor, and process to a smooth purée, in batches if necessary. (If using a food processor, strain off the cooking liquid and reserve. Purée the soup solids with enough cooking liquid to moisten them, then combine with the remaining liquid.)

4 Return the soup to the pan. Taste and adjust the seasoning. Gently reheat the soup over low heat for about 10 minutes until hot.

5 Ladle the soup into warm bowls and garnish with the chopped hard-cooked egg or croûtons.

COOK'S TIP

The rice gives the soup a little extra body, but a small amount of raw or cooked potato would do the same job.

Roasted Vegetable Soup

Mediterranean vegetables, roasted in olive oil and flavored with thyme, are the basis for this delicious soup.

NUTRITIONAL INFORMATION

Calories 163   Sugars 13g
Protein . . . . .5g   Fat 10g
Carbohydrate . . .15g   Saturates 3g

1 hr 10 mins   15 mins

SERVES 6

INGREDIENTS

2–3 tbsp olive oil

1½ lb/675 g ripe tomatoes, skinned, cored, and halved

3 large yellow bell peppers, halved, cored, and seeded

3 zucchini, halved lengthwise

1 small eggplant, halved lengthwise

4 garlic cloves, halved

2 onions, cut into eighths

pinch of dried thyme

4 cups vegetable bouillon

½ cup light cream

salt and pepper

shredded basil leaves, to garnish

1 Brush a large shallow baking dish with olive oil. Laying them cut-side down, arrange the tomatoes, bell peppers, zucchini, and eggplant in one layer (use two dishes, if necessary). Tuck the garlic cloves and onion pieces into the gaps and drizzle the vegetables with olive oil. Season lightly with salt and pepper and sprinkle with the thyme.

2 Place in a preheated oven at 375°F/ 190°C and bake the vegetables, uncovered, for 30–35 minutes, or until they are soft and browned around the edges. Let cool, then scrape out the eggplant flesh and remove the skin from the bell peppers.

3 Working in batches, put the eggplant and bell pepper flesh, together with the zucchini, into a food processor and chop to the consistency of salsa or pickle; do not purée. Alternatively, place in a bowl and chop together with a knife.

4 Combine the bouillon and chopped vegetable mixture in a pan and simmer over medium heat for about 20–30 minutes until all the vegetables are tender and the flavors have completely blended.

5 Stir the cream into the soup and simmer over low heat for about 5 minutes, stirring occasionally, until hot. Taste and adjust the seasoning, if necessary. Ladle the soup into warm bowls, garnish with basil and serve.

Italian Mixed Bean Soup

This thick, satisfying blend of beans and diced vegetables, based on an Italian favorite, makes an ideal simple supper.

NUTRITIONAL INFORMATION

Calories	192	Sugars	........10g
Protein	........10g	Fat	...........5g
Carbohydrate	...23g	Saturates	.......1g

 5 mins   25 mins

SERVES 4

I N G R E D I E N T S

1 medium onion, chopped

1 garlic clove, finely chopped

2 celery stalks, sliced

1 large carrot, diced

14 oz canned chopped tomatoes

⅔ cup Italian red wine

5 cups vegetable bouillon

1 tsp dried oregano

15 oz canned mixed beans and legumes

2 medium zucchini, diced

1 tbsp tomato paste

salt and pepper

TO SERVE

pesto sauce

crusty bread

COOK'S TIP
Use a jar of good quality pesto sauce from the food store as the garnish for this soup.

1 Place the prepared onion, garlic, celery, and carrot in a large pan. Stir in the tomatoes, red wine, vegetable bouillon, and oregano.

2 Bring the vegetable mixture to a boil, cover, and simmer for 15 minutes.

3 Stir the beans and zucchini into the mixture and continue to cook, uncovered, for a further 5 minutes.

4 Add the tomato paste to the mixture and season well with salt and pepper to taste.

5 Heat through, stirring occasionally, for a further 2–3 minutes, but do not let the mixture boil again.

6 Ladle the soup into warm bowls and garnish each portion with a spoonful of pesto. Serve with warm, crusty bread.

Orange & Artichoke Soup

Jerusalem artichokes have a delicious nutty flavor which combines well with the freshness of orange.

NUTRITIONAL INFORMATION

Calories	211	Sugars	. . . . .17g
Protein	. . . . .7g	Fat	. . . . .8g
Carbohydrate	. . .29g	Saturates	. . . . . . .4g

10 mins   30 mins

SERVES 4

INGREDIENTS

1 ½ lb/675 g Jerusalem artichokes

5 tbsp orange juice

2 tbsp butter

1 leek, chopped

1 garlic clove, crushed

1¼ cups vegetable bouillon

⅔ cup milk

2 tbsp chopped cilantro

⅔ cup unsweetened yogurt

grated orange rind, to garnish

1 Rinse the Jerusalem artichokes and place them in a large pan with 2 tablespoons of the orange juice and enough water to cover. Bring to a boil, reduce the heat, and cook for 20 minutes, or until the artichokes are tender.

2 Drain the artichokes, reserving 1¾ cups of the cooking liquid. Let the artichokes cool, then peel and place in a large bowl. Mash the flesh with a potato masher.

3 Melt the butter in a large pan. Add the leek and garlic and cook over low heat, stirring frequently, for 2–3 minutes, until the leek is soft.

4 Stir in the mashed artichoke, bouillon, milk, remaining orange juice, and reserved cooking water. Bring to a boil, then simmer for 2–3 minutes.

5 Remove a few pieces of the leek with a slotted spoon and reserve. Process the remainder of the mixture in a food processor for 1 minute until smooth. Alternatively, press through a strainer with the back of a spoon.

6 Return the soup to a clean pan and stir in the reserved leeks, cilantro, and yogurt and heat through. Transfer to individual soup bowls, garnish with orange rind and serve.

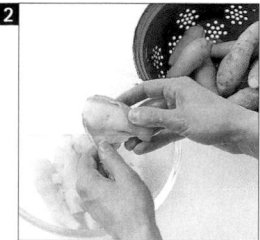

Jerusalem Artichoke Soup

Jerusalem artichokes are curious to look at but make a very tasty and satisfying winter soup.

NUTRITIONAL INFORMATION

Calories ....285 Sugars 5g
Protein ....5g Fat 24g
Carbohydrate ...16g Saturates 9g

 10 mins   30 mins

SERVES 6

I N G R E D I E N T S

1 lb/450 g Jerusalem artichokes

2 tsp butter

1 onion, finely chopped

½ cup peeled rutabaga, cubed

1 strip pared lemon zest

3 cups vegetable bouillon

3 tbsp heavy cream

1 tbsp fresh lemon juice, or to taste

4 tbsp lightly toasted pine nuts

1 Peel the Jerusalem artichokes and cut large ones into pieces. Drop the artichokes into a bowl of cold water to prevent discoloration.

2 Melt the butter in a large pan over medium heat. Add the onion and cook for about 3 minutes, stirring frequently, until just soft.

3 Drain the Jerusalem artichokes and add them to the pan with the rutabaga and lemon zest. Pour in the bouillon, season with a little salt and pepper, and stir to combine. Bring just to a boil, reduce the heat, and simmer gently for about 20 minutes until the vegetables are tender.

4 Let the soup cool slightly, then transfer to a blender or food processor and purée until smooth. (If using a food processor, strain off the cooking liquid and reserve. Purée the soup solids with just enough cooking liquid to moisten them, then combine with the remaining liquid.)

5 Return the soup to the pan, stir in the cream, and simmer for about 5 minutes until reheated. Add the lemon juice. Taste and adjust the seasoning, adding more lemon juice if wished. Ladle the soup into warm bowls and very gently place the pine nuts on top, dividing them evenly. Serve at once.

Bean Soup

Beans feature widely in Mexican cooking, and here pinto beans are used to give an interesting texture. Pinto beans require soaking overnight.

NUTRITIONAL INFORMATION

Calories 188   Sugars 9g
Protein ....13g   Fat 1g
Carbohydrate ...33g   Saturates 0.3g

 20 mins   3 hrs

SERVES 4

I N G R E D I E N T S

6 oz/175 g pinto beans

5 cups water

1½–2 cups carrots, finely chopped

1 large onion, finely chopped

2–3 garlic cloves, crushed

½–1 chili, seeded and finely chopped

4 cups vegetable bouillon

2 tomatoes, peeled and finely chopped

2 celery stalks, very thinly sliced

salt and pepper

1 tbsp chopped cilantro (optional)

C R O U T O N S

3 slices white bread, crusts removed

oil, for deep-frying

1–2 garlic cloves, crushed

1 Soak the beans overnight in cold water; drain, and place in a pan with the water. Bring to a boil and boil vigorously for 10 minutes. Lower the heat, cover, and simmer for 2 hours, or until the beans are tender.

2 Add the carrots, onion, garlic, chili, and bouillon and bring back to a boil. Cover and simmer for a further 30 minutes, until very tender.

3 Remove half the beans and vegetables with the cooking juices and press through a strainer or process in a food processor or blender until smooth.

4 Return the bean purée to the pan and add the tomatoes and celery. Simmer for 10–15 minutes, or until the celery is just tender, adding a little more bouillon or water if necessary.

5 Meanwhile, prepare the croûtons. Dice the bread. Heat the oil with the garlic in a small skillet and fry the croûtons until golden brown. Drain on paper towels.

6 Season the soup and stir in the chopped cilantro, if using. Transfer to a warm tureen and serve immediately with the croûtons.

VARIATION

Pinto beans are widely available, but if you cannot find them or you wish to vary the recipe, you can use cannellini beans or black-eyed peas as an alternative.

Split Pea & Parsnip Soup

This soup is surprisingly delicate. The yellow peas give it an appealing light color, while the parsnips add an aromatic flavor.

NUTRITIONAL INFORMATION

Calories	...270	Sugars	...5g
Protein	...16g	Fat	...7g
Carbohydrate	...39g	Saturates	...1g

  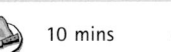

10 mins   1 hr

SERVES 4

I N G R E D I E N T S

generous 1 cup split yellow peas

1 tbsp olive oil

1 onion, finely chopped

1 small leek, finely chopped

3 garlic cloves, finely chopped

2 parsnips, sliced (about 8 oz/225 g)

8 cups water

10 fresh sage leaves or ¼ tsp dried sage

pinch of dried thyme

¼ tsp ground coriander

1 bay leaf

salt and pepper

freshly grated nutmeg

chopped fresh cilantro leaves or parsley, to garnish

1 Rinse the peas well under cold running water. Put in a pan and cover generously with water. Bring to a boil and boil for 3 minutes, skimming off the foam from the surface. Drain the peas.

2 Heat the oil in a large pan over medium heat. Add the onion and leek and cook, stirring occasionally, for about 3 minutes until just soft. Add the garlic and parsnips and continue cooking, stirring occasionally, for 2 minutes.

3 Add the peas, water, sage, thyme, coriander, and bay leaf. Bring almost to a boil, reduce the heat, cover, and simmer gently for about 40 minutes until the vegetables are very soft. Remove the bay leaf.

4 Remove the pan from the heat and let cool slightly, then transfer to a blender or food processor, and process to a smooth purée, in batches if necessary. (If using a food processor, strain off the cooking liquid and reserve. Purée the soup solids with enough cooking liquid to moisten them, then combine with the remaining liquid.)

5 Return the soup to the pan and thin with a little more water, if wished. Season generously with salt, pepper, and nutmeg. Place over low heat and simmer until reheated. Ladle into warmed soup plates and garnish with fresh cilantro leaves or parsley.

Bean & Pasta Soup

A dish with proud Mediterranean origins, this soup is a winter warmer.
Serve with warm, crusty bread and, if you like, a slice of cheese.

NUTRITIONAL INFORMATION

Calories	463	Sugars	.........5g
Protein	........13g	Fat	..........33g
Carbohydrate	...30g	Saturates	.......7g

 5–10 mins   1¼ hrs

SERVES 4

INGREDIENTS

generous 1 cup dried navy beans, soaked,
  drained and rinsed

4 tbsp olive oil

2 large onions, sliced

3 garlic cloves, chopped

2 cups canned chopped tomatoes

1 tsp dried oregano

1 tsp tomato paste

3½ cups water

generous 1 cup small pasta shapes, such
  as fusilli or conchigliette

4 ½ oz/125 g sun-dried tomatoes, drained
  and sliced thinly

1 tbsp chopped cilantro or flat-leaf parsley

2 tbsp freshly grated Parmesan

salt and pepper

1 Put the soaked beans into a large pan, cover with cold water, and bring them to a boil. Boil rapidly for 15 minutes to remove any harmful toxins. Drain the beans in a strainer.

2 Heat the oil in a pan over medium heat and cook the onions until they are just beginning to change color. Stir in the garlic and cook for 1 further minute. Stir in the chopped tomatoes, oregano, and the tomato paste and pour on the water. Add the drained beans, bring to a boil, and cover the pan. Simmer for about 45 minutes or until the beans are almost tender.

3 Add the pasta, season the soup with salt and pepper to taste, and stir in the sun-dried tomatoes. Return the soup to a boil, partly cover the pan, and continue cooking for 10 minutes, or until the pasta is nearly tender.

4 Stir in the chopped cilantro or parsley. Taste the soup and adjust the seasoning if necessary. Transfer to a warmed soup tureen to serve. Sprinkle with the cheese and serve hot.

Tomato & Pasta Soup

Plum tomatoes are ideal for making soups and sauces as they have denser, less watery flesh than rounder varieties.

NUTRITIONAL INFORMATION

Calories	503	Sugars	........16g
Protein	.........9g	Fat	..........28g
Carbohydrate	...59g	Saturates	......17g

 5 mins 50–55 mins

SERVES 4

INGREDIENTS

4 tbsp sweet butter

1 large onion, chopped

2½ cups vegetable bouillon

2 lb/900 g Italian plum tomatoes, skinned and roughly chopped

pinch of baking soda

3 cups dried fusilli

1 tbsp superfine sugar

150 ml/ ¼ pint heavy cream

salt and pepper

fresh basil leaves, to garnish

VARIATION

To make orange and tomato soup, simply use half the quantity of vegetable bouillon, topped up with the same amount of fresh orange juice, and garnish the soup with orange rind.

1 Melt the butter in a large pan, add the chopped onion, and cook for 3 minutes, stirring. Add 1½ cups of the vegetable bouillon to the pan, with the chopped tomatoes and baking soda. Bring the soup to a boil and simmer for 20 minutes.

2 Remove the pan from the heat and let the soup cool a little. Purée the soup in a blender or food processor and then pour it through a fine strainer back into the pan.

3 Add the remaining vegetable bouillon and the fusilli to the pan, and season to taste with salt and pepper.

4 Add the sugar to the pan, bring to a boil, then lower the heat and simmer for about 15 minutes.

5 Pour the soup into a warm tureen or individual warmed bowls, swirl the heavy cream around the surface of the soup, and garnish with fresh basil leaves. Serve immediately.

Yogurt & Spinach Soup

Whole young spinach leaves add vibrant color to this unusual soup.
Serve with hot, crusty bread for a nutritious light meal.

NUTRITIONAL INFORMATION

Calories	227	Sugars	........13g
Protein	........14g	Fat	...........7g
Carbohydrate	...29g	Saturates	......2g

 15 mins   30 mins

SERVES 4

I N G R E D I E N T S

2½ cups vegetable bouillon

4 tbsp long grain rice, rinsed and drained

4 tbsp water

1 tbsp cornstarch

2½ cups low-fat unsweetened yogurt

3 egg yolks, lightly beaten

juice of 1 lemon

12 oz/350 g young spinach leaves, washed
   and drained

salt and pepper

1 Pour the bouillon into a large pan, season, and bring to a boil. Add the rice and simmer for 10 minutes until barely cooked. Remove from the heat.

2 Combine the water and cornstarch to a smooth paste. Pour the yogurt into a second pan and stir in the cornstarch mixture. Bring the yogurt to a boil over low heat, stirring with a wooden spoon in one direction only. This will stabilize the yogurt and prevent it from separating or curdling on contact with the hot bouillon. When the yogurt has reached boiling point, stand the pan on a heat diffuser and simmer gently for 10 minutes. Remove the pan from the heat and set the mixture aside to cool slightly before stirring in the beaten egg yolks.

3 Pour the yogurt mixture into the bouillon, stir in the lemon juice, and stir to blend thoroughly. Keep the soup warm, but do not let it boil.

4 Blanch the washed and drained spinach leaves in a large pan of boiling, salted water for 2-3 minutes until they begin to soften, but have not wilted. Tip the spinach into a strainer, drain well, and stir it into the soup. Warm through. Taste the soup and adjust the seasoning if necessary.

5 Serve immediately in shallow soup plates, with hot, fresh, crusty bread.

Spanish Tomato Soup

This Mediterranean tomato soup is thickened with bread, as is traditional in some parts of Spain, and served with garlic bread.

NUTRITIONAL INFORMATION

Calories	297	Sugars	.........7g
Protein	.........8g	Fat	..........13g
Carbohydrate	...39g	Saturates	.......2g

 10 mins   20 mins

SERVES 4

INGREDIENTS

4 tbsp olive oil

1 onion, chopped

3 garlic cloves, crushed

1 green bell pepper, seeded and chopped

½ tsp chili powder

1 lb/450 g tomatoes, chopped

½ lb/225 g French or Italian bread, cubed

4 cups vegetable bouillon

GARLIC BREAD

4 slices ciabatta or French bread

4 tbsp olive oil

2 garlic cloves, crushed

¼ cups grated Cheddar cheese

chili powder, to garnish

1 Heat the olive oil in a large skillet. Add the onion, garlic, and bell pepper and sauté over low heat, stirring frequently, for 2–3 minutes, or until the onion is soft.

2 Add the chili powder and tomatoes and cook over medium heat until the mixture has thickened.

3 Stir in the bread cubes and bouillon and cook for 10–15 minutes, until the soup is thick and fairly smooth.

4 Meanwhile, prepare the garlic bread. Toast the bread slices under a medium broiler. Drizzle the oil over the top of the bread, rub with the garlic, sprinkle with the grated cheese, and return to the grill for a further 2–3 minutes, until the cheese is bubbling and melting. Sprinkle the bread with a little chili powder.

5 When the garlic bread is ready, ladle the soup into warmed individual soup bowls, and serve immediately with generous chunks of the bread.

VARIATION
Replace the green bell pepper with red or orange bell pepper, if you prefer.

Tomato & Bell Pepper Soup

Sweet red bell peppers and tangy tomatoes are blended together in a smooth vegetable soup that makes a perfect appetizer or light lunch.

NUTRITIONAL INFORMATION

Calories	52	Sugars	. . . . .9g
Protein	. . . . .3g	Fat	. . . . .0.4g
Carbohydrate	. . .10g	Saturates	. . . . . .0g

 15 mins   35 mins

SERVES 4

INGREDIENTS

2 large red bell peppers

1 large onion, chopped

2 stalks celery, trimmed and chopped

1 garlic clove, crushed

2½ cups vegetable bouillon

2 bay leaves

4 cups canned plum tomatoes

salt and pepper

2 scallions, finely shredded, to garnish

crusty bread, to serve

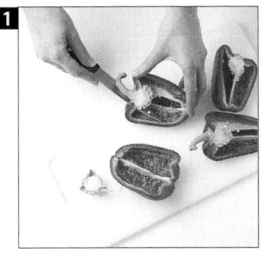 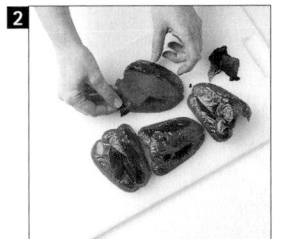 

1 Preheat the broiler to hot. Halve and seed the peppers, arrange them on the broiler rack, and cook, turning occasionally, for 8–10 minutes until soft and charred.

2 Let the bell peppers cool slightly, then carefully peel off the charred skin. Reserving a small piece for the garnish, chop the bell pepper flesh and place it in a large pan.

3 Mix in the onion, celery, and garlic. Add the bouillon and the bay leaves. Bring to a boil, cover, and simmer for 15 minutes. Remove from the heat.

4 Stir in the tomatoes and transfer to a blender. Process for a few seconds until the mixture is smooth, then return it to the pan.

5 Season the soup with salt and pepper to taste and heat for 3–4 minutes until piping hot. Ladle into warm bowls and garnish with the reserved bell pepper, cut into strips, and the shredded scallion. Serve with crusty bread.

COOK'S TIP

If you prefer a coarser, more robust soup, lightly mash the tomatoes with a wooden spoon and omit the blending process in step 4.

Spinach & Bean Curd Soup

This is a very colorful and delicious soup. If spinach is not in season, watercress or lettuce can be used instead.

NUTRITIONAL INFORMATION

Calories ....33 Sugar 1g
Protein ....4g Fat 2g
Carbohydrate ....1g Saturates 0.2g

🍲 15 mins   🕐 10 mins

SERVES 4

INGREDIENTS

1 block firm bean curd

4½ oz/125 g spinach leaves without stems

3 cups Vegetarian Stock (see page 8) or water

1 tbsp light soy sauce

salt and pepper

1 Using a sharp knife to avoid squashing it, cut the bean curd into small pieces about ¼ inch/5 mm thick.

2 Wash the spinach leaves under cold, running water and drain well.

3 Cut the spinach leaves into small pieces or shreds, discarding any discolored leaves and tough stalks. (If possible, use fresh young spinach leaves, which have not yet developed tough ribs. Otherwise, it is important to cut out all the ribs and stems for this soup.) Set the spinach aside until required.

4 In a preheated wok or large skillet, bring the Chinese bouillon or water to a rolling boil.

5 Add the bean curd cubes and light soy sauce, bring back to a boil, and simmer gently for about 2 minutes over medium heat.

6 Add the spinach and simmer for 1 more minute, stirring gently. Skim the surface of the soup to make it clear, and season to taste.

7 Transfer the soup into either a warm soup tureen or warmed individual serving bowls. Serve with chopsticks to pick up the spinach and chunks of bean curd, and a broad, shallow spoon for drinking the soup.

COOK'S TIP

Soup is an integral part of a Chinese meal; it is usually presented in a large bowl placed in the center of the table, and consumed as the meal progresses. It serves as a refresher between different dishes and as a beverage throughout the meal.

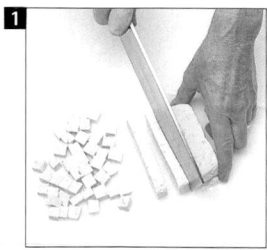

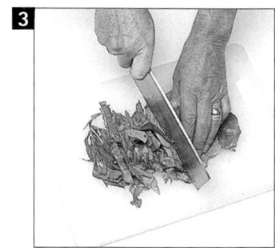

Broccoli & Cheese Soup

This richly flavored soup is popular with adults and children alike and, served with whole-wheat bread, makes a filling lunchtime snack.

NUTRITIONAL INFORMATION

Calories 249   Sugars 4g
Protein ....14g   Fat 15g
Carbohydrate ...16g   Saturates 9g

15 mins   20 mins

SERVES 6

I N G R E D I E N T S

2 tbsp butter

1 onion, chopped

1 lb/450 g potatoes, peeled and grated

2 fresh tarragon leaves

7½ cups vegetable bouillon

1½ lb/675 g broccoli, cut into small florets

6 oz/175 g colby cheese

1 tbsp chopped fresh parsley

salt and ground black pepper

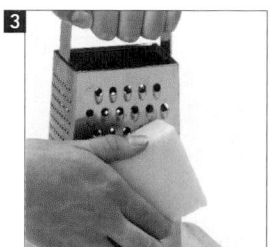

1 Chop the tarragon. Melt the butter in a large, heavy pan. Add the onion and cook, stirring occasionally, for 5 minutes, until soft. Add the grated potatoes and tarragon, season to taste with salt and pepper, and mix well. Pour in just enough of the bouillon to cover and bring to a boil. Lower the heat, cover, and simmer for 10 minutes.

2 Meanwhile, bring the remaining bouillon to a boil in another pan. Add the broccoli and cook for 6-8 minutes, until just tender.

3 Remove both pans from the heat, let cool slightly, then ladle the contents of both pans into a blender or food processor. Process until smooth, then pour the mixture into a clean pan. Grate in the cheese, add the parsley and heat gently to warm through, but do not let the soup boil. Ladle into warmed soup bowls and serve immediately.

Borscht

This is a lighter, easier version of the original Russian beet soup,
said to have been created by Antonin Carême, chef to Czar Alexander I.

NUTRITIONAL INFORMATION

Calories ....169 Sugars 12g
Protein ....3g Fat 12g
Carbohydrate ...13g Saturates 8g

25 mins   1¼ hrs

SERVES 6

INGREDIENTS

4 tbsp butter

1 onion, thinly sliced into rings

¾ lb/350 g raw beet, cut into thin batons

1 carrot, cut into thin batons

3 celery stalks, thinly sliced

2 tomatoes, skinned, seeded, and chopped

6¼ cups vegetable bouillon

1 tbsp white wine vinegar

1 tbsp sugar

fresh dill

1 cup white cabbage, shredded

1 raw beet, grated

salt and ground black pepper

⅔ cup sour cream, to garnish

rye bread, to serve

COOK'S TIP
It is not essential to add extra
beet toward the end of cooking,
but this helps to provide the
spectacular color of the soup
and freshens the flavor.

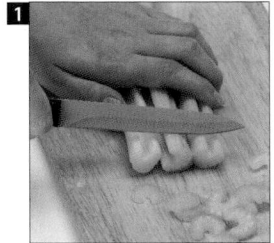

1 Slice the onion into rings and the celery stalks thinly. Melt the butter in a large, heavy pan. Add the onion and cook over low heat, stirring occasionally, for 3–5 minutes, until soft. Add the beet batons, carrot, celery stalks, and chopped tomatoes to the pan and cook, stirring frequently, for 4–5 minutes.

2 Snip two tablespoons worth of dill, add half to the pan with the bouillon, vinegar, and sugar, and season to taste with salt and pepper. Bring to a boil, lower the heat, and simmer for 35–40 minutes, until all the vegetables are tender.

3 Stir in the cabbage, cover, and simmer for 10 minutes. Stir in the grated beet, and cook for 10 minutes more.

4 Ladle the soup into warm bowls, garnish with a spoon of sour cream and the remaining dill, and serve immediately with rye bread.

Crécy Soup

The small French towns of Crécy-la-Chapelle and Crécy-en-Ponthieu both claim to be the originators of this classic soup.

NUTRITIONAL INFORMATION

Calories 208	Sugars 5g	
Protein 1g	Fat 18g	
Carbohydrate ...12g	Saturates 12g	

 20 mins   🕐 45 mins

SERVES 4

I N G R E D I E N T S

6 tbsp butter

2 shallots, finely chopped

3 carrots

pinch of sugar

2½ tbsp long grain rice

1 thyme sprig

3 cups vegetable bouillon

TO GARNISH

1 tbsp chopped fresh parsley

croûtons (see page 32)

2 Remove the pan from the heat and let the mixture cool slightly. Remove and discard the thyme sprig and then pour the soup into a blender or a food processor. Process the mixture until it becomes a smooth purée.

3 Return to a clean pan and reheat gently. Season to taste with salt and pepper, and whisk in the remaining butter in small pieces. Ladle into warm soup bowls, garnish with the parsley and croûtons, and serve immediately.

1 Slice the carrots. Melt 4 tbsp of the butter in a large, heavy pan. Add the shallots, carrots, the sugar, and a pinch of salt, cover, and cook over very low heat, stirring occasionally, for 10 minutes. Stir in the rice and thyme and pour in the bouillon. Bring to a boil, then lower the heat and simmer for 30 minutes.

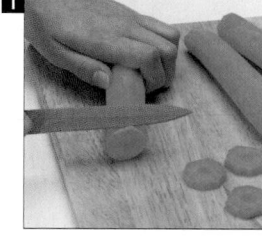

Creamy Tomato Soup

This quick and easy creamy soup has a lovely fresh tomato flavor.
The basil adds a special taste of summer.

NUTRITIONAL INFORMATION

Calories	286	Sugars	.........9g
Protein	.........5g	Fat	..........25g
Carbohydrate	....9g	Saturates	......12g

 10 mins   20 mins

SERVES 4

I N G R E D I E N T S

3 tbsp butter

1½ lb/675 g ripe tomatoes, preferably plum, roughly chopped

salt and pepper

3¾ cups hot vegetable bouillon

⅔ cup milk or light cream

¼ cup ground almonds

1 tsp sugar

2 tbsp shredded basil leaves

VARIATION
Very fine bread crumbs can be used instead of the ground almonds, if you prefer. Toast them in the same way as the almonds and add with the milk or cream in step 6.

1 Melt the butter in a large pan. Add the tomatoes and cook for 5 minutes until the skins start to wrinkle. Season to taste with salt and pepper.

2 Add the bouillon, bring to a boil, cover, and simmer for 10 minutes.

3 Meanwhile, under a preheated broiler, lightly toast the ground almonds until they are golden brown. This will take only 1-2 minutes, so watch them closely.

4 Remove the soup from the heat, place in a food processor, and blend the mixture to form a smooth consistency.

5 Pass the soup through a strainer to remove any tomato skin or pips.

6 Place the soup in the pan and return to the heat. Stir in the milk or cream, ground almonds, and sugar. Warm the soup through and add the shredded basil just before serving.

7 Transfer the creamy tomato soup to warm soup bowls and serve hot.

Broccoli & Potato Soup

This creamy soup has a delightful pale green coloring and rich flavor from the blend of tender broccoli and blue cheese.

NUTRITIONAL INFORMATION

Calories 452   Sugars 4g
Protein . . . . .14g   Fat 35g
Carbohydrate . . .20g   Saturates 19g

5–10 mins   35 mins

SERVES 4

INGREDIENTS

2 tbsp olive oil

2⅔ cups diced potatoes

1 onion, diced

2 cups broccoli florets

1 cup crumbled blue cheese

4½ cups vegetable bouillon

⅔ cup heavy cream

pinch of paprika

salt and pepper

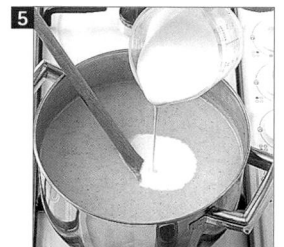

1 Heat the oil in a large pan and add the diced potatoes and onion. Sauté gently for 5 minutes, stirring constantly.

2 Reserve a few broccoli florets for the garnish and add the remaining broccoli to the pan. Add the crumbled blue cheese and bouillon.

3 Bring to a boil, then reduce the heat, cover the pan, and simmer for 25 minutes, until the potatoes are tender.

4 Transfer the soup to a food processor or blender in batches and process until the mixture is a smooth purée.

5 Return the purée to a clean pan and stir in the cream and a pinch of paprika. Season to taste.

6 Blanch the reserved broccoli florets in a little boiling water for approximately 2 minutes, then drain with a slotted spoon.

7 Pour the soup into warmed bowls and garnish with the broccoli florets and a sprinkling of paprika. Serve immediately.

COOK'S TIP

This soup freezes very successfully. Follow the method described here up to step 4, and freeze the soup after it has been puréed. Add the cream and paprika just before serving. Garnish and serve.

Cream Cheese & Herb Soup

Make the most of home-grown herbs to create this wonderfully creamy soup with its marvelous fresh aroma.

NUTRITIONAL INFORMATION

Calories ....275 Sugars 5g
Protein ....7g Fat 22g
Carbohydrate ...14g Saturates 11g

15 mins   35 mins

SERVES 4

I N G R E D I E N T S

2 tbsp butter or margarine

2 onions, chopped

3½ cups vegetable bouillon

3 tbsp coarsely chopped mixed herbs, such as parsley, chives, thyme, basil, and oregano

1 cup full-fat soft cheese

1 tbsp cornstarch

1 tbsp milk

chopped chives, to garnish

1 Melt the butter or margarine in a large, heavy pan. Add the onions and cook over medium heat for 2 minutes, then cover and turn the heat to low. Continue to cook the onions for 5 minutes, then remove the lid.

2 Add the vegetable bouillon and herbs to the pan. Bring to a boil over moderate heat. Lower the heat, cover, and simmer gently for 20 minutes.

3 Remove the pan from the heat. Transfer the soup to a food processor or blender and process for about 15 seconds, until smooth. Alternatively, press it through a strainer with the back of a wooden spoon. Return the soup to the pan.

4 Reserve a little of the cheese for garnish. Spoon the remaining cheese into the soup and whisk until it has melted and is incorporated.

5 Mix the cornstarch with the milk to a paste, then stir the mixture into the soup. Heat, stirring constantly, until thickened and smooth.

6 Pour the soup into warmed individual bowls. Spoon some of the reserved cheese into each bowl and garnish with chives. Serve at once.

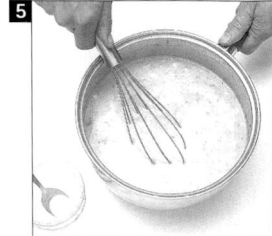

Mushroom Noodle Soup

A light, refreshing clear soup of mushrooms, cucumber, and small pieces of rice noodles, flavored with soy sauce and a touch of garlic.

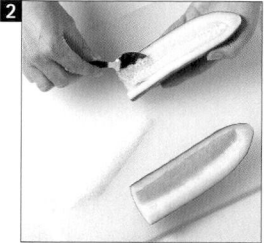

NUTRITIONAL INFORMATION

Calories	84	Sugars	.........1g
Protein	.........1g	Fat	...........8g
Carbohydrate	....3g	Saturates	.......1g

 5 mins   10 mins

SERVES 4

I N G R E D I E N T S

¼ lb/115 g flat or open-cup mushrooms

½ cucumber

2 scallions

1 garlic clove

2 tbsp vegetable oil

1 oz/25 g Chinese rice noodles

¾ tsp salt

1 tbsp soy sauce

1 Wash the mushrooms and pat them dry on kitchen towels. Slice thinly. Do not remove the mushroom peel as this adds more flavor.

2 Cut the cucumber in half lengthwise. Scoop out the seeds, using a teaspoon, and slice the cucumber thinly.

3 Chop the scallions finely and cut the garlic clove into thin strips.

4 Heat the vegetable oil in a large pan or wok.

5 Add the scallions and garlic to the pan or wok and stir-fry for 30 seconds. Add the mushrooms and stir-fry for a further 2–3 minutes.

6 Stir in 2½ cups of water. Break the noodles into short lengths and add to the pan. Bring the soup to a boil, stirring occasionally.

7 Add the cucumber slices, salt, and soy sauce and simmer for 2–3 minutes.

8 Serve the mushroom noodle soup in warmed bowls, distributing the noodles and vegetables evenly.

COOK'S TIP
Scooping the seeds out from the cucumber gives it a prettier effect when sliced, and also helps to reduce any bitterness, but if you prefer, you can leave them in.

Spinach & Mascarpone Soup

Spinach is the basis for this delicious soup, which has creamy mascarpone cheese stirred through it to give it a wonderful texture.

NUTRITIONAL INFORMATION

Calories 402   Sugars 2g
Protein . . . . .11g   Fat 36g
Carbohydrate . . .10g   Saturates 21g

15 mins   30 mins

SERVES 4

I N G R E D I E N T S

4 tbsp butter

1 bunch scallions, trimmed and chopped

2 celery stalks, chopped

¾ lb/350 g spinach or sorrel, or
 3 bunches watercress

3½ cups vegetable bouillon

1 x 8 oz tub mascarpone cheese

1 tbsp olive oil

2 slices thick-cut bread, cut into cubes

½ tsp caraway seeds

salt and pepper

sesame bread sticks, to serve

1 Melt half the butter in a very large pan. Add the scallions and celery, and cook them over medium heat, stirring frequently, for about 5 minutes, until soft.

2 Pack the spinach, sorrel, or watercress into the pan. Add the vegetable bouillon and bring to a boil, then reduce the heat, cover, and simmer for about 15–20 minutes.

3 Transfer the soup to a blender or food processor and process until smooth. Alternatively, rub it through a strainer. Return to the pan.

4 Add the mascarpone to the soup and heat gently, stirring constantly, until smooth and blended. Season to taste with salt and pepper.

5 Heat the remaining butter with the olive oil in a skillet. Add the bread cubes and fry, turning frequently, until golden brown, adding the caraway seeds toward the end of cooking, so that they do not burn.

6 Ladle the soup into warmed bowls. Sprinkle with the croûtons and serve with the sesame bread sticks.

VARIATION

Any leafy vegetable can be used to vary the flavor of this soup. For anyone who grows their own vegetables, it is the perfect recipe for experimenting with a glut of produce. Try young beet leaves or surplus lettuces for a change.

Lentil & Tomato Soup

This fresh-tasting and colorful soup is substantial enough to serve on its own with some crusty fresh bread for a light lunch or supper.

NUTRITIONAL INFORMATION

Calories	158	Sugars	.........6g
Protein	.........9g	Fat	...........4g
Carbohydrate	...24g	Saturates	.......1g

 20 mins   50 mins

SERVES 4

INGREDIENTS

1 tbsp corn or sunflower oil

1 onion, finely chopped

1 garlic glove, crushed

½ tsp ground cumin

½ tsp ground coriander

1 lb/450 g tomatoes, skinned, seeded and chopped

¾ cup red lentils, washed

5 cups vegetable bouillon

salt and ground black pepper

finely chopped fresh cilantro, to garnish

1 Heat the oil in a large pan. Add the onion and cook over low heat, stirring occasionally, for 5 minutes, until softened. Skin the tomatoes. Stir in the garlic, cumin, ground coriander, tomatoes, and lentils and cook, stirring constantly, for 4 minutes more.

2 Pour the bouillon into the pan, bring to a boil, then simmer gently for about 30–40 minutes or until the lentils are tender. Season the soup to taste with salt and pepper.

3 Remove the pan from the heat and let cool slightly, then process the soup in a blender or food processor to a purée. Return to the clean pan and reheat.

4 Serve the soup immediately in warm bowls, garnished with finely chopped fresh cilantro.

COOK'S TIP
Never season lentils with salt until they have finished cooking, or they will become tough.

Lettuce & Arugula Soup

Arugula has a distinctive flavor that blends well with lettuce in this delicious creamy soup. The rice adds body to the soup.

NUTRITIONAL INFORMATION

Calories ....253 Sugars 8g
Protein ....4g Fat 18g
Carbohydrate ...21g Saturates 10g

15 mins   55 mins

SERVES 4–6

I N G R E D I E N T S

1 tbsp butter

1 large sweet onion, halved and sliced

2 leeks, sliced

6¼ cups vegetable bouillon

6 tbsp white rice

2 carrots, thinly sliced

3 garlic cloves

1 bay leaf

2 heads soft round lettuce (about 1 lb/ 450 g), cored and chopped

¾ cup heavy cream

freshly grated nutmeg

3 oz arugula leaves, finely chopped

salt and pepper

1 Heat the butter in a large pan over medium heat and add the onion and leeks. Cover and cook for 3–4 minutes, stirring frequently, until the vegetables begin to soften.

2 Add the bouillon, rice, carrots, garlic, and bay leaf with a large pinch of salt. Bring just to a boil. Reduce the heat, cover, and simmer for 25–30 minutes, or until the rice and vegetables are tender. Remove the bay leaf.

3 Add the lettuce and cook for 10 minutes, until the leaves are soft, stirring occasionally.

4 Let the soup cool slightly, then transfer to a blender or food processor and purée until smooth, working in batches if necessary. (If using a food processor, strain off the cooking liquid and reserve. Purée the soup solids with enough cooking liquid to moisten them, then combine with the remaining liquid.)

5 Return the soup to the pan and place over medium-low heat. Stir in the cream and a grating of nutmeg. Simmer gently for about 5 minutes, stirring occasionally, until the soup is reheated. Add more water or cream if you prefer a thinner soup.

6 Add the arugula and simmer for 2–3 minutes, stirring occasionally, until it is wilted. Adjust the seasoning and ladle the soup into warm bowls.

French Onion Soup

This vegetarian version of the classic French onion soup is flavored with vegetable bouillon instead of the traditional beef bouillon.

NUTRITIONAL INFORMATION

Calories 417   Sugars 10g
Protein . . . . .16g   Fat 19g
Carbohydrate . . .41g   Saturates 9g

15 mins   1 hr 45 mins

SERVES 6

I N G R E D I E N T S

1 tbsp butter

2 tbsp olive oil

2 lb/1 kg large yellow onions, halved and sliced into half-circles

3 large garlic cloves, finely chopped

2 tbsp all-purpose flour

¾ cup dry white wine

8 cups vegetable bouillon

3 tbsp Cognac or brandy

6 slices French bread

1 cup grated Swiss cheese

salt and pepper

1 Melt the butter with the oil in a large, heavy pan over medium heat. Add the onions and cook, covered, for 10–12 minutes until they soften, stirring occasionally. Add the garlic and sprinkle with salt and pepper.

2 Reduce the heat a little and continue cooking, uncovered, for 30–35 minutes, or until the onions turn a deep, golden brown, stirring from time to time until they start to color, then stirring more frequently and scraping the bottom of the pan as they begin to stick.

3 Sprinkle over the flour and stir to blend. Stir in the white wine and bubble for 1 minute. Pour in the bouillon and bring to a boil, scraping the bottom of the pan and stirring to combine well.

4 Reduce the heat to low, add the Cognac or brandy, and simmer gently, stirring occasionally, for 45 minutes.

5 Toast the bread under a preheated hot broiler on one side. Turn over and top with the cheese, dividing it evenly. Broil until the cheese melts.

6 Place a piece of cheese toast in each of the 6 warmed bowls, then ladle the hot soup over. Serve at once.

Exotic Mushroom Soup

This soup has an intense, earthy flavor that brings to mind woodland aromas. It makes a memorable, rich-tasting appetizer.

NUTRITIONAL INFORMATION

Calories 130   Sugars 5g
Protein ....3g   Fat 9g
Carbohydrate ....6g   Saturates 5g

20 mins   1 hr

SERVES 4

INGREDIENTS

1 oz/25 g dried porcini mushrooms

1½ cups boiling water

4½ oz/125 g fresh porcini mushrooms

2 tsp olive oil

1 celery stalk, chopped

1 carrot, chopped

1 onion, chopped

3 garlic cloves, crushed

5 cups vegetable bouillon or water

leaves from 2 fresh thyme sprigs

1 tbsp butter

3 tbsp dry or medium sherry

2–3 tbsp sour cream

salt and pepper

chopped fresh parsley, to garnish

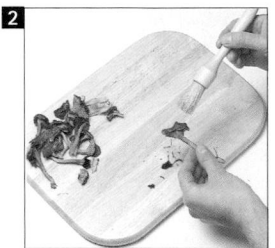  

1 Put the dried mushrooms in a bowl and pour the boiling water over them. Let soak for 10–15 minutes.

2 Brush or wash the fresh mushrooms. Trim and reserve the stems. Slice any large mushroom caps.

3 Heat the oil in a large pan over medium heat. Add the celery, carrot, onion, and mushroom stems. Cook, stirring frequently, for about 8 minutes until the onion begins to color. Stir in the garlic and continue cooking for 1 minute.

4 Add the vegetable bouillon or water and thyme leaves with a pinch of salt. Using a slotted spoon, transfer the soaked dried mushrooms to the pan. Strain the soaking liquid through a cheesecloth-lined strainer into the pan. Bring to a boil, reduce the heat, partially cover, and simmer gently for 30–40 minutes or until the carrots are tender.

5 Remove the pan from the heat and let cool slightly, then transfer the soup solids, with enough of the cooking liquid to moisten, to a blender or food processor, and process to a smooth purée. Return the soup to the pan, combine with the remaining cooking liquid, cover, and simmer gently.

6 Meanwhile, melt the butter in a skillet over medium heat. Add the fresh mushroom caps and season to taste with salt and pepper. Cook, stirring occasionally, for about 8 minutes until they start to color, stirring more frequently as the liquid evaporates. When the skillet becomes dry, add the sherry and cook briefly.

7 Add the mushrooms and sherry to the soup. Taste and adjust the seasoning, if necessary. Ladle into warmed soup bowls, put a spoon of sour cream in each, garnish with parsley, and serve.

Lettuce & Bean Curd Soup

This is a delicate, clear soup of shredded lettuce and small chunks of bean curd with sliced carrot and scallion.

NUTRITIONAL INFORMATION

Calories 113   Sugars 2g
Protein ....5g   Fat 8g
Carbohydrate ....3g   Saturates 1g

 5 mins   15 mins

SERVES 4

I N G R E D I E N T S

7 oz/200 g bean curd

2 tbsp vegetable oil

1 carrot, sliced thinly

½ inch/1 cm piece ginger root, cut into thin shreds

3 scallions, sliced diagonally

5 cups vegetable bouillon

2 tbsp soy sauce

2 tbsp dry sherry

1 tsp sugar

1 small romaine lettuce, shredded

salt and pepper

1 Using a sharp knife, cut the bean curd into small cubes.

2 Heat the vegetable oil in a preheated wok or large pan, then add the bean curd and stir-fry until browned. Remove it with a perforated spoon and drain on paper towels.

3 Add the carrot, ginger root, and scallions to the wok or pan and stir-fry for 2 minutes.

4 Add the vegetable bouillon, soy sauce, sherry, and sugar to the wok or pan. Stir well to mix all the ingredients. Bring to a boil and simmer for 1 minute. Add the romaine lettuce to the wok or pan and stir until it wilts.

5 Return the bean curd to the wok or pan to reheat. Season with salt and pepper to taste and serve the soup immediately in warmed bowls.

COOK'S TIP

For a pretty effect, score grooves along the length of the carrot with a sharp knife before slicing. This will create a flower effect as the carrot is cut into rounds. You could also try slicing the carrot on the diagonal to make longer slices.

Creamy Stilton Soup

Crisp, fresh celery and creamy Stilton cheese are a delicious combination, which works equally well in soup.

NUTRITIONAL INFORMATION

Calories	...381	Sugars	...6g
Protein	...10g	Fat	...35g
Carbohydrate	...7g	Saturates	...21g

 15 mins   40 mins

SERVES 4

INGREDIENTS

2 tbsp butter

1 onion, finely chopped

4 large stalks celery, peeled and finely chopped

1 large carrot, finely chopped

4 cups vegetable bouillon

3–4 thyme sprigs

1 bay leaf

½ cup heavy cream

1¼ cups crumbled Stilton cheese

freshly grated nutmeg

salt and pepper

1 Melt the butter in a large pan over medium-low heat. Add the onion and cook for 3–4 minutes, stirring frequently, until just soft. Add the celery and carrot and continue cooking for 3 minutes. Season lightly with salt and pepper.

2 Add the bouillon, thyme, and bay leaf and bring to a boil. Reduce the heat, cover, and simmer gently for about 25 minutes, stirring occasionally, until the vegetables are very tender.

3 Let the soup cool slightly and remove the thyme and bay leaf. Transfer the soup to a blender or food processor and purée until smooth, working in batches, if necessary. (If using a food processor, strain off the cooking liquid and reserve. Purée the soup solids with enough cooking liquid to moisten them, then combine with the remaining liquid.)

4 Return the puréed soup to the pan and stir in the cream. Simmer over low heat for 5 minutes.

5 Add the Stilton slowly, stirring constantly, until smooth. (Do not let the soup boil.) Taste and adjust the seasoning, adding salt, if needed, plenty of pepper, and nutmeg to taste.

6 Ladle into warm bowls, garnish with celery leaves, and serve.

VARIATION
Substitute grated sharp Cheddar or Swiss cheese for the Stilton.

Fava Bean & Mint Soup

Fresh fava beans are best for this delicious soup, but if they are unavailable, use frozen beans instead.

NUTRITIONAL INFORMATION

Calories	224	Sugars	.........4g
Protein	........12g	Fat	...........6g
Carbohydrate	...31g	Saturates	.......1g

 15 mins   40 mins

SERVES 4

INGREDIENTS

2 tbsp olive oil

1 red onion, chopped

2 garlic cloves, crushed

2⅔ cups diced potatoes

3 cups fava beans, thawed if frozen

3¾ cups vegetable bouillon

2 tbsp freshly chopped mint

mint sprigs and unsweetened yogurt, to garnish

1 Heat the olive oil in a large pan. Add the onion and garlic and sauté for 2–3 minutes, until softened.

2 Add the potatoes and cook, stirring constantly, for 5 minutes.

3 Stir in the beans and the bouillon. Cover and simmer for 30 minutes, or until the beans and potatoes are tender.

4 Remove a few vegetables with a slotted spoon and set aside. Place the remainder of the soup in a food processor or blender and process until smooth.

5 Return the soup to a clean pan and add the reserved vegetables and chopped mint. Stir thoroughly and heat through gently.

6 Transfer the soup to a warm tureen or individual serving bowls. Garnish with swirls of yogurt and sprigs of fresh mint, and serve immediately.

VARIATION
Use fresh cilantro and ½ teaspoon ground cumin as flavorings in the soup, if you prefer.

Green Soup

This fresh-tasting soup with green beans, cucumber, and watercress can be served warm, or chilled on a hot summer day.

NUTRITIONAL INFORMATION

Calories 121	Sugars 2g
Protein 2g	Fat 8g
Carbohydrate . . .10g	Saturates 1g

 5 mins   25 mins

SERVES 4

I N G R E D I E N T S

1 tbsp olive oil

1 onion, chopped

1 garlic clove, chopped

½ lb potato, cut into 1 inch/2.5 cm cubes

3 cups vegetable bouillon

1 small cucumber or ½ large cucumber, cut into chunks

1 bunch watercress

¾ cup green beans, trimmed and halved lengthwise

salt and pepper

1 Heat the oil in a large pan and cook the onion and garlic over medium heat for 3–4 minutes or until soft.

2 Add the cubed potato and cook for a further 2–3 minutes. Stir in the bouillon and bring to a boil. Lower the heat and simmer for 5 minutes.

3 Add the cucumber to the pan and cook for a further 3 minutes or until the potatoes are tender. Test by inserting the tip of a knife into the potato cubes—it should pass through easily.

4 Add the watercress and cook until just wilted. Remove from the heat and let cool slightly, then transfer to a food processor, and process to a smooth purée. Alternatively, before adding the watercress, mash the vegetables with a potato masher and push through a strainer, then chop the watercress finely and stir into the soup.

5 Bring a small pan of water to a boil and steam the beans for 3–4 minutes or until tender. Add the beans to the soup, season to taste with salt and pepper, and warm through. Ladle into warmed soup bowls and serve immediately, or let cool and then chill inthe refrigerator.

Beet & Potato Soup

A deep red soup makes a stunning appetizer—and it's easy in the microwave. A swirl of soured cream gives a very pretty effect.

NUTRITIONAL INFORMATION

Calories	120	Sugars	........11g
Protein	.........4g	Fat	...........2g
Carbohydrate	...22g	Saturates	......1g

20 mins   30 mins

SERVES 6

I N G R E D I E N T S

1 onion, chopped

3 cups diced potatoes

1 small cooking apple, peeled, cored, and grated

3 tbsp water

1 tsp cumin seeds

1 lb/450 g cooked beet, peeled and diced

1 bay leaf

pinch of dried thyme

1 tsp lemon juice

2½ cups hot vegetable bouillon

4 tbsp sour cream

salt and pepper

fresh dill sprigs, to garnish

1 Place the onion, potatoes, apple, and water in a large bowl. Cover and cook on HIGH power for 10 minutes.

2 Stir in the cumin seeds and cook on HIGH power for 1 minute.

3 Stir in the beet, bay leaf, thyme, lemon juice, and bouillon. Cover and cook on HIGH power for 12 minutes, stirring halfway through. Set aside, uncovered, for 5 minutes.

4 Remove and discard the bay leaf. Strain the vegetables and reserve the liquid in a pitcher.

5 Place the vegetables with a little of the reserved liquid in a food processor or blender and process to a smooth and creamy purée. Alternatively, either mash the vegetables with a potato masher or press through a strainer.

6 Pour the vegetable purée into a clean bowl with the reserved liquid and mix well. Season with salt and pepper to taste. Cover and cook on HIGH power for 4–5 minutes until piping hot.

7 Serve the soup in warmed bowls. Swirl 1 tablespoon of sour cream into each serving and garnish with a few sprigs of fresh dill.

Cauliflower & Broccoli Soup

Full of flavor, this creamy cauliflower and broccoli soup is simple to make and absolutely delicious to eat.

NUTRITIONAL INFORMATION

Calories 378	Sugars 14g
Protein 18g	Fat 26g
Carbohydrate ...20g	Saturates 7g

 10 mins   35 mins

SERVES 4

INGREDIENTS

3 tbsp vegetable oil

1 red onion, chopped

2 garlic cloves, crushed

2½ cups cauliflower florets

3 cups broccoli florets

1 tbsp all-purpose flour

2½ cups milk

1¼ cups vegetable bouillon

½ cup Swiss cheese

pinch of paprika

⅔ cup light cream

paprika and Swiss cheese shavings,
  to garnish

1 Heat the vegetable oil in a large, heavy pan. Add the prepared onion, garlic, cauliflower florets, and broccoli florets and sauté over low heat, stirring constantly, for about 3–4 minutes. Sprinkle the flour over the vegetables and cook, stirring constantly, for a further 1 minute.

2 Gradually stir in the milk and vegetable bouillon and bring to a boil, stirring constantly. Reduce the heat and simmer for 20 minutes.

3 Remove about a quarter of the vegetables with a slotted spoon and set aside. Put the remaining soup in a food processor or blender and process for about 30 seconds, until smooth. Alternatively, press the vegetables through a strainer with the back of a wooden spoon. Transfer the soup to a clean pan.

4 Return the reserved vegetable pieces to the soup. Stir in the grated Swiss cheese, paprika, and light cream and heat through over low heat, without boiling, for about 2–3 minutes, or until the cheese starts to melt.

5 Ladle the soup into warmed individual serving bowls, garnish with shavings of Swiss cheese, and dust with the paprika. Serve immediately.

COOK'S TIP

The soup must not start to boil after the cream has been added, otherwise it will curdle. Use unsweetened yogurt instead of the cream if preferred, but again do not allow it to boil.

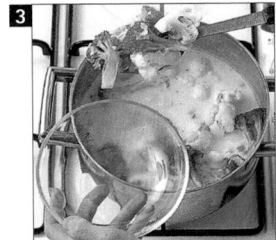

Orange & Pumpkin Soup

This thick, creamy soup has a wonderful, warming, golden color.
It is flavored with orange and thyme.

NUTRITIONAL INFORMATION

Calories 111   Sugars 4g
Protein ....2g   Fat 6g
Carbohydrate ....5g   Saturates 2g

 10 mins   35–40 mins

SERVES 4

INGREDIENTS

2 tbsp olive oil

2 medium onions, chopped

2 cloves garlic, chopped

2 lb/900 g pumpkin, peeled and cut into
    2.5 cm/1 inch chunks

6 cups boiling vegetable bouillon

finely grated zest and juice of 1 orange

3 tbsp fresh thyme, stalks removed

⅔ cup pint milk

salt and pepper

crusty bread, to serve

1 Heat the olive oil in a large pan. Add the onions to the pan and cook for 3–4 minutes or until soft. Add the garlic and pumpkin and cook for a further 2 minutes, stirring well.

2 Add the boiling vegetable bouillon, the orange zest and juice, and 2 tablespoons of the thyme to the pan. Let simmer, covered, for 20 minutes or until the pumpkin is tender.

3 Place the mixture in a food processor and blend until smooth. Alternatively, mash the mixture with a potato masher until smooth. Season to taste.

4 Return the soup to the pan and add the milk. Reheat the soup for about 3–4 minutes or until it is piping hot but not boiling.

5 Sprinkle with the remaining fresh thyme just before serving.

6 Divide the soup among 4 warm soup bowls and serve it with plenty of fresh crusty bread.

COOK'S TIP
Pumpkins are usually large vegetables. This soup freezes well, so make double the quantity and freeze for up to 3 months.

Chinese Vegetable Soup

This tasty vegetable broth would make an unusual first course for a dinner party or a delicious light lunch.

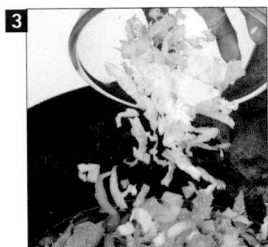

NUTRITIONAL INFORMATION

Calories 117	Sugars 2g	
Protein 6g	Fat 8g	
Carbohydrate 5g	Saturates 1g	

15 mins   10 mins

SERVES 4

INGREDIENTS

2 tbsp groundnut oil

8 oz/225 g marinated bean curd

2 garlic cloves

4 scallions

1 carrot

4 cups vegetable bouillon

1 tbsp Chinese rice wine

2 tbsp light soy sauce

1 tsp sugar

generous 1 cup Napa cabbage

salt and ground black pepper

1 Cut the bean curd into ½ inch/1 cm cubes. Slice the garlic, scallions and carrot thinly and shred the Napa cabbage. Set the vegetables aside.

COOK'S TIP

Always use a sharp knife when cutting bean curd because it is very easily squashed.

2 Heat the groundnut oil in a large wok or heavy skillet. Add the bean curd cubes and stir-fry for 4–5 minutes, until browned. Remove the bean curd from the wok or skillet with a slotted spoon and drain on paper towels.

3 Add the garlic, scallions, and carrot to the wok or skillet and stir-fry for

2 minutes. Pour in the bouillon, Chinese rice wine, and soy sauce and add the sugar and Napa cabbage. Continue to cook over medium heat for 1–2 minutes, until the soup is heated through.

4 Season to taste with salt and pepper, and add the bean curd. Ladle the soup into warm bowls and serve immediately.

Chili & Watercress Soup

This delicious soup is a wonderful blend of colors and flavors. It is very hot, so if you prefer a milder taste, omit the seeds from the chilies.

NUTRITIONAL INFORMATION

Calories 90	Sugars 1g	
Protein 7g	Fat 6g	
Carbohydrate 2g	Saturates 1g	

10 mins   15 mins

SERVES 4

INGREDIENTS

1 tbsp sunflower oil

9 oz/250 g smoked bean curd, sliced

3 oz/90 g shiitake mushrooms, sliced

2 tbsp chopped fresh cilantro

1 large bunch watercress

1 red chili, sliced finely, to garnish

BOUILLON

1 tbsp tamarind pulp

2 dried red chilies, chopped

2 kaffir lime leaves, torn in half

1 inch/2.5 cm piece ginger, chopped

2 inch/5 cm piece galangal, chopped

1 stalk lemon grass, chopped

1 onion, quartered

4 cups cold water

1 Put all the ingredients for the bouillon into a pan and bring to a boil.

2 Simmer the bouillon for 5 minutes. Remove from the heat and strain, reserving the bouillon.

3 Heat the sunflower oil in a wok or large, heavy skillet and cook the bean curd over high heat for about 2 minutes, stirring constantly so that the bean curd cooks evenly on both sides. Add the strained bouillon to the skillet.

4 Add the mushrooms and cilantro and boil for 3 minutes.

5 Add the watercress and boil for a further 1 minute.

6 Serve immediately, garnished with red chili slices.

VARIATION
You might like to try a mixture of different types of mushroom. Oyster, white, and straw mushrooms are all suitable.

Mushroom & Ginger Soup

Thai soups are very quickly and easily put together, and are cooked so that each ingredient can still be tasted in the finished dish.

NUTRITIONAL INFORMATION

Calories 74   Sugars 1g
Protein . . . . .3g   Fat 3g
Carbohydrate . . . .9g   Saturates 0.4g

 30 mins   🕐 15 mins

SERVES 4

I N G R E D I E N T S

½ oz/15 g dried Chinese mushrooms or
   ¼ lb/125 g field or crimini mushrooms

4 cups hot vegetable bouillon

¼ lb/115 g thread egg noodles

2 tsp sunflower oil

3 garlic cloves, crushed

1 inch/2.5 cm piece ginger,
   shredded finely

½ tsp mushroom catsup

1 tsp light soy sauce

1½ cups bean sprouts

cilantro leaves, to garnish

1 Soak the dried Chinese mushrooms (if using) for at least 30 minutes in 1¼ cups of the hot vegetable bouillon. Remove the stalks and discard, then slice the mushrooms. Reserve the bouillon.

2 Cook the noodles for 2–3 minutes in boiling water. Drain and rinse. Set them aside.

3 Heat the oil over high heat in a wok or large, heavy skillet. Add the garlic and ginger, stir, and add the mushrooms. Stir over high heat for 2 minutes.

4 Add the remaining vegetable bouillon with the reserved bouillon and bring to a boil. Add the mushroom catsup and soy sauce.

5 Stir in the beansprouts and cook until tender. Put some noodles in each bowl and ladle the soup on top. Garnish with cilantro leaves and serve immediately.

COOK'S TIP
Rice noodles contain no fat and are ideal for anyone on a low-fat diet.

Creamed Beet Soup

Here are two variations using the same vegetable: a creamy soup made with puréed cooked beet and a traditional clear soup, Bortsch.

NUTRITIONAL INFORMATION

Calories	106	Sugars	........11g
Protein	.........3g	Fat	..........5g
Carbohydrate	...13g	Saturates	.......3g

 25 mins   35-55 mins

SERVES 6

INGREDIENTS

BORTSCH

1 lb/450 g raw beet, peeled and grated

2 carrots, finely chopped

1 large onion, finely chopped

1 garlic clove, crushed

1 bouquet garni

4 cups vegetable bouillon

2–3 tsp lemon juice

salt and pepper

⅔ cup sour cream, to serve

CREAMED BEET SOUP

4 tbsp butter or margarine

2 large onions, finely chopped

1–2 carrots, chopped

2 celery stalks, chopped

1 lb/450 g cooked beetroot, diced

1–2 tbsp lemon juice

3½ cups vegetable bouillon

1¼ cups milk

salt and pepper

TO SERVE

grated cooked beet or 6 tbsp heavy cream, lightly whipped

1 To make bortsch, place the beet, carrots, onion, garlic, bouquet garni, bouillon, and lemon juice in a pan and season to taste with salt and pepper. Bring to a boil, cover the pan, and simmer for 45 minutes.

2 Press the soup through a fine strainer or a strainer lined with cheesecloth, then pour into a clean pan. Taste and adjust the seasoning and add a little extra lemon juice, if necessary.

3 Bring to a boil and simmer for 1–2 minutes. Serve with a spoonful of sour cream swirled through.

4 To make creamed beet soup, melt the butter or margarine in a pan. Add the onions, carrots, and celery, and sauté until just beginning to color.

5 Add the beet, 1 tbsp of the lemon juice, the bouillon, and the seasoning, and bring to a boil. Cover and simmer for 30 minutes, until tender.

6 Cool slightly, then press through a strainer or process in a food processor. Pour into a clean pan. Add the milk and bring to a boil. Adjust the seasoning and add extra lemon juice, if necessary. Top with grated beet or heavy cream.

Curried Parsnip Soup

Parsnips make a delicious soup as they have a slightly sweet flavor.
In this recipe, spices are added to complement this sweetness.

NUTRITIONAL INFORMATION

Calories	152	Sugars	. . . . .7g
Protein	. . . . .3g	Fat	. . . . .8g
Carbohydrate	. . .18g	Saturates	. . . . . . .3g

 10 mins   35 mins

SERVES 4

INGREDIENTS

1 tbsp vegetable oil

1 tbsp butter

1 red onion, chopped

3 parsnips, chopped

2 garlic cloves, crushed

2 tsp garam masala

½ tsp chili powder

1 tbsp all-purpose flour

3½ cups vegetable bouillon

grated zest and juice of 1 lemon

salt and pepper

lemon zest, to garnish

1 Heat the vegetable oil and butter in a large pan until the butter has melted. Add the onion, parsnips, and garlic and sauté, stirring frequently, for about 5–7 minutes, until the vegetables are soft, but not colored.

2 Add the garam masala and chili powder and cook, stirring constantly, for 30 seconds. Sprinkle in the flour, mixing well, and cook, stirring constantly, for a further 30 seconds.

3 Stir in the bouillon, lemon zest, and lemon juice and bring to a boil. Reduce the heat and simmer for 20 minutes.

4 Remove some of the vegetable pieces with a slotted spoon and reserve until required. Transfer the remaining soup and vegetables to a food processor or blender and process for about 1 minute, or until a smooth purée is formed. Alternatively, press the vegetables through a strainer with the back of a wooden spoon.

5 Return the soup to a clean pan and stir in the reserved vegetables. Heat the soup through for 2 minutes until piping hot.

6 Season to taste with salt and pepper, then transfer to soup bowls, garnish with grated lemon zest, and serve.

Mixed Bean Soup

This is a really hearty soup, filled with color, flavor, and goodness, which may be adapted to any vegetables that you have to hand.

NUTRITIONAL INFORMATION

Calories 190   Sugars 9g
Protein ....10g   Fat 4g
Carbohydrate ...30g   Saturates 0.5g

 10 mins   40 mins

SERVES 4

INGREDIENTS

1 tbsp vegetable oil

1 red onion, halved and sliced

1 cup diced potatoes

1 carrot, diced

1 leek, sliced

1 green chili, sliced

3 garlic cloves, crushed

1 tsp ground coriander

1 tsp chili powder

4 cups vegetable bouillon

1¼ cups mixed canned beans, such as red kidney, borlotti, black eyed, or flageolet, drained

salt and pepper

2 tbsp chopped fresh cilantro, to garnish

1 Heat the vegetable oil in a large pan. Add the onion, potatoes, carrot, and leek, and sauté, stirring constantly, for about 2 minutes, until the vegetables are slightly softened.

2 Add the chili and crushed garlic and cook for a further minute.

3 Stir in the ground coriander, chili powder, and vegetable bouillon.

4 Bring the soup to a boil, reduce the heat, and cook for 20 minutes, or until the vegetables are tender.

5 Stir in the beans, season well with salt and pepper, and cook, stirring occasionally, for a further 10 minutes.

6 Transfer the soup to a warm tureen or warmed individual bowls, garnish with chopped cilantro, and serve.

COOK'S TIP
Serve this soup with slices of warm corn bread or a cheese loaf.

Sweet Potato Soup

When there's a chill in the air, this vivid soup is just the thing to serve—
it's very warm and comforting.

NUTRITIONAL INFORMATION

Calories 57   Sugars 1.5g
Protein . . . . .2.3g   Fat 2.5g
Carbohydrate . . .6.6g   Saturates 0.8g

15 mins   1 hr 15 mins

SERVES 6

INGREDIENTS

¾ lb/350 g sweet potatoes

1 acorn squash

4 shallots

olive oil

5–6 garlic cloves, unpeeled

3¾ cups vegetable bouillon

½ cup light cream

salt and pepper

snipped chives, to garnish

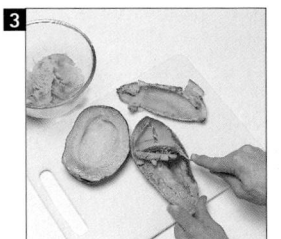

1 Cut the sweet potato, squash, and shallots in half lengthwise. Brush the cut sides with oil.

2 Put the vegetables, cut sides down, in a shallow roasting pan. Add the garlic cloves. Roast in a preheated oven, 375°F/190°C for about 40 minutes until tender and light brown.

3 When cool, scoop the flesh from the potato and squash halves and put in a pan with the shallots. Remove the garlic peel and add the soft insides to the other vegetables.

4 Add the bouillon and a pinch of salt. Bring just to a boil, then reduce the heat and simmer, partially covered, for about 30 minutes, stirring occasionally, until the vegetables are very tender.

5 Let the soup cool slightly, then transfer to a blender or food processor and purée until smooth, working in batches, if necessary. (If using a food processor, strain off the cooking liquid and reserve. Purée the soup solids with enough cooking liquid to moisten them, then combine with the remaining liquid.)

6 Return the soup to the pan and stir in the cream. Season to taste, then simmer for 5–10 minutes until completely heated through. Ladle into warm bowls and serve hot garnished with chives.

Corn & Spinach Soup

Fresh corn cobs are used in this unusual recipe. The spinach is added at the last minute so that its vibrant color is retained.

NUTRITIONAL INFORMATION

Calories ....347 Sugars 11g
Protein ....9g Fat 20g
Carbohydrate ...36g Saturates 10g

20 mins   35 mins

SERVES 4

INGREDIENTS

3 ears of corn, cooked

1 tsp butter

1 tsp oil

1 large onion, finely chopped

1 leek, thinly sliced

1 carrot, finely chopped

1 large potato, diced

5 cups water

½ cup heavy cream

½ cup milk

freshly grated nutmeg

6 oz spinach leaves, finely chopped

salt and pepper

1 Cut the kernels from the corn, without cutting all the way down to the cob. Using the back of a knife, scrape the cobs to extract the milky liquid, and set it aside.

2 Heat the butter and oil in a large pan over medium heat and add the onion and leek. Cover and cook for 3–4 minutes, stirring frequently, until soft.

3 Add the carrot, potato, and water with a large pinch of salt. Bring just to a boil and stir in the corn kernels and the liquid scraped from the cobs. Reduce the heat to low, cover, and simmer for about 25 minutes, or until the carrot and potato are tender.

4 Let the soup cool slightly, then transfer about half of it to a blender or food processor and purée until smooth.

5 Return the puréed soup to the pan, add the cream and milk, and stir to blend. Thin with a little more milk, if preferred. Season with salt, pepper, and nutmeg. Reheat over low heat.

6 Add the spinach and cook for 4–5 minutes, stirring frequently, just until the spinach is completely wilted. Taste and adjust the seasoning, if necessary, then ladle the soup into warm bowls and serve.

COOK'S TIP

To cut corn kernels off the cob, lay on its side on a cutting board and slice lengthwise, rotating until all kernels are removed. Then stand on its stem and scrape down to extract the remaining pulp and juice.

Carrot & Cumin Soup

Carrot soups are very popular and here cumin, tomato, potato, and celery give the soup both richness and depth.

NUTRITIONAL INFORMATION

Calories	114	Sugars	.........8g
Protein	.........3g	Fat	..........6g
Carbohydrate	...12g	Saturates	......4g

 15 mins   45 mins

SERVES 4–6

INGREDIENTS

3 tbsp butter or margarine

1 large onion, chopped

1–2 garlic cloves, crushed

3 cups carrots, sliced

3¾ cups vegetable bouillon

¾ tsp ground cumin

2 celery stalks, thinly sliced

1 cup potato, diced

2 tsp tomato paste

2 tsp lemon juice

2 fresh or dried bay leaves

about 1¼ cups skim milk

salt and pepper

celery leaves, to garnish

1 Melt the butter or margarine in a large pan. Add the onion and garlic and cook very gently until soft.

2 Add the carrots and cook gently for a further 5 minutes, stirring frequently and taking care they do not brown.

3 Add the bouillon, cumin, seasoning, celery, potato, tomato paste, lemon juice, and bay leaves and bring to a boil. Cover and simmer for about 30 minutes until the vegetables are tender.

4 Remove and discard the bay leaves, cool the soup a little, and then press it through a strainer or process in a food processor or blender until smooth.

5 Pour the soup into a clean pan, add the milk, and bring to a boil over low heat. Taste and adjust the seasoning if necessary.

6 Ladle into warmed bowls, garnish each serving with a small celery leaf and serve.

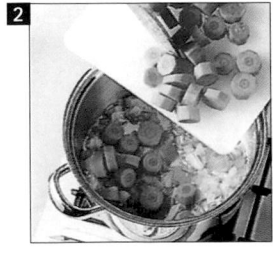

COOK'S TIP

This soup can be frozen for up to 3 months. Add the milk when reheating.

Avocado & Vegetable Soup

Avocado has a rich flavor and color which makes a creamy flavored soup.
It is best served chilled, but may be eaten warm as well.

NUTRITIONAL INFORMATION

Calories 167   Sugars 5g
Protein ....4g   Fat 13g
Carbohydrate ....8g   Saturates 3g

 15 mins   10 mins

SERVES 4

I N G R E D I E N T S

1 large, ripe avocado

2 tbsp lemon juice

1 tbsp vegetable oil

2 tbsp canned corn kernels, drained

2 tomatoes, peeled and seeded

1 garlic clove, crushed

1 leek, chopped

1 red chili, chopped

1¾ cups vegetable bouillon

⅔ cup milk

shredded leek, to garnish

  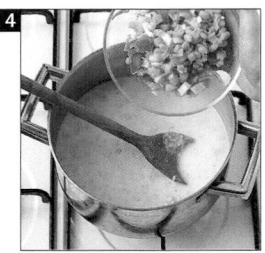

1 Peel the avocado and mash the flesh with a fork, stir in the lemon juice, and reserve until required.

2 Heat the vegetable oil in a large pan. Add the corn, tomatoes, garlic, leek, and chili and sauté over low heat for 2–3 minutes, or until the vegetables are soft.

3 Put half the vegetable mixture in a food processor or blender, together with the mashed avocado, and process until smooth. Transfer the mixture to a clean pan.

4 Add the vegetable bouillon, milk, and reserved vegetables and cook over low heat for 3–4 minutes, until hot.

5 Transfer to warmed individual serving bowls, garnish with shredded leek, and serve immediately.

COOK'S TIP

If serving chilled, transfer from the food processor to a bowl, stir in the vegetable bouillon and milk, cover, and chill in the refrigerator for at least 4 hours.

Tuscan Bean Soup

A thick and creamy soup that is based on a traditional Tuscan recipe. If you use dried beans, the preparation and cooking times will be longer.

NUTRITIONAL INFORMATION

Calories ....250 Sugars 4g
Protein ....13g Fat 10g
Carbohydrate ...29g Saturates 2g

 5 mins   10 mins

SERVES 4

I N G R E D I E N T S

8 oz/225 g dried lima beans, soaked overnight, or 3½–4 cups canned lima beans

1 tbsp olive oil

2 garlic cloves, crushed

1 vegetable bouillon cube, crumbled

⅔ cups milk

2 tbsp chopped fresh oregano

salt and pepper

1 If you are using dried beans that have been soaked overnight, drain them thoroughly. Bring a large pan of water to a boil, add the beans, and boil for 10 minutes. Cover the pan and simmer for a further 30 minutes or until the beans are tender. Drain the beans, reserving the cooking liquid. If you are using canned beans, drain them thoroughly and reserve the liquid.

2 Heat the oil in a large skillet and cook the garlic for 2–3 minutes or until just beginning to brown.

3 Add the beans and 1¾ cups of the reserved liquid to the pan, stirring. You may need to add a little water if there is insufficient liquid. Stir in the crumbled bouillon cube. Bring the mixture to a boil and then remove the pan from the heat.

4 Place the bean mixture in a food processor or blender and process until a smooth purée is formed. Alternatively, mash the bean mixture to a smooth consistency. Season the soup to taste with salt and pepper, and stir in the milk.

5 Pour the soup back into the pan and gently heat to just below boiling point. Stir in the chopped fresh oregano just before serving.

Cream of Artichoke Soup

A creamy soup with the unique, subtle flavoring of Jerusalem artichokes and a garnish of grated carrots for extra crunch.

NUTRITIONAL INFORMATION

Calories 19   Sugars 0g
Protein . . . . .0.4g   Fat 2g
Carbohydrate . . .0.7g   Saturates 0.7g

10–15 mins   55–60 mins

SERVES 6

I N G R E D I E N T S

1¾ lb/795 g Jerusalem artichokes

1 lemon, sliced thickly

4 tbsp butter or margarine

2 onions, chopped

1 garlic clove, crushed

5 cups vegetable bouillon

2 bay leaves

¼ tsp ground mace or ground nutmeg

1 tbsp lemon juice

⅔ cup light cream or unsweetened yogurt

salt and pepper

TO GARNISH

coarsely grated carrot

chopped fresh parsley or cilantro

1 Peel and slice the artichokes. Put into a bowl of water with the lemon slices.

2 Melt the butter or margarine in a large pan. Add the onions and garlic and sauté gently for 3–4 minutes until soft but not colored.

3 Drain the artichokes (discarding the lemon) and add to the pan. Mix well and cook gently for 2–3 minutes without letting color.

4 Add the bouillon, seasoning, bay leaves, mace or nutmeg, and lemon juice. Bring slowly to a boil, then cover and simmer gently for about 30 minutes until the vegetables are very tender.

5 Discard the bay leaves. Cool the soup slightly then press through a strainer or blend in a food processor until smooth.

If liked, a little of the soup may be only partially puréed and added to the rest of the puréed soup, to give extra texture.

6 Pour into a clean pan and bring to a boil. Adjust the seasoning and stir in the cream or yogurt. Reheat gently without boiling.

7 Ladle the soup into serving bowls and garnish with grated carrot and chopped parsley or cilantro to serve.

Eggplant Soup

In this satisfying soup, the eggplants are first roasted with carrots and parsnips, giving a special flavor. The lemon-garlic seasoning adds a kick.

NUTRITIONAL INFORMATION

Calories 117	Sugars 0g
Protein 6g	Fat 8g
Carbohydrate 5g	Saturates 1g

 15 mins   1¼ hrs

SERVES 6

I N G R E D I E N T S

1 tbsp olive oil, plus extra for brushing

1½ lb eggplant, halved lengthwise

1 carrot, halved

1 small parsnip, halved

2 onions, finely chopped

3 garlic cloves, finely chopped

4 cups vegetable bouillon

¼ tsp fresh thyme leaves, or a pinch of dried thyme

1 bay leaf

⅛ tsp ground coriander

1 tbsp tomato paste

⅔ cup light cream

freshly squeezed lemon juice

salt and pepper

L E M O N - G A R L I C
S E A S O N I N G

grated zest of ½ lemon

1 garlic clove, finely chopped

3 tbsp chopped fresh parsley

1 Oil a shallow roasting pan and add the eggplant, cut sides down, and the carrot and parsnip. Brush the vegetables with oil. Roast in a preheated oven at 400°F/200°C for 30 minutes, turning once.

2 When cool enough to handle, scrape the eggplant flesh away from the skin, or scoop it out, then roughly chop. Cut the parsnip and carrot into chunks.

3 Heat the oil in a large pan over medium-low heat. Add the onions and garlic and cook for about 5 minutes, stirring frequently, until soft. Add the eggplant, parsnip, carrot, bouillon, thyme, bay leaf, coriander, and tomato paste, with a little salt. Stir to combine. Cover and simmer for 30 minutes, or until the vegetables are very tender.

4 Let the soup cool slightly, then transfer to a blender or food processor and purée until smooth, working in batches if necessary. (If using a food processor, strain off the cooking liquid and reserve. Purée the soup solids with enough cooking liquid to moisten them, then combine with the remaining liquid.)

5 Return the puréed soup to the pan and stir in the cream. Reheat the soup over low heat for about 10 minutes until hot. Adjust the seasoning, adding lemon juice to taste.

6 To make the lemon-garlic seasoning, chop together the lemon zest, garlic, and parsley until very fine and well mixed. Ladle the soup into warm bowls, then garnish with the lemon-garlic seasoning.

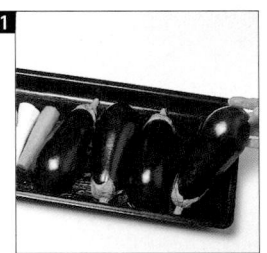

Spicy Vegetable Soup

Wake up the taste buds with a hint of curry spices in this easy-to-prepare vegetable soup. For a light lunch, serve with Indian bread.

NUTRITIONAL INFORMATION

Calories	75	Sugars	.........5g
Protein	.........3g	Fat	...........4g
Carbohydrate	....8g	Saturates	.......1g

15 mins   15 mins

SERVES 4

INGREDIENTS

1 tbsp sunflower or corn oil

10 oz/280 g leeks, thinly sliced

2 garlic cloves, finely chopped

½ tsp grated fresh ginger root

½ tsp ground cumin

½ tsp ground coriander

½ tsp ground turmeric

5 cups vegetable bouillon

1 lb/450 g tomatoes, finely diced

2 zucchini, cut into batons

salt and ground black pepper

3 tbsp chopped fresh cilantro, to garnish

1 Prepare the ingredients. Heat the sunflower or corn oil in a large pan. Add the sliced leeks, crushed garlic, and grated ginger, and cook, stirring occasionally, for 2 minutes. Stir in the cumin, ground coriander, and turmeric and cook, stirring constantly, for 30 seconds.

2 Pour in the bouillon and bring to a boil. Cover the pan and simmer for about 5 minutes.

3 Stir in the tomatoes and zucchini. Cover and simmer for a further 3 minutes.

4 Season the soup to taste with salt and pepper, then serve, garnished with the chopped cilantro.

COOK'S TIP
If you buy whole cumin and coriander seeds and grind them yourself with a pestle and mortar or spice mill, the flavor and aroma will be stronger.

Sweetcorn & Lentil Soup

This pale-coloured soup is made with corn kernels and green lentils.
Serve it with whole-wheat bread for a perfectly balanced light meal.

NUTRITIONAL INFORMATION

Calories 171   Sugars 9g
Protein . . . . .5g   Fat 2g
Carbohydrate . . .30g   Saturates 0.3g

 5 mins   30 mins

SERVES 4

INGREDIENTS

2 tbsp green lentils, washed

4 cups vegetable bouillon

½ inch/1 cm piece ginger root, chopped finely

2 tsp soy sauce

1 tsp sugar

1 tbsp cornstarch

3 tbsp dry sherry

1½ cups canned corn kernels

1 egg white

1 tsp sesame oil

salt and pepper

TO GARNISH

strips of scallion

strips of red chili

COOK'S TIP

Ginger should be smooth and fresh looking. Keep unused ginger in a plastic bag and store in the refrigerator.

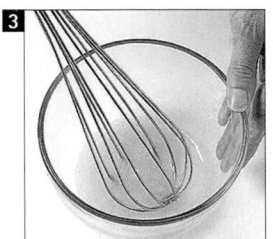

1 Place the lentils in a pan with the bouillon, ginger root, soy sauce, and sugar. Boil rapidly, uncovered, for 10 minutes. Skim the liquid. Reduce the heat, cover, and simmer for 15 minutes.

2 Mix the cornstarch with the sherry in a small bowl and add to the pan. Add the corn and its liquid. Simmer for a further 2 minutes.

3 Whisk the egg white lightly with the sesame oil. Pour the egg mixture into the soup in a thin stream, remove from the heat, and stir. The egg white will form white strands.

4 Season the soup to taste with salt and pepper. Pour into 4 warmed soup bowls and garnish with strips of scallion and chili before serving.

Saffron Noodle Soup

This soup has everything going for it—it is very low in fat, takes little time to make, looks intriguing, and has wonderful flavors and textures.

NUTRITIONAL INFORMATION

Calories	135	Sugars	.........3g
Protein	.........3g	Fat	...........1g
Carbohydrate	...29g	Saturates	.......0g

 10 mins   15 mins

SERVES 4

I N G R E D I E N T S

5 cups vegetable bouillon

2 tbsp light soy sauce

1½ tsp saffron threads

4 scallions, sliced into rings

2 zucchini, cut into batons

2 large tomatoes, skinned and chopped

1 garlic clove, finely chopped

4 oz/115 g rice noodles

ground black pepper

finely chopped garlic chives, to garnish

1 Prepare the ingredients. Pour the bouillon into a large pan, add the soy sauce, and bring to a boil. Crush the saffron with a mortar and pestle and stir it into the bouillon.

2 Add the scallions, zucchini, tomatoes, garlic, and rice noodles to the saffron bouillon, and bring back to a boil. Cover the pan and simmer the soup for 5 minutes.

3 Season the soup to taste with ground black pepper and serve immediately in warm bowls, garnished with the chopped garlic chives.

COOK'S TIP
Soy sauce is quite salty, so this soup is unlikely to need any additional salt. In the interests of healthy eating, you may prefer to use low-sodium soy sauce.

Potato & Split Pea Soup

Split green peas are sweeter than other varieties of split pea and reduce down to a purée when cooked, which acts as a thickener in soups.

NUTRITIONAL INFORMATION

Calories 260	Sugars 5g
Protein 11g	Fat 10g
Carbohydrate ...32g	Saturates 3g

5–10 mins   45 mins

SERVES 4

INGREDIENTS

2 tbsp vegetable oil

2 unpeeled, diced mealy potatoes

2 onions, diced

½ cup split green peas

4 cups vegetable bouillon

5 tbsp grated Swiss cheese

salt and pepper

CROUTONS

3 tbsp butter

1 garlic clove, crushed

1 tbsp chopped parsley

1 thick slice of white bread, cubed

1 Heat the vegetable oil in a large pan. Add the potatoes and onions and sauté over low heat, stirring constantly, for about 5 minutes.

2 Add the split green peas to the pan and stir to mix together well.

3 Pour the vegetable bouillon into the pan and bring it to a boil. Reduce the heat to low and simmer for 35 minutes, until the potatoes are tender and the split peas are cooked.

4 Meanwhile, make the croûtons. Melt the butter in a skillet. Add the garlic, parsley, and bread cubes to the skillet and cook, turning over frequently, for about 2 minutes, until the bread cubes are golden brown on all sides.

5 Stir the grated cheese into the soup and season to taste with salt and pepper. Heat gently until the cheese is starting to melt.

6 Pour the soup into warmed individual bowls and scatter the croûtons on top. Serve at once.

VARIATION

For a richly colored soup, red lentils could be used instead of split green peas. Add a large pinch of brown sugar to the recipe for extra sweetness if red lentils are used.

Dhal Soup

Dhal is a delicious Indian lentil dish. This soup is a variation of the theme, made with red lentils and spiced with curry powder.

NUTRITIONAL INFORMATION

Calories 284   Sugars 13g
Protein ....16g   Fat 9g
Carbohydrate ...38g   Saturates 5g

 5 mins   🕐 35 mins

SERVES 4

I N G R E D I E N T S

2 tbsp butter

2 garlic cloves, finely chopped

1 onion, chopped

½ tsp turmeric

1 tsp garam masala

¼ tsp chili powder

1 tsp ground cumin

2 lb canned, chopped tomatoes, drained

1 cup red lentils

2 tsp lemon juice

2½ cups vegetable bouillon

1¼ cups coconut milk

salt and pepper

chopped cilantro and lemon slices,
   to garnish

naan bread, to serve

1 Melt the butter in a large pan and sauté the garlic and onion for 2–3 minutes, stirring. Add the spices and cook for a further 30 seconds.

2 Stir in the tomatoes, red lentils, lemon juice, vegetable bouillon, and coconut milk, and bring to a boil.

3 Reduce the heat and simmer for 25–30 minutes until the lentils are tender and cooked.

4 Season to taste and spoon the soup into a warm tureen. Garnish and serve with warm naan bread.

COOK'S TIP
You can buy cans of coconut milk from stores and delicatessens. It can also be made by grating creamed coconut, which comes in the form of a solid bar, and mixing it with water.

Tomato & Rice Soup

This warming, comforting soup is easy to make from store cupboard ingredients. The rice adds a satisfying bite to the blended soup.

NUTRITIONAL INFORMATION

Calories	253	Sugars	........14g
Protein	.........5g	Fat	..........14g
Carbohydrate	...30g	Saturates	.......3g

10 mins   1 hr 10 mins

SERVES 4

INGREDIENTS

1 tbsp olive oil

1 large onion, finely chopped

2 garlic cloves, finely chopped or crushed

2 carrots, grated

1 stalk celery, thinly sliced

4 cups canned plum tomatoes in juice

1 tsp dark brown sugar, or to taste

3¾ cups vegetable bouillon or water

1 bay leaf

1 cup cooked white rice

2 tbsp chopped fresh dill

6 tbsp heavy cream

salt and pepper

fresh dill sprigs, to garnish

1 Heat the olive oil in a large pan over medium heat. Add the onion, cover, and cook for 3–4 minutes, stirring occasionally, until the onion is just soft.

2 Add the garlic, carrots, celery, tomatoes, brown sugar, and bouillon or water with the bay leaf to the pan. Reduce the heat, cover, and simmer for

1 hour, stirring occasionally. Remove and discard the bay leaf.

3 Let the soup cool slightly, then transfer to a blender or food processor and purée until smooth, working in batches if necessary. (If using a food processor, strain off the cooking liquid and reserve. Purée the soup solids with enough cooking liquid to moisten them, then combine with the remaining liquid.)

4 Return the soup to the pan and stir in the rice and dill. Season with salt, if needed, and pepper. Cook gently over medium-low heat for about 5 minutes, or until hot.

5 Stir in the cream. Taste the soup and adjust the seasoning, if necessary. Ladle into warm soup bowls and garnish each serving with a swirl of cream and dill sprigs. Serve at once.

Corn Soup with Chilies

A dried ancho chili adds a kick to this glowing Mexican corn soup.
The corn kernels are tossed in butter, giving the soup a roasted flavor.

NUTRITIONAL INFORMATION

Calories	.824	Sugars	.12g
Protein	.9g	Fat	.74g
Carbohydrate	.33g	Saturates	.45g

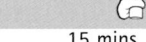   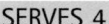

15 mins,
plus 15 mins
standing   1 hr

SERVES 4

INGREDIENTS

1 dried ancho chili

4 tbsp butter

3½ cups defrosted frozen corn kernels

1 large onion, finely chopped

1 large garlic clove, finely chopped

1 red bell pepper, cored, seeded, and finely
  chopped

1¼ cups vegetable bouillon or water

2½ cups whipping cream

½ tsp ground cumin

salt

chopped fresh cilantro or parsley, to garnish

1 Put the chili in a bowl and cover with boiling water. Let stand for about 15 minutes to soften.

2 Melt the butter in a skillet over medium-low heat. Add the corn and turn to coat. Cook for about 15 minutes, stirring frequently, until it starts to brown slightly. Add the onion, garlic, and bell pepper and cook for about 7–10 minutes, stirring frequently, until the onion is soft and the mixture starts to stick.

3 Transfer the mixture to a blender or food processor, add the bouillon, and purée until smooth.

4 Put the cream in a large pan, stir in the puréed vegetables, and bring almost to a boil. Add the cumin. Season with a little salt. Adjust the heat so the soup bubbles very gently and continue to cook until the mixture is reduced by about one-quarter.

5 Remove the ancho chili from its liquid and discard the core and the seeds.

(Wash your hands well after preparing chilies, as they can irritate the skin.) Put the chili into a blender or food processor with 4–5 tablespoons of the soaking water and purée until smooth.

6 Stir 2–4 tablespoons of the purée into the soup, according to taste, and continue cooking for a further 5 minutes.

7 Taste the soup and adjust the seasoning, if necessary. Ladle the soup into warm bowls, garnish with cilantro or parsley, and serve.

Indian Bean Soup

A thick and hearty soup, nourishing and substantial enough to serve as an entrée with whole-wheat bread.

NUTRITIONAL INFORMATION

Calories	237	Sugars	.........9g
Protein	.........9g	Fat	...........9g
Carbohydrate	...33g	Saturates	.......1g

20 mins   50 mins

SERVES 6

I N G R E D I E N T S

4 tbsp vegetable ghee or vegetable oil

2 onions, peeled and chopped

8 oz/225 g potatoes, cut into chunks

8 oz/225 g parsnips, cut into chunks

8 oz/225 g turnips or rutabagas, cut into chunks

2 celery stalks, sliced

2 zucchini, sliced

1 green bell pepper, seeded and cut into ½ inch/1 cm pieces

2 garlic cloves, crushed

2 tsp ground coriander

1 tbsp paprika

1 tbsp mild curry paste

5 cups vegetable bouillon

salt

1½ cups canned black-eyed peas, drained and rinsed

chopped cilantro, to garnish (optional)

1 Heat the ghee or oil in a pan, add all the prepared vegetables, except the zucchini and green bell pepper, and cook over moderate heat, stirring frequently, for 5 minutes. Add the garlic, ground coriander, paprika, and curry paste and cook, stirring constantly, for 1 minute.

2 Stir in the bouillon and season with salt to taste. Bring to a boil, cover, and simmer over low heat, stirring occasionally, for 25 minutes.

3 Stir in the black-eyed peas, sliced zucchini, and green bell pepper, then replace the lid and continue cooking for a further 15 minutes, or until all the vegetables are tender.

4 Process 1¼ cups of the soup mixture (about 2 ladlefuls) in a food processor or blender. Return the puréed mixture to the soup in the pan and reheat until piping hot. Sprinkle with chopped cilantro if using, and serve hot.

Baked Leek & Cabbage Soup

This unusual baked soup is perfect for lunch on a crisp, cold winter day—pop it in the oven and enjoy a brisk walk while it is cooking.

NUTRITIONAL INFORMATION

Calories	420	Sugars	.........8g
Protein	........24g	Fat	..........25g
Carbohydrate	...27g	Saturates	......15g

 15 mins　 1 hr 20 mins

SERVES 4

I N G R E D I E N T S

2 tbsp butter

2 large leeks, halved lengthwise and thinly sliced

1 large onion, halved and thinly sliced

3 garlic cloves, finely chopped

2 cups finely shredded green cabbage

4 cups vegetable bouillon

4 slices firm bread, cut in half, or 8 slices baguette

2 cups grated Swiss cheese

1 Melt the butter in a large pan over medium heat. Add the leeks and onion and cook for 4–5 minutes, stirring frequently, until just soft.

2 Add the garlic and cabbage, stir to combine, and continue cooking for about 5 minutes to wilt the cabbage.

3 Stir in the bouillon and simmer for 10 minutes. Taste and season with salt and pepper.

4 Arrange the bread in the base of a large, deep, 12 cups ovenproof dish. Sprinkle about half the grated cheese over the bread.

5 Ladle over the soup and top with the remaining grated cheese. Bake in a preheated oven at 350°F/180°C for 1 hour. Serve at once.

COOK'S TIP
A large soufflé dish or earthenware casserole at least 4 inches deep, or an enamelled cast-iron casserole, is good for baking the soup. If the soup fills the dish to the top, put a cookie sheet with a rim underneath to catch any overflow.

Curried Zucchini Soup

This soup can be frozen, so it is a good way to use up a glut of zucchini. Adding curry powder gives the flavor a lift.

NUTRITIONAL INFORMATION

Calories 147	Sugars 8g
Protein 6g	Fat 9g
Carbohydrate ...10g	Saturates 5g

 10 mins 30 mins

SERVES 4

INGREDIENTS

2 tsp butter

1 large onion, finely chopped

2 lb/900 g zucchini, sliced

2 cups vegetable bouillon

1 tsp curry powder

½ cup sour cream

salt and pepper

1 Melt the butter in a large pan over medium heat. Add the onion and cook for about 3 minutes until it begins to soften.

2 Add the bouillon, zucchini, and curry powder, along with a large pinch of salt if using unsalted bouillon. Bring the soup to a boil, reduce the heat, cover, and cook gently for about 25 minutes until the vegetables are tender.

COOK'S TIP
Bouillon made from a cube or liquid bouillon base is fine for this soup. In this case, you may wish to add a little more sour cream. The soup freezes well, but freeze it without the cream and add before serving.

3 Let the soup cool slightly, then transfer to a blender or food processor, working in batches if necessary. Purée the soup until just smooth, but still with green flecks. (If using a food processor, strain off the cooking liquid and reserve. Purée the soup solids with enough cooking liquid to moisten them, then combine with the remaining liquid.)

4 Return the soup to the pan and stir in the sour cream. Reheat gently over low heat until the soup is just hot, but do not let it boil.

5 Taste the soup, adjust the seasoning, if necessary, ladle into warm bowls, and serve immediately. If liked, garnish with sour cream and a little curry powder.

Roasted Pumpkin & Tomato Soup

This soup is a wonderful way to use fall harvest vegetables. Make it when sun-ripened tomatoes are still plentiful and pumpkins first appear.

NUTRITIONAL INFORMATION

Calories	180	Sugars	........11g
Protein	.........4g	Fat	..........12g
Carbohydrate	...13g	Saturates	.......5g

15 mins   1 hr 5 mins

SERVES 4

I N G R E D I E N T S

1–2 tbsp olive oil

2 lb/900 g peeled pumpkin flesh, cut into slices ¾ inch/2 cm thick

1 lb/450 g ripe tomatoes, skinned, cored, and thickly sliced

1 onion, chopped

2 garlic cloves, finely chopped

4 tbsp white wine

2 tbsp water

2½ cups vegetable bouillon

½ cup light cream

salt and pepper

snipped chives, to garnish

about 45 minutes, or until all the vegetables are tender.

3 Let the vegetables cool slightly, then transfer them to a blender or food processor. Add the cooking juices from the baking dish and as much bouillon as needed to cover the vegetables. Purée the vegetables until smooth, working in batches if necessary.

4 Pour the purée into a pan and stir in the remaining bouillon. Cook gently over medium heat, stirring occasionally, for about 15 minutes, or until heated through. Stir in the cream and continue cooking for 3–4 minutes.

5 Taste and adjust the seasoning, if necessary. Ladle the soup into warm bowls, garnish with chives, and serve.

1 Drizzle 1 tablespoon of the olive oil over the base of a large baking dish. Layer the pumpkin, tomatoes, onion, and garlic in 2 or 3 layers. Drizzle the top with the remaining olive oil, and pour over the wine and water. Season with a little salt and pepper.

2 Cover with aluminum foil and bake in a preheated oven at 375°F/190°C for

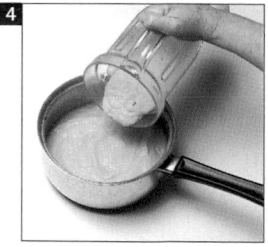

Leek, Potato & Carrot Soup

A quick, chunky soup, ideal for a snack or a quick lunch. Save some of the soup and purée it to make one portion of creamed soup for the next day.

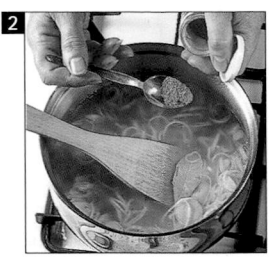

NUTRITIONAL INFORMATION

Calories ....156 Sugars 7g
Protein ....4g Fat 6g
Carbohydrate ...22g Saturates 0.7g

 10 mins   25 mins

SERVES 2

INGREDIENTS

1 leek, about 6 oz/175 g

1 tbsp sunflower oil

1 garlic clove, crushed

3 cups vegetable bouillon

1 bay leaf

¼ tsp ground cumin

1½ cups diced potatoes

generous ½ cup coarsely grated carrot

salt and pepper

chopped parsley, to garnish

PUREED SOUP

5–6 tbsp milk

1–2 tbsp heavy cream or sour cream

1 Trim off and discard some of the coarse green part of the leek, then slice thinly and rinse thoroughly in cold water. Drain well.

2 Heat the sunflower oil in a heavy pan. Add the leek and garlic and cook over low heat for about 2–3 minutes, until soft, but barely colored. Add the bouillon, bay leaf, and cumin and season to taste. Bring to a boil, stirring constantly.

3 Add the diced potato to the pan, cover, and simmer over low heat for 10–15 minutes. Keep a careful eye on the soup during the cooking time to make sure the potato cooks until it is just tender, but not broken up.

4 Add the grated carrot to the pan and simmer the soup for a further 2–3 minutes. Adjust the seasoning if necessary, discard the bay leaf, and serve the soup in warmed bowls, sprinkled liberally with the chopped parsley.

5 To make a puréed soup, first process the leftovers (about half the original soup) in a blender or food processor until smooth, or press through a strainer with the back of a wooden spoon, and then return to a clean pan. Add the milk to the pan, bring the soup to a boil, and simmer for 2–3 minutes.

6 Adjust the seasoning and stir in the heavy cream, or sour cream before serving the soup in warmed bowls, sprinkled with chopped parsley.

Green Vegetable Soup

This soup takes advantage of summer vegetables bursting with flavor.
If you find fresh small cannellini or other fresh beans, be sure to use them.

NUTRITIONAL INFORMATION

Calories	260	Sugars	. . . . .7g
Protein	. . . . .12g	Fat	. . . . .15g
Carbohydrate	. . .21g	Saturates	. . . . . .4g

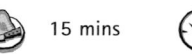 15 mins 45 mins

SERVES 6

INGREDIENTS

1 tbsp olive oil

1 onion, finely chopped

1 large leek, split and thinly sliced

1 celery stalk, thinly sliced

1 carrot, quartered and thinly sliced

1 garlic clove, finely chopped

6¼ cups water

1 potato, diced

1 parsnip, finely diced

1 small kohlrabi or turnip, diced

150 g/5½ oz green beans, cut in
  small pieces

5½ oz/150 g fresh or frozen peas

2 small zucchini, quartered lengthwise
  and sliced

14 oz/400 g can small cannellini beans,
  drained and rinsed

3½ oz/100 g spinach leaves, cut into
  thin ribbons

salt and pepper

PESTO

1 large garlic clove, very finely chopped

½ cup fresh basil leaves

1 cup freshly grated Parmesan cheese

4 tbsp extra virgin olive oil

1 Heat the oil in a large pan. Cook the onion and leek over low heat, stirring occasionally, for 5 minutes. Add the celery, carrot, and garlic, cover, and cook for a further 5 minutes.

2 Add the water, potato, parsnip, kohlrabi or turnip, and green beans. Bring to a boil, reduce the heat, cover, and simmer for 5 minutes.

3 Add the peas, zucchini, and small cannellini beans and season to taste.

Cover and simmer for about 25 minutes until all the vegetables are tender.

4 Meanwhile, make the pesto. Put all the ingredients in a food processor and process until smooth, scraping down the sides as necessary. Alternatively, pound together using a pestle and mortar.

5 Add the spinach to the soup and simmer for 5 minutes. Stir a spoon of the pesto into the soup. Ladle into bowls and pass the remaining pesto separately.

Vegetable Chili

This is a hearty and flavorful soup that is good on its own or spooned over cooked rice or baked potatoes for a more substantial meal.

NUTRITIONAL INFORMATION

Calories	.213	Sugars	.11g
Protein	.12g	Fat	.10g
Carbohydrate	.21g	Saturates	.5g

 10 mins   1¼ hrs

SERVES 5–6

INGREDIENTS

1 medium eggplant, peeled if wished, cut into 1 inch/2.5 cm slices

1 tbsp olive oil, plus extra for brushing

1 large red or yellow onion, finely chopped

2 red or yellow bell peppers, seeded and finely chopped

3–4 garlic cloves, finely chopped or crushed

4 cups canned chopped tomatoes

1 tbsp mild chili powder

½ tsp ground cumin

½ tsp dried oregano

2 small zucchini, quartered lengthwise and sliced

1½ cups canned kidney beans, drained and rinsed

2 cups water

1 tbsp tomato paste

6 scallions, finely chopped

1 cup grated Cheddar cheese

salt and pepper

1 Brush the eggplant slices on 1 side with olive oil. Heat half the oil in a large, heavy skillet over medium-high heat. Add the eggplant slices, oiled side up, and cook for 5–6 minutes until browned on 1 side. Turn the slices over, cook on the other side until browned, and then transfer to a plate. Cut the slices into bite-size pieces.

2 Heat the remaining oil in a large pan over medium heat. Add the onion and bell peppers and cook, stirring occasionally, for 3–4 minutes until the onion is just soft, but not browned. Add the garlic to the pan and continue cooking for 2–3 minutes or until the onion is just beginning to color.

3 Add the tomatoes, chili powder, cumin, and oregano. Season to taste with salt and pepper. Bring just to a boil, reduce the heat, cover, and simmer gently for 15 minutes.

4 Add the zucchini, eggplant pieces, and kidney beans. Stir in the water and tomato paste. Bring back to a boil, cover, and continue simmering for about 45 minutes or until the vegetables are tender. Taste and adjust the seasoning if necessary. If you prefer a hotter dish, stir in a little more chili powder.

5 Ladle the soup into warmed bowls and top with the chopped scallions and grated cheese.

Gazpacho

This Spanish soup is full of chopped and grated vegetables with a puréed tomato base. It requires chilling, so prepare well in advance.

NUTRITIONAL INFORMATION

Calories 140   Sugars 12g
Protein ....3g   Fat 9g
Carbohydrate ...13g   Saturates 1g

 30 mins, plus chilling   0 mins

SERVES 4

I N G R E D I E N T S

½ small cucumber

½ small green bell pepper, seeded and very finely chopped

1 lb/450 g ripe tomatoes, peeled or 2 cups canned chopped tomatoes

½ onion, coarsely chopped

2–3 garlic cloves, crushed

3 tbsp olive oil

2 tbsp white wine vinegar

1–2 tbsp lemon or lime juice

2 tbsp tomato paste

1¾ cups tomato juice

salt and pepper

TO SERVE

chopped green bell pepper

thinly sliced onion rings

garlic croûtons

1 Coarsely grate the cucumber into a large bowl and add the chopped green bell pepper.

2 Put the tomatoes, onion, and garlic in a food processor or blender, add the oil, vinegar, lemon or lime juice, and tomato paste and process until a smooth purée is formed. Alternatively, finely chop the tomatoes and finely grate the onion, then mix together and add the crushed garlic, oil, vinegar, lemon or lime juice, and tomato paste.

3 Add the tomato mixture to the bowl and mix well, then add the tomato juice and mix again.

4 Season to taste, cover the bowl with plastic wrap and chill thoroughly—for at least 6 hours and preferably longer so that the flavors have time to blend.

5 Prepare the side dishes of chopped green bell pepper, thinly sliced onion rings, and garlic croûtons and arrange them in individual serving bowls.

6 Ladle the soup into warmed bowls, preferably from a soup tureen set in the center of the table with the side dishes of bell pepper, onion rings, and croûtons placed around it. Hand the dishes round to allow the guests to help themselves.

Barley & Rice Soup

This hearty winter soup makes a warming lunch or supper when served with a crusty loaf of ciabatta.

NUTRITIONAL INFORMATION

Calories ....260 Sugars 8g
Protein ....9g Fat 6g
Carbohydrate ...46g Saturates 1g

15 mins   1½ hrs

SERVES 4–6

INGREDIENTS

½ cup pearl barley

½ cup long grain brown rice

1 lb/450 g Swiss chard, trimmed and soaked for 10 minutes

2 tbsp olive oil

1 large onion, finely chopped

2 carrots, finely chopped

2 celery stalks, finely chopped

2 garlic cloves, finely chopped

14 oz/400 g canned chopped plum tomatoes

1 bay leaf

1 tsp dried thyme

1 tsp herbes de Provence or dried oregano

4 cups chicken or vegetable stock

1 lb/450 g can cannellini beans, drained

2 tbsp chopped fresh parsley

salt and pepper

freshly grated Parmesan cheese, to serve

1 Bring a large pan of water to a boil. Add the barley and the brown rice and return to a boil. Reduce the heat and simmer gently for 30–35 minutes until just tender. Drain and set aside.

2 Drain the Swiss chard. Cut out the hard white stems. Slice the stems crosswise into very thin strips and set aside. Roll the leaves into a long cigar shape, shred thinly, and set aside.

3 Heat the oil in a large, heavy pan. Add the onion, carrots, and celery and cook, stirring frequently, for about 5 minutes until soft and beginning to color. Add the garlic and cook for a minute longer. Add the tomatoes with their juice, the bay leaf, thyme, and herbes de Provence. Reduce the heat, partially cover, and simmer for about 7 minutes until all the vegetables are soft.

4 Stir in the sliced white chard stems and the stock. Simmer gently for about 20 minutes. Add the shredded green chard and simmer for a further 15 minutes.

5 Stir in the beans and parsley with the cooked barley and brown rice. Season with salt and pepper. Bring back to a boil and simmer for a further 8–10 minutes. Remove the bay leaf and serve with Parmesan.

Vermicelli & Vegetable Soup

This wonderful combination of beans, vegetables, and vermicelli is made even richer by the addition of pesto and dried mushrooms.

NUTRITIONAL INFORMATION

Calories 225   Sugars 6g
Protein ....11g   Fat 5g
Carbohydrate ...36g   Saturates 1g

 15 mins   20 mins

SERVES 4

INGREDIENTS

1 small eggplant

2 large tomatoes

1 potato, peeled

1 carrot, peeled

1 leek

14½ oz canned cannellini beans

3¾ cups hot vegetable bouillon

2 tsp dried basil

½ oz/15 g dried porcini mushrooms, soaked for 10 minutes in enough warm water to cover

¼ cup vermicelli

3 tbsp pesto

freshly grated Parmesan cheese, to serve (optional)

1 Slice the eggplant into rings about ½ inch thick, then cut each ring into 4 pieces. Cut the tomatoes and potato into small dice. Cut the carrot into sticks about 1 inch long. Cut the leek into rings.

2 Place the cannellini beans and their liquid in a large pan. Add the eggplant, tomatoes, potatoes, carrot, and leek, stirring to mix.

3 Add the bouillon to the pan and bring to a boil. Reduce the heat and leave to simmer for 15 minutes.

4 Add the basil, dried mushrooms, their soaking liquid, and the vermicelli, and simmer for 5 minutes, or until all of the vegetables are tender.

5 Remove the pan from the heat and stir in the pesto. Serve with freshly grated Parmesan cheese, if using.

Fresh Tomato Soup

This soup, made with fresh tomatoes, tastes of summer, although it can be made at any time of year as long as the tomatoes are ripe.

NUTRITIONAL INFORMATION

Calories ....254 Sugars 13g
Protein ....3g Fat 21g
Carbohydrate ...14g Saturates 10g

15 mins   55 mins

SERVES 4

INGREDIENTS

2 lb/900 g ripe plum tomatoes, skinned

2 tsp olive oil

1 large sweet onion, finely chopped

1 carrot, finely chopped

1 stalk celery, finely chopped

2 garlic cloves, finely chopped or crushed

1 tsp fresh marjoram leaves, or ¼ tsp dried marjoram

2 cups water

4–5 tbsp heavy cream, plus extra to garnish

2 tbsp chopped fresh basil leaves

salt and pepper

1 Cut the tomatoes in half and scrape the seeds into a strainer set over a bowl to catch the juice. Reserve the juice and discard the seeds. Chop the tomato flesh into large chunks.

2 Heat the olive oil in a large pan. Add the onion, carrot, and celery and cook over medium-low heat for 3–4 minutes, stirring occasionally.

3 Add the tomatoes and their juice, with the garlic and marjoram. Cook for 2 minutes. Stir in the water, reduce the heat and simmer, covered, for about 45 minutes until the vegetables are very soft, stirring occasionally.

4 Let the soup cool slightly, then transfer to a blender or food processor and purée until smooth, working in batches, if necessary. (If using a food processor, strain off the cooking liquid and reserve. Purée the soup solids with enough cooking liquid to moisten them, then combine with the remaining liquid.)

5 Return the soup to the pan and place over medium-low heat. Add the cream and stir in the basil. Season with salt and pepper and heat through; do not let boil.

6 Ladle the soup into warm bowls and swirl a little extra cream into each serving. Serve at once.

COOK'S TIP

For the best flavor, this soup needs to be made with ripe tomatoes. If the tomatoes are pale and hard, leave them to ripen at room temperature for several days. This is especially important in winter when most tomatoes are picked before they are ripe.

Cheese & Vegetable Chowder

This hearty soup is wonderful made in the middle of winter with fresh seasonal vegetables. Use a really well-flavored sharp Cheddar cheese.

NUTRITIONAL INFORMATION

Calories	669	Sugars	........13g
Protein	........26g	Fat	..........49g
Carbohydrate	...33g	Saturates	......30g

15 mins   45 mins

SERVES 4

I N G R E D I E N T S

2 tbsp butter

1 large onion, finely chopped

1 large leek, split lengthwise and thinly sliced

1–2 garlic cloves, crushed

6 tbsp all-purpose flour

5 cups vegetable bouillon

3 carrots, finely diced

2 stalks celery, finely diced

1 turnip, finely diced

1 large potato, finely diced

3–4 sprigs fresh thyme, or ⅛ tsp dried thyme

1 bay leaf

1½ cups light cream

2¼ cups grated sharp Cheddar cheese

fresh chopped parsley, to garnish

salt and pepper

1 Melt the butter in a large, heavy pan over medium-low heat. Add the onion, leek, and garlic. Cover and cook for about 5 minutes, stirring frequently, until the vegetables start to soften.

2 Stir the flour into the vegetables and continue cooking for 2 minutes. Add a little of the bouillon and stir well, scraping the bottom of the pan to mix in the flour. Bring to a boil, stirring frequently, and slowly stir in the rest of the bouillon.

3 Add the carrots, celery, turnip, potato, thyme, and bay leaf. Reduce the heat, cover, and cook gently for about 35 minutes, stirring occasionally, until the vegetables are tender. Remove the bay leaf and the thyme sprigs.

4 Stir the light cream into the soup and simmer over very low heat for 5 minutes. Add the grated cheese a handful at a time, stirring constantly for 1 minute after each addition, to make sure it is completely melted.

5 Taste the soup and adjust the seasoning, adding salt if needed, and pepper to taste.

6 Serve immediately in warm bowls, garnished with fresh chopped parsley.

Cucumber & Tomato Soup

Although this chilled soup is not an authentic Indian dish, it is wonderful served as a "cooler" between hot, spicy courses.

NUTRITIONAL INFORMATION

Calories . . . . .73 Sugar 16g
Protein . . . . .2g Fats 1g
Carbohydrates . . .16g Saturates 0.2g

20 mins, plus chilling   0 mins

SERVES 6

I N G R E D I E N T S

4 tomatoes, peeled and seeded

3½ lb/1.5 kg watermelon, seedless if available

4 inch/10 cm piece cucumber, peeled and seeded

2 scallions, green part only, chopped

1 tbsp chopped fresh mint

salt and pepper

fresh mint sprigs, to garnish

1 Using a sharp knife, cut 1 tomato into ½ inch/1 cm dice.

2 Remove the rind from the melon, and remove the seeds if it is not seedless.

3 Put the 3 remaining tomatoes into a blender or food processor and, with the motor running, add the seeded cucumber, chopped scallions, and watermelon. Blend until smooth.

4 If not using a food processor, push the seeded watermelon through a strainer. Stir the diced tomatoes and mint into the melon mixture. Adjust the seasoning to taste. Chop the cucumber, scallions, and the 3 remaining tomatoes finely and add to the melon.

5 Chill the cucumber and tomato soup overnight in the refrigerator. Check the seasoning and transfer to a serving dish. Garnish with mint sprigs.

COOK'S TIP

Although this soup does improve if chilled overnight, it is also delicious as a quick appetizer if whipped up just before a meal, and served immediately.

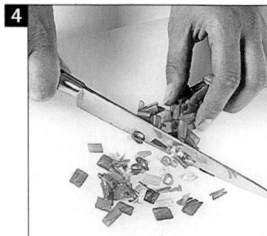

Melon & Ginger Soup

The zingy hot taste of fresh ginger blends perfectly with cool melon in this delicious and intriguing soup.

NUTRITIONAL INFORMATION

Calories	176	Sugars	........16g
Protein	.........2g	Fat	..........12g
Carbohydrate	...16g	Saturates	.......7g

 10 mins   0 mins

SERVES 4

INGREDIENTS

1 large ripe melon (about 2 lb/900 g)

¾ tsp grated peeled fresh ginger root, or more to taste

1 tbsp fresh lemon juice, or to taste

1 tsp sugar

½ cup whipping cream

salt

snipped fresh chives, to garnish

1 Halve the melon, discard the seeds, and scoop the flesh into a blender or food processor. Purée until smooth, scraping down the sides as necessary. (You may need to work in batches.)

2 Add the grated ginger, lemon juice, and sugar, with a pinch of salt and process to combine. Taste and add a little more ginger, if desired. Scrape into a bowl, cover and chill completely, usually for about 30 minutes, or until cold.

3 Add the cream and stir to combine well. Taste and adjust the seasoning, adding a little more salt and lemon juice if necessary.

4 To serve, divide the melon purée among four chilled bowls and garnish with chives.

COOK'S TIP
To determine the ripeness of melon, gently press the end opposite the stem—it should give a little, and there is usually a characteristic aroma on pressing that helps to confirm that it is ripe.

Iced Salsa Soup

A chunky mix of colorful vegetables, highlighted with Mexican flavors, this cold soup makes a lively appetizer at the start of any meal.

NUTRITIONAL INFORMATION

Calories	138	Sugars	........12g
Protein	.........5g	Fat	...........4g
Carbohydrate	...22g	Saturates	.......1g

 10 mins, plus chilling   12–15 mins

SERVES 4

INGREDIENTS

2 large corn ears or 1⅓ cups frozen corn kernels

1 tbsp olive oil

1 orange or red bell pepper, seeded and finely chopped

1 green bell pepper, seeded and finely chopped

1 sweet onion, such as Vidalia, finely chopped

3 ripe tomatoes, peeled, seeded, and chopped

½ tsp chili powder

½ cup water

2 cups tomato juice

chili paste (optional)

salt and pepper

TO GARNISH

3–4 scallions, finely chopped

fresh cilantro leaves

1 Cut the corn kernels from the cobs, or if using frozen corn, thaw and drain.

2 Heat the oil in a pan over medium-high heat. Add the bell peppers and cook, stirring briskly, for 3 minutes. Add the onion and continue cooking for about 2 minutes or until it starts to color slightly.

3 Add the tomatoes, corn, and chili powder. Continue cooking, stirring frequently, for 1 minute. Pour in the water and when it begins to boil, reduce the heat, cover, and cook for a further 4–5 minutes or until the bell peppers are just barely tender.

4 Transfer the mixture to a large container and stir in the tomato juice. Season with salt and pepper to taste and add more chili powder if wished. Cover with plastic wrap and chill in the refrigerator until cold.

5 Taste and adjust the seasoning. For a spicier soup, add a little chili paste to taste. For a thinner soup, add ice water.

6 Ladle the soup into chilled bowls and garnish with scallions and fresh cilantro leaves.

Avocado & Mint Soup

A rich and creamy pale green soup made with avocados and enhanced by a touch of chopped mint. Serve chilled in summer or hot in winter.

NUTRITIONAL INFORMATION

Calories	199	Sugars	.........3g
Protein	.........3g	Fat	..........18g
Carbohydrate	....7g	Saturates	.......6g

 15 mins, plus chilling   35 mins

SERVES 6

INGREDIENTS

3 tbsp butter or margarine

6 scallions, sliced

1 garlic clove, crushed

4 tbsp all-purpose flour

2½ cups vegetable bouillon

2 ripe avocados

2–3 tsp lemon juice

pinch of grated lemon zest

⅔ cups milk

⅔ cups light cream

1–1½ tbsp chopped mint

salt and pepper

mint sprigs, to garnish

MINTED GARLIC BREAD

½ cup & 1 tbsp butter

1–2 tbsp chopped mint

1–2 garlic cloves, crushed

1 whole-wheat or white French bread stick

1 Melt the butter or margarine in a large, heavy pan. Add the scallions and garlic clove to the pan and sauté over low heat, stirring occasionally, for about 3 minutes, until soft and translucent.

2 Stir in the flour and cook, stirring, for 1–2 minutes. Gradually stir in the bouillon, then bring to a boil. Simmer gently while preparing the avocados.

3 Peel the avocados, discard the pits, and chop coarsely. Add to the soup with the lemon juice and zest and seasoning. Cover and simmer for about 10 minutes, until tender.

4 Cool the soup slightly, then press through a strainer with the back of a spoon or process in a food processor or blender until a smooth purée forms. Pour into a bowl.

5 Stir in the milk and cream, adjust the seasoning, then stir in the mint. Cover and chill thoroughly.

6 To make the minted garlic bread, soften the butter and beat in the mint and garlic. Cut the loaf into slanting slices but leave a hinge on the bottom crust. Spread each slice with the butter and reassemble the loaf. Wrap in foil and place in a preheated oven, 350°F/180°C, for about 15 minutes.

7 Serve the soup garnished with a sprig of mint and accompanied by the minted garlic bread.

Watercress Vichyssoise

The addition of watercress to a traditional vichyssoise gives it a refreshing flavor and lovely cool color.

NUTRITIONAL INFORMATION

Calories	42	Sugars	.......0.8g
Protein	........2.1g	Fat	..........2.2g
Carbohydrate	...3.6g	Saturates	.......1g

 15 mins, plus chillling   35 mins

SERVES 6

INGREDIENTS

1 tbsp olive oil

3 large leeks, thinly sliced

2 cups finely diced potatoes

2½ cups vegetable bouillon

2 cups water

1 bay leaf

6 oz/175g prepared watercress

¾ cup light cream

salt and pepper

watercress leaves, to garnish

1 Heat the oil in a heavy pan over medium heat. Add the leeks and cook for about 3 minutes, stirring frequently, until they begin to soften.

2 Add the potato, bouillon, water, and bay leaf. Add salt if the bouillon is unsalted. Bring to a boil, then reduce the heat, cover, and cook gently for about 25 minutes until the vegetables are tender. Remove the bay leaf.

3 Add the watercress and continue to cook for another 2–3 minutes, stirring frequently, until the watercress is completely wilted.

4 Let the soup cool slightly, then transfer to a blender or food processor and purée until smooth, working in batches if necessary. (If using a food processor, strain off the cooking liquid and reserve. Purée the soup solids with enough cooking liquid to moisten them, then combine with the remaining liquid.)

5 Put the soup in a large bowl and stir in half the cream. Season with salt, if needed, and plenty of pepper. Let cool.

6 Refrigerate until cold. Taste and adjust the seasoning. Ladle into chilled bowls, drizzle the remaining cream on top, garnish with watercress leaves, and serve.

Wonton Soup

The recipe for the wonton skins makes 24 but the soup requires only half this quantity. The other half can be frozen ready for another time.

NUTRITIONAL INFORMATION

Calories 278	Sugars 2g	
Protein 10g	Fat 5g	
Carbohydrate ...50g	Saturates 1g	

45 mins   5 mins

SERVES 4

INGREDIENTS

WONTON SKINS

1 egg

6 tbsp water

1¾ cups all-purpose flour, plus extra for dusting

FILLING

¾ cup frozen chopped spinach, defrosted

½ oz/15 g pine nuts, toasted and chopped

¼ cup minced TVP

salt

SOUP

2½ cups vegetable bouillon

1 tbsp dry sherry

1 tbsp light soy sauce

2 scallions, chopped

1 To make the wonton skins, beat the egg lightly in a bowl and mix with the water. Stir in the flour to form a stiff dough. Knead lightly, then cover with a damp cloth and let rest for 30 minutes.

2 Roll the dough out into a large sheet about ¼ inch/1.5 mm thick. Cut out 24 x 3 inch/7 cm squares and dust each square lightly with flour. Only 12 squares are required for the soup, but the remainder can be frozen to use on another occasion.

3 To make the filling, squeeze out the excess water from the defrosted spinach. Mix the spinach with the pine nuts and TVP until thoroughly combined. Season the mixture with salt.

4 Divide the mixture into 12 equal portions. Using a teaspoon, place one portion in the center of each square. Seal the wontons by bringing the opposite corners of each square together and squeezing well.

5 To make the soup, bring the vegetable bouillon, dry sherry, and soy sauce to a boil, then add the wontons and boil rapidly for 2–3 minutes. Add the chopped scallions and serve the soup immediately in warmed bowls, dividing the wantons equally.

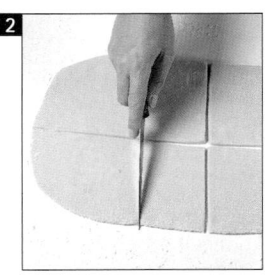

Vichyssoise

This is a classic creamy soup made from potatoes and leeks. To achieve the delicate pale color, be sure to use only the white parts of the leeks.

NUTRITIONAL INFORMATION

Calories . . . . . . .208 Sugars 5g
Protein . . . . .5g Fat 12g
Carbohydrate . . .20g Saturates 6g

15 mins, plus chillling   40 mins

SERVES 6

I N G R E D I E N T S

3 large leeks

3 tbsp butter or margarine

1 onion, thinly sliced

1 lb 2 oz/500 g potatoes, chopped

3½ cups vegetable bouillon

2 tsp lemon juice

pinch of ground nutmeg

¼ tsp ground coriander

1 bay leaf

1 egg yolk

⅔ cup light cream

salt and white pepper

freshly snipped chives, to garnish

1 Trim the leeks and remove most of the green part. Slice the white part of the leeks very finely.

2 Melt the butter or margarine in a pan. Add the leeks and onion and sauté, stirring occasionally, for about 5 minutes without browning.

3 Add the potatoes, vegetable bouillon, lemon juice, nutmeg, coriander, and bay leaf to the pan. Season to taste with salt and pepper and bring to a boil. Cover and simmer for about 30 minutes, until all the vegetables are very soft.

4 Cool the soup a little. Remove and discard the bay leaf and then press through a strainer or process in a food processor or blender until smooth. Pour into a clean pan.

5 Blend the egg yolk into the cream. Add a little of the soup to this mixture and then whisk it all back into the soup. Reheat the soup gently, without boiling. Adjust the seasoning to taste if necessary. Cool, and then chill thoroughly in the refrigerator.

6 Serve the chilled soup garnished with a sprinkling of freshly snipped chives.

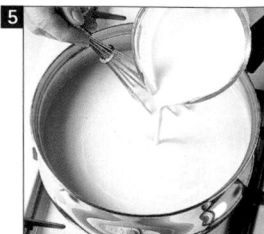

Iced Gazpacho

This delicious soup, with its brightly colored garnish of bell peppers, cucumber, and scallions, is perfect to serve at a summer lunch party.

NUTRITIONAL INFORMATION

Calories	164	Sugars	.........7g
Protein	.........3g	Fat	..........12g
Carbohydrate	...13g	Saturates	.......3g

20 mins, plus chilling   5 mins

SERVES 4–6

INGREDIENTS

2 ripe red bell peppers

1 cucumber

1 lb/450 g large, juicy tomatoes, skinned, seeded, and coarsely chopped

4 tbsp olive oil

2 tbsp sherry vinegar

salt and pepper

GARLIC CROUTONS

2 tbsp olive oil

1 garlic clove, halved

2 slices bread, crusts removed, cut into ¼ inch cubes

sea salt

TO GARNISH

diced green bell pepper

diced red bell pepper

finely diced seeded cucumber

chopped scallions

ice cubes

1 Cut the bell peppers in half and remove the cores and seeds, then coarsely chop. Peel the cucumber, cut it in half lengthwise, then cut into quarters. Remove the seeds with a teaspoon, then coarsely chop the flesh.

2 Put the chopped red bell peppers, cucumber, and tomatoes with the olive oil and sherry vinegar in a food processor and process until smooth. Season the soup with salt and pepper to taste. Transfer to a bowl, cover, and chill for at least 4 hours.

3 Meanwhile, make the garlic croûtons. Heat the oil in a skillet over medium-high heat. Add the garlic and sauté, stirring, for 2 minutes to flavor the oil.

4 Remove and discard the garlic. Add the diced bread and cook until golden on all sides. Drain well on crumpled paper towels and sprinkle with sea salt. Store in an airtight container if not using at once.

5 To serve, place each of the vegetable garnishes in bowls for guests to add to their soup. Taste the soup and adjust the seasoning if necessary. Put ice cubes into soup bowls and ladle the soup on top. Serve at once.

Onion & Artichoke Soup

This refreshing chilled soup is ideal for alfresco dining. It is very quick to make, but needs several hours in the refrigerator to chill thoroughly.

NUTRITIONAL INFORMATION

Calories	159	Sugars 2g
Protein	.........2g	Fat 15g
Carbohydrate	....5g	Saturates 6g

  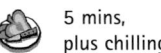

 5 mins, plus chilling 15 mins

SERVES 4

I N G R E D I E N T S

1 tbsp olive oil

1 onion, chopped

1 garlic clove, minced

28 oz canned artichoke hearts, drained

2½ cups hot vegetable bouillon

⅔ cup light cream

2 tbsp fresh thyme, stalks removed

2 sun-dried tomatoes, cut into strips

1 Heat the oil in a large pan and cook the chopped onion and minced garlic until just soft.

2 Using a sharp knife, coarsely chop the artichoke hearts. Add the artichoke pieces to the onion and garlic mixture in the pan. Pour in the hot bouillon, stirring.

3 Bring the mixture to a boil, then reduce the heat and let simmer, covered, for about 3 minutes.

4 Place the mixture in a food processor and blend until smooth. Alternatively, push the mixture through a strainer to remove any lumps.

5 Return the soup to the pan. Stir the light cream and fresh thyme into the soup.

6 Transfer the soup to a large bowl and cover, and then let chill in the refrigerator for about 3–4 hours.

7 Transfer the chilled soup to individual soup bowls and garnish with strips of sun-dried tomato. Serve with lots of fresh, crusty bread.

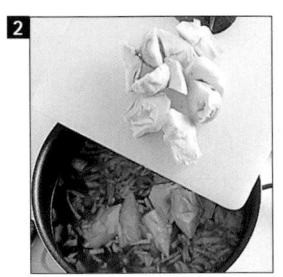

COOK'S TIP
Try adding 2 tablespoons of dry vermouth, such as Martini, to the soup in step 5.

Garlic & Almond Soup

This pretty, pale, chilled soup looks beautiful with its unusual garnish of sliced white grapes and a swirl of olive oil.

NUTRITIONAL INFORMATION

Calories	.513	Sugars	.3g
Protein	.15g	Fat	.34g
Carbohydrate	.40g	Saturates	.4g

 30 mins, plus chilling   0 mins

SERVES 4–6

I N G R E D I E N T S

14 oz day-old French bread, sliced

4 large garlic cloves

3–4 tbsp sherry vinegar

6 tbsp extra-virgin olive oil

2 cups ground almonds

4 cups water, chilled

sea salt and pepper

TO GARNISH

seedless white grapes, chilled and sliced

pepper

extra-virgin olive oil

1 Tear the bread into small pieces and put in a bowl. Pour over enough cold water to cover and soak for 10–15 minutes. Using your hands, squeeze the bread dry. Transfer the moist bread to a food processor.

2 Cut the garlic cloves in half lengthwise and use the tip of the knife to remove the pale green or white cores. Add to the food processor with 3 tablespoons of the sherry vinegar and 1 cup of the water, and process until blended. Add the oil and ground almonds and blend.

3 With the motor running, slowly pour in the remaining water until a smooth

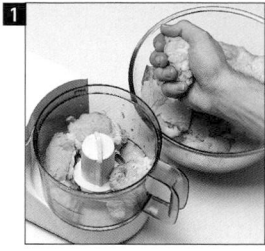  

soup forms. Add extra sherry vinegar to taste, and season with salt and pepper. Transfer the soup to a bowl, cover, and chill in the refrigerator for at least 4 hours.

4 To serve, adjust the seasoning. Ladle into bowls and float grapes on top. Garnish each with a sprinkling of pepper and a swirl of olive oil. Serve while still very cold.

COOK'S TIP

Instead of grapes, serve with Garlic Croûtons and diced vegetables (see the Gazpacho recipe on page 115). Alternatively, sprinkle with a dusting of paprika or very finely chopped fresh parsley just before serving.

Cold Cilantro Soup

This soup brings together Thai flavors for a cool, refreshing appetizer. It highlights fresh cilantro, now much more widely available.

NUTRITIONAL INFORMATION

Calories	79	Sugars	.........5g
Protein	.........3g	Fat	...........3g
Carbohydrate	...13g	Saturates	.......0g

15 mins, plus chilling 30 mins

SERVES 4

INGREDIENTS

2 tsp olive oil

1 large onion, finely chopped

1 leek, thinly sliced

1 garlic clove, thinly sliced

4 cups water

1 zucchini, about 7 oz/200 g, peeled and chopped

4 tbsp long grain white rice

2 inch/5 cm piece of lemon grass

2 lime leaves

2 cups fresh cilantro leaves and soft stems

chili paste, optional

salt and pepper

finely chopped red bell pepper and/or fresh red chilies, to garnish

1 Heat the oil in a large pan over medium heat. Add the onion, leek, and garlic and cook, stirring occasionally, for 4–5 minutes until the onion is soft, but not browned.

2 Add the water, zucchini, and rice with a pinch of salt and some pepper. Stir in the lemon grass and lime leaves. Bring just to a boil and reduce the heat to low. Cover and simmer for 15–20 minutes until the rice is soft and tender.

3 Add the fresh cilantro leaves and stems, pushing them down into the liquid. Continue cooking over low heat for 2–3 minutes until the leaves are wilted. Remove and discard the lemon grass and lime leaves.

4 Remove from the heat and let cool slightly, then transfer to a blender or food processor, and process to a smooth purée, working in batches if necessary. (If using a food processor, strain off the cooking liquid and reserve. Purée the soup solids with enough cooking liquid to moisten them, then combine with the remaining liquid.)

5 Scrape the soup into a large container. Season to taste with salt and pepper. Cover with plastic wrap and chill in the refrigerator until cold.

6 Taste and adjust the seasoning. For a spicier soup, stir in a little chili paste to taste. For a thinner soup, add a small amount of ice water. Ladle into chilled bowls and garnish with finely chopped red bell pepper and/or chilies.

Spiced Fruit Soup

This delicately flavored apple and apricot soup is gently spiced with ginger and allspice and finished with a swirl of sour cream.

NUTRITIONAL INFORMATION

Calories 147	Sugars 28g
Protein 3g	Fat 0.4g
Carbohydrate ... 29g	Saturates 0g

15 mins, plus chilling   25 mins

SERVES 4–6

INGREDIENTS

generous 1 cup dried apricots, soaked overnight, or no-soak dried apricots

1 lb 2 oz/500 g eating apples, peeled, cored, and chopped

1 small onion, chopped

1 tbsp lemon or lime juice

3 cups vegetable bouillon

⅔ cup dry white wine

¼ tsp ground ginger

pinch of ground allspice

salt and pepper

TO GARNISH

4–6 tbsp sour cream

ground ginger or ground allspice

1 Drain the apricots, if necessary, and chop coarsely.

2 Put the apricots in a pan and add the apples, onion, lemon or lime juice, and bouillon. Bring to a boil, cover, and simmer gently for about 20 minutes.

3 Set the soup aside to cool a little, then press through a strainer or process in a food processor or blender until a smooth purée. Pour the fruit soup into a clean pan.

4 Add the wine and spices to the soup and season to taste.

5 Bring back to a boil, then let cool. If the soup is too thick, add a little more bouillon or water. Transfer to a serving bowl and chill in the refrigerator for several hours.

6 To serve, garnish with sour cream and dust lightly with ginger or allspice.

VARIATION

Other fruits can be combined with apples to make fruit soups— try raspberries, blackberries, black currants, or cherries. If the fruits have a lot of seeds or pits, the soup should be strained after puréeing.

Vegetarian Hot & Sour Soup

This popular soup is easy to make and very filling. It can be eaten as a meal on its own or served as an appetizer before a light menu.

NUTRITIONAL INFORMATION

Calories	61	Sugars	.......1g
Protein	......5g	Fat	.........2g
Carbohydrate	...8g	Saturates	.....0.2g

🖐 30 mins 🕐 10 mins

SERVES 4

INGREDIENTS

4 Chinese dried mushrooms (if unavailable, use open-cup mushrooms)

4½ oz/125 g firm bean curd

2 oz/60 g canned bamboo shoots

2½ cups vegetable bouillon or water

½ cup peas

1 tbsp dark soy sauce

2 tbsp white wine vinegar

2 tbsp cornstarch

salt and pepper

sesame oil, to serve

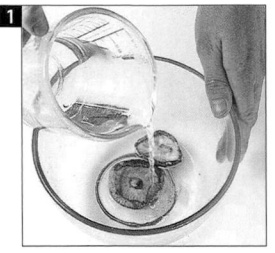

1 Place the Chinese dried mushrooms in a small bowl and cover with warm water. Leave them to soak for about 20–25 minutes.

2 Drain the mushrooms and squeeze out the excess water, reserving this. Remove the tough centers and cut the mushrooms into thin shreds. Shred the bean curd and bamboo shoots.

3 Bring the vegetable bouillon or water to a boil in a large pan. Add the mushrooms, bean curd, bamboo shoots, and peas. Simmer for 2 minutes.

4 Mix together the soy sauce, the white wine vinegar, and the cornstarch with 2 tablespoons of the liquid reserved from soaking the mushrooms.

5 Stir the soy sauce and cornstarch mixture into the soup with the remaining mushroom liquid. Bring the mixture to a boil and season to taste with salt and plenty of pepper. Simmer for a further 2 minutes.

6 Ladle the soup into warmed bowls and serve with a few drops of sesame oil sprinkled over the top of each.

COOK'S TIP

If you use open-cup mushrooms instead of dried mushrooms, add an extra ⅝ cup of vegetable bouillon or water to the soup, as these mushrooms do not need soaking.

Minestrone with Pesto

This version of minestrone contains cannellini beans—these need to be soaked overnight, so prepare in advance.

NUTRITIONAL INFORMATION

Calories	604	Sugars	.........3g
Protein	........26g	Fat	..........45g
Carbohydrate	...24g	Saturates	......11g

 10–15 mins 1¾ hrs

SERVES 6

I N G R E D I E N T S

¾ cup dried cannellini beans, soaked overnight

10 cups water or vegetable bouillon

1 large onion, chopped

1 leek, trimmed and sliced thinly

2 celery stalks, sliced very thinly

2 carrots, chopped

3 tbsp olive oil

2 tomatoes, peeled and coarsely chopped

1 zucchini, trimmed and sliced thinly

2 potatoes, diced

scant 1 cup elbow macaroni (or other small macaroni)

salt and pepper

4–6 tbsp freshly grated Parmesan, to serve

P E S T O

2 tbsp pine nuts

5 tbsp olive oil

2 bunches basil, stems removed

4–6 garlic cloves, crushed

1¼ cups grated Parmesan

1 Drain the soaked beans, rinse, and put in a pan with the water or vegetable bouillon (avoid using a very salty bouillon, or the beans will become tough during cooking.) Bring to a boil, cover, and simmer for 1 hour.

2 Add the onion, leek, celery, carrots, and oil. Cover and simmer for 4–5 minutes.

3 Add the tomatoes, zucchini, potatoes, macaroni, and seasoning. Cover again and continue to simmer for about 30 minutes or until very tender.

4 Meanwhile, make the pesto. Sauté the pine nuts in 1 tablespoon of the oil until pale brown, then drain. Put the basil into a food processor or blender with the nuts and garlic and process until well chopped. Alternatively, chop the basil finely by hand and pound with the crushed garlic using a pestle and mortar. Gradually add the remaining oil until smooth. Turn into a bowl, add the cheese and seasoning, and mix thoroughly.

5 Add 1½ tablespoons of the pesto to the soup and stir until it is well blended. Simmer the soup for a further 5 minutes and adjust the seasoning if necessary. Serve the soup very hot in warmed bowls, sprinkled with the freshly grated Parmesan cheese.

Cucumber Soup

Parsley tames the pungent garlic flavor of this traditional Balkan soup. The cucumber and yogurt make it a refreshing summer appetizer.

NUTRITIONAL INFORMATION

Calories	208	Sugars	........10g
Protein	.........8g	Fat	..........15g
Carbohydrate	...10g	Saturates	.......2g

15 mins, plus chilling   0 mins

SERVES 4

INGREDIENTS

1 large cucumber

½ cup walnut pieces, toasted (see Cook's Tip)

½ cup fresh parsley leaves

1 small garlic clove, very finely chopped

2 tbsp olive oil

4 tbsp water

1 tbsp fresh lemon juice

1¼ cups unsweetened strained yogurt

salt and pepper

fresh mint leaves, to garnish

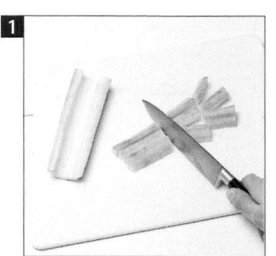

1 Peel the cucumber, slice lengthwise, and scoop out the seeds with a small, pointed spoon. Cut the flesh into 1 inch/2.5 cm pieces.

COOK'S TIP
Toasting the walnuts gives them extra flavor. Just heat them in a dry skillet over medium-low heat until they begin to color and smell aromatic.

2 Put the walnuts, parsley leaves, garlic, oil, and water in a blender or food processor with half of the cucumber and process to a smooth purée, stopping to scrape down the sides as necessary.

3 Add the remaining cucumber to the blender or processor with a pinch of salt and the lemon juice. Process briefly until smooth.

4 Scrape the purée into a large bowl and stir in the yogurt. Season to taste with salt and pepper and add a little more lemon juice, if wished.

5 Cover with plastic wrap and chill in the refrigerator for about 30 minutes or until cold. Taste and adjust the seasoning if necessary. Ladle into chilled bowls and garnish with mint leaves.

Walnut, Egg & Cheese Pâté

This unusual pâté, flavored with parsley and dill, can be served with crackers, crusty bread, or toast. The pâté requires chilling until set.

NUTRITIONAL INFORMATION

Calories . . . . . . .438 Sugars 2g
Protein . . . . .21g Fat 38g
Carbohydrate . . . .2g Saturates 18g

 20 mins   2 mins

SERVES 4

I N G R E D I E N T S

1 celery stalk

1–2 scallions

¼ cup shelled walnuts

1 tbsp chopped fresh parsley

1 tsp chopped fresh dill or ½ tsp dried dill

1 garlic clove, crushed

dash of Worcestershire sauce

½ cup cottage cheese

½ cup blue cheese, finely grated

1 hard-cooked egg

2 tbsp butter

salt and pepper

fresh herbs, to garnish

crackers, toast, or crusty bread and crudités, to serve

1 Finely chop the celery, slice the scallions very thinly, and chop the walnuts evenly. Place in a bowl.

2 Add the chopped herbs and garlic and Worcestershire sauce to taste and mix well, then stir the cottage cheese evenly through the mixture.

3 Stir the blue cheese into the pâté mixture. Finely chop the hard-cooked egg and stir it into the mixture. Season to taste with salt and pepper.

4 Melt the butter and stir it into the pâté, then spoon into 1 serving dish or 4 individual dishes. Smooth the top, but do not press down firmly. Chill until set.

5 Garnish with fresh herbs and serve with crackers, toast, or fresh, crusty bread and a few crudités, if liked.

COOK'S TIP
You can also use this as a stuffing for vegetables. Cut the tops off extra-large tomatoes, scoop out the seeds, and fill with the pâté, piling it well up, or spoon into the hollows of celery stalks cut into 2 inch/5 cm pieces.

Lentil Pâté

Red lentils are used in this spicy recipe for speed as they do not require presoaking. If you use other lentils, soak and precook them first.

NUTRITIONAL INFORMATION

Calories	267	Sugars	........12g
Protein	........14g	Fat	...........8g
Carbohydrate	...37g	Saturates	......1g

  25 mins   1¼ hrs

SERVES 4

INGREDIENTS

1 tbsp vegetable oil, plus extra for greasing

1 onion, chopped

2 garlic cloves, crushed

1 tsp garam masala

½ tsp ground coriander

3½ cups vegetable bouillon

1 cup red lentils

1 small egg

2 tbsp milk

2 tbsp mango chutney

2 tbsp chopped parsley

chopped parsley, to garnish

salad greens and warm toast, to serve

1 Heat the vegetable oil in a large pan and sauté the onion and garlic for 2–3 minutes, stirring. Add the spices and cook for a further 30 seconds. Stir in the vegetable bouillon and lentils and bring the mixture to a boil. Reduce the heat and simmer for 20 minutes or until the lentils are soft. Remove the pan from the heat and drain off any excess moisture.

2 Put the mixture in a food processor and add the egg, milk, mango chutney, and parsley. Blend until smooth.

3 Grease and line the base of a 1 lb loaf pan and spoon the mixture into the pan. Cover and cook in a preheated oven at 400°F/200°C for 40–45 minutes or until firm.

4 Let the pâté cool in the pan for 20 minutes, then transfer to the refrigerator to cool completely. Slice the pâté and garnish with chopped parsley. Serve with salad greens and warm toast.

VARIATION

Use other spices, such as chili powder or Chinese five-spice powder, to flavor the pâté, and add tomato relish or chili relish instead of the mango chutney, if you prefer.

Hummus & Garlic Toasts

Hummus is a real favorite spread on these garlic toasts for a delicious appetizer or as part of a nutritious light lunch.

NUTRITIONAL INFORMATION

Calories 731	Sugars 2g	
Protein 22g	Fat 55g	
Carbohydrate . . .39g	Saturates 8g	

 10–15 mins   5 mins

SERVES 4

I N G R E D I E N T S

1½ cups canned garbanzo
  beans (chickpeas)

juice of 1 large lemon

6 tbsp sesame seed paste (tahini)

2 tbsp olive oil

2 garlic cloves, finely chopped

salt and pepper

1 ciabatta loaf, sliced

2 garlic cloves, finely chopped

1 tbsp chopped fresh cilantro

4 tbsp olive oil

chopped fresh cilantro and black olives,
  to garnish

1 To make the hummus, firstly drain the garbanzo beans, reserving a little of the liquid. Put the garbanzo beans and liquid in a food processor and blend, gradually adding the reserved liquid and lemon juice. Blend well after each addition until smooth.

2 Stir in the sesame seed paste and all but 1 teaspoon of the olive oil. Add the garlic, season to taste, and blend again until smooth.

3 Spoon the hummus into a serving dish. Drizzle the remaining olive oil over the top, and garnish with chopped cilantro and olives. Let chill in the refrigerator while preparing the toasts.

4 Lay the slices of ciabatta on a broiler rack in a single layer.

5 Mix the garlic, cilantro, and olive oil together and drizzle over the bread slices. Cook under a hot broiler for 2–3 minutes until golden brown, turning once. Serve hot with the hummus.

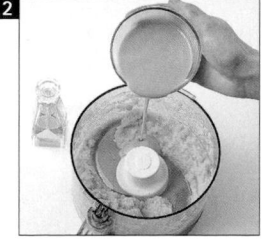

Mushroom & Garlic Soufflés

These individual soufflés make very impressive appetizers, but must be cooked just before serving to prevent them from sinking.

NUTRITIONAL INFORMATION

Calories	179	Sugars	.........3g
Protein	.........6g	Fat	..........14g
Carbohydrate	....8g	Saturates	.......8g

 10 mins   20 mins

SERVES 4

INGREDIENTS

4 tbsp butter

2¾ oz/75 g flat mushrooms, chopped

2 tsp lime juice

2 garlic cloves, crushed

2 tbsp chopped marjoram

3½ tbsp all-purpose flour

1 cup milk

salt and pepper

2 eggs, separated

1 Lightly grease the inside of 4⅝ cup/150 ml individual soufflé dishes with a little butter.

2 Melt 2 tablespoons of the butter in a skillet. Add the mushrooms, lime juice, and garlic and sauté for 2–3 minutes, then remove the mushroom mixture with a slotted spoon and transfer it to a mixing bowl. Stir in the marjoram.

3 Melt the remaining butter in a pan. Add the flour and cook for 1 minute, then remove from the heat. Stir in the milk and return to the heat. Bring to a boil, stirring until thickened.

4 Mix the sauce into the mushroom mixture and beat in the egg yolks.

5 Whisk the egg whites until they form peaks and fold into the mushroom mixture until fully incorporated.

6 Divide the mixture between the prepared soufflé dishes. Place the dishes on a cookie sheet and cook in a preheated oven, 400°F/200°C, for about 8–10 minutes, or until the soufflés are well risen, golden brown, and cooked through. Serve immediately.

COOK'S TIP

Insert a skewer into the center of the soufflés to test if they are cooked through—it should come out clean. If not, cook for a few minutes longer, but do not overcook otherwise they will become rubbery.

Stuffed Grape Leaves

These refreshing little parcels with their fragrant filling are a lovely way to start a summer meal. Serve them warm, the way the Greeks do.

NUTRITIONAL INFORMATION

Calories	407	Sugars	.........1g
Protein	.........5g	Fat	..........32g
Carbohydrate	...27g	Saturates	.......4g

🍳 20 mins 🕐 45 mins

SERVES 6

INGREDIENTS

8 oz/225 g grape leaves

4 scallions, finely chopped

2 shallots, finely chopped

¼ cup slivered almonds, toasted

3 tbsp chopped fresh parsley

3 tbsp chopped fresh mint

finely grated zest of 1 lemon

scant 1 cup long grain rice

½ cup olive oil

1¼ cups boiling vegetable bouillon

salt and ground black pepper

FOR THE DRESSING

½ cup extra virgin olive oil

3 tbsp lemon juice

1 tbsp chopped fresh mint

1 If using fresh grape leaves, blanch them in boiling water for 5 minutes, then refresh under cold water and pat dry. If using preserved grape leaves, rinse thoroughly and pat dry. Cut off the stalks and prepare the herbs.

2 Combine the scallions, shallots, almonds, parsley, mint, lemon zest, and rice in a bowl and add half the oil. Season to taste with salt. Spread out a grape leaf on a counter and place a spoonful of the filling near the stalk end. Fold the stalk end over, fold the sides in and roll up to make a neat parcel. Repeat with the remaining leaves and filling.

3 Line the base of a large pan with any remaining grape leaves and place the parcels on top in a single layer. Sprinkle with the remaining oil and pour in the bouillon. Place a plate on top of the leaves to keep them submerged, cover the pan, and simmer for 45 minutes. To make the dressing, pour the oil into a small serving bowl and season well with salt and pepper. Whisk in the lemon juice and stir in the mint. Serve the grape leaves warm or cold, with the dressing.

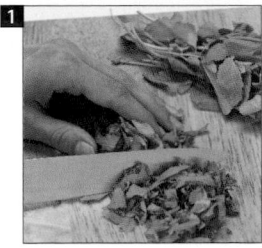

Phyllo Parcels

These crisp pastry parcels can be served as a main course with a potato salad and mixed salad greens or on their own as appetizers.

NUTRITIONAL INFORMATION

Calories 410   Sugars 5g
Protein . . . . .14g   Fat 19g
Carbohydrate . . .45g   Saturates 11g

15 mins, plus chilling   45 mins

SERVES 6

INGREDIENTS

4 tbsp butter

1 tbsp sunflower oil

4 leeks, sliced

2 onions, chopped

1 garlic clove, finely chopped

2 tsp chopped fresh thyme

2 tbsp light cream

1 cup grated Swiss cheese

12 sheet phyllo pastry, thawed if frozen

salt and ground black pepper

1 Melt half the butter with the oil in a large, heavy skillet. Add the leeks, onions, garlic, and thyme and season to taste with salt and pepper. Cook, stirring frequently, for 10 minutes. Stir in the cream and cook for 2–3 minutes more, until all the liquid has been absorbed. Remove the pan from the heat and let cool. Stir in the cheese, cover with plastic wrap, and chill in the refrigerator for 30 minutes.

2 Melt the remaining butter and brush a little on to a cookie sheet. Brush 2 sheets of phyllo with butter and place them one on top of the other. Place a heaped spoonful of the leek mixture close to 1 corner. Fold the corner over the filling, fold in the sides, and roll up the parcel. Place the parcel, seam side down, on the cookie sheet and make 5 more parcels in the same way.

3 Brush the pastry parcels with the remaining melted butter and bake in a preheated oven, 350°F/180°C, for 30 minutes, until crisp and golden. Serve immediately.

Mixed Bhajis

These small bhajis are often served as an accompaniment but are also delicious served as an appetizer with a small salad and yogurt sauce.

NUTRITIONAL INFORMATION

Calories 414	Sugars 7g	
Protein 9g	Fat 26g	
Carbohydrate . . .38g	Saturates 3g	

25 mins   30 mins

SERVES 4

INGREDIENTS

BHAJIS

1 cup gram (besan) flour

1 tsp baking soda

2 tsp ground coriander

1 tsp garam masala

1½ tsp turmeric

1½ tsp chili powder

2 tbsp chopped cilantro

1 small onion, halved and sliced

1 small leek, sliced

1 cup cooked cauliflower

9–12 tbsp cold water

salt and pepper

vegetable oil, for deep-frying

SAUCE

⅔ cup unsweetened yogurt

2 tbsp chopped mint

½ tsp turmeric

1 garlic clove, crushed

mint sprigs, to garnish

1 Strain the flour, baking soda, and salt to taste into a mixing bowl and add the spices and fresh cilantro. Mix together thoroughly.

2 Divide the mixture into 3 and place in separate bowls. Stir the onion into one bowl, the leek into another, and the cauliflower into the third bowl. Add 3–4 tbsp of water to each bowl and mix each to form a smooth paste.

3 Heat the vegetable oil in a deep fryer to 350°F/180°C or until a cube of bread browns in 30 seconds. Using 2 dessert spoons, form the mixture into rounds and cook each in the oil for 3–4 minutes, until browned.

4 Remove the bhajis with a slotted spoon, drain well on absorbent paper towels, and keep warm in the oven while cooking the remainder.

5 Mix the sauce ingredients together, garnish with mint sprigs, and serve with the warm bhajis.

Feta Cheese Tartlets

These crisp-baked bread cases, filled with sliced tomatoes, feta cheese, black olives, and quail's eggs, are quick to make and taste delicious.

NUTRITIONAL INFORMATION

Calories 570	Sugars 3g
Protein 14g	Fat 42g
Carbohydrate . . .36g	Saturates 23g

30 mins   10 mins

SERVES 4

INGREDIENTS

8 slices bread from a medium-cut large loaf

½ cup & 1 tbsp butter, melted

1 cup feta cheese, cut into small cubes

4 cherry tomatoes, cut into wedges

8 pitted black or green olives, halved

8 quail's eggs, hard-cooked

2 tbsp olive oil

1 tbsp wine vinegar

1 tsp whole-grain mustard

pinch of superfine sugar

salt and pepper

parsley sprigs, to garnish

1 Remove the crusts from the bread. Trim the bread into squares and flatten each piece with a rolling pin.

2 Brush the bread squares with melted butter, and then arrange them in bun or muffin pans. Press a piece of crumpled foil into each bread case to secure in place. Bake the cases in a preheated oven, 375°F/190°C, for about 10 minutes, or until crisp and browned.

3 Meanwhile, mix together the feta cheese, tomatoes, and olives. Shell the eggs and quarter them. Mix together the

olive oil, vinegar, mustard, and sugar. Season to taste with salt and pepper.

4 Remove the bread cases from the oven and discard the foil. Let cool.

5 Just before serving, fill the bread cases with the cheese and tomato mixture. Arrange the eggs on top and spoon over the dressing. Garnish with parsley sprigs.

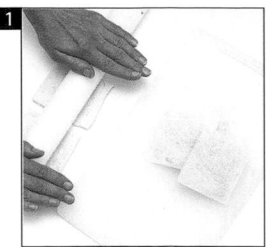

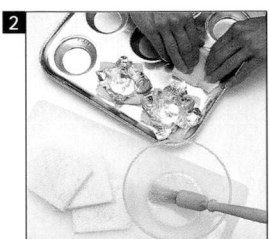

Spinach Phyllo Baskets

If you use frozen spinach, it only needs to be thawed and drained before being mixed with the cheeses and seasonings.

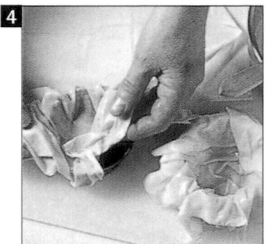

NUTRITIONAL INFORMATION

Calories	533	Sugars	.........3g
Protein	........24g	Fat	..........38g
Carbohydrate	...26g	Saturates	......22g

 55 mins   30 mins

SERVES 2

INGREDIENTS

3 cups fresh leaf spinach, washed and chopped roughly, or ½ cup thawed frozen spinach

2–4 scallions, trimmed and chopped, or 1 tbsp finely chopped onion

1 garlic clove, crushed

2 tbsp grated Parmesan cheese

¾ cup grated sharp Cheddar cheese

pinch of ground allspice

1 egg yolk

4 sheets phyllo pastry

2 tbsp butter, melted

salt and pepper

2 scallions, to garnish

1 If using fresh spinach, cook it in the minimum of boiling salted water for 3–4 minutes, until tender. Drain very thoroughly, using a potato masher to remove excess liquid, then chop and put into a bowl. If using frozen spinach, simply drain and chop.

2 Add the scallions or onion, garlic, cheeses, allspice, egg yolk, and seasoning, and mix well.

3 Grease 2 individual muffin pans, or alternatively use ovenproof dishes or pans about 5 inches/12 cm in diameter, and 1½ inches/4 cm deep. Cut the phyllo pastry sheets in half to make 8 pieces and brush each piece lightly with the melted butter.

4 Place one piece of phyllo pastry in a pan or dish and then cover with a second piece at right angles to the first. Add two more pieces at right angles, so that all the corners are in different places. Line the other pan in the same way.

5 Spoon the spinach mixture into the "baskets" and cook in a preheated oven, 350°F/180°C, for about 20 minutes, or until the pastry is golden brown. Garnish each basket with a scallion tassel and serve hot or cold.

6 Make the scallion tassels about 30 minutes before required. Trim off the root end and cut to a length of 2–3 inches/5–7 cm. Make a series of cuts from the green end to within ¾ inch/2 cm of the other end. Place in a bowl of iced water to open out. Drain well before use.

Leek & Tomato Timbales

Angel-hair pasta, known as cappellini, is mixed with fried leeks, sun-dried tomatoes, fresh oregano, and beaten eggs, and baked in ramekins.

NUTRITIONAL INFORMATION

Calories 331   Sugars 10g
Protein . . . . .10g   Fat 21g
Carbohydrate . . .26g   Saturates 9g

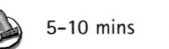

5–10 mins   50 mins

SERVES 4

INGREDIENTS

90 g/3 oz angel-hair pasta (cappellini)

2 tbsp butter

1 tbsp olive oil

1 large leek, sliced finely

2 oz/60 g sun-dried tomatoes in oil, drained and chopped

1 tbsp chopped fresh oregano or 1 tsp dried oregano

2 eggs, beaten

⅓ cup light cream

1 tbsp freshly grated Parmesan

salt and pepper

sprigs of oregano, to garnish

lettuce leaves, to serve

SAUCE

1 small onion, chopped finely

1 small garlic clove, crushed

¾ lb/350 g tomatoes, peeled and chopped

1 tsp mixed dried Italian herbs

4 tbsp dry white wine

1 Cook the pasta in plenty of boiling salted water for about 3 minutes until "al dente" (just tender). Drain and rinse with cold water to cool quickly.

2 Meanwhile, heat the butter and oil in a skillet. Gently sauté the leek until soft, about 5–6 minutes. Add the sun-dried tomatoes and oregano, and cook for a further 2 minutes, then remove the pan from the heat.

3 Add the leek mixture to the pasta. Stir in the beaten eggs, cream, and Parmesan. Season with salt and pepper. Divide between 4 greased ramekin dishes or dariole molds.

4 Place the dishes in a roasting pan with enough warm water to come halfway up their sides. Bake in a preheated oven, 350°F/180°C, for about 30 minutes, until set.

5 Meanwhile, make the tomato sauce. Sauté the onion and garlic in the remaining butter and oil until soft. Add the tomatoes, herbs, and wine. Cover and cook gently for about 20 minutes until pulpy. Blend in a food processor until smooth, or press through a strainer.

6 Run a knife or small spatula around the edge of the ramekins, then turn out the timbales on to 4 warm serving plates. Pour over a little sauce and garnish with oregano. Serve with the lettuce leaves.

Vegetable Fritters

These mixed vegetable fritters are coated in a light batter and deep-fried until golden. They are ideal with the sweet and sour dipping sauce.

 20 mins   🕐 20 mins

SERVES 4

I N G R E D I E N T S

¾ cup whole-wheat flour

pinch of cayenne pepper

4 tsp olive oil

12 tbsp cold water

1 cup broccoli florets

scant 1 cup cauliflower florets

¾ cup snow peas

1 large carrot, cut into batons

1 red bell pepper, seeded and sliced

2 egg whites, beaten

oil, for deep-frying

salt

S A U C E

⅔ cup pint pineapple juice

⅔ cup vegetable bouillon

2 tbsp white wine vinegar

2 tbsp light brown sugar

2 tsp cornstarch

2 scallions, chopped

1 Sift the flour and a pinch of salt into a mixing bowl and add the cayenne pepper. Make a well in the center and gradually beat in the oil and cold water to make a smooth batter.

2 Cook the vegetables in boiling water for 5 minutes and drain well.

3 Whisk the egg whites until they form peaks and gently fold them into the flour batter.

4 Dip the vegetables into the batter, turning to coat well. Drain off any excess batter. Heat the oil in a deep-fryer to 350°F/180°C or until a cube of bread browns in 30 seconds. Fry the coated vegetables, in batches, for 1–2 minutes, until golden. Remove from the oil with a slotted spoon and drain on paper towels.

5 Place all of the sauce ingredients in a pan and bring to a boil, stirring, until the sauce is thickened and clear. Serve with the fritters.

Heavenly Garlic Dip

Anyone who loves garlic will adore this dip—it is very potent! Serve it at a barbecue and dip raw vegetables or chunks of French bread into it.

NUTRITIONAL INFORMATION

Calories . . . . . . .344 Sugars 2g
Protein . . . . .6g Fat 34g
Carbohydrate . . . .3g Saturates 5g

15 mins   20 mins

SERVES 4

INGREDIENTS

2 bulbs garlic

6 tbsp olive oil

1 small onion, finely chopped

2 tbsp lemon juice

3 tbsp sesame seed paste (tahini)

2 tbsp chopped parsley

salt and pepper

TO SERVE

fresh vegetable crudités

French bread or warmed pocket breads

1 Separate the bulbs of garlic into individual cloves. Place them on a cookie sheet and roast in a preheated oven, 400°F/200°C, for 8–10 minutes. Set them aside to cool for a few minutes.

2 When they are cool enough to handle, peel the garlic cloves and then chop them finely.

3 Heat the olive oil in a pan or skillet and add the garlic and onion. Sauté over low heat, stirring occasionally, for 8–10 minutes, until soft. Remove the pan from the heat.

4 Mix in the lemon juice, sesame seed paste, and parsley. Season to taste with salt and pepper. Transfer the dip to a small heatproof bowl and keep warm at one side of the barbecue grill.

5 Serve with fresh vegetable crudités, or with chunks of French bread or warm pocket breads.

VARIATION

If you come across smoked garlic, use it in this recipe—it tastes wonderful. There is no need to roast the smoked garlic, so omit the first step. This dip can also be used to baste vegetarian burgers.

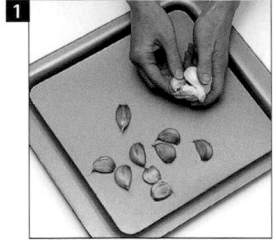

Mixed Bean Pâté

This is a really quick appetizer to prepare if canned beans are used. Choose a wide variety of beans for color and flavor.

NUTRITIONAL INFORMATION

Calories	126	Sugars	.........3g
Protein	.........5g	Fat	...........6g
Carbohydrate	...13g	Saturates	.......1g

 1 hr, plus chilling   0 mins

SERVES 4

I N G R E D I E N T S

1½–2 cups canned mixed beans, drained

2 tbsp olive oil

juice of 1 lemon

2 garlic cloves, crushed

1 tbsp chopped fresh cilantro

2 scallions, chopped

salt and pepper

shredded scallions, to garnish

1 Rinse the beans thoroughly under cold running water and drain well.

2 Transfer the beans to a food processor or blender and process until smooth. Alternatively, place the beans in a bowl and mash thoroughly by hand with a fork or potato masher.

3 Add the olive oil, lemon juice, garlic, cilantro, and scallions and blend until fairly smooth. Season with salt and pepper to taste.

4 Transfer the pâté to a serving bowl, cover, and chill in the refrigerator for at least 30 minutes.

5 Garnish the pâté with shredded scallions and serve.

Vegetable Medley

This is a colorful dish of shredded vegetables in a fresh garlic and honey dressing. It is delicious served with crusty bread.

NUTRITIONAL INFORMATION

Calories 209   Sugars 10g
Protein . . . . .2g   Fat 14g
Carbohydrate . . .20g   Saturates 2g

 15 mins   5 mins

SERVES 4

INGREDIENTS

2 tbsp olive oil

1 potato, cut into thin strips

1 fennel bulb, cut into thin strips

2 carrots, grated

1 red onion, cut into thin strips

chopped chives and fennel fronds, to
   garnish

DRESSING

3 tbsp olive oil

1 tbsp garlic wine vinegar

1 garlic clove, crushed

1 tsp Dijon mustard

2 tsp clear honey

salt and pepper

1 Heat the olive oil in a skillet, add the strips of potato and fennel, and cook them over medium heat for about 2–3 minutes, or until they are beginning to brown.

2 Remove the vegetables from the skillet with a slotted spoon and drain on paper towels.

3 Arrange the carrot, red onion, potato, and fennel in separate piles on a serving platter.

4 Mix the dressing ingredients together and pour over the vegetables. Toss well and sprinkle with chopped chives and fennel fronds. Serve immediately or leave in the refrigerator until required.

VARIATION
Use mixed, broiled bell peppers or shredded leeks in this dish for variety, or add bean sprouts and a segmented orange, if you prefer.

Avocado Cream Terrine

The smooth, rich taste of ripe avocados combines well with thick, creamy yogurt and light cream to make this impressive terrine.

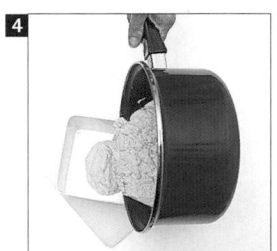

NUTRITIONAL INFORMATION

Calories	327	Sugars	.........3g
Protein	.........6g	Fat	..........32g
Carbohydrate	....4g	Saturates	.......8g

 15 mins, plus chilling   0 mins

SERVES 4

INGREDIENTS

2 ripe avocados

¼ cup cold water

2 tsp gelozone

1 tbsp lemon juice

4 tbsp low-fat mayonnaise

⅔ cup unsweetened yogurt

⅔ cup light cream

salt and pepper

mixed salad greens, to serve

TO GARNISH

cucumber slices

nasturtium flowers

1 Peel the avocados and remove and discard the pits. Put the flesh in a blender or food processor or a large bowl with the water, gelozone, lemon juice, mayonnaise, yogurt, and cream. Season to taste with salt and pepper.

2 Process for about 10–15 seconds or beat by hand, using a fork or whisk, until smooth.

3 Transfer the mixture to a small, heavy pan and heat very gently, stirring constantly, until it is just beginning to boil.

4 Pour the mixture into a 3¾ cup terrine, nonstick loaf pan, or plastic food storage box and smooth the surface. Let the mixture cool and set and then place in the refrigerator to chill completely for about 1½–2 hours.

5 Turn the terrine out of its container and cut into neat slices. Arrange a bed of salad greens on 4 serving plates, then place a slice of avocado terrine on top. Garnish with cucumber slices and nasturtium flowers.

Artichokes with Sauce

Always an elegant starter, globe artichokes are served here with a deliciously creamy and unusual orange-flavored sauce.

NUTRITIONAL INFORMATION

Calories . . . . . . .383 Sugars 7g
Protein . . . . .8g Fat 36g
Carbohydrate . . .10g Saturates 24g

 20 mins   25 mins

SERVES 4

INGREDIENTS

4 large globe artichokes

2 lemon slices

SAUCE MALTAISE

1 blood orange

¾ cup butter

2–3 tbsp lemon juice

3 tbsp water

3 egg yolks

salt and pepper

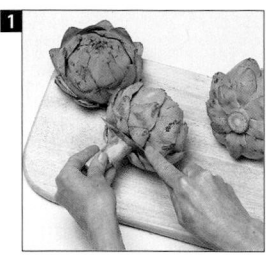

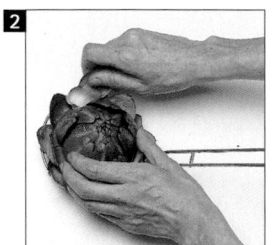

1 To prepare the globe artichokes, bring lightly salted water to a boil in a pan large enough to hold the 4 artichokes upright. Add the lemon slices. Break off the stems and trim the bases of the artichokes so they are flat and will sit upright on a plate.

2 Put the artichokes in the pan and place a heatproof plate on top. Lower the heat and simmer for 20–25 minutes, until you can easily pull a leaf out.

3 Meanwhile, make the sauce. Finely grate the zest from the orange and squeeze 2 tablespoons orange juice. Put the butter in a pan over medium heat and melt, skimming the surface.

4 Put 2 tablespoons of the lemon juice, the water, plus salt and pepper, in a bowl. Set it over a pan of simmering water, making sure the base of the bowl does not come into contact with the water. Whisk until heated.

5 Whisk in the egg yolks until they are thoroughly blended and warmed through. Then add the hot butter in a steady stream, whisking constantly, and continue to whisk the mixture until a thick, smooth sauce is formed.

6 Stir the grated orange zest and the orange juice into the sauce. Taste, and adjust the seasoning, adding a little extra lemon juice if necessary. Remove the sauce from the heat.

7 Drain the artichokes thoroughly. To serve, place each one on an individual plate with a ramekin of the warm Sauce Maltaise for dipping.

COOK'S TIP

Pull out the leaves, starting with the outer layer, dip the base of each leaf into the sauce, and scrape off the fleshy part with your teeth. Cut off the central core of purple leaves, which are inedible, and the hairy choke to reveal the delicious "heart."

Mini Vegetable Puff Pastries

These are ideal with a more formal meal as they take little time to prepare and look really impressive.

NUTRITIONAL INFORMATION

Calories	210	Sugars	.......2.3g
Protein	........3.8g	Fat	.........12.9g
Carbohydrate	..20.8g	Saturates	.....1.7g

 15 mins   25 mins

SERVES 4

I N G R E D I E N T S

PASTRY

1 lb/450 g puff pie dough

1 egg, beaten

FILLING

8 oz/225 g sweet potatoes, cubed

12–16 baby asparagus spears

2 tbsp butter or margarine

1 leek, sliced

2 small open-cup mushrooms, sliced

1 tsp lime juice

1 tsp chopped thyme

pinch of dried mustard

salt and pepper

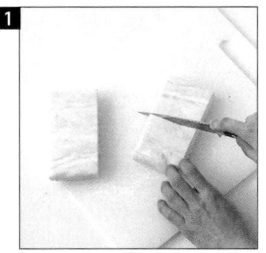 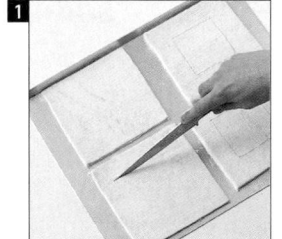 

1 Cut the pie dough into 4 equal pieces. Roll each piece out on a lightly floured surface to form a 5 inch/13 cm square. Place the pieces on a dampened cookie sheet and score a smaller 2½ inch/ 6 cm square inside.

2 Brush with beaten egg and cook in a preheated oven, 400°F/200°C, for 20 minutes or until risen and golden brown.

3 While the pie dough is cooking, start the filling. Cook the sweet potato in a pan of boiling water for 15 minutes, then drain well. Blanch the asparagus in a pan

of boiling water for 10 minutes or until tender. Drain and reserve.

4 Remove the pastry squares from the oven. Cut out the central square of pastry and lift out. Reserve.

5 Melt the butter or margarine in a pan and sauté the sliced leek and mushrooms for 2–3 minutes. Add the lime juice, thyme, and mustard and season well. Stir in the sweet potatoes and asparagus. Spoon into the pastry cases. Top with the reserved pastry squares and serve immediately.

COOK'S TIP

Use a colorful selection of any vegetables you have to hand for this recipe.

Buttered Nut & Lentil Dip

This tasty dip is very easy to make. It is perfect to have at barbecues, as it gives your guests something to nibble while they are waiting.

NUTRITIONAL INFORMATION

Calories ....395 Sugars 4g
Protein ....12g Fat 31g
Carbohydrate ...18g Saturates 10g

 5–10 mins   40 mins

SERVES 4

INGREDIENTS

4 tbsp butter

1 small onion, chopped

½ cup red lentils

1¼ cups vegetable bouillon

¾ cups blanched almonds

½ cup pine nuts

½ tsp ground coriander

½ tsp ground cumin

½ tsp grated ginger root

1 tsp chopped fresh cilantro

salt and pepper

sprigs of fresh coriander to garnish

TO SERVE

fresh vegetable crudités

bread sticks

VARIATION

Green or brown lentils can be used, but they will take longer to cook than red lentils. If you wish, substitute peanuts for the almonds. Ground ginger can be used instead of fresh—substitute ½ teaspoon and add it with the other spices.

1 Melt half the butter in a pan, add the onion and sauté over medium heat, stirring frequently, until it is golden brown in color.

2 Add the lentils and vegetable bouillon. Bring to a boil, then reduce the heat and simmer gently, uncovered, for about 25–30 minutes, until the lentils are tender. Drain well.

3 Melt the remaining butter in a small skillet. Add the almonds and pine nuts and cook them over low heat, stirring frequently, until golden brown. Remove the pan from the heat.

4 Put the lentils, the almonds, and the pine nuts into a food processor or blender, together with any butter remaining in the skillet. Add the ground coriander, cumin, ginger, and fresh cilantro. Process for about 15–20 seconds, until the mixture is smooth. Alternatively, press the lentils through a strainer with the back of a wooden spoon to purée them and then mix with the finely chopped nuts, spices and herbs.

5 Season the dip with salt and pepper and garnish with sprigs of fresh cilantro. Serve with fresh vegetable crudités and breadsticks.

Onions à la Grecque

This is a well-known method of cooking vegetables and is perfect with shallots or onions, served with a crisp salad.

10 mins   15 mins

SERVES 4

INGREDIENTS

1 lb/450 g shallots

3 tbsp olive oil

3 tbsp clear honey

2 tbsp garlic wine vinegar

3 tbsp dry white wine

1 tbsp tomato paste

2 celery stalks, sliced

2 tomatoes, seeded and chopped

salt and pepper

chopped celery leaves, to garnish

1 Peel the shallots. Heat the oil in a large pan, add the shallots and cook, stirring, for 3–5 minutes, or until they begin to brown.

2 Add the honey and cook over high heat for a further 30 seconds, then add the garlic wine vinegar and dry white wine, stirring well.

3 Stir in the tomato paste, the celery and the tomatoes, and bring the mixture to a boil. Cook over high heat for 5–6 minutes. Season to taste with salt and pepper and let cool slightly.

4 Garnish with chopped celery leaves and serve warm. Alternatively chill in the refrigerator before serving.

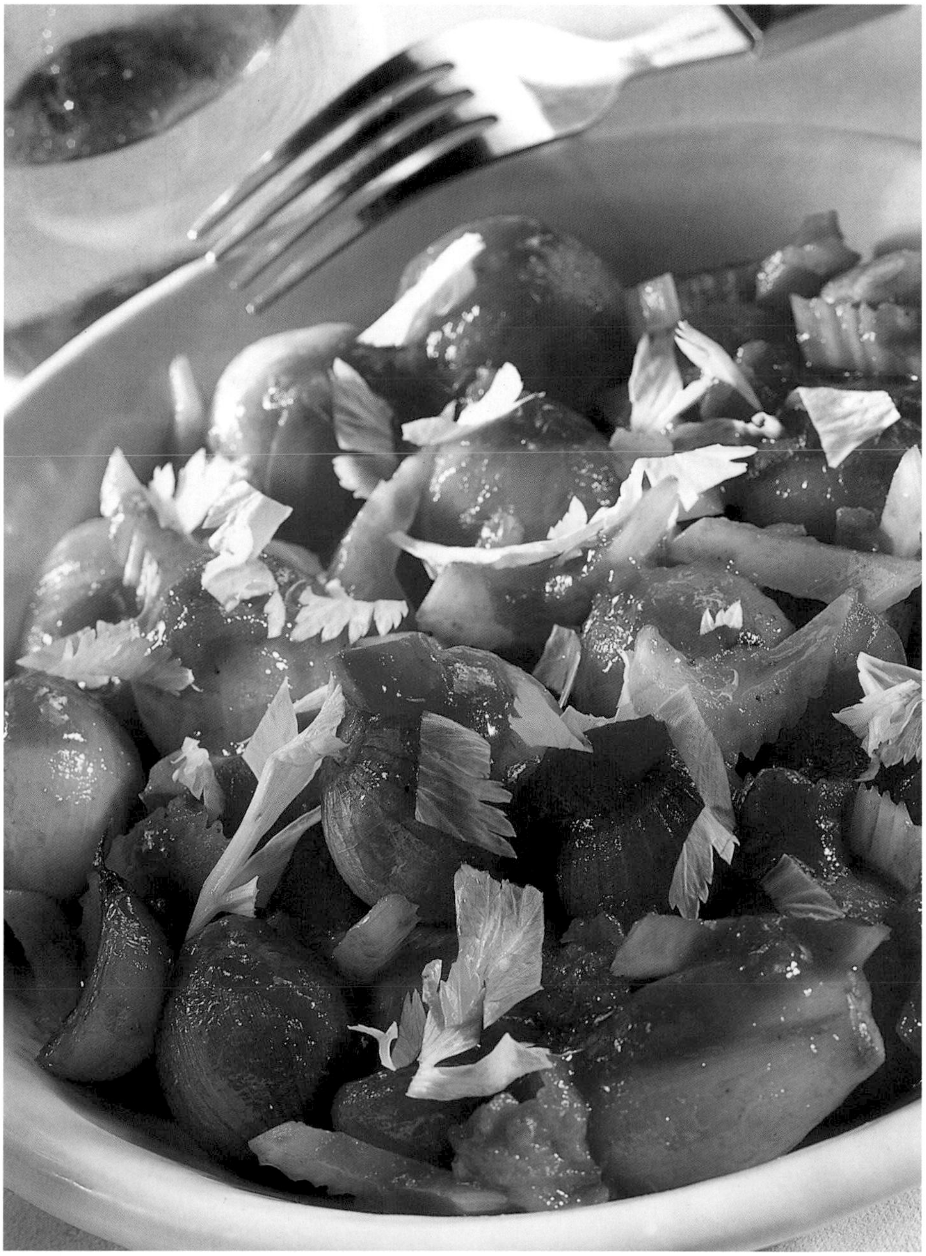

Bean Curd Tempura

Crispy coated vegetables and bean curd, accompanied by a sweet, spicy dip, give a real taste of Asia in this Japanese-style dish.

NUTRITIONAL INFORMATION

Calories	582	Sugars	........10g
Protein	........16g	Fat	..........27g
Carbohydrate	...65g	Saturates	.......4g

15 mins   20 mins

SERVES 4

INGREDIENTS

¼ lb/115 g baby zucchini

¼ lb/115 g baby carrots

¼ lb/115 g baby corn ears

¼ lb/115 g baby leeks

2 baby eggplants

8 oz/225 g bean curd

vegetable oil, for deep-frying

julienne strips of carrot, ginger root, and
   baby leek to garnish

noodles, to serve

BATTER

2 egg yolks

1¼ cups water

1½ cups all-purpose flour

DIPPING SAUCE

5 tbsp mirin or dry sherry

5 tbsp Japanese soy sauce

2 tsp clear honey

1 garlic clove, crushed

1 tsp grated ginger root

1   Slice the zucchini and carrots in half lengthwise. Trim the corn. Trim the leeks at both ends. Cut the eggplants into quarters lengthwise. Cut the bean curd into 1 inch/2.5 cm cubes.

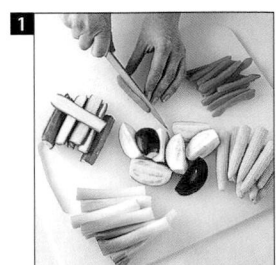

2   To make the batter, mix the egg yolks with the water. Sift in 1¼ cups of the flour and beat with a balloon whisk to form a thick batter. Don't worry if there are any lumps. Heat the oil for deep-frying to 350°F/180°C or until a cube of bread browns in 30 seconds.

3   Place the remaining flour on a large plate and toss the vegetables and bean curd until lightly coated.

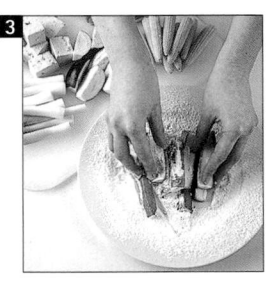

4   Dip the bean curd in the batter and deep-fry for 2–3 minutes, until lightly golden. Drain on paper towels and keep warm.

5   Dip the vegetables in the batter and deep-fry, a few at a time, for 3–4 minutes, until golden. Drain and place on a warmed serving plate.

6   To make the dipping sauce, mix all the ingredients together. Serve with the vegetables and bean curd, accompanied with noodles and garnished with julienne strips of vegetables.

Avocado Margherita

This classic Italian combination of tomatoes, basil, and mozzarella cheese is easy to prepare in this microwave oven recipe.

NUTRITIONAL INFORMATION

Calories 284	Sugars 3g
Protein 6g	Fat 27g
Carbohydrate 6g	Saturates 7g

 10 mins   7 mins

SERVES 4

INGREDIENTS

1 small red onion, sliced

1 garlic clove, crushed

1 tbsp olive oil

2 small tomatoes

2 avocados, halved and pitted

4 fresh basil leaves, torn into shreds

½ cup mozzarella cheese, thinly sliced

salt and pepper

TO GARNISH

mixed salad

fresh basil leaves

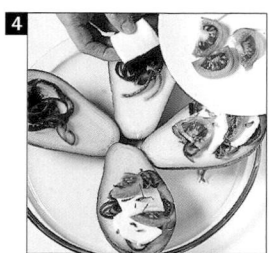

1 Place the onion, garlic, and olive oil in a bowl. Cover and cook on HIGH power for 2 minutes.

2 Meanwhile, peel the tomatoes by cutting a cross in the base of the tomatoes and placing them in a small bowl. Pour on boiling water and let stand for about 45 seconds. Drain and then plunge into cold water. The skins will slide off without too much difficulty.

3 Arrange the avocado halves on a plate, narrow ends toward the center. Spoon the onions into the hollows.

4 Cut the tomatoes into slices. Divide the tomatoes, basil, and thin slices of mozzarella between the four avocado halves, and season to taste with salt and pepper.

5 Cook on MEDIUM power for 5 minutes until the avocados are heated through and the cheese has melted. Serve immediately with a mixed salad garnished with basil leaves.

COOK'S TIP
This recipe is ideal for combination microwave ovens with a broiler. Arrange the avocados on the low rack of the broiler or on the turntable. Cook on combination grill 1 and LOW power for 8 minutes until browned and bubbling.

Hummus with Crudités

Making your own hummus couldn't be simpler and it tastes much better than the varieties you buy at the store.

NUTRITIONAL INFORMATION

Calories 311   Sugars 8g
Protein . . . . .11g   Fat 23g
Carbohydrate . . .16g   Saturates 3g

15 mins   0 mins

SERVES 4

INGREDIENTS

1 cup canned garbanzo beans (chickpeas), drained and rinsed

4 fl oz/125 ml sesame seed paste (tahini)

2 garlic cloves

½ cup lemon juice

2–3 tbsp water

1 tbsp olive oil

1 tbsp chopped fresh parsley

pinch of cayenne pepper

salt

FOR THE CRUDITÉS

4 carrots, cut into thin batons

4 celery sticks, cut into thin batons

4 radishes

½ small cauliflower, cut into florets

1 green bell pepper, seeded and cut into thin batons

1 red bell pepper, seeded and cut into thin batons

1 Prepare the ingredients. Place the drained garbanzo beans, sesame seed paste, garlic, and lemon juice in a blender or food processor and season to taste.

2 Process the ingredients, gradually adding water to the mixture as necessary until the consistency becomes smooth and creamy. Taste, and adjust the seasoning if necessary.

3 Transfer the mixture into a serving bowl and make a hollow in the center with the back of a spoon. Pour the olive oil into the hollow, then sprinkle the hummus with the chopped fresh parsley and the cayenne pepper.

4 Arrange the prepared raw vegetables on a large serving platter and serve immediately with the hummus.

Caponata

This Sicilian specialty varies slightly from one part of the island to the other, but it always contains eggplant, onion, celery, tomato, and capers.

NUTRITIONAL INFORMATION

Calories	178	Sugars	.......10g
Protein	.........2g	Fat	.........14g
Carbohydrate	...12g	Saturates	.......2g

10 mins   25 mins

SERVES 4

INGREDIENTS

4 tbsp olive oil

1 onion, sliced

2 celery stalks, sliced

1 eggplant, diced

5 plum tomatoes, chopped

1 garlic clove, finely chopped

3 tbsp red wine vinegar

1 tbsp sugar

12 black olives, pitted

2 tbsp capers

salt

3 tbsp chopped fresh flat-leaf parsley, to garnish

1 Heat 2 tablespoons of the oil in a large, heavy pan. Add the onion and celery and cook over low heat, stirring frequently, for 5 minutes, until soft. Add the remaining oil with the eggplant and continue to cook, stirring constantly, for 10 minutes.

2 Stir in the tomatoes, garlic, vinegar, and sugar. Cover the surface with a circle of waxed paper and simmer for 10 minutes.

3 Stir the olives and capers into the mixture and season to taste with salt.

4 Transfer the mixture to a serving dish and let cool to room temperature. Sprinkle the caponata with chopped parsley, and serve.

COOK'S TIP

Serve plenty of fresh, crusty bread with this delicous dish to soak up the juices.

Soft Dumplings in Yogurt

These are very light and make a good summer afternoon snack, as well as a good appetizer before any vegetarian meal.

NUTRITIONAL INFORMATION

Calories 476   Sugars 29g
Protein . . . . .11g   Fat 21g
Carbohydrate . . .64g   Saturates 3g

15 mins   20 mins

SERVES 4

INGREDIENTS

7 oz/200 g urid dhal powder

1 tsp baking powder

½ tsp ground ginger

1¼ cups water

oil, for deep-frying

2 cups unsweetened yogurt

⅓ cup sugar

MASALA

1¾ oz/50 g coriander seeds

1¾ oz/50 g white cumin seeds

1 oz/25 g crushed red chilies

3½ oz/100 g citric acid

chopped fresh red chilies, to garnish

3 Place the yogurt in a separate bowl. Add 1¾ cups water and the sugar and mix together with a whisk or fork. Set aside.

4 To make the masala, roast the coriander and the white cumin in a pan until a little darker in color and giving off their aroma. Grind coarsely in a food processor or in a mortar with a pestle. Add the crushed red chilies and citric acid and blend well together.

5 Sprinkle about 1 tablespoon of the masala over the dumplings and store the remainder in an airtight jar for future use. Garnish with chopped red chilies. Serve with the reserved yogurt mixture.

1 Place the powdered urid dhal in a large mixing bowl. Add the baking powder and ginger and stir to combine. Add the water and mix to form a paste.

2 Heat the oil in a deep pan. Pour in the batter, 1 tsp at a time, and deep-fry the dumplings until golden brown, lowering the heat when the oil gets too hot. Set the dumplings aside.

Tzatziki & Black Olive Dip

Tzatziki is a Greek dish, made with yogurt, mint, and cucumber.
It tastes superb with warm pocket bread.

NUTRITIONAL INFORMATION

Calories	.381	Sugars	.8g
Protein	11g	Fat	15g
Carbohydrate	52g	Saturates	.2g

 1 hr   3 mins

SERVES 4

INGREDIENTS

½ cucumber

1 cup thick unsweetened yogurt

1 tbsp chopped mint

salt and pepper

4 pocket breads

DIP

2 garlic cloves, crushed

¾ cup pitted black olives

4 tbsp olive oil

2 tbsp lemon juice

1 tbsp chopped parsley

TO GARNISH

mint sprigs

parsley sprigs

1 To make the tzatziki, peel the cucumber and chop it coarsely. Sprinkle with salt and let stand for 15–20 minutes. Rinse with cold water and drain well.

2 Mix the cucumber, yogurt, and mint together. Season to taste with salt and pepper and transfer to a serving bowl. Cover and chill for 20–30 minutes.

3 To make the black olive dip, put the crushed garlic and olives into a blender or food processor and process for 15–20 seconds. Alternatively, chop them very finely.

4 Add the olive oil, lemon juice, and parsley to the blender or food processor and process for a few more seconds. Alternatively, mix with the chopped garlic and olives and mash together. Season with salt and pepper.

5 Wrap the pocket breads in foil and either place over a barbecue grill for 2–3 minutes, turning once to warm through, or heat in the oven or under the broiler. Cut into pieces and serve with the tzatziki and black olive dip, garnished with sprigs of fresh mint and parsley.

COOK'S TIP

Sprinkling the cucumber with salt draws out some of its moisture, making it crisper. If you are in a hurry, you can omit this procedure.

Cheese, Garlic & Herb Pâté

This wonderful soft cheese pâté is fragrant with the aroma of fresh herbs and garlic. Serve with triangles of Melba toast for a perfect starter.

NUTRITIONAL INFORMATION

Calories	392	Sugars	.........1g
Protein	........17g	Fat	..........28g
Carbohydrate	...18g	Saturates	......18g

 20 mins   10 mins

SERVES 4

INGREDIENTS

1 tbsp butter

1 garlic clove, crushed

3 scallions, finely chopped

½ cup full-fat soft cheese

2 tbsp chopped mixed herbs, such as parsley, chives, marjoram, oregano, and basil

1½ cups finely grated sharp Cheddar cheese

pepper

4–6 slices of white bread from a medium-cut sliced loaf

mixed salad greens and cherry tomatoes, to serve

TO GARNISH

ground paprika

herb sprigs

1 Melt the butter in a small skillet and gently sauté the garlic and scallions together for 3–4 minutes, until soft. Let them cool.

2 Beat the soft cheese in a large mixing bowl until smooth, then add the garlic and scallions. Stir in the chopped mixed herbs, mixing well.

3 Add the Cheddar and work the mixture together to form a stiff paste. Cover and chill until ready to serve.

4 To make the Melba toast, toast the slices of bread on both sides, and then cut off the crusts. Using a sharp bread knife, cut through the slices horizontally to make very thin slices. Cut into triangles and then lightly toast the untoasted sides until golden.

5 Arrange the mixed salad greens on 4 serving plates with the cherry tomatoes. Pile the cheese pâté on top and sprinkle with a little paprika. Garnish with sprigs of fresh herbs and serve with the Melba toast.

Garlicky Mushroom Pakoras

Whole mushrooms are dunked in a spiced garlicky batter and deep-fried until golden. They are at their most delicious served piping hot.

NUTRITIONAL INFORMATION

Calories	297	Sugars	.........3g
Protein	.........5g	Fat	..........21g
Carbohydrate	...24g	Saturates	.......2g

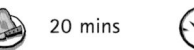

20 mins   10-15 mins

SERVES 4

I N G R E D I E N T S

1 cup gram (besan) flour

½ tsp salt

¼ tsp baking powder

1 tsp cumin seeds

½–1 tsp chili powder

¾ cup water

2 garlic cloves, crushed

1 small onion, finely chopped

vegetable oil, for deep-frying

1 lb/450 g white mushrooms, trimmed and wiped

lemon wedges and cilantro sprigs, to garnish

1 Put the gram flour, salt, baking powder, cumin, and chili powder into a bowl and mix well together. Make a well in the center of the mixture and gradually stir in the water, mixing thoroughly to form a batter.

2 Stir the garlic and onion into the batter and let the mixture infuse for 10 minutes. One-third fill a deep-fat fryer or pan with vegetable oil and heat to 350°F/180°C or until a cube of bread browns in 30 seconds. Lower the basket into the hot oil.

3 Meanwhile, mix the mushrooms into the batter, stirring to coat. Remove a few at a time and place them into the hot oil. Sauté for about 2 minutes, or until golden brown.

4 Remove the mushrooms from the pan with a slotted spoon and drain on paper towels while you are cooking the remainder in the same way.

5 Serve hot, sprinkled with coarse salt and garnished with lemon wedges and cilantro sprigs.

COOK'S TIP

Gram flour, also known as besan flour, is a pale yellow flour made from garbanzo beans (chickpeas). It is now readily available from larger food stores, as well as Indian food stores and some ethnic delicatessens.

Hyderabad Pickles

This is a very versatile dish that will go with almost anything and can be served warm or cold. It is perfect as an appetizer for a dinner party.

NUTRITIONAL INFORMATION

Calories	732	Sugars	.........6g
Protein	.........6g	Fat	..........75g
Carbohydrate	....8g	Saturates	......10g

30 mins, plus cooling

30 mins

SERVES 4

INGREDIENTS

2 tsp coriander seeds

2 tsp cumin seeds

2 tsp shredded coconut

2 tsp sesame seeds

1 tsp mixed mustard and onion seeds

1¼ cups vegetable oil

3 medium onions, sliced

1 tsp finely chopped ginger root

1 tsp crushed garlic

½ tsp turmeric

1½ tsp chili powder

1½ tsp salt

3 medium eggplants, halved lengthwise

1 tbsp tamarind paste

1¼ cups water

3 hard-cooked eggs, halved, to garnish

BAGHAAR

1 tsp mixed onion and mustard seeds

1 tsp cumin seeds

4 dried red chilies

⅔ cup vegetable oil

cilantro leaves

1 green chili, finely chopped

1 Dry-roast the coriander, cumin, coconut, sesame seeds, and mustard and onion seeds in a pan until lightly colored and the spices release their aroma. Grind in a pestle and mortar or food processor and set aside.

2 Heat the oil in a skillet and sauté the onions until golden. Reduce the heat and add the ginger, garlic, turmeric, chili powder, and salt, stirring. Let cool, then grind this mixture to form a paste.

3 Make 4 cuts across each eggplant half. Blend the spices with the onion paste. Spoon this mixture into the slits in the eggplants.

4 In a bowl, mix the tamarind paste and 3 tbsp water to make a fine paste and set aside.

5 For the baghaar, sauté the onion and mustard seeds, cumin seeds, and dried red chilies in the oil. Reduce the heat, place the eggplants in the baghaar, and stir gently. Stir in the tamarind paste and the remaining water and cook over medium heat for 15–20 minutes. Add the cilantro and the chopped green chili.

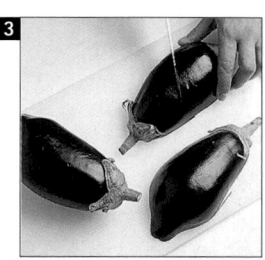

6 When cool, transfer to a serving dish and serve garnished with the hard-cooked eggs.

Vegetable & Nut Samosas

These delicious little fried pastries are really quite simple to make. Serve them hot or cold as an appetizer before an Indian meal.

NUTRITIONAL INFORMATION

Calories 343   Sugars 2g
Protein . . . . .5g   Fat 26g
Carbohydrate . . .24g   Saturates 5g

🧊 30 mins   🕐 40 mins

MAKES 12

INGREDIENTS

2¼ cups potatoes, diced

salt

1 cup frozen peas

3 tbsp vegetable oil

1 onion, chopped

1 inch/2.5 cm piece of ginger root, chopped

1 garlic clove, crushed

1 tsp garam masala

2 tsp mild curry paste

½ tsp cumin seeds

2 tsp lemon juice

½ cup unsalted cashews, coarsely chopped

vegetable oil, for shallow frying

cilantro sprigs, to garnish

mango chutney, to serve

PASTRY

1½ cups all-purpose flour

4 tsp butter

6 tbsp warm milk

1 Cook the potatoes in a pan of boiling, salted water for 5 minutes. Add the peas and cook for a further 4 minutes, or until the potatoes are tender. Drain well. Heat the oil in a skillet and sauté the onion, the potato and pea mixture, and the ginger, garlic, and spices for 2 minutes. Stir in the lemon juice and cook gently, uncovered, for 2 minutes. Remove from the heat, slightly mash the potato and peas, then add the cashews, mix well, and season to taste with salt.

2 To make the pastry, put the flour in a bowl and rub in the butter. Mix in the milk to form a dough. Knead lightly and divide into 6 portions. Form each into a ball and roll out to an 7 inch/18 cm round. Cut each one in half.

3 Divide the filling equally between the semicircles of pastry, spreading it out to within ¼ inch/5 mm of the edges. Brush the edges of the pastry all the way round with water and fold over to form triangular shapes, sealing the edges well together to enclose the filling completely.

4 Heat the vegetable oil in a skillet to 350°F/180°C or until a cube of bread browns in 30 seconds. Fry the samosas, a few at a time, turning frequently until golden brown and heated through. Drain on paper towels and keep warm while cooking the remainder. Garnish with cilantro sprigs and serve hot with mango chutney.

Vegetable-Topped Muffins

Roasted vegetables are delicious and attractive. Served on warm English muffins with a herb sauce, they are unbeatable.

NUTRITIONAL INFORMATION

Calories 740   Sugars 27g
Protein ....20g   Fat 45g
Carbohydrate ...67g   Saturates 17g

1¼ hrs   35 mins

SERVES 4

INGREDIENTS

1 red onion, cut into 8 wedges

1 eggplant, halved and sliced

1 yellow bell pepper, seeded and sliced

1 zucchini, sliced

¼ cup olive oil

1 tbsp garlic vinegar

2 tbsp vermouth

2 garlic cloves, crushed

1 tbsp chopped fresh thyme

2 tsp light brown sugar

4 English muffins, halved

SAUCE

2 tbsp butter

1 tbsp all-purpose flour

⅔ cup milk

5 tbsp vegetable bouillon

¾ cup grated Cheddar cheese

1 tsp whole-grain mustard

3 tbsp chopped fresh mixed herbs

salt and pepper

1 Arrange the onion, eggplant, yellow bell pepper, and zucchini in a shallow nonmetallic dish. Combine the olive oil, garlic vinegar, vermouth, garlic, thyme, and sugar and pour over the vegetables, turning to coat well. Let marinate for 1 hour.

2 Transfer the vegetables to a cookie sheet. Roast in a preheated oven, 400°F/200°C, for about 20–25 minutes or until the vegetables have softened.

3 Meanwhile, make the sauce. Melt the butter in a small pan and stir in the flour. Cook for 1 minute over low heat, stirring constantly, then remove the pan from the heat. Gradually stir in the milk and vegetable bouillon and return the pan to the heat. Bring to a boil, stirring constantly until thickened. Stir in the cheese, mustard, and mixed herbs and season well.

4 Cut the muffins in half and toast under a preheated broiler for 2–3 minutes until golden brown, then transfer to a serving plate. Spoon the roasted vegetables onto the muffins and pour the sauce over. Serve immediately.

Bruschetta

Traditionally, this Italian savory is enriched with olive oil. Here, sun-dried tomatoes are a good substitute and only a little oil is used.

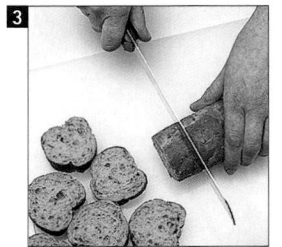

NUTRITIONAL INFORMATION

Calories 178   Sugars 2g
Protein ....8g   Fat 6g
Carbohydrate ...24g   Saturates 2g

 45 mins   5 mins

SERVES 4

I N G R E D I E N T S

2 oz/60 g dry-pack sun-dried tomatoes

1¼ cups boiling water

14 inch/35 cm long Granary or whole-wheat stick of French bread

1 large garlic clove, halved

¼ cup pitted black olives in brine, drained and quartered

2 tsp olive oil

2 tbsp chopped fresh basil

½ cup shredded low-fat Italian mozzarella cheese

salt and pepper

fresh basil leaves, to garnish

1 Place the sun-dried tomatoes in a heatproof bowl and pour over the boiling water.

2 Set aside for 30 minutes to let the tomatoes soften. Drain well and pat dry with paper towels. Slice into thin strips and set aside.

3 Trim and discard the ends from the bread and cut into 12 slices. Arrange on a broiler rack, place under a preheated hot broiler, and cook for 1–2 minutes on each side until lightly golden.

4 Rub both sides of each piece of bread with the cut sides of the garlic. Top with strips of sun-dried tomato and olives.

5 Brush lightly with olive oil and season well. Sprinkle with the basil and mozzarella cheese and return to the broiler for 1–2 minutes until the cheese is melted and bubbling.

6 Transfer to a warmed serving platter and garnish with fresh basil leaves.

COOK'S TIP

If you use sun-dried tomatoes packed in oil, drain them, rinse well in warm water and drain again on paper towels to remove as much oil as possible. Sun-dried tomatoes give a rich, full flavour to this dish, but thinly sliced fresh tomatoes can be used instead.

Dressed Artichoke Hearts

Artichoke hearts are truly a luxury and taste superb with this warm, nutty dressing. Use the leaves on another occasion, served with citrus vinaigrette.

NUTRITIONAL INFORMATION

Calories . . . . . . .287 Sugars 2g
Protein . . . . .7g Fat 18g
Carbohydrate . . .14g Saturates 2g

 15 mins   45 mins

SERVES 4

INGREDIENTS

1 bag mixed salad greens, such as lollo rosso, escarole, and lamb's lettuce

6 tbsp lemon juice

4 globe artichokes

5 tbsp Calvados

1 shallot, very finely chopped

1 tbsp red wine vinegar

3 tbsp walnut oil

salt and ground black pepper

TO GARNISH

½ cup shelled walnuts, chopped

1 tbsp finely chopped fresh parsley

VARIATION
This recipe also works well with good quality canned or bottled artichoke hearts. Drain and rinse well before using.

1 Place the salad greens in a bowl and set aside. Fill a bowl with cold water and add 2 tablespoons of the lemon juice. Prepare the artichokes one at a time. Twist off the artichoke stalk, cut the base flat and pull off all the dark outer leaves. Slice the artichoke in half horizontally and discard the top part. Trim around the base to remove the outer dark green layer and place in the acidulated water while you prepare the remainder.

2 Bring a large pan of water to a boil, add the remaining lemon juice, and cook the artichoke bases, covered, for 30–40 minutes or until tender. Drain, refresh under cold water, and drain again. Pull off the remaining leaves and scoop out and discard the chokes. Set the artichoke hearts aside.

3 Pour the Calvados into a small pan, add the shallot and a pinch of salt, and bring to just below boiling point. Lower the heat, carefully ignite the alcohol and continue to cook until the flames have died down. Stir in the vinegar and oil and cook, stirring constantly, for 1 minute. Remove the pan from the heat.

4 Spoon half the dressing over the salad greens and toss well to coat. Transfer the salad greens to a serving platter and top with the artichoke hearts. Spoon the remaining dressing over the artichoke hearts, garnish with the walnuts and parsley, and serve immediately.

Dolmas

Start a Greek meal with these vegetarian stuffed grape leaves.
You will need a large skillet with a lid to hold all the stuffed leaves.

NUTRITIONAL INFORMATION

Calories	82	Sugars	.........2g
Protein	.........1g	Fat	...........7g
Carbohydrate	....5g	Saturates	.......1g

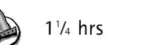 1¼ hrs   45 mins

SERVES 4

INGREDIENTS

8 oz/225 g grape leaves preserved in brine, about 40 in total

⅔ cup olive oil

4 tbsp lemon juice

1¼ cups water

lemon wedges, to serve

FILLING

scant ⅔ cup long grain rice, not basmati

1½ cups water

¼ cup currants

½ cup pine nuts, chopped

2 scallions, very finely chopped

1 tbsp very finely chopped fresh cilantro

1 tbsp very finely chopped fresh parsley

1 tbsp very finely chopped fresh dill

finely grated zest of ½ lemon

salt and pepper

1 Rinse the grape leaves under cold running water and place them in a heatproof bowl. Pour over enough boiling water to cover and let soak for 5 minutes. Drain well.

2 Meanwhile, place the rice and water in a pan with a pinch of salt and bring to a boil. Lower the heat, cover, and simmer for 10–12 minutes or until all the liquid is completely absorbed. Drain and let cool.

3 Stir the currants, pine nuts, scallions, cilantro, parsley, dill, and lemon zest into the cooled rice. Season to taste with salt and pepper.

4 Line the bottom of a large skillet with 3 or 4 of the thickest grape leaves or with any that are torn.

5 Put a grape leaf on the counter, vein side upward, with the pointed end facing away from you. Put a small, compact roll of the rice stuffing at the base of the leaf. Fold up the bottom end of the leaf.

6 Fold in each side to overlap in the center. Roll up the leaf around the filling. Squeeze lightly in your hand. Continue this process with the remaining leaves and stuffing mixture.

7 Place the leaf rolls in a single layer in the pan, seam side down. Combine the olive oil, lemon juice, and water and pour into the pan.

8 Fit a heatproof plate over the rolls and cover the pan. Simmer for 30 minutes.

9 Remove from the heat and let the stuffed grape leaves cool in the liquid. Serve chilled with lemon wedges.

Cauliflower Roulade

A light-as-air mixture of eggs and vegetables produces a stylish vegetarian dish that can be enjoyed hot or cold.

NUTRITIONAL INFORMATION

Calories 271	Sugars 4g
Protein 15g	Fat 20g
Carbohydrate 7g	Saturates 11g

 30 mins   40 mins

SERVES 4

INGREDIENTS

1 small cauliflower, divided into florets

4 eggs, separated

¾ cup grated Cheddar cheese

¼ cup cottage cheese

pinch of grated nutmeg

½ tsp mustard powder

salt and pepper

FILLING

1 bunch watercress, trimmed

4 tbsp butter

3½ tbsp all-purpose flour

¾ cup unsweetened yogurt

¼ cup grated Cheddar cheese

¼ cup cottage cheese

1 Line a jelly roll pan with baking parchment.

2 Steam the cauliflower until just tender, then drain under cold water. Process the cauliflower in a food processor or chop and press through a strainer.

3 Beat the egg yolks, then stir in the cauliflower, two-thirds of the Cheddar and the ¼ cup cottage cheese. Season with nutmeg, mustard, and salt and pepper. Whisk the egg whites until stiff but not dry, then fold them in.

4 Spread the mixture evenly in the pan. Bake the roulade in a preheated oven, 375°F/190°C, for about 20–25 minutes, until risen and golden.

5 Chop the watercress, reserving a few sprigs for garnish. Melt the butter in a small pan. Cook the watercress, stirring, for 3 minutes, until wilted. Blend in the flour, then stir in the yogurt and simmer for 2 minutes. Stir in the cheeses.

6 Turn out the roulade on to a damp dish cloth covered with a fresh sheet of baking parchment. Peel off the paper and let the steam escape for a minute. Using the new sheet of baking parchment to help you, roll up the roulade, starting from one narrow end.

7 Unroll the roulade, spread the filling to within 1 inch/2.5 cm of the edges, and roll it up again. Transfer to a cookie sheet, sprinkle with the remaining Cheddar cheese and return it to the oven for 5 minutes. Serve immediately if serving hot or allow to cool completely.

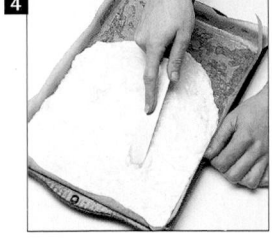

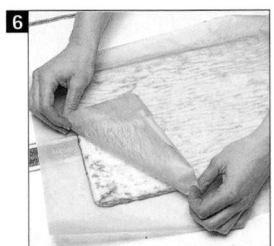

Sicilian Caramelized Onions

This is a typical Sicilian dish, combining honey and vinegar to give a delicate sweet and sour flavor. Serve hot or cold as an accompaniment.

  2 mins   15 mins

SERVES 4

I N G R E D I E N T S

12 oz baby or pickling onions

2 tbsp olive oil

2 fresh bay leaves, torn into strips

thinly pared zest of 1 lemon

1 tbsp soft brown sugar

1 tbsp honey

4 tbsp red wine vinegar

 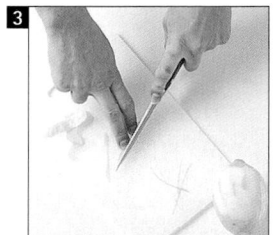 

1 Soak the onions in a bowl of boiling water—this will make them easier to peel. Using a sharp knife, peel and halve the onions.

2 Heat the oil in a large skillet. Add the bay leaves and onions to the skillet and cook for 5–6 minutes over medium-high heat, or until well browned all over.

3 Cut the lemon zest into short, thin sticks. Add to the skillet with the sugar and honey. Cook for 2–3 minutes, stirring occasionally, until the onions are lightly caramelized.

4 Add the red wine vinegar to the skillet, being careful because it will spit. Cook for about 5 minutes, stirring, or until the onions are tender and the liquid has all but disappeared.

5 Transfer the onions to a serving dish and serve at once.

COOK'S TIP

To make the onions easier to peel, place them in a large pan and pour over boiling water, then let stand for 10 minutes. Drain the onions thoroughly, and when they are cold enough to handle, peel them.

Minted Onion Bhajis

Gram flour (also known as besan flour) is a fine yellow flour made from garbanzo beans and is available from food stores and Asian stores.

NUTRITIONAL INFORMATION

Calories 251	Sugars 7g
Protein 7g	Fat 8g
Carbohydrate . . .39g	Saturates 1g

🥗 5 mins   🕐 15 mins

MAKES 12

I N G R E D I E N T S

¾ cup gram (besan) flour

¼ tsp cayenne pepper

¼–½ tsp ground coriander

¼–½ tsp ground cumin

1 tbsp chopped fresh mint

4 tbsp strained thick low-fat yogurt

¼ cup cold water

1 large onion, quartered and thinly sliced

vegetable oil, for frying

salt and pepper

sprigs of mint, to garnish

1 Put the gram flour into a bowl, add the cayenne pepper, coriander, cumin, and mint and season with salt and pepper to taste. Stir in the yogurt, water, and sliced onion and mix well together.

2 One-third fill a large, deep skillet with oil and heat until very hot. Drop heaped spoonfuls of the mixture, a few at a time, into the hot oil and use two forks to neaten the mixture into rough ball-shapes.

3 Fry the bhajis until golden brown and cooked through, turning frequently.

4 Drain the bhajis thoroughly on absorbent paper towels and keep them warm while cooking the remainder in the same way.

5 Arrange the bhajis on a platter and garnish with sprigs of fresh mint. Serve hot or warm.

COOK'S TIP

Gram flour is excellent for making batter and is used in India in place of flour. It can be made from ground split peas as well as garbanzo beans.

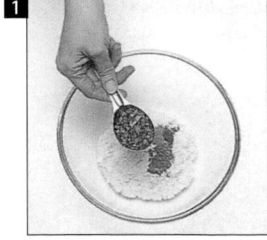

Roasted Cheese with Salsa

This delicious, warming Mexican dish is very satisfying—the salsa is cooked with the cheese for a wonderful mingling of textures.

NUTRITIONAL INFORMATION

Calories	476	Sugars	.........4g
Protein	........23g	Fat	.........13g
Carbohydrate	...70g	Saturates	.......7g

 15 mins   🕐 5–10 mins

SERVES 4

I N G R E D I E N T S

2 cups mozzarella, fresh romano or Mexican queso oaxaca

⅔ cup Salsa Cruda (see page 830), or other good salsa

½–1 onion, finely chopped

8 soft corn tortillas, to serve

1 To warm the corn tortillas ready for serving, heat a nonstick skillet, add a tortilla and heat through, sprinkling with a few drops of water as it heats. Wrap in kitchen foil to keep warm. Repeat the process with the remaining tortillas.

2 Cut chunks or slabs of the cheese and arrange in a shallow ovenproof dish or in individual dishes.

3 Spoon the salsa over the cheese to cover and place in either a preheated oven at 400°F/200°C or under a preheated broiler. Cook until the cheese melts and bubbles, lightly browning in spots.

4 Sprinkle with chopped onion to taste and serve with the warmed tortillas for dipping. Serve immediately as the melted cheese turns stringy when cold and becomes difficult to eat.

COOK'S TIP
Queso oaxaca is the authentic cheese to use, but mozzarella or romano make excellent substitutes since they produce the right effect when melted.

Frijoles

Beans take a starring role in both Mexican cuisine and vegetarian diets. This delicious recipe is known simply as frijoles, that is, beans.

NUTRITIONAL INFORMATION

Calories 213   Sugars 5g
Protein . . . . .14g   Fat 5g
Carbohydrate . . .31g   Saturates 1g

 15 mins   2 hrs

SERVES 6

INGREDIENTS

2 cups dried red kidney beans, soaked in cold water for 3 hours

2 onions, chopped

2 garlic cloves, chopped

2 fresh green chiles, seeded and chopped

1 bay leaf

2 tbsp corn oil

2 tomatoes, skinned, seeded and chopped

salt

1 Prepare the ingredients. Drain the beans and place in a large, heavy pan. Add sufficient cold water to cover the beans by about 1 inch/2.5 cm. Add half the onion, half the garlic, the chiles, and the bay leaf. Bring to a boil and boil vigorously for 15 minutes, then lower the heat and simmer for 30 minutes, adding more boiling water if the mixture begins to dry out.

2 Add 1 tablspoon of the oil and simmer for 30 minutes more, adding more boiling water if necessary. Season to taste with salt and simmer for another 30 minutes, but do not add any more water.

3 Meanwhile, heat the remaining oil in a skillet. Add the remaining onion and garlic and cook, stirring occasionally, for 5 minutes, until soft. Stir in the tomatoes and cook for an additional 5 minutes. Add 3 tablespoons of the cooked beans to the tomato mixture, mash thoroughly to a paste, and then stir the paste into the beans. Heat through gently, then serve.

COOK'S TIP

Some dried legumes, including red kidney beans, contain a toxin that is only destroyed by cooking. It is essential to boil the beans vigorously for 15 minutes, before simmering to finish cooking.

Mushroom Bites with Aïoli

These crispy morsels make delicious canapés and are wonderful warm snacks to serve at parties.

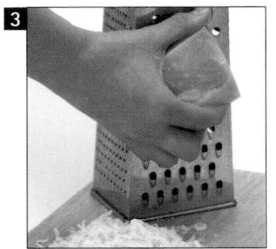

NUTRITIONAL INFORMATION

Calories	504	Sugars	.........1g
Protein	.........8g	Fat	..........46g
Carbohydrate	...15g	Saturates	.......8g

 20 mins   15 mins

SERVES 4

INGREDIENTS

1¾ cups fresh white bread crumbs

2 tbsp freshly grated Parmesan cheese

1 tsp paprika

½ lb/225 g white mushrooms

2 egg whites

FOR THE AÏOLI

4 garlic cloves, crushed

2 egg yolks

1 cup extra virgin olive oil

salt and ground black pepper

1 First make the aïoli. Put the garlic in a bowl, add a pinch of salt and mash with the back of a spoon. Add the egg yolks and beat with a whisk for 30 seconds to a minute, until creamy. Beat in the oil, one drop at a time. As the mixture begins to thicken, add the oil in a steady stream, beating constantly.

2 Season the aïoli to taste with salt and pepper, cover the bowl with plastic wrap, and chill in the refrigerator.

3 Grate the Parmesan and lightly whisk the egg whites. Combine the bread crumbs, Parmesan and paprika in a bowl. Dip each mushroom into the egg whites then into the breadcrumbs. Place on a baking sheet lined with baking paper.

4 Bake in a preheated oven, 375°F/190°C, for 15 minutes, until the coating is crisp and golden. Serve immediately with the aïoli.

VARIATION
Instead of aïoli, serve the mushrooms with a herb cream. Combine 4 tablespoons chopped, mixed, fresh herbs with ¾ cup sour cream, 1 finely chopped garlic clove and 1 tablespoon lemon juice. Season to taste with salt and pepper.

Antipasto Mushrooms

Traditionally, porcini mushrooms, also known as ceps, would be used for this dish, but you can make it with any of your favorite varieties.

NUTRITIONAL INFORMATION

Calories	.413	Sugars	.2g
Protein	.3g	Fat	.9g
Carbohydrate	.2g	Saturates	.1g

10 mins, plus cooling   30 mins

SERVES 4

INGREDIENTS

3 tbsp olive oil

2 garlic cloves, finely chopped

½ lb/225 g tomatoes, skinned, seeded and finely chopped

1 tbsp finely chopped fresh oregano

1 lb/450 g porcini or other mushrooms, thinly sliced

salt and ground black pepper

fresh flat-leaf parsley sprigs, to garnish

1 Prepare the ingredients. Heat 1 tbsp of the oil in a pan, add the garlic, and cook over low heat for 1 minute, stirring constantly. Add the tomatoes and oregano and season to taste with salt and pepper.

Continue to cook over low heat, stirring frequently, for about 20 minutes, or until pulpy and thickened.

2 Heat the remaining oil in a skillet. Add the mushrooms and cook over medium heat, stirring frequently, for about 5 minutes, or until tender. Stir the mushrooms into the tomato mixture and season with salt. Lower the heat, cover, and simmer for 10 minutes more.

3 Transfer the mushroom mixture to a bowl and let cool. Serve the dish at room temperature, with a garnish of flat-leaf parsley.

COOK'S TIP

Try to find sun-ripened tomatoes for this dish as they have a sweeter, fuller flavor than those ripened under glass.

Cheese & Bean Quesadillas

These bite-size rolls are made from flour tortillas filled with a delicious mixture of refried beans, melted cheese, cilantro, and salsa.

NUTRITIONAL INFORMATION

Calories 452	Sugars 11g	
Protein 18g	Fat 16g	
Carbohydrate ...62g	Saturates 7g	

 10 mins   10 mins

SERVES 4–6

INGREDIENTS

14 oz/400g canned refried beans

8 flour tortillas

1¾ cups grated Cheddar cheese

1 onion, chopped

½ bunch of fresh cilantro leaves, chopped

1 quantity Salsa Cruda (see page 830)

1 Place the beans in a small pan and set over low heat to warm through.

2 Meanwhile, make the tortillas pliable, by warming them gently in a lightly greased nonstick skillet.

3 Remove the tortillas from the skillet and quickly spread with a layer of warm beans. Top each tortilla with grated cheese, onion, fresh cilantro, and a spoonful of salsa. Roll up tightly.

4 Just before serving, heat the nonstick skillet over medium heat, sprinkling lightly with a couple of drops of water. Add the tortilla rolls, cover the skillet, and heat through until the cheese melts. Let it brown lightly, if wished.

5 Remove the tortilla rolls from the skillet and slice each roll, on the diagonal, into about 4 bite-size pieces. Serve the quesadillas at once.

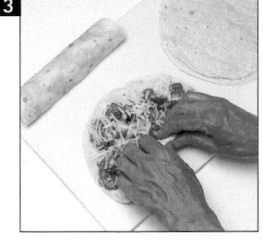

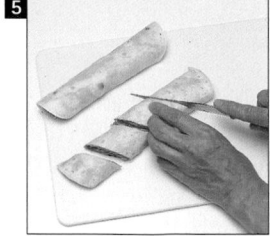

Vegetables with Sesame Dip

This tasty dip is great for livening up simply cooked vegetables. Varying the vegetables according to the season adds interest to the dish.

NUTRITIONAL INFORMATION

Calories 126   Sugars 7g
Protein . . . . .11g   Fat 6g
Carbohydrate . . . .8g   Saturates 1g

5 mins   20 mins

SERVES 4

INGREDIENTS

2½ cups small broccoli florets

2 cups small cauliflower florets

8 oz/225 g asparagus, sliced into 2 inch/ 5 cm lengths

2 small red onions, quartered

1 tbsp lime juice

2 tsp toasted sesame seeds

1 tbsp chopped fresh chives, to garnish

HOT SESAME SEED PASTE & GARLIC DIP

1 tsp sunflower oil

2 garlic cloves, crushed

½–1 tsp chili powder

2 tsp sesame seed paste (tahini)

⅔ cup low-fat unsweetened yogurt

2 tbsp chopped fresh chives

salt and pepper

1 Line the base of a steamer with baking parchment and arrange the broccoli florets, cauliflower florets, asparagus, and onion pieces on top.

2 Bring a wok or large pan of water to a boil, and place the steamer on top. Sprinkle the vegetables with lime juice and steam them for 10 minutes, or until they are just tender.

3 To make the Hot Sesame Seed Paste & Garlic Dip, heat the oil in a small nonstick pan, add the garlic, chili powder, and seasoning to taste, and cook gently for 2–3 minutes until the garlic is soft.

4 Remove the pan from the heat and stir in the sesame seed paste and yogurt. Return the pan to the heat and cook gently for 1–2 minutes without bringing to a boil. Stir in the chives.

5 Remove the vegetables from the steamer and place on a warmed serving platter. Sprinkle them with the sesame seeds and garnish with chopped chives. Serve with the hot dip.

Gazpacho Water Ice

Try serving this refreshing appetizer at a dinner party—it's certain to impress and contains virtually no fat.

NUTRITIONAL INFORMATION

Calories	33	Sugars	. . . . .6g
Protein	. . . . .1g	Fat	. . . . .1g
Carbohydrate	. . . .6g	Saturates	. . . . .0.2g

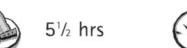

5½ hrs   0 mins

SERVES 4

I N G R E D I E N T S

1 lb/450 g tomatoes

2½ cups boiling water

4 scallions, chopped

2 celery stalks, chopped

1 small red bell pepper, chopped

1 garlic clove, crushed

1 tbsp tomato paste

1 tbsp chopped fresh parsley

salt and pepper

fresh parsley sprigs, to garnish

TO SERVE

shredded iceberg lettuce

breadsticks

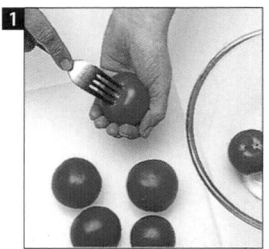 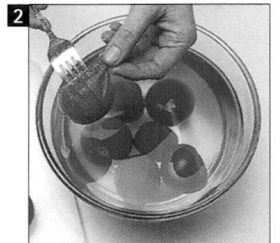 

1 Prick the skin of the tomatoes with a fork at the stalk end and place in a large heatproof bowl. Pour over enough boiling water to cover them. Let stand for 5–10 minutes. After this time, the skin should start peeling away from the flesh.

2 Skewer the tomatoes with a fork and peel away the skin. Slice the tomatoes in half, then scoop out and discard the seeds. Chop the flesh.

3 Place the chopped tomatoes, scallions, celery, bell pepper, garlic, and tomato paste in a food processor or blender. Blend for a few seconds until smooth. Alternatively, finely chop or mince the vegetables then mix with the tomato paste. Pour into a freezerproof container and freeze.

4 Remove from the freezer and let stand at room temperature for 30 minutes. Break up with a fork and place in a blender or food processor. Blend for a few seconds to break up the ice crystals and form a smooth mixture. Alternatively, beat with a wooden spoon until smooth.

5 Transfer the mixture to a mixing bowl and stir in the parsley and seasoning. Return to the freezer container and freeze for a further 30 minutes. Fork through the water ice again, garnish with parsley, and serve immediately with shredded iceberg lettuce and breadsticks.

Potato & Bean Pâté

This pâté is easy to prepare and may be stored in the refrigerator for up to two days. Serve with small toasts, Melba toast, or crudités.

NUTRITIONAL INFORMATION

Calories 84	Sugars 3g	
Protein 5.1g	Fat 0.5g	
Carbohydrate ..15.7g	Saturates 0.1g	

3 mins   10 mins

SERVES 4

INGREDIENTS

⅔ cup diced mealy potatoes

1½ cups mixed canned beans, such as borlotti beans, lima beans, and kidney beans, drained

1 garlic clove, crushed

2 tsp lime juice

1 tbsp chopped fresh cilantro

2 tbsp unsweetened yogurt

salt and pepper

chopped fresh cilantro, to garnish

COOK'S TIP

To make Melba toast, toast ready-sliced bread lightly on both sides under a preheated high broiler. Remove the crusts. Holding the bread flat, slide a sharp knife through the slice to split it horizontally. Cut into triangles and toast the untoasted side until the edges curl.

1 Cook the potatoes in a pan of boiling water for 10 minutes until tender. Drain well and mash.

2 Transfer the potato to a food processor or blender and add the beans, garlic, lime juice, and the cilantro.

3 Season the mixture and process for 1 minute to make a smooth purée.

Alternatively, mix the beans with the potato, garlic, lime juice, and cilantro and mash with a fork or a potato masher.

4 Turn the pâté into a bowl and add the yogurt. Mix well.

5 Spoon the pâté into a serving dish and garnish with the chopped cilantro. Serve at once or let chill.

Potato Skins with Guacamole

Although avocados do contain fat, if they are used in small quantities you can still enjoy their creamy texture.

NUTRITIONAL INFORMATION

Calories	399	Sugars	........4g
Protein	........10g	Fat	..........15g
Carbohydrate	...59g	Saturates	......4g

 45 mins   1¾ hrs

SERVES 4

INGREDIENTS

4 large baking potatoes

2 tsp olive oil

coarse sea salt and pepper

chopped fresh chives, to garnish

GUACAMOLE DIP

175 g/6 oz ripe avocado

1 tbsp lemon juice

2 ripe, firm tomatoes, chopped finely

1 tsp grated lemon zest

½ cup low-fat soft cheese with herbs and garlic

4 scallions, chopped finely

a few drops of Tabasco sauce

salt and pepper

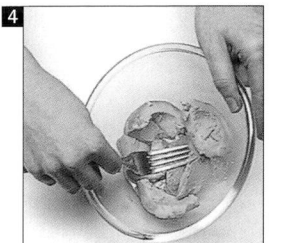

1 Bake the potatoes in a preheated oven at 400°F/200°C for 1¼ hours. Remove from the oven and let cool for 30 minutes. Reset the oven to 425°F/220°C.

2 Halve the potatoes lengthwise and scoop out 2 tablespoons of the flesh, then slice the potatoes in half again.

3 Place on a cookie sheet and brush the flesh side lightly with oil. Sprinkle with salt and pepper. Bake for 25 minutes until the potatoes are golden and crisp.

4 To make the guacamole dip, mash the avocado with the lemon juice. Add the remaining ingredients and mix.

5 Drain the potato skins on paper towels and transfer to a warmed serving platter. Garnish with chives. Pile the avocado mixture into a serving bowl.

COOK'S TIP
Mash the leftover potato flesh with unsweetened yogurt and seasoning, and serve as an accompaniment.

Marinated Fennel

Fennel has a wonderful anise flavor which is ideal for broiling or cooking on a barbecue. This marinated recipe is really delicious.

NUTRITIONAL INFORMATION

Calories	117	Sugars	.........3g
Protein	.........1g	Fat	...........11g
Carbohydrate	....3g	Saturates	.......2g

1¼ hrs   10 mins

SERVES 4

I N G R E D I E N T S

2 fennel bulbs

1 red bell pepper, seeded and cut into large dice

1 lime, cut into 8 wedges

M A R I N A D E

2 tbsp lime juice

4 tbsp olive oil

2 garlic cloves, crushed

1 tsp wholegrain mustard

1 tbsp chopped thyme

fennel fronds, to garnish

crisp salad, to serve

1 Cut off and reserve the fennel fronds for the garnish. Cut each of the bulbs into 8 pieces and place in a shallow dish. Add the bell pepper and mix well.

2 To make the marinade, combine the lime juice, olive oil, garlic, mustard, and thyme. Pour the marinade over the fennel and bell pepper and toss to coat thoroughly. Cover with plastic wrap and set aside to marinate for 1 hour.

3 Thread the fennel and bell pepper onto wooden skewers with the lime wedges. Cook the kabobs under a preheated medium broiler, turning and basting frequently with the marinade, for about 10 minutes. Alternatively, cook on a medium hot barbecue, turning and basting frequently, for about 10 minutes.

4 Transfer the kabobs to serving plates, garnish with fennel fronds, and serve immediately with a crisp salad.

COOK'S TIP

Soak the skewers in cold water for 20 minutes before using to prevent them from burning during broiling or grilling. You could substitute 2 tablespoons orange juice for the lime juice and add 1 tbsp honey, if you prefer.

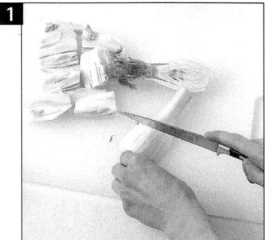

Rosy Melon & Strawberries

The combination of sweet melon and strawberries macerated in rosé wine and a hint of rose water is a delightful start to a special meal.

NUTRITIONAL INFORMATION

Calories	85	Sugars	.........14g
Protein	.........2g	Fat	...........0g
Carbohydrate	...14g	Saturates	.......0g

10 mins, plus chilling

0 mins

SERVES 4

INGREDIENTS

¼ honeydew melon

½ Charentais or Cantaloupe melon

⅔ cup rosé wine

2–3 tsp rose water

6 oz/175 g small strawberries, washed and hulled

rose petals, to garnish

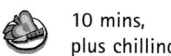

1 Scoop out the seeds from both melons with a spoon. Then carefully remove the skin, taking care not to remove too much flesh.

2 Cut the melon flesh into thin strips and place in a bowl. Pour over the wine and sufficient rose water to taste. Stir the melon and the liquid together gently to combine, cover, and let chill in the refrigerator for at least 2 hours.

3 Halve the strawberries and carefully mix them into the macerated melon. Let the melon and strawberries stand at room temperature for about 15 minutes for the flavors to develop before serving— if the melon is served too cold, there will be little flavor.

4 Arrange the melon and strawberries on individual serving plates and serve sprinkled with a few rose petals.

COOK'S TIP
Rose water is generally available from pharmacies and food stores as well as from specialist food suppliers.

Paprika Chips

These wafer-thin potato chips are great cooked over a barbecue grill and served with spicy vegetable kabobs.

NUTRITIONAL INFORMATION

Calories ....149 Sugars 0.6g
Protein ....2g Fat 8g
Carbohydrate ...17g Saturates 1g

 5 mins   25 mins

SERVES 4

INGREDIENTS

2 large potatoes

3 tbsp olive oil

½ tsp paprika

salt

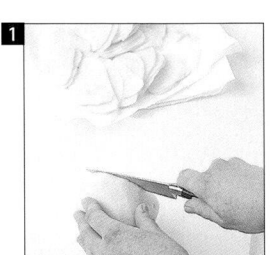

1 Using a sharp knife, slice the potatoes very thinly so that they are almost transparent. Drain the potato slices thoroughly and pat dry with paper towels.

2 Heat the oil in a large skillet and add the paprika, stirring constantly to ensure that the paprika doesn't catch light and burn.

3 Add the potato slices to the skillet and cook them in a single layer for about 5 minutes or until they just begin to curl slightly at the edges.

4 Remove the potato slices from the skillet using a slotted spoon.

5 Transfer the potato slices to paper towels and let them drain thoroughly.

6 Thread the potato slices on to several wooden kabob skewers.

7 Sprinkle the potato slices with a little salt and cook over a medium hot barbecue grill or under a medium broiler, turning frequently, for 10 minutes, until the potato slices begin to go crisp. Sprinkle with a little more salt, if preferred, and serve immediately.

VARIATION

You could use curry powder or any other spice to flavor the chips instead of the paprika, if you prefer.

Vegetarian Spring Rolls

These crisp little spring rolls are bursting with texture and flavor.
They are excellent served as an appetizer before a Chinese meal.

NUTRITIONAL INFORMATION

Calories 491	Sugars 2g
Protein 7g	Fat 34g
Carbohydrate . . .40g	Saturates 7g

 20 mins   20 mins

SERVES 4

I N G R E D I E N T S

1 oz fine cellophane noodles

2 tbsp peanut oil

2 garlic cloves, crushed

½ tsp. grated fresh ginger

⅔ cup oyster mushrooms, thinly sliced

2 scallions, finely chopped

½ cup beansprouts

1 small carrot, finely shredded

½ tsp sesame oil

1 tbsp light soy sauce

1 tbsp rice wine or dry sherry

¼ tsp ground black pepper

1 tbsp chopped fresh cilantro

1 tbsp chopped fresh mint

24 spring- (egg-) roll wrappers

½ tsp cornstarch

peanut oil for deep frying

2 Heat the peanut oil in a wok or wide pan over high heat. Add the garlic, ginger, oyster mushrooms, scallions, beansprouts, and carrot and stir-fry for about 1 minute until just soft.

3 Stir in the sesame oil, soy sauce, rice wine, pepper, cilantro, and mint, then remove from the heat. Stir in the rice noodles.

4 Arrange the spring- (egg-) roll wrappers on a counter, pointing diagonally. Mix the cornstarch with 1 tablespoon water and brush the edges of 1 wrapper with this. Spoon a little filling on to one pointed side of a wrapper.

5 Roll the point of the wrapper over the filling, then fold the side points inward over the filling. Continue to roll up the wrapper away from you, moistening the tip with more cornstarch mixture to secure to the roll.

6 Heat the oil in a wok or deep pan to 350°F/180°C, or until a cube of bread browns in 30 seconds. Add rolls in batches and deep fry for 2–3 minutes each until golden brown and crisp. Serve hot.

1 Place the noodles in a heatproof bowl, pour over enough boiling water to cover, and let stand for 4 minutes. Drain, rinse in cold water, then drain again. Cut into 2 inch lengths.

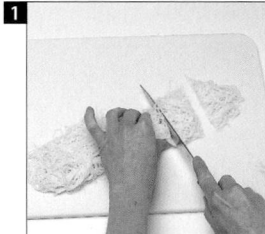 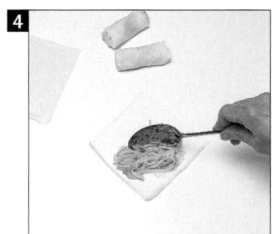 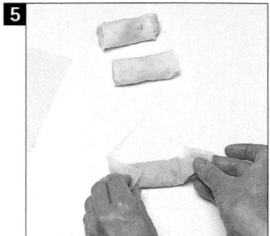

Imam Bayildi

In this Turkish dish, eggplant halves are baked with a deliciously aromatic topping of tomatoes and green bell pepper, and served chilled.

NUTRITIONAL INFORMATION

Calories 207   Sugars 2g
Protein . . . . .3g   Fat 12g
Carbohydrate . . .23g   Saturates 2g

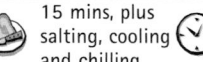

15 mins, plus salting, cooling and chilling   45 mins

SERVES 4

INGREDIENTS

2 medium eggplants, halved lengthwise

4 tbsp olive oil

2 onions, thinly sliced

2 garlic cloves, finely chopped

1 green bell pepper, seeded and sliced

2 cups canned chopped tomatoes

3 tbsp sugar

1 tsp ground coriander

2 tbsp chopped fresh cilantro

salt and ground black pepper

COOK'S TIP

Even after salting, eggplants tend to absorb a lot of oil, so you may need to add a little more before cooking the onions in step 2.

1 Halve the eggplants, slash the flesh 4 or 5 times and sprinkle generously with salt. Place in a strainer and let stand for 30 minutes. Rinse well and pat dry.

2 Heat the oil in a large, heavy skillet. Add the eggplants, cut side down, and cook for 5 minutes. Drain well and place in a casserole. Add the onions, garlic, and green bell pepper to the skillet and cook, stirring occasionally, for 10 minutes. Add the tomatoes, sugar, and ground coriander and season to taste with salt and pepper. Stir in the chopped fresh cilantro.

3 Spoon the mixture onto the eggplant halves, cover, and bake in a preheated oven, 355°F/190°C, for 30 minutes.

4 Remove from the oven and let cool, then chill in the refrigerator for 1 hour before serving.

Crispy Wontons

Mushroom-filled crispy wontons are served on skewers with a dipping sauce flavored with chilies.

NUTRITIONAL INFORMATION

Calories 302   Sugars 1g
Protein ....3g   Fat 25
Carbohydrate ...15g   Saturates 6g

45 mins   20 mins

SERVES 4

INGREDIENTS

8 wooden skewers, soaked in cold water for 30 minutes

1 tbsp vegetable oil

1 tbsp chopped onion

1 small garlic clove, chopped

½ tsp chopped ginger root

½ firmly packed cup chopped mushrooms

16 wonton skins (see page 113)

vegetable oil, for deep-frying

salt

SAUCE

2 tbsp vegetable oil

2 scallions, shredded thinly

1 red and 1 green chili, seeded and shredded thinly

3 tbsp light soy sauce

1 tbsp vinegar

1 tbsp dry sherry

pinch of sugar

1 Heat the vegetable oil in a preheated wok or skillet.

2 Add the onion, garlic, and ginger root to the wok or skillet and stir-fry for 2 minutes. Stir in the mushrooms and stir-fry for a further 2 minutes. Season well with salt and let cool.

3 Place 1 teaspoon of the cooled mushroom filling in the center of each wonton skin.

4 Bring two opposite corners of each wonton skin together to cover the mixture and pinch together to seal. Repeat with the remaining corners.

5 Thread 2 wontons on to each skewer. Heat enough oil in a large pan to deep-fry the wontons in batches until golden and crisp. Do not overheat the oil or the wontons will brown on the outside before they are properly cooked inside.

Remove the wontons with a perforated spoon and drain thoroughly on absorbent paper towels.

6 To make the sauce, heat the vegetable oil in a small pan until quite hot or until a small cube of bread dropped in the oil browns in a few seconds. Put the scallions and chilies in a bowl and pour the hot oil slowly on top. Mix in the remaining sauce ingredients.

7 Transfer the crispy wontons to a serving dish and serve with the dipping sauce.

Gado Gado

This is a well-known and very popular Indonesian salad of mixed vegetables with a peanut dressing.

NUTRITIONAL INFORMATION

Calories	392	Sugars	.........8g
Protein	.........9g	Fat	..........35g
Carbohydrate	....11g	Saturates	.......5g

🍳 🍳

 10 mins   🕐 25 mins

SERVES 4

I N G R E D I E N T S

1½ cups shredded white cabbage

¼ lb/115 g green beans, cut into three

¼ lb/115 g carrots, cut into matchsticks

scant cup cauliflower florets

1 cup beansprouts

D R E S S I N G

⅓ cup vegetable oil

½ cup unsalted peanuts

2 garlic cloves, crushed

1 small onion, finely chopped

½ tsp chili powder

½ tsp light brown sugar

1¾ cups water

juice of ½ lemon

salt

sliced scallions, to garnish

3 Remove from the skillet with a slotted spoon and drain on paper towels. Process in a food processor or crush with a rolling pin until a fine mixture is formed.

4 Leave 1 tbsp of oil in the skillet and cook the garlic and onion for 1 minute. Add the chili powder, sugar, a pinch of salt, and the water and bring to a boil.

5 Stir the peanuts into the sauce. Reduce the heat and simmer for 4–5 minutes, until the sauce thickens. Add the lemon juice and let cool.

6 Arrange the vegetables in a serving dish and spoon the peanut dressing into the center. Garnish with the sliced scallions and serve.

1 Cook the vegetables separately in a pan of salted boiling water for 4–5 minutes, drain well, and chill.

2 To make the dressing, heat the oil in a skillet and cook the peanuts, tossing frequently, for 3–4 minutes.

Seven-Spice Eggplant

This tasty Thai dish is really simple to make, and is perfect served with an authentic spicy chili dip.

NUTRITIONAL INFORMATION

Calories	169	Sugars 2g
Protein	.........2g	Fat 12g
Carbohydrate	...15g	Saturates 1g

 35 mins   20 mins

SERVES 4

I N G R E D I E N T S

1 lb eggplant, wiped

1 egg white

3½ tbsp cornstarch

1 tsp salt

1 tbsp Thai seven-spice seasoning

oil, for deep-frying

1 Using a sharp knife, slice the eggplant into thin rings.

2 Place the egg white in a small bowl and whip until light and foamy.

3 Mix together the cornstarch, salt, and seven-spice powder on a large plate.

4 Heat the oil for deep-frying in a large wok.

5 Dip each piece of eggplant into the beaten egg white then coat in the cornstarch and seven-spice mixture.

6 Deep-fry the eggplant slices, in batches, for 5 minutes, or until pale golden and crispy.

7 Transfer the eggplant to absorbent paper towels and let drain. Transfer to serving plates and serve hot.

Son-in-Law Eggs

This recipe is supposedly so called because it is an easy dish for a son-in-law to cook to impress his new mother-in-law!

NUTRITIONAL INFORMATION

Calories ....229 Sugars 8g
Protein ....9g Fat 18g
Carbohydrate ....8g Saturates 3g

15 mins   15 mins

SERVES 4

I N G R E D I E N T S

6 eggs, hard-cooked and shelled

4 tbsp sunflower oil

1 onion, sliced thinly

2 fresh red chilies, sliced

2 tbsp sugar

1 tbsp water

2 tsp tamarind pulp

1 tbsp liquid seasoning, such as Maggi

rice, to serve

1 Prick the hard-cooked eggs 2 or 3 times with a toothpick.

2 Heat the sunflower oil in a wok and cook the eggs until crispy and golden. Drain on absorbent paper towels.

3 Halve the eggs lengthwise and put on a serving dish.

4 Reserve one tablespoon of the oil, pour off the rest, then heat the tablespoonful in the wok.

5 Cook the onion and chilies over high heat until golden and slightly crisp. Drain on paper towels.

6 Heat the sugar, water, tamarind pulp (or lemon juice—see Cook's Tip), and liquid seasoning in the wok and simmer over low heat for 5 minutes, until the mixture has thickened.

7 Pour the tamarind sauce over the eggs and spoon over the onion and chili mix to garnish. Serve immediately with the rice.

COOK'S TIP

Tamarind pulp is sold in Asian stores, and is quite sour. If it is not available, use twice the amount of lemon juice in its place.

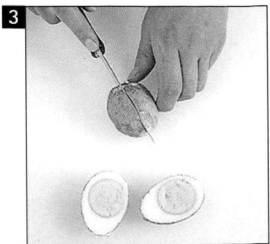

Bell Peppers & Rosemary

The flavor of broiled or roasted bell peppers is very different from when they are eaten raw, so do try them cooked in this way.

NUTRITIONAL INFORMATION

Calories 201	Sugars 6g
Protein 2g	Fat 19g
Carbohydrate 6g	Saturates 2g

20 mins   10 mins

SERVES 4

INGREDIENTS

4 tbsp olive oil

finely grated zest of 1 lemon

4 tbsp lemon juice

1 tbsp balsamic vinegar

1 tbsp crushed fresh rosemary, or
   1 tsp dried rosemary

2 garlic cloves, crushed

2 red bell peppers, halved and seeded

2 yellow bell peppers, halved and seeded

2 tbsp pine nuts

salt and pepper

fresh rosemary sprigs, to garnish

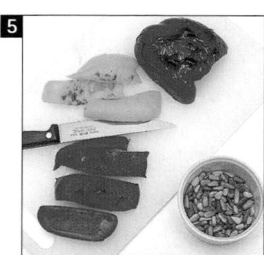

1 Mix together the olive oil, lemon zest, lemon juice, balsamic vinegar, rosemary, and garlic. Season with salt and pepper to taste.

2 Place the red and yellow bell peppers, skin side up, on the rack of a broiler pan, and then brush the olive oil mixture over them.

3 Broil the bell peppers for 3–4 minutes or until the skin begins to char, basting frequently with the olive oil mixture. Remove from the heat, cover with foil, and set aside for 5 minutes.

4 Meanwhile, sprinkle the pine nuts onto the broiler rack and toast them lightly for 2–3 minutes. Keep a close eye on them, as they tend to burn very quickly.

5 Peel the bell peppers, slice into strips, and place in a warmed serving dish. Sprinkle with the toasted pine nuts and drizzle over any remaining olive oil mixture. Garnish with fresh rosemary and serve immediately.

COOK'S TIP

A combination of red and yellow bell peppers looks attractive, but you could use all one color or substitute an orange bell pepper. However, do not use green bell peppers, which are not really sweet enough for this dish.

Little Golden Parcels

These little parcels will draw admiring gasps from your guests, but they are fairly simple to prepare.

NUTRITIONAL INFORMATION

Calories 320	Sugars 1g	
Protein 6g	Fat 21g	
Carbohydrate ...28g	Saturates 5g	

 35 mins   35 mins

SERVES 4

I N G R E D I E N T S

1 garlic clove, crushed

1 tsp chopped cilantro root

1 tsp pepper

1¼ cups boiled mashed potato

6 oz/175 g water chestnuts, chopped finely

1 tsp grated ginger root

2 tbsp ground roasted peanuts

2 tsp light soy sauce

½ tsp salt

½ tsp sugar

30 wonton sheets, defrosted

1 tsp cornstarch, made into a paste
   with a little water

vegetable oil, for deep-frying

fresh chives, to garnish

sweet chili sauce, to serve

VARIATION

If wonton sheets are not available, use spring roll sheets or phyllo pastry, and cut the large squares down to about 10 cm/4 inches square.

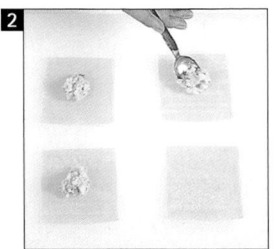

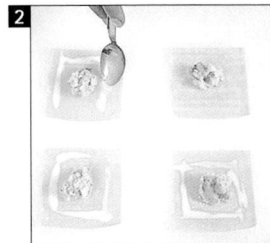

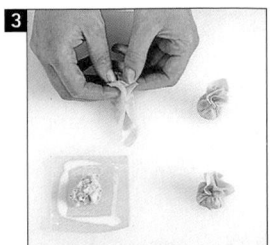

1 Mix together all the ingredients except the wonton sheets, cornstarch and vegetable oil.

2 Keeping the remainder of the wonton sheets covered with a damp cloth to prevent them drying out, lay 4 sheets out on a counter. Put a teaspoonful of the mixture on each. Make a line of the cornstarch paste around each sheet, about ½ inch/1 cm from the edge.

3 Bring all four corners to the center and press together to form little bags. Repeat with all the wonton sheets.

4 Heat 2 inches/5 cm of the oil in a pan until a light haze appears on top and cook the parcels, in batches of 3, until golden brown. Remove and drain on paper towels. Tie a chive around the neck of each bag to garnish, and serve with a sweet chili sauce for dipping.

Money Bags

These traditional steamed dumplings can be eaten on their own
or dipped in a mixture of soy sauce, sherry, and slivers of ginger root.

NUTRITIONAL INFORMATION

Calories	.315	Sugars	.3g
Protein	.8g	Fat	.8g
Carbohydrate	..56g	Saturates	.1g

 45 mins 20 mins

SERVES 4

I N G R E D I E N T S

3 Chinese dried mushrooms (if unavailable,
   use thinly sliced open-cup mushrooms)

1½ cups all-purpose flour

1 egg, beaten

5 tbsp water

1 tsp baking powder

¾ tsp salt

2 tbsp vegetable oil

2 scallions, chopped

scant ½ cup corn kernels

½ red chili, seeded and chopped

1 tbsp brown bean sauce

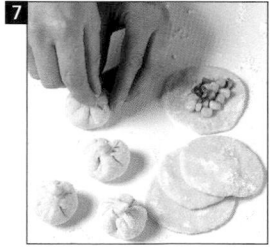

1 Place the dried mushrooms in a small bowl, cover with warm water and let soak for 20–25 minutes.

2 To make the wrappers, sift the all-purpose flour into a bowl. Add the beaten egg and mix in lightly. Stir in the water, baking powder, and salt and mix together to make a soft dough.

3 Knead the dough lightly on a floured board. Cover with a damp dish cloth and set aside for 5–6 minutes. This allows the baking powder time to activate, so that the dumplings swell when steaming.

4 Drain the mushrooms, squeezing them dry. Remove the tough centers and chop the mushrooms.

5 Heat the vegetable oil in a wok or large skillet and stir-fry the mushrooms, scallions, corn kernels, and chili for 2 minutes.

6 Stir in the brown bean sauce and remove from the heat.

7 Roll the dough into a large sausage and cut into 24 even-sized pieces. Roll each piece out into a thin round and place a teaspoonful of the filling in the center. Gather up the edges to a point, pinch together and twist to seal.

8 Stand the dumplings in an oiled steaming basket. Place over a pan of simmering water, cover, and steam for 12–14 minutes before serving.

Lentil Balls with Sauce

Crisp golden lentil balls are served in a sweet and sour sauce with bell peppers and pineapple chunks.

NUTRITIONAL INFORMATION

Calories	384	Sugars	........15g
Protein	.........17g	Fat	..........14g
Carbohydrate	...49g	Saturates	.......2g

 15 mins   35 mins

SERVES 4

INGREDIENTS

1½ cups red lentils

1¾ cups water

½ green chili, seeded and chopped

4 scallions, chopped finely

1 garlic clove, crushed

1 tsp salt

4 tbsp pineapple juice from can

1 egg, beaten

vegetable oil for deep-frying

rice or noodles, to serve

SAUCE

3 tbsp white wine vinegar

2 tbsp sugar

2 tbsp tomato paste

1 tsp sesame oil

1 tsp cornstarch

½ tsp salt

6 tbsp water

2 tbsp vegetable oil

½ red bell pepper, cut into chunks

½ green bell pepper, cut into chunks

2 canned pineapple rings, cut into chunks

1 Wash the lentils, then place them in a pan with the water and bring to a boil. Skim and boil rapidly for 10 minutes, uncovered. Reduce the heat to low and cook the lentils for a further 5 minutes, stirring occasionally, until you have a fairly dry mixture.

2 Remove the pan from the heat and stir in the chili, scallions, garlic, salt, and pineapple juice. Let the mixture cool for 10 minutes.

3 To make the sauce, mix together the vinegar, sugar, tomato paste, sesame oil, cornstarch, salt, and water.

4 Add the beaten egg to the lentil mixture. Heat the oil in a large pan or wok and deep-fry tablespoonfuls of the mixture in batches until crisp and golden. Remove with a perforated spoon and drain on paper towels.

5 Heat the 2 tablespoons of oil in a wok or skillet. Stir-fry the bell peppers for 2 minutes. Add the sauce mixture with the pineapple chunks. Bring to a boil, then reduce the heat and simmer for 1 minute, stirring constantly, until the sauce has thickened. Add the lentil balls and heat thoroughly, taking care not to break them up. Serve with rice or noodles.

Deep-Fried Chili Corn Balls

These small corn balls have a wonderful hot and sweet flavor, offset by the pungent cilantro.

NUTRITIONAL INFORMATION

Calories	248	Sugars	.........6g
Protein	.........6g	Fat	12
Carbohydrate	...30g	Saturates	.......5g

 15 mins   30 mins

SERVES 4

I N G R E D I E N T S

6 scallions, sliced

3 tbsp chopped fresh cilantro

1 cup canned corn kernels

1 tsp mild chili powder

1 tbsp sweet chili sauce

¼ cup shredded coconut

1 egg

⅓ cup cornmeal

oil, for deep-frying

extra sweet chili sauce, to serve

1 In a large bowl, mix together the scallions, cilantro, corn, chili powder, chili sauce, coconut, egg, and cornmeal until well blended.

2 Cover the bowl with plastic wrap and let stand for about 10 minutes.

3 Heat the oil for deep-frying in a large preheated wok or skillet to 350°F/180°C or until a cube of bread browns in 30 seconds.

4 Carefully drop spoonfuls of the chili and cornmeal mixture into the hot oil.

Deep-fry the chili corn balls, in batches, for 4–5 minutes or until crispy and a deep golden brown color.

5 Remove the chili corn balls with a slotted spoon, transfer to paper towels, and let drain thoroughly.

6 Transfer the chili corn balls to serving plates and serve with an extra sweet chili sauce for dipping.

COOK'S TIP

For safe deep-frying in a round-bottomed wok, place it on a wok rack so that it rests securely. Only half-fill the wok with oil. Never leave the wok unattended over high heat.

Eggplant Satay

Spicy, marinated eggplants and mushrooms are broiled on skewers and served with a satay sauce.

NUTRITIONAL INFORMATION

Calories	155	Sugars	.........2g
Protein	.........4g	Fat	..........14g
Carbohydrate	....3g	Saturates	.......3g

 2¼ hrs   🕐 25 mins

SERVES 4

INGREDIENTS

2 eggplants, cut into 1 inch/2.5 cm pieces

6 oz/175 g small crimini mushrooms

MARINADE

1 tsp cumin seeds

1 tsp coriander seeds

1 inch/2.5 cm piece ginger root, grated

2 garlic cloves, crushed lightly

½ stalk lemon grass, chopped roughly

4 tbsp light soy sauce

8 tbsp sunflower oil

2 tbsp lemon juice

PEANUT SAUCE

½ tsp cumin seeds

½ tsp coriander seeds

3 garlic cloves

1 small onion, puréed in a food processor or chopped very finely by hand

1 tbsp lemon juice

1 tsp salt

½ red chili, seeded and sliced

½ cup coconut milk

1 cup crunchy peanut butter

1 cup water

1 Thread the vegetables on to eight metal or presoaked wooden skewers.

2 For the marinade, grind the cumin and coriander seeds, ginger, garlic, and lemon grass. Stir-fry over high heat until fragrant. Remove from the heat and add the remaining marinade ingredients. Place the skewers in a dish and spoon the marinade over. Let marinate for at least 2 hours and up to 8 hours.

3 To make the sauce, grind the cumin and coriander seeds with the garlic. Add all the ingredients except the water. Transfer to a pan and stir in the water. Bring to a boil and cook until thick.

4 Cook the vegetable skewers under a preheated very hot broiler for 15–20 minutes. Brush with the marinade frequently and turn once. Serve with the peanut sauce.

Vegetable Rolls

In this recipe a mixed vegetable stuffing is wrapped in Napa cabbage and steamed until tender.

NUTRITIONAL INFORMATION

Calories	69	Sugars	.........1g
Protein	.........2g	Fat	...........5g
Carbohydrate	....3g	Saturates	.......1g

10 mins   20 mins

SERVES 4

INGREDIENTS

8 large Napa cabbage leaves

FILLING

2 baby corn cobs, sliced

1 carrot, finely chopped

1 celery stalk, chopped

4 scallions, chopped

4 water chestnuts, chopped

2 tbsp unsalted cashews, chopped

1 garlic clove, chopped

1 tsp grated fresh ginger root

1 oz/25 g canned bamboo shoots, drained, rinsed, and chopped

1 tsp sesame oil

2 tsp soy sauce

  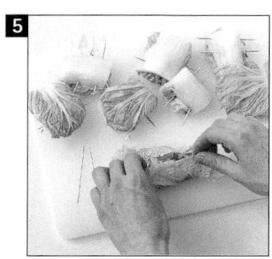

1 Place the Napa cabbage leaves in a large bowl and pour over boiling water to soften them. Let stand for 1 minute and drain thoroughly.

2 Mix together the baby corn cobs, chopped carrot, celery, scallions, water chestnuts, cashews, garlic, ginger, and bamboo shoots in a large bowl.

3 In a separate bowl, whisk together the sesame oil and soy sauce. Add this to the vegetables, and stir well until all the vegetables are thoroughly coated in the mixture.

4 Spread out the Napa cabbage leaves on a chopping board and divide the filling mixture between them, carefully spooning an equal quantity of the mixture on to each leaf.

5 Roll up the Napa cabbage leaves, folding in the sides, to make neat parcels. Secure the parcels with toothpicks.

6 Place in a small heatproof dish in a steamer, cover, and cook for 15–20 minutes, until the parcels are cooked.

7 Transfer the vegetable rolls to a warm serving dish and serve with a soy or chili sauce.

Rice Cubes with Satay Sauce

Plain rice cubes are a good foil to any piquant dipping sauce, and they are often served with satay, to complement the dipping sauce.

NUTRITIONAL INFORMATION

Calories 317	Sugars 3g	
Protein 10g	Fat 10g	
Carbohydrate . . .49g	Saturates 2g	

8¼ hrs   25 mins

SERVES 4

I N G R E D I E N T S

1½ cups jasmine rice

6 cups water

CILANTRO DIPPING SAUCE

1 garlic clove

2 tsp salt

1 tbsp black peppercorns

2 oz/60 g washed cilantro, including roots and stem

3 tbsp lemon juice

¾ cup coconut milk

2 tbsp peanut butter

2 scallions, chopped roughly

1 red chili, seeded and sliced

1 Grease and line a 8 x 4 x 1 inch /20 x 10 x 2.5 cm pan.

2 To make the sauce, grind together the garlic, salt, peppercorns, cilantro, and lemon juice in either a pestle and mortar or a blender.

3 Add the coconut milk, peanut butter, scallions, and chili. Grind finely. Transfer to a pan and bring to a boil, then let cool.

4 To cook the rice, do not rinse. Bring the water to a boil and add the rice.

Stir and return to a medium boil. Cook, uncovered, for 14–16 minutes until very soft. Drain thoroughly.

5 Put ½ cup of the cooked rice in a blender and purée until smooth. Alternatively, grind to a paste in a pestle and mortar.

6 Combine the puréed rice with the remaining cooked rice and spoon into

the lined pan. Level the surface and cover with a layer of plastic wrap. Compress the rice by using either a slightly smaller-sized pan or a small piece of board, and weigh this down with cans. Chill the rice in the refrigerator for at least 8 hours or preferably overnight.

7 Invert the pan on to a board. Cut the rice into cubes with a wet knife. Serve with the Cilantro Dipping Sauce.

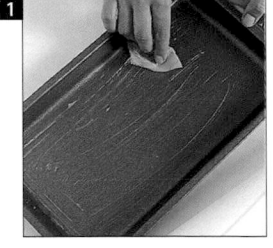

Asparagus Parcels

These small parcels are ideal as part of an entrée and irresistible as a quick snack with extra plum sauce for dipping.

NUTRITIONAL INFORMATION

Calories	194	Sugars	.........2g
Protein	.........3g	Fat	..........16g
Carbohydrate	....11g	Saturates	.......4g

5 mins   25 mins

SERVES 4

INGREDIENTS

3½ oz/100 g fine-tip asparagus

1 red bell pepper, seeded and thinly sliced

½ cup beansprouts

2 tbsp plum sauce

1 egg yolk

8 sheets phyllo pastry

oil, for deep-frying

1 Place the asparagus, bell pepper, and beansprouts in a large mixing bowl.

2 Add the plum sauce to the vegetables and mix until well combined.

3 Beat the egg yolk and set aside until required.

4 Lay the sheets of phyllo pastry out on a clean counter.

5 Place a little of the asparagus and red bell pepper filling at the top end of each phyllo pastry sheet. Brush the edges of the phyllo pastry with a little of the beaten egg yolk.

6 Roll up the phyllo pastry, tucking in the ends and enclosing the filling like a spring roll. Repeat with the remaining phyllo sheets.

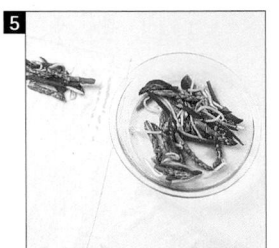
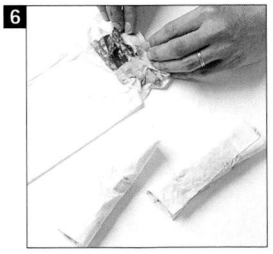

7 Heat the oil for deep-frying in a large preheated wok. Carefully cook the parcels, 2 at a time, in the hot oil for 4–5 minutes or until crispy.

8 Remove the parcels with a slotted spoon and let them drain on paper towels.

9 Transfer the parcels to warm serving plates and serve immediately.

COOK'S TIP
Be sure to use fine-tip asparagus as it is more tender than the larger stems.

Thai-Style Corn Fritters

These quick little fritters make a really appetizing first course, served with a spoonful of spicy chili relish and a squeeze of lime juice.

NUTRITIONAL INFORMATION

Calories	203	Sugars	.........3g
Protein	.........7g	Fat	...........7g
Carbohydrate	...29g	Saturates	.......1g

 15 mins   30 mins

SERVES 4

INGREDIENTS

½ cup all-purpose flour

1 large egg

2 tsp Thai green curry paste

5 tbsp coconut milk

1¾ cups canned or frozen corn kernels

4 scallions

1 tbsp chopped fresh cilantro

1 tbsp chopped fresh basil

salt and pepper

vegetable oil, for frying

TO SERVE

lime wedges

chili relish

1 Place the flour, egg, curry paste, coconut milk, and about half the corn kernels in a food processor and process until a smooth, thick batter forms. Pour into a bowl.

2 Finely chop the scallions and stir into the batter with the remaining corn, chopped cilantro, and basil. Season to taste with salt and pepper.

3 Heat a small amount of oil in a wide, heavy skillet. Drop in tablespoonfuls of the batter and cook for 2–3 minutes until golden brown.

4 Turn the fritters over and cook for a further 2–3 minutes until golden brown in color.

5 Fry in batches, making about 12–16 fritters, keeping the cooked fritters hot while you cook the remaining batter.

6 Serve the fritters hot with lime wedges and a chili relish.

COOK'S TIP

If you prefer to use fresh corn, strip the kernels from the cobs with a sharp knife, then cook in boiling water for about 4–5 minutes until just tender. Drain well before using as instructed.

Aïoli

This garlic mayonnaise features in many traditional Provençal recipes, but also makes a delicious dip, surrounded by a selection of vegetables.

NUTRITIONAL INFORMATION

Calories	239	Sugars	.........0g
Protein	.........1g	Fat	..........26g
Carbohydrate	....1g	Saturates	.......4g

 15 mins 0 mins

SERVES 6

INGREDIENTS

4 large garlic cloves or to taste

2 large egg yolks

1¼ cups extra virgin olive oil

1–2 tbsp lemon juice

1 tbsp fresh white bread crumbs

sea salt and pepper

TO SERVE (OPTIONAL)

a selection of raw vegetables, such as
sliced red bell peppers, zucchini slices,
whole scallions, and tomato wedges

a selection of blanched and cooled
vegetables, such as baby artichoke
hearts, cauliflower or broccoli florets,
or green beans

1 Finely chop the garlic on a cutting board. Add a pinch of sea salt to the garlic and use the tip and broad side of a knife to work the garlic and salt into a smooth paste.

2 Transfer the garlic paste to a food processor. Add the egg yolks and process until well blended, scraping down the side of the bowl with a rubber spatula, if necessary.

3 With the motor running, slowly pour in the olive oil in a steady stream through the feeder tube, processing until a thick mayonnaise forms.

4 Add 1 tablespoon of the lemon juice and the bread crumbs and process again. Taste and add more lemon juice if necessary. Season to taste with sea salt and pepper.

5 Place the aïoli in a bowl, cover, and chill until ready to serve. To serve, place the bowl of aïoli on a large platter and surround with a selection of raw and lightly blanched vegetables.

COOK'S TIP
The amount of garlic in a traditional Provençal aïoli is a matter of personal taste. Local cooks use 2 cloves per person as a rule of thumb, but this version is slightly milder, although still bursting with flavor.

Crudités with Cilantro Dip

Raw vegetables are the ideal healthy start to a meal, and this dip is the perfect accompaniment—full of flavor, but no fat.

NUTRITIONAL INFORMATION

Calories 67	Sugars 8g
Protein 7g	Fat 1g
Carbohydrate 9g	Saturates 0g

 10 mins 2 mins

SERVES 4

I N G R E D I E N T S

FOR THE CRUDITÉS

¼ lb/115 g baby corn ears

¼ lb/115 g young asparagus spears or sprue

1 head of endive, leaves separated

1 red bell pepper, seeded and sliced

1 orange bell pepper, seeded and sliced

8 radishes, trimmed

FOR THE DIP

1 tbsp hot water

1 tsp saffron threads

1 cup fat-free unsweetened yogurt

3 tbsp chopped fresh cilantro

1 tbsp chopped garlic chives

salt and pepper

fresh cilantro sprigs, to garnish

COOK'S TIP

For a really creamy dip, use low-fat strained Greek-style yogurt, or use equal quantities of strained yogurt and fat-free yogurt.

1 Blanch the baby corn ears and asparagus spears or sprue in separate pans of boiling water for 2 minutes. Drain, plunge into iced water, and drain again.

2 Arrange all the vegetables on a serving platter and cover with a damp dish cloth while you make the dip.

3 Put the tablespoonful of hot water into a small bowl. Lightly crush the saffron threads between your fingers and add them to the bowl. Set aside for about 3–4 minutes, until the water has turned a rich golden color.

4 Beat the yogurt until it becomes smooth, then beat in the infused saffron water. Stir in the chopped cilantro and chives and season to taste with salt and pepper. Serve the dip immediately with the vegetables.

Zucchini & Thyme Fritters

These tasty little fritters, flecked with green, are great to serve at a drinks party or as an appetizer. Dried chilies can be added to spice them up.

NUTRITIONAL INFORMATION

Calories 162	Sugars 2g
Protein 7g	Fat 6g
Carbohydrate ...20g	Saturates 2g

5–10 mins   20 mins

MAKES 16-30

INGREDIENTS

¾ cup self–rising flour

2 eggs, beaten

¼ cup milk

2 zucchini (total 10–12 oz/280–340 g)

2 tbsp fresh thyme

1 tbsp oil

salt and pepper

1 Strain the self-rising flour into a large bowl and make a well in the center. Add the eggs to the well and, using a wooden spoon, gradually draw in the flour.

2 Slowly add the milk to the mixture, stirring constantly until a thick batter is formed.

3 Meanwhile, wash the zucchini then grate them over a sheet of paper towel placed in a bowl to absorb some of the juices.

4 Add the zucchini, thyme, and salt and pepper to taste to the batter and mix thoroughly.

5 Heat the oil in a large, heavy skillet. Taking a tablespoon of the batter for a medium-sized fritter or half a tablespoon of batter for a smaller-sized fritter, spoon

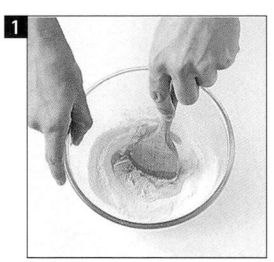

the mixture into the hot oil and cook the fritters, in batches, for 3–4 minutes on each side.

6 Remove the fritters with a perforated spoon and drain them thoroughly on absorbent paper towels. Keep each batch of fritters warm in the oven while making the rest. Transfer to warmed serving plates and serve hot.

VARIATION
Try adding ½ teaspoon of dried, crushed chilies to the batter in step 4 for spicier tasting fritters.

Orange-Dressed Asparagus

Try to use locally grown asparagus for this recipe—it is in season only for a short time in late spring and early summer, and the flavor is superb.

NUTRITIONAL INFORMATION

Calories 88   Sugars 6g
Protein . . . . .3g   Fat 6g
Carbohydrate . . . .6g   Saturates 1g

10 mins, plus standing   10 mins

SERVES 4

I N G R E D I E N T S

thinly pared zest and juice of 2 oranges

12 oz/350 g asparagus, trimmed

1 tablespoon lemon juice

1 scallion, finely chopped

1 garlic clove, finely chopped

2 tablespoons extra virgin olive oil

1 tablespoon white wine vinegar

1 Bring a small pan of water to a boil. Cut the orange zest into very thin strips, add to the pan, bring back to a boil and simmer for 1 minute. Drain, refresh under cold water, and drain again.

2 Bring water to a boil in an asparagus kettle or a deep pan (see Cook's Tip). Add the asparagus and cook for 5 minutes, or until crisp-tender. Drain, refresh under cold water, and drain again. Pat dry with paper towels.

3 Arrange the asparagus on a serving dish, cover, and chill until required.

4 To make the orange dressing, combine 5 tablespoons of the orange juice with the lemon juice, scallion, garlic, and orange zest. Let stand at room temperature for 15 minutes to let the flavors mingle. Whisk in the olive oil and vinegar.

5 Pour the orange dressing over the chilled asparagus and serve immediately.

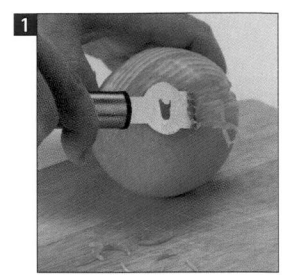

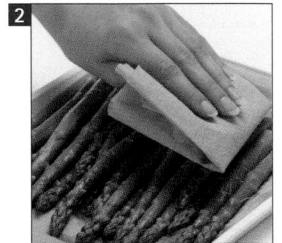

COOK'S TIP

An asparagus kettle is a tall, lidded pan with a basket, designed so that the stems cook in the water while the tips are gently steamed. If you don't have one, tie the asparagus loosely in a bundle and wedge upright in a deep pan. Cover with foil if the stems protrude.

Spicy Corn Fritters

Polenta can be found in most food stores or health food stores. Yellow in color, it acts as a binding agent in this recipe.

NUTRITIONAL INFORMATION

Calories 213   Sugars 6g
Protein . . . . .5g   Fat 8g
Carbohydrate . . .30g   Saturates 1g

 5 mins   15 mins

SERVES 4

I N G R E D I E N T S

1 cup canned or frozen corn kernels

2 red chilies, seeded and finely chopped

2 cloves garlic, crushed

10 lime leaves, finely chopped

2 tbsp chopped fresh cilantro

1 large egg

½ cup polenta

¾ cup fine green beans, finely sliced

groundnut oil, for frying

1 Place the corn kernels, chilies, garlic, lime leaves, cilantro, egg, and polenta in a large mixing bowl, and stir to combine thoroughly.

2 Add the sliced green beans to the ingredients in the bowl and mix well, using a wooden spoon.

3 Divide the mixture into small, evenly sized balls. Flatten the balls of mixture gently between the palms of your hands to form rounds.

4 Heat a little groundnut oil in a preheated wok or large skillet until really hot. Cook the fritters in batches, turning occasionally, until brown and crispy on the outside.

5 Let the fritters drain on absorbent paper towels while cooking the remaining fritters.

6 Transfer the cooked, drained fritters to warm serving plates and serve them immediately.

Spiced Corn & Nut Mix

A tasty mixture of buttery-spiced nuts, raisins, and popcorn to enjoy as a snack or with pre-dinner drinks.

NUTRITIONAL INFORMATION

Calories	372	Sugars	.........9g
Protein	.........8g	Fat	..........31g
Carbohydrate	...16g	Saturates	.......9g

🕒 5 mins   🕑 10 mins

SERVES 4

I N G R E D I E N T S

2 tbsp vegetable oil

½ cup unpopped corn

4 tbsp butter

1 garlic clove, crushed

½ cup unblanched almonds

½ cup unsalted cashews

½ cup unsalted peanuts

1 tsp vegetarian Worcestershire sauce

1 tsp curry powder or paste

¼ tsp chili powder

⅔ cup seedless raisins

salt

1 Heat the oil in a pan. Add the unpopped corn, stir well, then cover and cook over fairly high heat for 3-5 minutes, holding the pan lid firmly and shaking the pan frequently until the popping stops.

2 Turn the popped corn into a dish, discarding any unpopped corn kernels.

3 Melt the butter in a skillet and add the garlic, almonds, cashews, and peanuts, then stir in the Worcestershire sauce, the curry powder or paste, and the chili powder. Cook the mixture over medium heat, stirring frequently, for 2–3 minutes, until the nuts are lightly toasted.

4 Remove the pan from the heat and stir in the raisins and popped corn. Season with salt to taste and mix thoroughly. Transfer to a serving bowl and serve warm or cold.

VARIATION

Use a mixture of any unsalted nuts of your choice—walnuts, pecans, hazelnuts, Brazils, macadamia, and pine nuts. For a less fiery flavour, omit the curry and chili powder and add 1 tsp cumin seeds, 1 tsp ground coriander and ½ tsp paprika.

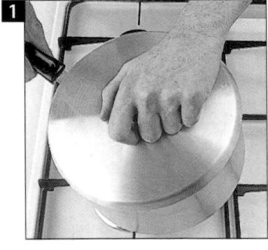

Crispy Seaweed

This tasty Chinese appetizer is not all that it seems—the "seaweed"
is in fact bok choi which is sautéed, salted, and tossed with pine nuts.

NUTRITIONAL INFORMATION

Calories	214	Sugars	........14g
Protein	.........6g	Fat	..........15g
Carbohydrate	...15g	Saturates	.......2g

 10 mins   5 mins

SERVES 4

I N G R E D I E N T S

2 lb 4 oz/1 kg bok choi

3½ cups peanut oil, for deep-frying

1 tsp salt

1 tbsp superfine sugar

2½ tbsp toasted pine nuts

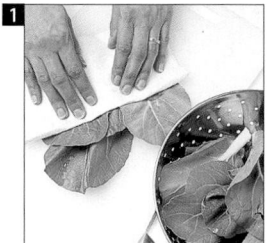

1 Rinse the bok choi leaves under cold running water and then pat dry thoroughly with paper towels.

2 Discarding any tough outer leaves, roll each bok choi leaf up, then slice through thinly so that the leaves are finely shredded. Alternatively, use a food processor to shred the bok choi.

3 Heat the peanut oil in a large wok or heavy skillet.

4 Carefully add the shredded bok choi leaves to the wok or skillet and cook for about 30 seconds or until they shrivel up and become crispy (you will probably need to do this in several batches, depending on the size of your wok).

5 Remove the crispy seaweed from the wok with a slotted spoon and drain on paper towels.

6 Transfer to a large bowl and toss with the salt, sugar, and pine nuts. Serve immediately on warm serving plates.

COOK'S TIP
The tough, outer leaves of bok choi are discarded as these will spoil the overall taste and texture of the dish. Use savoy cabbage instead of the bok choi if it is unavailable, drying the leaves thoroughly before frying.

Bell Peppers with Thyme

These bell peppers are wonderful served as an antipasto,
but they can also be used as an interesting side dish.

NUTRITIONAL INFORMATION

Calories . . . . .103 Sugars 14g
Protein . . . . .3g Fat 4g
Carbohydrate . . .16g Saturates 1g

15 mins   35 mins

SERVES 4

INGREDIENTS

2 each, red, yellow, and orange
  bell peppers, halved and seeded

4 tomatoes, halved

1 tbsp olive oil

3 garlic cloves, chopped

1 onion, sliced in rings

2 tbsp fresh thyme

salt and pepper

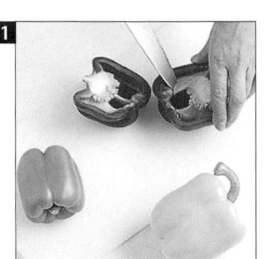
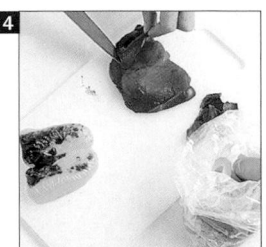

1 Place the bell peppers, cut-side down, on a cookie sheet and cook under a preheated broiler for 10 minutes.

2 Add the tomatoes to the cookie sheet and broil for 5 minutes, or until the skins of the bell peppers and tomatoes are charred.

3 Put the bell peppers into a plastic bag for 10 minutes to sweat, which will make the skin easier to peel. Meanwhile,

remove the tomato skins and then coarsely chop the flesh.

4 Peel the skins from the bell peppers and slice the flesh into strips.

5 Heat the oil in a large skillet and cook the garlic and onion for 3–4 minutes, or until softened.

6 Add the bell peppers and tomatoes to the skillet and cook for 5 minutes.

7 Stir in the fresh thyme and season to taste with salt and pepper.

8 Transfer the peppers to a serving bowl and serve warm, or let cool and then chill in the refrigerator.

COOK'S TIP

Preserve the bell peppers in the refrigerator by placing them in a sterilized jar and pouring olive oil over the top to seal.

Roman Artichokes

This is a traditional Roman dish. The artichokes are stewed in a mixture of olive oil with fresh herbs.

NUTRITIONAL INFORMATION

Calories 190   Sugars 0g
Protein . . . . .6g   Fat 11g
Carbohydrate . . .16g   Saturates 2g

🥗 10 mins   🕐 40 mins

SERVES 4

I N G R E D I E N T S

4 small globe artichokes

olive oil

4 garlic cloves, peeled

2 bay leaves

finely grated zest and juice of 1 lemon

2 tbsp fresh marjoram

lemon wedges, to serve

1 Using a sharp knife, carefully peel away the tough outer leaves surrounding the artichokes. Trim the stems to about 1 inch.

2 Using a knife, cut each artichoke in half and scoop out the heart.

3 Place the artichokes in a large, heavy pan. Pour over enough olive oil to half cover the artichokes in the pan.

4 Add the garlic cloves, bay leaves, and half of the grated lemon zest.

5 Start to heat the artichokes gently, then cover the pan and continue to cook over low heat for about 40 minutes. The artichokes should be stewed in the oil, not fried.

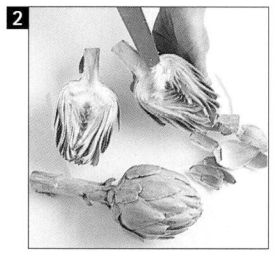

6 Once the artichokes are tender, remove them with a draining spoon and drain thoroughly. Remove the bay leaves.

7 Transfer the artichokes to warm serving plates. Serve immediately, garnished with a sprinkling of the remaining grated lemon zest, fresh marjoram, and lemon wedges.

COOK'S TIP

Use the oil used for cooking the artichokes for salad dressings— it will impart a lovely lemon and herb flavor.

Rice & Cheese Balls

The Italian name for this dish translates as "telephone wires," referring to the strings of melted mozzarella cheese hidden inside the risotto balls.

NUTRITIONAL INFORMATION

Calories 282   Sugars 2g
Protein . . . . .8g   Fat 11g
Carbohydrate . . .36g   Saturates 1g

 30 mins   25 mins

SERVES 4

INGREDIENTS

2 tbsp olive oil

1 medium onion, finely chopped

1 garlic clove, chopped

½ red bell pepper, diced

¾ cup risotto rice, washed

1 tsp dried oregano

1⅔ cup hot vegetable bouillon

½ scant cup dry white wine

3 oz/85 g mozzarella cheese

oil, for deep-frying

fresh basil sprig, to garnish

1 Heat the oil in a skillet and cook the onion and garlic for 3–4 minutes, or until just soft.

2 Add the bell pepper, rice, and oregano to the skillet. Cook for 2–3 minutes, stirring to coat the rice in the oil.

3 Mix the bouillon together with the wine and add to the pan a ladleful at a time, waiting for the liquid to be absorbed by the rice before you add the next ladleful of liquid.

4 Once all of the liquid has been absorbed and the rice is tender (it should take about 15 minutes in total,)

remove the skillet from the heat and let stand until cool enough to handle.

5 Cut the cheese into 12 pieces. Taking about a tablespoon of risotto, shape the mixture around the cheese pieces to make 12 balls.

6 Heat the oil until a piece of bread browns in 30 seconds. Cook the risotto balls in batches of 4 for 2 minutes, or until golden.

7 Remove the risotto balls with a draining spoon and drain thoroughly on absorbent paper towels. Garnish with a sprig of basil and serve hot.

  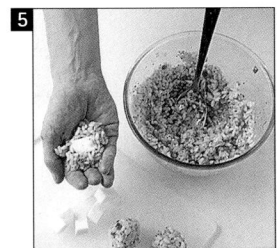

COOK'S TIP

Although mozzarella is the traditional cheese for this recipe and creates the stringy "telephone wire" effect, other cheeses may be used if you prefer.

Vegetable Spring Rolls

This version of vegetarian spring rolls is very quick and easy to make, using phyllo pastry to make the crisp cases.

NUTRITIONAL INFORMATION

Calories 189   Sugars 4g
Protein ....2g   Fat 16g
Carbohydrate ....11g   Saturates 5g

 10 mins   15 mins

SERVES 4

INGREDIENTS

½ lb/225 g carrots

1 red bell pepper

1 tbsp sunflower oil, plus extra for frying

scant 1 cup beansprouts

finely grated zest and juice of 1 lime

1 red chili, seeded and finely chopped

1 tbsp soy sauce

½ tsp arrowroot

2 tbsp chopped fresh cilantro

8 sheets phyllo pastry

2 tbsp butter

2 tsp sesame oil

TO SERVE

chili sauce

scallion tassels

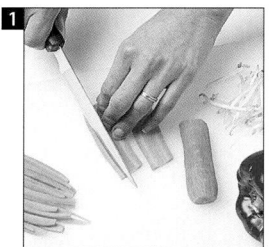

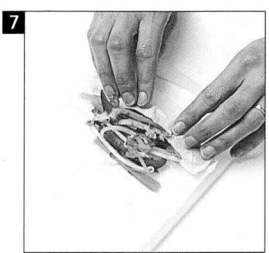

1 Using a sharp knife, cut the carrots into thin sticks. Seed the pepper and cut into thin slices.

2 Heat the sunflower oil in a large preheated wok.

3 Add the carrot, red bell pepper, and beansprouts and cook, stirring, for 2 minutes, or until soft. Remove the wok from the heat and toss in the lime zest and juice, and the red chili.

4 Mix the soy sauce with the arrowroot. Stir the mixture into the wok, return to the heat, and cook for 2 minutes or until the juices thicken.

5 Add the chopped fresh cilantro to the wok and mix well.

6 Lay the sheets of phyllo pastry out on a board. Melt the butter and sesame oil and brush each sheet with the mixture.

7 Spoon a little of the vegetable filling at the top of each sheet, fold over each long side, and roll up.

8 Add a little oil to the wok and cook the spring rolls in batches, for 2–3 minutes, or until crisp and golden.

9 Transfer the spring rolls to a serving dish, garnish, and serve hot with chili dipping sauce.

Tuscan Ciabatta

Using ripe tomatoes and the best olive oil will make this Tuscan dish absolutely delicious.

NUTRITIONAL INFORMATION

Calories 308	Sugars 3g
Protein 7g	Fat 15g
Carbohydrate . . .37g	Saturates 2g

10 mins   5 mins

SERVES 4

INGREDIENTS

¾ lb/340 g cherry tomatoes

4 sun-dried tomatoes

4 tbsp extra virgin olive oil

16 fresh basil leaves, shredded

8 slices ciabatta

2 garlic cloves, peeled

salt and pepper

1 Using a sharp knife, cut the cherry tomatoes in half.

2 Using a sharp knife, slice the sun-dried tomatoes into strips.

3 Place the cherry tomatoes and sun-dried tomatoes in a bowl.

COOK'S TIP

Ciabatta is an Italian rustic bread which is slightly holey and quite chewy. It is good in this recipe, as it absorbs the full flavor of the garlic and extra-virgin olive oil.

4 Add the olive oil and the shredded basil leaves to the tomatoes and toss to mix well. Season to taste with a little salt and pepper.

5 Using a sharp knife, cut the garlic cloves in half.

6 Lightly toast the ciabatta bread under a preheated broiler. Rub the garlic clove halves, cut-side down, over both sides of the toasted bread.

7 Top the ciabatta bread with the tomato mixture, and serve at once.

Bite-Sized Bhajis

Don't be surprised at the shape these form—they are odd but look lovely when arranged on a tray with the yogurt dipping sauce.

NUTRITIONAL INFORMATION

Calories	122	Sugars 2g
Protein	.........2g	Fat 10g
Carbohydrate	....6g	Saturates 1g

 15 mins   15 mins

MAKES 20

INGREDIENTS

2 heaped tbsp gram (besan) flour

½ tsp turmeric

½ tsp cumin seeds, ground

1 tsp garam masala

pinch of cayenne pepper

1 egg

1 large onion, quartered and sliced

1 tbsp chopped cilantro

3 tbsp bread crumbs (optional)

vegetable oil, for deep-frying

salt

SAUCE

1 tsp coriander seeds, ground

1½ tsp cumin seeds, ground

1 cup unsweetened yogurt

salt and pepper

1 Put the gram flour into a large bowl and mix in the turmeric, cumin, garam masala, and cayenne. Make a well in the center and add the egg. Stir to form a sticky mixture. Add the onion and sprinkle in a little salt. Add the cilantro and stir. If the mixture is not stiff enough, stir in the bread crumbs.

2 Heat the oil for deep-frying over medium heat until fairly hot—it should just be starting to smoke.

3 Push a teaspoonful of the mixture into the oil with a second teaspoon to form fairly round balls. The bhajis should firm up quite quickly. Cook in batches of 8–10, stirring so that they brown evenly. Drain on paper towels and keep them warm in the oven until ready to serve.

4 To make the sauce, roast the spices in a skillet. Remove from the heat and stir in the yogurt. Season well.

COOK'S TIP
Make sure that the pan and all the utensils are properly dried before use. Do not let any water come into contact with the hot oil or the oil will spit and splutter, which could be dangerous.

Crispy-Fried Vegetables

A hot and sweet dipping sauce makes the perfect accompaniment to fresh vegetables coated in a light batter and deep-fried.

NUTRITIONAL INFORMATION

Calories	258	Sugars	........11g
Protein	.........6g	Fat	...........9g
Carbohydrate	...39g	Saturates	......11g

 40 mins   10 mins

SERVES 4

INGREDIENTS

vegetable oil for deep-frying

1 lb/450 g selection of vegetables, such as cauliflower, broccoli, mushrooms, zucchini, bell peppers, and baby corn ears, cut into even-sized pieces

BATTER

¾ cup all-purpose flour

½ tsp salt

1 tsp superfine sugar

1 tsp baking powder

3 tbsp vegetable oil

¾ cup warm water

SAUCE

6 tbsp light malt vinegar

2 tbsp light soy sauce

2 tbsp water

1 tbsp soft brown sugar

pinch of salt

2 garlic cloves, crushed

2 tsp grated ginger root

2 red chilies, seeded and chopped finely

2 tbsp chopped fresh cilantro

1 To make the batter, strain the flour, salt, sugar, and baking powder into a bowl. Add the oil and most of the water. Whisk to make a smooth batter, adding extra water to give it the consistency of light cream. Chill for 20–30 minutes.

2 Meanwhile, make the sauce. Heat the vinegar, soy sauce, water, sugar, and salt until boiling. Remove from the heat and let cool.

3 Mix together the garlic, ginger, chilies, and cilantro. Add the cooled vinegar mixture and stir well to combine.

4 Heat the oil for deep-frying in a wok. Dip the vegetables in the batter and cook, in batches, until crisp and golden—about 2 minutes. Drain on paper towels.

5 Serve the vegetables accompanied by the dipping sauce.

Celery Root Rémoulade

Celery root served with a rémoulade sauce—a mustard-flavored mayonnaise—is a classically simple French dish.

NUTRITIONAL INFORMATION

Calories	236	Sugars	.........3g
Protein	.........3g	Fat	..........24g
Carbohydrate	....4g	Saturates	.......3g

 10 mins   0 mins

SERVES 4

INGREDIENTS

225 ml/8 fl oz mayonnaise (see page 8)

2 tsp lemon juice

1 tbsp Dijon mustard

½ lb/225 g celery root

1 shallot, grated

6 lettuce leaves

salt and ground black pepper

snipped fresh chives, to garnish

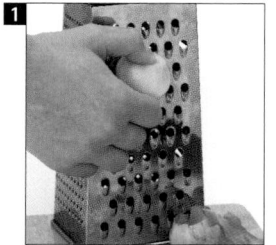

1 Grate the shallot and set aside. Combine the mayonnaise, lemon juice, and mustard in a large bowl and season to taste with salt and pepper. Peel the celery root and grate it into the mayonnaise.

2 Stir in the shallot and mix thoroughly, making sure the celery root is well coated in the dressing.

3 Line a salad bowl with the lettuce leaves and spoon the celery root mixture into the center. Sprinkle with the snipped chives and serve.

COOK'S TIP
Do not grate the celery root in advance, as it will discolor quickly on exposure to air.

Pear & Roquefort Salad

The sweetness of the pear is a perfect partner to the peppery "bite" of the radicchio and the piquancy of the cheese.

NUTRITIONAL INFORMATION

Calories ....94 Sugars 10g
Protein ....5g Fat 4g
Carbohydrate ...10g Saturates 3g

 10 mins   0 mins

SERVES 4

INGREDIENTS

2 oz/55 g Roquefort cheese

⅔ cup low-fat unsweetened yogurt

2 tbsp chopped fresh chives

few leaves of lollo rosso

few leaves of radicchio

few leaves of mâche

2 ripe pears

pepper

whole fresh chives, to garnish

1 Place the Roquefort cheese in a bowl and mash with a fork.

2 Gradually blend the yogurt into the cheese to make a smooth dressing. Add the chopped chives and season with pepper to taste.

3 Tear the lollo rosso, radicchio, and mâche leaves into manageable pieces. Arrange the salad greens on a large serving platter or divide them between individual serving plates.

4 Cut the pears into quarters and remove the cores. Cut the quarters into slices. Arrange the pear slices over the salad leaves.

5 Drizzle the Roquefort dressing over the pears and garnish with a few whole chives.

COOK'S TIP

Look out for bags of mixed salad greens, as these are generally more economical than buying lots of different greens separately.

Cress & Cheese Tartlets

These tasty and attractive individual tartlets are great served hot at lunchtime or cool for picnic food.

NUTRITIONAL INFORMATION

Calories . . . . .410 Sugars 4g
Protein . . . . .15g Fat 29g
Carbohydrate . . .24g Saturates 19g

 20 mins   25 mins

SERVES 4

I N G R E D I E N T S

generous ¾ cup all-purpose flour, plus extra
  for dusting

pinch of salt

6 tbsp butter or margarine

2–3 tbsp cold water

2 bunches of watercress

2 garlic cloves, crushed

1 shallot, chopped

1¼ cups grated Cheddar cheese

4 tbsp unsweetened yogurt

½ tsp paprika

1 Strain the flour into a mixing bowl and add the salt. Rub 2 tablespoons of the butter or margarine into the flour until the mixture resembles bread crumbs. Stir in enough of the cold water to make a smooth dough.

2 Roll the dough out on a lightly floured counter and use to line 4 x 4 inch/10 cm tartlet pans. Prick the bottoms of the tartlet shells with a fork and let chill in the refrigerator.

3 Heat the remaining butter or margarine in a skillet. Discard the stems from the watercress. Add the leaves to the pan with the garlic and shallot and cook for 1–2 minutes until wilted.

4 Remove the pan from the heat and stir in the grated Cheddar cheese, yogurt, and paprika.

5 Spoon the mixture into the tartlet shells and cook in a preheated oven, 350°F/180°C, for 20 minutes or until the filling is just firm. Turn out the tartlets and serve immediately, if serving hot. If serving cold, place on a wire rack to cool, then store in the refrigerator until required.

VARIATION
Use spinach instead of the watercress, making sure it is well drained before mixing with the remaining filling ingredients.

Spanish Tortilla

This classic Spanish dish is often served as part of a tapas selection.
A variety of cooked vegetables can be added to this recipe.

NUTRITIONAL INFORMATION

Calories 430   Sugars 6g
Protein . . . . .16g   Fat 20g
Carbohydrate . . .50g   Saturates 4g

 10 mins   35 mins

SERVES 4

I N G R E D I E N T S

2 lb/900 g waxy potatoes, thinly sliced

4 tbsp vegetable oil

1 onion, sliced

2 garlic cloves, crushed

1 green bell pepper, seeded and diced

2 tomatoes, seeded and chopped

2½ tbsp canned corn kernels, drained

6 large eggs, beaten

2 tbsp chopped fresh parsley

salt and pepper

1 Parboil the potatoes in a pan of lightly salted boiling water for 5 minutes. Drain well.

2 Heat the oil in a large skillet, add the potatoes and onion, and then sauté over low heat, stirring constantly, for 5 minutes until the potatoes have browned.

3 Add the garlic, bell pepper, tomatoes, and corn kernels, mixing well.

4 Pour in the eggs and add the parsley. Season to taste with salt and pepper. Cook for 10–12 minutes until the underside is cooked through.

5 Remove the skillet from the heat and continue to cook the tortilla under a preheated medium broiler for 5–7 minutes or until the tortilla is set and the top is golden brown.

6 Cut the tortilla into wedges or cubes, depending on your preference, and transfer to serving dishes. Serve with salad. In Spain tortillas are served either hot, cold, or warm.

COOK'S TIP

Ensure that the handle of your skillet is heatproof before placing it under the broiler and be sure to use an oven mitt when removing it because it will be very hot.

Baked Potatoes with Salsa

The cooked potato flesh is flavored with avocado and piled back into the shell with a salad garnish. It is then served with a hot tomato salsa.

NUTRITIONAL INFORMATION

Calories 71	Sugars 1.4g
Protein 2.3g	Fat 2.7g
Carbohydrate . . .10g	Saturates 0.5g

 10 mins   1 hr

SERVES 4

I N G R E D I E N T S

4 baking potatoes

1 large ripe avocado

1 tsp lemon juice

6 oz/175 g smoked bean curd, diced

2 garlic cloves, crushed

1 onion, chopped finely

1 tomato, chopped finely

1 bag mixed salad greens

fresh cilantro sprigs, to garnish

S A L S A

2 ripe tomatoes, seeded and diced

1 tbsp chopped cilantro

1 shallot, diced finely

1 green chili, diced

1 tbsp lemon juice

salt and pepper

3 Cut the potatoes in half lengthwise and scoop the flesh into a large bowl, leaving a thin layer of potato inside the shells.

4 Halve and pit the avocado. Using a spoon, scoop out the avocado flesh and add to the bowl. Stir in the lemon juice and mash the mixture together with a fork. Mix in the bean curd, garlic, onion, and tomato. Spoon the mixture into one half of the potato shells.

5 Arrange the salad greens on top of the guacamole mixture and place the other half of the potato shell on top.

6 To make the salsa, mix the tomatoes, cilantro, shallots, chili, and lemon juice in a bowl, and season with salt and pepper to taste.

7 Garnish the potatoes with sprigs of fresh cilantro and serve immediately with the salsa.

1 Scrub the potatoes and prick the skins with a fork. Rub a little salt into the skins and place them on a cookie sheet.

2 Cook in a preheated oven, 375°F/ 190°C, for 1 hour or until cooked through and the skins are crisp.

Dumplings in Yogurt Sauce

Adding a baghaar (seasoned oil dressing) just before serving makes this a mouth-watering accompaniment to any meal.

NUTRITIONAL INFORMATION

Calories 719   Sugars 9g
Protein . . . . .9g   Fat 60g
Carbohydrate . . .38g   Saturates 7g

   35 mins   35 mins

SERVES 4

I N G R E D I E N T S

D U M P L I N G S

½ cup gram (besan) flour

1 tsp chili powder

½ tsp baking soda

1 medium onion, finely chopped

2 green chilies

cilantro leaves

⅔ cup water

1¼ cup vegetable oil

salt

Y O G U R T   S A U C E

1¼ cup unsweetened yogurt

3 tbsp gram flour

150 ml/¼ pint water

1 tsp chopped root ginger

1 tsp crushed garlic

1½ tsp chili powder

½ tsp turmeric

1 tsp ground coriander

1 tsp ground cumin

S E A S O N E D   D R E S S I N G

⅔ cup vegetable oil

1 tsp white cumin seeds

6 dried red chilies

1 To make the dumplings, strain the gram flour into a large bowl. Add the chili powder, ½ teaspoon salt, baking soda, onion, green chilies, and cilantro and mix. Add the water and mix thoroughly to form a thick paste. Heat the oil in a skillet. Place teaspoonfuls of the paste in the oil and cook over medium heat, turning once, until a crisp golden brown. Set aside.

2 To make the sauce, place the unsweetened yogurt in a bowl and whisk with the gram flour and the water. Add all of the spices and 1½ teaspoons salt and mix well.

3 Press this mixture through a large strainer into a pan. Bring to a boil over low heat, stirring constantly. If the yogurt sauce becomes too thick, add a little extra water.

4 Pour the sauce into a deep serving dish and arrange all the dumplings on top. Set aside and keep warm.

5 To make the dressing, heat the oil in a skillet. Add the cumin seeds and the chilies and cook until darker in color and giving off their aroma. Pour the dressing over the dumplings and serve hot.

Samosas

Samosas, which are a sort of Indian pasty, make excellent snacks.
In India, they are popular snacks at roadside stands.

3 To make the filling, mash the boiled potatoes gently and mix with the ginger, garlic, white cumin seeds, onion and mustard seeds, salt, crushed red chilies, lemon juice, and green chilies.

4 Break small balls off the dough and roll each out very thinly to form a round. Cut in half, dampen the edges, and shape into cones. Fill the cones with a little of the filling, dampen the top and

bottom edges of the cones, and pinch together to seal. Set aside.

5 Fill a deep pan one-third full with oil and heat to 350°F/180°C or until a small cube of bread browns in 30 seconds. Carefully lower the samosas into the oil, a few at a time, and cook for 2-3 minutes, or until golden brown. Remove from the oil and drain thoroughly on paper towels. Serve hot or cold.

NUTRITIONAL INFORMATION

Calories	.261	Sugars	.0.4g
Protein	.2g	Fat	.23g
Carbohydrate	.13g	Saturates	.4g

🥔 40 mins   🕐 40 mins

MAKES 12

I N G R E D I E N T S

PASTRY

¾ cup self-rising flour

½ tsp salt

3 tbsp butter, cut into small pieces

4 tbsp water

FILLING

3 medium potatoes, boiled

1 tsp finely chopped ginger root

1 tsp crushed garlic

½ tsp white cumin seeds

½ tsp mixed onion and mustard seeds

1 tsp salt

½ tsp crushed red chilies

2 tbsp lemon juice

2 small green chilies, finely chopped

ghee or oil, for deep-frying

1 Strain the flour and salt into a bowl. Add the pieces of butter and rub into the flour until the mixture resembles fine bread crumbs.

2 Pour in the water and mix with a fork to form a dough. Pat it into a ball and knead for 5 minutes, or until smooth. Cover and let rise.

Potato Fritters with Relish

These are incredibly simple to make and sure to be popular served as a tempting snack or as an accompaniment to almost any Indian meal.

NUTRITIONAL INFORMATION

Calories 294	Sugars 4g
Protein 4g	Fat 24g
Carbohydrate ...18g	Saturates 3g

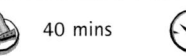

🥔 40 mins 🕐 15 mins

SERVES 8

INGREDIENTS

⅓ cup all-purpose whole-wheat flour

½ tsp ground coriander

½ tsp cumin seeds

¼ tsp chili powder

½ tsp ground turmeric

¼ tsp salt

1 egg

3 tbsp milk

¾ lb/350 g potatoes, peeled

1–2 garlic cloves, crushed

4 scallions, chopped

¼ cup corn kernels

vegetable oil, for shallow frying

ONION & TOMATO RELISH

1 onion, peeled

½ lb/225 g tomatoes

2 tbsp chopped cilantro

2 tbsp chopped mint

2 tbsp lemon juice

½ tsp roasted cumin seeds

¼ tsp salt

pinch of cayenne pepper

1 First make the relish. Cut the onion and tomatoes into small dice and place in a bowl with the remaining ingredients. Mix together well and let stand for at least 15 minutes before serving to let the flavors blend.

2 Place the flour in a bowl, stir in the spices and salt, and make a well in the center. Add the egg and milk and mix to form a fairly thick batter.

3 Coarsely grate the potatoes, place them in a strainer, and rinse well under cold running water. Drain and squeeze dry, then stir them into the batter with the garlic, scallions, and corn and mix to combine thoroughly.

4 Heat about ¼ inch/5 mm of vegetable oil in a large skillet and add a few tablespoonfuls of the mixture at a time, flattening each one to form a thin fritter. Cook over low heat, turning frequently, for 2–3 minutes, or until golden brown and cooked through.

5 Drain the fritters on absorbent paper towels and keep them hot while cooking the remaining mixture in the same way. Serve the potato fritters hot with the onion and tomato relish.

Falafel

These are a very tasty, well-known Middle Eastern dish of small garbanzo bean balls, spiced and deep-fried.

NUTRITIONAL INFORMATION

Calories	.491	Sugars	.3g
Protein	.15g	Fat	.30g
Carbohydrate	.43g	Saturates	.3g

  25 mins   10–15 mins

SERVES 4

I N G R E D I E N T S

1½ lb/675 g canned garbanzo beans (chickpeas), drained

1 red onion, chopped

3 garlic cloves, crushed

3–4 slices whole-wheat bread

2 small fresh red chilies

1 tsp ground cumin

1 tsp ground coriander

½ tsp turmeric

1 tbsp chopped cilantro, plus extra to garnish

1 egg, beaten

¾ cup whole-wheat bread crumbs

vegetable oil, for deep-frying

salt and pepper

tomato and cucumber salad and lemon wedges, to serve

1 Put the garbanzo beans, onion, garlic, whole-wheat bread, chilies, spices, and cilantro in a food processor and process for 30 seconds. Stir the mixture and season to taste with salt and pepper.

2 Remove the mixture from the food processor and shape into walnut-sized balls.

3 Place the beaten egg in a shallow bowl and place the whole-wheat bread crumbs on a plate. First dip the garbanzo bean balls into the egg to coat them thoroughly and then roll them in the bread crumbs, shaking off any excess crumbs.

4 Heat the oil for deep-frying to 350°F/180°C or until a cube of bread browns in 30 seconds. Cook the falafel, in batches if necessary, for 2–3 minutes, until crisp and browned. Carefully remove them from the oil with a slotted spoon and dry on absorbent paper towels.

5 Garnish the falafel with the reserved chopped cilantro and serve with a tomato and cucumber salad and lemon wedges.

Gnocchi with Tomato Sauce

These gnocchi or small dumplings are made with potato and flavored with spinach and nutmeg, then served in a tomato and basil sauce.

NUTRITIONAL INFORMATION

Calories 337   Sugars 4g
Protein ....9g   Fat 10g
Carbohydrate ...52g   Saturates 4g

 25 mins   1 hr

SERVES 4

INGREDIENTS

1 lb/450 g baking potatoes

3 oz/85 g spinach

1 tsp water

3 tbsp butter or margarine

1 small egg, beaten

¾ cup all-purpose flour

fresh basil sprigs, to garnish

TOMATO SAUCE

1 tbsp olive oil

1 shallot, chopped

1 tbsp tomato paste

1 cup canned chopped tomatoes

2 tbsp chopped basil

6 tbsp red wine

1 tsp superfine sugar

salt and pepper

1 Cook the potatoes in their skins in a pan of boiling salted water for 20 minutes. Drain well and press through a strainer into a bowl.

2 Cook the spinach in the water for 5 minutes or until wilted. Drain and pat dry with paper towels. Chop and stir into the potatoes.

3 Add the butter or margarine, egg, and half of the flour to the spinach mixture, mixing well. Turn out on to a floured surface, gradually kneading in the remaining flour to form a soft dough.

4 With floured hands, roll the dough into thin ropes and cut off ¾ inch/ 2 cm pieces. Press the center of each dumpling with your finger, drawing it toward you to curl the sides of the gnocchi. Cover the gnocchi with plastic wrap and let chill.

5 Heat the oil for the sauce in a pan and sauté the chopped shallot for 5 minutes. Add the tomato paste, tomatoes, basil, red wine, and sugar and season well. Bring to a boil and then simmer for 20 minutes.

6 Bring a pan of salted water to a boil and cook the gnocchi for 2–3 minutes or until they rise to the top of the pan. Drain well and transfer to serving dishes. Spoon the tomato sauce over the gnocchi. Garnish and serve.

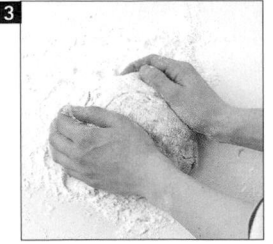

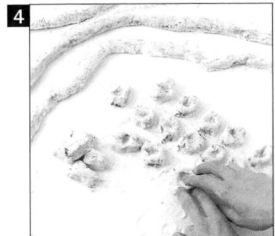

Indian-Style Omelet

Omelets are very versatile: they go with almost anything and you can also serve them at any time of the day.

NUTRITIONAL INFORMATION

Calories	132	Sugars	.........1g
Protein	.........7g	Fat	...........11g
Carbohydrate	....2g	Saturates	.......2g

 10 mins   20 mins

SERVES 4

INGREDIENTS

1 small onion, very finely chopped

2 fresh green chilies, seeded and finely chopped

2 tbsp finely chopped fresh cilantro leaves

4 eggs

1 tsp salt

2 tbsp vegetable oil

fresh basil sprigs, to garnish

toasted bread or crisp salad greens, to serve

1 Place the onion, chilies, and cilantro in a large mixing bowl and combine.

2 Whisk the eggs in a separate bowl. Stir the onion mixture into the eggs. Add the salt and whisk again.

3 Heat 1 tablespoon of the oil in a large, heavy skillet over medium heat. Place a ladleful of the omelet batter in the pan. Cook the omelet, turning once and pressing down with a flat spoon to make sure that the egg is cooked right through, until the omelet is just firm and golden brown in color.

4 Repeat the same process with the remaining batter. Set the omelets aside, as you make them, and keep warm while you make the remaining batches.

5 Serve the omelets hot, garnished with fresh basil sprigs and accompanied by toasted bread. Alternatively, simply serve the omelets with crisp salad greens for a light lunch.

COOK'S TIP

Whether free-range or intensively farmed, eggs are susceptible to bacteria. Store them in the refrigerator, with the pointed end downward, for up to 2 weeks, and never use cracked or dirty eggs. Bring them to room temperature about 30 minutes before using.

Creamy Stuffed Mushrooms

These oven-baked mushrooms are covered with a creamy potato and mushroom filling topped with melted cheese.

NUTRITIONAL INFORMATION

Calories 214	Sugars 1g
Protein 5g	Fat 17g
Carbohydrate 11g	Saturates 11g

20 mins, plus soaking time   40 mins

SERVES 4

INGREDIENTS

½ cup dried porcini

1½ cups mealy potatoes, diced

2 tbsp butter, melted

4 tbsp heavy cream

2 tbsp chopped fresh chives

8 large open-capped mushrooms

4 tbsp grated Swiss cheese

⅔ cup vegetable bouillon

salt and pepper

fresh chives, to garnish

1 Place the dried porcini in a small bowl. Add sufficient boiling water to cover and let soak for 20 minutes.

2 Meanwhile, cook the potatoes in a medium pan of lightly salted boiling water for 10 minutes until cooked through and tender. Drain thoroughly and mash until smooth.

3 Drain the soaked mushrooms and then chop them finely. Mix them into the mashed potato.

4 Thoroughly blend the butter, cream, and chives together and pour into the mushroom and potato mixture, mixing well. Season to taste with salt and pepper.

5 Remove the stems from the open-capped mushrooms. Chop the stems and stir them into the potato mixture.

6 Spoon the mixture into the open-capped mushrooms and sprinkle the grated cheese over the top.

7 Arrange the filled mushrooms in a shallow casserole and pour in the vegetable bouillon.

8 Cover the dish and cook in a preheated oven, 425°F/220°C, for 20 minutes, then remove the lid and cook for a further 5 minutes until the cheese topping is golden and bubbling.

9 Garnish the mushrooms with fresh chives and serve at once.

VARIATION

Use fresh mushrooms instead of the dried ones, if preferred, and stir chopped nuts into the mushroom stuffing mixture for extra crunch.

Lentils & Mixed Vegetables

The green lentils used in this recipe require soaking but are worth it for the flavor. If time is short, you could use red split peas instead.

NUTRITIONAL INFORMATION

Calories 386   Sugars 16g
Protein ....12g   Fat 23g
Carbohydrate ...35g   Saturates 12g

 45 mins   40–45 mins

SERVES 4

I N G R E D I E N T S

scant 1 cup green lentils

4 tbsp butter or margarine

2 garlic cloves, crushed

2 tbsp olive oil

1 tbsp cider vinegar

1 red onion, cut into 8

5–6 baby corn ears, halved lengthwise

1 yellow bell pepper, seeded and cut into strips

1 red bell pepper, seeded and cut into strips

¼ cup green beans, halved

½ cup vegetable bouillon

2 tbsp clear honey

salt and pepper

crusty bread, to serve

1 Soak the lentils in a large pan of cold water for 25 minutes. Bring to a boil, reduce the heat, and simmer for 20 minutes. Drain thoroughly.

2 Add 1 tablespoon of the butter or margarine, 1 of the garlic cloves, 1 tablespoon of olive oil, and the vinegar to the lentils and mix well.

3 Melt the remaining butter, garlic, and olive oil in a skillet and stir-fry the onion, corn ears, bell peppers and beans for 3–4 minutes.

4 Add the vegetable bouillon and bring to a boil. Boil for about 10 minutes, or until the liquid has evaporated.

5 Add the honey and season with salt and pepper to taste. Stir in the lentil mixture and cook for 1 minute to heat through. Spoon on to warmed serving plates and serve with crusty bread.

VARIATION
This pan-fry is very versatile: you can use a mixture of your favorite vegetables, if you prefer. Try zucchini, carrots, or snow peas.

Corn & Potato Fritters

These crisp little fritters make an ideal supper dish for two—topped with a poached egg or two, they are surprisingly filling.

NUTRITIONAL INFORMATION

Calories	639	Sugars	........17g
Protein	........28g	Fat	.........31g
Carbohydrate	...65g	Saturates	.......9g

20 mins   20 mins

SERVES 2

INGREDIENTS

2 tbsp oil

1 small onion, thinly sliced

1 garlic clove, crushed

¾ lb/350 g potatoes

scant cup canned corn kernels, drained

½ tsp dried oregano

1 egg, beaten

½ cup grated Dutch cheese

salt and pepper

2–4 eggs

2–4 tomatoes, sliced

parsley sprigs, to garnish

1 Heat 1 tablespoon of the oil in a nonstick skillet. Add the onion and garlic and sauté very gently, stirring frequently, until soft but only lightly colored. Remove the skillet from the heat.

2 Grate the potatoes coarsely into a bowl and mix in the corn kernels, oregano, beaten egg, and salt and pepper to taste. Add the sautéed onion.

3 Heat the remaining oil in the skillet. Divide the potato mixture in half and add to the skillet to make 2 oval-shaped fritters, shaping them with a spatula.

4 Cook the fritters over low heat for about 10 minutes, until golden brown underneath and almost cooked through, keeping them tidily in shape with the spatula and loosening so they don't stick.

5 Sprinkle each potato fritter with the grated cheese and place under a preheated moderately hot broiler until golden brown.

6 Meanwhile, poach 1 or 2 eggs for each person until just cooked. Transfer the fritters to warmed plates and top with the eggs and sliced tomatoes. Garnish with parsley and serve at once.

Stuffed Onions

Try to find onions that are all about the same size for even cooking and an attractive presentation. Serve this dish with rice and a salad.

NUTRITIONAL INFORMATION

Calories 190   Sugars 21g
Protein . . . . .7g   Fat 6g
Carbohydrate . . .28g   Saturates 1g

30 mins   40 mins

SERVES 6

I N G R E D I E N T S

¼ cup raisins

6 onions

1 tbsp sunflower oil

1 garlic clove, finely chopped

1 lb/450 g spinach, thick stalks removed

½ cup unsweetened yogurt

¼ cup pine nuts, toasted

pinch of freshly grated nutmeg

2 tbsp fresh whole-wheat bread crumbs

salt

1 Place the raisins in a small bowl, cover with water, and set aside. Meanwhile, cut a thin slice off the bases of the onions so that they stand level. Cut off a ½ inch/1 cm slice from the tops. Using a teaspoon or melon baller, carefully scoop out the onion flesh, leaving a shell ½ inch/1 cm thick. Set a steamer over a pan of boiling water and arrange the onion shells inside it. Cover tightly and steam for 10–15 minutes, until tender. Remove from the heat and set aside.

2 Finely chop the scooped-out onion flesh. Heat the oil in a heavy skillet. Add the chopped onion and cook, stirring occasionally, for 5 minutes, until soft. Stir in the garlic and cook for 2 minutes, then add the spinach. Cover and cook for 3 minutes, until the spinach has wilted. Season with salt and cook, uncovered, stirring occasionally, for about 5 minutes, until all the liquid has evaporated. Remove from the heat and let cool.

3 Drain the raisins and add them to the onion and spinach mixture with the yogurt, pine nuts, and nutmeg. Drain the onion shells, then spoon the spinach stuffing into them. Spread the remaining stuffing over the base of an ovenproof dish and stand the stuffed onions on top. Sprinkle the onions with the bread crumbs and bake in a preheated oven, 350°F/ 180°C, for 25 minutes.

4 Place the dish under a preheated broiler for 3-4 minutes, until the bread crumbs are crisp. Serve immediately.

Spanish Omelet

This is an incredibly adaptable dish and you can incorporate leftover and fresh vegetables of your choice.

NUTRITIONAL INFORMATION

Calories . . . . . . .376 Sugars 7g
Protein . . . . .19g Fat 22g
Carbohydrate . . .27g Saturates 8g

20 mins   20 mins

SERVES 4

INGREDIENTS

2 tbsp olive oil

1 Spanish onion, chopped

2 garlic cloves, finely chopped

1 red bell pepper, seeded and diced

½ lb/225 g zucchini, thinly sliced

2 tomatoes, skinned and diced

¾ lb/350 g diced boiled potatoes (optional)

6 eggs

4 tbsp milk

2 tsp chopped fresh tarragon

¾ cup grated Cheddar cheese

salt and ground black pepper

COOK'S TIP

If you do not have a skillet with a heatproof handle, cover the handle with a double layer of foil, but be very careful that the skillet doesn't slip out as you lift it.

1 Heat the oil in a large, heavy skillet with a flameproof handle. Add the onion and cook, stirring occasionally, for 5 minutes, until soft. Add the garlic, red bell pepper, and zucchini and cook, stirring frequently, for 5 minutes more. Add the tomatoes and potatoes and cook, stirring frequently, for 3 minutes.

2 Beat the eggs with the milk and chopped tarragon in a bowl and season to taste with salt and pepper. Pour the egg mixture into the skillet and cook, without stirring, until the eggs begin to set and the underside of the omelet is golden brown.

3 Sprinkle the cheese evenly over the surface and place the skillet under a preheated broiler. Cook for 3–4 minutes, until the cheese has melted and the top is golden brown. Cut into wedges to serve.

Garlic Mushrooms on Toast

This is so simple to prepare and looks great if you use a variety of mushrooms for shape and texture.

NUTRITIONAL INFORMATION

Calories 366	Sugars 2g
Protein 9g	Fat 18g
Carbohydrate . . .45g	Saturates 4g

 10 mins   10 mins

SERVES 4

I N G R E D I E N T S

3 tbsp margarine

2 garlic cloves, crushed

¾ lb/350 g mixed mushrooms,
    such as open-cap, white, oyster, and
    shiitake, sliced

8 slices French bread

1 tbsp chopped parsley

salt and pepper

1 Melt the margarine in a skillet. Add the crushed garlic and cook, stirring constantly, for 30 seconds.

2 Add the mushrooms and cook, turning occasionally, for 5 minutes.

3 Toast the French bread slices under a preheated medium broiler for 2–3 minutes, turning once. Transfer the toasts to a serving plate.

4 Toss the parsley into the mushrooms, mixing well, and season well with salt and pepper to taste.

5 Spoon the mushroom mixture over the bread and serve immediately.

COOK'S TIP
Always store mushrooms for a maximum of 24–36 hours in the refrigerator, in paper bags, as they sweat in plastic. Exotic mushrooms should be washed but cultivated varieties can simply be wiped clean with paper towels.

Pakoras

Pakoras are eaten all over India. They are made in many different ways and with a variety of fillings. Sometimes they are served with yogurt.

NUTRITIONAL INFORMATION

Calories 331	Sugars 5g	
Protein 9g	Fat 22g	
Carbohydrate . . .27g	Saturates 3g	

15 mins   15–20 mins

SERVES 4

I N G R E D I E N T S

6 tbsp gram (besan) flour

½ tsp salt

1 tsp chili powder

1 tsp baking powder

1½ tsp white cumin seeds

1 tsp pomegranate seeds

1¼ cups water

1 tbsp finely chopped fresh cilantro leaves

vegetables of your choice: cauliflower cut into small florets, onions cut into rings, sliced potatoes, sliced eggplants, or fresh spinach leaves

vegetable oil

COOK'S TIP

When cooking pakoras, it is important to use oil at the correct temperature. If the oil is too hot, the outside of the food will burn, as will the spices, before the inside is cooked. If the oil is too cool, the food will be soaked with oil before a crisp batter forms.

1 Strain the gram flour into a large mixing bowl. Add the salt, chili powder, baking powder, cumin, and pomegranate seeds, and blend together well. Pour in the water and beat thoroughly to form a smooth batter.

2 Add the cilantro and mix. Set the batter aside.

3 Dip the prepared vegetables of your choice into the batter, carefully shaking off any of the excess batter.

4 Heat enough oil to cover the pakoras in a deep, heavy pan. Place the battered vegetables in the oil and cook, in batches, turning once.

5 Repeat this process until all of the batter has been used up.

6 Transfer the battered vegetables to absorbent paper towels and drain thoroughly. Serve immediately on a warmed plate, with a sprig of fresh cilantro to garnish.

Broiled Potatoes with Lime

This dish is ideal with broiled or grilled foods, as the potatoes themselves may be cooked by either method.

NUTRITIONAL INFORMATION

Calories . . . . . . .253 Sugars 0.7g
Protein . . . . .1.8g Fat 22.2g
Carbohydrate . .12.4g Saturates 5.8g

10 mins   15–20 mins

SERVES 4

INGREDIENTS

1 lb/450 g potatoes, unpeeled and scrubbed

3 tbsp butter, melted

2 tbsp chopped fresh thyme

paprika, for dusting

LIME MAYONNAISE

⅔ cup mayonnaise

2 tsp lime juice

finely grated zest of 1 lime

1 garlic clove, crushed

pinch of paprika

salt and pepper

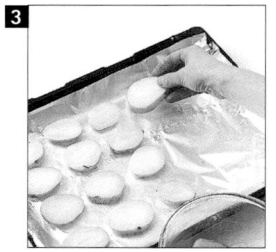  

1 Cut the potatoes into ½ inch/1 cm thick slices.

2 Cook the potatoes in a pan of boiling water for 5–7 minutes—they should still be quite firm. Remove the potatoes with a perforated spoon and drain thoroughly.

3 Line a broiler pan with aluminum foil, and place the potato slices on the foil.

4 Brush the potatoes with the melted butter and sprinkle the chopped thyme on top. Season to taste with salt and pepper.

5 Cook the potatoes under a preheated medium broiler for 10 minutes, turning them over once.

6 Meanwhile, combine the mayonnaise, lime juice, lime zest, garlic, paprika, and salt and pepper to taste, in a bowl.

7 Dust the hot potato slices with a little paprika and serve immediately with the lime mayonnaise.

COOK'S TIP
For an impressive side dish, thread the potato slices on to skewers and cook over a medium hot barbecue grill.

Spinach Crêpes

Serve these crêpes as a light lunch or supper dish, with a tomato and basil salad for a dramatic color contrast.

NUTRITIONAL INFORMATION

Calories	663	Sugars	.........9g
Protein	........32g	Fat	..........48g
Carbohydrate	...28g	Saturates	......18g

25 mins   25 mins

SERVES 4

I N G R E D I E N T S

⅔ cup whole-wheat flour

1 egg

⅔ cup unsweetened yogurt

3 tbsp water

1 tbsp vegetable oil, plus extra for brushing

7 oz/200 g frozen leaf spinach, thawed and puréed

pinch of grated nutmeg

salt and pepper

T O   G A R N I S H

lemon wedges

fresh cilantro sprigs

F I L L I N G

1 tbsp vegetable oil

3 scallions, thinly sliced

1 cup ricotta cheese

4 tbsp unsweetened yogurt

¾ cup grated Swiss cheese

1 egg, lightly beaten

1 cup unsalted cashew nuts

2 tbsp chopped fresh parsley

pinch of cayenne pepper

1 Strain the flour and salt into a bowl and tip in any bran left in the strainer. Whisk the egg with the yogurt, water, and oil. Gradually pour it onto the flour, beating constantly. Stir in the spinach and season with pepper and nutmeg to taste.

2 To make the filling, heat the oil in a pan and cook the scallions until translucent. Remove with a draining spoon and drain on paper towels. Beat the ricotta with the yogurt and half the Swiss cheese. Beat in the egg and stir in the cashew nuts and parsley. Season with salt and cayenne to taste.

3 Lightly brush a small, heavy skillet with oil and heat. Pour in 3–4 tablespoons of the crêpe batter and tilt the skillet so that it covers the base. Cook for about 3 minutes until bubbles appear in the center. Turn and cook the other side for about 2 minutes until lightly browned. Slide the crêpe onto a warmed plate, cover with foil, and keep warm while you cook the remainder. The batter should make 8–12 crêpes.

4 Spread a little filling over each crêpe and fold in half, and then half again, envelope style. Spoon the remaining filling into the opening.

5 Grease a shallow casserole and arrange the crêpes in a single layer. Sprinkle with the remaining cheese and cook in a preheated oven, 350°F/180°C, for about 15 minutes.

6 Serve the crêpes immediately on warmed plates, garnished with lemon wedges and cilantro sprigs.

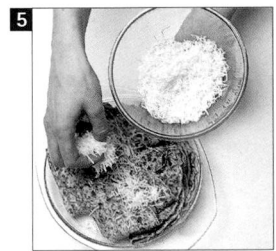

Sweet Potato Salad

This piquant salad is a meal in itself. Choose a mixture of colorful salad leaves with a range of sweet and bitter flavors.

NUTRITIONAL INFORMATION

Calories	143	Sugars	........19g
Protein	.........6g	Fat	...........1g
Carbohydrate	...29g	Saturates	.......1g

 10 mins   10 mins

SERVES 4

I N G R E D I E N T S

1 sweet potato, peeled and diced

4 baby carrots, halved

4 tomatoes

1 bag mixed salad leaves, such as frisée, arugula, radicchio, and oakleaf lettuce

4 celery stalks, chopped

1 cup canned borlotti beans, drained and rinsed

1 tbsp golden raisins

4 scallions, finely chopped

125 ml/4 fl oz Honey and Yogurt Dressing (see page 8)

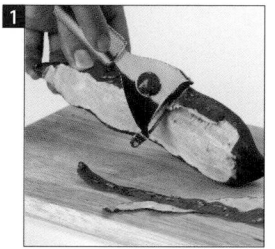

1 Peel and dice the sweet potato and cook it in a pan of boiling water until just tender. Drain and set aside in a bowl. Cook the carrots in a pan of boiling water for 1 minute. Drain and add to the bowl.

2 Drain and rinse the beans. Cut the tops off the tomatoes and scoop out the seeds. Chop the flesh and add to the bowl, mixing in the celery and beans.

3 Line a serving bowl with the salad leaves. Spoon the sweet potato and bean mixture on top.

4 Sprinkle with the golden raisins and scallions, spoon on the Honey and Yogurt dressing, and serve the salad immediately.

COOK'S TIP
Cook the sweet potato until it is just tender, otherwise it will absorb too much water and become unpleasantly soggy.

Hash Browns

Hash Browns are a popular recipe of fried potato squares, often served as brunch. This recipe includes extra vegetables.

NUTRITIONAL INFORMATION

Calories 339   Sugars 9g
Protein ....10g   Fat 21g
Carbohydrate ...29g   Saturates 7g

20 mins   45 mins

SERVES 4

I N G R E D I E N T S

1 lb/450 g waxy potatoes

1 carrot, diced

1 celery stalk, diced

¾ cup diced white mushrooms

1 onion, diced

2 garlic cloves, crushed

¼ cup frozen peas, thawed

⅔ cup freshly grated Parmesan cheese

4 tbsp vegetable oil

2 tbsp butter

salt and pepper

S A U C E

1¼ cups strained tomatoes

2 tbsp chopped fresh cilantro

1 tbsp Worcestershire sauce

½ tsp chili powder

2 tsp brown sugar

2 tsp mild mustard

5 tbsp vegetable bouillon

1 Cook the potatoes in a pan of lightly salted boiling water for 10 minutes. Drain and let cool. Meanwhile, cook the carrot in lightly salted boiling water for 5 minutes.

2 When the potatoes are cool enough to handle, grate them with a coarse grater.

3 Drain the carrot and add it to the grated potatoes, with the celery, mushrooms, onion, garlic, peas, and cheese. Season to taste with salt and pepper.

4 Put all of the sauce ingredients in a small pan and bring to a boil. Reduce the heat to low and simmer for 15 minutes.

5 Divide the potato mixture into 8 portions of equal size and shape into flattened rectangles with your hands.

6 Heat the oil and butter in a skillet and cook the hash browns in batches over low heat for 4–5 minutes on each side, until crisp and golden brown.

7 Transfer the hash browns to a serving plate and serve immediately with the tomato sauce

Bean Curd Burgers

Flavored with spices and served with a sesame-flavored relish, these delicious burgers are perfect for vegetarians.

NUTRITIONAL INFORMATION

Calories 471	Sugars 7g	
Protein 22g	Fat 12g	
Carbohydrate . . .74g	Saturates 2g	

 15 mins   20 mins

SERVES 4

I N G R E D I E N T S

1 small red onion, chopped finely

1 garlic clove, crushed

1 tsp ground cumin

1 tsp ground coriander

2 tbsp lemon juice

1½ cups canned garbanzo beans, drained and rinsed

2¾ oz/75 g soft silken bean curd, drained

¼ lb/115 g cooked potato, diced

4 tbsp freshly chopped cilantro

½ cup dry whole-wheat bread crumbs

1 tbsp vegetable oil

burger buns

2 medium tomatoes, sliced

1 large carrot, grated

salt and pepper

R E L I S H

1 tsp sesame-seed paste

4 tbsp low-fat unsweetened yogurt

1 inch/2.5 cm piece cucumber, finely chopped

1 tbsp chopped fresh cilantro

garlic salt, to season

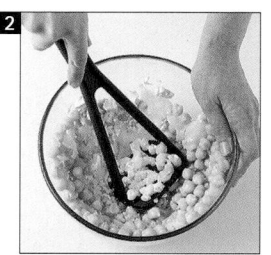  

1 Place the onion, garlic, spices, and lemon juice in a pan, bring to a boil, cover, and simmer for 5 minutes until the onions are softened.

2 Place the garbanzo beans, bean curd, and potato in a bowl and mash well. Stir in the onion mixture, the cilantro, and the seasoning, and mix together. Divide the mixture into 4 equal portions and form into patties 4 inch/10 cm across.

3 Sprinkle the bread crumbs on to a plate and press the burgers into the crumbs to coat both sides.

4 Heat the oil in a large skillet and cook the burgers for 5 minutes on each side until golden. Mix the relish ingredients together in a bowl and let chill. Place the sliced tomato and grated carrot on the buns and top each with a burger. Serve with the relish.

Vegetable Kabobs

These kabobs, made from a spicy vegetable mixture, are delightfully easy to make and taste delicious.

NUTRITIONAL INFORMATION

Calories 268   Sugars 1g
Protein . . . . .2g   Fat 25g
Carbohydrate . . . .9g   Saturates 3g

20 mins

25 mins

MAKES 12

INGREDIENTS

3½ cups potatoes, sliced

1 onion, sliced

½ medium cauliflower, cut into small florets

scant ½ cup peas

1 tbsp spinach paste

2–3 green chilies

1 tbsp fresh cilantro leaves

1 tsp finely chopped fresh ginger root

1 tsp crushed garlic

1 tsp ground coriander

1 pinch turmeric

1 tsp salt

1 cup bread crumbs

1¼ cups vegetable oil

fresh chili strips, to garnish

1 Place the potatoes, onion, and cauliflower florets in a pan of water and bring to a boil. Reduce the heat and simmer until the potatoes are cooked through. Remove the vegetables from the pan with a slotted spoon and drain thoroughly. Set aside.

2 Add the peas and spinach paste to the vegetables and mix, mashing down thoroughly with a fork.

3 Using a sharp knife, finely chop the green chilies and the fresh cilantro leaves.

4 Mix the chilies and cilantro leaves with the ginger, garlic, ground coriander, turmeric, and salt.

5 Blend the spice mixture into the vegetables, mixing with a fork to make a paste.

6 Scatter the bread crumbs on to a large plate.

7 Break off 10–12 small balls from the spice paste. Flatten them with the palm of your hand to make flat, round shapes.

8 Dip each kabob in the bread crumbs, coating well.

9 Heat the oil in a heavy skillet and shallow-fry the kabobs, in batches, until golden brown in color, turning occasionally. Transfer to warm serving plates and garnish with the fresh chili strips. Serve hot.

Buck Rarebit

This substantial version of cheese on toast—a creamy cheese sauce topped with a poached egg—makes a tasty, filling snack.

NUTRITIONAL INFORMATION

Calories 478	Sugars 2g
Protein 29g	Fat 34g
Carbohydrate ...14g	Saturates 20g

 10 mins   15–20 mins

SERVES 4

I N G R E D I E N T S

¾ lb/350 g sharp Cheddar

¼ lb/115 g Dutch or Swiss cheese

1 tsp mustard powder

1 tsp whole-grain mustard

2-4 tbsp brown ale, cider, or milk

½ tsp vegetarian Worcestershire sauce

4 thick slices white or whole-wheat bread

4 eggs

salt and pepper

TO GARNISH

tomato wedges

watercress sprigs

1 Grate the cheeses and place in a nonstick pan.

2 Add the mustards, seasoning, brown ale, cider, or milk, and the vegetarian Worcestershire sauce and mix well.

3 Heat the cheese mixture gently, stirring until it has melted and is completely thick and creamy. Remove from the heat and let cool a little.

4 Toast the slices of bread on each side under a preheated broiler then spread the rarebit mixture evenly over each piece.

Put under a moderate broiler until golden brown and bubbling.

5 Meanwhile, poach the eggs. If using a poacher, grease the cups, heat the water in the pan and, when just boiling, break the eggs into the cups. Cover and simmer for 4-5 minutes until just set. Alternatively, bring about 1½ inches/4 cm of water to a boil in a skillet or large pan and for each egg quickly swirl the water with a knife and drop the egg into the "hole" created. Cook for about 4 minutes until just set.

6 Top the rarebits with a poached egg and serve garnished with tomato wedges and sprigs of watercress.

VARIATION

For a change, you can use part or all Stilton or other blue cheese; the appearance is not so attractive but the flavor is very good.

Feta & Potato Patties

Served with a salad, these tasty patties make a satisfying light lunch and they are very easy to prepare, too.

NUTRITIONAL INFORMATION

Calories ....269 Sugars 1g
Protein ....9g Fat 16g
Carbohydrate ...24g Saturates 1g

 20 mins, plus chilling   35 mins

SERVES 4

INGREDIENTS

1 lb/450 g mealy potatoes, unpeeled

4 scallions, chopped

1 cup crumbled feta cheese

2 tsp chopped fresh thyme

1 egg, beaten

1 tbsp lemon juice

all-purpose flour, for dusting

3 tbsp sunflower or corn oil

salt and ground black pepper

VARIATION
These potato patties are also delicious made with goat cheese instead of feta.

1 Cook the potatoes in lightly salted boiling water for about 25 minutes, until tender. Drain and peel. Place the potatoes in a bowl and mash well with a potato masher or fork.

2 Add the scallions, feta, thyme, egg, and lemon juice and season to taste with salt and pepper. Mix thoroughly. Cover the bowl with plastic wrap and chill for 1 hour.

3 Take small handfuls of the potato mixture and roll into balls about the size of a walnut between the palms of your hands. Flatten each one slightly and dust all over with flour.

4 Heat the oil in a skillet and cook the potato patties, in batches if necessary, until golden brown on both sides. Drain on absorbent paper towels and serve immediately.

Paprika Potatoes

Baked potatoes are an easy and welcome snack on a cold day and here they are given a new twist with an interesting and colorful filling.

NUTRITIONAL INFORMATION

Calories 177	Sugars 6g	
Protein 6g	Fat 1g	
Carbohydrate ...38g	Saturates 0g	

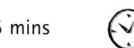

15 mins   1 hr 10 mins

SERVES 4

I N G R E D I E N T S

4 baking potatoes

½ cup vegetable bouillon

1 onion, finely chopped

1 garlic clove, finely chopped

½ cup unsweetened yogurt

2 tsp paprika

salt and ground black pepper

1 Prick the potatoes with a fork and bake in a preheated oven, 400°F/ 200°C , for about 1 hour, until tender.

2 Just before the potatoes are ready, pour the bouillon into a pan and add the onion and garlic. Bring to a boil and simmer for 5 minutes.

3 Remove the potatoes from the oven and cut a lengthwise slice from the top of each. Do not switch off the oven. Using a teaspoon, carefully scoop out the flesh, leaving a shell. Stir the potato flesh into the onion mixture, then add half the yogurt and 1½ teaspoons of the paprika

and season to taste with salt and pepper. Mix well and push through a strainer with the back of a wooden spoon.

4 Spoon the potato mixture into the potato shells and return to the oven for 10 minutes, until heated through. Top the potatoes with the remaining yogurt, sprinkle the remaining paprika over it, and serve immediately.

COOK'S TIP
If you like a crisp skin on baked potatoes, rub them all over with a little olive oil before baking.

Scrambled Bean Curd

These colorful, healthy open sandwiches take only a few minutes to prepare, but they look and taste very special.

NUTRITIONAL INFORMATION

Calories . . . . . . .392 Sugars 6g
Protein . . . . .16g Fat 22g
Carbohydrate . . .35g Saturates 4g

 5–10 mins   5 mins

SERVES 4

I N G R E D I E N T S

6 tbsp margarine

1 lb marinated, firm bean curd

1 red onion, chopped

1 red bell pepper, chopped

4 ciabatta rolls

2 tbsp chopped mixed herbs

salt and pepper

fresh herbs, to garnish

1 Melt the margarine in a skillet and crumble in the bean curd.

2 Add the chopped onion and bell pepper and cook for 3–4 minutes, stirring occasionally.

3 Meanwhile, slice the ciabatta rolls in half and toast under a hot broiler for about 2–3 minutes, turning once.

Remove the toasts and transfer to a serving plate.

4 Add the herbs to the bean curd mixture, combine, and season to taste with salt and pepper.

5 Spoon the bean curd mixture on to the toast and garnish with fresh herbs. Serve at once.

COOK'S TIP

Marinated bean curd adds extra flavor to this dish. Smoked bean curd could be used in its place.

Lentil Croquettes

These mildly spiced croquettes are an ideal light lunch served with a crisp salad and a sesame dip.

NUTRITIONAL INFORMATION

Calories	409	Sugars	.........5g
Protein	........19g	Fat	..........17g
Carbohydrate	...48g	Saturates	.......2g

 1¼ hrs 1 hr

SERVES 4

I N G R E D I E N T S

1 cup split red lentils

1 green bell pepper, seeded and finely chopped

1 red onion, finely chopped

2 garlic cloves, crushed

1 tsp garam masala

½ tsp chili powder

1 tsp ground cumin

2 tsp lemon juice

2 tbsp chopped unsalted peanuts

2½ cups water

1 egg, beaten

3 tbsp all-purpose flour

1 tsp ground turmeric

1 tsp chili powder

4 tbsp vegetable oil

salt and pepper

salad greens and herbs, to serve

1 Put the lentils in a large pan with the bell pepper, onion, garlic, garam masala, chili powder, ground cumin, lemon juice, and peanuts. Add the water and bring to a boil. Reduce the heat and simmer gently, stirring occasionally, for about 30 minutes or until all the liquid has been absorbed.

2 Remove the mixture from the heat and let cool slightly. Beat in the egg and season to taste with salt and pepper. Let cool completely.

3 With floured hands, form the mixture into 8 rectangles or ovals.

4 Combine the flour, turmeric, and chili powder on a small plate. Roll the croquettes in the spiced flour mixture to coat thoroughly.

5 Heat the oil in a large skillet. Add the croquettes, in batches, and cook, turning once, for about 10 minutes until crisp on both sides. Transfer to warmed serving plates and serve the croquettes immediately with crisp salad greens and fresh herbs.

Mixed Mushroom Patties

These appetizing little cakes are packed with creamy potato and a variety of mushrooms, and make a quick and satisfying snack.

NUTRITIONAL INFORMATION

Calories	298	Sugars	.......0.8g
Protein	.........5g	Fat	..........22g
Carbohydrate	...22g	Saturates	.......5g

 20 mins   25 mins

SERVES 4

I N G R E D I E N T S

1 lb/450 g diced mealy potatoes

2 tbsp butter

2 cups chopped mixed mushrooms

2 garlic cloves, crushed

1 small egg, beaten

1 tbsp chopped fresh chives, plus extra to garnish

flour, for dusting

vegetable oil, for frying

salt and pepper

salad, to serve

1 Cook the potatoes in a pan of lightly salted boiling water for 10 minutes or until cooked through.

2 Drain the potatoes well, mash with a potato masher or fork, and set aside.

COOK'S TIP

Prepare the patties in advance, cover, and let chill in the refrigerator for up to 24 hours, if you wish.

3 Meanwhile, melt the butter in a skillet. Add the mushrooms and garlic and cook over medium heat, stirring constantly, for 5 minutes. Drain well.

4 Stir the mushrooms and garlic into the potatoes, together with the beaten egg and chives.

5 Divide the mixture equally into 4 portions and shape them into round

patties. Toss them in the flour until the outsides of the patties are completely coated, shaking off any excess.

6 Heat the vegetable oil in a skillet. Add the mushroom patties and cook over medium heat for 10 minutes until they are golden brown, turning them over carefully halfway through to prevent them breaking up. Serve the patties immediately, with a simple crisp salad.

Stuffed Vegetable Snacks

In this recipe, eggplants are filled with a spicy bulgur and vegetable stuffing for a delicious light meal.

NUTRITIONAL INFORMATION

Calories ....360 Sugars 17g
Protein ....9g Fat 16g
Carbohydrate ...50g Saturates 2g

🧊 40 mins   🕐 30 mins

SERVES 4

I N G R E D I E N T S

4 medium eggplants

1 cup bulgur

1¼ cups boiling water

3 tbsp olive oil

2 garlic cloves, crushed

2 tbsp pine nuts

½ tsp ground turmeric

1 tsp chili powder

2 celery stalks, chopped

4 scallions, chopped

1 carrot, grated

¾ cup chopped white mushrooms

2 tbsp raisins

2 tbsp chopped fresh cilantro

salt

salad greens, to serve

1 Cut the eggplants in half lengthwise and scoop out the flesh with a teaspoon without piercing the "shells." Chop the flesh and set aside. Rub the insides of the eggplants with a little salt and set aside for 20 minutes.

2 Meanwhile, put the bulgur in a large bowl and pour the boiling water over it. Set aside for about 20 minutes or until the bulgur has softened and completely absorbed the water.

3 Heat the oil in a heavy skillet. Add the garlic, pine nuts, turmeric, chili powder, celery, scallions, carrot, mushrooms, and raisins and cook over low heat, stirring occasionally, for about 2–3 minutes.

4 Stir in the reserved eggplant flesh and cook for a further 2–3 minutes. Add the chopped cilantro, mixing well.

5 Remove the skillet from the heat and stir in the bulgur. Rinse the eggplant shells under cold water and pat dry with paper towels.

6 Spoon the bulgur filling into the eggplants and place in a roasting pan. Pour in a little boiling water and cook in a preheated oven, 350°F/180°C, for about 15–20 minutes until piping hot. Remove from the oven, transfer to a warmed serving plate, and serve immediately with salad greens.

Spicy Potato Fries

These home-made fries are flavored with spices and cooked in the oven.
Serve with Lime Mayonnaise (see page 219).

NUTRITIONAL INFORMATION

Calories	328	Sugars	.........2g
Protein	.........5g	Fat	...........11g
Carbohydrate	...56g	Saturates	.......7g

15 mins,
plus soaking
time

40 mins

SERVES 4

INGREDIENTS

4 large waxy potatoes

2 sweet potatoes

4 tbsp butter, melted

½ tsp chili powder

1 tsp garam masala

salt

1 Cut the potatoes and sweet potatoes into slices about ½ inch/1 cm thick, then cut them into fries.

2 Place the potatoes in a large bowl of cold salted water. Let soak for 20 minutes.

3 Remove the potato slices with a slotted spoon and drain thoroughly. Pat with paper towels until completely dry.

4 Pour the melted butter on to a cookie sheet. Transfer the potato slices to the cookie sheet.

5 Sprinkle with the chili powder and garam masala, turning the potato slices to coat them with the mixture.

6 Cook the fries in a preheated oven, 400°F/200°C, turning frequently, for 40 minutes, until they are browned and cooked through.

7 Drain the fries on paper towels to remove the excess oil, and serve.

COOK'S TIP

Rinsing the potatoes in cold water before cooking removes the starch, thus preventing them from sticking together. Soaking the potatoes in a bowl of cold salted water actually makes the cooked fries crisper.

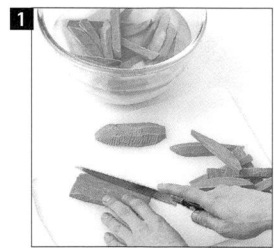

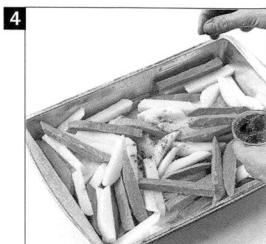

Mexican Refried Beans

Refried beans are a classic Mexican dish. They make a delicious snack served with warm tortillas and a quick onion relish.

NUTRITIONAL INFORMATION

Calories	.519	Sugars	.14g
Protein	.25g	Fat	.28g
Carbohydrate	.44g	Saturates	.9g

15 mins   15 mins

SERVES 4

I N G R E D I E N T S

2 tbsp olive oil

1 onion, finely chopped

3 garlic cloves, finely chopped

1 green chili, chopped

1½ cups canned red kidney beans, drained

1½ cups canned pinto beans, drained

2 tbsp chopped cilantro

⅔ cup vegetable bouillon

8 wheat tortillas

¼ cup grated Cheddar cheese

salt and pepper

R E L I S H

4 scallions, chopped

1 red onion, chopped

1 green chili, chopped

1 tbsp garlic-wine vinegar

1 tsp superfine sugar

1 tomato, chopped

1 Heat the olive oil in a large skillet. Add the onion and sauté for 3–5 minutes. Add the garlic and chili and cook for 1 minute.

2 Mash the beans with a potato masher and stir into the skillet with the cilantro.

3 Stir in the bouillon and cook the beans, stirring, for 5 minutes until soft and pulpy.

4 Place the tortillas on a cookie sheet and heat through in a warm oven for 1–2 minutes.

5 Mix together the relish ingredients in a serving bowl.

6 Spoon the beans into a serving dish and top with the cheese. Season well.

Roll the tortillas and serve with the relish and beans.

COOK'S TIP

Add a little more liquid to the beans when they are cooking if they begin to catch on the bottom of the skillet.

Vegetable Enchiladas

This warming Mexican dish consists of tortillas filled with a spicy vegetable mixture and topped with a hot tomato sauce.

NUTRITIONAL INFORMATION

Calories 264   Sugars 8g
Protein ....11g   Fat 13g
Carbohydrate ...28g   Saturates 5g

20 mins   50 mins

SERVES 4

INGREDIENTS

4 flour tortillas

½ cup grated Cheddar cheese

FILLING

3 oz/85 g spinach

2 tbsp olive oil

8 baby corn ears, sliced

¼ cup frozen peas, thawed

1 red bell pepper, diced

1 carrot, diced

1 leek, sliced

2 garlic cloves, crushed

1 red chili, chopped

salt and pepper

SAUCE

1¼ cups strained tomatoes

2 shallots, chopped

1 garlic clove, crushed

1¼ cups vegetable bouillon

1 tsp superfine sugar

1 tsp chili powder

1 To make the filling, blanch the spinach in a pan of boiling water for 2 minutes, drain well, and chop.

2 Heat the oil in a skillet and sauté the corn cobs, peas, bell pepper, carrot, leek, garlic, and chili for 3–4 minutes, stirring briskly. Stir in the spinach and season well with salt and pepper to taste.

3 Put all of the sauce ingredients in a pan and bring them to a boil, stirring constantly. Continue to cook over high heat for an additional 20 minutes, stirring, until the sauce has thickened and reduced by a third.

4 Spoon a quarter of the filling along the center of each tortilla. Roll the tortillas around the filling and place in an ovenproof dish, seam-side down.

5 Pour the tomato sauce over the tortillas and sprinkle the grated cheese on top. Cook in a preheated oven, 350°F/180°C, for 20 minutes or until the cheese is bubbling and golden. Serve the enchiladas immediately.

Feta Cheese Patties

Grated carrots, zucchini, and feta cheese are combined with
cumin seeds, poppy seeds, curry powder, and chopped fresh parsley.

NUTRITIONAL INFORMATION

Calories	217	Sugars	.........6g
Protein	.........6g	Fat	..........16g
Carbohydrate	...12g	Saturates	.......7g

15 mins   20 mins

SERVES 4

I N G R E D I E N T S

2 large carrots

1 large zucchini

1 small onion

2 oz /55 g feta cheese

4 tbsp all-purpose flour

¼ tsp cumin seeds

½ tsp poppy seeds

1 tsp medium curry powder

1 tbsp chopped fresh parsley

1 egg, beaten

2 tbsp butter

2 tbsp vegetable oil

salt and pepper

fresh herb sprigs, to garnish

1 Grate the carrots, zucchini, onion, and feta cheese coarsely, either by hand or process in a food processor.

2 Combine the flour, cumin seeds, poppy seeds, curry powder, and parsley in a large bowl. Season with salt and pepper.

3 Add the carrot and zucchini mixture to the seasoned flour, tossing well to combine. Stir in the beaten egg.

4 Heat the butter and vegetable oil in a large, heavy skillet. Place heaped tablespoonfuls of the patty mixture in the skillet, flattening them slightly with the back of the spoon. Cook over low heat for about 2 minutes on each side until crisp and golden brown. Drain on paper towels and keep warm. Cook more patties in the same way until all the mixture is used.

5 Serve immediately, garnished with sprigs of fresh herbs.

Bombay Bowl

You can use dried garbanzo beans for this popular snack, but the canned sort are quick and easy without sacrificing much flavor.

NUTRITIONAL INFORMATION

Calories	183	Sugars	.........6g
Protein	.........9g	Fat	...........3g
Carbohydrate	...33g	Saturates	.....0.3g

15 mins   15 mins

SERVES 4

INGREDIENTS

1½ cups canned garbanzo
   beans (chickpeas)

2 medium potatoes

1 medium onion

2 tbsp tamarind paste

6 tbsp water

1 tsp chili powder

2 tsp sugar

1 tsp salt

TO GARNISH

1 tomato, sliced

2 fresh green chilies, chopped

fresh cilantro leaves

1 Drain the can of garbanzo beans and place them in a bowl.

2 Using a sharp knife, cut the potatoes into even-sized dice.

3 Place the diced potatoes in a pan of water and boil until cooked through. Test by inserting the tip of a knife into the potatoes—they should feel soft and tender. Drain the potatoes and set them aside until required.

4 Using a sharp knife, finely chop the onion. Set aside until required.

5 Mix together the tamarind paste and water in a small mixing bowl.

6 Add the chili powder, sugar, and salt to the tamarind paste mixture and stir well to combine. Pour the mixture over the garbanzo beans.

7 Add the chopped onion and the diced potatoes, and stir to mix. Season to taste with a little salt.

8 Transfer the mixture to a serving bowl and garnish with tomatoes, chilies, and cilantro leaves.

COOK'S TIP

Cream-colored and resembling a filbert in appearance, garbanzo beans have a distinctive nutty flavor and slightly crunchy texture.

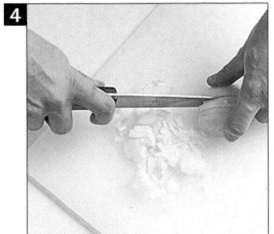

Stuffed Mushrooms

Use large open-cap mushrooms for this recipe, both for their delicious flavor and for their suitability for filling.

NUTRITIONAL INFORMATION

Calories ....273 Sugars 5g
Protein ....13g Fat 18g
Carbohydrate ...15g Saturates 5g

15 mins   25 mins

SERVES 4

I N G R E D I E N T S

8 open-cap mushrooms

1 tbsp olive oil

1 small leek, chopped

1 celery stalk, chopped

¼ lb/100 g firm bean curd, diced

1 zucchini, chopped

1 carrot, chopped

scant 2 cups whole-wheat bread crumbs

2 tbsp chopped fresh basil

1 tbsp tomato paste

2 tbsp pine nuts

¾ cup grated Cheddar cheese

⅔ cup vegetable bouillon

salt and pepper

salad, to serve

1 Remove the stems from the mushrooms and chop finely. Reserve the caps.

2 Heat the olive oil in a large, heavy skillet over medium heat. Add the chopped mushroom stems, leek, celery, bean curd, zucchini, and carrot and cook, stirring constantly, for 3–4 minutes.

3 Stir in the whole-wheat bread crumbs, chopped basil, tomato paste, and pine nuts. Season with salt and pepper to taste and mix thoroughly.

4 Divide the stuffing mixture evenly between the mushroom caps and sprinkle the grated cheese over the top. Arrange the mushrooms in a shallow ovenproof dish and pour the vegetable bouillon around them.

5 Cook in a preheated oven, 425°F/ 220°C, for 20 minutes or until the mushrooms are cooked through and the cheese has melted and browned. Remove the mushrooms from the dish and serve immediately with a salad.

Fritters with Garlic Sauce

Chunks of cooked potato are coated first in Parmesan cheese, then in a light batter before being fried until golden for a delicious hot snack.

NUTRITIONAL INFORMATION

Calories	599	Sugars	.........9g
Protein	........22g	Fat	..........39g
Carbohydrate	...42g	Saturates	......13g

 20 mins   20-25 mins

SERVES 4

I N G R E D I E N T S

1 lb/450 g waxy potatoes, cubed

1¼ cups freshly grated Parmesan cheese

vegetable oil, for deep-frying

S A U C E

2 tbsp butter

1 onion, halved and sliced

2 garlic cloves, crushed

¼ cup all-purpose flour

1¼ cups milk

1 tbsp chopped fresh parsley

B A T T E R

½ cup all-purpose flour

1 small egg

⅔ cup milk

1 To make the sauce, melt the butter in a pan and cook the sliced onion and garlic over low heat, stirring frequently, for 2–3 minutes. Add the flour and cook, stirring constantly, for 1 minute.

2 Remove from the heat and stir in the milk and parsley. Return to the heat and bring to a boil. Keep warm.

3 Meanwhile, cook the cubed potatoes in a pan of boiling water for 5–10 minutes, until just firm. Do not overcook or they will fall apart.

4 Drain the potatoes and toss them in the Parmesan cheese. If the potatoes are still slightly wet, the cheese sticks to them and coats them well.

5 To make the batter, place the flour in a mixing bowl and gradually beat in the egg and milk until smooth. Dip the potato cubes into the batter to coat them.

6 In a large pan, heat the oil to 350°F/180°C or until a cube of bread browns in 30 seconds. Add the fritters and cook for 3–4 minutes, or until golden.

7 Remove the fritters with a slotted spoon and drain well. Transfer them to a warm serving bowl and serve immediately with the garlic sauce.

Cheese & Onion Rostis

These grated potato patties are also known as straw patties, as they resemble a straw mat! Serve them with a tomato sauce or salad.

NUTRITIONAL INFORMATION

Calories 307	Sugars 4g
Protein 8g	Fat 13g
Carbohydrate ...42g	Saturates 6g

10 mins · 40 mins

SERVES 4

INGREDIENTS

2 lb/900 g potatoes

1 onion, grated

½ cup grated Swiss cheese

2 tbsp chopped parsley

1 tbsp olive oil

2 tbsp butter

salt and pepper

TO GARNISH

1 shredded scallion

1 small tomato, quartered

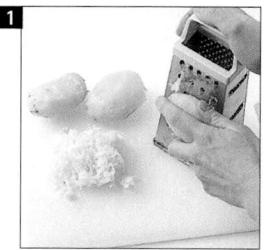

1 Parboil the potatoes in a pan of lightly salted boiling water for 10 minutes and let cool. Peel the potatoes, grate with a coarse grater, and place in a mixing bowl.

2 Stir in the onion, cheese, and parsley. Season well with salt and pepper. Divide the potato mixture into 4 portions of equal size and form them into patties.

3 Heat half of the olive oil and butter in a skillet. Cook two of the potato patties over high heat for 1 minute, then reduce the heat and cook for 5 minutes, until they are golden underneath. Turn them over and cook for another 5 minutes.

4 Repeat with the remaining oil and butter to cook the remaining patties. Transfer to warm individual serving plates. Garnish and serve immediately.

COOK'S TIP
The potato pattes should be flattened as much as possible during cooking, otherwise the outside will be cooked before the center.

Eggplant Timbale

This is a great way to serve pasta as an appetizer, wrapped in an eggplant mold. It looks really impressive, yet it is so easy to make.

NUTRITIONAL INFORMATION

Calories	291	Sugars	11g
Protein	8g	Fat	18g
Carbohydrate	25g	Saturates	4g

25 mins   40 mins

SERVES 4

INGREDIENTS

1 large eggplant

½ cup dried macaroni

1 tbsp vegetable oil

1 onion, chopped

2 garlic cloves, crushed

2 tbsp drained canned corn

2 tbsp frozen peas, thawed

3½ oz/100 g spinach

¼ cup grated Cheddar cheese

1 egg, beaten

8 oz/225 g canned, chopped tomatoes

1 tbsp chopped fresh basil

salt and pepper

SAUCE

4 tbsp olive oil

2 tbsp white wine vinegar

2 garlic cloves, crushed

3 tbsp chopped basil

1 tbsp superfine sugar

1 Cut the eggplant lengthwise into thin strips, using a potato peeler. Place in a bowl of salted boiling water and let stand for 3–4 minutes. Drain well.

2 Grease 4 x ⅔ cup ramekin dishes and line with the eggplant strips, leaving 1 inch/2.5 cm overlapping.

3 Bring a pan of lightly salted water to a boil. Add the pasta, bring back to a boil, and cook for 8–10 minutes until tender, but still firm to the bite. Drain.

4 Heat the oil in a pan and cook the onion and garlic for 2–3 minutes. Stir in the corn and peas and remove the pan from the heat.

5 Blanch the spinach, drain well, chop, and reserve. Add the pasta to the onion mixture with the cheese, egg, tomatoes, and basil. Season to taste and mix well. Half-fill each ramekin with some of the pasta. Place the spinach on top and then the remaining pasta mixture. Fold the eggplant over the pasta filling to cover. Put the ramekins in a roasting pan half-filled with boiling water, cover, and cook in a preheated oven, 350°F/180°C, for 20–25 minutes or until set.

6 Meanwhile, heat all the sauce ingredients in a pan. Turn out the ramekins and serve with the sauce.

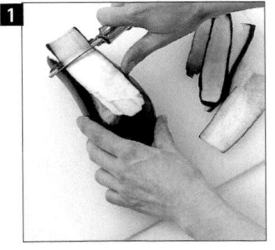
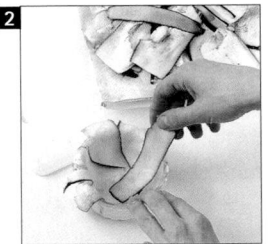

Vegetable Biryani

The Biryani originated in the North of India, and was a dish reserved for festivals. The vegetables are marinated in a yogurt-based marinade.

NUTRITIONAL INFORMATION

Calories 449	Sugars 18g	
Protein 12g	Fat 12g	
Carbohydrate ...79g	Saturates 6g	

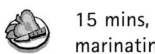

15 mins, plus marinating   1 hr 5 mins

SERVES 4

I N G R E D I E N T S

¾ lb/350 g cubed potato

¼ lb/100 g baby carrots

2 oz/50 g okra, thickly sliced

2 celery stalks, sliced

3 oz/85 g baby white mushrooms, halved

1 eggplant, halved and sliced

1¼ cups unsweetened yogurt

1 tbsp grated fresh ginger root

2 large onions, grated

4 garlic cloves, crushed

1 tsp turmeric

1 tbsp curry powder

2 tbsp butter

2 onions, sliced

1¼ cups basmati rice

chopped fresh cilantro, to garnish

1 Cook the potato cubes, carrots, and okra in a pan of boiling salted water for 7–8 minutes. Drain well and place in a large bowl. Mix with the celery, mushrooms, and eggplant.

2 Mix the unsweetened yogurt, ginger, grated onions, garlic, turmeric, and curry powder, and spoon over the vegetables. Let marinate in a cool place for at least 2 hours.

3 Heat the butter in a heavy skillet. Add the sliced onions to the skillet and cook over medium heat for 5–6 minutes, until they are soft and golden brown. Remove a few onions from the pan and reserve for the garnish.

4 Cook the rice in a large pan of boiling water for 7 minutes. Drain thoroughly and set aside.

5 Add the marinated vegetables to the onions and cook for 10 minutes.

6 Put half of the rice into a 8¾ cup/ 2 liter casserole dish. Spoon the vegetables on top and cover with the remaining rice.

7 Cover the dish and cook the biryani in a preheated oven, 375°F/190°C, for 20–25 minutes, or until the rice is tender and the biryani is heated through.

8 Spoon the biryani on to a warm serving plate. Garnish with the reserved onions and cilantro and serve.

Aloo Gobi

It is not surprising that this vegetable curry is so popular, as it looks attractive, smells wonderful, and tastes superb.

NUTRITIONAL INFORMATION

Calories 00   Sugars 0g
Protein ....00g   Fat 00g
Carbohydrate ...00g   Saturates 0g

20 mins   20 mins

SERVES 4

INGREDIENTS

1 lb/450 g potatoes

2 tbsp groundnut or sunflower oil

1 tsp cumin seeds

2 fresh green chilies, seeded and finely chopped

1 cauliflower, cut into florets

1 tsp ground cumin

1 tsp ground coriander

½ tsp ground turmeric

¼ tsp chili powder

salt

chopped fresh cilantro, to garnish

1 Cut the potatoes into 1 inch/2.5 cm pieces. Cook the potatoes in a large pan of boiling water for 10 minutes. Drain well.

2 Meanwhile, heat the oil in a large, heavy skillet. Add the cumin seeds and cook, stirring constantly, for about 1½ minutes, until the seeds begin to pop and give off their aroma.

3 Add the chili to the skillet and cook, stirring constantly, for a further 1 minute.

4 Add the cauliflower to the pan and cook, stirring constantly, for 5 minutes.

5 Add the potatoes, cumin, coriander, turmeric, and chili powder, and season to taste with salt and pepper. Cook, stirring frequently, for a further 10 minutes, until all the vegetables are tender.

6 Transfer the aloo gobi to a warm serving dish, garnish with the fresh cilantro, and serve immediately.

Vegetable-Stuffed Parathas

This bread can be quite rich and is usually made for special occasions. It can be eaten on its own or with a vegetable curry.

NUTRITIONAL INFORMATION

Calories 391	Sugars 2g
Protein 6g	Fat 24g
Carbohydrate . . .40g	Saturates 2.5g

🥔 25 mins   🕐 30–35 mins

SERVES 6

I N G R E D I E N T S

D O U G H

1¾ cups whole-wheat flour (ata or chapati flour)

½ tsp salt

scant 1 cup water

3½ oz/100 g vegetable ghee

2 tbsp ghee, for frying

F I L L I N G

1½ lb/675 g potatoes

½ tsp turmeric

1 tsp garam masala

1 tsp finely chopped fresh ginger root

1 tbsp fresh cilantro leaves

3 green chilies, finely chopped

1 tsp salt

1 To make the parathas, mix the flour, salt, water, and ghee in a bowl to form a dough.

2 Divide the dough into 6–8 equal portions. Roll each portion out on to a floured counter. Brush the middle of the dough portions with ½ teaspoon of ghee. Fold the dough portions in half and roll into a pipelike shape, then flatten with the palms of your hands and roll around a finger to form a coil. Roll out again, using flour to dust when necessary, to form a round about 7 inches/18 cm in diameter.

3 Place the potatoes in a pan of boiling water and cook until soft enough to be mashed.

4 Blend the turmeric, garam masala, ginger, cilantro leaves, chilies, and salt together in a bowl.

5 Add the spice mixture to the mashed potato and mix well. Spread about 1 tablespoon of the spicy potato mixture on each dough portion and cover with another rolled-out piece of dough. Seal the edges well.

6 Heat 2 teaspoons of ghee in a heavy skillet. Place the parathas gently in the pan, in batches, and cook, turning and moving them about gently with a flat spoon, until golden.

7 Remove the parathas from the skillet and serve immediately.

Vegetable Samosas

These Indian snacks are perfect for a quick or light meal. Served with a salad, they can be made in advance and frozen for ease.

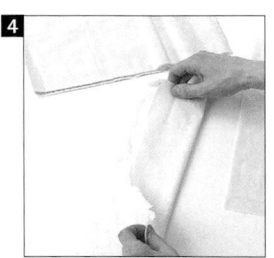

NUTRITIONAL INFORMATION

Calories 291	Sugars 2g	
Protein 4g	Fat 23g	
Carbohydrate . . .18g	Saturates 3g	

 20 mins   30 mins

MAKES 12

INGREDIENTS

FILLING

2 tbsp vegetable oil

1 onion, chopped

½ tsp ground coriander

½ tsp ground cumin

pinch of turmeric

½ tsp ground ginger

½ tsp garam masala

1 garlic clove, crushed

1½ cups diced potatoes

1 cup frozen peas, thawed

5½ oz/150 g spinach, chopped

PASTRY

12 oz/350 g phyllo pastry

vegetable oil, for deep-frying

1 To make the filling, heat the oil in a skillet. Add the onion and sauté, stirring frequently, for 1–2 minutes, until soft. Stir in all of the spices and garlic and cook for 1 minute.

2 Add the potatoes and cook over low heat, stirring frequently, for 5 minutes, until they begin to soften.

3 Stir in the peas and spinach and cook for another 3–4 minutes.

4 Lay the phyllo pastry sheets out on a clean counter and fold 12 sheets in half lengthwise.

5 Place 2 tablespoons of the vegetable filling at one end of each folded pastry sheet. Fold over one corner to make a triangle. Continue folding in this way to make a triangular package and seal the edges with water.

6 Repeat with the remaining pastry and the remaining filling.

7 Heat the oil for deep-frying to 350°F/180°C or until a cube of bread browns in 30 seconds. Fry the samosas, in batches, for 1–2 minutes until golden brown. Drain on absorbent paper towels and keep warm while cooking the remainder. Serve immediately.

Ciabatta Rolls

Sandwiches are always a welcome snack, but can be mundane.
These crisp rolls filled with roasted bell peppers and cheese are irresistible.

NUTRITIONAL INFORMATION

Calories 328	Sugars 6g
Protein 8g	Fat 19g
Carbohydrate ...34g	Saturates 9g

15 mins   10 mins

SERVES 4

INGREDIENTS

4 ciabatta rolls

2 tbsp olive oil

1 garlic clove, crushed

FILLING

1 red bell pepper

1 green bell pepper

1 yellow bell pepper

4 radishes, sliced

1 bunch of watercress

½ cup cream cheese

1 Slice the ciabatta rolls in half. Heat the olive oil and garlic in a pan. Pour the garlic and oil mixture over the cut surfaces of the rolls and set aside.

2 Halve and seed the bell peppers and place, skin side up, on a broiler rack. Cook under a preheated hot broiler for 8–10 minutes until just beginning to char. Remove the bell peppers from the broiler and place in a plastic bag. When cool enough to handle, peel and slice thinly.

3 Arrange the radish slices on 1 half of each roll with a few watercress leaves. Spoon the cream cheese on top. Pile the roasted bell peppers on top of the cream cheese and top with the other half of the roll. Serve immediately.

Feta & Spinach Omelet

This quick chunky omelet has pieces of potato cooked into the egg mixture and is then filled with feta cheese and spinach.

NUTRITIONAL INFORMATION

Calories 564   Sugars 6g
Protein ....30g   Fat 39g
Carbohydrate ...25g   Saturates 19g

20 mins   25-30 mins

SERVES 4

INGREDIENTS

6 tbsp butter

8 cups diced waxy potatoes

3 garlic cloves, crushed

1 tsp paprika

2 tomatoes, peeled, seeded, and diced

12 eggs

pepper

FILLING

8 oz/225 g baby spinach

1 tsp fennel seeds

¼ lb/115 g feta cheese, diced

4 tbsp unsweetened yogurt

VARIATION

Use any other cheese, such as blue cheese, instead of the feta, and blanched broccoli in place of the baby spinach, if you prefer.

1 Heat 2 tbsp of the butter in a skillet and cook the potatoes over low heat, stirring constantly, for 7–10 minutes until golden. Transfer to a bowl.

2 Add the garlic, paprika, and tomatoes to the pan and cook for another 2 minutes.

3 Whisk the eggs together and season with pepper. Pour the eggs into the potatoes and mix well.

4 Cook the spinach in boiling water for 1 minute, until just wilted. Drain and refresh under cold running water. Pat dry with paper towels. Stir in the fennel seeds, feta cheese, and yogurt.

5 Heat a quarter of the remaining butter in a 6 inch/15 cm omelet pan. Ladle a quarter of the egg and potato mixture into the pan. Cook, turning once, for 2 minutes, until set.

6 Transfer the omelet to a serving plate. Spoon a quarter of the spinach mixture on to one half of the omelet, then fold the omelet in half over the filling. Repeat to make 4 omelets.

Potato & Mushroom Bake

Use any mixture of mushrooms to hand for this creamy layered bake. It can be served straight from the dish in which it is cooked.

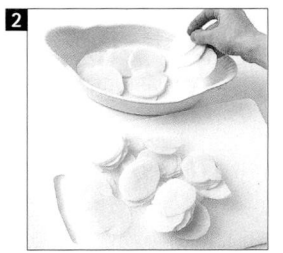

NUTRITIONAL INFORMATION

Calories ....304 Sugars 2g
Protein ....4g Fat 24g
Carbohydrate ...20g Saturates 15g

 15 mins   1 hr

SERVES 4

INGREDIENTS

2 tbsp butter

1 lb/450 g waxy potatoes, thinly sliced

2 cups sliced mixed mushrooms

1 tbsp chopped rosemary

4 tbsp chopped chives

2 garlic cloves, crushed

⅔ cup heavy cream

salt and pepper

snipped chives, to garnish

1 Grease a shallow round ovenproof dish with butter.

2 Parboil the sliced potatoes in a pan of boiling water for 10 minutes. Drain well. Layer a quarter of the potatoes in the base of the dish.

3 Arrange one-quarter of the mushrooms on top of the potatoes and sprinkle with one-quarter of the rosemary, chives, and garlic. Continue making layers in the same order, finishing with a layer of potatoes on top.

4 Pour the heavy cream over the top of the potatoes. Season to taste with salt and pepper.

5 Cook in a preheated oven, 375°F/ 190°C, for about 45 minutes, or until the bake is golden brown on top and piping hot.

6 Garnish with snipped chives and serve at once straight from the dish.

COOK'S TIP
For a special occasion, the bake may be made in a lined cake pan and then turned out to serve.

Three-Cheese Fondue

A hot cheese dip made from three different cheeses can be prepared easily and with guaranteed success in the microwave oven.

NUTRITIONAL INFORMATION

Calories 565	Sugars 1g	
Protein 29g	Fat 38g	
Carbohydrate ...15g	Saturates 24g	

 15 mins   10 mins

SERVES 4

I N G R E D I E N T S

1 garlic clove

1¼ cups dry white wine

2 cups grated mild Cheddar cheese

1 cup grated Swiss cheese

1 cup grated mozzarella cheese

2 tbsp cornstarch

pepper

TO SERVE

French bread

vegetables, such as zucchini, mushrooms, baby corn ears, and cauliflower

1 Bruise the garlic by placing the flat side of a knife on top and pressing down with the heel of your hand.

2 Rub the garlic around the inside of a large bowl. Discard the garlic.

3 Pour the wine into the bowl and heat, uncovered, on HIGH power for 3–4 minutes, until hot but not boiling.

4 Gradually add the Cheddar and Swiss cheeses, stirring well after each addition (see Cook's Tip), then add the mozzarella. Stir until all the cheese is completely melted.

5 Mix the cornstarch with a little water to form a smooth paste and stir it into the cheese mixture. Season to taste with pepper.

6 Cover and cook on MEDIUM power for 6 minutes, stirring twice during cooking, until the sauce is smooth.

7 Cut the French bread into bite-sized cubes and the vegetables into batons, slices, or florets. To serve, keep the fondue warm over a spirit lamp or reheat as necessary in the microwave oven. Dip in cubes of French bread and batons, slices, or florets of vegetables.

COOK'S TIP

Make sure you add the cheese to the wine gradually, mixing well in between each addition, to prevent the mixture from curdling.

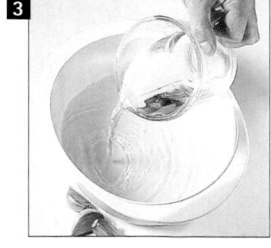

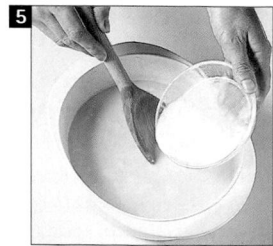

Stuffed Tomatoes

These attractive tomatoes, with a mushroom and fresh herb filling, would be wonderful served as part of a light buffet lunch in late summer.

NUTRITIONAL INFORMATION

Calories	78	Sugars	.........5g
Protein	.........3g	Fat	...........6g
Carbohydrate	....6g	Saturates	.......1g

20 mins   35 mins

SERVES 4

INGREDIENTS

4 large tomatoes

2 tbsp finely chopped fresh basil

4 tsp olive oil

10 oz/280 g white mushrooms, very finely chopped

1 small onion, very finely chopped

2 garlic cloves, very finely chopped

1 tablespoon chopped fresh parsley

1 cup vegetable bouillon

1 tbsp freshly grated Parmesan cheese

salt and ground black pepper

fresh basil sprigs, to garnish

  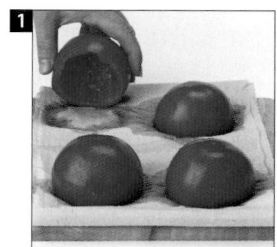

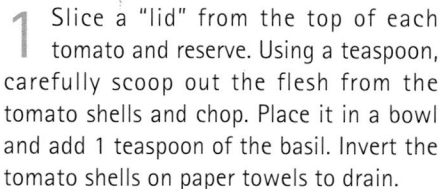

1 Slice a "lid" from the top of each tomato and reserve. Using a teaspoon, carefully scoop out the flesh from the tomato shells and chop. Place it in a bowl and add 1 teaspoon of the basil. Invert the tomato shells on paper towels to drain.

2 Heat 1 tbsp of the oil in a skillet. Add the mushrooms, onion, garlic, parsley, and remaining basil and season with pepper to taste. Cover and cook over low heat for 2 minutes, then remove the lid and cook, stirring occasionally, for 8-10 minutes more. Meanwhile, bring the bouillon to a boil in a pan and cook until

reduced by about three-quarters. Stir in the chopped tomato mixture and cook for 3-4 minutes more until thickened. Push the mixture through a strainer with a wooden spoon and stir it into the mushroom mixture. Stir in the Parmesan.

3 Stand the tomatoes in an ovenproof dish and season the insides with salt. Fill each tomato with stuffing and replace the "lids." Brush with the remaining oil and bake in a preheated oven, 350°F/180°C, for about 15 minutes, or until tender and cooked through. Serve warm, garnished with basil sprigs.

COOK'S TIP
Check for any seeds remaining in the tomato shells after you have scooped out the flesh and remove them.

Cheese & Potato Slices

This recipe takes a while to prepare, but it is well worth the effort.
The golden potato slices coated in bread crumbs and cheese are delicious.

NUTRITIONAL INFORMATION

Calories	560	Sugars	.........3g
Protein	........19g	Fat	..........31g
Carbohydrate	...55g	Saturates	.......7g

 10 mins   40 mins

SERVES 4

INGREDIENTS

2 lb/900 g large waxy potatoes, unpeeled and thickly sliced

1 cup fresh white bread crumbs

½ cup grated Parmesan cheese

1½ tsp chili powder

2 eggs, beaten

oil, for deep frying

chili powder, for dusting (optional)

1 Cook the sliced potatoes in a pan of boiling water for about 10–15 minutes, or until they are just tender. Drain thoroughly.

2 Mix the bread crumbs, cheese, and chili powder together in a bowl, then transfer to a shallow dish. Pour the beaten eggs into a separate shallow dish.

COOK'S TIP

The cheese and potato slices may be coated in the bread crumb mixture in advance and then stored in the refrigerator until ready to use.

3 Dip the potato slices first in egg and then roll them in the bread crumbs to coat completely.

4 Heat the oil in a large pan to 350°F/180°C, or until a cube of bread browns in 30 seconds. Cook the cheese and potato slices, in several batches, for 4–5 minutes or until they are a golden brown color.

5 Remove the cheese and potato slices from the oil with a slotted spoon and drain thoroughly on paper towels. Keep the cheese and potato slices warm while you cook the remaining batches.

6 Transfer the cheese and potato slices to warm individual serving plates. Dust lightly with chili powder, if using, and serve immediately.

Corn & Bell Pepper Crêpes

These light-as-air crêpes are very appetizing, so it's fortunate that they are so easy to make. For best results, use a heavy skillet or griddle.

NUTRITIONAL INFORMATION

Calories 239   Sugars 6g
Protein ....8g   Fat 6g
Carbohydrate ....4g   Saturates 1g

15 mins   20 mins

SERVES 4

I N G R E D I E N T S

1 cup frozen corn kernels, thawed

4 tbsp cornmeal

4 tbsp all-purpose flour

1 tbsp very finely chopped fresh parsley

1 small red bell pepper, seeded and very finely chopped

1 small egg yolk

½ tsp superfine sugar

2 egg whites

1 tbsp olive oil

1 Process half the corn kernels in a food processor until finely chopped. Scrape into a bowl and add the remaining corn kernels, cornmeal, flour, parsley, and chopped bell pepper. Beat the egg yolk with the sugar in a small bowl, then add it to the corn mixture and stir thoroughly.

2 Beat the egg whites in a clean bowl until they stand in soft peaks (see Cook's Tip). Gently fold half the egg whites into the corn mixture, then fold in the remaining egg whites.

3 Heat half the olive oil in a heavy skillet. Drop spoonfuls of the batter into the skillet, spacing them out well, and cook for 3 minutes, until the undersides are golden brown. Flip the crêpes over carefully with a spatula and cook the other sides for about 3 minutes, until golden brown. Transfer the crêpes to a plate and keep warm while you cook the remaining batter, adding more olive oil to the skillet if necessary. Serve immediately.

COOK'S TIP
Remove the eggs from the refrigerator about 30 minutes before using so that the whites will whisk fully and easily.

Spinach & Cheese Crêpes

Ricotta cheese and spinach are made for each other and feature in many Italian recipes. Here they are combined in a delicious filling for crêpes.

NUTRITIONAL INFORMATION

Calories	630	Sugars	........10g
Protein	........36g	Fat	..........38g
Carbohydrate	...38g	Saturates	.......2g

 25 mins   45 mins

serves 4-6

I N G R E D I E N T S

1 tbsp sunflower oil, plus extra for brushing

1 quantity crêpe batter (see page 8)

½ quantity hot cheese sauce (see page 9), made with Parmesan cheese

¼ lb/115 g thinly sliced mozzarella cheese

F I L L I N G

1¾ lb/750 g spinach, coarse stalks removed

2 tbsp butter

1 x 8 oz tub ricotta cheese

1 egg, lightly beaten

pinch of freshly grated nutmeg

salt and ground black pepper

VARIATION

If you like, substitute ½ cup buckwheat flour for half the all-purpose flour, when making the crêpe batter.

1 Brush a crêpe pan with oil, cook 12 crêpes, and keep warm. Cook the spinach in a heavy pan, with just the water clinging to the leaves after washing, for 7 minutes. Drain and squeeze out any excess moisture.

2 Coarsely chop the spinach, place in a blender or food processor with the butter, and process to a smooth purée. Add the ricotta cheese and process until blended. Scrape into a bowl, stir in the egg, and season to taste with nutmeg, salt, and pepper. Brush an ovenproof dish with a little oil. Divide the spinach mixture between the crêpes, roll up and place, seam side down, in the dish.

3 Pour the cheese sauce over the crêpes and cover with the thinly sliced mozzarella. Bake in a preheated oven, 425°F/220°C, for 15-20 minutes, until the topping is melted and golden. Serve immediately.

Sausages & Mash

Cheesy sausages served with sweet-potato mash turn simple fare into a sophisticated lunch or supper dish.

NUTRITIONAL INFORMATION

Calories ....909 Sugars 15g
Protein ....2g Fat 65g
Carbohydrate ...63g Saturates 36g

 30 mins   40 mins

SERVES 4

INGREDIENTS

FOR THE SAUSAGES

2 cups fresh whole-wheat bread crumbs

1½ cups grated Monterey Jack cheese

1 leek, finely chopped

2 tbsp finely chopped fresh parsley

1 tbsp finely chopped fresh marjoram

1 tbsp whole-grain mustard

2 eggs

½ cup uncolored dried bread crumbs

corn oil, for deep-frying

FOR THE MASH

1½ lb/675 g sweet potatoes

½ cup butter

1 onion, grated

½ cup heavy cream

pinch of freshly grated nutmeg

salt and ground black pepper

1 For the mash, cook the unpeeled sweet potatoes in a large pan of lightly salted boiling water for 25-30 minutes, until tender.

2 Meanwhile, make the sausage mix. Combine the fresh bread crumbs, cheese, leek, parsley, marjoram, and mustard in a bowl. Separate 1 egg and add the yolk with the remaining egg to the mixture. Season to taste with pepper and knead lightly until the mixture comes together. Using your fingers, form it into 8 sausage shapes.

3 When the sweet potatoes are tender, drain and let cool slightly, then peel and mash well with a potato masher. Heat the butter in a small skillet. Add the onion and cook over very low heat for 5 minutes. Pour the onion mixture into the mashed potatoes, add the cream, and beat well with a wooden spoon. Season to taste with nutmeg, salt, and pepper. Keep warm while you finish the sausages.

4 Heat the oil for deep-frying to 350-375°F/180-190°C or until a cube of bread browns in 30 seconds. Whisk the egg white in a shallow dish until foamy. Place the dried bread crumbs in another shallow dish. Dip the sausages, first in the egg white, then in the bread crumbs to coat thoroughly. Shake off any excess. Deep-fry the sausages, in batches, for about 2 minutes. Drain on paper towels and keep warm while you cook the remainder.

5 When all the sausages are cooked, serve them immediately on warmed plates with the sweet potato mash.

  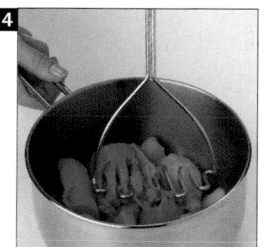

Potato & Mushroom Hash

This is a quick one-pan dish which is ideal for a quick snack. Packed with color and flavor, you can add any other vegetable you have to hand.

NUTRITIONAL INFORMATION

Calories	378	Sugars	........14g
Protein	........18g	Fat	..........26g
Carbohydrate	...20g	Saturates	......7g

 10 mins   35 mins

SERVES 4

I N G R E D I E N T S

1½ lb/675 g cubed potatoes

1 tbsp olive oil

2 garlic cloves, crushed

1 green bell pepper, cubed

1 yellow bell pepper, cubed

3 tomatoes, diced

3 oz/85 g white mushrooms, halved

1 tbsp vegetarian Worcester sauce

2 tbsp chopped basil

salt and pepper

fresh basil sprigs, to garnish

warm crusty bread, to serve

1 Cook the potatoes in a pan of boiling salted water for 7–8 minutes. Drain well and reserve.

2 Heat the olive oil in a large, heavy skillet and cook the potatoes for 8–10 minutes, stirring until browned.

3 Add the garlic and bell peppers to the skillet and cook for 2–3 minutes.

4 Stir the tomatoes and mushrooms into the mixture and continue to cook, stirring, for a further 5–6 minutes.

5 Stir in the Worcester sauce and basil and season well.

6 Transfer the hash to a warmed serving dish, garnish with the fresh basil, and serve at once with crusty bread.

COOK'S TIP
Most brands of Worcester sauce contain anchovies. If cooking for vegetarians, make sure you choose a vegetarian variety.

Vegetable Jambalaya

This spicy rice dish is a vegetarian version of the traditional jambalaya.
Packed with a variety of vegetables, it is both colorful and nutritious.

NUTRITIONAL INFORMATION

Calories	181	Sugars	8g
Protein	6g	Fat	7g
Carbohydrate	25g	Saturates	1g

 10 mins   55 mins

SERVES 4

I N G R E D I E N T S

75 g/2¾ oz brown rice (see Cook's Tip)

2 tbsp olive oil

2 garlic cloves, crushed

1 red onion, cut into eight

1 eggplant, diced

1 green bell pepper, diced

5–6 baby corn ears, halved lengthwise

½ cup frozen peas

1 cup small broccoli florets

⅔ cup vegetable bouillon

8 oz/225 g can chopped tomatoes

1 tbsp tomato paste

1 tsp creole seasoning

½ tsp chili flakes

salt and pepper

1 Cook the rice in a large pan of salted boiling water for 20 minutes, or until cooked through. Drain, rinse with boiling water, drain again, and set aside.

2 Heat the oil in a heavy skillet and cook the garlic and onion, stirring constantly, for 2–3 minutes. Add the eggplant, bell pepper, corn, peas, and broccoli to the skillet and cook, stirring occasionally, for a further 2–3 minutes.

3 Stir in the vegetable bouillon and the canned tomatoes, tomato paste, creole seasoning, and chili flakes.

4 Season to taste and cook over low heat for 15–20 minutes, or until the vegetables are tender.

5 Stir the brown rice into the vegetable mixture and cook, mixing well, for 3–4 minutes, or until hot.

6 Transfer the vegetable jambalaya to a warm serving dish and serve at once.

COOK'S TIP

Use a mixture of different kinds of rice, such as wild or red rice, to add color and texture to this dish. Cook the rice in advance, following the instructions on the packet, for a speedier recipe.

Potato & Spinach Triangles

These small pasties are made with crisp phyllo pastry and filled with a tasty spinach and potato mixture flavored with chili and tomato.

NUTRITIONAL INFORMATION

Calories 514   Sugars 4g
Protein . . . . .9g   Fat 37g
Carbohydrate . . .37g   Saturates 8g

 25 mins   35 mins

SERVES 4

INGREDIENTS

2 tbsp butter, melted, plus extra
for greasing

1½ cups finely diced waxy potatoes

1 lb/450 g young spinach

1 tomato, seeded and chopped

¼ tsp chili powder

½ tsp lemon juice

½ lb/225 g phyllo pastry, thawed if frozen

salt and pepper

crisp salad, to serve

LEMON MAYONNAISE

⅔ cup mayonnaise

2 tsp lemon juice

zest of 1 lemon

1 Lightly grease a cookie sheet with a little butter.

2 Cook the potatoes in a pan of lightly salted boiling water for 10 minutes, or until cooked through. Drain thoroughly and place in a mixing bowl.

3 Meanwhile, put the spinach in a pan with 2 tablespoonfuls of water. Cover and cook over low heat for 2 minutes, until wilted. Drain the spinach thoroughly, squeezing out excess moisture, and add to the potato.

4 Stir in the chopped tomato, chili powder, and lemon juice. Season to taste with salt and pepper.

5 Lightly brush 8 sheets of phyllo pastry with melted butter. Spread out 4 of the sheets and lay the other 4 on top of each. Cut them into rectangles about 8 x 4 inches/20 x 10 cm.

6 Spoon the potato and spinach mixture on to one end of each rectangle. Fold a corner of the pastry over the filling, fold the pointed end back over the pastry strip, then fold over the remaining pastry to form a triangle.

7 Place the triangles on a cookie sheet and bake in a preheated oven, 375°F/190°C, for 20 minutes, or until golden brown.

8 To make the lemon mayonnaise, mix the mayonnaise, lemon juice, and lemon zest together in a small bowl. Serve the potato and spinach triangles warm or cold with the lemon mayonnaise and a crisp salad.

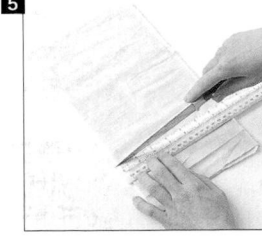

Red Onion Bruschetta

Garlic-flavored toast is topped with a melt-in-the-mouth mixture of caramelized onions, olives, and melted goat cheese.

 10 mins   20 mins

SERVES 4

INGREDIENTS

6 tbsp extra virgin olive oil

4 red onions, thickly sliced

2 tbsp balsamic vinegar

8 black olives, pitted and chopped

1 tsp fresh thyme leaves

¼ lb/115 g goat cheese, sliced

4 thick slices of country-style bread, such as ciabatta

4 garlic cloves

1 Heat 2 tablespoons of the olive oil in a large, heavy skillet. Add the onions to the skillet and cook over low heat, stirring occasionally, for about 5 minutes or until soft. Increase the heat to medium and cook, stirring occasionally, until the onions have begun to color. Add the balsamic vinegar to the pan and cook, stirring constantly, until it has almost completely evaporated. Stir in the olives and thyme leaves.

2 Toast the bread on 1 side only. Rub the toasted sides with the garlic cloves. Place the bread, toasted side down, on the broiler rack and drizzle with the remaining olive oil. Toast the second side.

3 Divide the onion mixture among the slices of toast and top with the goat cheese. Return the toast to the broiler for 2 minutes, or until the cheese has melted. Serve immediately.

VARIATION
To make little party snacks, use a slender French stick or 2 sfilatini (thin ciabatta) .

Oeufs au Nid

Soft-cooked eggs sitting in a bed of mashed potato look just as if they are resting in a nest, and they taste superb.

NUTRITIONAL INFORMATION

Calories	673	Sugars	.........4g
Protein	........18g	Fat	..........49g
Carbohydrate	...42g	Saturates	......30g

15 mins   40 mins

SERVES 4

INGREDIENTS

4 tbsp grated colby cheese

2 lb/900 g mealy potatoes, unpeeled

¾ cup butter

1 cup milk

4 eggs

salt and ground black pepper

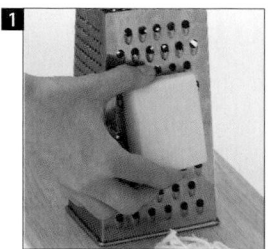

1 Grate the cheese and set aside. Cook the potatoes in lightly salted boiling water for about 25 minutes, until tender. Drain and peel. Mash the potatoes in a bowl with ½ cup of the butter until no lumps remain. Season to taste with salt and pepper. Pour in half the milk and beat vigorously with a whisk or wooden spoon. Continue whisking, adding more milk if necessary, until the potato is light and smooth.

COOK'S TIP

Don't be tempted to beat the potatoes in a food processor, as this will make them sticky and will fail to incorporate enough air to make a light mash.

2 Use a little of the remaining butter to grease an ovenproof dish. Spoon the mashed potato into the dish and make 4 hollows with the back of a spoon. Dot a little butter in each of the hollows and crack in the eggs. Season the eggs with salt and pepper.

3 Using the prongs of a fork, make grooves around each egg to create a "nest." Sprinkle the grated cheese over the eggs and bake them in a preheated oven, 400°F/200°C, for 15 minutes, or until the whites are set, but the yolks are still runny. Serve immediately.

Carrot & Potato Soufflé

Hot soufflés have a reputation for being difficult to make, but this one is both simple and impressive. Make sure you serve it as soon as it is ready.

NUTRITIONAL INFORMATION

Calories	294	Sugars	.........6g
Protein	........10g	Fat	..........9g
Carbohydrate	...46g	Saturates	.......4g

  15 mins   40 mins

SERVES 4

I N G R E D I E N T S

2 tbsp butter, melted

4 tbsp fresh whole-wheat bread crumbs

3 mealy potatoes, baked in their skins

2 carrots, grated

2 eggs, separated

2 tbsp orange juice

¼ tsp grated nutmeg

salt and pepper

carrot curls, to garnish

 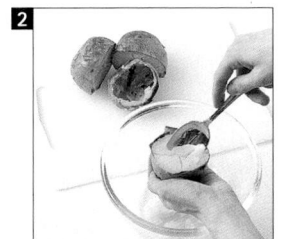 

1 Brush the inside of an 3¾ cup soufflé dish with the butter. Sprinkle about three-quarters of the bread crumbs over the base and sides.

2 Cut the baked potatoes in half and scoop the flesh into a mixing bowl.

3 Add the carrots, egg yolks, orange juice, and nutmeg to the potato flesh. Season to taste with salt and pepper.

4 In a separate bowl, whisk the egg whites until soft peaks form, then gently fold into the potato mixture with a metal spoon until well incorporated.

5 Gently spoon the potato and carrot mixture into the prepared soufflé dish. Sprinkle the remaining bread crumbs over the top of the mixture.

6 Cook in a preheated oven, 400°F/ 200°C, for 40 minutes, until risen and golden. Do not open the oven door during the cooking time, otherwise the soufflé will sink. Serve the soufflé immediately, garnished with carrot curls.

COOK'S TIP
To bake the potatoes, prick the skins and cook in a preheated oven, 375°F/ 190°C, for about 1 hour.

Vegetable Stir-Fry

A range of delicious flavors are captured in this simple recipe, which is ideal if you are in a hurry.

NUTRITIONAL INFORMATION

Calories	138	Sugars	.........5g
Protein	.........3g	Fat	..........12g
Carbohydrate	....5g	Saturates	.......2g

 5 mins   25 mins

SERVES 4

INGREDIENTS

3 tbsp vegetable oil

8 pearl onions, halved

1 eggplant, cubed

½ lb/225 g zucchini, sliced

½ lb/225 g open-cap mushrooms, halved

2 cloves garlic, crushed

2 cups canned chopped tomatoes

2 tbsp sundried tomato paste

2 tbsp soy sauce

1 tsp sesame oil

1 tbsp Chinese rice wine or dry sherry

freshly ground black pepper

fresh basil leaves, to garnish

COOK'S TIP

Basil has a very strong flavor which is perfect with vegetables and Chinese flavorings. Instead of using basil simply as a garnish in this dish, try adding a handful of fresh basil leaves to the stir-fry in step 4.

1 Heat the vegetable oil in a large preheated wok or skillet.

2 Add the pearl onions and eggplant and cook for 5 minutes, until golden and just beginning to soften.

3 Add the sliced zucchini, mushrooms, garlic, chopped tomatoes, and sundried tomato paste to the wok and cook for about 5 minutes. Reduce the heat and simmer for 10 minutes, or until the vegetables are tender, but not soft.

4 Add the soy sauce, sesame oil, and rice wine or sherry to the wok, bring back to a boil, and cook for 1 minute.

5 Season the vegetable stir-fry with freshly ground black pepper and scatter with fresh basil leaves. Serve immediately on warm serving plates.

Stuffed Globe Artichokes

This imaginative and attractive recipe for artichokes stuffed with nuts, tomatoes, olives, and mushrooms, has been adapted for the microwave.

NUTRITIONAL INFORMATION

Calories 248   Sugars 8g
Protein . . . . .5g   Fat 19g
Carbohydrate . . .16g   Saturates 2g

30 mins   25 mins

SERVES 4

INGREDIENTS

4 globe artichokes

8 tbsp water

4 tbsp lemon juice

1 onion, chopped

1 garlic clove, crushed

2 tbsp olive oil

3 cups white mushrooms, chopped

½ cup pitted black olives, sliced

2 oz/60 g sun-dried tomatoes in oil, drained and chopped

1 tbsp chopped fresh basil

1 cup fresh white bread crumbs

¼ cup pine nuts, toasted

oil from the jar of sun-dried tomatoes for drizzling

salt and pepper

1 Cut the stalks and lower leaves off the artichokes. Snip off the leaf tips with scissors. Place 2 artichokes in a large bowl with half the water and half the lemon juice. Cover and cook on HIGH power for 10 minutes, turning the artichokes over halfway through, until a leaf pulls away easily from the base. Let stand, covered, for 3 minutes before draining. Turn the artichokes upside down and let cool. Repeat to cook the remaining artichokes.

2 Place the onion, garlic, and olive oil in a bowl. Cover and cook on HIGH power for 2 minutes, stirring once. Add the mushrooms, olives, and sun-dried tomatoes. Cover and cook on HIGH power for 2 minutes.

3 Stir in the basil, bread crumbs, and pine nuts. Season the mixture to taste with salt and pepper.

4 Turn the artichokes the right way up and carefully pull the leaves apart. Remove the purple-tipped central leaves.

Using a teaspoon, scrape out the hairy choke and discard.

5 Divide the stuffing into 4 equal portions and spoon into the center of each artichoke. Push the leaves back around the stuffing.

6 Arrange the stuffed artichokes in a shallow dish and drizzle over a little oil from the jar of sun-dried tomatoes. Cook on HIGH power for 7–8 minutes to reheat, turning the artichokes around halfway through.

Baked Fennel Gratinati

Fennel is a common ingredient in Italian cooking. In this elegant dish its distinctive flavor is offset by the smooth Béchamel Sauce.

NUTRITIONAL INFORMATION

Calories 426	Sugars 9g
Protein 13g	Fat 35g
Carbohydrate ...16g	Saturates 19g

 5–10 mins 45 mins

SERVES 4

INGREDIENTS

4 fennel bulbs

2 tbsp butter

2/3 cup dry white wine

Béchamel sauce (see page 6), enriched with 2 egg yolks

½ cup fresh white bread crumbs

3 tbsp freshly grated Parmesan cheese

salt and pepper

fennel fronds, to garnish

1 Remove any bruised or tough outer stalks of fennel and cut each bulb in half. Put into a pan of lightly salted boiling water and simmer for 20 minutes until tender, then drain.

2 Butter a casserole liberally and arrange the drained fennel in it.

3 Stir the wine into the Béchamel sauce and season with salt and pepper to taste. Pour over the fennel.

4 Sprinkle evenly with the bread crumbs and then the Parmesan.

5 Bake in a preheated oven, 400°F/ 200°C, for 20 minutes until the top is golden. Serve immediately, garnished with fennel fronds.

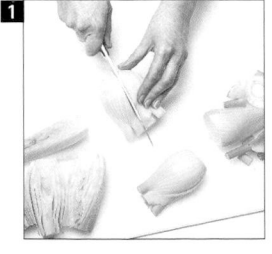 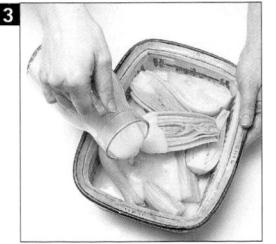 

Summer Stir-Fry

Not only are stir-fries quick and easy, they are also a great way to cook vegetables, because their flavor, color, and texture are preserved.

NUTRITIONAL INFORMATION

Calories	105	Sugars	.........5g
Protein	.........5g	Fat	...........7g
Carbohydrate	....6g	Saturates	.......1g

 15 mins   10 mins

SERVES 4

I N G R E D I E N T S

2 tbsp groundnut or sunflower oil

1 inch/2.5 cm pieces fresh root ginger, finely chopped

2 garlic cloves, finely chopped

1 cup green beans

1 cup snow peas

1 cup broccoli florets

1 cup carrots, thinly sliced diagonally

1 cup asparagus spears, thinly sliced diagonally

½ red bell pepper, thinly sliced

½ orange bell pepper, thinly sliced

½ yellow bell pepper, thinly sliced

2 celery stalks, thinly sliced

3 scallions, thinly sliced diagonally

salt

Chinese chives, to garnish

1 Prepare the vegetables. Heat half the oil in a wok or heavy skillet. Add the ginger and garlic and stir-fry for a few seconds, then add the green beans and continue to stir-fry for 2 minutes.

2 Add the snow peas and stir-fry them for 1 minute, then add the broccoli florets, carrots, and asparagus and stir-fry for a further 2 minutes.

3 Add the remaining oil to the wok or skillet with the mixed bell peppers, celery, and scallions and continue to stir-fry for an additional 2-3 minutes, or until all the vegetables are crisp-tender and heated through.

4 Season the stir-fry to taste with salt and serve immediately, garnished with Chinese chives.

COOK'S TIP
Cutting vegetables into diagonal slices maximizes their surface area so that they cook more rapidly and evenly.

Garlic & Pine Nut Tarts

A crisp lining of bread is filled with garlic butter and pine nuts to make an unusual and delightful light meal.

NUTRITIONAL INFORMATION

Calories	435	Sugars 1g
Protein	.........6g	Fat 39g
Carbohydrate	...17g	Saturates 20g

 20 mins   15 mins

SERVES 4

INGREDIENTS

4 slices whole-wheat or Granary bread

½ cup pine nuts

¾ cup butter

5 garlic cloves, peeled and halved

2 tbsp chopped fresh oregano

4 pitted black olives, halved

oregano leaves, to garnish

1 Using a rolling pin, flatten the bread slightly. Using a cookie cutter, cut out 4 circles of bread to fit your individual tart pans—they should measure about 4 inches/10 cm across. Reserve the offcuts of bread and place them in the refrigerator until required.

2 Meanwhile, place the pine nuts on a cookie sheet. Toast the pine nuts

under a preheated broiler for 2–3 minutes or until golden.

3 Put the bread offcuts, pine nuts, butter, garlic, and oregano into a food processor and blend for about 20 seconds. Alternatively, pound the ingredients by hand in a mortar with a pestle. The mixture should have a rough texture.

4 Spoon the pine nut and butter mixture into the lined pans and top with the olive halves. Bake in a preheated oven, 400°F/200°C, for 10–15 minutes or until golden.

5 Transfer the tarts to serving plates and serve warm, garnished with the fresh oregano leaves.

VARIATION

Use 7 oz/200 g puff pie dough to line 4 tart pans. Leave to chill for 20 minutes then line with foil and bake blind for 10 minutes. Remove the foil and bake for 3–4 minutes or until the dough is set. Continue from step 2, adding 2 tablespoons breadcrumbs to the mixture.

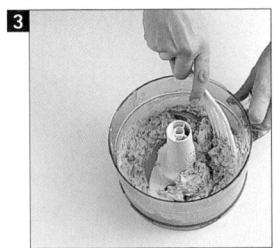

Mushroom & Onion Quiche

For the best flavor, use a mixture of several different types of mushrooms to make this delicious light quiche.

NUTRITIONAL INFORMATION

Calories	640	Sugars	........11g
Protein	........11g	Fat	..........48g
Carbohydrate	...44g	Saturates	......28g

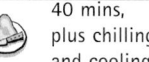

40 mins, plus chilling and cooling

1¼ hrs

SERVES 4-6

INGREDIENTS

butter, for greasing

all-purpose flour, for dusting

1 quantity rich shortcrust pie dough (see page 8), chilled

FOR THE FILLING

2 tbsp sweet butter

3 red onions, halved and sliced

¾ lb/350 g mixed exotic mushrooms, such as porcini, morels, chanterelles, and oyster

2 tsp chopped fresh thyme

1 egg

2 egg yolks

½ cup heavy cream

salt and ground black pepper

1 Lightly grease a 9 inch/23 cm loose-based quiche pan. Roll out the dough on a lightly floured surface, line the pan, and prick the base. Chill for 30 minutes. Line with foil and baking beans and bake blind in a preheated oven, 375°F/190°C, for 25 minutes. Remove the foil or paper and beans and cool on a wire rack.

2 To make the filling, melt the butter in a large, heavy skillet. Add the onions, cover, and cook over very low heat, stirring occasionally, for 20 minutes. Add the mushrooms and thyme and cook, stirring occasionally, for 10 minutes more. Spoon the mixture into the cooled pie shell and place the pan on a cookie sheet.

3 Lightly beat the egg with the egg yolks and cream and season to taste with salt and pepper. Pour the mixture over the mushroom filling and bake in a preheated oven, 350°F/180°C, for 20 minutes, until the filling is set and golden. Serve hot or at room temperature.

COOK'S TIP

If you are in a hurry, you can use ready-prepared shortcrust pie dough. Make sure that you thaw frozen pie dough thoroughly before use.

Thai-Style Omelet

In Thailand, egg dishes such as this one are eaten as part of an entrée or as a snack, depending on the time of day.

NUTRITIONAL INFORMATION

Calories ....304 Sugars 7g
Protein ....11g Fat 24g
Carbohydrate ....11g Saturates 4g

 10 mins   10 mins

SERVES 4

INGREDIENTS

3 tbsp vegetable oil

1 garlic clove, finely chopped

1 small onion, finely chopped

1 small eggplant, diced

½ small green bell pepper, seeded and chopped

1 tomato, diced

1 large dried Chinese black mushroom, soaked, drained, and sliced

1 tbsp light soy sauce

½ tsp sugar

¼ tsp ground black pepper

2 large eggs

salad greens, tomato wedges, and cucumber slices, to garnish

1 Heat half the vegetable oil in a pan and cook the garlic over high heat for 30 seconds. Add the onion and eggplant and stir-fry until golden.

2 Add the green bell pepper and stir-fry for a further minute.

3 Stir in the diced tomato, sliced mushroom, soy sauce, sugar, and black pepper. Remove from the pan and keep hot.

4 Beat the eggs lightly. Heat the remaining oil, swirling to coat the pan. Pour in the eggs and swirl to set around the pan. When the egg is set, spoon the filling into the center. Fold in the sides of the omelet to make a neat, square package.

5 Slide the omelet carefully onto a warmed dish and garnish with salad greens, tomato wedges, and cucumber slices. Serve hot.

COOK'S TIP

If you heat the pan thoroughly before adding the oil, and heat the oil before adding the ingredients, you should not have a problem with ingredients sticking to the pan.

Jacket Potatoes with Beans

Baked jacket potatoes, topped with a tasty mixture of beans in a spicy sauce, provide a deliciously filling, high-fiber dish.

NUTRITIONAL INFORMATION

Calories 378   Sugars 9g
Protein ....15g   Fat 9g
Carbohydrate ...64g   Saturates 1g

 15 mins   1¼ hrs

SERVES 6

INGREDIENTS

4lb/1.8 kg potatoes

4 tbsp vegetable ghee or oil

1 large onion, chopped

2 garlic cloves, crushed

1 tsp ground turmeric

1 tbsp cumin seeds

2 tbsp mild or medium curry paste

¾ lb/350 g cherry tomatoes

1½ cups canned black-eyed peas,
 drained and rinsed

1½ cups canned red kidney beans,
 drained and rinsed

1 tbsp lemon juice

2 tbsp tomato paste

⅔ cup water

2 tbsp chopped fresh mint or cilantro

salt and pepper

1 Scrub the potatoes and prick several times with a fork. Place in a preheated oven, 350°F/180°C, and then cook for 1–1¼ hours, or until the potatoes feel soft when gently squeezed.

2 About 20 minutes before the end of cooking time, prepare the topping. Heat the ghee or oil in a pan, then add the onion and cook over low heat, stirring frequently, for 5 minutes. Add the garlic, turmeric, cumin seeds, and curry paste and cook gently for 1 minute.

3 Stir in the tomatoes, black-eyed peas, red kidney beans, lemon juice, tomato paste, water, and chopped mint. Season to taste with salt and pepper, then cover and simmer over low heat, stirring frequently, for 10 minutes.

4 When the potatoes are cooked, cut them in half and mash the flesh lightly with a fork. Spoon the prepared bean mixture on top. Place on warmed serving plates and serve immediately.

VARIATION
Instead of cutting the potatoes in half, cut a cross in each and squeeze gently to open out. Spoon some of the prepared filling into the cross and place any remaining filling to the side.

Thai-Style Noodle Röstis

These unusual röstis, flavored with fresh lemon grass and coconut, look wonderful layered up with beansprouts, red onion, and avocado.

NUTRITIONAL INFORMATION

Calories	365	Sugars	.........2g
Protein	.........4g	Fat	..........25g
Carbohydrate	...29g	Saturates	.......2g

 5 mins   10 mins

SERVES 4

INGREDIENTS

4½ oz vermicelli rice noodles

2 scallions, finely shredded

1 lemon grass stalk, finely shredded

3 tbsp finely shredded fresh coconut

salt and pepper

vegetable oil for frying

TO SERVE

generous 1 cup beansprouts

1 small red onion, thinly sliced

1 avocado, thinly sliced

2 tbsp lime juice

2 tbsp rice wine

1 tsp chili sauce

1 Break the rice noodles into short pieces and soak in hot water for 4 minutes, or according to the packet directions. Drain thoroughly and pat dry with paper towels.

2 Stir together the noodles, scallions, lemon grass, and coconut.

3 Heat a small amount of oil until very hot in a heavy skillet. Brush a 3½ inch round cookie cutter with oil and place in the pan. Spoon a small amount of noodle mixture into the cutter to just cover the base of the skillet, then press down lightly with the back of a spoon.

4 Fry for 30 seconds, then carefully remove the cutter and continue frying the rosti until it is golden brown, turning it over once. Remove and drain on paper towels. Repeat with the remaining noodles, to make about 12 rostis.

5 To serve, arrange the noodles in stacks, with beansprouts, onion, and avocado between the layers.

6 Mix the lime juice, rice wine, and chili sauce together and spoon over the stacks just before serving.

Gnocchi with Tomato Sauce

Freshly made potato gnocchi are delicious, especially when they are topped with a fragrant tomato sauce.

NUTRITIONAL INFORMATION

Calories 216   Sugars 5g
Protein . . . . .5g   Fat 6g
Carbohydrate . . .39g   Saturates 1g

 30 mins   45 mins

SERVES 4

INGREDIENTS

¾ lb/350 g mealy potatoes, halved

⅔ cup self-rising flour, plus extra for dusting

2 tsp dried oregano

2 tbsp vegetable oil

1 large onion, chopped

2 garlic cloves, chopped

2 cups canned chopped tomatoes

½ vegetable bouillon cube dissolved in scant ½ cup boiling water

2 tbsp fresh basil, shredded, plus whole leaves to garnish

salt and pepper

Parmesan cheese, freshly grated, to serve

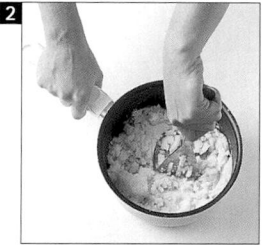  

1 Bring a large pan of water to a boil. Add the potatoes and cook for 12–15 minutes or until tender. Drain and let cool.

2 Peel and then mash the potatoes with the salt and pepper, sifted flour, and oregano. Mix together with your hands to form a dough.

3 Heat the oil in a skillet, add the onions and garlic, and cook for 3–4 minutes. Add the tomatoes and bouillon and cook, uncovered, for 10 minutes. Season with salt and pepper to taste.

4 Roll the potato dough into a sausage about 1 inch/2.5 cm in diameter. Cut the sausage into 1 inch/2.5 cm lengths. Flour your hands, then press a fork into each piece to create a series of ridges on one side and the indent of your index finger on the other side.

5 Bring a large pan of water to a boil, add the gnocchi, in batches, and cook for 2–3 minutes. They should rise to the surface when cooked. Remove from the pan with a slotted spoon, drain well, and keep warm while you are cooking the remaining batches.

6 Stir the basil into the tomato sauce and pour over the gnocchi. Garnish with basil leaves and season with pepper to taste. Sprinkle with grated Parmesan and serve immediately.

VARIATION
The gnocchi can also be served with a pesto sauce made from fresh basil leaves, pine nuts, garlic, olive oil, and romano or Parmesan cheese.

Mixed Rice, Nuts, & Raisins

This is one of the most popular nut mixtures in India and is very tasty. Make a large quantity and store it in an airtight container.

NUTRITIONAL INFORMATION

Calories ....568 Sugars 28g
Protein ....6g Fat 39g
Carbohydrate ...51g Saturates 4g

 15 mins, plus soaking   🕐 15–20 mins

SERVES 4

I N G R E D I E N T S

300 ml/½ pint vegetable oil

2 tsp onion seeds

6 curry leaves

7 oz/200 g flaked rice

2 tbsp peanuts

¼ cup raisins

⅓ cup sugar

2 tsp salt

2 tsp chili powder

1¾ oz/50 g sev (optional)

1¾ oz/50 g chana dhal, soaked in cold water for 3 hours

1 Heat the oil in a pan. Add the onion seeds and the curry leaves and fry, stirring constantly, until the onion seeds are crisp and golden.

2 Add the flaked rice to the mixture in the pan and cook until crisp and golden (do not let it burn).

3 Remove the mixture from the pan and drain on paper towels so that any excess oil is soaked up.

4 Fry the peanuts in the remaining oil, stirring constantly.

5 Add the peanuts to the flaked rice mixture, stirring to mix well.

6 Add the raisins, sugar, salt, and chili powder and mix together. Mix in the sev (if using). Transfer to a serving dish.

7 Reheat the oil remaining in the pan. Drain the soaked chana dhal, add to the pan, and fry until golden. Add to the other ingredients in the serving dish and mix together.

8 This dish can be eaten straight away but will keep well stored in an airtight container until you need it.

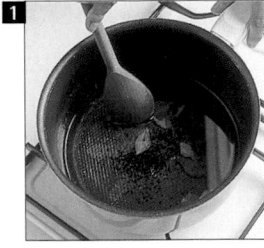  

COOK'S TIP
Sev are very thin sticks made of gram flour which can be bought in Indian and Pakistani stores.

Paglia e Fieno

This simple pasta dish, which literally means "straw and hay," makes a quick and easy, light summer lunch that is surprisingly tasty.

NUTRITIONAL INFORMATION

Calories 823   Sugars 7g
Protein . . . . .23g   Fat 43g
Carbohydrate . . .94g   Saturates 26g

 15 mins   12 mins

SERVES 4

I N G R E D I E N T S

1 lb/450 g mixed plain and green dried tagliarini or spaghetti

4 tbsp sweet butter

2 lb/900 g fresh peas, shelled

¾ cup heavy cream

½ cup freshly grated romano cheese, plus extra to serve

pinch of freshly grated nutmeg

salt and ground black pepper

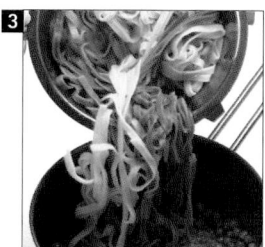

1 Bring a large pan of lightly salted water to a boil. Add the pasta to the pan, bring back to a boil, and simmer for 8–10 minutes, until tender, but still firm to the bite.

2 Meanwhile, melt the butter in a heavy pan. Add the peas and cook over low heat, stirring frequently, for 4–5 minutes. Pour in ½ cup of the cream, bring to a boil and simmer for 1 minute.

3 When the pasta is al dente, drain well and add to the peas. Pour in the extra cream, add the romano, and season to taste with nutmeg, salt, and pepper. Toss well, then transfer to a warm serving dish and serve immediately.

COOK'S TIP
Although peas freeze exceptionally well, they have neither the flavor nor the texture of fresh peas, so it is really only worth making this dish when fresh peas are in season.

Mediterranean Crêpes

A rich tomato and herb filling makes these crêpes irresistible.
They make an impressive light supper dish served with a crisp salad.

NUTRITIONAL INFORMATION

Calories	00	Sugars	. . . . .0g
Protein	. . . . .00g	Fat	. . . . .00g
Carbohydrate	. . .00g	Saturates	. . . . . . .0g

  25 mins   about 1¼ hrs

SERVES 4-6

I N G R E D I E N T S

1 tbsp sunflower oil, plus extra for brushing

1 quantity crêpe batter (see page 8)

FOR THE FILLING

2 tbsp olive oil

1 onion, chopped

2 garlic cloves, finely chopped

1 small eggplant, diced

1 red bell pepper, seeded and diced

4 tomatoes, skinned and diced

1 tbsp sun-dried tomato paste

1 tbsp chopped fresh parsley

2 tsp chopped fresh thyme

salt and ground black pepper

FOR THE TOPPING

2 tbsp butter, melted

3 tbsp freshly grated Parmesan cheese

1 Brush a crêpe pan with a little sunflower oil and heat well. Add a little of the batter and quickly tilt and rotate the pan to cover the base with a thin layer. Cook for about 1 minute, until the underside is golden. Flip over the crêpe with a spatula and cook the second side for about 30 seconds, until golden. Slide the crêpe out on to a warm plate. Cook the remaining batter in the same way to make 12 crêpes, stacking them on the plate interleaved with waxed paper.

2 To make the filling for the crêpes, heat the oil in a heavy skillet. Add the onion and cook, stirring occasionally, for 5 minutes, until soft. Add the garlic, eggplant, and red bell pepper and continue to cook, stirring occasionally, for 10 minutes. Stir in the tomatoes, sun-dried tomato paste, parsley, and thyme, season to taste with salt and pepper, cover, and simmer for 15 minutes.

3 Lightly brush an ovenproof dish with oil. Divide the filling between the crêpes, roll up, and place, seam side down, in the dish.

4 Brush the crêpes with melted butter, sprinkle with the Parmesan and bake in a preheated oven, 375°F/190°C, for 15 minutes. Serve immediately.

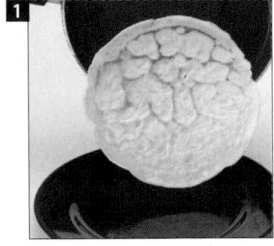

Deep-Fried Diamond Pastries

This simple-to-make snack will retain its crispness if stored in an airtight container. Serve with drinks or at coffee time.

NUTRITIONAL INFORMATION

Calories	465	Sugars	.......0.6g
Protein	.........4g	Fat	..........38g
Carbohydrate	...29g	Saturates	.......4g

15 mins   15-20 mins

SERVES 4

INGREDIENTS

generous 1 cup all-purpose flour

1 tsp baking powder

½ tsp salt

1 tbsp black cumin seeds

½ cup water

1¼ cups oil

1 Place the flour in a large mixing bowl. Add the baking powder, salt, and the black cumin seeds and stir to mix.

2 Add the water to the dry ingredients and mix together until combined to form a soft, elastic dough.

3 Roll out the dough on to a clean counter to about ¼ inch/6 mm thick.

4 Using a sharp knife, score the dough to form diamond shapes. Reroll the trimmings and cut out more diamond shapes until the dough has been used up.

5 Heat the oil in a large pan to 350°F/180°C or until a cube of bread browns in 30 seconds.

6 Carefully place the pastry diamonds in the oil, in batches if necessary, and deep-fry until golden brown.

7 Remove the diamond pastries with a slotted spoon and drain on paper towels. Serve with a dhal for dipping or store and serve when required.

COOK'S TIP
Black cumin seeds are used here for their strong aromatic flavour—do not be tempted to use white cumin seeds as a substitute.

Vegetable Dim Sum

Dim sum are small Chinese parcels which may be filled with any variety of fillings, steamed or fried, and served with a dipping sauce.

NUTRITIONAL INFORMATION

Calories	295	Sugars	.........1g
Protein	.........5g	Fat	..........22g
Carbohydrate	...20g	Saturates	.......6g

15 mins

15 mins

SERVES 4

I N G R E D I E N T S

2 scallions, chopped

2 tbsp green beans, chopped

½ small carrot, finely chopped

1 red chili, chopped

¼ cup beansprouts, chopped

1 oz/25 g white mushrooms, chopped

¼ cup unsalted cashew nuts, chopped

1 small egg, beaten

2 tbsp cornstarch

1 tsp light soy sauce

1 tsp hoisin sauce

1 tsp sesame oil

32 wonton wrappers

oil, for deep-frying

1 tbsp sesame seeds

COOK'S TIP

If preferred, arrange the wontons on a heatproof plate and then steam in a steamer for 5–7 minutes for a healthier cooking method.

1 Mix all of the vegetables together in a bowl. Add the nuts, egg, cornstarch, soy sauce, hoisin sauce, and sesame oil to the bowl. Mix well.

2 Lay the wonton wrappers out on a chopping board and spoon small quantities of the mixture into the center of each. Gather the wrapper around the filling at the top, to make little parcels, leaving the top open.

3 Heat the oil for deep-frying in a wok to 350°F/180°C or until a cube of bread browns in 30 seconds. Cook the wontons, in batches, for 1–2 minutes or until golden brown. Drain on paper towels and keep warm while cooking the remaining wontons.

4 Sprinkle the sesame seeds over the wontons. Serve the vegetable dim sum with a soy or plum dipping sauce.

Mexican-Style Pizzas

Ready-made individual pizza doughs are covered with a chili-tomato sauce and topped with kidney beans, cheese, and jalapeño chilies.

NUTRITIONAL INFORMATION

Calories	350	Sugars	.........8g
Protein	........18g	Fat	..........10g
Carbohydrate	...49g	Saturates	......3g

10 mins   20 mins

SERVES 4

I N G R E D I E N T S

4 ready-made, precooked individual
pizza crusts

1 tbsp olive oil

1 cup canned chopped tomatoes with garlic
and herbs

2 tbsp tomato paste

1 cup canned kidney beans, drained and
rinsed

⅔ cup corn kernels, thawed if frozen

1–2 tsp chili sauce

1 large red onion, shredded

1 cup grated reduced-fat sharp
Cheddar cheese

1 large green chili, seeded and sliced
into rings

salt and pepper

1 Arrange the pizza crusts on a cookie sheet and brush them lightly with the olive oil.

2 Combine the chopped tomatoes, tomato paste, kidney beans, and corn kernels in a large bowl and add chili sauce to taste. Season the mixture to taste with salt and pepper.

3 Spread the tomato and kidney bean mixture evenly over each pizza crust to cover.

4 Top each pizza with shredded onion and sprinkle with some grated Cheddar cheese and a few slices of fresh green chili to taste.

5 Bake in a preheated oven, 425°F/ 220°C, for about 20 minutes until the vegetables are tender, the cheese has melted, and the dough is crisp and golden.

6 Remove the pizzas from the cookie sheet and transfer to serving plates. Serve immediately.

COOK'S TIP
Serve a Mexican-style salad with this pizza. Arrange sliced tomatoes, fresh cilantro leaves, and a few slices of a small, ripe avocado on a platter. Sprinkle with fresh lime juice and coarse sea salt.

Cottage Potatoes

Give the humble potato a surprising kick with this spiced cheese filling.
Serve with a tomato and onion salad or on a bed of mixed salad greens.

NUTRITIONAL INFORMATION

Calories	271	Sugars	.........4g
Protein	........11g	Fat	...........6g
Carbohydrate	...29g	Saturates	.......1g

 10 mins   1 hr

SERVES 4

INGREDIENTS

4 baking potatoes

2 tsp sun-dried tomato paste

½ tsp ground coriander

1 tbsp olive oil

3–4 scallions, finely chopped

1–2 fresh green chilies, seeded and finely
  chopped

1 cup low-fat cottage cheese

1 tbsp tequila

1 tbsp finely chopped fresh cilantro

salt and ground black pepper

lime wedges and fresh cilantro sprigs,
  to garnish

1 Cut a cross in the middle of each potato and prick the skins with a fork. Wrap the potatoes individually in foil and bake in a preheated oven, 400°F/200°C, for about 1 hour, or until they are soft and cooked through.

2 Meanwhile, combine the sun-dried tomato paste and ground coriander in a small bowl. Season to taste with salt and pepper. Just before the potatoes are ready, heat the oil in a small pan and add the scallions and chopped chilies. Cook, stirring occasionally, for 2–3 minutes until soft. Stir in the sun-dried tomato paste mixture and tequila and cook for 1 minute more. Remove from the heat and stir in the chopped cilantro.

3 Place the cottage cheese in a bowl and add the tomato mixture. Stir in to blend thoroughly.

4 Unwrap the potatoes and squeeze gently to open out the cut side. Divide the cottage cheese equally among the potatoes and serve, garnished with lime wedges and cilantro sprigs.

COOK'S TIP

Speed up this recipe by cooking the potatoes in the microwave. Prick them all over with a fork and arrange on a paper towel in the oven. Cook on High for 6 minutes, turn them over and cook on High for 8 minutes more. Wrap each potato in foil and leave to stand for 5 minutes.

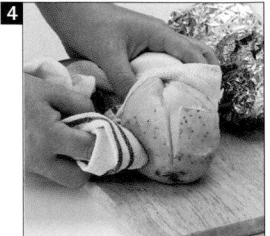

Pasta with Low-Fat Pesto

Pesto is a wonderfully versatile sauce but is usually very high in fat. The fat content in this recipe is about a quarter of that of traditional pesto.

NUTRITIONAL INFORMATION

Calories 288	Sugars 3g
Protein 15g	Fat 7g
Carbohydrate ...44g	Saturates 1g

5 mins   8–10 mins

SERVES 4

I N G R E D I E N T S

8 oz/225 g dried linguine or spaghetti

2 oz/55 g fresh basil leaves

1 oz/25 g fresh flat-leaf parsley sprigs

1 garlic clove, coarsely chopped

¼ cup pine nuts

½ cup low-fat soft cheese

2 tbsp freshly grated Parmesan cheese

salt and ground black pepper

fresh basil sprigs, to garnish

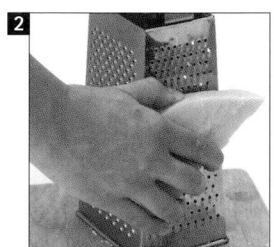

1 Bring a large pan of lightly salted water to a boil. Add the pasta, bring back to a boil and cook for 8–10 minutes, until tender but still firm to the bite. Drain and return to the pan.

2 Meanwhile, put half the basil, half the parsley, the garlic, pine nuts, and soft cheese into a blender or food processor and process until smooth. Add the remaining basil and parsley, together with the Parmesan, and season to taste. Process again briefly.

3 Add the pesto sauce to the drained pasta and toss thoroughly with 2 forks to combine.

4 Transfer the pasta to 4 warm plates and serve immediately, garnished with basil sprigs.

COOK'S TIP
If the pesto is too thick, you can dilute it with a little of the pasta cooking water—but remember to reserve it when you drain the pasta.

Spanish Potato Omelet

Adding garlic and onions to an omelet gives it extra flavor, while the potatoes give it body, making it a very satisfying snack meal.

NUTRITIONAL INFORMATION

Calories .... .300	Sugars 3g
Protein 9g	Fat .... .21g
Carbohydrate ...20g	Saturates 4g

20 mins   35 mins

SERVES 6

I N G R E D I E N T S

½ cup olive oil

1½ lb/675 g potatoes, sliced

1 large onion, sliced

1 large garlic clove, crushed

6 large eggs

salt and pepper

1 Heat a 10 inch skillet, preferably non-stick, over high heat. Pour in the oil and heat. Lower the heat, add the potatoes, onion, and garlic and cook for 15–20 minutes, stirring frequently, until the potatoes are tender.

2 Beat the eggs together in a large bowl and season generously with salt and pepper. Using a slotted spoon, transfer the potatoes and onion to the bowl of eggs. Pour the excess oil left in the skillet into a heatproof pitcher, then scrape off the crusty bits from the base of the pan.

3 Reheat the skillet. Add about 2 tablespoons of the oil reserved in the pitcher. Pour in the potato mixture, smoothing the vegetables into an even layer. Cook for about 5 minutes, shaking the skillet occasionally, or until the base of the omelet is set.

4 Shake the pan and use a spatula to loosen the side of the omelet. Place a large plate face down over the pan. Carefully invert the omelet onto the plate.

5 If you are not using a nonstick skillet, add 1 tablespoon of the reserved oil to the skillet and swirl around. Gently slide the omelet back into the skillet, cooked-side up. Use the spatula to "tuck down" the edge. Continue cooking over medium heat for 3–5 minutes until set.

6 Remove the skillet from the heat and slide the omelet onto a serving plate. Let it cool for at least 5 minutes before cutting. Serve hot, warm, or at room temperature with salad.

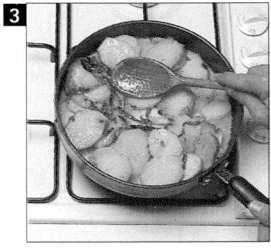

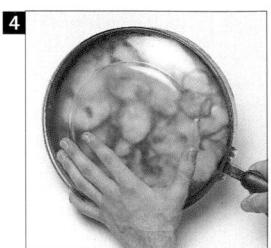

Spinach & Herb Frittata

If you find the prospect of turning over a Spanish tortilla daunting, try this Italian version of a flat omelet—it finishes cooking under a broiler.

NUTRITIONAL INFORMATION

Calories	145	Sugars	.........0g
Protein	.........8g	Fat	..........12g
Carbohydrate	....1g	Saturates	......13g

 15 mins   12 mins

SERVES 6–8

I N G R E D I E N T S

4 tbsp olive oil

6 scallions, sliced

9 oz/250 g young spinach leaves, any coarse stems removed, rinsed

6 large eggs

3 tbsp finely chopped mixed fresh herbs, such as flat-leaf parsley, thyme, and cilantro

2 tbsp freshly grated Parmesan cheese, plus extra for garnishing

salt and pepper

fresh parsley sprigs, to garnish

1 Heat a 10 inch/25 cm skillet, preferably nonstick with a flameproof handle, over medium heat. Add the oil and heat. Add the scallions and cook for about 2 minutes.

2 Add the spinach and cook until it just wilts.

3 Beat the eggs in a large bowl and season to taste with salt and pepper. Using a draining spoon, transfer the spinach and onions to the bowl of eggs and stir in the herbs. Pour the excess oil left in the skillet into a heatproof pitcher, then scrape off the crusty sediment from the bottom of the skillet.

4 Reheat the skillet. Add 2 tablespoons of the reserved oil. Pour in the egg mixture, smoothing it into an even layer. Cook, shaking the skillet occasionally, for 6 minutes or until the base is set when you lift up the side with a spatula.

5 Sprinkle the top of the frittata with the Parmesan. Place the skillet under a preheated broiler and cook for about 3 minutes or until the excess liquid is set and the cheese is golden.

6 Remove the skillet from the heat and slide the frittata onto a serving plate.

7 Let stand for at least 5 minutes before cutting and garnishing with extra Parmesan and parsley. Serve hot, warm, or at room temperature.

Soufflé Omelet

Sweet cherry tomatoes, mushrooms, and peppery arugula leaves make a mouthwatering filling for these light, fluffy omelets.

NUTRITIONAL INFORMATION

Calories	146	Sugars	2g
Protein	10g	Fat	11g
Carbohydrate	2g	Saturates	2g

1¼ hrs   45 mins

SERVES 4

INGREDIENTS

6 oz/175 g cherry tomatoes

½ lb/225 g mixed mushrooms, such as white, crimini, shiitake, and oyster

4 tbsp vegetable bouillon

small bunch of fresh thyme

4 eggs, separated

½ cup water

4 egg whites

4 tsp olive oil

1 oz/25 g arugula leaves

salt and pepper

fresh thyme sprigs, to garnish

1 Halve the tomatoes and place them in a pan. Wipe the mushrooms with paper towels, trim if necessary, and slice if large. Place the mushrooms in the pan with the tomatoes.

2 Add the bouillon, and thyme still tied together, to the pan. Bring to a boil, cover, and simmer for 5–6 minutes until tender. Drain, remove the thyme, and discard. Keep the mixture warm.

3 Meanwhile, separate the eggs and whisk the egg yolks with the water until foamy. In a clean, grease-free bowl, whisk the 8 egg whites until stiff and dry.

4 Spoon the egg yolk mixture into the egg whites and, using a metal spoon, fold together until well mixed. Take care not to knock out too much of the air.

5 For each omelet, brush a small omelet pan with 1 teaspoon of the oil and heat until hot. Pour in a quarter of the egg mixture and cook for 4–5 minutes until the mixture has set.

6 Finish cooking the omelet under a preheated medium broiler for 2–3 minutes.

7 Transfer the omelet to a warm serving plate. Fill the omelet with a few arugula leaves and a quarter of the mushroom and tomato mixture. Flip over the top of the omelet, garnish with sprigs of thyme, and serve.

Tomato & Onion Bake

This nourishing and flavorful bake is just the right thing for a weekend lunch on a cold winter day.

NUTRITIONAL INFORMATION

Calories	00	Sugars	.........0g
Protein	........00g	Fat	..........00g
Carbohydrate	...00g	Saturates	.......0g

 10 mins   1 hour

SERVES 4

INGREDIENTS

4 tbsp butter, plus extra for greasing

2 large onions, thinly sliced

1 lb/450 g tomatoes, skinned and sliced

2 cups fresh white bread crumbs

4 eggs

salt and ground black pepper

1 Grease an ovenproof dish with butter. Melt 3 tablespoons§ of the butter in a heavy skillet. Add the onions and cook over low heat, stirring occasionally, for 5 minutes, until soft.

2 Layer the onions, tomatoes, and bread crumbs in the dish, seasoning each layer with salt and pepper to taste. Dot the remaining butter on top and bake in a preheated oven, 350°F/180°C, for 40 minutes.

3 Make 4 hollows in the mixture with the back of a spoon. Crack 1 egg into each hollow. Return the dish to the oven and bake for 15 minutes more, until the eggs are just set. Serve immediately.

VARIATION

For a more substantial and spicier dish, add 2 seeded and sliced red bell peppers to the skillet once the onions have softened, and cook for 10 minutes more. Stir in a pinch of cayenne pepper before making the layers as above.

Leek & Onion Tartlets

Rather like mini quiches, these flavorful tartlets are delicious served warm or cold and are excellent picnic food.

NUTRITIONAL INFORMATION

Calories 575	Sugars 5g	
Protein 11g	Fat 47g	
Carbohydrate . . .28g	Saturates 28g	

30 mins, plus chilling and cooling   40 mins

SERVES 6

I N G R E D I E N T S

butter, for greasing

all-purpose flour, for dusting

1 quantity rich shortcrust pie dough (see page 8)

FOR THE FILLING

2 tbsp sweet butter

1 onion, thinly sliced

1 lb/450 g leeks, thinly sliced

2 tsp chopped fresh thyme

½ cup grated Swiss cheese

3 eggs

1¼ cups heavy cream

salt and ground black pepper

1 Lightly grease 6 x 10 cm/4 in tartlet pans with butter. Roll out the dough on a lightly floured surface and stamp out 6 rounds with a 5 inch/13 cm cutter, re-rolling as necessary. Gently ease the dough into the tartlet pans and prick the bases. Chill for 30 minutes. Line the pastry cases with foil or waxed paper and baking beans, place them on a cookie sheet, and bake blind in a preheated oven, 375°F/190°C, for 8 minutes. Remove the foil and beans and bake for a further 2 minutes. Transfer the pans to a wire rack to cool.

2 Meanwhile, make the filling. Melt the butter in a heavy skillet. Add the onion and cook, stirring occasionally, for 5 minutes, until soft. Add the leeks and thyme and continue to cook, stirring occasionally, for 10 minutes, until soft. Divide the leek and onion mixture among the tartlet cases, then sprinkle with the grated Swiss cheese.

3 Lightly beat the eggs with the cream and season to taste. Place the tartlet pans on a cookie sheet and divide the egg mixture among them. Bake in a preheated oven, 350°F/180°C, for 15 minutes, or until the filling is set and golden brown.

4 Transfer to a wire rack to cool slightly before removing from the pans.

Bean Burgers

These tasty veggie burgers are both delicious and nutritious—good news if you are cooking for children.

NUTRITIONAL INFORMATION

Calories ....00 Sugars 0g
Protein ....00g Fat 00g
Carbohydrate ...00g Saturates 0g

15 mins

20 mins

SERVES 4

INGREDIENTS

1 tbsp sunflower oil, plus extra for brushing

1 onion, finely chopped

1 garlic clove, finely chopped

1 tsp ground coriander

1 tsp ground cumin

5 oz/115 g white mushrooms, finely chopped

1½ cups canned red pinto or red kidney beans, drained and rinsed

2 tbsp chopped fresh flat-leaf parsley

all-purpose flour, for dusting

salt and ground black pepper

burger buns and salad, to serve

1 Heat the oil in a heavy skillet. Add the onion and cook, stirring occasionally, for 5 minutes, until soft. Add the garlic, coriander, and cumin and cook, stirring frequently, for 1 minute more. Add the mushrooms and continue to cook, stirring constantly, for 4–5 minutes until all the liquid has evaporated. Transfer the mixture to a bowl.

2 Place the beans in a small bowl and mash with a potato masher or fork.

Stir the beans into the mushroom mixture with the parsley and season to taste with salt and pepper.

3 Dust with flour. Divide the mixture into 4 portions and shape each into a flat, round patty. Brush with oil and cook under a preheated broiler for 4–5 minutes on each side. Serve immediately in burger buns with salad.

VARIATION
Substitute 4 oz/115 g mixed, finely chopped zucchini and carrot for the mushrooms.

Tomato Soufflés

These individual soufflés are cooked in tomato shells to make an intriguing and attractive dish.

NUTRITIONAL INFORMATION

Calories 179	Sugars 5g	
Protein 7g	Fat 13g	
Carbohydrate 8g	Saturates 7g	

 30 mins 30 mins

SERVES 6

I N G R E D I E N T S

6 beef tomatoes, halved

2 tbsp butter

4 tbsp all-purpose flour

2 tbsp heavy cream

2 tbsp freshly grated Parmesan cheese

½ tsp mustard powder

pinch of grated nutmeg

5 egg whites

4 egg yolks

salt and ground black pepper

1 Scoop out the flesh and seeds of the tomatoes with a teaspoon. Place the shells upside down on paper towels to drain. Place the flesh and seeds in a small pan and simmer gently for 3 minutes. Rub the mixture through a fine strainer into a small bowl and reserve.

2 Melt the butter in a small pan. Stir in the flour and cook, stirring constantly, for 1 minute. Remove the pan from the heat and gradually stir in the reserved tomato and the cream. Return the pan to the heat and cook, stirring constantly, for 2 minutes, until smooth and thickened. Remove the pan from the heat and stir in the cheese and mustard and season to taste with nutmeg, salt, and pepper. Let cool for 10 minutes.

3 Whisk the egg whites in a grease-free bowl until they form stiff peaks. Beat the egg yolks into the tomato mixture, 1 at a time. Fold 2 tablespoons of the egg whites into the mixture, then fold in the remainder. If necessary, pat dry the insides of the tomato shells, then divide the soufflé mixture among them.

4 Place on a cookie sheet and bake in a preheated oven, 425°F/220°C, for 5 minutes. Lower the oven temperature to 400°F/200°C and bake for 15-20 minutes more, until golden brown on top. Serve the soufflés immediately.

Leek & Herb Soufflé

Hot soufflés look very impressive if served as soon as they come out of the oven, otherwise they will sink quite quickly.

NUTRITIONAL INFORMATION

Calories	182	Sugars	.........4g
Protein	.........8g	Fat	..........15g
Carbohydrate	....5g	Saturates	.......2g

 15 mins   50 mins

SERVES 4

INGREDIENTS

12 oz/350 g baby leeks

1 tbsp olive oil

½ cup vegetable bouillon

½ cup walnuts

2 eggs, separated

2 tbsp chopped mixed herbs

2 tbsp unsweetened yogurt

salt and pepper

1 Using a sharp knife, chop the leeks finely. Heat the oil in a skillet. Add the leeks and sauté over medium heat, stirring occasionally, for 2–3 minutes.

2 Add the vegetable bouillon to the skillet, lower the heat, and simmer gently for a further 5 minutes.

3 Place the walnuts in a food processor and process until finely chopped. Add the leek mixture to the nuts and process briefly to form a purée. Transfer to a mixing bowl.

4 Mix together the egg yolks, the herbs, and the yogurt until thoroughly combined. Pour the egg mixture into the leek purée. Season with salt and pepper to taste and mix well.

5 In a separate, grease-free mixing bowl, whisk the egg whites until firm peaks form.

6 Fold the egg whites into the leek mixture. Spoon the mixture into a lightly greased 3½ cup soufflé dish and place on a warmed cookie sheet.

7 Cook the soufflé in a preheated oven, 350°F/180°C, for 35–40 minutes, or until well risen, set, and golden brown on top. Serve immediately.

COOK'S TIP

Placing the soufflé dish on a warm cookie sheet helps to cook the soufflé from the bottom, thus aiding its cooking and lightness.

Fresh Tomato Tarts

These tomato-flavored tarts should be eaten as fresh as possible to enjoy the flaky and crisp buttery puff pastry.

NUTRITIONAL INFORMATION

Calories	217	Sugars	. . . . .3g
Protein	. . . . .5g	Fat	. . . . .14g
Carbohydrate	. . .18g	Saturates	. . . . . . .1g

 35 mins   20 mins

SERVES 6

I N G R E D I E N T S

9 oz/250 g ready-made puff pie dough, thawed if frozen

1 egg, beaten

2 tbsp pesto (see page 121)

6 plum tomatoes, sliced

salt and pepper

fresh thyme leaves, to garnish (optional)

1 On a lightly floured counter, roll out the pie dough to a rectangle measuring 12 x 10 inches/30 x 25 cm.

2 Cut the rectangle in half and divide each half into 3 pieces to make 6 even-size rectangles. Chill in the refrigerator for 20 minutes.

3 Lightly score the edges of the pie dough rectangles and brush with the beaten egg.

4 Spread the pesto over the rectangles, dividing it equally among them, leaving a 1 inch/2.5 cm border around each one.

5 Arrange the tomato slices along the center of each rectangle on top of the pesto.

6 Season well with salt and pepper to taste and lightly sprinkle with fresh thyme leaves, if using.

7 Bake the tarts in a preheated oven, 400°F/200°C, for 15–20 minutes, until well risen and golden brown.

8 Transfer the tomato tarts to warm serving plates straight from the oven and serve while they are still piping hot and crisp.

VARIATION
Instead of individual tarts, roll the dough out to form 1 large rectangle. Spoon over the Pesto and arrange the tomatoes over the top.

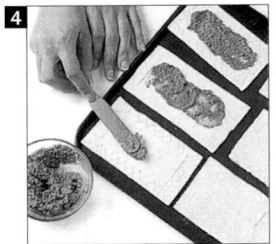

Hot Chile Pasta

Chilies are not usually associated with Italian cooking, but some regions of the country grow fiery hot chiles that are nicknamed "little devils."

NUTRITIONAL INFORMATION

Calories	320	Sugars	.........7g
Protein	........10g	Fat	...........4g
Carbohydrate	...61g	Saturates	.......0g

 10 mins   15 mins

SERVES 6

INGREDIENTS

2 garlic cloves, finely chopped

2 fresh red chiles

1¼ lb/550 g strained tomatoes or crushed plum tomatoes

1 cup canned chopped plum tomatoes

¾ cup dry white wine

4 tsp sun-dried tomato paste

1 lb/450 g dried gemelli

3 tbsp chopped fresh flat leaf parsley

salt and ground black pepper

freshly grated Parmesan cheese, to serve (optional)

1 Put the garlic, whole chiles, strained or crushed tomatoes, chopped tomatoes, white wine, and sun-dried tomato paste into a large, heavy pan and bring to a boil, stirring occasionally. Lower the heat, cover, and simmer while you cook the pasta.

2 Bring a large pan of lightly salted water to a boil. Add the pasta, bring back to a boil, and simmer for 8–10 minutes, until tender, but still firm to the bite. Drain well and place in a large warm serving dish.

3 Remove the chiles from the sauce. If you like a hot, spicy flavor, chop 1 or both and return to the sauce. If you prefer a milder flavor, discard them. Season to taste with salt and pepper, then pour the sauce on to the pasta. Add the parsley and serve immediately, with the Parmesan.

COOK'S TIP

Gemelli, which means "twins," are made from two short pieces of pasta twisted together. You can use any small pasta shapes for this dish.

Artichoke-Heart Soufflé

This exquisite dish is perfect for entertaining, but for maximum impact, be sure to serve it as soon as the dish comes out of the oven.

NUTRITIONAL INFORMATION

Calories 350   Sugars 5g
Protein ....18g   Fat 24g
Carbohydrate ...18g   Saturates 3g

 20 mins   40 mins

SERVES 4

I N G R E D I E N T S

4 tbsp butter, plus extra for greasing

½ cup all-purpose flour

1¼ cups milk

pinch of freshly grated nutmeg

2 tbsp light cream

½ cup grated Swiss cheese

6 canned artichoke hearts, drained and mashed

4 egg yolks

5 egg whites

salt and ground black pepper

1 Grease a 7½ cup soufflé dish with butter. Tie a double strip of waxed paper around the dish so that it protrudes about 5 cm/2 inches above the rim. Melt the butter in a heavy pan. Add the flour and cook, stirring constantly, for 2 minutes. Remove the pan from the heat and gradually stir in the milk. Return to the heat and bring to a boil, whisking constantly, for 2 minutes, until thickened and smooth. Remove from the heat, season to taste with nutmeg, salt, and pepper, and beat in the cream, Swiss cheese, and mashed artichoke hearts. Beat in the egg yolks, 1 at a time.

2 Whisk the egg-whites in a grease-free bowl until they form stiff peaks. Fold 2 tablespoons of the egg whites into the artichoke mixture to loosen, then gently fold in the remainder.

3 Pour the mixture into the soufflé dish and bake in a preheated oven, 190°C/375°F, for 35 minutes, until the soufflé is well risen and the top is golden brown. Serve immediately.

VARIATION

For spinach soufflé, substitute 8 oz/ 225 g cooked, drained and chopped spinach for the artichoke hearts.

Three-Cheese Soufflé

This soufflé is very simple to make, yet it has a delicious flavor and melts in your mouth. Choose three alternative cheeses, if preferred.

NUTRITIONAL INFORMATION

Calories	447	Sugars	.........1g
Protein	........22g	Fat	..........23g
Carbohydrate	...41g	Saturates	......11g

 10 mins   55 mins

SERVES 4

INGREDIENTS

2 tbsp butter

2 tsp all-purpose flour

2 lb/900 g mealy potatoes

8 eggs, separated

4 tbsp grated Swiss cheese

4 tbsp crumbled blue cheese

4 tbsp grated sharp Cheddar

salt and pepper

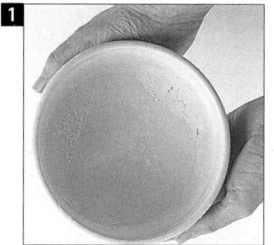

1 Butter a 10 cup soufflé dish and dust with the flour. Set aside.

2 Cook the potatoes in a pan of boiling water until tender. Mash until very smooth and then transfer to a mixing bowl to cool.

3 Beat the egg yolks into the potato and stir in the Swiss cheese, blue cheese, and Cheddar, mixing well. Season to taste with salt and pepper.

4 Whisk the egg whites until standing in peaks, then gently fold them into the potato mixture with a metal spoon until fully incorporated.

5 Spoon the potato mixture into the prepared soufflé dish.

6 Cook in a preheated oven, 425°F/ 220°C, for 35–40 minutes until risen and set. Serve immediately.

COOK'S TIP
Insert a fine skewer into the center of the soufflé; it should come out clean when the soufflé is fully cooked through.

Spicy Vegetable Fritters

These crisp, attractive little vegetable fritters, served with a spicy hot chili dip, make a fantastic snack.

NUTRITIONAL INFORMATION

Calories	290	Sugars	.........6g
Protein	.........6g	Fat	..........12g
Carbohydrate	...33g	Saturates	......10g

15 mins   10 mins

SERVES 4–6

I N G R E D I E N T S

1 cup all-purpose flour

1 tsp ground coriander

1 tsp ground cumin

1 tsp turmeric

1 tsp salt

½ tsp ground black pepper

2 garlic cloves, finely chopped

1 inch/2.5 cm piece fresh ginger, chopped

2 small green chilies, finely chopped

1 tbsp chopped fresh cilantro

about 1 cup water

1 onion, chopped

1 potato, coarsely grated

½ cup corn kernels

1 small eggplant, diced

1 cup Chinese broccoli, cut into short lengths

coconut oil for deep frying

S W E E T   C H I L I   D I P

2 bird's-eye red chilies, finely chopped

4 tbsp sugar

4 tbsp rice vinegar

1 tbsp light soy sauce

1 Make the dip by mixing together all the ingredients thoroughly until the sugar is dissolved. Cover and let stand until needed.

2 For the fritters, place the flour in a bowl and stir in the coriander, cumin, turmeric, salt, and pepper. Add the garlic, ginger, chilies, and cilantro with just enough cold water to make a thick batter.

3 Add the onion, potato, corn, eggplant, and broccoli to the batter and stir well to distribute evenly.

4 Heat the oil in a wok to 375°F/190°C, or until a cube of bread browns in 40 seconds.

5 Drop tablespoons of the batter into the hot oil and fry until golden brown and crisp, turning once. Cook in batches, if necessary, and keep any cooked fritters hot in a warm oven.

6 Drain the fritters thoroughly on paper towels, and serve immediately, with the sweet chili dip.

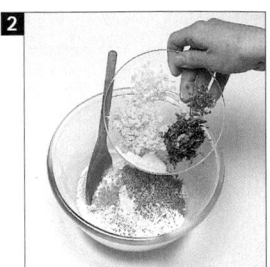

Sweet Potato Patties

Enticing little tasty mouthfuls of sweet potato, served hot and sizzling from the skillet with a delicious fresh tomato sauce.

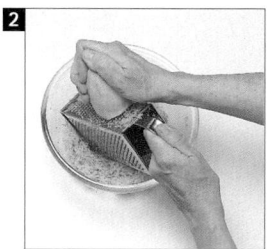

NUTRITIONAL INFORMATION

Calories	349	Sugars	.........9g
Protein	.........4g	Fat	..........24g
Carbohydrate	...32g	Saturates	.......3g

 15 mins   15 mins

SERVES 4

I N G R E D I E N T S

1 lb/450 g sweet potatoes

2 garlic cloves, crushed

1 small fresh green chili, chopped

2 fresh cilantro sprigs, chopped

1 tbsp dark soy sauce

all-purpose flour, for shaping

vegetable oil, for frying

sesame seeds, for sprinkling

S O Y - T O M A T O   S A U C E

2 tsp vegetable oil

1 garlic clove, finely chopped

1½ tsp finely chopped fresh ginger root

3 tomatoes, peeled and chopped

2 tbsp dark soy sauce

1 tbsp lime juice

2 tbsp chopped fresh cilantro

1 To make the soy-tomato sauce, heat the oil in a wok and stir-fry the garlic and ginger for about 1 minute. Add the tomatoes and stir-fry for a further 2 minutes. Remove from the heat and stir in the soy sauce, lime juice, and chopped cilantro. Set aside and keep warm.

2 Peel the sweet potatoes and grate finely (you can do this quickly with a food processor). Place the garlic, chili, and cilantro in a mortar and crush to a smooth paste with a pestle. Stir in the soy sauce and mix with the sweet potatoes.

3 Divide the mixture into 12 equal portions. Dip into flour and pat into a flat, round patty shape.

4 Heat a shallow layer of oil in a wide skillet. Cook the sweet potato patties in batches over high heat until golden, turning once.

5 Drain on paper towels and sprinkle with sesame seeds. Serve hot, with a spoonful of the soy-tomato sauce.

COOK'S TIP
Although deeper in color than light soy sauce, dark soy sauce is not so strongly flavored and is sweeter.

Spinach Patties

"Nudo" or naked is the word used to describe this mixture, which can also be made into thin crêpes or used as a filling for tortelloni.

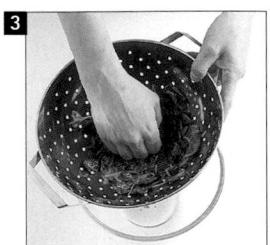

NUTRITIONAL INFORMATION

Calories	360	Sugars	.........3g
Protein	........17g	Fat	..........29g
Carbohydrate	....8g	Saturates	......18g

20 mins   30 mins

SERVES 4

INGREDIENTS

1 lb/450 g fresh spinach

1 x 8 oz tub ricotta cheese

1 egg, beaten

2 tsp fennel seeds, lightly ground

½ cup finely grated romano or Parmesan cheese

3½ tbsp all-purpose flour, mixed with 1 tsp dried thyme

5 tbsp butter

2 garlic cloves, minced

salt and pepper

1 Wash the spinach and trim off any long stalks. Place in a pan, cover, and cook for 4–5 minutes, or until wilted. This will probably have to be done in batches as the volume of spinach is quite large. Place in a strainer and let drain and cool.

COOK'S TIP

Once it is washed, spinach holds enough water on the leaves to cook without adding any extra liquid. If you use frozen spinach instead of fresh, simply defrost it and squeeze out the excess water.

2 Mash the ricotta and beat in the egg and the fennel seeds. Season with plenty of salt and pepper, then stir in the romano or Parmesan cheese.

3 Squeeze as much excess water as possible from the spinach, then finely chop the leaves. Stir the spinach into the cheese mixture.

4 Taking about 1 tablespoon of the spinach and cheese mixture, shape it into a ball, then flatten it slightly to form a patty. Gently roll in the seasoned flour.

Continue this process until all of the mixture has been used up.

5 Half fill a large skillet with water and bring to a boil. Carefully add the patties and cook for 3–4 minutes, or until they rise to the surface. Remove with a draining spoon.

6 Melt the butter in a pan. Add the garlic and cook for 2–3 minutes. Pour the garlic butter over the patties and season with freshly ground black pepper, then serve at once.

Sweet Potato & Leek Patties

Sweet potatoes have very dense flesh and a delicious, sweet, earthy taste, which contrasts well with the pungent flavor of the ginger.

NUTRITIONAL INFORMATION

Calories	403	Sugars	. . . . .34g
Protein	. . . . .8g	Fat	. . . . .12g
Carbohydrate	. . .67g	Saturates	. . . . . .2g

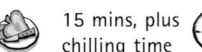

15 mins, plus chilling time

40 mins

SERVES 4

INGREDIENTS

2 lb/900 g sweet potato

4 tsp sunflower oil

2 leeks, trimmed and finely chopped

1 garlic clove, crushed

2 tsp finely chopped fresh ginger root

scant cup canned corn kernels, drained

2 tbsp low-fat unsweetened yogurt

generous ½ cup whole-wheat flour

salt and pepper

ginger sauce

2 tbsp white wine vinegar

2 tsp superfine sugar

1 red chili, seeded and chopped

1 inch/2.5 cm piece fresh ginger root, cut into thin strips

2 tbsp ginger wine

4 tbsp vegetable bouillon

1 tsp cornstarch

TO SERVE

lettuce leaves

1 scallion, shredded

1 Peel the potatoes. Cut into thick cubes and boil for 10–15 minutes. Drain well and mash. Let cool.

2 Heat 2 tsp of oil and sauté the leeks, garlic, and ginger for 2–3 minutes. Stir into the potato with the corn, unsweetened yogurt, and seasoning. Form into 8 patties and toss in the flour. Chill for 30 minutes. Place the patties on a preheated broiler rack and lightly brush with oil. Broil for 5 minutes, then turn over, brush with oil, and broil for another 5 minutes.

3 Place the vinegar, sugar, chili, and ginger in a pan and simmer for 5 minutes. Stir in the wine. Blend the bouillon and cornstarch and add to the sauce, stirring until thickened. Serve the patties with lettuce and scallions, and the sauce.

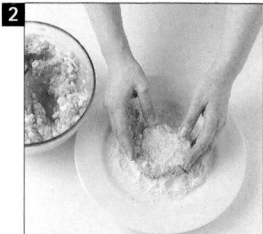

Roasted Summer Vegetables

This appetizing and colorful mixture of Mediterranean vegetables makes a sensational summer lunch.

NUTRITIONAL INFORMATION

Calories 142   Sugars 13g
Protein ....4g   Fat 7g
Carbohydrate ...18g   Saturates 1g

 10 mins   🕐 20-25 mins

SERVES 4

INGREDIENTS

2 tbsp olive oil

1 fennel bulb, cut into wedges

2 red onions, cut into wedges

2 beef tomatoes, cut into wedges

1 eggplant, thickly sliced

2 zucchini, thickly sliced

1 yellow bell pepper, seeded and cut into chunks

1 red bell pepper, seeded and cut into chunks

1 orange bell pepper, seeded and cut into chunks

4 garlic cloves

4 fresh rosemary sprigs

ground black pepper

crusty bread, to serve (optional)

COOK'S TIP

You can also serve this dish as an accompaniment. This quantity will serve 8 people.

1 Prepare the vegetables. Brush an ovenproof dish with a little oil. Arrange the fennel, onions, tomatoes, eggplant, zucchini, and bell peppers in the dish and tuck the garlic cloves and rosemary sprigs among them. Drizzle with the remaining oil and season to taste with pepper.

2 Roast the vegetables in a preheated oven, 400°F/200°C, for 10 minutes.

3 Turn the vegetables over, return the dish to the oven, and roast for a further 10-15 minutes, or until the vegetables are tender and beginning to turn golden brown.

4 Serve the vegetables straight from the dish or transfer to a warm serving platter. Serve immediately, with crusty bread, if you like, to soak up the juices.

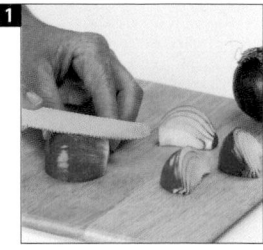 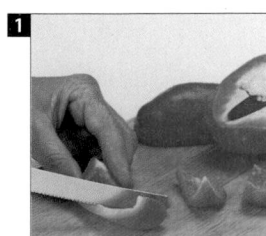 

Filled Pocket Breads

Pocket breads are warmed over hot coals, then split and filled
with a Greek salad tossed in a fragrant rosemary dressing.

NUTRITIONAL INFORMATION

Calories	456	Sugars	.........4g
Protein	........13g	Fat	..........25g
Carbohydrate	...49g	Saturates	.......7g

 15 mins   10 mins

SERVES 4

I N G R E D I E N T S

½ iceberg lettuce, roughly chopped

2 large tomatoes, cut into wedges

3 inch/7.5 cm piece of cucumber, cut
into chunks

¼ cup pitted black olives

¼ lb/115 g feta cheese

4 pocket breads

D R E S S I N G

6 tbsp olive oil

3 tbsp red wine vinegar

1 tbsp crushed rosemary

½ tsp superfine sugar

salt and pepper

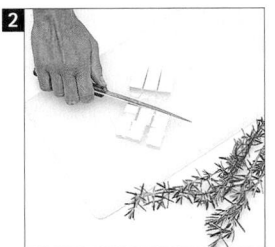

1 To make the salad, combine the
lettuce, tomatoes, cucumber, and
black olives.

2 Cut the feta cheese into chunks and
add to the salad. Toss gently.

3 To make the dressing, whisk together
the olive oil, red wine vinegar,
rosemary, and sugar. Season to taste with
salt and pepper. Place in a small pan or
heatproof bowl and heat very gently or
place on the side of a barbecue grill to
warm through gently.

4 Wrap the individual pocket breads
tightly in foil and place on a barbecue
grill over hot coals for 2–3 minutes, turning
once, to warm through.

5 Unwrap the pocket breads and split
them open. Fill with the Greek salad
mixture and drizzle over the warm
dressing. Serve immediately.

COOK'S TIP
Substitute different herbs
for the rosemary—either oregano
or basil would make a delicious
alternative. Pack plenty of the
salad into the pocket breads—
they taste much better when
they are full to bursting.

Cauliflower Cheese Surprise

The surprise is all the other delicious ingredients cooked with the cauliflower in this version of the well-known family favorite.

NUTRITIONAL INFORMATION

Calories	549	Sugars	.......20g
Protein	........24g	Fat	.........32g
Carbohydrate	...43g	Saturates	......17g

 15 mins   15 mins

SERVES 4

INGREDIENTS

2 tbsp sunflower oil

2 onions, chopped

¼ lb/115 g mushrooms, chopped

4 tomatoes, skinned and chopped

scant cup canned corn kernels, drained

1 large cauliflower, cut into florets

2½ cups Cheese Sauce (see page 304), made with ½ cup Cheddar and ½ cup Swiss cheese

4 tbsp freshly grated Parmesan cheese

4 tbsp dry bread crumbs

salt and ground black pepper

1 Heat the sunflower oil in a heavy skillet. Add the onions and cook over low heat, stirring occasionally, for 5 minutes, until soft. Add the mushrooms and cook, stirring occasionally, for 5 minutes. Add the tomatoes and corn, mix well, and heat through.

2 Meanwhile, cook the cauliflower in a pan of lightly salted boiling water for 5–10 minutes, until just tender. Drain well and keep warm.

3 Stir ⅝ cup of the cheese sauce into the onion and corn mixture, then spoon it into a large, flameproof dish. Top with cauliflower and pour the remaining cheese sauce over it.

4 Combine the grated Parmesan and the bread crumbs and sprinkle them over the top. Place under a preheated broiler for 3-5 minutes, until lightly browned. Serve the cauliflower cheese immediately, on warmed plates.

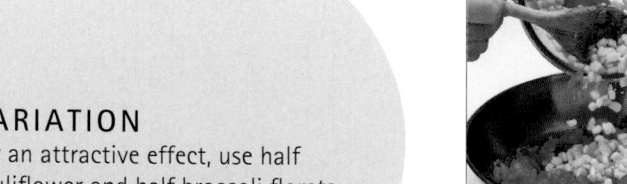

VARIATION
For an attractive effect, use half cauliflower and half broccoli florets.

Lattice Pie

This pretty pie, with its lattice effect revealing the pale green spinach filling, looks every bit as good as it tastes. Serve warm or cold.

NUTRITIONAL INFORMATION

Calories	930	Sugars	.........8g
Protein	........28g	Fat	..........59g
Carbohydrate	...78g	Saturates	......33g

30 mins   1 hr

SERVES 4–6

I N G R E D I E N T S

butter, for greasing

all-purpose flour, for dusting

2 x quantity rich shortcrust pie dough (see page 8), chilled

lightly beaten egg, to glaze

F O R   T H E   F I L L I N G

1 lb/450 g frozen spinach, thawed

2 tbsp olive oil

1 large onion, chopped

2 garlic cloves, finely chopped

2 eggs, lightly beaten

1 x 8 oz tub ricotta cheese

½ cup freshly grated Parmesan cheese

pinch of freshly grated nutmeg

salt and ground black pepper

1 To make the filling, drain the spinach and squeeze out as much moisture as possible. Heat the oil in a large, heavy skillet. Add the onion and cook, stirring occasionally, for 5 minutes, until soft. Add the garlic and spinach to the skillet and continue to cook, stirring occasionally, for a further 10 minutes.

2 Remove the skillet from the heat, let the mixture cool slightly, transfer to a bowl, then beat in the eggs and cheeses. Season to taste with nutmeg, salt, and pepper.

3 Lightly grease a 9 inch/23 cm loose-based quiche pan with butter. Roll out two-thirds of the dough on a lightly floured surface and use to line the quiche pan, leaving the dough overhanging the sides. Spoon in the spinach mixture, spreading it evenly over the base.

4 Roll out the remaining dough on a lightly floured surface and cut into ¼ inch/5 mm strips. Arrange the strips in a lattice pattern on top of the pie, pressing the ends securely to seal. Trim any excess pastry. Brush with the egg glaze and bake in a preheated oven, 400°F/200°C, for about 45 minutes, until golden brown.

5 Transfer the pie to a wire rack to cool slightly before removing from the pan.

Egg Curry

This curry can be made very quickly. It can either be served as a side dish or, with parathas, as a light lunch.

NUTRITIONAL INFORMATION

Calories 189   Sugars 3g
Protein . . . . .7g   Fat 16g
Carbohydrate . . . .4g   Saturates 3g

 10 mins   15 mins

SERVES 4

I N G R E D I E N T S

4 tbsp vegetable oil

1 medium onion, sliced

1 fresh red chili, finely chopped

½ tsp chili powder

½ tsp fresh ginger root, finely chopped

½ tsp fresh garlic, crushed

4 medium eggs

1 firm tomato, sliced

fresh cilantro leaves

parathas, to serve (optional)

1 Heat the oil in a large, heavy pan. Add the sliced onion to the pan and fry over medium heat, stirring occasionally, for about 5 minutes, until it is just soft and a light golden color.

2 Lower the heat. Add the fresh red chili, the chili powder, the chopped ginger, and the crushed garlic to the pan and fry over low heat, stirring constantly, for about 1 minute.

3 Add the eggs and tomatoes to the pan and continue cooking, stirring to break up the eggs when they begin to cook, for a further 3–5 minutes.

4 Sprinkle the fresh cilantro leaves over the curry and transfer it to warm serving plates.

5 Serve the egg curry immediately, with parathas to accompany it, if you wish.

COOK'S TIP

Both the leaves and the finely chopped stems of cilantro are used in Indian cooking, to flavor dishes and as edible garnishes. It has a very distinctive and pronounced taste.

Layered Vegetable Bake

Simple to prepare, this tasty bake makes a superb meal in itself, or it can be served as an accompaniment.

NUTRITIONAL INFORMATION

Calories	174	Sugars	.........4g
Protein	.........5g	Fat	...........4g
Carbohydrate	...33g	Saturates	.......1g

 10 mins   1½ hrs

SERVES 4

INGREDIENTS

1 tbsp olive oil, for brushing

1½ lb/675 g potatoes, thinly sliced

8 fresh basil leaves

2 leeks, sliced

2 beefsteak tomatoes, sliced

1 garlic clove, finely chopped

1¼ cups vegetable bouillon

salt and ground black pepper

  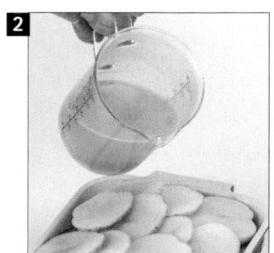

1 Brush a large ovenproof dish with a little of the olive oil. Place a layer of potato slices in the base, sprinkle with half the basil leaves, and cover with a layer of leeks. Top with a layer of tomato slices. Repeat these layers until all the vegetables are used up, ending with a layer of potatoes.

2 Stir the chopped garlic into the bouillon and season to taste with salt and pepper. Pour the bouillon over the vegetables and brush the top with the remaining olive oil.

3 Bake in a preheated oven, 350°F/ 180°C, for 1½ hours, or until the vegetables are tender and the topping is golden brown. Serve immediately, on warmed plates.

COOK'S TIP
Try to find sun-ripened tomatoes, which have a sweeter and fuller flavor than those grown under glass.

Savory Bell Pepper Bread

This flavorful bread contains only the minimum amount of fat.
Serve with a bowl of hot soup for a filling and nutritious light meal.

NUTRITIONAL INFORMATION

Calories	468	Sugars	........11g
Protein	........16g	Fat	...........5g
Carbohydrate	...97g	Saturates	......1g

2 hrs   50 mins

SERVES 4

INGREDIENTS

1 small red bell pepper

1 small green bell pepper

1 small yellow bell pepper

2 oz/60 g dry-pack sun-dried tomatoes

¼ cup boiling water

2 tsp dried yeast

1 tsp superfine sugar

⅔ cup tepid water

3 cups strong white bread flour

2 tsp dried rosemary

2 tbsp tomato paste

⅔ cup low-fat unsweetened yogurt

1 tbsp coarse salt

1 tbsp olive oil

1 Preheat the oven to 425°F/220°C and the broiler to hot. Halve and seed the bell peppers, arrange on the broiler rack, and cook until the skin is charred. Let cool for 10 minutes, peel off the skin, and chop the flesh. Slice the tomatoes into strips, place in a bowl, pour over the boiling water, and let soak.

2 Place the yeast and sugar in a small pitcher, pour over the tepid water, and let stand for 10–15 minutes until foamy. Strain the flour into a bowl and add 1 tsp dried rosemary. Make a well in the center and pour in the yeast.

3 Add the tomato paste, tomatoes and soaking liquid, bell peppers, yogurt, and half the salt. Mix to form a soft dough. Turn out on to a lightly floured surface and knead for 3–4 minutes until smooth and elastic. Place in a lightly floured bowl, cover, and let rise in a warm room for 40 minutes until doubled in size.

4 Knead the dough again and place in a lightly greased 9 inch/23 cm round spring-clip cake pan. Using a wooden spoon, form "dimples" in the surface. Cover and let stand for 30 minutes. Brush with the olive oil and sprinkle with the dried rosemary and coarse salt. Bake for 35–40 minutes, cool for 10 minutes and release from the pan. Let cool on a rack and serve.

COOK'S TIP

For a quick, filling snack, serve the bread with a bowl of hot soup in winter, or a crisp leaf salad in summer.

Onion & Mozzarella Tarts

These individual tarts are delicious served either hot or cold and are great for school lunches or as picnic food.

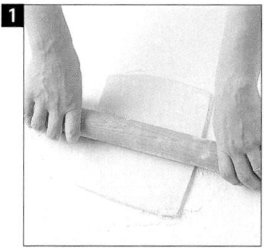

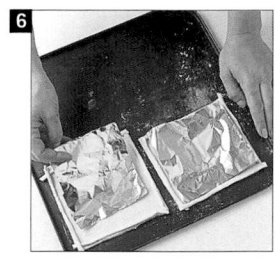

NUTRITIONAL INFORMATION

Calories 327	Sugars 3g	
Protein 5g	Fat 23g	
Carbohydrate ...25g	Saturates 9g	

45 mins | 45 mins

SERVES 4

I N G R E D I E N T S

9 oz/250 g packet puff pie dough, thawed if frozen

2 red onions

1 red bell pepper

8 cherry tomatoes, halved

¼ lb/100 g mozzarella cheese, cut into chunks

8 sprigs thyme

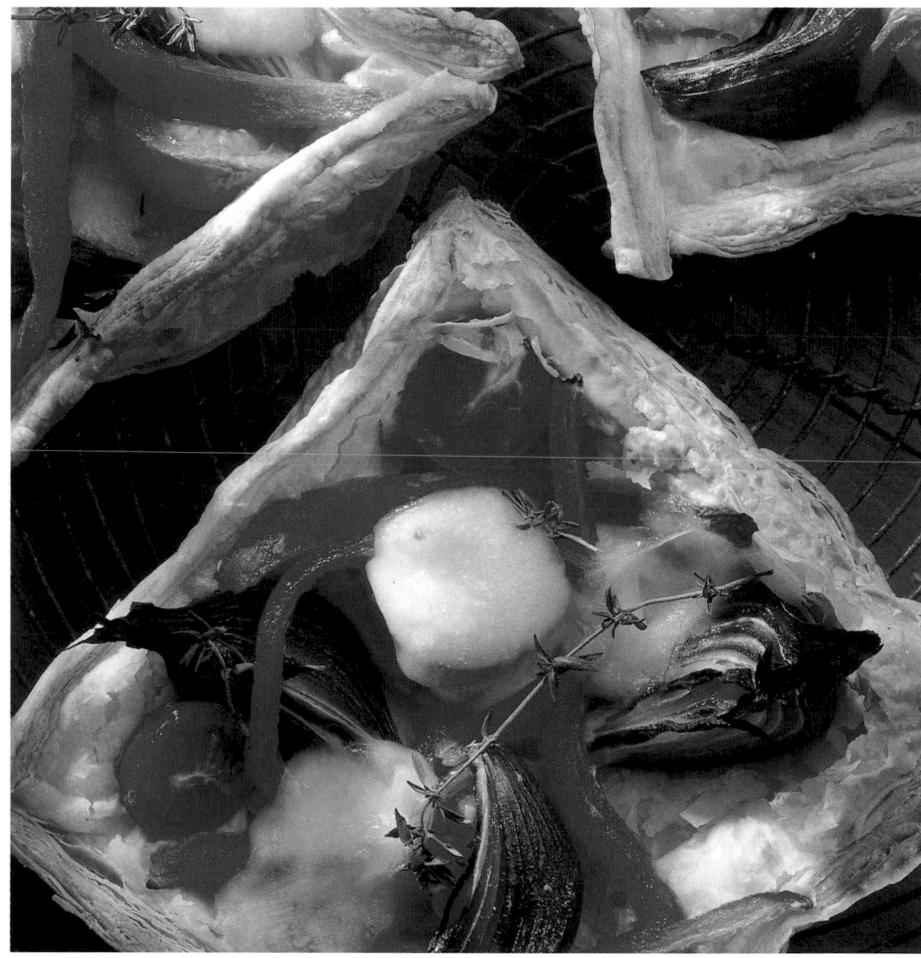

1 Roll out the pie dough on a lightly floured surface to make 4 squares, each 3 inches/7.5 cm wide. Using a sharp knife, trim the edges of the dough, reserving the trimmings. Chill the dough squares in the refrigerator for about 30 minutes.

2 Place the dough squares on a cookie sheet. Brush a little water along the edge of each square and use the reserved dough trimmings to make a rim around each tart.

3 Cut the red onions into thin wedges and halve and seed the bell pepper.

4 Place the onions and bell pepper in a roasting pan. Cook under a preheated broiler for 15 minutes or until the bell pepper skin is blackened and charred.

5 Place the roasted bell pepper halves in a plastic bag and set aside to sweat for 10 minutes, then peel off the skin and cut the flesh into strips.

6 Line the dough squares with foil. Bake in a preheated oven, 400°F/200°C, for 10 minutes. Remove the foil squares and bake the squares for a further 5 minutes.

7 Divide the onions, bell pepper strips, tomatoes, and cheese among the tarts and sprinkle with the fresh thyme.

8 Return to the oven for 15 minutes or until the tarts are golden and the cheese is melted. Transfer the tarts to warm serving plates if serving hot, or to a cooling tray if serving cold.

Baked Potatoes with Pesto

This is an easy but very filling meal. The potatoes are baked until fluffy, then they are mixed with a tasty pesto filling and baked again.

NUTRITIONAL INFORMATION

Calories	444	Sugars	.........3g
Protein	........10g	Fat	..........28g
Carbohydrate	...40g	Saturates	......13g

10 mins   1½ hrs

SERVES 4

I N G R E D I E N T S

4 large baking potatoes

⅔ cup heavy cream

⅓ cup vegetable bouillon

1 tbsp lemon juice

2 garlic cloves, crushed

3 tbsp chopped basil

2 tbsp pine nuts

2 tbsp grated Parmesan cheese

salt and pepper

1 Scrub the potatoes well and prick the skins with a fork. Rub a little salt into the skins and place on a cookie sheet.

2 Cook in a preheated oven, 375°F/ 190°C, for 1 hour, or until the potatoes are cooked through and the skins are crisp.

3 Remove the potatoes from the oven and cut them in half lengthwise. Using a spoon, scoop the potato flesh into a mixing bowl, leaving a thin shell of potato inside the skins. Mash the potato flesh with a fork.

4 Meanwhile, mix the cream and bouillon in a pan and simmer over low heat for about 8–10 minutes, or until reduced by half.

5 Stir in the lemon juice, garlic, and chopped basil and season to taste with salt and pepper. Stir the mixture into the mashed potato flesh, together with the pine nuts.

6 Spoon the mixture back into the potato shells and sprinkle the Parmesan cheese on top. Return the potatoes to the oven for 10 minutes, or until the cheese has browned, and serve.

VARIATION
Add full-fat soft cheese or thinly sliced mushrooms to the mashed potato flesh in step 5, if you prefer.

Vegetable Calzone

These pizza-dough parcels are great for making in advance and freezing—they can be defrosted when required for a quick snack.

NUTRITIONAL INFORMATION

Calories	446	Sugars	........10g
Protein	........16g	Fat	...........8g
Carbohydrate	...82g	Saturates	.......2g

  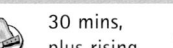

30 mins, plus rising   40 mins

MAKES 4

INGREDIENTS

DOUGH

450 g/1 lb strong white flour

2 tsp active dried yeast

1 tsp superfine sugar

⅔ cup vegetable bouillon

⅔ cup strained tomatoes

beaten egg

FILLING

1 tbsp vegetable oil

1 onion, chopped

1 garlic clove, crushed

2 tbsp chopped sun-dried tomatoes

100 g/3½ oz spinach, chopped

3 tbsp canned and drained corn kernels

4 green beans, cut into three

1 tbsp tomato paste

1 tbsp chopped oregano

2 oz/50 g sliced mozzarella cheese

salt and pepper

1 Strain the flour into a bowl. Add the dried yeast and sugar and beat in the vegetable bouillon and strained tomatoes to make a smooth dough.

2 Knead the dough on a lightly floured surface for 10 minutes, then place in a clean, lightly oiled bowl and let rise in a warm place for 1 hour.

3 Heat the oil in a skillet and sauté the onion for 2–3 minutes. Stir in the garlic, tomatoes, spinach, corn, and beans and cook for 3–4 minutes. Add the tomato paste and oregano and season well.

4 Divide the risen dough into 4 equal portions and roll each portion out on a floured surface to form an 7 inch/18 cm circle. Spoon a quarter of the filling mixture on to one half of each circle and top with the sliced mozzarella cheese.

5 Fold the dough over to encase the filling, pressing the edge firmly with a fork to seal. Glaze the dough with the beaten egg.

6 Put the calzone on a lightly greased cookie sheet and cook in a preheated oven, 425°F/220°C, for 25–30 minutes until risen and golden. Serve warm.

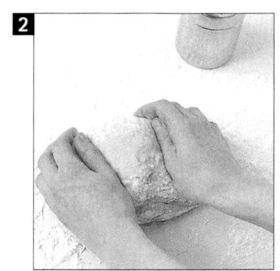

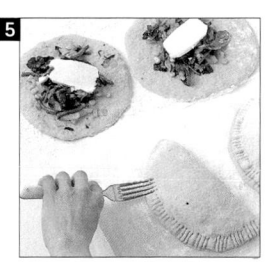

Golden Macaroni Cheese

Always a useful store-cupboard stand-by, macaroni cheese can still be a little dull, but adding some extra ingredients livens it up.

NUTRITIONAL INFORMATION

Calories 618	Sugars 12g
Protein 29g	Fat 32g
Carbohydrate . . .58g	Saturates 18g

15 mins   20 mins

SERVES 4

I N G R E D I E N T S

scant 2 cups dried elbow macaroni

1 onion, sliced

4 cherry tomatoes, halved

4 hard-cooked eggs, quartered

3 tbsp dried bread crumbs

2 tbsp finely grated brick cheese

salt

C H E E S E   S A U C E

3 tbsp butter

⅓ cup all-purpose flour

2½ cups milk

1 cup grated brick cheese

pinch of cayenne pepper

1 Bring a large pan of lightly salted water to a boil. Add the macaroni and onion, bring back to a boil, and cook for 8-10 minutes, until the pasta is tender, but still firm to the bite. Drain well and tip the macaroni and onion into an ovenproof dish.

2 To make the cheese sauce, melt the butter in a pan. Stir in the flour and cook, stirring constantly, for 1-2 minutes. Remove the pan from the heat and gradually whisk in the milk.

3 Return the pan to the heat and bring to a boil, whisking constantly. Simmer for about 2 minutes, until the sauce is thick and glossy.

4 Remove the pan from the heat, stir in the cheese, and season to taste with cayenne and salt.

5 Pour the sauce over the macaroni, add the hard-cooked eggs, and mix lightly. Arrange the tomato halves on top. Mix together the bread crumbs and finely grated brick cheese and sprinkle over the surface.

6 Cook under a preheated broiler for 3-4 minutes, until the topping is golden brown and bubbling. Serve the macaroni cheese immediately.

COOK'S TIP

Always remove the pan from the heat before stirring in the grated cheese, or the sauce will become rubbery.

Penne with Walnut Sauce

Pasta is wonderfully versatile and goes with a wide range of vegetables. Here it is served in a creamy sauce with walnuts and herbs.

NUTRITIONAL INFORMATION

Calories 635   Sugars 8g
Protein ....19g   Fat 29g
Carbohydrate ...82g   Saturates 8g

15 mins   35 mins

SERVES 4

INGREDIENTS

2 tbsp butter

3 tbsp olive oil

2 red onions, thinly sliced

1 lb/450 g zucchini, thinly sliced

3½ cups dried penne

½ cup chopped walnuts

3 tbsp chopped fresh flat-leaf parsley

2 tbsp crème fraîche (see page 8)

2 tbsp freshly grated Parmesan cheese

salt and ground black pepper

1 Melt the butter with the olive oil in a large, heavy skillet. Add the sliced red onions, cover, and cook over low heat, stirring occasionally, for 5 minutes, until soft. Add the zucchini to the skillet, cover, and continue to cook, stirring occasionally, for 15-20 minutes, until the vegetables are very tender.

2 Bring a large pan of lightly salted water to a boil. Add the pasta to the pan, bring back to a boil, and simmer for 8-10 minutes, until the pasta is tender, but still firm to the bite.

3 Meanwhile, stir the walnuts, parsley, and crème fraîche into the zucchini mixture and add salt and pepper to taste.

4 When the pasta is al dente, drain it and tip into a serving dish. Add the zucchini mixture and toss well. Sprinkle over the grated Parmesan and serve the pasta immediately.

COOK'S TIP
For perfect pasta, start checking for tenderness, by breaking off a small piece and biting it, when it has been cooking for about 7 minutes. As soon as it is ready, turn off the heat and drain.

Spinach & Ricotta Shells

This is a classic combination in which the smooth, creamy cheese balances the sharper taste of the spinach.

NUTRITIONAL INFORMATION

Calories 672	Sugars 10g	
Protein 23g	Fat 26g	
Carbohydrate ...93g	Saturates 8g	

5 mins   40 mins

SERVES 4

INGREDIENTS

14 oz/400 g dried lumache rigate grande pasta

5 tbsp olive oil

1 cup fresh white bread crumbs

½ cup milk

10½ oz/300 g frozen spinach, thawed and drained

1 cup ricotta cheese

pinch of freshly grated nutmeg

2 cups canned chopped tomatoes, drained

1 garlic clove, crushed

salt and pepper

1 Bring a large pan of lightly salted water to a boil. Add the lumache and 1 tablespoon of the olive oil, bring back to a boil, and cook for 8–10 minutes until just tender, but still firm to the bite. Drain the pasta, refresh under cold water and set aside until required.

2 Put the bread crumbs, the milk, and 3 tablespoons of the remaining olive oil in a food processor and process to combine.

3 Add the spinach and ricotta cheese to the food processor and process to a smooth mixture. Transfer the mixture to a bowl, stir in the nutmeg, and season with salt and pepper to taste.

4 Mix together the tomatoes, garlic, and the remaining tablespoon of oil and spoon the mixture into the base of a large ovenproof dish.

5 Using a teaspoon, fill the lumache with the spinach and ricotta mixture and arrange on top of the tomato mixture in the dish.

6 Cover and bake in a preheated oven, 350°F/180°C, for 20 minutes. Serve the stuffed pasta shells hot, straight from the dish.

COOK'S TIP

Ricotta is a creamy Italian cheese traditionally made from sheeps' milk whey. It is soft and white, with a smooth texture and a slightly sweet flavor. It should be used within 2–3 days of purchase.

Eggplant Sandwiches

These unusual and delicious grilled sandwiches are made
from two slices of eggplant with a cheese and tomato filling.

NUTRITIONAL INFORMATION

Calories 270   Sugars 4g
Protein . . . . .10g   Fat 15g
Carbohydrate . . .25g   Saturates 7g

5 mins   10–15 mins

SERVES 2

INGREDIENTS

1 large eggplant

1 tbsp lemon juice

3 tbsp olive oil

1 cup grated mozzarella cheese

2 sun-dried tomatoes, chopped

salt and pepper

TO SERVE

Italian bread, such as focaccia or ciabatta

mixed salad greens

slices of tomato

1 Slice the eggplant into thin rounds, using a very sharp knife.

2 Combine the lemon juice and olive oil in a small bowl and season the mixture with salt and pepper to taste.

3 Brush the eggplant slices with the oil and lemon juice mixture and grill over medium hot coals for 2–3 minutes, without turning, until they are golden on the underside.

4 Turn half of the eggplant slices over and sprinkle with cheese and chopped sun-dried tomatoes.

5 Place the remaining eggplant slices on top of the cheese and tomatoes,

turning them over so that the pale side is now uppermost.

6 Grill for 1–2 minutes, then carefully turn the whole sandwich over and grill for another 1–2 minutes, basting with the oil mixture.

7 Serve the eggplant sandwiches with Italian bread, mixed salad greens, and a few slices of tomato.

VARIATION

Try feta cheese instead of mozzarella but omit the salt from the basting oil because feta is quite salty. A creamy goat cheese would be equally delicious.

Corn Patties

These are a delicious addition to any party buffet, and very simple to prepare. Serve with a sweet chili sauce.

  10 mins   10 mins

SERVES 6

I N G R E D I E N T S

1½ cups canned corn kernels, drained

1 onion, finely chopped

1 tsp curry powder

1 garlic clove, crushed

1 tsp ground coriander

2 scallions, chopped

3 tbsp all-purpose flour

½ tsp baking powder

1 large egg

4 tbsp sunflower oil

salt

1 Mash the drained corn kernels lightly in a medium-sized bowl. Add the onion, curry powder, garlic, ground coriander, scallions, flour, baking powder, and egg. Stir well to combine thoroughly and season to taste with salt.

2 Heat the sunflower oil in a skillet. Drop tablespoonfuls of the mixture carefully on to the hot oil, far enough apart for them not to run into each other as they cook.

3 Cook for about 4–5 minutes, turning each patty once, until they are golden brown and firm to the touch. Take care not to turn them too soon, or they will break up in the skillet.

4 Carefully remove the patties from the skillet with a slice and drain them well on absorbent paper towels. Serve immediately while still warm.

COOK'S TIP

To make this dish more attractive, you can serve the patties on large leaves, like those shown in the photograph. Be sure to cut the scallions on the diagonal, as shown, for a more elegant appearance.

 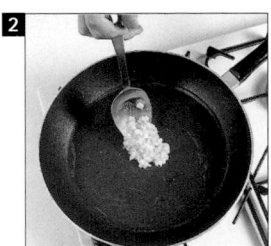 

Spinach Frittata

This Italian dish may be made with many flavorings. Spinach is used as the main ingredient in this recipe for color and flavor.

NUTRITIONAL INFORMATION

Calories 307   Sugars 4g
Protein . . . . .15g   Fat 25g
Carbohydrate . . . .6g   Saturates 8g

🍲 20 mins   🕐 20 mins

SERVES 4

I N G R E D I E N T S

1 lb/450 g spinach

2 tsp water

4 eggs, beaten

2 tbsp light cream

2 garlic cloves, crushed

⅓ cup canned corn kernels, drained

1 celery stalk, chopped

1 fresh red chili, chopped

2 tomatoes, seeded and diced

2 tbsp olive oil

2 tbsp butter

4 tbsp pecan halves

2 tbsp grated romano cheese

1 oz/25 g Fontina cheese, cubed

a pinch of paprika

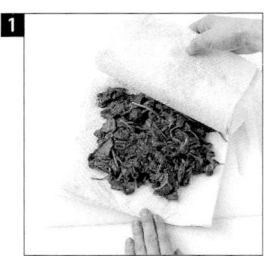  

1 Cook the spinach in 2 teaspoons of water in a covered pan for 5 minutes. Drain thoroughly and pat dry on absorbent paper towels.

2 Beat the eggs in a bowl and stir in the spinach, light cream, garlic, corn, celery, chili, and tomatoes until the ingredients are well mixed.

3 Heat the olive oil and butter in an 8 inch/20 cm heavy skillet over medium heat.

4 Spoon the egg mixture into the skillet and sprinkle with the pecan halves, romano and Fontina cheeses, and paprika. Cook, without stirring, over medium heat for 5–7 minutes or until the underside of the frittata is brown.

5 Put a large plate over the pan and invert to turn out the frittata. Slide it back into the skillet and cook the other side for a further 2–3 minutes. Serve the frittata straight from the skillet or transfer to a serving plate.

COOK'S TIP
Be careful not to burn the underside of the frittata during the initial cooking stage—this is why it is important to use a heavy skillet. Add a little extra oil to the pan when you turn the frittata over, if required.

Potato-Filled Naan Breads

This is a filling Indian sandwich. Spicy potatoes fill the naan breads, which are served with a cool cucumber raita and lime pickle.

NUTRITIONAL INFORMATION

Calories	244	Sugars	.........7g
Protein	.........8g	Fat	...........8g
Carbohydrate	...37g	Saturates	......1g

 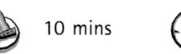

10 mins   25 mins

SERVES 4

INGREDIENTS

½ lb/225 g waxy potatoes, scrubbed and diced

1 tbsp vegetable oil

1 onion, chopped

2 garlic cloves, crushed

1 tsp ground cumin

1 tsp ground coriander

½ tsp chili powder

1 tbsp tomato paste

3 tbsp vegetable bouillon

3 oz/85 g young spinach, shredded

4 small or 2 large naan breads

lime pickle, to serve

RAITA

⅔ cup low-fat unsweetend yogurt

4 tbsp diced cucumber

1 tbsp chopped fresh mint

1 Cook the diced potatoes in a pan of boiling water for 10 minutes. Drain thoroughly.

2 Heat the vegetable oil in a separate pan and cook the onion and garlic over low heat, stirring frequently, for 3 minutes. Add the spices and cook for a further 2 minutes.

3 Stir in the potatoes, tomato paste, vegetable bouillon, and spinach. Cook for 5 minutes until the potatoes are tender.

4 Warm the naan breads in a preheated oven, 300°F/150°C, for about 2 minutes.

5 To make the raita, combine the yogurt, cucumber, and mint in a small bowl.

6 Remove the naan breads from the oven. Using a sharp knife, cut a pocket in the side of each bread. Spoon the spicy potato mixture into each pocket.

7 Serve the filled naan breads immediately, accompanied by the raita and lime pickle.

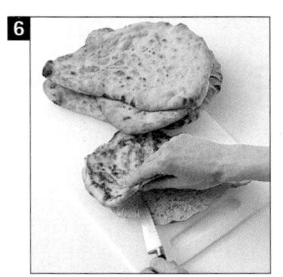

COOK'S TIP

To give the raita a much stronger flavor, make it in advance and chill in the refrigerator until ready to serve.

Mexican Eggs

In this unusual recipe, the eggs are cooked nestling in a spicy tomato, bell pepper, and red wine sauce.

NUTRITIONAL INFORMATION

Calories	156	Sugars	.........6g
Protein	.........8g	Fat	...........8g
Carbohydrate	....7g	Saturates	.......2g

 10 mins   50 mins

SERVES 4

I N G R E D I E N T S

1 tbsp corn or sunflower oil

1 red bell pepper, seeded and cut into batons

1 yellow bell pepper, seeded and cut into batons

1 garlic clove, finely chopped

2 fresh red chilies, seeded and finely chopped

1 tsp ground coriander

1 tsp ground cumin

½ cup red wine

4 cups canned chopped tomatoes

1 tsp muscovado sugar

4 eggs

salt and ground black pepper

2 tbsp chopped fresh cilantro, to garnish

1 Heat the oil in a large skillet. Add the bell peppers and garlic and cook over medium heat, stirring occasionally, for about 2 minutes, until soft.

2 Add the chopped red chilies, the coriander, and the cumin to the pan and continue to cook, stirring constantly, for 1 minute more. Pour in the red wine, bring the mixture to a boil and simmer for 3 minutes.

3 Stir in the tomatoes with their can juice and the sugar, lower the heat, and simmer gently for 20-25 minutes, until thickened. Season to taste with salt and pepper.

4 Using a large spoon, make 4 hollows in the tomato mixture. Break an egg into each hollow, cover the pan, and cook for 10-15 minutes, until the eggs are set. Sprinkle with the chopped cilantro and serve immediately.

COOK'S TIP

Although chili seeds themselves contain no capsaicin—the substance that makes chillies hot—it is very concentrated in the flesh surrounding them, so removing the seeds reduces the heat.

Pasta, Grains, & Pulses

Pasta, grains, and pulses are fantastically versatile staple foods and a perfect base for vegetarian recipes—they go wonderfully well with all sorts of vegetables, cheese, and nuts, so the scope for making colorful, tasty, and highly nutritious dishes is endless. Pasta, grains such as rice, and pulses—lentils and beans—all come in a variety of shapes, colors, and textures, making them ideal for all sorts of exciting recipes, from quick dishes cooked on the hob, such as Pesto Pasta, to hearty bakes like Brown Rice Gratin, which are great served hot, straight from the oven, when a warming supper is called for.

Summertime Tagliatelle

This is a really fresh-tasting dish, made with zucchini and cream, which is ideal with a crisp white wine and some crusty bread.

NUTRITIONAL INFORMATION

Calories 502	Sugars 5g	
Protein 16g	Fat 30g	
Carbohydrate ...44g	Saturates 9g	

 10 mins   20 mins

SERVES 4

I N G R E D I E N T S

1½ lb/675 g zucchini

6 tbsp olive oil

3 garlic cloves, crushed

3 tbsp chopped fresh basil

2 fresh red chilies, seeded and sliced

juice of 1 large lemon

5 tbsp light cream

4 tbsp grated Parmesan cheese

8 oz/225 g dried tagliatelle

salt and pepper

crusty bread, to serve

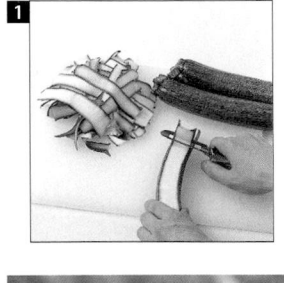

1 Using a swivel vegetable peeler, slice the zucchini into thin ribbons.

2 Heat the oil in a skillet and cook the garlic for 30 seconds.

COOK'S TIP

Lime juice could be used instead of the lemon. As limes are usually smaller, squeeze the juice from 2 fruits.

3 Add the zucchini ribbons and cook over low heat, stirring constantly, for 5–7 minutes.

4 Stir in the basil, chilies, lemon juice, cream, and Parmesan cheese and season with salt and pepper to taste. Keep warm over very low heat while the pasta is cooking.

5 Bring a large pan of lightly salted water to a boil. Add the pasta, bring back to a boil, and cook for 8–10 minutes until tender, but still firm to the bite. Drain thoroughly and put the pasta in a warm serving bowl.

6 Pile the zucchini mixture on top of the pasta and serve with crusty bread.

Pasta with Nuts & Cheese

Simple and inexpensive, this tasty dish is fairly quick and easy to prepare, but looks and tastes very impressive.

NUTRITIONAL INFORMATION

Calories 531	Sugars 4g	
Protein 20g	Fat 35g	
Carbohydrate . . .35g	Saturates 16g	

 10 mins   30 mins

SERVES 4

I N G R E D I E N T S

½ cup pine nuts

12 oz/350 g dried pasta shapes

2 zucchini, sliced

1 cup broccoli, broken into florets

1 cup full-fat soft cheese

⅔ cup milk

1 tbsp chopped fresh basil

¼ lb/115 g white mushrooms, sliced

⅔ cup crumbled blue cheese

salt and pepper

sprigs of fresh basil, to garnish

salad greens, to serve

1 Scatter the pine nuts onto a cookie sheet and broil, turning occasionally, until lightly browned all over. Set aside.

2 Cook the pasta in plenty of boiling salted water for 8–10 minutes or until it is just tender.

3 Meanwhile, cook the zucchini and broccoli in a small amount of boiling, lightly salted water for about 5 minutes or until just tender.

4 Put the soft cheese into a pan and heat gently, stirring constantly. Add the milk and stir to mix. Add the basil and mushrooms and cook gently for 2–3 minutes. Stir in the blue cheese and season to taste.

5 Drain the pasta and the vegetables and mix together. Pour over the cheese and mushroom sauce and add the pine nuts. Toss gently to mix. Garnish with basil sprigs and serve immediately with salad greens.

Tagliatelle with Mushrooms

This dish can be prepared in a moment—the intense flavors are sure to make this a popular recipe.

NUTRITIONAL INFORMATION

Calories 501	Sugars 3g
Protein 15g	Fat 31g
Carbohydrate . . .43g	Saturates 11g

15 mins   20 mins

SERVES 4

INGREDIENTS

2 tbsp walnut oil

1 bunch scallions, sliced

2 garlic cloves, sliced thinly

½ lb/225 g mushrooms, sliced

1 lb/450 g fresh green and white tagliatelle

½ lb/225 g frozen chopped leaf spinach, thawed and drained

¼ lb/115 g full-fat soft cheese with garlic and herbs

4 tbsp light cream

½ cup chopped, unsalted pistachio nuts

2 tbsp shredded fresh basil

salt and pepper

sprigs of fresh basil, to garnish

Italian bread, to serve

1 Gently heat the walnut oil in a wok or skillet and sauté the scallions and garlic for 1 minute or until just soft. Add the mushrooms to the skillet, stir well, cover, and cook gently for 5 minutes or until soft.

2 Meanwhile, bring a large pan of lightly salted water to a boil and cook the pasta for 3–5 minutes or until just tender. Drain the pasta thoroughly and return to the pan.

3 Add the spinach to the mushrooms and heat through for 1–2 minutes. Add the cheese and let melt slightly. Stir in the cream and continue to heat without letting boil.

4 Pour the vegetable mixture over the pasta, season to taste, and mix well. Heat gently, stirring, for 2–3 minutes.

5 Transfer the pasta into a warmed serving bowl and sprinkle over the pistachio nuts and shredded basil. Garnish with fresh basil sprigs and serve with Italian bread.

Pasta Omelet

This is a superb way of using up any leftover short pasta shapes, such as penne, macaroni, or conchiglie.

NUTRITIONAL INFORMATION

Calories	460	Sugars	.........3g
Protein	........16g	Fat	..........34g
Carbohydrate	...23g	Saturates	.......6g

10 mins   15–20 mins

SERVES 2

I N G R E D I E N T S

4 tbsp olive oil

1 small onion, chopped

1 fennel bulb, thinly sliced

¼ lb/115 g diced potato

1 garlic clove, chopped

4 eggs

1 tbsp chopped fresh flat-leaf parsley

pinch of chili powder

¼ lb/115 g cooked short pasta

2 tbsp stuffed green olives, halved

salt and pepper

fresh marjoram sprigs, to garnish

tomato salad, to serve

1 Heat half of the oil in a heavy skillet over low heat. Add the onion, fennel, and potato and cook, stirring occasionally, for 8–10 minutes until the potato is just tender.

2 Stir in the garlic and cook for 1 minute. Remove the skillet from the heat, transfer the vegetables to a plate, and set aside.

3 Beat the eggs until they are foamy. Stir in the parsley and season with salt, pepper, and a pinch of chili powder.

4 Heat 1 tbsp of the remaining oil in a clean skillet. Add half of the egg mixture to the skillet, then add the cooked vegetables, pasta, and half of the olives. Pour in the remaining egg mixture and cook until the sides begin to set.

5 Lift up the edges of the omelet with a spatula to let the uncooked egg spread underneath. Cook, shaking the skillet occasionally, until the underside is a light golden brown color.

6 Slide the omelet out of the skillet onto a plate. Wipe the pan with paper towels and heat the remaining oil. Carefully invert the omelet into the pan and cook until the other side is a golden brown color.

7 Slide the omelet onto a warmed serving dish and garnish with the remaining olives and the sprigs of marjoram. Cut the omelet into wedges and serve with a tomato salad.

Penne & Vegetables

The sweet cherry tomatoes in this recipe add color and flavor
and are complemented by the black olives and mixed bell peppers.

NUTRITIONAL INFORMATION

Calories 380	Sugars 6g
Protein 8g	Fat 16g
Carbohydrate ...48g	Saturates 7g

 10 mins   25 mins

SERVES 4

INGREDIENTS

2 cups dried penne

2 tbsp olive oil

2 tbsp butter

2 garlic cloves, crushed

1 green bell pepper, seeded and
thinly sliced

1 yellow bell pepper, seeded and
thinly sliced

16 cherry tomatoes, halved

1 tbsp chopped oregano

½ cup dry white wine

2 tbsp quartered, pitted black olives

3 oz/85 g arugula

salt and pepper

fresh oregano sprigs, to garnish

VARIATION

If arugula is unavailable, spinach
makes a good substitute. Follow
the same cooking instructions
as for arugula.

1 Bring a pan of lightly salted water to
a boil. Add the pasta, bring back to a
boil, and cook for 8–10 minutes until
tender, but still firm to the bite. Drain.

2 Heat the oil and butter in a pan.
Sauté the garlic for 30 seconds. Add
the bell peppers and cook, stirring
occasionally, for 3–4 minutes.

3 Stir in the cherry tomatoes, oregano,
wine, and olives and cook for
3–4 minutes. Season with salt and pepper
and stir in the arugula until just wilted.

4 Transfer the pasta to a serving dish,
spoon over the sauce, and garnish.

Spaghetti with Ricotta

This light but nutritious pasta dish has a delicate flavor ideally suited for a summer lunch.

NUTRITIONAL INFORMATION

Calories	701	Sugars	........12g
Protein	........17g	Fat	..........40g
Carbohydrate	...73g	Saturates	......15g

  5 mins   25 mins

SERVES 4

INGREDIENTS

¾ lb/350 g dried spaghetti

3 tbsp butter

2 tbsp chopped fresh flat-leaf parsley

1 cup freshly ground almonds

½ cup ricotta cheese

pinch of freshly grated nutmeg

pinch of ground cinnamon

⅔ cup crème fraîche

2 tbsp olive oil

½ cup hot vegetable bouillon

1 tbsp pine nuts

salt and pepper

fresh flat-leaf parsley sprigs, to garnish

1 Bring a pan of lightly salted water to a boil. Add the spaghetti, bring back to a boil, and cook for 8–10 minutes until tender, but still firm to the bite.

2 Drain the pasta, return to the pan, and toss with the butter and chopped parsley. Set aside and keep warm.

3 To make the sauce, combine the ground almonds, ricotta cheese, nutmeg, cinnamon, and crème fraîche in a small pan and stir over low heat to a thick paste. Gradually stir in the oil. When the oil has been fully incorporated, gradually stir in the hot vegetable bouillon, until smooth. Season to taste with pepper.

4 Transfer the spaghetti to a warm serving dish, pour the sauce over it, and toss together well (see Cook's Tip). Sprinkle over the pine nuts, garnish with the sprigs of fresh flat-leaf parsley, and serve immediately.

COOK'S TIP
Use 2 large forks to toss spaghetti or other long pasta, so that it is thoroughly coated with the sauce. Special spaghetti forks are available from some cookware departments and kitchen stores.

Spinach & Nut Pasta

Use any pasta shapes that you have for this recipe—fusilli were used here. Multicolored pasta is visually the most attractive to use.

NUTRITIONAL INFORMATION

Calories 603   Sugars 5g
Protein ....12g   Fat 41g
Carbohydrate ...46g   Saturates 6g

 5 mins   15 mins

SERVES 4

INGREDIENTS

2 cups dried pasta shapes

½ cup olive oil

2 garlic cloves, crushed

1 onion, quartered and sliced

3 large flat mushrooms, sliced

½ lb/225 g spinach

2 tbsp pine nuts

5 tbsp dry white wine

salt and pepper

Parmesan shavings, to garnish

1 Bring a large pan of lightly salted water to a boil. Add the pasta, bring back to a boil, and cook for 8–10 minutes until the pasta is tender, but still firm to the bite. Drain well.

2 Meanwhile, heat the oil in a large pan. Add the garlic and onion and cook over low heat, stirring occasionally, for 1 minute.

3 Add the sliced mushrooms to the pan and cook over medium heat, stirring occasionally, for 2 minutes.

4 Lower the heat, add the spinach, and cook, stirring occasionally, for about 4–5 minutes or until the spinach has just wilted.

5 Stir in the pine nuts and wine, season to taste with salt and pepper, and cook for 1 minute.

6 Transfer the pasta to a warm serving bowl and toss the sauce into it, mixing well. Garnish with shavings of Parmesan cheese and serve immediately.

COOK'S TIP

Grate a little nutmeg over the dish for extra flavor, because this spice has a particular affinity with spinach.

Tagliatelle with Garlic Butter

Pasta is not difficult to make yourself, just a little time-consuming.
The pasta only takes a couple of minutes to cook and tastes wonderful.

NUTRITIONAL INFORMATION

Calories 642	Sugars 2g	
Protein 16g	Fat 29g	
Carbohydrate ...84g	Saturates 13g	

45 mins   5 mins

SERVES 4

INGREDIENTS

3 cups strong white flour, plus extra
  for dredging

2 tsp salt

4 eggs, beaten

3 tbsp olive oil

5 tbsp butter, melted

3 garlic cloves, finely chopped

2 tbsp chopped, fresh parsley

pepper

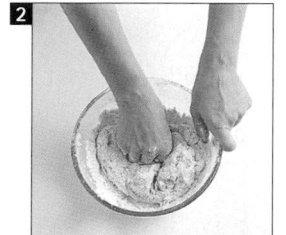
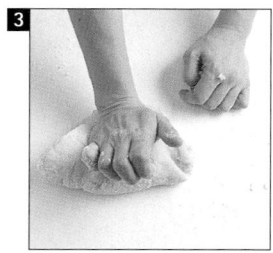

1 Sift the flour into a large bowl and stir in the salt.

2 Make a well in the middle of the dry ingredients and add the eggs and 2 tablespoons of oil. Using a wooden spoon, stir in the eggs, gradually drawing in the flour. After a few minutes the dough will be too stiff to use a spoon and you will need to use your fingers.

3 Once all of the flour has been incorporated, turn the dough out on to a floured surface and knead for about 5 minutes, or until smooth and elastic. If you find the dough is too wet, add a little more flour and continue kneading. Cover with plastic wrap and let rest for at least 15 minutes.

4 The basic dough is now ready; roll out the pasta thinly and create the pasta shapes required. This can be done by hand or using a pasta machine. Results from a machine are usually neater and thinner, but not necessarily better.

5 To make the tagliatelle by hand, fold the thinly rolled pasta sheets into 3 and cut out long, thin stips, about ½ inch/1 cm wide.

6 To cook, bring a pan of water to a boil, add the remaining 1 tbsp of oil, and the pasta. It will take 2–3 minutes to cook, and the texture should have a slight bite to it. Drain.

7 Mix together the butter, garlic, and parsley. Stir into the pasta, season with a little pepper to taste, and serve immediately.

COOK'S TIP
Generally allow about
1½ cups fresh pasta or about
1 cup dried pasta per person.

Lemon Spaghetti

Steaming vegetables helps to preserve their nutritional content and lets them retain their bright, natural colors and crunchy texture.

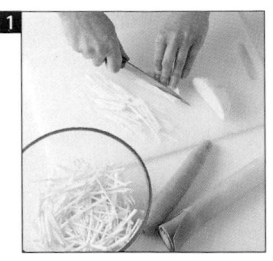

NUTRITIONAL INFORMATION

Calories ....133 Sugars 8g
Protein ....8g Fat 1g
Carbohydrate ...25g Saturates 0.2g

 10 mins   25 mins

SERVES 4

INGREDIENTS

½ lb/225 g celery root

2 medium carrots

2 medium leeks

1 small red bell pepper

1 small yellow bell pepper

2 garlic cloves

1 tsp celery seeds

1 tbsp lemon juice

10½ oz/300 g spaghetti

salt

chopped celery leaves, to garnish

LEMON DRESSING

1 tsp finely grated lemon zest

1 tbsp lemon juice

4 tbsp low-fat unsweetened yogurt

salt and pepper

2 tbsp chopped fresh chives

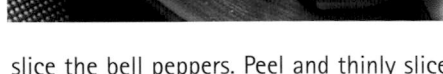

1 Peel the celery root and carrots, cut into thin batons, and place in a bowl. Trim and slice the leeks, rinse under cold running water to flush out any trapped dirt, then shred finely. Halve, seed, and slice the bell peppers. Peel and thinly slice the garlic.

2 Add all of the vegetables to the bowl with the celery root and the carrots. Toss the vegetables with the celery seeds and lemon juice.

3 Bring a large pan of lightly salted water to a boil. Add the pasta, bring back to a boil, and cook for 8–10 minutes until tender, but still firm to the bite. Drain and keep warm.

4 Meanwhile, bring another large pan of water to a boil, put the vegetables in a steamer, and place over the boiling water. Cover and steam for 6–7 minutes or until tender.

5 Meanwhile, combine all the ingredients for the lemon dressing.

6 Transfer the spaghetti and vegetables to a warmed serving bowl and mix with the dressing. Garnish with chopped celery leaves and serve.

Vegetable Pasta Salad

A combination of vegetables tossed in a tomato dressing, served on a bed of assorted salad leaves, makes a tasty entrée or an appetizing side dish.

NUTRITIONAL INFORMATION

Calories 197	Sugars 5g	
Protein 10g	Fat 5g	
Carbohydrate ...30g	Saturates 1g	

 10 mins   15 mins

SERVES 4

I N G R E D I E N T S

2 cups penne

1 tbsp olive oil

salt and pepper

1 oz/25 g pitted black olives, drained and sliced in rings

1 oz/25 g dry-pack sun-dried tomatoes, soaked, drained, and chopped

14 oz/400 g canned artichoke hearts, drained and halved

¼ lb/115g baby zucchini, trimmed and sliced

¼ lb/115g baby plum tomatoes, halved

assorted baby salad leaves

shredded basil leaves, to garnish

DRESSING

4 tbsp strained tomatoes

2 tbsp low-fat unsweetened yogurt

1 tbsp unsweetened orange juice

1 small bunch fresh basil, shredded

 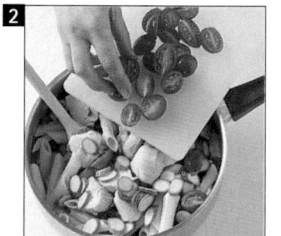 

1 Cook the penne according to the directions on the packet. Do not overcook the pasta—it should still have "bite." Drain well and return to the pan. Stir in the olive oil, salt and pepper, olives, and sun-dried tomatoes. Let cool.

2 Gently mix the artichokes, zucchini, and plum tomatoes into the cooked pasta. Arrange the salad leaves in a serving bowl.

3 To make the dressing, mix all the ingredients together and toss into the vegetables and pasta.

4 Spoon the mixture on top of the salad leaves and garnish with shredded basil leaves.

VARIATION

Try making this dish with other pasta shapes, or a mixture—look out for farfalle (bows) and rotelle (spoked wheels).

Spicy Pasta Wheels

Wheel-shaped pasta looks very attractive, and tastes great tossed in a basic red wine sauce spiced up with fresh red chilies.

NUTRITIONAL INFORMATION

Calories . . . . . . .490 Sugars 3g
Protein . . . . .13g Fat 16g
Carbohydrate . . .77g Saturates 2g

 30 mins   25 mins

SERVES 4

I N G R E D I E N T S

5 tbsp olive oil

3 garlic cloves, minced

2 fresh red chilies, chopped

1 green chili, chopped

⅞ cup Red Wine Sauce (see page 7)

3½ cups dried rotelle

salt and pepper

warm Italian bread, to serve

3 Stir the Red Wine Sauce into the pan and season with salt and pepper to taste. Simmer gently over low heat for 20 minutes.

4 Bring a large pan of lightly salted water to a boil. Add the rotelle and the remaining oil and cook for 8 minutes, or until just tender, but still firm to the bite. Drain the pasta.

5 Toss the rotelle in the spicy sauce, then transfer to a warm serving dish. Serve with warm Italian bread.

1 Make the Red Wine Sauce (see page 7).

2 Heat 4 tbsp of the olive oil in a pan. Add the garlic and chilies and cook for 3 minutes.

COOK'S TIP

Take care when using fresh chilies, as they can burn your skin. Handle them as little as possible—wear protective gloves. Always wash your hands thoroughly afterward and don't touch your face or eyes before you have washed your hands.

Cream & Sage Tagliarini

This simple, creamy, blue cheese and fresh sage pasta sauce is a classic Italian recipe.

NUTRITIONAL INFORMATION

Calories 880	Sugars 3g
Protein 35g	Fat 49g
Carbohydrate . . .79g	Saturates 27g

 10 mins   25 mins

SERVES 4

I N G R E D I E N T S

2 tbsp butter

2 cups roughly crumbled
  Gorgonzola cheese

⅝ cup heavy cream

2 tbsp dry white wine

1 tsp cornstarch

4 fresh sage sprigs, finely chopped

14 oz dried tagliarini

2 tbsp olive oil

salt and white pepper

1 Melt the butter in a heavy pan. Stir in 1½ cups of the Gorgonzola cheese and melt, over low heat, for about 2 minutes.

2 Add the cream, wine, and cornstarch and beat with a whisk until fully incorporated.

3 Stir in the sage and season to taste with salt and white pepper. Bring to a boil over low heat, whisking constantly, until the sauce thickens. Remove from the heat and set aside.

4 Bring a large pan of lightly salted water to a boil. Add the tagliarini and 1 tbsp of the olive oil. Cook the pasta for 12–14 minutes, or until just tender, then drain thoroughly and toss in the remaining olive oil. Transfer the pasta to a serving dish and keep warm.

5 Return the pan containing the sauce to low heat to reheat the sauce, whisking constantly. Spoon the Gorgonzola sauce over the tagliarini, then generously sprinkle over the remaining cheese, and serve immediately.

COOK'S TIP
When buying Gorgonzola, always check that it is creamy yellow with delicate green veining. Avoid hard or discolored cheese. If you find Gorgonzola too strong or rich, you could substitute Danish blue.

Pasta & Chili Tomatoes

The pappardelle and vegetables are tossed in a delicious chili and tomato sauce for a quick and economical meal.

NUTRITIONAL INFORMATION

Calories ....353 Sugars 7g
Protein ....10g Fat 24g
Carbohydrate ...26g Saturates 4g

 15 mins   20 mins

SERVES 4

INGREDIENTS

10 oz/280 g dried pappardelle

3 tbsp peanut oil

2 garlic cloves, crushed

2 shallots, sliced

½ lb/225 g green beans, sliced

¼ lb/115 g cherry tomatoes, halved

1 tsp chili flakes

4 tbsp crunchy peanut butter

⅔ cup coconut milk

1 tbsp tomato paste

sliced scallions, to garnish

1 Bring a large pan of lightly salted water to a boil. Add the pappardelle, bring back to a boil, and cook for 8–10 minutes until tender, but still firm to the bite. Drain thoroughly and set aside.

2 Meanwhile, heat the peanut oil in a large, heavy skillet or preheated wok. Add the garlic and shallots and stir-fry for 1 minute.

3 Add the green beans and drained pasta to the skillet or wok and stir-fry for 5 minutes. Add the cherry tomatoes and mix well.

4 Combine the chili flakes, peanut butter, coconut milk, and tomato paste. Pour the chili mixture into the skillet or wok, toss well to combine, and heat through.

5 Transfer to warm serving dishes and garnish with scallion slices. Serve immediately.

VARIATION

Try using egg noodles for this dish, instead of the pappardelle. Follow the instructions on the packet for cooking the noodles, then toss them in the wok with the sauce.

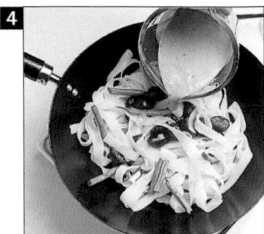

Pasta & Vegetable Sauce

The different shapes and textures of the vegetables make a mouthwatering presentation in this light and summery dish.

NUTRITIONAL INFORMATION

Calories	389	Sugars	.........4g
Protein	........16g	Fat	..........20g
Carbohydrate	...38g	Saturates	......11g

 10 mins   30 mins

SERVES 4

I N G R E D I E N T S

2 cups dried gemelli or other pasta shapes

1 broccoli head, cut into florets

2 zucchini, sliced

½ lb/225 g asparagus spears

¼ lb/115 g snow peas

1 cup frozen peas

2 tbsp butter

3 tbsp vegetable bouillon

4 tbsp heavy cream

freshly grated nutmeg

2 tbsp chopped fresh parsley

2 tbsp freshly grated Parmesan cheese

salt and pepper

1 Bring a large pan of lightly salted water to a boil. Add the pasta, bring back to a boil, and cook for 8–10 minutes or until tender, but still firm to the bite. Drain the pasta, return to the pan, cover, and keep warm.

2 Steam the broccoli, zucchini, asparagus, and snow peas over a pan of boiling salted water until they are just beginning to soften. Remove the pan from the heat and refresh the vegetables in cold water. Drain and set aside.

3 Bring a small pan of lightly salted water to a boil. Add the frozen peas and cook for 3 minutes. Drain the peas, refresh in cold water, then drain again. Set aside with the other vegetables.

4 Put the butter and vegetable bouillon in a pan over medium heat. When the butter has melted, add the vegetables, reserving a few of the asparagus spears, and toss carefully with a wooden spoon until they have heated through, taking care not to break them up.

5 Stir in the cream and heat through without bringing to a boil. Season to taste with salt, pepper, and a little freshly grated nutmeg.

6 Transfer the pasta to a warmed serving dish and stir in the chopped parsley. Spoon over the vegetable sauce.

7 Sprinkle over the grated Parmesan cheese, then arrange the reserved asparagus spears in a pattern on top and serve immediately.

Pasta & Cheese Molds

These delicious individual pasta molds are served with a tasty tomato sauce, flavored with bay leaf.

NUTRITIONAL INFORMATION

Calories 517   Sugars 8g
Protein . . . . .19g   Fat 27g
Carbohydrate . . .47g   Saturates 13g

45 mins   50 mins

SERVES 4

I N G R E D I E N T S

1 tbsp butter or margarine, softened

½ cup dried white bread crumbs

6 oz/175 g tricolour spaghetti

1¼ cups Béchamel sauce (see page 6)

1 egg yolk

1 cup grated Swiss cheese

salt and pepper

fresh flat-leaf parsley, to garnish

T O M A T O   S A U C E

2 tsp olive oil

1 onion, chopped finely

1 bay leaf

⅔ cup dry white wine

⅔ cup strained tomatoes

1 tbsp tomato paste

1 Grease four ¾ cup molds or ramekins with the butter or margarine. Evenly coat the insides with half of the bread crumbs.

2 Break the spaghetti into 2 inch/5 cm lengths. Bring a pan of lightly salted water to a boil and cook the spaghetti for 5-6 minutes or until just tender. Drain well and put in a bowl.

3 Mix the Béchamel sauce, egg yolk, cheese, and seasoning into the cooked pasta and pack the mixture into the molds.

4 Sprinkle over the remaining bread crumbs and place the molds on a cookie sheet. Bake in a preheated oven, 425°F/220°C, for 20 minutes until golden brown. Let stand for 10 minutes.

5 Meanwhile, make the sauce. Heat the olive oil in a pan and sauté the onion and bay leaf for 2-3 minutes or until the onion is just soft.

6 Stir in the wine, strained tomatoes, tomato paste, and seasoning. Bring the sauce to a boil and simmer for 20 minutes or until thickened. Remove from the heat and discard the bay leaf.

7 Run a spatula around the inside of the molds. Turn out on to serving plates, garnish, and serve with the tomato sauce.

Vegetable Cannelloni

This dish is made with prepared cannelloni tubes, but may also be made by rolling ready-bought lasagna sheets.

NUTRITIONAL INFORMATION

Calories	594	Sugars	........12g
Protein	........13g	Fat	..........38g
Carbohydrate	...52g	Saturates	.......7g

10 mins   45 mins

SERVES 4

INGREDIENTS

1 eggplant

½ cup olive oil

8 oz/225 g spinach

2 garlic cloves, crushed

1 tsp ground cumin

1¼ cups chopped mushrooms

12 cannelloni tubes

salt and pepper

TOMATO SAUCE

1 tbsp olive oil

1 onion, chopped

2 garlic cloves, crushed

28 oz/800 g canned chopped tomatoes

1 tsp superfine sugar

2 tbsp chopped fresh basil

2 oz/55 g sliced mozzarella

1 Cut the eggplant into small dice. Heat the oil in a skillet. Add the eggplant and cook over moderate heat, stirring frequently, for 2–3 minutes.

2 Add the spinach, garlic, cumin, and mushrooms and reduce the heat. Season to taste with salt and pepper and cook, stirring constantly, for 2–3 minutes. Spoon the mixture into the cannelloni tubes and arrange in a casserole in a single layer.

3 To make the sauce, heat the olive oil in a pan and cook the onion and garlic for 1 minute. Add the tomatoes, sugar, and basil and bring to a boil. Reduce the heat and simmer gently for about 5 minutes. Spoon the sauce over the cannelloni tubes.

4 Arrange the sliced mozzarella on top of the sauce and cook in a preheated oven, 375°F/190°C, for about 30 minutes or until the cheese is bubbling and golden brown. Serve immediately.

Vegetable & Pasta Parcels

These small parcels are very easy to make and can be filled with your favorite mixture of succulent mushrooms.

NUTRITIONAL INFORMATION

Calories 333   Sugars 1g
Protein . . . . .7g   Fat 30g
Carbohydrate . . .10g   Saturates 13g

 20 mins   20 mins

SERVES 4

I N G R E D I E N T S

FILLING

2 tbsp butter or margarine

2 garlic cloves, crushed

1 small leek, chopped

2 celery stalks, chopped

7 oz/200 g open-cap mushrooms, chopped

1 egg, beaten

2 tbsp grated Parmesan cheese

salt and pepper

RAVIOLI

4 sheets phyllo pastry

2 tbsp margarine

oil, for deep-frying

 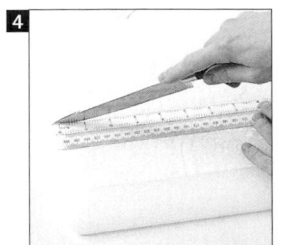 

1 To make the filling, melt the butter or margarine in a skillet and sauté the garlic and leek for 2–3 minutes, or until soft but not brown.

2 Add the celery and mushrooms and cook for a further 4–5 minutes until all of the vegetables are tender.

3 Turn off the heat and stir in the egg and grated Parmesan cheese. Season with salt and pepper to taste.

4 Lay the pastry sheets on a cutting board and cut each into nine squares.

5 Spoon a little of the filling into the center of the squares and brush the edges of the pastry with butter or margarine. Lay another square on top and seal the edges to make a parcel.

6 Heat the oil for deep-frying to 350°F/180°C or until a cube of bread browns in 30 seconds. Fry the ravioli, in batches, for 2–3 minutes or until golden brown. Carefully remove from the oil with a slotted spoon and pat dry on absorbent paper towels. Transfer to a warm serving plate and serve immediately.

Filled Eggplants

Combined with tomatoes and a topping of melting mozzarella cheese, pasta makes a tasty filling for baked eggplant shells.

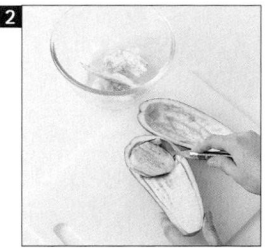

NUTRITIONAL INFORMATION

Calories	342	Sugars	.........6g
Protein	.........11g	Fat	..........16g
Carbohydrate	...40g	Saturates	.......4g

 25 mins   55 mins

SERVES 4

INGREDIENTS

2 cups dried penne or other short
  pasta shapes

4 tbsp olive oil, plus extra for brushing

2 eggplants

1 large onion, chopped

2 garlic cloves, crushed

14 oz/400 g canned chopped tomatoes

2 tsp dried oregano

2 oz/55 g mozzarella cheese, thinly sliced

⅓ cup freshly grated Parmesan cheese

5 tbsp dry bread crumbs

salt and pepper

salad greens, to serve

1 Bring a large pan of lightly salted water to a boil. Add the pasta and 1 tablespoon of the olive oil, bring back to a boil, and cook for 8–10 minutes or until the pasta is just tender, but still firm to the bite. Drain, return to the pan, cover, and keep warm.

2 Cut the eggplants in half lengthwise and score around the inside with a sharp knife, being careful not to pierce the shells. Scoop out the flesh with a spoon. Brush the insides of the shells with olive oil. Chop the flesh and set aside.

3 Heat the remaining oil in a skillet. Sauté the onion over low heat for 5 minutes, until soft. Add the garlic and sauté for 1 minute. Add the chopped eggplant and cook, stirring frequently, for 5 minutes. Add the tomatoes and oregano and season to taste with salt and pepper. Bring to a boil and simmer for 10 minutes until thickened. Remove the skillet from the heat and stir in the pasta.

4 Brush a cookie sheet with oil and arrange the eggplant shells in a single layer. Divide half of the tomato and pasta mixture among them. Sprinkle over the slices of mozzarella, then pile the remaining tomato and pasta mixture on top.

5 Mix together the grated Parmesan cheese and the bread crumbs and sprinkle over the top, patting lightly into the mixture.

6 Bake in a preheated oven, 400°F/ 200°C, for approximately 25 minutes or until the topping is golden brown. Serve hot with a selection of mixed fresh salad greens.

Tomato & Pasta Bake

This pasta dish is baked in the oven and cut into slices for serving.
It looks and tastes terrific and is perfect when you want to impress.

NUTRITIONAL INFORMATION

Calories 179   Sugars 6g
Protein ....8g   Fat 10g
Carbohydrate ...16g   Saturates 3g

10 mins   1 hr 5 mins

Serves 8

INGREDIENTS

1 cup pasta shapes, such as penne or
 casareccia

1 tbsp olive oil

1 leek, chopped

3 garlic cloves, crushed

1 green bell pepper, chopped

2 cups canned chopped tomatoes

2 tbsp chopped, pitted black olives

2 eggs, beaten

1 tbsp chopped basil

TOMATO SAUCE

1 tbsp olive oil

1 onion, chopped

1 cup canned chopped tomatoes

1 tsp caster sugar

2 tbsp tomato paste

⅔ cup vegetable bouillon

salt and pepper

1 Cook the pasta in a pan of boiling salted water for 8 minutes. Drain thoroughly.

2 Meanwhile, heat the olive oil in a pan and sauté the leek and garlic for 2 minutes, stirring constantly. Add the pepper, tomatoes, and olives to the pan and cook for a further 5 minutes.

3 Remove the pan from the heat and stir in the pasta, beaten eggs, and basil. Season well, and spoon into a lightly greased 2 pint/1 litre heatproof bowl.

4 Place the bowl in a roasting pan and half-fill the pan with boiling water. Cover the bowl, and cook in a preheated oven, 350°F/180°C, for 40 minutes, until set.

5 To make the sauce, heat the olive oil in a pan and sauté the onion for 2 minutes. Add the remaining ingredients to the pan and cook for a further 10 minutes. Put the sauce in a food processor or blender and blend until smooth. Return to a clean pan and heat through again until hot.

6 Turn the pasta out of the bowl on to a warm plate. Slice and serve with the tomato sauce.

Eggplant Lasagna

This filling eggplant, zucchini, and mozzarella lasagna is one of many variations of a classic Italian dish.

1¼ hrs   1 hr

SERVES 4

I N G R E D I E N T S

2 lb/900 g eggplants

4 tsp salt

8 tbsp olive oil

2 tbsp garlic and herb butter or margarine

1 lb/450 g zucchini, sliced

2 cups grated mozzarella

2½ cups strained tomatoes

6 sheets precooked green lasagna

2½ cups Béchamel sauce (see page 6)

¾ cup grated Parmesan

1 tsp dried oregano

pepper

 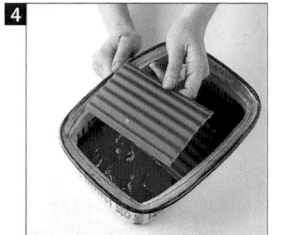 

1 Thinly slice the eggplants. Layer the slices in a bowl, sprinkling with the salt as you go. Let stand for 30 minutes. Rinse well in cold water and pat dry with paper towels.

2 Heat 4 tbsp of olive oil in a skillet and sauté half of the eggplant slices for 6–7 minutes or until they are lightly golden all over. Drain thoroughly on paper towels. Repeat with the remaining eggplant slices and oil.

3 Melt the garlic and herb butter or margarine in the skillet and sauté the zucchini slices for about 5–6 minutes until golden brown. Drain thoroughly on paper towels.

4 Place half of the eggplant and zucchini slices in the bottom of a large ovenproof dish. Season to taste with pepper and sprinkle over half of the grated mozzarella. Spoon over half of the strained tomatoes and top with 3 sheets of lasagna.

5 Arrange the remaining eggplant and zucchini slices on top. Season with pepper and top with the remaining grated mozzarella, strained tomatoes, and another layer of 3 sheets of lasagna.

6 Spoon over the Béchamel sauce and top with the grated Parmesan and a sprinkling of oregano. Place on a cookie sheet and bake in a preheated oven, 425°F/220°C, for 30–35 minutes or until golden brown.

Eggplant & Linguine

Prepare the marinated eggplants well in advance so—when you are ready to eat—all you have to do is cook the pasta.

NUTRITIONAL INFORMATION

Calories 378   Sugars 3g
Protein ....12g   Fat 30g
Carbohydrate ...16g   Saturates 3g

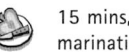
15 mins, plus marinating   15 mins

SERVES 4

INGREDIENTS

⅔ cup vegetable bouillon

⅔ cup white wine vinegar

2 tsp balsamic vinegar

3 tbsp olive oil

fresh oregano sprig

1 lb/450 g eggplants, peeled and thinly sliced

14 oz/400 g dried linguine

MARINADE

2 tbsp extra virgin olive oil

2 garlic cloves, crushed

2 tbsp chopped fresh oregano

2 tbsp finely chopped roasted almonds

2 tbsp diced red bell pepper

2 tbsp lime juice

grated zest and juice of 1 orange

salt and pepper

  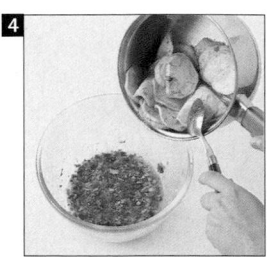

1 Put the vegetable bouillon, wine vinegar, and balsamic vinegar into a pan and bring to a boil over low heat. Add 2 teaspoons of the olive oil and the sprig of oregano and simmer gently for about 1 minute.

2 Add the eggplant slices to the pan, remove from the heat, and let stand for 10 minutes.

3 Meanwhile, make the marinade. Combine the olive oil, garlic, fresh oregano, almonds, red bell pepper, lime juice, orange zest, and juice in a large bowl and season to taste with salt and pepper.

4 Carefully remove the eggplant slices from the pan with a slotted spoon, and drain well. Add the eggplant slices to the marinade, mixing well to coat. Cover with plastic wrap and let stand in the refrigerator for about 12 hours.

5 Bring a large pan of lightly salted water to a boil. Add half of the remaining olive oil and the linguine. Bring back to a boil and cook for 8–10 minutes until the pasta is just tender, but still firm to the bite.

6 Drain the pasta thoroughly and toss with the remaining oil while it is still warm. Arrange the pasta on a serving plate with the eggplant slices and the marinade and serve immediately.

Vegetable Pasta Nests

These large pasta nests look impressive when presented filled with broiled mixed vegetables and they taste simply delicious.

NUTRITIONAL INFORMATION

Calories 392	Sugars 1g
Protein 6g	Fat 28g
Carbohydrate ...32g	Saturates 9g

 25 mins   40 mins

SERVES 4

INGREDIENTS

6 oz/175 g dried spaghetti

1 eggplant, halved and sliced

1 zucchini, diced

1 red bell pepper, seeded and chopped diagonally

6 tbsp olive oil

2 garlic cloves, crushed

butter, for greasing

4 tbsp butter or margarine, melted

1 tbsp dry white bread crumbs

salt and pepper

fresh parsley sprigs, to garnish

1 Bring a large pan of water to a boil. Add the spaghetti, bring back to a boil, and cook for 8–10 minutes until tender, but still firm to the bite. Drain the spaghetti and set aside until required.

2 Place the eggplant, zucchini, and bell pepper on a cookie sheet.

3 Combine the oil and garlic and pour over the vegetables, tossing them to coat all over.

4 Cook the vegetables under a preheated hot broiler for about 10 minutes, turning, until tender and lightly charred. Set aside and keep warm.

5 Lightly grease 4 large, shallow muffin pans and divide the spaghetti among them. Using 2 forks, curl the spaghetti to form nests.

6 Brush the pasta nests with melted butter or margarine and sprinkle with the bread crumbs. Bake in a preheated oven, 400°F/200°C, for 15 minutes or until lightly golden. Remove the pasta nests from the pans and transfer to warm individual serving plates. Divide the broiled vegetables among the pasta nests, season, and garnish.

COOK'S TIP

The Italian term, al dente means "to the bite" and describes cooked pasta that is not too soft, but still has a bite to it.

Three-Cheese Bake

Serve this dish while the cheese is still hot and melted, because cooked cheese turns very rubbery if it is allowed to cool down.

NUTRITIONAL INFORMATION

Calories 710   Sugars 6g
Protein ....34g   Fat 30g
Carbohydrate ...80g   Saturates 16g

5 mins   1 hr

SERVES 4

I N G R E D I E N T S

butter, for greasing

3½ cups dried penne pasta

2 eggs, beaten

1½ cups ricotta cheese

4 fresh basil sprigs

1 cup grated mozzarella or halloumi cheese

scant 1 cup freshly grated Parmesan cheese

salt and pepper

fresh basil leaves, to garnish (optional)

selection of cooked vegetables, to serve

1 Lightly grease a large casserole with a little butter.

2 Bring a pan of lightly salted water to a boil. Add the pasta, bring back to a boil, and cook for 8–10 minutes until just tender, but still firm to the bite. Drain the pasta, set aside, and keep warm.

3 Beat the eggs into the ricotta cheese and season to taste.

4 Spoon half of the pasta into the bottom of the prepared dish and cover with half of the basil leaves.

5 Spoon over half of the ricotta cheese mixture. Sprinkle over the mozzarella or halloumi cheese and top with the remaining basil leaves. Cover with the remaining pasta and then spoon over the remaining ricotta cheese mixture. Lightly sprinkle the freshly grated Parmesan cheese over the top.

6 Bake in a preheated oven, 375°F/ 190°C, for 30–40 minutes until golden brown and the cheese topping is hot and bubbling.

7 Garnish with fresh basil leaves, if liked, and serve immediately with a selection of cooked vegetables.

Vegetable Lasagna

This colorful and tasty lasagna has layers of sliced eggplants and vegetables in tomato sauce, all topped with a rich cheese sauce.

NUTRITIONAL INFORMATION

Calories	544	Sugars	........18g
Protein	........20g	Fat	.........26g
Carbohydrate	...61g	Saturates	......12g

  35 mins   55 mins

SERVES 4

I N G R E D I E N T S

1 eggplant, sliced

3 tbsp olive oil

2 garlic cloves, crushed

1 red onion, halved and sliced

3 mixed bell peppers, seeded and diced

½ lb/225 g mixed mushrooms, sliced

2 celery stalks, sliced

1 zucchini, diced

½ tsp chili powder

½ tsp ground cumin

2 tomatoes, chopped

1¼ cups strained tomatoes

2 tbsp chopped basil

8 no-precook lasagna verdi sheets

salt and pepper

C H E E S E S A U C E

2 tbsp butter or margarine

1 tbsp flour

⅔ cup vegetable bouillon

1¼ cups milk

¾ cup grated Cheddar cheese

1 tsp Dijon mustard

1 tbsp chopped basil

1 egg, beaten

1 Place the eggplant slices in a colander, sprinkle them with salt, and let stand for 20 minutes. Rinse under cold water, drain, and reserve.

2 Heat the oil in a pan and sauté the garlic and onion for 1–2 minutes. Add the bell peppers, mushrooms, celery, and zucchini and cook, stirring constantly, for 3–4 minutes.

3 Stir in the spices and cook for 1 minute. Mix in the chopped tomatoes, strained tomatoes, and basil and season to taste with salt and pepper.

4 For the sauce, melt the butter in a pan, stir in the flour, and cook for 1 minute. Remove from the heat, stir in the bouillon and milk, return to the heat, and add half the cheese and all the mustard. Boil, stirring, until thickened. Stir in the basil. Remove from the heat and stir in the egg.

5 Place half the lasagna sheets in an ovenproof dish. Top with half the vegetable mixture then half the eggplants. Repeat the layers and spoon the cheese sauce over the top.

6 Sprinkle the lasagna with the remaining cheese and cook in a preheated oven, 350°F/180°C, for 40 minutes, until the top is golden brown.

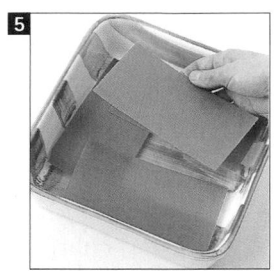

Eggplant Pasta Cake

This recipe would make a stunning dinner party dish, yet it contains simple ingredients and is easy to make.

NUTRITIONAL INFORMATION

Calories 201	Sugars 4g	
Protein 14g	Fat 7g	
Carbohydrate . . .22g	Saturates 4g	

55 mins   35 mins

SERVES 4

INGREDIENTS

butter, for greasing

1 medium eggplant

3 cups dried tricolor pasta shapes

½ cup low-fat soft cheese with garlic and herbs

1½ cups strained tomatoes

scant ¾ cup freshly grated Parmesan cheese

1½ tsp dried oregano

2 tbsp dry white bread crumbs

salt and pepper

1 Grease and line an 8 inch/20 cm round spring-form cake pan.

2 Trim the eggplant and cut lengthwise into slices about ¼ inch/5 mm thick. Place in a bowl, sprinkle with salt, and let stand for 30 minutes to remove any bitter juices. Rinse well under cold running water and drain.

3 Bring a pan of water to a boil and blanch the eggplant slices for 1 minute. Drain and pat dry with paper towels. Set aside.

4 Bring a large pan of lightly salted water to a boil. Add the pasta shapes, bring back to a boil, and cook for 8–10 minutes, until tender, but still firm to the bite. Drain well and return to the pan. Add the soft cheese and allow it to melt over the pasta.

5 Stir in the strained tomatoes, Parmesan, and oregano, and season to taste with salt and pepper. Set aside.

6 Arrange the eggplant slices over the base and sides of the pan, overlapping them and leaving no gaps. Pile the pasta mixture into the pan, packing it down, and sprinkle with the bread crumbs. Bake in a preheated oven, 375°F/190°C, for 20 minutes. Remove from the oven and let stand for 15 minutes.

7 Loosen the cake round the edge with a spatula and release from the pan. Turn out the pasta cake, eggplant side uppermost, and serve hot.

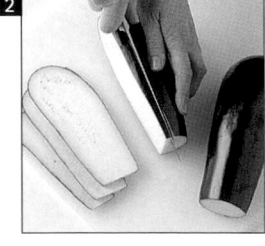

Mushroom & Pasta Pie

Lightly cooked vermicelli is pressed into a quiche pan and baked with a creamy mushroom filling.

NUTRITIONAL INFORMATION

Calories	557	Sugars	.........5g
Protein	........15g	Fat	..........36g
Carbohydrate	...47g	Saturates	......19g

 10 mins   1 hr 10 mins

SERVES 4

INGREDIENTS

½ lb/225 g vermicelli or spaghetti

1 tbsp olive oil

2 tbsp butter, plus extra for greasing

salt and pepper

tomato and basil salad, to serve

SAUCE

4 tbsp butter

1 onion, chopped

5½ oz/150 g white mushrooms, trimmed

1 green bell pepper, cored, seeded, and
   sliced into thin rings

⅔ cup milk

3 eggs, beaten lightly

2 tbsp heavy cream

1 tsp dried oregano

pinch of finely grated nutmeg

1 tbsp freshly grated Parmesan

1 Cook the pasta in a large pan of salted boiling water, adding the olive oil, for 8–10 minutes or until tender. Drain the pasta, return to the pan, add the butter, and shake the pan well.

2 Grease a 8 inch/20 cm loose-based quiche pan. Press the pasta onto the base and around the sides to form a shell.

3 Heat the butter in a skillet over medium heat and sauté the onion until it is translucent. Remove with a slotted spoon and spread in the pie shell.

4 Add the mushrooms and bell pepper rings to the skillet and turn them in the oil until glazed. Sauté for 2 minutes on each side, then arrange in the pie shell

5 Beat together the milk, eggs, and cream, stir in the dried oregano, and season to taste with nutmeg and pepper. Pour the mixture carefully over the vegetables and sprinkle the grated Parmesan cheese over the top.

6 Bake the pie in the preheated oven, 350°F/180°C, for 40–45 minutes, or until the filling is set.

7 Slide the pie carefully onto a serving plate and serve warm.

Linguine with Pesto Sauce

Make the pesto sauce in advance and use fresh linguine, which cooks in just two or three minutes, to make a really speedy and delicious meal.

NUTRITIONAL INFORMATION

Calories 860	Sugars 4g	
Protein 30g	Fat 50g	
Carbohydrate ...77g	Saturates 12g	

15 mins, plus chilling   10–15 mins

SERVES 4

INGREDIENTS

14 oz/400 g dried or fresh linguine

freshly grated Parmesan cheese, to serve (optional)

PESTO SAUCE

5½ oz/150 g Parmesan cheese in a wedge

3 garlic cloves, or to taste

3 cups fresh basil leaves

5 tbsp pine nuts

⅔ cup fruity extra-virgin olive oil

salt and pepper

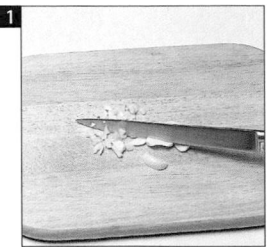

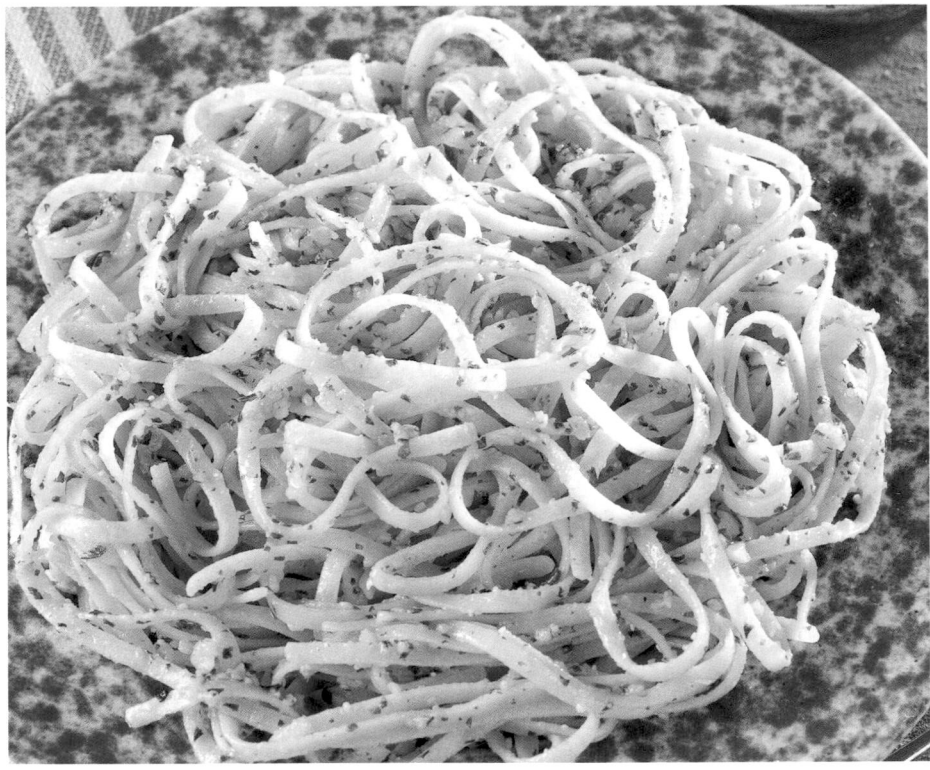

VARIATION

Blanched almonds can be used instead of pine nuts. To make a creamy dip to serve with sliced zucchini and bell pepper strips, stir 4 tablespoons of the pesto sauce into 4 tablespoons thick unsweetened yogurt.

1 To make the pesto sauce, cut the rind off the Parmesan and finely grate the cheese. Set aside. Cut each garlic clove in half lengthwise and use the tip of the knife to lift out the green core, which can have a bitter flavor if the cloves are old. Coarsely chop the garlic.

2 Rinse the basil leaves and pat dry with paper towels. Put the basil in a food processor and add the pine nuts, grated cheese, chopped garlic, and olive oil. Process for about 30 seconds, just until well blended.

3 Add pepper and extra salt to taste, but cautiously—remember, the cheese is salty. Cover with plastic wrap and chill for up to 5 days.

4 Bring a large pan of water to a boil. Add ½ teaspoon salt and the linguine and cook according to the packet instructions. Drain well, reserving a few tablespoons of cooking water.

5 Return the linguine to the pan over low heat and stir in the sauce. Toss until well coated and the sauce is heated though. Stir in a couple of tablespoons of the reserved cooking water if the sauce seems too thick.

6 Serve at once with grated Parmesan for sprinkling over the top, if desired.

Italian Pasta Salad

Tomatoes and mozzarella cheese are a classic Italian combination. Here they are joined with pasta and avocado for an extra touch of luxury.

NUTRITIONAL INFORMATION

Calories 541	Sugars 5g	
Protein 12g	Fat 43g	
Carbohydrate . . .29g	Saturates 10g	

 15 mins   15 mins

SERVES 4

I N G R E D I E N T S

2 tbsp pine nuts

1½ cups dried fusilli

1 tbsp olive oil

6 tomatoes

½ lb/225 g mozzarella cheese

1 large avocado

2 tbsp lemon juice

3 tbsp chopped fresh basil

salt and pepper

fresh basil sprigs, to garnish

D R E S S I N G

6 tbsp extra virgin olive oil

2 tbsp white wine vinegar

1 tsp whole-grain mustard

pinch of sugar

1 Spread the pine nuts out on a cookie sheet and toast them under a preheated broiler for 1–2 minutes. Remove and let cool.

2 Bring a large pan of lightly salted water to a boil. Add the pasta, bring back to a boil, and cook for 8–10 minutes or until tender, but still firm to the bite. Drain the pasta and refresh in cold water. Drain again and let cool.

3 Thinly slice the tomatoes and the mozzarella cheese.

4 Cut the avocado in half lengthwise, carefully remove the pit, then peel. Cut the flesh into thin slices lengthwise and sprinkle with lemon juice to prevent it turning brown.

5 To make the dressing, whisk together the oil, vinegar, mustard, and sugar in a small bowl and season to taste with salt and pepper.

6 Arrange the tomatoes, mozzarella cheese, and avocado alternately in overlapping slices on a large serving platter, leaving room in the center.

7 Toss the pasta with half of the dressing and the chopped basil and season to taste with salt and pepper. Spoon the pasta into the center of the platter and pour over the remaining dressing. Sprinkle over the pine nuts, garnish with fresh sprigs of basil, and serve immediately.

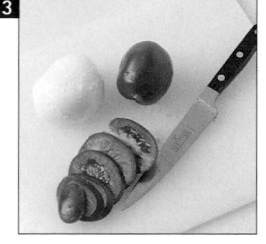

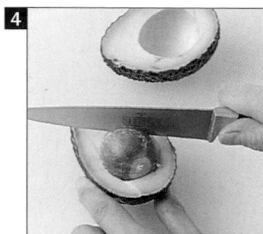

Garlicky Spaghetti

This easy and satisfying Roman dish originated as a cheap meal for poor people, but has now become a favorite in restaurants and trattorias.

NUTRITIONAL INFORMATION

Calories 669	Sugars 4g	
Protein 14g	Fat 33g	
Carbohydrate . . .84g	Saturates 5g	

5 mins   5–10 mins

SERVES 4

INGREDIENTS

½ cup olive oil

3 garlic cloves, crushed

1 lb/450 g fresh spaghetti

3 tbsp coarsely chopped fresh parsley

salt and pepper

1 Reserve 1 tbsp of the olive oil and heat the remainder in a medium pan. Add the garlic and a pinch of salt and cook over low heat, stirring constantly, until golden brown, then remove the pan from the heat. Do not let the garlic burn as this will taint its flavor. (If it does burn, you will have to start all over again!)

2 Meanwhile, bring a large pan of lightly salted water to a boil. Add the spaghetti and remaining olive oil and cook for 2–3 minutes, or until tender but still firm to the bite. Drain the spaghetti thoroughly and return to the pan.

3 Add the olive oil and garlic mixture to the spaghetti and toss to coat thoroughly. Season to taste with pepper, then add the chopped fresh parsley and toss to coat again.

4 Transfer the spaghetti to a warm serving dish and serve immediately.

COOK'S TIP

Oils produced by different countries—mainly Italy, Spain, and Greece—have their own characteristic flavors. Some produce an oil which has a hot, peppery taste while others have a green flavor.

Three-Cheese Macaroni

Based on a traditional family favorite, this pasta bake has plenty of flavor. Serve with a crisp salad for a quick, tasty supper.

NUTRITIONAL INFORMATION

Calories	672	Sugars	........10g
Protein	........31g	Fat	.........44g
Carbohydrate	...40g	Saturates	......23g

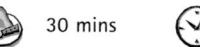

30 mins   45 mins

SERVES 4

INGREDIENTS

2½ cups Béchamel sauce (see page 6)

2 cups macaroni

1 egg, beaten

1 cup grated sharp Cheddar

1 tbsp whole-grain mustard

2 tbsp chopped fresh chives

4 tomatoes, sliced

1 cup grated brick cheese

½ cup grated blue cheese

2 tbsp sunflower seeds

salt and pepper

snipped fresh chives, to garnish

1 Make the Béchamel sauce, transfer it into a bowl, and cover with plastic wrap to prevent a skin forming on the surface of the sauce. Set aside.

2 Bring a pan of salted water to a boil and cook the macaroni for 8–10 minutes or until just tender. Drain well and place in a lightly greased ovenproof dish.

3 Stir the beaten egg, Cheddar cheese, mustard, and chives into the Béchamel sauce and season to taste with salt and pepper.

4 Spoon the sauce over the macaroni, making sure it is well covered. Arrange the sliced tomatoes in a layer over the top.

5 Sprinkle the brick and blue cheeses and the sunflower seeds evenly over the pasta bake. Put the dish on a cookie sheet and bake in a preheated oven, 375°F/190°C, for 25–30 minutes or until the topping is bubbling and golden.

6 Garnish the pasta bake with snipped chives and serve immediately on warmed plates.

Pear & Walnut Pasta

This is quite an unusual combination of ingredients in a savory dish, but is absolutely wonderful tossed into a fine pasta, such as spaghetti.

NUTRITIONAL INFORMATION

Calories	508	Sugars	.........9g
Protein	.........15g	Fat	..........27g
Carbohydrate	...50g	Saturates	......11g

  10 mins   20 mins

SERVES 4

INGREDIENTS

8 oz/225 g dried spaghetti

2 small ripe pears, peeled and sliced

⅔ cup vegetable stock

6 tbsp dry white wine

2 tbsp butter

1 tbsp olive oil

1 red onion, quartered and sliced

1 garlic clove, crushed

½ cup walnut halves

2 tbsp chopped fresh oregano

1 tbsp lemon juice

3 oz/85 g dolcelatte cheese

salt and pepper

fresh oregano sprigs, to garnish

1 Bring a large pan of lightly salted water to a boil. Add the pasta, bring back to a boil, and cook for 8–10 minutes until tender, but still firm to the bite. Drain thoroughly, set aside, and keep warm until required.

2 Meanwhile, place the pears in a pan and pour in the stock and wine. Poach the pears over low heat for about 10 minutes until tender. Remove the pears with a draining spoon and reserve the cooking liquid. Set the pears aside.

3 Heat the butter and oil in a pan until the butter melts. Add the onion and garlic and cook over low heat, stirring frequently, for 2–3 minutes.

4 Stir in the walnut halves, chopped oregano, and lemon juice. Stir in the reserved pears with 4 tablespoons of the poaching liquid.

5 Crumble the dolcelatte cheese into the pan and cook over low heat, stirring occasionally, for 1–2 minutes or until the cheese is just beginning to melt. Season with salt and pepper to taste.

6 Add the pasta and toss in the sauce, using 2 forks. Transfer to a serving dish, garnish with oregano, and serve.

Walnut & Olive Pasta

This mouthwatering dish would make an excellent light, vegetarian lunch for four or a good appetizer for six.

NUTRITIONAL INFORMATION

Calories 833	Sugars 5g
Protein 20g	Fat 66g
Carbohydrate . . .44g	Saturates 15g

 15 mins   10 mins

Serves 4–6

INGREDIENTS

2 thick slices whole-wheat bread, crusts removed

1¼ cups milk

2½ cups shelled walnuts

2 garlic cloves, minced

1 cup pitted black olives

⅔ cup freshly grated Parmesan cheese

8 tbsp extra virgin olive oil

⅝ cup heavy cream

1 lb/450 g fresh fettuccine

salt and pepper

2–3 tbsp chopped fresh parsley

  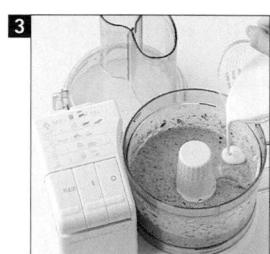

1 Put the bread in a shallow dish. Pour over the milk and let soak until the liquid has been absorbed.

2 Spread the walnuts out on a cookie sheet and toast in a preheated oven at 375°F/190°C for about 5 minutes, or until golden. Let cool.

3 Put the soaked bread, walnuts, garlic, olives, Parmesan cheese, and 6 tbsp of the olive oil in a food processor and work to make a paste. Season to taste with salt and black pepper and stir in the cream.

4 Bring a large pan of lightly salted water to a boil. Add the fettuccine and 1 tbsp of the remaining oil and cook for 2–3 minutes, or until tender but still firm to the bite. Drain the fettuccine thoroughly and toss with the remaining olive oil.

5 Divide the fettuccine between individual serving plates and spoon the olive, garlic, and walnut sauce on top. Sprinkle over the fresh parsley, and serve.

COOK'S TIP
Parmesan quickly loses its pungency and bite. It is better to buy small quantities and grate it yourself. Wrapped in foil, it will keep in the refrigerator for several months.

Mozzarella & Broccoli Pasta

This colorful dish provides a mouthwatering contrast in the crisp *al dente* texture of the broccoli and the creamy cheese sauce.

NUTRITIONAL INFORMATION

Calories 472	Sugars 6g
Protein 15g	Fat 24g
Carbohydrate ...52g	Saturates 14g

 10 mins   25 mins

SERVES 4

I N G R E D I E N T S

4 tbsp butter

1 large onion, finely chopped

1 lb/450 g dried ribbon pasta

1 lb/450 g broccoli, broken into flowerets

⅝ cup boiling vegetable bouillon

1 tbsp all-purpose flour

⅝ cup light cream

½ cup grated mozzarella cheese

freshly grated nutmeg

salt and white pepper

fresh apple slices, to garnish

1 Melt half of the butter in a large pan over medium heat. Add the onion and cook for 4 minutes.

2 Add the broccoli and pasta to the pan and cook, stirring constantly, for 2 minutes. Add the vegetable bouillon, then bring back to a boil and simmer for an additional 12 minutes. Season well with salt and white pepper.

3 Meanwhile, melt the remaining butter in a pan over medium heat. Sprinkle over the flour and cook, stirring constantly, for 2 minutes. Gradually stir in the cream and bring to simmering point, but do not boil. Add the grated cheese and season to taste with salt and a little freshly grated nutmeg.

4 Drain the pasta and broccoli mixture and pour over the cheese sauce. Cook, stirring occasionally, for about 2 minutes. Transfer the pasta and broccoli mixture to a warm, large, deep serving dish and serve garnished with slices of fresh apple.

VARIATION

This dish would also be delicious and look just as colorful made with Cape broccoli, which is actually a purple variety of cauliflower and not broccoli at all.

Macaroni & Corn Crêpes

These vegetable crêpes can be filled with your favorite vegetables—
try shredded parsnips with a tablespoon of mustard.

NUTRITIONAL INFORMATION

Calories 702   Sugars 4g
Protein . . . . .13g   Fat 50g
Carbohydrate . . .55g   Saturates 23g

🍯 15 mins   🕐 40 mins

SERVES 4

I N G R E D I E N T S

2 corn ears

4 tbsp butter

4 oz/115 g red bell peppers, seeded and
finely diced

2½ cups dried short-cut macaroni

⅔ cup heavy cream

¼ cup all-purpose flour

4 egg yolks

4 tbsp olive oil

salt and pepper

TO SERVE

oyster mushrooms

fried leeks

1 Bring a pan of water to a boil, add the corn ears, and cook for about 8 minutes. Drain thoroughly and refresh under cold running water for 3 minutes. Carefully cut away the kernels onto paper towels and let dry.

2 Melt 2 tablespoons of the butter in a skillet. Add the bell peppers and cook over low heat for 4 minutes. Drain and pat dry with paper towels.

3 Bring a large pan of lightly salted water to a boil. Add the macaroni, bring back to a boil, and cook for about 12 minutes or until the macaroni is tender, but still firm to the bite. Drain the macaroni thoroughly and let cool in cold water until required.

4 Beat the cream with the flour, a pinch of salt, and the egg yolks in a bowl until smooth. Add the corn kernels and bell peppers. Drain the macaroni and then toss into the corn and cream mixture. Season with pepper to taste.

5 Heat the remaining butter with the oil in a large skillet. Drop spoonfuls of the mixture into the pan and press down until the mixture forms flat crêpes. Cook until golden on both sides, and all the mixture is used up. Serve immediately with oyster mushrooms and sautéed leeks.

Macaroni Cheese & Tomato

This is a really simple, family dish which is inexpensive and easy to prepare and cook. Serve with a salad or fresh green vegetables.

NUTRITIONAL INFORMATION

Calories	592	Sugars	.........6g
Protein	........28g	Fat	..........29g
Carbohydrate	...57g	Saturates	......17g

 15 mins   35–40 mins

SERVES 4

I N G R E D I E N T S

2 cups dried elbow-macaroni

1½ cups grated Cheddar cheese

generous 1 cup grated Parmesan cheese

1 tbsp butter or margarine, plus extra
    for greasing

4 tbsp fresh white bread crumbs

1 tbsp chopped fresh basil

T O M A T O   S A U C E

1 tbsp olive oil

1 shallot, finely chopped

2 garlic cloves, crushed

1 lb 2 oz/500 g canned chopped tomatoes

1 tbsp chopped fresh basil

salt and pepper

1 To make the tomato sauce, heat the oil in a heavy pan. Add the shallots and garlic and cook, stirring constantly, for 1 minute. Add the tomatoes and basil and season with salt and pepper to taste. Cook over medium heat, stirring constantly, for 10 minutes.

2 Meanwhile, bring a large pan of lightly salted water to a boil. Add the macaroni, bring back to a boil, and cook for 8 minutes or until tender, but still firm to the bite. Drain well.

3 Combine the grated Cheddar and Parmesan in a bowl. Grease a deep, casserole. Spoon one-third of the tomato sauce into the bottom of the dish, cover with one-third of the macaroni, and then top with one-third of the mixed cheeses. Season to taste with salt and pepper. Repeat these layers twice, ending with a layer of grated cheese.

4 Combine the bread crumbs and basil and sprinkle evenly over the top. Dot the topping with the butter or margarine and cook in a preheated oven, 375°F/190°C, for 25 minutes or until the the topping is golden brown and bubbling. Serve immediately.

Spinach Lasagna

Always check the seasoning of vegetables—you can always add a little more to a recipe, but you cannot take it out once it has been added.

NUTRITIONAL INFORMATION

Calories	720	Sugars	.........9g
Protein	........31g	Fat	..........52g
Carbohydrate	...36g	Saturates	......32g

🍴 20 mins   🕐 40 mins

SERVES 4

INGREDIENTS

½ cup butter, plus extra for greasing

2 garlic cloves, finely chopped

¼ lb/115 g shallots

½ lb/225 g exotic mushrooms, such as chanterelles

1 lb/450 g spinach, cooked, drained, and finely chopped

2 cups grated Cheddar cheese

¼ tsp freshly grated nutmeg

1 tsp chopped fresh basil

scant ½ cup all-purpose flour

2½ cups hot milk

⅔ cup grated mellow hard cheese

8 sheets precooked lasagna

salt and pepper

1 Lightly grease a large ovenproof dish with a little butter and set aside.

2 Melt 4 tablespoons of the butter in a skillet. Add the garlic, shallots, and exotic mushrooms and sauté over low heat, stirring frequently, for 3 minutes. Stir in the spinach, Cheddar cheese, nutmeg, and basil. Season with salt and pepper to taste and set aside.

3 Melt the remaining butter in another skillet over low heat. Add the flour and cook, stirring constantly, for 1 minute. Gradually stir in the hot milk, whisking constantly until smooth. Stir in ¼ cup of the mellow hard cheese and season to taste with salt and pepper.

4 Spread half of the mushroom and spinach mixture over the bottom of the prepared dish. Cover with a layer of half the lasagna sheets and then with half of the cheese sauce.

5 Repeat the layering process, then sprinkle over the remaining mellow hard cheese.

6 Bake in a preheated oven, at 400°F/200°C, for about 30 minutes or until the topping is golden brown and bubbling. Serve hot straight from the dish.

VARIATION

You could substitute 4 bell peppers for the spinach. Roast in a preheated oven, at 400°F/200°C, for 20 minutes. Rub off the skins under cold water, seed, and chop before using.

Vegetable Ravioli

It is important not to overcook the vegetable filling or it will become sloppy and unexciting, instead of firm to the bite and delicious.

NUTRITIONAL INFORMATION

Calories	622	Sugars	.......10g
Protein	......12g	Fat	........40g
Carbohydrate	...58g	Saturates	......6g

🕑 1½ hrs   ⏲ 55 mins

SERVES 4

INGREDIENTS

1 lb/450 g Basic Pasta Dough
  (see page 321)

1 tbsp olive oil

6 tbsp butter

⅔ cup light cream

¾ cup freshly grated Parmesan cheese

fresh basil sprigs, to garnish

STUFFING

2 large eggplants

3 large zucchini

6 large tomatoes

1 large green bell pepper

1 large red bell pepper

3 garlic cloves

1 large onion

½ cup olive oil

2 tbsp tomato paste

½ tsp chopped fresh basil

salt and pepper

1 First, make the stuffing. Cut the eggplants and zucchini into 1 inch/ 2.5 cm chunks. Put the eggplant pieces in a strainer, sprinkle liberally with salt, and let stand for 20 minutes. Rinse and drain.

2 Blanch the tomatoes in boiling water for 2 minutes. Drain, peel, and chop the flesh. Core and seed the bell peppers and cut into 1 inch/2.5 cm dice. Chop the garlic and onion.

3 Heat the olive oil in a pan. Add the chopped garlic and onion to the pan and sauté over low heat, stirring occasionally, for 3 minutes.

4 Stir in the eggplants, zucchini, tomatoes, bell peppers, tomato paste, and basil. Season with salt and pepper to taste, cover, and simmer for 20 minutes, stirring frequently.

5 Roll out the pasta dough and cut out 3 inch/7.5 cm circles with a plain cutter. Put a spoonful of the vegetable stuffing on each circle. Dampen the edges slightly and fold the pasta circles over, pressing together to seal.

6 Bring a pan of salted water to a boil. Add the ravioli and the oil, bring back to a boil, and cook for 3–4 minutes. Drain and transfer to an ovenproof dish, dotting each layer with butter. Pour over the cream and sprinkle over the Parmesan cheese. Bake in a preheated oven, 400°F/200°C, for 20 minutes. Garnish with basil and serve.

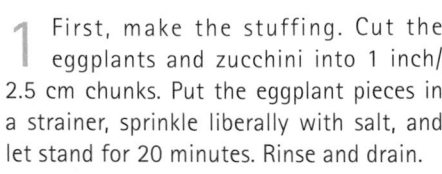

Goat Cheese & Penne Salad

This superb and substantial salad is a delicious combination of goat's cheese with the slightly bitter taste of radicchio.

NUTRITIONAL INFORMATION

Calories	634	Sugars	........13g
Protein	........18g	Fat	..........51g
Carbohydrate	...27g	Saturates	......13g

1½ hrs   15 mins

SERVES 4

INGREDIENTS

2¼ cups dried penne

1 head radicchio, torn into pieces

1 lettuce, torn into pieces

7 tbsp chopped walnuts

2 ripe pears, cored and diced

1 fresh basil sprig

1 bunch of watercress, trimmed

2 tbsp lemon juice

4 tbsp olive oil

3 tbsp garlic vinegar

4 tomatoes, quartered

1 small onion, sliced

1 large carrot, grated

9 oz/250 g goat cheese, diced

salt

1 Bring a large pan of lightly salted water to a boil. Add the pasta, bring back to a boil, and cook for 8–10 minutes or until tender, but still firm to the bite. Drain the pasta, refresh under cold running water, drain thoroughly again, and set aside to cool.

2 Place the radicchio and lettuce in a large salad bowl and mix together well. Top with the pasta, walnuts, pears, basil, and watercress.

3 Combine the lemon juice, olive oil, and the vinegar in a measuring cup. Pour the dressing over the salad ingredients and toss to coat the salad greens well.

4 Add the tomato quarters, onion slices, grated carrot, and diced goat cheese and toss together, using 2 forks, until well mixed. Cover the salad with plastic wrap and chill in the refrigerator for about 1 hour before serving.

COOK'S TIP
Radicchio is a variety of endive originating in Italy. It has a slightly bitter flavor.

Tortelloni

These tasty little squares of pasta stuffed with mushrooms and cheese are surprisingly filling. This recipe makes 36 tortelloni.

NUTRITIONAL INFORMATION

Calories 360   Sugars 1g
Protein ....9g   Fat 21g
Carbohydrate ...36g   Saturates 12g

1¼ hrs   25 mins

SERVES 4

INGREDIENTS

about 10½ oz/300 g Pasta Dough (see page XXX), rolled out to thin sheets

5 tbsp butter

2 oz shallots, finely chopped

3 garlic cloves, crushed

1 cup mushrooms, wiped and finely chopped

½ celery stalk, finely chopped

5 tbsp grated romano cheese, plus extra to garnish

1 tbsp vegetable oil

salt and pepper

1 Using a serrated pasta cutter, cut 2 inch/5 cm squares from the sheets of fresh pasta. To make 36 tortelloni you will need 72 squares. Once the pasta is cut, cover the squares with plastic wrap to prevent them drying out.

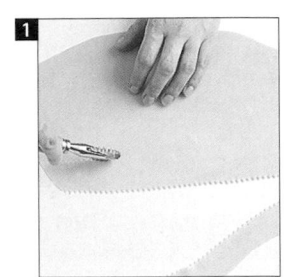

2 Heat 3 tablespoons of the butter in a skillet. Add the shallots, 1 crushed garlic clove, the mushrooms, and celery and cook for 4–5 minutes.

3 Remove the skillet from the heat, stir in the cheese, and season with salt and pepper to taste.

4 Spoon ½ teaspoon of the mixture onto the middle of 36 pasta squares. Brush the edges of the squares with water and top with the remaining 36 squares. Press the edges together to seal. Let rest for 5 minutes.

5 Bring a large pan of water to a boil, add the oil, and cook the tortelloni, in batches, for 2–3 minutes. The tortelloni will rise to the surface when cooked and the pasta should be tender, but still firm to the bite. Remove from the pan with a slotted spoon and drain thoroughly.

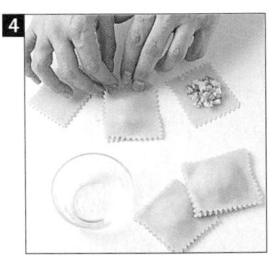

6 Meanwhile, melt the remaining butter in a pan over low heat. Add the remaining garlic and plenty of pepper and cook for 1–2 minutes. Transfer the tortelloni to serving plates and pour the garlic butter over them. Garnish with grated romano and serve immediately.

Basil & Tomato Pasta

Roasting the tomatoes gives a sweeter, smoother flavor to the sauce. Italian plum or flavia tomatoes are ideal for this dish.

NUTRITIONAL INFORMATION

Calories	177	Sugars	.........4g
Protein	.........5g	Fat	..........4g
Carbohydrate	...31g	Saturates	......1g

10 mins

25–35 mins

SERVES 4

INGREDIENTS

1 tbsp olive oil

2 sprigs rosemary

2 cloves garlic, unpeeled

1 lb/450 g tomatoes, halved

1 tbsp sun-dried tomato paste

12 fresh basil leaves, plus extra to garnish

salt and pepper

1½ lb/675 g fresh farfalle or ¾ lb dried farfalle

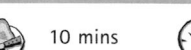

1 Place the oil, rosemary, garlic, and tomatoes, skin side up, in a shallow roasting pan.

2 Drizzle with oil and cook under a preheated broiler for 20 minutes, or until the tomato skins are slightly charred.

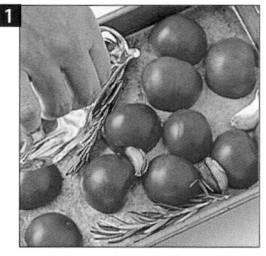
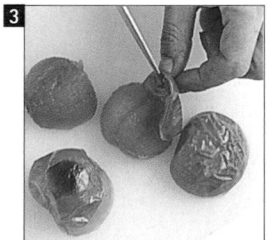

3 Peel the skin from the tomatoes. Coarsely chop the tomato flesh and place in a pan.

4 Squeeze the pulp from the garlic cloves and mix with the tomato flesh and sun-dried tomato paste.

5 Roughly tear the fresh basil leaves into smaller pieces and then stir them into the sauce. Season with a little salt and pepper to taste.

6 Cook the farfalle in a pan of boiling, lightly salted water according to the instructions on the packet, or until it is cooked through, but still has bite. Drain the pasta thoroughly.

7 Gently heat through the tomato and basil sauce.

8 Transfer the farfalle to serving plates and serve with the sauce, garnished with basil leaves.

COOK'S TIP
This sauce tastes just as good when served cold in a pasta salad.

Chili Tagliatelle

Pasta is cooked in a deliciously fresh and slightly spicy tomato sauce which is excellent for lunch or a light supper.

NUTRITIONAL INFORMATION

Calories ....306 Sugars 7g
Protein ....8g Fat 12g
Carbohydrate ...45g Saturates 7g

15 mins   35 mins

SERVES 4

INGREDIENTS

3 tbsp butter

1 onion, finely chopped

1 garlic clove, minced

2 small red chilies, seeded and diced

1 lb/450 g fresh tomatoes, skinned, seeded, and diced

¾ cup vegetable bouillon

2 tbsp tomato paste

1 tsp sugar

salt and pepper

1½ lb/675 g fresh green and white tagliatelle, or ¾ lb dried

1 Melt the butter in a large pan. Add the onion and garlic and cook for 3–4 minutes, or until soft.

2 Add the chilies and continue cooking for about 2 minutes more.

3 Add the tomatoes and bouillon, then reduce the heat and let simmer for 10 minutes, stirring.

4 Pour the sauce into a food processor and blend for 1 minute, or until smooth. Alternatively, push the sauce through a strainer.

5 Return the sauce to the pan and add the tomato paste, sugar, and salt and pepper to taste. Gently reheat over low heat, until piping hot.

6 Cook the tagliatelle in a pan of boiling water according to the instructions on the packet or until it is cooked, but still has bite. Drain the tagliatelle and transfer to serving plates. Serve immediately with the tomato sauce.

VARIATION

Try using a different shape of pasta, such as penne, for this recipe,then put it in an ovenproof dish, top it with some grated cheese, and bake it for a warming winter feast.

Penne & Apple Salad

This gorgeous crisp salad, dressed in garlic mayonnaise, is perfect to serve as part of a summer buffet lunch alfresco.

NUTRITIONAL INFORMATION

Calories	858	Sugars 35g
Protein	........11g	Fat 64g
Carbohydrate	...64g	Saturates 8g

20 mins, plus chilling

10–15 mins

SERVES 4

I N G R E D I E N T S

2 large lettuces

2½ cups dried penne

1 tbsp olive oil

8 red eating apples

juice of 4 lemons

1 head of celery, sliced

¾ cup shelled, halved walnuts

1⅛ cups fresh garlic mayonnaise
  (see Cook's Tip, right)

salt

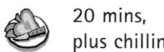

1 Wash, drain, and pat dry the lettuce leaves with paper towels. Transfer them to the refrigerator for 1 hour, until crisp.

2 Meanwhile, bring a large pan of lightly salted water to a boil. Add the pasta and olive oil and cook until tender, but still firm to the bite. Drain the pasta and refresh under cold running water. Drain thoroughly and set aside.

3 Core and dice the apples, then place them in a small bowl and sprinkle with the lemon juice. Mix together the pasta, celery, apples, and walnuts halves and toss the mixture in the garlic mayonnaise (see Cook's Tip, right). Add more mayonnaise, if liked.

4 Line a salad bowl with the lettuce leaves and spoon the pasta salad into the lined bowl. Serve when required.

COOK'S TIP

To make garlic mayonnaise, beat 2 egg yolks with a pinch of salt and 6 crushed garlic cloves. Beat in 1½ cups of olive oil, 1–2 tsp at a time. When ¼ of the oil has been used, add 1–2 tbsp white wine vinegar. Beat in the rest of the oil in a thin stream. Add 1 tsp Dijon mustard, and season.

Traditional Cannelloni

You can buy ready made dried pasta tubes. However, if using fresh pasta, you must cut out squares and roll them yourself.

NUTRITIONAL INFORMATION

Calories	342	Sugars	.........6g
Protein	........15g	Fat	..........15g
Carbohydrate	...38g	Saturates	.......8g

 50 mins 30 mins

SERVES 4

I N G R E D I E N T S

20 tubes dried cannelloni (about 7 oz/ 200 g) or 20 square sheets of fresh pasta (about ¾ lb/350 g)

generous 1 cup ricotta cheese

150 g/5½ oz frozen spinach, thawed

½ small red bell pepper, seeded and diced

2 scallions, chopped

butter, for greasing

⅔ cup hot vegetable or bouillon

1 quantity Tomato Sauce (see page 7), made with 2 tbsp chopped fresh basil instead of parsley

⅓ cup freshly grated Parmesan or romano cheese

salt and pepper

VARIATION

If you would prefer a creamier version, omit the bouillon and the tomato sauce and replace with Béchamel sauce (see page 6).

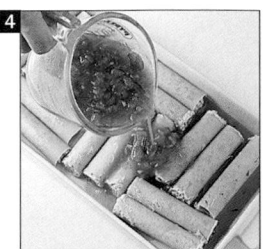

1 If necessary, precook dried cannelloni. Bring a large pan of water to a boil, add the pasta, bring back to a boil, and cook for 3–4 minutes. Cook in batches if this is easier.

2 Combine the ricotta, spinach, bell pepper, and scallions in a bowl and season to taste with salt and pepper.

3 Lightly grease a casserole, large enough to contain all of the pasta tubes in a single layer, with a little butter. Spoon the ricotta mixture into the pasta tubes and place them into the prepared casserole. If you are using fresh sheets of pasta, spread the ricotta mixture along one side of each fresh pasta square and roll up to form a tube.

4 Combine the vegetable bouillon and the tomato sauce and pour it over the pasta tubes.

5 Sprinkle the Parmesan or romano cheese over the cannelloni and bake in a preheated oven, 375°F/190°C, for 20–25 minutes or until the pasta is cooked through and the topping is golden and bubbling. Serve immediately.

Mushroom Lasagna

Layers of pasta, tomatoes and mushrooms are baked in a creamy sauce for a filling, colorful and truly scrumptious supper.

NUTRITIONAL INFORMATION

Calories	628	Sugars	........10g
Protein	24	Fat	..........41g
Carbohydrate	43	Saturates	......23g

 45 mins   40 mins

SERVES 4

INGREDIENTS

40 g/1½ oz dried porcini mushrooms

2 tbsp olive oil

1 onion, finely chopped

2 cups canned chopped tomatoes

1 lb/450 g white mushrooms, thinly sliced

4 tbsp butter, plus extra for greasing

1 garlic clove, finely chopped

1 tbsp lemon juice

6 sheets no-precook lasagna

½ tsp Dijon mustard

¾ quantity cheese sauce, made with Cheddar cheese (see page 304)

4 tbsp freshly grated Parmesan cheese

salt and ground black pepper

1 Place the porcini mushrooms in a small bowl, cover with boiling water, and let soak for 30 minutes. Meanwhile, heat the olive oil in a small skillet. Add the onion and cook, stirring occasionally, for 5 minutes, until softened. Add the tomatoes and cook, stirring frequently, for 7–8 minutes. Season the mixture to taste with salt and pepper and set aside.

2 Drain the porcini mushrooms and slice. Melt half the butter in a large, heavy skillet. Add the porcini and white mushrooms and cook until they start to give off their juices. Add the garlic and lemon juice and season to taste with salt and pepper. Cook over low heat, stirring occasionally, until the liquid has almost evaporated.

3 Lightly grease an ovenproof dish with butter. Stir the mustard into the cheese sauce, then spread a layer of the sauce over the base of the dish. Place a layer of lasagna on top, cover with the mushrooms, another layer of sauce, another layer of lasagna, the tomato mixture, and, finally, another layer of sauce. Sprinkle with the cheese and dot with the remaining butter.

4 Bake in a preheated oven, 400°F/200°C, for 20 minutes. Let the lasagna stand for 5 minutes before serving.

Patriotic Pasta

The ingredients of this dish have the same bright colors as the Italian flag—red, white, and green—hence its name.

NUTRITIONAL INFORMATION

Calories 325   Sugars 5g
Protein ....8g   Fat 13g
Carbohydrate ...48g   Saturates 2g

 5 mins   15 mins

SERVES 4

INGREDIENTS

1 lb/450 g dried farfalle

3 tbsp olive oil

1 lb/450 g cherry tomatoes

3 oz/85 g arugula

salt and pepper

romano cheese, to garnish

1 Bring a large pan of lightly salted water to a boil. Add the farfalle, bring back to a boil, and cook for 8–10 minutes or until tender, but still firm to the bite. Drain the farfalle thoroughly and return to the pan.

2 Cut the cherry tomatoes in half and trim the arugula.

3 Heat the olive oil in a large, heavy pan. Add the tomatoes to the pan and cook for 1 minute.

4 Add the drained farfalle and the arugula to the tomatoes in the pan and stir very gently over low heat until thoroughly mixed and warmed through—the arugula should only just have wilted. Season the mixture to taste with salt and pepper.

5 Meanwhile, using a vegetable peeler, shave thin slices of romano cheese.

6 Transfer the farfalle and vegetables to a warmed serving dish. Garnish with the romano cheese shavings and serve the pasta immediately.

COOK'S TIP

Romano cheese is a hard sheep's-milk cheese which resembles Parmesan and is often used for grating over a variety of dishes. It has a sharp flavor and is used only in small quantities.

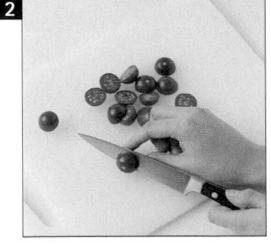

Pasta with Alfredo Sauce

This simple, traditional dish can be made with any long pasta, but is especially good with flat noodles, such as fettuccine or tagliatelle.

NUTRITIONAL INFORMATION

Calories	627	Sugars	.........2g
Protein	........18g	Fat	..........41g
Carbohydrate	...51g	Saturates	......23g

 5 mins   10 mins

SERVES 4

INGREDIENTS

2 tbsp butter

⅞ cup heavy cream

1 lb fresh fettuccine

1 tbsp olive oil

1 cup freshly grated Parmesan cheese, plus extra to serve

pinch of freshly grated nutmeg

salt and pepper

fresh parsley sprigs, to garnish

1 Put the butter and ⅝ cup of the cream in a large pan and bring to a boil over medium heat. Reduce the heat, then simmer gently for about 1½ minutes, or until slightly thickened.

2 Meanwhile, bring a large pan of lightly salted water to a boil. Add the fettuccine and olive oil and cook for 2–3 minutes, or until tender, but still firm to the bite. Drain the fettuccine thoroughly and then pour over the cream sauce.

3 Toss the fettuccine in the sauce over low heat until thoroughly coated.

4 Add the remaining cream, the Parmesan cheese, and nutmeg to the fettuccine mixture and season with salt and pepper. Toss thoroughly to coat while gently heating through.

5 Transfer the fettucine mixture to a warm serving plate and garnish with fresh sprigs of parsley. Serve immediately, handing around extra grated Parmesan cheese separately.

VARIATION

This classic Roman dish is delicious served with the addition of fresh peas. Add 1 cup shelled cooked peas with the Parmesan cheese in step 4.

Macaroni Bake

This warming and satisfying dish would make an excellent supper for a mid-week family meal on a cold winter evening.

NUTRITIONAL INFORMATION

Calories 728	Sugars 11g
Protein 17g	Fat 42g
Carbohydrate ...75g	Saturates 23g

15 mins   45 mins

SERVES 4

INGREDIENTS

4 cups dried short-cut macaroni

1 tbsp olive oil

4 tbsp butter or margarine

1 lb/450 g potatoes, thinly sliced

1 lb/450 g onions, sliced

2 cups grated mozzarella cheese

⅔ cup heavy cream

salt and pepper

crusty whole-wheat bread and butter, to serve

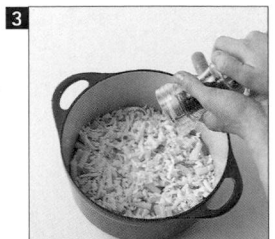

1 Bring a large pan of lightly salted water to a boil. Add the macaroni and olive oil, bring back to a boil, and cook for about 12 minutes or until tender but still firm to the bite. Drain the macaroni thoroughly and set aside.

2 Melt the butter or margarine in a large flameproof casserole, then remove the pan from the heat.

3 Make alternate layers of potatoes, onions, macaroni, and grated mozzarella in the dish, seasoning well with salt and pepper between each layer, and finishing with a layer of cheese on top. Finally, pour the cream over the top layer of cheese.

4 Bake in a preheated oven, 400°F/200°C, for 25 minutes. Remove the dish from the oven and carefully brown the top of the bake under a preheated hot broiler.

5 Serve the bake straight from the dish with crusty whole-wheat bread and butter as an entrée. Alternatively, serve as a vegetable accompaniment with your favorite entrée.

VARIATION

For a stronger flavor, use mozzarella affumicata, a smoked version of this cheese, or Swiss cheese, instead of the normal mozzarella.

Eggplant & Artichoke Pasta

Delicious Mediterranean vegetables, cooked in rich tomato sauce, make an ideal topping for nutty whole-wheat pasta.

NUTRITIONAL INFORMATION

Calories	492	Sugars	........13g
Protein	........15g	Fat	..........16g
Carbohydrate	...77g	Saturates	.......5g

 10 mins   40 mins

SERVES 4

I N G R E D I E N T S

2 tbsp olive oil

1 large, red onion, chopped

2 garlic cloves, minced

1 tbsp lemon juice

4 baby eggplant, cut into quarters

2½ cups strained tomatoes

2 tsp superfine sugar

2 tbsp tomato paste

14 oz canned artichoke hearts, drained and halved

1 cup pitted black olives

¾ lb/340 g dried spaghetti

2 tbsp butter

salt and pepper

fresh basil sprigs, to garnish

olive bread, to serve

and stir in the superfine sugar and tomato paste. Bring to a boil, then lower the heat and simmer, stirring occasionally, for 20 minutes.

3 Gently stir in the artichoke hearts and black olives and cook for 5 minutes.

4 Meanwhile, bring a large pan of lightly salted water to a boil. Add the spaghetti and the remaining oil and cook for 7–8 minutes, or until tender, but still firm to the bite.

5 Drain the spaghetti and toss with the butter. Transfer the spaghetti to a large serving dish.

6 Pour the vegetable sauce over the spaghetti and garnish with the sprigs of fresh basil. Serve immediately with olive bread.

1 Heat 1 tbsp of the olive oil in a large skillet. Add the onion, garlic, lemon juice, and eggplant and cook over low heat for 4–5 minutes, or until the onion and eggplant are lightly golden brown.

2 Pour in the strained tomatoes, season to taste with salt and black pepper,

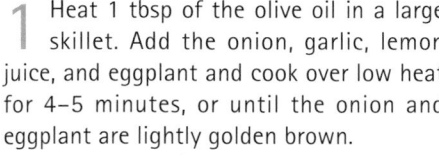

Mushroom Pasta with Port

This easy vegetarian dish is ideal for busy people with little time to spare, but very good taste!

NUTRITIONAL INFORMATION

Calories 763	Sugars 11g	
Protein 17g	Fat 38g	
Carbohydrate . . .93g	Saturates 20g	

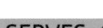

10 mins   35 mins

SERVES 4

I N G R E D I E N T S

4 tbsp butter

2 tbsp olive oil

6 shallots, sliced

6 cups sliced white mushrooms

1 tsp all-purpose flour

⅝ cup heavy cream

2 tbsp port

4 oz sun-dried tomatoes, chopped

freshly grated nutmeg

1 lb/450 g dried spaghetti

1 tbsp freshly chopped parsley

salt and pepper

6 triangles of fried white bread, to serve

VARIATION

If you like the sound of this recipe but don't have any port available, you can use 2 tbsp of dry white wine instead.

1 Heat the butter and 1 tbsp of the olive oil in a large pan. Add the shallots and cook over medium heat for 3 minutes. Add the mushrooms and cook over low heat for 2 minutes. Season to taste with salt and black pepper, then sprinkle over the flour and cook, stirring constantly, for 1 minute.

2 Gradually stir in the cream and port, then add the sun-dried tomatoes and a pinch of grated nutmeg, and cook over low heat for 8 minutes.

3 Meanwhile, bring a large pan of lightly salted water to a boil. Add the spaghetti and remaining olive oil and cook for 12–14 minutes, or until tender, but still firm to the bite.

4 Drain the spaghetti and return to the pan. Pour over the mushroom sauce and cook for 3 minutes. Transfer the spaghetti and mushroom sauce to a large serving plate and sprinkle over the chopped parsley. Serve with crispy triangles of fried bread.

Beet Cannolicchi

Quick and simple, this colorful, warm salad works equally well as a tasty appetizer or as a main dish for a light lunch.

NUTRITIONAL INFORMATION

Calories 449	Sugars 13g	
Protein 13g	Fat 16g	
Carbohydrate ...70g	Saturates 2g	

 10 mins   25 mins

SERVES 4

INGREDIENTS

2¾ cups dried ditalini rigati

5 tbsp olive oil

2 garlic cloves chopped

14 oz/400 g canned chopped tomatoes

14 oz/400 g cooked beets, diced

2 tbsp chopped fresh basil leaves

1 tsp mustard seeds

salt and pepper

TO SERVE

mixed salad greens, tossed in olive oil

4 Italian plum tomatoes, sliced

1 Bring a large pan of lightly salted water to a boil. Add the pasta and 1 tablespoon of the oil. Bring back to a boil and cook for 8–10 minutes until tender, but still firm to the bite. Drain and set aside.

2 Heat the remaining olive oil in a large pan. Add the garlic and cook over low heat for 3 minutes. Add the chopped tomatoes and cook for 10 minutes.

3 Remove the pan from the heat and carefully add the beets, basil, mustard seeds, and pasta. and season to taste with salt and pepper.

4 Serve while still warm on a bed of mixed salad greens, tossed in olive oil, and sliced plum tomatoes.

COOK'S TIP
To cook raw beets, trim off the leaves about 2 inches above the roots and ensure that the skin is not broken. Boil in very lightly salted water for 30–40 minutes until tender. Set aside to cool and then rub off the skin.

Pesto Pasta

This low-fat version of the traditional rich Italian pesto, combined with pasta and vegetables, makes a healthy and satisfying meal.

🧊 1 hr   🕐 30 mins

SERVES 4

I N G R E D I E N T S

3¼ cups sliced crimini mushrooms

⅔ cup fresh vegetable bouillon

6 oz/175 g asparagus, trimmed and cut into 2 inch/5 cm lengths

10½ oz/300 g green and white tagliatelle

14 oz/400g canned artichoke hearts, drained and halved

grissini, to serve

P E S T O

2 large garlic cloves, crushed

½ cup fresh basil leaves

6 tbsp low-fat unsweetened yogurt

2 tbsp freshly grated Parmesan cheese

salt and pepper

T O   G A R N I S H

shredded fresh basil leaves

Parmesan shavings

1 Place the mushrooms in a pan with the bouillon. Bring to a boil, cover, and simmer for 3–4 minutes until just tender. Drain and set aside, reserving the cooking liquid to use in soups if wished.

2 Bring a small pan of water to a boil and cook the asparagus for 3–4 minutes until just tender. Drain and set aside until required.

3 Bring a large pan of lightly salted water to a boil. Add the pasta, bring back to a boil, and cook until tender, but still firm to the bite: 8–10 minutes for dried pasta or 2–3 minutes for fresh tagliatelle. Drain, return to the pan, and keep warm.

4 Meanwhile, make the pesto. Place all of the ingredients in a blender or food processor and process for a few seconds until smooth. Alternatively, finely chop the basil and mix all the ingredients together.

5 Add the mushrooms, asparagus, and artichoke hearts to the pasta and cook, stirring, over low heat for 2–3 minutes. Remove from the heat and mix with the pesto.

6 Transfer to a warm bowl. Garnish with basil and Parmesan and serve.

Vegetable & Pasta Stir-Fry

Prepare all the vegetables and cook the pasta in advance, then the dish can be cooked in a few minutes.

NUTRITIONAL INFORMATION

Calories	575	Sugars	........13g
Protein	........15g	Fat	..........17g
Carbohydrate	...94g	Saturates	.......2g

 15 mins   25 mins

SERVES 4

I N G R E D I E N T S

4 cups dried whole-wheat pasta shells or other short pasta shapes

1 tbsp olive oil

2 carrots, thinly sliced

¼ lb/115 g baby corn ears

3 tbsp corn oil

1 inch piece fresh ginger root, thinly sliced

1 large onion, thinly sliced

1 garlic clove, thinly sliced

3 celery stalks, thinly sliced

1 small red bell pepper, cored, seeded, and cut into short, thin sticks

1 small green bell pepper, cored, seeded, and cut into short, thin sticks

1 tsp cornstarch

2 tbsp water

3 tbsp soy sauce

3 tbsp dry sherry

1 tsp honey

a dash of hot pepper sauce (optional)

salt

1 Bring a large pan of lightly salted water to a boil. Add the pasta and olive oil and cook until tender, but still firm to the bite. Drain, then return to the pan and keep warm.

2 Bring a pan of lightly salted water to a boil. Add the carrots and corn and cook for 2 minutes. Drain, then refresh in cold water and drain again.

3 Heat the corn oil in a preheated wok or large skillet. Add the ginger and stir-fry over medium heat for 1 minute to flavor the oil. Remove the ginger with a draining spoon and discard.

4 Add the onion, garlic, celery, and bell peppers to the pan and stir-fry for 2 minutes. Add the carrots and baby corn and stir-fry for 2 minutes. Stir in the cooked pasta.

5 Mix together the cornstarch and water to make a smooth paste. Stir in the soy sauce, sherry, and honey. Pour the cornstarch mixture into the pasta and cook, stirring occasionally, for 2 minutes. Stir in a dash of pepper sauce, if liked.

6 Transfer to a warm serving dish and serve immediately.

Spicy Fried Noodles

This is a simple idea to add an extra kick to egg noodles, which accompany many entrées in Thailand.

NUTRITIONAL INFORMATION

Calories . . . . .568 Sugars 3g
Protein . . . . .16g Fat 19g
Carbohydrate . . .90g Saturates 4g

15 mins • 3–5 mins

SERVES 4

I N G R E D I E N T S

1 lb/450 g medium egg noodles

1 cup beansprouts

small bunch chives

3 tbsp sunflower oil

1 garlic clove, crushed

4 fresh green chilies, seeded, sliced, and
   soaked in 2 tbsp rice vinegar

salt

1 Place the noodles in a bowl, cover with boiling water, and soak for 10 minutes. Drain and set aside.

2 Pick over the beansprouts and soak in cold water while you cut the chives into 1 inch/2.5cm pieces. Set a few chives aside for the garnish. Drain the beansprouts thoroughly.

3 Heat the oil in a preheated wok or large, heavy skillet. Add the crushed garlic and stir; then add the chilies and stir-fry for about 1 minute, until fragrant.

4 Add the beansprouts, stir, and then add the noodles. Stir in salt to taste and add the chives. Using 2 spoons or a wok scoop, lift and toss the noodles for 1 minute, until the beansprouts and noodles are heated through.

5 Transfer the noodle mixture to a warm serving dish, garnish with the reserved chive pieces, and serve immediately.

COOK'S TIP

Soaking a chili in rice vinegar has the effect of distributing the hot chili flavor throughout the dish. To reduce the heat, you can slice the chili more thickly before soaking.

Chow Mein

Egg noodles are cooked and then stir-fried with a colorful variety of vegetables to make this well-known and ever-popular dish.

NUTRITIONAL INFORMATION

Calories 669	Sugars 9g	
Protein 19g	Fat 23g	
Carbohydrate ..100g	Saturates 4g	

 15 mins 10 mins

SERVES 4

INGREDIENTS

1 lb/450 g egg noodles

4 tbsp vegetable oil

1 onion, thinly sliced

2 carrots, cut into thin sticks

¼ lb/115 g white mushrooms, quartered

1½ cups snow peas

½ cucumber, cut into sticks

¼ lb/115 g spinach, shredded

2 cups beansprouts

2 tbsp dark soy sauce

1 tbsp sherry

1 tsp salt

1 tsp sugar

1 tsp cornstarch

1 tsp sesame oil

1 Cook the egg noodles according to the instructions on the packet. Drain and rinse under cold running water until cool. Set aside.

2 Heat 3 tablespoons of the vegetable oil in a preheated wok or skillet. Add the onion and carrots and stir-fry for 1 minute, then add the mushrooms, snow peas, and cucumber and stir-fry for an additional 1 minute.

3 Stir in the remaining vegetable oil and add the drained noodles, together with the spinach and beansprouts.

4 Blend together all the remaining ingredients and pour over the noodles and vegetables.

5 Stir-fry until the noodle mixture is thoroughly heated through, transfer to a warm serving dish, and serve.

COOK'S TIP
For a spicy hot chow mein, add 1 tablespoon chili sauce or substitute chili oil for the sesame oil.

Thai-Style Stir-Fried Noodles

This dish is considered the Thai national dish, as it is made and eaten everywhere—a one-dish, fast food for eating on the move.

NUTRITIONAL INFORMATION

Calories 407   Sugars 11g
Protein . . . . .14g   Fat 16g
Carbohydrate . . .56g   Saturates 3g

 15 mins   5 mins

SERVES 4

INGREDIENTS

½ lb/225 g dried rice noodles

2 red chilies, seeded and finely chopped

2 shallots, finely chopped

2 tbsp sugar

2 tbsp tamarind water

1 tbsp lime juice

2 tbsp light soy sauce

1 tbsp sunflower oil

1 tsp sesame oil

6 oz/175 g diced smoked bean curd

pepper

2 tbsp chopped roasted peanuts, to garnish

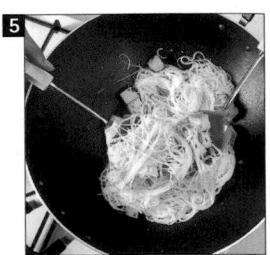

COOK'S TIP

This is a quick one-dish meal that is very useful if you are catering for a single vegetarian in the family.

1 Cook the rice noodles as directed on the pack, or soak them in boiling water for 5 minutes.

2 Grind together the chilies, shallots, sugar, tamarind water, lime juice, light soy sauce, and pepper to taste.

3 Heat the sunflower and sesame oils together in a preheated wok or large, heavy skillet over high heat. Add the bean curd and stir-fry for 1 minute.

4 Add the chili mixture, bring to a boil, and continue to cook, stirring constantly, for about 2 minutes, until the sauce has thickened.

5 Drain the rice noodles and add them to the chili mixture. Use 2 spoons to lift and stir the noodles until they are no longer steaming.

6 Serve the hot noodles immediately, garnished with the chopped peanuts.

Stir-Fried Japanese Noodles

This quick dish is an ideal lunchtime meal, packed with mixed mushrooms in a sweet sauce.

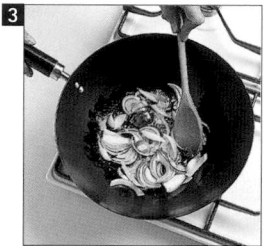

NUTRITIONAL INFORMATION

Calories 379	Sugars 8g
Protein 12g	Fat 13g
Carbohydrate . . .53g	Saturates 3g

 15 mins 15 mins

SERVES 4

I N G R E D I E N T S

½ lb/225 g Japanese egg noodles

2 tbsp sunflower oil

1 red onion, sliced

1 clove garlic, crushed

1 lb/450 g mixed mushrooms (shiitake, oyster, brown cap)

¾ lb/350 g bok choi

2 tbsp sweet sherry

6 tbsp vegetable bouillon

4 scallions, sliced

1 tbsp toasted sesame seeds

1 Place the Japanese egg noodles in a large bowl. Pour over enough boiling water to cover and let the noodles soak for 10 minutes.

2 Meanwhile, heat the sunflower oil in a large preheated wok.

3 Add the red onion and garlic to the wok and cook for 2–3 minutes, or until soft.

4 Add the mushrooms to the wok and cook for about 5 minutes, or until the mushrooms have softened.

5 Drain the soaked egg noodles thoroughly.

6 Add the bok choi, drained noodles, sweet sherry, and bouillon to the wok.

7 Toss all of the ingredients together and cook for 2–3 minutes or until the liquid is just bubbling.

8 Transfer the mushroom noodles to warm serving bowls and scatter with sliced scallions and toasted sesame seeds. Serve immediately.

COOK'S TIP

The variety of mushrooms in large food stores has improved and a good mixture should be easily obtainable. If not, use the more common white and flat mushrooms.

Hot & Sour Noodles

This simple, fast-food dish is sold from street food stands in Thailand, with many and varied additions.

NUTRITIONAL INFORMATION

Calories	337	Sugars	.........1g
Protein	........10g	Fat	...........11g
Carbohydrate	...53g	Saturates	.......1g

5 mins   8 mins

SERVES 4

INGREDIENTS

9 oz/250 g dried medium egg noodles

1 tbsp sesame oil

1 tbsp chili oil

1 garlic clove, crushed

2 scallions, finely chopped

scant 1 cup sliced white mushrooms

1½ oz/40 g dried Chinese black mushrooms, soaked, drained, and sliced

2 tbsp lime juice

3 tbsp light soy sauce

1 tsp sugar

shredded Napa cabbage, to serve

TO GARNISH

2 tbsp chopped fresh cilantro

2 tbsp chopped, toasted peanuts

COOK'S TIP

Thai chili oil is very hot, so if you want a milder flavor, use vegetable oil for the initial cooking instead, then add a final drizzle of chili oil just for seasoning.

1 Cook the noodles in a large pan of boiling water for 3–4 minutes or according to the packet instructions. Drain well, return to the pan, toss with the sesame oil, and set aside.

2 Heat the chili oil in a large skillet or wok and quickly stir-fry the garlic, onions, and white mushrooms for 2 minutes until just soft.

3 Add the black mushrooms, lime juice, soy sauce, and sugar and continue stir-frying until boiling. Add the noodles and toss to mix.

4 Make a bed of shredded Napa cabbage on a serving platter and spoon the noodle mixture on top. Garnish with the fresh cilantro and chopped peanuts and serve immediately.

Chilled Noodles & Peppers

This is a convenient dish to serve when you are arriving home just before family or friends. Quick to prepare and assemble, it is ready in minutes.

NUTRITIONAL INFORMATION

Calories 260	Sugars 4g	
Protein 4g	Fat 21g	
Carbohydrate ...15g	Saturates 4g	

5 mins

15 mins

SERVES 4–6

INGREDIENTS

9 oz/250 g ribbon noodles, or Chinese egg noodles

1 tbsp sesame oil

1 red bell pepper

1 yellow bell pepper

1 green bell pepper

6 scallions, cut into matchstick strips

salt

DRESSING

5 tbsp sesame oil

2 tbsp light soy sauce

1 tbsp sesame seed paste (tahini)

4–5 drops hot pepper sauce

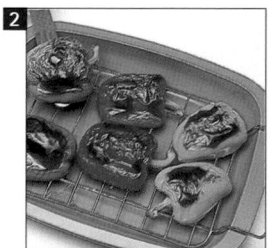 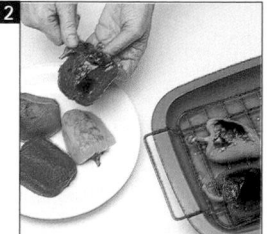 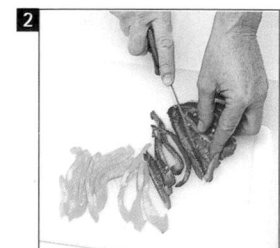

1 Preheat the broiler to medium. Cook the noodles in a large pan of boiling, salted water until they are almost tender. Drain them in a colander, run cold water through them, and drain thoroughly. Tip the noodles into a bowl, stir in the sesame oil, cover, and chill.

2 Cook the bell peppers under the broiler, turning them over frequently, until they are blackened on all sides. Plunge into cold water, then skin them. Cut in half, remove the core and seeds, and cut the flesh into thick strips. Set them aside in a covered container.

3 To make the dressing, mix together the sesame oil, light soy sauce, sesame seed paste, and hot pepper sauce until well combined.

4 Pour the dressing on the noodles, reserving 1 tablespoon, and toss well.

5 Turn the noodles into a serving dish, arrange the grilled bell peppers over the noodles, and spoon on the reserved dressing. Scatter on the scallion strips, and serve immediately.

COOK'S TIP

If you have time, another way of skinning bell peppers is to first broil them, then place in a plastic bag, seal and leave for about 20 minutes. The skin will then peel off easily.

Spicy Japanese Noodles

These noodles are highly spiced with chili and flavored with sesame seeds for a nutty taste which is a true delight.

NUTRITIONAL INFORMATION

Calories	.381	Sugars	.12g
Protein	.11g	Fat	.13g
Carbohydrate	.59g	Saturates	.2g

5 mins   15 mins

SERVES 4

INGREDIENTS

1 lb/450 g fresh Japanese noodles

1 tbsp sesame oil

1 tbsp sesame seeds

1 tbsp sunflower oil

1 red onion, sliced

1½ cups snow peas

2 carrots, thinly sliced

3 cups white cabbage, shredded

3 tbsp sweet chili sauce

2 scallions, sliced, to garnish

1 Bring a large pan of water to a boil. Add the Japanese noodles to the pan and cook for 2–3 minutes. Drain the noodles thoroughly.

2 Toss the noodles with the sesame oil and sesame seeds.

3 Heat the sunflower oil in a large, preheated wok.

4 Add the onion slices, snow peas, carrot slices, and shredded cabbage to the wok and cook for about 5 minutes.

5 Add the sweet chili sauce to the wok and cook, stirring occasionally, for a further 2 minutes.

6 Add the sesame noodles to the wok, toss well to combine, and heat through for a further 2–3 minutes.

7 Transfer the Japanese noodles and spicy vegetables to warm serving bowls and garnish with sliced scallions. Serve immediately. If you prefer, you can serve the noodles separately with the sauce spooned on top.

COOK'S TIP

If fresh Japanese noodles are difficult to get hold of, use dried rice noodles or thin egg noodles instead.

Asian Vegetable Noodles

This dish has a mild, nutty flavor from the peanut butter and dry-roasted peanuts.

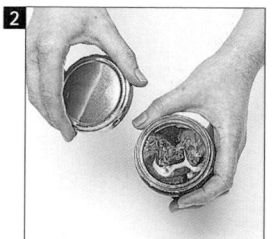

NUTRITIONAL INFORMATION

Calories 193	Sugars 5g	
Protein 7g	Fat 12g	
Carbohydrate ...14g	Saturates 2g	

10 mins   15 mins

SERVES 4

INGREDIENTS

6 oz/175 g green thread noodles or multi-colored spaghetti

1 tsp sesame oil

2 tbsp crunchy peanut butter

2 tbsp light soy sauce

1 tbsp white wine vinegar

1 tsp clear honey

1 cup white radish, grated

1 cup carrot, grated

1 cup cucumber, shredded finely

1 bunch scallions, shredded finely

1 tbsp dry-roasted peanuts, crushed

TO GARNISH

carrot flowers

scallion tassels

1 Bring a large pan of water to a boil, add the noodles or spaghetti, and cook according to the packet instructions. Drain well and rinse in cold water. Let stand in a bowl of cold water until required.

2 To make the peanut butter sauce, put the sesame oil, peanut butter, soy sauce, vinegar, honey, and seasoning into a small screw-top jar. Seal and shake well to mix thoroughly.

3 Drain the noodles or spaghetti well, place in a large serving bowl, and mix in half the peanut sauce.

4 Using 2 forks, toss in the white radish, carrot, cucumber, and scallions. Sprinkle with crushed peanuts and garnish with carrot flowers and scallion tassels.

5 Serve the noodles with the remaining peanut sauce.

COOK'S TIP

There are many varieties of Asian noodles available from Asian markets, delicatessens, and food stores. Try rice noodles, which contain very little fat and require little cooking; usually soaking in boiling water is sufficient.

Crispy Noodles & Bean Curd

This dish requires a certain amount of care and attention to get the crispy noodles properly cooked, but it is well worth the effort.

NUTRITIONAL INFORMATION

Calories 242	Sugars 2g
Protein 13g	Fat 17g
Carbohydrate ...10g	Saturates 3g

35 mins   25 mins

SERVES 4

INGREDIENTS

6 oz/175 g thread egg noodles

2½ cups sunflower oil, for deep-frying

2 tsp grated lemon zest

1 tbsp light soy sauce

1 tbsp rice vinegar

1 tbsp lemon juice

1½ tbsp sugar

9 oz/250 g marinated bean curd, diced

2 garlic cloves, crushed

1 red chili, sliced finely

1 red bell pepper, diced

4 eggs, beaten

red chili flower, to garnish

1 Blanch the egg noodles briefly in hot water, to which a little of the oil has been added. Drain the noodles and spread out to dry for at least 30 minutes. Cut into threads about 3 inches/7 cm long.

2 Combine the lemon zest, light soy sauce, rice vinegar, lemon juice, and sugar in a small bowl. Set the mixture aside until required.

3 Heat the sunflower oil in a wok or large, heavy skillet, and test the temperature with a few strands of the noodles. They should swell to many times their original size, but if they do not, wait a little longer until the oil is hot enough; otherwise they will be tough and stringy, not puffy and light.

4 Cook the noodles in batches. As soon as they turn a pale gold color, scoop them out and drain on plenty of absorbent paper towels. Let cool.

5 Reserve 2 tablespoons of the oil and drain off the rest. Heat the reserved oil in the wok or skillet.

6 Add the marinated bean curd to the wok or skillet and cook quickly over high heat to seal.

7 Add the crushed garlic cloves, sliced red chili, and diced red bell pepper to the wok. Stir-fry for 1–2 minutes.

8 Add the reserved vinegar mixture to the wok, stir to mix well, and add the beaten eggs, stirring until they are set.

9 Serve the bean curd mixture with the crispy fried noodles, garnished with a red chili flower.

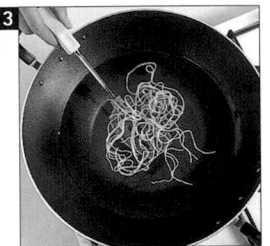

Fried Vegetable Noodles

In this recipe, noodles are first boiled and then deep-fried for a crisply textured dish, and tossed with vegetables.

NUTRITIONAL INFORMATION

Calories	229	Sugars	.........4g
Protein	.........5g	Fat	..........15g
Carbohydrate	...20g	Saturates	.......2g

5 mins   25 mins

SERVES 4

INGREDIENTS

12 oz/350 g dried egg noodles

2 tbsp peanut oil

2 garlic cloves, crushed

½ tsp ground star anise

1 carrot, cut into very thin sticks

1 green bell pepper, cut into very thin sticks

1 onion, quartered and sliced

1 cup broccoli florets

3 oz/85 g canned bamboo shoots

1 celery stalk, sliced

1 tbsp light soy sauce

⅔ cup vegetable bouillon

oil, for deep-frying

1 tsp cornstarch

2 tsp water

1 Cook the noodles in a pan of boiling water for 1–2 minutes. Drain well and rinse under cold running water. Let the noodles drain thoroughly in a strainer until required.

2 Heat the peanut oil in a preheated wok until smoking. Reduce the heat, add the crushed garlic and ground star anise, and cook for 30 seconds. Add the remaining vegetables and cook for 1–2 minutes.

3 Add the soy sauce and vegetable bouillon to the wok and cook over low heat for 5 minutes.

4 Heat the oil for deep-frying in a separate wok to 350°F/180°C, or until a cube of bread browns in 30 seconds.

5 Using a fork, twist the drained noodles and form them into rounds. Deep-fry them in batches until crisp, turning once. Let drain on paper towels.

6 Blend the cornstarch with the water to form a paste and stir into the vegetables. Bring to a boil, stirring, until the sauce is thickened and clear.

7 Arrange the noodles on a warm serving plate, spoon the vegetables on top, and serve immediately.

Home-Made Noodles

These noodles are simple to make; you do not need a pasta-making machine as they are rolled out by hand.

NUTRITIONAL INFORMATION

Calories 294   Sugars 3g
Protein . . . . .7g   Fat 15g
Carbohydrate . . .35g   Saturates 2g

🌀 🌀 🌀 🌀

20 mins   15 mins

SERVES 2–4

I N G R E D I E N T S

N O O D L E S

¾ cup all-purpose flour

2 tbsp cornstarch

½ tsp salt

½ cup boiling water

5 tbsp vegetable oil

S T I R - F R Y

1 zucchini, cut into thin sticks

1 celery stalk, cut into thin sticks

1 carrot, cut into thin sticks

1½ cup open-cup mushrooms, sliced

1 cup broccoli florets and stalks, peeled and
  thinly sliced

1 leek, sliced

1½ cups beansprouts

1 tbsp soy sauce

2 tsp rice wine vinegar

½ tsp sugar

2 Make the noodles by breaking off small pieces of dough and rolling into balls. Roll each ball across a very lightly oiled counter with the palm of your hand to form thin noodles. Do not worry if some of the noodles break into shorter lengths. Set the noodles aside.

3 Heat 3 tablespoons of vegetable oil in a wok. Add the noodles in batches and cook over high heat for 1 minute. Reduce the heat and cook for a further 2 minutes. Remove and drain on absorbent paper towels. Set aside.

4 Heat the remaining vegetable oil in the wok. Add the zucchini, celery, and carrot, and stir-fry for 1 minute. Add the mushrooms, broccoli, and leek, and stir-fry for a further minute.

5 Add the beansprouts, soy sauce, rice wine vinegar, and sugar to the pan and mix well until thoroughly heated.

6 Add the noodles and continue to cook over high heat until they are heated through, tossing with 2 forks to mix the ingredients. Serve immediately.

1 To prepare the noodles, sift the flour, cornstarch, and salt into a bowl. Make a well in the center and pour in the boiling water and 1 teaspoon of oil. Mix quickly to make a soft dough. Cover and let stand for 5–6 minutes.

Sesame Hot Noodles

Plain egg noodles are tossed in a dressing made with sesame oil, soy sauce, peanut butter, cilantro, lime, chili, and sesame seeds.

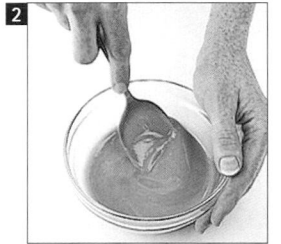

NUTRITIONAL INFORMATION

Calories	300	Sugars	.........1g
Protein	.........7g	Fat	..........21g
Carbohydrate	...21g	Saturates	.......3g

 5 mins   10 mins

SERVES 4

I N G R E D I E N T S

18 oz/500 g dried medium egg noodles

3 tbsp sunflower oil

2 tbsp sesame oil

1 garlic clove, crushed

1 tbsp smooth peanut butter

1 small green chili, seeded and very finely chopped

3 tbsp toasted sesame seeds

4 tbsp light soy sauce

½ tbsp lime juice

salt and pepper

4 tbsp chopped fresh cilantro

1 Place the noodles in a large pan of boiling water, then immediately remove from the heat. Cover and let stand for 6 minutes, stirring once halfway through the time. At the end of 6 minutes the noodles will be perfectly cooked. Alternatively, cook the noodles following the packet instructions.

2 Meanwhile, make the dressing. Mix together the sunflower oil, sesame oil, crushed garlic, and peanut butter in a mixing bowl until smooth.

3 Add the chopped green chili, sesame seeds, and light soy sauce to the other dressing ingredients. Add the lime juice, according to taste, and mix well. Season with salt and pepper.

4 Drain the noodles thoroughly, then place in a warmed serving bowl.

5 Add the dressing and chopped fresh cilantro to the noodles and toss well to mix. Serve hot as an entrée or as an accompaniment.

COOK'S TIP
If you are cooking the noodles ahead of time, toss the cooked, drained noodles in 2 teaspoons of sesame oil, then turn into a bowl. Cover and keep warm until required.

Noodle & Mango Salad

Fruit combines well with the peanut dressing, colorful mixed bell peppers, and chili in this delicious hot salad.

NUTRITIONAL INFORMATION

Calories 368   Sugars 11g
Protein ....11g   Fat 26g
Carbohydrate ...24g   Saturates 5g

15 mins   5 mins

SERVES 4

INGREDIENTS

9 oz/250 g thread egg noodles

2 tbsp peanut oil

4 shallots, sliced

2 cloves garlic, crushed

1 red chili, seeded and sliced

1 red bell pepper, seeded and sliced

1 green bell pepper, seeded and sliced

1 ripe mango, sliced into thin strips

¼ cup salted peanuts, chopped

DRESSING

4 tbsp peanut butter

generous ⅓ cup coconut milk

1 tbsp tomato paste

1 Place the egg noodles in a large dish or bowl. Pour over enough boiling water to cover the noodles and let stand for 10 minutes.

2 Heat the peanut oil in a large preheated wok or skillet.

3 Add the shallots, crushed garlic, chili, and bell pepper slices to the wok or skillet and cook for 2–3 minutes.

4 Drain the egg noodles thoroughly in a strainer. Add the drained noodles and mango slices to the wok or skillet and heat through for about 2 minutes, tossing the noodles to heat them through.

5 Transfer the noodle and mango salad to warmed serving dishes and scatter with chopped peanuts.

6 To make the dressing, mix together the peanut butter, coconut milk, and tomato paste.

7 Spoon the dressing over the noodle salad and serve immediately.

COOK'S TIP

If preferred, gently heat the peanut dressing before pouring over the noodle salad.

Zucchini & Basil Risotto

An easy way of livening up a simple risotto is to use a flavored olive oil—here a basil-flavored oil heightens the taste of the dish.

NUTRITIONAL INFORMATION

Calories	460	Sugars	.........5g
Protein	........13g	Fat	..........18g
Carbohydrate	...64g	Saturates	.......7g

5–10 mins   35 mins

SERVES 4

INGREDIENTS

4 tbsp basil-flavored extra virgin olive oil, plus extra for drizzling

4 zucchini, diced

1 yellow bell pepper, seeded and diced

2 garlic cloves, finely chopped

1 large onion, finely chopped

3½ cups risotto rice

4 tbsp dry white vermouth

scant 7 cups vegetable bouillon, simmering

2 tbsp sweet butter, at room temperature

large handful of fresh basil leaves, torn, plus a few leaves to garnish

1 cup freshly grated Parmesan cheese

1 Heat half the oil in a large skillet over high heat. When very hot, but not smoking, add the zucchini and yellow bell pepper and stir-fry for 3 minutes until lightly golden. Stir in the garlic and cook for about 30 seconds longer. Transfer to a plate and set aside.

2 Heat the remaining oil in a large heavy pan over medium heat. Add the onion and cook, stirring occasionally, for about 2 minutes until soft. Add the rice and cook, stirring frequently, for about 2 minutes until the rice is translucent and well coated with the olive oil.

3 Pour in the vermouth; it will bubble and steam rapidly and evaporate almost immediately. Add a ladleful (about 1 cup) of the simmering bouillon and cook, stirring constantly, until the bouillon is completely absorbed.

4 Continue adding the bouillon, about half a ladleful at a time, letting each addition be absorbed before adding the next. This should take 20–25 minutes. The risotto should have a creamy consistency and the rice should be tender, but still firm to the bite.

5 Stir in the zucchini mixture with any juices, the butter, basil, and grated Parmesan. Drizzle with a little oil and garnish with basil. Serve hot.

White Radish Curry

This is rather an unusual recipe for a vegetarian curry using mooli, a long white radish. The dish is good served hot with chapatis.

NUTRITIONAL INFORMATION

Calories 384   Sugars 4g
Protein ....3g   Fat 38g
Carbohydrate ....9g   Saturates 4g

 10 mins   20 mins

SERVES 4

I N G R E D I E N T S

1 lb/450 g white radish, preferably with leaves

1 tbsp moong dhal

2½ cups water

⅔ cup vegetable oil

1 medium onion, thinly sliced

1 tsp crushed garlic

1 tsp crushed dried red chilies

1 tsp salt

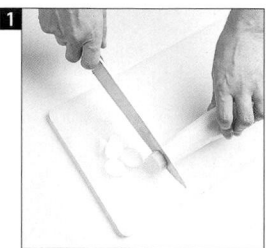

1 Rinse, peel, and roughly slice the white radish, with its leaves, if using.

2 Place the white radish, the leaves, if using, and the moong dhal in a large pan and pour over the water. Bring to a boil and cook over medium heat until the white radish has softened.

3 Drain the white radish mixture thoroughly and squeeze out any excess water, using your hands.

4 Heat the oil in a heavy pan. Add the onion, garlic, crushed red chilies, and salt and cook over medium heat, stirring from time to time, for about 5–7 minutes, until the onions have softened and turned light golden brown in color.

5 Stir the white radish mixture into the spiced onion mixture and combine well. Reduce the heat and continue cooking, stirring frequently, for about 3–5 minutes.

6 Transfer the white radish curry to individual warmed serving plates and serve hot with chapatis

COOK'S TIP

The vegetable used in this recipe, white radish, looks a bit like a parsnip without the tapering end and is now sold in most food stores, as well as in Indian grocery stores.

Kofta Kabobs

Traditionally, koftas are made from a spicy meat mixture, but this bean and wheat version makes a tasty vegetarian alternative.

NUTRITIONAL INFORMATION

Calories	598	Sugars	.........7g
Protein	........26g	Fat	..........17g
Carbohydrate	...90g	Saturates	.......3g

🍲 1 hr 20 mins 🕐 1½ hrs

SERVES 4

INGREDIENTS

1 cup adzuki beans

1 cup bulgur wheat

2 cups vegetable bouillon

3 tbsp olive oil, plus extra for brushing

1 onion, finely chopped

2 garlic cloves, crushed

1 tsp ground coriander

1 tsp ground cumin

2 tbsp chopped fresh cilantro

3 eggs, beaten

1 cup dried bread crumbs

salt and pepper

TABBOULEH

1 cup bulgur wheat

2 tbsp lemon juice

1 tbsp olive oil

6 tbsp chopped parsley

4 scallions, finely chopped

2 oz/60 g cucumber, finely chopped

3 tbsp chopped mint

1 extra-large tomato, finely chopped

TO SERVE

black olives

pocket bread

1 Cook the adzuki beans in boiling water for 40 minutes, until tender. Drain, rinse, and let cool. Cook the bulgur wheat in the bouillon for 10 minutes, until the bouillon is absorbed. Set aside.

2 Heat 1 tablespoon of the olive oil in a skillet and sauté the onion, garlic, and spices for 4–5 minutes.

3 Transfer to a bowl, together with the beans, cilantro, seasoning, and eggs and mash with a potato masher or fork. Add the bread crumbs and bulgur wheat and stir well to combine. Cover and chill for 1 hour, until firm.

4 To make the tabbouleh, soak the bulgur wheat in 1¾ cups of boiling water for 15 minutes or until all the water has been absorbed. Combine with the remaining ingredients then cover and chill until required.

5 With wet hands, mold the kofta mixture into 32 oval shapes.

6 Press on to skewers, brush with oil, and broil for 5–6 minutes until golden. Turn, brush with oil again, and broil for 5–6 minutes. Drain on paper towels. Garnish and serve with the tabbouleh, black olives, and pocket bread.

Deep South Rice & Beans

Cajun spices add a flavor of the Deep South to this colorful rice and red kidney bean salad.

NUTRITIONAL INFORMATION

Calories 336   Sugars 8g
Protein ....7g   Fat 13g
Carbohydrate ...51g   Saturates 2g

10 mins   15 mins

SERVES 4

INGREDIENTS

1 cup long grain rice

4 tbsp olive oil

1 small green bell pepper, seeded and chopped

1 small red bell pepper, seeded and chopped

1 onion, finely chopped

1 small red or green chili, seeded and finely chopped

2 tomatoes, chopped

1 cup canned red kidney beans, rinsed and drained

1 tbsp chopped fresh basil

2 tsp chopped fresh thyme

1 tsp Cajun spice

salt and pepper

fresh basil leaves, to garnish

1 Cook the rice in plenty of boiling, lightly salted water for about 12 minutes, until just tender. Rinse under cold water, drain well, and set aside.

2 Meanwhile, heat the olive oil in a skillet, add the green and red bell peppers and the onion, and cook gently for about 5 minutes, until soft.

3 Add the chili and tomatoes and cook for a further 2 minutes.

4 Add the vegetable mixture and the drained red kidney beans to the cooked rice, and stir thoroughly but gently to combine.

5 Add the chopped fresh herbs and the Cajun spice to the rice mixture and stir again to combine.

6 Season the salad to taste with salt and pepper, and serve, garnished with fresh basil leaves.

Milanese Risotto

Italian rice is a round, short-grained variety with a nutty flavor, which is essential for a good risotto. Arborio is a good one to use.

NUTRITIONAL INFORMATION

Calories	631	Sugars	.........1g
Protein	........16g	Fat	..........29g
Carbohydrate	...77g	Saturates	......17g

 10 mins   35 mins

SERVES 4

INGREDIENTS

2 good pinches of saffron threads

1 large onion, chopped finely

1–2 garlic cloves, crushed

6 tbsp butter

2 cups arborio rice

⅔ cup dry white wine

5 cups boiling vegetable bouillon

1¼ cups grated Parmesan

salt and pepper

1 Put the saffron in a small bowl, cover with 3–4 tablespoons of boiling water, and let soak.

2 Sauté the chopped onion and the garlic in 4 tablespoons of the butter until they are soft but not colored. Add the rice and continue to cook for 2–3 minutes or until all of the grains are coated in butter and just beginning to color lightly.

3 Add the wine to the rice and simmer gently, stirring from time to time, until it is all absorbed.

4 Add the boiling bouillon a ladleful at a time, cooking until the liquid is fully absorbed before adding more, and stirring frequently.

5 When all the bouillon has been absorbed (this should take about 20 minutes), the rice should be tender but not soft and soggy. Add the saffron liquid, Parmesan, remaining butter, and salt and pepper to taste. Let simmer for 2 minutes until piping hot and thoroughly mixed.

6 Cover the pan tightly and let stand for 5 minutes off the heat. Give a good stir and serve at once.

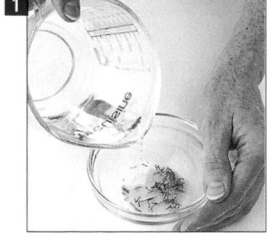

Spiced Basmati Pilau

The whole spices are not meant to be eaten and may be removed before serving. Omit the broccoli and mushrooms for a plain, spiced pilau.

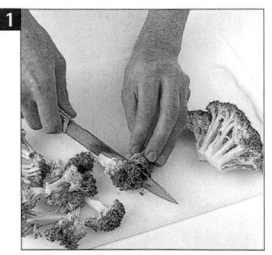

NUTRITIONAL INFORMATION

Calories	450	Sugars	.........3g
Protein	.........9g	Fat	..........15g
Carbohydrate	...76g	Saturates	.......2g

 20 mins   25 mins

SERVES 4

INGREDIENTS

2½ cups basmati rice

6 oz/175 g broccoli, trimmed

6 tbsp vegetable oil

2 large onions, chopped

½ lb/225 g sliced mushrooms

2 garlic cloves, crushed

6 cardamom pods, split

6 whole cloves

8 black peppercorns

1 cinnamon stick or piece of cassia bark

1 tsp ground turmeric

5 cups boiling vegetable bouillon or water

salt and pepper

⅓ cup seedless raisins

½ cup unsalted pistachios, coarsely chopped

VARIATION

For added richness, you could stir a spoonful of vegetable ghee through the rice mixture just before serving. A little diced red bell pepper and a few cooked peas forked through at step 4 add a colorful touch.

1 Place the rice in a strainer and wash well under cold running water. Drain. Trim off most of the broccoli stalk and cut into small florets, then quarter the stalk lengthwise and cut diagonally into 1 cm/½ inch pieces.

2 Heat the oil in a large pan. Add the onions and broccoli stalks and cook over low heat, stirring frequently, for 3 minutes. Add the mushrooms, rice, garlic, and spices and cook for 1 minute, stirring, until the rice is coated in oil.

3 Add the boiling bouillon and season to taste with salt and pepper. Stir in the broccoli florets and return the mixture to a boil. Cover, reduce the heat, and cook over low heat for 15 minutes without uncovering the pan.

4 Remove the pan from the heat and let the pilau stand for 5 minutes without uncovering. Remove the whole spices, add the raisins and pistachios, and gently fork through to fluff up the grains. Serve the pilau hot.

Tabbouleh Salad

This kind of salad is eaten widely throughout the Middle East. The flavor improves as it is kept, so it tastes even better on the second day.

NUTRITIONAL INFORMATION

Calories 637   Sugars 8g
Protein . . . . .20g   Fat 41g
Carbohydrate . . .50g   Saturates 11g

1½ hrs   5–10 mins

SERVES 2

I N G R E D I E N T S

¾ cup bulgur wheat

2½ cups boiling water

1 red bell pepper, seeded and halved

3 tbsp olive oil

1 garlic clove, crushed

grated zest of ½ lime

about 1 tbsp lime juice

1 tbsp chopped mint

1 tbsp chopped parsley

3–4 scallions, trimmed and thinly sliced

8 pitted black olives, halved

½ cup large salted peanuts or
   cashew nuts

1–2 tsp lemon juice

2–3 oz/60–90 g Swiss cheese

salt and pepper

mint sprigs, to garnish

warm pocket bread or crusty rolls, to serve

1 Put the bulgur wheat into a bowl and cover with the boiling water to reach about 1 inch/2.5 cm above the bulgar. Let soak for up to 1 hour, until most of the water is absorbed and is cold.

2 Meanwhile, put the halved red bell pepper, skin side upward, on a broiler rack and cook under a preheated moderate broiler until the skin is thoroughly charred and blistered. Let cool slightly.

3 When the bell pepper is cool enough to handle, peel off the skin and discard the seeds, then cut the bell pepper flesh into narrow strips.

4 Whisk together the oil, garlic, and lime zest and juice. Season to taste with salt and pepper and whisk until thoroughly blended. Add 4½ teaspoons of the dressing to the bell peppers and mix lightly.

5 Drain the soaked bulgur wheat thoroughly, squeezing it in a dry cloth to make it even drier, then place in a bowl.

6 Add the chopped herbs, scallions, olives, and peanuts or cashew nuts to the bulgar and toss well to combine. Add the lemon juice to the remaining dressing, and stir through the salad. Spoon the salad on to 2 serving plates.

7 Cut the cheese into narrow strips and mix with the bell pepper strips. Spoon alongside the bulgar salad. Garnish with mint sprigs and serve with warm pocket bread or crusty rolls.

 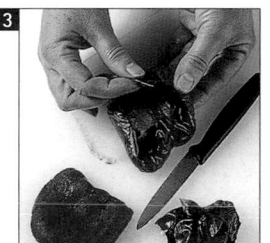 

Thai Jasmine Rice

Every Thai meal has as its centerpiece a big bowl of steaming, fluffy Thai jasmine rice, to which salt should not be added.

NUTRITIONAL INFORMATION

Calories 239	Sugars 0g	
Protein 5g	Fat 2g	
Carbohydrate ...54g	Saturates 0.6g	

 5 mins   10–15 mins

SERVES 4

INGREDIENTS

OPEN PAN METHOD

generous 1 cup Thai jasmine rice

4 cups water

ABSORPTION METHOD

generous 1 cup Thai jasmine rice

2 cups water

1 For the open pan method, rinse the rice in a strainer under cold running water and let drain.

2 Bring the water to a boil. Add the rice, stir once, and return to a medium boil. Cook, uncovered, for 8–10 minutes, until the rice is tender.

3 Drain thoroughly and fork through lightly before serving.

4 For the absorption method, rinse the rice under cold running water.

5 Put the rice and water into a pan and bring to a boil. Stir once and then cover the pan tightly. Lower the heat as much as possible. Cook the rice for 10 minutes, and let rest for a further 5 minutes.

6 Fork through lightly and serve the rice immediately.

COOK'S TIP

Thai jasmine rice can be frozen. Freeze in a plastic sealed container. Frozen rice is ideal for stir-fry dishes, as the process seems to separate the grains.

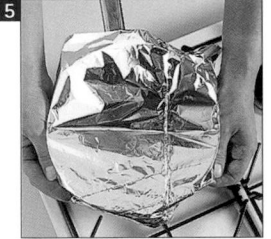

Couscous Royale

Serve this stunning dish as a centerpiece for a North African-style feast; it will prove to be a truly memorable meal.

NUTRITIONAL INFORMATION

Calories	329	Sugars	........31g
Protein	.........6g	Fat	..........13g
Carbohydrate	...50g	Saturates	.......6g

 25 mins   45 mins

SERVES 6

I N G R E D I E N T S

3 carrots

3 zucchini

¾ lb/350 g pumpkin or squash

5 cups vegetable bouillon

2 cinnamon sticks, broken in half

2 tsp ground cumin

1 tsp ground coriander

pinch of saffron strands

2 tbsp olive oil

pared zest and juice of 1 lemon

2 tbsp clear honey

3 cups precooked couscous

4 tbsp butter or margarine, softened

1 cup large seedless raisins

salt and pepper

cilantro, to garnish

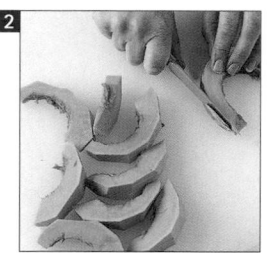

1 Cut the carrots and zucchini into 3 inch/7 cm pieces and cut these in half lengthwise.

2 Trim the pumpkin or squash, remove the seeds with a spoon, and discard them. Peel and cut into pieces the same size as the carrots and zucchini.

3 Put the bouillon, spices, saffron, and carrots in a large pan. Bring to a boil, skim off any scum, and add the olive oil. Simmer for 15 minutes.

4 Add the lemon zest and juice to the pan, together with the clear honey, zucchini and pumpkin or squash. Season well. Bring back to a boil and simmer for an additional 10 minutes.

5 Meanwhile, soak the couscous according to the packet instructions. Transfer it to a steamer or large strainer lined with cheesecloth and place over the vegetable pan. Cover and steam as directed. Stir in the butter.

6 Pile the couscous on to a warmed serving plate. Drain the vegetables, reserving the bouillon, lemon zest, and cinnamon. Arrange the vegetables on top of the couscous. Put the raisins on top and spoon over 6 tablespoons of the reserved bouillon. Keep warm.

7 Return the remaining bouillon to the heat and boil for 5 minutes until it has reduced slightly. Remove the lemon rind and cinnamon stick from the sauce and discard them.

8 Garnish the dish with sprigs of fresh cilantro and serve immediately, handing the sauce separately.

Risotto Verde

Baby spinach and fresh herbs are the basis of this colorful, refreshing risotto that tastes of summer.

NUTRITIONAL INFORMATION

Calories 374	Sugars 5g	
Protein 10g	Fat 9g	
Carbohydrate ...55g	Saturates 2g	

 5 mins   45 mins

SERVES 4

I N G R E D I E N T S

7½ cups vegetable bouillon

2 tbsp olive oil

2 garlic cloves, crushed

2 leeks, shredded

2 cups risotto rice

1¼ cups dry white wine

4 tbsp chopped fresh mixed herbs

½ lb/225 g young spinach

3 tbsp low-fat unsweetened yogurt

salt and pepper

shredded leek, to garnish

1 Pour the bouillon into a large pan and bring to a boil. Reduce the heat to a simmer.

2 Meanwhile, heat the oil in a separate pan and cook the garlic and leeks, stirring occasionally, for 2–3 minutes until soft, but not browned.

3 Stir in the rice and cook, stirring constantly, until translucent and well coated with oil.

4 Pour in half of the wine and a little of the hot bouillon; it will bubble and steam rapidly. Cook over gentle heat until all of the liquid has been absorbed.

5 Add the remaining bouillon and wine and cook over low heat for 25 minutes or until the rice is creamy.

6 Stir in the chopped mixed herbs and spinach, season to taste, and cook for a further 2 minutes.

7 Stir in the unsweetened yogurt, garnish with the shredded leek, and serve the risotto immediately.

COOK'S TIP

Do not hurry the process of cooking the risotto as the rice must absorb the liquid slowly in order for it to reach the correct consistency.

Rice with Fruit & Nuts

Here is a tasty and filling rice dish that is nice and spicy and includes fruits for a refreshing flavor and toasted nuts for a crunchy texture.

NUTRITIONAL INFORMATION

Calories	423	Sugars	........19g
Protein	........10g	Fat	..........17g
Carbohydrate	...62g	Saturates	.......2g

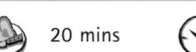 20 mins 1 hr

SERVES 6

INGREDIENTS

4 tbsp vegetable ghee or vegetable oil

1 large onion, chopped

2 garlic cloves, crushed

1 inch/2.5 cm piece of fresh ginger root, chopped

1 tsp chili powder

1 tsp cumin seeds

1 tbsp mild or medium curry powder or paste

1½ cups brown rice

3¾ cups boiling vegetable bouillon

2 cups canned chopped tomatoes

1½ cups ready-to-eat dried apricots or peaches, cut into slivers

1 red bell pepper, seeded and diced

¾ cup frozen peas

1–2 small, slightly green bananas

½–¾ cup toasted nuts, such as almonds, cashews, and hazelnuts or pine nuts

salt and pepper

fresh cilantro sprigs, to garnish

1 Heat the ghee or oil in a large pan. Add the onion and cook over low heat for 3 minutes. Stir in the garlic, ginger, spices, and rice and cook gently, stirring constantly, for 2 minutes until the rice is coated in the spiced oil.

2 Pour in the boiling bouillon, add the chopped tomatoes, and season with salt and pepper to taste. Bring to a boil, then reduce the heat, cover, and simmer gently for 40 minutes or until the rice is almost cooked and most of the liquid has been absorbed.

3 Add the slivered apricots or peaches, diced red bell pepper, and peas. Cover and continue cooking for 10 minutes. Remove from the heat and let stand for 5 minutes without uncovering.

4 Peel and slice the bananas. Uncover the rice mixture and fork through to mix the ingredients and fluff up the rice. Add the toasted nuts and sliced bananas and toss lightly.

5 Transfer to a serving platter, garnish with fresh cilantro sprigs, and serve.

Fried Rice with Spicy Beans

This rice is really colorful and crunchy with the addition of corn kernels and red kidney beans.

NUTRITIONAL INFORMATION

Calories	363	Sugars	.........3g
Protein	........10g	Fat	...........11g
Carbohydrate	...61g	Saturates	.......2g

 10 mins   25 mins

SERVES 4

INGREDIENTS

3 tbsp sunflower oil

1 onion, finely chopped

generous 1 cup long grain rice

1 green bell pepper, seeded and diced

1 tsp chili powder

2½ cups boiling water

¾ cup canned corn kernels

1 cup canned red kidney beans, drained and rinsed

2 tbsp chopped fresh cilantro, plus extra for garnish (optional)

1 Heat the sunflower oil in a large preheated wok.

2 Add the onion and stir-fry over medium heat for about 2 minutes or until soft.

3 Lower the heat, add the rice, green bell pepper and chili powder, and stir-fry for 1 minute.

4 Pour in the boiling water. Bring back to a boil, then reduce the heat, and simmer for 15 minutes.

5 Stir in the corn kernels, kidney beans, and cilantro and heat through, stirring occasionally.

6 Transfer to a warmed serving bowl and serve hot, sprinkled with extra cilantro, if wished.

COOK'S TIP

For perfect fried rice, the raw rice should ideally be soaked in a bowl of water for a short time before cooking to remove excess starch. Short grain Asian rice can be substituted for the long grain rice.

Refried Bean Nachos

A Mexican classic, refried beans and tortilla crisps are topped with luscious melted cheese, salsa, and assorted toppings.

NUTRITIONAL INFORMATION

Calories 287   Sugars 2g
Protein . . . . .15g   Fat 15g
Carbohydrate . . .22g   Saturates 7g

 15 mins   15 mins

SERVES 6–8

I N G R E D I E N T S

1½ cups canned refried beans

1½ cups canned pinto beans, drained

large pinch of ground cumin

large pinch of mild chili powder

6 oz/175 g tortilla chips

2 cups grated cheese, such as Cheddar

salsa of your choice

1 avocado, pitted, diced, and tossed with
    lime juice

½ small onion or 3–5 scallions, chopped

2 ripe tomatoes, diced

handful of shredded lettuce

3–4 tbsp chopped fresh cilantro

sour cream, to serve

1 Place the refried beans in a pan with the pinto beans, cumin, and chili powder. Add enough water to make a thick soup-like consistency, stirring gently so that the beans do not lose their texture.

2 Heat the bean mixture over medium heat until hot, then reduce the heat, and keep the mixture warm while you prepare the rest of the dish.

3 Arrange half the tortilla chips in the bottom of a flameproof casserole or gratin dish, and cover with the bean mixture. Sprinkle with the cheese and bake in a preheated oven, 400°F/200°C, until the cheese melts.

4 Alternatively, place the casserole under a preheated broiler and broil for 5–7 minutes or until the cheese melts and lightly sizzles in places.

5 Arrange the salsa, avocado, onion, tomato, lettuce, and fresh cilantro on top of the melted cheese. Surround with the remaining tortilla chips and serve immediately with sour cream.

VARIATION
Replace the sour cream with strained unsweetened yogurt as an alternative.

Cashew Nut Paella

This vegetarian version of paella is packed with vegetables and nuts for a truly delicious and simple dish.

NUTRITIONAL INFORMATION

Calories	406	Sugars	.........8g
Protein	........10g	Fat	..........22g
Carbohydrate	...44g	Saturates	.......6g

 15 mins   🕐 35 mins

SERVES 4

INGREDIENTS

2 tbsp olive oil

1 tbsp butter

1 red onion, chopped

⅔ cup risotto rice

1 tsp ground turmeric

1 tsp ground cumin

½ tsp chili powder

3 garlic cloves, crushed

1 fresh green chili, seeded and sliced

1 green bell pepper, seeded and diced

1 red bell pepper, seeded and diced

¾ cup baby corn ears, halved lengthwise

2 tbsp pitted black olives

1 large tomato, seeded and diced

2 cups vegetable bouillon

¾ cup unsalted cashew nuts

½ cup frozen peas

2 tbsp chopped fresh parsley

pinch of cayenne pepper

salt and pepper

fresh herbs, to garnish

1 Heat the olive oil and butter in a large skillet or paella pan until the butter has melted.

2 Add the onion and cook over medium heat, stirring constantly, for about 2–3 minutes until soft.

3 Stir in the rice, turmeric, cumin, chili powder, garlic, sliced chili, green and red bell peppers, corn cobs, olives, and tomato and cook over medium heat, stirring occasionally, for 1–2 minutes.

4 Pour in the bouillon and bring the mixture to a boil. Reduce the heat and cook gently, stirring constantly, for 20 minutes.

5 Add the cashew nuts and peas and cook, stirring occasionally, for a further 5 minutes. Season to taste and sprinkle with parsley and cayenne pepper.

6 Transfer the paella to warm serving plates, garnish with fresh herbs, and serve immediately.

Mushroom & Cheese Risotto

Make this creamy risotto with Italian arborio rice and freshly grated Parmesan cheese for the best results.

NUTRITIONAL INFORMATION

Calories ....358 Sugars 3g
Protein ....11g Fat 14g
Carbohydrate ...50g Saturates 5g

 20 mins   40 mins

SERVES 4

INGREDIENTS

2 tbsp olive or vegetable oil

2 cups risotto rice

2 garlic cloves, crushed

1 onion, chopped

2 celery stalks, chopped

1 red or green bell pepper, seeded and chopped

3¼ cups sliced mushrooms

1 tbsp chopped fresh oregano or 1 tsp dried oregano

4 cups vegetable bouillon

2 oz/55 g sun-dried tomatoes in olive oil, drained and chopped (optional)

⅔ cup finely grated Parmesan cheese

salt and pepper

TO GARNISH

fresh flat-leaf parsley sprigs

fresh bay leaves

1 Heat the oil in a wok or large skillet. Add the rice and cook, stirring constantly, for 5 minutes.

2 Add the garlic, onion, celery, and bell pepper and cook, stirring constantly, for 5 minutes. Add the mushrooms and cook for 3–4 minutes.

3 Stir in the oregano and bouillon. Heat until just boiling, then reduce the heat, cover, and simmer gently for about 20 minutes or until the rice is tender and creamy.

4 Add the sun-dried tomatoes, if using, and season to taste with salt and pepper. Stir in half of the grated Parmesan cheese and top with the remaining cheese.

5 Garnish with flat-leaf parsley and bay leaves, and serve immediately.

Mixed Mushroom Risotto

This creamy risotto is flavored with a mixture of exotic and cultivated mushrooms and thyme.

NUTRITIONAL INFORMATION

Calories	364	Sugars	.........1g
Protein	.........15g	Fat	..........16g
Carbohydrate	...44g	Saturates	.......6g

15 mins   30 mins

SERVES 4

INGREDIENTS

2 tbsp olive oil

1 large onion, finely chopped

1 garlic clove, minced

½ lb/225 g mixed exotic and cultivated mushrooms, such as porcini, oyster, and white, wiped and sliced if large

1⅓ cups risotto rice, washed

pinch saffron threads

scant 3 cups hot vegetable bouillon

4 tbsp dry white wine

1 cup grated Parmesan cheese, plus extra for serving

2 tbsp chopped thyme

salt and pepper

COOK'S TIP

Exotic mushrooms each have their own distinctive flavors and make a change from white mushrooms. However, they can be quite expensive, so you can always use a mixture with crimini or white mushrooms instead.

1 Heat the olive oil in a large skillet. Add the onions and garlic to the skillet and sauté for 3–4 minutes, or until soft but not brown.

2 Add the mushrooms to the skillet and cook for an additional 3 minutes, or until they are just beginning to brown.

3 Add the rice and saffron threads to the skillet and stir to coat the rice thoroughly in the oil.

4 Mix together the bouillon and the wine and add to the skillet, a ladleful at a time. Stir the rice mixture and let the liquid be fully absorbed before adding more liquid, a ladleful at a time.

5 When all of the wine and bouillon is incorporated, the rice should be cooked. Test by tasting a grain—if it is still crunchy, add a little more water and continue cooking. It should take at least 15 minutes to cook.

6 Stir in the grated cheese and thyme, and season with black pepper.

7 Transfer the risotto to serving dishes and serve sprinkled with extra Parmesan cheese.

Green Risotto

A simple rice dish cooked with green vegetables and herbs.
This recipe has been adapted for the microwave.

NUTRITIONAL INFORMATION

Calories	344	Sugars	........4g
Protein	........13g	Fat	..........10g
Carbohydrate	...54g	Saturates	.......4g

 15 mins   20 mins

SERVES 4

INGREDIENTS

1 onion, chopped

2 tbsp olive oil

1 cup risotto rice

3 cups hot vegetable bouillon

¾ lb/350 g mixed green vegetables, such as
asparagus, thin green beans, snow peas,
zucchini, broccoli florets, frozen peas

2 tbsp chopped fresh parsley

¾ cup fresh Parmesan cheese,
shaved thinly

salt and pepper

1 Place the onion and olive oil in a large bowl. Cover and cook on HIGH power for 2 minutes.

2 Add the rice and stir until thoroughly coated in the oil. Pour in about ⅓ cup of the hot bouillon. Cook, uncovered, for 2 minutes, until the liquid has been absorbed. Pour in another ⅓ cup of the bouillon and cook, uncovered, on HIGH power for 2 minutes. Repeat once more.

3 Chop or slice the vegetables into even-sized pieces. Stir into the rice with the remaining bouillon.

4 Cover and cook on HIGH power for 8 minutes, stirring occasionally, until most of the liquid has been absorbed and the rice is just tender.

5 Stir in the chopped parsley and season generously to taste with salt and pepper.

6 Let the risotto stand, covered, for about 5 minutes. The rice should be tender and creamy.

7 Scatter the Parmesan cheese over the risotto before serving.

COOK'S TIP
For extra texture, stir in a few toasted pine nuts or coarsely chopped cashew nuts at the end of the cooking time.

Rice-Stuffed Mushrooms

Flat mushrooms are ideal for baking. They are filled with more strongly flavored exotic mushrooms, although you can use the ordinary varieties.

NUTRITIONAL INFORMATION

Calories 168	Sugars 1g
Protein 7g	Fat 3g
Carbohydrate ...23g	Saturates 1g

25 mins   35 mins

SERVES 4

INGREDIENTS

4 large flat mushrooms

¼ lb/100 g assorted exotic mushrooms, sliced

4 dry-pack, sun-dried tomatoes, shredded

⅔ cup dry red wine

4 scallions, trimmed and finely chopped

½ cup cooked red rice

2 tbsp freshly grated Parmesan cheese

4 thick slices granary bread

salt and pepper

scallion, shredded, to garnish

1 Preheat the oven to 375°F/190°C. Peel the flat mushrooms, pull out the stalks, and set aside. Finely chop the stalks and place in a pan.

2 Add the exotic mushrooms to the pan along with the sun-dried tomatoes and red wine.

3 Bring to a boil, cover, and gently simmer the tomatoes and mushrooms for 2–3 minutes until just tender. Drain, reserving the cooking liquid, and place in a small bowl.

4 Gently stir in the chopped scallions and cooked rice. Season well, and spoon into the flat mushrooms, pressing the mixture down gently. Sprinkle with the grated Parmesan.

5 Arrange the mushrooms in an ovenproof baking dish and pour the reserved cooking juices around them. Bake in the oven for 20–25 minutes until they are just cooked.

6 Trim the crusts from the bread and toast each side under a hot broiler.

7 Drain the mushrooms and place each one on a piece of toast. Garnish with scallions and serve.

Pesto Rice with Garlic Bread

Try this combination of two types of rice with the richness of pine nuts, basil, and freshly grated Parmesan.

NUTRITIONAL INFORMATION

Calories 918   Sugars 2g
Protein . . . . .18g   Fat 64g
Carbohydrate . . .73g   Saturates 19g

 20 mins   40 mins

SERVES 4

INGREDIENTS

1½ cups mixed long-grain and wild rice

fresh basil sprigs, to garnish

tomato and orange salad, to serve

PESTO DRESSING

½ oz/15 g fresh basil

1 cup pine nuts

2 garlic cloves, crushed

6 tbsp olive oil

¾ cup freshly grated Parmesan

salt and pepper

GARLIC BREAD

2 small granary or whole-wheat French breadsticks

6 tbsp butter or margarine, softened

2 garlic cloves, crushed

1 tsp dried mixed herbs

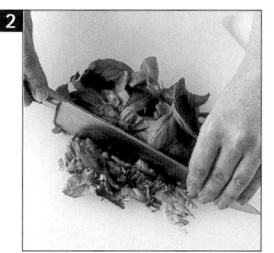

1 Place the rice in a pan and cover with water. Bring to a boil and cook for 15–20 minutes. Drain well and keep warm.

2 Meanwhile, make the pesto dressing. Remove the basil leaves from the stalks and finely chop the leaves. Reserve ¼ cup of the pine nuts and finely chop the remainder. Mix with the chopped basil and the rest of the dressing ingredients. Alternatively, put all the ingredients in a food processor or blender and blend for a few seconds until smooth. Set aside.

3 To make the garlic bread, slice the bread at 1 inch/2.5 cm intervals, taking care not to slice all the way through. Mix the butter or margarine with the garlic, herbs, and seasoning. Spread thickly between each slice.

4 Wrap the bread in foil and bake in a preheated oven, 400°F/200°C, for 10–15 minutes.

5 To serve, toast the reserved pine nuts under a preheated medium broiler for 2–3 minutes until golden. Toss the pesto dressing into the hot rice and pile into a warmed serving dish. Sprinkle with toasted pine nuts and garnish with basil sprigs. Serve with the garlic bread and a tomato and orange salad.

Rice with Black Beans

Any kind of bean cooking liquid is delicious for cooking rice—black beans are particularly good for their startling gray color and earthy flavor.

NUTRITIONAL INFORMATION

Calories ....252 Sugars 2g
Protein ....5g Fat 8g
Carbohydrate ...43g Saturates 1g

 15 mins   15 mins

SERVES 4

I N G R E D I E N T S

1 onion, chopped

5 garlic cloves, chopped

1 cup vegetable bouillon

2 tbsp vegetable oil

scant 1 cup long grain rice

1 cup liquid from cooking black beans (including some black beans, too)

½ tsp ground cumin

salt and pepper

TO GARNISH

3–5 scallions, thinly sliced

2 tbsp chopped fresh cilantro leaves

VARIATION
Instead of black beans, use pinto beans or garbanzo beans. Proceed as above and serve with any savory spicy sauce.

1 Put the onion in a blender or food processor with the garlic and bouillon and process to a chunky sauce.

2 Heat the oil in a heavy pan. Add the rice and cook over low heat, stirring constantly, until it is golden. Add the onion mixture, with the cooking liquid from the black beans (adding any beans, too.) Add the cumin and season to taste with salt and pepper.

3 Cover the pan and cook over low heat for about 10 minutes or until the rice is just tender. The rice should be a grayish color and taste delicious.

4 Fluff up the rice with a fork, re-cover, and let rest for about 5 minutes.

5 Serve sprinkled with thinly sliced scallions and the chopped fresh cilantro leaves.

Rice with Lime

The tangy citrus taste of lime is marvelous with all sorts of rice dishes. You could add wild rice to this dish, if desired.

NUTRITIONAL INFORMATION

Calories	227	Sugars	.........1g
Protein	.........4g	Fat	...........7g
Carbohydrate	...39g	Saturates	.......1g

5 mins   15 mins

SERVES 4

INGREDIENTS

2 tbsp vegetable oil

1 small onion, finely chopped

3 garlic cloves, finely chopped

scant 1 cup long grain rice

2 cups vegetable bouillon

juice of 1 lime

1 tbsp chopped fresh cilantro

1 Heat the oil in a heavy pan or flameproof casserole. Add the onion and garlic and cook gently, stirring occasionally, for 2 minutes.

2 Add the rice and cook for a further minute, stirring constantly. Pour in the bouillon, increase the heat, and bring the rice to a boil. Reduce the heat to a very low simmer.

3 Cover and cook the rice for about 10 minutes or until it is just tender and the liquid is absorbed.

4 Sprinkle in the lime juice and fork the rice to fluff up and to mix the juice in. Sprinkle with the chopped cilantro and serve immediately.

Vegetable Couscous

Couscous is a semolina grain which is very quick and easy to cook, and it makes a pleasant change from rice or pasta.

NUTRITIONAL INFORMATION

Calories 280	Sugars 13g
Protein 10g	Fat 7g
Carbohydrate ...47g	Saturates 1g

 20 mins   40 mins

SERVES 4

INGREDIENTS

2 tbsp vegetable oil

1 large onion, coarsely chopped

1 carrot, chopped

1 turnip, chopped

2½ cups vegetable bouillon

scant 1 cup couscous

2 tomatoes, peeled and quartered

2 zucchini, chopped

1 red bell pepper, seeded and chopped

¾ cup green beans, chopped

grated zest of 1 lemon

pinch of ground turmeric (optional)

1 tbsp finely chopped fresh cilantro
  or parsley

salt and pepper

fresh flat-leaf parsley sprigs, to garnish

1 Heat the oil in a large pan and cook the onion, carrot, and turnip for 3–4 minutes. Add the bouillon, bring to a boil, cover, and simmer for 20 minutes.

2 Meanwhile, put the couscous in a bowl and moisten with a little boiling water, stirring, until the grains have swollen and separated.

3 Add the tomatoes, zucchini, bell pepper, and green beans to the pan.

4 Stir the lemon zest into the couscous, add the turmeric, if using, and mix thoroughly. Put the couscous in a steamer and position it over the pan of vegetables. Simmer the vegetables so that the couscous steams for 8–10 minutes.

5 Pile the couscous on to warmed serving plates. Ladle the vegetables over the top, together with some of their cooking liquid.

6 Scatter the vegetable couscous with the chopped cilantro or parsley and serve at once, garnished with the flat leaf parsley sprigs.

Risotto in Shells

An eggplant is halved and filled with a risotto mixture, topped with cheese, and baked to make a snack or quick meal for two.

NUTRITIONAL INFORMATION

Calories .... .444   Sugars .... .20g
Protein .... .13g   Fat .... .23g
Carbohydrate ...50g   Saturates 8g

 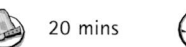

20 mins   55 mins

SERVES 2

INGREDIENTS

⅓ cup mixed long grain and wild rice

1 large eggplant

1 tbsp olive oil

1 small onion, finely chopped

1 garlic clove, crushed

½ small red bell pepper, seeded and chopped

2 tbsp water

¼ cup raisins

¼ cup cashew nuts, roughly chopped

½ tsp dried oregano

½ cup grated sharp Cheddar or Parmesan cheese

salt and pepper

oregano or parsley to garnish

1 Cook the rice in boiling salted water for about 15 minutes, until just tender. Drain, rinse, and drain again.

2 Bring a large pan of water to a boil. Cut the stem off the eggplant and cut the eggplant in half lengthwise. Cut out the flesh from the center carefully, leaving about a ½ inch/1.5 cm shell. Blanch the shells in the boiling water for 3–4 minutes. Drain thoroughly, then chop the eggplant flesh finely.

3 Heat the olive oil in a pan or skillet. Add the onion and garlic and cook over low heat until beginning to soften, then add the bell pepper and eggplant flesh and continue cooking for 2–3 minutes. Add the water to the pan and cook for a further 2–3 minutes.

4 Remove the pan from the heat, stir the raisins, chopped cashew nuts, dried oregano, and cooked rice into the eggplant mixture, and season to taste with salt and pepper.

5 Place the eggplant shells in an ovenproof dish and spoon in the rice mixture, piling it up well. Cover and cook in a preheated oven, 375°F/190°C, for 20 minutes.

6 Remove the lid and sprinkle the grated Cheddar or Parmesan cheese over the rice, covering it evenly. Place the dish under a preheated moderate broiler and cook for 3–4 minutes, until golden brown and bubbling. Serve hot, garnished with oregano or parsley.

Special Fried Rice

In this simple recipe, cooked rice is fried with vegetables and cashew nuts. It can either be eaten on its own or served as an accompaniment.

NUTRITIONAL INFORMATION

Calories . . . . . . .355 Sugars 6g
Protein . . . . .9g Fat 15g
Carbohydrate . . .48g Saturates 3g

 10 mins   30 mins

SERVES 4

I N G R E D I E N T S

1 cup long grain rice

½ cup cashew nuts

1 carrot

½ cucumber

1 yellow bell pepper

2 scallions

2 tbsp vegetable oil

1 garlic clove, crushed

1 cup frozen peas, thawed

1 tbsp soy sauce

1 tsp salt

cilantro leaves, to garnish

1 Bring a large pan of water to a boil. Add the rice to the pan and simmer for 15 minutes. Tip the rice into a strainer and rinse; drain thoroughly.

2 Heat a wok or large, heavy skillet, add the cashew nuts, and dry-fry, stirring constantly, until lightly browned. Remove and set aside.

3 Cut the carrot in half along the length, then slice thinly into semi-circles. Halve the cucumber and remove the seeds, using a teaspoon, then dice the flesh. Seed and slice the bell pepper and chop the scallions.

4 Heat the oil in a wok or large skillet. Add the prepared vegetables and the garlic. Stir-fry for 3 minutes. Add the rice, peas, soy sauce, and salt. Continue to stir-fry until the vegetables are well mixed and thoroughly heated.

5 Stir in the reserved cashew nuts. Transfer the rice to a warmed serving dish, garnish with the cilantro leaves, and serve immediately.

COOK'S TIP

You can replace any of the vegetables in this recipe with others suitable for a stir-fry, and using leftover rice makes this a perfect last-minute dish.

Spinach & Nut Pilau

Fragrant basmati rice is cooked with porcini mushrooms, spinach, and pistachio nuts in this easy microwave recipe.

NUTRITIONAL INFORMATION

Calories	403	Sugars	.........7g
Protein	........10g	Fat	..........15g
Carbohydrate	...62g	Saturates	.......2g

55 mins   15–20 mins

SERVES 4

INGREDIENTS

⅓ oz dried porcini mushrooms

1¼ cups hot water

1 onion, chopped

1 garlic clove, crushed

1 tsp grated ginger root

½ fresh green chili, seeded and chopped

2 tbsp oil

1¼ cups basmati rice

1 large carrot, grated

¾ cup vegetable bouillon

½ tsp ground cinnamon

4 cloves

½ tsp saffron strands

½ lb/225 g fresh spinach, long stalks removed

½ cup pistachio nuts

1 tbsp chopped cilantro

salt and pepper

cilantro leaves, to garnish

1 Place the porcini mushrooms in a small bowl. Pour over the hot water and let soak for 30 minutes.

2 Place the onion, garlic, ginger, chili, and oil in a large bowl. Cover and cook on HIGH power for 2 minutes. Rinse the rice, then stir it into the bowl, together with the carrot. Cover and cook on HIGH power for 1 minute.

3 Strain and coarsely chop the mushrooms. Add the mushroom soaking liquid to the bouillon to make 1¾ cups. Pour on to the rice.

4 Stir in the mushrooms, cinnamon, cloves, saffron, and ½ teaspoon salt. Cover and cook on HIGH power for 10 minutes, stirring once. Let the mixture stand, covered, for 10 minutes.

5 Place the spinach in a large bowl. Cover and cook on HIGH power for 3½ minutes, stirring once. Drain well and chop the spinach coarsely.

6 Stir the spinach, pistachio nuts, and chopped cilantro into the rice.

7 Season to taste with salt and pepper and garnish with cilantro leaves. Serve immediately.

Pilau Rice

Plain boiled rice is eaten by most people in India every day, but for entertaining, a more interesting rice dish, such as this, is served.

NUTRITIONAL INFORMATION

Calories 265	Sugars 0g	
Protein 4g	Fat 10g	
Carbohydrate ...43g	Saturates 6g	

 5 mins   25 mins

SERVES 4

INGREDIENTS

1 cup basmati rice

2 tbsp vegetable ghee

3 green cardamoms

2 cloves

3 peppercorns

½ tsp salt

½ tsp saffron

1¾ cups water

1 Rinse the rice twice under running water and set aside until required.

2 Heat the ghee in a pan. Add the cardamoms, cloves, and peppercorns to the pan and cook, stirring constantly, for about 1 minute.

3 Add the rice and stir-fry over medium heat for a further 2 minutes.

4 Add the salt, saffron, and water to the rice mixture and reduce the heat.

Cover the pan and simmer over low heat until the water has been absorbed.

5 Transfer the pilau rice to a serving dish and serve hot.

COOK'S TIP

The most expensive of all spices, saffron strands are the stamens of a type of crocus. They give dishes a rich, golden color, as well as adding a distinctive, slightly bitter taste. Saffron is sold as a powder or in the more expensive strands.

Eggplant & Rice Rolls

Slices of eggplant are blanched and stuffed with a savory rice and nut mixture, and baked in a piquant tomato and wine sauce.

NUTRITIONAL INFORMATION

Calories	142	Sugars	.........3g
Protein	.........6g	Fat	...........9g
Carbohydrate	....9g	Saturates	.......3g

 30 mins   1 hr 5 mins

SERVES 4

I N G R E D I E N T S

3 eggplants (total weight about 1½ lb/675 g)

⅓ cup mixed long-grain and wild rice

4 scallions, trimmed and thinly sliced

3 tbsp chopped cashew nuts or toasted chopped hazelnuts

2 tbsp capers

1 garlic clove, crushed

2 tbsp grated Parmesan cheese

1 egg, beaten

1 tbsp olive oil

1 tbsp balsamic vinegar

2 tbsp tomato paste

⅔ cup water

⅔ cup white wine

salt and pepper

cilantro sprigs, to garnish

1 Using a sharp knife, cut off the stem end of each eggplant, then cut off and discard a strip of skin from opposite sides of each eggplant. Cut each eggplant into thin slices to give a total of 16 slices.

2 Blanch the eggplant slices in boiling water for 5 minutes, then drain on paper towels.

3 Cook the rice in boiling salted water for about 12 minutes or until just tender. Drain and place in a bowl. Add the scallions, nuts, capers, garlic, cheese, and egg, season to taste with salt and pepper, and stir well to combine.

4 Spread a thin layer of rice mixture over each slice of eggplant and roll up carefully, securing with a wooden toothpick. Place the rolls in a greased ovenproof dish and brush each one with the olive oil.

5 Mix together the vinegar, tomato paste, and water and pour over the eggplant rolls. Cook in a preheated oven, at 350°F/180°C, for about 40 minutes or until tender and most of the liquid has been absorbed. Transfer the rolls to a serving dish.

6 Add the wine to the pan juices, heat gently until the sediment loosens, and then simmer gently for 2–3 minutes. Adjust the seasoning and strain the sauce over the eggplant rolls. Let cool and then chill thoroughly.

7 Garnish the eggplant rolls with sprigs of cilantro and serve.

Kitchouri

The traditional breakfast plate of kedgeree reputedly has its roots in this Indian flavored rice dish, adopted by English colonists.

NUTRITIONAL INFORMATION

Calories 318   Sugars 5g
Protein . . . . .12g   Fat 10g
Carbohydrate . . .48g   Saturates 6g

 10 mins   30 mins

SERVES 4

INGREDIENTS

2 tbsp vegetable ghee or butter

1 red onion, finely chopped

1 garlic clove, crushed

½ celery stalk, finely chopped

1 tsp turmeric

½ tsp garam masala

1 green chili, seeded and finely chopped

½ tsp cumin seeds

1 tbsp chopped cilantro

generous ½ cup basmati rice, rinsed under cold water

generous ½ cup green lentils

1¼ cups vegetable juice

2½ cups vegetable bouillon

COOK'S TIP

This is a versatile dish, and can be served as a great-tasting and satisfying one-pot meal. It can also be served as a winter lunch dish with tomatoes and yogurt.

1 Heat the ghee or butter in a large heavy pan. Add the onion, garlic, and celery to the pan and cook for about 5 minutes, until soft.

2 Add the turmeric, garam masala, chopped green chili, cumin seeds, and cilantro. Cook over moderate heat, stirring constantly, for about 1 minute, until fragrant.

3 Add the rice and lentils and cook for 1 minute, until the rice is translucent.

4 Pour the vegetable juice and bouillon into the pan and bring to a boil over medium heat.

5 Cover and simmer over low heat, stirring occasionally, for about 20 minutes, or until the lentils are cooked (they should be tender when pressed between two fingers). Transfer the kitchouri to a warmed serving dish and serve immediately.

Green Rice

Based on the Mexican dish Arroz Verde, this recipe is perfect for bell pepper and chili lovers. Serve with iced lemonade to quell the fire!

NUTRITIONAL INFORMATION

Calories 445	Sugars 6g
Protein 13g	Fat 12g
Carbohydrate ...76g	Saturates 2g

 25 mins   🕐 30 mins

SERVES 4

I N G R E D I E N T S

2 large green bell peppers

2 fresh green chilies

2 tbsp, plus 1 tsp vegetable oil

1 large onion, finely chopped

1 garlic clove, crushed

1 tbsp ground coriander

scant 1¾ cups long grain rice

3 cups vegetable bouillon

2 cups frozen peas

6 tbsp chopped cilantro

1 egg, beaten

salt and pepper

cilantro, to garnish

T O S E R V E

tortilla chips

lime wedges

3 Stir in the ground coriander, rice, and bouillon. Bring to a boil, cover, and simmer for 10 minutes. Add the peas, bring back to a boil, cover, and simmer for a further 5 minutes, until the rice is tender. Remove from the heat and let stand, covered, for 10 minutes.

4 Season to taste with salt and pepper and add the fresh cilantro. Pile into a warmed serving dish and keep warm.

5 Heat the remaining vegetable oil in a small omelet pan. Pour in the egg and cook over medium heat for 1–2 minutes on each side, until set. Slide the omelet on to a plate, roll up loosely, and slice into thin rounds.

6 Arrange the omelet strips on top of the rice. Garnish with cilantro and serve immediately with tortilla chips and lime wedges.

1 Halve, core, and seed the bell peppers. Cut the flesh into small cubes. Seed and finely chop the chilies.

2 Heat 2 tablespoons of the oil in a pan and sauté the onion, garlic, bell peppers, and chilies for 5–6 minutes, until soft, but not browned.

Gnocchi Romana

This is a traditional Italian recipe but, if you prefer a less rich version, you can simply omit the eggs.

NUTRITIONAL INFORMATION

Calories 709	Sugars 9g	
Protein 32g	Fat 41g	
Carbohydrate . . .58g	Saturates 25g	

 1¼ hrs 45 mins

SERVES 4

INGREDIENTS

scant 4 cups milk

pinch of freshly grated nutmeg

6 tbsp butter, plus extra for greasing

1¼ cups semolina

generous 1 cup freshly grated
    Parmesan cheese

2 eggs, beaten

½ cup grated Swiss cheese

salt and pepper

fresh basil sprigs, to garnish

1 Pour the milk into a pan and bring to a boil. Remove the pan from the heat and stir in the freshly grated nutmeg and 2 tablespoons of the butter. Season to taste with salt and pepper.

2 Gradually stir the semolina into the milk, whisking to prevent lumps forming, and return the pan to low heat. Simmer, stirring constantly, for about 10 minutes or until very thick.

3 Beat ⅔ cup of Parmesan cheese into the semolina mixture, then beat in the eggs. Continue beating the mixture until smooth. Let the mixture cool slightly.

4 Spread out the cooled semolina mixture in an even layer on a sheet of

baking parchment or in a large, oiled baking pan, smoothing the surface with a damp spatula—it should be about ½ inch/ 1 cm thick. Let cool completely, then chill in the refrigerator for 1 hour.

5 Once chilled, cut out circles of gnocchi, measuring about 1½ inches/ 4 cm in diameter, using a plain, greased dough cutter.

6 Grease a shallow ovenproof dish or 4 individual ovenproof dishes. Lay the gnocchi trimmings in the base of the

dish or dishes and arrange the circles of gnocchi on top, slightly overlapping each other.

7 Melt the remaining butter and drizzle it over the gnocchi. Sprinkle over the remaining grated Parmesan cheese, then sprinkle over the Swiss cheese.

8 Bake the gnocchi in a preheated oven, 400°F/200°C, for 25–30 minutes, until the top is crisp, golden brown, and bubbling. Serve at once, garnished with the basil leaves.

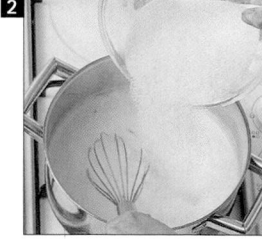

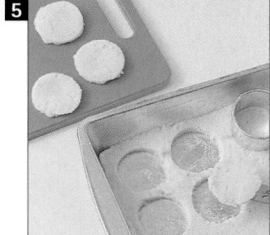

Spinach & Ricotta Gnocchi

Try not to handle the mixture too much when making gnocchi, as this will make the dough a little heavy.

NUTRITIONAL INFORMATION

Calories 712	Sugars 15g	
Protein 29g	Fat 59g	
Carbohydrate . . .16g	Saturates 33g	

20 mins   15 mins

SERVES 4

I N G R E D I E N T S

2 lb 4 oz spinach

1½ x 8 oz/225 g tubs ricotta

1½ cups grated romano

3 eggs, beaten

¼ tsp freshly grated nutmeg

all-purpose flour, to mix

9 tbsp sweet butter

¼ cup pine nuts

½ cup raisins

salt and pepper

1 Wash and drain the spinach well and cook in a covered pan without any extra liquid until soft, about 8 minutes. Place the spinach in a colander and press well to remove as much liquid as possible. Either rub the spinach through a strainer or purée in a blender.

2 Combine the spinach purée with the ricotta, half of the romano, the eggs, nutmeg, and seasoning to taste, mixing lightly but thoroughly. Work in enough flour, lightly and quickly, to make the mixture easy to handle.

3 Shape the dough quickly into small lozenge shapes, and dust lightly with a little flour.

4 Add a dash of oil to a large pan of salted water and bring to a boil. Add the gnocchi carefully and boil for about 2 minutes or until they float to the surface. Using a perforated spoon, transfer the gnocchi to a buttered ovenproof dish. Keep warm.

5 Melt the butter in a skillet. Add the pine nuts and raisins and sauté until the nuts start to brown slightly, but do not let the butter burn.

6 Pour the mixture over the gnocchi and serve sprinkled with the remaining grated romano.

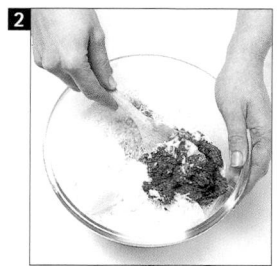

Kidney Bean Risotto

The combination of brown rice and kidney beans provides
a perfect nutritional balance, as well as tasting wonderful.

NUTRITIONAL INFORMATION

Calories 456	Sugars 9g
Protein 14g	Fat 20g
Carbohydrate ...61g	Saturates 2g

 20 mins 1 hr

SERVES 4

I N G R E D I E N T S

4 tbsp olive oil

1 onion, chopped

2 garlic cloves, finely chopped

scant 1 cup brown rice

2½ cups vegetable bouillon

1 red bell pepper, seeded and chopped

2 celery stalks, sliced

½ lb/225 g crimini mushrooms, thinly sliced

1½ cups canned red kidney beans, drained
and rinsed

3 tbsp chopped fresh parsley, plus extra to
garnish

½ cup cashew nuts

salt and ground black pepper

1 Heat half the oil in a large, heavy pan. Add the onion and cook, stirring occasionally, for 5 minutes, until soft.

VARIATION
You could also make this dish with a mixture of long grain and wild rice. Follow the packet instructions for cooking.

Add half the garlic and cook, stirring frequently, for 2 minutes, then add the rice and stir for 1 minute until the grains are thoroughly coated with the oil.

2 Add the vegetable bouillon and a pinch of salt and bring to a boil, stirring constantly. Lower the heat, cover, and simmer for 35-40 minutes, until all the liquid has been absorbed.

3 Meanwhile, heat the remaining oil in a heavy skillet. Add the red bell

pepper and celery and cook, stirring frequently, for 5 minutes. Add the mushrooms and the remaining garlic and cook, stirring frequently, for 4-5 minutes.

4 Stir the rice into the skillet and add the kidney beans, parsley, and cashew nuts. Season to taste with salt and pepper and cook, stirring constantly, until the risotto is piping hot.

5 Transfer to a warm serving dish, sprinkle with extra parsley and serve.

Risotto alla Rustica

A proper risotto is thoroughly delicious, but it cannot be hurried if it is to acquire its characteristic creamy texture.

NUTRITIONAL INFORMATION

Calories 519	Sugars 6g	
Protein 8g	Fat 16g	
Carbohydrate . . .89g	Saturates 7g	

5 mins   30 mins

SERVES 4

INGREDIENTS

3½ cups vegetable bouillon

3 tbsp butter

2 tbsp olive oil

1 onion, finely chopped

2 shallots, finely chopped

1 garlic clove, finely chopped

1⅞ cups risotto rice

¼ cup dry white wine

4 plum tomatoes, skinned

1 rosemary sprig, finely chopped

1 tbsp chopped fresh parsley

4 basil leaves, torn

2 tbsp light cream

salt and ground black pepper

1 Pour the bouillon into a large pan, bring to a boil, then lower the heat to a simmer and keep hot. Meanwhile, melt 2 tablespoons of the butter with the olive oil in a large, heavy pan over low heat. Add the onion, shallots, and garlic and cook, stirring occasionally, for 5 minutes.

2 Add the rice and stir for about 1 minute to the coat the grains with the butter and oil. Pour in the wine, bring to a boil and cook, stirring, until almost all the liquid has evaporated. Add the tomatoes, breaking them up with a fork, and the rosemary, parsley, and basil.

3 Add the hot bouillon, a large ladleful at a time, stirring until each addition is absorbed into the rice. Continue adding bouillon in this way, cooking until the rice is creamy, but the grains are still firm. This will take about 20 minutes.

4 Stir in the remaining butter and season to taste with salt and pepper. Stir in the cream and serve immediately.

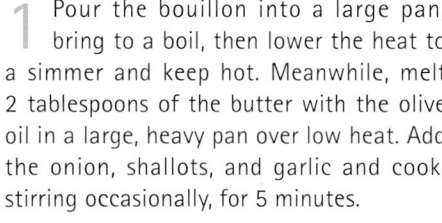

Lemon Risotto

This simple risotto has a wonderful fresh aroma and taste—serve it as an appetizer for six to eight people, or as an entrée for four.

NUTRITIONAL INFORMATION

Calories 442	Sugars 3g
Protein 6g	Fat 15g
Carbohydrate ...68g	Saturates 6g

10 mins   35 mins

SERVES 6-8

INGREDIENTS

2–3 lemons

2 tbsp olive oil

2 shallots, finely chopped

2⅔ cups risotto rice

½ cup dry white vermouth

4 cups vegetable bouillon, simmering

1 tbsp very finely chopped fresh
 flat-leaf parsley

2 tbsp butter

TO GARNISH

thin strips of pared lemon zest

fresh parsley sprigs

TO SERVE

Parmesan cheese shavings

avocado slices

1 Finely grate the zest from 2 lemons. Roll the zestless lemons backward and forward on a board, then squeeze scant ½ cup juice. If you don't have enough, squeeze another lemon. Set the zest and juice aside.

2 Heat the olive oil in a heavy pan. Add the shallots and cook, stirring, for about 3 minutes until soft. Add the rice and stir until all the grains are well coated.

3 Stir in the vermouth and cook until it evaporates. Lower the heat to medium–low. Add the lemon juice and a ladleful of simmering bouillon. Stir, then simmer, stirring occasionally, until all the liquid is absorbed.

4 Add another ladleful of bouillon and stir, then simmer until absorbed. Continue adding the bouillon in this way,

letting it be absorbed after each addition, until it has all been incorporated and the risotto is creamy in texture.

5 Stir in the lemon zest and parsley. Add the butter, cover, remove from the heat, and let stand for 5 minutes. Stir well and then garnish with lemon strips and parsley. Serve with Parmesan cheese and avocado slices.

Cumin Rice

Cumin seeds add a distinctive flavor to this colorful rice dish.
Serve as a side dish with any simple vegetable recipe.

NUTRITIONAL INFORMATION

Calories	258	Sugars	........4g
Protein	.........5g	Fat	..........9g
Carbohydrate	...49g	Saturates	....,...5g

 20 mins   20 mins

SERVES 4

I N G R E D I E N T S

2 tbsp butter

1 tbsp vegetable oil

1 green bell pepper, seeded and sliced

1 red bell pepper, seeded and sliced

3 scallions, thinly sliced

3–4 garlic cloves, finely chopped

scant 1 cup long grain rice

1½ tsp cumin seeds

½ tsp dried oregano or marjoram, crushed

2 cups vegetable bouillon

1 Heat the butter and vegetable oil together in a heavy pan or flameproof casserole. Add the green and red bell peppers and cook, stirring occasionally, until soft.

2 Add the scallions, garlic, rice, and cumin seeds. Cook, stirring constantly, for about 5 minutes or until the rice turns slightly golden.

3 Add the oregano or marjoram and the bouillon to the pan or casserole, bring to a boil, then reduce the heat, and simmer gently for about 5–10 minutes, or until the rice is tender.

4 Cover with a clean dish cloth and remove from the heat. Let stand for about 10 minutes. Fluff up the rice with a fork and serve.

VARIATION
Fold through a portion or two of black beans for protein, and serve with a simple vegetable curry.

Baked Semolina Gnocchi

Semolina has a similar texture to polenta, but is slightly grainier. These gnocchi, which are flavored with cheese and thyme, are easy to make.

NUTRITIONAL INFORMATION

Calories 259   Sugars 0g
Protein ....9g   Fat 16g
Carbohydrate ...20g   Saturates 10g

15 mins   30 mins

SERVES 4

INGREDIENTS

1¾ cups vegetable bouillon

1¼ cups semolina

1 tbsp thyme, stalks removed

1 egg, beaten

½ cup grated Parmesan cheese

3½ tbsp butter

2 garlic cloves, crushed

salt and pepper

1 Place the bouillon in a large pan and bring to a boil. Add the semolina in a steady trickle, stirring continuously. Keep stirring for 3–4 minutes until the mixture is thick enough to hold a spoon upright. Set aside and let cool slightly.

2 Add the thyme leaves, egg, and half of the cheese to the semolina mixture, and season well to taste with salt and pepper.

3 Spread the semolina mixture on to a board to a thickness of about ½ inch/12 mm, and let stand until it has cooled and set.

4 When the semolina is cold, cut it into 1 inch/2.5 cm squares, reserving any offcuts.

5 Grease an ovenproof dish, placing the reserved offcuts in the bottom. Arrange the semolina squares on top and sprinkle with the remaining cheese.

6 Melt the butter in a pan, add the garlic, and season with pepper to taste. Pour the butter mixture over the gnocchi. Bake in a preheated oven, at 425°F/220°C, for 15–20 minutes until the gnocchi are puffed up and golden. Serve the gnocchi hot.

VARIATION
Try adding ½ tablespoon of sun-dried tomato paste or 2 oz/50 g finely chopped mushrooms, fried in butter, to the semolina mixture in step 2. Follow the same cooking method.

Spiced Semolina

A south Indian savory snack which is very quick and easy to prepare, this should be served warm. It has a really lovely aroma.

NUTRITIONAL INFORMATION

Calories 556   Sugars 2g
Protein ....9g   Fat 41g
Carbohydrate ...40g   Saturates 5g

 5 mins   15 mins

SERVES 4

INGREDIENTS

⅔ cup vegetable oil

1 tsp mixed onion and mustard seeds

4 dried red chilies

4 curry leaves (fresh or dried)

8 tbsp coarse semolina

½ cup cashew nuts

1 tsp salt

⅔ cup water

1 Heat the vegetable oil in a large, heavy skillet over fairly low heat.

2 Add the mixed onion and mustard seeds, dried red chilies, and curry leaves and cook, stirring constantly, for about 1 minute.

3 Reduce the heat to low and add the semolina and the cashew nuts. Stir-fry for about 5 minutes, moving the mixture around the skillet all the time to prevent it from catching and burning on the base.

4 Add the salt to the pan, mixing well, and continue to stir-fry over low heat, keeping the mixture moving all the time.

5 Add the water and cook, stirring constantly, until the mixture is beginning to thicken.

6 Serve the spiced semolina warm as a delicious snack with Indian tea.

COOK'S TIP

Curry leaves are very similar in appearance to bay leaves but are very different in flavor. They can be bought both fresh and dried. They are mainly used to flavor lentil dishes and vegetable curries.

Chili Polenta Chips

Polenta is used in Italy in the same way as potatoes and rice. It has little flavor, but combined with butter, garlic, and herbs, it is transformed.

NUTRITIONAL INFORMATION

Calories 365   Sugars 1g
Protein . . . . .8g   Fat 12g
Carbohydrate . . .54g   Saturates 5g

🥄 🥄

🍞 5 mins   🕐 20 mins

SERVES 4

I N G R E D I E N T S

2 cups instant polenta

2 tsp chili powder

1 tbsp olive oil

⅔ cup sour cream

1 tbsp chopped parsley

salt and pepper

1 Place 6 cups of water in a pan and bring to a boil. Add 2 teaspoons of salt, then add the polenta in a steady stream, stirring constantly.

2 Reduce the heat slightly and continue stirring for about 5 minutes. It is essential to stir the polenta, otherwise it will stick and burn. The polenta should have a thick consistency at this point and should be stiff enough to hold the spoon upright in the pan.

3 Add the chili powder to the polenta mixture and stir well. Season to taste with a little salt and pepper.

4 Spread the polenta out on to a board or cookie sheet to about 1½ inch/4 cm thick. Let cool and set.

5 Cut the cooled polenta mixture into thin wedges.

6 Heat 1 tablespoon of oil in a skillet. Add the polenta wedges and cook for 3–4 minutes on each side or until golden and crispy. Alternatively, brush with melted butter and broil for 6–7 minutes until golden. Drain the cooked polenta on paper towels.

7 Mix the sour cream with parsley and place in a bowl.

8 Serve the polenta with the sour cream and parsley dip.

COOK'S TIP

Easy-cook instant polenta is widely available in food stores and is quick to make. It will keep for up to 1 week in the refrigerator. The polenta can also be baked in a preheated oven, at 400°F/200°C, for 20 minutes.

Biryani with Onions

An assortment of vegetables cooked with tender rice, flavored and colored with bright yellow turmeric and other warming Indian spices.

NUTRITIONAL INFORMATION

Calories	223	Sugars	........18g
Protein	.........8g	Fat	...........4g
Carbohydrate	...42g	Saturates	......1g

1¼ hrs   25 mins

SERVES 4

I N G R E D I E N T S

scant 1 cup basmati rice, rinsed

¼ cup red lentils, rinsed

1 bay leaf

6 cardamom pods, split

1 tsp ground turmeric

6 cloves

1 tsp cumin seeds

1 cinnamon stick, broken

1 onion, chopped

2 cups cauliflower, small florets

1 large carrot, diced

scant 1 cup frozen peas

⅓ cup golden raisins

2½ cups vegetable bouillon

salt and pepper

naan bread, to serve

C A R A M E L I Z E D   O N I O N S

2 tsp vegetable oil

1 medium red onion, shredded

1 medium onion, shredded

2 tsp superfine sugar

1 Place the rice, lentils, bay leaf, spices, onion, cauliflower, carrot, peas, and golden raisins in a large pan. Season with salt and pepper to taste and mix well.

2 Add the bouillon, bring to a boil, cover, and simmer for 15 minutes, stirring occasionally, until the rice is tender. Remove from the heat and let stand, covered, for 10 minutes to absorb the bouillon. Discard the bay leaf, cardamom pods, cloves, and cinnamon stick.

3 Heat the oil in a skillet and cook the onions over medium heat for 3–4 minutes until just soft. Add the sugar, increase the heat, and cook, stirring constantly, for a further 2–3 minutes until the onions are golden.

4 Gently combine the rice and vegetables and transfer to warm serving plates. Spoon over the caramelized onions and serve immediately with plain, warmed naan bread.

Curried Rice Patties

Substantial and flavorful, these patties are rich in protein and delicious. Leave the rice with a little bite to give extra texture.

NUTRITIONAL INFORMATION

Calories 311	Sugars 4g	
Protein 7g	Fat 11g	
Carbohydrate . . .50g	Saturates 2g	

1¼ hrs   55 mins

SERVES 4–6

I N G R E D I E N T S

⅓ cup basmati rice

2 tbsp olive oil

1 red onion, finely chopped

2 garlic cloves

2 tsp curry powder

½ tsp crushed dried chili flakes

1 small red bell pepper, seeded and diced

1 cup frozen peas, thawed

1 small leek, finely chopped

1 tomato, peeled, seeded, and chopped

1 cup canned garbanzo beans (chickpeas), rinsed and drained

1½ cups fresh white bread crumbs

1–2 tbsp chopped fresh cilantro or mint

1 egg, lightly beaten

vegetable oil, for frying

salt and pepper

cucumber slices, to garnish

lime wedges, to serve

D R E S S I N G

½ cup sesame seed paste (tahini)

2 garlic cloves, crushed

½ tsp ground cumin

pinch of cayenne pepper

5 tbsp lemon juice

drizzle of extra-virgin olive oil

1 To make the dressing, process the sesame seed paste, garlic, cumin, cayenne, and lemon juice in a food processor until creamy. Slowly pour in the oil, then gradually add enough water to make a creamy dressing (about ½ cup).

2 Bring a pan of water to a boil. Add ½ teaspoon of the salt and sprinkle in the rice; simmer for 15–20 minutes until the rice is just tender. Drain, rinse, and set aside.

3 Heat the olive oil in a large pan. Add the onion and garlic and cook until beginning to soften. Stir in the curry powder and chili flakes and cook for 2 minutes. Add the red bell pepper, peas, leek, and tomato and cook gently for about 7 minutes until tender. Set aside.

4 Process the garbanzo beans in a food processor until smooth. Add half the vegetables and process again. Transfer to a large bowl and add the remaining vegetable mixture, bread crumbs, cilantro, and egg. Mix well. Stir in the rice and season to taste with salt and pepper. Chill for 1 hour in the refrigerator, then shape into 4–6 patties.

5 Cook the patties in oil for 6–8 minutes until golden. Garnish with cucumber slices and serve with the dressing and lime wedges.

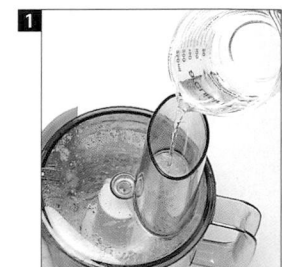

Brown Rice Gratin

This dish is extremely versatile and could be made with any vegetables that you have to hand and basmati rice instead of brown.

NUTRITIONAL INFORMATION

Calories 321   Sugars 6g
Protein . . . . .10g   Fat 18g
Carbohydrate . . .32g   Saturates 9g

🍚 15 mins   🕐 1 hr

SERVES 4

INGREDIENTS

½ cup brown rice

2 tbsp butter or margarine, plus extra for greasing

1 red onion, chopped

2 garlic cloves, crushed

1 carrot, cut into thin batons

1 zucchini, sliced

¾ cup baby corn ears, halved lengthwise

2 tbsp sunflower seeds

3 tbsp chopped fresh mixed herbs

1 cup grated mozzarella cheese

2 tbsp whole-wheat bread crumbs

salt and pepper

1 Cook the rice in a pan of lightly salted boiling water for 20 minutes until tender. Drain well.

2 Lightly grease a 3¾ cup casserole with butter or margarine.

3 Melt the butter or margarine in a skillet. Cook the onion over low heat, stirring, for 2 minutes or until soft.

4 Add the garlic, carrot, zucchini, and baby corn ears and cook, stirring constantly, for a further 5 minutes until the vegetables are soft.

5 Combine the drained rice with the sunflower seeds and mixed herbs and stir into the skillet. Stir in half of the mozzarella cheese and season with salt and pepper to taste.

6 Spoon the mixture into the prepared casserole and top with the bread crumbs and remaining cheese.

7 Cook in a preheated oven, 350°F/180°C, for about 25–30 minutes or until the cheese has begun to turn golden. Serve immediately.

Egg Fried Rice

In this classic Chinese dish, boiled rice is sautéed with peas, scallions, and egg, and flavored with soy sauce.

NUTRITIONAL INFORMATION

Calories	203	Sugars	.........1g
Protein	.........9g	Fat	...........11g
Carbohydrate	...19g	Saturates	.......2g

 20 mins   10 mins

SERVES 4

INGREDIENTS

¾ cup long-grain rice

3 eggs, beaten

2 tbsp vegetable oil

2 garlic cloves, crushed

4 scallions, chopped

1 cup cooked peas

1 tbsp light soy sauce

pinch of salt

shredded scallion, to garnish

1 Cook the rice in a pan of boiling water for 10–12 minutes, until almost cooked, but not soft. Drain well, rinse under cold water, and drain again.

2 Place the beaten eggs in a pan and cook over low heat, stirring until softly scrambled.

COOK'S TIP
The rice is rinsed under cold water to wash out the starch and prevent it from sticking together.

3 Heat the vegetable oil in a preheated wok or large skillet, swirling the oil around the bottom of the wok until it is really hot.

4 Add the crushed garlic, scallions, and peas and sauté, stirring occasionally, for 1–2 minutes. Stir the rice into the wok, mixing to combine.

5 Add the beaten eggs and the light soy sauce to the wok or skillet, add a pinch of salt, and stir thoroughly to mix the egg into the rice mixture.

6 Transfer the egg fried rice to warmed individual serving bowls, then garnish with the shredded scallion, and serve immediately.

Fried Spicy Rice

Ginger and garlic give this beautifully aromatic rice dish a lovely flavor. If desired, you can add a few peas to it for extra color.

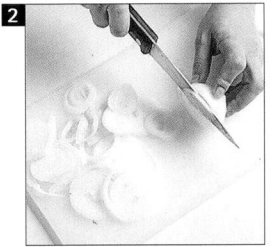  

NUTRITIONAL INFORMATION

Calories 507   Sugars 2g
Protein . . . . .9g   Fat 11g
Carbohydrate . . .99g   Saturates 6g

🍲 10 mins   🕐 35 mins

SERVES 4

INGREDIENTS

2¾ cups rice

1 medium onion

2 tbsp vegetable ghee

1 tsp finely chopped ginger root

1 tsp crushed garlic

1 tsp salt

1 tsp black cumin seeds

3 whole cloves

3 whole green cardamoms

2 cinnamon sticks

4 peppercorns

3 cups water

1 Rinse the rice thoroughly under cold running water.

2 Using a sharp knife, cut the onion into thin slices.

3 Heat the ghee in a large pan. Add the onion and sauté over medium heat, stirring occasionally, until crisp and a golden brown color.

4 Add the ginger, garlic, and salt to the onions in the pan, stirring to combine.

5 Remove half of the spicy onions from the pan and set aside.

6 Add the rice, black cumin seeds, cloves, cardamoms, cinnamon sticks, and peppercorns to the pan and stir-fry for 3-5 minutes.

7 Add the water to the pan and bring to a boil over medium heat. Reduce the heat, cover, and simmer until steam comes out through the lid. Check to see whether the rice is cooked and the liquid has been absorbed—if not, cook a little longer.

8 Transfer the fried spicy rice to a warmed serving dish and serve immediately, garnished with the reserved sautéed onions.

Caribbean Rice & Peas

Depending on whether you are on an eastern or western Caribbean island, this dish is known as rice and peas or peas and rice!

NUTRITIONAL INFORMATION

Calories . . . . . . .349 Sugars 3g
Protein . . . . .11g Fat 6g
Carbohydrate . . .67g Saturates 4g

 10 mins   1½ hrs

SERVES 4

I N G R E D I E N T S

¼ lb/115 g dried gunga peas, soaked overnight in cold water to cover

1¼ cups long grain rice

3 cups water

2 oz/55 g creamed coconut

1 onion, chopped

2 garlic cloves, finely chopped

1 small red bell pepper, seeded and chopped

1 tbsp fresh thyme leaves

1 bay leaf

½ tsp ground allspice

salt and ground black pepper

COOK'S TIP

Gunga peas go by a variety of names, including pigeon, Congo, and Jamaica peas. Fresh gunga peas, sometimes known as Cajun peas, also feature in Caribbean cooking.

1 Drain the gunga peas and put them in a large pan. Add enough cold water to cover them by about 1 inch/2.5 cm. Bring to a boil and simmer for about 1 hour, until tender. Drain the peas and return them to the pan.

2 Add the rice, water, creamed coconut, onion, garlic, red bell pepper, thyme, bay leaf, and allspice and season to taste with salt and pepper. Bring to a boil, stirring constantly, until the creamed coconut has melted, then lower the heat and simmer for 20 minutes.

3 Uncover the pan and continue to cook for about 5 minutes, until any excess liquid has evaporated. Gently fork through the rice to fluff up the grains, then serve it immediately.

Stuffed Bell Peppers

Use a mixture of bell peppers for a colorful display at the supper table and serve with a mixed leaf salad.

25 mins, plus standing   40 mins

SERVES 4

I N G R E D I E N T S

4 large red, yellow, or orange bell peppers

2 cups vegetable bouillon

1 cup long-grain rice

2 tbsp olive oil

1 onion, chopped

2 garlic cloves, finely chopped

¼ lb/115 g crimini mushrooms, chopped

4 tomatoes, skinned and chopped

1 carrot, diced

1 tbsp chopped fresh parsley

⅔ cup goat cheese, crumbled

½ cup pine nuts

¼ cup freshly grated Parmesan cheese

salt and ground black pepper

1 Cut the bell peppers in half lengthwise and seed them. Blanch them in a large pan of boiling water for 5 minutes, then remove from the pan with a slotted spoon and place upside down to drain.

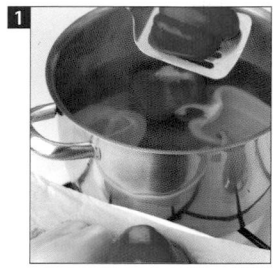

2 Pour the bouillon into another pan, add the rice, and bring to a boil. Lower the heat, cover, and simmer for 15 minutes. Remove the pan from the heat and let stand, still covered, for 5 minutes.

3 Meanwhile, heat the olive oil in a large skillet. Add the onion and cook, stirring occasionally, for 5 minutes, until softened. Add the garlic, mushrooms, tomatoes, and carrot and season to taste with salt and pepper. Cover and cook for a further 5 minutes.

4 Stir the rice, parsley, crumbled goat cheese, and pine nuts into the vegetable mixture. Place the bell pepper halves, cut side up, in a roasting pan or ovenproof dish. Divide the rice and vegetable mixture among them.

5 Sprinkle the tops of the bell peppers with the grated Parmesan cheese and bake in a preheated oven, 375°F/190°C, for about 20 minutes, until the cheese is golden brown and melted. Serve immediately, on warmed serving plates.

Lentil & Rice Casserole

This is a really hearty dish, perfect for cold days when a filling hot dish is just what you need to keep the winter out.

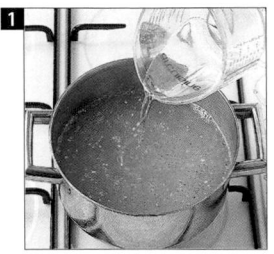

NUTRITIONAL INFORMATION

Calories 312   Sugars 9g
Protein . . . . .20g   Fat 2g
Carbohydrate . . .51g   Saturates 0.4g

 15 mins   40 mins

SERVES 4

INGREDIENTS

1 cup split red lentils

generous ¼ cup long grain rice

5 cups vegetable stock

1 leek, cut into chunks

3 garlic cloves, crushed

14 oz/400 g canned chopped tomatoes

1 tsp ground cumin

1 tsp chili powder

1 tsp garam masala

1 red bell pepper, deseeded and sliced

3½ oz/100 g small broccoli florets

8 baby corn cobs, halved lengthwise

2 oz/55 g green beans, halved

1 tbsp shredded fresh basil

salt and pepper

fresh basil sprigs, to garnish

VARIATION
You can vary the rice in this recipe—use brown or wild rice, if you prefer.

1 Place the lentils, rice, and vegetable stock in a large flameproof casserole and cook over low heat, stirring occasionally, for 20 minutes.

2 Add the leek, garlic, tomatoes and their can juice, ground cumin, chili powder, garam masala, sliced bell pepper, broccoli, corn cobs, and green beans to the casserole.

3 Bring the mixture to a boil, reduce the heat, cover, and simmer for a further 10–15 minutes or until all the vegetables are tender.

4 Add the shredded basil and season with salt and pepper to taste.

5 Garnish with fresh basil sprigs and serve immediately.

Stuffed Rice Crêpes

Dosas (crêpes) are widely eaten in southern India. The rice and urid dhal need to soak and ferment, so prepare well in advance.

NUTRITIONAL INFORMATION

Calories 748	Sugars 1g	
Protein 10g	Fat 47g	
Carbohydrate ...76g	Saturates 5g	

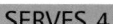
15 mins   40–45 mins

SERVES 4

INGREDIENTS

1 cup rice and ¼ cup urid dhal, or 1¾ cups ground rice and ½ cup urid dhal flour (ata)

2–2½ cups water

1 tsp salt

4 tbsp vegetable oil

FILLING

generous 5 cups diced potatoes

3 fresh green chilies, chopped

½ tsp turmeric

1 tsp salt

⅔ cup vegetable oil

1 tsp mixed mustard and onion seeds

3 dried chilies

4 curry leaves

2 tbsp lemon juice

1 To make the dosas, soak the rice and urid dhal for 3 hours, then grind the to a smooth consistency, adding water if necessary. Let stand for a further 3 hours to ferment. Alternatively, if you are using ground rice and urid dhal flour (ata), mix together in a bowl. Add the water and salt and stir until a batter is formed.

2 Heat about 1 tbsp of oil in a large, nonstick skillet. Using a ladle, spoon the batter into the skillet. Tilt the skillet to spread the mixture over the base. Cover and cook over medium heat for about 2 minutes. Remove the lid and turn the dosa over very carefully. Pour a little oil around the edge, then cover and cook for another 2 minutes. Repeat with the remaining batter.

3 To make the filling, place the potatoes chilies, turmeric, and salt in a pan of boiling water and cook until the potatoes are just soft. Drain and mash lightly.

4 Heat the vegetable oil in a pan and cook the mustard and onion seeds, dried red chilies, and curry leaves, stirring constantly, for about 1 minute. Pour the spice mixture over the mashed potatoes, then sprinkle over the lemon juice and stir well to combine.

5 Spoon the potato filling on one half of each of the dosas and fold the other half over it. Transfer to a warmed serving dish and serve hot.

Asian-Style Millet Pilau

Millet makes an interesting alternative to rice, which is the more traditional ingredient for a pilau. Serve with a crisp Asian salad.

NUTRITIONAL INFORMATION

Calories	660	Sugars	........28g
Protein	.........15g	Fat	..........27g
Carbohydrate	...94g	Saturates	.......5g

20 mins   30 mins

SERVES 4

INGREDIENTS

1½ cups millet grains

1 tbsp vegetable oil

1 bunch of scallions, white and green parts, chopped

1 garlic clove, crushed

1 tsp grated fresh ginger root

1 orange bell pepper, seeded and diced

2½ cups water

1 orange

⅔ cup chopped pitted dates

2 tsp sesame oil

1 cup roasted cashew nuts

2 tbsp pumpkin seeds

salt and pepper

Asian salad vegetables, to serve

1 Place the millet in a large pan and toast over medium heat, shaking the pan occasionally, for 4–5 minutes until the grains begin to crack and pop.

2 Heat the oil in another pan. Add the scallions, garlic, ginger, and bell pepper and cook over medium heat, stirring frequently, for 2–3 minutes until just soft, but not browned. Add the millet and pour in the water.

3 Using a vegetable peeler, pare the zest from the orange and add the zest to the pan. Squeeze the juice from the orange into the pan. Season to taste with salt and pepper.

4 Bring to a boil, reduce the heat, cover, and cook gently for 20 minutes until all the liquid has been absorbed. Remove the pan from the heat, stir in the dates and sesame oil, and let stand for 10 minutes.

5 Remove and discard the orange zest and stir in the roasted cashew nuts. Pile the pilau into a warmed serving dish, garnish with a sprinkling of the pumpkin seeds, and serve immediately with Asian salad vegetables.

Green Herb Rice

This is a deliciously different way to serve plain rice for a special occasion or to liven up a simple meal.

NUTRITIONAL INFORMATION

Calories	652	Sugars	.........9g
Protein	........15g	Fat	..........17g
Carbohydrate	...116g	Saturates	.......6g

1hr 10 mins   35 mins

SERVES 4

INGREDIENTS

2 tbsp olive oil

2¾ cups basmati or Thai jasmine rice (see page 386), soaked for 1 hour, washed and drained

3 cups coconut milk

1 tsp salt

1 bay leaf

2 tbsp cilantro

2 tbsp chopped mint

2 green chilies, seeded and finely chopped

1 Heat the oil in a pan, add the rice, and stir over medium heat until it becomes translucent.

2 Add the coconut milk, salt, and bay leaf. Bring to a boil and cook until all the liquid is absorbed.

3 Reduce the heat to very low, cover the pan tightly, and cook the rice for 10 minutes, taking great care that it does not catch and burn on the base of the pan.

4 Remove the bay leaf and stir in the cilantro, mint, and green chilies. Fork through the rice gently to fluff up the grains. Transfer to a warm serving dish and serve immediately.

COOK'S TIP

The contrasting colors of this dish make it particularly attractive, and it can be made to look even more interesting with a carefully chosen garnish. Two segments of fresh lime complement the cilantro perfectly.

Vegetable Pilau

This is a delicious way of cooking rice and vegetables together, and the saffron gives it a beautiful aroma. Serve this with any kabob.

NUTRITIONAL INFORMATION

Calories	557	Sugars	.........9g
Protein	........11g	Fat	..........14g
Carbohydrate	..104g	Saturates	.......7g

20 mins   55 mins

SERVES 6

INGREDIENTS

2 potatoes, each cut into 12 pieces

1 eggplant, cut into 6

2 carrots, sliced

½ cup green beans, chopped

4 tbsp vegetable ghee

2 onions, sliced

¾ cup unsweetened yogurt

2 tsp finely chopped fresh ginger root

2 tsp crushed garlic

2 tsp garam masala

2 tsp black cumin seeds

½ tsp turmeric

3 black cardamom pods

3 cinnamon sticks

2 tsp salt

1 tsp chili powder

½ tsp saffron strands

1¼ cups milk

3 cups basmati rice

5 tbsp lemon juice

TO GARNISH

4 green chilies, chopped

cilantro leaves, chopped

1 Prepare the vegetables. Heat the ghee in a skillet. Add the potatoes, eggplant, carrots, and beans and cook, turning frequently, until soft. Remove from the pan and set aside.

2 Add the onions and cook, stirring frequently, until soft. Add the yogurt, ginger, garlic, garam masala, 1 teaspoon black cumin seeds, turmeric, 1 cardamom pod, 1 cinnamon stick, 1 teaspoon salt, and the chili powder and cook for 3–5 minutes. Return the vegetables to the pan and cook for 4–5 minutes.

3 Put the saffron and milk in a pan and bring to a boil, stirring. Remove from the heat and let stand.

4 In a pan of boiling water, half-cook the rice with 1 teaspoon salt, 2 cinnamon sticks, 2 black cardamom pods, and 1 teaspoon black cumin seeds. Drain the rice, leaving half in the pan, while transferring the other half to a bowl.

5 Pour the vegetable mixture on top of the rice in the pan. Pour half of the lemon juice and half of the saffron milk over the vegetables and rice, then cover with the remaining rice and pour the remaining lemon juice and saffron milk over the top.

6 Garnish with chilies and cilantro, cover, and cook over low heat for about 20 minutes. Serve hot.

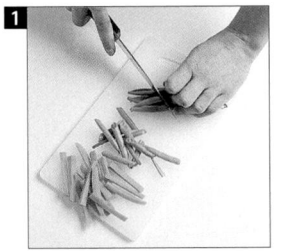

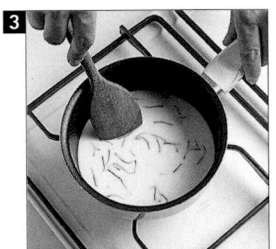

Refried Beans

The beans in this Mexican dish are cooked once and then literally refried to a delicious, thick purée, which tastes wonderful topped with cheese.

 5–10 mins, plus soaking   3 hrs

SERVES 4–6

INGREDIENTS

1 quantity Mexican beans, with their cooking liquid (see page 449)

½ cup vegetable oil

1–2 onions, chopped

½ tsp ground cumin

salt

2¼ cups grated Cheddar cheese (optional)

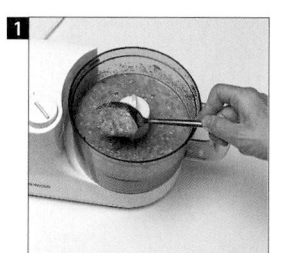  

1   Put two-thirds of the cooked beans, with their cooking liquid, in a food processor or blender and process to a purée. Stir in the remaining whole beans and set the mixture aside.

2   Heat the vegetable oil in a heavy skillet. Add the onions and cook until they are very soft. Sprinkle with cumin and salt to taste.

3   Ladle in a cupful of the bean mixture, and cook, stirring, until the beans reduce down to a thick mixture; the beans will darken slightly as they cook.

4   Continue adding the bean mixture to the pan, a ladleful at a time, stirring and reducing down the liquid before adding the next ladleful. You should end up with a thick, chunky purée.

5   If you are using the grated Cheddar cheese, sprinkle it over the beans and cover tightly so that the heat in the pan melts the cheese. Alternatively, place the dish under a preheated broiler until the cheese is melted and bubbling.

6   Serve the refried beans immediately on warmed serving plates. Crisp salad greens go well with this dish.

Polenta

Polenta is prepared in a variety of ways and can be served hot or cold, sweet or savory.

NUTRITIONAL INFORMATION

Calories	.661	Sugars	.5g
Protein	.15g	Fat	.34g
Carbohydrate	.68g	Saturates	.12g

1¼ hrs   1 hr

SERVES 4

INGREDIENTS

7 cups water

1½ tsp salt

1¾ cups polenta or cornmeal flour

2 beaten eggs (optional)

2 cups fresh fine white
  bread crumbs (optional)

vegetable oil, for cooking and oiling

2 quantities basic tomato sauce
  (see page 7)

MUSHROOM SAUCE

3 tbsp olive oil

½ lb/225 g mushrooms, sliced

2 garlic cloves, crushed

⅔ cup dry white wine

4 tbsp heavy cream

2 tbsp chopped fresh mixed herbs

salt and pepper

1 Bring the water and salt to a boil in a large pan and gradually sprinkle in the polenta or cornmeal flour, stirring all the time to prevent lumps forming. Simmer the mixture very gently, stirring frequently, until the polenta becomes very thick and starts to draw away from the sides of the pan, about 30–35 minutes. It is likely to splatter, in which case partially cover the pan with a lid.

2 Thoroughly oil a shallow pan, about 11 x 7 inches/28 x 18 cm, and spoon in the polenta. Spread out evenly, using a wet wooden spoon or spatula. Let cool, then let stand for a few hours at room temperature, if possible.

3 Cut the polenta into 30–36 squares. Heat the vegetable oil in a skillet and cook the pieces, in batches, until golden brown all over, turning several times—this will take about 5 minutes. Alternatively, dip each piece of polenta in beaten egg and coat in bread crumbs before cooking in the hot vegetable oil.

4 To make the mushroom sauce, heat the olive oil in a pan and cook the mushrooms with the crushed garlic for 3–4 minutes. Add the wine, season well, and simmer for 5 minutes. Add the cream and chopped herbs and simmer for 1–2 minutes.

5 Serve the polenta with either the tomato sauce or mushroom sauce.

Chana Dhal & Rice

Saffron is used to flavor this dish, which makes it rather special.
It is absolutely delicious served with any curry.

NUTRITIONAL INFORMATION

Calories 479	Sugars 7g	
Protein 12g	Fat 14g	
Carbohydrate ...80g	Saturates 8g	

 3¼ hrs   1 hr

SERVES 6

INGREDIENTS

3½ oz/100 g chana dhal

4 tbsp ghee

2 medium onions, sliced

1 tsp finely chopped ginger root

1 tsp crushed garlic

½ tsp turmeric

2 tsp salt

½ tsp chili powder

1 tsp garam masala

5 tbsp unsweetened yogurt

5 cups water

⅔ cup milk

1 tsp saffron

3 tbsp lemon juice

2 fresh green chilies

fresh cilantro leaves

3 black cardamoms

3 black cumin seeds

2¾ cups basmati rice

1 Rinse and soak the chana dhal for 3 hours. Rinse the rice under running water and let stand.

2 Heat the ghee in a skillet. Add the onion and sauté until golden brown. Using a slotted spoon, remove half of the onion with a little of the ghee and set aside in a bowl.

3 Add the ginger, garlic, turmeric, 1 tsp of the salt, the chili powder, and the garam masala to the mixture remaining in the pan and stir-fry for 5 minutes. Stir in the yogurt and add the chana dhal and ⅝ cup of water. Cook, covered, for 15 minutes. Set aside.

4 Meanwhile, boil the milk with the saffron and set aside with the reserved sautéed onion, lemon juice, green chilies, and cilantro leaves.

5 Boil the rest of the water and add the salt, black cardamoms, black cumin seeds, and the rice, and cook, stirring, until the rice is half-cooked. Drain, and place half of the sautéed onion, saffron, lemon juice, green chilies, and cilantro on top of the chana dhal mixture. Place the remaining rice on top of this and the rest of the sautéed onion, saffron, lemon juice, chilies, and cilantro on top of the rice.

6 Cover tightly with a lid and cook for 20 minutes over very low heat. Mix with a slotted spoon before transferring to a warmed serving dish. Serve immediately.

Spiced Rice & Lentils

This is a lovely combination of rice and masoor dhal and is simple to cook. You can add a knob of sweet butter before serving, if liked.

NUTRITIONAL INFORMATION

Calories	394	Sugars	.........3g
Protein	........14g	Fat	...........8g
Carbohydrate	...70g	Saturates	.......1g

🍚 5 mins   🕐 30 mins

SERVES 4

INGREDIENTS

1 cup basmati rice

6 oz/175 g masoor dhal

2 tbsp vegetable ghee

1 small onion, sliced

1 tsp finely chopped ginger root

1 tsp crushed garlic

½ tsp turmeric

2½ cups water

1 tsp salt

1 Combine the rice and dhal and rinse thoroughly in cold running water. Set aside until required.

2 Heat the ghee in a large pan. Add the onion and cook, stirring occasionally, for about 2 minutes.

3 Reduce the heat, add the ginger, garlic, and turmeric to the pan and stir-fry for 1 minute.

4 Add the rice and dhal to the mixture in the pan and blend together, mixing gently, but thoroughly.

5 Add the water to the mixture in the pan and bring it to a boil over medium heat. Reduce the heat, cover, and cook for 20–25 minutes, until the rice is tender and the liquid is absorbed.

6 Just before serving, add the salt and mix to combine.

7 Transfer the spiced rice and lentils to a large warmed serving dish and serve immediately.

COOK'S TIP

Many Indian recipes specify using ghee as the cooking fat. This is because it is similar to clarified butter in that it can be heated to a very high temperature without burning. Ghee adds a nutty flavour to dishes and a glossy shine to sauces.

Vegballs with Chili Sauce

These tasty, nutty morsels are delicious served with a fiery, tangy sauce that counteracts the richness of the peanuts.

NUTRITIONAL INFORMATION

Calories	615	Sugars	........13g
Protein	........23g	Fat	..........43g
Carbohydrate	...37g	Saturates	.......8g

25 mins   30 mins

SERVES 4

I N G R E D I E N T S

3 tbsp groundnut oil

1 onion, finely chopped

1 celery stalk, chopped

1 tsp dried mixed herbs

225 g/8 oz roasted unsalted peanuts, ground

175 g/6 oz canned garbanzo beans, drained and mashed

1 tsp yeast extract

1 cup fresh whole-wheat bread crumbs

1 egg yolk

3½ tbsp all-purpose flour

strips of fresh red chili, to garnish

HOT CHILI SAUCE

2 tsp groundnut oil

1 large red chili, seeded and finely chopped

2 scallions, finely chopped

2 tbsp red wine vinegar

1 cup canned chopped tomatoes

2 tbsp tomato paste

2 tsp superfine sugar

salt and pepper

rice and salad greens, to serve

1 Heat 1 tablespoon of the oil in a skillet and gently sauté the onion and celery for 3–4 minutes, or until soft but not browned.

2 Place all the other ingredients, except the remaining oil and the flour, in a mixing bowl and add the onion and celery. Stir well to combine.

3 Divide the mixture into 12 portions and roll into small balls. Coat all over with the flour.

4 Heat the remaining oil in a skillet. Add the garbanzo bean and peanut balls and cook over medium heat, turning frequently but carefully, for 15 minutes, until cooked through and golden. Drain well on absorbent paper towels.

5 Meanwhile, make the hot chili sauce. Heat the groundnut oil in a small skillet and gently sauté the chili and scallions for 2–3 minutes. Stir in the remaining ingredients and season to taste with salt and pepper. Bring to a boil and simmer for 5 minutes.

6 Serve the garbanzo bean and peanut balls with the hot chili sauce, rice, and crisp salad greens.

Red Bean Stew & Dumplings

There's nothing better on a cold day than a hearty dish topped with dumplings. This recipe is very quick and easy to prepare.

NUTRITIONAL INFORMATION

Calories 508   Sugars 15g
Protein ....22g   Fat 12g
Carbohydrate ...83g   Saturates 4g

 20 mins   40 mins

SERVES 4

INGREDIENTS

1 tbsp vegetable oil

1 red onion, sliced

2 celery sticks, chopped

3½ cups vegetable bouillon

1 cup carrots, diced

1 cup potatoes, diced

1 cup zucchini, diced

4 tomatoes, peeled and chopped

¾ cup split red lentils

1½ cups canned kidney beans, rinsed
   and drained

1 tsp paprika

salt and pepper

DUMPLINGS

1 cup all-purpose flour

½ tsp salt

2 tsp baking powder

1 tsp paprika

1 tsp dried mixed herbs

1 oz/25 g vegetable suet

7 tbsp water

sprigs of flat-leaf parsley to garnish

1 Heat the vegetable oil in a flameproof casserole or a large pan. Add the onion and celery and cook over low heat, stirring frequently, for 3–4 minutes or until just soft.

2 Pour in the bouillon and stir in the carrots and potatoes. Bring to a boil, cover, and cook for 5 minutes.

3 Stir in the zucchini, tomatoes, lentils, kidney beans, paprika, and seasoning. Bring to a boil, cover, and cook for 5 minutes.

4 Meanwhile, make the dumplings. Sift the flour, salt, baking powder, and paprika into a bowl. Stir in the herbs and suet. Bind together with the water to form a soft dough. Divide into 8 portions and roll gently to form balls.

5 Uncover the stew, stir, then add the dumplings, pushing them slightly into the stew. Cover, reduce the heat so the stew simmers, and cook for a further 15 minutes, until the dumplings have risen and are cooked through.

6 Serve immediately on warmed plates, garnished with flat-leaf parsley.

Creamy Vegetable Curry

Vegetables are cooked in a mildly spiced curry sauce with yogurt and fresh cilantro stirred in just before serving.

NUTRITIONAL INFORMATION

Calories	423	Sugars	........24g
Protein	........16g	Fat	..........19g
Carbohydrate	...50g	Saturates	.......7g

 20 mins 25 mins

SERVES 4

I N G R E D I E N T S

2 tbsp sunflower oil

1 onion, sliced

2 tsp cumin seeds

2 tbsp ground coriander

1 tsp ground turmeric

2 tsp ground ginger

1 tsp chopped fresh red chili

2 garlic cloves, chopped

2 cups canned chopped tomatoes

3 tbsp powdered coconut mixed with
    1¼ cups boiling water

1 small cauliflower, broken into florets

2 zucchini, sliced

2 carrots, sliced

1 potato, diced

1½ cups canned garbanzo beans, drained
    and rinsed

½ cup thick unsweetened yogurt

2 tbsp mango chutney

3 tbsp chopped fresh cilantro

salt and pepper

fresh herbs, to garnish

1 Heat the oil in a pan and cook the onion until soft. Add the cumin, ground coriander, turmeric, ginger, chili, and garlic and cook for 1 minute.

2 Add the tomatoes and the coconut mixture and mix well.

3 Add the cauliflower, zucchini, carrots, diced potato, and garbanzo beans and season to taste with salt and pepper. Cover and simmer for 20 minutes, until the vegetables are tender.

4 Stir in the yogurt, mango chutney, and fresh cilantro and heat through gently, but do not boil.

5 Transfer to a warm serving dish, garnish and serve with rice.

Fragrant Curry

There are many different ways of cooking garbanzo beans, but this version is probably one of the most delicious and popular.

NUTRITIONAL INFORMATION

Calories 313	Sugars 5g	
Protein 8g	Fat 19g	
Carbohydrate . . .29g	Saturates 2g	

 10 mins   20 mins

I N G R E D I E N T S

6 tbsp vegetable oil

2 medium onions, sliced

1 tsp finely chopped ginger root

1 tsp ground cumin

1 tsp ground coriander

1 tsp crushed garlic

1 tsp chili powder

2 fresh green chilies

cilantro leaves

150 ml/¼ pint water

1 large potato

1½ cups canned garbanzo beans, drained

1 tbsp lemon juice

COOK'S TIP
Using canned garbanzo beans saves time, but you can use dried garbanzo beans if you prefer. Soak them overnight, then boil them for 15-20 minutes, or until soft.

1 Heat the vegetable oil in a large pan. Add the onions and cook over medium heat, stirring occasionally, for 5–8 minutes, until golden brown.

2 Reduce the heat, add the ginger, ground cumin, ground coriander, garlic, chili powder, fresh green chilies, and cilantro leaves to the pan, and stir-fry for 2 minutes.

3 Add the water to the mixture in the pan and stir well to mix.

4 Using a sharp knife, cut the potato into small dice. Add the potato and garbanzo beans to the mixture in the pan. Lower the heat, cover, and simmer, stirring occasionally, for 5-7 minutes.

5 Sprinkle the lemon juice over the curry and stir again.

6 Transfer the garbanzo bean curry to warmed individual serving dishes and serve immediately. Warm naan breads go well with this dish.

Semolina Fritters

Based on a gnocchi recipe, these delicious cheese-flavored fritters are accompanied by a fruity home-made apple relish.

NUTRITIONAL INFORMATION

Calories . . . . . . .682 Sugars 40g
Protein . . . . .19g Fat 32g
Carbohydrate . . .85g Saturates 11g

30 mins   40-45 mins

SERVES 4

INGREDIENTS

2½ cups milk

1 small onion

1 celery stalk

1 bay leaf

2 cloves

1½ cups semolina

1 cup grated sharp Cheddar cheese

½ tsp dried mustard powder

2 tbsp all-purpose flour

1 egg, beaten

1 cup dried white bread crumbs

6 tbsp vegetable oil

salt and pepper

celery leaves, to garnish

coleslaw, to serve

RELISH

2 celery stalks, chopped

2 small eating apples, cored and diced

¾ cup golden raisins

¾ cup ready-to-eat dried apricots, chopped

6 tbsp cider vinegar

pinch of ground cloves

½ tsp ground cinnamon

1 Pour the milk into a pan and add the onion, celery, bay leaf, and cloves. Bring to a boil, remove from the heat and let stand for 15 minutes.

2 Strain into another pan, bring to a boil, and sprinkle in the semolina, stirring constantly. Reduce the heat and simmer for 5 minutes, until very thick, stirring occasionally to prevent it sticking.

3 Remove the pan from the heat. Beat in the cheese, mustard, and seasoning. Place in a greased bowl and let cool.

4 To make the relish, put all the ingredients in a pan, bring to a boil,

cover, and simmer gently for 20 minutes, until tender. Let cool.

5 Put the flour, egg, and bread crumbs on separate plates. With floured hands, divide the cooled semolina mixture into 8 and press into 2½ inch/6 cm rounds.

6 Coat lightly in flour, then in egg, and finally in bread crumbs. Heat the oil in a large skillet and gently cook the fritters for 3–4 minutes on each side, until golden. Drain on paper towels.

7 Garnish the fritters with celery leaves and serve immediately with the apple relish and coleslaw.

Fragrant Coconut Rice

This fragrant, sweet rice is delicious served with a variety of vegetable dishes as part of a Chinese menu.

NUTRITIONAL INFORMATION

Calories 306	Sugars 2g	
Protein 5g	Fat 6g	
Carbohydrate ...61g	Saturates 4g	

 5 mins   15 mins

SERVES 4

INGREDIENTS

1⅓ cups long-grain white rice

2½ cups water

½ tsp salt

generous ⅓ cup coconut milk

¼ cup shredded coconut

1 Rinse the rice thoroughly under cold running water until the water runs completely clear.

2 Drain the rice thoroughly in a strainer set over a large bowl. This is to remove some of the starch and to prevent the grains from sticking together.

3 Place the drained rice in a wok with the water.

4 Add the salt and coconut milk to the wok and bring to a boil.

5 Cover the wok with a lid or a lid made of foil, curved into a domed shape and resting on the sides of the wok. Reduce the heat and let simmer for 10 minutes.

6 Remove the lid from the wok and fluff up the rice with a fork—all of the liquid should have been absorbed and the rice grains should be tender. If not, add a little more water to the wok, replace the lid, and continue to simmer for an additional few minutes until all the liquid has been absorbed.

7 Spoon the rice into a warm serving bowl and scatter with the shredded coconut. Serve immediately.

COOK'S TIP

Coconut milk is not the liquid found inside coconuts—that is called coconut water. Coconut milk is made from the white coconut flesh soaked in water and milk and then squeezed to extract all of the flavor. You can make your own or buy it in cans.

Midweek Curry Special

This easy curry is always enjoyed. Double the quantities for a great dish if you're cooking for a crowd.

NUTRITIONAL INFORMATION

Calories	403	Sugars	........19g
Protein	........19g	Fat	..........15g
Carbohydrate	...51g	Saturates	.......3g

20 mins   40–45 mins

SERVES 4

I N G R E D I E N T S

2 tbsp vegetable oil

2 garlic cloves, crushed

1 large onion, chopped

1 large carrot, sliced

1 apple, cored and chopped

2 tbsp medium-hot curry powder

1 tsp finely grated ginger root

2 tsp paprika

3½ cups vegetable bouillon

2 tbsp tomato paste

½ small cauliflower, broken into florets

1½ cups canned garbanzo beans, rinsed and drained

¼ cup golden raisins

2 tbsp cornstarch

2 tbsp water

4 hard-cooked eggs

salt and pepper

paprika, to garnish

C U C U M B E R   D I P

3 inch/7.5 cm piece of cucumber, chopped

1 tbsp chopped mint

⅔ cup unsweetened yogurt

mint sprigs, to garnish

1 Heat the vegetable oil in a large pan. Add the garlic, onion, carrot, and apple and cook, stirring frequently, for 4–5 minutes, until soft.

2 Add the curry powder, ginger, and paprika to the pan and cook for 1 minute. Stir in the vegetable stock and tomato paste.

3 Add the cauliflower, garbanzo beans, and golden raisins. Bring to a boil, stirring, then reduce the heat, cover the pan, and simmer for 25–30 minutes, or until all the vegetables are tender.

4 Blend the cornstarch with the water to a smooth paste and add to the curry, stirring until thickened. Cook over low heat for a further 2 minutes. Season to taste with salt and pepper.

5 To make the dip, mix together the cucumber, mint, and yogurt in a small serving bowl.

6 Ladle the curry on to 4 warmed serving plates. Shell and quarter the eggs and arrange them on top of the curry. Sprinkle with a little paprika. Garnish the dip with mint and serve with the curry.

Lentil & Vegetable Biryani

A delicious mix of vegetables, basmati rice, and continental lentils produces a wholesome and nutritious dish.

NUTRITIONAL INFORMATION

Calories	516	Sugars	.........9g
Protein	........20g	Fat	..........19g
Carbohydrate	...72g	Saturates	.......3g

 20 mins   45 mins

SERVES 6

I N G R E D I E N T S

1 cup continental lentils

4 tbsp vegetable ghee or oil

2 onions, quartered and sliced

2 garlic cloves, crushed

1 inch/2.5 cm piece of ginger root, chopped

1 tsp ground turmeric

½ tsp chili powder

1 tsp ground coriander

2 tsp ground cumin

3 tomatoes, peeled and chopped

1 eggplant, trimmed and cut in
  ½ inch/1 cm pieces

7½ cups boiling vegetable bouillon

1 red or green bell pepper, seeded and
  diced

1⅞ cups basmati rice

1 cup green beans, halved

2 cups cauliflower florets

½ lb/115 g mushrooms, sliced or quartered

½ cup unsalted cashews

3 hard-cooked eggs, shelled, and
  cilantro sprigs, to garnish

1 Rinse the lentils under cold running water and drain. Heat the ghee or oil in a pan, add the onions, and cook gently for 2 minutes. Stir in the garlic, ginger, and spices and cook gently, stirring frequently, for 1 minute.

2 Add the lentils, tomatoes, eggplant, and 2 cups of the bouillon, mix well, then cover and simmer gently for 20 minutes.

3 Add the red or green bell pepper and cook for a further 10 minutes, or until the lentils are tender and all the liquid has been absorbed.

4 Meanwhile, rinse the rice under cold running water. Drain and place in another pan with the remaining bouillon. Bring to a boil, add the green beans, cauliflower, and mushrooms, then cover and cook gently for 15 minutes, or until the rice and vegetables are tender. Remove from the heat and let stand, covered, for 10 minutes.

5 Add the lentil mixture and the cashews to the cooked rice and mix lightly together. Pile the biryani on to a warm serving platter and garnish with wedges of hard-cooked egg and cilantro sprigs. Serve hot.

Dry Moong Dhal

This dhal has a baghaar (seasoned dressing) of butter, dried red chilies and white cumin seeds. It is simple to cook and tastes very good.

NUTRITIONAL INFORMATION

Calories	304	Sugars	.........1g
Protein	.........9g	Fat	..........21g
Carbohydrate	...21g	Saturates	......14g

 5 mins   🕐 30-35 mins

SERVES 4

INGREDIENTS

5½ oz/150 g moong dhal

1 tsp finely chopped ginger root

½ tsp ground cumin

½ tsp ground coriander

1 tsp fresh garlic, crushed

½ tsp chili powder

2½ cups water

1 tsp salt

BAGHAAR

8 tbsp sweet butter

5 dried red chilies

1 tsp white cumin seeds

TO SERVE

chapati

vegetable curry

1 Rinse the lentils under cold running water and place them in a large pan. Add the ginger, ground cumin, ground coriander, garlic, and chili powder, and stir to mix well.

2 Pour in enough of the water to cover the lentil mixture. Cook over medium heat, stirring frequently, until the lentils are soft but not mushy.

3 Stir in the salt, transfer to a serving dish, and keep warm.

4 Meanwhile, make the baghaar. Melt the butter in a heavy pan over fairly low heat. Add the dried red chilies and white cumin seeds and cook, stirring constantly, until they begin to pop and give off their aroma.

5 Pour the baghaar over the lentils and serve immediately with chapati and a vegetable curry.

COOK'S TIP

Moong dhal are teardrop-shaped yellow split lentils, more popular in northern India than in the south. Dried red chilies are the quickest way to add heat to a dish.

Vegetable & Lentil Koftas

A mixture of vegetables, nuts, and lentils is shaped into small balls and baked in the oven with a sprinkling of aromatic garam masala.

NUTRITIONAL INFORMATION

Calories 679	Sugars 20g
Protein 29g	Fat 33g
Carbohydrate ...73g	Saturates 5g

🍶 30 mins   🕐 50 mins

SERVES 4

INGREDIENTS

6 tbsp vegetable ghee or oil

1 onion, finely chopped

2 carrots, finely chopped

2 celery stalks, finely chopped

2 garlic cloves, crushed

1 fresh green chili, seeded and finely chopped

4½ tsp curry powder or paste

1¾ cups split red lentils

2½ cups vegetable bouillon

2 tbsp tomato paste

1 cup fresh whole-wheat bread crumbs

¾ cup unsalted cashews, finely chopped

2 tbsp chopped cilantro

1 egg, beaten

salt and pepper

garam masala, for sprinkling

YOGURT DRESSING

1 cup unsweetened yogurt

1–2 tbsp chopped cilantro

1–2 tbsp mango chutney, chopped if necessary

1 Heat 4 tablespoons of ghee or oil in a large pan and gently sauté the onion, carrots, celery, garlic, and chili, stirring frequently, for 5 minutes. Add the curry powder or paste and the lentils and cook, stirring constantly, for 1 minute.

2 Add the bouillon and tomato paste and bring to a boil. Reduce the heat, cover, and simmer for 20 minutes, or until the lentils are tender and all the liquid has been absorbed.

3 Remove from the heat and cool slightly. Add the bread crumbs, nuts, cilantro, egg, and seasoning to taste. Mix well and let cool. Shape into rounds about the size of golf balls (use 2 spoons to help shape the rounds).

4 Place the balls on a lightly greased cookie sheet, drizzle with the remaining oil, and sprinkle with a little garam masala, to taste. Cook in a preheated oven, at 350°F/180°C, for 15-20 minutes, or until piping hot and lightly golden in color.

5 Meanwhile, to make the yogurt dressing, mix all the ingredients together in a bowl. Serve the koftas hot with the yogurt dressing.

Black-Eyed Peas

This Indian dish is very good served with chapatis and a vegetable curry. The beans need to be soaked overnight so prepare well in advance.

NUTRITIONAL INFORMATION

Calories	757	Sugars	.........5g
Protein	.........10g	Fat	..........69g
Carbohydrate	...26g	Saturates	.......7g

 15 mins, plus soaking   1 hr

SERVES 4

I N G R E D I E N T S

¾ cup black-eyed peas

1¼ cups vegetable oil

2 medium onions, sliced

1 tsp finely chopped fresh ginger root

1 tsp crushed garlic

1 tsp chili powder

1½ tsp salt

1½ tsp ground coriander

1½ tsp ground cumin

⅔ cup water

2 fresh green chilies, finely chopped

fresh cilantro leaves

1 tbsp lemon juice

1 Rinse the black-eyed peas, place them in a bowl, cover with cold water, and let soak overnight.

2 Drain the peas, place in a pan, and add water to cover. Bring to a boil over low heat, then simmer gently for about 30 minutes. Drain the peas thoroughly and set aside.

3 Heat the oil in a heavy pan. Add the onions and cook, stirring frequently, for 5–8 minutes, until golden brown. Add the ginger, garlic, chili powder, salt, ground coriander, and ground cumin and stir-fry the mixture over low heat for about 3–5 minutes.

4 Add the water to the pan, cover, and simmer until all of the water has completely evaporated.

5 Add the black-eyed peas, green chilies, and cilantro leaves to the onions and stir-fry for 3-5 minutes.

6 Transfer the black-eyed peas to a serving dish, sprinkle over the lemon juice, and serve immediately. Alternatively, let the beans cool and serve cold.

COOK'S TIP
Black-eyed peas are oval-shaped, gray or beige beans with a dark dot in the center. They have a slightly smoky flavor. They are sold canned, as well as dried.

Midweek Medley

Canned garbanzo beans are used in this dish, but you could use black-eyed peas or red kidney beans, if preferred.

NUTRITIONAL INFORMATION

Calories	480	Sugars	.........8g
Protein	........11g	Fat	..........38g
Carbohydrate	...25g	Saturates	......13g

15 mins   20–25 mins

SERVES 4

I N G R E D I E N T S

1 large eggplant

2 zucchini

6 tbsp vegetable ghee or oil

1 large onion, quartered and sliced

2 garlic cloves, crushed

1–2 fresh green chilies, seeded and chopped, or 1–2 tsp minced chili

2 tsp ground coriander

2 tsp cumin seeds

1 tsp ground turmeric

1 tsp garam masala

2 cups canned chopped tomatoes

1¼ cups vegetable bouillon or water

salt and pepper

1½ cups canned garbanzo beans, drained and rinsed

2 tbsp chopped mint

½ cup heavy cream

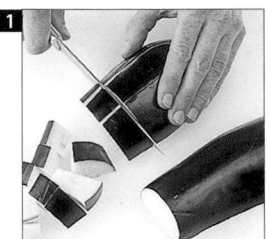

1 Trim the leaf end off the eggplant and cut it into cubes. Trim the zucchini and cut into slices.

2 Heat the vegetable ghee or oil in a pan and sauté the eggplant, zucchini, onion, garlic, and chilies over low heat, stirring frequently, for about 5 minutes, If necessary, add a little more oil to the pan.

3 Stir in the spices and cook for 30 seconds. Add the tomatoes and bouillon and season with salt and pepper to taste, then continue to cook for an additional 10 minutes.

4 Add the drained garbanzo beans to the pan and continue to cook for a further 5 minutes.

5 Stir in the mint and cream and reheat gently. Taste and adjust the seasoning, if necessary. Transfer to a warm serving dish and serve hot with plain or pilau rice, or with parathas, if preferred.

Aloo Chat

Aloo Chat is one of a variety of Indian foods served at any time of the day. The garbanzo beans need to be soaked overnight.

NUTRITIONAL INFORMATION

Calories . . . . . . .262 Sugars 6g
Protein . . . . .13g Fat 4g
Carbohydrate . . .46g Saturates 0.5g

35 mins   1 hr 5 mins

SERVES 4

I N G R E D I E N T S

1 cup garbanzo beans, soaked overnight in cold water and drained

1 dried red chili

1 lb/450 g waxy potatoes, boiled in their skins and peeled

1 tsp cumin seeds

2 tsp salt

1 tsp black peppercorns

½ tsp dried mint

½ tsp chili powder

½ tsp ground ginger

2 tsp mango powder

½ cup unsweetened yogurt

oil, for deep frying

4 poppadoms

1 Boil the garbanzo beans with the chili in plenty of water for about 1 hour until tender, then drain.

2 Cut the potatoes into 1 inch/2.5 cm dice and mix into the garbanzo beans while they are still warm. Set aside.

3 Grind together the cumin, salt, and peppercorns in a spice grinder or with a pestle and mortar. Stir in the mint, chili powder, ginger, and mango powder.

4 Put a small pan or skillet over low heat and add the spice mix. Cook, stirring, until the spices give off their aroma and then immediately remove the pan from the heat.

5 Stir half of the spice mix into the garbanzo bean and potato mixture and stir the other half into the yogurt.

6 Cook the poppadoms according to the instructions on the packet. Drain on plenty of paper towels. Break into bite-size pieces and stir into the potatoes and garbanzo beans, spoon over the spiced yogurt, and serve immediately.

VARIATION
Instead of garbanzo beans, diced tropical fruits can be stirred into the potatoes and spice mix; add a little lemon juice to balance the sweetness.

Vegetarian Paella

This recipe, full of Mediterranean vegetables, is one of the many different variations of this popular Spanish dish.

NUTRITIONAL INFORMATION

Calories .... 359 Sugars 8g
Protein .... 10g Fat 14g
Carbohydrate ... 52g Saturates 2g

 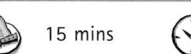

15 mins   40 mins

SERVES 4

I N G R E D I E N T S

¼ tsp saffron threads

3 tbsp hot water

6 tbsp olive oil

1 Spanish onion, sliced

3 garlic cloves, finely chopped

1 red bell pepper, seeded and sliced

1 orange bell pepper, seeded and sliced

1 large eggplant, cut into cubes

1¼ cups risotto rice

2½ cups vegetable bouillon (see page 6)

1 lb/450 g tomatoes, skinned and chopped

4 oz/115 g mushrooms, sliced

4 oz/115 g green beans, halved

1½ cups canned pinto beans or
   garbanzo beans

COOK'S TIP

Risotto rice is rounder than long grain rice and can absorb a lot of liquid without becoming soggy. Spanish rice, which would be more authentic in this dish, is similar but is not so widely available.

1 Put the saffron and hot water in a small bowl and let stand. Meanwhile, heat the oil in a large, heavy skillet or a paella pan. Add the onion and cook, stirring occasionally, for 5 minutes, until soft. Add the garlic, bell peppers, and eggplant and cook, stirring occasionally, for 5 minutes more.

2 Add the rice and stir for about 1 minute, until the grains are coated in oil. Add the bouillon, tomatoes, saffron, and soaking water to the pan and season to taste with salt and pepper. Bring to a boil, lower the heat, and simmer, shaking the pan frequently and stirring the mixture occasionally, for 15 minutes.

3 Stir in the mushrooms, green beans, and pinto beans or garbanzo beans with their can juices. Cook for 10 minutes more, then serve.

Stuffed Cabbage Rolls

Bathed in a tomato sauce, these cabbage rolls are stuffed with a nutty filling of pearl barley and zucchini to make a satisfying entrée.

NUTRITIONAL INFORMATION

Calories	224	Sugars	........19g
Protein	.........6g	Fat	...........5g
Carbohydrate	...43g	Saturates	.......1g

🥔 30 mins   🕐 1 hr 10 mins

SERVES 4

INGREDIENTS

8 large or 12 medium green cabbage leaves

4 cups pints water

½ cup pearl barley

2 tbsp chopped fresh parsley

2 garlic cloves, coarsely chopped

4 cups canned chopped tomatoes

4 tbsp red wine vinegar

1 tbsp sunflower or corn oil, plus extra for brushing

2 zucchini, diced

3 scallions, sliced

2 tbsp brown sugar

salt and ground black pepper

1 Cut out the thick stems from the cabbage leaves, then blanch the leaves in a large pan of boiling water for 1 minute. Drain the leaves well and spread out to dry.

2 Bring the measured water to a boil in a large pan. Add the barley and half the chopped parsley, cover the pan, and simmer for 45 minutes, until the liquid has been absorbed.

3 Meanwhile, put the garlic, 1 can of tomatoes, and the vinegar in a blender or food processor and process to a smooth purée. Scrape into a bowl and set aside.

4 Heat the oil in a large skillet. Add the zucchini and the remaining parsley and cook, stirring frequently, for 3 minutes. Add the scallions and cook briefly, then add the tomato purée mixture. Cook for about 10 minutes, until thickened, then transfer to a large bowl.

5 Add the cooked barley to the bowl, season to taste, and stir well. Lightly brush an ovenproof dish with oil. Place a spoonful of the barley mixture at the stem end of a cabbage leaf. Roll up, tucking in the sides, and place, seam side down, in the dish. Stuff and roll the remaining cabbage leaves in the same way, placing them in the dish in a single layer.

6 Sprinkle the brown sugar over the cabbage rolls and pour the remaining tomatoes, with their can juice, on top. Cover with foil and bake in a preheated oven, 375°F/190°C, for 30 minutes, or until tender. Serve straight from the dish.

 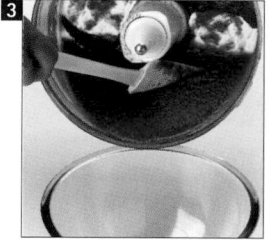 

Saucy Borlotti Beans

Fresh sage, a herb used frequently in Mediterranean cooking, adds a subtle flavor to these pink and white speckled beans.

NUTRITIONAL INFORMATION

Calories	84	Sugars	.........6g
Protein	.........4g	Fat	...........3g
Carbohydrate	...10g	Saturates	.......0g

20 mins   30 mins

SERVES 4–6

INGREDIENTS

1¼ lb/560 g fresh borlotti beans

4 large leaves fresh sage, torn

1 tbsp olive oil

1 large onion, thinly sliced

1¼ cups good-quality bottled or homemade tomato sauce (see page 269) for pasta

salt and pepper

shredded fresh sage leaves, to garnish

1 Shell the borlotti beans. Bring a pan of water to a boil, add the beans and the torn sage leaves to the pan, bring back to a boil, and simmer for about 12 minutes or until the beans are tender. Drain and set aside.

2 Heat the olive oil in a large, heavy skillet over medium heat. Add the onion and cook, stirring occasionally, for about 5 minutes until translucent and soft, but not browned.

3 Stir the tomato sauce into the pan with the cooked borlotti beans and the torn fresh sage leaves.

4 Increase the heat and bring to a boil, stirring. Lower the heat, partially cover, and simmer for about 10 minutes or until the sauce has slightly reduced.

5 Adjust the seasoning, transfer to a serving bowl, and serve hot, garnished with fresh sage leaves.

VARIATION

If fresh borlotti beans are unavailable, use 20 oz/600 g of canned beans instead. Drain and rinse, then add with the sage and tomato sauce in Step 2.

Mexican Beans

A pot of beans, bubbling away on the stove, is the basic everyday food of Mexico—delicious and healthy.

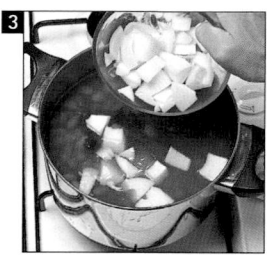

NUTRITIONAL INFORMATION

Calories 282   Sugars 1g
Protein ....18g   Fat 1g
Carbohydrate ...50g   Saturates 0g

 15 mins, plus soaking   2½ hrs

SERVES 4–6

INGREDIENTS

2½ cups dried pinto or borlotti beans

fresh mint sprig

fresh thyme sprig

fresh flat-leaf parsley sprig

1 onion, cut into chunks

salt

TO SERVE

warmed flour or corn tortillas

shreds of scallion

1 Pick through the beans and remove any pieces of grit or stones. Put the beans in a bowl, cover with cold water, and let soak overnight. If you want to cut down on soaking time, bring the beans to a boil, boil for 5 minutes, then remove from the heat, cover, and let stand for 2 hours.

2 Drain the beans, place in a pan, and cover with fresh water. Add the mint, thyme, and parsley sprigs. Bring to a boil, then reduce the heat to very low, cover, and simmer gently for about 2 hours until the beans are tender. The best way to check that they are done is to sample a bean every so often after 1¾ hours cooking time.

3 Add the onion chunks and continue to cook until the onion and beans are very tender.

4 To serve as a side dish, drain, season with salt, and serve in a bowl lined with warmed corn or flour tortillas, garnished with scallion shreds.

COOK'S TIP
If using the beans for refried beans, do not drain because the liquid is required for the recipe.

Fruity Coconut Rice

The coconut, dried fruit, nuts, seeds, and spices in this pale yellow rice make this a tasty accompaniment with a lovely texture.

NUTRITIONAL INFORMATION

Calories	578	Sugars	........17g
Protein	.........8g	Fat	..........31g
Carbohydrate	....71g	Saturates	......15g

5 mins   35 mins

SERVES 4

INGREDIENTS

3 oz/90 g creamed coconut

3 cups boiling water

1 tbsp sunflower oil (or olive oil for a stronger flavour)

1 onion, thinly sliced or chopped

1½ cups long-grain rice

¼ tsp turmeric

6 whole cloves

1 cinnamon stick

½ tsp salt

¾ cup raisins or golden raisins

½ cup walnut or pecan halves, roughly chopped

2 tbsp pumpkin seeds (optional)

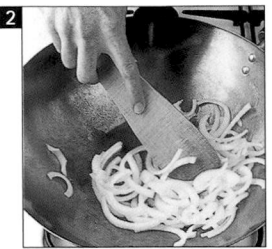

1 Blend the creamed coconut with half the boiling water until smooth, then stir in the remainder until well blended.

2 Heat the oil in a preheated wok, add the onion, and stir-fry gently for 3–4 minutes until the onion begins to soften.

3 Rinse the rice thoroughly under cold running water, drain well, and add to the wok with the turmeric. Cook for 1–2 minutes, stirring all the time.

4 Add the coconut milk, cloves, cinnamon stick, and salt to the wok and bring to a boil. Cover and simmer very gently for 10 minutes.

5 Add the raisins, nuts, and pumpkin seeds, if using, and mix well. Cover the wok again and continue to cook for a further 5-8 minutes or until all the liquid has been absorbed and the rice is tender. Remove from the heat and let stand, still tightly covered, for 5 minutes. Remove the cinnamon stick and serve.

COOK'S TIP

The addition of coconut milk gives the cooked rice a slightly sticky consistency and a special taste.

Lentils Simmered with Fruit

Although this might seem an unusual combination, when you taste this traditional Mexican dish you will discover just how delicious it is.

NUTRITIONAL INFORMATION

Calories	23	Sugars	........18g
Protein	........10g	Fat	..........7g
Carbohydrate	...36g	Saturates	.......1g

 5 mins   🕐 45 mins

SERVES 4

I N G R E D I E N T S

⅔ cup brown or green lentils

about 4 cups water

2 tbsp vegetable oil

3 small to medium onions, chopped

4 garlic cloves, coarsely chopped

1 large tart apple, coarsely chopped

about ¼ ripe pineapple, peeled and coarsely chopped

2 tomatoes, seeded and diced

1 almost ripe banana, cut into bite-size pieces

cayenne pepper

salt

fresh parsley sprig, to garnish

1 Put the lentils in a pan and add the water. Bring to a boil, then reduce the heat, and simmer gently for about 40 minutes until the lentils are tender. Do not let them become mushy.

2 Meanwhile, heat the oil in a skillet and cook the onions and garlic over low heat for 10 minutes until lightly browned. Add the apple and continue to cook until golden. Add the pineapple, heat through, stirring, then add the tomatoes. Cook over medium heat until thickened, stirring occasionally.

3 Drain the lentils, reserving ½ cup of the cooking liquid. Add the drained lentils to the sauce, stirring in the reserved liquid if necessary. Heat through for a minute to mingle the flavors.

4 Add the banana to the skillet, then season to taste with cayenne pepper and salt. Transfer the lentils to a warmed serving dish, garnish with the parsley sprig, and serve immediately.

VARIATION
Instead of lentils, prepare the dish using cooked pinto or borlotti beans.

Egg & Lentil Curry

A nutritious meal that is easy and relatively quick to make. The curried lentil sauce would also be delicious served with cooked vegetables.

NUTRITIONAL INFORMATION

Calories ....298 Sugars 6g
Protein ....17g Fat 17g
Carbohydrate ...20g Saturates 4g

10 mins   35 mins

SERVES 4

INGREDIENTS

3 tbsp vegetable ghee or oil

1 large onion, chopped

2 garlic cloves, chopped

1 inch/2.5 cm piece of ginger root, chopped

½ tsp minced chili or chili powder

1 tsp ground coriander

1 tsp ground cumin

1 tsp paprika

½ cup split red lentils

1¾ cups vegetable bouillon

1 cup canned chopped tomatoes

6 eggs

¼ cup coconut milk

salt

2 tomatoes, cut into wedges, and
  cilantro sprigs, to garnish

parathas, chapattis, or naan bread, to serve

1 Heat the ghee or oil in a pan, add the onion, and sauté gently for 3 minutes. Stir in the garlic, ginger, chili, and spices and cook gently, stirring frequently, for 1 minute. Stir in the lentils, bouillon, and chopped tomatoes and bring to a boil. Reduce the heat, cover, and simmer, stirring occasionally, for 30 minutes, until the lentils are tender.

2 Meanwhile, place the eggs in a pan of cold water and bring to a boil. Reduce the heat and simmer for 10 minutes. Drain and cover immediately with cold water.

3 Stir the coconut milk into the lentil mixture and season well with salt to taste. Process the mixture in a blender or food processor until smooth. Return to the pan and warm through over low heat, stirring constantly.

4 Shell the hard-cooked eggs and cut them in half lengthwise. Arrange 3 halves, in a petal design, on each of 4 warmed serving plates. Spoon the hot lentil sauce over the eggs, adding enough to flood the plate.

5 Arrange a tomato wedge and a cilantro sprig between each halved egg. Serve the curry hot with parathas, chapattis, or naan bread.

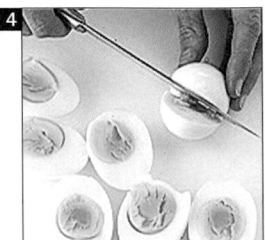

Spinach & Chana Dhal

An attractive-looking dish, this makes a good accompaniment to almost any recipe. For a contrast in color and taste, serve with a tomato curry.

NUTRITIONAL INFORMATION

Calories	175	Sugars	.........1g
Protein	.........6g	Fat	..........12g
Carbohydrate	...12g	Saturates	.......1g

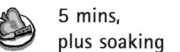

5 mins, plus soaking   45 mins

SERVES 6

I N G R E D I E N T S

4 tbsp chana dhal

6 tbsp vegetable oil

1 tsp mixed onion and mustard seeds

4 dried red chilies

14–15 oz/400-425 g canned spinach, drained

1 tsp finely chopped fresh ginger root

1 tsp ground coriander

1 tsp ground cumin

1 tsp salt

1 tsp chili powder

2 tbsp lemon juice

1 fresh green chili, seeded and finely chopped, to garnish

1 Soak the chana dhal in a bowl of warm water for 3–8 hours.

2 Place the dhal in a pan, cover with water, and bring to a boil. Lower the heat and simmer gently for 30 minutes. Drain well.

3 Heat the oil in another pan. Add the mixed onion and mustard seeds and dried red chilies and cook, stirring constantly, until they turn a shade darker.

4 Add the drained spinach to the pan, mixing gently. Add the ginger, ground coriander, ground cumin, salt, and chili powder. Reduce the heat and gently stir-fry the mixture for 7-10 minutes.

5 Add the drained dhal to the pan and blend into the spinach mixture well, stirring gently so that it does not break up.

6 Transfer the mixture to a warmed serving dish. Sprinkle over the lemon juice and garnish with the chopped green chili. Serve immediately.

COOK'S TIP
Very similar in appearance to moong dhal—the yellow split peas—chana dhal have slightly less shiny grains.

Kabli Chana Sag

Pulses such as garbanzo beans are widely used in India. They need to be soaked overnight so prepare well in advance.

NUTRITIONAL INFORMATION

Calories 217   Sugars 5g
Protein . . . . .12g   Fat 9g
Carbohydrate . . .25g   Saturates 1g

🥧🥧🥧

🍲 10 mins   🕐 1–2 hrs

SERVES 6

INGREDIENTS

1 cup garbanzo beans, soaked overnight and drained

5 cloves

1 inch/2.5 cm piece of cinnamon stick

2 garlic cloves

3 tbsp sunflower oil

1 small onion, sliced

3 tbsp lemon juice

1 tsp coriander seeds

2 tomatoes, peeled, seeded, and chopped

1 lb/450 g spinach, rinsed and any tough stems removed

1 tbsp chopped fresh cilantro

TO GARNISH

fresh cilantro sprigs

lemon slices

beans are tender when tested with a toothpick. Skim off any foam that comes to the surface.

2 Meanwhile, heat 1 tablespoon of the oil in a heavy pan. Crush the remaining garlic clove. Put it into the pan with the onion and cook over moderate heat, stirring occasionally, for about 5 minutes.

3 Remove the cloves, cinnamon, and garlic from the pan of garbanzo beans and discard. Drain the garbanzo beans. Place ⅓ cup of the garbanzo beans in a food processor with the onion and garlic, the lemon juice, and 1 tablespoon of the oil and process until smooth. Alternatively, blend together with a fork in a bowl. Stir this purée into the remaining beans.

4 Heat the remaining oil in a large skillet, add the coriander seeds, and stir for 1 minute until they give off their aroma. Add the tomatoes, stir, and add the spinach. Cover and cook over moderate heat for 1 minute. The spinach should be wilted, but not soggy. Stir in the chopped cilantro and remove from the heat.

5 Transfer the garbanzo beans to a warmed serving dish and spoon over the spinach mixture. Garnish with the cilantro sprigs and slices of lemon and serve immediately.

1 Put the garbanzo beans into a pan with enough water to cover. Add the cloves, cinnamon, and 1 whole unpeeled garlic clove that has been lightly crushed with the back of a knife to release the juices. Bring to a boil, reduce the heat, and simmer for 1–2 hours or until the garbanzo

Curried Rice with Bean Curd

Cooked rice is combined with marinated bean curd, vegetables, and peanuts to make this deliciously rich curry.

NUTRITIONAL INFORMATION

Calories ....598 Sugars 2g
Protein ....16g Fat 25
Carbohydrate ...81g Saturates 4g

🥄 15 mins   🕐 15 mins

SERVES 4

INGREDIENTS

1 tsp coriander seeds

1 tsp cumin seeds

1 tsp ground cinnamon

1 tsp cloves

1 whole star anise

1 tsp cardamom pods

1 tsp white peppercorns

1 tbsp oil

6 shallots, chopped very roughly

6 garlic cloves, chopped very roughly

2 inch/5 cm piece lemon grass, sliced

4 fresh red chilies, seeded and chopped

grated zest of 1 lime

1 tsp salt

3 tbsp sunflower oil

9 oz/250 g marinated bean curd, cut into
    1 inch/2.5cm cubes

1 cup green beans, cut into
    1 inch/2.5cm lengths

5–6 cups cooked rice (1¾ cups raw weight)

3 shallots, diced finely and deep-fried

1 scallion, chopped finely

2 tbsp chopped roast peanuts

1 tbsp lime juice

1 To make the curry paste, grind together the seeds and spices in a pestle and mortar or spice grinder.

2 Heat the sunflower oil in a preheated wok until it is really hot. Add the shallots, garlic, and lemon grass and cook over low heat until soft, about 5 minutes. Add the chilies, together with the dry spices, then stir in the grated lime zest and salt.

3 To make the curry, heat the oil in a wok or large, heavy skillet. Cook the bean curd over high heat for 2 minutes to seal. Stir in the curry paste and green beans. Add the rice and stir over high heat for about 3 minutes more.

4 Transfer to a warmed serving dish. Sprinkle with the deep-fried shallots, scallion, and peanuts, and squeeze over the lime juice. Serve hot.

Chinese Vegetable Rice

This tasty rice can either be served as a meal or as an accompaniment to other vegetable recipes.

NUTRITIONAL INFORMATION

Calories	228	Sugars	.........5g
Protein	.........5g	Fat	...........7g
Carbohydrate	...37g	Saturates	.......1g

5 mins   25 mins

SERVES 4

INGREDIENTS

1¾ cups long-grain white rice

1 tsp turmeric

2 tbsp sunflower oil

½ lb/450 g zucchini, sliced

1 red bell pepper, seeded and sliced

1 green bell pepper, seeded and sliced

1 green chili, seeded and finely chopped

1 medium carrot, coarsely grated

1½ cups beansprouts

6 scallions, sliced, plus extra to garnish (optional)

2 tbsp soy sauce

salt

1 Place the rice and turmeric in a pan of lightly salted water and bring to a boil. Reduce the heat and let simmer until the rice is just tender. Drain the rice thoroughly and press out any excess water with paper towels. Set aside until required.

2 Heat the sunflower oil in a large preheated wok.

3 Add the zucchini to the wok and cook for about 2 minutes.

4 Add the bell peppers and chili to the wok and cook for 2–3 minutes.

5 Add the cooked rice to the mixture in the wok, a little at a time, tossing well after each addition.

6 Add the carrots, beansprouts, and scallions to the wok and cook for a further 2 minutes.

7 Drizzle with soy sauce and serve at once, garnished with extra scallions, if desired.

COOK'S TIP

For real luxury, add a few saffron strands infused in boiling water instead of the turmeric.

Split Peas with Vegetables

Here is a simple, yet nourishing and flavorful way of cooking yellow split peas. Vary the choice of vegetables and spices according to taste.

NUTRITIONAL INFORMATION

Calories	490	Sugars	.........8g
Protein	........21g	Fat	..........19g
Carbohydrate	...63g	Saturates	.......3g

4¼ hrs   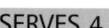 1 hr

SERVES 4

I N G R E D I E N T S

1 cup dried yellow split peas

5 cups water

½ tsp ground turmeric (optional)

1 lb/450 g new potatoes

5 tbsp vegetable oil

2 onions, coarsely chopped

6 oz/175 g white mushrooms

1 tsp ground coriander

1 tsp ground cumin

1 tsp chili powder

1 tsp garam masala

scant 1 cup vegetable bouillon

½ cauliflower, broken into florets

¾ cup frozen peas

6 oz/175 g cherry tomatoes, halved

salt and pepper

fresh mint sprigs, to garnish

1 Place the split peas in a bowl, add the water, and let soak for at least 4 hours or overnight.

2 Place the peas and the soaking liquid in a large pan, stir in the turmeric, if using, and bring to a boil. Skim off any scum that rises to the surface, half-cover the pan, and simmer gently for 20 minutes or until the peas are tender and almost dry. Remove the pan from the heat and set aside.

3 Meanwhile, cut the potatoes into ¼ inch/5 mm thick slices. Heat the oil in a flameproof casserole, add the onions, potatoes, and mushrooms, and cook over low heat, stirring frequently, for 5 minutes. Stir in the spices and fry, stirring frequently, for 1 minute, then season with salt and pepper to taste, and add the bouillon and cauliflower florets.

4 Cover the pan and simmer, stirring occasionally, for 25 minutes or until the potatoes are tender. Add the split peas (and any of the cooking liquid) and the frozen peas. Bring to a boil, cover, and continue cooking for 5 minutes.

5 Stir in the halved cherry tomatoes and cook for 2 minutes. Taste and adjust the seasoning, if necessary. Serve hot, garnished with mint sprigs.

VARIATION

Chana dhal (popular with vegetarians because of its high protein content) may be used instead of yellow split peas, if preferred. Chana dhal is similar to yellow split peas, although the grains are smaller and the flavor sweeter.

Toovar Dhal

Dried pulses and lentils can be cooked in similar ways, but the soaking and cooking times do vary, so check the pack for instructions.

NUTRITIONAL INFORMATION

Calories	195	Sugars	.........4g
Protein	........11g	Fat	...........5g
Carbohydrate	...28g	Saturates	.......3g

 10 mins   50 mins

SERVES 6

I N G R E D I E N T S

2 tbsp vegetable ghee

1 large onion, finely chopped

1 garlic clove, crushed

1 tbsp grated fresh ginger root

1 tbsp cumin seeds, ground

2 tsp coriander seeds, ground

1 dried red chili

1 inch/2.5 cm piece of cinnamon stick

1 tsp salt

½ tsp ground turmeric

1 cup split yellow peas, soaked in cold water for 1 hour and drained

2 cups canned plum tomatoes

1¼ cups water

2 tsp garam masala

COOK'S TIP

Use a nonstick pan if you have one, because the mixture is quite dense and does stick to the base of the pan occasionally. If the dhal is overstirred, the split peas will break up and the dish will not have much texture or bite.

1 Heat the ghee in a large pan, add the onion, garlic, and ginger and sauté for 3–4 minutes until the onion has softened slightly.

2 Add the cumin, coriander, chili, cinnamon, salt, and turmeric, then stir in the split peas until well mixed.

3 Add the tomatoes, with their can juices, breaking up the tomatoes slightly with the back of a spoon.

4 Add the water and bring to a boil. Reduce the heat to very low and simmer the split peas, uncovered, stirring occasionally, for about 40 minutes until most of the liquid has been absorbed and the split peas are tender. Skim the surface occasionally with a slotted spoon to remove any scum.

5 Gradually stir in the garam masala, tasting after each addition, until it is to your taste. Serve hot.

Onion Dhal

This dhal is semidry when cooked, so it is best to serve it with a curry that has a sauce. Ordinary onions can be used as a substitute.

NUTRITIONAL INFORMATION

Calories	232	Sugars	.........1g
Protein	.........6g	Fat	..........17g
Carbohydrate	...15g	Saturates	.......2g

5 mins   30 mins

SERVES 4

INGREDIENTS

½ cup masoor dhal

6 tbsp vegetable oil

1 small bunch scallions, chopped

1 tsp finely chopped ginger root

1 tsp crushed garlic

½ tsp chili powder

½ tsp turmeric

1¼ cups water

1 tsp salt

1 fresh green chili, finely chopped

fresh cilantro leaves

1 Rinse the lentils thoroughly and set aside until required.

2 Heat the oil in a heavy pan. Add the scallions to the pan and cook over medium heat, stirring frequently, until lightly browned.

3 Reduce the heat and add the ginger, garlic, chili powder, and turmeric. Briefly stir-fry the scallions with the spices. Add the lentils and stir to blend.

4 Add the water to the lentil mixture, reduce the heat to low, and cook for 20–25 minutes.

5 When the lentils are thoroughly cooked and tender, add the salt and stir gently to mix well.

6 Transfer the onion dhal to a serving dish. Garnish with the chopped green chilies and fresh cilantro leaves and serve immediately.

COOK'S TIP
Masoor dhal are small, round, pale orange split lentils. They turn a pale yellow color when cooked.

Murkha Dhal

In this dhal recipe, the garlic is intended to burn in the base of the pan, and this flavor permeates the dish.

NUTRITIONAL INFORMATION

Calories	372	Sugars	.........7g
Protein	........18g	Fat	..........16g
Carbohydrate	...42g	Saturates	......10g

 5 mins   55 mins

SERVES 4

I N G R E D I E N T S

4 tbsp butter

2 tsp black mustard seeds

1 onion, finely chopped

2 garlic cloves, finely chopped

1 tbsp grated ginger root

1 tsp turmeric

2 green chilies, seeded and finely chopped

1¼ cups red lentils

4 cups water

1¾ cups coconut milk

1 tsp salt

1 Melt the butter in a large, heavy pan over moderate heat. Add the mustard seeds and cover the pan. When you can hear the seeds popping, add the onion, garlic, and grated ginger. Cook, uncovered, for about 7–8 minutes, until the onion is soft and the garlic is brown.

2 Stir in the turmeric and green chilies and cook for 1–2 minutes, until the chilies soften a little.

3 Add the lentils and cook, stirring frequently, for 2 minutes, until the lentils begin to turn translucent.

4 Stir in the water, coconut milk, and salt. Bring to a boil, then reduce the heat and simmer for 40 minutes, or until the desired consistency is reached. However, if you intend to reheat the dhal later rather than eat it straight away, cook it for only 30 minutes to allow for reheating time.

5 Transfer the dhal to a warmed serving dish and serve immediately, while piping hot.

COOK'S TIP

There are many types of lentils used in India, but the two most common are red lentils and green or beige lentils. Red lentils are very useful, as they cook in a relatively short time to form a homogeneous mass. Green and beige lentils stay more separate when cooked.

Oil-Dressed Dhal

This dhal is given a baghaar (seasoned oil dressing), just before serving, of ghee, onion, and a combination of spicy seeds.

NUTRITIONAL INFORMATION

Calories	173	Sugars	.........3g
Protein	.........8g	Fat	...........8g
Carbohydrate	...20g	Saturates	.......5g

5 mins   30 mins

SERVES 4

INGREDIENTS

scant ½ cup masoor dhal

3 tbsp moong dhal

1¾ cups water

1 tsp finely chopped ginger root

1 tsp crushed garlic

2 red chilies, chopped

1 tsp salt

BAGHAAR

2 tbsp ghee

1 medium onion, sliced

1 tsp mixed mustard and onion seeds

1 Rinse the lentils thoroughly and place in a large pan. Pour over the water, stirring. Add the ginger, garlic, and red chilies and bring to a boil over medium heat. Half cover with a lid and simmer for about 15–20 minutes, until they are soft enough to be mashed.

2 Mash the lentils and add more water if necessary to form a thick sauce.

3 Add the salt to the lentil mixture and stir well. Transfer the lentils to a heatproof serving dish.

4 Just before serving, melt the ghee in a small pan. Add the onion and sauté over medium heat, stirring frequently, for about 5–8 minutes, until golden brown. Add the mustard and onion seeds and stir to mix well.

5 Pour the onion mixture over the lentils while it is still hot. Stir the mixture to combine thoroughly and serve the oil-dressed dhal immediately.

COOK'S TIP

This dish makes a a very good accompaniment, especially for a dry curry. It also freezes well—simply re-heat it in a pan or covered in the oven.

Tarka Dhal

This is just one version of many dhals that are served throughout India; as many people are vegetarian, dhals form a staple part of the diet.

NUTRITIONAL INFORMATION

Calories 183   Sugars 4g
Protein ....8g   Fat 8g
Carbohydrate ...22g   Saturates 5g

10 mins   25 mins

SERVES 4

INGREDIENTS

2 tbsp ghee

2 shallots, sliced

1 tsp yellow mustard seeds

2 garlic cloves, crushed

8 fenugreek seeds

1 tsp grated fresh ginger root

½ tsp salt

generous ½ cup red lentils

1 tbsp tomato paste

2½ cups water

2 tomatoes, peeled and chopped

1 tbsp lemon juice

4 tbsp chopped fresh cilantro

½ tsp garam masala

½ tsp chili powder

1 Heat half of the ghee in a large pan and add the shallots. Cook for 2–3 minutes over high heat, then add the mustard seeds. Cover the pan until the seeds begin to pop.

2 Immediately remove the lid from the pan and add the garlic, fenugreek, ginger, and salt.

3 Stir once and add the lentils, tomato paste, and water. Bring to a boil, then lower the heat and simmer gently for 10 minutes.

4 Stir in the tomatoes, lemon juice, and chopped cilantro and simmer for 4–5 minutes until the lentils are tender.

5 Transfer to a serving dish. Heat the remaining ghee in a pan. Remove from the heat and stir in the garam masala and chili powder. Pour over the tarka dhal and serve.

COOK'S TIP

The flavors in a dhal can be altered to suit your particular taste; for example, for extra heat, add more chili powder or chilies, or add fennel seeds for a pleasant anise flavor.

Risotto with Asparagus

Using the best asparagus available turns this simple recipe, an Italian classic, into a gourmet treat for lunch or supper.

NUTRITIONAL INFORMATION

Calories 494   Sugars 3g
Protein . . . . 15g   Fat 23g
Carbohydrate . . . . . 61g   Saturates 11g

5–10 mins   30–35 mins

SERVES 6

INGREDIENTS

2 lb/900 g fresh asparagus, washed

2 tbsp sunflower or other vegetable oil

6 tbsp sweet butter

2 shallots or 1 small onion, chopped finely

2 cups risotto or carnaroli rice

6¼ cups light vegetable bouillon, simmering

1 cup freshly grated Parmesan cheese

salt and pepper

Parmesan shavings, to garnish (optional)

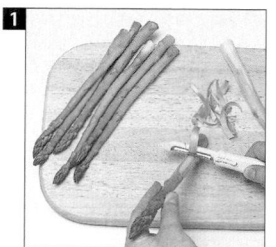

1 Lightly peel the stems of the asparagus and trim off the woody ends. Cut the tips off each stalk and set them aside, then cut the remaining stems into 1 inch/2.5 cm pieces.

2 Add the asparagus stem pieces to a pan of boiling water and boil for 2 minutes. Add the asparagus tips and boil for about 1 minute, or until tender-crisp. Do not overcook. Rinse under cold running water and set aside.

3 Heat the oil with half the butter in a large, heavy pan. Add the shallots and cook gently for 2 minutes until soft. Add the rice and cook, stirring frequently, for about 2 minutes, or until the rice is translucent and well coated.

4 Add a ladleful of the simmering bouillon and cook, stirring constantly, until the liquid is completely absorbed.

5 Continue adding the bouillon, about half a ladleful at a time, letting each addition be absorbed before adding the next. This should take about 20–25 minutes. The risotto should have a creamy consistency and the rice should be tender, but al dente, or firm to the bite.

6 Heat the asparagus tips in the bouillon, then stir the stems into the risotto with the last ladleful of bouillon, the remaining butter, and the grated Parmesan cheese.

7 Remove the pan from the heat, then stir in the asparagus tips and season if necessary. Transfer the risotto to a warmed serving dish and serve with Parmesan cheese shavings, if wished.

Green Fried Rice

Spinach is used in this recipe to give the rice a wonderful green coloring. Tossed with the carrot strips, it is a really appealing dish.

NUTRITIONAL INFORMATION

Calories 139	Sugars 2g
Protein 3g	Fat 7g
Carbohydrate ...18g	Saturates 1g

5 mins   20 mins

SERVES 4

INGREDIENTS

scant 1 cup long-grain rice

2 tbsp vegetable oil

2 garlic cloves, crushed

1 tsp grated fresh ginger root

1 carrot, cut into matchsticks

1 zucchini, diced

½ lb/225 g young spinach

2 tsp light soy sauce

2 tsp light brown sugar

1 Cook the rice in a pan of boiling water for about 15 minutes. Drain the rice well, rinse under cold running water, and then drain thoroughly again. Set aside until required.

2 Heat the oil in a preheated wok or a large, heavy skillet.

3 Add the crushed garlic and grated fresh ginger root to the wok or skillet and stir-fry for about 30 seconds.

4 Add the carrot matchsticks and diced zucchini to the mixture in the wok and stir-fry for about 2 minutes, so the vegetables still retain their crunch.

5 Add the spinach and stir-fry for 1 minute, until wilted.

6 Add the rice, soy sauce, and sugar to the wok and mix together well.

7 Transfer the green fried rice to serving dishes and serve immediately.

COOK'S TIP
Light soy sauce has more flavor than the sweeter, dark soy sauce, which gives the food a rich, reddish color.

Chatuchak Fried Rice

An excellent way to use up left-over rice. Pop it in the freezer as soon as it is cool, and it will be ready to reheat at any time.

NUTRITIONAL INFORMATION

Calories 241	Sugars 5g	
Protein 7g	Fat 5g	
Carbohydrate . . . 46g	Saturates 1g	

 25 mins   15 mins

SERVES 4

I N G R E D I E N T S

1 tbsp sunflower oil

3 shallots, chopped finely

2 garlic cloves, crushed

1 red chili, seeded and chopped finely

1 inch/2.5 cm piece ginger root,
  shredded finely

½ green bell pepper, seeded and
  sliced finely

5½ oz/150 g baby aubergines, quartered

3 oz/90 g sugar snap peas or snow peas,
  trimmed and blanched

9–12 baby sweetcorn, halved lengthwise
  and blanched

1 tomato, cut into 8 pieces

1 cup beansprouts

7 cups cooked jasmine rice

2 tbsp tomato catsup

2 tbsp light soy sauce

TO GARNISH

fresh cilantro leaves

lime wedges

1 Heat the oil in a wok or a large, heavy skillet over high heat.

2 Add the shallots, garlic, chili, and ginger to the wok or skillet. Stir until the shallots have softened, then add the green bell pepper and quartered baby eggplants and stir well.

3 Add the sugar snap peas or the snow peas, baby sweetcorn, tomato, and beansprouts. Stir-fry for 3 minutes.

4 Add the cooked jasmine rice to the wok, and lift and stir with two spoons for about 4–5 minutes, until no more steam is released.

5 Stir the tomato catsup and soy sauce into the mixture in the wok.

6 Serve the Chatuchak fried rice immediately on warmed plates, garnished with cilantro leaves and lime wedges to squeeze over.

Fennel Risotto with Vodka

The alcohol in the vodka cooks out, but leaves a pleasant, tantalizing flavor which complements the cool sweetness of the fennel.

NUTRITIONAL INFORMATION

Calories 385	Sugars 4g	
Protein 10g	Fat 10g	
Carbohydrate ..55g	Saturates 3g	

5 mins   30–35 mins

SERVES 4–6

I N G R E D I E N T S

2 large fennel bulbs

2 tbsp vegetable oil

6 tbsp sweet butter

1 large onion, finely chopped

1¾ cups risotto or carnaroli rice

⅔ cup vodka (or lemon-flavored vodka, if you can find it)

5⅔ cups light vegetable bouillon, simmering

⅔ cup freshly grated Parmesan cheese

5–6 tbsp lemon juice

salt and pepper

1   Trim the fennel, reserving the fronds for the garnish, if wished. Cut the bulbs in half lengthwise, then remove the V-shaped cores and chop the flesh coarsely. (If you like, add any of the fennel trimmings to the bouillon for extra flavor.)

2   Heat the oil and half the butter in a large, heavy pan over medium heat. Add the onion and fennel and cook for about 2 minutes, stirring frequently, until the vegetables are soft. Add the rice and cook for about 2 minutes, stirring frequently, until the rice is translucent and well coated with oil and butter.

3   Pour the vodka into the rice. It will bubble rapidly and evaporate almost immediately. Add a ladleful of the bouillon. Cook, stirring constantly, until the ladleful of liquid is absorbed.

4   Continue stirring in the bouillon, about half a ladleful at a time, letting each addition be completely absorbed by the rice before adding the next. This should take about 20–25 minutes. The finished risotto should have a creamy consistency and the rice should be just tender, but firm to the bite.

5   Stir in the remaining butter, grated Parmesan cheese, and lemon juice. Remove from the heat, cover, and let stand for 1 minute.

6   Garnish the risotto with a few of the reserved fennel fronds, and serve.

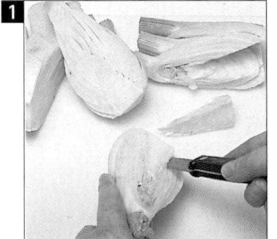

Fragrant Jasmine Rice

Jasmine rice has a delicate flavor and it can be served completely plain.
This simple dish just has the light tang of lemon and soft scent of basil.

NUTRITIONAL INFORMATION

Calories	384	Sugars	.........0g
Protein	.........7g	Fat	...........4g
Carbohydrate	...86g	Saturates	.......1g

 15 mins 15 mins

SERVES 4

INGREDIENTS

2 cups jasmine rice

3½ cups water

zest of ½ lemon, finely grated

2 tbsp fresh sweet basil, chopped

1 Wash the rice in several changes of cold water until the water runs clear. Bring the water to a boil in a large pan, then add the rice.

2 Bring back to a rolling boil. Turn the heat to a low simmer, cover the pan, and simmer for a further 12 minutes.

3 Remove the pan from the heat and let stand, covered, for 10 minutes. It is important to leave the pan tightly covered while the rice steams inside, so that the grains cook evenly and become fluffy and separate.

4 Fluff up the rice with a fork, then stir in the lemon zest. Serve sprinkled with basil leaves.

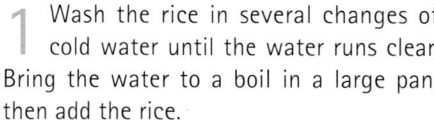

Vegetable Fried Rice

This dish can be served as part of a substantial meal for a number of people or as a vegetarian meal in itself for four.

NUTRITIONAL INFORMATION

Calories 175   Sugars 3g
Protein . . . . .3g   Fat 10g
Carbohydrate . . .20g   Saturates 2g

 10 mins   20 mins

SERVES 4

I N G R E D I E N T S

⅔ cup long-grain white rice

3 tbsp peanut oil

2 garlic cloves, crushed

½ tsp Chinese five-spice powder

½ cup green beans

1 green bell pepper, seeded and chopped

4 baby corn cobs, sliced

1 oz/25 g canned bamboo shoots, drained and chopped

3 tomatoes, skinned, seeded, and chopped

½ cup cooked peas

1 tsp sesame oil

VARIATION
Use a selection of vegetables of your choice in this recipe, cutting them to a similar size in order to ensure that they cook in the same amount of time.

1 Bring a large pan of water to a boil, then add the rice to the pan and cook for about 15 minutes. Drain the rice well, rinse under cold running water, and drain thoroughly again.

2 Heat the peanut oil in a preheated wok or large skillet. Add the crushed garlic and the Chinese five-spice powder to the wok or skillet and cook for 30 seconds, stirring constantly.

3 Add the green beans, chopped green bell pepper, and sliced corn cobs, and cook the ingredients in the wok for 2 minutes.

4 Stir the bamboo shoots, tomatoes, peas, and rice into the mixture in the wok and cook for 1 further minute.

5 Sprinkle with sesame oil and transfer to serving dishes. Serve immediately.

Risotto Primavera

This is a nice way to use those first green vegetables that signal the spring (*la primavera* in Italian.) Feel free to add other favorite vegetables.

NUTRITIONAL INFORMATION

Calories	.381	Sugars	.3g
Protein	.13g	Fat	.19g
Carbohydrate	.43g	Saturates	.8g

15 mins   40 mins

SERVES 6–8

INGREDIENTS

8 oz/225 g fresh thin asparagus spears

4 tbsp olive oil

1½ cups young green beans, cut into 1 inch/2.5 cm pieces

1½ cups young zucchini, quartered and cut into 1 inch/2.5 cm lengths

2 cups shelled fresh peas

1 onion, finely chopped

1–2 garlic cloves, finely chopped

3 cups risotto rice

scant 7 cups vegetable bouillon, simmering

4 scallions, cut into 1 inch/2.5 cm lengths

4 tbsp sweet butter

1⅓ cups freshly grated Parmesan cheese

2 tbsp chopped fresh chives

2 tbsp shredded fresh basil

salt and pepper

scallions, to garnish (optional)

2 Heat 2 tablespoons of the olive oil in a large skillet over high heat until very hot. Add the asparagus, green beans, zucchini, and peas and stir-fry for 3–4 minutes until they are bright green and just beginning to soften. Set aside.

3 Heat the remaining olive oil in a large heavy pan over medium heat. Add the onion and cook for about 1 minute until it begins to soften. Stir in the garlic and cook for a further 30 seconds. Add the rice to the pan and cook, stirring frequently, for 2 minutes until it is translucent and coated with oil.

4 Add a ladleful (about 1 cup) of the hot bouillon; the bouillon will bubble rapidly. Cook, stirring constantly, until the bouillon is absorbed.

5 Continue adding the bouillon, about half a ladleful at a time, letting each addition be completely absorbed before adding the next, but never letting the rice cook "dry." This should take 20–25 minutes. The risotto should have a creamy consistency and the rice should be tender, but still firm to the bite.

6 Stir in the stir-fried vegetables and scallions with a little more bouillon. Cook for 2 minutes, stirring frequently, then season with salt and pepper. Stir in the butter, Parmesan, chives, and basil.

7 Remove the pan from the heat, cover, and let stand for about 1 minute. Transfer the risotto to a warmed serving dish, garnish with scallions, if wished, and serve immediately.

1 Trim the woody ends of the asparagus and cut off the tips. Cut the stems into 1 inch/2.5 cm pieces and set aside with the tips.

Stir-Fries Casseroles, & Bakes

Stir-fries, casseroles, and bakes are ideal for busy vegetarian cooks, as the effort goes into the preparation but the rest takes care of itself. Stir-fries are simply wonderful—they take only a few minutes to prepare, they are endlessly adaptable, and the ingredients retain all their goodness because they are cooked so quickly. They are also the ultimate in "one-pot" cooking—ideally a wok, as these are designed to distribute heat evenly and efficiently, but a heavy skillet is also fine. Casseroles and bakes can be prepared, often in advance, and left to cook, leaving you to get on with something else—or just relax!

Bean Curd & Peanut Sauce

This is a very sociable dish if put in the center of the table where people can help themselves with toothpicks.

NUTRITIONAL INFORMATION

Calories ....338 Sugars 9g
Protein ....16g Fat 22g
Carbohydrate ...21g Saturates 4g

 5 mins   20 mins

SERVES 4

INGREDIENTS

1 lb/450 g marinated or plain firm
   bean curd

2 tbsp rice vinegar

2 tbsp sugar

1 tsp salt

3 tbsp smooth peanut butter

½ tsp chili flakes

3 tbsp barbecue sauce

4 cups sunflower oil

2 tbsp sesame oil

BATTER

4 tbsp all-purpose flour

2 eggs, beaten

4 tbsp milk

½ tsp baking powder

½ tsp chili powder

COOK'S TIP

Bean curd is made from puréed soy beans. It is white, with a soft, cheese-like texture, and is sold in blocks, either fresh or vacuum-packed. Although it has a bland flavor, it blends well with other ingredients, and absorbs the flavors of spices and sauces.

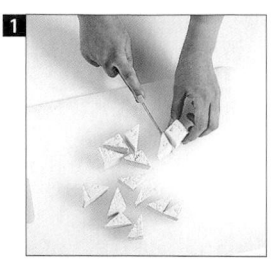 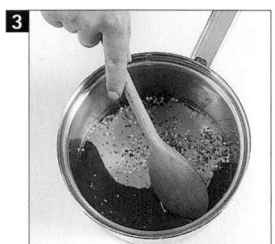 

1 Cut the bean curd into 1 inch/2.5 cm triangles. Set aside until required.

2 Combine the rice vinegar, sugar, and salt in a pan. Bring to a boil and then simmer for 2 minutes.

3 Remove the sauce from the heat and add the smooth peanut butter, chili flakes, and barbecue sauce, stirring well until thoroughly blended.

4 To make the batter, sift the all-purpose flour into a bowl, make a well in the center, and add the eggs. Draw in the flour, adding the milk slowly. Stir in the baking powder and chili powder.

5 Heat both the sunflower oil and sesame oil in a deep-fryer or large pan until a light haze appears on top.

6 Dip the bean curd triangles into the batter and deep-fry until golden brown. You may need to do this in batches. Drain on paper towels.

7 Transfer the bean curd triangles to a warm serving dish and serve with the peanut sauce.

Bean Curd with Mushrooms

Chunks of cucumber and smoked bean curd, stir-fried with straw mushrooms, snow peas, and corn in a yellow bean sauce.

NUTRITIONAL INFORMATION

Calories	130	Sugars	.........2g
Protein	.........9g	Fat	...........9g
Carbohydrate	....3g	Saturates	.......1g

 15 mins   10 mins

SERVES 4

I N G R E D I E N T S

1 large cucumber

1 tsp salt

8 oz/225 g smoked bean curd

2 tbsp vegetable oil

¾ cup snow peas

10–12 baby corn ears

1 celery stalk, sliced diagonally

15 oz/425 g can straw mushrooms, drained

2 scallions, cut into strips

½ inch/1 cm piece ginger root, chopped

1 tbsp yellow bean sauce

1 tbsp light soy sauce

1 tbsp dry sherry

1 Halve the cucumber lengthwise and remove the seeds, using a teaspoon or melon baller.

2 Cut the cucumber into cubes, place in a strainer, and sprinkle over the salt. Let drain for 10 minutes, then rinse thoroughly in cold water to remove the salt and drain thoroughly on absorbent paper towels.

3 Cut the smoked bean curd into bite-sized cubes, using a very sharp knife to avoid squashing the bean curd.

4 Heat the vegetable oil in a wok or large skillet until smoking.

5 Add the bean curd, snow peas, baby corn, and celery to the wok. Stir until the bean curd is lightly browned. Add the straw mushrooms, scallions, and ginger, and stir-fry for a further minute.

6 Stir in the cucumber, yellow bean sauce, light soy sauce, dry sherry, and 2 tbsp of water. Stir-fry for 1 minute and ensure that all the vegetables are coated in the sauces before serving.

COOK'S TIP
Straw mushrooms are available in cans from Asian suppliers and some food stores. If unavailable, substitute ½ lb/225 g baby white mushrooms.

Spicy Bean Curd Triangles

Marinated bean curd is ideal in this recipe for added flavor, although the spicy coating is very tasty with plain bean curd.

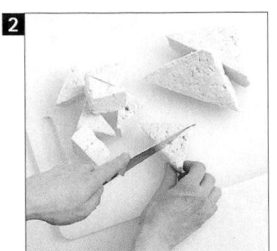

NUTRITIONAL INFORMATION

Calories ......224 Sugars 17g
Protein ....10g Fat 13g
Carbohydrate ...18g Saturates 2g

 1¼ hrs   10 mins

SERVES 4

I N G R E D I E N T S

1 tbsp sea salt

4½ tsp Chinese five-spice powder

3 tbsp light brown sugar

2 garlic cloves, crushed

1 tsp grated fresh ginger root

1lb/450 g firm bean curd

vegetable oil, for deep-frying

2 leeks, shredded and halved

shredded leek, to garnish

1 Mix together the salt, Chinese five-spice powder, sugar, garlic, and ginger in a bowl and transfer to a plate.

2 Cut the bean curd cakes in half diagonally to form two triangles. Cut each triangle in half and then in half again to form 16 triangles.

3 Roll the bean curd triangles in the spice mixture, turning to coat thoroughly. Let stand for 1 hour.

4 Heat the vegetable oil for deep-frying in a wok until it is almost smoking.

5 Reduce the heat slightly, add the bean curd triangles to the wok, and cook for 5 minutes, until golden brown.

Remove the bean curd from the wok with a slotted spoon, set aside, and keep warm until required.

6 Add the leeks to the wok and cook for 1 minute. Remove from the wok and drain on paper towels.

7 Arrange the leeks on a warm serving plate and place the bean curd on top.

8 Garnish with the fresh shredded leek and serve immediately.

COOK'S TIP

Cook the bean curd in batches and keep each batch warm until all of the bean curd has been cooked and is ready to serve.

Vegetable & Nut Stir-Fry

A colorful selection of vegetables, stir-fried in a creamy peanut sauce and sprinkled with nuts to serve.

NUTRITIONAL INFORMATION

Calories	325	Sugars	.........6g
Protein	........11g	Fat	..........21g
Carbohydrate	...26g	Saturates	.......4g

🥄 10 mins 🕐 15 mins

SERVES 4

INGREDIENTS

3 tbsp crunchy peanut butter

⅔ cup water

1 tbsp soy sauce

1 tsp sugar

1 carrot

½ red onion

4 baby zucchini

1 red bell pepper

9 oz/250 g egg thread noodles

¼ cup peanuts, chopped roughly

2 tbsp vegetable oil

1 tsp sesame oil

1 small green chili, seeded and sliced thinly

1 garlic clove, sliced thinly

8 oz/225 g can water chestnuts, drained and sliced

2 cups beansprouts

salt

3 Bring a large pan of water to a boil and add the egg noodles. Remove from the heat immediately and let stand for 4 minutes, stirring occasionally to separate the noodles.

4 Heat a wok or large skillet, add the peanuts, and dry-fry them, stirring constantly, until they are beginning to brown. Remove with a perforated spoon and set aside until required.

5 Add the vegetable and sesame oils to the pan and heat. Add the carrot, onion, zucchini, bell pepper, chili, and garlic, and stir-fry for 2–3 minutes. Add the water chestnuts, beansprouts, and peanut sauce. Bring to a boil and heat thoroughly. Season with salt to taste.

6 Drain the noodles and serve with the vegetable and nut stir-fry. Sprinkle with the reserved peanuts.

1 Gradually blend the peanut butter with the water in a small bowl. Stir in the soy sauce and sugar. Set aside.

2 Cut the carrot into thin matchsticks and slice the red onion. Slice the zucchini on the diagonal and cut the bell pepper into chunks.

Bean Curd Stir-Fry

Bean curd is a low-fat source of high-quality protein and, although it is naturally bland, it readily absorbs the flavors of other ingredients.

NUTRITIONAL INFORMATION

Calories 135   Sugars 5g
Protein ....11g   Fat 7g
Carbohydrate ....7g   Saturates 3g

 10 mins, plus marinating   12 mins

SERVES 4

INGREDIENTS

8 oz/225 g firm bean curd, cut into bite-size pieces

1 tbsp groundnut or sunflower oil

2 scallions, chopped

1 garlic clove, finely chopped

1½ cups snow peas

10–12 baby corn ears, halved

¼ lb/115 g shiitake mushrooms, thinly sliced

2 tbsp finely chopped cilantro leaves

MARINADE

2 tbsp dark soy sauce

1 tbsp Chinese rice wine

2 tsp brown sugar

½ tsp Chinese five-spice powder

1 fresh red chili, seeded and finely chopped

2 scallions, finely chopped

1 tbsp grated fresh ginger root

COOK'S TIP

Always use a sharp knife for cutting bean curd—a blunt knife will squash it.

1 Combine all the marinade ingredients in a shallow, nonmetallic dish, whisking well to mix. Add the bean curd and turn to coat. Cover with plastic wrap and let marinate in the refrigerator for 2 hours, turning once or twice.

2 Drain the bean curd and reserve the marinade. Heat the oil in a wok or large skillet. Add the bean curd and stir-fry for 2–3 minutes, until golden. Remove and set aside. Add the scallions and garlic and stir-fry for 2 minutes, then add the corn cobs and stir-fry for 1 minute. Add the snow peas and mushrooms and stir-fry for 2 minutes more.

3 Return the bean curd to the wok or skillet and add the marinade. Cook gently for 1–2 minutes until heated through. Sprinkle with the chopped cilantro and serve immediately.

Bean Curd with Bell Peppers

Bean curd is perfect for marinating as it readily absorbs flavors for a great tasting entrée.

NUTRITIONAL INFORMATION

Calories 267   Sugars 2g
Protein . . . . .9g   Fat 23g
Carbohydrate . . . .5g   Saturates 3g

25 mins   15 mins

SERVES 4

INGREDIENTS

12 oz/350 g firm bean curd

2 cloves garlic, crushed

4 tbsp soy sauce

1 tbsp sweet chili sauce

6 tbsp sunflower oil

1 onion, sliced

1 green bell pepper, seeded and diced

1 tbsp sesame oil

1 Using a sharp knife, cut the bean curd into bite-sized pieces. Place the bean curd in a shallow, nonmetallic dish.

2 Mix together the garlic, soy sauce, and sweet chili sauce and drizzle over the bean curd. Toss well to coat and let marinate for about 20 minutes.

3 Meanwhile, heat the sunflower oil in a large preheated wok.

4 Add the onion to the wok and cook over high heat until brown and crispy. Remove the onion with a slotted spoon and let drain on paper towels.

5 Add the bean curd to the hot oil and cook for about 5 minutes.

6 Remove all but 1 tablespoon of the sunflower oil from the wok. Add the bell pepper to the wok and cook for 2–3 minutes, or until soft.

7 Return the bean curd and onions to the wok and heat through, stirring occasionally.

8 Drizzle with sesame oil. Transfer to serving plates and serve immediately.

COOK'S TIP
If you are in a real hurry, buy ready-marinated bean curd from your food store.

Green Bean Stir-Fry

These beans are simply cooked in a spicy, hot sauce for a tasty and very easy recipe.

NUTRITIONAL INFORMATION

Calories 86	Sugars 4g
Protein 2g	Fat 6g
Carbohydrates 6g	Saturates 1g

 5 mins   5 mins

SERVES 4

INGREDIENTS

1 lb/450 g thin green beans

2 fresh red chilies

2 tbsp peanut oil

½ tsp ground star anise

1 garlic clove, crushed

2 tbsp light soy sauce

2 tsp clear honey

½ tsp sesame oil

1 Using a sharp knife, cut the green beans in half.

2 Slice the fresh chilies, removing the seeds first if you prefer a milder dish.

3 Heat the oil in a preheated wok or large skillet until it is almost smoking.

4 Lower the heat slightly, add the halved green beans to the wok, and cook for 1 minute.

5 Add the sliced red chilies, star anise, and garlic to the wok and cook for a further 30 seconds.

6 Mix together the soy sauce, honey, and sesame oil in a small bowl.

7 Stir the sauce mixture into the wok. Cook for 2 minutes, tossing the beans to ensure that they are thoroughly coated in the sauce.

8 Transfer the mixtureto a warm serving dish and serve immediately.

VARIATION

This recipe is surprisingly delicious made with Brussels sprouts instead of green beans. Trim the sprouts, then shred them finely. Cook the sprouts in hot oil for 2 minutes, then proceed with the recipe from step 4.

Chinese Braised Vegetables

Quickly prepared and packed with flavor, this dish is stir-fried to begin with before the vegetables are briefly braised to finish them off.

NUTRITIONAL INFORMATION

Calories 150   Sugars 2g
Protein . . . . .12g   Fat 13g
Carbohydrates . . . .7g   Saturates 4g

 10 mins   10 mins

SERVES 4

INGREDIENTS

¼ oz/10 g Chinese dried mushrooms

3 tbsp groundnut or sunflower oil

8 oz/225 g firm bean curd, cut into cubes

1½ cups Napa cabbage, shredded

3 oz/75 g canned sliced bamboo shoots, drained and rinsed

3 oz/75 g straw mushrooms, halved

1¼ cups snow peas

½ tsp muscovado sugar

1 tbsp dark soy sauce

dash of sesame oil

1 Put the dried mushrooms in a small bowl, cover with cold water, and let stand for 20 minutes. Drain, then cut off and discard any hard stems.

2 Heat the groundnut or sunflower oil in a wok or skillet. Add the bean curd and stir-fry for 2–4 minutes, until browned all over. Remove from the skillet with a slotted spoon and set aside.

3 Add the Chinese mushrooms, Napa cabbage, bamboo shoots, straw mushrooms, and snow peas to the skillet and stir-fry for 2 minutes.

4 Return the bean curd to the skillet and add the sugar and soy sauce. Stir for 1 minute, then cover and braise for 3 minutes. Sprinkle with a dash of sesame oil before serving.

COOK'S TIP
Firm, marinated, and smoked bean curd are all suitable for stir-frying.

Bell Peppers with Chestnuts

This is a crisp and colorful recipe, topped with crisp, shredded leeks for both flavor and color.

NUTRITIONAL INFORMATION

Calories	192	Sugars	.........5g
Protein	.........3g	Fat	..........14g
Carbohydrate	...13g	Saturates	......13g

 5 mins   15 mins

SERVES 4

INGREDIENTS

8 oz/225 g leeks

oil, for deep-frying

3 tbsp peanut oil

1 yellow bell pepper, seeded and diced

1 green bell pepper, seeded and diced

1 red bell pepper, seeded and diced

7 oz/200 g canned water chestnuts, drained and sliced

2 cloves garlic, crushed

3 tbsp light soy sauce

1 To make the garnish, finely slice the leeks into thin strips.

2 Heat the oil for deep-frying in a wok or large, heavy skillet. Add the sliced leeks and cook for 2–3 minutes, or until crispy. Set aside until required.

3 Heat the 3 tablespoons of peanut oil in the wok or skillet.

4 Add the yellow, green, and red bell peppers to the wok and cook over high heat for about 5 minutes, or until they are just beginning to brown at the edges and to soften.

5 Add the sliced water chestnuts, garlic, and light soy sauce to the wok and cook all of the vegetables for a further 2–3 minutes.

6 Spoon the bell pepper stir-fry on to warm serving plates, garnish with the crispy leeks, and serve.

COOK'S TIP

Add 1 tablespoon of hoisin sauce with the soy sauce in step 6 for extra flavor and spice.

Stir-Fried Greens

Eat your greens in this most delicious way—stir-fried, so that they retain all their color, crunch and flavor.

NUTRITIONAL INFORMATION

Calories	116	Sugars	.........3g
Protein	.........5g	Fat	...........9g
Carbohydrate	....5g	Saturates	.......1g

 5 mins   🕐 10 mins

SERVES 4

I N G R E D I E N T S

8 scallions

2 celery stalks

1 cup white radish

1½ cup sugar snap peas or snow peas

1½ cup Napa cabbage

6 oz/175 g bok choi or spinach

2 tbsp vegetable oil

1 tbsp sesame oil

2 garlic cloves, chopped finely

3 tbsp light soy sauce

1 tsp finely grated fresh ginger root

pepper

1 Slice the scallions and celery finely. Cut the white radish into matchstick strips. Trim the sugar snap peas or snow peas. Shred the Napa cabbage and the bok choi or spinach.

2 Heat the vegetable oil and sesame oil together in a wok or large skillet. Add the garlic and cook for about 1 minute.

3 Add the scallions, celery, white radish, and sugar snap peas or snow peas to the wok or skillet and stir-fry for about 2 minutes.

4 Add the shredded Napa cabbage and bok choi or spinach to the wok or skillet, and continue to stir-fry for about 1 minute.

5 Stir the light soy sauce into the vegetables with the grated ginger. Cook for 1 minute. Season with pepper to taste, transfer to a warm serving dish, and serve at once.

VARIATION
Any variety—and any amount—of fresh vegetables can be used in this dish. Just make sure that harder vegetables, such as carrots, are cut very finely so that they cook quickly.

Bamboo with Spinach

In this recipe, spinach is fried with spices and then braised in a soy-flavored sauce with bamboo shoots for a rich, delicious dish.

NUTRITIONAL INFORMATION

Calories 105	Sugars 1g
Protein 3g	Fat 9g
Carbohydrate 3g	Saturates 2g

 5 mins   🕐 10 mins

SERVES 4

I N G R E D I E N T S

3 tbsp peanut oil

8 oz/225 g spinach, chopped

6 oz/175 g canned bamboo shoots, drained and rinsed

1 garlic clove, crushed

2 fresh red chilies, sliced

pinch of ground cinnamon

1¼ cups vegetable bouillon

pinch of sugar

pinch of salt

1 tbsp light soy sauce

1 Heat the peanut oil in a preheated wok or large skillet, swirling the oil around the bottom of the wok until it is really hot.

2 Add the spinach and bamboo shoots to the wok and cook for 1 minute.

3 Add the garlic, chilies, and cinnamon to the mixture in the wok and cook for a further 30 seconds.

4 Stir in the bouillon, sugar, salt, and light soy sauce, cover, and cook over medium heat for 5 minutes, or until the vegetables are cooked through and the sauce has reduced. If there is too much cooking liquid, blend a little cornstarch with double the quantity of cold water and stir into the sauce.

5 Transfer the bamboo shoots and spinach to a serving dish and serve.

COOK'S TIP

Fresh bamboo shoots are rarely available in the West and, in any case, are extremely time-consuming to prepare. Canned bamboo shoots are quite satisfactory, as they are used to provide a crunchy texture, rather than for their flavor, which is fairly insipid.

Bamboo with Bell Peppers

This dish has a wonderfully strong ginger flavor which is integral to Chinese cooking. The mixed bell peppers give the dish a burst of color.

NUTRITIONAL INFORMATION

Calories 101   Sugars 5g
Protein . . . . .3g   Fat 6g
Carbohydrate . . . .9g   Saturates 1g

 5 mins   15 mins

SERVES 4

INGREDIENTS

2 tbsp peanut oil

8 oz/225 g canned bamboo shoots, drained and rinsed

2 tsp finely chopped fresh ginger root

1 small red bell pepper, seeded and thinly sliced

1 small green bell pepper, seeded and thinly sliced

1 small yellow bell pepper, seeded and thinly sliced

1 leek, sliced

½ cup vegetable bouillon

1 tbsp light soy sauce

2 tsp light brown sugar

2 tsp Chinese rice wine or dry sherry

1 tsp cornstarch

2 tsp water

1 tsp sesame oil

1 Heat the peanut oil in a preheated wok or large skillet, swirling the oil around the bottom until it is really hot.

2 Add the bamboo shoots, ginger, bell peppers, and leek to the wok and cook for 2–3 minutes.

3 Stir in the vegetable bouillon, soy sauce, light brown sugar, and Chinese rice wine or sherry and bring to a boil, stirring. Reduce the heat and simmer for 4–5 minutes, or until the vegetables begin to soften.

4 Blend the cornstarch with the water to form a smooth paste.

5 Stir the cornstarch paste into the wok or skillet. Bring to a boil and cook, stirring constantly, until the sauce thickens and clears.

6 Sprinkle the sesame oil over the vegetables and cook for 1 minute, then transfer to a warm serving dish and serve immediately.

Gingered Broccoli

Ginger and broccoli are a perfect combination of flavors and make an exceptionally tasty side dish.

NUTRITIONAL INFORMATION

Calories 118   Sugars 3g
Protein . . . . .8g   Fat 7g
Carbohydrate . . . .6g   Saturates 1g

 5 mins   15 mins

SERVES 4

I N G R E D I E N T S

2 inch/5 cm piece fresh ginger root

2 tbsp peanut oil

1 garlic clove, crushed

7 cups broccoli florets

1 leek, sliced

2¾ oz/75 g canned water chestnuts, halved

½ tsp superfine sugar

½ cup vegetable bouillon

1 tsp dark soy sauce

1 tsp cornstarch

2 tsp water

1 Using a sharp knife, finely chop the ginger. (Alternatively, cut the ginger into larger strips, to be discarded later, for a slightly milder ginger flavor.)

2 Heat the peanut oil in a preheated wok. Add the garlic and ginger and cook for 30 seconds.

3 Add the broccoli, leek, and water chestnuts to the wok and cook for a further 3–4 minutes.

4 Add the sugar, bouillon, and dark soy sauce to the wok, reduce the heat, and simmer for 4–5 minutes, or until the broccoli is almost cooked.

5 Blend the cornstarch with the water to form a smooth paste and stir it into the wok.

6 Bring to a boil and cook, stirring, for 1 minute or until thickened.

7 If using larger strips of ginger, remove from the wok and discard.

8 Transfer the vegetables to a warm serving dish and serve immediately.

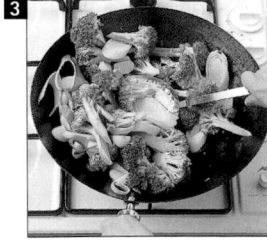  

VARIATION

Use spinach instead of the broccoli, if you prefer. Add the spinach leaves half way through step 3. Reduce the cooking time in step 4 to 3–4 minutes.

Bamboo with Cucumber

A simple stir-fried side dish of canned bamboo shoots and sliced cucumber is the perfect accompaniment to a Chinese entrée.

NUTRITIONAL INFORMATION

Calories 101   Sugars 0.2g
Protein . . . . .3g   Fat 7g
Carbohydrate . . . .7g   Saturates 1g

20 mins   10 mins

SERVES 4

INGREDIENTS

½ cucumber

2 tbsp sesame oil

4 shallots, chopped finely

1 garlic clove, sliced finely

12 oz/350 g canned bamboo shoots, drained

1 tbsp dry sherry

1 tbsp soy sauce

2 tsp cornstarch

1 tsp sesame seeds

salt

TO GARNISH

2 red chili flowers (see page 8)

sliced scallions

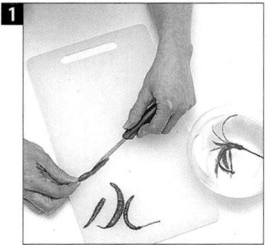  

1 Slice the cucumber thinly and sprinkle with salt. Let stand for 10–15 minutes, then rinse with cold water. Prepare the chili and scallion garnish.

2 Heat the sesame oil in a wok or skillet and add the shallots and garlic. Stir-fry for 2 minutes, until golden.

3 Add the bamboo shoots and the cucumber to the wok or skillet and stir-fry for 2–3 minutes.

4 Blend together the dry sherry, soy sauce, and cornstarch. Add to the bamboo shoots and cucumber in the wok, stirring to combine.

5 Cook for 1–2 minutes to thicken slightly, then add the sesame seeds and stir through.

6 Transfer the vegetables to a warmed serving dish. Garnish with the chili flowers and the chopped scallion and serve immediately.

COOK'S TIP
Salting the cucumber before it is stir-fried draws out some of its moisture so that it stays crisp. Add some very finely sliced carrot to this dish to add some extra color, if you like.

Lemon Napa Cabbage

Stir-fried Napa cabbage leaves is served with a tangy sauce made of grated lemon zest, lemon juice, and ginger.

NUTRITIONAL INFORMATION

Calories 120	Sugars 0g
Protein 5g	Fat 8g
Carbohydrate 8g	Saturates 1g

 5 mins 10 mins

SERVES 4

INGREDIENTS

1 lb/450 g Napa cabbage

3 tbsp vegetable oil

½ inch/1 cm piece ginger root, grated

1 tsp salt

1 tsp sugar

½ cup water or vegetable bouillon

1 tsp grated lemon zest

1 tbsp cornstarch

1 tbsp lemon juice

1 Separate the Napa cabbage leaves, wash, and drain thoroughly. Pat dry with absorbent paper towels

2 Cut the Napa cabbage leaves into 2 inch/5 cm wide slices.

3 Heat the oil in a wok, add the grated ginger root followed by the Napa cabbage leaves, and stir-fry for 2–3 minutes or until the leaves begin to wilt.

4 Add the salt and sugar, and mix well until the leaves soften. Remove the leaves with a slotted spoon and set aside.

5 Add the water or bouillon to the wok with the lemon zest. Bring to a boil.

6 Meanwhile, mix the cornstarch to a smooth paste with the lemon juice, then add to the wok. Simmer, stirring constantly, for about 1 minute to make a smooth sauce.

7 Return the cooked Napa cabbage leaves to the wok and mix thoroughly to coat the leaves in the lemon sauce. Arrange the leaves on a warm serving plate and serve them immediately.

COOK'S TIP

If Napa cabbage leaves are unavailable, substitute slices of savoy cabbage. Cook for 1 extra minute to soften the leaves.

Spicy Mushrooms

A mixture of mushrooms, common in Western cooking, has been used in this recipe for a richly flavored dish.

NUTRITIONAL INFORMATION

Calories	103	Sugars	........4g
Protein	.........3g	Fat	...........8g
Carbohydrate	....5g	Saturates	.......2g

 5 mins   10 mins

SERVES 4

INGREDIENTS

2 tbsp peanut oil

2 garlic cloves, crushed

3 scallions, chopped

10½ oz/300 g white mushrooms

2 large open-cap mushrooms, sliced

4½ oz/125 g oyster mushrooms

1 tsp chili sauce

1 tbsp dark soy sauce

1 tbsp hoisin sauce

1 tbsp wine vinegar

½ tsp ground Szechuan pepper

1 tbsp dark brown sugar

1 tsp sesame oil

chopped fresh parsley, to garnish

1 Heat the peanut oil in a preheated wok or large skillet until it is almost smoking.

2 Reduce the heat slightly, then add the garlic and scallions to the wok or skillet and cook for 30 seconds.

3 Add the mushrooms to the wok with the chili, soy, and hoisin sauces, wine vinegar, Szechuan pepper, and sugar. Cook for 4–5 minutes, until the mushrooms are cooked through. Stir constantly to prevent the mixture sticking to the wok.

4 Sprinkle the sesame oil on top of the mixture in the wok. Transfer to a warm serving dish, garnish with parsley, and serve immediately.

COOK'S TIP

If Chinese dried mushrooms are available, add a small quantity to this dish for texture. Wood ears are widely used and are available dried from Chinese food stores. They should be rinsed, soaked in warm water for 20 minutes, and rinsed again before use.

TVP & Vegetable Stir-Fry

TVP, like bean curd, absorbs all of the flavors in a dish, making it ideal for this recipe, which is packed with classic Chinese flavorings.

NUTRITIONAL INFORMATION

Calories 167	Sugars 8g	
Protein 12g	Fat 9g	
Carbohydrate . . .10g	Saturates 1g	

 30 mins   10 mins

SERVES 4

INGREDIENTS

1 tbsp grated fresh ginger root

1 tsp ground ginger

1 tbsp tomato paste

2 tbsp sunflower oil

1 clove garlic, crushed

2 tbsp soy sauce

¾ lb/350 g TVP or soy cubes

2 cups sliced carrots

1½ cups green beans, sliced

4 stalks celery, sliced

1 red bell pepper, seeded and sliced

boiled rice, to serve

COOK'S TIP

Ginger root will keep for several weeks in a cool, dry place. Ginger root can also be kept frozen—break off lumps as needed.

1 Place the grated fresh ginger root, ground ginger, tomato paste, 1 tbsp of the sunflower oil, garlic, soy sauce, and the TVP or soy cubes in a large bowl. Mix well to combine, stirring carefully so that you don't break up the TVP or soy cubes. Cover the mixture and let marinate for 20 minutes.

2 Heat the remaining sunflower oil in a large preheated wok.

3 Add the marinated TVP or soy mixture to the wok and stir-fry for about 2 minutes.

4 Add the carrots, green beans, celery, and red pepper to the wok and stir-fry for a further 5 minutes.

5 Transfer the stir-fry to warm serving dishes and serve immediately with freshly cooked boiled rice.

Vegetables with Hoisin

This spicy vegetable stir-fry has rice added to it and it can be served as a meal in itself.

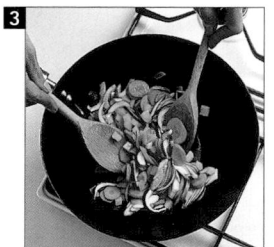

NUTRITIONAL INFORMATION

Calories	120	Sugars	.........6g
Protein	.........4g	Fat	...........6g
Carbohydrate	...12g	Saturates	.......1g

20 mins   10 mins

SERVES 4

I N G R E D I E N T S

1 red onion

1 carrot

1 yellow bell pepper

2 tbsp sunflower oil

1 cup cooked brown rice

2¼ cups snow peas

1¾ cups beansprouts

4 tbsp hoisin sauce

1 tbsp snipped fresh chives

1 Using a sharp knife, thinly slice the red onion. Thinly slice the carrot. Seed and dice the yellow bell pepper.

2 Heat the sunflower oil in a large preheated wok or heavy skillet.

3 Add the red onion slices, carrot, and yellow bell pepper to the wok and cook for about 3 minutes.

4 Add the cooked brown rice, snow peas, and beansprouts to the mixture in the wok and cook for a further 2 minutes. Stir briskly to ensure that the ingredients are well mixed and the rice grains are separated.

5 Stir the hoisin sauce into the vegetables and mix until well combined and completely heated through.

6 Transfer the vegetable stir-fry to warm serving dishes and scatter with the snipped fresh chives. Serve immediately.

COOK'S TIP

Hoisin sauce is a dark brown, reddish sauce made from soy beans, garlic, chili, and various other spices, and is commonly used in Chinese cookery. It may also be used as a dipping sauce.

Carrots with Pineapple

If you can use fresh pineapple, the flavor of this dish is even better and the texture crisper.

NUTRITIONAL INFORMATION

Calories 125   Sugars 17g
Protein ....1g   Fat 6g
Carbohydrate ...18g   Saturates 1g

5 mins   15 mins

SERVES 4

INGREDIENTS

1 tbsp sunflower oil

1 tbsp olive oil

1 small onion, finely sliced

1 inch/2.5 cm piece ginger root, peeled and grated

1–2 garlic cloves, crushed

1 lb/450 g carrots, thinly sliced

7 oz/200 g canned pineapple in natural juice, chopped, or 9 oz/250 g fresh pineapple, chopped

2-3 tbsp pineapple juice (from the can or fresh)

salt and coarsely ground black pepper

freshly chopped parsley or dill, to garnish

1 Heat the sunflower oil and the olive oil together in a wok. Add the onion, ginger, and garlic to the wok and stir-fry briskly for 2–3 minutes.

2 Add the carrots and continue to stir-fry, lowering the heat a little, for about 5 minutes.

3 Add the pineapple and the pineapple juice to the wok with plenty of seasoning, and continue to stir-fry for about 5-6 minutes, or until the carrots are tender-crisp and the liquid has almost evaporated.

4 Adjust the seasoning, adding plenty of black pepper, and transfer the stir-fry to a warmed serving dish.

5 Sprinkle the stir-fry with the chopped fresh parsley or dill and serve as a vegetable accompaniment.

6 Alternatively, you can let the carrots cool and serve them as a delicious salad, tossed in 2-4 tbsp of French dressing to taste.

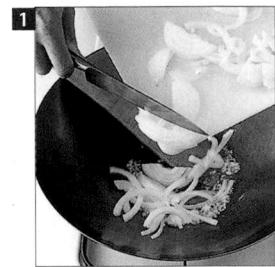

COOK'S TIP

If using canned pineapple, make sure it is in natural juice, not syrup: the sweet taste of the syrup will ruin the fresh flavor of this dish. Most fruits can now be bought canned in natural juice, which gives a much fresher, lighter taste.

Carrot & Orange Stir-Fry

Carrots and oranges have long been combined in Asian cooking, the orange juice bringing out the sweetness of the carrots.

NUTRITIONAL INFORMATION

Calories 341	Sugars 26g	
Protein 10g	Fat 21g	
Carbohydrate . . .28g	Saturates 4g	

 10 mins   10 mins

SERVES 4

INGREDIENTS

2 tbsp sunflower oil

2¼ cups grated carrots

8 oz/225 g leeks, shredded

2 oranges, peeled and segmented

2 tbsp tomato catsup

1 tbsp raw brown sugar

2 tbsp light soy sauce

½ cup chopped peanuts

1 Heat the sunflower oil in a large preheated wok.

2 Add the grated carrot and leeks to the wok and cook for 2–3 minutes, or until the vegetables have just softened.

3 Add the orange segments to the wok and heat through gently, ensuring that you do not break up the orange segments as you stir the mixture.

4 Mix the tomato catsup, brown sugar, and light soy sauce together in a small bowl.

5 Add the tomato and sugar mixture to the wok and cook for a further 2 minutes.

6 Transfer the stir-fry to warm serving bowls and scatter with the chopped peanuts. Serve immediately.

VARIATION
Cut the carrots into fine julienne strips for a slightly crunchier texture to this dish.

Napa Cabbage in Honey

Napa cabbage is rather similar to lettuce in that the leaves are delicate with a sweet flavor.

NUTRITIONAL INFORMATION

Calories	121	Sugars	6g
Protein	5g	Fat	7g
Carbohydrate	10g	Saturates	1g

5 mins   10 mins

SERVES 4

INGREDIENTS

1 lb/450 g Napa cabbage

1 tbsp peanut oil

1 tsp grated fresh ginger root

2 garlic cloves, crushed

1 fresh red chili, sliced

1 tbsp Chinese rice wine or dry sherry

4½ tsp light soy sauce

1 tbsp clear honey

½ cup orange juice

1 tbsp sesame oil

2 tsp sesame seeds

orange zest, to garnish

COOK'S TIP

Single-flower honey has a better, more individual flavor than blended honey. Acacia honey is typically Chinese, but you could also try clover, lemon blossom, lime flower, or orange blossom honey.

1 Separate the Napa cabbage and shred the leaves finely, using a sharp knife.

2 Heat the peanut oil in a preheated wok. Add the ginger, garlic, and chili to the wok and cook the mixture for about 30 seconds.

3 Add the Napa cabbage, Chinese rice wine or sherry, soy sauce, honey, and orange juice to the wok. Reduce the heat and let simmer for 5 minutes.

4 Add the sesame oil to the wok, sprinkle the sesame seeds on top, and mix to combine.

5 Transfer to a warm serving dish, garnish with the orange zest and serve immediately.

Stir-Fried Spinach

This is an easy recipe to make as a quick accompaniment to an entrée. The water chestnuts give a delicious crunch to the greens.

NUTRITIONAL INFORMATION

Calories 85   Sugars 2g
Protein . . . . .4g   Fat 4g
Carbohydrate . . . .9g   Saturates 1g

 5 mins   10 mins

SERVES 4

INGREDIENTS

1 tbsp sunflower oil

1 garlic clove, halved

2 scallions, sliced finely

8 oz/225 g canned water chestnuts, drained and sliced finely

1 lb/450 g spinach, any tough stalks removed

1 tsp sherry vinegar

1 tsp light soy sauce

pepper

1 Heat the sunflower oil in a wok or large, heavy skillet over high heat, swirling the oil around the base of the wok until it is really hot.

2 Add the halved garlic clove and cook, stirring, for 1 minute. If the garlic should brown, remove it immediately.

3 Add the scallions and water chestnuts and stir-fry for 2–3 minutes.

4 Add the spinach leaves to the wok and stir to combine.

5 Add the sherry vinegar, soy sauce, and a sprinkling of pepper. Cook, stirring, until the spinach is tender, then remove the garlic from the wok.

6 Using a slotted spoon, drain off the excess liquid from the wok and serve the stir-fried greens immediately.

COOK'S TIP

Several types of Asian greens (for example, choi sam and bok choi) are widely available and any of these can be successfully substituted for the spinach.

Eight Jewel Vegetables

This recipe, as the title suggests, is a colorful mixture of eight vegetables, cooked in a black bean and soy sauce.

NUTRITIONAL INFORMATION

Calories	110	Sugars	.........3g
Protein	.........4g	Fat	...........8g
Carbohydrate	....7g	Saturates	.......1g

 5 mins   10 mins

SERVES 4

INGREDIENTS

2 tbsp peanut oil

6 scallions, sliced

3 garlic cloves, crushed

1 green bell pepper, seeded and diced

1 red bell pepper, seeded and diced

1 fresh red chili, sliced

2 tbsp chopped water chestnuts

1 zucchini, chopped

4½ oz/125 g oyster mushrooms

3 tbsp black bean sauce

2 tsp Chinese rice wine or dry sherry

4 tbsp dark soy sauce

1 tsp dark brown sugar

2 tbsp water

1 tsp sesame oil

1 Heat the peanut oil in a preheated wok or large skillet until it is almost smoking.

2 Lower the heat then add the scallions and garlic, and cook for about 30 seconds.

3 Add the red and green bell peppers, fresh red chili, water chestnuts, and zucchini to the wok or skillet and cook for 2–3 minutes, or until the vegetables are just beginning to soften.

4 Add the oyster mushrooms, black bean sauce, Chinese rice wine or dry sherry, dark soy sauce, dark brown sugar, and water to the wok and cook for a further 4 minutes.

5 Sprinkle the stir-fry with sesame oil and serve immediately.

COOK'S TIP

Eight jewels or treasures form a traditional part of the Chinese New Year celebrations, which start in the last week of the old year. The Kitchen God, an important figure, is sent to give a report to heaven, returning on New Year's Eve in time for the feasting.

Sherry & Soy Vegetables

This is a simple yet tasty side dish which also makes a delicious light snack or even an entrée for two.

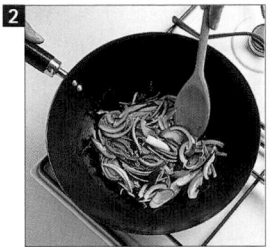
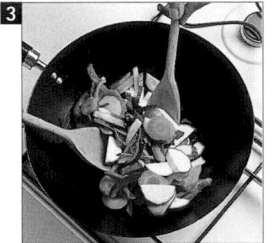

NUTRITIONAL INFORMATION

Calories	374	Sugars	10g
Protein	14g	Fat	25g
Carbohydrate	20g	Saturates	5g

10 mins   15 mins

SERVES 4

I N G R E D I E N T S

2 tbsp sunflower oil

1 red onion, sliced

2 carrots, thinly sliced

1½ cups zucchini, sliced diagonally

1 red bell pepper, seeded and sliced

1 small head Napa cabbage, shredded

1½ cups beansprouts

8 oz/225 g canned bamboo shoots, drained

1 cup cashew nuts, toasted

S A U C E

3 tbsp medium sherry

3 tbsp light soy sauce

1 tsp ground ginger

1 clove garlic, crushed

1 tsp cornstarch

1 tbsp tomato paste

1 Heat the sunflower oil in a large preheated wok.

2 Add the red onion and cook for 2–3 minutes or until softened.

3 Add the carrots, zucchini, and bell pepper slices to the wok and cook for a further 5 minutes.

4 Add the Napa cabbage, beansprouts, and bamboo shoots and heat through for 2–3 minutes, or until the cabbage leaves begin to wilt. Stir in the toasted cashew nuts.

5 Combine the sherry, soy sauce, ginger, garlic, cornstarch, and tomato paste. Pour over the vegetables and toss well. Let simmer for 2–3 minutes or until the juices start to thicken. Serve immediately.

VARIATION
Use any mixture of fresh vegetables that you have to hand in this very versatile dish.

Muttar Paneer

Paneer is a delicious fresh, soft cheese frequently used in Indian cooking. It is easily made at home, but must be made the day before it's required.

NUTRITIONAL INFORMATION

Calories	550	Sugars 25g
Protein	........19g	Fat 39g
Carbohydrate	...33g	Saturates 12g

15 mins 25 mins

SERVES 6

I N G R E D I E N T S

⅔ cup vegetable oil

2 onions, chopped

2 garlic cloves, crushed

1 inch/2.5 cm piece of ginger root, chopped

1 tsp garam masala

1 tsp ground turmeric

1 tsp chili powder

1 lb/450 g frozen peas

1 cup canned chopped tomatoes

½ cup vegetable bouillon

salt and pepper

2 tbsp chopped cilantro

P A N E E R

11 cups milk

5 tbsp lemon juice

1 garlic clove, crushed (optional)

1 tbsp chopped cilantro (optional)

1 To make the paneer, bring the milk to a rolling boil in a large pan. Remove from the heat and stir in the lemon juice. Return to the heat for about 1 minute until the curds and whey separate. Remove from the heat. Line a strainer with double thickness cheesecloth and pour the mixture through the cheesecloth, adding the garlic and cilantro, if using. Squeeze all the liquid from the curds and let drain.

2 Transfer to a dish, cover with a plate and a heavy weight, and let stand overnight in the refrigerator.

3 Cut the pressed paneer into small cubes. Heat the oil in a large skillet. Add the paneer and cook until golden on all sides. Remove from the pan and drain on paper towels.

4 Pour off some of the oil, leaving about 4 tablespoons in the pan. Add the onions, garlic, and ginger and cook gently, stirring frequently, for 5 minutes. Stir in the spices and cook gently for 2 minutes. Add the peas, tomatoes, and bouillon and season with salt and pepper. Cover and simmer, stirring occasionally, for 10 minutes, until the onion is tender.

5 Add the paneer cubes and continue to cook for a further 5 minutes. Taste and adjust the seasoning, if necessary. Sprinkle with the chopped cilantro and serve at once.

Bubble & Squeak

Bubble and squeak is best known as sautéed mashed potato and leftover greens served as an accompaniment.

 15 mins   40 mins

SERVES 4

I N G R E D I E N T S

2⅔ cups mealy diced potatoes

1½ cups Savoy cabbage, shredded

5 tbsp vegetable oil

2 leeks, chopped

1 garlic clove, crushed

8 oz/225 g smoked bean curd, cubed

salt and pepper

shredded cooked leek, to garnish

1 Cook the diced potatoes in a pan of lightly salted boiling water for 10 minutes, until tender. Drain and mash the potatoes.

2 Meanwhile, in a separate pan, blanch the cabbage in boiling water for 5 minutes. Drain well and add to the potato.

3 Heat the oil in a heavy-based skillet. Add the leeks and garlic and cook gently for 2–3 minutes. Stir into the potato and cabbage mixture.

4 Add the smoked bean curd and season well with salt and pepper. Cook over medium heat for 10 minutes.

5 Carefully turn the whole mixture over and continue to cook over medium heat for another 5–7 minutes, or until crispy underneath.

6 Serve immediately, garnished with shredded leek.

COOK'S TIP
This vegetarian version is a perfect entrée, as the smoked bean curd cubes added to the basic bubble and squeak mixture make it very substantial and nourishing.

Tomato Curry

This vegetarian tomato curry is served topped with a few hard-cooked eggs. It is a lovely accompaniment to any Indian meal.

NUTRITIONAL INFORMATION

Calories 170   Sugars 3g
Protein . . . . .6g   Fat 15g
Carbohydrate . . . .3g   Saturates 2g

 25 mins   15 mins

SERVES 4

INGREDIENTS

2 cups canned tomatoes

1 tsp finely chopped ginger root

1 tsp crushed garlic

1 tsp chili powder

1 tsp salt

½ tsp ground coriander

½ tsp ground cumin

4 tbsp vegetable oil

½ tsp onion seeds

½ tsp mustard seeds

½ tsp fenugreek seeds

pinch of white cumin seeds

3 dried red chilies

2 tbsp lemon juice

3 eggs, hard-cooked

fresh cilantro leaves

1 Place the tomatoes in a large mixing bowl. Add the ginger, garlic, chili powder, salt, ground coriander, and ground cumin and blend well.

2 Heat the vegetable oil in a pan. Add the onion, the mustard, fenugreek and white cumin seeds, and the dried red chilies, and stir-fry for about 1 minute, until they give off their aroma. Remove the pan from the heat.

3 Add the tomato mixture to the spicy oil mixture and return the pan to the heat. Stir-fry for about 3 minutes.

4 Reduce the heat and continue to cook, half covered with a lid, stirring frequently, for 7–10 minutes.

5 Sprinkle over 1 tbsp of the lemon juice. Taste, and add the remaining lemon juice if required.

6 Transfer the tomato curry to a warmed serving dish, set aside, and keep warm until required.

7 Shell the hard-cooked eggs and cut them into quarters. Add them to the tomato curry, pushing them in gently, yolk end downward.

8 Garnish with the fresh cilantro leaves and serve hot.

Potato & Cauliflower Curry

Potatoes and cauliflower go very well together. Served with a dhal and rice or bread, this dish makes a perfect vegetarian meal.

NUTRITIONAL INFORMATION

Calories 426	Sugars 6g	
Protein 4g	Fat 35g	
Carbohydrate ...26g	Saturates 4g	

 10 mins 25 mins

SERVES 4

INGREDIENTS

⅔ cup vegetable oil

½ tsp white cumin seeds

4 dried red chilies

2 onions, sliced

1 tsp finely chopped fresh ginger root

1 tsp crushed garlic

1 tsp chili powder

1 tsp salt

pinch of turmeric

1½ lb/675g potatoes, chopped

½ cauliflower, cut into small florets

2 green chilies, optional

1 tbsp fresh cilantro leaves

⅔ cup water

1 Heat the oil in a large, heavy pan. Add the white cumin seeds and dried red chilies, stirring to mix thoroughly.

2 Add the onions and cook over medium heat, stirring occasionally, for about 5–8 minutes, until golden brown.

3 Mix the ginger, garlic, chili powder, salt, and turmeric together. Add the spice mixture to the onions and cook for about 2 minutes.

4 Add the potatoes and cauliflower to the pan and stir to coat thoroughly with the spice mixture.

5 Reduce the heat and add the green chilies (if using), the cilantro leaves, and the water to the pan. Cover and simmer for about 10–15 minutes, or until the vegetables are cooked through and very tender.

6 Transfer the potato and cauliflower curry to warmed serving plates and serve immediately.

COOK'S TIP
Ground ginger is no substitute for the fresh root. It is less aromatic and flavorsome and cannot be used in sautéed dishes, as it burns easily at the high temperatures required.

Green Curry with Bean Curd

Green curry paste will keep for up to three weeks in the refrigerator. Serve the curry over rice or noodles.

NUTRITIONAL INFORMATION

Calories 237   Sugars 4g
Protein . . . . .16g   Fat 17g
Carbohydrate . . . .5g   Saturates 3g

 20 mins   15–20 mins

SERVES 4

INGREDIENTS

1 tbsp sunflower oil

6 oz/175 g marinated or plain bean curd, cut into diamonds

6 scallions, cut into 1 inch/2.5 cm pieces

⅔ cup coconut milk

grated zest of 1 lime

½ oz/15 g fresh basil leaves

¼ tsp liquid seasoning, such as Maggi

GREEN CURRY PASTE

2 tsp coriander seeds

1 tsp cumin seeds

1 tsp black peppercorns

4 large green chilies, seeded

2 shallots, quartered

2 garlic cloves,

2 tbsp chopped cilantro

grated zest of 1 lime

1 tbsp roughly chopped galangal

1 tsp ground turmeric

salt

2 tbsp oil

TO GARNISH

cilantro leaves

2 green chilies, thinly sliced

1 To make the green curry paste, grind together the coriander and cumin seeds with the black peppercorns in a food processor or in a mortar with a pestle.

2 Blend the remaining ingredients together and add the ground spice mixture. The curry paste can be stored in a clean, dry jar for up to 3 weeks in the refrigerator, or it can be frozen in a suitable container.

3 Heat the oil in a wok or large, heavy skillet. Add the bean curd and stir over high heat for about 2 minutes until sealed on all sides. Add the scallions and stir-fry for 1 minute. Remove the bean curd and scallions and reserve.

4 Put half the coconut milk into the wok or skillet and bring to a boil. Add 6 tablespoons of the curry paste and the lime zest, and cook for 1 minute, until fragrant. Add the reserved bean curd and scallions to the wok or skillet.

5 Add the remaining coconut milk and simmer for about 7–8 minutes. Stir in the fresh basil leaves and liquid seasoning. Let the curry simmer for a further minute before serving, garnished with cilantro leaves and chilies.

Green Bean & Potato Curry

You can use fresh or canned green beans for this semi-dry vegetable curry, served with an oil-dressed dhal for flavor and color.

NUTRITIONAL INFORMATION

Calories	690	Sugars	.........4g
Protein	.........3g	Fat	..........69g
Carbohydrate	...16g	Saturates	.......7g

 15 mins 30 mins

SERVES 4

INGREDIENTS

1¼ cups vegetable oil

1 tsp white cumin seeds

1 tsp mustard and onion seeds

4 dried red chilies

3 fresh tomatoes, sliced

1 tsp salt

1 tsp finely chopped fresh ginger root

1 tsp fresh garlic, crushed

1 tsp chili powder

½ lb/450 g green beans

2⅔ cups diced potatoes

1¼ cups water

1 tbsp chopped fresh cilantro

2 green chilies, finely chopped

boiled rice, to serve

1 Heat the vegetable oil in a large, heavy pan. Add the white cumin seeds, mustard and onion seeds, and dried red chilies to the pan, stirring well.

2 Add the tomatoes to the pan and cook the mixture for 3-5 minutes.

3 Mix together the salt, ginger, garlic, and chili powder, and spoon into the pan. Blend the whole mixture together thoroughly.

4 Add the green beans and potatoes to the pan and cook for about 5 minutes.

5 Add the water to the pan, then reduce the heat and let simmer for 10-15 minutes, stirring occasionally.

6 Garnish the green bean and potato curry with chopped cilantro leaves and green chilies, and serve hot with cooked rice.

Spicy Mixed Vegetable Curry

You can vary the vegetables used in this recipe according to personal preferences—experiment!

NUTRITIONAL INFORMATION

Calories	408	Sugars	20
Protein	........11g	Fat	..........24g
Carbohydrate	...39g	Saturates	.......3g

30 mins   45 mins

SERVES 4

I N G R E D I E N T S

½ lb/225 g turnips or rutabaga, peeled

1 eggplant, leaf end trimmed

¾ lb/350 g new potatoes, scrubbed

½ lb/225 g cauliflower

½ lb/225 g white mushrooms, wiped

1 large onion, peeled

½ lb/225 g carrots

6 tbsp vegetable ghee or oil

2 garlic cloves, peeled and crushed

2 inch/5 cm piece of ginger root, peeled and chopped

1–2 fresh green chilies, seeded and chopped

1 tbsp paprika

2 tsp ground coriander

1 tbsp mild or medium curry powder or paste

2 cups vegetable bouillon

2 cups canned chopped tomatoes

salt

1 green bell pepper, seeded and sliced

1 tbsp cornstarch

⅔ cup coconut milk

2–3 tbsp ground almonds

cilantro sprigs, to garnish

1 Using a sharp knife, cut the turnips or rutabaga, eggplant, and potatoes into ½ inch/1 cm cubes.

2 Divide the cauliflower into small florets. Leave the mushrooms whole, or slice thickly. Slice the onion and carrots.

3 Heat the ghee or oil in a large pan, add the onion, turnip, potato, and cauliflower and cook gently for 3 minutes, stirring frequently.

4 Add the garlic, ginger, chili, and spices and cook for 1 minute, stirring.

5 Add the bouillon, tomatoes, eggplant, and mushrooms and season with salt. Cover and simmer gently for about 30 minutes or until the vegetables are tender, stirring occasionally. Add the green bell pepper, cover, and continue cooking for a further 5 minutes.

6 Blend the cornstarch with the coconut milk to a smooth paste, and stir into the mixture. Add the ground almonds and simmer for 2 minutes, stirring all the time. Taste and adjust the seasoning, if necessary. Serve hot, garnished with cilantro sprigs.

Spinach & Cheese Curry

This vegetarian curry is full of protein and iron. Paneer is a type of cheese that you can easily make at home the day before it is needed.

NUTRITIONAL INFORMATION

Calories 578	Sugars 4g
Protein 10g	Fat 58g
Carbohydrate 4g	Saturates 7g

 20–30 mins   25 mins

SERVES 4

INGREDIENTS

1¼ cups vegetable oil

½ lb/225 g paneer, cubed (see page 496)

3 tomatoes, sliced

1 tsp ground cumin

1½ tsp ground chili powder

1 tsp salt

1 lb/450 g spinach

3 green chilies

pooris or boiled rice, to serve

1 Heat the vegetable oil in a large, heavy skillet. Add the cubed paneer and cook, stirring occasionally, until it is golden brown.

2 Remove the paneer from the skillet with a slotted spoon and drain on absorbent paper towels.

3 Add the tomatoes to the remaining oil in the pan and stir-fry, breaking them up with a spoon, for 5 minutes.

4 Add the ground cumin, the chili powder, and the salt to the skillet and mix well to combine.

5 Add the spinach leaves to the skillet and stir-fry over low heat for about 7–10 minutes until wilted.

6 Add the green chilies and return the paneer to the pan. Cook, stirring constantly, for a further 2 minutes.

7 Transfer to warmed serving plates and serve immediately with pooris or plain boiled rice.

VARIATION

You could use frozen spinach in this recipe. It should be completely thawed and squeezed as dry as possible before using.

Potato Curry

Served hot with pooris, this curry makes an excellent brunch with mango chutney as the perfect accompaniment.

NUTRITIONAL INFORMATION

Calories	390	Sugars	.......0.7g
Protein	.........2g	Fat	..........34g
Carbohydrate	...19g	Saturates	.......4g

10 mins   25 mins

SERVES 4

INGREDIENTS

3 medium potatoes

⅔ cup vegetable oil

1 tsp onion seeds

½ tsp fennel seeds

4 curry leaves

1 tsp ground cumin

1 tsp ground coriander

1 tsp chili powder

pinch of turmeric

1 tsp salt

1½ tsp dried mango powder

1 Peel the potatoes and rinse in cold water. Using a sharp knife, cut each potato into 6 slices.

2 Cook the potato slices in a pan of boiling water until they are just cooked, but not mushy (test with a sharp knife.) Drain and set aside until required.

3 Heat the vegetable oil in a separate, heavy pan over moderate heat. Reduce the heat and add the onion seeds, fennel seeds, and curry leaves and stir thoroughly.

4 Remove the pan from the heat and add the ground cumin, coriander, chili powder, turmeric, salt, and dried mango powder, stirring well to combine.

5 Return the pan to low heat and cook the mixture, stirring constantly, for about 1 minute.

6 Pour this mixture over the cooked potatoes, mix together, and stir-fry over low heat for about 5 minutes.

7 Transfer the potato curry to serving dishes and serve immediately.

COOK'S TIP

Traditionally, Semolina Dessert (see page 928) is served to follow Potato Curry.

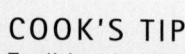

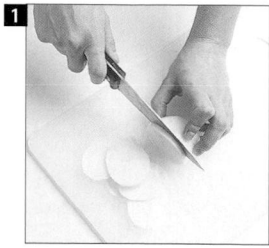

Potato Stir-Fry

In this sweet and sour dish, tender vegetables are simply stir-fried with spices and coconut milk, and flavored with lime.

NUTRITIONAL INFORMATION

Calories	138	Sugars	.........5g
Protein	.........2g	Fat	...........6g
Carbohydrate	...20g	Saturates	.......1g

 10 mins   20 mins

SERVES 4

I N G R E D I E N T S

4 waxy potatoes

2 tbsp vegetable oil

1 yellow bell pepper, diced

1 red bell pepper, diced

1 carrot, cut into matchstick strips

1 zucchini, cut into matchstick strips

2 garlic cloves, crushed

1 red chili, sliced

1 bunch scallions, halved lengthwise

8 tbsp coconut milk

1 tsp chopped lemon grass

2 tsp lime juice

finely grated zest of 1 lime

1 tbsp chopped fresh cilantro

1 Using a sharp knife, cut the potatoes into small dice.

2 Bring a large pan of water to a boil and cook the diced potatoes for 5 minutes. Drain thoroughly.

3 Heat the oil in a wok or large skillet, swirling the oil around the base of the wok until it becomes really hot.

4 Add the potatoes, diced bell peppers, carrot, zucchini, garlic, and chili to the wok and stir-fry the vegetables for about 2–3 minutes.

5 Stir in the scallions, the coconut milk, the chopped lemon grass, and the lime juice and stir-fry the mixture for a further 5 minutes.

6 Add the lime zest and cilantro and stir-fry for 1 minute. Transfer to a warmed serving dish and serve hot.

COOK'S TIP

Check that the potatoes are not overcooked in step 2, otherwise the potato pieces will disintegrate when they are stir-fried in the wok.

Sweet & Sour Vegetables

Serve this dish with plain noodles or fluffy white rice for a filling and flavorful Asian meal.

NUTRITIONAL INFORMATION

Calories	401	Sugars	. . . . .16g
Protein	. . . . .14g	Fat	. . . . .9g
Carbohydrate	. . .70g	Saturates	. . . . . . .2g

10 mins

15 mins

SERVES 4

INGREDIENTS

1 tbsp peanut oil

2 garlic cloves, crushed

1 tsp grated ginger root

6–8 baby corn ears

¾ cup snow peas

1 carrot, cut into matchsticks

1 green bell pepper, seeded and cut into matchsticks

8 scallions

2 oz/50 g canned bamboo shoots

½ lb/225 g marinated firm bean curd, cubed

2 tbsp dry sherry or Chinese rice wine

2 tbsp rice vinegar

2 tbsp clear honey

1 tbsp light soy sauce

⅔ cup vegetable bouillon

1 tbsp cornstarch

noodles or boiled rice, to serve

1 Heat the oil in a preheated wok until it is almost smoking. Add the garlic and the grated ginger root and cook over medium heat, stirring frequently, for 30 seconds.

2 Add the baby corn ears, the snow peas, and the carrot and pepper matchsticks, and stir-fry for about 5 minutes, or until the vegetables are tender, but still crisp.

3 Add the scallions, bamboo shoots, and bean curd and cook for 2 minutes.

4 Stir in the sherry or Chinese rice wine, the rice vinegar, honey, soy sauce, vegetable bouillon, and cornstarch and bring to a boil. Reduce the heat to low and simmer for 2 minutes until heated through.

5 Transfer to warmed serving dishes and serve immediately.

Sweet & Sour Cauliflower

A sweet and sour sauce gives a wonderful flavor to vegetables,
as in this tasty recipe.

NUTRITIONAL INFORMATION

Calories 154	Sugars 16g	
Protein 6g	Fat 7g	
Carbohydrate ...17g	Saturates 1g	

 5 mins   20 mins

SERVES 4

INGREDIENTS

1 lb/450 g cauliflower florets

2 tbsp sunflower oil

1 onion, sliced

½ lb/225 g carrots, sliced

1½ cups snow peas

1 ripe mango, sliced

1 cup beansprouts

3 tbsp chopped fresh cilantro

3 tbsp fresh lime juice

1 tbsp clear honey

6 tbsp coconut milk

1 Bring a large pan of water to a boil. Add the cauliflower to the pan and cook for 2 minutes. Drain the cauliflower thoroughly.

2 Heat the sunflower oil in a large preheated wok.

3 Add the onion and carrots to the wok and cook for about 5 minutes.

4 Add the drained cauliflower and snow peas to the wok and cook for 2–3 minutes.

5 Add the mango and beansprouts to the wok and cook for about 2 minutes.

6 Mix together the chopped cilantro, lime juice, honey, and coconut milk in a bowl.

7 Add the cilantro and coconut mixture to the wok and cook for about 2 minutes or until the juices are bubbling.

8 Transfer the sweet and sour cauliflower stir-fry to serving dishes and serve immediately.

VARIATION
Use broccoli instead of the cauliflower as an alternative, if you prefer.

Spiced Eggplant

This is a spicy and sweet dish, flavored with mango chutney and heated up with chilies for a really wonderful combination of flavors.

NUTRITIONAL INFORMATION

Calories 208	Sugars 17g
Protein 1g	Fat 15g
Carbohydrate ...17g	Saturates 2g

 5 mins 25 mins

SERVES 4

INGREDIENTS

3 tbsp peanut oil

2 onions, sliced

2 cloves garlic, chopped

2 eggplants, diced

2 red chilies, seeded and very finely chopped

2 tbsp raw brown sugar

6 scallions, sliced

3 tbsp mango chutney

oil, for deep-frying

2 cloves garlic, sliced, to garnish

1 Heat the peanut oil in a large preheated wok or heavy skillet, swirling the oil around the bottom of the wok until it is really hot.

2 Add the onions and chopped garlic to the wok, stirring well.

3 Add the diced eggplant and chilies to the wok and cook for 5 minutes.

4 Add the raw brown sugar, scallions, and mango chutney to the wok, stirring well.

5 Reduce the heat, cover, and let simmer, stirring from time to time, for 15 minutes or until the eggplant is tender.

6 Transfer the stir-fry to serving bowls and keep warm.

7 Heat the oil for deep-frying in the wok and quickly cook the slices of garlic, until they brown slightly.

8 Garnish the stir-fry with the deep-fried garlic and serve immediately on warm plates.

COOK'S TIP

The "hotness" of chilies varies enormously so always use with caution, but as a general guide the smaller they are the hotter they will be. The seeds are the hottest part and so are usually discarded.

Spinach with Mushrooms

For best results, use straw mushrooms, available in cans from Asian stores. If these are unavailable, use white mushrooms instead.

NUTRITIONAL INFORMATION

Calories	201	Sugars	. . . . .8g
Protein	. . . . .7g	Fat	. . . . .15g
Carbohydrate	. . .10g	Saturates	. . . . . . .2g

  5 mins   10 mins

SERVES 4

I N G R E D I E N T S

¼ cup pine nuts

1 lb/450 g fresh spinach leaves

1 red onion

2 garlic cloves

3 tbsp vegetable oil

15 oz/425 g canned straw mushrooms, drained

¼ cup raisins

2 tbsp soy sauce

salt

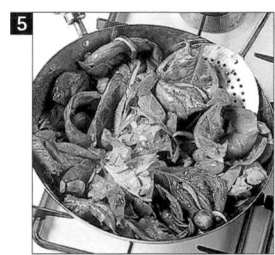

1 Heat a wok or large, heavy skillet and dry-fry the pine nuts until they are lightly browned. Remove with a perforated spoon and set aside until required.

2 Wash the spinach thoroughly, picking the leaves over and removing long stalks. Drain thoroughly and pat dry with absorbent paper towels.

3 Using a sharp knife, slice the red onion and the garlic.

4 Heat the oil in the wok or skillet. Add the onion and garlic slices and stir-fry for 1 minute until slightly softened.

5 Add the spinach and mushrooms, and continue to stir-fry until the leaves have wilted. Drain off any excess liquid.

6 Stir in the raisins, reserved pine nuts, and soy sauce. Stir-fry until thoroughly heated and all the ingredients are well combined.

7 Season to taste with salt, transfer to a warm serving dish, and serve.

COOK'S TIP

Soak the raisins in 2 tablespoons dry sherry before using. This helps to plump them up as well as adding extra flavor to the stir-fry.

Vegetable Pasta Stir-Fry

East meets West in this delicious dish. Prepare all the vegetables and cook the pasta in advance, then the dish can be cooked in a few minutes.

NUTRITIONAL INFORMATION

Calories . . . . . . .383 Sugars 18g
Protein . . . . .14g Fat 23g
Carbohydrate . . .32g Saturates 8g

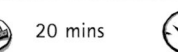 20 mins   30 mins

SERVES 4

INGREDIENTS

4 cups dried whole-wheat pasta shells, or other short pasta shapes

1 tbsp olive oil

2 carrots, thinly sliced

10–12 baby corn ears

3 tbsp peanut oil

1 inch/2.5 cm piece fresh ginger root, thinly sliced

1 large onion, thinly sliced

1 garlic clove, thinly sliced

3 celery stalks, thinly sliced

1 small red bell pepper, seeded and sliced into matchstick strips

1 small green bell pepper, seeded and sliced into matchstick strips

salt

steamed snow peas, to serve

SAUCE

1 tsp cornstarch

2 tbsp water

3 tbsp soy sauce

3 tbsp dry sherry

1 tsp clear honey

dash of hot pepper sauce (optional)

1 Cook the pasta in a large pan of boiling, lightly salted water, adding the tablespoon of olive oil. When tender, but still firm to the bite, drain the pasta, return to the pan, cover, and keep warm.

2 Cook the carrots and baby corn cobs in boiling, salted water for 2 minutes. Drain, plunge into cold water to prevent further cooking, and drain again.

3 Heat the peanut oil in a large skillet over medium heat. Add the ginger and stir-fry for 1 minute, to flavor the oil. Remove with a slotted spoon and discard.

4 Add the onion, garlic, celery, and bell peppers to the oil and stir-fry over medium heat for 2 minutes. Add the carrots and baby corn ears, and stir-fry for a further 2 minutes, then stir in the reserved pasta.

5 Put the cornstarch in a small bowl and mix to a smooth paste with the water. Stir in the soy sauce, the sherry, and the honey.

6 Pour the sauce into the pan, stir well, and cook for 2 minutes, stirring once or twice. Taste the sauce and season with hot pepper sauce if wished. Serve with a steamed green vegetable, such as snow peas.

Winter Vegetable Stir-Fry

Ordinary winter vegetables are given extraordinary treatment in this lively stir-fry, just the thing for perking up jaded palates.

NUTRITIONAL INFORMATION

Calories	175	Sugars	.........7g
Protein	.........6g	Fat	..........13g
Carbohydrate	....9g	Saturates	.......2g

 5 mins   ⏲ 10 mins

SERVES 4

INGREDIENTS

3 tbsp sesame oil

¼ cup blanched almonds

1 large carrot, cut into thin strips

1 large turnip, cut into thin strips

1 onion, sliced finely

1 garlic clove, crushed

3 celery stalks, sliced finely

8 Brussels sprouts, trimmed and halved

1 cup cauliflower, broken into florets

1 cup white cabbage, shredded

2 tsp sesame seeds

1 tsp grated fresh ginger root

½ tsp medium chili powder

1 tbsp chopped fresh cilantro

1 tbsp light soy sauce

salt and pepper

sprigs of fresh cilantro, to garnish

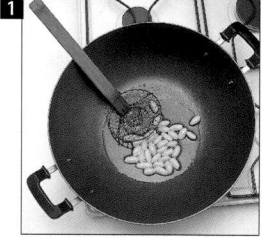  

1 Heat the oil in a wok or large skillet. Stir-fry the almonds until lightly browned, then lift them out and drain on absorbent paper towels.

2 Add all the vegetables to the wok or skillet, except for the cabbage, and stir-fry the vegetables briskly for 3–4 minutes.

3 Add the cabbage, sesame seeds, ginger, and chili powder and cook, stirring, for 2 minutes. Season to taste.

4 Add the chopped cilantro, soy sauce, and almonds, stirring gently to mix. Serve the vegetables, garnished with cilantro sprigs.

COOK'S TIP
As well as adding protein, vitamins, and useful fats to the diet, nuts and seeds add important flavor and texture to vegetarian meals. Sesame seeds are also a good source of vitamin E and calcium.

Vegetable Chop Suey

A classic Chinese dish found on all take-away menus, this recipe is quick to prepare and makes a tasty meal.

NUTRITIONAL INFORMATION

Calories 129	Sugars 19g	
Protein 5g	Fat 12g	
Carbohydrate ...21g	Saturates 2g	

 10 mins   6 mins

SERVES 4

INGREDIENTS

2 tbsp peanut oil

1 onion, chopped

3 garlic cloves, chopped

1 green bell pepper, diced

1 red bell pepper, diced

¾ cup broccoli florets

1 zucchini, sliced

⅓ cup green beans

1 carrot, cut into matchsticks

1 cup beansprouts

2 tsp light brown sugar

2 tbsp light soy sauce

½ cup vegetable bouillon

salt and pepper

noodles, to serve

COOK'S TIP

The clever design of a wok, with its spherical base and high sloping sides, enables the food to be tossed so that it is cooked quickly and evenly. It is essential to heat the wok sufficiently before you add the ingredients to ensure quick and even cooking.

1 Heat the peanut oil in a preheated wok until it is almost smoking. Add the chopped onion and garlic to the wok and stir-fry for 30 seconds.

2 Add the diced bell peppers, broccoli florets, sliced zucchini, green beans and carrot matchsticks to the pan and continue to stir-fry for a further 2–3 minutes.

3 Stir in the beansprouts, the light brown sugar, the soy sauce, and the vegetable bouillon and toss to combine thoroughly. Season the mixture with salt and pepper to taste and continue to cook for a further 2 minutes.

4 Transfer the vegetables to warmed serving plates and serve immediately with noodles.

Braised Napa Cabbage

Shredded white cabbage can be used instead of the Napa cabbage for this delicious braised dish.

NUTRITIONAL INFORMATION

Calories 138	Sugars 4g	
Protein 6g	Fat 9g	
Carbohydrate ...10g	Saturates 1g	

5 mins   5 mins

SERVES 4

INGREDIENTS

1 lb/450 g Napa cabbage or white cabbage

3 tbsp vegetable oil

½ tsp Szechuan red peppercorns

5–6 small dried red chilies, seeded and chopped

½ tsp salt

1 tbsp sugar

1 tbsp light soy sauce

1 tbsp rice vinegar

a few drops sesame oil (optional)

1 Shred the Napa cabbage or white cabbage crosswise into thin pieces. (If Napa cabbage is unavailable, the best alternative to use in this recipe is a firm-packed white cabbage, not the dark green type of cabbage. Cut out the thick core of the cabbage with a sharp knife before you shred it.)

2 Heat the vegetable oil in a preheated wok or large skillet, add the Szechuan red peppercorns and dried red chilies, and stir for a few seconds.

3 Add the shredded Napa cabbage or white cabbage to the peppercorns and chilies and stir-fry them for about 1 minute.

4 Add the salt to the mixture in the wok or skillet and continue stirring for another minute.

5 Add the sugar, light soy sauce, and rice vinegar, blend well and braise for one more minute.

6 Finally, sprinkle on the sesame oil, if using. Serve the braised Napa cabbage hot or cold.

COOK'S TIP

Szechuan red peppercorns are not true peppers, but reddish brown dry berries with a pungent, aromatic odour that distinguishes them from the hotter black peppercorns. Roast them briefly in the oven or dry-fry them. Grind them in a blender and store in a jar until needed.

Leeks with Bean Sauce

This is a simple side dish, cooked in a delicious yellow bean sauce, which is ideal served with a vegetarian entrée.

NUTRITIONAL INFORMATION

Calories	131	Sugars	3g
Protein	6g	Fat	9g
Carbohydrate	7g	Saturates	2g

 5 mins   10 mins

SERVES 4

INGREDIENTS

1 lb/450 g leeks

15 baby corn ears

6 scallions

3 tbsp peanut oil

½ lb/225 g Napa cabbage, shredded

4 tbsp yellow bean sauce

1 Using a sharp knife, slice the leeks, halve the baby corn ears, and thinly slice the scallions.

2 Heat the oil in a large preheated wok or skillet until smoking.

COOK'S TIP

Yellow bean sauce adds an authentic Chinese flavor to stir-fries. It is made from crushed salted soya beans mixed with flour and spices to make a thick paste. It is mild in flavor and is excellent with a range of vegetables.

3 Add the leeks, shredded Napa cabbage, and baby corn ears to the wok or skillet.

4 Cook the vegetables over high heat for about 5 minutes or until the edges of the vegetables are slightly brown.

5 Add the scallions to the wok or skillet, stirring to combine.

6 Add the yellow bean sauce to the wok or skillet and cook the mixture over low heat, stirring occasionally, for a further 2 minutes, or until the vegetables are heated through and thoroughly coated in the sauce.

7 Transfer the vegetables and sauce to warm serving dishes and serve immediately.

Green & Black Bean Stir-Fry

A terrific side dish, the variety of greens in this recipe make it as attractive as it is tasty.

NUTRITIONAL INFORMATION

Calories 88	Sugars 2g	
Protein 2g	Fat 7g	
Carbohydrate 4g	Saturates 4g	

 5 mins   10 mins

SERVES 4

I N G R E D I E N T S

8 oz/225 g fine green beans, sliced

4 shallots, sliced

3½ oz/100 g shiitake mushrooms, thinly sliced

1 clove garlic, crushed

1 iceberg lettuce, shredded

1 tsp chili oil

2 tbsp butter

4 tbsp black bean sauce

1 Using a sharp knife, slice the fine green beans, shallots, and shiitake mushrooms. Crush the garlic with a pestle and mortar and shred the lettuce.

2 Heat the chili oil and butter in a large preheated wok or skillet.

3 Add the green beans, shallots, garlic, and mushrooms to the wok and cook for 2–3 minutes.

4 Add the shredded lettuce to the wok or skillet and cook until the leaves have wilted.

5 Stir the black bean sauce into the mixture in the wok and heat through, tossing gently to mix, until the sauce is bubbling.

6 Transfer the green and black bean stir-fry to a warm serving dish and serve immediately.

Stir-Fried Beansprouts

Be sure to use fresh beansprouts, rather than the canned variety, for this crunchy-textured dish.

NUTRITIONAL INFORMATION

Calories	98	Sugars	........2g
Protein	.........2g	Fat	..........9g
Carbohydrate	....3g	Saturates	.......1g

5 mins | 5 mins

SERVES 4

INGREDIENTS

3 cups fresh beansprouts

2–3 scallions

1 medium red chili (optional)

3 tbsp vegetable oil

½ tsp salt

½ tsp sugar

1 tbsp light soy sauce

a few drops sesame oil (optional)

1 Rinse the beansprouts in cold water, discarding any husks or small pieces that float to the top.

2 Drain the beansprouts well on absorbent paper towels.

3 Using a sharp knife, cut the scallions into short pieces.

4 Thinly shred the red chili, if using, discarding the seeds.

5 Heat the vegetable oil in a preheated wok, swirling the oil around the base of the wok until it is really hot.

6 Add the beansprouts, scallions, and chili, if using, to the wok, and stir-fry the mixture for about 2 minutes.

7 Add the salt, sugar, soy sauce, and sesame oil, if using, to the mixture in the wok and stir well to blend thoroughly. Serve the beansprouts immediately, or let cool and serve chilled.

COOK'S TIP

The red chili gives a bite to this dish—leave the seeds in for an even hotter taste. If you prefer a milder, sweeter flavor, use red pepper instead of the chili pepper. Core, seed, and cut into strips in the same way.

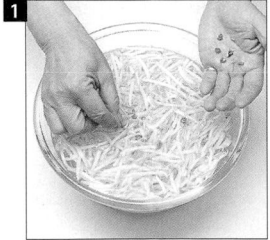

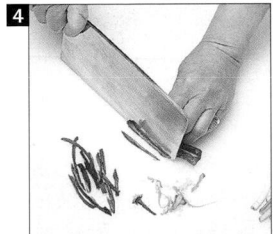

Cabbage & Walnut Stir-Fry

This is a really quick, one-pan dish using white and red cabbage for color and flavor.

NUTRITIONAL INFORMATION

Calories 422	Sugars 9g	
Protein 13g	Fat 37g	
Carbohydrate ...10g	Saturates 5g	

 10 mins   10 mins

SERVES 4

INGREDIENTS

¾ lb/350 g white cabbage

¾ lb/350 g red cabbage

4 tbsp peanut oil

1 tbsp walnut oil

2 garlic cloves, crushed

8 scallions, trimmed

½ lb/225 g firm bean curd, cubed

2 tbsp lemon juice

1 cup walnut halves

2 tsp Dijon mustard

2 tsp poppy seeds

salt and pepper

1 Using a sharp knife, shred the white and red cabbages thinly and set aside until required.

2 Heat the peanut and walnut oils in a preheated wok. Add the garlic, cabbage, scallions, and bean curd and cook for 5 minutes, stirring.

3 Add the lemon juice, walnuts, and mustard, season with salt and pepper, and cook for a further 5 minutes or until the cabbage is tender.

4 Transfer the stir-fry to a warm serving bowl, sprinkle with poppy seeds and serve immediately.

VARIATION
Sesame seeds could be used instead of the poppy seeds and drizzle 1 teaspoon of sesame oil over the dish just before serving, if you wish.

Cauliflower with Greens

This is a delicious way to cook cauliflower with a lovely texture and flavor—even without the greens.

NUTRITIONAL INFORMATION

Calories ....49 Sugars 2g
Protein ....2g Fat 3g
Carbohydrate ....3g Saturates 0.5g

5 mins   5 mins

SERVES 4

INGREDIENTS

1½ cups cauliflower, cut into florets

1 garlic clove

½ tsp turmeric

1 tbsp cilantro root or stem

1 tbsp sunflower oil

2 scallions, cut into 1 inch/2.5 cm pieces

¼ lb/125 g Asian greens, such as bok choi or mustard greens, tough stalks removed

1 tsp yellow mustard seeds

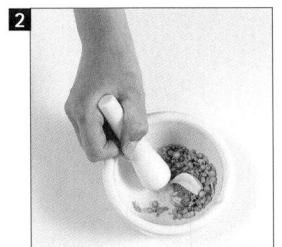

1 Blanch the cauliflower, rinse in cold running water, and drain. Set aside until required.

2 Grind together the garlic, turmeric, and cilantro root or stem in a pestle and mortar or spice grinder.

COOK'S TIP

Pestle and mortars are available in wood or stone. The stone mortar gives a finer grind than the wooden mortar. A coffee grinder can be used , but will need a thorough clean afterwards, as some of the spices used in Chinese cooking can be quite pungent!

3 Heat the sunflower oil in a wok or large, heavy skillet.

4 Add the scallions to the wok or skillet and cook over high heat for 2 minutes, stirring constantly.

5 Add the Asian greens and continue to stir-fry for 1 minute. Remove the mixture from the pan, keep warm, and set aside until required.

6 Return the wok or skillet to the heat and add the mustard seeds. Stir until the seeds start to pop,

7 Add the turmeric and cilantro mixture and the blanched cauliflower to the pan, and stir until the cauliflower is thoroughly coated.

8 Serve the cauliflower with the greens on a warmed serving plate.

Butternut Squash Stir-Fry

Butternut squash is as its name suggests, deliciously buttery and nutty in flavor. If the squash is not in season, use sweet potatoes instead.

NUTRITIONAL INFORMATION

Calories	301	Sugars	. . . . .4g
Protein	. . . . .9g	Fat	. . . . .22g
Carbohydrate	. . .19g	Saturates	. . . . . . .4g

 5 mins   25 mins

SERVES 4

I N G R E D I E N T S

2 lb/900 g butternut squash, peeled

3 tbsp peanut oil

1 onion, sliced

2 cloves garlic, crushed

1 tsp coriander seeds

1 tsp cumin seeds

2 tbsp chopped fresh cilantro

generous ⅓ cup coconut milk

½ cup water

⅔ cup salted cashew nuts

T O   G A R N I S H

freshly grated lime zest

fresh cilantro

lime wedges

1 Slice the butternut squash into small, bite-sized cubes, using a sharp knife.

2 Heat the peanut oil in a large preheated wok.

3 Add the butternut squash, onion, and garlic and cook for 5 minutes.

4 Stir in the coriander seeds, cumin seeds, and fresh cilantro and cook for 1 minute.

5 Add the coconut milk and water to the wok and bring to a boil. Cover the wok and let simmer for 10–15 minutes, or until the squash is tender.

6 Add the cashew nuts and stir to combine.

7 Transfer the stir-fry to warm serving dishes and garnish with freshly grated lime zest, fresh cilantro, and lime wedges. Serve hot.

COOK'S TIP

If you do not have coconut milk, grate some creamed coconut into the dish with the water in step 5.

Braised Vegetables

This colorful selection of braised vegetables makes a splendid light meal or an accompaniment to a main dish.

NUTRITIONAL INFORMATION

Calories 170   Sugars 8g
Protein . . . . .7g   Fat 10g
Carbohydrate . . .14g   Saturates 1g

 10 mins   10 mins

SERVES 4

INGREDIENTS

3 tbsp sunflower oil

1 garlic clove, crushed

1 Napa cabbage, thickly shredded

2 onions, peeled and cut into wedges

2½ cups broccoli florets

2 large carrots, peeled and cut into thin julienne strips

12 baby or dwarf corn ears, halved if large

¾ cup snow peas, halved

3 oz/90 g Chinese or oyster mushrooms, sliced

1 tbsp grated ginger root

¾ cup vegetable bouillon

2 tbsp light soy sauce

1 tbsp cornstarch

salt and pepper

½ tsp sugar

COOK'S TIP

This dish also makes an ideal vegetarian main meal. Double the quantities, to serve 4–6, and serve with noodles or Green Rice (see page 427).

1 Heat the oil in a wok. Add the garlic, cabbage, onions, broccoli, carrots, corn, snow peas, mushrooms, and ginger and stir-fry for 2 minutes.

2 Add the vegetable bouillon, cover, and cook for a further 2-3 minutes.

3 Blend together the soy sauce and the cornstarch and season to taste with salt and pepper.

4 Remove the braised vegetables from the wok with a slotted spoon and keep warm. Add the soy sauce mixture to the wok juices, mixing well. Bring to a boil, stirring constantly, until the mixture thickens slightly. Stir in the sugar.

5 Return the vegetables to the wok and toss in the slightly thickened sauce. Cook gently to just heat through then serve immediately.

Vegetable Stir-Fry with Eggs

This is a true classic which never fades from popularity. A delicious warm salad with a peanut sauce.

NUTRITIONAL INFORMATION

Calories ....269 Sugars 12g
Protein ....12g Fat 19g
Carbohydrate ...14g Saturates 3g

10 mins

15 mins

SERVES 4

INGREDIENTS

2 eggs

3 small carrots

¾ lb/350 g white cabbage

2 tbsp vegetable oil

1 red bell pepper, seeded and thinly sliced

1½ cups beansprouts

1 tbsp tomato catsup

2 tbsp soy sauce

½ cup salted peanuts, chopped

1 Bring a small pan of water to a boil. Add the eggs to the pan and cook for about 7 minutes. Remove the eggs from the pan and let cool under cold running water for 1 minute. Peel the shell from the eggs and then cut the eggs into quarters.

2 Peel and coarsely grate the carrots. Remove any outer leaves from the white cabbage and cut out the stem, then shred the leaves very finely, either with a sharp knife or by using the fine slicing blade on a food processor.

3 Heat the vegetable oil in a large preheated wok or large skillet.

4 Add the carrots, white cabbage, and bell pepper to the wok and cook for 3 minutes, then add the bean sprouts and cook for a further 2 minutes.

5 Combine the tomato catsup and soy sauce in a small bowl and add to the wok or skillet, stirring thoroughly to coat the vegetables.

6 Add the chopped peanuts to the wok and cook for 1 minute.

7 Transfer the stir-fry to warm serving plates, garnish with the hard-cooked egg quarters, and serve immediately.

COOK'S TIP
The eggs are cooled in cold water immediately after cooking in order to prevent the egg yolk blackening around the edges.

Stir-Fried Mixed Vegetables

The Chinese carefully select vegetables to achieve a harmonious balance of contrasting colors and textures.

NUTRITIONAL INFORMATION

Calories 534   Sugars 8g
Protein . . . . .14g   Fat 45g
Carbohydrate . . .19g   Saturates 5g

5 mins   5 mins

SERVES 4

INGREDIENTS

¾ cup snow peas

1 small carrot

¼ lb/125 g Napa cabbage

60 g/2 oz black or white mushrooms

2 oz canned bamboo shoots, rinsed and drained

3-4 tbsp vegetable oil

1½ cups fresh beansprouts

1 tsp salt

1 tsp sugar

1 tbsp light soy sauce

a few drops sesame oil (optional)

dip sauce, to serve (optional)

COOK'S TIP

Put some rice on to cook while you are preparing the stir-fry. Serve the stir-fry on a bed of rice and scatter a few toasted cashew nuts on top for a perfectly balanced and incredibly quick, nutritious meal.

1 Prepare the vegetables: top and tail the snow peas, and cut the carrot, Napa cabbage, mushrooms, and bamboo shoots into roughly the same shape and size as the snow peas.

2 Heat the vegetable oil in a preheated wok or large skillet and add the carrot. Stir-fry for a few seconds.

3 Add the snow peas and the Napa cabbage to the wok or skillet and stir-fry for a further minute.

4 Add the beansprouts, mushrooms, and bamboo shoots to the other vegetables and continue to stir-fry for another minute.

5 Add the salt and sugar, continue stirring for another minute, then add the light soy sauce, blending well.

6 Sprinkle the vegetables with sesame oil (if using) and serve hot or cold, with a dip sauce, if liked, or with rice and toasted cashew nuts (see Cook's Tip.)

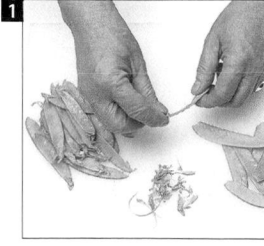

Vegetable Sesame Stir-Fry

Sesame seeds add a delicious flavor to any recipe and are particularly good with vegetables in this soy and rice wine or sherry sauce.

NUTRITIONAL INFORMATION

Calories	118	Sugars	.........2g
Protein	.........3g	Fat	...........9g
Carbohydrate	....5g	Saturates	.......1g

5 mins   10 mins

SERVES 4

I N G R E D I E N T S

2 tbsp vegetable oil

3 garlic cloves, crushed

1 tbsp sesame seeds, plus extra to garnish

2 celery stalks, sliced

2 baby corn ears, sliced

1 cup white mushrooms, sliced

1 leek, sliced

1 zucchini, sliced

1 small red bell pepper, sliced

1 fresh green chili, sliced

2 oz/60 g Napa cabbage, shredded

rice or noodles, to serve

S A U C E

½ tsp Chinese curry powder

2 tbsp light soy sauce

1 tbsp Chinese rice wine or dry sherry

1 tsp sesame oil

1 tsp cornstarch

4 tbsp water

1 Heat the vegetable oil in a preheated wok or heavy skillet, swirling the oil around the bottom of the wok until it is almost smoking.

2 Lower the heat slightly, add the garlic and sesame seeds, and cook for 30 seconds.

3 Add the celery, baby corn ears, mushrooms, leek, zucchini, bell pepper, chili, and Napa cabbage and cook for 4–5 minutes, until the vegetables are beginning to soften.

4 To make the sauce, mix together the Chinese curry powder, light soy sauce, Chinese rice wine, or dry sherry, sesame oil, cornstarch, and water.

5 Stir the sauce mixture into the wok until well combined with the other ingredients.

6 Bring to a boil and cook, stirring constantly, until the sauce thickens and clears.

7 Cook for 1 minute, then spoon into a warm serving dish and garnish with sesame seeds.

8 Serve the vegetable sesame stir-fry immediately with rice or noodles.

Mixed Vegetable Balti

Any combination of vegetables or pulses can be used in this recipe.
It would make a good dish for an informal vegetarian supper party.

NUTRITIONAL INFORMATION

Calories	207	Sugars	......6g
Protein	......8g	Fat	......9g
Carbohydrate	...24g	Saturates	......1g

10 mins   1 hr

SERVES 4

I N G R E D I E N T S

1⅓ cups split yellow peas

3 tbsp vegetable oil

1 tsp onion seeds

2 onions, sliced

1 cup zucchini, sliced

¼ lb/115 g potatoes, cut into ½ inch/
  1 cm cubes

1 cup carrots, sliced

1 small eggplant, sliced

1 cup tomatoes, chopped

1¼ cups water

3 garlic cloves, chopped

1 tsp ground cumin

1 tsp ground coriander

1 tsp salt

2 fresh green chilies, sliced

½ tsp garam masala

2 tbsp chopped fresh cilantro

1 Put the split peas into a pan and cover with lightly salted water. Bring to a boil and simmer for 30 minutes. Drain the peas and keep warm.

2 Heat the oil in a karahi or wok, add the onion seeds, and cook until they start popping.

3 Add the onions and stir-fry over medium heat until golden brown.

4 Add the zucchini, potatoes, carrots, and eggplant to the pan. Stir-fry the vegetables for about 2 minutes.

5 Stir in the tomatoes, water, garlic, cumin, ground coriander, salt, chilies, garam masala, and reserved split peas.

6 Bring to a boil, then lower the heat, and simmer for about 15 minutes or until all the vegetables are tender.

7 Add the chopped fresh cilantro to the vegetable mixture and stir well to combine thoroughly.

8 Transfer the balti to a warmed serving dish and serve immediately.

Potato & Tomato Calzone

These pizza dough Italian pasties are best served hot with a salad for a delicious lunch or supper dish.

NUTRITIONAL INFORMATION

Calories 524	Sugars 8g
Protein 17g	Fat 8g
Carbohydrate ..103g	Saturates 2g

🥔 1½ hrs   🕐 35 mins

SERVES 4

INGREDIENTS

DOUGH

4 cups white bread flour

1 tsp active dry yeast

1¼ cups vegetable bouillon

1 tbsp clear honey

1 tsp caraway seeds

skim milk, for glazing

FILLING

1 tbsp vegetable oil

1⅓ cups diced waxy potatoes

1 onion, halved and sliced

2 garlic cloves, crushed

1½ oz/40 g sun-dried tomatoes

2 tbsp chopped fresh basil

2 tbsp tomato paste

2 celery stalks, sliced

½ cup grated mozzarella cheese

1 To make the dough, sift the flour into a large mixing bowl and stir in the yeast. Make a well in the center of the mixture. Stir in the vegetable bouillon, honey, and caraway seeds, and bring the mixture together to form a dough.

2 Turn the dough out on to a lightly floured counter and knead for 8 minutes until smooth. Place the dough in a lightly oiled mixing bowl, then cover and let rise in a warm place for 1 hour or until it has doubled in size.

3 Meanwhile, make the filling. Heat the oil in a skillet and add all the remaining ingredients except for the cheese. Cook for about 5 minutes, stirring.

4 Divide the risen dough into 4 pieces. On a lightly floured counter, roll them out to form four 7 inch/18 cm circles. Spoon equal amounts of the filling on to one half of each circle. Sprinkle the grated cheese over the filling. Brush the edge of the dough with milk and fold the dough over to form 4 semicircles, pressing to seal the edges.

5 Place on a nonstick cookie sheet and brush with milk. Cook in a preheated oven, 425°F/220°C, for 30 minutes until golden and risen.

Apricot Slices

These vegan slices are ideal for children's lunches. They are full of flavor and made with healthy ingredients.

NUTRITIONAL INFORMATION

Calories	198	Sugars	13g
Protein	4g	Fat	9g
Carbohydrate	25g	Saturates	2g

 50 mins 1 hr

MAKES 12

INGREDIENTS

PASTRY

7 tbsp margarine, cut into
small pieces, plus extra for greasing

2 cups whole-wheat flour

½ cup finely ground mixed nuts

4 tbsp water

soy milk, to glaze

FILLING

1 cup dried apricots

grated rind of 1 orange

1½ cups apple juice

1 tsp ground cinnamon

generous ⅓ cup raisins

1 Lightly grease a 9 inch/23 cm square cake pan. To make the dough, place the flour and nuts in a mixing bowl and rub in the margarine with your fingers until the mixture resembles bread crumbs. Stir in the water and bring together to form a dough. Wrap and set aside to chill in the refrigerator for 30 minutes.

2 To make the filling, place the apricots, orange rind, and apple juice in a pan and bring to a boil. Simmer for 30 minutes until the apricots are mushy. Cool slightly, then process in a food processor or blender to a purée. Alternatively, press the mixture through a fine strainer. Stir in the cinnamon and raisins.

3 Divide the dough in half, roll out 1 half, and use to line the base of the pan. Spread the apricot purée over the top and brush the edges of the dough with water. Roll out the rest of the dough to fit over the top of the apricot purée. Press down and seal the edges.

4 Prick the top of the dough with a fork and brush with soy milk. Bake in a preheated oven, 400°F/200°C, for 20–25 minutes until the pastry is golden. Set aside to cool slightly before cutting into 12 bars. Serve the slices either warm or cold.

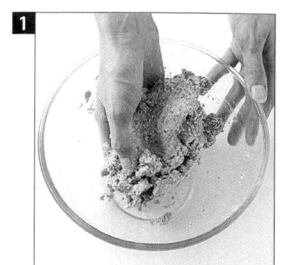

COOK'S TIP
These slices will keep in an airtight container for 3–4 days.

Cheese & Potato Strudel

This bread has a delicious cheese and garlic flavor and is best eaten straight from the oven, as soon as it is the right temperature.

SERVES 8

INGREDIENTS

butter, for greasing

6 cups white bread flour, plus extra for dusting

1 cup mealy potatoes, diced

2 envelopes (5 tsp) active dry yeast

2 cups vegetable bouillon

2 garlic cloves, crushed

2 tbsp chopped fresh rosemary

1 cup grated Swiss cheese

1 tbsp vegetable oil

1 tbsp salt

1 Lightly grease and flour a cookie sheet. Cook the potatoes in a pan of boiling water for 10 minutes or until soft. Drain well and mash.

2 Transfer the mashed potatoes to a large mixing bowl, stir in the yeast, flour, and bouillon, and mix to form a smooth dough. Add the garlic, rosemary, and ¾ cup of the cheese and knead the dough for 5 minutes. Make a hollow in the dough, pour in the oil, and knead the dough again.

3 Cover the dough and let stand in a warm place for 1½ hours or until doubled in size.

4 Knead the dough again and divide it into 3 equal portions. Roll each portion into a sausage shape about 14 inches/35 cm long.

5 Press one end of each of the sausage shapes firmly together, then carefully braid the dough, without breaking it, and fold the remaining ends under, sealing them firmly.

6 Place the strudel on the cookie sheet, cover with oiled plastic wrap, and let rise for 30 minutes.

7 Sprinkle the remaining cheese over the top of the strudel and cook in a preheated oven, 375°F/190°C, for 40 minutes or until the base of the loaf sounds hollow when tapped. Serve while it is still warm.

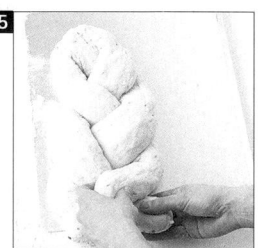

Cheese & Chive Biscuits

These tea-time classics have been given a healthy twist by the use of low-fat soft cheese and reduced-fat Cheddar cheese.

NUTRITIONAL INFORMATION

Calories 297   Sugars 3g
Protein . . . . .13g   Fat 7g
Carbohydrate . . .49g   Saturates 4g

 10 mins   20 mins

MAKES 10

INGREDIENTS

generous 1½ cups self-rising flour

1 tsp powdered mustard

½ tsp cayenne pepper

½ tsp salt

½ cup low-fat soft cheese with added herbs

2 tbsp snipped fresh chives, plus extra to garnish

scant ½ cup skim milk, plus 2 tbsp for brushing

generous ½ cup grated reduced-fat sharp Cheddar cheese

low-fat soft cheese, to serve

1 Strain the flour, mustard, cayenne pepper, and salt into a mixing bowl.

2 Add the soft cheese to the mixture and mix together until well incorporated. Stir in the snipped chives.

3 Make a well in the center of the ingredients and gradually pour in the ½ cup of milk, stirring as you pour, until the mixture forms a soft dough.

4 Turn the dough onto a floured counter and knead lightly. Roll out until ¾ inch/2 cm thick, and use a 2 inch/5 cm plain dough cutter to stamp out as many circles as you can. Transfer the circles to a cookie sheet.

5 Reknead the dough trimmings together and roll out again. Stamp out more circles—you should be able to make 10 biscuits in total.

6 Brush the biscuits with the remaining milk and sprinkle with the grated cheese. Bake in a preheated oven, 400°F/200°C, for 15–20 minutes until risen and golden.

7 Transfer to a wire rack to cool. Serve warm with low-fat soft cheese, garnished with chives.

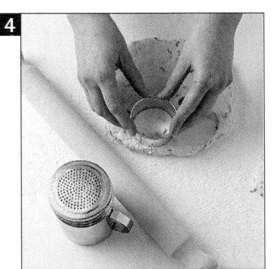

VARIATION

For sweet biscuits, omit the mustard, cayenne pepper, chives, and grated cheese. Replace the flavored soft cheese with plain low-fat soft cheese. Add ½ cup currants and 2 tablespoons of superfine sugar. Serve with low-fat soft cheese and fruit spread.

Herb Focaccia

Rich with olive oil, this bread is so delicious it would turn a simple salad or bowl of soup into a positive feast.

NUTRITIONAL INFORMATION

Calories 210	Sugars 1g	
Protein 6g	Fat 5g	
Carbohydrate 5g	Saturates 1g	

2 hrs   15 mins

MAKES 1 LOAF

I N G R E D I E N T S

3½ cups unbleached white bread flour, plus extra for dusting

1 envelope active dry yeast

1½ tsp salt

½ tsp sugar

1¼ cups lukewarm water

3 tbsp extra virgin olive oil, plus extra for greasing

4 tbsp finely chopped fresh herbs

polenta or cornmeal, for sprinkling

coarse sea salt, for sprinkling

1 Combine the flour, yeast, salt, and sugar in a bowl and make a well in the center. Gradually stir in most of the water and 2 tablespoons of the olive oil to make a dough. Gradually add the remaining water, if necessary, drawing in all the flour.

2 Turn out onto a lightly floured counter and knead. Transfer to a bowl and lightly knead in the herbs for 10 minutes until soft but not sticky. Wash the bowl and lightly coat with olive oil.

3 Shape the dough into a ball, put it in the bowl, and turn the dough over. Cover tightly with a dish cloth or lightly greased plastic wrap and let rise in a warm place until the dough has doubled in volume. Meanwhile, sprinkle polenta over a cookie sheet.

4 Turn the dough out onto a lightly floured counter and knead lightly. Cover with the upturned bowl and let stand for 10 minutes.

5 Roll out and pat the dough into a 10 inch/25 cm circle, about ½ inch/ 1 cm thick, and carefully transfer it to the prepared cookie sheet. Cover with a dish cloth and let rise again for 15 minutes.

6 Using a lightly oiled finger, poke indentations all over the surface of the loaf. Drizzle the remaining olive oil over and sprinkle lightly with sea salt. Bake in a preheated oven, 450°F/ 230°C, for 15 minutes or until golden brown and the loaf sounds hollow when tapped on the bottom. Transfer to a wire rack to cool completely.

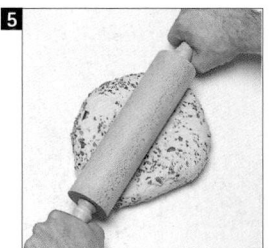

Garlic Bread

A perennial favorite, garlic bread is perfect with a range of barbecue meals, and works especially well with chargrilled vegetables.

NUTRITIONAL INFORMATION

Calories 261	Sugars 1g	
Protein 3g	Fat 22g	
Carbohydrate . . .15g	Saturates 14g	

 10 mins   15 mins

SERVES 4

I N G R E D I E N T S

¾ cup butter, softened

3 cloves garlic, crushed

2 tbsp chopped, fresh parsley

pepper

1 large or 2 small sticks of French bread

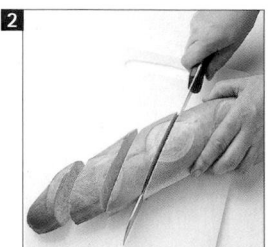
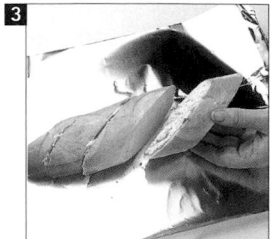

1 Mix together the butter, garlic, and parsley in a bowl until well combined. Season with pepper to taste and mix well.

2 Cut the French bread into thick slices. Spread the garlic and parsley flavored butter over one side of each slice and reassemble the loaf on a large sheet of thick aluminum foil.

3 Wrap the bread well in foil and grill over hot coals for about 10–15 minutes until the butter melts and the bread is piping hot.

4 Serve as an accompaniment to a wide range of dishes.

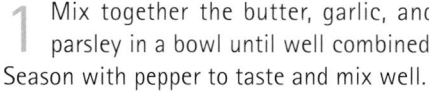

Mediterranean Bread

Many of the flavors of the Mediterranean are captured in this rustic loaf. It is a perfect accompaniment for pasta dishes, stews, and casseroles.

NUTRITIONAL INFORMATION

Calories	222	Sugars	.........1g
Protein	.........5g	Fat	..........12g
Carbohydrate	...26g	Saturates	.......2g

 25 mins, plus rising   40 mins

SERVES 4

INGREDIENTS

3½ cups all-purpose flour, plus extra for dusting

1 envelope active dry yeast

1 tsp salt

1 tbsp coriander seeds, lightly crushed

2 tsp dried oregano

scant 1 cup lukewarm water

3 tbsp olive oil, plus extra for greasing

5½ oz/150 g sun-dried tomatoes in oil, drained, patted dry and chopped

3 oz/85 g feta cheese, drained, patted dry, and cubed

1 cup black olives, patted dry, pitted, and sliced

1 Combine the flour, yeast, salt, coriander seeds, and oregano and make a well in the center. Gradually add most of the water and the oil to make a dough. Gradually add the remaining water, if needed, drawing in all the flour.

2 Turn out onto a lightly floured counter and knead for 10 minutes, gradually kneading in the tomatoes, cheese, and olives. Wash the bowl and lightly coat it with oil.

3 Shape the dough into a ball, put it in the bowl, and turn the dough over. Cover tightly and set the dough aside until it doubles in volume.

4 Turn the dough out onto a lightly floured counter. Knead lightly, then shape into a ball. Place on a lightly floured cookie sheet. Cover and let rise until it doubles in volume again.

5 Lightly sprinkle the top of the loaf with flour. Using a sharp knife, cut 3 shallow slashes in the top. Bake in a preheated oven, 450°F/230°C, for 20 minutes. Lower the temperature to 400°F/200°C and bake for a further 20 minutes or until the loaf sounds hollow when you tap the base. Transfer to a wire rack to cool completely. This loaf will keep well for up to 3 days stored in an airtight container.

Fougasse

This distinctive-looking bread, with its herringbone slits, is baked daily throughout Provence. It is best eaten on the day it is baked.

NUTRITIONAL INFORMATION

Calories 161   Sugars 1g
Protein . . . . .5g   Fat 0g
Carbohydrate . . .36g   Saturates 0g

 1¾ hrs   25 mins

MAKES 2 LARGE LOAVES

I N G R E D I E N T S

6½ cups unbleached white bread flour, plus extra for dusting

1 envelope active dry yeast

2 tsp salt

1 tsp sugar

2 cups lukewarm water

olive oil, for greasing

1 Combine the flour, yeast, salt, and sugar in a bowl and make a well in the center. Gradually stir in most of the water to make a dough. Gradually add the remaining water, if necessary, drawing in all the flour.

2 Turn out onto a lightly floured counter and knead for 10 minutes until smooth and elastic. Wash the bowl and lightly coat with olive oil.

3 Shape the dough into a ball, put it in the bowl, and turn the dough over. Cover the bowl tightly with a dish cloth or lightly oiled plastic wrap and let rise in a warm place until the dough has doubled in volume.

4 Punch down the dough and turn out onto a lightly floured counter. Knead lightly, then cover with the upturned bowl, and let stand for 10 minutes.

5 Put a roasting pan of water in the bottom of the oven while it preheats to 450°F/230°C, then lightly flour a cookie sheet.

6 Divide the dough into 2 pieces and roll each one into a 12 inch oval, ½ inch/1 cm thick. Using a sharp knife, cut 5 x 3 inch/7.5 cm slices on an angle in a herringbone pattern on each of the dough ovals. Cut all the way through the dough, using the tip of the knife to open the slits.

7 Spray the loaves with cold water. Bake for 20 minutes, turn upside down, and continue baking for 5 minutes until the loaves sound hollow when tapped on the bottom. Transfer to wire racks to cool.

Olive Rolls

These rustic-style bread rolls depend on fruity olive oil and good-quality olives. You could use any of the Flavored Olives on page 845.

You could use any of the Flavored Olives on page 845.

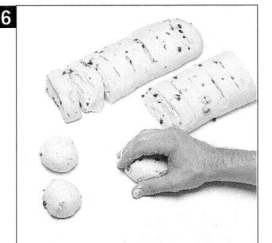

NUTRITIONAL INFORMATION

Calories	181	Sugars	1g
Protein	6g	Fat	3g
Carbohydrate	35g	Saturates	0.5g

 1¾ hrs   30 mins

MAKES 16 ROLLS

I N G R E D I E N T S

1 cup olives in brine or oil, drained

6½ cups unbleached white bread flour, plus extra for dusting

1½ tsp salt

1 envelope active dry yeast

2 cups lukewarm water

2 tbsp extra virgin olive oil, plus extra for brushing

4 tbsp finely chopped fresh oregano, parsley, or thyme leaves or 1 tbsp dried mixed herbs

1 Pit the olives with an olive or cherry pitter and finely chop. Pat off the excess brine or olive oil with paper towels. Set aside.

2 Combine the flour, salt, and yeast in a bowl and make a well in the center. Gradually stir in most of the water and the olive oil to make a dough. Gradually add the remaining water, if necessary, drawing in all the flour.

3 Lightly knead in the chopped olives and herbs. Turn out the dough onto a lightly floured counter and knead for 10 minutes until smooth and elastic. Wash the bowl and lightly coat with oil.

4 Shape the dough into a ball, put it in the bowl, and turn over so it is coated. Cover tightly with a dish cloth or lightly oiled plastic wrap and let rise until it has doubled in volume. Dust a cookie sheet with flour.

5 Turn out the dough onto a lightly floured counter and knead lightly. Roll the dough into 8 inch/20 cm sausages on a very lightly floured counter.

6 Cut the dough into 16 even pieces. Shape each piece into a ball and place on the prepared cookie sheet. Cover and let rise for 15 minutes.

7 Lightly brush the top of each roll with olive oil. Bake in a preheated oven, 425°F/220°C, for about 25–30 minutes or until the rolls are golden brown. Transfer to a wire rack and let cool completely before serving.

Spicy Oven Bread

This is a Western-style bread with an Indian touch. It is very quick once the dough is made and is a quite rich and very tasty mix.

NUTRITIONAL INFORMATION

Calories	445	Sugars	.........1g
Protein	.........6g	Fat	..........26g
Carbohydrate	...49g	Saturates	......17g

 1½ hrs   10 mins

SERVES 8

INGREDIENTS

½ tsp active dried yeast

1¼ cups warm water

3 cups strong white flour

1 tsp salt

1 cup butter, melted and cooled

½ tsp garam masala

½ tsp coriander seeds, ground

1 tsp cumin seeds, ground

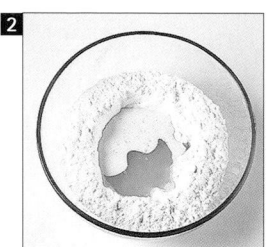

1 Mix the yeast with a little of the warm water until it starts to foam and is completely dissolved.

2 Put the flour and salt into a large bowl, make a well in the center, and add the yeast mixture and ½ cup of the melted butter. Blend the yeast and butter together before drawing in the flour and kneading lightly. Add the water gradually until a firm dough is obtained; you may not need it all.

3 Turn the dough out on to a floured counter and knead it for about 10 minutes, until smooth and elastic.

4 Put the dough into an oiled bowl and turn it over so that it is coated with the oil. Cover and let rise in a warm place for 30 minutes, until doubled in size.

Alternatively, let the dough stand in the refrigerator overnight.

5 Knead the dough again and divide into 8 balls. Roll each one out to a 6 inch/15 cm round. Place on a floured cookie sheet. Sprinkle with flour and let rise for 20 minutes.

6 Mix the spices together with the remaining melted butter.

7 Brush each bread with the spice and butter mixture and cover with foil. Place the cookie sheet on the middle shelf of a preheated oven, 425°F/220°C, for 5 minutes. Remove the foil, brush each bread with the spice and butter mixture once again, and cook for a further 5 minutes.

8 Remove from the oven and wrap in a clean dish cloth until ready to eat.

Sun-Dried Tomato Loaf

This delicious tomato bread is great with cheese or soup or for making an unusual sandwich. This recipe makes one loaf.

NUTRITIONAL INFORMATION

Calories 403   Sugars 5g
Protein ....12g   Fat 2g
Carbohydrate ...91g   Saturates 0.3g

 1¾ hrs   35 mins

SERVES 4

I N G R E D I E N T S

2 tsp dried yeast

1 tsp granulated sugar

1¼ cups lukewarm water

3 cups white bread flour

1 tsp salt

2 tsp dried basil

2 tbsp sun-dried tomato paste or
   tomato paste

vegan margarine, for greasing

12 sun-dried tomatoes in oil, drained and
   cut into strips

1 Place the yeast and sugar in a bowl and mix with ½ cup of the water. Let the mixture ferment in a warm place for 15 minutes.

2 Strain the flour and salt into a bowl. Make a well in the center and add the basil, yeast mixture, tomato paste, and half of the remaining water. Using a wooden spoon, draw the flour into the liquid and mix to form a dough, adding the rest of the water gradually.

3 Turn out onto a floured counter and knead for 5 minutes. Cover with oiled plastic wrap and let stand in a warm place for 30 minutes or until doubled in size.

 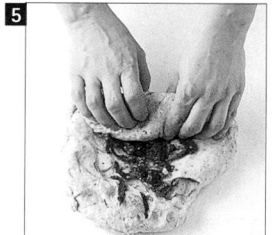 

4 Lightly grease a 2 lb/900 g loaf pan with vegan margarine.

5 Remove the dough from the bowl and knead in the sun-dried tomatoes. Knead again for 2–3 minutes.

6 Place the dough in the pan and let rise for 30–40 minutes or until it has doubled in size again. Bake in a preheated oven, 375°F/190°C, for 30–35 minutes or until the loaf is golden and the base sounds hollow when tapped. Cool on a wire rack.

COOK'S TIP
You could make mini sun-dried tomato loaves for children. Divide the dough into 8 equal portions, leave to rise, and bake in mini-loaf pans for 20 minutes. Alternatively, make 12 small rounds, leave to rise, and bake for 12–15 minutes.

Roasted Bell Pepper Bread

Bell peppers become wonderfully sweet and mild when they are roasted, and make this bread delicious.

NUTRITIONAL INFORMATION

Calories	426	Sugars	.........4g
Protein	........12g	Fat	...........4g
Carbohydrate	...90g	Saturates	.......1g

 1¾ hrs   1 hr 5 mins

SERVES 4

I N G R E D I E N T S

vegan margarine, for greasing

1 red bell pepper, halved and seeded

1 yellow bell pepper, halved and seeded

2 sprigs rosemary

1 tbsp olive oil

2 tbsp dried yeast

1 tsp granulated sugar

1¼ cups lukewarm water

3 cups white bread flour

1 tsp salt

1 Grease a 9 inch/23 cm deep circular cake pan with vegan margarine.

2 Place the bell peppers and rosemary in a shallow roasting pan. Pour over the oil and roast in a preheated oven, 400°F/200°C, for 20 minutes or until slightly charred. Remove the skin from the bell peppers and cut the flesh into slices.

3 Place the yeast and sugar in a small bowl and mix with ½ cup of lukewarm water. Let the mixture ferment in a warm place for 15 minutes.

4 Strain the flour and salt together into a large bowl. Stir in the yeast mixture and the remaining water and mix to form a smooth dough.

5 Knead the dough for about 5 minutes until smooth. Cover with oiled plastic wrap and let rise for about 30 minutes or until doubled in size.

6 Cut the dough into 3 equal portions. Roll the portions into circles slightly larger than the cake pan.

7 Place 1 circle in the bottom of the pan so that it reaches up the sides of the pan by about ¾ inch/2 cm. Top with half of the bell pepper mixture.

8 Place the second circle of dough on top, followed by the remaining bell pepper mixture. Place the last circle of dough on top, pushing the edges of the dough down the sides of the pan.

9 Cover the dough with oiled plastic wrap and let rise for 30–40 minutes. Return to the oven and bake for 45 minutes until golden or the bottom sounds hollow when lightly tapped. Transfer to a wire rack to cool slightly, then cut into slices and serve warm.

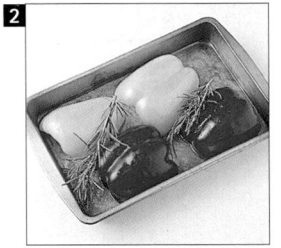 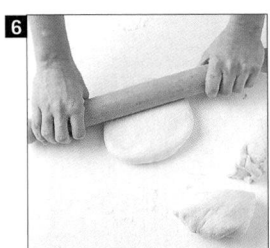 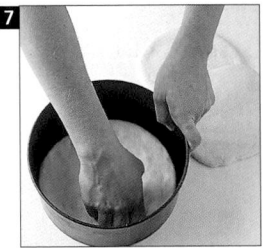

Roman Focaccia

Roman focaccia makes a delicious snack on its own or served with a selection of vegetarian cheeses and salad for a quick supper.

NUTRITIONAL INFORMATION

Calories 119   Sugars 2g
Protein . . . . .3g   Fat 2g
Carbohydrate . . .24g   Saturates 0.3g

 1 hr   45 mins

MAKES 16 SQUARES

I N G R E D I E N T S

2 tsp dried yeast

1 tsp granulated sugar

1¼ cups lukewarm water

3 cups white bread flour

2 tsp salt

3 tbsp fresh rosemary, chopped

2 tbsp olive oil

1 lb/450 g mixed red and white onions, sliced into rings

4 garlic cloves, sliced

1 Place the yeast and the sugar in a bowl and mix with ½ cup of the water. Let the mixture ferment in a warm place for 15 minutes.

2 Strain the flour with the salt into a large bowl. Add the yeast mixture, half of the rosemary, and the remaining water, and mix to form a smooth dough. Knead the dough for 4 minutes.

3 Cover the dough with oiled plastic wrap and let rise for 30 minutes or until doubled in size.

4 Meanwhile, heat the oil in a large pan. Add the onions and garlic and cook over low heat for 5 minutes or until soft. Cover the pan and continue to cook

for a further 7–8 minutes or until the onions are lightly caramelized.

5 Knead the dough again for 1–2 minutes, then roll out to a square. It should be no more than ¼ inch/5 mm thick because it will rise during cooking. Place the dough on a large cookie sheet, pushing out the edges until even.

6 Spread the onions evenly over the dough, and sprinkle the surface with the remaining rosemary.

7 Bake in a preheated oven, 400°F/ 200°C, for 25–30 minutes or until a golden brown color. Cut the focaccia into 16 squares and serve immediately while it is still warm.

Garlic & Sage Bread

This freshly made herb bread is an ideal accompaniment to salads and soups and is suitable for vegans.

NUTRITIONAL INFORMATION

Calories	207	Sugars	.........3g
Protein	.........9g	Fat	...........2g
Carbohydrate	...42g	Saturates	.......0g

 1¼ hrs   ⊙ 30 mins

SERVES 6

I N G R E D I E N T S

vegetable oil, for greasing

2¼ cups strong brown bread flour

1 package active dry yeast (2¼ tsp)

3 tbsp chopped fresh sage

2 tsp sea salt

3 garlic cloves, finely chopped

1 tsp honey

⅔ cup lukewarm water

1 Grease a cookie sheet. Strain the flour into a large mixing bowl and stir in the bran remaining in the strainer.

2 Stir in the active dry yeast, chopped sage, and half of the sea salt. Reserve 1 teaspoon of the chopped garlic for sprinkling and stir the remainder into the bowl. Add the honey and lukewarm water and mix together thoroughly to form a dough.

3 Turn the dough out onto a lightly floured counter and knead it for about 5 minutes until smooth and elastic (alternatively, use an electric mixer with a dough hook.)

4 Place the dough in a greased bowl, cover with lightly oiled plastic wrap, and let rise in a warm place until doubled in size.

5 Knead the dough again for a few minutes. Roll it into a long sausage and then shape it into a ring. Place on the cookie sheet. Cover and let rise for 30 minutes or until springy to the touch. Sprinkle with the remaining sea salt and garlic.

6 Bake the loaf in a preheated oven, 400°F/200°C, for 25–30 minutes. Transfer to a wire rack to cool completely before serving.

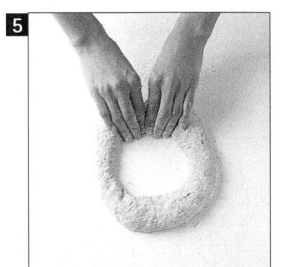

COOK'S TIP

Roll the dough into a long sausage and then curve it into a circular shape. You can omit the sea salt for sprinkling, if you prefer.

Sweet Potato Bread

This is a great-tasting loaf, colored light orange by the sweet potato. Added sweetness from the honey is offset by the tangy orange rind.

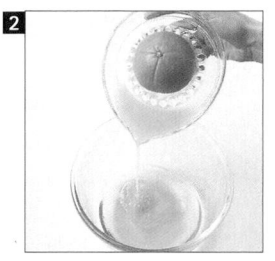

NUTRITIONAL INFORMATION

Calories	267	Sugars	.........7g
Protein	.........4g	Fat	...........9g
Carbohydrate	...45g	Saturates	.......4g

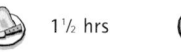

1½ hrs   1¼ hrs

SERVES 8

I N G R E D I E N T S

5 tbsp butter, plus extra for greasing

1½ cups sweet potatoes, diced

⅔ cup lukewarm water

2 tbsp honey

2 tbsp vegetable oil

3 tbsp orange juice

scant ½ cup semolina

2 cups white bread flour

1 package (2¼ tsp) active dry yeast

1 tsp ground cinnamon

grated rind of 1 orange

1 Lightly grease a 1½ lb/675 g loaf pan. Cook the sweet potatoes in a pan of boiling water for about 10 minutes or until soft. Drain thoroughly and mash until smooth.

2 Meanwhile, mix the water, honey, oil, and orange juice together in a large mixing bowl.

3 Add the mashed sweet potatoes, semolina, three-quarters of the flour, the yeast, ground cinnamon, and grated orange zest and mix thoroughly to form a dough. Let stand for about 10 minutes.

4 Dice the butter and knead it into the dough with the remaining flour. Knead for about 5 minutes until smooth.

5 Place the dough in the prepared loaf pan. Cover and let rise in a warm place for 1 hour or until doubled in size.

6 Cook the loaf in a preheated oven, 375°F/190°C, for 45–60 minutes, or until it is golden and the base sounds hollow when tapped.

7 Serve the bread while it is still warm, cut into slices.

Olive Oil Bread with Cheese

This flat cheese bread is similar to focaccia. It is delicious served with antipasto or simply on its own. This recipe makes one loaf.

NUTRITIONAL INFORMATION

Calories 586	Sugars 3g
Protein 22g	Fat 26g
Carbohydrate ...69g	Saturates 12g

 1 hr   30 mins

SERVES 4

I N G R E D I E N T S

4 tsp dried yeast

1 tsp granulated sugar

1 cup lukewarm water

2½ cups white bread flour

1 tsp salt

3 tbsp olive oil

7 oz/200 g romano cheese, cubed

½ tbsp fennel seeds, lightly crushed

1 Mix the yeast with the sugar and a generous ⅓ cup of the lukewarm water. Let stand in a warm place for about 15 minutes until foamy.

2 Mix the flour with the salt. Add 1 tablespoon of the oil, the yeast mixture, and the remaining water, to form a smooth dough. Knead the dough for 4 minutes.

COOK'S TIP

Romano is a hard, quite salty cheese, which is sold in most large food stores and Italian delicatessens. If you cannot obtain romano, use sharp Cheddar or Parmesan cheese instead.

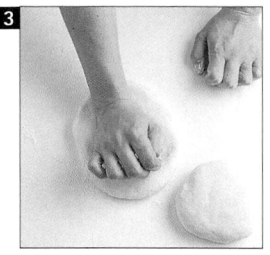

3 Divide the dough into 2 equal portions. Roll out each portion to a form a circle ¼ inch/6 mm thick. Place 1 circle on a cookie sheet.

4 Scatter the cheese and half of the fennel seeds evenly over the circle.

5 Place the second circle on top and squeeze the edges together to seal so that the filling does not leak during the cooking time.

6 Using a sharp knife, make a few slashes in the top of the dough and brush with the remaining olive oil.

7 Sprinkle with the remaining fennel seeds and set the loaf aside to rise for 20–30 minutes.

8 Bake in a preheated oven, 400°F/ 200°C, for 30 minutes or until golden brown. Remove from the oven and serve while still warm.

Italian Bruschetta

It is important to use a good quality olive oil for this recipe. Serve the bruschetta with vegetable kabobs for a really summery taste.

NUTRITIONAL INFORMATION

Calories 415	Sugars 2g	
Protein 8g	Fat 24g	
Carbohydrate . . .45g	Saturates 4g	

10 mins   10 mins

SERVES 4

I N G R E D I E N T S

1 ciabatta loaf or small stick of
  French bread

1 plump clove garlic

extra virgin olive oil

freshly grated Parmesan cheese (optional)

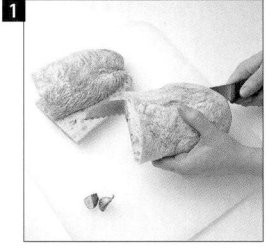

1 Slice the bread in half crosswise and again lengthwise to give 4 portions.

2 Do not peel the garlic clove, but cut it in half.

3 Grill the bread over hot coals for 2–3 minutes on both sides or until it is golden brown.

4 Rub the garlic, cut side down, all over the toasted surface of the bread.

5 Drizzle the olive oil over the bread and serve hot as an accompaniment. If using Parmesan cheese, sprinkle the cheese over the bread.

6 Return the bread to the grill, cut side up, for 1–2 minutes or until the cheese just begins to melt. Serve hot.

COOK'S TIP

As ready-grated Parmesan quickly loses its pungency and "bite," it is better to buy small quantities of the cheese in one piece and grate it yourself as needed. Tightly wrapped in plastic wrap or foil, it will keep in the refrigerator for several months.

Cheese & Tomato Bake

A juicy combination of vegetables concealed beneath a crisp topping needs only a mixed leaf salad to make a substantial family supper dish.

NUTRITIONAL INFORMATION

Calories 324   Sugars 11g
Protein ....14g   Fat 22g
Carbohydrate ...19g   Saturates 11g

15 mins   40 mins

SERVES 4

INGREDIENTS

2 tbsp olive oil

2 onions, sliced

1 garlic clove, finely chopped

3 cups sliced zucchini

1 tsp chopped fresh thyme

1 tbsp torn fresh basil leaves

4 beefsteak tomatoes, skinned and sliced

½ quantity cheese sauce (see page 304), made with Cheddar cheese

½ cup grated Cheddar cheese

1 tbsp fresh bread crumbs

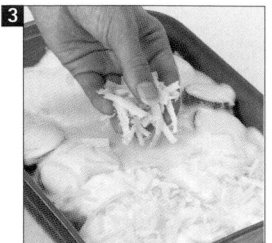

1 Heat the oil in a skillet. Add the onions and cook, stirring occasionally, for 5 minutes, until soft. Add the garlic, zucchini, thyme, and basil and season to taste with salt and pepper. Cook, stirring occasionally, for 5 minutes.

2 Spoon half the onion and zucchini mixture into a large ovenproof dish. Arrange the tomato slices on top and cover with the remaining onion and zucchini mixture. Pour in the cheese sauce.

3 Combine the grated Cheddar and bread crumbs in a small bowl, then sprinkle over the vegetables. Bake in a preheated oven, 350°F/180°C, for 30 minutes. Serve immediately.

Lentil and Mushroom Pie

This is a good dish for entertaining as it is tasty and filling and the phyllo topping looks hugely appetizing and attractive.

NUTRITIONAL INFORMATION

Calories	439	Sugars	.........2g
Protein	........18g	Fat	...........9g
Carbohydrate	...75g	Saturates	.......4g

 25 mins, plus cooling   1½ hrs

SERVES 6

I N G R E D I E N T S

1 cup Puy or green lentils

2 bay leaves

6 shallots, sliced

5 cups vegetable bouillon

2 tbsp butter

1¼ cups long grain rice

2 tbsp chopped fresh parsley

2 tsp chopped fresh fennel or savory

8 oz/225 g field mushrooms

1 egg, beaten

8 sheets phyllo pastry, thawed if frozen

melted butter, for brushing

3 hard-cooked eggs, sliced

salt and ground black pepper

  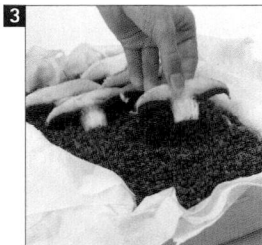

1 Put the lentils, bay leaves, and half the shallots in a large, heavy pan, add half the bouillon, bring to a boil, and simmer for 25 minutes, until tender. Season to taste with salt and pepper and let cool.

2 Melt the butter in a heavy pan. Add the remaining shallots to the pan and cook, stirring occasionally, for 5 minutes, until soft. Stir in the rice and cook, stirring constantly, for 1 minute, then add the remaining bouillon. Season to taste and bring to a boil. Lower the heat, cover, and simmer for 15 minutes. Remove the pan from the heat and let cool.

3 Brush the inside of an ovenproof dish with melted butter and arrange the phyllo sheets in it with the sides overlapping, brushing each sheet with melted butter. Stir the parsley and fennel or savory into the cooled rice mixture, then beat in the raw egg. Make layers of rice, hard-cooked egg, lentils, and mushrooms in the dish, seasoning each layer with salt and pepper. Bring up the phyllo sheets and scrunch into folds on top of the pie.

4 Brush with melted butter and chill for 15 minutes. Bake in a preheated oven, 375°F/190°C, for 45 minutes. Let the pie stand for 10 minutes before serving.

Cheese, Herb & Onion Rolls

A great texture and flavor are achieved by mixing white and granary flours together with minced onion, grated cheese, and fresh herbs.

NUTRITIONAL INFORMATION

Calories 529   Sugars 2g
Protein . . . . .24g   Fat 7g
Carbohydrate . . .98g   Saturates 4g

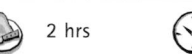

2 hrs   15 mins

SERVES 4

INGREDIENTS

1½ cups strong white flour

1½ tsp salt

1 tsp dried mustard powder

good pinch of pepper

1¾ cups granary or malted wheat flour

2 tbsp chopped fresh mixed herbs

2 tbsp finely chopped scallions

1–1½ cups grated low-fat sharp
    Cheddar cheese

½ oz/15 g fresh yeast; or 1½ tsp dried yeast
    plus 1 tsp caster sugar or 1 package
    active dry yeast plus 1 tbsp oil

1¼ cups warm water

1 Strain the white flour with the salt, mustard, and pepper into a bowl. Mix in the granary flour, herbs, scallions, and most of the cheese.

2 Blend the fresh yeast with the warm water or, if using dried yeast, dissolve the sugar in the water, sprinkle the yeast on top, and let stand in a warm place for about 10 minutes until foamy. Add the yeast mixture of your choice to the dry ingredients and mix to form a firm dough, adding more flour if necessary.

3 Knead until smooth and elastic. Cover with an oiled plastic bag and let rise in a warm place for 1 hour or until doubled in size. Knock back and knead the dough until smooth. Divide into 10–12 pieces and shape into round or long rolls, coils, or knots.

4 Alternatively, make one large plaited loaf. Divide the dough into 3 even pieces and roll each into a long thin sausage and join at one end. Beginning at the joined end, plait to the end and secure. Place on greased cookie sheets, cover with an oiled sheet of plastic wrap, and let rise until doubled in size. Remove the plastic wrap.

5 Sprinkle with the rest of the cheese. Bake in a preheated oven at 400°F/200°C for 15–20 minutes for the rolls, or 30–40 minutes for the loaf.

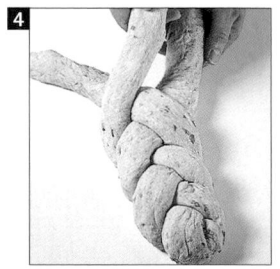

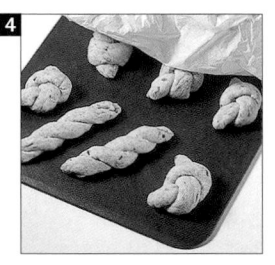

Olive Cake

This simple savory cake makes a delicious snack to nibble with a glass of chilled sparkling wine.

NUTRITIONAL INFORMATION

Calories 214   Sugars 2g
Protein . . . . .5g   Fat 13g
Carbohydrate . . .21g   Saturates 3g

 5 mins   1 hr

MAKES 12–15 SLICES

I N G R E D I E N T S

2 cups pitted black or green olives,
  or a mixture

2 cups self-rising flour

4 large eggs

1 tbsp caster sugar

½ cup milk

½ cup olive oil

butter, for greasing

salt and pepper

1 Lightly butter an 8 inch/20 cm cake pan, 2 inches/5 cm deep. Line the base with a circle of baking parchment. Put the olives in a small bowl and toss in 2 tablespoons of the measured flour.

2 Break the eggs into a bowl and lightly whisk. Stir in the sugar and season with salt and pepper to taste. Stir in the milk and olive oil.

3 Strain the remaining flour into the bowl, add the coated olives, and stir together. Spoon the mixture into the prepared pan and smooth the surface.

4 Bake the olive cake in a preheated oven at 400°F/200°C for 45 minutes. Lower the temperature to 325°F/160°C and continue baking for 15 minutes until the cake is well risen and golden.

5 Remove from the oven and let cool in the pan on a wire rack for 20 minutes. Remove from the pan, peel off the lining paper, and let cool completely. Store in an airtight container.

Mexican Chili Corn Pie

This bake of corn and kidney beans, flavored with chili and fresh cilantro, is topped with crispy cheese cornbread.

 25 mins 20 mins

SERVES 4

INGREDIENTS

1 tbsp corn oil

2 garlic cloves, crushed

1 red bell pepper, seeded and diced

1 green bell pepper, seeded and diced

1 celery stalk, diced

1 tsp hot chili powder

2 cups canned chopped tomatoes

1½ cups canned corn kernels, drained

1 cup canned kidney beans, drained and rinsed

2 tbsp chopped cilantro

salt and pepper

cilantro sprigs, to garnish

tomato and avocado salad, to serve

TOPPING

¾ cup cornmeal

1 tbsp all-purpose flour

½ tsp salt

2 tsp baking powder

1 egg, beaten

6 tbsp milk

1 tbsp corn oil

1 cup grated sharp Cheddar cheese

1 Heat the corn oil in a large skillet and gently cook the garlic and the diced bell peppers and celery for 5–6 minutes until just soft.

2 Stir in the chili powder, tomatoes, corn kernels, beans, and seasoning. Bring to a boil and simmer the mixture for 10 minutes. Stir in the cilantro and spoon into an ovenproof dish.

3 To make the topping, mix together the cornmeal, flour, salt, and baking powder. Make a well in the center, add the egg, milk, and oil and beat until a smooth batter is formed.

4 Spoon over the bell pepper and corn mixture and sprinkle with the grated cheese. Bake in a preheated oven, at 425°F/220°C, for 25–30 minutes, until golden and firm.

5 Garnish with the cilantro sprigs and serve the pie immediately with a tomato and avocado salad.

Vegetable Hotpot

In this recipe, a variety of vegetables are cooked under a layer of potatoes, topped with cheese, and cooked until golden brown.

NUTRITIONAL INFORMATION

Calories 279	Sugars 12g	
Protein 10g	Fat 11g	
Carbohydrate ...34g	Saturates 4g	

 25 mins   🕐 1 hr

SERVES 4

INGREDIENTS

1½ lb/675 g potatoes, thinly sliced

2 tbsp vegetable oil

1 red onion, halved and sliced

1 leek, sliced

2 garlic cloves, crushed

1 carrot, cut into chunks

1 cup broccoli florets

scant 1 cup cauliflower florets

2 small turnips, quartered

¼ cup all-purpose flour

3 cups vegetable bouillon

⅔ cup dry hard cider

1 eating apple, cored and sliced

2 tbsp chopped sage

pinch of cayenne pepper

½ cup grated Cheddar cheese

salt and pepper

1 Cook the potato slices in a pan of boiling water for 10 minutes. Drain thoroughly and reserve.

2 Heat the vegetable oil in a flameproof casserole. Add the onion, leek, and garlic to the oil and sauté, stirring occasionally, for 2–3 minutes.

3 Add the remaining vegetables and cook, stirring constantly, for a further 3–4 minutes.

4 Stir in the flour and cook for 1 minute. Gradually add the bouillon and cider and bring to a boil. Add the apple, sage, and cayenne pepper and season well.

5 Remove from the heat and transfer the vegetables to an ovenproof dish.

6 Arrange the potato slices on top of the vegetable mixture to cover.

7 Sprinkle the grated cheese on top of the potato slices and cook in a preheated oven, 375°F/190°C, for about 30–35 minutes or until the potato is golden brown and beginning to go crisp around the edges. Serve the vegetable hotpot immediately, straight from the dish.

Mushroom Tarts

Different varieties of mushrooms are becoming more widely available in food stores, so use this recipe to make the most of them.

NUTRITIONAL INFORMATION

Calories 494	Sugars 2g	
Protein 9g	Fat 35g	
Carbohydrate ...38g	Saturates 18g	

🍄 🍄 🍄

🥘 15 mins   🕐 20 mins

SERVES 4

INGREDIENTS

1 lb/450 g phyllo pastry, thawed if frozen

½ cup butter, melted

1 tbsp hazelnut oil

4 tbsp pine nuts

¾ lb/350 g mixed mushrooms, such as white, crimini, oyster, and shiitake

2 tsp chopped fresh parsley

½ lb/225 g soft goat cheese

salt and pepper

fresh parsley sprigs to garnish

lettuce, tomatoes, cucumber, and scallions, to serve

1 Cut the sheets of phyllo pastry into 4 inch/10 cm squares and line 4 individual tart pans, brushing each layer with melted butter. Line the pans with baking parchment and baking beans. Bake in a preheated oven, 400°F/200°C, for 6–8 minutes until golden.

2 Remove the tarts from the oven and carefully take out the foil or baking parchment and baking beans. Reduce the oven temperature to 350°F/180°C.

3 Put any remaining butter into a large pan with the hazelnut oil and cook the pine nuts until golden brown. Remove from the pan and drain on paper towels.

4 Add the mushrooms to the pan and cook gently, stirring frequently, for about 4–5 minutes. Add the parsley and season to taste with salt and pepper.

5 Spoon one-quarter of the goat cheese into the base of each cooked phyllo tart. Divide the mushrooms equally among them and sprinkle the pine nuts evenly over the top.

6 Return the tarts to the oven for about 5 minutes to heat through.

7 Garnish the tarts with sprigs of parsley. Serve with lettuce, tomatoes, cucumber, and scallions.

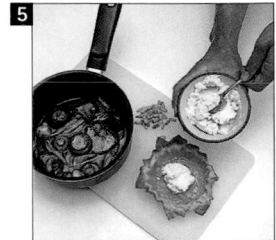

Beans & Pasta Casserole

A satisfying winter dish, this hearty casserole with a crunchy topping is a slow-cooked, one-pot meal.

NUTRITIONAL INFORMATION

Calories	400	Sugars	.........2g
Protein	........26g	Fat	..........20g
Carbohydrate	...32g	Saturates	......10g

 15 mins, plus soaking   3½ hrs

SERVES 4

INGREDIENTS

1¼ cups dried navy beans, soaked overnight and drained

2 cups dried penne

6 tbsp olive oil

3½ cups vegetable bouillon

2 large onions, sliced

2 garlic cloves, chopped

2 bay leaves

1 tsp dried oregano

1 tsp dried thyme

5 tbsp red wine

2 tbsp tomato paste

2 celery stalks, sliced

1 fennel bulb, sliced

1⅝ cups sliced mushrooms

8 oz tomatoes, sliced

1 tsp dark muscovado sugar

4 tbsp dry white bread crumbs

salt and pepper

salad greens and crusty bread, to serve

1 Put the navy beans in a large pan and add sufficient cold water to cover. Bring to a boil and continue to boil vigorously for 20 minutes. Drain, set aside, and keep warm.

2 Bring a large pan of lightly salted water to a boil. Add the penne and 1 tbsp of the olive oil to the pan and cook for about 3 minutes. Drain the pasta and set aside, keeping it warm.

3 Put the beans in a large, flameproof casserole. Add the vegetable bouillon and stir in the remaining olive oil, the onions, garlic, bay leaves, dried oregano and thyme, red wine, and tomato paste.

4 Bring to a boil, then cover and cook in a preheated oven at 350°F/180°C for 2 hours.

5 Add the penne, celery, fennel, mushrooms, and tomatoes to the casserole and season to taste with salt and pepper. Stir in the muscovado sugar and sprinkle over the bread crumbs. Cover the dish and cook in the oven for a further hour.

6 Serve the bean and pasta casserole hot with salad greens and crusty bread.

Cold-Weather Casserole

Heart-warming, comfort food on a chilly evening, this is a rich casserole of root vegetables, served with tasty parsley dumplings.

NUTRITIONAL INFORMATION

Calories . . . . . . .345 Sugars 7g
Protein . . . . .9g Fat 17g
Carbohydrate . . .43g Saturates 10g

🍲 🍲

❄ 20 mins   🕐 1¼ hrs

SERVES 6

INGREDIENTS

4 tbsp butter or margarine

2 leeks, sliced

2 carrots, sliced

2 potatoes, cut into bite-size pieces

1 rutabaga, cut into bite-size pieces

2 zucchini, sliced

1 fennel bulb, halved and sliced

2 tbsp all-purpose flour

1½ cups canned lima beans

2½ cups vegetable bouillon

2 tbsp tomato paste

1 tsp dried thyme

2 bay leaves

salt and ground black pepper

PARSLEY DUMPLINGS

¾ cup self-rising flour

2 oz/55 g vegetarian suet

2 tbsp chopped fresh parsley

about 4 tbsp water

1 Melt the butter in a large, heavy pan. Add the leeks, carrots, potatoes, rutabaga, zucchini, and fennel and cook, stirring occasionally, for 10 minutes.

2 Stir in the flour and cook, stirring constantly, for 1 minute. Add the can juice from the beans, the bouillon, tomato paste, thyme, and bay leaves and season to taste. Bring to a boil, stirring, then cover and simmer for 10 minutes.

3 Meanwhile, make the dumplings. Strain the flour with a pinch of salt into a bowl. Stir in the suet and chopped parsley, then add enough water to bind to a soft dough. Divide the dough into 8 pieces and roll into balls.

4 Add the beans and the dumplings to the pan, then cover and simmer for a further 30 minutes. Remove and discard the bay leaf before serving.

Vegetable & Lentil Casserole

This easy, one-pot dish cooks slowly so that the flavors mingle deliciously. Use Puy lentils if possible for their superior flavor.

NUTRITIONAL INFORMATION

Calories	273	Sugars	........10g
Protein	........18g	Fat	...........2g
Carbohydrate	....5g	Saturates	.......0g

 15 mins 2 hrs

SERVES 4

I N G R E D I E N T S

1 onion

4 cloves

1⅓ cups Puy or green lentils

1 bay leaf

6–7 cups vegetable bouillon or water

2 leeks, sliced

2 potatoes, diced

2 carrots, chopped

3 zucchini, sliced

1 celery stick, chopped

1 red bell pepper, seeded and chopped

1 tbsp lemon juice

salt and ground black pepper

1 Spike the onion with the cloves. Put the lentils in a large casserole, add the onion and bay leaf, and pour in the vegetable bouillon or water. Cover and bake in a preheated oven, 350°F/180°C, for 1 hour.

2 Remove the casserole from the oven. Take out the onion and discard the cloves. Slice the onion and return it to the casserole with the leeks, potatoes, carrots, zucchini, celery, and red bell pepper.

3 Stir thoroughly and season to taste with salt and pepper. Cover and return to the oven for a further hour.

4 Discard the bay leaf. Stir the lemon juice into the casserole and serve it immediately on warmed serving plates.

COOK'S TIP
Unlike other pulses, lentils do not require soaking before they are cooked.

Indian Curry Feast

This vegetable curry is quick and easy to prepare and it tastes superb.
A colorful Indian salad and mint raita make perfect accompaniments.

NUTRITIONAL INFORMATION

Calories	473	Sugars	........18g
Protein	........19g	Fat	...........9g
Carbohydrate	...84g	Saturates	.......1g

 25-30 mins   55 mins

SERVES 4

INGREDIENTS

1 tbsp vegetable oil

2 garlic cloves, crushed

1 onion, chopped

3 celery stalks, sliced

1 apple, cored and chopped

1 tbsp medium-strength curry powder

1 tsp ground ginger

1½ cups canned garbanzo beans

1 cup dwarf green beans, sliced

2 cups cauliflower, broken into florets

1½ cups potatoes, cut into cubes

3 cups sliced mushrooms

2½ cups vegetable bouillon

1 tbsp tomato paste

¼ cup golden raisins

scant 1 cup basmati rice

1 tbsp garam masala

MINT RAITA

⅔ cup unsweetened yogurt

1 tbsp chopped mint plus extra for garnish

1 Heat the oil in a large pan. Add the garlic, onion, celery, and apple to the pan and cook over medium heat, stirring frequently, for 3–4 minutes. Add the curry powder and ginger, and cook gently for 1 more minute.

2 Drain the garbanzo beans and add to the onion mixture, together with the green beans, cauliflower, potatoes, mushrooms, bouillon, tomato paste, and golden raisins.

3 Bring to a boil, reduce the heat, cover, and simmer for 35–40 minutes.

4 Meanwhile, make the raita. Mix the yogurt and mint together. Transfer to a small serving bowl, then cover and chill in the refrigerator.

5 Cook the rice in a large pan of boiling, lightly salted water for about 12 minutes, or until just tender. Drain, rinse with boiling water, and drain again.

6 Just before serving, stir the garam masala into the curry. Divide between four warmed serving plates and serve with the rice. Garnish the raita with fresh mint and hand the bowl separately.

Bean Curd Casserole

In this quick recipe, all the cooking is done in a microwave—there is not a wok in sight!

NUTRITIONAL INFORMATION

Calories . . . . .222 Sugars 3g
Protein . . . . .11g Fat 13g
Carbohydrate . . .16g Saturates 2g

 1¼ hrs   15 mins

SERVES 4

I N G R E D I E N T S

9½ oz/275 g smoked bean curd, cubed

2 tbsp soy sauce

1 tbsp dry sherry

1 tsp sesame oil

4 dried Chinese mushrooms

9 oz/250 g egg noodles

1 carrot, cut into thin sticks

1 celery stalk, cut into thin sticks

10–12 baby corn ears, halved lengthwise

2 tbsp oil

1 zucchini, sliced

4 scallions, chopped

1½ cups snow peas, each cut into 3 pieces

2 tbsp black bean sauce

1 tsp cornstarch

salt and pepper

1 tbsp toasted sesame seeds, to garnish

1 Marinate the bean curd in the soy sauce, sherry, and sesame oil for 30 minutes.

2 Place the mushrooms in a small bowl and pour over boiling water to cover. Let soak for 20 minutes.

3 Place the egg noodles in a large bowl. Pour over enough boiling water to cover by 1 inch/2.5 cm. Add ½ teaspoon salt, cover the bowl, and cook on HIGH power for 4 minutes.

4 Place the carrot, celery, corn, and oil in a large bowl. Cover and cook on HIGH power for 1 minute.

5 Drain the mushrooms, reserving 1 tablespoon of the liquid. Squeeze out any excess water from the mushrooms and discard the hard cores. Cut the mushrooms into thin slices.

6 Add the mushrooms to the bowl of vegetables with the zucchini, scallions, and snow peas. Mix well. Cover and cook on HIGH power for 4 minutes, stirring every minute. Add the black bean sauce to the vegetables, stirring to coat the vegetables in the sauce.

7 Mix the cornstarch with the reserved mushroom water and stir into the bowl with the bean curd and marinade.

8 Cover and cook on HIGH power for 2–3 minutes until heated through and the sauce has thickened slightly.

9 Season with salt and pepper to taste. Drain the noodles, then garnish the vegetables with sesame seeds and serve with the noodles.

Garbanzo Bean Hotpot

This is an economical and trouble-free dish that is packed with goodness and tastes simply wonderful.

NUTRITIONAL INFORMATION

Calories 438	Sugars 14g	
Protein 19g	Fat 13g	
Carbohydrate ...66g	Saturates 2g	

15 mins   2½ hrs

SERVES 4

INGREDIENTS

225 g/8 oz dried garbanzo beans, soaked overnight in water to cover

3 tbsp olive oil

1 large onion, sliced

2 garlic cloves, finely chopped

2 leeks, sliced

1½ cups carrots, sliced

4 turnips, sliced

4 celery stalks, sliced

⅔ cup bulgur wheat

2 cups canned chopped tomatoes

2 tbsp snipped fresh chives, plus extra to garnish

salt and ground black pepper

COOK'S TIP

Remember to check the water level regularly and have boiling water to hand to top up the pan if necessary.

1 Drain the garbanzo beans and place in a heavy pan. Add enough water to cover, bring to a boil, and simmer for 1½ hours.

2 Meanwhile, heat the oil in a large pan. Add the onion and cook, stirring occasionally, for 5 minutes, until soft. Add the garlic, leeks, carrots, turnips, and celery and cook, stirring occasionally, for 5 minutes.

3 Stir in the bulgur, tomatoes, and chives, season to taste with salt and pepper, and bring to a boil. Spoon the mixture into a heatproof bowl and cover with a lid or circle of foil.

4 When the garbanzo beans have been cooking for 1½ hours, set a steamer over the pan. Place the bowl in the steamer, cover tightly, and cook for 40 minutes. Remove the bowl from the steamer, drain the garbanzo beans, then stir them into the vegetable and bulgur mixture. Transfer the hotpot to a warm serving dish and serve immediately, garnished with the extra chives.

Kenyan Dengu

This mildly spiced mung bean stew is economical, filling, and easy to make—perfect for a midweek family supper.

NUTRITIONAL INFORMATION

Calories 254   Sugars 8g
Protein . . . . .17g   Fat 6g
Carbohydrate . . .34g   Saturates 1g

15 mins   1 hr 40 mins

SERVES 4

I N G R E D I E N T S

8 oz/225 g mung beans, soaked overnight in water to cover

2 tbsp sunflower oil

1 onion, chopped

2 garlic cloves, finely chopped

2 tbsp tomato paste

1 red bell pepper, seeded and diced

1 green bell pepper, seeded and diced

1 fresh red chili, seeded and finely chopped

1¼ cups vegetable bouillon or water

1 Drain the mung beans, place in a pan, and cover with water. Bring to a boil, cover, and simmer for 1–1¼ hours, or until the beans are tender. Drain the beans well, return to the pan and mash thoroughly until smooth.

2 Heat the sunflower oil in another pan. Add the chopped onion and cook, stirring occasionally, for 10 minutes, until soft and golden.

3 Add the chopped garlic and cook for 2 minutes, then add the tomato paste to the pan and continue to cook, stirring constantly, for a further 3 minutes. Stir in the mashed beans.

4 Add the bell peppers, chili, and vegetable bouillon or water, stir well, and simmer gently for 10 minutes. Transfer the bean stew to a warm serving dish and serve immediately.

VARIATION
If you like, stir in ½ lb/225 g shredded spinach leaves 3-4 minutes before the end of cooking in step 3.

Potato & Lemon Casserole

This is based on a Moroccan dish in which potatoes are spiced with coriander and cumin and cooked in a lemon sauce.

NUTRITIONAL INFORMATION

Calories 338	Sugars 8g
Protein 5g	Fat 23g
Carbohydrate ...29g	Saturates 2g

 15 mins 35 mins

SERVES 4

INGREDIENTS

scant ½ cup olive oil

2 red onions, cut into 8 wedges

3 garlic cloves, crushed

2 tsp ground cumin

2 tsp ground coriander

pinch of cayenne pepper

1 carrot, thickly sliced

2 small turnips, quartered

1 zucchini, sliced

1 lb 2 oz/500 g potatoes, thickly sliced

juice and rind of 2 large lemons

1¼ cups vegetable stock

2 tbsp chopped fresh cilantro

salt and pepper

COOK'S TIP

Check the vegetables while they are cooking, because they may begin to stick to the pan. Add a little more boiling water or stock if necessary.

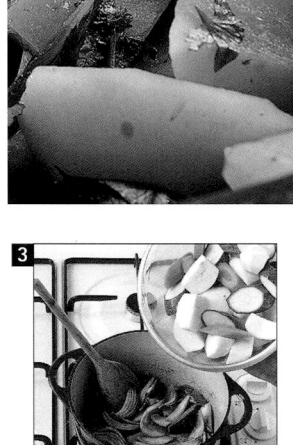

1 Heat the olive oil in a flameproof casserole. Add the onion and sauté over medium heat, stirring frequently, for 3 minutes.

2 Add the garlic and cook for 30 seconds. Stir in the cumin, ground coriander, and cayenne and cook, stirring constantly, for 1 minute.

3 Add the carrot, turnips, zucchini, and potatoes and stir to coat in the oil.

4 Add the lemon juice and rind and the vegetable stock. Season to taste with salt and pepper. Cover and cook over medium heat, stirring occasionally, for 20–30 minutes until tender.

5 Remove the lid, sprinkle in the chopped fresh cilantro and stir well. Serve immediately.

Chinese Vegetable Casserole

This mixed vegetable casserole is very versatile and is delicious with any combination of vegetables of your choice.

NUTRITIONAL INFORMATION

Calories 218   Sugars 4g
Protein . . . . .7g   Fat 14g
Carbohydrate . . .12g   Saturates 2g

 5 mins   30 mins

SERVES 4

I N G R E D I E N T S

4 tbsp vegetable oil

2 carrots, sliced

1 zucchini, sliced

4 baby corn ears, halved lengthwise

1 cup cauliflower florets

1 leek, sliced

4½ oz/125 g water chestnuts, halved

8 oz/225 g firm bean curd, cubed

1¼ cups vegetable bouillon

1 tsp salt

2 tsp dark brown sugar

2 tsp dark soy sauce

2 tbsp dry sherry

1 tbsp cornstarch

2 tbsp water

1 tbsp chopped fresh cilantro, to garnish

1 Heat the oil in a preheated wok until it is almost smoking. Lower the heat slightly, add the carrots, zucchini, corn ears, cauliflower, and leek to the wok, and cook for 2–3 minutes.

2 Stir in the water chestnuts, bean curd, vegetable bouillon, salt, sugar, soy sauce, and dry sherry and bring to a boil. Reduce the heat, cover, and simmer for 20 minutes.

3 Blend the cornstarch with the water to form a smooth paste.

4 Stir the cornstarch mixture into the wok. Bring the sauce to a boil and cook, stirring constantly until it thickens and clears.

5 Transfer the casserole to a warm serving dish, sprinkle with chopped cilantro and serve immediately.

COOK'S TIP
If there is too much liquid remaining, boil vigorously for 1 minute before adding the cornstarch to reduce it slightly.

Italian Vegetable Stew

In spite of the formidable list of ingredients, this flavorful stew is very simple to make—simply put the ingredients in a pot, and cook!

NUTRITIONAL INFORMATION

Calories	307	Sugars	........15g
Protein	.........5g	Fat	..........24g
Carbohydrate	...20g	Saturates	.......3g

 30 mins   35–40 mins

SERVES 4

I N G R E D I E N T S

1 red onion, sliced

2 leeks, sliced

4 garlic cloves, finely chopped

1 small acorn squash, diced

1 eggplant, sliced

1 small celery root, diced

2 turnips, sliced

2 plum tomatoes, chopped

1 carrot, sliced

1 zucchini, sliced

2 red bell peppers, seeded and cut
   into strips

1 fennel bulb, sliced

6 oz/175 g chard or spinach beet, chopped

2 bay leaves

½ tsp fennel seeds

½ tsp chili powder

pinch of dried thyme

pinch of dried oregano

pinch of sugar

½ cup extra virgin olive oil

1 cup vegetable bouillon

handful fresh basil leaves, torn

4 tbsp chopped fresh flat-leaf parsley

salt ground black pepper

2 tbsp freshly grated Parmesan cheese, to
   serve (optional)

1 Put the onion, leeks, garlic, squash, eggplant, celery root, turnips, tomatoes, carrot, zucchini, bell peppers, fennel, chard or spinach beet, bay leaves, fennel seeds, chili powder, thyme, oregano, sugar, olive oil, vegetable bouillon, and half the basil leaves in a large, heavy pan. Mix well and bring to a boil.

2 Lower the heat, cover the pan, and simmer the vegetables for about 30 minutes, until tender.

3 Sprinkle in the remaining basil and the parsley and season to taste with salt and pepper. Serve immediately, sprinkled with the Parmesan, if you like.

Black Bean Casserole

This colorful Chinese-style casserole is made with bean curd and vegetables and flavored with black bean sauce.

NUTRITIONAL INFORMATION

Calories 513	Sugars 5g
Protein 19g	Fat 25g
Carbohydrate . . .56g	Saturates 4g

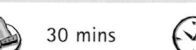

 30 mins   30 mins

SERVES 4

I N G R E D I E N T S

6 Chinese dried mushrooms

9½ oz/275 g bean curd

3 tbsp vegetable oil

1 carrot, cut into thin strips

1½ cups snow peas

10–12 baby corn ears, halved lengthwise

8 oz/225 g canned sliced bamboo shoots, drained

1 red bell pepper, cut into chunks

1 cup Napa cabbage, shredded

1 tbsp soy sauce

1 tbsp black bean sauce

1 tsp sugar

1 tsp cornstarch

vegetable oil for deep-frying

9 oz/250 g Chinese rice noodles

salt

1 Soak the dried mushrooms in a bowl of warm water for 20–25 minutes. Drain and squeeze out the excess water, reserving the liquid. Remove the tough centers and slice the mushrooms thinly.

2 Cut the bean curd into cubes, then boil in a pan of lightly salted water for 2–3 minutes to firm up, and drain.

3 Heat half the vegetable oil in a pan. Add the bean curd and cook until lightly browned. Remove and drain on paper towels.

4 Add the remaining vegetable oil and stir-fry the mushrooms, carrot, snow peas, baby corn, bamboo shoots, and bell pepper for 2–3 minutes. Add the Napa cabbage and bean curd, and continue to stir-fry for a further 2 minutes.

5 Stir in the soy and black bean sauces and the sugar, and season with a little salt. Add 6 tbsp of the reserved mushroom liquid mixed with the cornstarch. Bring to a boil, reduce the heat, cover, and braise for about 2–3 minutes, until the sauce thickens slightly.

6 Heat the oil for deep-frying in a large pan. Deep-fry the noodles, in batches, until puffed up and lightly golden. Drain and serve with the casserole.

Bean Curd Casserole

Bean curd is ideal for absorbing all the other flavors in this dish. If marinated bean curd is used, it will add a flavor of its own.

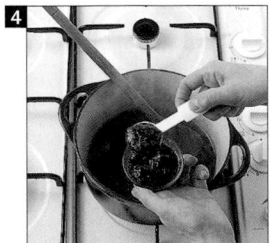

NUTRITIONAL INFORMATION

Calories	228	Sugars	.........3g
Protein	........16g	Fat	..........15g
Carbohydrate	....7g	Saturates	.......2g

 5 mins   15 mins

SERVES 4

I N G R E D I E N T S

1 lb/450 g firm bean curd

2 tbsp peanut oil

8 scallions, cut into batons

2 celery stalks, sliced

1¼ cups broccoli florets

1 cup zucchini, sliced

2 garlic cloves, thinly sliced

1 lb/450 g baby spinach

rice, to serve

S A U C E

scant 2 cups vegetable bouillon

2 tbsp light soy sauce

3 tbsp hoisin sauce

½ tsp chili powder

1 tbsp sesame oil

VARIATION

This recipe has a green vegetable theme, but you can alter the color and flavor by adding your favorite vegetables. Add 2¾ oz/75 g fresh or canned and drained straw mushrooms with the vegetables in step 2.

1 Cut the bean curd into 1 inch/2.5 cm cubes and set aside until required.

2 Heat the peanut oil in a preheated wok or large skillet.

3 Add the scallion batons, sliced celery, broccoli florets, zucchini slices, garlic, baby spinach, and bean curd to the oil in the wok or skillet and stir-fry for 3–4 minutes until heated through.

4 To make the sauce, mix together the vegetable bouillon, soy sauce, hoisin sauce, chili powder, and sesame oil in a flameproof casserole and bring to a boil.

5 Add the stir-fried vegetables and bean curd to the pan, reduce the heat, cover, and simmer for 10 minutes.

6 Transfer the bean curd and vegetables to a serving dish and serve with rice.

Curry Pasties

These pasties, which are suitable for vegans, are a delicious combination of vegetables and spices. They can be eaten either hot or cold.

NUTRITIONAL INFORMATION

Calories 455   Sugars 5g
Protein . . . . .8g   Fat 27g
Carbohydrate . . .48g   Saturates 5g

20 mins, plus 30 mins chilling time   1 hr

SERVES 4

INGREDIENTS

2 cups all-purpose whole-wheat flour

⅓ cup vegetarian margarine, cut into small pieces

4 tbsp water

2 tbsp oil

1½ cups diced root vegetables, such as potatoes, carrots, and parsnips

1 small onion, chopped

2 garlic cloves, finely chopped

½ tsp curry powder

½ tsp ground turmeric

½ tsp ground cumin

½ tsp whole-grain mustard

5 tbsp vegetable bouillon

soy milk, to glaze

1 Place the flour in a mixing bowl and rub in the margarine with your fingertips until the mixture resembles bread crumbs. Stir in the water and bring together to form a soft dough. Wrap and let chill in the refrigerator for 30 minutes.

2 To make the filling, heat the oil in a large pan. Add the diced root vegetables, chopped onion, and garlic, and cook, stirring occasionally, for 2 minutes. Stir in all of the spices, turning the vegetables to coat them thoroughly. Cook the vegetables, stirring constantly, for another minute.

3 Add the bouillon to the pan and bring to a boil. Cover and simmer, stirring occasionally, for about 20 minutes, until the vegetables are tender and the liquid has been absorbed. Let cool.

4 Divide the dough into 4 portions. Roll each portion into a 6 inch/15 cm round. Place the filling on one half of each round.

5 Brush the edges of each round with soy milk, then fold over and press the edges together to seal. Place on a cookie sheet. Bake in a preheated oven, 400°F/200°C, for 25–30 minutes until golden brown.

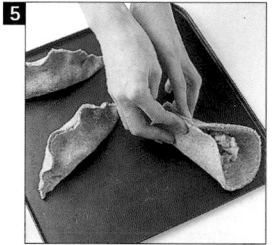

Garbanzo Bean Roast

This pastry case with a garbanzo bean stuffing is delicious. Served with a sherry sauce, it makes a tasty and impressive entrée.

NUTRITIONAL INFORMATION

Calories	795	Sugars	.........9g
Protein	........24g	Fat	..........48g
Carbohydrate	...66g	Saturates	.......3g

 20 mins, plus cooling   30 mins

SERVES 4

INGREDIENTS

2 cups canned garbanzo beans, drained

1 tsp yeast extract

1½ cups chopped walnuts

2½ cups fresh white bread crumbs

1 onion, finely chopped

1½ cups mushrooms, sliced

¼ cup canned corn kernels, drained

2 garlic cloves, crushed

2 tbsp dry sherry

2 tbsp vegetable bouillon

1 tbsp chopped cilantro

8 oz/225 g prepared puff pie dough

1 egg, beaten

2 tbsp milk

salt and pepper

SAUCE

1 tbsp vegetable oil

1 leek, thinly sliced

4 tbsp dry sherry

⅔ cup vegetable bouillon

1 Blend the garbanzo beans, yeast extract, nuts, and bread crumbs in a food processor for 30 seconds. In a skillet, sauté the onion and mushrooms in their own juices for 3–4 minutes. Stir in the garbanzo bean mixture, corn, and garlic. Add the sherry, bouillon, cilantro, and seasoning and bind the mixture together. Remove from the heat and let cool.

2 Roll the pie dough out on a floured surface to form a 14 inch x 12 inch/35.5 cm x 30 cm rectangle. Shape the garbanzo bean mixture into a loaf shape and wrap the pie dough around it, sealing the edges. Place seam-side down on a dampened cookie sheet and score the top in a criss-cross pattern. Mix the egg and milk and brush over the pie dough. Cook in a preheated oven, 400°F/200°C, for 25–30 minutes.

3 To make the sauce, heat the oil in a pan and sauté the leek for 5 minutes. Add the sherry and bouillon, bring to a boil, and simmer for 5 minutes.

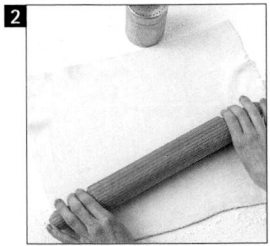

Layered Vegetable Gratin

In this tasty recipe an assortment of vegetables are cooked in a light nutmeg sauce with a potato and cheese topping.

NUTRITIONAL INFORMATION

Calories 236   Sugars 9g
Protein ....9g   Fat 9g
Carbohydrate ...31g   Saturates 3g

 25 mins   1½ hrs

SERVES 6

I N G R E D I E N T S

2 carrots

2 cups baby parsnips

1 fennel bulb

1 lb/450 g potatoes

6 tbsp low-fat spread

4 tbsp all-purpose flour

1¼ cups skim milk

½ tsp ground nutmeg

1 egg, beaten

¼ cup freshly grated Parmesan cheese

salt and pepper

T O   S E R V E

crusty bread

tomato salad

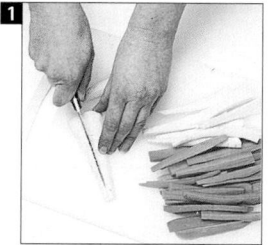 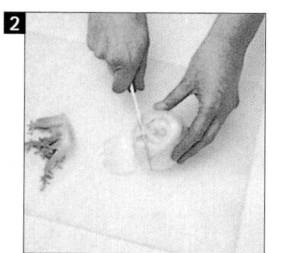 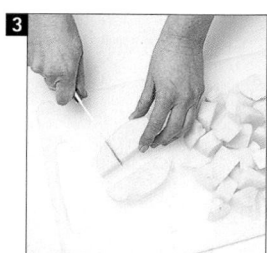

1 Cut the carrots and parsnips into thin strips lengthwise. Cook in boiling water for 5 minutes. Drain well and transfer to an ovenproof baking dish.

2 Thinly slice the fennel and cook in boiling water for 2–3 minutes. Drain well and add to the carrots and parsnips. Season to taste with salt and pepper.

3 Peel and dice the potatoes into ¾ inch/2 cm cubes. Cook in boiling water for 6 minutes. Drain well.

4 Gently melt half the low-fat spread and stir in the flour. Remove from the heat and gradually mix in the milk.

5 Return to the heat and stir until thickened. Season and stir in the ground nutmeg. Cool for 10 minutes.

6 Beat in the egg and spoon over the vegetables. Arrange the potatoes on top and sprinkle over the cheese.

7 Dot the cheesy potatoes with the remaining low-fat spread. Bake the gratin in a preheated oven at 350°F/180°C for 1 hour until all the vegetables are tender and the topping is a light golden color.

8 Serve the vegetable gratin as an entrée with wedges of crusty bread and a tomato salad, or as an accompaniment to a light entrée.

Mushroom & Spinach Puffs

These puffs, filled with garlic, mushrooms, and spinach, are easy to make and bake to an appealing golden brown.

NUTRITIONAL INFORMATION

Calories	467	Sugars	.........4g
Protein	.........8g	Fat	..........38g
Carbohydrate	...24g	Saturates	......18g

 20 mins   30 mins

SERVES 4

I N G R E D I E N T S

2 tbsp butter

1 red onion, halved and sliced

2 garlic cloves, crushed

3 cups sliced open-cap mushrooms

6 oz young spinach

pinch of nutmeg

4 tbsp heavy cream

8 oz/225 g ready-made puff pie dough,
   defrosted if frozen

1 egg, beaten

salt and pepper

2 tsp poppy seeds

1 Melt the butter in a skillet. Add the onion and garlic and sauté over low heat, stirring, for 3–4 minutes, until the onion has softened.

2 Add the mushrooms, spinach, and nutmeg and cook them over medium heat, stirring occasionally, for 2–3 minutes.

3 Stir in the heavy cream, mixing thoroughly. Season with salt and pepper to taste and remove the pan from the heat. Let the mixture stand.

4 Roll out the pastry on a lightly floured surface and cut it into four 6 inch/15 cm rounds, using a bowl or a saucer as a guide.

5 Dampen the pastry edges. Put a quarter of the filling onto one half of each round and fold the pastry over to encase it. Press down to seal the edges and brush with the beaten egg. Sprinkle with the poppy seeds.

6 Place the puffs on a dampened cookie sheet and cook in a preheated oven, 400°F/200°C, for 20 minutes, until the pastry is risen and golden brown in color. Serve immediately.

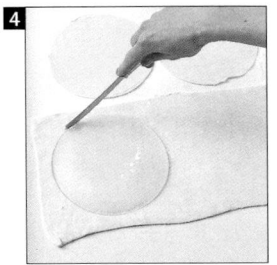

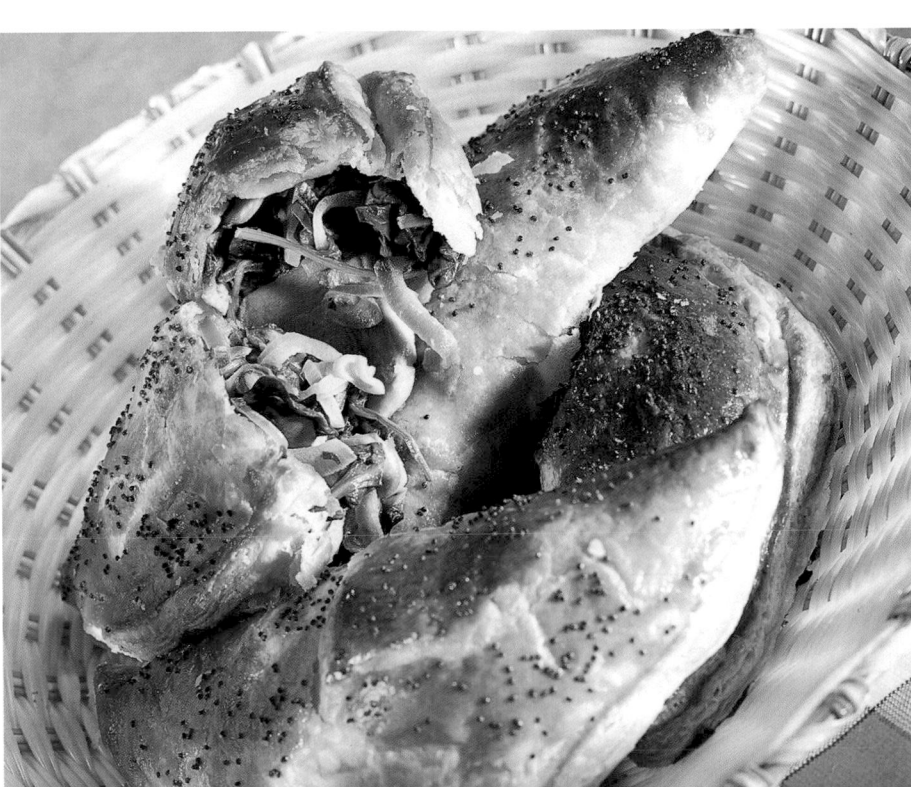

COOK'S TIP

The cookie sheet is dampened so that steam forms with the heat of the oven, which helps the dough to rise and set.

Gratin of Mixed Vegetables

This gratin is very quick to make using canned artichoke and celery hearts. The Swiss and romano cheeses add an unusual touch.

NUTRITIONAL INFORMATION

Calories	150	Sugars	........3g
Protein	.........7g	Fat	..........12g
Carbohydrate	....8g	Saturates	.......5g

 15 mins   1¼ hrs

SERVES 6

INGREDIENTS

2 parsnips, sliced

2 tbsp olive oil

1 eggplant, diced

1 garlic clove, finely chopped

2 tsp chopped fresh thyme

2 tsp butter

2 shallots, chopped

4 canned artichoke hearts, drained

4 canned celery hearts, sliced

½ cup grated Swiss cheese

½ cup freshly grated romano cheese

1 Steam the parsnips over a pan of simmering water for about 4 minutes, until just tender. Let cool.

2 Heat the oil in a heavy skillet. Add the eggplant and cook, stirring frequently, for 5 minutes. Add the garlic and thyme, season to taste with salt, and cook for 3 minutes. Using a slotted spoon, transfer the eggplant mixture to a dish. Add the butter to the pan. When it has melted, add the shallots and a pinch of salt and cook over very low heat, stirring occasionally, for 7–10 minutes.

3 Combine the shallots with the eggplant. Cut each artichoke heart into 8 pieces and add to the eggplant mixture with the parsnips, celery hearts, Swiss cheese, and half the romano. Mix well and spoon into an ovenproof dish. Sprinkle with the remaining romano and bake in a preheated oven, 350°F/180°C, for 45 minutes. Serve at once.

COOK'S TIP

To chop garlic, place a clove on a cutting board, lay the flat side of a cook's knife on top, and hit it with your fist. Remove the papery skin and chop the clove. Sprinkle a little salt on the garlic and work it into the clove with the flat side of the knife blade to release the juices.

Lentil & Vegetable Shells

These stuffed eggplants are delicious served hot or cold, topped with unsweetened yogurt or cucumber raita.

NUTRITIONAL INFORMATION

Calories	386	Sugars	.........9g
Protein	........14g	Fat	..........24g
Carbohydrate	...30g	Saturates	.......3g

🥗🥗🥗

🍲 25 mins   🕐 1 hr

SERVES 6

INGREDIENTS

1½ cups European lentils

3½ cups water

2 garlic cloves, crushed

3 well-shaped eggplants

⅔ cup vegetable oil, plus extra for brushing

2 onions, chopped

4 tomatoes, chopped

2 tsp cumin seeds

1 tsp ground cinnamon

2 tbsp mild curry paste

1 tsp minced chili

2 tbsp chopped mint

salt and pepper

unsweetened yogurt and mint sprigs,
    to serve

1 Rinse the lentils under cold running water. Drain them and place in a pan with the water and garlic. Cover and simmer for 30 minutes.

2 Cook the eggplants in a pan of boiling water for 5 minutes. Drain, then plunge into cold water for 5 minutes. Drain again, then cut the eggplants in half lengthwise, scoop out most of the flesh, and reserve, leaving a ½ inch/1 cm thick border to form a shell.

3 Place the eggplant shells in a shallow greased ovenproof dish, brush with a little oil, and sprinkle with salt and pepper. Cook in a preheated oven, 375°F/190°C, for 10 minutes. Meanwhile, heat half the remaining oil in a skillet, add the onions and tomatoes, and cook gently for 5 minutes. Chop the reserved eggplant flesh, add to the skillet with the spices, and cook gently for 5 minutes. Season with salt.

4 Stir in the lentils, most of the remaining oil, reserving a little for later, and the chopped mint. Spoon the mixture into the shells. Drizzle with the remaining oil and bake for 15 minutes.

5 Serve hot or cold, topped with a spoonful of unsweetened yogurt and mint sprigs.

COOK'S TIP

Choose nice plump eggplants, rather than thin tapering ones, as they retain their shape better when filled and baked with a stuffing.

Potato & Eggplant Gratin

Similar to a simple moussaka, this recipe is made up of layers of eggplant, tomato, and potato baked with a yogurt topping.

NUTRITIONAL INFORMATION

Calories 409	Sugars 17g	
Protein 28g	Fat 14g	
Carbohydrate . . .45g	Saturates 3g	

 25 mins   🕐 1¼ hrs

SERVES 4

INGREDIENTS

1 lb/450 g waxy potatoes, sliced

1 tbsp vegetable oil

1 onion, chopped

2 garlic cloves, crushed

1 lb/450 g bean curd, diced

2 tbsp tomato paste

½ cup all-purpose flour

1¼ cups vegetable bouillon

2 large tomatoes, sliced

1 eggplant, sliced

2 tbsp chopped fresh thyme

scant 2 cups unsweetened yogurt

2 eggs, beaten

salt and pepper

salad, to serve

1 Cook the sliced potatoes in a pan of boiling water for 10 minutes, until tender, but not breaking up. Drain and then set aside.

2 Heat the oil in a skillet. Add the onion and garlic and cook, stirring occasionally, for 2–3 minutes.

3 Add the bean curd, tomato paste, and flour, and cook for 1 minute. Gradually stir in the bouillon and bring to a boil, stirring. Reduce the heat and simmer for 10 minutes.

4 Arrange a layer of the potato slices in the base of a deep ovenproof dish. Spoon the bean curd mixture evenly on top. Layer the sliced tomatoes, then the eggplant, and finally, the remaining potato slices, on top of the bean curd mixture, making sure that it is completely covered. Sprinkle with thyme.

5 Mix the yogurt and beaten eggs together in a bowl and season to taste with salt and pepper. Spoon the yogurt topping over the sliced potatoes to cover them completely.

6 Bake in a preheated oven, 375°F/ 190°C, for about 35–45 minutes or until the topping is browned. Serve with a crisp salad.

VARIATION

You can use marinated or smoked bean curd for extra flavor, if you wish.

Vegetable Jalousie

This is a really easy dish to make, but looks impressive. The mixture of vegetables gives the dish a wonderful color and flavor.

NUTRITIONAL INFORMATION

Calories ....660 Sugars 7g
Protein ....11g Fat 45g
Carbohydrate ...53g Saturates 15g

 25 mins   45 mins

SERVES 4

INGREDIENTS

1 lb/450 g puff pie dough

1 egg, beaten

FILLING

2 tbsp butter or margarine

1 leek, shredded

2 garlic cloves, crushed

1 red bell pepper, seeded and sliced

1 yellow bell pepper, seeded and sliced

1 cup sliced mushrooms

2¾ oz/75 g small asparagus spears

2 tbsp all-purpose flour

6 tbsp vegetable bouillon

6 tbsp milk

4 tbsp dry white wine

1 tbsp chopped oregano

salt and pepper

1 Melt the butter or margarine in a skillet and sauté the leek and garlic, stirring frequently, for 2 minutes. Add the remaining vegetables and cook, stirring, for 3–4 minutes.

2 Add the flour and cook for 1 minute. Remove the pan from the heat and stir in the vegetable bouillon, milk, and white wine. Return the pan to the heat and bring to a boil, stirring, until thickened. Stir in the oregano and season with salt and pepper to taste.

3 Roll out half of the pastry on a lightly floured surface to form a rectangle 15 x 6 inches/38 x 15 cm.

4 Roll out the other half of the pastry to the same shape, but a little larger all round. Transfer the smaller rectangle to a cookie sheet lined with dampened baking parchment.

5 Spoon the filling evenly on top of the smaller rectangle, leaving a ½ inch/ 1 cm clear margin around the edges.

6 Using a sharp knife, cut parallel diagonal slits across the larger rectangle to within 1 inch/2.5 cm of each of the long edges.

7 Brush the edges of the smaller rectangle with beaten egg and place the larger rectangle on top, pressing the edges firmly together to seal.

8 Brush the whole jalousie with egg to glaze and bake in a preheated oven, 400°F/200°C, for about 30–35 minutes, until well risen and golden. Transfer the jalousie to a warmed serving dish and serve immediately.

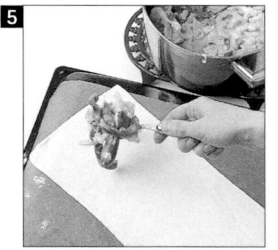

Italian Vegetable Tart

This mouthwateringly attractive tart is full of Mediterranean flavors—spinach, red bell peppers, ricotta cheese, and pine nuts.

NUTRITIONAL INFORMATION

Calories ....488 Sugars 7g
Protein ....13g Fat 40g
Carbohydrate ...21g Saturates 19g

30 mins   30 mins

SERVES 6

I N G R E D I E N T S

½ lb/225 g frozen phyllo pastry, thawed

½ cup butter, melted

12 oz/350 g frozen spinach, thawed

2 eggs

⅔ cup light cream

1 cup ricotta cheese

1 red bell pepper, seeded and sliced into strips

½ cup pine nuts

salt and pepper

1 Use the sheets of phyllo pastry to line an 8 inch/20 cm quiche pan, brushing each layer with melted butter.

2 Put the spinach into a strainer and squeeze out the excess moisture with the back of a spoon or your hand. Form the spinach into 8–9 small balls and arrange them in the prepared quiche pan.

3 Beat the eggs, cream, and ricotta cheese together until thoroughly blended. Season to taste with salt and pepper and pour over the spinach.

4 Put the remaining butter into a pan. Add the red bell pepper strips and

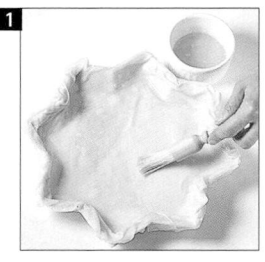  

sauté over low heat, stirring frequently, for about 4–5 minutes, until soft. Arrange the strips on the tart.

5 Scatter the pine nuts over the surface and bake in a preheated oven at 375°F/190°C for about 20–25 minutes, until the filling has set and the pastry is golden brown. Serve the tart immediately or let cool completely and serve at room temperature.

VARIATION

If you are not fond of bell peppers, you could use mushrooms instead. Exotic mushrooms would be especially delicious. Add a few sliced sun-dried tomatoes for extra color and flavor.

Potato-Topped Lentil Bake

A wonderful mixture of red lentils, bean curd, and vegetables is cooked beneath a crunchy potato topping for a really hearty meal.

NUTRITIONAL INFORMATION

Calories ....627 Sugars 7g
Protein ....26g Fat 30g
Carbohydrate ...66g Saturates 13g

 10 mins   1½ hrs

SERVES 4

INGREDIENTS

TOPPING

4½ cups diced mealy potatoes

2 tbsp butter

1 tbsp milk

½ cup chopped pecan nuts

2 tbsp chopped thyme

thyme sprigs, to garnish

FILLING

1¼ cups red lentils

¼ cup butter

1 leek, sliced

2 garlic cloves, crushed

1 celery stalk, chopped

1¼ cups broccoli florets

6 oz/175 g smoked bean curd, cubed

2 tsp tomato paste

salt and pepper

VARIATION
You can use almost any combination of your favorite vegetables in this dish.

1 To make the topping, cook the diced potatoes in a pan of boiling water for 10–15 minutes, or until cooked through. Drain well, add the butter and milk, and mash thoroughly. Stir in the chopped pecan nuts and the chopped thyme and set aside.

2 Cook the lentils in boiling water for 20–30 minutes, or until tender. Drain and set aside.

3 Melt the butter in a skillet. Add the leek, garlic, celery, and broccoli. Fry over medium heat, stirring frequently, for 5 minutes, until soft.

4 Add the bean curd cubes. Stir in the lentils, together with the tomato paste. Season with salt and pepper to taste, then turn the mixture into the base of a shallow ovenproof dish.

5 Spoon the mashed potato on top of the lentil mixture, spreading to cover it completely.

6 Cook the lentil bake in a preheated oven, 400°F/200°C, for about 30–35 minutes, or until the topping is golden brown. Remove the bake from the oven, garnish with sprigs of fresh thyme, and serve hot.

Vegetable Crumble

Always a family favorite, the crisp, crunchy topping contrasts with the creamy mixture of vegetables beneath.

NUTRITIONAL INFORMATION

Calories	523	Sugars	........14g
Protein	........21g	Fat	..........30g
Carbohydrate	...45g	Saturates	......13g

 15 mins   40 mins

SERVES 4

I N G R E D I E N T S

1 cauliflower, cut into florets

2 tbsp sunflower oil

4 tbsp all-purpose flour

1½ cups milk

1½ cups canned corn kernels, drained

2 tbsp chopped fresh parsley

1 tsp chopped fresh thyme

1¼ cups grated Cheddar cheese

salt and ground black pepper

C R U M B L E   T O P P I N G

scant ½ cup whole-wheat flour

2 tbsp butter

¼ cup rolled oats

¼ cup blanched almonds, chopped

1 Cook the cauliflower in a large pan of lightly salted boiling water for 5 minutes. Drain well, reserving the cooking water.

2 Heat the oil in a pan and stir in the flour. Cook, stirring constantly, for 1 minute. Remove the pan from the heat and gradually stir in the milk and ⅔ cup of the reserved cooking water. Return the pan to the heat and bring to a boil, stirring constantly. Cook, stirring constantly, for about 3 minutes, until thickened. Remove the pan from the heat.

3 Stir the corn, parsley, thyme, and half the Cheddar into the sauce and season to taste with salt and pepper. Fold in the cauliflower, then spoon the mixture into an ovenproof dish.

4 To make the crumble topping, place the flour in a bowl and rub in the butter with your fingertips until the mixture resembles bread crumbs. Stir in the oats, almonds, and remaining Cheddar, then sprinkle the mixture evenly over the vegetables. Bake in a preheated oven, 375°F/190°C, for 30 minutes. Serve immediately.

Lentil Roast

The perfect dish to serve for Sunday lunch. Roast vegetables make a succulent accompaniment.

NUTRITIONAL INFORMATION

Calories	400	Sugars	.........2g
Protein	........26g	Fat	..........20g
Carbohydrate	...32g	Saturates	......10g

15 mins   1 hr 20 mins

SERVES 6

INGREDIENTS

1¼ cups red lentils

2 cups vegetable bouillon

1 bay leaf

1 tbsp butter or margarine, softened

2 tbsp dried whole-wheat bread crumbs

2 cups grated sharp Cheddar cheese

1 leek, finely chopped

2 cups white mushrooms, finely chopped

1½ cups fresh whole-wheat bread crumbs

2 tbsp chopped parsley

1 tbsp lemon juice

2 eggs, lightly beaten

salt and pepper

flat-leaf parsley sprigs, to garnish

mixed roasted vegetables, to serve

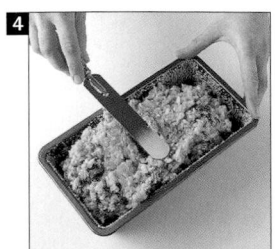

1 Put the lentils, bouillon, and bay leaf in a pan. Bring to a boil, cover, and simmer gently for 15–20 minutes, until all the liquid is absorbed and the lentils have softened. Discard the bay leaf.

2 Base-line a 2 lb/900 g loaf pan with baking parchment. Grease with the butter or margarine and sprinkle with the dried bread crumbs.

3 Stir the grated cheese, chopped leek and mushrooms, bread crumbs, and parsley into the lentils.

4 Bind the mixture together with the lemon juice and eggs. Season with salt and pepper. Spoon into the prepared loaf pan and smooth the top.

5 Bake in a preheated oven, 375°F/190°C, for about 1 hour, until golden.

6 Loosen the loaf with a spatula and turn on to a warmed serving plate.

7 Garnish with parsley and serve sliced, with roasted vegetables.

Chili Bean Curd

A tasty Mexican-style dish with a melt-in-the-mouth combination of bean curd and avocado, served with a tangy tomato sauce.

 30 mins 35 mins

SERVES 4

INGREDIENTS

½ tsp chili powder

1 tsp paprika

2 tbsp all-purpose flour

8 oz/225 g bean curd, cut into ½ inch/1 cm pieces

2 tbsp vegetable oil

1 onion, finely chopped

1 garlic clove, crushed

1 large red bell pepper, seeded and finely chopped

1 large ripe avocado

1 tbsp lime juice

4 tomatoes, peeled, seeded, and chopped

1 cup grated Cheddar cheese

8 soft flour tortillas

⅔ cup sour cream

salt and pepper

cilantro sprigs to garnish

pickled green jalapeño chilies, to serve

SAUCE

3½ cups sugocasa

3 tbsp chopped parsley

3 tbsp chopped cilantro

1 Mix the chili powder, paprika, flour, and salt and pepper on a plate and coat the bean curd pieces.

2 Heat the oil in a skillet and gently cook the bean curd for 3–4 minutes, until golden. Remove with a slotted spoon, drain on paper towels, and set aside.

3 Add the onion, garlic, and bell pepper to the oil and cook for 2–3 minutes, until just soft. Drain and set aside.

4 Halve the avocado, peel, and remove the pit. Slice lengthwise, put in a bowl with the lime juice, and toss to coat.

5 Add the bean curd and onion mixture and gently stir in the chopped tomatoes and half the grated Cheddar cheese. Spoon one-eighth of the filling down the center of each tortilla, top with sour cream, and roll up.

6 Arrange the tortillas, seam-side down, in a shallow ovenproof dish in a single layer.

7 To make the sauce, mix together all the ingredients. Spoon the sauce over the tortillas, sprinkle with the remaining grated cheese, and bake in a preheated oven, 375°F/190°C, for 25 minutes, until the cheese is golden brown and bubbling.

8 Garnish the chili bean curd with cilantro sprigs and serve immediately with pickled jalapeño chilies.

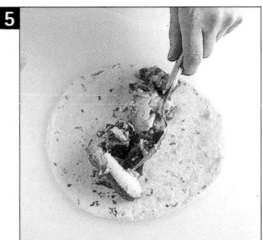
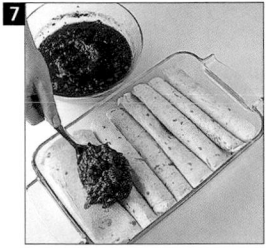

Layered Pies

These individual pies of layered potato, eggplant, and zucchini baked in a tomato sauce can be made in advance, so are good for entertaining.

NUTRITIONAL INFORMATION

Calories ....427 Sugars 8g
Protein ....22g Fat 21g
Carbohydrate ...41g Saturates 8g

40 mins   1 hr 20 mins

SERVES 4

INGREDIENTS

3 large waxy potatoes, thinly sliced

1 small eggplant, thinly sliced

1 zucchini, sliced

3 tbsp vegetable oil

1 onion, diced

1 green bell pepper, seeded and diced

1 tsp cumin seeds

2 tbsp chopped fresh basil

1 cup canned chopped tomatoes

salt and pepper

6 oz/175 g mozzarella cheese, sliced

8 oz/225 g bean curd, sliced

1 cup fresh white bread crumbs

2 tbsp grated Parmesan cheese

fresh basil leaves, to garnish

1 Cook the sliced potatoes in a pan of boiling water for 5 minutes. Drain and set aside.

2 Put the eggplant slices on a plate, sprinkle with salt, and let stand for 20 minutes. Meanwhile, blanch the zucchini in a pan of boiling water for 2-3 minutes. Drain and set aside.

3 Meanwhile, heat 2 tablespoons of the oil in a skillet. Add the onion and cook over low heat, stirring occasionally, for 2-3 minutes until soft. Add the bell pepper, cumin seeds, basil, and canned tomatoes. Season to taste with salt and pepper and simmer for 30 minutes.

4 Rinse the eggplant slices thoroughly under cold running water and pat dry with paper towels. Heat the remaining oil in a large skillet. Add the eggplant slices and cook over medium heat for 3-5 minutes, turning to brown both sides. Drain and set aside.

5 Arrange half of the potato slices in the base of 4 small loose-based tart pans. Cover with half of the zucchini slices, half of the eggplant slices, and half of the mozzarella slices. Lay the bean curd on top and spoon over the tomato sauce. Repeat the layers of vegetables and cheese in the same order.

6 Combine the bread crumbs and grated Parmesan cheese and sprinkle over the top. Cook in a preheated oven, 375°F/ 190°C, for 25-30 minutes or until golden. Garnish the pies with fresh basil leaves and serve immediately.

Provençal Bean Stew

Bursting with Mediterranean flavors, this colorful stew is delicious served with slices of warm garlic bread.

NUTRITIONAL INFORMATION

Calories	420	Sugars	........11g
Protein	........22g	Fat	..........9g
Carbohydrate	...64g	Saturates	.......1g

 20 mins   2½ hours

SERVES 4

INGREDIENTS

1¾ cups dried pinto beans, soaked overnight in water to cover

2 tbsp olive oil

2 onions, sliced

2 garlic cloves, finely chopped

1 red bell pepper, seeded and sliced

1 yellow bell pepper, seeded and sliced

2 cups canned chopped tomatoes

2 tbsp tomato paste

1 tbsp torn fresh basil leaves

2 tsp chopped fresh thyme

2 tsp chopped fresh rosemary

1 bay leaf

salt and pepper

⅓ cup black olives, pitted and halved

2 tbsp chopped fresh parsley, to garnish

1 Drain the beans and place in a large pan. Add cold water to cover and bring to a boil. Boil for 15 minutes, then cover and simmer for 1¼ hours, until almost tender. Drain, reserving 1¼ cups of the cooking liquid.

2 Heat the olive oil in a heavy pan. Add the onions and cook, stirring occasionally, for 5 minutes, until soft. Add the garlic and bell peppers and cook, stirring frequently, for 10 minutes.

3 Add the tomatoes with their can juice, the tomato paste, basil, thyme, rosemary, bay leaf, and beans and season to taste with salt and pepper. Cover and simmer for 40 minutes. Add the olives and simmer for 5 minutes more.

4 Transfer the stew to a warm serving dish, sprinkle with the parsley and serve immediately.

VARIATION
You could substitute other beans for the pinto beans in this recipe, such as borlotti, cannellini, or haricot, or use a mixture of different types.

Mushroom Gougère

A gougère is a savory round of choux pastry, usually flavored with cheese. This dish is equally good served warm or cold.

NUTRITIONAL INFORMATION

Calories 490   Sugars 4g
Protein ....14g   Fat 39g
Carbohydrate ...21g   Saturates 13g

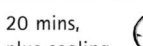

20 mins, plus cooling

1 hr

SERVES 4

I N G R E D I E N T S

C H O U X   P A S T R Y

½ cup strong white flour

4 tbsp butter, plus extra for greasing

⅔ cup water

2 eggs

½ cup grated Swiss cheese

F I L L I N G

2 tbsp olive oil

1 onion, chopped

8 oz/225 g crimini mushrooms, sliced

2 garlic cloves, finely chopped

1 tbsp all-purpose flour

⅔ cup vegetable bouillon

¾ cup walnuts, chopped

2 tbsp chopped fresh parsley

salt and pepper

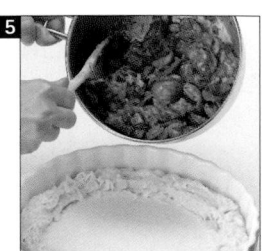

1 To make the choux pastry, strain the flour with a pinch of salt on to a sheet of waxed paper. Heat the butter and water in a heavy pan until the butter melts, but do not let the water boil. Add the flour all at once and beat vigorously with a wooden spoon until the mixture is smooth and comes away from the sides of the pan.

2 Remove the pan from the heat and let cool for 10 minutes, then gradually beat in the eggs until smooth and glossy. Beat in the cheese. Grease a round ovenproof dish with butter and spoon the choux pastry around the sides.

3 To make the filling, heat the oil in a large, heavy skillet. Add the onion and cook, stirring occasionally, for 5 minutes, until soft. Add the mushrooms and garlic and cook for 2 minutes. Stir in the flour and cook, stirring, for 1 minute, then gradually stir in the bouillon. Bring to a boil, stirring constantly, and cook for 3 minutes, until thickened.

4 Reserve 2 tablespoons of the walnuts and stir the remainder into the mushroom mixture with the parsley. Season to taste with salt and pepper.

5 Spoon the mushroom filling into the center of the dish and sprinkle the reserved walnuts over it. Bake in a preheated oven, 400°F/200°C, for about 40 minutes, until risen and golden brown. Serve immediately.

Green Vegetable Gougère

A tasty, simple supper dish of choux pastry and crisp green vegetables.
The choux pastry ring can be filled with all kinds of vegetables.

 30 mins   40 mins

SERVES 4

I N G R E D I E N T S

1 cup all-purpose flour

½ cup plus 1 tbsp butter

1¼ cups water

4 eggs, beaten

¾ cup Swiss cheese, grated

salt and pepper

1 tbsp milk

FILLING

2 tbsp garlic and herb butter or margarine

2 tsp olive oil

2 leeks, shredded

2 cups green cabbage, finely shredded

1½ cups beansprouts

½ tsp grated lime zest

1 tbsp lime juice

celery salt and pepper

lime slices, to garnish

1 Strain the flour on to a piece of baking parchment. Cut the butter into dice and put in a pan with the water. Heat until the butter has melted.

2 Do not let the water boil, and tip in the flour all at once. Beat until the mixture becomes thick. Remove from the heat and continue to beat until the mixture is glossy and comes away from the sides of the pan.

3 Transfer to a mixing bowl and cool for 10 minutes. Gradually beat in the eggs, a little at a time, making sure they are thoroughly incorporated after each addition. Stir in ½ cup of the cheese and season with salt and pepper.

4 Place spoonfuls of the mixture in a 9 inch/23 cm circle on a dampened cookie sheet. Brush with milk and sprinkle with the remaining cheese.

5 Bake in a preheated oven, 425°F/ 220°C, for 30–35 minutes, until golden and crisp. Transfer to a warmed serving plate.

6 Meanwhile, make the filling. Heat the butter or margarine and the olive oil in a large skillet and stir-fry the leeks and cabbage for 2 minutes. Add the beansprouts, lime zest, and juice and stir-fry for 1 minute. Season to taste.

7 Pile into the center of the pastry ring. Garnish with lime slices and serve.

Vegetable Strudels

These strudels look really impressive and are perfect if friends are coming round or for a more formal dinner party dish.

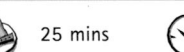 25 mins   30 mins

SERVES 4

INGREDIENTS

FILLING

2 tbsp vegetable oil

2 tbsp butter

¾ finely cup diced potatoes

1 leek, shredded

2 garlic cloves, crushed

1 tsp garam masala

½ tsp chili powder

½ tsp turmeric

¼ cup okra, sliced

1½ cups sliced white mushrooms

2 tomatoes, diced

8 oz/225 g firm bean curd, diced

salt and pepper

FILLING

¾ lb/350 g phyllo pastry

2 tbsp butter, melted

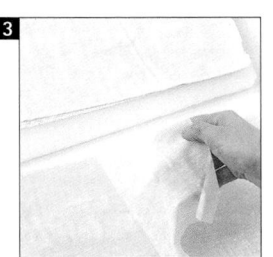
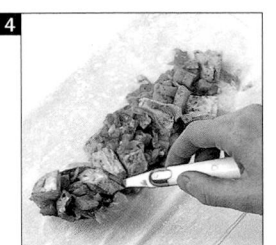

1 To make the filling, heat the vegetable oil and butter in a skillet. Add the potatoes and leek to the skillet and cook, stirring constantly, for 2–3 minutes. Add the garlic and spices, okra, mushrooms, tomatoes, and bean curd, and season to taste with salt and pepper. Cook, stirring, for 5–7 minutes, or until the mixture is tender.

2 Lay the pastry out on a cutting board and brush each individual sheet with melted butter. Place 3 sheets on top of one another; repeat to make 4 stacks.

3 Spoon a quarter of the filling along the center of each stack and brush the edges with melted butter. Fold the short edges in and roll up lengthwise to form a cigar shape. Brush the outside with melted butter. Place the strudels on a greased cookie sheet.

4 Cook in a preheated oven, 375°F/ 190°C, for 20 minutes, or until the strudels are golden brown and crisp. Transfer them to a warm serving dish and serve immediately.

Bread & Butter Savory

Quick, simple, nutritious, and a pleasure to eat—what more could you ask for an inexpensive midweek meal?

NUTRITIONAL INFORMATION

Calories	472	Sugars	.........7g
Protein	........22g	Fat	..........33g
Carbohydrate	...25g	Saturates	......20g

 30 mins   45 mins

SERVES 4

I N G R E D I E N T S

¼ cup butter or margarine

1 bunch scallions, sliced

6 slices of white or whole-wheat bread, crusts removed

1½ cups sharp Cheddar cheese, grated

2 eggs

scant 2 cups milk

salt and pepper

flat-leaf parsley sprigs, to garnish

1 Lightly grease a 2½ pint/1.5 liter ovenproof dish with a little of the butter or margarine.

2 Melt the remaining butter or margarine in a small pan. Add the scallions and cook over medium heat, stirring occasionally, until soft and golden.

3 Meanwhile, cut the bread into triangles and place half of them in the base of the dish. Cover with the sliced scallions and top with half the grated Cheddar cheese.

4 Beat together the eggs and milk and season to taste with salt and pepper. Layer the remaining triangles of bread in the dish and carefully pour over the milk mixture. Let soak for 15–20 minutes.

5 Sprinkle the remaining cheese over the soaked bread. Bake in a preheated oven, 375°F/190°C, for 35–40 minutes, until puffed up and golden brown.

6 Garnish with flat-leaf parsley and serve immediately.

VARIATION

You can vary the vegetables used in this savory bake, depending on what you have to hand. Shallots, mushrooms, or tomatoes are all suitable.

Cheese & Potato Layer Bake

This is a quick dish to prepare and it can be left to cook in the oven without needing any more attention.

NUTRITIONAL INFORMATION

Calories . . . . . . .766 Sugars 14g
Protein . . . . .44g Fat 40g
Carbohydrate . . .60g Saturates 23g

25 mins   45 mins

SERVES 4

INGREDIENTS

2 lb/900 g unpeeled waxy potatoes,
    cut into wedges

2 tbsp butter

1 red onion, halved and sliced

2 garlic cloves, crushed

¼ cup all-purpose flour

2½ cups milk

14 oz/400 g canned artichoke hearts in
    brine, drained and halved

1 generous cup frozen mixed
    vegetables, thawed

1¼ cups Swiss cheese, grated

1¼ cups sharp cheese, grated

½ cup Gorgonzola cheese, crumbled

⅓ cup Parmesan cheese, freshly grated

8 oz/225 g bean curd, sliced

2 tbsp chopped fresh thyme

salt and pepper

fresh thyme sprigs, to garnish

1 Cook the potato wedges in a pan of boiling water for 10 minutes. Drain thoroughly.

2 Meanwhile, melt the butter in a pan. Add the sliced onion and garlic and cook over low heat, stirring frequently, for 2–3 minutes.

3 Stir the flour into the pan and cook for 1 minute. Gradually add the milk and bring to a boil, stirring constantly.

4 Reduce the heat. Add the artichoke hearts, mixed vegetables, half of each of the 4 cheeses, and the bean curd to the pan, mixing well. Stir in the thyme and season with salt and pepper to taste.

5 Arrange a layer of parboiled potato wedges in the base of a shallow ovenproof dish. Spoon the vegetable mixture over the top and cover with the remaining potato wedges. Sprinkle the rest of the 4 cheeses over the top.

6 Cook in a preheated oven, 400°F/ 200°C for 30 minutes, or until the potatoes are cooked and the top is golden brown. Serve the bake garnished with fresh thyme sprigs.

White Nut Phyllo Parcels

These crisp, buttery parcels, filled with nuts and pesto, and served with cranberry sauce, would make a wonderful Sunday lunch.

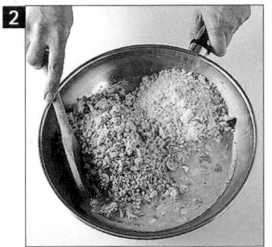
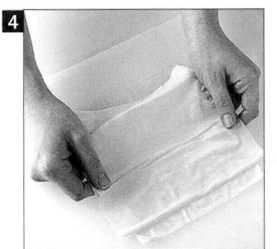
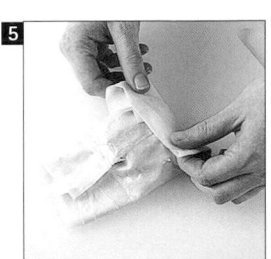

NUTRITIONAL INFORMATION

Calories 1100	Sugars 9g	
Protein 29g	Fat 80g	
Carbohydrate ...73g	Saturates 15g	

 15 mins 25 mins

SERVES 4

I N G R E D I E N T S

3 tbsp butter or margarine

1 large onion, finely chopped

2 cups mixed white nuts, such as pine nuts, unsalted cashew nuts, blanched almonds, and unsalted peanuts, finely chopped

1½ cups fresh white bread crumbs

½ tsp ground mace

1 egg, beaten

salt and pepper

1 egg yolk

3 tbsp pesto sauce

2 tbsp chopped basil

9 tbsp butter or margarine, melted

16 sheets phyllo pastry

fresh basil sprigs to garnish

TO SERVE

cranberry sauce

steamed vegetables

1 Melt the butter or margarine in a skillet, add the onion, and gently cook for 2–3 minutes, until soft but not brown.

2 Remove from the heat and stir in the nuts, two-thirds of the bread crumbs, the mace, and beaten egg. Season to taste with salt and pepper. Set aside.

3 Place the remaining bread crumbs in a bowl and stir in the egg yolk, pesto sauce, basil, and 1 tablespoon of the melted butter or margarine. Mix well.

4 Brush 1 sheet of phyllo pastry with melted butter or margarine. Fold in half and brush again. Repeat with a second sheet and lay it on top of the first one so that it forms a cross.

5 Put one-eighth of the nut mixture in the centre of the pastry. Top with one-eighth of the pesto mixture. Fold over the edges, brushing with more butter or margarine, to form a parcel. Brush the top with butter or margarine and transfer to a cookie sheet. Make eight parcels in the same way and brush with the remaining butter or margarine.

6 Bake in a preheated oven at 425°F/ 220°C for 15–20 minutes, until golden. Transfer to serving plates, garnish with basil sprigs, and serve with cranberry sauce and steamed vegetables.

Green Easter Pie

This traditional Easter risotto pie is from the Piedmont region in northern Italy. Serve it warm or chilled in slices.

NUTRITIONAL INFORMATION

Calories	392	Sugars	.........3g
Protein	........17g	Fat	..........17g
Carbohydrate	...41g	Saturates	.......5g

25 mins   50 mins

SERVES 4

I N G R E D I E N T S

butter, for greasing

3 oz/85 g arugula leaves

2 tbsp olive oil

1 onion, chopped

2 garlic cloves, chopped

1 cup risotto rice

3 cups hot vegetable bouillon

½ cup dry white wine

⅔ cup freshly grated Parmesan cheese

1 cup frozen peas, thawed

2 tomatoes, diced

4 eggs, beaten

3 tbsp chopped fresh marjoram

salt and pepper

1 cup fresh bread crumbs

1 Lightly grease a 9 inch/23 cm deep cake pan and line the base.

2 Using a sharp knife, coarsely chop the arugula leaves.

3 Heat the oil in a skillet and cook the onion and garlic over low heat for 4–5 minutes or until soft.

4 Add the rice to the skillet, mix well to combine, then begin adding the bouillon a ladleful at a time. Wait until each ladleful of bouillon has been absorbed before adding the next.

5 Continue to cook the mixture, adding the wine, until the rice is tender. This will take at least 15 minutes. Remove the skillet from the heat.

6 Stir in the Parmesan cheese, peas, arugula leaves, tomatoes, eggs, and 2 tablespoons of the marjoram. Season to taste with salt and pepper.

7 Spoon the risotto into the prepared pan and level the surface by pressing down with the back of a wooden spoon.

8 Top with the bread crumbs and the remaining marjoram.

9 Bake in a preheated oven, 350°F/180°C, for 30 minutes or until set. Cut into slices and serve.

Root Croustades

This colorful combination of grated root vegetables and mixed bell peppers would make a stunning dinner-party dish.

NUTRITIONAL INFORMATION

Calories	304	Sugars	........17g
Protein	.........6g	Fat	..........19g
Carbohydrate	...28g	Saturates	.......3g

 2½ hrs   1¼ hrs

SERVES 4

INGREDIENTS

1 orange bell pepper

1 red bell pepper

1 yellow bell pepper

3 tbsp olive oil

2 tbsp red wine vinegar

1 tsp French mustard

1 tsp clear honey

salt and pepper

fresh flat-leaf parsley sprigs, to garnish

green vegetables, to serve

CROUSTADES

1½ cups potatoes, coarsely grated

1½ cups carrots, coarsely grated

2¼ cups celery root, coarsely grated

1 garlic clove, crushed

1 tbsp lemon juice

2 tbsp butter or margarine, melted

1 egg, beaten

1 tbsp vegetable oil

1 Place the bell peppers on a cookie sheet and bake in a preheated oven, 375°F/190°C, for 35 minutes, turning after 20 minutes.

2 Cover with a dish cloth and let cool for 10 minutes.

3 Peel the skin from the cooked bell peppers; cut in half and discard the seeds. Thinly slice the flesh into strips and place in a shallow dish.

4 Put the oil, vinegar, mustard, honey and seasoning in a small screw-top jar and shake well to mix. Pour over the bell pepper strips, mix well, and let marinate for 2 hours.

5 To make the croustades, put the grated potatoes, carrots, and celery root in a mixing bowl and toss in the crushed garlic and lemon juice.

6 Mix in the melted butter or margarine and the egg. Season to taste with salt and pepper. Divide the mixture into 8 and pile on to 2 cookie sheets lined with baking parchment, forming each into a 4 inch/10 cm round. Brush with oil.

7 Bake in a preheated oven, 425°F/220°C, for 30–35 minutes, until the croustades are crisp around the edges and golden. Carefully transfer to a warmed serving dish.

8 Heat the bell peppers and the marinade for 2–3 minutes until warmed through. Spoon the bell peppers over the croustades, garnish with flat-leaf parsley and serve at once.

Spicy Potato & Nut Terrine

This delicious baked terrine has a base of mashed potato flavored with nuts, cheese, herbs, and spices.

NUTRITIONAL INFORMATION

Calories 1100	Sugars 13g	
Protein 34g	Fat 93g	
Carbohydrate . . .31g	Saturates 22g	

15 mins   1 hr 20 mins

SERVES 4

I N G R E D I E N T S

2 tbsp butter, plus extra for greasing

1½ cups mealy potatoes, diced

2 cups shelled pecan nuts

2 cups unsalted cashew nuts

1 onion, finely chopped

2 garlic cloves, crushed

2 cups open-cap mushrooms, diced

2 tbsp chopped fresh mixed herbs

1 tsp paprika

1 tsp ground cumin

1 tsp ground coriander

4 eggs, beaten

½ cup full-fat soft cheese

⅔ cup freshly grated Parmesan cheese

salt and pepper

S A U C E

3 large tomatoes, peeled, seeded, and chopped

2 tbsp tomato paste

5 tbsp red wine

1 tbsp red wine vinegar

pinch of superfine sugar

1 Lightly grease a 2 lb/900 g loaf pan with a little butter and line it with baking parchment.

2 Cook the potatoes in a large pan of lightly salted boiling water for 10 minutes or until cooked through. Drain and mash thoroughly.

3 Finely chop the pecan and cashew nuts or process in a food processor. Mix the nuts with the onion, garlic, and mushrooms. Melt the butter in a skillet and cook the nut mixture for 5–7 minutes. Add the herbs and spices. Stir in the eggs, cheeses, and potatoes and season to taste with salt and pepper.

4 Spoon the mixture into the prepared loaf pan, pressing it down quite firmly. Cook in a preheated oven, 375°F/190°C, for 1 hour or until set.

5 To make the sauce, mix the tomatoes, tomato paste, wine, wine vinegar, and sugar in a pan and bring to a boil, stirring constantly. Cook for 10 minutes, or until the tomatoes have reduced. Press the sauce through a strainer or process in a food processor for 30 seconds. Turn the terrine out of the pan onto a serving plate and cut into slices. Serve with the tomato sauce.

Roasted Bell Pepper Terrine

Serve this terrine for Sunday lunch with Italian bread and a green salad. You can use a hot broiler instead of a barbecue to cook the vegetables.

NUTRITIONAL INFORMATION

Calories	196	Sugars	.........6g
Protein	.........6g	Fat	..........14g
Carbohydrate	...13g	Saturates	.......3g

 30 mins   30 mins

SERVES 8

INGREDIENTS

3 cups fava beans

6 red bell peppers, halved and seeded

3 small zucchini, sliced lengthwise

1 eggplant, sliced lengthwise

3 leeks, halved lengthwise

6 tbsp olive oil, plus extra for greasing

salt and pepper

6 tbsp light cream

2 tbsp chopped fresh basil

1 Grease a 5 cup/1.5 liter terrine. Blanch the fava beans in boiling water for 1–2 minutes and pop them out of their skins. It is not essential to do this, but the effort is worthwhile as the beans taste a lot sweeter.

2 Roast the red bell peppers over a hot grill, turning, until the skin is black—about 10–15 minutes. Remove and put into a plastic bag. Seal and set aside.

3 Brush the zucchini, eggplant, and leeks with 5 tablespoons of the olive oil, and season with salt and pepper to taste. Cook over the hot grill until tender, about 8–10 minutes, turning once.

4 Purée the fava beans in a blender or food processor with 1 tablespoon of the olive oil, the cream, and seasoning. Alternatively, chop and then press through a strainer.

5 Remove the red bell peppers from the bag, peel them, and put a layer along the bottom and up the sides of the terrine.

6 Spread a third of the bean purée over the bell pepper. Cover with the eggplant slices and spread over half of the remaining bean purée.

7 Sprinkle over the basil. Top with zucchini and the remaining bean purée. Lay the leeks on top. Add any remaining pieces of red bell pepper. Put a piece of foil, folded 4 times, on the top and weigh down with cans.

8 Chill until required. Turn out on to a serving platter, slice and serve with Italian bread and salad greens.

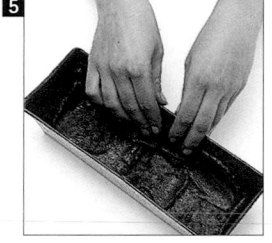

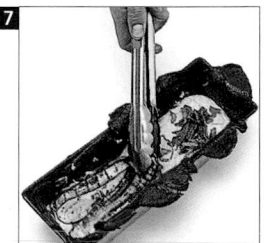

Mushroom & Nut Crumble

A filling, tasty dish that is ideal for a warming family supper.
The crunchy topping is flavored with three different types of nuts.

NUTRITIONAL INFORMATION

Calories	779	Sugars	.........5g
Protein	........16g	Fat	..........59g
Carbohydrate	...48g	Saturates	......14g

20 mins   55 mins

SERVES 4

I N G R E D I E N T S

6 cups open-cap mushrooms, sliced

6 cups crimini mushrooms, sliced

1¾ cups vegetable bouillon

4 tbsp butter or margarine

1 large onion, finely chopped

1 garlic clove, crushed

8 tbsp all-purpose flour

salt and pepper

4 tbsp heavy cream

2 tbsp chopped fresh parsley

fresh herbs, to garnish

C R U M B L E   T O P P I N G

1 generous ½ cup medium oatmeal

½ cup whole-wheat flour

⅓ cup ground almonds

¼ cup finely chopped walnuts

½ cup finely chopped unsalted shelled
  pistachio nuts

1 tsp dried thyme

salt and pepper

6 tbsp butter or margarine, softened

1 tbsp fennel seeds

1 Put the mushrooms and bouillon in a large pan, bring to a boil, cover, and simmer for 15 minutes, until tender. Drain, reserving the bouillon.

2 In another pan, melt the butter or margarine and cook the onion and garlic for 2–3 minutes, until just soft. Stir in the flour and cook for 1 minute.

3 Remove from the heat and gradually stir in the reserved mushroom bouillon. Return to the heat and cook, stirring, until thickened. Add the mushrooms, seasoning, cream, and parsley, stir to combine, and spoon into a shallow ovenproof dish.

4 To make the topping, mix together in a bowl the medium oatmeal, flour, nuts, and thyme and season with plenty of salt and pepper to taste.

5 Using a fork, mix in the butter or margarine until the topping resembles coarse bread crumbs.

6 Sprinkle the topping mixture evenly over the mushrooms and then sprinkle with the fennel seeds. Bake in a preheated oven, 375°F/190°C, for about 25–30 minutes, or until the topping is golden and crisp. Garnish with fresh herbs and serve immediately.

Vegetable Toad-in-the-Hole

This satisfying dish can be cooked in a single large dish or in four individual muffin pans.

NUTRITIONAL INFORMATION

Calories	.313	Sugars	.9g
Protein	.9g	Fat	.18g
Carbohydrate	.31g	Saturates	.7g

15 mins

55 mins

SERVES 4

INGREDIENTS

BATTER

¾ cup all-purpose flour

salt

2 eggs, beaten

¾ cup milk

2 tbsp whole-grain mustard

2 tbsp vegetable oil

FILLING

2 tbsp butter

2 garlic cloves, crushed

1 onion, cut into eight

3 oz/85 g baby carrots, halved lengthwise

⅔ cup green beans

¼ cup canned corn kernels, drained

2 tomatoes, seeded and cut into chunks

1 tsp whole-grain mustard

1 tbsp chopped fresh mixed herbs

salt and pepper

1 To make the batter, strain the flour and a pinch of salt into a bowl. Beat in the eggs and milk to make a batter. Stir in the mustard and let stand.

2 Pour the oil into a shallow ovenproof dish and heat in a preheated oven, 400°F/200°C, for 10 minutes.

3 To make the filling, melt the butter in a skillet and sauté the garlic and onion, stirring constantly, for 2 minutes. Cook the carrots and beans in a pan of boiling water for 7 minutes, or until tender. Drain well.

4 Add the corn and tomatoes to the skillet with the mustard and chopped mixed herbs. Season well and add the carrots and beans.

5 Remove the heated dish from the oven and pour in the batter. Spoon the vegetables into the center, return to the oven, and cook for 30–35 minutes, until the batter has risen and set. Serve the vegetable toad-in-the-hole immediately.

Elizabethan Artichoke Pie

The filling of Jerusalem artichokes, grapes, onion, dates, and hard-cooked eggs is an unusual but delicious blend of flavors.

NUTRITIONAL INFORMATION

Calories 136	Sugars 8g
Protein 6g	Fat 6g
Carbohydrate ...16g	Saturates 3g

 1¼ hrs   55 mins

SERVES 6

I N G R E D I E N T S

¾ lb/350 g Jerusalem artichokes

2 tbsp butter or margarine

1 onion, chopped

1–2 garlic cloves, crushed

about 30 white seedless grapes, halved

⅓ cup dates, roughly chopped

2 hard-cooked eggs, sliced

1 tbsp chopped fresh mixed herbs or
    1 tsp dried herbs

4–6 tbsp light cream or unsweetened
    yogurt

SHORTCRUST PIE DOUGH

2¼ cups all-purpose flour

good pinch of salt

6 tbsp butter or margarine

6 tbsp white vegetable fat

4–6 tbsp cold water

beaten egg or milk, to glaze

1 To make the pie dough, strain the flour and salt into a bowl, rub in the butter or margarine and vegetable fat until the mixture resembles fine bread crumbs, then add sufficient water to mix to a pliable dough. Knead lightly. Wrap in foil or plastic wrap and chill for 30 minutes.

2 Peel the artichokes, plunging them immediately into salted water to prevent discoloration. Drain, cover with fresh water, bring to a boil, and simmer for 10–12 minutes until just tender. Drain.

3 Heat the butter or margarine in a pan and cook the onion and garlic until soft but not colored. Remove from the heat and stir in the grapes and dates.

4 Roll out almost two-thirds of the pie dough and use to line an 8 inch/ 20 cm pie dish. Slice the artichokes and arrange in the pie dish, then cover with slices of egg and then with the onion mixture, seasoning, and herbs.

5 Roll out the remaining pastry, dampen the edges, and use to cover the pie; press the edges firmly together, then trim and crimp. Roll out the trimmings and cut into narrow strips. Arrange a lattice over the top of the pie, dampening the strips to attach them.

6 Glaze with beaten egg or milk and make 2–3 holes in the lid. Bake in a preheated oven at 400°F/200°C for 40–50 minutes until golden. Gently heat the cream or yogurt and pour into the pie through the holes in the lid, then serve immediately.

Nutty Harvest Loaf

This attractive and nutritious loaf is also utterly delicious.
Served with a fresh tomato sauce, it can be eaten hot or cold with salad.

NUTRITIONAL INFORMATION

Calories	554	Sugars	........12g
Protein	........16g	Fat	..........37g
Carbohydrate	...43g	Saturates	......16g

 20 mins 1½ hrs

SERVES 4

INGREDIENTS

2 tbsp butter, plus extra for greasing

1 lb/450 g mealy potatoes, diced

1 onion, chopped

2 garlic cloves, crushed

1 cup unsalted peanuts

1½ cups fresh white bread crumbs

1 egg, beaten

2 tbsp chopped fresh cilantro

⅔ cup vegetable bouillon

generous 1 cup mushrooms, sliced

2 oz sun-dried tomatoes in oil,
   drained and sliced

salt and pepper

SAUCE

⅔ cup crème fraîche

2 tsp tomato paste

2 tsp honey

2 tbsp chopped fresh cilantro

1 Grease a 1 lb/450 g loaf pan. Cook the potatoes in a pan of boiling water for 10 minutes, until cooked through. Drain well, mash, and set aside.

2 Melt half of the butter in a skillet. Add the onion and garlic and cook gently for 2–3 minutes until soft. Finely chop the nuts or process them in a food processor for 30 seconds with the bread crumbs.

3 Mix the chopped nuts and bread crumbs into the potatoes with the egg, cilantro, and vegetable bouillon. Stir in the onion and garlic and season.

4 Melt the remaining butter in the skillet, add the sliced mushrooms, and cook for 2–3 minutes.

5 Press half of the potato mixture into the base of the prepared loaf pan. Spoon the mushrooms on top and sprinkle with the sun-dried tomatoes. Spoon the remaining potato mixture on top and smooth the surface. Cover with foil and bake in a preheated oven, 375°F/190°C, for 1 hour or until firm to the touch.

6 Meanwhile, mix the sauce ingredients together. Cut the nutty harvest loaf into slices and serve with the sauce.

Roasted Bell Pepper Tart

This tastes truly delicious, the flavor of roasted vegetables being entirely different from that of boiled or fried.

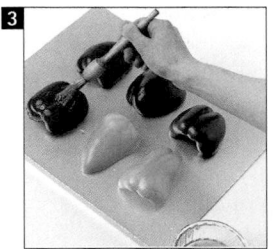

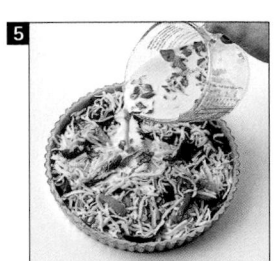

NUTRITIONAL INFORMATION

Calories 237   Sugars 3g
Protein ....6g   Fat 15g
Carbohydrate ...20g   Saturates 4g

 25 mins   40 mins

SERVES 8

I N G R E D I E N T S

PIE DOUGH

1 generous cup all-purpose flour

pinch of salt

6 tbsp butter or margarine

2 tbsp green olives, pitted and finely chopped

3 tbsp cold water

FILLING

1 red bell pepper

1 green bell pepper

1 yellow bell pepper

2 garlic cloves, crushed

2 tbsp olive oil

1 scant cup mozzarella cheese, grated

2 eggs

⅔ cup milk

1 tbsp chopped fresh basil

salt and pepper

1 To make the pastry, strain the flour and salt into a bowl. Rub in the butter or margarine until the mixture resembles bread crumbs. Add the chopped olives and cold water, bringing the mixture together to form a dough.

2 Roll the dough out on a floured counter and use to line an 8 inch/ 20 cm loose-based quiche pan. Prick the base with a fork and let chill.

3 Cut the bell peppers in half lengthwise, seed them, and place, skin side uppermost, on a cookie sheet. Mix the garlic and oil and brush over the bell peppers. Cook in a preheated oven, 400°F/200°C, for 20 minutes, or until beginning to char slightly.

4 Let the bell peppers cool slightly, then thinly slice them. Arrange the slices in the pie shell, layering with the grated mozzarella cheese.

5 Beat the eggs and milk and add the basil. Season and pour over the bell peppers. Put the tart on a cookie sheet and bake in the oven for 20 minutes, or until set. Serve hot or cold.

Spinach Roulade

A delicious savory roll, stuffed with mozzarella and broccoli. Serve as an entrée or as an appetizer, in which case it would easily serve six.

NUTRITIONAL INFORMATION

Calories 287	Sugars 8g	
Protein 23g	Fat 12g	
Carbohydrate 8g	Saturates 6g	

 15 mins   25 mins

SERVES 4

I N G R E D I E N T S

1 lb/450 g small fresh spinach leaves

2 tbsp water

4 eggs, separated

salt and pepper

½ tsp ground nutmeg

1¼ cups sugocasa, to serve

F I L L I N G

1¾ cups small broccoli florets

¼ cup Parmesan cheese, freshly grated

1½ cups mozzarella cheese, grated

1 Wash the spinach and pack, still wet, into a large pan. Add the water. Cover the pan with a tight-fitting lid and cook the spinach over high heat for 4–5 minutes, until reduced and soft. Drain thoroughly, squeezing out excess water. Chop finely and pat dry.

2 Mix the spinach with the egg yolks, seasoning, and nutmeg. Whisk the egg whites until very foamy but not too stiff, and fold into the spinach mixture.

3 Grease and base-line a 13 x 9/ 32 x 23 cm inch jelly roll pan, then line with baking parchment to come 1 inch/2.5 cm above the sides of the pan.

Spread the spinach mixture in the pan and smooth the surface with a wet spatula. Bake in a preheated oven, 425°F/220°C, for 12–15 minutes, or until firm to the touch and golden brown.

4 Meanwhile, cook the broccoli florets in lightly salted boiling water for 4–5 minutes, until just tender. Drain and keep the florets warm.

5 Sprinkle Parmesan on a sheet of baking parchment. Turn the base on to it and peel away the lining paper. Sprinkle with mozzarella and top with broccoli.

6 Hold one end of the paper and roll up the spinach base like a jelly roll. Heat the sugocasa and spoon on to warmed serving plates. Slice the roulade and place on top of the sugocasa.

Cauliflower & Broccoli Tart

This really is a tasty flan. The delicious herb pie shell may be made in advance and frozen until required.

NUTRITIONAL INFORMATION

Calories	252	Sugars	.........3g
Protein	.........7g	Fat	..........16g
Carbohydrate	...22g	Saturates	.......5g

  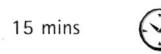

15 mins   50 mins

SERVES 4

INGREDIENTS

PASTRY

1½ cups all-purpose flour, plus extra
    for dusting

pinch of salt

½ tsp paprika

1 tsp dried thyme

6 tbsp margarine

3 tbsp water

FILLING

¾ cup cauliflower florets

1 cup broccoli florets

1 onion, cut into 8 wedges

2 tbsp butter or margarine

1 tbsp all-purpose flour

6 tbsp vegetable bouillon

½ cup milk

¾ cup Cheddar cheese, grated

salt and pepper

paprika, to garnish

1 To make the dough, strain the flour and salt into a bowl. Add the paprika and thyme and rub in the margarine. Stir in the water and bind to form a dough.

2 Roll out on a floured counter and line a 7 inch/18 cm loose-bottomed quiche pan. Prick the base and line with baking parchment. Fill with baking beans and bake in a preheated oven, 375°F/190°C, for 15 minutes. Remove the parchment and beans and return the pie shell to the oven for 5 minutes.

3 To make the filling, cook the vegetables in a pan of lightly salted boiling water for 10–12 minutes until tender. Drain and reserve.

4 Melt the butter in a pan. Add the flour and cook, stirring constantly, for 1 minute. Remove from the heat, stir in the bouillon and milk, and return to the heat. Bring to a boil, stirring constantly, and add ½ cup of the cheese. Season to taste with salt and pepper.

5 Spoon the cauliflower, broccoli, and onion into the pie shell. Pour over the sauce and sprinkle with the remaining grated cheese. Return the pie to the oven for 10 minutes until the cheese is golden and bubbling. Garnish with paprika and serve immediately.

Cheese Enchiladas

Mole sauce makes a delicious enchilada—a good reason to make yourself a big pot of Mole Poblano (see page 853).

(see page 853)

NUTRITIONAL INFORMATION

Calories	668	Sugars	.........6g
Protein	........24g	Fat	..........33g
Carbohydrate	...73g	Saturates	......13g

 15 mins   30 mins

SERVES 4

INGREDIENTS

8 corn tortillas

vegetable oil, for greasing

2 cups mole sauce

2 cups grated cheese, such as Cheddar, mozzarella, asiago or Mexican queso Oaxaco, one type or a mixture

1 cup vegetable bouillon

5 scallions, thinly sliced

2–3 tbsp chopped fresh cilantro

handful of romaine lettuce leaves, shredded

1 avocado, pitted, diced, and tossed in lime juice

4 tbsp sour cream

salsa of your choice

1 Heat the tortillas in a lightly greased nonstick skillet; wrap the heated tortillas in aluminum foil as you work to keep them warm.

2 Dip the tortillas into the mole sauce, and pile up on a plate. Fill the inside of the top sauced tortilla with a few spoonfuls of cheese. Roll up and place in a shallow ovenproof dish. Repeat this process with the remaining tortillas, reserving a handful of the cheese to sprinkle over the top.

3 Pour the rest of the mole sauce over the rolled tortillas. Pour the bouillon over the top, sprinkle with the reserved grated cheese, and cover the dish with foil.

4 Bake in a preheated oven, 375°F/ 190°C, until the tortillas are very hot and the cheese filling has melted.

5 Arrange the sliced scallions, cilantro, shredded lettuce, diced avocado, and sour cream on top. Add the salsa of your choice to taste and serve immediately.

Broccoli Enchiladas

These delicious and very nutritious enchiladas are cooked
in a mild chili sauce, and served with a hot salsa.

NUTRITIONAL INFORMATION

Calories . . . . . . .605 Sugars 7g
Protein . . . . .37g Fat 33g
Carbohydrate . . .42g Saturates 18g

20 mins

30 mins

SERVES 4

INGREDIENTS

4½ cups broccoli florets

1 x 8 oz tub ricotta cheese

1 garlic clove, chopped

½ tsp ground cumin

1½ cups grated Cheddar cheese

6–8 tbsp freshly grated Parmesan cheese

1 egg, lightly beaten

salt and pepper

4–6 flour tortillas

vegetable oil, for greasing

1 quantity Mild Red Chili Sauce
(see page 855)

1 cup vegetable bouillon

½ onion, finely chopped

3–4 tbsp chopped fresh cilantro

3 tomatoes, diced

hot salsa, to serve

1 Bring a pan of salted water to a boil, add the broccoli, bring back to a boil, and blanch for 1 minute. Drain, refresh under cold running water, then drain again. Cut off the stems, peel, and chop. Dice the heads.

2 Mix the broccoli with the ricotta cheese, garlic, cumin, and half the Cheddar and Parmesan in a bowl. Mix in the egg and season with salt and pepper.

3 Heat the tortillas in a lightly greased nonstick skillet, then wrap them in foil to keep warm.

4 Fill the tortillas with the broccoli mixture, rolling them up. Arrange the tortilla rolls in an ovenproof dish, then pour the Mild Red Chili Sauce over the top. Pour over the bouillon.

5 Top with the remaining grated cheeses and bake in a preheated oven at 375°F/190°C for about 30 minutes.

6 Serve the enchiladas sprinkled with the chopped onion, fresh cilantro, and diced tomatoes. Serve with a hot salsa.

Potatoes with Goat Cheese

This makes a really hearty and satisfying vegetarian entrée, or a luscious side dish. Goat cheese is a traditional food of Mexico.

NUTRITIONAL INFORMATION

Calories	725	Sugars	.........4g
Protein	........30g	Fat	..........43g
Carbohydrate	...56g	Saturates	.....28g

🥔 2 mins   🕐 35 mins

SERVES 4

INGREDIENTS

2¾ lbs/1.25 kg baking potatoes, peeled and cut into chunks

pinch of salt

pinch of sugar

scant 1 cup crème fraîche

½ cup vegetable bouillon

3 garlic cloves, finely chopped

a few shakes of bottled chipotle salsa, or 1 dried chipotle chile, reconstituted, seeded, and thinly sliced

8 oz/225 g goat cheese, sliced

1½ cups grated mozzarella or Cheddar cheese

⅔ cup grated Parmesan or romano cheese

1 Put the potatoes in a pan of water with the salt and sugar. Bring to a boil and cook for about 10 minutes until they are half cooked.

2 Combine the crème fraîche with the bouillon, garlic, and salsa or chile.

3 Arrange half the potatoes in a casserole. Pour half the crème fraîche sauce over the potatoes and cover with the goat cheese. Top with the remaining potatoes and sauce.

4 Sprinkle with the grated mozzarella or Cheddar cheese, then with the grated Parmesan or romano.

5 Bake in a preheated oven, 350°F/ 180°C, for about 25 minutes, until the potatoes are tender and the cheese topping is lightly golden and has become crisp in places. Serve immediately straight from the casserole.

Spicy Black-Eye Peas

This is a hearty casserole of black-eye peas in a rich, sweet tomato sauce flavored with molasses and mustard.

NUTRITIONAL INFORMATION

Calories 233   Sugars 21g
Protein ....11g   Fat 4g
Carbohydrate ...42g   Saturates 1g

 15 mins   2 hrs

SERVES 4

INGREDIENTS

2 cups black-eye peas, soaked overnight in cold water

1 tbsp vegetable oil

2 onions, chopped

1 tbsp clear honey

2 tbsp molasses

4 tbsp dark soy sauce

1 tsp dry mustard powder

4 tbsp tomato paste

scant 2 cups vegetable bouillon

1 bay leaf

1 sprig each of fresh rosemary, thyme, and sage

1 small orange

pepper

1 tbsp cornstarch

2 red bell peppers, seeded and diced

2 tbsp chopped fresh flat-leaf parsley, to garnish

crusty bread, to serve

2 Meanwhile, heat the oil in a skillet and cook the onions over low heat, stirring occasionally, for 5 minutes. Stir in the honey, molasses, soy sauce, mustard, and tomato paste. Pour in the bouillon, bring to a boil, and pour over the peas.

3 Tie the bay leaf and herbs together with string and add to the casserole. Using a vegetable peeler, pare off 3 pieces of orange zest and mix into the peas. Season with pepper, cover, and cook in a preheated oven, 300°F/150°C, for 1 hour.

4 Extract the juice from the orange and blend with the cornstarch to form a paste. Remove the casserole from the oven and stir the cornstarch paste into the peas, along with the red bell peppers. Cover, return to the oven, and cook for 1 further hour, until the sauce is rich and thick and the peas are tender. Discard the herbs and orange zest.

5 Garnish the casserole with chopped fresh parsley and serve immediately with crusty bread.

1 Rinse the peas and place in a pan. Cover with water, bring to a boil, and boil rapidly for 15 minutes. Drain and place in a casserole dish.

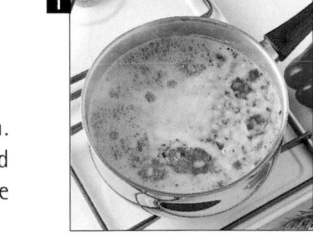  

Lentil & Red Bell Pepper Tart

This savory tart combines lentils and red bell peppers in a tasty whole-wheat shell. The tart is suitable for vegans.

NUTRITIONAL INFORMATION

Calories 374	Sugars 5g	
Protein 13g	Fat 17g	
Carbohydrate . . .44g	Saturates 7g	

 15–20 mins 50 mins

SERVES 6

INGREDIENTS

PIE DOUGH

1¾ cups whole-wheat flour

⅓ cup vegan margarine, cut into small pieces

4 tbsp water

FILLING

¾ cup red lentils, rinsed

1¼ cups vegetable bouillon

1 tbsp vegan margarine

1 onion, chopped

2 red bell peppers, seeded, and diced

1 tsp yeast extract

1 tbsp tomato paste

3 tbsp chopped fresh parsley

pepper

1 To make the pie dough, strain the flour in a mixing bowl and add any bran remaining in the strainer. Rub in the vegan margarine with your fingertips until the mixture resembles fine bread crumbs. Stir in the water and bring together to form a dough. Wrap and chill in the refrigerator for 30 minutes.

2 Meanwhile, make the filling. Put the lentils in a pan with the bouillon, bring to a boil, and then simmer for 10 minutes until the lentils are tender and can be mashed to a paste.

3 Melt the margarine in a small pan, add the chopped onion and diced red bell peppers, and cook over low heat, stirring occasionally, until just soft.

4 Add the lentil paste, yeast extract, tomato paste, and parsley. Season with pepper. Mix until well combined.

5 On a lightly floured surface, roll out the dough and line a 9½ inch/24 cm loose-bottomed flan pan. Prick the base of the pie shell with a fork and spoon in the lentil mixture.

6 Bake in a preheated oven, 400°F/ 200°C, for 30 minutes, until the filling is firm. Serve immediately.

VARIATION

Add corn kernels to the flan in step 4 for a colorful and tasty change, if you prefer.

Artichoke & Cheese Tart

Artichoke hearts are delicious to eat and are delicate in flavor and appearance. They are ideal for cooking in a cheese-flavored pie shell.

NUTRITIONAL INFORMATION

Calories	276	Sugars	.........3g
Protein	........10g	Fat	..........19g
Carbohydrate	...18g	Saturates	......10g

 15 mins   30 mins

SERVES 8

INGREDIENTS

1½ cups all-purpose whole-wheat flour, plus extra for dusting

pinch of salt

2 garlic cloves, crushed

6 tbsp butter or margarine

3 tbsp water

FILLING

2 tbsp olive oil

1 red onion, halved and sliced

10 canned artichoke hearts

scant 1 cup Cheddar cheese, grated

½ cup Gorgonzola cheese, crumbled

2 eggs, beaten

1 tbsp chopped fresh rosemary

⅔ cup milk

salt and pepper

1 To make the dough, strain the flour into a mixing bowl, add a pinch of salt and the garlic. Rub in the butter or margarine with the fingertips until the mixture resembles bread crumbs. Stir in the water and bring the mixture together to form a dough.

2 Roll out the dough on a lightly floured counter to fit an 8 inch/20 cm quiche pan. Prick the dough with a fork.

3 Heat the oil in a skillet. Add the onion and cook over medium heat, stirring occasionally, for 3 minutes. Add the artichoke hearts and cook, stirring frequently, for a further 2 minutes.

4 Combine the grated Cheddar, crumbled Gorgonzola, beaten eggs, chopped rosemary, and milk in a large bowl. Remove the artichoke and onion mixture from the pan with a draining spoon and transfer to the cheese mixture, stirring gently. Season to taste with salt and pepper.

5 Spoon the artichoke and cheese mixture into the pie shell and cook in a preheated oven, 400°F/200°C, for 25 minutes or until cooked and set. Serve the tart hot or cold.

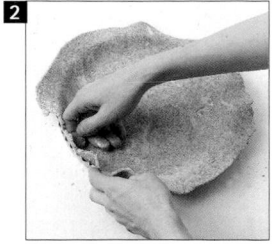

Mushroom Vol-au-Vent

A simple mixture of creamy, tender mushrooms in a crisp, rich pastry case, this dish will make an impression at any dinner party.

NUTRITIONAL INFORMATION

Calories 688	Sugars 2g
Protein 10g	Fat 52g
Carbohydrate ...45g	Saturates 22g

 25 mins   50 mins

SERVES 4

INGREDIENTS

500 g/1 lb 2 oz puff pie dough, thawed
if frozen

1 egg, beaten, for glazing

FILLING

2 tbsp butter or margarine

1½ lb/675 g mixed mushrooms,
such as open-cap, field, white, crimini,
shiitake, pied de mouton, sliced

6 tbsp dry white wine

4 tbsp heavy cream

2 tbsp chopped fresh chervil

salt and pepper

fresh chervil sprigs, to garnish

1 Roll out the puff pie dough on a lightly floured counter to make an 8 inch/20 cm square.

2 Using a sharp knife, mark a square 1 inch/2.5 cm from the pie dough edge, cutting halfway through the dough.

3 Score the top in a diagonal pattern. Knock up the edges of the pie dough with a kitchen knife and place on a cookie sheet. Brush the top with beaten egg, taking care not to let the egg run into the cut. Bake in a preheated oven, 425°F/220°C, for 35 minutes.

4 Cut out the central square. Discard the soft pastry inside the case, leaving the base intact. Return to the oven, with the square, for 10 minutes.

5 Meanwhile, make the filling. Melt the butter or margarine in a skillet and stir-fry the sliced mushrooms over high heat for 3 minutes.

6 Add the wine and cook, stirring occasionally, for 10 minutes, until the mushrooms have softened. Stir in the cream and chervil and season to taste with salt and pepper.

7 Pile into the pastry case. Top with the pastry square, garnish with sprigs of chervil, and serve.

Spinach & Ricotta Pie

This puff pastry pie looks extremely impressive, but it is actually fairly easy to make. Serve it hot or cold.

NUTRITIONAL INFORMATION

Calories	545	Sugars	.........3g
Protein	........19g	Fat	..........42g
Carbohydrate	...25g	Saturates	......13g

25 mins   50 mins

SERVES 4

I N G R E D I E N T S

8 oz/225 g fresh spinach

¼ cup pine nuts

½ cup ricotta cheese

2 large eggs, beaten

scant ½ cup ground almonds

½ cup freshly grated Parmesan cheese

9 oz puff pie dough, thawed if frozen

1 small egg, beaten

1 Rinse the spinach and place in a large pan with just the water clinging to the leaves after washing. Cook over low heat for 4–5 minutes until wilted. Drain thoroughly. When the spinach is cool enough to handle, squeeze out the excess liquid with your hands.

COOK'S TIP

Spinach must be washed very thoroughly in several changes of water to get rid of the grit and soil that can be trapped in it. Cut off any thick central ribs.

2 Place the pine nuts on a cookie sheet and lightly toast under a preheated broiler for 2–3 minutes or until golden.

3 Place the ricotta, spinach, and eggs in a bowl and mix together. Add the pine nuts, beat well, then stir in the ground almonds and Parmesan cheese.

4 Roll out the puff pie dough on a lightly floured counter and make 2 squares 8 inches/20 cm wide. Trim the edges, reserving the pastry trimmings.

5 Place 1 dough square on a cookie sheet. Spoon the spinach mixture on

top, keeping within ½ inch/1 cm of the edge of the square. Brush the edges with beaten egg and place the second square over the top.

6 Using a round-bladed knife, press the edges together by tapping along the sealed edge. Use the pie dough trimmings to make a few leaves to decorate the pie.

7 Brush the pie with the beaten egg and bake in a preheated oven, 425°F/220°C, for 10 minutes. Reduce the oven temperature to 375°F/190°C and bake for a further 25–30 minutes. Remove from the oven, let cool a little, and serve.

Cheese-Topped Risotto Tart

Risotto, combined with spinach and mozzarella cheese, makes a mouthwatering filling for this tart.

NUTRITIONAL INFORMATION

Calories	827	Sugars	.........4g
Protein	........29g	Fat	..........48g
Carbohydrate	...72g	Saturates	......30g

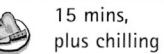

🕒 15 mins, plus chilling   ⏱ 35 mins

SERVES 6–8

I N G R E D I E N T S

SHORTCRUST PIE DOUGH

1⅓ cups all-purpose flour

½ tsp salt

1 tsp superfine sugar

½ cup sweet butter, diced

1 egg yolk, beaten with 2 tbsp iced water

FILLING

1 quantity Basic Cheesy Rice with Parmesan (see page 9), still warm

9 oz/250 g fresh spinach, cooked, drained very well, and chopped

2 tbsp heavy cream

2 cups grated mozzarella, preferably buffalo

¾ cup Parmesan cheese, freshly grated

1 To make the shortcrust pie dough, strain the flour, salt, and sugar into a large bowl and sprinkle over the butter. Rub the butter into the flour until the mixture forms coarse crumbs. Sprinkle in the egg mixture and stir to make a dough. Gather the dough into a ball, wrap in plastic wrap, and chill for at least 1 hour.

2 Gently roll out the pastry to a thickness of about ⅛ inch/3 mm, then use to line a lightly greased tart pan (9–10 inch/23–25 cm) with a removable base. Prick the bottom with a fork and chill for 1 hour.

3 Cover the tart shell with baking parchment and fill with baking beans. Bake blind in a preheated oven at 400°F/200°C for about 20 minutes until the pastry is set and the edge is golden. Remove the beans and parchment and set aside. Reduce the oven temperature to 350°F/180°C.

4 Put the cheesy rice in a bowl and stir in the spinach, cream, half the mozzarella, and half the Parmesan. Spoon into the tart shell and smooth the top. Sprinkle the remaining cheeses evenly over the tart.

5 Bake for 12–15 minutes or until cooked through and golden. Remove the tart from the oven, cool slightly on a wire rack, then serve warm.

Basic Pizza Dough

Traditionally, pizza bases are made from bread dough; this recipe will give you a base similar to an Italian pizza.

NUTRITIONAL INFORMATION

Calories 182	Sugars 2g
Protein 5g	Fat 3g
Carbohydrate ...36g	Saturates 0.5g

 1½ hrs   0 mins

SERVES 4

INGREDIENTS

½ oz/15 g fresh yeast or 1 tsp dried or active dry yeast

6 tbsp lukewarm water

½ tsp sugar

1 tbsp olive oil

1½ cups all-purpose flour, plus extra for dusting

1 tsp salt

1 Combine the fresh yeast with the water and sugar in a bowl. If using dried yeast, sprinkle it over the surface of the water and whisk in until dissolved.

2 Let stand in a warm place for 10–15 minutes until foamy on the surface. Stir in the olive oil.

3 Sift the flour and salt into a large bowl. If using active dry yeast, stir it in. Make a well in the center and pour in the yeast liquid, or water and oil (without the sugar for active dry yeast).

4 Using either floured hands or a wooden spoon, mix together to form a dough. Turn out onto a floured counter and knead for about 5 minutes or until smooth and elastic.

5 Place the dough in a large greased plastic bag and let rise in a warm place for about 1 hour or until doubled in size. An airing cupboards is often the best place for this process, as the temperature remains constant.

6 Turn out onto a lightly floured counter and punch down the dough with your fist—this releases any air bubbles, which would make the pizza uneven. Knead again 4 or 5 times. The dough is now ready to use.

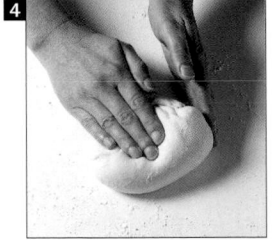

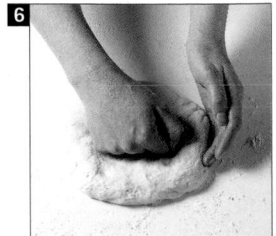

Biscuit Base

This is a quicker alternative to a bread dough base for pizza. If you do not have time to wait for bread dough to rise, a biscuit base is ideal.

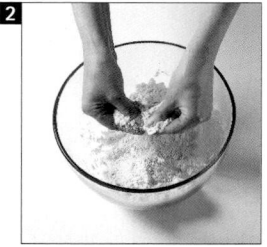
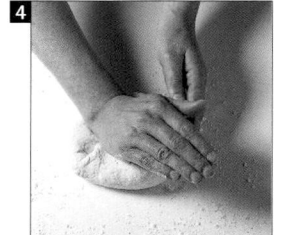

NUTRITIONAL INFORMATION

Calories 215   Sugars 3g
Protein . . . . .5g   Fat 7g
Carbohydrate . . .35g   Saturates 4g

 20 mins   0 mins

SERVES 4

INGREDIENTS

1 generous cup self-rising flour

½ tsp salt

2 tbsp butter

½ cup milk

1 Sift the flour and salt into a large mixing bowl.

2 Rub in the butter with your fingertips until it resembles fine bread crumbs.

3 Make a well in the center of the flour and butter mixture and pour in nearly all of the milk at once. Mix in quickly with a knife. Add the remaining milk only if necessary to mix to a soft dough.

4 Turn the dough out on to a floured counter and knead by turning and pressing with the heel of your hand 3 or 4 times.

5 Either roll out or press the dough into a 10 inch/25 cm circle on a lightly greased cookie sheet or pizza pan. Push up the edge slightly all round to form a ridge and use immediately.

Potato Base

This is an unusual pizza base made from mashed potatoes and flour and is a great way to use up any leftover boiled potatoes.

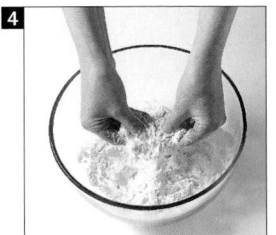

NUTRITIONAL INFORMATION

Calories	170	Sugars	1g
Protein	4g	Fat	3g
Carbohydrate	34g	Saturates	1g

 15 mins   0 mins

SERVES 4

INGREDIENTS

8 oz/225 g boiled potatoes

4 tbsp butter or margarine

¾ cup self-rising flour

½ tsp salt

1 If the potatoes are hot, mash them, then stir in the butter until melted and distributed evenly throughout the potatoes. Let cool.

2 Strain the flour and salt together and stir into the mashed potato to form a soft dough.

3 If the potatoes are cold, mash them without adding the butter.

4 Strain the flour and salt into a bowl. Rub in the butter with your fingertips until the mixture resembles fine bread crumbs, then stir the flour and butter mixture into the mashed potatoes to form a soft dough.

5 This potato base is rather tricky to lift before it is cooked, so it is better to roll it out directly on to the cookie sheet. Press the dough into a 10 inch/25 cm circle on a lightly greased cookie sheet or pizza pan, pushing up the edge slightly all round to form a ridge before adding the topping of your choice.

6 If the base is not required for cooking immediately, cover it with plastic wrap and chill it for up to 2 hours.

Tomato Sauce

This is a basic topping sauce for pizzas. Using canned chopped tomatoes for this dish saves time.

NUTRITIONAL INFORMATION

Calories 41   Sugars 3g
Protein . . . . .1g   Fat 3g
Carbohydrate . . . .3g   Saturates 0.4g

5 mins   25 mins

SERVES 4

INGREDIENTS

1 small onion, chopped

1 garlic clove, crushed

1 tbsp olive oil

1 cup canned chopped tomatoes

2 tsp tomato paste

½ tsp sugar

½ tsp dried oregano

1 bay leaf

salt and pepper

1 Cook the onion and garlic gently in the oil for 5 minutes or until soft but not browned.

2 Add the tomatoes, tomato paste, sugar, oregano, bay leaf, and salt and pepper to taste. Stir well.

3 Bring the sauce to a boil, cover, and let simmer gently for 20 minutes, stirring occasionally, until you have a thickish sauce.

4 Remove the bay leaf and season to taste. Let cool completely before using. This sauce keeps well in a screw-top jar in the refrigerator for up to 1 week.

Special Tomato Sauce

This sauce is made with fresh tomatoes. Use the plum variety whenever available and always choose the ripest ones for the best flavor.

NUTRITIONAL INFORMATION

Calories	.81	Sugars	.6g
Protein	1g	Fat	.6g
Carbohydrate	.6g	Saturates	1g

 10 mins   35 mins

SERVES 4

INGREDIENTS

1 small onion, chopped

1 small red bell pepper, seeded and chopped

1 garlic clove, crushed

2 tbsp olive oil

½ lb/225 g tomatoes

1 tbsp tomato paste

1 tsp soft brown sugar

2 tsp chopped fresh basil

½ tsp dried oregano

1 bay leaf

salt and pepper

1 Fry the onion, bell pepper, and garlic gently in the oil for 5 minutes until soft but not browned.

2 Cut a cross in the base of each tomato and place them in a bowl. Pour on boiling water and let stand for about 45 seconds. Drain, and then plunge in cold water. The skins will slide off easily.

3 Chop the tomatoes, discarding any hard green cores.

4 Add the tomatoes to the onion mixture along with the tomato paste, sugar, herbs, and salt and pepper to taste. Stir well. Bring to a boil, cover, and let simmer gently for about 30 minutes, stirring occasionally, until you have a thickish sauce.

5 Remove the bay leaf and adjust the seasoning to taste. Let cool completely before using.

6 This sauce will keep well stored in a screw-top jar in the refrigerator for up to 1 week.

 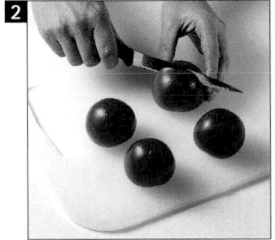 

Pizza Margherita

Pizza means "pie" in Italian. The fresh bread dough is not difficult to make but it does take a little time.

NUTRITIONAL INFORMATION

Calories ....456 Sugars 7g
Protein ....16g Fat 13g
Carbohydrate ...74g Saturates 5g

1 hr   45 mins

SERVES 4

INGREDIENTS

½ oz/15 g fresh yeast

½ tsp sugar

6 tbsp lukewarm water

1 tbsp olive oil

1½ cups all-purpose flour

1 tsp salt

TOPPING

2 cups canned tomatoes, chopped

2 garlic cloves, crushed

2 tsp dried basil

1 tbsp olive oil

2 tbsp tomato paste

scant cup mozzarella cheese, chopped

scant ½ cup Parmesan cheese, freshly grated

salt and pepper

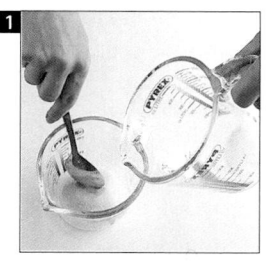

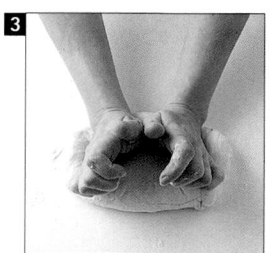

1 Combine the yeast, sugar, and 4 tablespoons of the water. Stand in a warm place for 15 minutes until foamy.

2 Mix the flour with the salt and make a well in the center. Add the oil, the yeast mixture, and the remaining water. Using a wooden spoon, mix to form a smooth dough.

3 Turn the dough out onto a floured counter and knead for 4–5 minutes or until smooth.

4 Return the dough to the bowl, cover with an oiled sheet of plastic wrap, and let rise for 30 minutes or until doubled in size.

5 Knock the air out of the dough and knead again for 2 minutes. Stretch it with your hands, then place it on an oiled cookie sheet, pushing out the edges until even. The dough should be no more than ¼ inch/5 mm thick because it will rise during cooking.

6 To make the topping, place the tomatoes, garlic, dried basil, olive oil, and salt and pepper to taste in a large skillet and simmer over low heat for about 20 minutes or until the sauce has thickened. Stir in the tomato paste and let cool slightly.

7 Spread the topping evenly over the pizza dough almost to the edge. Top with the chopped mozzarella and grated Parmesan cheese.

8 Bake in a preheated oven, 400°F/ 200°C, for 20–25 minutes until the topping is golden and bubbling. Serve hot.

Mushroom Pizza

Juicy mushrooms and stringy mozzarella top this pizza. Use exotic mushrooms or a combination of exotic and cultivated mushrooms.

NUTRITIONAL INFORMATION

Calories	302	Sugars	.........7g
Protein	........10g	Fat	..........12g
Carbohydrate	...41g	Saturates	.......4g

1¼ hrs   45 mins

SERVES 4

INGREDIENTS

1 quantity Basic Pizza Dough (see page 602)

TOPPING

½ lb/225 g mushrooms

2 cups canned chopped tomatoes

2 garlic cloves, crushed

1 tsp dried basil

1 tbsp olive oil

salt and pepper

2 tbsp tomato paste

1½ cups mozzarella cheese, grated

basil leaves, to garnish

1 Knead the Basic Pizza Dough on a lightly floured counter for 2 minutes.

2 Roll out the dough to form an oval or a circular shape, then place it on an oiled cookie sheet, pushing out the edges until even. The dough should be no more than ¼ inch/5 mm thick because it will rise during cooking.

3 Using a sharp knife, cut the mushrooms into slices.

4 To make the topping, place the tomatoes, garlic, dried basil, olive oil, and salt and pepper in a large pan and simmer for 20 minutes or until the sauce has thickened. Stir in the tomato paste and let cool slightly.

5 Spread the sauce over the pizza dough, top with the mushrooms, and scatter over the mozzarella.

6 Bake in a preheated oven, 400°F/ 200°C, for 25 minutes. Garnish with basil leaves.

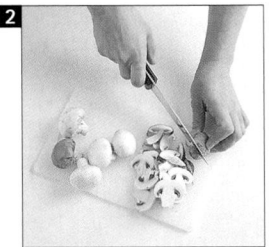

COOK'S TIP

To intensify the mushroom flavor, you could add a few dried porcini mushrooms, as they have a very concentrated flavour. Soak them in hot water before use. They are expensive, but you will need only a few.

Gorgonzola & Pumpkin Pizza

Blue Gorgonzola cheese and juicy pears combine to give a colorful pizza. The whole-wheat base adds a nutty flavor and texture.

NUTRITIONAL INFORMATION

Calories	470	Sugars	. . . . .5g
Protein	. . . . .17g	Fat	. . . . .15g
Carbohydrate	. . .72g	Saturates	. . . . . . .6g

 1¼ hrs   35 mins

SERVES 4

I N G R E D I E N T S

PIZZA DOUGH

2 tsp dried yeast

1 tsp sugar

1 cup lukewarm water

1¼ cups whole-wheat all-purpose flour

1¼ cups white bread flour

1 tsp salt

1 tbsp olive oil

TOPPING

1 lb/450 g pumpkin or squash, peeled and cubed

1 tbsp olive oil

1 pear, cored, peeled, and sliced

1 cup Gorgonzola cheese, crumbled

1 sprig fresh rosemary, to garnish

1 Place the yeast and sugar in a pitcher and mix with 4 tablespoons of the lukewarm water. Let the yeast mixture stand in a warm place for 15 minutes or until foamy.

2 Combine both of the flours with the salt and make a well in the center. Add the oil, the yeast mixture, and the remaining water. Using a wooden spoon, mix to form a dough.

3 Turn the dough out onto a floured counter and knead for 4–5 minutes or until smooth.

4 Return the dough to the bowl, cover with an oiled sheet of plastic wrap, and let rise for 30 minutes or until doubled in size.

5 Remove the dough from the bowl. Knead the dough for 2 minutes. Using a rolling pin, roll out the dough to form a long oval shape, then place it on an oiled cookie sheet, pushing out the edges until even. The dough should be no more than ¼ inch/5 mm thick because it will rise during cooking.

6 To make the topping, place the pumpkin in a shallow roasting pan. Drizzle with the olive oil and cook under a preheated broiler for 20 minutes or until soft and lightly golden.

7 Top the dough with the pear and the pumpkin, brushing with the oil from the pan. Scatter over the Gorgonzola. Bake in a preheated oven, 400°F/200°C, for 15 minutes or until the base is golden. Garnish with rosemary.

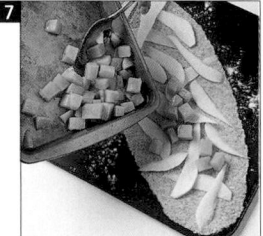

Roasted Vegetable Pizza

Wonderfully colorful vegetables are roasted in olive oil with thyme and garlic. The goat cheese adds a nutty, piquant flavour.

NUTRITIONAL INFORMATION

Calories . . . . . . .387 Sugars 9g
Protein . . . . .10g Fat 21g
Carbohydrate . . .42g Saturates 5g

2½ hrs   40 mins

SERVES 4

I N G R E D I E N T S

2 baby zucchini, halved lengthwise

2 baby eggplants, quartered lengthwise

½ red bell pepper, seeded and cut into 4 strips

½ yellow bell pepper, seeded and cut into 4 strips

1 small red onion, cut into wedges

2 garlic cloves, unpeeled

4 tbsp olive oil

1 tbsp red wine vinegar

1 tbsp chopped fresh thyme

salt and pepper

1 quantity Basic Pizza Dough (see page 602)

Basic Tomato Sauce (see page 605)

3 oz/90 g goat cheese

fresh basil leaves, to garnish

1 Place all of the prepared vegetables in a large roasting pan. Mix together the olive oil, vinegar, thyme, and plenty of seasoning and pour over, coating well.

2 Roast the vegetables in a preheated oven, at 400°F/200°C, for 15–20 minutes or until the skins have started to blacken in places, turning them over half-way through. Let rest for 5 minutes after roasting.

3 Carefully peel off the skins from the roasted bell peppers and the garlic cloves. Slice the garlic.

4 Roll out or press the dough, using a rolling pin or your hands, into a 10 inch/25 cm circle on a lightly floured counter. Place on a large greased cookie sheet or pizza pan and raise the edge a little to make a rim. Cover and let rise slightly for 10 minutes in a warm place. Spread with the tomato sauce almost to the edge.

5 Arrange the roasted vegetables on top and dot with the cheese. Drizzle the oil and juices from the roasting pan over the pizza, and season.

6 Bake in a preheated oven, at 400°F/200°C, for 18–20 minutes, or until the edge is crisp and golden, then serve immediately, garnished with basil leaves.

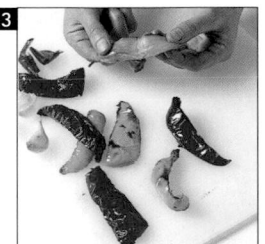

Bell Pepper & Onion Pizza

The vibrant colors of the bell peppers and red onion make this a delightful pizza. Served cut into fingers, it is ideal for a party or buffet.

NUTRITIONAL INFORMATION

Calories 380   Sugars 19g
Protein . . . . .7g   Fat 17g
Carbohydrate . . .53g   Saturates 2g

 25 mins   25 mins

SERVES 8

I N G R E D I E N T S

1 quantity Basic Pizza Dough (see page 602)

2 tbsp olive oil, plus extra for drizzling

½ red bell pepper, seeded and thinly sliced

½ green bell pepper, seeded and thinly sliced

½ yellow bell pepper, seeded and thinly sliced

1 small red onion, thinly sliced

1 garlic clove, crushed

Basic Tomato Sauce (see page 605)

3 tbsp raisins

4 tbsp pine nuts

1 tbsp chopped fresh thyme

salt and pepper

1 Roll out or press the dough, using a rolling pin or your hands, on a lightly floured counter to fit a 12 x 7 inch/ 30 x 18 cm greased jelly roll pan. Place the dough in the pan and push up the edges slightly.

2 Cover with plastic wrap and set the dough aside in a warm place for about 10 minutes to rise slightly.

3 Heat the oil in a large skillet. Add the bell peppers, onion, and garlic and cook gently for 5 minutes until they have softened. Let cool.

4 Spread the tomato sauce over the base of the pizza almost to the edge.

5 Sprinkle over the raisins and top with the cooled bell pepper mixture. Add the pine nuts and thyme. Drizzle with a little olive oil and season to taste with salt and pepper.

6 Bake in a preheated oven, 400°F/ 200°C, for 18–20 minutes, or until the edges are crisp and golden. Cut into fingers and serve immediately.

Mushroom & Walnut Pizza

Exotic mushrooms make a delicious pizza topping when mixed with walnuts and Roquefort cheese.

NUTRITIONAL INFORMATION

Calories .... .499	Sugars 9g	
Protein 13g	Fat .... .32g	
Carbohydrate ...42g	Saturates ..... .11g	

 10 mins 25 mins

SERVES 4

I N G R E D I E N T S

1 quantity Basic Pizza Dough (see page 602) or 1 x 10 inch/25 cm pizza base

Basic Tomato Sauce (see page 605)

½ cup soft cheese

1 tbsp chopped fresh mixed herbs, such as parsley, oregano, and basil

½ lb/225 g exotic mushrooms, such as oyster, shiitake, or porcini, or ¼ lb/115 g each exotic and white mushrooms

2 tbsp olive oil, plus extra for drizzling

¼ tsp fennel seeds

4 tbsp coarsely chopped walnuts

scant ½ cup blue cheese, crumbled

salt and pepper

fresh flat-leaf parsley sprig, to garnish

1 Roll out or press the pizza dough, using a rolling pin or your hands, into a 10 inch/25 cm circle on a lightly floured counter.

2 Place the pizza base on a large, greased cookie sheet or pizza pan and push up the edge a little with your fingers to form a rim.

3 Carefully spread the tomato sauce almost to the edge of the pizza dough. Dot with the soft cheese and chopped fresh herbs.

4 Wipe and slice the mushrooms. Heat the oil in a large skillet or wok and stir-fry the mushrooms and fennel seeds for 2–3 minutes. Spread over the pizza dough with the chopped walnuts.

5 Scatter the blue cheese over the pizza, drizzle with a little olive oil, and season with salt and pepper to taste.

6 Bake in a preheated oven, 400°F/200°C, for 18–20 minutes or until the edge is crisp and golden.

7 Serve the pizza immediately, garnished with a sprig of flat-leaf parsley.

Florentine Pizza

A pizza adaptation of Eggs Florentine—sliced hard-cooked eggs on freshly cooked spinach, with a crunchy almond topping.

NUTRITIONAL INFORMATION

Calories . . . . . . .474 Sugars 7g
Protein . . . . .19g Fat 26g
Carbohydrate . . .43g Saturates 7.5g

 20 mins   20 mins

SERVES 4

INGREDIENTS

1 quantity Basic Pizza Dough (see page 602) or 1 x 10 inch/25 cm pizza base

3 tbsp olive oil, plus extra for drizzling

2 tbsp freshly grated Parmesan cheese

Basic Tomato Sauce (see page 605)

6 oz/175 g fresh spinach

1 small red onion, thinly sliced

¼ tsp freshly grated nutmeg

2 hard-cooked eggs

¼ cup fresh white bread crumbs

½ cup grated Jarlsberg, Cheddar, or Swiss cheese, grated

2 tbsp sliced almonds

salt and pepper

1 Roll out or press the dough, using a rolling pin or your hands, into a 10 inch/25 cm circle on a lightly floured counter. Brush with the olive oil and sprinkle with the Parmesan. Place on a large greased cookie sheet or pizza pan and push up the edge slightly. Spread the tomato sauce almost to the edge.

2 Remove the stalks from the spinach and wash the leaves thoroughly in plenty of cold water. Drain well and pat off the excess water with paper towels.

3 Heat the remaining oil and cook the onion for 5 minutes until softened. Add the spinach and cook until just wilted. Drain off any excess liquid. Arrange on the pizza and sprinkle over the nutmeg.

4 Shell and slice the eggs. Arrange the slices of egg on top of the spinach.

5 Combine the bread crumbs, cheese, and almonds and sprinkle over. Drizzle with a little olive oil and season to taste.

6 Bake in a preheated oven, 400°F/ 200°C, for 18–20 minutes or until the edge is crisp and golden. Serve the pizza immediately.

Tomato & Ricotta Pizza

This is a traditional dish from the Calabrian Mountains in southern Italy, where it is made with naturally sun-dried tomatoes and ricotta cheese.

NUTRITIONAL INFORMATION

Calories	274	Sugars	.........4g
Protein	.........8g	Fat	...........11g
Carbohydrate	...38g	Saturates	.......4g

 1¼ hrs   30 mins

SERVES 4

INGREDIENTS

1 quantity Basic Pizza Dough (see page 602)

TOPPING

4 tbsp sun-dried tomato paste

⅔ cup ricotta cheese

10 sun-dried tomatoes in oil, drained

1 tbsp fresh thyme

salt and pepper

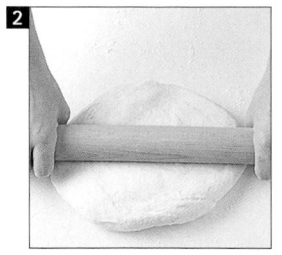

1 Knead the Basic Pizza Dough on a lightly floured counter for 2 minutes.

2 Using a rolling pin, roll out the dough to form a circle, then carefully transfer it to an oiled cookie sheet, pushing out the edges until even. The dough should be no more than about 1/4 inch/5 mm thick because it will rise during cooking.

3 Spread the sun-dried tomato paste evenly over the dough, then add spoonfuls of ricotta cheese, dotting them over the pizza.

4 Cut the drained sun-dried tomatoes into strips and arrange these on top of the pizza.

5 Sprinkle the thyme over the top of the pizza and season with salt and pepper to taste. Bake in a preheated oven, 400°F/200°C, for 30 minutes or until piping hot and the crust is golden. Serve the pizza at once.

COOK'S TIP

Sun-dried tomatoes are also available in packets. Soak them in a small bowl of hot water until softened before using. You can use the tomato-flavored water for stocks and soups.

Giardiniera Pizza

As the name implies, this colorful pizza should be topped with fresh vegetables from the garden, especially in the summer months.

NUTRITIONAL INFORMATION

Calories 362	Sugars 10g	
Protein 13g	Fat 15g	
Carbohydrate ...48g	Saturates 5g	

 15 mins   20 mins

SERVES 4

INGREDIENTS

6 spinach leaves

Bread Dough Base (see page 602) or
   1 x 10 inch/25 cm pizza base

Basic Tomato Sauce (see page 605)

1 tomato, sliced

1 celery stalk, thinly sliced

½ green bell pepper, seeded and
   thinly sliced

1 baby zucchini, sliced

1 oz/25 g asparagus tips

2½ tbsp corn, thawed if frozen

4 tbsp peas, thawed if frozen

4 scallions, trimmed and chopped

1 tbsp chopped fresh mixed herbs

½ cup grated mozzarella cheese

2 tbsp freshly grated Parmesan cheese

1 canned artichoke heart

olive oil, for drizzling

salt and pepper

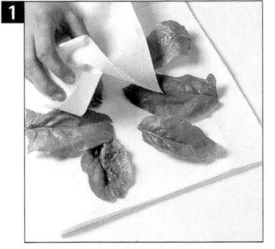  

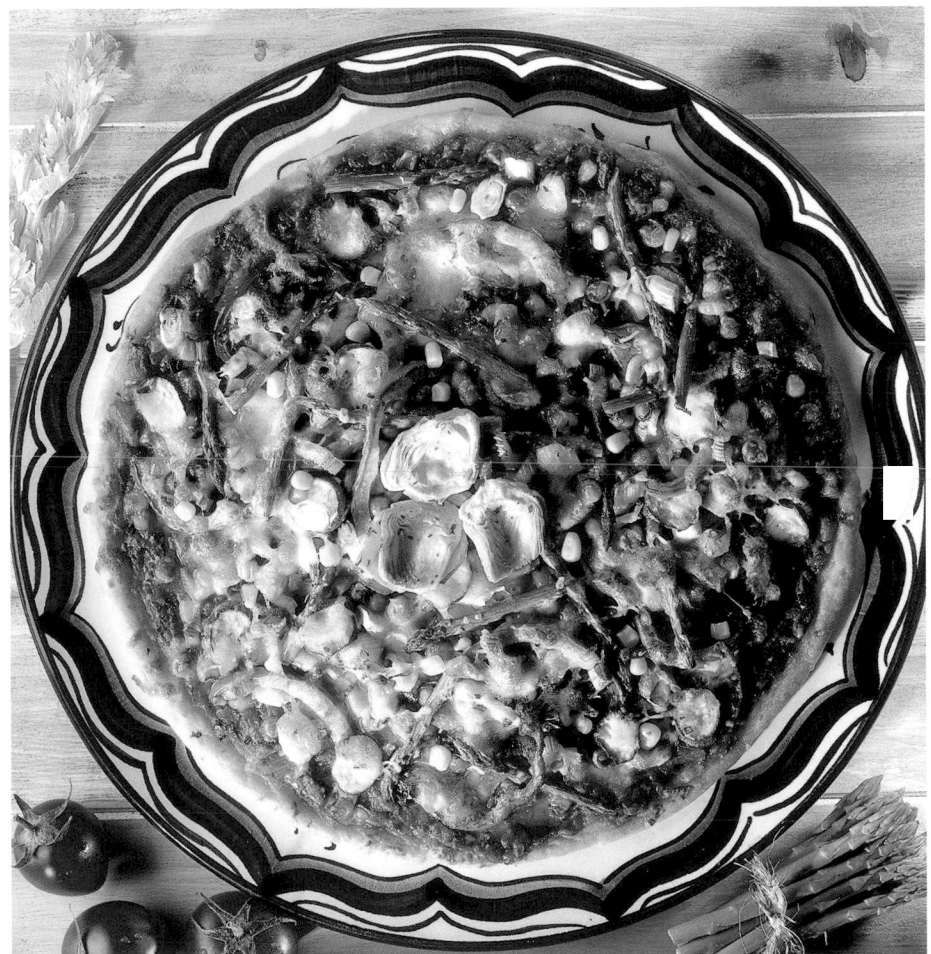

1 Remove any tough stalks from the spinach and wash the leaves in cold water. Pat dry with paper towels.

2 Roll out or press the pizza base, using a rolling pin or your hands, into a 10 inch/25 cm circle on a lightly floured counter. Place the round on a large greased cookie sheet or pizza pan and push up the edge a little. Spread with the tomato sauce.

3 Arrange the spinach leaves on the sauce, followed by the tomato slices. Top with the remaining vegetables and the fresh mixed herbs.

4 Combine the cheeses and sprinkle over the pizza. Place the artichoke heart in the center. Drizzle the pizza with a little olive oil and season to taste.

5 Bake in a preheated oven, 400°F/ 200°C, for 18–20 minutes or until the edges are crisp and golden brown. Serve immediately.

Pizza Biancas

Simple, fresh flavors are the highlight of this thin pizza.
For the best results, use buffalo mozzarella imported from Italy.

NUTRITIONAL INFORMATION

Calories	1191	Sugars	.........5g
Protein	........60g	Fat	..........40g
Carbohydrate	..158g	Saturates	......21g

1½ hrs   15 mins

MAKES TWO 9 INCH/23 CM PIZZAS

I N G R E D I E N T S

3½ cups all-purpose flour, plus extra
   for dusting

1 envelope active dry yeast

1 tsp salt

1 tbsp extra virgin olive oil, plus extra
   for greasing

T O P P I N G

2 zucchini

10½ oz/300 g buffalo mozzarella

1½–2 tbsp finely chopped fresh rosemary,
   or ½ tbsp dried rosemary

1 To make the crust, heat 1 cup water in the microwave on HIGH for 1 minute or until it reads 125°F/52°C on an instant-read thermometer. Alternatively, heat the water in a pan over low heat until it is lukewarm.

2 Stir the flour, yeast, and salt together and make a well in the center. Stir in most of the water with the olive oil to make a dough. Add the remaining water, if necessary, to form a soft dough.

3 Turn out onto a lightly floured counter and knead for about 10 minutes until smooth but still soft. Wash the bowl and lightly coat with olive oil. Shape the dough into a ball, put in the bowl, and turn the

dough over so it is coated. Cover and set aside until doubled in size.

4 Turn the dough out onto a lightly floured counter. Quickly knead a few times, then cover with the upturned bowl, and set aside for 10 minutes.

5 Meanwhile, using a vegetable peeler, cut long, thin strips of zucchini. Drain and dice the mozzarella.

6 Divide the dough in half and shape each half into a ball. Cover 1 ball and roll out the other into a 9 inch/23 cm

round. Place the round on a lightly floured cookie sheet.

7 Scatter half the mozzarella over the base. Add half the zucchini strips and sprinkle with half the rosemary. Repeat with the remaining dough and remaining topping ingredients.

8 Bake in a preheated oven, 425°F/ 220°C, for 15 minutes or until crispy. Serve immediately.

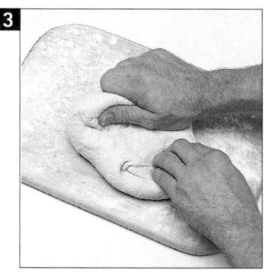

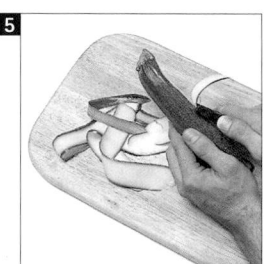

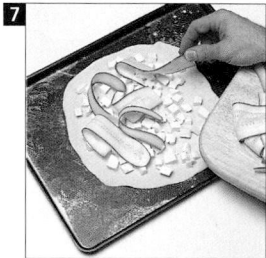

Ratatouille & Lentil Pizza

Ratatouille and lentils on a whole-wheat bread base are topped with cheese and sunflower seeds for a really healthy pizza.

NUTRITIONAL INFORMATION

Calories 377   Sugars 6g
Protein ....11g   Fat 19g
Carbohydrate ...44g   Saturates 5g

  2½ hrs   55 mins

SERVES 4

INGREDIENTS

4 tbsp green lentils

½ small eggplant, diced

1 small onion, sliced

1 garlic clove, crushed

3 tbsp olive oil

½ zucchini, sliced

½ red bell pepper, seeded and sliced

½ green bell pepper, seeded and sliced

1 cup canned chopped tomatoes

1 tbsp chopped fresh oregano or 1 tsp dried

2 tbsp water

salt and pepper

1 quantity Basic Pizza Dough (see page 602), made with whole-wheat flour

2 oz/60 g colby cheese, thinly sliced

1 tbsp sunflower seeds

olive oil, for drizzling

3 Cook the onion and garlic in the oil for 3 minutes. Add the zucchini, bell peppers, and eggplant. Cover, and let cook over low heat for about 5 minutes.

4 Add the chopped tomatoes, drained lentils, oregano, 2 tablespoons of water, and seasoning. Cover and simmer for 15 minutes, stirring occasionally, adding more water if necessary.

5 Roll out or press the dough, using a rolling pin or your hands, into a 10 inch/25 cm circle on a lightly floured counter. Place on a large greased cookie sheet or pizza pan and push up the edge slightly.

6 Cover and let the dough rise slightly for 10 minutes in a warm place.

7 Spread the ratatouille over the pizza dough almost to the edge. Arrange the cheese slices on top and sprinkle over the sunflower seeds. Drizzle with a little olive oil and season with a little salt and pepper to taste.

8 Bake in a preheated oven, at 400°F/200°C, for 18–20 minutes, or until the edge is crisp and golden brown. Serve immediately.

1 Soak the green lentils in hot water for 30 minutes. Drain and rinse, then cover with fresh water and simmer over a low heat for 10 minutes.

2 Place the eggplant in a strainer, sprinkle with a little salt, and let the bitter juices drain for about 20 minutes. Rinse well and pat dry with paper towels.

Bean Curd Pizza

Chunks of bean curd, marinated in ginger and soy sauce, impart something of an Asian flavor to this pizza.

NUTRITIONAL INFORMATION

Calories 596   Sugars 17g
Protein . . . . .33g   Fat 23g
Carbohydrate . . .66g   Saturates 9g

1 hr   35 mins

SERVES 4

INGREDIENTS

4 cups milk

1 tsp salt

2⅔ cups semolina

1 tbsp soy sauce

1 tbsp dry sherry

½ tsp grated fresh ginger root

9 oz/250 g bean curd, cut into chunks

2 eggs

½ cup Parmesan cheese, grated

Basic Tomato Sauce (see page 605)

3 baby corn ears, cut into 4

½ cup snow peas, trimmed and cut into 4

4 scallions, trimmed and cut into
    1 inch/2.5 cm strips

2 oz/60 g mozzarella cheese, thinly sliced

2 tsp sesame oil

salt and pepper

1 Bring the milk to a boil with the salt. Sprinkle the semolina over the surface, stirring all the time. Cook for 10 minutes over low heat, stirring occasionally, taking care not to let it burn. Remove from the heat and let the mixture cool until tepid.

2 Mix the soy sauce, sherry, and ginger together in a bowl, add the bean curd, and stir gently to coat. Let marinate in a cool place for 20 minutes.

3 Beat the eggs with a little pepper. Add to the semolina with the Parmesan and mix well. Place on a large greased cookie sheet or pizza pan and pat into a 10 inch/25 cm round, using the back of a metal spoon. Spread the tomato sauce almost to the edge.

4 Blanch the corn cobs and snow peas in a pan of boiling water for 1 minute, drain thoroughly, and place on the pizza with the drained bean curd. Top with the scallions and slices of cheese. Drizzle over the sesame oil and season with salt and pepper.

5 Bake in a preheated oven, at 400°F/ 200°C, for 18–20 minutes, or until the edge is crisp and golden. Serve the pizza immediately.

Tomato & Olive Pizzas

Halved ciabatta bread or baguettes are a ready-made pizza base.
The colors of the tomatoes and cheese contrast beautifully on top.

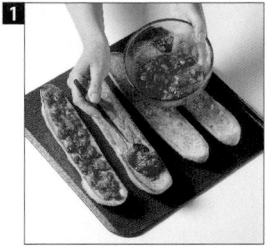

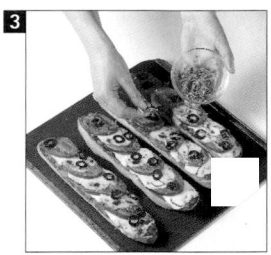

NUTRITIONAL INFORMATION

Calories 181	Sugars 4g
Protein 7g	Fat 10g
Carbohydrate ...18g	Saturates 4g

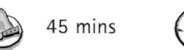 45 mins   🕑 25 mins

SERVES 4

I N G R E D I E N T S

2 loaves of ciabatta or 2 baguettes

Basic Tomato Sauce (see page 605)

4 plum tomatoes, sliced thinly lengthwise

5½ oz/150 g mozzarella cheese,
  thinly sliced

10 black olives, cut into rings

8 fresh basil leaves, shredded

olive oil, for drizzling

salt and pepper

1 Cut the bread in half lengthwise and toast the cut side of the bread lightly. Carefully spread the toasted bread with the tomato sauce.

2 Arrange the tomato and mozzarella slices alternately along the length.

3 Top with the olive rings and half of the basil. Drizzle over a little olive oil and season with salt and pepper.

4 Either place under a preheated medium broiler and cook until the cheese is melted and bubbling, or bake in a preheated oven, 400°F/200°C, for 15–20 minutes.

5 Sprinkle over the remaining basil and serve immediately.

Tomato & Bell Pepper Pizza

This pizza is made with a dough base flavored with cheese and topped with a delicious tomato sauce and roasted bell peppers.

NUTRITIONAL INFORMATION

Calories 611   Sugars 8g
Protein . . . . .14g   Fat 38g
Carbohydrate . . .56g   Saturates 21g

1½ hrs   55 mins

SERVES 4

INGREDIENTS

generous 1½ cups all-purpose flour

1 cup butter, diced

½ tsp salt

scant ½ cup dried Parmesan cheese

1 egg, beaten

2 tbsp water

2 tbsp olive oil

1 large onion, finely chopped

1 garlic clove, chopped

14 oz/400 g canned chopped tomatoes

4 tbsp concentrated tomato paste

1 red bell pepper, halved

5 sprigs fresh thyme, stalks removed

6 black olives, pitted and halved

⅓ cup freshly grated Parmesan cheese

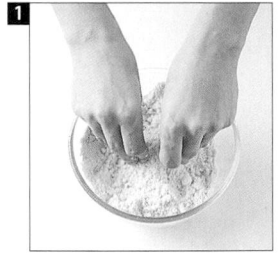  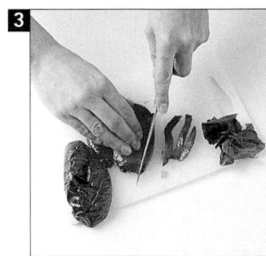

1 Strain the flour into a bowl. Rub in the butter with your fingertips until the mixture resembles bread crumbs. Stir in the salt and dried Parmesan. Mix in the egg and 1 tablespoon of the water with a round-bladed knife. Add more water if necessary to make a soft dough. Cover with plastic wrap and chill for 30 minutes.

2 Meanwhile, heat the oil in a skillet and cook the onions and garlic for about 5 minutes or until golden. Add the tomatoes and cook for 8–10 minutes. Stir in the tomato paste.

3 Place the bell pepper, skin side up, on a cookie sheet and cook under a preheated broiler for 15 minutes until charred. Place in a plastic bag and let sweat for 10 minutes. Peel off the skin and slice the flesh into thin strips.

4 Roll out the dough to fit a 9-inch/ 23-cm loose-bottomed fluted tart pan. Line with foil and bake in a preheated oven, 400°F/200°C, for 10 minutes or until just set. Remove the foil and bake for a further 5 minutes until lightly golden. Let cool slightly.

5 Spoon the tomato sauce evenly over the dough and top with the bell pepper strips, thyme, olives, and fresh Parmesan. Return to the oven for 15 minutes or until the dough is crisp. Serve warm or cold.

Garlic Mushroom Pizza

This pizza dough is flavored with garlic and herbs and topped with mixed mushrooms and melting cheese for a really delicious pizza.

NUTRITIONAL INFORMATION

Calories 541	Sugars 5g
Protein 16g	Fat 15g
Carbohydrate . . .91g	Saturates 6g

 45 mins   30 mins

SERVES 4

I N G R E D I E N T S

D O U G H

4 cups white bread flour, plus extra for dusting

2 tsp active dry yeast

2 garlic cloves, crushed

2 tbsp chopped fresh thyme

2 tbsp olive oil, plus extra for brushing

1¼ cups lukewarm water

T O P P I N G

2 tbsp butter or margarine

4¾ cups sliced mixed mushrooms

2 garlic cloves, crushed

2 tbsp chopped fresh parsley, plus extra to garnish

2 tbsp tomato paste

6 tbsp sieved tomatoes

salt and pepper

¾ cup grated mozzarella cheese

1 Put the flour, yeast, garlic, and thyme in a bowl. Make a well in the center and gradually stir in the oil and water. Bring together to form a soft dough.

2 Turn the dough onto a floured counter and knead for 5 minutes or until smooth. Roll into a 14 inch/35 cm round. Brush a cookie sheet with a little oil and place the dough base on it. Set aside in a warm place for 20 minutes or until the dough puffs up.

3 Meanwhile, make the topping. Melt the margarine or butter in a skillet and cook the mushrooms, garlic, and parsley over low heat for 5 minutes.

4 Combine the tomato paste and sieved tomatoes and spoon onto the pizza base, leaving a ½ inch/1 cm edge of dough. Spoon the mushroom mixture on top. Season to taste with salt and pepper and sprinkle the cheese on top.

5 Cook the pizza in a preheated oven, 375°F/190°C, for 20–25 minutes or until the base is crisp and the cheese has melted. Garnish with chopped parsley and serve the pizza immediately.

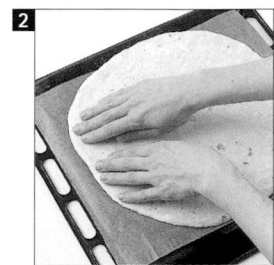

Barbecues

If you thought grills were strictly for the meat-eaters, this chapter will prove you wrong. Vegetables taste fantastic cooked over hot coals—if you've never tried grilled corn-on-the-cob, you are really missing out, and vegetable skewers in a tasty marinade are  great served with rice or couscous, salad, and garlic bread. Home-made vegetarian burgers and sausages work really well on the grill too—cook them in a hinged rack so that you can turn them over easily. And for dessert, try Charcooked Pineapple, Stuffed Pears, or Apple Skewers served with a toffee sauce—this one is perfect for a Hallowe'en supper!

Tasty Barbecue Sauce

Just the thing for brushing on to vegetable kabobs and burgers, this sauce is easy and quick to make.

NUTRITIONAL INFORMATION

Calories 100	Sugars 9g
Protein 1g	Fat 6g
Carbohydrate . . .10g	Saturates 1g

 5 mins   40 mins

SERVES 4

I N G R E D I E N T S

2 tbsp butter or margarine

1 garlic clove, crushed

1 onion, finely chopped

2 cups canned chopped tomatoes

1 tbsp dark muscovado sugar

1 tsp hot chili sauce

1–2 gherkins

1 tbsp capers, drained

salt and pepper

1 Melt the butter or margarine in a pan and cook the garlic and onion for 8–10 minutes, until well browned.

2 Add the chopped tomatoes, sugar and chili sauce. Bring to a boil, then reduce the heat and simmer gently for 20–25 minutes, until thick and pulpy.

3 Chop the gherkins and capers finely. Add to the sauce, stirring to mix, and continue to cook the sauce over low heat for 2 minutes.

4 Taste the sauce and season with a little salt and pepper.

5 Use this barbecue sauce as a baste for vegetarian kabobs and burgers, or as an accompaniment to grilled foods such as vegetable kabobs.

COOK'S TIP

To make sure that the sauce has a good color, it is important to brown the onions really well to begin with. When fresh tomatoes are cheap and plentiful, they can be used instead of canned ones. Peel and chop 1 lb/450 g.

Citrus & Herb Marinades

Choose one of these marinades to give a marvelous flavor to grilled food.
The nutritional information is for Orange & Marjoram only.

NUTRITIONAL INFORMATION

Calories	269	Sugars	.........3g
Protein	........0.4g	Fat	...........6g
Carbohydrate	....3g	Saturates	.......1g

 20 mins   0 mins

SERVES 4

INGREDIENTS

ORANGE & MARJORAM

1 orange

½ cup olive oil

4 tbsp dry white wine

4 tbsp white wine vinegar

1 tbsp snipped fresh chives

1 tbsp chopped fresh marjoram

salt and pepper

THAI-SPICED LIME

1 lemon grass stalk

finely grated zest and juice of 1 lime

4 tbsp sesame oil

2 tbsp light soy sauce

pinch of ground ginger

1 tbsp chopped fresh cilantro

salt and pepper

BASIL & LEMON

finely grated zest of 1 lemon

4 tbsp lemon juice

1 tbsp balsamic vinegar

2 tbsp red wine vinegar

2 tbsp virgin olive oil

1 tbsp chopped fresh oregano

1 tbsp chopped fresh basil

salt and pepper

1 To make the Orange & Marjoram marinade, remove the zest from the orange with a zester, or grate it finely, then squeeze the juice.

2 Mix the orange zest and juice with all the remaining ingredients in a small bowl, whisking together to combine. Season with salt and pepper.

3 To make the Thai-spiced Lime marinade, bruise the lemon grass by crushing it with a rolling pin. Mix the remaining ingredients together in a small bowl and add the lemon grass.

4 To make the Basil & Lemon marinade, whisk all the ingredients together in a small bowl. Season to taste with salt and pepper.

5 Keep the marinades covered with plastic wrap or store them in screw-top jars, ready for using as marinades or bastes for vegetable kabobs, chargrilled vegetables, and so on.

Three Favorite Dressings

You can rely on any of these dressings to bring out the best in your salads. The nutritional information is for the Mustard & Vinegar dressing.

NUTRITIONAL INFORMATION

Calories	245	Sugars	.......0.5g
Protein	.........0g	Fat	.......27g
Carbohydrate	...0.5g	Saturates	.......4g

 45 mins   0 mins

SERVES 4

INGREDIENTS

WHOLE-GRAIN MUSTARD & CIDER VINEGAR

½ cup olive oil

4 tbsp cider vinegar

2 tsp whole-grain mustard

½ tsp superfine sugar

salt and pepper

GARLIC & PARSLEY

1 small garlic clove

1 tbsp fresh parsley

⅔ cup light cream

4 tbsp unsweetened yogurt

1 tsp lemon juice

pinch of superfine sugar

salt and pepper

RASPBERRY & HAZELNUT

4 tbsp raspberry vinegar

4 tbsp light olive oil

4 tbsp hazelnut oil

½ tsp superfine sugar

2 tsp chopped fresh chives

salt and pepper

1 To make the Whole-grain Mustard & Cider Vinegar Dressing, whisk all the ingredients together in a small bowl.

2 To make the Garlic & Parsley Dressing, crush the garlic clove and finely chop the fresh parsley.

3 Mix the garlic and parsley with the remaining ingredients, then whisk together until combined. Cover and chill for 30 minutes.

4 To make the Raspberry & Hazelnut Vinaigrette, whisk all the ingredients together until combined.

5 Keep the dressings covered with plastic wrap or sealed in screw-top jars. Chill until ready for use.

Mixed Vegetables

The wonderful aroma of vegetables as they are chargrilled over hot coals will set the tastebuds tingling.

NUTRITIONAL INFORMATION

Calories	155	Sugars	.........6g
Protein	.........2g	Fat	..........12g
Carbohydrate	....7g	Saturates	.......7g

🔥

🥘 10 mins   🕐 25 mins

SERVES 6

I N G R E D I E N T S

8 baby eggplants

4 zucchini

2 red onions

4 tomatoes

salt and pepper

1 tsp balsamic vinegar, to serve

B A S T E

6 tbsp butter

2 tsp walnut oil

2 garlic cloves, chopped

4 tbsp dry white wine or hard cider

1 To prepare the vegetables, cut the eggplants in half. Trim and cut the zucchini in half lengthwise. Thickly slice the onion and halve the tomatoes.

2 Season all of the vegetables with salt and pepper to taste.

3 To make the baste, melt the butter with the oil in a pan. Add the garlic and cook gently for 1–2 minutes. Remove the pan from the heat and stir in the wine or cider.

4 Add the vegetables to the pan and toss them in the baste mixture. You may need to do this in several batches to ensure that all of the vegetables are coated thoroughly and evenly.

5 Remove the vegetables from the baste mixture, reserving any excess baste. Place the vegetables on an oiled rack over medium hot coals. Grill the vegetables for 15–20 minutes, basting with the reserved baste mixture and turning once or twice during cooking.

6 Transfer the vegetables to warm serving plates and serve immediately, sprinkled with balsamic vinegar.

Cheeseburgers in Buns

Ground soy and seasonings combine to make these tasty vegetarian burgers, which are topped with cheese.

NUTRITIONAL INFORMATION

Calories 551	Sugars 4g
Protein 29g	Fat 24g
Carbohydrate . . .57g	Saturates 5g

1¼ hrs   10 mins

SERVES 4

I N G R E D I E N T S

5½ oz/150 g dehydrated ground soy

1¼ cups vegetable bouillon

1 small onion, finely chopped

1 cup all-purpose flour

1 egg, beaten

1 tbsp chopped fresh herbs

1 tbsp mushroom catsup or soy sauce

salt and pepper

2 tbsp vegetable oil

4 burger buns

4 cheese slices

B A R B E C U E S A U C E

2 tbsp tomato catsup

3 tbsp sweet relish

1 tbsp vegetarian Worcestershire sauce

2 tsp Dijon mustard

1 tbsp white wine vinegar

2 tbsp fruity brown sauce

T O G A R N I S H

dill pickles

tomato slices

T O S E R V E

lettuce, cucumber, and scallion salad

1 Put the ground soy into a large bowl. Pour in the vegetable bouillon and let soak for about 15 minutes until it has been absorbed.

2 Meanwhile, make the barbecue sauce. Combine the tomato catsup, relish, vegetarian Worcestershire sauce, and mustard. Stir in the vinegar and fruity brown sauce, then cover, and chill until required.

3 Add the onion, flour, beaten egg, and chopped herbs to the soy and mix thoroughly. Stir in the mushroom catsup or soy sauce and season to taste with salt and pepper, stirring to mix again.

4 Form the mixture into 8 burgers. Cover and chill until ready to cook.

5 Brush the burgers with oil and grill over hot coals, turning once. Allow about 5 minutes on each side. Alternatively, cook under a preheated broiler.

6 Split the buns and top with a burger. Lay a cheese slice on top and garnish with barbecue sauce, dill pickle, and tomato slices. Serve with a salad made with lettuce, scallions, and sliced cucumber.

Mushroom Burgers

Home-made vegetarian burgers are much tastier—and usually much healthier—than ready-made ones.

NUTRITIONAL INFORMATION

Calories	164	Sugars	.........5g
Protein	.........7g	Fat	...........5g
Carbohydrate	...24g	Saturates	.......1g

20 mins, plus chilling

about 20 mins

SERVES 4

INGREDIENTS

2 tsp sunflower oil, plus extra for brushing

1 firmly packed cup mushrooms, finely chopped

¼ cup peanuts

1 carrot, chopped

1 onion, chopped

1 zucchini, chopped

2 cups fresh white bread crumbs

1 tbsp chopped fresh parsley

1 tsp yeast extract

1 tbsp all-purpose flour

1 Heat the oil in a heavy skillet and cook the mushrooms, stirring constantly for about 8 minutes, until all the moisture has evaporated. Using a slotted spoon, transfer them to a large bowl.

2 Put the carrot, onion, zucchini, and peanuts in a food processor and process until finely chopped. Scrape into the bowl and stir in the breadcrumbs, parsley, and yeast extract. Lightly flour your hands and shape the mixture into 4 burgers. Place on a plate, cover with plastic wrap, and chill in the refrigerator for at least 1 hour and up to 1 day.

3 Brush the burgers with oil and cook on a hot grill for 8–10 minutes.

Stuffed Tomatoes

These grilled tomato cups are filled with a delicious Greek-style combination of herbs, nuts, and raisins.

NUTRITIONAL INFORMATION

Calories	156	Sugars	........10g
Protein	.........3g	Fat	...........7g
Carbohydrate	...22g	Saturates	.....0.7g

🐷 🐷

🍲 10 mins   🕐 10 mins

SERVES 4

I N G R E D I E N T S

4 beef tomatoes

salt and pepper

5 cups cooked rice

8 scallions, chopped

3 tbsp chopped fresh mint

2 tbsp chopped fresh parsley

3 tbsp pine nuts

3 tbsp raisins

2 tsp olive oil

1 Cut the tomatoes in half, then scoop out and discard the seeds.

2 Stand the tomatoes upside down on absorbent paper towels for a few moments to let the juices drain out. Turn the tomato shells the right way up and sprinkle the insides with seasoning.

3 Mix together the rice, scallions, mint, parsley, pine nuts, and raisins, then divide the rice mixture between the tomato cups.

4 Drizzle a little olive oil over the stuffed tomatoes, then grill on an oiled rack over medium-hot coals for about 10 minutes until they are tender and cooked through.

5 Transfer the grilled tomatoes to serving plates and serve immediately.

COOK'S TIP

Tomatoes are a popular barbecue grill vegetable. Try broiling slices of beef tomato and slices of onion, brushed with a little oil, and topped with sprigs of fresh herbs, or thread cherry tomatoes on to skewers and grill for 5-10 minutes.

Buttered Corn Cobs

There are a number of ways of cooking corn on a barbecue grill.
Leaving on the husks protects the tender corn kernels.

NUTRITIONAL INFORMATION

Calories	79	Sugars	........2g
Protein	........3g	Fat	..........2g
Carbohydrate	...14g	Saturates	.....0.2g

 10 mins   20–30 mins

SERVES 4

INGREDIENTS

4 ears of corn, with husks

scant ½ cup butter

1 tbsp chopped fresh parsley

1 tsp chopped fresh chives

1 tsp chopped fresh thyme

grated zest of 1 lemon

salt and pepper

 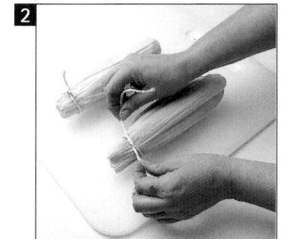 

1 To prepare the ears of corn, peel back the husks and remove the silken hairs.

2 Fold back the husks and secure them in place with string if necessary.

3 Blanch the ears in a large pan of boiling water for about 5 minutes. Remove the ears with a perforated spoon and drain thoroughly.

4 Grill the ears over medium–hot coals for 20–30 minutes, turning frequently to cook evenly.

5 Meanwhile, soften the butter and beat in the parsley, chives, thyme, lemon zest, and salt and pepper to taste.

6 Transfer the ears to serving plates, remove the string and pull back the husks. Serve with the herb butter.

COOK'S TIP
If you are unable to get fresh ears, frozen ears can be cooked on a barbecue grill. Spread some of the herb butter on to a sheet of double thickness foil. Wrap the ears in the foil and grill among the coals for 20–30 minutes.

Turkish Kabobs

A spicy garbanzo bean sauce is served with colorful, grilled vegetable kabobs—perfect for lunch on a warm summer day.

NUTRITIONAL INFORMATION

Calories	303	Sugars	........13g
Protein	........13g	Fat	..........15g
Carbohydrate	...30g	Saturates	.......2g

15 mins   15 mins

SERVES 4

INGREDIENTS

SAUCE

4 tbsp olive oil

3 garlic cloves, crushed

1 small onion, finely chopped

1½ cups canned garbanzo beans, rinsed and drained

1¼ cups unsweetened yogurt

1 tsp ground cumin

½ tsp chili powder

lemon juice

salt and pepper

KABOBS

1 eggplant

1 red bell pepper, seeded

1 green bell pepper, seeded

4 plum tomatoes

1 lemon, cut into wedges

8 small bay leaves

olive oil, for brushing

1 To make the sauce, heat the olive oil in a small skillet. Add the garlic and chopped onion and cook over medium heat, stirring occasionally, for about 5 minutes, until the onion is soft and has turned golden brown.

2 Put the garbanzo beans and yogurt into a blender or food processor and add the cumin, chili powder, and onion mixture. Process for about 15 seconds until smooth. Alternatively, mash the garbanzo beans with a potato masher and stir in the yogurt, ground cumin, chili powder, and onion mixture.

3 Scrape the puréed mixture into a bowl and season to taste with lemon juice, salt, and pepper. Cover with plastic wrap and chill in the refrigerator until ready to serve.

4 To prepare the kabobs, cut the vegetables into large chunks and thread them onto 4 skewers, placing a bay leaf and a lemon wedge at both ends of each kabob.

5 Brush the kabobs with olive oil and cook them on the grill, turning frequently, for 5–8 minutes. Alternatively, cook under a preheated broiler.

6 Heat the garbanzo sauce. Transfer the kabobs to serving plates and serve immediately, with the sauce.

Vegetables with Pesto

These chargrilled Mediterranean vegetables are served with a very special creamy pesto sauce.

NUTRITIONAL INFORMATION

Calories	313	Sugars	........11g
Protein	........10g	Fat	.........24g
Carbohydrate	...15g	Saturates	.......6g

30 mins | 8 mins

SERVES 4

INGREDIENTS

1 red onion

1 fennel bulb

4 baby eggplants

4 baby zucchini

1 orange bell pepper

1 red bell pepper

2 beefsteak tomatoes, halved

2 tbsp olive oil

salt and pepper

CREAMY PESTO

2 oz/55 g fresh basil leaves

1½ tbsp pine nuts

1 garlic clove

¼ cup freshly grated Parmesan cheese

¼ cup extra virgin olive oil

⅔ cup unsweetened Greek yogurt

coarse sea salt

1 First, make the creamy pesto. Put the basil, pine nuts, garlic, and a pinch of sea salt in a mortar and pound to a paste with a pestle. Gradually work in the Parmesan, then gradually stir in the oil. Place the yogurt in a small serving bowl and stir in 3–4 tablespoons of the pesto. Cover with plastic wrap and chill in the refrigerator until required.

2 Cut the onion and fennel into wedges and halve and seed the bell peppers.

3 Prepare the vegetables. Brush the onion, fennel, eggplants, zucchini, bell peppers, and tomatoes with olive oil and season to taste with salt and pepper.

4 Cook the eggplants and bell peppers on a hot grill for 3 minutes, add the zucchini, onion, and tomatoes, and cook, turning occasionally and brushing with more oil if necessary, for 5 minutes more. Serve immediately with the creamy pesto.

VARIATION
If baby vegetables are not available, cut 2 eggplants into slices and cut 2 zucchini in half lengthwise instead.

Grilled Bean Pot

Cook this tasty vegetable and TVP casserole conventionally,
then keep it piping hot over the grill.

NUTRITIONAL INFORMATION

Calories	381	Sugars	. . . . .17g
Protein	. . . . .21g	Fat	. . . . .19g
Carbohydrate	. . .34g	Saturates	. . . . . . .3g

10 mins   1 hr

SERVES 4

INGREDIENTS

¼ cup butter or margarine

1 large onion, chopped

2 garlic cloves, crushed

2 carrots, sliced

2 celery stalks, sliced

1 tbsp paprika

2 tsp ground cumin

2 cups canned chopped tomatoes

1½ cups canned mixed beans, rinsed
   and drained

⅔ cup vegetable bouillon

1 tbsp molasses sugar or molasses

12 oz/350 g TVP or soy cubes

salt and pepper

crusty French bread, to serve

VARIATION

If you prefer, cook the casserole
in a preheated oven, 375°F/
190°C from step 3, but keep
the dish covered. Instead of
mixed beans you could use just
one type of canned beans.

1 Melt the butter or margarine in a large flameproof casserole and cook the onion and the garlic over medium heat, stirring occasionally, for about 5 minutes, until golden brown.

2 Add the sliced carrots and celery and cook, stirring occasionally, for a further 2 minutes, then stir in the paprika and ground cumin.

3 Add the tomatoes and beans. Pour in the bouillon and add the sugar or molasses. Bring to a boil, then reduce the heat and simmer, uncovered, stirring occasionally, for 30 minutes.

4 Add the TVP or soy cubes to the casserole, cover, and cook, stirring occasionally, for a further 20 minutes.

5 Season to taste with salt and pepper, then transfer the casserole to the grill, setting it to one side to keep hot.

6 Ladle the bean pot onto plates and serve immediately with crusty French bread.

Greek Vegetable Kabobs

A complete meal on a skewer, these tasty kabobs include vegetables, cheese, and, perhaps surprisingly, nectarines in a colorful combination.

NUTRITIONAL INFORMATION

Calories 428	Sugars 15g	
Protein 19g	Fat 23g	
Carbohydrate . . .40g	Saturates 4g	

20 mins, plus cooling   35 mins

SERVES 4

INGREDIENTS

8 new potatoes, washed but not peeled

2 onions, cut into wedges

1 eggplant, cut into 8 pieces

8 thick slices cucumber

1 red bell pepper, seeded and cut into 8 pieces

1 yellow bell pepper, seeded and cut into 8 pieces

½ lb/225 g halloumi cheese, cut into 8 cubes

2 nectarines, pitted and cut into quarters

8 white mushrooms

2 tbsp olive oil

2 tsp chopped fresh thyme

2 tsp chopped fresh rosemary

salt

1 quantity Tzatziki (see page 147), to serve

1 Prepare the vegetables and cheese. Cook the potatoes and onion wedges in a pan of lightly salted boiling water for about 20 minutes, until just tender. Drain and let cool. Meanwhile, blanch the eggplant pieces in boiling water for 2 minutes, add the cucumber, and simmer for 1 minute more. Add the red and yellow bell peppers and simmer for 2 minutes, then drain and let all the vegetables cool.

2 Place the cooled vegetables, cheese, nectarines, and mushrooms in a bowl, add the olive oil and chopped herbs, and toss to coat thoroughly. Thread the vegetables, cheese, nectarines, and mushrooms on to skewers.

3 Cook the kabobs on a hot grill, turning frequently, for 15 minutes. Serve immediately with the tzatziki.

COOK'S TIP
Halloumi, a ewe's milk cheese, is perfect for grills because it softens and chars without melting.

Nutty Rice Burgers

Serve these burgers in toasted sesame seed rolls. If you wish, add a slice of cheese to top the burger at the end of cooking.

NUTRITIONAL INFORMATION

Calories 517	Sugars 5g
Protein 16g	Fat 26g
Carbohydrate . . .59g	Saturates 6g

1¼ hrs   30 mins

SERVES 4

INGREDIENTS

1 tbsp sunflower oil

1 small onion, finely chopped

1⅓ cups mushrooms, finely chopped

2 cups cooked brown rice

1¾ cups bread crumbs

¾ cup chopped walnuts

1 egg, lightly beaten

2 tbsp brown fruity sauce

dash of Tabasco sauce

salt and pepper

vegetable oil, for basting

6 individual cheese slices (optional)

TO SERVE

onion slices

tomato slices

6 sesame seed burger buns

1 Heat the oil in a large pan and cook the onions for 3–4 minutes until they just begin to soften. Add the mushrooms and cook for a further 2 minutes.

2 Remove the pan from the heat. Transfer to a bowl and stir the cooked rice, bread crumbs, walnuts, egg, brown fruity sauce, and a dash of Tabasco sauce into the vegetables. Season to taste with salt and pepper and mix well.

3 Shape the mixture into 4 burgers, pressing the mixture together with your fingers. Let chill in the refrigerator for at least 30 minutes.

4 Grill the burgers on an oiled rack over medium–hot coals for 5–6 minutes on each side, turning once and frequently basting with oil. Alternatively, cook under a preheated broiler.

5 If liked, top the burgers with a slice of cheese 2 minutes before the end of the cooking time. Grill or broil the onion and tomato slices for 3–4 minutes until they are just beginning to color.

6 Toast the sesame seed buns at the side of the grill or under the broiler. Serve the burgers in the buns, with the onions and tomatoes.

Cajun Vegetables

These delicious slices of sweet potatoes and chunks of corn are basted with butter and coated in cajun spice—a great side dish.

NUTRITIONAL INFORMATION

Calories 244	Sugars 7g	
Protein 5g	Fat 8g	
Carbohydrate ...41g	Saturates 4g	

 10 mins   12–15 mins

SERVES 4

INGREDIENTS

4 corn ears

2 sweet potatoes

2 tbsp butter, melted

CAJUN SPICE

2 tsp paprika

1 tsp ground cumin

1 tsp ground coriander

1 tsp ground black pepper

½–1 tsp chili powder

1 To make the Cajun spice mix, combine all the spices in a small bowl.

2 Prepare the vegetables. Cut the corn ears into quarters and the sweet potato into thick slices. Brush the corn ear pieces and sweet potato slices with melted butter and sprinkle with some of the Cajun spice mix.

3 Cook on a medium grill, turning frequently, for 12–15 minutes. Brush with more melted butter and sprinkle with more spice mixture during cooking.

COOK'S TIP
The flesh of sweet potatoes varies in color from white to orange. Not only are the orange-flesh varieties more attractive, they also contain more nutrients.

Chargrilled Eggplants

The wonderful flavor and texture of chargrilled eggplants is hard to beat. Try serving the slices with pesto or minty cucumber sauce.

NUTRITIONAL INFORMATION

Calories ....336 Sugars 6g
Protein ....6g Fat 32g
Carbohydrate ....6g Saturates 5g

15 mins   10 mins

SERVES 4

INGREDIENTS

1 large eggplant

3 tbsp olive oil

1 tsp sesame oil

salt and pepper

PESTO

1 clove garlic

¼ cup pine nuts

½ oz/15 g fresh basil leaves

2 tbsp freshly grated Parmesan cheese

6 tbsp olive oil

salt and pepper

CUCUMBER SAUCE

⅔ cup unsweetened yogurt

2 inch/5 cm piece cucumber

½ tsp mint sauce

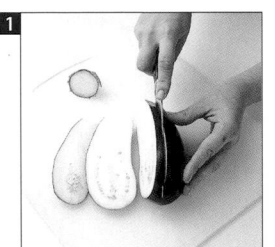

1 Remove the stalk from the eggplant, then cut it lengthwise with a sharp knife to make 8 thin slices.

2 Lay the slices on a plate or board and sprinkle them liberally with salt to remove the bitter juices. Let stand.

3 Meanwhile, prepare the baste. Combine the olive and sesame oils, season with pepper, and set aside.

4 To make the pesto, put the garlic, pine nuts, basil, and cheese in a food processor until finely chopped. With the machine running, gradually add the oil in a thin stream. Season to taste.

5 To make the minty cucumber sauce, place the yogurt in a mixing bowl. Remove the seeds from the cucumber and dice the flesh finely. Stir into the yogurt with the mint sauce.

6 Rinse the eggplant slices and pat them dry on absorbent paper towels.

7 Baste the eggplant slices with the oil mixture and grill over hot coals for about 10 minutes, turning once. The eggplant should be golden and tender.

8 Transfer the eggplant slices to serving plates and serve with either the cucumber sauce or the pesto.

Prune & Apricot Skewers

Try serving these unusual skewers as a starter, with a garnish of salad greens and some fresh crusty bread to soak up any juices.

NUTRITIONAL INFORMATION

Calories 292   Sugars 46g
Protein . . . . .5g   Fat 6g
Carbohydrate . . .48g   Saturates 1g

🧊 15 mins   🕐 25 mins

SERVES 4

I N G R E D I E N T S

1 cup prunes, pitted

1½ cup dried apricots, pitted

2 inch/5 cm piece cinnamon stick

1 cup white wine

2 tbsp chili sauce

2 tbsp sunflower oil

1 lb/450 g baby onions

1 Prepare the onions and fruit. Place the prunes, apricots, cinnamon stick, and wine in a heavy pan and bring to a boil. Lower the heat and simmer for 5 minutes. Drain, reserving the cooking liquid, and let the fruit cool.

2 Return the cooking liquid to the pan, bring back to a boil, and boil until reduced by about half. Remove the pan from the heat and discard the cinnamon stick. Stir in the chili sauce and oil.

3 Thread the prunes, apricots, and onions on to skewers. Cook on a medium grill, turning and brushing frequently with the wine mixture, for 10 minutes. Serve immediately.

Indian Kabobs

Vegetables, fruit, and cheese, brushed with a spicy glaze, need no more than a plate of salad to make a delicious vegetarian meal.

NUTRITIONAL INFORMATION

Calories	160	Sugars	........22g
Protein	.........7g	Fat	...........6g
Carbohydrate	...22g	Saturates	.......1g

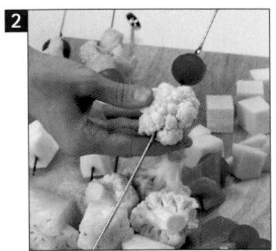

15 mins   10–12 mins

SERVES 4

I N G R E D I E N T S

8 cherry tomatoes

1 orange bell pepper, seeded and cut into chunks

8 cauliflower florets

3 pineapple slices, cut into quarters

1 mango, peeled, pitted, and cut into cubes

6 oz/175 g paneer, cut into cubes

salad and bread or rice, to serve

G L A Z E

2 tbsp lime juice

2 tbsp chili sauce

1 tbsp vegetable oil

1 tbsp clear honey

1 tbsp water

pinch of ground cumin

salt and ground black pepper

COOK'S TIP

Paneer is a soft Indian cheese made by curdling milk with lemon juice, before straining and pressing flat. Most Indian cooks make their own, but it is available from Indian stores. Bean curd could be used as a substitute.

1 Prepare the ingredients. Combine all the ingredients for the glaze in a small bowl, mixing well. Set aside.

2 Thread the tomatoes, orange bell pepper chunks, cauliflower florets, pineapple pieces, mango cubes, and paneer cubes on to 4 skewers.

3 Brush the kabobs with the glaze and cook on a medium grill, turning and brushing frequently with the glaze, for 10–12 minutes.

4 Serve the kabobs with a simple salad and either fresh crusty bread or some plain cooked rice.

Mixed Fruit Kabobs

You can use almost any firm-fleshed fruit to make these colorful, quick, and easy grilled kabobs.

NUTRITIONAL INFORMATION

Calories	185	Sugars	........37g
Protein	.........3g	Fat	............1g
Carbohydrate	...38g	Saturates	.......0g

20 mins, plus marinating   5-7 mins

SERVES 4

INGREDIENTS

2 nectarines

1 mango, peeled, halved, and pitted

2 kiwi fruit

4 red plums, halved and pitted

2 bananas, peeled and thickly sliced

8 strawberries, hulled

1 tbsp clear honey

3 tbsp Cointreau

1 Halve and stone the nectarines. Cut the pieces in half again and place on a large, shallow dish. Cut the mango flesh into chunks and add to the dish with the kiwi fruit, plums, bananas, and strawberries.

2 Combine the honey and Cointreau in a bowl, mixing well. Pour the mixture over the fruit and toss lightly to coat. Cover with plastic wrap and let marinate for 1 hour.

3 Drain the fruit, reserving the honey and Cointreau marinade. Thread the fruit on to skewers and cook on a medium grill, turning and brushing frequently with the reserved marinade, for 5–7 minutes. Serve immediately.

Tropical Grilled Fruit

This delicious variation of a hot fruit salad includes wedges of tropical fruits, dusted with dark brown, treacly sugar, and a pinch of spice.

NUTRITIONAL INFORMATION

Calories 120   Sugars 20g
Protein ....1g   Fat 3g
Carbohydrate ...21g   Saturates 1g

15 mins, plus standing   5 mins

SERVES 4

INGREDIENTS

1 baby pineapple

1 ripe papaya

1 ripe mango

2 kiwi fruit

4 finger bananas

4 tbsp dark rum

1 tsp ground allspice

2 tbsp lime juice

4 tbsp dark muscovado sugar

LIME "BUTTER"

4 tbsp low-fat spread

½ tsp finely grated lime peel

1 tbsp confectioners' sugar

1 Quarter the pineapple, trimming away most of the leaves, and place in a shallow dish. Peel the papaya, cut it in half, and scoop out the seeds. Cut the flesh into thick wedges and place with the pineapple.

2 Peel the mango, cut either side of the smooth, central flat pit, and remove the pit. Slice the flesh into thick wedges. Peel the kiwi fruit and cut in half. Peel the bananas. Add all of these fruits to the dish.

3 Sprinkle over the rum, allspice, and lime juice, cover, and let stand at room temperature for 30 minutes, turning occasionally, to let the flavors develop.

4 Meanwhile, make the butter. Place the low-fat spread in a small bowl and beat in the lime zest and sugar until well mixed. Let chill until required.

5 Preheat the broiler to hot. Drain the fruit, reserving the juices, and arrange in the broiler pan. Sprinkle with the sugar and broil for 3–4 minutes until hot, bubbling, and beginning to char.

6 Transfer the fruit to a serving plate and spoon over the juices. Serve with the lime butter.

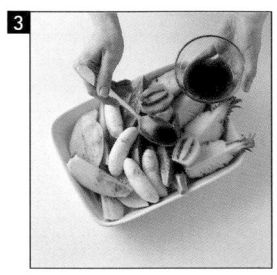

VARIATION
Serve with a light sauce of 1¼ cups tropical fruit juice thickened with 2 tsp arrowroot.

Mini Kabobs

Cubes of smoked bean curd are speared on bamboo satay sticks
with crisp vegetables and marinated with lemon juice and olive oil.

NUTRITIONAL INFORMATION

Calories	322	Sugars	.........9g
Protein	........13g	Fat	..........24g
Carbohydrate	...13g	Saturates	.......7g

25 mins   15–20 mins

SERVES 6

INGREDIENTS

10½ oz/300 g smoked bean curd, cubed

1 large red bell pepper, seeded and diced

1 large yellow bell pepper, seeded
and diced

6 oz/175 g white mushrooms

1 small zucchini, sliced

finely grated zest and juice of 1 lemon

3 tbsp olive oil

1 tbsp chopped fresh parsley

1 tsp superfine sugar

salt and pepper

fresh parsley sprigs, to garnish

SAUCE

1 cup cashew nuts

1 tbsp butter

1 garlic clove, crushed

1 shallot, finely chopped

1 tsp ground coriander

1 tsp ground cumin

1 tbsp superfine sugar

1 tbsp unsweetened shredded coconut

⅔ cup unsweetened yogurt

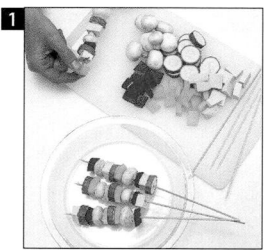

1 Thread the bean curd cubes, red and yellow bell peppers, mushrooms, and zucchini onto bamboo satay sticks. Arrange them in a shallow dish.

2 Combine the lemon zest and juice, olive oil, parsley, and sugar. Season to taste with salt and pepper. Pour over the kabobs and brush them with the mixture. Let stand for 10 minutes.

3 To make the sauce, sprinkle the cashew nuts in a single layer on a cookie sheet and toast them under a hot broiler until lightly browned.

4 Melt the butter in a pan and cook the garlic and shallot over low heat until soft. Transfer to a blender or food processor and add the toasted cashew nuts, coriander, cumin, sugar, coconut, and yogurt. Process for about 15 seconds or until combined.

5 Place the kabobs under a preheated broiler and cook, turning and basting with the lemon juice mixture, until lightly browned. Garnish with sprigs of parsley and serve with the cashew nut sauce.

Colorful Kabobs

Brighten up a barbecue grill meal with these colorful vegetable kabobs. They are basted with an aromatic, flavored oil.

NUTRITIONAL INFORMATION

Calories . . . . .131 Sugars 7g
Protein . . . . .2g Fat 11g
Carbohydrate . . . .8g Saturates 2g

15 mins   15 mins

SERVES 4

INGREDIENTS

1 red bell pepper, seeded

1 yellow bell pepper, seeded

1 green bell pepper, seeded

1 small onion

8 cherry tomatoes

100 g/¼ lb exotic mushrooms

SEASONED OIL

6 tbsp olive oil

1 garlic clove, crushed

½ tsp mixed dried herbs or herbes de Provence

1 Cut the bell peppers into 1 inch/ 2.5 cm pieces.

2 Peel the onion and cut it into wedges, leaving the root end just intact to help keep the wedges together.

COOK'S TIP

To make walnut sauce, process 1 cup of walnuts in a food processor to a smooth paste. With the machine running, add ⅔ cup heavy cream and 1 tablespoon of olive oil. Season to taste with salt and pepper.

3 Thread the bell pepper pieces, onion wedges, tomatoes, and mushrooms on to skewers, alternating the colors of the bell peppers.

4 To make the seasoned oil, mix together the olive oil, garlic, and mixed herbs or herbes de Provence in a small bowl. Brush the mixture liberally over the kabobs.

5 Grill the kabobs over medium–hot coals for 10–15 minutes, brushing with the seasoned oil and turning the skewers frequently.

6 Transfer the kabobs on to warmed serving plates and serve immediately.

7 If you wish, serve the kabobs with a rich walnut sauce (see Cook's Tip, left).

Roast Leeks

Use a good-quality French or Italian olive oil for this deliciously simple yet sophisticated vegetable accompaniment.

NUTRITIONAL INFORMATION

Calories	71	Sugars	2g
Protein	2g	Fat	6g
Carbohydrate	3g	Saturates	1g

 5 mins 7 mins

SERVES 6

INGREDIENTS

4 leeks

3 tbsp olive oil

2 tsp balsamic vinegar

sea salt and pepper

1 Cut the leeks in half lengthwise, making sure that you hold the knife straight, so that the leek is held together by the root. Brush each leek liberally with the olive oil.

2 Cook the leeks over a hot grill for 6–7 minutes, turning once.

3 Remove the leeks from the grill and brush them lightly with the balsamic vinegar. Season to taste with salt and pepper and serve hot or warm.

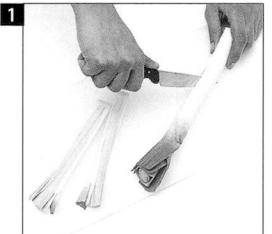

Grilled Corn

Corn ears are delicious grilled. They taste particularly delicious served with this creamy blue cheese dressing.

NUTRITIONAL INFORMATION

Calories 255	Sugars 4g	
Protein 12g	Fat 14g	
Carbohydrate ...20g	Saturates 8g	

🦪

🍲 15 mins   🕐 15–20 mins

SERVES 6

INGREDIENTS

1¼ cups crumbled Danish Blue (Danablu) cheese

1½ cups curd cheese

½ cup unsweetened Greek yogurt

6 corn ears in their husks

salt and pepper

1 Place the Danish Blue in a bowl and beat with a wooden spoon until creamy. Beat in the curd cheese until thoroughly combined. Gradually beat in the yogurt and season to taste with salt and pepper. Cover with plastic wrap and chill in the refrigerator until required.

2 Fold back the husks on each corn ear and remove the silks. Smooth the husks back into place. Cut 6 pieces of foil, each large enough to enclose a corn ear. Wrap the ears in the foil.

3 Cook the ears on a hot grill, turning frequently, for 15–20 minutes. Unwrap the corn ears and discard the foil. Peel back the husk on 1 side of each ear and trim off with a sharp knife or kitchen scissors. Serve immediately, with the cheese dressing.

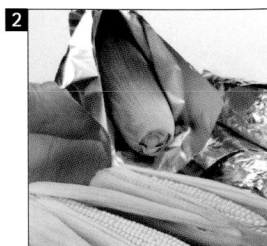

Stuffed Tomato Parcels

An unusual filling for stuffed tomatoes, spinach and cheese are given extra flavor with toasted sunflower seeds.

NUTRITIONAL INFORMATION

Calories 248   Sugars 9g
Protein ....16g   Fat 16g
Carbohydrate ....11g   Saturates 6g

15 mins, plus cooling   20 mins

SERVES 4

INGREDIENTS

1 tbsp olive oil

2 tbsp sunflower seeds

1 onion, finely chopped

1 garlic clove, finely chopped

1 lb/450 g spinach, thick stalks removed and leaves shredded

4 beefsteak tomatoes

1½ cups diced mozzarella cheese

pinch of freshly grated nutmeg

salt and pepper

1 Heat the oil in a heavy pan. Add the sunflower seeds to the pan and cook, stirring constantly, for 2 minutes, until golden.

2 Add the onion and cook over low heat, stirring occasionally, for 5 minutes, until soft but not brown. Add the garlic and spinach, cover, and cook for a further 2–3 minutes until the spinach has wilted.

3 Remove from the heat and season to taste with nutmeg, salt, and pepper. Let cool.

4 Cut off and reserve a thin slice from the top of each tomato and scoop out the flesh with a teaspoon, taking care not to pierce the shell. Chop the flesh and stir it into the spinach mixture with the cheese.

5 Fill each of the tomato shells with some of the spinach and cheese mixture and replace the tops. Cut 4 squares of foil, each large enough to enclose a tomato. Place 1 tomato in the center of each square and fold up the sides to enclose securely.

6 Cook the stuffed tomatoes on a hot grill, turning them occasionally, for 10 minutes. Serve immediately, in the foil parcels.

Spicy Caribbean Kabobs

Bring a taste of the tropics to your barbecue with these sizzling vegetable kabobs in a spicy hot marinade.

NUTRITIONAL INFORMATION

Calories 250	Sugars 10g	
Protein 5g	Fat 13g	
Carbohydrate 3g	Saturates 2g	

20 mins, plus marinating   15 mins

SERVES 4

INGREDIENTS

115 g/4 oz chayote, peeled, pitted, and cut into 2.5 cm/1 inch cubes

1 plantain, peeled and cut into thick slices

1 corn ear cut into 2.5 cm/1 inch thick slices

1 eggplant, cut into chunks

1 red bell pepper, seeded and cut into chunks

1 green bell pepper, seeded and cut into chunks

1 onion, cut into wedges

8 white mushrooms

4 cherry tomatoes

MARINADE

⅔ cup tomato juice

4 tbsp sunflower oil

4 tbsp lime juice

3 tbsp dark soy sauce

1 shallot, finely chopped

2 garlic cloves, finely chopped

1 fresh green chili, seeded and finely chopped

½ tsp ground cinnamon

pepper

1 Prepare the vegetables. Blanch the chayote in boiling water for 2 minutes. Drain, refresh in cold water, and drain again. Place it in a large bowl with the plantain, corn ear eggplant, red and green bell peppers, onion, mushrooms, and tomatoes.

2 Combine the tomato juice, sunflower oil, lime juice, soy sauce, shallot, garlic, chili, and cinnamon in a pitcher and season to taste with pepper. Pour the marinade over the vegetables, tossing to coat. Cover with plastic wrap and let marinate for 3 hours.

3 Drain the vegetables, reserving the marinade. Thread the vegetables on to skewers. Cook on a hot grill, turning and brushing frequently with the reserved marinade, for 10–15 minutes.

Potato Fans

These garlic-flavored potatoes are baked in foil on the grill. They need plenty of time to cook, but otherwise they take care of themselves.

NUTRITIONAL INFORMATION

Calories	235	Sugars	.........2g
Protein	.........6g	Fat	...........4g
Carbohydrate	...46g	Saturates	.......1g

  5 mins   1 hr

SERVES 6

I N G R E D I E N T S

6 large potatoes, scrubbed but not peeled

2 tbsp garlic-flavored olive oil

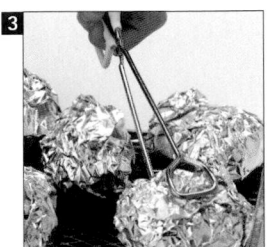

1 Make a series of cuts across the potatoes almost all the way through. Cut out 6 squares of foil, each large enough to enclose a potato.

2 Place a potato on each square of foil and brush generously with the garlic flavored oil. Fold up the sides to enclose the potatoes entirely.

3 Cook on a hot grill, turning occasionally, for 1 hour. To serve, open the foil parcels and gently pinch the potatoes to open up the fans.

COOK'S TIP

If you do not have any garlic-flavored oil, pour 2 tablespoons olive oil into a bowl, add 1 lightly crushed garlic clove, cover with plastic wrap and let infuse for 2 hours, then use as above.

Cheese & Red Onion Kabobs

Red onions have a mild, sweet flavor and retain their attractive color when cooked. Here, they are grilled with tart apples and salty cheese.

NUTRITIONAL INFORMATION

Calories	449	Sugars	........13g
Protein	........21g	Fat	..........34g
Carbohydrate	...16g	Saturates	.......2g

10 mins, plus marinating   10–15 mins

SERVES 4

INGREDIENTS

3 red onions, cut into wedges

1 lb/450g halloumi cheese, cut into 1 inch/2.5 cm cubes

2 tart eating apples, cored and cut into wedges

4 tbsp olive oil

1 tbsp cider vinegar

1 tbsp Dijon mustard

1 garlic clove, finely chopped

1 tsp finely chopped sage

salt and pepper

COOK'S TIP

If you like, you could serve these kabobs with Mild Mustard Sauce (see page 8).

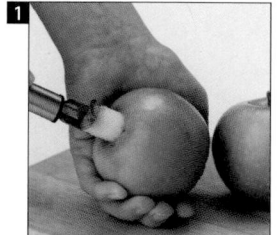

1 Prepare the ingredients. Place the onions, cheese, and apples in a large, shallow, nonmetallic dish. Combine the oil, vinegar, mustard, and the chopped garlic and sage in a pitcher and season to taste.

2 Pour the marinade over the onions, cheese, and apples, tossing to coat. Cover with plastic wrap and let marinate for 2 hours.

3 Drain the marinated onions, cheese, and apples, reserving the marinade for basting the skewers as they cook. Thread the onions, cheese, and apples alternately on to skewers.

4 Cook the kabobs on a hot grill, turning and brushing frequently with the reserved marinade, for 10–15 minutes. Serve immediately.

Toffee Fruit Kabobs

Serve these fruit kabobs with a sticky toffee sauce. They are perfect for fall celebrations such as Hallowe'en.

NUTRITIONAL INFORMATION

Calories	656	Sugars 48g
Protein	.........2g	Fat 52g
Carbohydrate	...48g	Saturates 34g

10 mins   5 mins

SERVES 4

INGREDIENTS

2 dessert apples, cored and cut into wedges

2 firm pears, cored and cut into wedges

juice of ½ lemon

2 tbsp light muscovado sugar

¼ tsp ground allspice

2 tbsp unsalted butter, melted

TOFFEE SAUCE

9 tbsp butter

¾ cup light muscovado sugar

6 tbsp heavy cream

1 Toss the apple and pears in the lemon juice to prevent any discoloration.

2 Mix the sugar and allspice together and sprinkle over the fruit. Thread the fruit pieces on to skewers.

3 To make the toffee sauce, place the butter and sugar in a pan and heat, stirring gently, until the butter has melted and the sugar has dissolved.

4 Add the cream to the pan and bring to a boil. Boil for 1–2 minutes, then let cool slightly.

5 Meanwhile, place the fruit kabobs over hot coals and grill for about 5 minutes, turning and basting frequently with the melted butter, until the fruit is just tender. Transfer the kabobs to warm serving plates.

6 Pour over the slightly cooled toffee sauce and serve the fruit kabobs immediately.

COOK'S TIP

Firm apples that will keep their shape are needed for this dish. Soft apples and pears will become mushy as they cook.

Baked Bananas

The orange-flavored cream can be prepared in advance, but do not make up the banana packets until just before you need to cook them.

NUTRITIONAL INFORMATION

Calories	380	Sugars	........40g
Protein	.........2g	Fat	..........18g
Carbohydrate	...43g	Saturates	.....11g

🧊 30 mins   🕐 10 mins

SERVES 4

I N G R E D I E N T S

4 bananas

2 passion fruit

4 tbsp orange juice

4 tbsp orange-flavored liqueur

O R A N G E - F L A V O R E D
C R E A M

⅔ cup heavy cream

3 tbsp confectioners' sugar

2 tbsp orange-flavored liqueur

1 To make the orange-flavored cream, pour the heavy cream into a mixing bowl and sprinkle with the confectioners' sugar. Whisk the mixture until it is standing in soft peaks. Carefully fold in the orange-flavored liqueur and chill in the refrigerator until required.

2 Peel the bananas and place each one on a sheet of aluminum foil.

3 Cut the passion fruit in half and squeeze the juice of each half over each banana. Spoon over the orange juice and liqueur.

4 Fold the aluminum foil over the top of the bananas so that they are completely enclosed.

5 Place the packets on a cookie sheet and bake the bananas in a preheated oven, 350°F/180°C, for about 10 minutes or until they are just tender (test by inserting a toothpick.)

6 Transfer the foil packets to warm, individual serving plates. Open out the foil packets at the table and then serve immediately with the chilled orange-flavored cream.

VARIATION

Leave the bananas in their skins for a really quick dessert. Split the banana skins and pop in 1–2 squares of chocolate. Wrap the bananas in aluminum foil and bake for 10 minutes or until the chocolate has just melted.

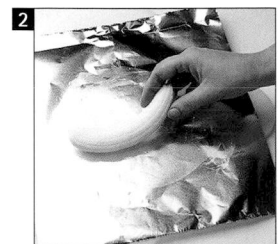

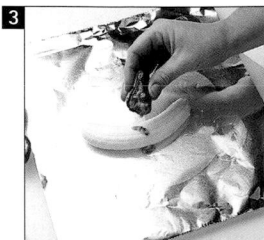

Exotic Fruit Parcels

Delicious pieces of exotic fruit are warmed through in a deliciously scented sauce to make a delicious grilled dessert.

NUTRITIONAL INFORMATION

Calories	43	Sugars	.........9g
Protein	.........2g	Fat	..........0.3g
Carbohydrate	....9g	Saturates	.....0.1g

🖐 🖐

🍮 10 mins, plus marinating   🕐 15–20 mins

.SERVES 4

INGREDIENTS

1 papaya

1 mango

1 star fruit

1 tbsp grenadine

3 tbsp orange juice

light cream or low-fat unsweetened yogurt, to serve

1 Cut the papaya in half, scoop out the seeds, and discard them. Peel the papaya and cut the flesh into thick slices.

2 Prepare the mango by cutting it lengthwise in half either side of the central pit.

3 Score each mango half in a criss-cross pattern. Push each mango half inside out to separate the cubes and cut them away from the peel.

4 Using a sharp knife, thickly slice the star fruit.

5 Place all of the fruit in a bowl and mix them together.

6 Mix the grenadine and orange juice together and pour over the fruit. Let marinate for at least 30 minutes.

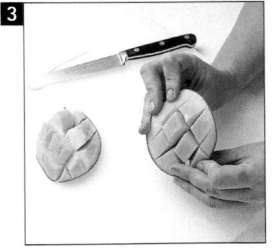

7 Divide the fruit among 4 double thickness squares of foil and gather up the edges to form a parcel that encloses the fruit.

8 Place the foil parcel on a rack set over warm coals and grill the fruit for 15–20 minutes.

9 Serve the fruit in the parcel, with the cream or low-fat unsweetened yogurt.

COOK'S TIP

Grenadine is a sweet syrup made from pomegranates. If you prefer you could use pomegranate juice instead. To extract the juice, cut the pomegranate in half and squeeze gently with a lemon squeezer—do not press too hard or the juice may become bitter.

Fruit with Maple Syrup

Slices of juicy fruit are coated in a rich maple syrup sauce as they cook in little parcels on the grill.

NUTRITIONAL INFORMATION

Calories ....383 Sugars 33g
Protein ....2g Fat 24g
Carbohydrate ...42g Saturates 16g

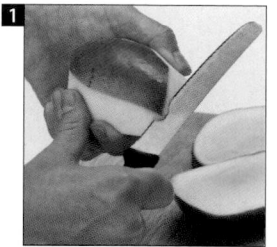

20 mins   10 mins

SERVES 4

INGREDIENTS

1 papaya, halved and seeded

2 bananas

2 peaches, peeled and pitted

1 ogen melon, halved and seeded

1 mango, peeled, pitted, and sliced

½ cup sweet butter, diced

4 tbsp maple syrup

pinch of ground allspice

1 Cut out 4 large squares of foil. Cut the papaya into thick slices and peel off the skin. Peel the bananas and cut in half lengthwise. Slice the peach halves. Cut the melon halves into thin wedges, then cut the flesh away from the rind. Divide the fruit among the foil squares.

2 Dice the butter. Put the butter and maple syrup in a food processor and process until thoroughly combined and smooth. Divide the flavored butter between the piles of fruit and sprinkle with a little allspice. Fold up the sides of the foil to enclose the fruit securely.

3 Cook the fruit parcels over medium-hot coals, turning occasionally, for 10 minutes. Serve immediately.

Stuffed Pears

It has long been known that sprinkling strawberries with pepper brings out their flavor, and this is just as effective with other fruit.

NUTRITIONAL INFORMATION

Calories	184	Sugars	........42g
Protein	.........1g	Fat	...........3g
Carbohydrate	...42g	Saturates	.......2g

 20 mins   20 mins

SERVES 4

I N G R E D I E N T S

2 tsp sweet butter

4 firm dessert pears

2 tbsp lemon juice

4 tbsp rosehip syrup

1 tsp green peppercorns, lightly crushed

1¼ cups redcurrants

4 tbsp superfine sugar

vanilla ice cream, to serve

1 Cut 4 squares of foil, each large enough to enclose the pears, and grease with the butter. Halve and core the pears, but do not peel them. Brush the cut surfaces with lemon juice. Place 2 pear halves on each of the foil squares, brush them with the rosehip syrup, and sprinkle with the pepper.

2 Put the redcurrants in a bowl and sprinkle with the sugar. Spoon the redcurrant mixture into the cavities of the pears. Fold up the sides of the foil to enclose the pears securely.

3 Cook the pears on a hot grill for 20 minutes. Serve with ice cream.

VARIATION
Substitute your own favorite soft fruit, such as blackcurrants or blueberries, for the redcurrants.

Banana Sizzles

Bananas are particularly sweet and delicious when grilled—
and conveniently come with their own protective wrapping.

NUTRITIONAL INFORMATION

Calories 284	Sugars 37g	
Protein 2g	Fat 12g	
Carbohydrate ...41g	Saturates 8g	

10 mins   6–8 mins

SERVES 4

INGREDIENTS

3 tbsp butter, softened

2 tbsp dark rum

1 tbsp orange juice

4 tbsp muscovado sugar

pinch of ground cinnamon

4 bananas

1 Beat the butter with the rum, orange, sugar, and cinnamon in a small bowl until thoroughly combined and smooth.

2 Place the bananas, without peeling, on a hot grill and cook, turning frequently, for 6–8 minutes, until the skins are blackened.

3 Transfer the bananas to serving plates, slit the skins, and cut partially through the flesh lengthwise. Divide the flavored butter between the bananas and serve.

VARIATION

You can also cook the bananas wrapped in foil. Cut them in half lengthwise without peeling. Spread the flavored butter on the cut surfaces and reassemble the bananas. Wrap in foil parcels and cook on a medium grill for 5–10 minutes.

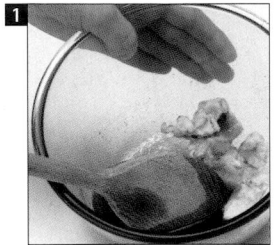
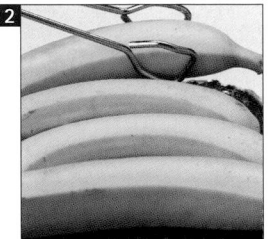
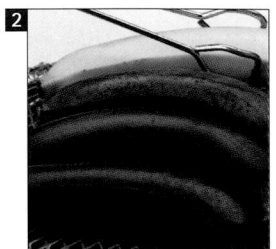

Zucchini & Cheese Parcels

These delicately flavored, melt-in-the mouth stuffed zucchini are cooked in the grill embers and need no attention.

NUTRITIONAL INFORMATION

Calories	...172	Sugars	...6g
Protein	...9g	Fat	...12g
Carbohydrate	...8g	Saturates	...1g

 10 mins   30 mins

SERVES 4

INGREDIENTS

8 zucchini

1 tbsp olive oil, plus extra for brushing

4 oz/155 g feta cheese, cut into strips

1 tbsp fresh mint

pepper

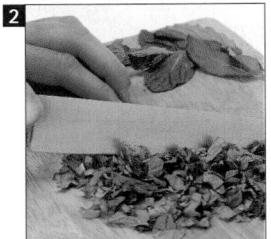
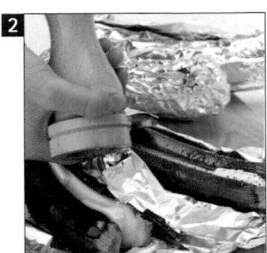

1 Cut 8 rectangles of foil, each large enough to enclose a zucchini, and brush lightly with oil. Cut a slit along the length of each zucchini and place them on the foil rectangles.

2 Insert strips of feta into the zucchini slits, drizzle with the olive oil, sprinkle with the mint, and season to taste with pepper. Fold in the sides of the foil securely to enclose the zucchini.

3 Bake the zucchini in the grill embers for 30 minutes. Unwrap and serve immediately.

VARIATION
Substitute mozzarella or fontina for the feta cheese.

Chargrilled Vegetables

This medley of bell peppers, zucchini, eggplant, and red onion can be served on its own or as an unusual side dish.

NUTRITIONAL INFORMATION

Calories 66   Sugars 7g
Protein . . . . .2g   Fat 3g
Carbohydrate . . . .7g   Saturates 0.5g

15 mins   15 mins

SERVES 4

INGREDIENTS

1 large red bell pepper

1 large green bell pepper

1 large orange bell pepper

1 large zucchini

4 baby eggplants

2 medium red onions

2 tbsp lemon juice

1 tbsp olive oil

1 garlic clove, crushed

1 tbsp chopped fresh rosemary or
   1 tsp dried rosemary

salt and pepper

TO SERVE

cracked wheat, cooked

tomato and olive relish

 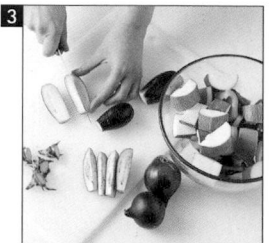 

1 Halve and seed the bell peppers and cut into even-size pieces, about 1 inch/2.5 cm wide.

2 Trim the zucchini, cut them in half lengthwise, and slice into 1 inch/2.5 cm pieces. Place the bell peppers and zucchini in a large bowl.

3 Trim the eggplants and quarter them lengthwise. Peel the onions, then cut each of them into 8 even-size wedges.

Add the eggplants and onions to the bell peppers and zucchini.

4 In a small bowl, whisk the lemon juice together with the olive oil, garlic, and rosemary. Season to taste with salt and pepper. Pour the mixture over the vegetables and stir to coat evenly.

5 Thread the vegetables onto 8 metal or pre-soaked wooden skewers. Grill over hot coals, turning frequently, for about 8–10 minutes, or until the vegetables are soft and beginning to char. Alternatively, arrange the kabobs on the broiler rack and cook under a preheated broiler, turning frequently, for about 10–12 minutes until the vegetables are lightly charred and just soft.

6 Drain the vegetable kabobs and serve immediately on a bed of cracked wheat, accompanied with a tomato and olive relish.

Chargrilled Vegetable Platter

Chargrilling is a popular way of cooking vegetables in the Mediterranean because it intensifies the flavor of the sun-ripened produce.

NUTRITIONAL INFORMATION

Calories	157	Sugars	........6g
Protein	.........5g	Fat	..........10g
Carbohydrate	...15g	Saturates	.......2g

10 mins   15–20 mins

SERVES 4–6

I N G R E D I E N T S

4½ lb/2 kg mixed fresh vegetables, such as eggplants, endive, zucchini, fennel, bell peppers, scallions

garlic-flavored olive oil

salt and pepper

fresh basil leaves, to garnish

1 Prepare the vegetables as necessary. Trim the ends of the eggplants and cut into ¼-inch slices. Cut each head of endive in half lengthwise.

2 Trim the ends from the zucchini and cut the zucchini into ¼-inch slices. Remove the fronds from the fennel and slice thickly across the grain.

3 Cut the bell peppers into quarters, then remove the cores and seeds. Trim the top green part of the scallions, and cut in half lengthwise if large.

4 As each vegetable is prepared, put it in a large bowl, drizzle with the garlic oil, and season lightly with salt and pepper. Using your hands, toss the vegetables together, so they are just lightly coated with oil; the vegetables should not be dripping in oil.

5 Heat a large, ridged cast-iron skillet over high heat and lightly brush with olive oil. Add a batch of vegetables—enough to fit in the pan in a single layer. Cook the vegetables on one side over medium-high heat until they are starting to turn limp.

6 Brush the half-cooked vegetables with a little more oil, then turn them.

Continue cooking until they are tender—the exact cooking times will depend on the age and thickness of the vegetables.

7 Transfer to a large platter and repeat with the remaining vegetables.

8 While still hot, sprinkle the vegetables with salt and pepper. Garnish with basil leaves and serve.

  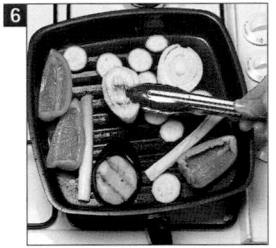

Fruit Parcels

Cooking fruit in a foil parcel is a good idea for dessert, as it keeps the fruit wonderfully moist and needs no attention.

NUTRITIONAL INFORMATION

Calories 112   Sugars 28g
Protein . . . . .2g   Fat 0g
Carbohydrate . . .28g   Saturates 0g

15 mins   4 mins

SERVES 4

INGREDIENTS

2 oranges

2 eating apples

juice of 1 lemon

2 pears

4 tsp muscovado sugar

1 Peel the oranges, carefully removing all the pith. Cut each horizontally into 6 slices.

2 Core the apples, but do not peel. Cut each horizontally into 6 slices. Brush the slices with lemon juice.

3 Peel and core the pears, then cut each of them horizontally into 6 slices. Brush the slices with lemon juice.

4 Cut out 4 large squares of foil. Divide the fruit slices equally among the squares and sprinkle each pile with 1 teaspoon of the sugar. Fold up the sides of the squares to enclose the fruit securely.

5 Cook the parcels on a medium grill for about 4 minutes. Serve immediately.

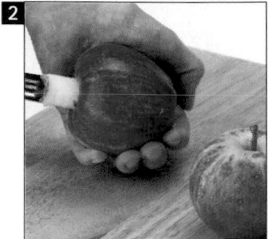

Chargrilled Pineapple

Fresh pineapple slices are cooked on the grill, and brushed
with a buttery fresh ginger and brown sugar baste.

NUTRITIONAL INFORMATION

Calories 461   Sugars 44g
Protein . . . . .5g   Fat 30g
Carbohydrate . . .45g   Saturates 20g

10 mins   10 mins

SERVES 4

I N G R E D I E N T S

1 pineapple

B U T T E R

9 tbsp butter

¾ cup light muscovado sugar

1 tsp finely grated fresh ginger root

T O P P I N G

1 cup unsweetened yogurt

½ tsp ground cinnamon

1 tbsp light muscovado sugar

1 Prepare the pineapple by cutting off the spiky top. Peel the pineapple with a sharp knife, remove the "eyes," and cut the flesh into thick slices.

2 To make the ginger-flavored butter, put the butter, sugar, and ginger into a small pan and heat gently until melted. Transfer to a heatproof bowl and keep warm at the side of the grill, ready for basting the fruit.

3 To prepare the topping, mix together the yogurt, cinnamon, and sugar. Cover and chill until ready to serve.

4 Grill the pineapple slices, brushing them well with the ginger butter baste, for about 2 minutes on each side.

5 Serve the pineapple with a little extra ginger butter sauce poured over. Top with a spoonful of the spiced yogurt.

VARIATION
If you prefer, substitute ½ teaspoon ground ginger for the grated ginger root. Light muscovado sugar gives the best flavor, but you can use ordinary soft brown sugar instead.

Grape Leaf Packets

A wonderful combination of soft cheese, chopped dates, ground almonds, and lightly sautéed nuts is encased in grape leaves.

NUTRITIONAL INFORMATION

Calories 459   Sugars 8g
Protein . . . . .12g   Fat 42g
Carbohydrate . . . .9g   Saturates 20g

25 mins   15 mins

SERVES 4

INGREDIENTS

1¼ cups full-fat soft cheese

½ cup ground almonds

2 tbsp chopped pitted dates

salt and pepper

2 tbsp butter

4 tbsp sliced almonds

12–16 grape leaves

grilled baby corn, to serve

TO GARNISH

fresh rosemary sprigs

tomato wedges

1 Beat the soft cheese in a large bowl until smooth. Add the ground almonds and chopped dates and mix together thoroughly. Season to taste with salt and pepper.

2 Melt the butter in a small skillet. Add the almonds and cook over very low heat, stirring constantly, for 2–3 minutes, until golden brown. Remove from the heat and let cool for a few minutes.

3 Mix the sliced almonds into the soft cheese mixture, stirring well to combine thoroughly.

4 Soak the grape leaves in water, if specified on the packet. Drain them, lay them out on a counter and spoon an equal amount of the soft cheese mixture onto each. Fold over the leaves to enclose the filling.

5 Wrap the grape leaf packets in foil, 1 or 2 per foil package. Place over the grill to heat through for about 8–10 minutes, turning once. Serve with grilled baby corn and garnish with sprigs of rosemary and tomato wedges.

Grilled Potato Wedges

Serve this tasty potato dish with grilled kabobs, bean burgers, or vegetarian sausages.

NUTRITIONAL INFORMATION

Calories	257	Sugars 1g
Protein	.........3g	Fat 16g
Carbohydrate	...26g	Saturates 5g

 10 mins   30–35 mins

SERVES 4

INGREDIENTS

3 large baking potatoes, scrubbed

4 tbsp olive oil

2 tbsp butter

2 garlic cloves, chopped

1 tbsp chopped fresh rosemary

1 tbsp chopped fresh parsley

1 tbsp chopped fresh thyme

salt and pepper

Barbecue Sauce (see page 624), to serve

1 Bring a large pan of water to a boil. Add the potatoes and parboil them for 10 minutes. Drain the potatoes and refresh under cold water, then drain them again thoroughly.

2 Transfer the potatoes to a cutting board. When the potatoes are cold enough to handle, cut them into thick wedges, but do not peel.

3 Heat the oil and butter in a small pan together with the garlic. Cook gently until the garlic begins to brown, then remove the pan from the heat.

4 Stir the herbs and salt and pepper to taste into the mixture in the pan.

5 Brush the herb mixture all over the potato wedges.

6 Grill the potatoes over hot coals for 10–15 minutes, or until the potato wedges are just tender. Turn the potatoes once or twice during cooking, brushing liberally with any of the remaining herb and butter mixture.

7 Transfer the garlic potato wedges to a warm serving plate and serve as an appetizer or as a side dish.

COOK'S TIP

You may find it easier to grill these potatoes in a hinged rack or in a specially designed roasting pan.

Cheese & Onion Baguettes

Part-baked baguettes are split and filled with a tasty cheese and onion mixture, then wrapped in foil and cooked over the grill.

NUTRITIONAL INFORMATION

Calories 715	Sugars 5g
Protein 21g	Fat 41g
Carbohydrate . . .70g	Saturates 25g

15 mins   20 mins

SERVES 4

I N G R E D I E N T S

4 part-baked baguettes

2 tbsp tomato relish

4 tbsp butter

8 scallions, finely chopped

9 tbsp cream cheese

1 cup colby cheese, grated

1 tsp snipped fresh chives

pepper

T O   S E R V E

mixed salad leaves

herbs

COOK'S TIP

If there's no room on the grill, and you want to eat these at the same time as the rest of the food, bake them in a preheated oven, at 400°F/200°C, for 15 minutes.

1 Split the part-baked baguettes in half lengthwise, without cutting right through. Spread a little tomato relish on each split baguette.

2 Melt the butter in a skillet and add the chopped scallions. Sauté them over medium heat, stirring frequently, for 5 minutes, until soft and golden. Remove from the heat and let cool slightly.

3 Beat the cream cheese in a mixing bowl to soften it. Mix in the scallions, with any remaining butter. Add the grated cheese and snipped chives and mix well. Season to taste with pepper.

4 Divide the cheese mixture between the baguettes, spread it over the cut surfaces and sandwich the baguettes together again. Wrap each baguette tightly in aluminum foil.

5 Heat the baguettes over the grill for about 10–15 minutes, turning them occasionally. Peel back the foil to check that they are cooked and if the cheese mixture has melted.

6 Serve the baguettes with salad leaves and garnished with fresh herbs.

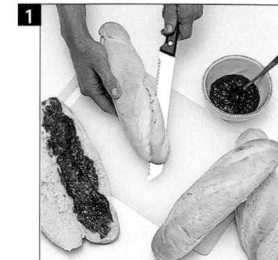

Sidekick Vegetables

Colorful vegetables are grilled over hot coals to make this unusual hot salad, which is served with a spicy chili sauce on the side.

NUTRITIONAL INFORMATION

Calories	224	Sugars	........14g
Protein	.........4g	Fat	..........15g
Carbohydrate	...21g	Saturates	.......2g

🍴 15 mins   🕐 30 mins

SERVES 4

I N G R E D I E N T S

1 red bell pepper, seeded

1 orange or yellow bell pepper, seeded

2 zucchini

2 corn ears

1 eggplant

olive oil, for brushing

salt and pepper

handful of chopped fresh thyme, rosemary, and parsley

lime or lemon wedges, to serve

D R E S S I N G

2 tbsp olive oil

1 tbsp sesame oil

1 garlic clove, crushed

1 small onion, finely chopped

1 celery stalk, finely chopped

1 small fresh green chili, seeded and chopped

4 tomatoes, chopped

2 inch/5 cm piece of cucumber, chopped

1 tbsp tomato paste

1 tbsp lime or lemon juice

salt and pepper

1 To make the dressing, heat the olive and sesame oils together in a pan or skillet. Add the garlic and onion, and cook over low heat, stirring occasionally, for about 3 minutes until soft.

2 Add the celery, chili, and tomatoes to the pan and cook, stirring frequently, for 5 minutes.

3 Stir in the chopped cucumber, tomato paste, and lime or lemon juice, and simmer over low heat for 8–10 minutes until thick and pulpy. Season to taste with salt and pepper.

4 Cut the vegetables into thick slices and brush with a little olive oil.

5 Cook the vegetables over the hot coals of the grill for about 5–8 minutes, turning over once. Sprinkle the vegetables with salt and pepper and fresh herbs as they cook.

6 Divide the vegetables among 4 serving plates and spoon some of the dressing onto the side. Serve immediately, sprinkled with a few more chopped herbs and accompanied by the lime or lemon wedges.

Marinated Brochettes

These bean curd and mushroom brochettes are marinated in a lemon, garlic, and herb mixture so that they soak up a delicious flavor.

NUTRITIONAL INFORMATION

Calories 192   Sugars 0.5g
Protein . . . . .11g   Fat 16g
Carbohydrate . . . .1g   Saturates 2g

15 mins, plus marinating   6 mins

SERVES 4

INGREDIENTS

1 lemon

1 garlic clove, crushed

4 tbsp olive oil

4 tbsp white wine vinegar

1 tbsp chopped fresh herbs, such as rosemary, parsley, and thyme

salt and pepper

10½ oz/300 g smoked bean curd

12 oz/350 g mushrooms

fresh herbs, to garnish

TO SERVE

mixed salad greens

cherry tomatoes, halved

1 Finely grate the zest from the lemon and squeeze out the juice.

2 Add the garlic, olive oil, vinegar, and chopped herbs and mix well. Season to taste with salt and pepper.

3 Slice the bean curd into large chunks with a sharp knife. Thread the pieces onto metal or wooden skewers, alternating them with the mushrooms.

4 Place the brochettes in a shallow, nonmetallic dish and pour over the marinade. Cover with plastic wrap and chill in the refrigerator for 1–2 hours, turning the brochettes occasionally.

5 Remove the brochettes from the dish, reserving the marinade. Cook on a medium hot grill, brushing them frequently with the marinade and turning often, for about 6 minutes until cooked through and golden brown. Alternatively, cook under a preheated broiler, turning them frequently and brushing with the reserved marinade.

6 Transfer to warmed serving plates, garnish with herbs, and serve with mixed salad greens and cherry tomatoes.

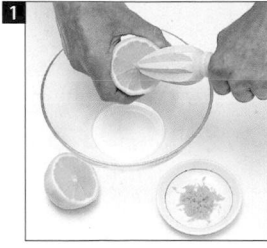 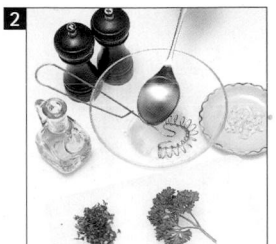 

Eggplant & Potato Rolls

Partially cooked in advance, these attractive little aubergine rolls with a tasty sweet-potato filling are baked in foil parcels.

NUTRITIONAL INFORMATION

Calories	452	Sugars	........14g
Protein	........17g	Fat	..........27g
Carbohydrate	...39g	Saturates	......11g

30 mins   45–50 mins

SERVES 4–6

INGREDIENTS

1 lb/450 g sweet potatoes

4 scallions, chopped

1½ cups diced Swiss cheese

1 red bell pepper, seeded and chopped

1 garlic clove, crushed

1 tsp chopped fresh thyme

salt and pepper

4 tbsp all-purpose flour

1½ tsp paprika

1½ tsp curry powder

1½ tsp celery salt

1 tsp superfine sugar

1 tbsp garlic granules

4 large eggplants

3 tbsp olive oil, plus extra for brushing

1 Cook the potatoes in a large pan of lightly salted water for 20 minutes, or until tender. Drain and let cool, then peel and mash in a large bowl until smooth. Add the scallions, cheese, red bell pepper, garlic, and thyme and season to taste.

2 Place the flour on a plate and stir in the paprika, curry powder, celery salt, sugar, and garlic granules. Slice each eggplant lengthwise into quarters and dust with the seasoned flour. Heat half the oil in a large, heavy skillet. Add the eggplant slices, in batches, and cook until just golden brown, adding more oil as necessary. Remove with a slotted spoon and let cool.

3 Place a spoonful of the sweet potato mixture on each eggplant slice and roll up. Cut out 4 x 12 inch/30 cm squares of foil and brush each one with oil. Place 4 eggplant rolls on each square and fold up the sides to enclose the rolls. Cook on a medium–hot grill, turning occasionally, for 25–30 minutes. Unwrap the parcels and transfer the rolls to a serving dish.

COOK'S TIP

Salting the eggplants helps to prevent them soaking up so much oil during cooking. Place the slices in a strainer, sprinkling each layer liberally with salt, and leave to drain for 30 minutes. Rinse thoroughly and pat dry with paper towels before coating with seasoned flour.

Eggplants with Tzatziki

This makes a delicious appetizer for a barbecue party or can be served as part of a vegetarian barbecue meze.

NUTRITIONAL INFORMATION

Calories 137	Sugars 4g
Protein 5g	Fat 11g
Carbohydrate 5g	Saturates 4g

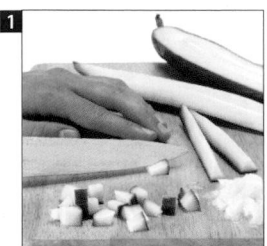

🕐 15 mins   🕑 10 mins

SERVES 4

INGREDIENTS

1 cup unsweetened Greek yogurt

½ cucumber, diced

4 scallions, finely chopped

1 garlic clove, finely chopped

3 tbsp chopped fresh mint

salt and pepper

2 tbsp olive oil

2 eggplants, thinly sliced

 First, make the tzatziki. Dice the cucumber. Place the yogurt in a bowl and beat well until smooth. Stir in the cucumber, scallions, garlic, and mint. Season to taste with salt and pepper. Transfer to a serving bowl, cover with plastic wrap, and chill in the refrigerator.

VARIATION

An alternative dip to serve with the eggplant slices can be made very quickly by combining 1¼ cups sour cream with 2 very finely chopped garlic cloves. Season to taste with salt and pepper and chill before serving.

 Season the olive oil to taste with plenty of salt and pepper, then brush the eggplant slices generously with the seasoned oil.

3 Cook the eggplants on a hot grill for 5 minutes on each side, brushing with more oil, if necessary. Serve immediately with the tsatziki.

Pumpkin Parcels

This spicy side dish is perfect to serve at a Hallowe'en party, although it is equally delicious on a summer evening.

NUTRITIONAL INFORMATION

Energy	118	Sugar	........3g
Protein	.........1g	Fat	...........11g
Carbohydrates	....4g	Saturates	.......4g

 10 mins   25–30 mins

SERVES 4

INGREDIENTS

1½ lb/675 g pumpkin or squash

2 tbsp sunflower oil

2 tbsp butter

½ tsp chili sauce

grated zest of 1 lime

2 tsp lime juice

1 Halve the pumpkin or squash and scoop out the seeds. Rinse the seeds and reserve. Cut the pumpkin into thin wedges and peel.

2 Heat the oil and butter together in a large pan, stirring constantly, until melted. Stir in the chili sauce, lime zest, and juice.

3 Add the pumpkin or squash and seeds to the pan and toss to coat all over in the flavored butter.

4 Divide the mixture between 4 double thickness sheets of foil and fold over the foil to enclose the mixture completely.

5 Grill the foil parcels over hot coals for 15–25 minutes, or until the pumpkin or squash is tender.

6 Transfer the foil parcels to warm serving plates. Open the parcels at the table and serve at once.

VARIATION
Add 2 teaspoons of curry paste to the oil instead of the lime and chili. Use butternut squash when pumpkin is not available.

Spicy Sweet Potato Slices

Serve these as an accompaniment to other grill dishes or with a spicy dip as an appetizer while the other dishes are being cooked.

NUTRITIONAL INFORMATION

Calories ....178 Sugars 0.8g
Protein ....2g Fat 6g
Carbohydrate ...32g Saturates 0.7g

10 mins   25 mins

SERVES 4

INGREDIENTS

1 lb/450 g sweet potatoes, unpeeled

2 tbsp sunflower oil

1 tsp chili sauce

salt and pepper

1 Bring a large pan of water to a boil. Add the sweet potatoes and parboil them for 10 minutes. Drain thoroughly and transfer to a cutting board.

2 Peel the potatoes and cut them into thick slices.

3 Mix together the sunflower oil, chili sauce, and salt and pepper to taste in a small bowl.

4 Brush the spicy mixture liberally over one side of the potatoes. Place the potatoes, oil side down, over medium–hot coals and grill for 5–6 minutes.

5 Lightly brush the tops of the potatoes with the oil, then turn them over and grill for another 5 minutes or until crisp and golden.

6 Transfer the potatoes to a warm serving dish and serve at once, with a dip if liked (see Cook's Tip, left).

COOK'S TIP

For a simple spicy dip, combine ⅔ cup sour cream with ½ teaspoon of sugar, ½ teaspoon of Dijon mustard, and salt and pepper to taste. Chill until required.

Barbecue Mushrooms

Large mushrooms have more flavor than the smaller white ones. Serve these mushrooms as part of a vegetarian barbecue.

NUTRITIONAL INFORMATION

Calories 148   Sugars 1g
Protein ....11g   Fat 7g
Carbohydrate ....11g   Saturates 3g

10 mins   15 mins

SERVES 4

INGREDIENTS

12 open-cap mushrooms

4 tsp olive oil

4 scallions, chopped

1¾ cups fresh brown bread crumbs

1 tsp chopped fresh oregano

4 oz/100 g low-fat sharp Cheddar cheese

1 Remove the stems from the mushrooms, reserving the caps. Chop the stems finely.

2 Heat half the oil in a skillet. Add the mushroom stems and scallions and cook over low heat, stirring occasionally, for 5 minutes.

3 Transfer the mushroom stems and scallions to a large bowl with a slotted spoon and add the bread crumbs and oregano. Mix well.

4 Crumble the cheese into small pieces in a small bowl. Add the cheese to the bread crumb mixture and mix well. Carefully spoon the stuffing mixture into the mushroom caps.

5 Drizzle the remaining oil over the stuffed mushrooms. Cook the mushrooms on an oiled rack over medium–hot coals for 10 minutes or until cooked through. Alternatively, arrange on a cookie sheet and bake in a preheated oven, 350°F/180°C for about 20 minutes or until cooked through.

6 Transfer the mushrooms to serving plates and serve hot.

VARIATION

For a change, replace the cheese with chopped hard-cooked egg, or chopped olives. Mop up the juices with some crusty bread.

Vegetarian Sausages

The delicious cheese flavor will make these sausages a hit with vegetarians, who need not feel left out when it comes to a barbecue.

NUTRITIONAL INFORMATION

Calories	.213	Sugars	.4g
Protein	.8g	Fat	.12g
Carbohydrate	.19g	Saturates	.4g

50 mins   25 mins

MAKES 8

I N G R E D I E N T S

1 tbsp sunflower oil

1 small onion, finely chopped

¾ cup mushrooms, finely chopped

½ red bell pepper, seeded and finely chopped

1½ cups canned cannellini beans, rinsed and drained

2¾ cups fresh bread crumbs

scant 1 cup colby cheese, grated

1 tsp dried mixed herbs

1 egg yolk

seasoned all-purpose flour

vegetable oil, to baste

T O   S E R V E

hot dog rolls

slices of fried onion

1 Heat the oil in a pan. Cook the onion, mushrooms, and red bell pepper over low heat for 5 minutes or until they are soft.

2 Mash the beans in a bowl with a potato masher. Add the onion, mushroom mixture, bread crumbs, cheese, herbs, and egg yolk and mix together well.

3 Press the mixture together with your fingers and shape into 8 sausages. Roll each sausage in the seasoned flour to coat evenly. Let chill in the refrigerator for at least 30 minutes.

4 Grill the sausages on a sheet of oiled foil set over medium–hot coals for about 15–20 minutes, turning and basting frequently with oil, until golden. Alternatively, cook under a preheated broiler, basting with the oil.

5 Split a hot dog roll and insert a layer of fried onions. Place the sausage in the roll and serve immediately.

Summer Vegetable Parcels

You can use any baby vegetables you like—patty pan squash, corn cobs, and plum tomatoes look attractive and add color.

NUTRITIONAL INFORMATION

Calories	299	Sugars	.........8g
Protein	.........3g	Fat	..........25g
Carbohydrate	...17g	Saturates	......16g

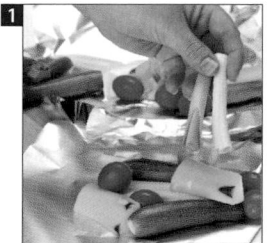
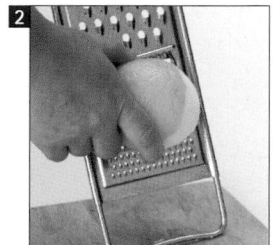
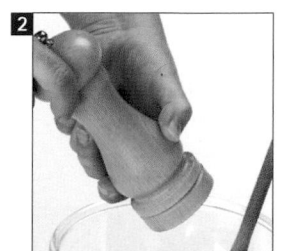

 15 mins   25–30 mins

SERVES 4

INGREDIENTS

2 lb/900 g mixed baby vegetables, such as carrots, patty pan squash, corn ears, plum tomatoes, leeks, zucchini, and onions

½ cup sweet butter

3 tbsp chopped mixed fresh herbs, such as parsley, thyme, and chervil

2 garlic cloves

grated zest and juice of 1 lemon

salt and pepper

1 Cut out 4 x 12 inch/30 cm squares of foil and divide the vegetables equally among them.

2 Zest the lemon. Put the butter, herbs, garlic, and lemon zest in a food processor and process until blended, then season to taste with salt and pepper. Alternatively, beat in a bowl until blended.

3 Divide the butter equally between the vegetables, dotting it on top. Fold up the sides of the foil to enclose the vegetables, sealing securely. Cook on a medium–hot grill, turning occasionally, for 25–30 minutes. Open the parcels, sprinkle with the lemon juice, and serve.

COOK'S TIP
Use a double thickness of foil to make parcels for cooking on the grill so that they don't tear when you turn them.

Grilled Bean Burgers

These tasty burgers are ideal for a grill in the summer, but they are equally delicious cooked indoors at any time of year.

NUTRITIONAL INFORMATION

Calories ....443 Sugars 12g
Protein ....17g Fat 14g
Carbohydrate ...68g Saturates 2g

15 mins   1 hr 5 mins

SERVES 6

I N G R E D I E N T S

¾ cup dried adzuki beans

¾ cup dried black-eye peas

6 tbsp vegetable oil

1 large onion, finely chopped

1 tsp yeast extract

¾ cup grated carrot

1½ cup fresh whole-wheat bread crumbs

2 tbsp whole-wheat flour

salt and pepper

B A R B E C U E   S A U C E

½ tsp chili powder

1 tsp celery salt

2 tbsp light muscovado sugar

2 tbsp red wine vinegar

2 tbsp vegetarian Worcestershire sauce

3 tbsp tomato paste

dash of Tabasco sauce

T O   S E R V E

6 whole-wheat burger buns, toasted

mixed salad

jacket potato fries

1 Place the beans and peas in separate pans, cover with water, and bring to a boil, then boil for 15 minutes. Cover and simmer the adzuki beans for 25 minutes and the black-eye peas for 35 minutes. Drain the beans and peas and rinse well.

2 Transfer to a mixing bowl and lightly mash together with a potato masher or fork. Set aside.

3 Heat 1 tablespoon of the oil in a skillet and gently cook the onion for 3–4 minutes, until soft. Mix into the beans with the yeast extract, grated carrot, bread crumbs, and seasoning. Bind the mixture together well.

4 With wet hands, divide the mixture into 6 and form into burgers 3½ inches/8 cm in diameter. Put the flour on a plate and use to coat the burgers.

5 To make the barbecue sauce, mix all the ingredients together until they are well blended.

6 Cook the burgers on a medium–hot grill for 3–4 minutes on each side, brushing with the remaining oil from time to time.

7 Serve the burgers in the toasted buns with a mixed salad, jacket potato fries, and a spoonful of the barbecue sauce.

Vegetarian Brochettes

In this lovely colorful recipe, the bean curd absorbs the flavor of the mustard and honey glaze.

NUTRITIONAL INFORMATION

Calories 174	Sugars 9g
Protein 10g	Fat 10g
Carbohydrate 11g	Saturates 3g

20 mins | 8–10 mins

SERVES 4

INGREDIENTS

2 zucchini

1 yellow bell pepper, seeded and cut into quarters

8 oz/225 g firm bean curd, cut into 1 inch/2.5 cm cubes

4 cherry tomatoes

4 baby onions

8 white mushrooms

GLAZE

2 tbsp olive oil

1 tbsp Meaux mustard

1 tbsp clear honey

salt and pepper

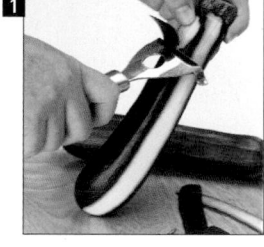

1 Peel off strips of skin along the length of the zucchini to leave alternate yellow and green stripes, then cut each zucchini into 8 thick slices. Cut each of the yellow bell pepper quarters in half.

2 Thread the pieces of bell pepper, zucchini slices, bean curd cubes, cherry tomatoes, baby onions, and white mushrooms on to 4 skewers.

3 Combine the olive oil, mustard and honey in a pitcher and season with salt and pepper.

4 Brush the brochettes with the honey mixture and cook on a medium–hot grill, turning and brushing frequently with the honey mixture, for 8–10 minutes. Serve the brochettes immediately.

Bean Curd Skewers

Although bean curd is rather bland on its own, it develops
a fabulous flavor when it is marinated in garlic and herbs.

NUTRITIONAL INFORMATION

Calories 149   Sugars 5g
Protein ....13g   Fat 9g
Carbohydrate ....5g   Saturates 1g

🍲 40 mins   🕐 15 mins

SERVES 4

I N G R E D I E N T S

12 oz/350 g bean curd

1 red bell pepper

1 yellow bell pepper

2 zucchini

8 white mushrooms

lemon slices, to garnish

M A R I N A D E

grated zest and juice of ½ lemon

1 garlic clove, crushed

½ tsp chopped fresh rosemary

½ tsp chopped fresh thyme

1 tbsp walnut oil

1 To make the marinade, combine the lemon zest and juice, garlic, rosemary, thyme, and oil in a shallow dish.

2 Drain the bean curd, pat it dry on paper towels, and cut it into squares with a sharp knife. Add to the marinade and toss to coat. Cover and let marinate for 20–30 minutes.

3 Meanwhile, seed and cut the bell peppers into 1 inch/2.5 cm pieces.

Blanch in boiling water for 4 minutes, refresh in cold water, and drain.

4 Using a canelle knife or potato peeler, remove strips of peel from the zucchini. Cut the zucchini into 1 inch/ 2.5 cm chunks.

5 Remove the bean curd from the marinade, reserving the liquid. Thread it onto 8 skewers, alternating with the bell peppers, zucchini, and white mushrooms.

6 Grill the skewers over medium–hot coals for about 6 minutes, turning and basting with the reserved marinade. Alternatively, cook under a preheated broiler. Transfer the skewers to warmed individual serving plates, garnish with slices of lemon, and serve.

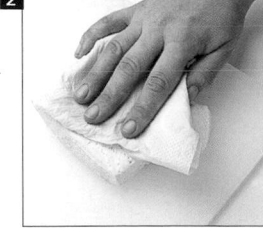

Grilled Baked Apples

When they are wrapped in foil, apples bake to perfection on the grill and make a delightful finale to any meal.

NUTRITIONAL INFORMATION

Calories 294   Sugars 30g
Protein . . . . .3g   Fat 18g
Carbohydrate . . .31g   Saturates 7g

15 mins   25–30 mins

SERVES 4

I N G R E D I E N T S

4 medium cooking apples

4 tbsp chopped walnuts

4 tbsp ground almonds

2 tbsp molasses sugar

8 cherries, chopped

2 tbsp chopped preserved ginger

1 tbsp Amaretto liqueur (optional)

2 tbsp butter

light cream or unsweetened yogurt, to serve

1 Core the apples and, using a sharp knife, score each around the middle to prevent the skins from splitting while they are grilling.

2 To make the filling, combine the walnuts, almonds, sugar, cherries, ginger, and amaretto liqueur, if using, in a small bowl.

3 Spoon the filling mixture into each apple, pushing it down into the hollowed-out core. Mound a little of the filling mixture on top of each apple.

4 Place each apple on a large square of double thickness aluminum foil and generously dot all over with the butter. Wrap up the foil so that each apple is completely enclosed.

5 Grill the foil packets over hot coals for 25–30 minutes or until the apples are tender.

6 Transfer the apples to warm, individual serving plates. Serve immediately with plenty of light cream or thick unsweetened yogurt.

COOK'S TIP
If the coals are dying down, place the foil packets directly on them, raking them up around the apples. Grill for 25–30 minutes.

Coconut Apples

This is a variation of the popular dessert of baked apples, but instead of being filled with dried fruit, they are layered with jam and coconut.

NUTRITIONAL INFORMATION

Calories 312   Sugars 32g
Protein . . . . .2g   Fat 20g
Carbohydrate . . .32g   Saturates 17g

10 mins   15–20 mins

SERVES 4

I N G R E D I E N T S

2 tsp sweet butter

4 tbsp ginger and apple jam

1 cup shredded coconut

pinch of ground cinnamon

4 cooking apples

heavy cream or vanilla ice cream, to serve (optional)

1 Cut 4 squares of foil, each large enough to enclose one apple, and lightly grease with the butter. Combine the jam and coconut in a small bowl and stir in cinnamon to taste.

2 Core the apples, but don't peel them. Cut each apple horizontally into 3 slices. Spread the mixture between the apple slices and reassemble the apples. Place 1 apple on each sheet of foil and fold up the sides to enclose securely.

3 Cook the apples on a hot grill for 15–20 minutes. Serve immediately with cream or ice cream, if you like.

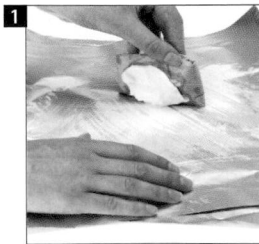  

VARIATION

Substitute large, firm pears for the apples.

Caramelized Fruit

Strawberries work surprisingly well in a chargrilled fruit salad. Choose large, ripe berries, don't hull them, and turn frequently while cooking.

NUTRITIONAL INFORMATION

Calories	234	Sugars	........49g
Protein	.........2g	Fat	..........10g
Carbohydrate	...49g	Saturates	.......0g

15 mins, plus marinating   5 mins

SERVES 4

INGREDIENTS

⅔ cup medium sherry

½ cup superfine sugar

1 ogen melon, halved and seeded

4 peaches, peeled, halved, and pitted

½ lb/225 g strawberries

1 To peel peaches, make a tiny nick in the skin with the point of a sharp knife. Place the in a bowl and cover with boiling water. Leavefor 15-30 seconds, then remove with a slotted spoon. Peel off the skin.

2 Combine the sherry with the sugar in a large bowl, stirring until the sugar has dissolved.

3 Cut the melon halves into wedges and cut the flesh away from the skin. Add the melon wedges, peach halves, and strawberries to the bowl, tossing gently to coat. Cover with plastic wrap and let marinate for 1 hour.

4 Drain the fruit, and reserve the marinade. Cook the melon and peaches on a hot grill for 3 minutes, then add the strawberries and cook for 2 minutes more. Turn the fruit and brush frequently with the reserved marinade.

Totally Tropical Pineapple

The delicious aroma of fresh pineapple and rum as this succulent dessert is cooking will transport your imagination to a Caribbean beach.

NUTRITIONAL INFORMATION

Calories 206   Sugars 20g
Protein . . . . .1g   Fat 12g
Carbohydrate . . .20g   Saturates 7g

 15 mins   6–8 mins

SERVES 4

INGREDIENTS

1 pineapple

3 tbsp dark rum

2 tbsp muscovado sugar

1 tsp ground ginger

4 tbsp melted sweet butter

1 Using a sharp knife, cut off the crown of the pineapple, then cut the fruit into ³/₄ inch/2 cm thick slices. Cut away the peel from each slice and flick out the "eyes" with the point of the knife. Stamp out the cores with an apple corer or small dough cutter.

2 Combine the rum, sugar, ginger, and butter in a bowl, stirring until the sugar has dissolved. Brush the pineapple rings with the mixture.

3 Cook the pineapple rings on a hot grill for about 3–4 minutes, turn over, and cook for a further 3–4 minutes.

4 Serve the pineapple rings immediately with the remaining rum mixture poured over them.

VARIATION

If you prefer, you can cut the pineapple into cubes or quarter slices and thread on skewers before brushing with the rum mixture and cooking.

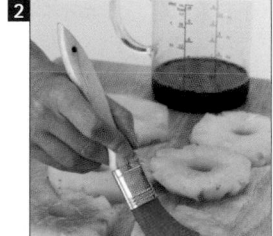

Panettone with Strawberries

Panettone is a sweet Italian bread. It is delicious toasted on the grill and topped with mascarpone and marinated strawberries.

NUTRITIONAL INFORMATION

Calories 475	Sugars 20g
Protein 7g	Fat 31g
Carbohydrate ...36g	Saturates 19g

5 mins, plus chilling

2 mins

SERVES 4

INGREDIENTS

½ lb/225 g strawberries

2 tbsp superfine sugar

6 tbsp Marsala wine

½ tsp ground cinnamon

4 slices panettone

4 tbsp mascarpone cheese

1 Hull and slice the strawberries top to bottom, and place them in a bowl. Add the sugar, Marsala wine, and ground cinnamon to the strawberries.

2 Toss the strawberries in the sugar and cinnamon mixture until they are well coated. Let chill in the refrigerator for at least 30 minutes.

3 When ready to serve, transfer the slices of panettone to a rack set over medium–hot coals. Grill the panettone for about 1 minute on each side or until golden brown.

4 Remove the panettone from the grill and transfer to serving plates. Top the panettone with the mascarpone cheese and the marinated strawberries, and serve immediately.

COOK'S TIP
Mascarpone is an Italian soft cheese with a rich, creamy texture, which tastes like very heavy cream. It will melt into the panettone, making it quite delicious..

Mincemeat-Stuffed Pears

Pears quickly go soft and lose their shape when they are cooked, so choose fruit with good firm flesh for this recipe.

NUTRITIONAL INFORMATION

Calories	187	Sugars	........29g
Protein	.........1g	Fat	...........7g
Carbohydrate	...31g	Saturates	.......3g

 10 mins 25–30 mins

SERVES 4

I N G R E D I E N T S

4 firm pears

1 tsp lemon juice

2 tbsp vegetarian mincemeat

5 tbsp cake crumbs or 4 amaretti biscuits, crushed

1 tbsp butter

vanilla ice cream, to serve

1 Using a sharp knife, cut the pears in half. Using a teaspoon, scoop out the core and discard.

2 Brush the cut surface of each of the pear halves with a little lemon juice to prevent discoloration.

3 Mix together the mincemeat and cake crumbs or crushed amaretti biscuits.

4 Divide the mixture among the pear halves, spooning it into a mound where the core has been removed.

5 Place 2 pear halves on a large square of double thickness foil and generously dot all over with the butter.

6 Wrap up the foil around the pears so that they are completely enclosed.

7 Transfer the foil parcels to a rack set over hot coals. Grill for 25–30 minutes or until the pears are hot and just tender.

8 Transfer the cooked pears to individual serving plates.

9 Serve the pears with 2 scoops of ice cream per serving.

VARIATION

Use vegetarian mincemeat to stuff apples instead of pears and bake them on the grill in the same way.

Special Peach Melba

The elegant simplicity of this dessert makes it the perfect end to a special occasion barbecue party.

NUTRITIONAL INFORMATION

Calories 234	Sugars 49g	
Protein 2g	Fat 0g	
Carbohydrate . . .49g	Saturates 0g	

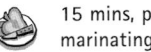

15 mins, plus marinating   3–5 mins

SERVES 4

INGREDIENTS

2 large peaches, peeled, halved, and pitted

1 tbsp light brown sugar

1 tbsp Amaretto liqueur

1 lb/450 g raspberries

1 cup confectioners' sugar

1 pint vanilla ice cream (2 cups)

1 Put the peach halves in a large, shallow dish and sprinkle with the brown sugar. Pour the Amaretto over them, cover with plastic wrap, and let stand for 1 hour.

2 Meanwhile, using the back of a wooden spoon, press the raspberries through a fine strainer set over a bowl. Discard the contents of the strainer. Stir the confectioners' sugar into the raspberry purée. Cover the bowl with plastic wrap and chill in the refrigerator until required.

3 Drain the peach halves, reserving the marinade. Cook on a hot grill, turning and brushing frequently with the reserved marinade, for 3–5 minutes.

4 Put 2 scoops of ice cream in each of 4 sundae glasses, top with a peach half, and spoon over the raspberry sauce.

Salads & Side Dishes

Forget limp lettuce leaves and dull vegetables—this chapter has some wonderful ideas for really unusual salads and side dishes. Salads are often served as an accompaniment, but put together the right ingredients, and a salad can be a meal in itself. Salads are also perfect to serve as part of a summer buffet lunch or picnic, or for a healthy packed lunch, and even to satisfy your mid-winter need for a warming dish. And try accompanying your entrée with a really different side dish—cauliflower and broccoli in a lemony cheese sauce, spiced up with ginger and cilantro, or a spicy Mexican sauce garnished with chocolate!

Tropical Rice Salad

Rice salads are always popular and this colorful, fruity mixture is perfect as part of a summer buffet lunch or on a picnic.

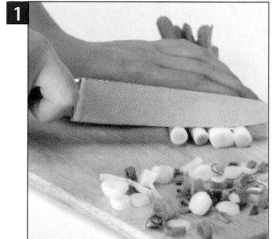

NUTRITIONAL INFORMATION

Calories	300	Sugars	........26g
Protein	.........5g	Fat	...........7g
Carbohydrate	...57g	Saturates	.......0g

 20 mins   15 mins

SERVES 4

INGREDIENTS

generous ½ cup long grain rice, rinsed

8 oz/225 g can pineapple pieces in natural juice

scant 1 cup canned corn kernels, drained

2 red bell peppers, seeded and diced

4 scallions, thinly sliced

3 tbsp golden raisins

salt and ground black pepper

DRESSING

1 tbsp groundnut oil

1 tbsp hazelnut oil

1 tbsp light soy sauce

1 garlic clove, finely chopped

1 tsp chopped fresh ginger root

1 Cook the rice in a pan of lightly salted boiling water for about 15 minutes, or until just tender. Drain well and rinse with cold water. Place the rice in a serving bowl.

2 Drain the pineapple pieces, reserving the juice in a pitcher. Add the pineapple, corn, red bell peppers, scallions, and golden raisins to the rice and mix together lightly.

3 Add all the dressing ingredients to the fruit juice, whisking well, and season to taste with salt and pepper. Pour the dressing over the salad and toss to coat.

Red & Green Salad

Beet and orange is a classic combination and here they are combined with tender, baby spinach leaves to make a dramatic warm salad.

NUTRITIONAL INFORMATION

Calories	173	Sugars	........19g
Protein	.........5g	Fat	...........9g
Carbohydrate	...20g	Saturates	.......1g

 10 mins   5 mins

SERVES 4

INGREDIENTS

3 tbsp extra virgin olive oil

juice of 1 orange

1 tsp superfine sugar

1 tsp fennel seeds

3 cups diced cooked beets

4 oz/115 g young spinach leaves

salt and pepper

1 Heat the olive oil in a small, heavy pan. Add the orange juice, sugar, and fennel seeds and season to taste with salt and pepper. Stir over medium heat until the sugar has dissolved.

2 Add the beets to the pan and stir gently to coat with the dressing. Remove the pan from the heat.

3 Arrange the spinach leaves in a salad bowl. Spoon the warm beets on top and serve.

COOK'S TIP
To cook raw beet, trim the tops, leaving about 2 inches/5 cm, and rinse under cold running water. Do not trim or peel the root. Simmer in a pan of lightly salted water for about 1 hour, until tender. Drain and cool, then rub off the skin and trim the leaves and root.

Sweet Potato & Nut Salad

Pecan nuts with their slightly bitter flavor are mixed with sweet potatoes to make a sweet and sour salad with an interesting texture.

NUTRITIONAL INFORMATION

Calories	.... .330	Sugars	.... .5g
Protein	.... .4g	Fat	.... .20g
Carbohydrate	...36g	Saturates	.... .2g

 25 mins   10 mins

SERVES 4

INGREDIENTS

2¾ cups diced sweet potatoes

2 celery stalks, sliced

1 firmly packed cup celery root, grated

2 scallions, sliced

½ cup pecan nuts, chopped

2 heads Belgian endive, separated

1 tsp lemon juice

thyme sprigs, to garnish

DRESSING

4 tbsp vegetable oil

1 tbsp garlic wine vinegar

1 tsp soft light brown sugar

2 tsp chopped thyme

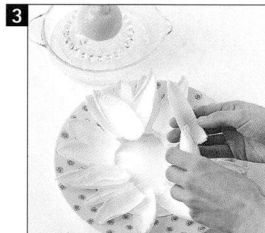

COOK'S TIP
Sweet potatoes do not store as well as ordinary potatoes. It is best to store them in a cool, dark place (not the refrigerator) and use within 1 week of purchase.

1 Cook the sweet potatoes in a large pan of boiling water for 10–15 minutes, until tender. Drain thoroughly and let cool.

2 When the potatoes have cooled, stir in the sliced celery, celery root, scallions, and pecan nuts.

3 Line a salad plate with the endive leaves and sprinkle with lemon juice.

4 Spoon the sweet potato mixture into the center of the leaves.

5 In a small bowl, whisk together the vegetable oil, garlic wine vinegar, sugar, and chopped thyme, then pour the dressing over the salad.

6 Serve the sweet potato and nut salad immediately, garnished with fresh thyme sprigs.

Three-Bean Salad

Fresh thin green beans are combined with soybeans and red kidney beans in a chive and tomato dressing to make a tasty salad.

NUTRITIONAL INFORMATION

Calories	276	Sugars	.........7g
Protein	........18g	Fat	..........15g
Carbohydrate	...18g	Saturates	......4g

 10 mins   5 mins

SERVES 6

INGREDIENTS

3 tbsp olive oil

1 tbsp lemon juice

1 tbsp tomato paste

1 tbsp light malt vinegar

1 tbsp chopped fresh chives, plus extra to garnish

1½ cups thin green beans, cut into thirds

1½ cups canned soybeans, rinsed and drained

1½ cups canned red kidney beans, rinsed and drained

2 tomatoes, chopped

4 scallions, trimmed and chopped

1 cup feta cheese, cut into cubes

salt and pepper

mixed salad greens, to serve

1 Put the olive oil, lemon juice, tomato paste, light malt vinegar, and chopped fresh chives into a large bowl and mix thoroughly. Set aside until required.

2 Cook the thin green beans in a small pan of lightly salted boiling water for 4–5 minutes. Drain, refresh under cold water to prevent any further cooking, and drain well again. Pat dry with absorbent paper towels.

3 Add all the beans to the dressing, stirring well to mix.

4 Add the tomatoes, scallions, and feta cheese to the bean mixture, tossing gently to coat in the dressing. Season to taste with salt and pepper.

5 Arrange the salad greens on serving plates. Pile the bean salad on top, garnish with extra chives, and serve.

COOK'S TIP
For a more substantial light meal, top the salad with 2–3 sliced hard-cooked eggs and serve with crusty bread to soak up the juices.

Multicolored Salad

The beet adds a rich color to this dish, tinting the potato an appealing pink. Mixed with cucumber it is a really vibrant salad.

NUTRITIONAL INFORMATION

Calories 174	Sugars 8g
Protein 4g	Fat 6g
Carbohydrate ...27g	Saturates 1g

15-20 mins   20 mins

SERVES 4

INGREDIENTS

1 lb/450 g waxy potatoes, diced

4 small cooked beets, sliced

½ small cucumber, thinly sliced

2 large dill pickles, sliced

1 red onion, halved and sliced

dill sprigs, to garnish

DRESSING

1 garlic clove, crushed

2 tbsp olive oil

2 tbsp red wine vinegar

2 tbsp chopped fresh dill

salt and pepper

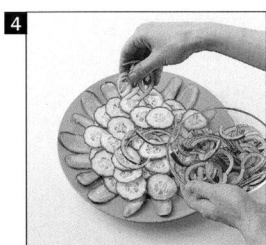

VARIATION

Line the salad platter with 2 heads of Belgian endive, separated into leaves, and arrange the cucumber, dill pickle, and red onion slices on top of the leaves.

1 Cook the diced potatoes in a pan of boiling water for about 15 minutes, or until just tender. Drain and let cool.

2 When cool, mix the diced potato and beets together gently in a bowl and set aside.

3 To make the dressing, whisk together the garlic, olive oil, vinegar, and chopped dill and season to taste with salt and pepper.

4 When you are ready to serve the salad, line a large serving platter with the slices of cucumber, the sliced dill pickles, and the sliced red onion.

5 Spoon the potato and beet mixture on top of the other vegetables in the center of the platter.

6 Pour the dressing over the salad and serve immediately, garnished with fresh dill sprigs.

Three-Way Potato Salad

Small new potatoes, served warm in a delicious dressing. The nutritional information is for the potato salad with the curry dressing only.

NUTRITIONAL INFORMATION

Calories 310	Sugars 12g
Protein 6g	Fat 19g
Carbohydrate . . .31g	Saturates 4g

10–20 mins   20 mins

SERVES 4

I N G R E D I E N T S

1 lb/450 g new potatoes (for each dressing)

herbs, to garnish

LIGHT CURRY DRESSING

1 tbsp vegetable oil

1 tbsp medium curry paste

1 small onion, chopped

1 tbsp mango chutney, chopped

6 tbsp unsweetened yogurt

3 tbsp light cream

2 tbsp mayonnaise

salt and pepper

1 tbsp light cream, to garnish

VINAIGRETTE DRESSING

6 tbsp hazelnut oil

3 tbsp cider vinegar

1 tsp whole-grain mustard

1 tsp superfine sugar

few basil leaves, torn

PARSLEY CREAM

⅔ cup sour cream

3 tbsp light mayonnaise

4 scallions, finely chopped

1 tbsp chopped fresh parsley

1 To make the Light Curry Dressing, heat the vegetable oil in a pan. Add the curry paste and onion and cook, stirring frequently, until the onion is soft. Remove from the heat and let cool slightly.

2 Mix together the mango chutney, yogurt, cream, and mayonnaise. Add the curry mixture and blend together. Season with salt and pepper.

3 To make the Vinaigrette Dressing, whisk the oil, vinegar, mustard, sugar, and basil together in a small pitcher or bowl. Season with salt and pepper.

4 To make the Parsley Cream, combine the mayonnaise, sour cream, scallions, and parsley, mixing well. Season with salt and pepper.

5 Cook the potatoes in lightly salted boiling water until just tender. Drain well and let cool for 5 minutes, then add the chosen dressing, tossing to coat.

6 Serve the salads garnished with fresh herbs, spooning a little light cream on to the potatoes if you have used the curry dressing.

Hot Lentil Salad

A robust vinaigrette dressing is served with this warm salad.
If you prefer, you can serve the salad cold.

NUTRITIONAL INFORMATION

Calories ......125 Sugars 3g
Protein ....6g Fat 6g
Carbohydrate ...12g Saturates 1g

 10 mins   50 mins

SERVES 6-8

INGREDIENTS

1 cup Puy lentils, cooked

4 tbsp olive oil

1 small onion, sliced

4 stalks celery, sliced

2 cloves garlic, crushed

2 zucchini, trimmed and diced

¾ cup green beans, trimmed and cut into
   short lengths

½ red bell pepper, seeded and diced

½ yellow bell pepper, seeded and diced

1 tsp Dijon mustard

1 tbsp balsamic vinegar

salt and pepper

1 Place the lentils in a large mixing or serving bowl. The lentils can still be warm, if wished.

2 Heat the oil in a pan and cook the onion and celery for 2–3 minutes until soft but not brown.

3 Stir the garlic, zucchini, and green beans into the pan and cook for a further 2 minutes.

4 Add the bell peppers to the pan and cook for 1 minute.

5 Stir the mustard and the balsamic vinegar into the pan and mix until warm and well combined.

6 Pour the warm mixture over the lentils and toss together to mix well. Season with salt and pepper to taste and serve immediately.

COOK'S TIP

To cook the lentils, rinse them well and place in a large pan. Cover with plenty of cold water and bring to a boil. Boil rapidly for 10 minutes, then reduce the heat and simmer for 35 minutes until the lentils are tender. Drain well.

Sweet Potato Salad

This hot, fruity salad combines sweet potato and fried bananas with colorful mixed bell peppers, tossed in a honey-based dressing.

NUTRITIONAL INFORMATION

Calories	424	Sugars	........29g
Protein	.........5g	Fat	..........17g
Carbohydrate	...68g	Saturates	.......8g

 15 mins 20 mins

SERVES 4

INGREDIENTS

2¾ cups diced sweet potatoes

4 tbsp butter

1 tbsp lemon juice

1 garlic clove, crushed

1 red bell pepper, seeded and diced

1 green bell pepper, seeded and diced

2 bananas, thickly sliced

2 thick slices white bread, crusts removed, diced

salt and pepper

DRESSING

2 tbsp clear honey

2 tbsp chopped chives

2 tbsp lemon juice

2 tbsp olive oil

1 Cook the sweet potatoes in a pan of boiling water for 10–15 minutes, until tender. Drain thoroughly and reserve.

2 Meanwhile, melt the butter in a skillet. Add the lemon juice, garlic, and bell peppers and cook, stirring constantly, for 3 minutes.

3 Add the banana slices to the skillet and cook for 1 minute. Remove the bananas from the skillet with a slotted spoon and stir into the potatoes.

4 Add the bread cubes to the skillet and cook, stirring frequently, for 2 minutes, until golden brown on all sides.

5 Mix the dressing ingredients together in a small pan and heat until the honey is runny.

6 Spoon the potato mixture into a serving dish and season to taste. Pour over the dressing and sprinkle the croûtons over the top. Serve immediately.

COOK'S TIP
Use firm, slightly underripe bananas in this recipe as they won't turn soft and mushy when they are cooked.

Goat Cheese Salad

A delicious hot salad of melting goat cheese over sliced tomato and basil on a base of hot ciabatta bread.

NUTRITIONAL INFORMATION

Calories	379	Sugars	.........3g
Protein	........15g	Fat	..........23g
Carbohydrate	...30g	Saturates	......10g

 10 mins 6 mins

SERVES 4

I N G R E D I E N T S

3 tbsp olive oil

1 tbsp white wine vinegar

1 tsp black olive paste

1 garlic clove, crushed

1 tsp chopped fresh thyme

1 ciabatta loaf

4 small tomatoes

12 fresh basil leaves

9 oz/250 g goat cheese

TO SERVE

mixed salad leaves, including arugula and radicchio

COOK'S TIP

Many French goat cheeses are widely available. Those labeled chèvre or pur chèvre must be made purely from goat's milk. The goat's milk in mi-chèvre cheeses is mixed with up to 75 percent cow's milk.

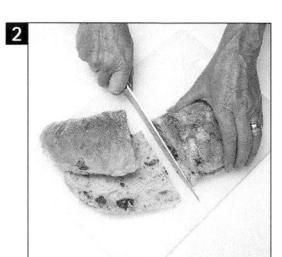

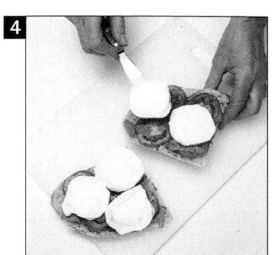

1 Mix the olive oil, white wine vinegar, black olive paste, garlic, and chopped thyme together in a screw-top jar and shake vigorously.

2 Cut the ciabatta loaf in half horizontally then in half again vertically to make 4 pieces.

3 Drizzle some of the dressing over the bread, then arrange the tomatoes and basil leaves on the top.

4 Cut each roll of goat cheese into 6 slices and places 3 slices on each piece of ciabatta.

5 Brush with some of the dressing and bake in a preheated oven, 450°F/230°C, for 5–6 minutes until turning brown at the edges.

6 Pour the remaining dressing over the mixed salad leaves and serve with the baked ciabatta bread.

Cheese, Nut & Pasta Salad

Use colorful salad greens to provide visual contrast to match the contrasts of taste and texture.

NUTRITIONAL INFORMATION

Calories	694	Sugars	1g
Protein	22g	Fat	57g
Carbohydrate	24g	Saturates	15g

15 mins   15–20 mins

SERVES 4

INGREDIENTS

2 cups dried pasta shells

1 tbsp olive oil

1 cup shelled and halved walnuts

mixed salad greens, such as radicchio, escarole, arugula, corn salad, and frisée

2 cups crumbled dolcelatte cheese

salt

DRESSING

2 tbsp walnut oil

4 tbsp extra-virgin olive oil

2 tbsp red wine vinegar

salt and pepper

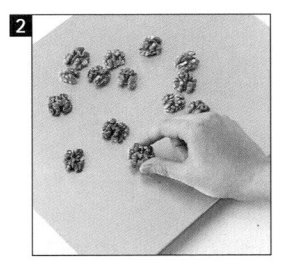
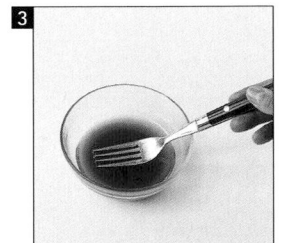

1 Bring a large pan of lightly salted water to a boil. Add the pasta shells and olive oil and cook until just tender, but still firm to the bite. Drain the pasta and refresh under cold running water, drain thoroughly again, and set aside.

2 Spread out the shelled walnut halves on to a cookie sheet and toast under a preheated broiler for 2–3 minutes. Let cool while you make the dressing.

3 To make the dressing, whisk together the walnut oil, olive oil, and vinegar in a small bowl, and season to taste.

4 Arrange the salad greens in a large serving bowl. Pile the cooled pasta in the middle of the salad greens and sprinkle over the dolcelatte cheese. Pour the dressing over the pasta salad, then scatter over the walnut halves and toss together to mix. Serve immediately.

COOK'S TIP

Dolcelatte is a semisoft, blue-veined cheese from Italy. Its texture is creamy and smooth and the flavor is delicate, but piquant. You could substitute Roquefort as an alternative. Whichever cheese you choose, it is essential that it is of the best quality and in peak condition.

Carrot & Nut Coleslaw

This simple salad has a dressing made from poppy seeds pan-fried in sesame oil to bring out their flavor and aroma.

NUTRITIONAL INFORMATION

Calories	220	Sugars	.........7g
Protein	.........4g	Fat	..........19g
Carbohydrate	...10g	Saturates	.......3g

 15 mins   5–10 mins

SERVES 4

INGREDIENTS

1 large carrot, grated

1 small onion, finely chopped

2 celery stalks, chopped

¼ small hard white cabbage, shredded

1 tbsp chopped fresh parsley

4 tbsp sesame oil

½ tsp poppy seeds

½ cup cashew nuts

2 tbsp white wine vinegar or apple vinegar

salt and pepper

fresh parsley sprigs, to garnish

1 In a large salad bowl, combine the carrot, onion, celery, and cabbage. Stir in the chopped parsley and season to taste with salt and pepper.

2 Heat the sesame oil in a pan with a lid. Add the poppy seeds and cover the pan. Cook over medium-high heat until the seeds start to make a popping sound. Remove the pan from the heat and let cool.

3 Spread out the cashew nuts on a cookie sheet. Place them under a preheated medium-hot broiler and toast until lightly browned, being careful not to burn them. Remove from the heat and let cool.

4 Add the white wine or apple vinegar to the oil and poppy seed mixture, then pour the poppy seed dressing over the vegetable mixture. Add the cooled cashew nuts. Toss together to coat well.

5 Garnish the salad with sprigs of fresh parsley and serve immediately.

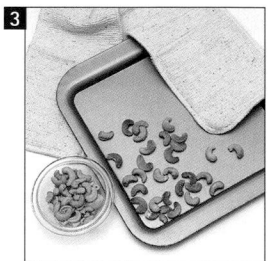

Hot Salad

This quickly made dish is ideal for a cold winter night. Serve with crusty bread, fresh rolls, or garlic bread.

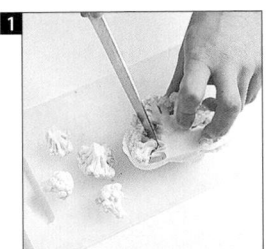

NUTRITIONAL INFORMATION

Calories	154	Sugars	13g
Protein	4g	Fat	9g
Carbohydrate	14g	Saturates	6g

 10 mins   10 mins

SERVES 4

I N G R E D I E N T S

½ medium-sized cauliflower

1 green bell pepper

1 red bell pepper

½ cucumber

4 carrots

2 tbsp butter

salt and pepper

crusty bread, rolls or garlic bread, to serve

D R E S S I N G

3 tbsp olive oil

1 tbsp white wine vinegar

1 tbsp light soy sauce

1 tsp superfine sugar

salt and pepper

1 Cut the cauliflower into small florets, using a sharp knife. Seed the bell peppers and cut the flesh into thin slices. Cut the cucumber into thin slices. Thinly slice the carrots lengthwise.

2 Melt the butter in a large, heavy pan. Add the cauliflower florets, bell peppers, cucumber, and carrots and cook over medium heat, stirring constantly, for 5–7 minutes, until tender, but still firm to the bite. Season with salt and pepper. Lower the heat, cover with a lid, and simmer for 3 minutes.

3 Meanwhile, make the dressing. Whisk together all the ingredients until thoroughly combined.

4 Transfer the vegetables to a serving dish, pour over the dressing, toss to mix well, and serve immediately.

VARIATION
You can replace the vegetables in this recipe with any of your choice, such as broccoli, scallions, and zucchini.

Green & White Salad

This potato, arugula, and apple salad is flavored with creamy, salty goat cheese—perfect with salad leaves.

NUTRITIONAL INFORMATION

Calories	282	Sugars	........10g
Protein	.........8g	Fat	..........17g
Carbohydrate	...26g	Saturates	.......5g

 15 mins   20 mins

SERVES 4

INGREDIENTS

2 large potatoes, unpeeled and sliced

2 green eating apples, diced

1 tsp lemon juice

¼ cup walnut pieces

1 cup goat cheese, cubed

arugula leaves

salt and pepper

DRESSING

2 tbsp olive oil

1 tbsp red wine vinegar

1 tsp clear honey

1 tsp fennel seeds

1 Cook the potato slices in a pan of lightly salted boiling water for about 15 minutes, or until just tender. Drain and let cool. Transfer the cooled potatoes to a serving bowl.

2 Toss the diced apples in the lemon juice, then drain them, add them to the bowl with the cold potatoes, and stir gently to mix.

3 Add the walnut pieces, the cubed goat cheese, and the arugula leaves to the potatoes and apples, then toss the salad to mix.

4 In a small bowl, whisk the olive oil, red wine vinegar, clear honey, and fennel seeds together until well combined. and pour the dressing over the salad. Serve immediately.

COOK'S TIP

Serve this salad immediately to prevent the apple from discoloring. Alternatively, prepare all of the other ingredients in advance and add the apple at the last minute.

Moroccan Salad

Couscous is a type of semolina made from durum wheat. It is wonderful in salads, as it readily takes up the flavor of the dressing.

NUTRITIONAL INFORMATION

Calories	195	Sugars	........15g
Protein	.........8g	Fat	...........2g
Carbohydrate	...40g	Saturates	.....0.3g

 30-35 mins   0 mins

SERVES 6

INGREDIENTS

1 cup couscous

1 bunch scallions, finely chopped

1 small green bell pepper, seeded and chopped

4 inch/10 cm piece of cucumber, chopped

¾ cup canned garbanzo beans, rinsed and drained

½ cup golden raisins or raisins

2 oranges

salt and pepper

mint sprigs, to garnish

lettuce leaves, to serve

DRESSING

finely grated zest of 1 orange

1 tbsp chopped fresh mint

⅔ cup unsweetened yogurt

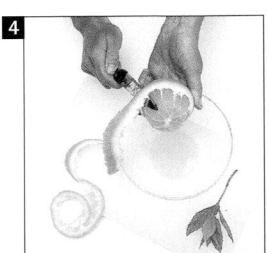

1 Put the couscous into a bowl and pour over boiling water to cover. Let it soak for about 15 minutes to swell the grains, then stir gently with a fork to separate them.

2 Add the scallions, green bell pepper, cucumber, garbanzo beans, and golden raisins or raisins to the couscous, stirring to combine. Season with salt and pepper.

3 To make the dressing, place the orange zest, mint, and yogurt in a bowl and mix together until well combined. Pour over the couscous mixture and stir to mix well.

4 Using a sharp serrated knife, remove the zest and pith from the oranges. Cut the flesh into segments, removing all the membrane.

5 Arrange the lettuce leaves on 4 serving plates. Divide the couscous mixture between the plates and arrange the orange segments on top. Garnish with sprigs of fresh mint and serve.

Grapefruit & Coconut Salad

This salad is quite deceptive—it is, in fact, surprisingly filling, even though it looks very light.

NUTRITIONAL INFORMATION

Calories	201	Sugars	. . . . .13g
Protein	. . . . .3g	Fat	. . . . .15g
Carbohydrate	. . .14g	Saturates	. . . . . . .9g

10 mins

10 mins

SERVES 4

INGREDIENTS

1¼ cups grated coconut

2 tsp light soy sauce

2 tbsp lime juice

2 tbsp water

2 tsp sunflower oil

1 garlic clove, halved

1 onion, finely chopped

2 large ruby grapefruits, peeled and segmented

1 cup alfalfa sprouts

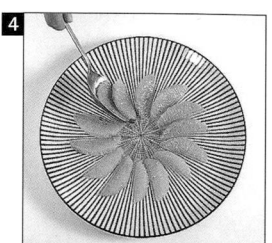

COOK'S TIP
Alfalfa sprouts can be bought in trays or packets from most food stores, but it is very easy to grow your own, and you will have a constant and cheap supply.

1 Toast the grated coconut in a dry skillet over low heat, stirring constantly, for about 3 minutes, or until it is golden brown. Transfer the toasted coconut to a bowl.

2 Add the light soy sauce, lime juice, and water to the toasted coconut and mix together well.

3 Heat the oil in a pan and sautée the garlic and onion until soft. Stir the onion into the coconut mixture. Remove and discard the garlic.

4 Divide the grapefruit segments between 4 plates. Sprinkle each with a quarter of the alfalfa sprouts and spoon over a quarter of the coconut mixture.

Eggplant Salad

A salad with a difference from Sicily. It has a real bite, both from the sweet-sour sauce, and from the texture of the celery.

NUTRITIONAL INFORMATION

Calories	390	Sugars	........15g
Protein	.........8g	Fat	..........33g
Carbohydrate	...16g	Saturates	.......5g

 1½ hrs   25 mins

SERVES 4

INGREDIENTS

2 large eggplants, about 2 lb/1 kg

6 tbsp olive oil

1 small onion, chopped finely

2 garlic cloves, crushed

6–8 celery stalks, cut into ½ inch slices

2 tbsp capers

12–16 green olives, pitted and sliced

2 tbsp pine nuts

1 oz/25 g bitter or dark chocolate, grated

4 tbsp wine vinegar

1 tbsp brown sugar

salt and pepper

2 hard-cooked eggs, sliced, to serve

celery leaves or curly endive, to garnish

1 Cut the eggplant into 1 inch/2.5 cm cubes and sprinkle liberally with 2–3 tablespoons of salt. Let stand for 1 hour to extract the bitter juices, then rinse off the salt thoroughly under cold water, drain, and dry on paper towels.

2 Heat most of the oil in a skillet and cook the eggplant cubes until golden brown all over. Drain on paper towels then put in a large bowl.

3 Add the onion and garlic to the skillet with the remaining oil and cook very gently until just soft.

4 Add the celery to the skillet and cook for a few minutes, stirring frequently, until the celery is lightly colored but still crisp. Add the celery to the eggplants with the capers, olives, and pine nuts and mix together lightly.

5 Add the chocolate, vinegar, and sugar to the residue in the skillet. Heat gently until melted, then bring to a boil. Season with salt and pepper to taste. Pour over the salad and mix lightly. Cover, let cool, and then chill thoroughly.

6 Serve the eggplant salad with sliced hard-cooked eggs and garnish with celery leaves or curly endive.

Mixed Bean & Apple Salad

Use any mixture of beans you have to hand in this recipe, but the wider the variety, the more colorful the salad.

NUTRITIONAL INFORMATION

Calories	183	Sugars	.........8g
Protein	.........6g	Fat	...........7g
Carbohydrate	...26g	Saturates	.......1g

 20 mins 20 mins

SERVES 4

INGREDIENTS

½ lb new potatoes, scrubbed and quartered

1½ cups mixed canned beans, such as red kidney beans, small cannellini beans, and borlotti beans, drained and rinsed

1 red eating apple, diced and tossed in 1 tbsp lemon juice

1 yellow bell pepper, seeded and diced

1 shallot, sliced

½ fennel bulb, sliced

oakleaf lettuce leaves

DRESSING

1 tbsp red wine vinegar

2 tbsp olive oil

1½ tsp mild yellow mustard

1 garlic clove, crushed

2 tsp chopped fresh thyme

VARIATION

Use Dijon or whole-grain mustard in place of mild yellow mustard for a different flavor.

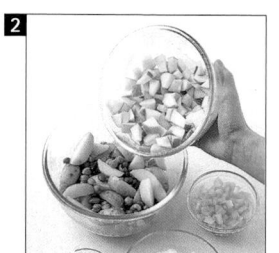

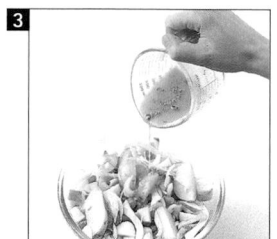

1 Cook the quartered potatoes in a pan of boiling water for 15 minutes until tender. Drain and transfer to a large bowl.

2 Add the mixed beans to the potatoes, with the diced apple, yellow bell pepper, shallot, and fennel. Mix thoroughly, taking care not to break up the cooked potatoes.

3 To make the dressing, whisk all the dressing ingredients together until thoroughly combined, then pour it over the potato salad.

4 Line a serving plate or salad bowl with the oakleaf lettuce leaves and spoon the potato mixture into the center. Serve the salad immediately.

Quick Bean Salad

This attractive-looking garbanzo bean salad makes a delicious light but satisfying meal in summer.

NUTRITIONAL INFORMATION

Calories	...139	Sugars	...5g
Protein	...8g	Fat	...3g
Carbohydrate	...21g	Saturates	...0.4g

 10 mins   0 mins

SERVES 4

INGREDIENTS

1½ cups canned garbanzo beans

4 carrots

1 bunch scallions

1 medium cucumber

½ tsp salt

½ tsp pepper

3 tbsp lemon juice

1 red bell pepper

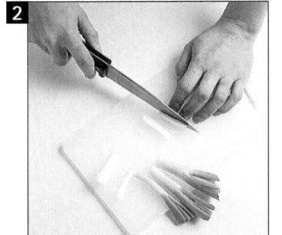

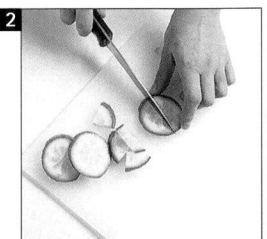

1 Drain the garbanzo beans thoroughly and place them in a salad bowl.

2 Using a sharp knife, peel and slice the carrots, cut the scallions into small pieces, and cut the cucumber into thick quarters.

3 Add the carrots, scallions, and cucumber to the garbanzo beans and mix. Season with the salt and pepper and sprinkle with the lemon juice.

4 Toss the salad ingredients together gently using 2 serving spoons.

5 Using a sharp knife, slice the red bell pepper thinly.

6 Arrange the slices of red bell pepper on top of the salad.

7 Serve the salad immediately or chill in the refrigerator until required.

COOK'S TIP
Using canned garbanzo beans rather than the dried ones speeds up the preparation time.

Salad with Garlic Dressing

This is a very quick and refreshing salad using a whole range of colorful ingredients, which make it look as good as it tastes.

NUTRITIONAL INFORMATION

Calories	82	Sugars	.........5g
Protein	.........2g	Fat	...........6g
Carbohydrate	....5g	Saturates	......1g

10 mins   0 mins

SERVES 4

I N G R E D I E N T S

¾ cup cucumber, cut into batons

6 scallions, halved

2 tomatoes, seeded and cut into 8 wedges

1 yellow bell pepper, seeded and cut into strips

2 celery stalks, cut into strips

4 radishes, quartered

3 oz/85 g arugula

1 tbsp chopped fresh mint, to garnish

D R E S S I N G

2 tbsp lemon juice

1 garlic clove, crushed

⅔ cup low-fat unsweetened yogurt

2 tbsp olive oil

salt and pepper

1 To make the salad, gently mix together the cucumber batons, scallions, tomato wedges, yellow bell pepper strips, celery strips, radishes, and arugula in a large serving bowl.

2 To make the dressing, stir the lemon juice, garlic, unsweetened yogurt, and olive oil together in a small bowl until they are thoroughly combined. Season with salt and pepper to taste.

3 Spoon the garlic dressing over the salad and toss carefully to mix, coating all the vegetables. Sprinkle the salad with chopped mint and serve.

COOK'S TIP
Arugula has a distinctive warm, peppery flavor which is ideal in green salads. If arugula is unavailable, mâche makes a good substitute.

Pasta Salad

All the ingredients of pesto sauce are included in this salad, which has a fabulous summery taste, perfect for alfresco eating.

NUTRITIONAL INFORMATION

Calories 432	Sugars 3g
Protein 14g	Fat 29g
Carbohydrate ...30g	Saturates 6g

25 mins   15 mins

SERVES 4

INGREDIENTS

2 cups fusilli

4 tomatoes

⅓ cup black olives

¼ cup sun-dried tomatoes in oil

2 tbsp pine nuts

2 tbsp grated Parmesan cheese

fresh basil, to garnish

VINAIGRETTE

½ oz/15 g basil leaves

1 clove garlic

2 tbsp grated Parmesan cheese

4 tbsp extra virgin olive oil

2 tbsp lemon juice

salt and pepper

1 Cook the pasta in a pan of lightly salted boiling water for 8–10 minutes or until just tender. Drain the pasta, rinse under cold water, then drain again thoroughly. Transfer to a large bowl.

2 To make the vinaigrette, place the basil leaves, garlic, cheese, oil, and lemon juice in a food processor and season to taste. Process until the leaves are well chopped and the ingredients are combined. Alternatively, finely chop the basil leaves by hand and combine with the other ingredients. Pour the vinaigrette over the pasta and toss to coat.

3 Cut the tomatoes into wedges. Pit and halve the olives. Slice the sun-dried tomatoes. Place the pine nuts on a cookie sheet and broil until golden.

4 Add the fresh and sun-dried tomatoes and the olives to the pasta and mix.

5 Transfer the pasta to a serving dish, scatter over the Parmesan and pine nuts, and garnish with basil leaves.

COOK'S TIP

Sun-dried tomatoes have a strong, intense flavor. They are most frequently found packed in oil with herbs and garlic. Do not waste the oil, which has an excellent flavor—use it in salad dressings.

Tomato & Basil Salad

These extra-large tomatoes make an excellent salad, especially when combined with basil, garlic, kiwi fruit, onion rings, and new potatoes.

NUTRITIONAL INFORMATION

Calories 167	Sugars 4g	
Protein 2g	Fat 11g	
Carbohydrate ...16g	Saturates 2g	

35 mins   15 mins

SERVES 8

INGREDIENTS

1 lb/450 g tiny new or salad
   potatoes, scrubbed

4–5 extra-large tomatoes

2 kiwi fruit

1 onion, sliced very thinly

2 tbsp roughly chopped fresh basil leaves

fresh basil leaves, to garnish

DRESSING

4 tbsp virgin olive oil

2 tbsp balsamic vinegar

1 garlic clove, crushed

2 tbsp mayonnaise or sour cream

salt and pepper

1 Cook the potatoes in their skins in a pan of salted water for about 10–15 minutes or until just tender. Drain the potatoes thoroughly.

COOK'S TIP
Ordinary tomatoes can be used for this salad, but make sure they are firm and bright red. You will need 8–10 ordinary-sized tomatoes.

2 To make the dressing, whisk together the oil, vinegar, garlic, and salt and pepper to taste until completely emulsified. Transfer half of the dressing to another bowl and whisk in the mayonnaise or sour cream.

3 Add the creamy dressing to the warm potatoes and toss thoroughly, then let get cold.

4 Wipe the tomatoes and slice thinly. Peel the kiwi fruit and cut into thin slices. Layer the tomatoes with the kiwi fruit, slices of onion, and chopped basil in a fairly shallow dish, leaving a space in the center for the potatoes.

5 Spoon the potatoes in their dressing into the center of the tomato salad.

6 Drizzle a little of the dressing over the tomatoes, or serve separately in a bowl or pitcher. Garnish the salad with fresh basil leaves. Cover the dish with plastic wrap and chill until ready to serve.

Coconut Couscous Salad

The nutty taste of toasted coconut really stands out in this delicious dish. It's perfect for picnics or for a healthy packed lunch.

NUTRITIONAL INFORMATION

Calories 330	Sugars 18g
Protein 7g	Fat 7g
Carbohydrate ...63g	Saturates 3g

 1½ hrs   15 mins

SERVES 4

I N G R E D I E N T S

2 cups precooked couscous

1 cup no-soak dried apricots

1 small bunch fresh chives

2 tbsp unsweetened shredded coconut

1 tsp ground cinnamon

salt and pepper

shredded mint leaves, to garnish

D R E S S I N G

1 tbsp olive oil

2 tbsp unsweetened orange juice

½ tsp finely grated orange zest

1 tsp whole-grain mustard

1 tsp clear honey

2 tbsp chopped fresh mint leaves

1 Soak the couscous according to the instructions on the packet. Bring a large pan of water to a boil. Transfer the couscous to a steamer or large strainer lined with cheesecloth and place over the water. Cover and steam as directed. Remove from the heat, place in a heatproof bowl, and let cool.

2 Slice the apricots into thin strips and place in a small bowl. Using scissors, snip the chives over the apricots.

3 When the couscous is cool, mix in the apricots, chives, coconut, and cinnamon. Season well.

4 To make the dressing, mix all the ingredients together and season. Pour over the couscous and mix until thoroughly combined. Cover and let chill for 1 hour to let the flavors develop, then serve the salad, garnished with the shredded mint leaves.

VARIATION
To serve this salad hot, when the couscous has been steamed, mix in the apricots, chives, coconut, cinnamon, and seasoning along with 1 tbsp olive oil. Transfer to a warmed serving bowl and serve.

Red Hot Slaw

As well as being an exciting side dish, this colorful salad makes an unusual filling for jacket potatoes.

NUTRITIONAL INFORMATION

Calories	169	Sugars	........16g
Protein	........11g	Fat	..........7g
Carbohydrate	...17g	Saturates	......3g

🍲

🥗 1 hr   🕐 0 mins

SERVES 4

INGREDIENTS

½ small red cabbage

1 large carrot

2 red-skinned apples

1 tbsp lemon juice

1 medium red onion

scant 1 cup grated reduced-fat colby cheese

TO GARNISH

fresh red chili strips

carrot strips

DRESSING

3 tbsp reduced-calorie mayonnaise

3 tbsp low-fat unsweetened yogurt

1 garlic clove, crushed

1 tsp paprika

1–2 tsp chili powder

pinch of cayenne pepper (optional)

salt and pepper

1 Cut the red cabbage in half and remove the central core. Finely shred the leaves and place in a large bowl. Peel and coarsely grate or finely shred the carrot and mix it into the cabbage.

2 Core the apples and finely dice, leaving on the skins. Place in another bowl and toss in the lemon juice to help prevent the apple from browning. Mix the apple into the cabbage and carrot.

3 Peel and finely shred or grate the onion. Stir into the other vegetables with the cheese and mix together.

4 To make the dressing, mix together the mayonnaise, yogurt, garlic, and paprika in a small bowl. Add chili powder according to taste and the cayenne pepper (if using)—remember this will add more spice to the dressing. Season to taste with salt and pepper.

5 Add the dressing to the vegetables and toss well to mix. Cover and chill in the refrigerator for 1 hour to let the flavors to develop.

6 Serve garnished with strips of fresh red chili and carrot.

Potato & Tomato Salad

Potato salad is always a favorite, but it is even more delicious with the addition of sun-dried tomatoes and fresh parsley.

NUTRITIONAL INFORMATION

Calories 425	Sugars 6g	
Protein 6g	Fat 27g	
Carbohydrate ...43g	Saturates 5g	

 10 mins, plus chilling   12 mins

SERVES 4

INGREDIENTS

1 lb/450 g baby potatoes, unpeeled, or larger potatoes, halved

8 sun-dried tomatoes

4 tbsp unsweetened yogurt

4 tbsp mayonnaise

2 tbsp flat-leaf parsley, chopped

salt and pepper

1 Rinse and clean the potatoes and place them in a large pan of water. Bring to a boil and cook for 8–12 minutes, or until just tender. (The cooking time will vary according to the size of your potatoes.)

2 Using a sharp knife, cut the sun-dried tomatoes into thin slices.

3 To make the dressing, mix together the yogurt and mayonnaise in a bowl and season to taste with a little salt and pepper. Stir in the sun-dried tomato slices and the chopped flat-leaf parsley.

4 Remove the potatoes with a draining spoon and drain them thoroughly,

then set them aside to cool. If you are using larger potatoes, cut them into 2 inch chunks.

5 Pour the dressing over the potatoes and toss to mix.

6 Leave the potato salad to chill in the refrigerator for about 20 minutes, then serve as an appetizer or as an accompaniment.

COOK'S TIP

It is easier to cut the larger potatoes once they are cooked. Although smaller pieces of potato will cook more quickly, they tend to disintegrate and become mushy.

Roast Bell Pepper Salad

Serve this colorful salad chilled as an antipasto, or warm as a side dish. Garlic bread makes a delicious accompaniment.

NUTRITIONAL INFORMATION

Calories 141	Sugars 8g
Protein 1g	Fat 11g
Carbohydrate 9g	Saturates 2g

 20 mins   20 mins

SERVES

I N G R E D I E N T S

4 large mixed red, green, and yellow bell peppers

4 tbsp olive oil

1 large red onion, sliced

2 garlic cloves, crushed

4 tomatoes, peeled and chopped

pinch of sugar

1 tsp lemon juice

salt and pepper

1 Trim and halve the bell peppers and remove the seeds.

2 Place the bell peppers, skin-side up, under a preheated hot broiler. Cook until the skins char. Rinse under cold water and remove the skins.

3 Trim off any thick membranes and slice thinly.

4 Heat the oil in a skillet and sauté the onion and garlic until soft. Add the bell peppers and tomatoes and cook over low heat for 10 minutes.

5 Remove from the heat, add the sugar and lemon juice, and season to taste. Serve immediately or let cool (the flavors will develop as the salad cools.)

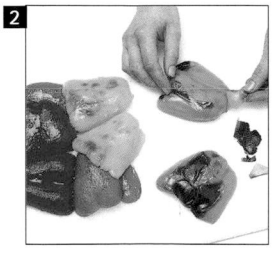

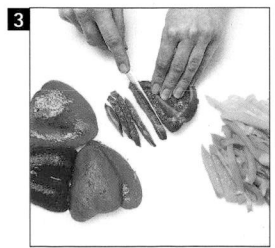

Orange & Fennel Salad

Fresh, juicy oranges and the sharp anise flavor of fennel combine to make this refreshing Spanish salad.

NUTRITIONAL INFORMATION

Calories	136	Sugars	........19g
Protein	.........3g	Fat	..........6g
Carbohydrate	...19g	Saturates	.......1g

 30 mins   0 mins

SERVES 4

INGREDIENTS

4 large oranges

1 large bulb fennel

2 tsp fennel seeds

2 tbsp extra virgin olive oil

freshly squeezed orange juice, to taste

finely chopped fresh parsley, to garnish

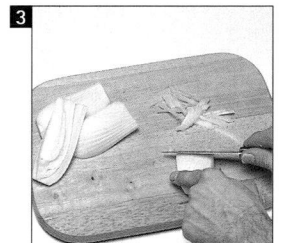

1 Using a small serrated knife, remove the zest and pith from 1 orange, cutting carefully from the top to the bottom of the orange so it retains its shape. Work over a small bowl to catch the juices.

2 Peel the remaining oranges the same way, reserving all the juices. Cut the oranges horizontally into ¼ inch slices and arrange in an attractive serving bowl; reserve the juices.

3 Cut the fronds from the fennel bulb, cut the bulb in half lengthwise and then into quarters. Cut crosswise into the very thin slices. Immediately place in the bowl of oranges and toss with a little of the reserved juice to prevent browning.

4 Sprinkle the fennel seeds over the oranges and fennel.

5 Whisk the olive oil with the remaining reserved orange juice, plus extra fresh orange juice to taste. Pour over the oranges and fennel and toss gently.

6 Cover the salad with plastic wrap and chill until ready to serve.

7 Just before serving, remove from the refrigerator and sprinkle with parsley. Serve chilled.

VARIATION
Replace the fennel with a finely sliced onion or a large bunch of scallions, finely chopped. This version is from Spain, where orange-colored oranges would be used, but in Sicily the dish is made with blood-red oranges.

Hot & Spicy Rice Salad

Serve this spicy Indian-style dish with a low-fat unsweetened yogurt raita for a delightfully refreshing contrast.

NUTRITIONAL INFORMATION

Calories 329   Sugars 27g
Protein ....8g   Fat 8g
Carbohydrate ...59g   Saturates 1g

30 mins   25 mins

SERVES 4

INGREDIENTS

2 tsp vegetable oil

1 onion, finely chopped

1 fresh red chili, seeded and finely chopped

8 cardamom pods

1 tsp ground turmeric

1 tsp garam masala

1¾ cups basmati rice, rinsed

3 cups boiling water

1 orange bell pepper, chopped

2 cups cauliflower florets, divided into small sprigs

4 ripe tomatoes, peeled, seeded, and chopped

scant 1 cup seedless raisins

¼ cup toasted sliced almonds

salt and pepper

raita of low-fat unsweetened yogurt, onion, cucumber, and mint, to serve

1 Heat the oil in a large nonstick pan. Add the onion, chili, cardamom pods, turmeric, and garam masala and cook over low heat for 2–3 minutes until the vegetables are just soft.

2 Stir in the rice, boiling water, orange bell pepper, and cauliflower. Season to taste with salt and pepper.

3 Cover with a tight-fitting lid and bring to a boil. Lower the heat and simmer for exactly 15 minutes, without lifting the lid.

4 Uncover the pan and fork through the rice. Stir in the tomatoes and raisins.

5 Cover the pan again, turn off the heat, and let the rice salad stand for 15 minutes, then remove and discard the cardamom pods.

6 Pile the rice onto a warmed serving platter and sprinkle over the toasted sliced almonds.

7 Serve the rice salad immediately, with the yogurt raita.

Cool Cucumber Salad

This cooling salad is another good foil for a highly spiced meal. Omit the green chile, if preferred.

NUTRITIONAL INFORMATION

Calories 11   Sugars 2g
Protein . . . . .0.4g   Fat 0g
Carbohydrate . . . .2g   Saturates 0g

1¼ hrs   0 mins

SERVES 4

INGREDIENTS

1 medium cucumber

1 green chile (optional)

fresh cilantro leaves, finely chopped

2 tbsp lemon juice

½ tsp salt

1 tsp sugar

fresh mint leaves and red bell pepper strips, to garnish

1 Using a sharp knife, slice the cucumber thinly. Arrange the cucumber slices on a round serving plate.

2 Using a sharp knife, chop the green chili (if using.) Scatter the chopped chile over the cucumber.

3 To make the dressing, mix together the chopped cilantro, lemon juice, salt, and sugar.

4 Place the cucumber in the refrigerator and let chill for at least 1 hour, or until required.

5 When ready to serve, transfer the cucumber to a serving dish. Pour the salad dressing over the cucumber just before serving and garnish with fresh mint and red bell pepper strips.

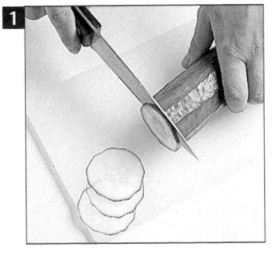
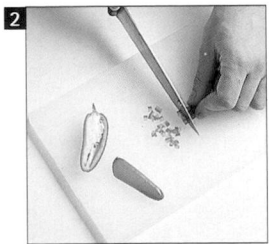

Indian Potato Salad

There are many hot Indian-flavored potato dishes which are served with curry, but this fruity salad is delicious chilled.

NUTRITIONAL INFORMATION

Calories	175	Sugars	........8g
Protein	.........6g	Fat	..........1g
Carbohydrate	...38g	Saturates	.....0.3g

 25 mins   20 mins

SERVES 4

INGREDIENTS

generous 5 cups diced mealy potatoes

¾ cup small broccoli florets

1 small mango, diced

4 scallions, sliced

salt and pepper

small cooked spiced poppadoms, to serve

DRESSING

½ tsp ground cumin

½ tsp ground coriander

1 tbsp mango chutney

⅔ cup low-fat unsweetened yogurt

1 tsp chopped fresh ginger root

2 tbsp chopped fresh cilantro

1 Cook the potatoes in a pan of boiling water for 10 minutes or until tender. Drain and place in a mixing bowl.

2 Meanwhile, blanch the broccoli florets in a separate pan of boiling water for 2 minutes. Drain the broccoli well and add to the potatoes in the bowl.

3 When the potatoes and broccoli have cooled, add the diced mango and sliced scallions to the bowl. Season to taste with salt and pepper and mix carefully to combine thoroughly.

4 In a small bowl, stir all of the dressing ingredients together.

5 Spoon the dressing over the potato mixture and mix together, taking care not to break up the potatoes and broccoli.

6 Serve the salad immediately, accompanied by the small cooked spiced poppadoms.

COOK'S TIP

Mix the dressing ingredients together in advance and let chill in the refrigerator for a few hours in order for a stronger flavor to develop.

Sweet Potato Salad

This unusual and filling salad, with its peppery yogurt dressing and lovely mix of textures, is best served warm.

NUTRITIONAL INFORMATION

Calories	192	Sugars	........23g
Protein	.........7g	Fat	..........4g
Carbohydrate	...33g	Saturates	.......1g

10 mins   15 mins

SERVES 4

INGREDIENTS

1 sweet potato, peeled and diced

2 carrots, sliced

3 tomatoes, seeded and chopped

½ cup canned garbanzo beans, drained

8 iceberg lettuce leaves

1 tbsp golden raisins

1 tbsp chopped walnuts

1 small onion, thinly sliced into rings

DRESSING

6 tbsp unsweetened yogurt

1 tbsp clear honey

1 tsp coarsely ground black pepper

salt

1 Cook the diced sweet potato in a large pan of boiling water for 10 minutes. Add the carrots and cook for a further 3-5 minutes until the sweet potato is tender, but still firm to the bite. Drain well and place in a bowl.

2 Add the tomatoes and garbanzo beans to the sweet potato and carrots and mix thoroughly.

3 Line a salad bowl with the lettuce leaves and spoon the vegetable mixture into the center. Sprinkle with the golden raisins, walnuts, and onion rings.

4 To make the dressing, combine the yogurt, honey, and black pepper in a small serving bowl, whisking thoroughly with a fork. Season to taste with salt.

5 Serve the salad warm and hand the yogurt and honey dressing separately.

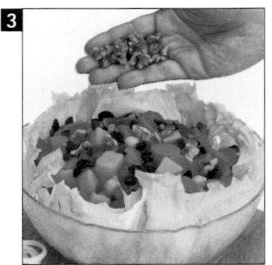

Fruity Coleslaw

This tangy coleslaw is packed with apples and nuts. It has a lovely olive oil, cider vinegar, and honey dressing.

NUTRITIONAL INFORMATION

Calories	234	Sugars	........30g
Protein	.........3g	Fat	..........12g
Carbohydrate	...30g	Saturates	.......2g

 10 mins   0 mins

SERVES 6

INGREDIENTS

½ small red cabbage, thinly shredded

½ small white cabbage, thinly shredded

1 cup dried dates, pitted and chopped

1 red eating apple

2 green eating apples

4 tbsp lemon juice

¼ cup pine nuts, toasted

DRESSING

5 tbsp olive oil

2 tbsp cider vinegar

1 tsp clear honey

salt and ground black pepper

1 Put the shredded red and white cabbage and the dates into a salad bowl and toss well to mix.

COOK'S TIP

A good way to mix salad dressings is to put all the ingredients into a screw-top jar, put on the lid, and shake vigorously to combine.

2 Core the apples, but do not peel them. Thinly slice them and place in another bowl. Add the lemon juice and toss well to coat to prevent the apples from turning brown. Add them to the salad bowl.

3 To make the dressing, whisk together the olive oil, vinegar, and honey in a small bowl and season to taste with salt and pepper. Pour the dressing over the salad and toss. Sprinkle with the pine nuts, toss lightly, and serve.

Coleslaw

Homemade coleslaw tastes far superior to any that you can buy.
If you make it in advance, add the sunflower seeds just before serving.

NUTRITIONAL INFORMATION

Calories	224	Sugars	.........8g
Protein	.........3g	Fat	.........20g
Carbohydrate	....8g	Saturates	......3g

10 mins   5 mins

SERVES 4

I N G R E D I E N T S

⅔ cup low-fat mayonnaise

⅔ cup low-fat unsweetened yogurt

dash of Tabasco sauce

1 medium head of white cabbage

4 carrots

1 green bell pepper

2 tbsp sunflower seeds

salt and pepper

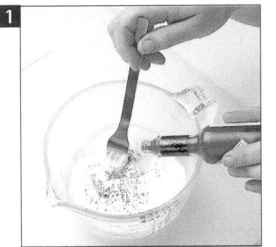 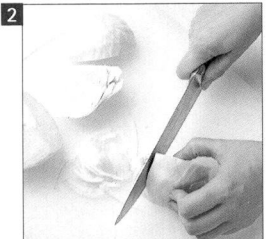 

1 To make the dressing, combine the mayonnaise, yogurt, Tabasco sauce, and salt and pepper to taste in a small bowl. Let chill until required.

2 Cut the cabbage in half and then into quarters. Remove and discard the tough center stem. Shred the cabbage leaves finely. Wash the leaves and dry them thoroughly.

3 Peel the carrots and shred using a food processor or a mandolin. Alternatively, coarsely grate the carrot.

4 Quarter and seed the bell pepper and cut the flesh into thin strips.

5 Combine the vegetables in a large bowl and toss to mix. Pour over the dressing and toss until the vegetables are coated. Chill until required.

6 Just before serving, place the sunflower seeds on a cookie sheet and toast them in the oven or under the broiler until golden brown. Transfer the salad to a large serving dish, scatter with sunflower seeds, and serve.

VARIATION
To give the coleslaw a slightly different flavor and texture, add one or more of the following ingredients: raisins, grapes, grated apple, chopped walnuts, cubes of cheese, or roasted peanuts.

Mango & Wild Rice Salad

The very slight edge that counteracts the sweetness of the fruit makes a juicy ripe mango the perfect choice for a summery salad.

NUTRITIONAL INFORMATION

Calories	320	Sugars	........10g
Protein	.........6g	Fat	..........20g
Carbohydrate	...30g	Saturates	......2g

15 mins 1¼ hrs

SERVES 4

INGREDIENTS

generous ½ cup wild rice

¾ cup basmati rice

3 tbsp hazelnut oil

1 tbsp sherry vinegar

1 ripe mango

3 celery stalks

¾ cup dried apricots, chopped

½ cup sliced almonds, toasted

2 tbsp chopped, fresh cilantro or mint

salt and pepper

fresh cilantro or mint sprigs, to garnish

1 Cook the wild rice and basmati rice in separate pans of lightly salted boiling water. Cook the wild rice for 45–50 minutes and the basmati rice for 10–12 minutes. Drain, rinse, and drain again. Place both rices in a large bowl.

2 Whisk together the oil and vinegar and season to taste with salt and pepper. Pour over the rice and toss well.

3 Cut the mango in half lengthwise, as close to the pit as possible. Remove and discard the pit.

4 Peel the skin from the mango and cut the flesh into slices.

5 Thinly slice the celery and add to the cooled rice with the mango, apricots, almonds, and chopped herbs. Toss together and transfer to a serving dish.

6 Garnish the salad with cilantro or mint sprigs and serve.

COOK'S TIP

To toast almonds, place them on a cookie sheet in a preheated oven, 350°F/180°C, for 5–10 minutes. Alternatively, toast them under the broiler, turning frequently and keeping a close eye on them because they will quickly burn.

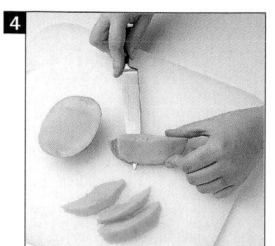

Mixed Salad Greens

Make this green leafy salad with as many varieties of salad greens and edible flowers as you can find to give an unusual effect.

NUTRITIONAL INFORMATION

Calories	51	Sugars	0.1g
Protein	0.1g	Fat	6g
Carbohydrate	1g	Saturates	1g

5 mins   0 mins

SERVES 4

I N G R E D I E N T S

½ head frisée

½ head oakleaf lettuce or quattro stagione

few leaves of radicchio

1 head Belgian endive

small bunch arugula leaves

few fresh basil or flat-leaf parsley sprigs

edible flowers, to garnish (optional)

F R E N C H   D R E S S I N G

1 tbsp white wine vinegar

pinch of sugar

½ tsp Dijon mustard

3 tbsp extra virgin olive oil

salt and pepper

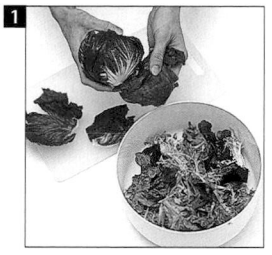
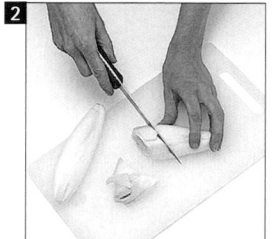

1 Tear the frisée, oakleaf lettuce, and radicchio into pieces. Place the salad greens in a large serving bowl or in individual bowls if you prefer.

2 Cut the endive into diagonal slices and add to the bowl with the arugula leaves, basil, or parsley.

3 To make the dressing, beat the white wine vinegar, sugar, and Dijon mustard in a small bowl until the sugar has dissolved. Gradually beat in the olive oil until the dressing is creamy and thoroughly mixed. Season to taste with salt and pepper.

4 Pour the dressing over the salad and toss thoroughly. Sprinkle a mixture of edible flowers over the top and serve.

COOK'S TIP
Violas, rock geraniums, nasturtiums, chive flowers, and pot marigolds add vibrant colors and a sweet flavor to any salad. Use it as a centerpiece at a dinner party, or to liven up a simple everyday meal.

Beet Salad

This simple salad has a delicate, subtle flavor that will not overpower the entrée. The beet looks wonderful with lamb's lettuce leaves.

NUTRITIONAL INFORMATION

Calories 339   Sugars 6g
Protein . . . . .3g   Fat 33g
Carbohydrate . . . .7g   Saturates 7g

 10 mins   0 mins

SERVES 4

INGREDIENTS

175 g/6 oz lamb's lettuce

4 small beets, cooked and diced

2 tbsp chopped walnuts

DRESSING

2 tbsp lemon juice

2 garlic cloves, finely chopped

1 tbsp Dijon mustard

pinch of sugar

½ cup sunflower oil

½ cup sour cream

salt and ground black pepper

1 To make the sour cream dressing, combine the lemon juice, garlic, mustard, and sugar in a bowl and season to taste with salt and pepper. Gradually whisk in the sunflower oil. Lightly beat the sour cream, then whisk it into the dressing.

2 Put the lamb's lettuce in a bowl and pour about one-third of the dressing over it. Toss to coat, then divide the lettuce among 4 plates.

3 Top each portion of lamb's lettuce with the diced beets and drizzle over the remaining dressing.

4 Garnish the salad with a sprinkling of chopped walnuts and serve immediately.

COOK'S TIP

You can prepare the dressing in advance, but do not pour it on to the salad until you are ready to serve because the lamb's lettuce will become soggy.

Egg & Fennel Salad

This is a very refreshing salad. The subtle liquorice flavor of fennel combines well with the cucumber and mint.

NUTRITIONAL INFORMATION

Calories	90	Sugars	.........7g
Protein	.........4g	Fat	...........5g
Carbohydrate	....7g	Saturates	.......1g

10 mins   0 mins

SERVES 4

INGREDIENTS

1 fennel bulb

lemon juice

2 small oranges

1 small or ½ a large cucumber

1 tbsp chopped mint

1 tbsp virgin olive oil

2 hard-cooked eggs

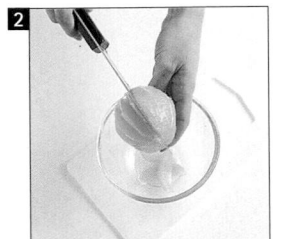
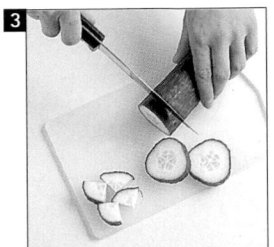

 Using a sharp knife, trim the outer leaves from the fennel. Slice the fennel bulb thinly then quickly place in a bowl of water and sprinkle with lemon juice (see Cook's Tip.)

 Grate the zest of the oranges over a bowl. Using a sharp knife, pare away the orange peel, then segment the orange by carefully slicing between each line of pith. Do this over the bowl in order to retain the juice.

3 Using a sharp knife, cut the cucumber into ½ inch/12 mm rounds, then cut each round into quarters. Drain the sliced fennel, mix with the orange segments and juice, add the sliced cucumber and the chopped mint, and mix gently to combine.

4 Pour the olive oil over the fennel and cucumber salad and toss well.

5 Peel and quarter the hard-cooked eggs and use these to decorate the top of the salad. Serve at once.

COOK'S TIP
Fennel will discolor if it is left for any length of time without a dressing. To prevent any discoloration, place it in a bowl of water and sprinkle with lemon juice.

Spinach & Garlic Salad

This robust salad goes especially well with pasta dishes. Roasting garlic gives it a deliciously sweet flavor.

NUTRITIONAL INFORMATION

Calories ....228 Sugars 2g
Protein ....6g Fat 21g
Carbohydrate ....3g Saturates 2g

5 mins   15 mins

SERVES 4

INGREDIENTS

12 garlic cloves

4 tbsp olive oil

1 lb/450 g baby spinach leaves

½ cup chopped walnuts or pine nuts

2 tbsp lemon juice

salt and ground black pepper

1 Do not peel the garlic. Place the cloves in an ovenproof dish, add 2 tbsp of the olive oil, and toss well to coat. Roast in a preheated oven, 375°F/190°C, for 15 minutes.

2 Transfer the garlic and oil to a salad bowl. Add the spinach, walnuts or pine nuts, lemon juice, and remaining oil. Toss well to coat and season to taste with salt and pepper.

3 Serve the salad immediately while the garlic is still warm—the diners squeeze the softened garlic out of the skins at the table.

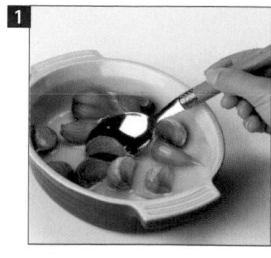  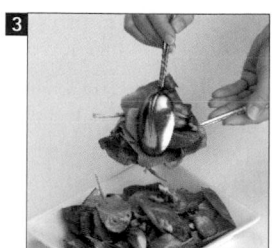

VARIATION
Substitute young sorrel leaves for the spinach for a delicious lemony flavor.

Beansprout Salad

This is a very light dish and is ideal served either on its own for a summer meal or as an appetizer.

NUTRITIONAL INFORMATION

Calories	70	Sugars	.........5g
Protein	.........4g	Fat	...........3g
Carbohydrate	....7g	Saturates	.....0.5g

10 mins   1 min

SERVES 4

INGREDIENTS

4 cups beansprouts

1 small cucumber

1 green bell pepper, seeded and cut into matchsticks

1 carrot, cut into matchsticks

2 tomatoes, finely chopped

1 celery stalk, cut into matchsticks

1 garlic clove, crushed

dash of chili sauce

2 tbsp light soy sauce

1 tsp wine vinegar

2 tsp sesame oil

16 fresh chives

1 Blanch the beansprouts in boiling water for 1 minute. Drain well and rinse under cold water, then drain thoroughly again.

2 Cut the cucumber in half lengthwise. Scoop out the seeds with a teaspoon and discard. Cut the flesh into matchsticks with a sharp knife and mix with the beansprouts, green bell pepper, carrot, tomatoes, and celery in a large glass bowl.

3 Mix together the crushed garlic, chili sauce, soy sauce, wine vinegar, and sesame oil in a small bowl.

4 Pour the dressing over the vegetables, tossing well to coat the salad thoroughly.

5 Spoon the salad on to 4 individual serving plates. Garnish with fresh chives and serve immediately.

VARIATION

You could substitute cooked, cooled green beans or snow peas for the cucumber. Vary the beansprouts for a different flavor. Try adzuki bean or alfalfa sprouts, as well as the better-known mung and soy bean sprouts.

Coronation Salad

The curried mayonnaise dressing for this dish is based on one invented for the coronation of Queen Elizabeth II.

NUTRITIONAL INFORMATION

Calories 236   Sugars 24g
Protein ....7g   Fat 5g
Carbohydrate ...43g   Saturates 1g

25 mins   0 mins

SERVES 4

INGREDIENTS

1 red bell pepper

½ cup golden raisins

1 celery stalk, sliced

½ cup corn kernels

1 Granny Smith apple, diced

16 white seedless grapes,
    washed and halved

3 cups cooked basmati rice
    (1 cup uncooked)

1 romaine lettuce, washed and drained

1 tsp paprika to garnish

DRESSING

4 tbsp low-fat mayonnaise

2 tsp mild curry powder

1 tsp lemon juice

1 tsp paprika

pinch of salt

1 Seed and chop the red bell pepper, then combine the golden raisins, red bell pepper, celery, corn, apple, and grapes in a large bowl. Stir in the cooked rice and mix well.

2 To make the dressing, put the mayonnaise, curry powder, lemon juice, paprika, and salt into a small bowl and mix well to combine.

3 Pour the dressing over the salad and gently mix until evenly coated.

4 Line the serving plate with romaine lettuce leaves and spoon on the salad. Sprinkle over the paprika and serve.

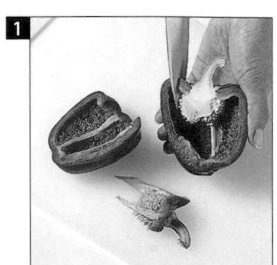

COOK'S TIP

Mayonnaise can be bought in varying thicknesses, from the type that you spoon out of the jar to the pouring variety. If you need to thin down mayonnaise for a dressing, simply add water little by little until the desired consistency is reached.

Cool Bean Salad

This is ideal for serving at a barbecue, for accompanying one of the hotter Indian curries, or for serving as part of a salad buffet at parties.

NUTRITIONAL INFORMATION

Calories	98	Sugars	........5g
Protein	.........9g	Fat	...........1g
Carbohydrate	...14g	Saturates	.....0.3g

 15 mins   15 mins

SERVES 4

INGREDIENTS

1 red onion, thinly sliced

2 cups beans, fresh or frozen

⅔ cup unsweetened yogurt

1 tbsp chopped fresh mint

1½ tsp lemon juice

1 garlic clove, halved

½ cucumber, peeled, halved, and sliced

salt and ground white pepper

1 Rinse the red onion slices briefly under cold running water and drain them thoroughly.

2 Cook the fava beans in a small pan of boiling water until tender: 8–10 minutes for fresh beans, 5–6 minutes for frozen.

3 Drain, rinse under cold running water, and drain again.

4 If you wish, shell the beans from their white outer shells to leave the sweet green bean.

5 Combine the unsweetened yogurt, chopped mint, lemon juice, garlic, and seasoning in a bowl.

6 Combine the onion, cucumber, and fava beans. Toss them in the yogurt dressing until well coated. Remove and discard the garlic halves.

7 Spoon the salad onto a serving plate and serve immediately.

COOK'S TIP
Rinsing the onion under cold running water takes the edge off the raw taste, as it washes away some of the juices. The same technique can be used on other pungent vegetables and salads, such as scallions, bitter cucumbers, and chilies.

Caesar Salad

Caesar Cardini, not Caesar Augustus, created this salad in the United States in the 1920s, and it is now regarded as a classic.

NUTRITIONAL INFORMATION

Calories ....280 Sugars 2g
Protein ....11g Fat 21g
Carbohydrate ...14g Saturates 5g

15 mins, plus cooling   20 mins

SERVES 4

INGREDIENTS

1 garlic clove, halved

1 romaine lettuce

½ cup coarsely grated Parmesan cheese

GARLIC CROUTONS

3 tbsp olive oil

1 large garlic clove, halved

4 slices whole-wheat bread, crusts removed and diced

DRESSING

1 egg

1 tsp vegetarian Worcestershire sauce

2 tbsp lemon juice

2 tsp Dijon mustard

2 tbsp olive oil

salt and ground black pepper

VARIATION
Some people, such as the elderly, the very young, invalids and pregnant women, should avoid raw or lightly cooked eggs because of the risk of salmonella. As an alternative, omit the softly cooked egg from the dressing and add quartered hard-cooked eggs to the salad.

1 First make the garlic croûtons. Pour the olive oil into a small pan and add the garlic. Heat gently for 5 minutes. Remove and discard the garlic. Place the cubes of bread in a bowl and pour in the oil. Toss well, then spread out on a cookie sheet. Bake the croûtons in a preheated oven, 375°F/190°C, for 10 minutes until crisp. Remove from the oven and let cool.

2 To make the dressing, boil the egg for 1 minute. Crack it into a bowl and scoop out any remaining egg white from the shell. Whisk in the Worcestershire sauce, lemon juice, mustard, and oil and season to taste with salt and pepper.

3 Rub the inside of a salad bowl with the garlic halves, then discard them.

4 Arrange the lettuce leaves in the salad bowl and sprinkle with the grated Parmesan cheese. Drizzle the dressing over the salad and sprinkle the garlic croûtons on top. Toss the salad at the table and serve at once.

Potatoes in Italian Dressing

The warm potatoes quickly absorb the wonderful flavors of olives, tomatoes, and olive oil. This salad is good served warm or cold.

NUTRITIONAL INFORMATION

Calories	239	Sugars	.........2g
Protein	.........4g	Fat	..........10g
Carbohydrate	...36g	Saturates	.......1g

  15 mins 15 mins

SERVES 4

INGREDIENTS

1¾ lb/790 g waxy potatoes

1 shallot

2 tomatoes

1 tbsp chopped fresh basil

salt

ITALIAN DRESSING

1 tomato, skinned and chopped finely

4 black olives, pitted and chopped finely

4 tbsp olive oil

1 tbsp wine vinegar

1 garlic clove, crushed

salt and pepper

1 Cook the potatoes in a pan of boiling salted water for 15 minutes or until they are tender. Drain well, chop roughly, and put into a bowl.

2 Chop the shallot. Cut the tomatoes into wedges and add the shallot and tomatoes to the potatoes.

3 To make the Italian dressing, put all the ingredients into a screw-top jar and shake the jar to mix the ingredients thoroughly.

4 Pour the Italian dressing over the potato mixture and toss thoroughly to coat the vegetables.

5 Transfer the salad to a serving dish and sprinkle with the basil.

COOK'S TIP
Be sure to use a really good quality extra virgin olive oil for the Italian dressing to give a really fruity flavor to the potatoes.

Sicilian Eggplant Salad

This colorful cooked salad from Sicily, with its Mediterranean flavors, was first brought to Italy by the Moors.

NUTRITIONAL INFORMATION

Calories 217	Sugars 12g
Protein 2g	Fat 18g
Carbohydrate . . .13g	Saturates 3g

10 mins

25 mins

SERVES 4

INGREDIENTS

6 tbsp olive oil

1 onion, chopped

2 garlic cloves, chopped

2 celery stalks, chopped

1 lb eggplant

2 cups canned tomatoes, chopped

⅓ cup green olives, pitted and chopped

2 tbsp granulated sugar

2⅓ cups red wine vinegar

¼ cup capers, drained

salt and pepper

1 tbsp flat-leaf parsley, coarsely chopped, to garnish

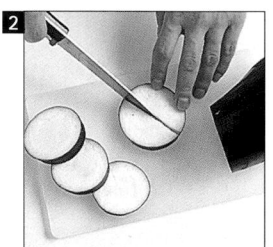

1 Heat 2 tablespoons of the oil in a large skillet. Add the prepared onions, garlic, and celery to the skillet and cook, stirring, for 3–4 minutes.

2 Using a sharp knife, slice the eggplant into thick rounds, then cut each round into 4 pieces.

3 Add the eggplant pieces to the skillet with the remaining olive oil and cook for 5 minutes, or until golden.

4 Add the chopped tomatoes and olives and the sugar to the skillet, stirring until the sugar has dissolved.

5 Add the red wine vinegar, then reduce the heat, and let simmer for 10–15 minutes, or until the sauce is thick and the eggplant pieces are tender.

6 While the skillet is still on the heat, stir in the capers. Season to taste with salt and pepper.

7 Transfer to serving plates and garnish with the chopped flat-leaf parsley.

COOK'S TIP

This salad is best served cold the day after it is made, which lets the flavors mingle and be fully absorbed.

Gazpacho Rice Salad

All the flavors of a zesty Spanish gazpacho—garlic, tomatoes, bell peppers and cucumber, combined with rice—make a great summer salad.

NUTRITIONAL INFORMATION

Calories	253	Sugars	........15g
Protein	.........7g	Fat	...........5g
Carbohydrate	...46g	Saturates	.......1g

 30 mins   35 mins

SERVES 4

INGREDIENTS

7 tbsp extra virgin olive oil

1 onion, finely chopped

4 garlic cloves, finely chopped

1 cup long grain white rice

1½ cups vegetable bouilon or water

1½ tsp dried thyme

3 tbsp sherry vinegar

1 tsp Dijon mustard

1 tsp clear honey

1 red bell pepper, seeded and chopped

½ yellow bell pepper, seeded and chopped

½ green bell pepper, seeded and chopped

1 red onion, finely chopped

½ cucumber, peeled, seeded, and chopped (optional)

3 tomatoes, seeded and chopped

2–3 tbsp chopped flat-leaf parsley

salt and pepper

TO SERVE

12 cherry tomatoes, halved

12 black olives, pitted and coarsely chopped

1 tbsp slivered almonds, toasted

---

1 Heat 2 tablespoons of the olive oil in a large pan. Add the onion and cook, stirring frequently, for 2 minutes, or until beginning to soften. Stir in half the garlic and cook for a further minute.

2 Add the rice, stir to coat, and cook for about 2 minutes until translucent. Stir in the bouillon and half the thyme and bring to a boil. Season to taste.

3 Cover and simmer gently for about 20 minutes until tender. Stand, still covered, for about 15 minutes; uncover and cool completely.

4 Whisk the vinegar with the remaining garlic and thyme, the mustard, honey, and salt and pepper in a large bowl. Gradually whisk in the remaining olive oil. Using a fork, gently fluff the rice into the vinaigrette.

5 Add the bell peppers, red onion, cucumber, tomatoes, and parsley; toss and adjust the seasoning.

6 Transfer the salad to a serving bowl and garnish with the halved tomatoes, black olives, and toasted almonds. Serve warm.

Potato Salad

You can use leftover cold potatoes, cut into bite-size pieces, for this salad, but tiny new potatoes are best for maximum flavor.

NUTRITIONAL INFORMATION

Calories	275	Sugars	........8g
Protein	.........5g	Fat	..........13g
Carbohydrate	...38g	Saturates	......2g

20 mins   20 mins

SERVES 4

INGREDIENTS

1½ lb/675 g tiny new potatoes

8 scallions

1 hard-cooked egg (optional)

generous 1 cup low-fat mayonnaise

1 tsp paprika

salt and pepper

TO GARNISH

2 tbsp chopped fresh chives

pinch of paprika

1 Bring a large pan of lightly salted water to a boil. Add the potatoes and cook for 10–15 minutes or until they are just tender.

2 Drain the potatoes in a colander and rinse them under cold running water until they are completely cold. Drain them again thoroughly. Transfer to a mixing bowl and set aside until required.

3 Trim and slice the scallions thinly on the diagonal.

4 Shell and chop the hard-cooked egg (if using.)

5 Mix together the mayonnaise, paprika, and salt and pepper to taste in a bowl until well blended. Pour the mixture over the potatoes.

6 Add the sliced scallions and chopped egg, if using, and then toss them together gently.

7 Transfer the potato salad to a serving bowl, and sprinkle with chopped chives and a pinch of paprika. Cover and chill in the refrigerator until required.

COOK'S TIP
To make a lighter dressing, use a mixture of half mayonnaise and half unsweetened yogurt.

Pesto Risotto-Rice Salad

This is a cross between a risotto and a rice salad—using Italian arborio rice produces a slightly heavier, stickier result.

NUTRITIONAL INFORMATION

Calories	406	Sugars	.........5g
Protein	.........7g	Fat	..........28g
Carbohydrate	...34g	Saturates	.......5g

45 mins   30 mins

SERVES 4–6

INGREDIENTS

3 tbsp extra virgin olive oil, plus extra for drizzling

1 onion, finely chopped

1 cup arborio rice

2 cups boiling water

6 sun-dried tomatoes in oil, drained and cut into thin slivers

½ small red onion, very thinly sliced

3 tbsp lemon juice

PESTO

2 oz/55 g fresh basil leaves

2 garlic cloves, finely chopped

2 tbsp pine nuts, lightly toasted

½ cup extra virgin olive oil

½ cup freshly grated Parmesan cheese

salt and pepper

TO GARNISH

fresh basil leaves

Parmesan shavings

1 To make the pesto, put the basil, garlic, and pine nuts in a food processor and process for 30 seconds. With the motor running, gradually add the olive oil through the feeder tube until a smooth paste forms. Add the cheese and pulse until blended, but still with texture. Scrape into a small bowl and season to taste.

2 Heat 1 tablespoon of the oil in a pan and cook the chopped onion until soft. Stir in the rice and cook, stirring occasionally, for 2 minutes. Stir in the water and season. Cover and simmer for 20 minutes until the rice is tender and the water absorbed. Cool slightly.

3 Put the sun-dried tomatoes and sliced onion in a bowl, and add the lemon juice and 2 tablespoons of oil. Fork in the hot rice and stir in the pesto. Toss to combine. Adjust the seasoning if necessary. Cover and cool to room temperature.

4 Fork the rice mixture into a shallow serving bowl. Drizzle with some olive oil and garnish with basil leaves and Parmesan shavings. Serve the salad at room temperature, not chilled.

Mexican Potato Salad

The flavors of Mexico are echoed in this dish, in which potato slices are topped with tomatoes and chiles and served with guacamole.

NUTRITIONAL INFORMATION

Calories 260   Sugars 6g
Protein ....6g   Fat 9g
Carbohydrate ...41g   Saturates 2g

20 mins   20 mins

SERVES 4

INGREDIENTS

2¾ lb/1.25 kg waxy potatoes, sliced

1 ripe avocado

1 tsp olive oil

1 tsp lemon juice

1 garlic clove, crushed

1 onion, chopped

2 large tomatoes, sliced

1 green chile, chopped

1 yellow bell pepper, seeded and sliced

2 tbsp chopped fresh cilantro

salt and pepper

lemon wedges, to garnish

1 Cook the potato slices in a pan of boiling water for 10–15 minutes, or until tender. Drain and let cool.

VARIATION
You can omit the green chili from this salad if you do not like hot dishes.

2 Meanwhile, cut the avocado in half and remove the pit. Mash the avocado flesh with a fork (you could also scoop the avocado flesh from the 2 halves using a spoon and then mash it.)

3 Add the olive oil, lemon juice, garlic, and chopped onion to the avocado flesh and stir to mix. Cover the bowl with plastic wrap, to minimize discoloration, and set aside.

4 Mix the tomatoes, chile, and yellow bell pepper together and transfer to a salad bowl with the potato slices.

5 Arrange the avocado mixture on top of the salad and sprinkle with the chopped fresh cilantro.

6 Season to taste with salt and pepper and serve garnished with the lemon wedges.

Potato & Apple Salad

Baby new potatoes are perfect for salads, as they look tempting and have a wonderful nutty flavor and texture.

NUTRITIONAL INFORMATION

Calories	.219	Sugars	.6g
Protein	.4g	Fat	11g
Carbohydrate	.29g	Saturates	.2g

 10 mins   20 mins

SERVES 6

INGREDIENTS

2 lb/900 g baby new potatoes

2 green eating apples

4 scallions, chopped

4 celery stalks, chopped

⅔ cup mayonnaise (see page 8)

salt and ground black pepper

2 Core and chop the apples and add them to the salad bowl with the scallions and celery.

3 Add the mayonnaise to the potato and apple mixture and season to taste with salt and pepper.

1 Cook the unpeeled potatoes in a large pan of lightly salted boiling water for 20 minutes, until tender. Drain well and place in a salad bowl.

4 Stir well to mix, then let cool and let the flavors develop. Serve the salad at room temperature.

VARIATION
Stir 1 tablespoon snipped fresh chives into the mayonnaise before adding it to the salad in step 3.

Roast Vegetable Salad

A colorful collection of Mediterranean vegetables makes a wonderful salad for a hot summer day. Serve at room temperature or just warm.

NUTRITIONAL INFORMATION

Calories 249	Sugars 13g
Protein 3g	Fat 19g
Carbohydrate ...17g	Saturates 3g

25 mins | 35 mins

SERVES 6

INGREDIENTS

6 tbsp olive oil

2 eggplants

1 yellow bell pepper, seeded and quartered

1 red bell pepper, seeded and quartered

1 orange bell pepper, seeded and quartered

6 shallots

3 red onions, quartered

6 plum tomatoes, quartered

6 fresh basil leaves

FOR THE DRESSING

4 tbsp olive oil

1 tbsp red wine vinegar

salt and ground black pepper

1 Pour the oil into a large roasting pan. Add the eggplants, bell peppers, shallots, onions, and tomatoes and toss well to coat. Roast in a preheated oven, 450°F/230°C, for 20 minutes, turning occasionally. Using a slotted spoon, transfer the bell peppers, shallots, onions, and tomatoes to a serving platter.

2 Return the eggplants to the oven and continue to roast, turning once, for 15 minutes more. Remove from the oven and let stand until cool enough to handle. Cut the eggplants into bite-size pieces and add to the vegetable platter.

3 To make the dressing, combine the oil, vinegar, and garlic, whisking well with a fork. Season to taste with salt and pepper and pour the dressing over the vegetables. Sprinkle the salad with the basil and serve.

Mixed Bean Salad

You can use a mixture of any canned beans to make this crunchy, colorful and very filling salad.

NUTRITIONAL INFORMATION

Calories	198	Sugars	.........6g
Protein	........10g	Fat	...........6g
Carbohydrate	...26g	Saturates	.......1g

30 mins   15–20 mins

SERVES 8

INGREDIENTS

1½ cups canned flageolet beans, drained

1½ cups canned red kidney beans, drained

1¼ cups canned lima beans, drained

1 small red onion, thinly sliced

1 cup dwarf green beans, topped and tailed

1 red bell pepper, halved and seeded

salt

DRESSING

4 tbsp olive oil

2 tbsp sherry vinegar

2 tbsp lemon juice

1 tsp light muscovado sugar

1 tsp chili sauce (optional)

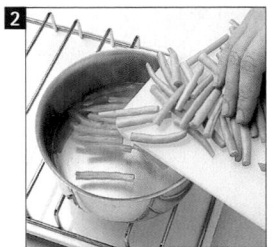

1 Put the canned beans in a large mixing bowl. Add the sliced onion and mix together.

2 Cut the dwarf green beans in half and cook in lightly salted boiling water for about 8 minutes until just tender. Refresh under cold water and drain again. Add to the mixed beans and onions.

3 Place the bell pepper halves, cut side down, on a broiler rack and cook until the skin blackens and chars. Let the bell peppers cool slightly then put them into a plastic bag for about 10 minutes. Peel away the skin from the bell peppers and discard. Roughly chop the bell pepper flesh and add it to the beans.

4 To make the dressing, place the oil, sherry vinegar, lemon juice, sugar, and chili sauce (if using) in a screw-top jar and shake vigorously.

5 Pour the dressing over the mixed bean salad and toss well. Let chill in the refrigerator until required.

VARIATION
Use any combination of beans in this salad. For a distinctive flavor, add 1 teaspoon of curry paste instead of the chili sauce.

Chinese Hot Salad

This salad can also be eaten cold—add 3-4 tablespoons French dressing as the vegetables cool, toss well, and serve cold or chilled.

NUTRITIONAL INFORMATION

Calories	192	Sugars	........13g
Protein	.........5g	Fat	..........9g
Carbohydrate	...20g	Saturates	.......1g

 5 mins   10 mins

SERVES 4

INGREDIENTS

1 tbsp dark soy sauce

1½–2 tsp bottled sweet chili sauce

2 tbsp sherry

1 tbsp brown sugar

1 tbsp wine vinegar

2 tbsp sunflower oil

1 garlic clove, crushed

4 scallions, thinly sliced diagonally

2 zucchini, cut into julienne strips about 1½ inches long

250 g/9 oz carrots, cut into julienne strips about 4 cm/1½ inches long

1 red or green bell pepper, cored, seeded, and thinly sliced

14 oz/400 g canned beansprouts, well drained

1 cup green or fine beans, cut into 2 inch lengths

1 tbsp sesame oil

salt and pepper

1–2 tsp sesame seeds, to garnish

1 Combine the soy sauce, chili sauce, sherry, sugar, vinegar, and seasoning in a small bowl.

2 Heat the 2 tablespoons of sunflower oil in a wok or large, heavy skillet, swirling the oil around the base of the skillet until it is really hot.

3 Add the garlic and scallions to the wok and stir-fry for 1-2 minutes.

4 Add the zucchini, carrots, and bell peppers and stir-fry for 1-2 minutes, then add the soy sauce mixture and bring to a boil.

5 Add the beansprouts and green beans and stir-fry for 1-2 minutes, making sure all the vegetables are thoroughly coated with the sauce.

6 Drizzle the sesame oil over the vegetables in the wok and stir-fry for about 30 seconds.

7 Serve the salad hot, sprinkled with sesame seeds.

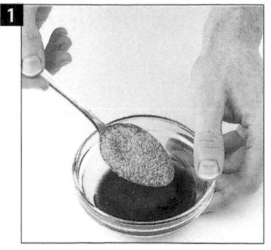

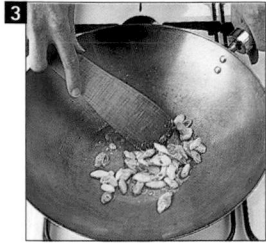

Zucchini & Mint Salad

This salad uses lots of green-colored ingredients which look and taste wonderful with the minty yogurt dressing.

NUTRITIONAL INFORMATION

Calories 49	Sugars 5g
Protein 4g	Fat 1g
Carbohydrate 6g	Saturates 0g

30 mins   7–8 mins

SERVES 4

INGREDIENTS

2 zucchini, cut into batons

¾ cup green beans, cut into thirds

1 green bell pepper, seeded and cut into strips

2 celery stalks, sliced

1 bunch of watercress

DRESSING

scant 1 cup unsweetened yogurt

1 garlic clove, crushed

2 tbsp chopped fresh mint

pepper

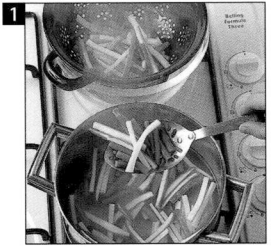 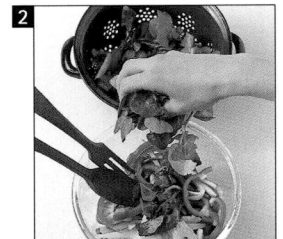 

1 Cook the zucchini batons and beans in a pan of lightly salted boiling water for 7–8 minutes. Drain, rinse under cold running water, and drain again. Let cool completely.

2 Mix the zucchini and beans with the green bell pepper strips, celery, and watercress in a large serving bowl.

3 To make the dressing, combine the natural yogurt, garlic, and chopped fresh mint in a small bowl. Season with pepper to taste.

4 Spoon the dressing onto the salad and serve immediately.

COOK'S TIP
The salad must be served as soon as the yogurt dressing has been added—the dressing will start to separate if it is kept for any length of time.

Mushroom Salad

This easy salad is a useful, year-round accompaniment that goes well with a wide variety of main courses.

NUTRITIONAL INFORMATION

Calories	74	Sugars 4g
Protein	. . . . .2g	Fat 6g
Carbohydrate	. . . .4g	Saturates 1g

 10 mins, plus marinating   0 mins

SERVES 4

INGREDIENTS

½ cucumber, cut into chunks

2 cups white mushrooms, thinly sliced

1 small lettuce, torn

4 tomatoes, sliced

1 tbsp chopped fresh cilantro

FOR THE DRESSING

2 tbsp olive oil

1 tbsp white wine vinegar

1 bay leaf

1 garlic clove, finely chopped

1 fresh tarragon sprig

1 fresh rosemary sprig

salt and ground black pepper

1 First make the dressing. Combine the oil, vinegar, bay leaf, garlic, tarragon, and rosemary in a large bowl, whisking well. Season to taste with salt and pepper.

2 Add the cucumber and mushrooms to the dressing, tossing well to mix. Cover with plastic wrap and let marinate for 30 minutes.

3 Place the lettuce in a salad bowl. Using a slotted spoon, transfer the mushrooms and cucumber to the salad bowl and add the tomatoes. Sprinkle with the cilantro.

4 Strain the dressing and discard the contents of the strainer. Pour the dressing over the salad and serve at once.

COOK'S TIP

To clean mushrooms, wipe with damp paper towels or brush with a small vegetable brush. Never immerse them in water.

Cheesy Pasta Salad

This delicious salad, packed with carbohydrate, protein, and vitamins, is hearty enough to be served as an entrée.

NUTRITIONAL INFORMATION

Calories	759	Sugars	.........3g
Protein	........17g	Fat	..........56g
Carbohydrate	...43g	Saturates	......17g

  15 mins 8-10 mins

SERVES 4

INGREDIENTS

2 cups dried fusilli

¼ lb/100g mixed salad leaves, such as oakleaf lettuce, radina, baby spinach, arugula, and lamb's lettuce

2 cups diced dolcelatte cheese

4 tbsp sunflower oil

2 tbsp walnut oil

2 tbsp red wine vinegar

1 cup lightly toasted walnut halves

salt and ground black pepper

1 Cook the pasta in a large pan of lightly salted boiling water for 8-10 minutes, until it is tender but still firm to the bite. Drain, rinse with cold water, and drain again.

2 Place the salad leaves in a serving bowl and add the pasta. Sprinkle the cheese on top.

3 Combine the sunflower oil, walnut oil, and wine vinegar in a pitcher and season to taste with salt and pepper.

4 Pour the dressing over the salad, toss lightly to coat the ingredients, then top with the walnuts.

VARIATION

You can substitute another piquant cheese for the dolcelatte, such as Stilton, goat cheese, or feta.

Fruity Wild Rice Salsa

Wild rice has a nutty flavor and a good texture, ideal for salsas and salads, and goes well with the black beans in this dish.

NUTRITIONAL INFORMATION

Calories 467	Sugars 15g
Protein 10g	Fat 20g
Carbohydrate ...49g	Saturates 4g

2¼ hrs   1 hr

SERVES 4–6

INGREDIENTS

scant 1 cup small black beans, soaked overnight in cold water

1 onion, studded with 4 cloves

¾ cup wild rice

2 garlic cloves

2 cups boiling water

1 red onion, finely chopped

2 fresh red chilies, seeded and thinly sliced

1 red bell pepper, seeded and chopped

1 small mango or papaya, peeled and diced

2 oranges, segments removed and juice reserved

4 passion fruits, pulp and juice

juice of 3–4 limes

½ tsp ground cumin

1 tbsp maple syrup or brown sugar

⅔ cup extra virgin olive oil

1 small bunch fresh cilantro, leaves stripped from stems and chopped

lime slices, to garnish

1 Drain the beans and put in a large pan with the clove-studded onion. Cover with cold water by at least 2 inches/5 cm. Bring to a boil, lower the heat, and simmer for 1 hour until the beans are tender. Remove and discard the onion, rinse the beans under cold running water, and drain.

2 Meanwhile, put the wild rice and garlic in a pan and pour in the boiling water. Cover and simmer over low heat for 30–50 minutes. Cool slightly and discard the garlic cloves.

3 Put the beans in a large bowl and fork in the wild rice. Add the onion, chilies, bell pepper, mango, orange segments and their juice, and the passion fruit pulp and juice. Toss well together.

4 Combine the lime juice, cumin, and maple syrup or sugar. Whisk in the olive oil and half the cilantro, then pour over the rice mixture, and toss well. Cover let stand for up to 2 hours.

5 Spoon into a serving bowl, sprinkle with the remaining cilantro, and serve garnished with lime slices.

Red Rice Salad

This hearty salad is made with red rice, originally from France. It has an earthy flavor, which goes well with the other robust ingredients.

NUTRITIONAL INFORMATION

Calories	192	Sugars	.........5g
Protein	.........6g	Fat	...........5g
Carbohydrate	...33g	Saturates	.......1g

1½ hrs   30 mins

SERVES 6–8

INGREDIENTS

1 tbsp olive oil

1 cup red rice

1 cup water

1½ cups canned red kidney beans, drained and rinsed

1 small red bell pepper, seeded and diced

1 small red onion, finely chopped

2 small cooked beets (not in vinegar), peeled and diced

6–8 red radishes, thinly sliced

2–3 tbsp chopped fresh chives

salt and pepper

fresh chives, to garnish

HOT DRESSING

2 tbsp horseradish

1 tbsp Dijon mustard

1 tsp sugar

¼ cup red wine vinegar

½ cup extra virgin olive oil

1 Put the olive oil and red rice in a heavy pan and place over medium heat. Add the water and 1 teaspoon of salt. Bring to a boil, reduce the heat, cover, and simmer gently until the rice is tender and all the water has been absorbed. (There are several varieties of red rice, which differ in cooking times, so follow the packet instructions.) Remove the pan from the heat and set aside to cool to room temperature.

2 To make the dressing, put the horseradish, Dijon mustard, and sugar into a small bowl and whisk thoroughly to combine. Whisk in the red wine vinegar, then gradually whisk in the oil to form a smooth dressing.

3 In a large bowl, combine the kidney beans, red bell pepper, onion, beet, radishes, and chives and toss together. Season with salt and pepper to taste.

4 Using a fork, fluff the rice into the bowl with the vegetables. Pour over the dressing and toss the salad well. Cover and let stand for about 1 hour. Spoon the salad into a large shallow serving bowl, garnish with fresh chives, and serve immediately.

Mango Chutney

Everyone's favorite chutney, this has a sweet and sour taste. It is best made well in advance and stored for at least 2 weeks before use.

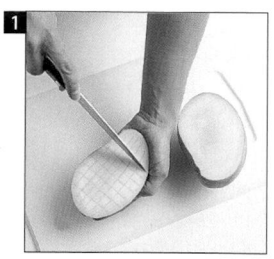

NUTRITIONAL INFORMATION

Calories	2819	Sugars	.......731g
Protein	........12g	Fat	...........2g
Carbohydrate	..734g	Saturates	.......1g

 10–15 mins   1 hr 5 mins

MAKES 1 QUANTITY

I N G R E D I E N T S

2 lb/900 g mangoes

4 tbsp salt

2½ cups water

2½ cups sugar

2 cups vinegar

2 tsp finely chopped ginger root

2 tsp crushed garlic

2 tsp chili powder

2 cinnamon sticks

¾ cup raisins

⅔ cup dates, pitted

1 Using a sharp knife, peel, halve and pit the mangoes. Cut the mango flesh into cubes. Place the mango flesh in a large bowl. Add the salt and water and let stand overnight. Drain the liquid from the mangoes and set aside.

2 Place the sugar and vinegar in a large pan and bring to a boil over low heat, stirring constantly.

3 Gradually add the mango cubes, stirring to coat them in the mixture.

4 Add the ginger, garlic, chili powder, cinnamon sticks, raisins, and dates to the pan and bring the mixture to a boil again, stirring occasionally. Reduce the heat and cook for about 1 hour, or until the mixture thickens. Remove from the heat and let cool.

5 Remove the cinnamon sticks from the chutney and discard.

6 Spoon the chutney into clean dry jars and cover tightly with lids. Let stand in a cool place for the flavors to develop.

COOK'S TIP

When choosing mangoes, select ones that are shiny with unblemished skins. To test if they are ripe, gently cup the mango in your hand and squeeze—it should give slightly to the touch if it is ready for eating.

Tamarind Chutney

A mouth-watering chutney which is extremely popular all over India and is served with various vegetarian snacks, particularly with samosas.

NUTRITIONAL INFORMATION

Calories 8   Sugars 1g
Protein ....0.3g   Fat 0.3g
Carbohydrate ....1g   Saturates 0g

 10 mins   0 mins

SERVES 6

INGREDIENTS

2 tbsp tamarind paste

5 tbsp water

1 tsp chile powder

½ tsp ground ginger

½ tsp salt

1 tsp sugar

finely chopped cilantro leaves,
   to garnish

1 Place the tamarind paste in a medium-size mixing bowl.

2 Gradually add the water to the tamarind paste, gently whisking with a fork to form a smooth, runny paste.

3 Add the chile powder and the ginger to the mixture and blend well.

4 Add the salt and the sugar and mix well.

5 Transfer the chutney to a serving dish and garnish with the cilantro.

COOK'S TIP

Vegetable dishes are often given a sharp, sour flavor with the addition of tamarind. This is made from the semidried, compressed pulp of the tamarind fruit. You can buy bars of the pungent-smelling pulp in Indian and Asian grocery stores.

Mixed Bell Pepper Pooris

These pooris are easy to make and so good to eat served with a scrumptious topping of spicy mixed bell peppers and yogurt.

NUTRITIONAL INFORMATION

Calories	386	Sugars	.........6g
Protein	.........5g	Fat	..........32g
Carbohydrate	...21g	Saturates	.......4g

55 mins · 15 mins

SERVES 6

INGREDIENTS

POORIS

¾ cup oz all-purpose whole-wheat flour

1 tbsp vegetable ghee or oil

pinch of salt

5 tbsp hot water

vegetable oil, for shallow frying

cilantro sprigs, to garnish

unsweetened yogurt, to serve

TOPPING

4 tbsp vegetable ghee or oil

1 large onion, quartered and thinly sliced

½ red bell pepper, seeded and thinly sliced

½ green bell pepper, seeded and thinly sliced

¼ eggplant, cut lengthwise into 6 wedges and thinly sliced

1 garlic clove, crushed

1 inch/2.5 cm piece of ginger root, chopped

½–1 tsp minced chili

2 tsp mild or medium curry paste

1 cup canned chopped tomatoes

salt

1 To make the pooris, put the flour in a bowl with the ghee or oil and salt. Add hot water and mix to form a fairly soft dough. Knead gently, cover with a damp cloth, and let stand for 30 minutes.

2 Meanwhile, prepare the topping. Heat the ghee or oil in a large pan. Add the onion, bell peppers, eggplant, garlic, ginger, chili, and curry paste and cook gently for 5 minutes. Stir in the tomatoes and salt to taste and simmer gently, uncovered, for 5 minutes, stirring occasionally until the sauce thickens. Remove from the heat.

3 Knead the dough on a floured surface and divide into 6. Roll each piece to a round about 6 inches/15 cm in diameter. Cover each one as you finish rolling to prevent drying out.

4 Heat about ½ inch/1 cm of vegetable oil in a large skillet. Add the pooris, one at a time, and cook them for about 15 seconds on each side, until puffed and golden, turning frequently. Drain on absorbent paper towels and keep warm while you are cooking the remainder in the same way.

5 Reheat the vegetable mixture. Place a poori on each serving plate and top with the vegetable mixture. Add a spoonful of yogurt to each, garnish with the cilantro sprigs, and serve.

Peshwari Naan

A tandoor oven throws out a ferocious heat; this bread is traditionally cooked on its side wall, where the heat is slightly less intense.

NUTRITIONAL INFORMATION

Calories	420	Sugars	........13g
Protein	........11g	Fat	..........9g
Carbohydrate	...77g	Saturates	.......3g

3¾ hrs   30 mins

SERVES 6

INGREDIENTS

¼ cup lukewarm water

pinch of sugar

½ tsp active dry yeast

4½ cups white bread flour, plus extra for dusting

½ tsp salt

¼ cup unsweetened yogurt

2 tart eating apples, peeled, cored, and diced

vegetable oil, for brushing

scant ½ cup golden raisins

½ cup sliced almonds

1 tbsp fresh cilantro leaves

2 tbsp grated coconut

1 Combine the water and sugar in a bowl and sprinkle over the yeast. Let stand for 5–10 minutes, until the yeast has dissolved and the mixture is foamy.

2 Put the flour and salt into a bowl and make a well in the center. Add the yeast mixture and yogurt. Draw in the flour until it is all absorbed. Mix thoroughly, adding enough lukewarm water to form a soft dough. Turn out onto a floured board and knead for 10 minutes until smooth. Put into an oiled bowl, cover, and let rise for 3 hours in a warm place.

3 Meanwhile, line the broiler pan with foil, shiny side up.

4 Put the apples into a pan with a little water. Bring to a boil, mash them down, reduce the heat, and simmer for 20 minutes, mashing occasionally.

5 Divide the dough into 4 pieces and roll each piece out to an 8 inch/20 cm oval. Pull one end out into a teardrop shape, about ¼ inch/5 mm thick. Lay on a floured surface and prick the dough all over with a fork.

6 Brush both sides of the bread with oil. Place 1 oval under a preheated broiler at the highest setting. Cook for 3 minutes, turn the bread over, using tongs, and cook for a further 3 minutes. It should have dark brown spots all over.

7 Spread a teaspoonful of the apple purée all over the bread, then sprinkle over a quarter of the golden raisins, sliced almonds, cilantro leaves, and the coconut. Broil the remaining 3 ovals of dough and spread with the apple purée and flavorings in the same way.

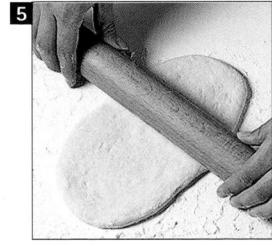

Gram Flour Bread

This filling bread goes well with any vegetarian curry and lime pickle.
Store the gram flour in a cool, dark place in an airtight container.

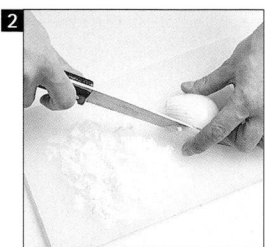

NUTRITIONAL INFORMATION

Calories 112   Sugars 1g
Protein . . . . .3g   Fat 2g
Carbohydrate . . .21g   Saturates 0g

 30 mins   15 mins

SERVES 4–6

INGREDIENTS

generous ¾ cup whole-wheat flour (ata or
   chapati flour), plus extra for dusting

⅔ cup gram flour

½ tsp salt

1 small onion

fresh cilantro leaves, very finely chopped

2 fresh green chilies, seeded and
   very finely chopped

⅔ cup water

2 tsp ghee

COOK'S TIP

In Indian kitchens, gram
flour is used to make breads,
bhajis, and batters and to thicken
sauces and stabilize yogurt
when it is added to hot dishes.

1 Strain the whole-wheat and gram
   flours together into a large mixing
bowl. Add the salt to the flours and mix
together thoroughly.

2 Chop the onion very finely. Blend the
   onion, cilantro, and chilies into the
flour mixture.

3 Add the water and mix to form a soft
   dough. Cover the dough with a clean
dish cloth or plastic wrap and let stand for
about 15 minutes.

4 Turn out the dough and knead
   thoroughly for 5–7 minutes. Divide
the dough into 8 equal portions.

5 Roll out the dough portions to rounds
   about 7 inches/18 cm in diameter on
a lightly floured surface.

6 Place the dough portions individually
   in a skillet and cook over medium
heat, turning over three times and lightly
greasing each side with a little of the ghee
each time.

7 Transfer the gram flour bread to
   serving plates and serve hot.

Chapati

This Indian bread contains no fat, but some people like
to brush the chapatis with a little melted butter before serving.

NUTRITIONAL INFORMATION

Calories 61   Sugars 0.5g
Protein . . . . .2g   Fat 0.3g
Carbohydrate . . .13g   Saturates 0g

40 mins   25 mins

MAKES 10–12

INGREDIENTS

1½ cups whole-wheat flour (ata or
  chapati flour)

½ tsp salt

¾ cup water

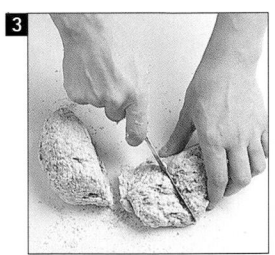

1 Place the flour in a large mixing bowl. Add the salt and mix to combine.

2 Make a well in the center of the flour and gradually pour in the water, mixing well with your fingers to form a supple dough.

3 Knead the dough for about 7–10 minutes. Ideally, set the dough aside and let rise for 15-20 minutes, but if time is short roll it out straight away. Divide the dough into 10-12 equal portions. Roll out each piece to form a round on a well-floured surface.

4 Place a heavy skillet over high heat. When steam starts to rise from the skillet, lower the heat to medium.

5 Place a chapati in the skillet and when it starts to bubble turn it over. Carefully press down on the chapati with a clean dish cloth or a flat spoon, and turn it over once again.

6 Remove the chapati from the pan, set aside, and keep warm while you make the others. Repeat the process until all of the chapatis are cooked. If possible, serve immediately (see Cook's Tip.)

COOK'S TIP
Ideally, chapatis should be eaten as they come out of the skillet, but if that is not practical keep them warm after cooking by wrapping them up in foil. In India, chapatis are sometimes cooked on a naked flame, which makes them puff up.

Naan Bread

There are many ways of making naan bread, but this recipe is very easy to follow. Naan bread should be served immediately after cooking.

NUTRITIONAL INFORMATION

Calories	152	Sugars	.........1g
Protein	.........3g	Fat	...........7g
Carbohydrate	...20g	Saturates	.......4g

2¼ hrs   10 mins

SERVES 8

I N G R E D I E N T S

1 tsp sugar

1 tsp fresh yeast

⅔ cup warm water

1½ cups all-purpose flour

1 tbsp ghee

1 tsp salt

4 tbsp sweet butter

1 tsp poppy seeds

1 Put the sugar, yeast, and warm water in a small bowl or pitcher, and mix thoroughly until the yeast has completely dissolved. Let stand for about 10 minutes, or until the mixture is foamy.

2 Place the flour in a large mixing bowl. Make a well in the center of the flour, add the ghee and salt, and pour in the yeast mixture. Mix thoroughly to form a dough, using your hands and adding more water if required.

3 Turn the dough out on to a floured counter and knead for about 5 minutes, or until smooth.

4 Return the dough to the bowl, cover, and let rise in a warm place for 1½ hours, or until doubled in size.

5 Turn the dough out on to a floured counter and knead for a further 2 minutes. Break off small balls with your hand and pat into rounds about 5 inches /12 cm diameter and ½ inch/1 cm thick.

6 Place the dough rounds on a greased sheet of foil and broil under a very hot preheated broiler for about 7–10 minutes, turning them over twice, and brushing with the butter and sprinkling with the poppy seeds.

7 Serve warm immediately, or keep wrapped in foil until required.

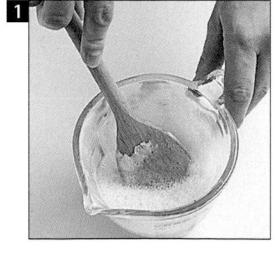

Poori

Although pooris are deep-fried, they are very light.
The nutritional information supplied is for each poori.

NUTRITIONAL INFORMATION

Calories ....165 Sugars 0.7g
Protein ....3g Fat 10g
Carbohydrate ...17g Saturates 1g

   35 mins   15-20 mins

MAKES 10

INGREDIENTS

1½ cups whole-wheat flour (ata or chapati flour)

½ tsp salt

⅔ cup water

2½ cups vegetable oil

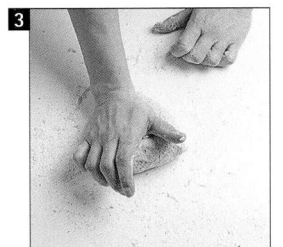

1 Place the flour and salt in a large mixing bowl and stir to combine.

2 Make a well in the center of the flour. Gradually pour in the water and mix together to form a dough, adding more water if necessary.

3 Knead the dough until it is smooth and elastic and let rise in a warm place for about 15 minutes.

4 Divide the dough into about 10 equal portions and with lightly oiled or floured hands pat each into a smooth ball.

5 On a lightly oiled or floured counter, roll out each of the balls to form a thin round.

6 Heat the vegetable oil in a deep skillet. Deep-fry the rounds, in batches, turning once, until they are golden brown in color.

7 Remove the pooris from the pan and drain. Serve hot.

COOK'S TIP
You can serve pooris either piled one on top of the other or spread out in a layer on a large serving platter so that they remain puffed up.

Parathas

These triangular shaped breads are so easy to make and are the perfect addition to most Indian meals. Serve hot, spread with a little butter.

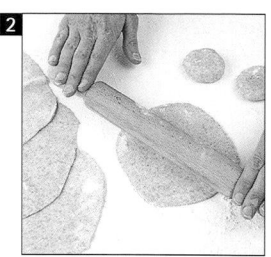
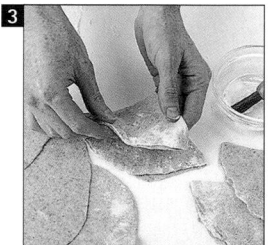

NUTRITIONAL INFORMATION

Calories	127	Sugars	.......0.5g
Protein	.........3g	Fat	..........4g
Carbohydrate	...22g	Saturates	.....0.4g

 50 mins   10 mins

SERVES 6

INGREDIENTS

⅔ cup all-purpose whole-wheat flour

⅔ cup all-purpose flour

pinch of salt

1 tbsp vegetable oil, plus extra for greasing

5 tbsp tepid water

1 Place the flours and the salt in a bowl. Drizzle 1 tablespoon of oil over the flour, add the tepid water, and mix to form a soft dough, adding a little more water, if necessary. Knead on a lightly floured counter until smooth, then cover and let stand for 30 minutes.

2 Knead the dough on a floured counter and divide into 6 equal pieces. Shape each one into a ball. Roll out on a floured surface to a 6 inch/15 cm round and brush very lightly with oil.

VARIATION

For added flavor, try brushing the parathas with a garlic- or chilli-flavored oil as they are cooking.

3 Fold in half, and then in half again to form a triangle. Roll out to form an 7 inch/18 cm triangle (when measured from point to center top), dusting with extra flour as necessary.

4 Brush a large, heavy skillet with a little oil and heat until hot, then add one or two parathas and cook for about 1–1½ minutes. Brush the surfaces very lightly with oil, then turn and cook the other sides for 1½ minutes until completely cooked through.

5 Place the cooked parathas on a plate and cover with foil, or place between the folds of a clean dish cloth to keep warm, while you are cooking the remainder in the same way, greasing the pan between cooking each batch.

Spinach Poori

These little nibbles are very satisfying to make and they will still be little puffballs when you get to the table.

🍲 1 hr   🕐 10 mins

SERVES 6

INGREDIENTS

1 cup whole-wheat flour

1 cup all-purpose flour

½ tsp salt

2 tbsp vegetable oil

¼ lb/115 g chopped fresh or frozen spinach, blanched, puréed, and all excess water squeezed out

4 tbsp water

oil, for deep-frying

RELISH

2 tbsp chopped mint

2 tbsp unsweetened yogurt

½ red onion, sliced and rinsed

½ tsp cayenne pepper

1 Strain the flours and salt together into a bowl. Drizzle over the oil and rub in with the fingertips until the mixture resembles fine bread crumbs.

2 Add the spinach and water, and stir in to make a stiff dough. Turn out and knead for 10 minutes until smooth. Form the dough into a ball. Put into an oiled bowl, turn to coat, cover with plastic wrap, and let stand for 30 minutes.

3 Meanwhile make the relish. Combine the mint, yogurt, and onion, transfer to a serving bowl, and strain the cayenne over the top.

4 Knead the dough again and divide into 12 small balls. Remove 1 ball and keep the rest covered. Roll this ball out into a 5 inch/12 cm circle.

5 Put the oil for deep frying into a wok or wide skillet to a depth of 1 inch/2.5 cm. Heat the oil until a haze appears—it must be very hot.

6 Have ready a plate lined with absorbent paper towels. Put 1 poori on the surface of the oil—if it sinks, it should rise up immediately and sizzle; if it doesn't, the oil isn't hot enough. Keep the poori submerged in the oil, using the back of a slotted spoon. The poori will puff up immediately. Turn it over and cook the other side for 5–10 seconds.

7 As soon as the poori is cooked, remove and drain on paper towels. Repeat with the remaining balls of dough, and serve immediately.

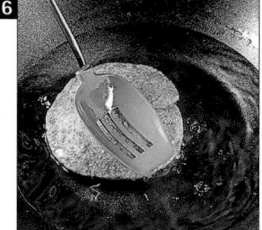

Baby Cauliflowers

Whole baby cauliflowers, coated with a brick cheese and poppy seed sauce, are cooked to perfection in the microwave oven.

NUTRITIONAL INFORMATION

Calories 173   Sugars 6g
Protein . . . . .8g   Fat 11g
Carbohydrate . . .10g   Saturates 6g

30 mins   15 mins

SERVES 4

INGREDIENTS

½ onion, studded with 4 cloves

½ carrot

1 bouquet garni

1 cup milk

4 baby cauliflowers

3 tbsp water

1 tbsp butter

2 tbsp all-purpose flour

½ cup grated brick cheese

1 tbsp poppy seeds

pinch of paprika

salt and pepper

parsley to garnish

1 Place the onion in a bowl with the carrot, bouquet garni, and milk. Heat on HIGH power for 2½–3 minutes, then let the milk stand for 20 minutes to let the flavors infuse.

2 Trim the base and leaves from the cauliflowers and scoop out the stem using a small sharp knife, leaving the cauliflowers intact. Place the cauliflowers upside down in a large dish. Add the water, cover, and cook on HIGH power for 5 minutes, until just tender. Let stand for 2–3 minutes.

3 Put the butter in a bowl and cook on HIGH power for 30 seconds, until melted. Stir in the flour. Cook on HIGH power for 30 seconds.

4 Strain the milk into a pitcher, discarding the vegetables. Gradually add to the flour and butter, beating well between each addition. Cover and cook on HIGH power for 3 minutes, stirring every 30 seconds after the first minute, until the sauce has thickened.

5 Stir the cheese and poppy seeds into the sauce and season with salt and pepper to taste. Cover and cook on HIGH power for 30 seconds.

6 Drain the cauliflowers and arrange on a plate or in a shallow dish. Pour over the sauce and sprinkle with a little paprika. Cook on HIGH power for 1 minute to reheat. Serve garnished with fresh parsley.

Dry Split Okra

This is an unusual way of cooking this delicious vegetable. The dish is dry when cooked, and should be served hot with chapatis and a dhal.

NUTRITIONAL INFORMATION

Calories	190	Sugars	.........4g
Protein	.........3g	Fat	..........18g
Carbohydrate	....5g	Saturates	.......2g

10 mins   20 mins

SERVES 4

INGREDIENTS

1 lb/450 g okra

⅔ cup vegetable oil

¼ lb dried onions

2 tsp dried mango powder

1 tsp ground cumin

1 tsp chili powder

1 tsp salt

1 Prepare the okra by cutting the ends off and discarding them. Carefully split the okra down the middle without cutting through completely.

2 Heat the oil in a large pan. Add the dried onions and sautée until crisp.

3 Remove the onions from the pan with a slotted spoon and drain thoroughly on paper towels. When cool enough to handle, roughly tear the onions and place in a large bowl.

4 Add the dried mango powder, ground cumin, chili powder, and salt to the onions and blend well together.

5 Spoon the onion and spice mixture into the split okra.

6 Re-heat the oil in the pan. Gently add the okra to the hot oil and cook over low heat for about 10-12 minutes. Transfer to a serving dish and serve at once.

COOK'S TIP
Ground cumin has a warm, pungent, aromatic flavor and is used extensively in Indian cooking. It is a good storecupboard standby.

Herby Potatoes & Onion

Sautéed potatoes are a classic favorite; here they are given extra flavor by sautéing them in butter with onion, garlic, and herbs.

NUTRITIONAL INFORMATION

Calories	413	Sugars	. . . . .4g
Protein	. . . . .5g	Fat	. . . . .26g
Carbohydrate	. . .42g	Saturates	. . . . . .17g

 10 mins   50 mins

SERVES 4

INGREDIENTS

2 lb/900 g waxy potatoes, cut into cubes

9 tbsp butter

1 red onion, cut into 8

2 garlic cloves, crushed

1 tsp lemon juice

2 tbsp chopped thyme

salt and pepper

1 Cook the cubed potatoes in a pan of boiling water for 10 minutes, then drain thoroughly.

2 Melt the butter in a large, heavy skillet and add the red onion wedges, garlic, and lemon juice. Cook, stirring constantly, for 2–3 minutes.

3 Add the potatoes to the pan and mix well to coat in the butter mixture.

4 Reduce the heat, cover, and cook for 25–30 minutes, or until the potatoes are golden brown and tender.

5 Sprinkle the chopped thyme over the top of the potatoes and season to taste with salt and pepper.

6 Transfer to a warm serving dish and serve immediately.

COOK'S TIP

Keep checking the potatoes and stirring throughout the cooking time to ensure that they do not burn or stick to the base of the skillet.

Sweet Hot Carrots & Beans

Take care not to overcook the vegetables in this tasty dish—they are definitely at their best served tender-crisp.

NUTRITIONAL INFORMATION

Calories 268	Sugars 16g
Protein 5g	Fat 19g
Carbohydrate . . .19g	Saturates 3g

10 mins   15 mins

SERVES 4

INGREDIENTS

1 lb/450 g young carrots

½ lb green beans

1 bunch of scallions

4 tbsp vegetable ghee or vegetable oil

1 tsp ground cumin

1 tsp ground coriander

3 cardamom pods, split and seeds removed

2 dried red chilies

2 garlic cloves, crushed

1–2 tsp honey

1 tsp lemon or lime juice

½ cup sweet, toasted cashews

1 tbsp chopped fresh cilantro or parsley

salt and pepper

TO GARNISH

slices of lime or lemon

fresh cilantro sprigs

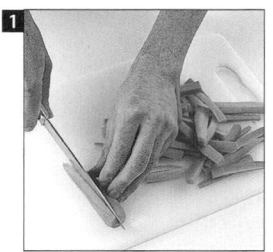

1 Cut the carrots lengthwise into quarters and then in half crosswise if very long. Trim the beans. Cut the scallions into 2 inch/5 cm pieces.

2 Cook the carrots and beans in a pan of lightly salted boiling water for 5–6 minutes until they are just tender-crisp. Drain well.

3 Heat the ghee or oil in a large skillet, add the scallions, carrots, beans, cumin, ground coriander, cardamom seeds, and whole dried chilies. Cook over low heat, stirring frequently, for 2 minutes.

4 Stir in the garlic, honey, and lemon or lime juice and continue cooking, stirring occasionally, for a further 2 minutes. Season to taste with salt and pepper. Remove and discard the chilies.

5 Sprinkle the vegetables with the cashews and chopped cilantro and mix together lightly.

6 Serve at once, garnished with lime or lemon slices and cilantro sprigs.

Spicy Potatoes & Onions

Masala aloo are potatoes cooked in a spicy mixture called baghaar.
Semi-dry when cooked, they go well with almost any curry.

NUTRITIONAL INFORMATION

Calories 313   Sugars 5g
Protein . . . . .2g   Fat 25g
Carbohydrate . . .21g   Saturates 3g

10–15 mins   10 mins

SERVES 4

INGREDIENTS

6 tbsp vegetable oil

2 medium-sized onions, finely chopped

1 tsp finely chopped fresh ginger root

1 tsp crushed garlic

1 tsp chili powder

1½ tsp ground cumin

1½ tsp ground coriander

1 tsp salt

14 oz/450 g canned new potatoes

1 tbsp lemon juice

BAGHAAR

3 tbsp oil

3 dried red chilies

½ tsp onion seeds

½ tsp mustard seeds

½ tsp fenugreek seeds

TO GARNISH

fresh cilantro leaves

1 green chili, finely chopped

1 Heat the oil in a large, heavy pan. Add the onions and cook, stirring, until golden brown. Reduce the heat, add the ginger, garlic, chili powder, ground cumin and coriander, salt, and potatoes and stir-fry for about 1 minute. Remove the pan from the heat and set aside until required.

2 Drain the water from the potatoes. Add the potatoes to the onion and spice mixture and heat through. Sprinkle in the lemon juice and mix well.

3 To make the baghaar, heat the oil in a separate pan. Add the chilies, onion seeds, mustard seeds, and fenugreek seeds and cook until the seeds turn a shade darker. Remove the pan from the heat and pour the baghaar over the potatoes.

4 Garnish with cilantro leaves and chilies, then serve.

Pommes Anna

This is a classic potato dish, which may be left to cook unattended while the remainder of the meal is being prepared, so it is ideal with stews.

NUTRITIONAL INFORMATION

Calories	237	Sugars	.........1g
Protein	.........4g	Fat	..........13g
Carbohydrate	...29g	Saturates	.......8g

⏱ 15 mins   🕐 2 hrs

SERVES 4

I N G R E D I E N T S

5 tbsp butter, melted

1½ lb/675 g waxy potatoes

4 tbsp chopped mixed herbs

salt and pepper

chopped fresh herbs, to garnish

1 Brush a shallow 4 cup ovenproof dish with a little of the melted butter.

2 Slice the potatoes thinly and pat dry with paper towels.

3 Arrange a layer of potato slices in the prepared dish until the base is covered. Brush with a little butter and sprinkle with a quarter of the chopped mixed herbs. Season to taste.

4 Continue layering the potato slices, brushing each layer with melted butter and sprinkling with herbs, until they are all used up.

5 Brush the top layer of potato slices with butter. Cover the dish and cook in a preheated oven, 375°F/190°C, for 1½ hours.

6 Turn out on to a warm ovenproof platter and return to the oven for another 25–30 minutes, until golden.

7 Serve at once, garnished with fresh herbs.

COOK'S TIP

Make sure that the potatoes are sliced very thinly so that they are almost transparent. This will ensure that they cook thoroughly.

Boston Beans

These are the original baked beans, and you will find that they are much tastier than the canned variety.

NUTRITIONAL INFORMATION

Calories	217	Sugars	........11g
Protein	........14g	Fat	...........11g
Carbohydrate	...40g	Saturates	.......0g

10 mins   5½ hrs

SERVES 8

INGREDIENTS

1 lb/450 g dried navy beans, soaked overnight in cold water to cover

2 onions, chopped

2 large tomatoes, skinned and chopped

2 tsp American mustard

2 tbsp treacle

salt and ground black pepper

COOK'S TIP
Serve these beans with chunks of whole-wheat bread or toast for a perfectly balanced light lunch or supper dish.

1 Drain the beans and place in a large pan. Add enough cold water to cover, bring to a boil, and simmer for 15 minutes. Drain, reserving 1¼ cups of the cooking liquid. Transfer the beans to a large casserole and add the onions.

2 Return the reserved cooking liquid to the pan and add the tomatoes. Bring to a boil and simmer for 10 minutes. Remove the pan from the heat, stir in the mustard and treacle, and season to taste with salt and pepper.

3 Pour the tomato mixture into the casserole and bake in a preheated oven, 275°F/140°C, for 5 hours. Serve the beans immediately.

Fava Beans with Savory

This is a traditional combination—summer savory is often grown with fava beans to protect them against black fly.

NUTRITIONAL INFORMATION

Calories	180	Sugars	.........2g
Protein	.........8g	Fat	..........13g
Carbohydrate	...10g	Saturates	.......8g

15 mins   20 mins

SERVES 4

INGREDIENTS

2 lb/900 g fava beans,

1 fresh summer savory sprig

4 tbsp butter or vegetarian margarine

1 tbsp lemon juice

1 tbsp chopped fresh summer savory

salt and ground black pepper

1 Reserve 1 pod and shell the remaining fava beans. Bring a large pan of lightly salted water to a boil and add the beans, the reserved pod, and the sprig of summer savory. Cover and simmer for 10-15 minutes, until the beans are tender.

2 Drain the beans and discard the pod and sprig of summer savory.

3 Melt the butter or margarine in the pan, add the lemon juice and beans, and season to taste with pepper. Toss the beans gently to coat.

4 Transfer the beans to a warm serving dish. Sprinkle them with the chopped summer savory and serve immediately.

COOK'S TIP
If using mature fava beans, skin them before tossing them in the melted butter or margarine.

Kashmiri Spinach

This is an imaginative way to serve spinach, which adds a little zip to it. It is a very simple dish, which will complement almost any curry.

NUTRITIONAL INFORMATION

Calories 81   Sugars 2g
Protein . . . . .4g   Fat 7g
Carbohydrate . . . .2g   Saturates 1g

5 mins   25 mins

SERVES 4

I N G R E D I E N T S

1 lb/450 g spinach or Swiss chard or young leaf spinach

2 tbsp mustard oil

¼ tsp garam masala

1 tsp yellow mustard seeds

2 scallions, sliced

1 Remove any tough stalks from the spinach, and rinse it several times in cold running water.

2 Heat the mustard oil in a preheated wok or large, heavy skillet until it smokes.

3 Add the garam masala and mustard seeds to the oil. Cover the skillet quickly—you will hear the mustard seeds popping inside.

4 When the popping has ceased, remove the cover and add the scallions and spinach. Cook, stirring constantly, until the spinach has wilted.

5 Continue cooking the spinach, uncovered, over medium heat for 10–15 minutes, until most of the water has evaporated. If using frozen spinach, it will not need to cook for so long—cook it until most of the water has evaporated.

6 Remove the spinach and scallions with a slotted spoon, draining off any remaining liquid. (It is best to eat this dish as dry as possible.)

7 Transfer the Kashmiri spinach to a warmed serving dish and serve immediately, while it is still piping hot.

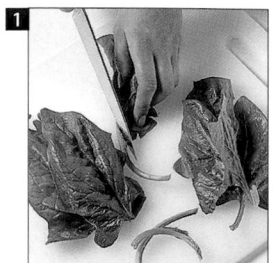

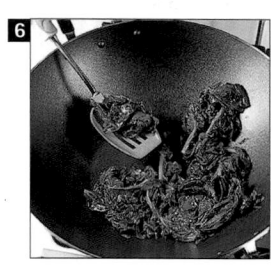

COOK'S TIP

Mustard oil is made from mustard seeds and is very fiery when raw. However, when it is heated to this smoking stage, it loses a lot of the fire and takes on a delightful sweet quality.

Seasonal Vegetables

These vegetables are ideal for a special occasion, such as Christmas Day. Do not start cooking them too early, as they take little time to cook.

NUTRITIONAL INFORMATION

Calories . . . . . . .434 Sugars 20g
Protein . . . . .7g Fat 19g
Carbohydrate . . .62g Saturates 5g

  20 mins   1 hr 40 mins

SERVES 8

INGREDIENTS

CRISPY ROAST POTATOES

4½ lb/2 kg potatoes

vegetable oil, for roasting

salt

HONEY-GLAZED CARROTS

2¼ lb/1 kg carrots

1 tbsp clear honey

2 tbsp butter

2 tsp sesame seeds, toasted

SPICED WINTER CABBAGE

1 hard white cabbage

2 eating apples, peeled, cored, and chopped

few drops of lemon juice

2 tbsp butter

freshly grated nutmeg

salt

1 To make Crispy Roast Potatoes, peel the potatoes and cut them into large, even-sized chunks. Put them into a large pan of cold water with ½ tsp salt. Bring to a boil, and then reduce the heat. Cover and simmer for about 8–10 minutes to parboil them. Drain thoroughly.

2 Heat about ¾ cup vegetable oil in a large roasting pan until very hot. Add the potatoes, basting thoroughly. Roast in a preheated oven, 400°F/200°C, for about 1 hour, basting occasionally, until crisp and golden brown.

3 To make Honey-Glazed Carrots, put the carrots into a pan and barely cover with water. Add the honey and butter. Cook, uncovered, for about 15 minutes, until the liquid has just evaporated and the carrots are glazed. Serve sprinkled with toasted sesame seeds.

4 To maked Spiced Winter Cabbage, shred the cabbage just before cooking it to retain the vitamins. Add the chopped apples and lemon juice, and cook in a small amount of water in a covered pan over medium heat for about 6 minutes. Drain thoroughly.

5 Season the cabbage to taste with salt and add the butter, tossing to melt.

6 Transfer to a warmed serving dish, sprinkle with freshly grated nutmeg, and serve immediately.

Sweet & Sour Vegetables

This is a dish of Persian origin, not Chinese as it sounds. Eggplants are sautéed and mixed with tomatoes, mint, sugar, and vinegar.

NUTRITIONAL INFORMATION

Calories	218	Sugars	........12g
Protein	.........3g	Fat	..........17g
Carbohydrate	...14g	Saturates	.......3g

45 mins   30 mins

SERVES 4

I N G R E D I E N T S

2 large eggplants

6 tbsp olive oil

4 garlic cloves, crushed

1 onion, cut into eight

4 large tomatoes, seeded and chopped

3 tbsp chopped mint

⅔ cup vegetable bouillon

4 tsp brown sugar

2 tbsp red wine vinegar

1 tsp chili flakes

salt and pepper

fresh mint sprigs to garnish

1 Using a sharp knife, cut the eggplants into cubes. Put them in a colander, sprinkle with plenty of salt, and let stand for 30 minutes. Rinse under cold running water to remove all traces of the salt and drain thoroughly. This process removes all the bitter juices from the eggplants. Pat dry with absorbent paper towels.

2 Heat the oil in a large, heavy skillet. Add the eggplant and sauté over medium heat, stirring, for 1-2 minutes, until beginning to color.

3 Stir in the garlic and onion wedges and cook, stirring constantly, for a further 2-3 minutes.

4 Stir in the tomatoes and mint and the bouillon. Lower the heat, cover the pan, and simmer for about 15-20 minutes, or until the eggplants are tender.

5 Add the sugar, vinegar, and chili flakes, then season with salt and pepper according to taste and cook for a further 2-3 minutes, stirring constantly.

6 Transfer to a warmed serving dish, garnish the eggplants with fresh mint sprigs, and serve immediately.

Chili Roast Potatoes

Small new potatoes are scrubbed and boiled in their skins,
then coated in a chili mixture and roasted to perfection in the oven.

NUTRITIONAL INFORMATION

Calories 178	Sugars 2g	
Protein 2g	Fat 11g	
Carbohydrate ...18g	Saturates 1g	

 5–10 mins   30 mins

SERVES 4

I N G R E D I E N T S

1 lb/450 g small new potatoes, scrubbed

⅔ cup vegetable oil

1 tsp chili powder

½ tsp caraway seeds

1 tsp salt

1 tbsp chopped basil

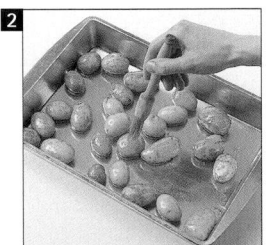

1 Cook the potatoes in a pan of boiling water for 10 minutes, then drain them thoroughly.

2 Pour a little of the oil into a shallow roasting pan to coat the base. Heat the oil in a preheated oven, 400°F/200°C, for 10 minutes. Add the potatoes to the pan and brush them with the hot oil.

3 In a small bowl, mix together the chili powder, caraway seeds, and salt. Sprinkle the mixture over the potatoes, turning to coat them all over.

4 Add the remaining oil to the pan and roast in the oven for about 15 minutes, or until the potatoes are cooked through.

5 Using a slotted spoon, remove the potatoes from the oil, draining them well, and transfer them to a warmed serving dish. Garnish the potatoes with a sprinkling of chopped basil and serve immediately.

VARIATION
Use any other spice of your choice, such as curry powder or paprika, for a variation in flavor.

Potatoes Dauphinois

This is a classic potato dish of layered potatoes, cream, garlic, onion, and cheese. Serve with pies, bakes, and casseroles.

NUTRITIONAL INFORMATION

Calories 580   Sugars 5g
Protein . . . . .10g   Fat 46g
Carbohydrate . . .34g   Saturates 28g

🍲 25 mins   🕐 1½ hrs

SERVES 4

INGREDIENTS

1 tbsp butter

1½ lb/675 g waxy potatoes, sliced

2 garlic cloves, crushed

1 red onion, sliced

¾ cup grated Swiss cheese

1¼ cups heavy cream

salt and pepper

1 Lightly grease a 4 cup/1 liter shallow ovenproof dish with the butter.

2 Arrange a single layer of potato slices in the base of the prepared dish.

3 Top the potato slices with half the garlic, half the sliced red onion, and one-third of the grated Swiss cheese. Season to taste with a little salt and pepper to taste.

4 Repeat the layers in exactly the same order, finishing with a layer of potatoes topped with grated cheese.

5 Pour the heavy cream over the top of the potatoes and cook them in a preheated oven, 350°F/180°C, for about 1½ hours, or until the potatoes are cooked through and the top is golden brown and crispy. Serve the potatoes at once, straight from the dish.

COOK'S TIP

There are many versions of this classic potato dish, but the recipes always contain heavy cream, making it a rich and very filling side dish or accompaniment. This recipe must be cooked in a shallow dish to ensure there is plenty of crispy topping.

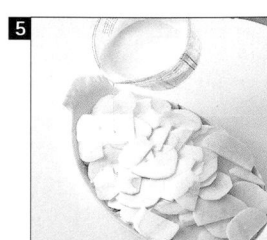

Vegetables in Saffron Sauce

Here is a quick and simple, delicately spiced and delicious way to cook eggplants and onion.

NUTRITIONAL INFORMATION

Calories . . . . . . .350 Sugars 14g
Protein . . . . .3g Fat 31g
Carbohydrate . . .15g Saturates 14g

25 mins   20 mins

SERVES 4

INGREDIENTS

a good pinch of saffron strands, finely crushed

1 tbsp boiling water

1 large eggplant

3 tbsp vegetable oil

1 large onion, coarsely chopped

2 garlic cloves, crushed

1 inch/2.5 cm piece of ginger root, chopped

1½ tbsp mild or medium curry paste

1 tsp cumin seeds

⅔ cup heavy cream

⅔ cup strained Greek yogurt

2 tbsp mango chutney, chopped if necessary

salt and pepper

1 Place the saffron in a small bowl, add the boiling water, and let infuse for 5 minutes. Cut the eggplant lengthwise into quarters, then cut into ½ inch/1 cm thick slices.

2 Heat the oil in a large skillet, add the onion, and cook gently for 3 minutes. Stir in the eggplant, garlic, ginger, curry paste, and cumin and cook gently for 3 minutes.

3 Stir in the saffron water, cream, yogurt, and chutney and cook, stirring frequently, for 8-10 minutes, until the eggplant is cooked through and tender.

4 Season with salt and pepper to taste and serve hot.

COOK'S TIP
Yogurt adds a creamy texture and pleasant tartness to this sauce. If you are worried about it curdling on heating, add a tablespoonful at a time and stir it in well before adding another.

Brindil Bhaji

This is one of the most delicious—and easiest—of the Indian bhaji dishes and has a wonderful sweet spicy flavor.

NUTRITIONAL INFORMATION

Calories 117	Sugars 8g	
Protein 3g	Fat 8g	
Carbohydrate 9g	Saturates 5g	

20 mins   20 mins

SERVES 4

I N G R E D I E N T S

1 lb/450 g eggplants, sliced

2 tbsp vegetable ghee

1 onion, thinly sliced

2 garlic cloves, sliced

1 inch/2.5 cm piece of fresh ginger root, grated

½ tsp ground turmeric

1 dried red chili

½ tsp salt

2 cups canned tomatoes

1 tsp garam masala

fresh cilantro sprigs, to garnish

1 Cut the eggplant slices into finger-width strips.

2 Heat the vegetable ghee in a heavy pan. Add the onion and cook over medium heat, stirring constantly, for 7–8 minutes, until very soft and just beginning to color.

3 Add the garlic and eggplant strips, increase the heat, and cook, stirring constantly, for 2 minutes. Stir in the ginger, turmeric, chili, salt, and tomatoes, with their can juices. Use the back of a wooden spoon to break up the tomatoes. Lower the heat and simmer, uncovered, for 15–20 minutes, until the eggplants are very soft.

4 Stir in the garam masala and simmer for a further 4–5 minutes.

5 Transfer the brindil bhaji to a warmed serving plate, garnish with fresh cilantro sprigs, and serve immediately.

VARIATION

Other vegetables can be used instead of the eggplants. Try zucchini, potatoes, or bell peppers, or any combination of these vegetables, using the same sauce.

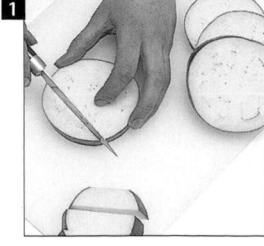

Curried Okra

Okra, also known as bhindi and ladies' fingers, are a favorite Indian vegetable. They are now widely available.

NUTRITIONAL INFORMATION

Calories 156   Sugars 5g
Protein ....5g   Fat 12g
Carbohydrate ....6g   Saturates 2g

 10 mins   20 mins

SERVES 4

I N G R E D I E N T S

1 lb/450 g fresh okra

4 tbsp vegetable ghee or oil

1 bunch scallions, sliced

2 garlic cloves, crushed

2 inch/5 cm piece of ginger root, chopped

1 tsp minced chili

1½ tsp ground cumin

1 tsp ground coriander

1 tsp ground turmeric

1 cup canned chopped tomatoes

⅔ cup vegetable bouillon

salt and pepper

1 tsp garam masala

chopped cilantro, to garnish

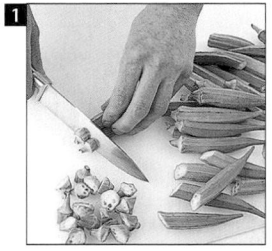

1 Wash the okra, trim off the stalks, and pat dry. Heat the ghee or oil in a large pan, add the scallions, garlic, ginger, and chili, and cook over low heat, stirring frequently, for 1 minute.

2 Stir in the ground spices and cook gently for 30 seconds, then add the chopped tomatoes, vegetable bouillon, and okra. Season with salt and pepper to taste and simmer, stirring and turning the mixture occasionally, for about 15 minutes, until the okra is cooked, but still a little crisp.

3 Sprinkle the okra with the garam masala, taste, and adjust the seasoning, if necessary.

4 Transfer the curried okra to a warm serving dish, garnish with the chopped cilantro, and serve hot.

COOK'S TIP

If preferred, slice the okra into rings, add to the mixture (step 2), cover, and cook until tender-crisp, stirring occasionally. When you buy fresh okra, make sure that the pods are not shriveled or do not have any brown spots.

Gingered Potatoes

This is a simple, spicy dish which is ideal with a simple entrée.
The cashew nuts and celery add extra crunch.

NUTRITIONAL INFORMATION

Calories 325	Sugars 1g
Protein 5g	Fat 21g
Carbohydrate ...30g	Saturates 9g

20 mins   30 mins

SERVES 4

I N G R E D I E N T S

1½ lb/675 g waxy potatoes, cubed

2 tbsp vegetable oil

4 tsp grated fresh ginger root

1 fresh green chili, chopped

1 celery stalk, chopped

¼ cup cashew nuts

a few strands of saffron

3 tbsp boiling water

5 tbsp butter

celery leaves, to garnish

1 Cook the potatoes in a pan of boiling water for 10 minutes, then drain them thoroughly.

2 Heat the oil in a heavy skillet and add the potatoes. Cook over medium heat, stirring constantly, for 3–4 minutes.

COOK'S TIP

Use a non-stick, heavy skillet as the potato mixture is fairly dry and may stick to an ordinary pan.

3 Add the grated ginger, the chopped chili and celery, and the cashew nuts and cook for 1 minute.

4 Meanwhile, place the saffron strands in a small bowl. Add the boiling water and let soak for 5 minutes.

5 Add the butter to the pan, lower the heat, and stir in the saffron mixture. Cook over low heat for 10 minutes, or until the potatoes are tender.

6 Transfer to a warm serving dish, garnish with celery leaves, and serve.

Sesame Stir-Fry

This wonderfully quick and easy stir-fry can be served either as part of a Chinese meal or as a simple vegetable accompaniment.

NUTRITIONAL INFORMATION

Calories	165	Sugars	.........2g
Protein	.........6g	Fat	..........13g
Carbohydrate	....6g	Saturates	.......2g

10 mins   12 mins

SERVES 4

INGREDIENTS

3 tbsp groundnut or sunflower oil

1 tbsp sesame oil

12 garlic cloves, finely chopped

3 cups broccoli florets

1½ cups snow peas or sugar snap peas

1 head Napa cabbage, shredded

6 scallions, chopped

2 tbsp dark soy sauce

2 tbsp Chinese rice wine

3 tbsp water

1 tbsp sesame seeds, toasted, to garnish

1 Heat both oils in a large, heavy skillet or wok. Add the garlic and stir-fry for 30 seconds. Add the broccoli and stir-fry for 3 minutes.

2 Add the snow peas or sugar snaps and stir-fry for 2 minutes,

3 Add the Napa cabbage and scallions and continue to stir-fry for a further 2 minutes.

4 Stir in the soy sauce and Chinese rice wine and cook, stirring constantly, for 3-4 minutes.

5 Transfer the stir-fry to a warm serving dish, sprinkle with the toasted sesame seeds, and serve immediately.

VARIATION

Use only half the Napa cabbage and add 1 cup thinly sliced carrots and 10 baby corn ears with the broccoli in step 1.

Cheese Crisp-Topped Mash

Liven up mashed potato by topping it with a crisp mixture flavored with herbs, mustard, and onion, which turns crunchy on baking.

NUTRITIONAL INFORMATION

Calories 451	Sugars 5g	
Protein 13g	Fat 19g	
Carbohydrate . . .60g	Saturates 12g	

 25 mins 30 mins

SERVES 4

INGREDIENTS

2 lb/900 g mealy potatoes, diced

2 tbsp butter

2 tbsp milk

½ cup grated sharp cheese or blue cheese

CRISP TOPPING

3 tbsp butter

1 onion, cut into chunks

1 garlic clove, crushed

1 tbsp whole-grain mustard

3 cups fresh whole-wheat bread crumbs

2 tbsp chopped fresh parsley

salt and pepper

1 Cook the potatoes in a pan of lightly salted boiling water for 10 minutes or until cooked through.

2 Meanwhile, make the crisp topping. Melt the butter in a skillet. Add the onion, garlic, and whole-grain mustard and cook gently for 5 minutes, stirring constantly, until the onion chunks have softened.

3 Put the bread crumbs and parsley in a mixing bowl and stir in the onion. Season to taste with salt and pepper.

4 Drain the potatoes thoroughly and place them in a mixing bowl. Add the butter and milk, then mash until smooth. Stir in the grated cheese while the potato is still hot.

5 Spoon the mashed potato into a shallow casserole and sprinkle with the crisp topping.

6 Cook in a preheated oven, 400°F/200°C, for 10–15 minutes until the crisp topping is golden brown and crunchy. Serve immediately.

COOK'S TIP

For extra crunch, add freshly cooked vegetables, such as celery and peppers, to the mashed potato in step 4.

Sautéed Cauliflower

A dry dish flavored with a few herbs, this is a very versatile accompaniment to curries and rice dishes.

NUTRITIONAL INFORMATION

Calories	135	Sugars	.........3g
Protein	.........4g	Fat	..........12g
Carbohydrate	....4g	Saturates	.......1g

 5 mins   20 mins

SERVES 4

INGREDIENTS

4 tbsp vegetable oil

½ tsp onion seeds

½ tsp mustard seeds

½ tsp fenugreek seeds

4 dried red chilies

1 small cauliflower, cut into small florets

1 tsp salt

1 green bell pepper, seeded and diced

1 Heat the oil in a large, heavy pan over moderate heat.

2 Add the onion seeds, mustard seeds, fenugreek seeds, and the dried red chilies to the pan, stirring to mix.

3 Reduce the heat and gradually add the cauliflower florets and the salt to the pan. Stir-fry the mixture for 7–10 minutes, thoroughly coating the cauliflower in the spices.

4 Add the diced green bell pepper to the pan and stir-fry over low heat for about 3–5 minutes.

5 Transfer the sautéed cauliflower to a warmed serving dish and serve hot.

Lemon Beans

Use a variety of beans if possible, although this recipe is perfectly acceptable with just one type of bean.

NUTRITIONAL INFORMATION

Calories 285   Sugars 6g
Protein ....9g   Fat 19g
Carbohydrate ...18g   Saturates 6g

 5 mins   20 mins

SERVES 4

INGREDIENTS

2 lb/900 g mixed green beans, such as fava beans, green beans, pole beans

5 tbsp butter or margarine

4 tsp all-purpose flour

1¼ cups vegetable bouillon

5 tbsp dry white wine

6 tbsp light cream

3 tbsp chopped mixed herbs

2 tbsp lemon juice

grated zest of 1 lemon

salt and pepper

1 Cook the beans in a pan of boiling salted water for 10 minutes, or until tender. Drain and place in a warmed serving dish.

VARIATION

Use lime zest and juice instead of lemon for an alternative citrus flavor. Replace the light cream with unsweetened yogurt for a healthier version of this dish.

2 Meanwhile, melt the butter in a pan. Add the flour and cook, stirring constantly, for 1 minute. Remove the pan from the heat and gradually stir in the bouillon and wine. Return the pan to the heat and bring to a boil, stirring.

3 Remove the pan from the heat once again and stir in the light cream, mixed herbs, and lemon juice and zest. Season with salt and pepper to taste. Pour the sauce over the beans, mixing well to coat thoroughly. Serve immediately.

Spanish Potatoes

This type of dish is usually served as part of Spanish tapas, and is delicious with salad or a simply cooked entrée.

NUTRITIONAL INFORMATION

Calories	176	Sugars	.........9g
Protein	.........5g	Fat	...........6g
Carbohydrate	...27g	Saturates	.......1g

 20 mins   35 mins

SERVES 4

I N G R E D I E N T S

2 tbsp olive oil

1 lb/450 g small new potatoes, halved

1 onion, halved and sliced

1 green bell pepper, seeded and cut into strips

1 tsp chili powder

1 tsp prepared mustard

1¼ cups strained tomatoes

1¼ cups vegetable bouillon

salt and pepper

chopped parsley, to garnish

1 Heat the olive oil in a large, heavy skillet. Add the halved new potatoes and the sliced onion and cook, stirring frequently, for 4–5 minutes, until the onion slices are soft and translucent.

2 Add the green bell pepper strips, chili powder, and mustard to the pan and cook for another 2–3 minutes.

3 Stir the strained tomatoes and the vegetable bouillon into the pan and bring to a boil. Reduce the heat and simmer for about 25 minutes, or until the potatoes are tender.

4 Transfer the potatoes to a warmed serving dish. Sprinkle the parsley over the top and serve immediately.

5 Alternatively, let the Spanish potatoes cool completely and serve cold, at room temperature.

COOK'S TIP
In Spain, tapas are traditionally served with a glass of chilled sherry or some other aperitif.

Italian Zucchini

This tasty method of cooking zucchini, in a vegetable bouillon with a touch of fresh marjoram, really brings out their full flavor.

NUTRITIONAL INFORMATION

Calories 10	Sugars 3g
Protein 3g	Fat 6g
Carbohydrate . . .10g	Saturates 1g

 10 mins   20 mins

SERVES 4

INGREDIENTS

2 tbsp olive oil

1 large onion, chopped

1 garlic clove, finely chopped

5 zucchini, sliced

⅔ cup vegetable bouillon

1 tsp chopped fresh marjoram

salt and ground black pepper

1 tbsp chopped fresh flat-leaf parsley, to garnish

1 Heat the oil in a heavy skillet. Add the onion and garlic and cook, stirring occasionally, for 5 minutes, until soft.

2 Add the zucchini and cook, stirring frequently, for 3-4 minutes, until they are just beginning to brown.

3 Add the bouillon and marjoram and season to taste with salt and pepper. Simmer for about 10 minutes, until almost all the liquid has evaporated. Transfer to a warm serving dish, sprinkle with the parsley, and serve immediately.

Cauliflower Fritters

This makes an unusual accompaniment to bakes or gratins and could also be served as an appetizer with a dipping sauce.

NUTRITIONAL INFORMATION

Calories 253   Sugars 3g
Protein ....10g   Fat 13g
Carbohydrate ...26g   Saturates 2g

15 mins   15 mins

SERVES 4

INGREDIENTS

1 large cauliflower, cut into florets

1 cup all-purpose flour

pinch of dried thyme

2 eggs, separated

⅔ cup water

4 tbsp milk

sunflower or corn oil, for deep-frying

salt

1 Blanch the cauliflower in a large pan of boiling water for 5 minutes. Drain well and pat dry with paper towels.

2 Strain the flour with a pinch of salt into a bowl and add the thyme, egg yolks, and water. Beat well with a wooden spoon until smooth. Beat in the milk.

3 In a separate, grease-free bowl, whisk the egg whites until stiff peaks form.

Gently fold a little of the egg white into the batter, then fold in the rest.

4 Heat the oil in a deep-fryer or pan to 350-375°F/180-190°C or until a cube of bread browns in 30 seconds. Dip the cauliflower florets in the batter to coat, then cook, in batches, until golden brown.

5 Drain the cauliflower fritters on paper towels and serve immediately.

COOK'S TIP
Reheat the oil between batches, as the temperature will drop during cooking.

Okra Bhaji

This is a very mild-tasting, rich curry, which would be an ideal accompaniment to a tomato-based curry.

NUTRITIONAL INFORMATION

Calories	173	Sugars	........11g
Protein	.........6g	Fat	...........11g
Carbohydrate	...13g	Saturates	.......5g

 25 mins   35 mins

SERVES 4

I N G R E D I E N T S

1 tbsp sunflower oil

1 tsp black mustard seeds

1 tsp cumin seeds

1 tsp coriander seeds, ground

½ tsp turmeric

1 green chili, seeded and finely chopped

1 red onion, finely sliced

2 garlic cloves, crushed

1 orange bell pepper, seeded and thinly sliced

1 lb/450 g okra, trimmed and blanched

1 cup vegetable juice

⅔ cup light cream

1 tbsp lemon juice

salt

1 Heat the oil in a preheated wok or large, heavy skillet. Add the mustard seeds and cover the wok or skillet until they start to pop.

2 Stir in the cumin seeds, ground coriander, turmeric, and chili. Stir constantly for 1 minute, until the spices are giving off their aroma.

3 Add the onion, garlic, and bell pepper, and cook, stirring frequently, for about 5 minutes, until soft.

4 Add the blanched okra to the pan and stir to combine all the ingredients thoroughly.

5 Pour in the vegetable juice, bring to a boil, and cook over high heat, stirring occasionally, for 5 minutes.

6 When most of the liquid has evaporated, check the seasoning and add salt if necessary.

7 Add the cream, bring to a boil again, and continue to cook the mixture over high heat for about 12 minutes, until it is almost dry.

8 Sprinkle the lemon juice over the okra bhaji, transfer to a warmed serving dish and serve immediately.

COOK'S TIP

Okra have a unique glutinous quality which, when they are added to curries and casseroles, disperses in the sauce and thickens it wonderfully—and naturally!

Carrot & Orange Bake

Poppy seeds add texture and flavor to this recipe and counteract the slightly sweet flavor of the carrots.

NUTRITIONAL INFORMATION

Calories	138	Sugars	........31g
Protein	.........2g	Fat	...........1g
Carbohydrate	...32g	Saturates	.....0.2g

20 mins   40 mins

SERVES 4

I N G R E D I E N T S

1½ lb/675 g carrots, cut into thin strips

1 leek, sliced

1¼ cups fresh orange juice

2 tbsp clear honey

1 garlic clove, crushed

1 tsp apple spice

2 tsp chopped thyme

1 tbsp poppy seeds

salt and pepper

thyme sprigs and orange zest, to garnish

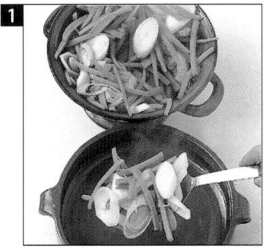

1 Cook the carrots and leek in a pan of boiling lightly salted water for 5–6 minutes. Drain well and transfer to a shallow ovenproof dish until required.

2 Mix together the orange juice, honey, garlic, apple spice, and thyme and pour the mixture over the vegetables. Season with salt and pepper to taste.

3 Cover the ovenproof dish with a lid and cook the vegetables in a preheated oven, 350°F/180°C, for about 25–30 minutes, or until all the vegetables are tender.

4 Remove the lid and sprinkle with poppy seeds. Transfer the bake to a warmed serving dish, garnish with the fresh thyme sprigs and orange zest, and serve immediately.

COOK'S TIP
Lemon or lime juice could be used instead of the orange juice, if you prefer. Garnish with lemon or lime zest.

Palak Paneer

Paneer—curd cheese—figures widely on Indian menus. It is combined with all sorts of ingredients, but most popularly with spinach and vegetables.

NUTRITIONAL INFORMATION

Calories 287	Sugars 7g
Protein 12g	Fat 18g
Carbohydrate ...22g	Saturates 11g

 20 mins   40 mins

SERVES 6

INGREDIENTS

2 tbsp vegetable ghee

1 onion, sliced

1 garlic clove, crushed

1 dried red chili

1 tsp ground turmeric

1 lb/450 g waxy potatoes, cut into 1 inch/2.5 cm cubes

2 cups canned tomatoes, drained

⅔ cup water

½ lb fresh spinach

1 lb/450 g paneer, cut into 1 inch/2.5 cm cubes

1 tsp garam masala

1 tbsp chopped cilantro

1 tbsp chopped parsley

salt and pepper

naan bread, to serve

VARIATION
Fresh Italian romano cheese can be used as a substitute for Indian paneer.

1 Heat the ghee in a pan. Add the onion and cook over low heat, stirring frequently, for 10 minutes, until very soft. Add the garlic and chili and cook for a further 5 minutes.

2 Add the turmeric, salt, potatoes, canned tomatoes, and water to the pan and bring to a boil.

3 Simmer for 10–15 minutes, until the potatoes are cooked.

4 Stir in the spinach, cheese cubes, garam masala, and chopped cilantro and parsley.

5 Simmer for a further 5 minutes and season well. Serve with naan bread.

Mixed Vegetables

This is one of my favorite vegetarian recipes. You can make it with any vegetables you choose, but the combination below is excellent.

NUTRITIONAL INFORMATION

Calories 669   Sugars 17g
Protein ....7g   Fat 57g
Carbohydrate ...36g   Saturates 8g

5 mins   45 mins

SERVES 4

INGREDIENTS

1¼ cups vegetable oil

1 tsp mustard seeds

1 tsp onion seeds

½ tsp white cumin seeds

3–4 curry leaves, chopped

1 lb/450 g onions, finely chopped

3 tomatoes, chopped

½ red and ½ green bell pepper, sliced

1 tsp finely chopped fresh ginger root

1 tsp fresh garlic, crushed

1 tsp chili powder

¼ tsp turmeric

1 tsp salt

2 cups water

1 lb/450 g potatoes, and cut into pieces

½ cauliflower, cut into small florets

4 carrots, sliced

3 green chilies, finely chopped

1 tbsp fresh cilantro leaves

1 tbsp lemon juice

1 Heat the oil in a large pan. Add the mustard, onion, and white cumin seeds and the curry leaves and cook until they turn a shade darker.

2 Add the onions and cook over medium heat until golden brown.

3 Add the tomatoes and bell peppers and cook for about 5 minutes.

4 Add the ginger, garlic, chili powder, turmeric, and salt, and mix well.

5 Add 1¼ cups of the water to the pan. Cover and let simmer for 10–12 minutes, stirring occasionally. Add the potatoes, cauliflower, carrots, green chilies, and cilantro leaves and cook for about 5 minutes.

6 Add the remaining water and the lemon juice. Stir, cover and let simmer for about 15 minutes, stirring occasionally.

7 Transfer the mixed vegetables to serving plates and serve immediately.

Cheese & Potato Pie

This really is a great side dish, perfect for serving with entrées cooked in the oven.

NUTRITIONAL INFORMATION

Calories	295	Sugars	.........5g
Protein	........13g	Fat	..........17g
Carbohydrate	...24g	Saturates	......11g

15 mins   1½ hrs

SERVES 4

INGREDIENTS

1 lb/450 g potatoes

1 leek, sliced

3 garlic cloves, crushed

½ cup grated Cheddar cheese

½ cup grated mozzarella cheese

⅓ cup grated Parmesan cheese

2 tbsp chopped fresh parsley

⅔ cup light cream

⅔ cup milk

salt and pepper

chopped fresh flat-leaf parsley, to garnish

1 Cook the potatoes in a pan of boiling salted water for 10 minutes. Drain well.

2 Cut the potatoes into thin slices. Arrange a layer of potatoes in the base of an ovenproof dish. Layer with a little of the leek, garlic, cheeses, and parsley. Season to taste with salt and pepper.

3 Repeat the layers until all of the ingredients have been used, finishing with a layer of cheese. Mix the cream and milk together and season with salt and pepper to taste. Pour over the potato layers.

4 Cook the potatoes in a preheated oven, 325°F/160°C, for 1–1¼ hours, or until the cheese is golden brown and bubbling and the potatoes are cooked right through and tender.

5 Garnish the potatoes with chopped fresh flat-leaf parsley and serve immediately.

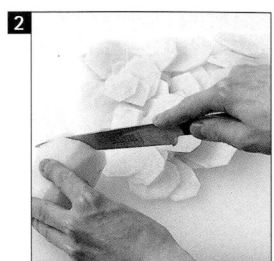

COOK'S TIP

Potatoes make a very good basis for a vegetable accompaniment. They are a good source of complex carbohydrate and contain a number of vitamins. From the point of view of flavor, they combine well with a vast range of other ingredients.

Steamed Vegetables Parcels

Baby vegetables are cooked whole so that they lose none of their flavor, color, texture, or goodness. Serve them still wrapped in their parcels.

NUTRITIONAL INFORMATION

Calories 170   Sugars 9g
Protein . . . . .3g   Fat 12g
Carbohydrate . . . .11g   Saturates 8g

 15 mins   8-10 mins

SERVES 4

INGREDIENTS

¼ lb/115 g green beans

¾ cup snow peas

12 baby carrots

8 baby onions or shallots

12 baby turnips

8 radishes

4 tbsp sweet butter or vegetarian margarine

4 thinly pared strips of lemon zest

4 tsp finely chopped fresh chervil

4 tbsp dry white wine

salt and ground black pepper

 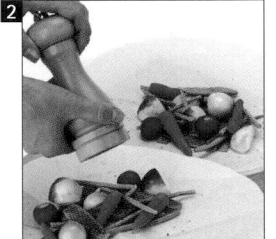 

1 Cut out 4 double thickness rounds of waxed paper about 12 inches/30 cm in diameter.

2 Divide the green beans, snow peas, carrots, onions or shallots, turnips, radishes and lemon zest among the rounds, placing them on one half. Season to taste with salt and pepper and dot with the butter. Sprinkle with the chervil and drizzle with the wine. Fold over the double layer of paper, twisting the edges together to seal.

3 Bring a large pan of water to a boil and place a steamer on top. Put the parcels in the steamer, cover tightly, and steam for 8–10 minutes, then remove the parcels from the steamer and serve them immediately, to be unwrapped at table.

VARIATION
Substitute 4 tablespoons olive oil for the butter or margarine, chopped fresh mint for the chervil, and cherry tomatoes for the radishes.

Spiced Lentils with Spinach

This dish is a good accompaniment to a carbohydrate-based entrée, or a complete meal in itself, served with rice and a side salad.

NUTRITIONAL INFORMATION

Calories ....179 Sugars 3g
Protein ....11g Fat 5g
Carbohydrate ...24g Saturates 1g

 15 mins   35 mins

SERVES 4–6

I N G R E D I E N T S

2 tbsp olive oil

1 large onion, finely chopped

1 large garlic clove, crushed

½ tbsp ground cumin

½ tsp ground ginger

generous 1 cup Puy lentils

about 2½ cups vegetable bouillon

¼ lb/115 g young spinach leaves

2 tbsp fresh mint leaves

1 tbsp fresh cilantro leaves

1 tbsp fresh flat-leaf parsley leaves

freshly squeezed lemon juice

salt and pepper

strips of lemon zest, to garnish

COOK'S TIP

This recipe uses green lentils from Puy in France because they are good at keeping their shape even after long cooking. You can, however, also use orange or brown lentils, but it is necessary to watch them while they cook or they will quickly turn to a mush.

1 Heat the oil in a large skillet over medium heat. Add the onion and cook, stirring occasionally, for about 6 minutes. Stir in the garlic, cumin, and ginger and cook, stirring occasionally, until the onion starts to brown.

2 Stir in the lentils. Pour in enough bouillon to cover the lentils by 1 inch/ 2.5 cm and bring to a boil. Lower the heat and simmer for 20–30 minutes until the lentils are tender.

3 Meanwhile, rinse the spinach leaves in several changes of cold water and shake dry. Finely chop the mint, cilantro, and parsley leaves.

4 If there isn't any bouillon left in the skillet, add a little extra. Add the spinach and stir through until it just wilts. Stir in the mint, cilantro, and parsley. Adjust the seasoning, adding lemon juice and salt and pepper. Transfer to a serving bowl and serve, garnished with lemon zest.

Vegetable Ratatouille

Ratatouille is a classic dish of vegetables cooked in a tomato and herb sauce. Here it is topped with diced potatoes and cheese.

NUTRITIONAL INFORMATION

Calories	287	Sugars	........13g
Protein	........14g	Fat	...........4g
Carbohydrate	...53g	Saturates	......2g

  15 mins   25 mins

SERVES 4

INGREDIENTS

2 onions

1 garlic clove

1 red bell pepper

1 green bell pepper

1 eggplant

2 zucchini

4 cups canned chopped tomatoes

1 bouquet garni

2 tbsp tomato paste

2 lb/900 g potatoes

¾ cup grated reduced-fat sharp
   Cheddar cheese

salt and pepper

2 tbsp snipped fresh chives, to garnish

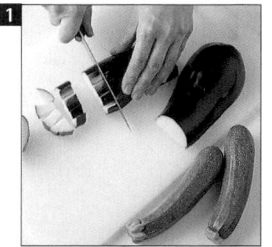 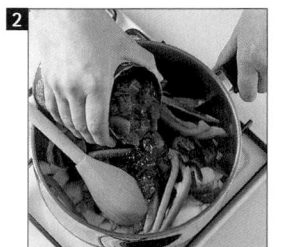 

1 Peel and finely chop the onions and garlic. Rinse, seed, and slice the bell peppers. Rinse, trim, and cut the eggplant into small dice. Rinse, trim, and thinly slice the zucchini.

2 Place the onion, garlic, and bell peppers in a pan. Add the tomatoes, bouquet garni, tomato paste, and salt and pepper to taste. Bring to a boil, cover, and simmer for 10 minutes, stirring halfway through. Stir in the eggplant and zucchini and cook, uncovered, for a further 10 minutes, stirring occasionally.

3 Meanwhile, peel the potatoes and cut into 1 inch/2.5 cm cubes. Place the potatoes into another pan and cover with water. Bring to a boil and cook for 10–12 minutes until tender. Drain and set aside.

4 Transfer the vegetables to a heatproof gratin dish. Arrange the cooked potatoes evenly over the vegetables.

5 Preheat the broiler to medium. Sprinkle the cheese over the potatoes and broil for 5 minutes until golden and bubbling. Serve, garnished with chives.

VARIATION
You can vary the vegetables in this dish depending on seasonal availability and personal preference. Try broccoli, carrots, or corn, if you prefer.

Gnocchi with Herb Sauce

These little potato dumplings are a traditional Italian appetizer or side dish. Served with a salad and bread, they also make a substantial entrée.

NUTRITIONAL INFORMATION

Calories	.619	Sugars	.3g
Protein	.11g	Fat	.30g
Carbohydrate	.81g	Saturates	.9g

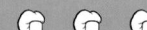

30 mins   30 mins

SERVES 6

INGREDIENTS

2 lb/900 g old potatoes, cut into ½ inch pieces

4 tbsp butter or margarine

1 egg, beaten

2 cups all-purpose flour

salt

SAUCE

½ cup olive oil

2 garlic cloves, very finely chopped

1 tbsp chopped fresh oregano

1 tbsp chopped fresh basil

salt and pepper

TO SERVE (OPTIONAL)

freshly grated Parmesan

mixed salad

warm ciabatta

1 Cook the potatoes in a pan of boiling salted water for about 10 minutes or until tender. Drain well.

2 Press the hot potatoes through a strainer into a large bowl. Add 1 tsp of salt, the butter or margarine, the egg, and 1 cup of the flour. Stir the mixture well to bind together.

3 Turn on to a lightly floured surface and knead, gradually adding the remaining flour, until a smooth, soft, slightly sticky dough is formed.

4 Flour the hands and roll the dough into ¾ inch/2 cm thick rolls. Cut each roll into ¾ inch/2 cm pieces. Press the top of each piece with the floured prongs of a fork and spread out on a floured dish cloth.

5 Bring a large pan of salted water to a gentle simmer. Add the gnocchi to the pan and cook them, in batches if necessary, for about 2–3 minutes, or until they rise to the surface.

6 Remove the gnocchi with a perforated spoon and put in a warmed, greased serving dish. Cover and keep warm.

7 To make the sauce, put the oil, garlic, and seasoning in a pan and cook, stirring, for 3–4 minutes until the garlic is golden. Remove from the heat and stir in the herbs. Pour over the gnocchi and serve, sprinkled with Parmesan and accompanied by salad and warm ciabatta, if desired.

Potato & Spinach Gnocchi

These small potato dumplings are flavored with spinach, cooked in boiling water, and served with a simple tomato sauce.

NUTRITIONAL INFORMATION

Calories	315	Sugars	.........7g
Protein	.........8g	Fat	...........8g
Carbohydrate	...56g	Saturates	.......1g

   20 mins   30 mins

SERVES 4

INGREDIENTS

1⅔ cups diced mealy potatoes

6 oz/175 g spinach

1 egg yolk

1 tsp olive oil

1 cup all-purpose flour

salt and pepper

spinach leaves, to garnish

SAUCE

1 tbsp olive oil

2 shallots, chopped

1 garlic clove, crushed

1¼ cups strained tomatoes

2 tsp soft light brown sugar

1 Cook the diced potatoes in a pan of boiling water for 10 minutes or until cooked through. Drain the potatoes and mash them.

2 Meanwhile, in a separate pan, blanch the spinach in a little boiling water for 1–2 minutes. Drain the spinach and shred the leaves.

3 Transfer the mashed potato to a lightly floured cutting board and make a well in the center. Add the egg yolk, olive oil, spinach, and a little of the flour. Quickly mix the ingredients into the potato, adding more flour as you go, until you have a firm dough. Divide the mixture into very small dumplings.

4 Cook the gnocchi, in batches, in a pan of boiling salted water for about 5 minutes or until they rise to the surface.

5 Meanwhile, make the sauce. Put the oil, shallots, garlic, strained tomatoes, and sugar into a pan and cook over low heat for 10–15 minutes or until the sauce has thickened.

6 Drain the gnocchi using a perforated spoon and transfer to warm serving dishes. Spoon the sauce over the gnocchi and garnish with the fresh spinach leaves.

VARIATION
Add chopped fresh herbs and cheese to the gnocchi dough instead of the spinach, if you prefer.

Potatoes with Almonds

This oven-cooked dish has a subtle, creamy, almond flavor and a pale yellow color as a result of being cooked with turmeric.

NUTRITIONAL INFORMATION

Calories 531   Sugars 6g
Protein . . . . .7g   Fat 46g
Carbohydrate . . .24g   Saturates 23g

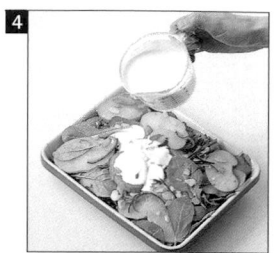

 5 mins   40–45 mins

SERVES 4

INGREDIENTS

1¼ lb/560 g potatoes, unpeeled and sliced

1 tbsp vegetable oil

1 red onion, halved and sliced

1 garlic clove, crushed

½ cup almond slivers

½ tsp turmeric

¼ lb/115 g arugula leaves

1¼ cups heavy cream

salt and pepper

1 Cook the sliced potatoes in a pan of boiling water for 10 minutes. Drain them thoroughly.

2 Heat the vegetable oil in a heavy skillet. Add the onion and garlic and cook over medium heat, stirring frequently, for 3–4 minutes.

3 Add the almonds, turmeric, and potato slices to the skillet and cook, stirring constantly, for 2–3 minutes. Stir in the arugula leaves.

4 Transfer the potato and almond mixture to a shallow, ovenproof dish. Pour the heavy cream evenly over the top of the potatoes and season to taste with salt and pepper.

5 Cook in a preheated oven, at 375°F/190°C, for 20 minutes, or until the potatoes are cooked through. Transfer to a warmed serving dish and serve them immediately.

Greek Beans

This dish contains many Greek flavors such as lemon, garlic, oregano, and olives, for a really flavorful recipe.

NUTRITIONAL INFORMATION

Calories 115	Sugars 4g
Protein 6g	Fat 4g
Carbohydrate ...15g	Saturates 0.6g

 5 mins 1 hr

SERVES 4

INGREDIENTS

2 cups canned navy beans, drained

1 tbsp olive oil

3 garlic cloves, crushed

1¾ cups vegetable bouillon

1 bay leaf

2 sprigs oregano

1 tbsp tomato paste

juice of 1 lemon

1 small red onion, chopped

¼ cup pitted black olives, halved

salt and pepper

1 Put the navy beans in a flameproof casserole dish.

2 Add the olive oil and crushed garlic and cook over gentle heat, stirring occasionally, for 4–5 minutes.

3 Stir in the vegetable bouillon, bay leaf, oregano, tomato paste, lemon juice, and red onion.

4 Cover the casserole and simmer for about 1 hour or until the sauce has thickened.

5 Stir in the black olives, and season with salt and pepper to taste. The beans are delicious served warm or cold.

VARIATION

You can substitute other canned beans for the navy beans—try cannellini or garbanzo beans or black-eyed peas instead. Rinse them before use as canned beans often have sugar or salt added.

Potato Hash

This recipe is a variation of the hearty American dish, which was traditionally served to seagoing New Englanders.

NUTRITIONAL INFORMATION

Calories	302	Sugars	........5g
Protein	........15g	Fat	..........10g
Carbohydrate	...40g	Saturates	.......4g

10 mins   30 mins

SERVES 4

INGREDIENTS

2 tbsp butter

1 red onion, halved and sliced

1 carrot, diced

¼ cup green beans, halved

generous 5 cups diced waxy potatoes

½ cup all-purpose flour

1¼ cups vegetable bouillon

½ lb bean curd, diced

salt and pepper

chopped fresh parsley, to garnish

1 Melt the butter in a large, heavy skillet. Add the onion, carrot, green beans, and potatoes, and cook over fairly low heat, stirring constantly, for about 5–7 minutes, or until the vegetables begin to turn golden brown.

2 Add the flour to the skillet and cook, stirring constantly, for 1 minute. Gradually pour in the bouillon, stirring constantly.

3 Reduce the heat to low and simmer for 15 minutes, or until the potatoes are tender.

4 Add the diced bean curd to the skillet and continue cooking for another 5 minutes. Season to taste with salt and pepper.

5 Sprinkle the chopped parsley over the top of the potato hash to garnish and then serve hot, straight from the skillet.

COOK'S TIP

A traditional hash dish is always made from chopped fresh ingredients, such as bell peppers, onion, and celery.

Spinach & Cauliflower Bhaji

This excellent vegetable dish goes well with most Indian food—
and it is simple and quick to cook, too.

NUTRITIONAL INFORMATION

Calories	212	Sugars	........12g
Protein	........10g	Fat	..........13g
Carbohydrate	...14g	Saturates	.......2g

 10 mins   25 mins

SERVES 4

I N G R E D I E N T S

1 cauliflower

1 lb/450 g fresh spinach, washed, or
½ lb/225 g frozen spinach, thawed

4 tbsp vegetable ghee or oil

2 large onions, coarsely chopped

2 garlic cloves, crushed

1 inch/2.5 cm piece of ginger root, chopped

1¼ tsp cayenne pepper, or to taste

1 tsp ground cumin

1 tsp ground turmeric

2 tsp ground coriander

2 cups canned chopped tomatoes

1¼ cups vegetable bouillon

salt and pepper

1 Divide the cauliflower into small florets, discarding the hard central stalk. Trim the stalks from the spinach leaves. Heat the ghee or oil in a large pan, add the onions and cauliflower florets, and cook over low heat, stirring frequently, for about 3 minutes.

2 Add the garlic, ginger, and spices and cook gently, stirring occasionally, for 1 minute. Stir in the tomatoes and the

vegetable bouillon and season to taste with salt and pepper. Bring to a boil, cover the pan, reduce the heat, and simmer gently for 8 minutes.

3 Add the spinach to the pan, stirring and turning to wilt the leaves. Cover and simmer gently, stirring frequently, for about 8-10 minutes, until the spinach and the cauliflower are tender. Transfer to a warmed serving dish and serve hot.

COOK'S TIP
When buying cauliflower, look for firm, white curds with no discoloration or signs of wilting.

Long Beans with Tomatoes

Indian meals often need some green vegetables to complement
the spicy dishes and to set off the richly flavored sauces.

NUTRITIONAL INFORMATION

Calories 76	Sugars 3g	
Protein 2g	Fat 6g	
Carbohydrate 4g	Saturates 3g	

15 mins

25 mins

SERVES 6

I N G R E D I E N T S

1 lb/450 g green beans, cut into
   2 inch/5 cm lengths

2 tbsp vegetable ghee

1 inch/2.5 cm piece of fresh
   ginger root, grated

1 garlic clove, crushed

1 tsp ground turmeric

½ tsp cayenne pepper

1 tsp ground coriander

4 tomatoes, peeled, seeded, and diced

⅔ cup vegetable bouillon

1 Blanch the beans briefly in boiling
   water, drain, refresh under cold
running water, and drain again.

2 Melt the ghee in a large pan over
   moderate heat. Add the grated ginger
and crushed garlic, stir, and add the

COOK'S TIP
Ginger graters are an invaluable
piece of equipment to have when
cooking Indian food. These small,
flat graters, made of either bamboo
or china, can be held directly over
the pan while you grate.

turmeric, cayenne, and ground coriander.
Stir over low heat for about 1 minute
until fragrant.

3 Add the diced tomatoes, tossing them
   until they are thoroughly coated in
the spice mix.

4 Add the vegetable bouillon to the
   pan, bring to a boil, and simmer over

medium-high heat, stirring occasionally,
for about 10 minutes until the sauce has
reduced and thickened.

5 Add the beans, reduce the heat to
   moderate, and heat through, stirring
constantly, for 5 minutes.

6 Transfer to a warmed serving dish and
   serve immediately.

Souffléd Cheesy Potato Fries

These small potato chunks are mixed in a creamy cheese sauce and deep-fried in oil until deliciously golden brown.

NUTRITIONAL INFORMATION

Calories 614	Sugars 2g
Protein 12g	Fat 46g
Carbohydrate . . .40g	Saturates 18g

20 mins   25 mins

SERVES 4

I N G R E D I E N T S

2 lb/900 g potatoes, cut into chunks

⅔ cup heavy cream

¾ cup grated Swiss cheese

pinch of cayenne pepper

2 egg whites

vegetable oil, for deep-frying

salt and pepper

chopped flat-leaf parsley and grated
   cheese, to garnish

1 Cook the potatoes in a pan of lightly salted boiling water for about 10 minutes. Drain thoroughly and pat dry with absorbent paper towels. Set aside until required.

2 Mix the heavy cream and Swiss cheese in a large bowl. Stir in the cayenne pepper and season with salt and pepper to taste.

3 Whisk the egg whites until stiff peaks form. Gently fold into the cheese mixture until fully incorporated.

4 Add the cooked potatoes, turning to coat thoroughly in the mixture.

5 In a deep pan, heat the oil to 350°F/180°C or until a cube of bread browns in 30 seconds. Remove the potatoes from the cheese mixture with a slotted spoon and cook in the oil, in batches if necessary, for 3–4 minutes, or until golden.

6 Transfer the potatoes to a warmed serving dish and garnish with parsley and grated cheese. Serve immediately.

VARIATION
Add other flavorings, such as grated nutmeg or curry powder, to the cream and cheese.

Easy Cauliflower & Broccoli

Whole baby cauliflowers are used in this recipe. Try to find them if you can, but if not use large bunches of florets instead.

NUTRITIONAL INFORMATION

Calories	433	Sugars	.........2g
Protein	.........8g	Fat	..........44g
Carbohydrate	....3g	Saturates	.......9g

 10 mins   20 mins

SERVES 4

INGREDIENTS

2 baby cauliflowers

½ lb/225 g broccoli

salt and pepper

SAUCE

8 tbsp olive oil

4 tbsp butter or margarine

2 tsp grated ginger root

juice and zest of 2 lemons

5 tbsp chopped cilantro

5 tbsp grated Cheddar cheese

1 Using a sharp knife, cut the cauliflowers in half and the broccoli into very large florets.

2 Cook the cauliflower and broccoli in a pan of boiling, salted water for 10 minutes. Drain well, transfer to a shallow ovenproof dish, and keep warm until required.

3 To make the sauce, put the oil and butter or margarine in a pan and heat gently until the butter melts.

4 Add the grated ginger root, lemon juice, lemon zest, and chopped cilantro and simmer for 2–3 minutes, stirring occasionally.

5 Season the sauce with salt and pepper to taste, then pour over the vegetables in the dish and sprinkle the cheese on top.

6 Cook under a preheated hot broiler for 2–3 minutes, or until the cheese is bubbling and golden. Let cool for 1–2 minutes and then serve.

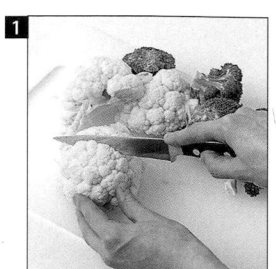

COOK'S TIP

Lime or orange could be used instead of the lemon for a fruity and refreshing sauce.

Saffron-Flavored Potatoes

Saffron is made from the dried stigma of the crocus and is native to Greece. It is very expensive, but only a very small amount is needed.

NUTRITIONAL INFORMATION

Calories 197   Sugars 4g
Protein ....4g   Fat 6g
Carbohydrate ...30g   Saturates 1g

  20 mins   40 mins

SERVES 4

I N G R E D I E N T S

1 tsp saffron strands

6 tbsp boiling water

1½ lb/675 g waxy potatoes, unpeeled and cut into wedges

1 red onion, cut into 8 wedges

2 garlic cloves, crushed

1 tbsp white wine vinegar

2 tbsp olive oil

1 tbsp whole-grain mustard

5 tbsp vegetable bouillon

5 tbsp dry white wine

2 tsp chopped rosemary

salt and pepper

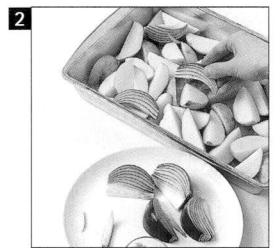  

1 Place the saffron strands in a small bowl and pour over the boiling water. Let soak for about 10 minutes.

2 Place the potatoes in a roasting pan, together with the red onion wedges and crushed garlic.

3 Add the vinegar, oil, mustard, vegetable bouillon, white wine, rosemary, and saffron water to the potatoes and onion in the pan. Season to taste with salt and pepper.

4 Cover the roasting pan with aluminum foil and bake in a preheated oven, 400°F/200°C, for about 30 minutes.

5 Remove the foil and cook the potatoes for another 10 minutes until crisp, browned, and cooked through. Serve them hot.

COOK'S TIP
Turmeric may be used instead of saffron to provide the yellow color in this recipe. However, it is worth using saffron, if possible, for the lovely nutty flavor it gives a dish.

Eggplant Bhaji

The panch poran spice mix used here is one of many traditional spice mixes used in Indian cooking and originated in the Bengal state.

NUTRITIONAL INFORMATION

Calories 170	Sugars 4g
Protein 2g	Fat 17g
Carbohydrate 4g	Saturates 2g

5 mins   25 mins

SERVES 4

INGREDIENTS

2 tbsp mustard oil

4 tbsp sunflower oil

1 tsp panch poran spice mix

6 baby eggplants, quartered, or
    2 eggplants, cut into 1 inch/
    2.5 cm cubes

¼ tsp cayenne

1 tsp coriander seeds, ground

½ tsp turmeric

1 cup canned chopped tomatoes in juice

½ tsp sugar

2 tsp lime juice

salt

1 Heat the mustard oil in a wok or large skillet until it just starts to smoke. Reduce the heat and add the sunflower oil. Add the panch poran mix to the skillet, stir once, then add the eggplant pieces.

2 Add the cayenne, ground coriander seeds, and turmeric to the wok or skillet and stir over high heat for 2–3 minutes, until the eggplant is sealed on all sides.

3 Add the chopped tomatoes, together with their can juices, to the wok or skillet and bring to a boil.

4 Simmer for 15 minutes, or until the bhaji is nearly dry. Stir once or twice. Remove from the heat and stir in the sugar, a pinch of salt, and the lime juice.

5 Transfer to a warmed serving dish, and serve immediately.

COOK'S TIP

Most Asian cooks do not salt eggplants. The eggplants available for most of the year are so fresh that they do not have any bitter juices, especially the plump, shiny ones that have been left on the plant until they are sweet.

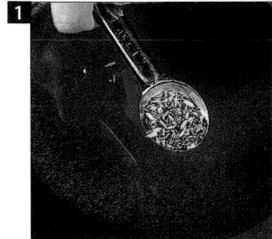

Candied Sweet Potatoes

A taste of the Caribbean is introduced in this recipe, where sweet potatoes are cooked with sugar and lime with a dash of brandy.

NUTRITIONAL INFORMATION

Calories ....348 Sugars 21g
Protein ....3g Fat 9g
Carbohydrate ...67g Saturates 6g

 15 mins   25 mins

SERVES 4

INGREDIENTS

1½ lb/675 g sweet potatoes, sliced

3 tbsp butter

1 tbsp lime juice

½ cup soft dark brown sugar

1 tbsp brandy

grated zest of 1 lime

lime wedges, to garnish

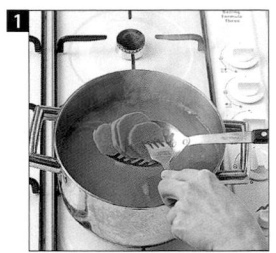

1 Cook the sweet potatoes in a pan of boiling water for about 5 minutes. Test that the potatoes have softened by pricking with a fork. Remove them with a perforated spoon and drain thoroughly.

2 Melt the butter in a large skillet. Add the lime juice and brown sugar and heat gently, stirring, to dissolve the sugar.

3 Stir the sweet potatoes and the brandy into the sugar and lime juice mixture. Cook over low heat for about 10 minutes or until the potato slices are cooked through.

4 Sprinkle the lime zest over the top of the sweet potatoes and mix well.

5 Transfer to a serving plate, garnish with lime wedges, and serve at once.

COOK'S TIP
Sweet potatoes have a pinkish skin and either white, yellow, or orange flesh. It doesn't matter which type is used.

Indian Potatoes & Peas

This quick and easy-to-prepare Indian dish can be served either as an accompaniment or on its own with chapatis.

NUTRITIONAL INFORMATION

Calories	434	Sugars	.........6g
Protein	.........5g	Fat	..........35g
Carbohydrate	...28g	Saturates	.......4g

 15 mins   25 mins

SERVES 4

I N G R E D I E N T S

⅔ cup vegetable oil

3 medium onions, sliced

1 tsp crushed garlic

1 tsp finely chopped fresh ginger root

1 tsp chili powder

½ tsp turmeric

1 tsp salt

2 fresh green chilies, finely chopped

1¼ cups water

1½ lb/675 g potatoes

1 cup peas

TO GARNISH

fresh cilantro leaves

chopped red chilies

COOK'S TIP

Turmeric is an aromatic root which is dried and ground to produce the distinctive bright yellow-orange powder used in many Indian dishes. It has a warm, aromatic smell and a full, somewhat musty taste.

1 Heat the vegetable oil in a large, heavy-based skillet.

2 Add the onions and cook, stirring occasionally, until golden brown.

3 Mix together the garlic, ginger, chili powder, turmeric, salt, and chilies. Add the spice mixture to the pan.

4 Stir in ⅔ cup of the water, then cover and cook until the onions are cooked right through.

5 Meanwhile, cut the potatoes into six slices each, using a sharp knife.

6 Add the potato slices to the mixture in the pan and cook for 5 minutes.

7 Add the peas and the remaining water to the pan, then cover and cook for 7–10 minutes.

8 Transfer the potatoes and peas to serving plates and serve, garnished with fresh cilantro leaves.

Spicy Corn

This dish is an ideal accompaniment to a wide range of Indian dishes and would also go well with a Western-style casserole.

NUTRITIONAL INFORMATION

Calories ....162 Sugars 6g
Protein ....2g Fat 11g
Carbohydrate ...15g Saturates 7g

 10 mins   10 mins

SERVES 4

INGREDIENTS

1 cup frozen or canned corn kernels

1 tsp ground cumin

1 tsp crushed garlic

1 tsp ground coriander

1 tsp salt

2 fresh green chiles

1 medium onion, finely chopped

3 tbsp sweet butter

4 red chiles, crushed

½ tsp lemon juice

1 tbsp fresh cilantro leaves, plus extra to garnish

1 Thaw frozen corn, if using, or drain canned corn, and set aside.

2 Place the cumin, garlic, coriander, salt, 1 fresh green chile, and the onion in a mortar or a food processor and grind to form a smooth paste.

3 Heat the butter in a large skillet. Add the onion and spice mixture and cook over medium heat, stirring occasionally, for about 5–7 minutes.

4 Add the crushed red chiles to the skillet and stir to combine.

5 Add the corn to the skillet and stir-fry for another 2 minutes.

6 Finely chop the remaining green chili and add to the skillet with the lemon juice and the fresh cilantro leaves, stirring to combine.

7 Transfer the spicy corn mixture to a warmed serving dish. Garnish with extra fresh cilantro leaves and serve hot.

COOK'S TIP
Coriander is available ground or as seeds and is one of the essential ingredients in Indian cooking. Coriander seeds are often dry roasted before use to develop their flavor.

Spiced Potatoes & Spinach

This is a classic Indian accompaniment for curries, and is very quick and easy to cook. Serve with a protein-based curry such as dhal.

NUTRITIONAL INFORMATION

Calories ....176 Sugars 4g
Protein ....6g Fat 9g
Carbohydrate ...18g Saturates 1g

 10 mins   20 mins

SERVES 4

INGREDIENTS

3 tbsp vegetable oil

1 red onion, sliced

2 garlic cloves, crushed

½ tsp chili powder

2 tsp ground coriander

1 tsp ground cumin

⅔ cup vegetable bouillon

1¾ cups potatoes, diced

1 lb/450 g young spinach

1 red chili, sliced

salt and pepper

1 Heat the oil in a heavy skillet. Add the onion and garlic and sauté over medium heat, stirring occasionally, for 2–3 minutes.

COOK'S TIP
Besides adding extra color to a dish, red onions have a sweeter, less pungent flavor than other varieties.

2 Add the chili powder and the ground coriander and cumin and cook, stirring constantly, for another 30 seconds.

3 Add the vegetable bouillon, diced potatoes, and spinach, and bring to a boil. Reduce the heat, cover the skillet, and simmer for about 10 minutes, or until

the potatoes are cooked right through and tender.

4 Uncover and season to taste with salt and pepper, then add the chili and cook for another 2–3 minutes. Transfer to a warmed serving dish and serve immediately.

Curried Roast Potatoes

This is the kind of Indian-inspired dish that would fit easily into any vegetarian menu, or how about serving with a curry in place of rice?

NUTRITIONAL INFORMATION

Calories .... .297	Sugars 2g	
Protein 3g	Fat .... .19g	
Carbohydrate ...30g	Saturates ...... .12g	

5 mins   30–35 mins

SERVES 4

INGREDIENTS

2 tsp cumin seeds

2 tsp coriander seeds

6 tbsp butter

1 tsp ground turmeric

1 tsp black mustard seeds

2 garlic cloves, crushed

2 dried red chilies

1¾ lb/790 g baby new potatoes

1 Grind the cumin and coriander seeds together in a mortar with a pestle or spice grinder. Grinding them fresh like this captures all of the flavor before it has a chance to dry out.

2 Melt the butter gently in a roasting pan and add the turmeric, mustard seeds, garlic, and chilies and the ground cumin and coriander seeds. Stir well to combine evenly. Place in a preheated oven at 400°F/200°C for 5 minutes.

3 Remove the pan from the oven—the spices should be very fragrant at this stage—and add the potatoes. Stir well so that the butter and spice mix coats the potatoes completely.

4 Return to the oven and bake for 20–25 minutes. Stir occasionally to ensure that the potatoes are coated evenly. Test the potatoes with a skewer—if they drop off the end of the skewer when lifted, they are done. Transfer to a serving dish and serve immediately.

COOK'S TIP
Baby new potatoes are now available all year round from food stores. However, they are not essential for this recipe. Red or white old potatoes can be substituted, cut into 1 inch/2.5 cm cubes.

Bombay Potatoes

Although virtually unknown in India, this dish is a very popular item on Indian restaurant menus in other parts of the world.

NUTRITIONAL INFORMATION

Calories	307	Sugars	........9g
Protein	.........9g	Fat	...........9g
Carbohydrate	...51g	Saturates	.......5g

5 mins   1 hr 10 mins

SERVES 4

I N G R E D I E N T S

2 lb/900 g waxy potatoes

2 tbsp vegetable ghee

1 tsp panch poran spice mix

3 tsp ground turmeric

2 tbsp tomato paste

1¼ cups unsweetened yogurt

salt

chopped cilantro, to garnish

1 Put the whole potatoes into a large pan of salted cold water, bring to a boil, then simmer until the potatoes are just cooked, but not tender; the time depends on the size of the potato, but an average-sized one should take about 15 minutes.

2 Heat the ghee in a pan over medium heat and add the panch poran, turmeric, tomato paste, yogurt, and salt to the pan. Bring to a boil and simmer the mixture, uncovered, for 5 minutes.

3 Drain the potatoes and cut each one into 4 pieces. Add the potatoes to the pan, cover, and cook briefly.

4 Transfer the mixture to an ovenproof casserole, cover, and cook in a preheated oven, 350°F/180°C, for about 40 minutes, or until the potatoes are tender and the sauce has thickened a little.

5 Sprinkle the potatoes with chopped cilantro and serve immediately.

COOK'S TIP

Panch poran spice mix can be bought from Asian or Indian grocery stores, or make your own from equal quantities of cumin seeds, fennel seeds, mustard seeds, nigella seeds, and fenugreek seeds.

Colcannon

This is an old Irish recipe, which is delicious served with an entrée—although you may be tempted to eat it just as it is!

NUTRITIONAL INFORMATION

Calories 102	Sugars 4g	
Protein 4g	Fat 4g	
Carbohydrate . . .14g	Saturates 2g	

20 mins   20 mins

SERVES 4

INGREDIENTS

½ lb/225 g green cabbage, shredded

5 tbsp milk

1½ cup diced mealy potatoes

1 large leek, chopped

pinch of grated nutmeg

1 tbsp butter, melted

salt and pepper

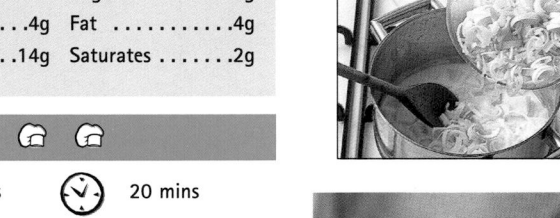

1 Cook the shredded cabbage in a pan of boiling salted water for 7–10 minutes. Drain thoroughly and set aside.

2 Meanwhile, in a separate pan, bring the milk to a boil and add the potatoes and leek. Reduce the heat and simmer for 15–20 minutes, or until they are cooked through.

3 Stir in the grated nutmeg and thoroughly mash the potatoes and leek together.

4 Add the drained cabbage to the mashed potato and leek mixture and mix well.

5 Spoon the mixture into a warmed serving dish, making a hollow in the center with the back of a spoon.

6 Pour the melted butter into the hollow and serve the colcannon immediately.

COOK'S TIP
There are many different varieties of cabbage, which produce hearts at varying times of year, so you can be sure of being able to make this delicious cabbage dish all year round.

Eggplant Bake

This is an unusual "back-to-front" dish, in that the eggplant is first baked in the oven, then cooked in a pan.

NUTRITIONAL INFORMATION

Calories	140	Sugars	.........5g
Protein	.........3g	Fat	..........12g
Carbohydrate	....6g	Saturates	.......1g

 10 mins   55 mins

SERVES 4

INGREDIENTS

2 medium eggplants

4 tbsp vegetable oil

1 medium onion, sliced

1 tsp white cumin seeds

1 tsp chili powder

1 tsp salt

3 tbsp unsweetened yogurt

½ tsp mint sauce

mint leaves, to garnish

1 Rinse the eggplants under cold running water and pat thoroughly dry with absorbent paper towels.

2 Place the eggplants side by side in an ovenproof dish or roasting pan. Bake in a preheated oven, 325°F/160°C, for 45 minutes. Remove the baked eggplants from the oven and let cool.

3 Using a teaspoon, scoop out the eggplant flesh and set aside.

4 Heat the vegetable oil in a heavy pan over low heat. Add the sliced onion and the white cumin seeds to the pan and cook, stirring constantly, for 1-2 minutes.

5 Add the chili powder, salt, yogurt, and mint sauce to the pan and stir well to combine.

6 Add the eggplant flesh to the onion and yogurt mixture and continue to cook over medium heat, stirring constantly, for about 5–7 minutes, or until all of the liquid has been absorbed and the mixture is quite dry.

7 Transfer the eggplant and yogurt mixture to a warmed serving dish.

8 Serve the eggplant bake immediately, garnished with the fresh mint leaves.

Potatoes Lyonnaise

In this classic French recipe, sliced potatoes are cooked with onions to make a delicious accompaniment to an entrée.

NUTRITIONAL INFORMATION

Calories	277	Sugars	........4g
Protein	.........5g	Fat	..........12g
Carbohydrate	...40g	Saturates	.......4g

 10 mins   25 mins

SERVES 6

INGREDIENTS

2¾ lb/1.25 kg potatoes

4 tbsp olive oil

2 tbsp butter

2 onions, sliced

2–3 garlic cloves, crushed (optional)

salt and pepper

chopped fresh parsley, to garnish

1 Slice the potatoes into ¼ inch/5 mm slices. Put in a large pan of lightly salted water and bring to a boil. Cover and simmer gently for about 10–12 minutes, until just tender. Avoid boiling too rapidly or the potatoes will break up and lose their shape. When cooked, drain well.

2 While the potatoes are cooking, heat the oil and butter in a very large skillet. Add the onions and garlic, if using, and cook over medium heat, stirring frequently, until the onions are soft.

3 Add the cooked potato slices to the skillet and cook with the onions and garlic, carefully stirring occasionally, for about 5–8 minutes until the potatoes are well browned.

4 Season to taste with salt and pepper. Sprinkle over the chopped parsley to serve. If wished, transfer the potatoes and onions to a large ovenproof dish and keep warm in a low oven until ready to serve.

COOK'S TIP
If the potatoes blacken slightly as they are boiling, add a spoonful of lemon juice to the cooking water.

Braised Belgian Endive

Belgian endive is a much underrated vegetable, yet it looks attractive and provides a refreshing, slightly bitter contrast to a rich entrée.

NUTRITIONAL INFORMATION

Calories 40	Sugars 2g
Protein 1g	Fat 3g
Carbohydrate 4g	Saturates 2g

15 mins   50 mins

SERVES 6

INGREDIENTS

2 cups vegetable bouillon

1 bay leaf

6 fresh parsley sprigs

2 fresh thyme sprigs

12 heads Belgian endive

4 tbsp lemon juice

6 tbsp fresh parsley leaves

5 tbsp light cream

salt and ground black pepper

1 Pour the bouillon into a large pan and bring to a boil. Tie the bay leaf, parsley, and thyme together, add to the pan, cover, and simmer for 10 minutes. Add the endive and lemon juice, cover again, and simmer for 20–25 minutes, until the endive is tender.

2 Transfer the endive to a warm serving dish and keep warm. Remove and discard the herbs. Bring the liquid back to a boil and continue to boil, uncovered, for about 15 minutes, until reduced to about ⁵/₈ cup.

3 Meanwhile, blanch the parsley leaves in boiling water for 1 minute, then drain and put in a food processor. Process until very finely chopped. With the motor running, gradually add the cooking liquid.

4 Transfer to a small pan, stir in the cream, and season to taste with salt and pepper. Heat through gently, but do not let the sauce boil. Pour the sauce over the endive and serve at once.

COOK'S TIP

To prepare Belgian endive, remove the core at the base with a sharp knife and cut off any wilted or damaged leaves.

Caramelized New Potatoes

This simple recipe is best served with a plainly cooked entrée, because it is fairly sweet and has delicious juices.

NUTRITIONAL INFORMATION

Calories	289	Sugars	........18g
Protein	.........3g	Fat	..........13g
Carbohydrate	...43g	Saturates	.......8g

 5 mins   20 mins

SERVES 4

INGREDIENTS

1½ lb/675 g new potatoes, scrubbed

4 tbsp dark brown sugar

5 tbsp butter

1 tbsp orange juice

1 tbsp chopped fresh parsley or cilantro

salt and pepper

orange zest curls, to garnish

1 Cook the new potatoes in a pan of boiling water for 10 minutes, or until almost tender. Drain thoroughly.

2 Melt the sugar in a large, heavy skillet over low heat, stirring constantly.

3 Add the butter and orange juice to the skillet, stirring the mixture constantly as the butter melts.

4 Add the potatoes to the orange and butter mixture and continue to cook, turning the potatoes frequently until they are completely coated in the caramel.

5 Sprinkle the chopped parsley or cilantro over the potatoes and season according to taste with salt and pepper.

6 Transfer to a serving dish, garnish with orange zest, and serve at once.

VARIATION
Lemon or lime juices may be used instead of the orange juice, if preferred. Garnish the finished dish with pared lemon or lime zest.

Garlic Mash

A delicious change from plain mash, serve this garlic mash with stuffed vegetables, casseroles, and stews.

NUTRITIONAL INFORMATION

Calories .... .347   Sugars 3g
Protein .... .6g   Fat .... .18g
Carbohydrate ...41g   Saturates ...... .12g

 15 mins   30 mins

SERVES 4

INGREDIENTS

2 lb/900 g mealy potatoes, cut into chunks

8 garlic cloves, crushed

¾ cup milk

6 tbsp butter

pinch of freshly grated nutmeg

salt and ground black pepper

1 Put the potatoes in a large pan. Add enough cold water to cover and a pinch of salt. Bring to a boil and cook for 10 minutes. Add the garlic and cook for 10–15 minutes more, until the potatoes are tender.

2 Drain the potatoes and garlic thoroughly, reserving 3 tablespoons of the cooking liquid.

3 Return the reserved liquid to the pan, add the milk, and bring to simmering point. Add the butter and return the potatoes and garlic to the pan. Mash thoroughly with a potato masher.

4 Season to taste with nutmeg, salt and pepper and beat the potato mixture with a wooden spoon until light and fluffy. Serve immediately.

VARIATION
Substitute light cream for the milk and 8 tablespoons extra virgin olive oil for the butter.

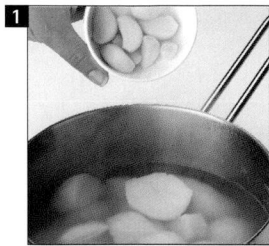

Fried Spiced Potatoes

Deliciously good and a super accompaniment to almost any entrée, although rather high in calories!

NUTRITIONAL INFORMATION

Calories	430	Sugars	.........7g
Protein	.........4g	Fat	..........35g
Carbohydrate	...26g	Saturates	......11g

 15 mins   30 mins

SERVES 6

INGREDIENTS

2 onions, quartered

2 inch/5 cm piece of ginger root, finely chopped

2 garlic cloves

2–3 tbsp mild or medium curry paste

4 tbsp water

1¾ lb/750 g new potatoes

vegetable oil, for deep frying

3 tbsp vegetable ghee or oil

⅔ cup strained Greek yogurt

⅔ cup heavy cream

3 tbsp chopped mint

salt and pepper

½ bunch scallions, chopped, to garnish

1 Place the onions, ginger, garlic, curry paste, and water in a blender or food processor and process until smooth.

2 Cut the potatoes into quarters and pat dry with paper towels. Heat the oil in a deep fryer to 350°F/180°C, or until a cube of bread browns in 30 seconds, and cook the potatoes, in batches, for about 5 minutes or until golden brown, turning frequently. Remove from the pan and drain on paper towels.

3 Heat the ghee or oil in a large skillet, add the curry and onion mixture, and cook gently, stirring constantly, for 2 minutes. Add the yogurt, cream, and 2 tablespoons of mint and mix well.

4 Add the fried potatoes and stir until coated in the sauce. Cook, stirring frequently, for 5–7 minutes, or until heated through and sauce has thickened.

5 Season with salt and pepper to taste and sprinkle with the remaining mint and sliced scallions. Serve at once.

COOK'S TIP
When buying new potatoes, look for the freshest you can find. The skin should be beginning to rub off. Cook them as soon after purchase as possible, but if you have to store them, keep them in a cool, dark well-ventilated place.

Chinese Potato Sticks

These potato sticks are a variation of the great Western favorite, flavored with soy sauce and chile.

NUTRITIONAL INFORMATION

Calories 326	Sugars 1g	
Protein 4g	Fat 22g	
Carbohydrate ...29g	Saturates 3g	

10 mins   15 mins

SERVES 4

INGREDIENTS

1½ lb/675 g medium potatoes

8 tbsp vegetable oil

1 fresh red chile, halved

1 small onion, quartered

2 garlic cloves, halved

2 tbsp soy sauce

pinch of salt

1 tsp wine vinegar

1 tbsp coarse sea salt

pinch of chile powder

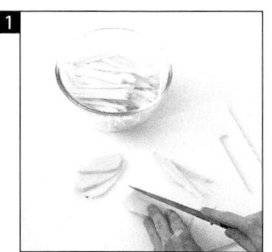

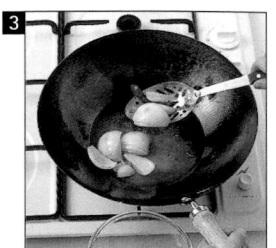

1 Peel the potatoes and cut into thin slices along their length. Cut the slices into very thin sticks.

2 Blanch the potato sticks for 2 minutes in a pan of boiling water. Drain, rinse under cold water, then drain well again. Pat the potato sticks thoroughly dry with paper towels.

3 Heat the vegetable oil in a preheated wok until it is almost smoking. Add the red chile, onion, and garlic to the wok and stir-fry for 30 seconds. Remove the chile, onion, and garlic with a slotted spoon and discard.

4 Add the potato sticks to the oil and cook for 3–4 minutes, or until golden.

5 Add the soy sauce, salt, and vinegar to the wok. Reduce the heat and cook for 1 minute, or until the potatoes are crisp, then remove them with a slotted spoon and let drain on paper towels.

6 Transfer the potato sticks to a serving dish. Sprinkle with the sea salt and chile powder and serve.

VARIATION

Sprinkle other flavorings, such as curry powder, over the cooked potato sticks, or serve with a chile dip.

Spicy Indian Potatoes

Indian cooking has many variations of spicy potatoes. In this recipe, spinach is added for both color and flavor.

NUTRITIONAL INFORMATION

Calories 65   Sugars 1.9g
Protein . . . . .2.5g   Fat 3.4g
Carbohydrate . . .6.5g   Saturates 0.4g

 10 mins   40 mins

SERVES 4

I N G R E D I E N T S

½ tsp coriander seeds

1 tsp cumin seeds

4 tbsp vegetable oil

2 cardamom pods

1 tsp fresh ginger root, grated

1 red chili, chopped

1 onion, chopped

2 garlic cloves, crushed

1 lb/450 g new potatoes, quartered

⅔ cup vegetable bouillon

1½ lb/675 g spinach, chopped

4 tbsp unsweetened yogurt

salt

1 Grind the coriander and cumin seeds using a pestle and mortar.

2 Heat the oil in a skillet. Add the ground coriander and cumin seeds to the skillet together with the cardamom pods and grated ginger and cook for about 2 minutes.

3 Add the chopped chili, onion, and garlic to the skillet. Cook for another 2 minutes, stirring frequently.

4 Add the potatoes to the skillet, together with the vegetable bouillon.

Cook gently for about 30 minutes or until the potatoes are cooked through, stirring occasionally.

5 Add the spinach to the skillet and cook for another 5 minutes.

6 Remove the skillet from the heat and stir in the yogurt. Season with salt and pepper to taste. Transfer the potatoes and spinach to a serving dish and serve.

VARIATION
Use frozen spinach instead of fresh spinach, if you prefer. Defrost the frozen spinach and drain it thoroughly before adding it to the dish, otherwise it will turn soggy.

Vegetable Medley

Serve this crisp and colorful vegetable dish as an accompaniment or as an entrée with pocket bread, chapatis, or naan.

NUTRITIONAL INFORMATION

Calories	190	Sugars	........17g
Protein	.........7g	Fat	..........7g
Carbohydrate	...27g	Saturates	......1g

10 mins   20 mins

SERVES 4

I N G R E D I E N T S

1 cup young, tender green beans

8 baby carrots

6 baby turnips

½ small cauliflower

2 tbsp vegetable oil

2 large onions, sliced

2 garlic cloves, finely chopped

300 ml/½ pint low-fat unsweetened yogurt

1 tbsp cornstarch

2 tbsp tomato paste

large pinch of chili powder

salt

1 Top and tail the beans and snap them in half. Cut the carrots in half and the turnips in quarters. Divide the cauliflower into florets, discarding the thickest part of the stalk. Steam the vegetables over boiling, salted water for 3 minutes, then turn them into a colander and plunge them at once in a large bowl of cold water to prevent further cooking.

2 Heat the vegetable oil in a skillet and sautée the onions until they are translucent. Stir in the garlic and cook for 1 further minute.

3 Mix together the yogurt, cornstarch, and tomato paste to form a smooth paste. Stir this paste into the onions in the skillet and cook for 1–2 minutes until the sauce is well blended.

4 Drain the vegetables well, then gradually stir them into the sauce, taking care not to break them up. Season with salt and chili powder to taste, cover, and simmer gently for 5 minutes, until the vegetables are just tender. Taste and adjust the seasoning if necessary. Serve immediately.

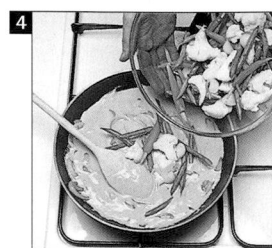

Peas with Baby Onions

This is a delightful dish with a subtle creamy flavor, and is perfect made with the first fresh peas of the season.

NUTRITIONAL INFORMATION

Calories	317	Sugars	.........6g
Protein	.........8g	Fat	..........23g
Carbohydrate	...22g	Saturates	......14g

🥄 20 mins 🕐 25 mins

SERVES 4

I N G R E D I E N T S

1 tbsp sweet butter

1 cup baby onions

2 lb/900 g fresh peas, shelled

½ cup water

2 tbsp all-purpose flour

⅔ cup heavy cream

1 tbsp chopped fresh parsley

1 tbsp lemon juice

salt and ground black pepper

1 Melt the butter in a large, heavy pan. Add the whole baby onions and cook, stirring occasionally, for 5 minutes. Add the peas and cook, stirring constantly, for a further 3 minutes, then add the measured water and bring to a boil. Lower the heat, partially cover, and simmer for 10 minutes.

2 Beat the flour into the cream. Remove the pan from the heat, stir in the cream mixture and parsley, and season to taste with salt and pepper.

3 Return the pan to the heat and cook, stirring gently but constantly, for about 3 minutes, until thickened.

4 Stir the lemon juice into the sauce and serve the peas immediately.

VARIATION
Substitute 2½ lb/1.125 kg young fava beans for the peas and cook as above.

Casseroled Potatoes

This delicious potato dish is cooked in the oven with leeks and wine. It is very quick and simple to make.

NUTRITIONAL INFORMATION

Calories 187   Sugars 2g
Protein . . . . .4g   Fat 3g
Carbohydrate . . .31g   Saturates 2g

 10 mins   50 mins

SERVES 4

I N G R E D I E N T S

1½ lb/675 g waxy potatoes, cut into chunks

1 tbsp butter

2 leeks, sliced

⅔ cup dry white wine

⅔ cup vegetable bouillon

1 tbsp lemon juice

2 tbsp chopped mixed fresh herbs

salt and pepper

T O   G A R N I S H

grated lemon zest

mixed fresh herbs, optional

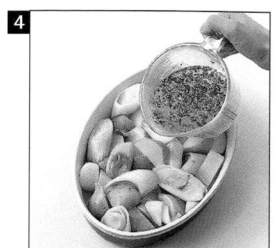

1 Cook the potato chunks in a pan of boiling water for 5 minutes. Drain them thoroughly.

2 Meanwhile, melt the butter in a skillet and sauté the leeks for 5 minutes or until they have softened.

3 Spoon the partly cooked potatoes and leeks into an ovenproof dish.

4 In a measuring pitcher, mix together the wine, vegetable bouillon, lemon juice, and chopped mixed herbs. Season to taste with salt and pepper, then pour the mixture over the potatoes.

5 Cook in a preheated oven, 375°F/ 190°C, for 35 minutes or until the potatoes are tender.

6 Garnish the potato casserole with lemon zest and fresh herbs, if using, and serve as an accompaniment to a casserole or vegetable bake.

COOK'S TIP

Cover the ovenproof dish halfway through cooking if the leeks start to brown on the top.

Lemony & Herby Potatoes

Choose from these two divine recipes for new potatoes. To check if new potatoes are fresh, rub the skin; the skin will come off easily if fresh.

NUTRITIONAL INFORMATION

Calories .... .226	Sugars 2g
Protein 5g	Fat 5g
Carbohydrate ...42g	Saturates 3g

20 mins   35 mins

SERVES 4

INGREDIENTS

LEMONY NEW POTATOES

2¼ lb/1 kg new potatoes

1 oz/25 g butter

1 tbsp finely grated lemon zest

2 tbsp lemon juice

1 tbsp chopped fresh dill or chives

salt and pepper

extra chopped fresh dill or chives,
   to garnish

HERBY NEW POTATOES

2¼ lb/1 kg new potatoes

3 tbsp light olive oil

1 tbsp white wine vinegar

pinch of dry mustard

pinch of superfine sugar

salt and pepper

2 tbsp chopped mixed fresh herbs,
   such as parsley, chives, marjoram,
   basil, and rosemary

extra chopped fresh mixed herbs, to garnish

1 For the Lemony New Potatoes, either scrub the potatoes well or remove the skins by scraping them off with a sharp knife. Cook the potatoes in plenty of lightly salted boiling water for about 15 minutes until just tender.

2 While the potatoes are cooking, melt the butter over low heat. Add the lemon zest, juice, and herbs. Season with salt and pepper.

3 Drain the cooked potatoes and transfer to a serving bowl.

4 Pour over the lemony butter mixture and stir gently to mix. Garnish with extra herbs and serve hot or warm.

5 For the Herby New Potatoes, prepare and cook the potatoes as described in step 1. Whisk the olive oil, vinegar, mustard, sugar, and seasoning together in a small bowl. Add the chopped herbs and mix well.

6 Drain the potatoes and pour over the oil and vinegar mixture, stirring to coat evenly. Garnish with extra fresh herbs and serve warm or cold.

Potatoes en Papillotes

New potatoes are perfect for this recipe. The potatoes and vegetables are wrapped in waxed paper and sealed, then steamed in the oven.

NUTRITIONAL INFORMATION

Calories	85	Sugars	4g
Protein	2g	Fat	0.5g
Carbohydrate	15g	Saturates	0.1g

 10 mins   35 mins

SERVES 4

INGREDIENTS

1 lb/450 g small new potatoes

1 carrot, cut into thin sticks

1 fennel bulb, sliced

½ cup green beans

1 yellow bell pepper, cut into strips

16 tbsp dry white wine

4 rosemary sprigs

salt and pepper

rosemary sprigs, to garnish

1 Cut 4 squares of waxed paper measuring about 10 inches/25 cm in size.

2 Divide the vegetables equally between the 4 paper squares, placing them in the center.

3 Bring the edges of the paper together and scrunch them together to encase the vegetables, leaving the top open.

4 Place the parcels in a shallow roasting pan and spoon 4 tablespoons of white wine into each parcel. Add a rosemary sprig and season.

5 Fold the top of each parcel over to seal it. Cook in a preheated oven, 375°F/190°C, for 30–35 minutes or until the vegetables are tender.

6 Transfer the sealed parcels to 4 individual serving plates and garnish with rosemary sprigs.

7 Open the parcels at the table for the full aroma of the vegetables to be appreciated.

COOK'S TIP

If small new potatoes are unavailable, use larger potatoes, halved or quartered to ensure that they cook through in the specified cooking time.

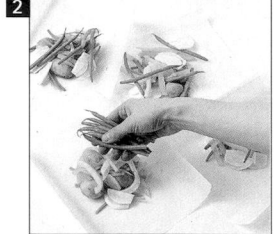

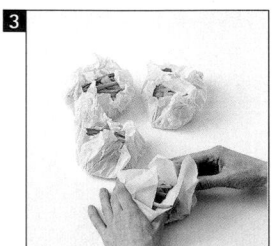

Trio of Potato Purées

These small molds filled with layers of flavored potato look very impressive. They are ideal with a vegetable casserole.

NUTRITIONAL INFORMATION

Calories	170	Sugars	.........5g
Protein	.........7g	Fat	...........6g
Carbohydrate	...24g	Saturates	......3g

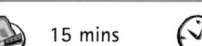 15 mins   🕐 1¼ hrs

SERVES 4

I N G R E D I E N T S

1 tbsp butter, plus extra for greasing

2½ cups mealy potatoes, chopped

1 cup rutabaga, chopped

1 carrot, chopped

1 lb/450 g spinach

1 tbsp skim milk

¼ cup all-purpose flour

1 egg

½ tsp ground cinnamon

1 tbsp orange juice

¼ tsp grated nutmeg

salt and pepper

carrot thin sticks, to garnish

1 Lightly grease four ²/₃ cup/150 ml ramekins with butter.

2 Cook the potatoes in a pan of boiling water for 10 minutes. In separate pans cook the rutabaga and carrot in boiling water for 10 minutes. Blanch the spinach in boiling water for 5 minutes. Drain the vegetables. Add the milk and butter to the potatoes and mash until smooth. Stir in the flour and egg.

3 Divide the potato mixture into 3 bowls. Spoon the rutabaga into one bowl and mix well. Spoon the carrot into the second bowl and mix well. Spoon the spinach into the third bowl and mix well.

4 Add the cinnamon to the rutabaga and potato mixture and season to taste. Stir the orange juice into the carrot and potato mixture. Stir the nutmeg into the spinach and potato mixture.

5 Spoon a layer of the rutabaga and potato mixture into each of the ramekins and smooth over the top. Cover each with a layer of spinach and potato mixture, then top with the carrot and potato mixture. Cover the ramekins with foil and place in a roasting pan. Half-fill the pan with boiling water and cook in a preheated oven, 350°F/180°C, for 40 minutes or until set.

6 Turn the molds out on to serving plates. Garnish with the carrot sticks and serve immediately.

Glazed Baby Onions

These onions are bathed in a rich, intensely flavored glaze, making them a good accompaniment to a nut roast.

NUTRITIONAL INFORMATION

Calories 81	Sugars 8g
Protein 1g	Fat 4g
Carbohydrate 11g	Saturates 1g

 10 mins   25 mins

SERVES 4–6

INGREDIENTS

1 lb/450 g baby onions

2 tbsp olive oil

2 large garlic cloves, crushed

1¼ cups vegetable bouillon

1 tbsp fresh thyme leaves

1 tbsp brown sugar

2 tbsp red wine vinegar

about 1½ tsp balsamic vinegar

salt and pepper

fresh thyme sprigs, to garnish

1 Put the baby onions in a large heatproof bowl, pour over enough boiling water to cover, and let stand for 2 minutes. Drain well.

2 Using a small knife and your fingers, peel off the skins, which should slip off easily.

3 Heat the olive oil in a large skillet over medium heat. Add the onions and cook, stirring constantly, for about 8 minutes until they are golden all over.

4 Add the garlic and cook, stirring, for 2 minutes. Add the bouillon, thyme leaves, sugar, and wine vinegar, stirring until the sugar has dissolved.

5 Bring to a boil, then lower the heat, and simmer gently for 10 minutes or until the onions are tender when you pierce them with the tip of a sharp knife and the cooking liquid is reduced to a syrupy glaze.

6 Stir in the balsamic vinegar. Season to taste with salt and pepper and add extra balsamic vinegar, if desired.

7 Transfer to a serving dish and serve the onions either hot or cold, garnished with fresh thyme sprigs.

VARIATION

For extra texture, stir in 2 tablespoons toasted pine nuts just before serving. Do not add them earlier or they will become soft.

Vegetables à la Grecque

A la Grecque is the French term for cooked vegetables left to cool in their highly flavored cooking liquid and then served cold.

NUTRITIONAL INFORMATION

Calories	67	Sugars	.........4g
Protein	.........2g	Fat	...........4g
Carbohydrate	....6g	Saturates	.......1g

 12¼ hrs   35–40 mins

SERVES 4–6

I N G R E D I E N T S

½ lb/225 g small pickling onions

½ lb/225 g mushrooms

½ lb/225 g zucchini

2 cups water

5 tbsp olive oil

2 tbsp lemon juice

2 strips lemon zest

2 large garlic cloves, thinly sliced

½ Spanish onion, finely chopped

1 bay leaf

15 black peppercorns, lightly crushed

10 coriander seeds, lightly crushed

pinch of dried oregano

finely chopped fresh flat-leaf parsley or cilantro, to garnish

focaccia, to serve

1 Put the small pickling onions in a heatproof bowl and pour over boiling water to cover. Let stand for 2 minutes, then drain. Peel and set aside.

2 Trim the mushroom stems. Cut the mushrooms into halves or quarters, if they are large, or leave whole if small. Trim the zucchini, cut off strips of the peel for a decorative finish, then cut into ¼ inch/5 mm slices. Set the mushrooms and zucchini aside.

3 Put the water, olive oil, lemon juice and zest, garlic, Spanish onion, bay leaf, peppercorns, coriander seeds, and oregano in a pan over high heat and bring to a boil. Lower the heat and simmer for 15 minutes.

4 Add the small onions and continue to simmer for 5 minutes. Add the mushrooms and zucchini and simmer for a further 2 minutes. Using a slotted spoon,

transfer all the vegetables to a heatproof dish or casserole.

5 Return the liquid to a boil and boil until reduced to about 6 tablespoons. Pour the liquid over the vegetables and let cool completely.

6 Cover with plastic wrap and chill for at least 12 hours.

7 To serve, put the vegetables and cooking liquid in a serving dish and sprinkle the fresh herbs over them. Serve with chunks of focaccia.

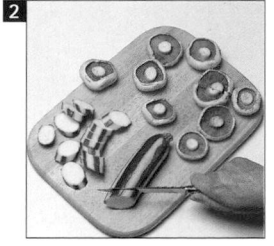

Chinese Vegetables

The Chinese are known for their colorful, crisp vegetables, quickly stir-fried. In this recipe, they are tossed in a tasty soy and hoisin sauce.

NUTRITIONAL INFORMATION

Calories	137	Sugars	.........7g
Protein	.........8g	Fat	..........7g
Carbohydrate	...10g	Saturates	......11g

5 mins   10 mins

SERVES 4

INGREDIENTS

2 tbsp peanut oil

4½ cups broccoli florets

1 tbsp chopped fresh ginger root

2 onions, each cut into 4 pieces

3 celery stalks, sliced

6 oz/175 g young spinach

1½ cups snow peas

6 scallions, quartered

2 garlic cloves, crushed

2 tbsp light soy sauce

2 tsp superfine sugar

2 tbsp dry sherry

1 tbsp hoisin sauce

⅔ cup vegetable bouillon

1 Heat the peanut oil in a preheated wok until it is almost smoking.

2 Add the broccoli florets, chopped ginger root, onions, and celery to the wok and cook for 1 minute.

3 Add the spinach, snow peas, scallions, and garlic and cook for 3–4 minutes.

4 Mix together the soy sauce, superfine sugar, sherry, hoisin sauce, and vegetable bouillon.

5 Pour the bouillon mixture into the wok, mixing thoroughly to coat all the vegetables.

6 Cover the wok and cook over medium heat for 2–3 minutes, or until the vegetables are cooked through, but are still crisp.

7 Transfer the Chinese vegetables to a warm serving dish and serve them immediately. If liked, use the vegetables to fill pancakes (see Cook's Tip, below.)

COOK'S TIP

You could use this mixture to fill Chinese pancakes. They are available from Chinese food stores and can be reheated in a steamer in 2–3 minutes.

Deep-Fried Zucchini

These crisp zucchini slices are so irresistible that you should always make more than you think you will need—they disappear very quickly!

NUTRITIONAL INFORMATION

Calories	299	Sugars	.........4g
Protein	.........4g	Fat	..........18g
Carbohydrate	...33g	Saturates	.......2g

 5 mins, plus standing   5 mins

SERVES 4

INGREDIENTS

5 tbsp cornstarch

1 tsp salt

pinch of cayenne pepper, or to taste

⅔ cup water

2 lb zucchini

vegetable oil, for frying

sea salt, to serve

fresh herb sprigs, such as basil, flat-leaf
   parsley, or sage, to garnish

1 Sift the cornstarch, salt, and cayenne pepper into a large mixing bowl and make a well in the center. Pour in the water and beat until just blended to make a thin batter. The batter may have a few lumps but this does not matter. Let stand for 20 minutes.

2 Meanwhile, cut the zucchini into ¼ inch slices. Heat the oil in a deep skillet or deep-fat fryer to 375°F/190°C or until a cube of bread sizzles in 20 seconds.

3 Stir the batter. Working in batches, put some zucchini slices in the batter and stir around until coated. Using a slotted spoon, remove the slices from the batter, shaking off the excess.

4 Drop the coated zucchini slices into the hot fat and cook for about 45–60 seconds, or until just golden brown on each side. Immediately remove from the fat and drain well on crumpled paper towels. Sprinkle with sea salt and keep warm if not serving straight away.

5 Repeat this process with the remaining slices. You can serve them garnished with a variety of herbs, according to what is available.

VARIATION
Cook red onion rings, coated with the batter.

Saffron Rice

This is the classic way to serve rice, paired with saffron, so that each brings out the best in the other.

NUTRITIONAL INFORMATION

Calories	63	Sugars	.......0.1g
Protein	........1.4g	Fat	...........2g
Carbohydrate	....11g	Saturates	.....0.2g

15 mins   25 mins

SERVES 8

INGREDIENTS

12 saffron threads, crushed lightly

2 tbsp warm water

1¾ cups water

1¼ cups basmati rice

1 tbsp toasted slivered almonds

1 Put the saffron threads into a bowl with the warm water and let stand for 10 minutes. They need to be crushed before soaking to ensure that the maximum flavor and color is extracted at this stage.

2 Put the water and rice into a medium pan and set it over the heat to boil. Add the saffron and saffron water and stir.

3 Bring back to a gentle boil, stir again, and let the rice simmer, uncovered, for about 10 minutes, until all the water has been absorbed.

4 Cover the pan tightly, reduce the heat as much as possible, and let stand for 10 minutes. Do not remove the lid. This ensures that the grains separate and that the rice is not soggy.

5 Alternatively, you can soak the rice overnight and drain thoroughly before cooking. Follow the cooking instructions in steps 2, 3, and 4, but reduce the cooking time by 3–4 minutes to compensate for the presoaking.

6 Remove the rice from the heat and transfer to a warmed serving dish. Fork through the rice gently and sprinkle over the toasted almonds before serving.

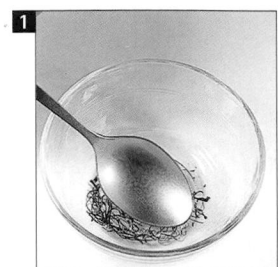

COOK'S TIP

Saffron, grown in Europe and the Middle East, is the most ancient of spices and continues to be the most expensive—literally worth its weight in gold. It is still harvested and sorted by hand and is a treasured commodity.

Ratatouille

This slow-cooked Provençal vegetable stew makes a delicious side dish, and is also lovely served with crusty bread to mop up the juices.

NUTRITIONAL INFORMATION

Calories 157	Sugars 11g	
Protein 4g	Fat 9g	
Carbohydrate . . .14g	Saturates 1g	

 40 mins   45 mins

SERVES 4–6

INGREDIENTS

1 large eggplant, about 10 oz/300 g

5 tbsp olive oil

2 large onions, thinly sliced

2 large garlic cloves, crushed

4 zucchini, sliced

4 cups canned chopped tomatoes

1 tsp sugar

1 bouquet garni of 2 fresh thyme sprigs, 2 large fresh parsley sprigs, 1 fresh basil sprig, and 1 bay leaf, tied in a 3 inch/ 7.5 cm piece of celery

salt and pepper

fresh basil leaves, to garnish

1 Coarsely chop the eggplant, then place in a colander. Sprinkle with salt and let stand for 30 minutes to drain. Rinse well under cold running water to remove all traces of the salt and pat dry with paper towels.

2 Heat the olive oil in a large heavy flameproof casserole over medium heat. Add the onions, lower the heat, and cook, stirring occasionally, for 10 minutes until soft and light golden brown.

3 Add the garlic and continue to cook for 2 minutes until the onions are very tender and lightly browned.

4 Add the eggplant, zucchini, tomatoes with their can juices, sugar, and bouquet garni. Season with salt and pepper to taste. Bring to a boil, then lower the heat to very low, cover, and simmer for 30 minutes.

5 Taste and adjust the seasoning if necessary. Remove and discard the bouquet garni. Garnish the vegetable stew with basil leaves and serve immediately.

COOK'S TIP

This is equally good served hot, at room temperature, or chilled. To make a vegetarian meal, serve it over cooked couscous or with tabbouleh.

Bean Curd Sandwiches

Slices of bean curd are sandwiched together with a cucumber and cream cheese filling and coated in batter.

NUTRITIONAL INFORMATION

Calories 398	Sugars 8g
Protein 13g	Fat 24g
Carbohydrate ...35g	Saturates 7g

 40 mins   15 mins

MAKES 28

INGREDIENTS

4 Chinese dried mushrooms (if unavailable, use thinly sliced open-cup mushrooms)

9½ oz/275 g bean curd

½ cucumber, grated

½ inch/1 cm piece ginger root, grated

4 tbsp cream cheese

salt and pepper

BATTER

1 cup all-purpose flour

1 egg, beaten

½ cup water

½ tsp salt

2 tbsp sesame seeds

vegetable oil for deep-frying

SAUCE

⅔ cup unsweetened yogurt

2 tsp honey

2 tbsp chopped fresh mint

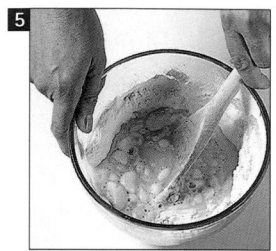

1 Place the dried mushrooms in a small bowl and cover with warm water. Let soak for 20–25 minutes.

2 Drain the mushrooms, squeezing out the excess water. Remove the tough centers and chop the mushrooms.

3 Drain the bean curd thoroughly and slice it thinly, then cut each slice to make 1 inch/2.5 cm squares.

4 Squeeze the excess liquid from the grated cucumber and then mix the cucumber with the mushrooms, grated ginger, and cream cheese. Season well with salt and pepper. Use as a filling to sandwich slices of bean curd together, making about 28 sandwiches.

5 To make the batter, sift the flour into a bowl. Beat in the egg, water, and salt to make a thick batter. Stir in the sesame seeds. Heat the oil in a wok. Coat the sandwiches in the batter and deep-fry in batches until golden. Remove and drain on absorbent paper towels.

6 To make the dipping sauce, combine the yogurt, honey, and mint. Serve with the bean curd sandwiches.

Coconut Potatoes

A colorful way to serve potatoes that is quick and easy to make.
Serve it with a spicy curry and cool, crisp salad greens.

NUTRITIONAL INFORMATION

Calories	93	Sugars	.......1.5g
Protein	........2.8g	Fat	.........4.8g
Carbohydrate	..10.3g	Saturates	.....4.0g

10 mins   15 mins

SERVES 4

INGREDIENTS

1½ lb/675 g potatoes

1 onion, thinly sliced

2 fresh red bird-eye chilies, finely chopped

½ tsp salt

½ tsp ground black pepper

3 oz/85 g creamed coconut

1½ cups vegetable bouillon

fresh cilantro or basil, chopped, to garnish

3 Bring to a boil, stirring, then lower the heat, cover the pan, and simmer gently, stirring occasionally, until the potatoes are tender.

4 Taste, and adjust the seasoning if necessary.

5 Transfer to a warm serving dish, sprinkle with chopped cilantro or basil, and serve immediately while hot.

1 Peel the potatoes thinly. Use a sharp knife to cut into ¾ inch/2 cm chunks.

2 Place the potatoes in a pan with the onion, chilies, salt, pepper, and creamed coconut. Stir in the bouillon.

COOK'S TIP
If the potatoes are thin-skinned, or a new variety, simply wash or scrub to remove any dirt and cook with the skins on. This adds extra dietary fiber and nutrients to the finished dish and cuts down on the preparation time. Baby new potatoes can be cooked whole.

Indonesian Onions

This is Indonesia's most popular garnish, but it also makes a tasty accompaniment to many vegetarian dishes.

NUTRITIONAL INFORMATION

Calories	76	Sugars	.........4g
Protein	.........1g	Fat	...........6g
Carbohydrate	....6g	Saturates	.......1g

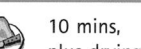

10 mins, plus drying   20 mins

SERVES 6

INGREDIENTS

1 lb/450 g small onions

groundnut or sunflower oil, for deep-frying

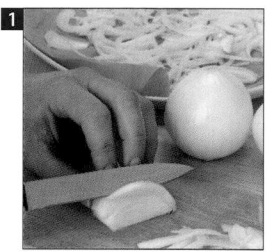 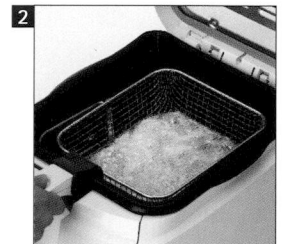 

1 Using a sharp knife, slice the onions as thinly and evenly as possible. Spread out the slices on paper towels in a well-ventilated place and let dry out for up to 2 hours.

2 Heat the oil in a wok or deep-fryer to 350–375°F/180–190°C or until a cube of bread browns in 30 seconds. Add the dried onion slices, in batches, and fry until crisp and golden.

3 Remove the onions with a slotted spoon and drain them on paper towels. Cook the remaining onion slices in the same way.

COOK'S TIP

It is important that the onions are well dried before frying or they will not become crisp. Small onions tend to be less watery than large ones.

Pesto Potatoes

Pesto sauce is more commonly used as a pasta sauce but is delicious served over potatoes as well.

NUTRITIONAL INFORMATION

Calories	531	Sugars	.........3g
Protein	.........13g	Fat	..........38g
Carbohydrate	...36g	Saturates	.......8g

 15 mins   15 mins

SERVES 4

I N G R E D I E N T S

2 lb/900 g small new potatoes

2¾ oz/75 g fresh basil

2 tbsp pine nuts

3 garlic cloves, crushed

½ cup olive oil

¾ cup freshly grated Parmesan cheese and romano cheese, mixed

salt and pepper

fresh basil sprigs, to garnish

1 Cook the potatoes in a pan of salted boiling water for 15 minutes or until tender. Drain well, transfer to a warm serving dish, and keep warm until required.

2 Meanwhile, put the basil, pine nuts, garlic, and a little salt and pepper to taste in a food processor. Blend for 30 seconds, adding the oil gradually, until the mixture is smooth.

3 Remove the mixture from the food processor and place in a mixing bowl. Stir in the grated Parmesan and romano cheeses and mix together.

4 Spoon the pesto sauce over the potatoes and mix well. Garnish with fresh basil sprigs and serve immediately.

Pepperonata

A delicious mixture of colorful bell peppers and onions,
cooked with tomatoes and herbs for a rich side dish.

NUTRITIONAL INFORMATION

Calories	206	Sugars	........19g
Protein	.........5g	Fat	..........12g
Carbohydrate	...21g	Saturates	.......2g

15 mins   40 mins

SERVES 4

INGREDIENTS

4 tbsp olive oil

1 onion, halved and finely sliced

2 red bell peppers, cut into strips

2 green bell peppers, cut into strips

2 yellow bell peppers, cut into strips

2 garlic cloves, crushed

4 cups canned chopped tomatoes, drained

2 tbsp chopped cilantro

2 tbsp chopped pitted black olives

salt and pepper

COOK'S TIP

Stir the vegetables occasionally
during the 30 minutes cooking
time to prevent them sticking to
the bottom of the pan. If the liquid
has not evaporated by the end of the
cooking time, remove the lid and boil
rapidly until the dish is dry.

1 Heat the olive oil in a large skillet.
Add the sliced onion and sauté for
5 minutes, stirring constantly, until just
beginning to color.

2 Add the red, green, and yellow bell
pepper strips and the crushed garlic
and cook for a further 3–4 minutes.

3 Stir in the tomatoes and chopped
cilantro and season to taste with salt
and pepper. Cover the skillet and cook the
vegetables gently for about 30 minutes or
until the mixture is dry.

4 Stir in the pitted black olives and
serve the pepperonata immediately.

Roasted Green Chilies

Mild chilies are cooked in a delicious garlic- and cumin-flavored cream sauce in this unusual side dish.

NUTRITIONAL INFORMATION

Calories 150	Sugars 5g	
Protein 5g	Fat 12g	
Carbohydrate 6g	Saturates 7g	

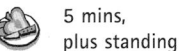 5 mins, plus standing 30 mins

SERVES 4–6

INGREDIENTS

4 large fresh mild green chilies, such as anaheim or poblano, or a combination of 4 green bell peppers and 2 jalapeños

2 tbsp butter

1 onion, finely chopped

3 garlic cloves, finely chopped

¼ tsp ground cumin

1 cup light cream

1 cup vegetable bouillon

salt and pepper

1 lime, halved, to serve

1 Roast the mild chilies, or the combination of bell peppers and jalapeños, in a heavy, ungreased skillet or under a preheated broiler until the skins are charred. Place in a plastic bag, twist to seal well, and let stand for 20 minutes to let the skins loosen.

2 Remove the seeds from the chilies and bell peppers, if using, and peel off the skins. Slice the flesh and set aside.

3 Melt the butter in a large skillet, add the onion and garlic, and sauté for about 3 minutes until soft. Sprinkle with the cumin and season with salt and pepper to taste.

4 Stir in the sliced chilies and pour in the cream and bouillon. Cook over medium heat, stirring constantly, until the liquid reduces in volume and forms a richly flavored sauce.

5 Transfer to a serving dish and serve warm, squeezing over lime juice at the last minute.

VARIATION
Add an equal amount of corn kernels with the chilies—they add a delicious sweetness to the dish.

Potatoes in Green Sauce

Earthy potatoes, served in a tangy spicy tomatillo sauce and topped with scallions and sour cream, are delicious.

NUTRITIONAL INFORMATION

Calories 61	Sugars 1.4g	
Protein 2g	Fat 1.4g	
Carbohydrate . .10.6g	Saturates 0.2g	

5 mins   25 mins

SERVES 5

INGREDIENTS

2¼ lb/1 kg small waxy potatoes

1 onion, halved and unpeeled

8 garlic cloves, unpeeled

1 fresh green chili

8 tomatillos, outer husks removed, or small
    tart tomatoes

1 cup vegetable bouillon

1 tsp ground cumin

1 fresh thyme sprig or generous pinch
    of dried thyme

1 fresh oregano sprig or generous
    pinch of dried oregano

2 tbsp vegetable or extra virgin
    olive oil

1 zucchini, coarsely chopped

1 bunch of fresh cilantro, chopped

salt

1 Put the potatoes in a pan of lightly salted water. Bring to a boil and cook for about 15 minutes or until almost tender. Do not overcook them. Drain and set aside.

2 Meanwhile lightly char the onion, garlic, chili, and tomatillos or tomatoes in a heavy, ungreased skillet. Let stand, and when cool enough to handle, peel and chop the onion, garlic, and chili. Chop the tomatillos or tomatoes. Put in a blender or food processor with half the bouillon and process to form a purée. Add the cumin, thyme, and oregano.

3 Heat the oil in the skillet. Add the purée and cook over medium heat, stirring constantly, for 5 minutes to reduce slightly and concentrate the flavors.

4 Add the potatoes and zucchini to the purée and pour in the remaining bouillon. Add about half of the chopped cilantro and cook for a further 5 minutes or until the zucchini is tender.

5 Transfer to a serving bowl and serve sprinkled with the remaining chopped cilantro to garnish.

Puff Potato Pie

This pie with its rich filling is a great alternative to serving potatoes as a side dish with any meal. Alternatively, serve with salad for a light lunch.

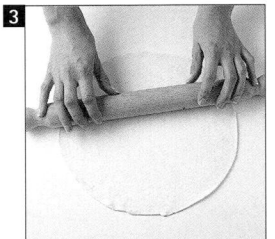

NUTRITIONAL INFORMATION

Calories	198	Sugars	.......1.4g
Protein	........3.7g	Fat	.........12.4g
Carbohydrate	..19.8g	Saturates	.....2.9g

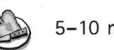 5–10 mins   50 mins

SERVES 6

INGREDIENTS

1½ lb/675 g potatoes, peeled and thinly sliced

2 scallions, finely chopped

1 red onion, finely chopped

⅔ cup heavy cream

1 lb/450 g fresh ready-made puff pie dough

2 eggs, beaten

salt and pepper

1 Bring a large pan of water to a boil, and add the sliced potatoes. Bring back to a boil and then simmer for a few minutes. Drain the potato slices and let cool. Dry off any excess moisture with paper towels.

2 In a bowl, mix together the scallions, red onion, and the cooled potato slices. Stir in 2 tablespoons of the cream and plenty of seasoning.

3 Divide the pie dough in half and roll out one piece to a 9 inch/23 cm round. Roll the remaining pie dough to a 10 inch/25 cm round.

4 Lightly grease a cookie sheet. Place the smaller pastry circle on to the cookie sheet and top with the potato mixture, leaving a 1 inch/2.5 cm border. Brush this border with a little of the beaten egg.

5 Top with the larger circle, then seal and crimp the edges. Cut a steam vent in the top of the pie and, using the back of a knife, mark with a pattern. Brush with beaten egg and bake in a preheated oven, 400°F/200°C, for 30 minutes.

6 Mix the remaining beaten egg and cream and pour into the pie through the steam vent. Return to the oven for 15 minutes, then let cool for 30 minutes.

Two Classic Salsas

A Mexican meal is not complete without an accompanying salsa. These two salsas are ideal for seasoning any traditional dish.

NUTRITIONAL INFORMATION

Calories	21	Sugars	. . . . .3g
Protein	. . . . .1g	Fat	. . . . .0g
Carbohydrate	. . . .4g	Saturates	. . . . . . .0g

 5 mins   0 mins

SERVES 4–6

I N G R E D I E N T S

JALAPEÑO SALSA

1 onion, finely chopped

2–3 garlic cloves, finely chopped

4–6 tbsp coarsely chopped pickled jalapeño chilies

juice of ½ lemon

about ¼ tsp ground cumin

salt

SALSA CRUDA

6–8 ripe tomatoes, finely chopped

about ½ cup tomato juice

3–4 garlic cloves, finely chopped

½–1 bunch fresh cilantro leaves, coarsely chopped

pinch of sugar

3–4 fresh green chilies, such as jalapeño or serrano, seeded and finely chopped

½–1 tsp ground cumin

3–4 scallions, finely chopped

salt

1 To make the jalapeño salsa, put the onion in a bowl with the garlic, jalapeños, lemon juice, and cumin. Season to taste with salt and stir together. Cover with plastic wrap and chill in the refrigerator until required.

2 To make a chunky-textured salsa cruda, stir all the ingredients together in a bowl and season with salt to taste. Cover with plastic wrap and chill in the refrigerator until required.

3 To make a smoother-textured salsa, process the ingredients in a blender or food processor until smooth. Scrape into a bowl, cover with plastic wrap, and chill as above.

Orange & White Coulis

Steaming is a healthy way to cook and is ideally suited to vegetables, as it helps to preserve valuable vitamins and minerals.

NUTRITIONAL INFORMATION

Calories	99	Sugars	........12g
Protein	.........3g	Fat	...........3g
Carbohydrate	...16g	Saturates	.......1g

 15 mins 10 mins

SERVES 4

I N G R E D I E N T S

ORANGE COULIS

⅔ cup freshly squeezed orange juice

2 cups carrots, thinly sliced

4 tbsp unsweetened yogurt or ricotta cheese

pinch of ground coriander

1 tsp lemon juice

salt and ground white pepper

WHITE COULIS

⅔ cup vegetable bouillon

2 cups parsnips, thinly sliced

4 tbsp unsweetened yogurt or ricotta cheese

pinch of freshly grated nutmeg

1 tsp lemon juice

salt and ground white pepper

1 To make the orange coulis, pour the orange juice into a small pan and bring to a boil. Place the carrots in a steamer on top of the pan, cover tightly, and steam for 10 minutes.

2 To make the white coulis, place the vegetable bouillon in a small pan and bring to a boil. Place the parsnips in a steamer on top of the pan, cover tightly, and steam for 10 minutes.

3 Transfer the carrots and orange juice to a blender or food processor and process to a smooth purée. Scrape into a bowl and stir in the unsweetened yogurt or ricotta cheese, ground coriander, and lemon juice and season to taste with salt and pepper.

4 Transfer the parsnips and bouillon to a blender or food processor and process to a smooth purée. Scrape into a bowl and stir in the unsweetened yogurt or ricotta cheese, nutmeg, and lemon juice and season to taste with salt and pepper.

5 Spoon the coulis decoratively on to serving plates and serve immediately.

VARIATION
To make a green coulis, steam a green vegetable, such as shredded cabbage or Brussels sprouts, over ⅝ cup vegetable bouillon, then process and combine with yogurt, 1 tbsp chopped fresh mint, and lemon juice, as above.

Chargrilled Vegetables

You can cook this colorful collection of vegetables under the broiler or on the grill. They look fabulous served with Salsa Verde.

NUTRITIONAL INFORMATION

Calories 172	Sugars 6g
Protein 2g	Fat 12g
Carbohydrate ...15g	Saturates 2g

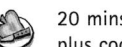

20 mins, plus cooling

15 mins

SERVES 6

INGREDIENTS

2 sweet potatoes, sliced

3 zucchini, halved lengthwise

3 red bell peppers, seeded and cut into quarters

olive oil, for brushing

salt

SALSA VERDE

2 fresh green chilies, halved and seeded

8 scallions, coarsely chopped

2 garlic cloves, coarsely chopped

1 tbsp capers

bunch of fresh parsley, coarsely chopped

grated zest and juice of 1 lime

4 tbsp lemon juice

6 tbsp olive oil

1 tbsp green Tabasco sauce

ground black pepper

COOK'S TIP

If using capers bottled in vinegar, rinse them before using. If using salted capers, simply brush them with your fingertips to remove some of the salt.

1 Cook the sweet potato slices in boiling water for 5 minutes. Drain and let cool. Sprinkle the zucchini with salt and let stand for 30 minutes. Rinse and pat dry with paper towels.

2 Meanwhile, make the salsa verde. Put the chilies, scallions, and garlic in a food processor and process briefly. Add the capers and parsley and pulse until finely chopped. Transfer the mixture into a serving bowl.

3 Stir in the lime zest and juice, lemon juice, olive oil, and Tabasco. Season to taste with pepper, cover with plastic wrap, and chill in the refrigerator until required.

4 Brush the sweet potato slices, zucchini, and bell peppers with olive oil and spread out on a broiler rack or grill. Broil, turning once and brushing with more olive oil, for 8-10 minutes, until tender and lightly charred. Serve the vegetables immediately with the salsa verde.

Vegetables in Coconut Milk

This is a deliciously crunchy way to prepare a mixture of raw vegetables and would be ideal as a buffet dish for a party.

NUTRITIONAL INFORMATION

Calories 201	Sugars 10g	
Protein 9g	Fat 13g	
Carbohydrate . . .13g	Saturates 3g	

5 mins

5 mins

SERVES 4

I N G R E D I E N T S

1 fresh red chili, seeded and chopped

1 tsp coriander seeds

1 tsp cumin seeds

2 garlic cloves, crushed

juice of 1 lime

generous 1 cup coconut milk

2 cups beansprouts

1 cup white cabbage, shredded

1½ cups snow peas, trimmed

1 cup carrots, thinly sliced

1 cup cauliflower florets

3 tbsp peanut butter

grated or shaved coconut, to serve

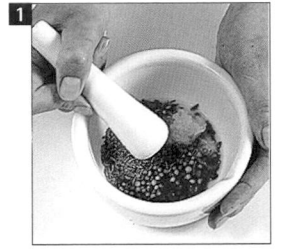

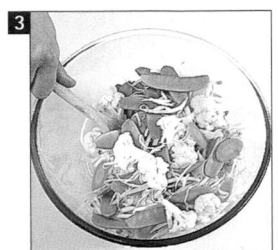

1 Grind the chili, coriander and cumin seeds, garlic, and lime juice in a mortar with a pestle or in a food processor until a smooth paste is formed.

2 Put the spice paste into a medium pan and heat gently for about 1 minute or until fragrant. Add the coconut milk and stir constantly until just about to boil.

3 Combine the beansprouts, shredded white cabbage, snow peas, sliced carrots, and cauliflower florets in a large mixing bowl.

4 Stir the peanut butter into the coconut mixture until well blended and then pour into the bowl, stirring to coat the vegetables. Serve garnished with grated or shaved coconut.

COOK'S TIP
If you prefer, the cauliflower, carrots, and snow peas may be blanched first for less bite.

Lightly Fried Bread

This is perfect with egg dishes and vegetable curries. Allow 2 portions of bread per person. The nutritional information is for each portion.

NUTRITIONAL INFORMATION

Calories 133   Sugars 1g
Protein ....3g   Fat 7g
Carbohydrate ...17g   Saturates 4g

 35 mins   20–25 mins

MAKES 10

INGREDIENTS

1¾ cups whole-wheat (ata or chapati) flour

½ tsp salt

1 tbsp ghee

1¼ cups water

1 Place the flour and the salt in a large mixing bowl and mix to combine.

2 Make a well in the center of the flour. Add the ghee and rub in well. Gradually pour in the water and work until a soft dough is formed. Let the dough rise for 10–15 minutes.

3 Carefully knead the dough for about 5–7 minutes. Divide the dough into about 10 equal portions.

4 On a lightly floured surface, roll out each dough portion to form a flat round shape.

5 Using a sharp knife, lightly draw lines in a criss-cross pattern on each rolled-out dough portion.

6 Heat a heavy skillet. Gently place the dough portions, one by one, into the skillet.

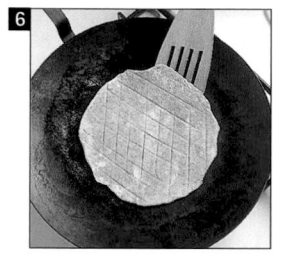

7 Cook the bread for about 1 minute, then turn over and spread with 1 teaspoon of ghee. Turn the bread over again and cook gently, moving it around the pan with a spatula, until golden brown. Turn the bread over once again, then remove from the pan and keep warm while you cook the remaining batches.

COOK'S TIP

In India, breads are cooked on a tava, a traditional flat griddle. A large skillet makes an adequate substitute.

Italian Potato Wedges

These oven-cooked potato wedges use classic pizza ingredients and are delicious served with a simple vegetable dish or with a dip.

NUTRITIONAL INFORMATION

Calories	115	Sugars	.........4g
Protein	.........6g	Fat	...........5g
Carbohydrate	...13g	Saturates	.......3g

 15 mins   35 mins

SERVES 4

I N G R E D I E N T S

2 large waxy potatoes, unpeeled

4 large ripe tomatoes, peeled and seeded

⅔ cup vegetable bouillon

2 tbsp tomato paste

1 small yellow bell pepper, cut into strips

4½ oz/125 g white mushrooms, quartered

1 tbsp chopped fresh basil

½ cup grated cheese

salt and pepper

1 Cut each of the potatoes into 8 equal wedges. Parboil the potatoes in a pan of boiling water for 15 minutes. Drain well and place in a shallow ovenproof dish.

2 Chop the tomatoes and add to the dish. Mix together the vegetable bouillon and tomato paste, then pour the mixture over the potatoes and tomatoes.

3 Add the yellow bell pepper strips, quartered mushrooms, and chopped basil. Season well with salt and pepper.

4 Sprinkle the grated cheese over the top and cook in a preheated oven, 375°F/190°C, for 15–20 minutes until the topping is golden brown. Serve at once.

Sauté of Summer Vegetables

The freshness of lightly cooked summer vegetables is enhanced by the aromatic flavor of a tarragon and white wine dressing.

NUTRITIONAL INFORMATION

Calories 217   Sugars 8g
Protein . . . . .2g   Fat 18g
Carbohydrate . . . .9g   Saturates 9g

10 mins   10–15 mins

SERVES 4

INGREDIENTS

½ lb/225 g baby carrots, scrubbed

1 cup string beans

2 zucchini, trimmed

1 bunch of large scallions

1 bunch of radishes

4 tbsp butter

2 tbsp light olive oil

2 tbsp white wine vinegar

4 tbsp dry white wine

1 tsp superfine sugar

1 tbsp chopped fresh tarragon

salt and pepper

fresh tarragon sprigs, to garnish

1 Cut the carrots in half lengthwise, slice the beans and zucchini, and halve the scallions and radishes, so that all the vegetables are cut to even-size pieces.

2 Melt the butter in a large, heavy skillet or wok. Add all the vegetables and cook them over medium heat, stirring frequently, until they are tender, but still crisp and firm to the bite.

3 Meanwhile, pour the olive oil, vinegar, and white wine into a small pan and add the sugar. Place over low heat, stirring until the sugar has dissolved. Remove the pan from the heat and then add the chopped tarragon.

4 When the vegetables are just cooked, pour over the "dressing." Stir through, tossing the vegetables well to coat. Season to taste with salt and pepper and then transfer to a warmed serving dish.

5 Garnish with sprigs of fresh tarragon and serve the sauté immediately.

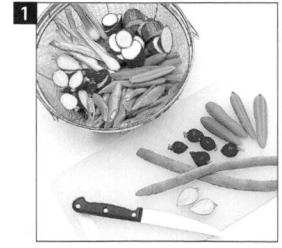

Rösti

This popular Swiss dish is a kind of crispy potato crêpe and is a great favorite with children—serve with vegetarian sausages and a salad.

NUTRITIONAL INFORMATION

Calories . . . . . . .267 Sugars 1g
Protein . . . . .5g Fat 11g
Carbohydrate . . .38g Saturates 6g

15 mins, plus cooling and chilling

30 mins

SERVES 4

INGREDIENTS

2 lb/900 g potatoes

2–4 tbsp sweet butter or
  vegetarian margarine

1–2 tbsp olive oil

salt and ground black pepper

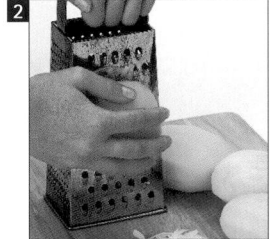

1 Cook the unpeeled potatoes in a pan of water for 10 minutes. Drain and let cool. Chill in the refrigerator for 30 minutes or longer.

2 Peel and coarsely grate the potatoes. Melt 2 tablespoons of the butter or margarine with 1 tablespoon of the olive oil in a heavy 9 inch/23 cm skillet over medium heat. Spread out the grated potato evenly in the skillet, lower the heat, and cook for 10 minutes.

3 Cover the pan with a plate and invert the pan and the plate. Slide the potato back into the pan to cook the second side. Cook for 10 minutes more, adding more butter and olive oil if necessary. Season to taste with salt and pepper and serve immediately.

COOK'S TIP
Chilling the parboiled potatoes is not essential, but it makes it much easier to grate them.

Honey-Fried Spinach

This stir-fry is the perfect accompaniment to bean curd dishes and it is wonderfully quick and simple to make.

NUTRITIONAL INFORMATION

Calories	146	Sugars	.........9g
Protein	.........4g	Fat	...........9g
Carbohydrate	...10g	Saturates	.......2g

 5 mins   15 mins

SERVES 4

INGREDIENTS

4 scallions

3 tbsp peanut oil

¾ lb/350 g shiitake mushrooms, sliced

2 garlic cloves, crushed

¾ lb/350 g young leaf spinach

2 tbsp dry sherry

2 tbsp honey

1 Using a sharp knife, thickly slice the scallions on the diagonal.

2 Heat the peanut oil in a large preheated wok or in a skillet with a heavy base.

3 Add the shiitake mushrooms to the wok or skillet and stir-fry for about 5 minutes or until soft.

4 Stir the crushed garlic into the wok or skillet. Add the baby leaf spinach and stir-fry for a further 2–3 minutes or until the spinach leaves have just begun to wilt.

5 Combine the dry sherry with the honey in a small bowl, stirring until thoroughly mixed. Drizzle the sherry and honey mixture over the spinach in the wok or skillet and heat through over low heat, stirring gently to coat the spinach leaves thoroughly in the mixture.

6 Transfer the stir-fry to warm serving dishes, scatter with the scallions, and serve immediately.

COOK'S TIP

Single-flower honey has a better, more individual flavor than blended honey. Acacia honey is typically Chinese, but you could also try clover, lemon blossom, lime flower, or orange blossom.

Broccoli & Black Bean Sauce

Broccoli works well with the black bean sauce and Napa cabbage in this recipe, while the almonds add extra crunch and flavor.

NUTRITIONAL INFORMATION

Calories 139	Sugars 3g
Protein 7g	Fat 10g
Carbohydrate 5g	Saturates 1g

🥔 5 mins   🕐 15 mins

SERVES 4

I N G R E D I E N T S

1 lb/450 g broccoli florets

2 tbsp sunflower oil

1 onion, sliced

2 garlic cloves, thinly sliced

¼ cup sliced almonds

1 head Napa cabbage, shredded

4 tbsp black bean sauce

1 Bring a large pan of water to a boil. Add the broccoli florets to the pan and cook for 1 minute. Drain, rinse in cold water to prevent any further cooking, and drain thoroughly again.

2 Meanwhile, heat the sunflower oil in a large preheated wok.

3 Add the onion and garlic slices to the wok and stir-fry until just beginning to brown.

4 Add the drained broccoli florets and the sliced almonds and stir-fry for a further 2–3 minutes.

5 Add the shredded Napa cabbage to the wok and stir-fry for a further 2 minutes.

6 Stir the black bean sauce into the vegetables, tossing to coat them thoroughly, and cook until the juices are just beginning to bubble.

7 Transfer the vegetables to warm serving bowls and serve immediately.

VARIATION
Use unsalted cashew nuts instead of the almonds, if preferred.

Crisp Pickled Vegetables

The fresh red chilies in this recipe ensure that these crisp pickled vegetables have a kick as well as a bite!

NUTRITIONAL INFORMATION

Calories 108   Sugars 5g
Protein . . . . .3g   Fat 7g
Carbohydrate . . . .5g   Saturates 1g

20 mins   10 mins

SERVES 6–8

I N G R E D I E N T S

½ small cauliflower

½ cucumber

2 medium carrots

1½ cups green beans

½ small Napa cabbage

2¼ cups rice vinegar

1 tbsp sugar

1 tsp salt

3 garlic cloves

3 shallots

3 bird's-eye red chilies

5 tbsp peanut oil

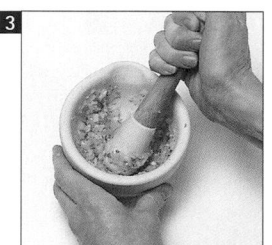

COOK'S TIP

To make simple carrot flowers, peel the carrot thinly as usual, then use a small sharp knife to cut narrow "channels" down the length of it at regular intervals. Slice the carrot as usual and the slices will resemble flowers.

1 Trim the cauliflower. Peel and seed the cucumber. Peel the carrots. Top and tail the beans. Trim the cabbage. Cut all the vegetables into bite-size pieces. If you have time, cut the carrots into flower shapes (see Cook's Tip, left.)

2 Place the rice vinegar, sugar, and salt in a large pan and bring almost to a boil. Add the vegetables, lower the heat, and simmer for 3–4 minutes until they are just tender, but still crisp inside. Remove the pan from the heat and let the vegetables and vinegar cool.

3 Peel the garlic and shallots and seed the chilies. Place in a mortar and pestle and grind until a smooth paste is formed.

4 Heat the oil in a wok and stir-fry the spice paste gently for 1–2 minutes. Add the vegetables with the vinegar and cook for an additional 2 minutes to reduce the liquid slightly.

5 Remove the wok from the heat and let the vegetables cool.

6 Serve cold, or pack into jars and store in the refrigerator for up to 2 weeks.

Chipotle Salsa

This garlicky chipotle and tomato salsa is incredibly quick to prepare, so if possible leave it until the last minute and serve it freshly made.

NUTRITIONAL INFORMATION

Calories	34	Sugars	.........5g
Protein	.........2g	Fat	..........0.5g
Carbohydrate	....6g	Saturates	.......0g

 10 mins   0 mins

MAKES ABOUT 12 CUPS

I N G R E D I E N T S

1 lb ripe juicy tomatoes, diced

3–5 garlic cloves, finely chopped

½ bunch fresh cilantro leaves, coarsely chopped

1 small onion, chopped

1–2 tsp adobo marinade from canned chipotle chilies

½–1 tsp sugar

lime juice, to taste

salt, to taste

pinch of cinnamon (optional)

pinch of ground allspice (optional)

pinch of ground cumin (optional)

1 Put the tomatoes, garlic, and cilantro in a blender or food processor.

2 Process the mixture until it is smooth, then add the onion, adobo marinade, and sugar.

3 Add the lime juice, and salt to taste. Add the cinnamon, allspice, or cumin, if desired.

4 Serve at once, or cover and chill until ready to serve. (Salsa is at its best when served freshly made.)

COOK'S TIPS
To simplify preparation, the fresh tomatoes can be replaced with 2 cups canned chopped tomatoes. Canned chipotle chilies are available from specialist Mexican stores.

Fennel with Tomatoes

Full of Italian flavors, this simple-to-prepare dish makes an excellent accompaniment for an extra special meal.

NUTRITIONAL INFORMATION

Calories	43	Sugars	. . . . .3g
Protein	. . . . .1g	Fat	. . . . .3g
Carbohydrate	. . . .4g	Saturates	. . . . . . .0g

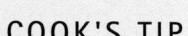

10 mins   25 mins

SERVES 6

I N G R E D I E N T S

2 fennel bulbs

1 tbsp olive oil

1 onion, thinly sliced

2 tomatoes, skinned and chopped

½ cup black olives, pitted

2 tbsp torn fresh basil leaves

ground black pepper

1 Cut off and chop the fennel fronds. Cut the bulbs in half lengthwise, then slice thinly.

2 Heat the oil in a heavy skillet. Add the onion to the skillet and cook over low heat, stirring occasionally, for 5 minutes, until soft.

3 Add the fennel slices and cook, stirring occasionally, for a further 10 minutes.

4 Increase the heat and add the tomatoes and olives. Cook, stirring frequently, for 10 minutes, then stir in the basil and season to taste with pepper.

5 Transfer the vegetables to a warm serving dish, garnish with the fennel fronds, and serve immediately.

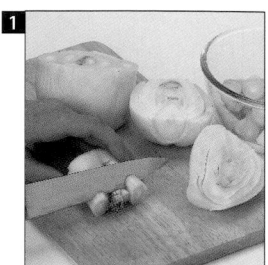

COOK'S TIP

Do not slice the fennel too much in advance, as the cut surfaces discolor on exposure to air. Alternatively, put the slices in a bowl of water acidulated with 2 tablespoons lemon juice and drain before using.

Braised Red Cabbage

A delicious sharp-sweet taste and an eye-catching color make this a vegetable accompaniment with attitude.

NUTRITIONAL INFORMATION

Calories 170	Sugars 28g
Protein 3g	Fat 4g
Carbohydrate ...29g	Saturates 0g

10 mins   55 mins

SERVES 6

I N G R E D I E N T S

2 tbsp sunflower oil

2 onions, thinly sliced

2 eating apples, peeled, cored, and thinly sliced

2 lb/900 g red cabbage, cored and shredded

4 tbsp red wine vinegar

2 tbsp sugar

¼ tsp ground cloves

½ cup raisins

½ cup red wine

2 tbsp redcurrant jelly

salt and ground black pepper

1 Heat the oil in a large, heavy pan. Add the onions and cook, stirring occasionally, for 10 minutes, until soft and golden. Stir in the apples and cook for 3 minutes.

2 Add the cabbage, vinegar, sugar, cloves, raisins, and red wine and season to taste with salt and pepper. Bring to a boil, stirring occasionally. Lower the heat, cover, and cook, stirring occasionally, for 40 minutes, until the cabbage is tender and most of the liquid has been absorbed.

3 Stir in the redcurrant jelly, transfer the red cabbage to a warm serving dish, and serve immediately.

COOK'S TIP

You can also braise the cabbage, in a preheated oven, 350°F/180°C, for about 1 hour.

Oven-Dried Tomatoes

The name may not have quite the same enticing ring to it as "sun-dried tomatoes," but the result is excellent!

NUTRITIONAL INFORMATION

Calories 81	Sugars 2g	
Protein 0.5g	Fat 8g	
Carbohydrate 2g	Saturates 1g	

15 mins   2½ hrs

MAKES 1 x 9 fl oz/250 ml JAR

INGREDIENTS

2¼ lb/1 kg large, juicy full-flavored tomatoes

sea salt

extra-virgin olive oil

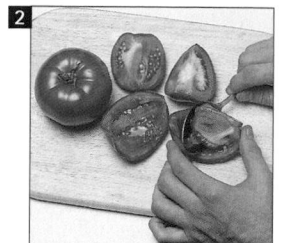

1 Using a sharp knife, cut each of the tomatoes into quarters lengthwise.

2 Using a teaspoon, scoop out the seeds and discard. If the tomatoes are large, cut each quarter in half lengthwise again.

3 Sprinkle sea salt in a roasting pan and arrange the tomato slices, skin-side down, on top. Roast in a preheated oven at 250°F/120°C for 2½ hours, or until the edges are just starting to look charred and the flesh is dry but still pliable. The exact roasting time and yield will depend on the size and juiciness of the tomatoes. Check the tomatoes at 30-minute intervals after 1½ hours.

4 Remove the dried tomatoes from the pan and let cool completely. Put into a 9 fl oz preserving jar and pour over enough olive oil to cover. Seal tightly, and store the tomatoes in the refrigerator for up to 2 weeks.

COOK'S TIP

Serve these oven-dried tomatoes with slices of buffalo mozzarella: drizzle with olive oil and sprinkle with coarsely ground black pepper and finely torn basil leaves.

Flavored Olives

You are sure to find Mediterranean stands selling all kinds of flavored olives. This nutritional analysis is based on a portion of 3 Provençal olives.

NUTRITIONAL INFORMATION

Calories	53	Sugars	.........0g
Protein	.........0g	Fat	...........6g
Carbohydrate	....0g	Saturates	.......1g

🍖

🥘 10–15 mins   🕐 0 mins

MAKES 1 x 2¼ CUPS

I N G R E D I E N T S

fresh herb sprigs, to serve

P R O V E N C A L O L I V E S

3 dried red chilies

1 tsp black peppercorns

2⅔ cups black Niçoise olives in brine

2 lemon slices

1 tsp black mustard seeds

1 tbsp garlic-flavored olive oil

fruity extra virgin olive oil

C A T A L A N O L I V E S

½ broiled red or orange bell pepper

1⅓ cups black olives in brine

1⅓ cups pimento-stuffed olives in brine

1 tbsp capers in brine, rinsed

pinch of dried chili flakes

4 tbsp chopped fresh cilantro leaves

1 bay leaf

fruity extra virgin olive oil

G R E E K O L I V E S

½ large lemon

2⅔ cups kalamata olives in brine

4 fresh thyme sprigs

1 shallot, very finely chopped

1 tbsp fennel seeds, lightly crushed

1 tsp dried dill

fruity extra virgin olive oil

1 To make the Provençal olives, place the dried red chilies and black peppercorns in a mortar, and lightly crush. Drain and rinse the olives, then pat dry with paper towels. Put all the ingredients in a 2¼ cup preserving jar, pouring in enough olive oil to cover.

2 Seal the jar and let stand for at least 10 days before serving, shaking the jar daily.

3 To make the Catalan olives, finely chop the bell pepper. Drain and rinse both types of olives, then pat dry with paper towels. Put all the ingredients into a 2¼ cup preserving jar, pouring in enough olive oil to cover. Seal and marinate as in Step 2.

4 To make the Greek olives, cut the lemon into 4 slices, then cut each slice into wedges. Drain and rinse the olives, then pat dry with paper towels.

5 Slice each olive lengthwise on 1 side down to the pit. Put all the ingredients in a 2¼ cup preserving jar, pouring in olive oil to cover. Seal and marinate as in Step 2.

6 To serve, spoon the olives into a bowl and garnish with fresh herbs.

Rouille

This is a great way to use up the remains of a good, country-style loaf—sliced white bread just won't give the same result.

NUTRITIONAL INFORMATION

Calories 40   Sugars 0.5g
Protein ....1g   Fat 3g
Carbohydrate ....3g   Saturates 0.5g

 10 mins   0 mins

MAKES ABOUT 175 g/ 6 oz

INGREDIENTS

2 slices day-old country-style white bread

2 large garlic cloves

2 small red chilies

pinch of salt

3 tbsp extra-virgin olive oil

1 tbsp tomato paste

cayenne pepper (optional)

pepper

1 Cut the crusts off the bread. Put the bread in a bowl, pour over water to cover, and let soak for 30 seconds, or until soft. Squeeze the bread dry, reserving 2 tablespoons of the soaking liquid.

2 Coarsely chop the garlic and chilies. Put them in a mortar with a pinch of salt and pound with a pestle until they form a paste.

3 Add the paste to the squeezed bread, then continue working in the mortar until the ingredients blend together. Transfer to a bowl and slowly add the olive oil, beating constantly. If you find the mixture begining to separate, add a little of the reserved soaking liquid and continue beating.

4 Add the tomato paste and cayenne pepper to taste. Adjust seasoning. Spread on croûtes and use to float on the surface of soup.

COOK'S TIP

If the sauce appears to be separating after it has stood for a while, stir in 1 tablespoon hot water. If it appears too thin to spread on croûtes, beat in a little extra soaked bread.

Greek Strained Yogurt

Genuine Greek or Greek-style strained yogurt is readily available in food stores, but it is much cheaper and more fun to make your own.

NUTRITIONAL INFORMATION

Calories	40	Sugars	.......0.5g
Protein	.........1g	Fat	...........3g
Carbohydrate	....3g	Saturates	.....0.5g

  15 mins, plus draining and standing   0 mins

MAKES ABOUT 2¼ CUPS

INGREDIENTS

4½ cups unsweetened yogurt

½ tsp salt, or to taste

OPTIONAL TOPPINGS

fruity extra-virgin olive oil

orange-blossom or lavender-flavored honey

finely grated lemon zest

coriander seeds, crushed

powdered paprika

very finely chopped fresh mint or cilantro

1 Place a 50 x 30 inch piece of cheesecloth in a pan, cover with water, and bring to a boil. Remove the pan from the heat and, using a wooden spoon, lift out the cheesecloth. Wearing rubber gloves, wring the cloth dry.

2 Fold the cloth into a double layer and use it to line a strainer set over a large bowl. Put the yogurt in a bowl and stir in the salt, then spoon it into the center of the cloth.

3 Tie the cloth so it is suspended above the bowl. If your sink is deep enough, gather up the corners of the cloth and tie it to the faucet. If not, lay a broom handle across 2 chairs and put the bowl between the chairs. Tie the cloth to the broom handle. Remove the strainer and let the yogurt drain into the bowl for at least 12 hours.

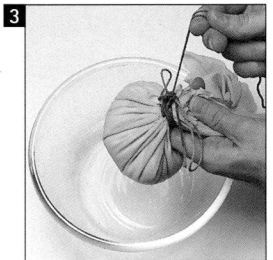

4 Transfer the thickened drained yogurt to a nylon strainer sitting over a bowl. Cover lightly with plastic wrap and keep in the refrigerator for another 24 hours until soft and creamy. This yogurt will keep refrigerated for up to 5 days.

5 To serve, taste and add extra salt if needed. Spoon the yogurt into a bowl and sprinkle with the topping of your choice, or a combination of toppings.

Cooked Chipotle Salsa

Unusually, this salsa is cooked. It uses dried chipotle chilies—be sure to read the warning in the Cook's Tip before you embark on this recipe!

NUTRITIONAL INFORMATION

Calories	102	Sugars	17g
Protein	2g	Fat	3g
Carbohydrate	19g	Saturates	0.5g

5 mins   30 mins

MAKES ABOUT 16 fl oz/450 ml

INGREDIENTS

3 dried chipotle chilies

1 onion, finely chopped

2 cups canned tomatoes, including their juices

2–3 tbsp dark brown sugar

2–3 garlic cloves, finely chopped

pinch of ground cinnamon

pinch of ground cloves or allspice

large pinch of ground cumin

juice of ½ lemon

1 tbsp extra-virgin olive oil

lemon zest strips, to garnish

1 Place the chilies in a pan with enough water to cover. Protecting your face against fumes and making sure the kitchen is well ventilated, bring the chilies and water to a boil. Cook for about 5 minutes, then remove from the heat, cover, and let stand until soft.

2 Remove the chilies from the water with a slotted spoon. Cut away and discard the stem and seeds, then either scrape the flesh from the skins or chop up the whole chilies.

3 Put the onions in a pan with the tomatoes and sugar and cook over medium heat, stirring, until thickened.

4 Remove from the heat and add the garlic, cinnamon, cloves, cumin, lemon juice, olive oil, and prepared chipotle chilies. Season with salt to taste and let cool. Serve the salsa garnished with lemon zest.

COOK'S TIPS

Do not inhale the fumes given off by the boiling chilies as they can irritate your lungs. This salsa freezes extremely well. Freeze in an ice-cube tray, then pop the cubes out and store in a plastic bag, ready to use for individual portions.

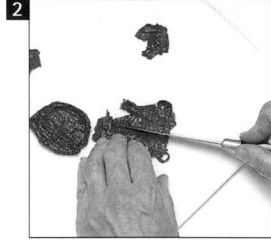  

Hot Mexican Salsas

These salsas capture the inimitable tangy, spicy flavor of Mexico. Choose from a fresh minty fruit salsa, charred chili salsa, or a spicy "green" salsa.

NUTRITIONAL INFORMATION

Calories	59	Sugars	.......12g
Protein	........1g	Fat	..........0g
Carbohydrate	...12g	Saturates	......0g

 10 mins   5 mins

SERVES 4–6

I N G R E D I E N T S

TROPICAL FRUIT SALSA

½–1 fresh green chili

½–1 fresh red chili

½ pineapple, peeled, cored, and diced

1 mango, peeled, pitted, and diced

½ red onion, chopped

1 tbsp sugar

juice of 1 lime

3 tbsp chopped fresh mint

salt

CHARRED CHILI SALSA

2–3 fresh green chilies

1 green bell pepper

2 garlic cloves, finely chopped

juice of ½ lime

1 tsp salt

2–3 tbsp extra virgin olive oil

pinch each dried oregano and ground cumin

SALSA VERDE

2 cups canned tomatillos, drained

1–2 fresh green chilies

1 green bell pepper, seeded and chopped

1 small onion, chopped

1 bunch fresh cilantro, finely chopped

½ tsp ground cumin

salt

1 To make the tropical fruit salsa, seed the green chili and chop both chilies. Combine all the ingredients in a large bowl and season with salt to taste. Cover the bowl with plastic wrap and chill in the refrigerator until required.

2 For the charred chili salsa, char the chilies and green bell pepper in an ungreased skillet. Cool, seed, peel, and chop. Combine the chilies and green bell pepper with the garlic, lime juice, salt, and oil in a bowl. Top with oregano and cumin.

3 For the salsa verde, drain and chop the tomatillos. Seed and finely chop the chilies and seed and chop the green bell pepper. Combine all the ingredients in a bowl and season with salt to taste. If a smoother sauce is preferred, blend the ingredients in a food processor, then spoon into a bowl to serve.

Marinated Chipotle Salsa

This fiery, spicy salsa will add a kick to all sorts of vegetarian dishes, and is of course perfect to serve as part of a Mexican menu.

NUTRITIONAL INFORMATION

Calories	84	Sugars	........13g
Protein	.........2g	Fat	...........2g
Carbohydrate	...15g	Saturates	.....0.5g

🍲 10 mins   🕐 35 mins

SERVES 4–6

I N G R E D I E N T S

6 dried chipotle chilies

6 tbsp tomato catsup

¾ lb/790 g ripe tomatoes, diced

1 large onion, chopped

5 garlic cloves, chopped

2 tbsp cider vinegar

1¼ cups water

1 tbsp extra-virgin olive oil

2 tbsp sugar, preferably molasses sugar

pinch of salt

¼ tsp ground allspice

¼ tsp ground cloves

¼ tsp ground cinnamon

¼ tsp ground cumin

3-4 tbsp lime juice or combination of pineapple and lemon juice

pepper

1 Place the chipotles in a pan with enough water to cover. Bring to a boil, taking care not to inhale the fumes given off as they can irritate your lungs. Simmer, covered, for 20 minutes, then remove from the heat and let cool.

2 Remove the chilies from the water. Cut away and discard the stem and seeds, then either scrape the flesh from the skins or chop up the whole chilies.

3 Place the catsup and tomatoes in a pan with the onion, chilies, garlic, vinegar, water, olive oil, sugar, salt, allspice, cloves, cinnamon, and cumin. Bring to a boil. Reduce the heat and simmer for about 15 minutes until the mixture has thickened.

4 Season with salt and pepper to taste, then stir in the fruit juice and use as required.

Fresh Pineapple Salsa

This sweet fruity salsa is fresh and fragrant, a wonderful foil to spicy dishes and perfect with food cooked on the grill.

NUTRITIONAL INFORMATION

Calories	37	Sugars	08
Protein	.........1g	Fat	..........0.5g
Carbohydrate	....8g	Saturates	.......0g

 15 mins 0 mins

SERVES 4

INGREDIENTS

½ ripe pineapple

juice of 1 lime or lemon

1 garlic clove, finely chopped

1 scallion, thinly sliced

½–1 fresh green or red chili, seeded and finely chopped

½ red bell pepper, seeded and chopped

3 tbsp chopped fresh mint

3 tbsp chopped fresh cilantro

pinch of salt

pinch of sugar

1 Using a long, sharp knife, cut off the top and bottom of the pineapple. Place the pineapple upright on a board, then slice off the skin, cutting downward. If any "eyes" still remain, cut them out with a small, pointed knife.

2 Cut the pineapple flesh into slices about ½ inch/1 cm thick, halve the slices, and remove the cores. Dice the flesh. Reserve any juice that accumulates as you cut the pineapple.

3 Place the pineapple and any juice in a bowl and stir in the lime juice, garlic, scallion, chili, and red bell pepper. Stir in the chopped fresh mint and cilantro. Add the salt and sugar and stir well to combine all the ingredients. Cover with plastic wrap and chill until ready to serve.

COOK'S TIP
A fresh pineapple is ripe if it has a sweet aroma. The flesh will still be fairly firm to touch. Fresh-looking leaves are a sign of good condition.

Mole Verde

This gorgeous Mexican sauce is based on toasted pumpkin seeds,
so it is as nutritious as it is tasty.

NUTRITIONAL INFORMATION

Calories	.319	Sugars	.6g
Protein	12g	Fat	.25g
Carbohydrate	12g	Saturates	.4g

10 mins   20 mins

SERVES 4

INGREDIENTS

2 cups toasted pumpkin seeds

4 cups vegetable bouillon

several pinches of ground cloves

8–10 tomatillos, diced, or use 1 cup
    mild tomatillo salsa

½ onion, chopped

½ fresh green chili, seeded and diced

3 garlic cloves, chopped

½ tsp fresh thyme leaves

½ tsp fresh marjoram leaves

3 tbsp vegetable oil

3 bay leaves

4 tbsp chopped fresh cilantro

salt and pepper

fresh green chili slices, to garnish

1 Grind the toasted pumpkin seeds in a food processor. Add half the vegetable bouillon, the cloves, tomatillos, onion, chili, garlic, thyme, and marjoram and blend to a purée.

2 Heat the oil in a heavy skillet and add the puréed pumpkin seed mixture and the bay leaves. Cook over medium-high heat for about 5 minutes until the mixture has thickened.

3 Remove from the heat and add the rest of the bouillon and the cilantro. Cook until it thickens, then remove from the heat.

4 Remove the bay leaves and process until smooth again. Add salt and pepper to taste.

5 Transfer to a bowl, garnish with chili slices, and serve.

VARIATION
Make a tamale dough and
poach in the mole as dumplings,
making a filling snack.

Mole Poblano

This great Mexican celebration dish, ladled out at fiestas, baptisms, and weddings, is known for its combination of chilies and chocolate.

NUTRITIONAL INFORMATION

Calories	152	Sugars	........10g
Protein	.........4g	Fat	...........8g
Carbohydrate	...17g	Saturates	.......1g

 20 mins   15 mins

SERVES 4

INGREDIENTS

3 mulato chilies

3 mild ancho chilies

5–6 New Mexico or California chilies

1 onion, chopped

5 garlic cloves, chopped

1 lb/450 g ripe tomatoes

2 tortillas, preferably stale, cut into
   small pieces

pinch of cloves

pinch of fennel seeds

⅛ tsp each ground cinnamon, coriander,
   and cumin

3 tbsp lightly toasted sesame seeds or
   sesame seed paste (tahini)

3 tbsp slivered or coarsely ground
   blanched almonds

2 tbsp raisins

1 tbsp peanut butter, optional

2 cups vegetable bouillon

3–4 tbsp grated dark chocolate, plus extra
   for garnishing

2 tbsp mild chili powder

3 tbsp vegetable oil

about 1 tbsp lime juice

salt and pepper

1 Using metal tongs, toast each chili over an open flame for a few seconds until the color darkens. Alternatively, roast the chilies in an ungreased skillet over medium heat, turning constantly, for about 30 seconds.

2 Place the toasted chilies in a bowl or a pan and pour boiling water over to cover. Cover and let soften for at least 1 hour or overnight. Once or twice lift the lid and rearrange the chilies so that they soak evenly.

3 Remove with a slotted spoon. Discard the stems and seeds and cut the flesh into pieces. Place in a blender.

4 Add the onion, garlic, tomatoes, tortillas, cloves, fennel seeds, cinnamon, coriander, cumin, sesame seeds, almonds, raisins, and peanut butter if using, then process to combine. With the motor running, add enough bouillon through the feed tube to make a smooth paste. Stir in the remaining bouillon, chocolate, and chili powder.

5 Heat the oil in a heavy pan until it is smoking, then pour in the mole mixture. It will splatter and pop as it hits theoil. Cook for about 10 minutes, stirring occasionally.

6 Season with salt, pepper, and lime juice, garnish with grated chocolate, and serve.

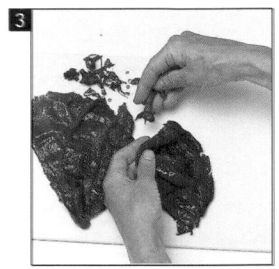

Hot Sauce of Dried Chilies

Preserved in an attractive bottle, this hot sauce would make an excellent gift for a chili-loving friend.

NUTRITIONAL INFORMATION

Calories	9	Sugars	.........1g
Protein	.........5g	Fat	...........5g
Carbohydrate	....1g	Saturates	.......0g

5 mins, plus cooling   5 mins

MAKES ABOUT 1 CUP

INGREDIENTS

10 dried arbol chilies, stems removed (see Cook's Tip)

1 cup cider or white wine vinegar

½ tsp salt

1 Place the chilies in a mortar and crush finely with a pestle.

2 Put the vinegar in a pan and add the chilies and salt. Stir to combine, then bring to a boil.

3 Remove from the heat and let cool and infuse. Pour into a bowl and serve. The sauce will keep for up to a month, covered, in the refrigerator.

COOK'S TIP

Arbol are dried long hot red chilies, with a dusty heat that is reminiscent of the Mexican desert. If arbol chilies are not available, use any hot dried chili, or chili flakes, such as cayenne.

Mild Red Chili Sauce

In this delicious recipe, the chilies are first roasted, either over a naked flame or under a broiler, to give them a delicious smoky flavor.

NUTRITIONAL INFORMATION

Calories . . . . .24 Sugars 0.5g
Protein . . . . .2g Fat 1g
Carbohydrate . . . .2g Saturates 0g

 10 mins, plus cooling   15 mins

MAKES ABOUT 1½ CUPS

I N G R E D I E N T S

5 large fresh mild chilies, such as New Mexico or ancho

2 cups vegetable bouillon

1 tbsp masa harina or 1 crumbled corn tortilla, puréed with enough water to make a thin paste

large pinch of ground cumin

1–2 garlic cloves, finely chopped

juice of 1 lime

salt, to taste

1 Using metal tongs, roast each chili over an open flame until the color darkens on all sides. Alternatively, place under a preheated broiler, turning them frequently. Do not let burn.

2 Put the chilies in a bowl and pour boiling water over them. Cover and let cool.

3 Meanwhile, put the bouillon in a pan and bring to a simmer.

4 When the chilies have cooled and are swelled up and softened, remove from the water with a slotted spoon. Remove the seeds from the chilies, then cut or tear the flesh into pieces and place in a blender or food processor. Process to form a purée, then mix in the hot bouillon.

5 Put the chili and bouillon mixture in a pan. Add the masa harina or puréed tortilla, cumin, garlic, and lime juice. Bring to a boil and cook for a few minutes, stirring, until the sauce has thickened. Adjust the seasoning and serve.

Hot Tomato Sauce

This fresh green chili and tomato sauce is an unusual accompaniment, but it is also good served as an appetizer with corn chips.

NUTRITIONAL INFORMATION

Calories	17	Sugars	........2g
Protein	.........1g	Fat	..........0.5g
Carbohydrate	....3g	Saturates	.......0g

5 mins   0 mins

SERVES 4

INGREDIENTS

2–3 fresh green chilies, such as jalapeño or serrano

1 cup canned chopped tomatoes

1 scallion, thinly sliced

2 garlic cloves, chopped

2–3 tbsp cider vinegar

¼–⅓ cup water

large pinch of dried oregano

large pinch of ground cumin

large pinch of sugar

large pinch of salt

1 Slice the chilies open, remove the seeds if desired, then chop the chilies.

2 Put the chilies in a blender or food processor together with the tomatoes, scallion, garlic, vinegar, water, oregano, cumin, sugar, and salt. Process until smooth.

3 Adjust the seasoning and chill until ready to serve. The sauce will keep for up to a week, covered, in the refrigerator.

COOK'S TIP

If you have sensitive skin, it may be advisable to wear rubber gloves when preparing chilies, as the oil in the seeds and flesh can cause irritation. Make sure that you do not touch your eyes when handling cut chilies.

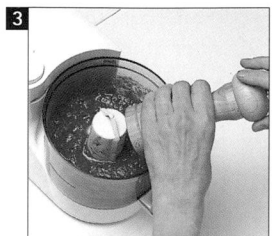

Quick Tomato Sauce

This tomato sauce is very quick and very versatile—it can be served over pasta or form the basis for spicy bean casseroles.

NUTRITIONAL INFORMATION

Calories	58	Sugars	.........3g
Protein	.........1g	Fat	...........6g
Carbohydrate	....5g	Saturates	.....0.5g

 5 mins   15 mins

SERVES 4–6

INGREDIENTS

2 tbsp vegetable or olive oil

1 onion, thinly sliced

5 garlic cloves, thinly sliced

2 cups canned tomatoes, diced, plus their juices, or 1½ lb/675 g fresh diced tomatoes

several shakes of mild chili powder

1½ cups vegetable bouillon

salt and pepper

pinch of sugar (optional)

1 Heat the oil in a large skillet. Add the onion and garlic and cook, stirring, until just softened.

2 Add the tomatoes, chili powder to taste, and the bouillon. Cook over medium-high heat for 10 minutes or until the tomatoes have reduced slightly and the flavor is more concentrated.

3 Season with salt, pepper, and sugar to taste and serve warm.

VARIATION
For a hotter kick, add a ½ teaspoon of finely chopped fresh chili with the onion.

Sesame Seed Chutney

This chutney is delicious served with spiced rice dishes and also makes an unusual filling to spread in sandwiches.

NUTRITIONAL INFORMATION

Calories 120   Sugars 0g
Protein . . . . .4g   Fat 12g
Carbohydrate . . .0.2g   Saturates 2g

10 mins   5 mins

SERVES 4

I N G R E D I E N T S

8 tbsp sesame seeds

2 tbsp water

½ bunch of fresh cilantro

3 fresh green chilies, chopped

1 tsp salt

2 tsp lemon juice

chopped fresh red chili, to garnish

1 Place the sesame seeds in a large, heavy pan and dry-roast them, stirring constantly. Set the sesame seeds aside and let cool.

2 Once cooled, place the sesame seeds in a food processor or mortar and grind well to form a fine powder.

3 Add the water to the ground sesame seeds and mix thoroughly to form a smooth paste.

4 Finely chop the cilantro. Add the chilies and cilantro to the sesame seed paste and grind again.

5 Add the salt and lemon juice to the mixture and grind once again.

6 Remove the mixture from the food processor or mortar and transfer to a serving dish. Garnish with chopped red chili and serve.

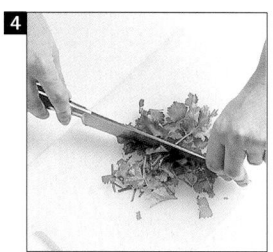

COOK'S TIP

Dry roasting brings out the flavor of spices and takes just a few minutes. You will be able to tell when the spices are ready because of the wonderful fragrance that develops. Stir the spices constantly to ensure that they do not burn.

Sautéed Eggplants

This makes a good alternative to a raita. The eggplants are sautéed until crisp, then given a baghaar, or seasoned oil dressing.

NUTRITIONAL INFORMATION

Calories	215	Sugars	.........4g
Protein	.........3g	Fat	..........21g
Carbohydrate	....5g	Saturates	.......2g

 5 mins   15 mins

SERVES 4

INGREDIENTS

1 cup unsweetened yogurt

5 tbsp water

1 tsp salt

1 medium eggplant

2/3 cup oil

1 tsp white cumin seeds

6 dried red chilies

1 Place the yogurt in a bowl and beat with a fork. Add the water and salt to the yogurt and mix well.

2 Using a sharp knife, slice the eggplant thinly.

3 Heat the oil in a large, heavy skillet. Add the eggplant slices and cook, in batches if necessary, over medium heat, turning occasionally, until they begin to turn crisp. Remove from the pan, drain on paper towels, transfer to a serving plate, and keep warm.

4 When all of the eggplant slices have been sautéed, lower the heat, and add the white cumin seeds and the dried red chilies to the skillet. Cook, stirring constantly, for 1 minute, then remove from the heat.

5 Spoon the thinned yogurt on top of the sautéed eggplant slices, then pour over the white cumin and red chili mixture. Serve immediately.

COOK'S TIP
Rich in protein and calcium, yogurt plays an important part in Indian cooking. It is used as a marinade, as a creamy flavoring in curries and sauces, and as a cooling accompaniment to hot dishes.

Raitas

Raitas are easy to prepare, very versatile, and have a cooling effect which will be appreciated if you are serving hot, spicy dishes.

NUTRITIONAL INFORMATION

Calories 33	Sugars 5g	
Protein 3g	Fat 0.4g	
Carbohydrate 5g	Saturates 0.3g	

 10 mins   5 mins

SERVES 4

INGREDIENTS

MINT RAITA

scant 1 cup low-fat unsweetened yogurt

¼ cup water

1 small onion, finely chopped

½ tsp mint sauce

½ tsp salt

3 fresh mint leaves, to garnish

CUCUMBER RAITA

½ lb/225 g cucumber

1 medium onion

½ tsp salt

½ tsp mint sauce

1¼ cups low-fat unsweetened yogurt

⅔ cup water

fresh mint leaves, to garnish

EGGPLANT RAITA

1 medium eggplant

1 tsp salt

1 small onion, finely chopped

2 fresh green chilies, seeded and finely chopped

scant 1 cup low-fat unsweetened yogurt

3 tbsp water

1 To make the mint raita, place the yogurt in a bowl and whisk with a fork. Gradually whisk in the water. Add the onion, mint sauce, and salt and blend together. Garnish with mint leaves.

2 To make the cucumber raita, peel and slice the cucumber. Chop the onion finely. Place the cucumber and onion in a large bowl, then add the salt and the mint sauce. Add the yogurt and the water, place the mixture in a blender, and blend well. Serve garnished with mint leaves.

3 To make the eggplant raita, remove the top end of the eggplant and chop the rest into small pieces. Boil in a pan of water until soft, then drain and mash. Add the salt, onion, and green chilies to the eggplant, mixing well. Whisk the yogurt with the water, add to the mixture, and mix thoroughly.

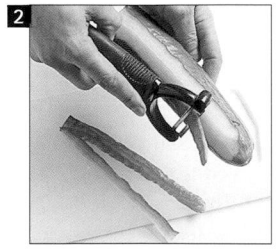

Tomato Salsa

This salad is used extensively in Mexican cooking and served as a dip or a relish, and is eaten as an accompaniment to almost any dish.

NUTRITIONAL INFORMATION

Calories	10	Sugars	.........2g
Protein	........0.4g	Fat	..........0.1g
Carbohydrate	....2g	Saturates	......0g

 10 mins   0 mins

SERVES 4

INGREDIENTS

4 ripe red tomatoes

1 medium red onion or 6 scallions

1–2 garlic cloves, crushed (optional)

2 tbsp chopped fresh cilantro

½ red or green chili (optional)

finely grated zest of ½–1 lemon or lime

1–2 tbsp lemon or lime juice

pepper

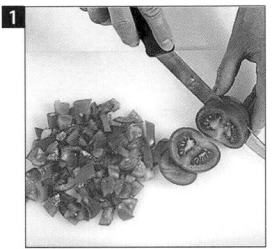

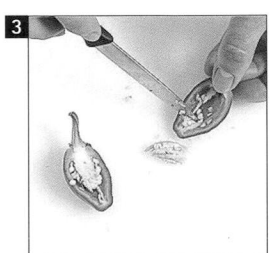

1 Chop the tomatoes fairly finely and evenly, and put into a bowl. They must be firm and a good strong red color for the best results, but if preferred, they may be peeled by placing them in boiling water for about 20 seconds and then plunging into cold water. The skins should then slip off easily when they are nicked with a knife.

2 Peel and slice the red onion thinly, or trim the scallions and cut into thin slanting slices; add to the chopped tomatoes with the garlic and coriander and mix lightly.

3 Remove the seeds from the red or green chili, chop the flesh very finely, and add to the salad. Treat the chilies with care; do not touch your eyes or face after handling them until you have washed your hands thoroughly. Chili juices can burn.

4 Add the lemon or lime zest and juice to the salsa, and mix well. Transfer the salsa to a serving bowl and sprinkle with pepper.

COOK'S TIP
If you don't like the distinctive flavor of fresh cilantro, you can replace it with flat-leaf parsley instead.

Desserts

As long as you are happy to include dairy foods in your vegetarian diet, the sky is the limit as far as desserts are concerned. In fact, many of the sumptuous desserts in this chapter are made from fresh and dried fruits, nuts, eggs, yogurt—good, wholesome foods, in fact, transformed into wonderful treats for when you have the urge for something indulgent. If you still have half a mind on your health, choose unrefined, organic ingredients where possible. These are all readily available in food stores—even chocolate! But whether you choose a healthy Creamy Fruit Parfait or a hearty Spiced Steamed Pudding—just enjoy it!

Mango Ice Cream

This delicious ice cream with its refreshing tang of mango and lime makes the perfect ending to a hot and spicy meal.

NUTRITIONAL INFORMATION

Calories	275	Sugars	........25g
Protein	.........2g	Fat	..........19g
Carbohydrate	...26g	Saturates	......11g

5¾ hrs   5 mins

SERVES 6

I N G R E D I E N T S

⅔ cup light cream

2 egg yolks

½ tsp cornstarch

1 tsp water

2 x 14 oz/400 g cans mango slices
in syrup, drained

1 tbsp lime or lemon juice

⅔ cup heavy cream

mint sprigs, to decorate

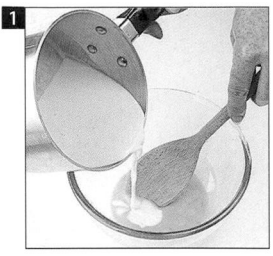
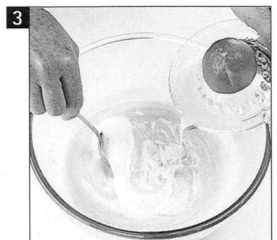
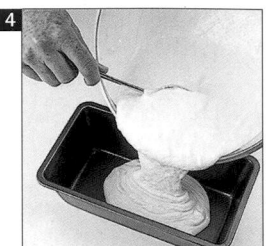

1 Heat the light cream in a pan until hot (but do not let it boil.) Place the egg yolks in a bowl with the cornstarch and water and mix together until smooth. Pour the hot cream on to the egg yolk mixture, stirring all the time.

2 Return the mixture to the pan and place over very low heat, whisking or stirring all the time, until the mixture thickens and coats the back of a wooden spoon. (Do not try and hurry this process or the mixture will overcook and spoil.) Pour into a bowl.

3 Process the mango slices in a blender or food processor until smooth. Mix with the custard and stir in the lime juice. Whip the heavy cream until softly peaking and fold into the mango mixture until thoroughly combined.

4 Transfer the mixture to a loaf pan or shallow freezerproof container. Cover and freeze for 2–3 hours, or until half-frozen and still mushy in the center. Turn the mixture into a bowl and mash well with a fork until smooth. Return to the container, cover, and freeze until firm.

5 Transfer the container of ice cream to the main compartment of the refrigerator for about 30 minutes before serving to let it soften slightly. Scoop or spoon the ice cream into serving dishes and decorate with mint sprigs.

COOK'S TIP

Use the drained mango syrup for adding to fruit salads or for mixing into drinks.

Ricotta Ice Cream

The ricotta cheese adds a creamy flavor, while the nuts add a crunchy texture. This ice cream needs to be chilled in the freezer overnight.

NUTRITIONAL INFORMATION

Calories 438   Sugars 39g
Protein . . . . .13g   Fat 25g
Carbohydrate . . .40g   Saturates 9g

🍨 20 mins   🕐 0 mins

SERVES 6

INGREDIENTS

⅓ cup pistachio nuts

⅓ cup walnuts or pecan nuts

⅓ cup toasted chopped hazelnuts

grated zest of 1 orange

grated zest of 1 lemon

2 tbsp candied or preserved ginger

2 tbsp candied cherries

¼ cup dried apricots

¼ cup raisins

1 lb ricotta

2 tbsp Maraschino, Amaretto or brandy

1 tsp vanilla extract

4 egg yolks

½ cup superfine sugar

TO DECORATE

whipped cream

a few candied cherries, pistachio nuts, or mint leaves

3 Stir the ricotta evenly through the fruit mixture, then beat in the liqueur and vanilla extract.

4 Put the egg yolks and sugar in a bowl and whisk hard until very thick and creamy. Use an electric hand whisk if you have one, otherwise whisking over a pan of gently simmering water speeds up the process. Let cool if necessary.

5 Carefully fold the ricotta mixture evenly through the beaten eggs and sugar until smooth.

6 Line a 7 x 5 inch/18 x 12 cm inch loaf pan with a double layer of plastic wrap or baking parchment. Pour in the ricotta mixture, level the top, cover with more plastic wrap or baking parchment, and freeze until firm—at least overnight.

7 To serve, remove the ice cream from the pan and peel off the paper.

8 Transfer the ice cream to a serving dish and decorate with whipped cream, candied cherries, pistachio nuts, and/or mint leaves. Serve in slices.

1 Roughly chop the pistachio nuts and walnuts and mix with the toasted hazelnuts, orange rind, and lemon zest.

2 Finely chop the candied or preserved ginger, cherries, apricots, and raisins, and add them to the bowl.

Potato & Nutmeg Biscuits

These have a slightly different texture from traditional biscuits, but they are just as delicious served warm and spread with butter.

NUTRITIONAL INFORMATION

Calories 135	Sugars 6g	
Protein 3g	Fat 4g	
Carbohydrate ...23g	Saturates 2g	

5 mins   25 mins

SERVES 8

INGREDIENTS

butter, for greasing

1⅓ cups diced mealy potatoes

⅓ cup all-purpose flour

1½ tsp baking powder

½ tsp grated nutmeg

⅓ cup golden raisins

1 egg, beaten

3 tbsp heavy cream

2 tsp soft light brown sugar

COOK'S TIP

For extra convenience, make a batch of biscuits in advance and open-freeze them. Thaw thoroughly and warm in a moderate oven when ready to serve.

1 Line and grease a cookie sheet. Cook the diced potatoes in a pan of boiling water for 10 minutes or until soft.

2 Drain and mash the potatoes, transfer to a large mixing bowl, and stir in the flour, baking powder, and nutmeg. Stir in the golden raisins, egg, and cream, and beat with a spoon until smooth.

3 Shape the mixture into 8 rounds, ¾ inch/2 cm thick, and place on the cookie sheet.

4 Cook in a preheated oven, 400°F/ 200°C, for about 15 minutes or until the biscuits have risen and are golden. Sprinkle the biscuits with sugar and serve warm, spread with butter.

Pear Tart

Pears are a very popular fruit in Italy. In this recipe from Trentino they are flavored with almonds, cinnamon, raisins, and apricot jam.

NUTRITIONAL INFORMATION

Calories	629	Sugars	........70g
Protein	.........7g	Fat	..........21g
Carbohydrate	..109g	Saturates	......13g

🍰🍰🍰

🍮 1½ hrs 🕐 50 mins

SERVES 6

INGREDIENTS

2 cups all-purpose flour

pinch of salt

½ cup superfine sugar

½ cup plus 1 tbsp diced butter

1 egg

1 egg yolk

few drops of vanilla extract

2–3 tsp water

strained confectioners' sugar, for sprinkling

FILLING

4 tbsp apricot jam

1 cup amaretti or ratafia cookies, crumbled

1¾–2¼ lb/850–1 kg pears, peeled and cored

1 tsp ground cinnamon

¾ cup raisins

4 tbsp soft brown or raw brown sugar

2 Using your fingers, gradually work the flour into the other ingredients to give a smooth dough, adding more water if necessary. Wrap in plastic wrap and chill for 1 hour or until firm. Alternatively, put all the ingredients into a food processor and process until the dough forms a smooth ball around the blade.

3 Roll out three-quarters of the dough and use to line a shallow 10 inch/25 cm cake pan or deep quiche pan. Spread the jam over the base and sprinkle with the crushed cookies.

4 Slice the pears very thinly. Arrange over the cookies in the pie shell.

Sprinkle with cinnamon, then with raisins, and finally with brown sugar.

5 Roll out a thin sausage shape using one-third of the remaining pie dough, and place around the edge of the pie. Roll the remainder of the pie dough into 8 or 10 thin sausages and arrange in a lattice over the pie, 4 or 5 strips in each direction, attaching them to the strip around the edge.

6 Cook in a preheated oven, at 400°F/200°C, for 50 minutes until golden and cooked through. Let cool, then serve warm or chilled, sprinkled with strained confectioners' sugar.

1 Sift the flour and salt on to a flat surface, make a well in the center, and add the sugar, butter, egg, egg yolk, vanilla extract, and most of the water.

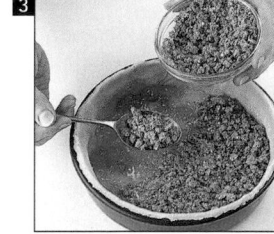

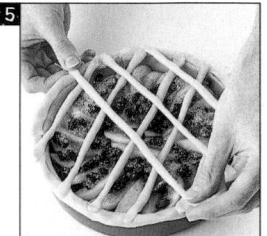

Eggless Sponge

This is a healthy, but still absolutely delicious variation of the classic sponge layer cake and is suitable for vegans.

NUTRITIONAL INFORMATION

Calories . . . . .273 Sugars 27g
Protein . . . . .3g Fat 9g
Carbohydrate . . .49g Saturates 1g

 1¼ hrs   30 mins

MAKES 1 X 8" CAKE

I N G R E D I E N T S

vegan margarine, for greasing

1¾ cups whole-wheat self-rising flour

2 tsp baking powder

¾ cup superfine sugar

6 tbsp sunflower oil

1 cup water

1 tsp vanilla extract

4 tbsp strawberry or raspberry
    reduced-sugar spread

superfine sugar, for dusting

1 Grease two 8-inch/20-cm layer pans and line them with baking parchment.

2 Sift the self-rising flour and baking powder into a large mixing bowl, stirring in any bran remaining in the strainer. Stir in the superfine sugar.

VARIATION

To make a chocolate-flavored sponge, replace 2 tablespoons of the flour with unsweetened cocoa. To make a citrus-flavored sponge, add the grated zest of ½ lemon or orange to the flour in step 2. To make a coffee-flavored sponge, replace 2 teaspoons of the flour with instant coffee powder.

3 Pour in the sunflower oil, water, and vanilla extract.

4 Mix well with a wooden spoon for about 1 minute until the mixture is smooth and combined, then divide among the prepared pans.

5 Bake in a preheated oven, 350°F/ 180°C, for 25–30 minutes or until the cakes spring back when lightly touched in the center.

6 Let the sponge cakes cool slightly in the pans before turning them out, then transfer to a wire rack and let cool completely.

7 Remove the baking parchment and place one sponge cake on a serving plate. Cover with the reduced-sugar spread and place the other sponge on top.

8 Dust the sponge cake with a little superfine sugar before serving.

Scottish Shortbread

Many recipes for shortbread contain rice flour; combined with all-purpose flour, it produces a delicate, crisp shortbread cookie.

NUTRITIONAL INFORMATION

Calories	164	Sugars	.........6g
Protein	.........2g	Fat	...........9g
Carbohydrate	...20g	Saturates	.......6g

10 mins   50–60 mins

MAKES 16 WEDGES

INGREDIENTS

2 cups all-purpose flour

½ cup rice flour

¼ tsp salt

¾ cup sweet butter, at room temperature

4 tbsp superfine sugar

3 tbsp confectioners' sugar, strained

¼ tsp vanilla extract (optional)

sugar, for sprinkling

2 Using an electric mixer, beat the butter for about 1 minute in a large bowl until creamy. Add the sugars and continue beating for 1–2 minutes until very light and fluffy. If using, beat in the vanilla.

3 Using a wooden spoon, stir the flour mixture into the butter and sugar until well blended. Turn on to a lightly floured counter and knead lightly to blend completely.

4 Divide the dough evenly between the 2 pans, smoothing the surface. Using a fork, press ¾ inch/2 cm radiating lines around the edge of the dough. Lightly sprinkle the surfaces with a little sugar, then prick the surface lightly with the fork.

5 Using a sharp knife, mark each dough round into 8 wedges. Bake in a preheated oven at 250°F/120°C for 50–60 minutes until pale golden and crisp. Cool in the pans on a wire rack for about 5 minutes.

6 Carefully remove the side of each pan and slide the bottoms on to a heatproof surface. Using the knife marks as a guide, cut each shortbread into 8 wedges while still warm. Cool completely on the wire rack, sprinkle with sugar, then store in airtight containers.

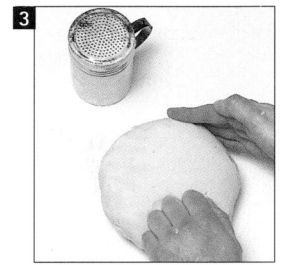

1 Lightly grease two 8–9 inch/20–23 cm cake or tart pans with removable bases. Sift the all-purpose flour, rice flour, and salt into a bowl and set aside.

Yogurt Cookies

Yogurt is a suitable alternative to buttermilk, providing just the acidity needed to produce perfect biscuits.

NUTRITIONAL INFORMATION

Calories 109	Sugars 5g	
Protein 3g	Fat 4g	
Carbohydrate . . .17g	Saturates 2g	

15 mins   10 mins

MAKES 16 SCONES

I N G R E D I E N T S

2 cups all-purpose flour, plus extra for dusting

1 tsp salt

1 tbsp baking powder

4 tbsp sweet butter, chilled, plus extra for greasing

5 tbsp sugar

1 egg

6 tbsp low-fat unsweetened yogurt

1 Sift together the flour, salt, and baking powder. Cut the butter into small pieces, and rub it into the dry ingredients until the mixture resembles dry bread crumbs. Stir in the sugar.

2 Beat together the egg and yogurt and stir it quickly into the dry ingredients.

Mix to form a thick dough and knead until it is smooth and free from cracks.

3 Lightly flour a pastry board or counter and rolling pin and roll out the dough to a thickness of ¾ inch/1.5 cm.

4 Cut out rounds with a 2 inch/5 cm dough cutter, gather up the trimmings, and roll them out again. Cut out as many more rounds as possible.

5 Grease a cookie sheet lightly with butter and heat it in the oven. Transfer the dough rounds to the sheet and dust lightly with flour.

6 Bake the cookies in the oven for 10 minutes, 350°F/180°C, or until they are well risen and golden brown.

7 Transfer the cookies to a wire rack to cool, but serve while still warm.

VARIATION

For spiced cookies add up to 1½ teaspoons ground ginger or cinnamon to the flour. For savory cookies, omit the sugar. At the end of step 1, stir in up to a scant ½ cup grated sharp Cheddar cheese.

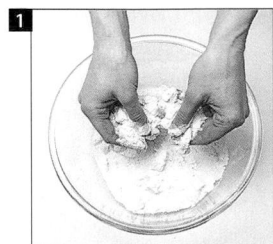 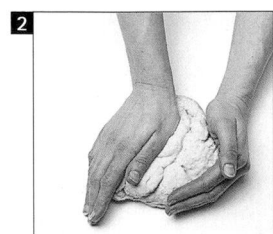 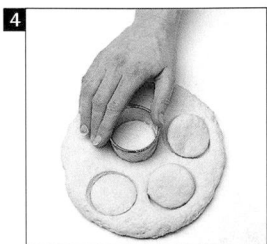

Carrot & Ginger Cake

This melt-in-your-mouth version of a favorite cake
has only a fraction of the fat of the traditional cake.

NUTRITIONAL INFORMATION

Calories 249	Sugars 28g	
Protein 7g	Fat 6g	
Carbohydrate ...46g	Saturates 1g	

 15 mins   1¼ hrs

SERVES 10

I N G R E D I E N T S

butter, for greasing

2 cups all-purpose flour

1 tsp baking powder

1 tsp baking soda

2 tsp ground ginger

½ tsp salt

¾ cup molasses sugar

1⅔ cups grated carrots

2 pieces chopped preserved ginger

1 tbsp grated fresh ginger root

generous ⅓ cup seedless raisins

2 eggs, beaten

3 tbsp corn oil

juice of 1 orange

F R O S T I N G

1 cup low-fat soft cheese

4 tbsp confectioners' sugar

1 tsp vanilla extract

T O   D E C O R A T E

grated carrot

finely chopped preserved ginger

ground ginger

1 Preheat the oven to 350°F/180°C. Grease and line an 8 inch/20 cm round cake pan with baking parchment.

2 Sift the flour, baking powder, baking soda, ground ginger, and salt into a bowl. Stir in the sugar, carrots, preserved ginger, fresh ginger root, and raisins. Beat together the eggs, oil, and orange juice, then pour into the bowl. Mix the ingredients together well.

3 Spoon the mixture into the pan and bake in the oven for 1–1¼ hours until firm to the touch or until a toothpick inserted into the center of the cake comes out clean.

4 To make the frosting, place the soft cheese in a bowl and beat to soften. Strain in the confectioners' sugar and add the vanilla extract. Mix well.

5 Remove the cake from the pan and smooth the frosting over the top. Decorate the cake and serve.

Fruity Muffins

The perfect choice for people on a low-fat diet,
these little cakes contain no butter, just a little corn oil.

NUTRITIONAL INFORMATION

Calories	162	Sugars	........11g
Protein	.........4g	Fat	...........4g
Carbohydrate	...28g	Saturates	......1g

 10 mins   30 mins

MAKES 10 MUFFINS

INGREDIENTS

2 cups self-rising whole-wheat flour

2 tsp baking powder

2 tbsp molasses sugar

¾ cup no-soak dried apricots,
  finely chopped

1 medium banana, mashed with 1 tbsp
  orange juice

1 tsp finely grated orange zest

1¼ cups skim milk

1 egg, beaten

3 tbsp corn oil

2 tbsp rolled oats

fruit spread, honey, or maple syrup, to serve

1 Place 10 paper muffin cases in a deep patty pan. Sift the flour and baking powder into a mixing bowl, adding any husks that remain in the strainer. Stir in the sugar and chopped apricots.

VARIATION

If you like dried figs, they make a deliciously crunchy alternative to the apricots; they also go very well with the flavor of orange. Other no-soak dried fruits, chopped finely, can be used as well.

2 Make a well in the center and add the banana, orange zest, milk, beaten egg, and oil. Mix together well to form a thick batter. Divide the batter evenly among the 10 paper cases.

3 Sprinkle with a few rolled oats and bake in a preheated oven, 400°F/ 200°C, for 25–30 minutes until well risen

and firm to the touch or until a toothpick inserted into the center comes out clean.

4 Transfer the muffins to a wire rack to cool slightly.

5 Serve the muffins while still warm with a little fruit spread, honey, or maple syrup.

Chocolate & Pineapple Cake

Decorated with thick yogurt and canned pineapple, this is a low-fat cake, but it is by no means lacking in flavor.

10 mins   25 mins

SERVES 9

INGREDIENTS

⅔ cup low-fat spread, plus extra for greasing

scant ¾ cup superfine sugar

generous ¾ cup self-rising flour, strained

3 tbsp unsweetened cocoa, strained

1½ tsp baking powder

2 eggs

8 oz/225 g can pineapple pieces in natural juice

½ cup low-fat thick unsweetened yogurt

about 1 tbsp confectioners' sugar

grated chocolate, to decorate

1 Lightly grease an 8 inch/20 cm square cake pan with a little low-fat spread.

2 Place the low-fat spread, superfine sugar, flour, unsweetened cocoa, baking powder, and eggs in a large mixing bowl. Beat with a wooden spoon or electric hand whisk until smooth.

3 Pour the cake mixture into the prepared pan and level the surface. Bake in a preheated oven, 325°F/190°C, for 20–25 minutes or until springy to the touch. Let the cake cool slightly in the pan before transferring to a wire rack to cool completely.

4 Drain and chop the pineapple pieces, then drain again. Reserve a little pineapple for decoration, then stir the remainder into the yogurt, and sweeten to taste with confectioners' sugar.

5 Spread the pineapple and yogurt mixture over the cake and decorate with the reserved pineapple pieces. Sprinkle with the grated chocolate.

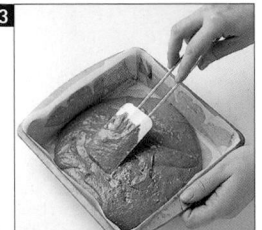

Coconut Bananas

This elaborate dessert is the perfect finale for a Chinese banquet.
Bananas are cooked in a citrus-flavored butter and served with coconut.

NUTRITIONAL INFORMATION

Calories	514	Sugars	........70g
Protein	.........4g	Fat	..........21g
Carbohydrate	...75g	Saturates	......14g

10 mins   10 mins

SERVES 4

INGREDIENTS

3 tbsp shredded fresh coconut

4 tbsp sweet butter

1 tbsp grated ginger root

grated zest of 1 orange

4 tbsp superfine sugar

4 tbsp fresh lime juice

6 bananas

6 tbsp orange liqueur (Cointreau or Grand
  Marnier, for example)

3 tsp toasted sesame seeds

lime slices, to decorate

ice cream, to serve (optional)

1 Heat a small, nonstick skillet until hot. Add the shredded coconut and cook, stirring constantly, for 1 minute until lightly colored. Remove the coconut from the pan and let cool.

2 Melt the butter in a large skillet and add the ginger, orange zest, sugar, and lime juice. Mix well.

3 Peel and slice the bananas in half lengthwise (and halve them again if they are very large.)

4 Place the bananas, cut-side down, in the butter mixture and cook for 1–2 minutes or until the sauce mixture starts to become sticky. Turn the bananas to coat thoroughly in the sauce.

5 Remove the bananas and sauce and place on heated serving plates. Keep warm.

6 Return the pan to the heat and add the orange liqueur, blending well. Ignite with a taper, let the flames die down, then pour the liqueur over the bananas.

7 Sprinkle with the reserved coconut and sesame seeds and serve at once, decorated with slices of lime.

COOK'S TIP

For a very special treat try serving this with a flavored ice cream such as coconut, ginger, or praline.

Banana & Lime Cake

A substantial cake that is ideal served with coffee. The mashed bananas help to keep the cake moist, and the lime frosting gives it extra zest.

NUTRITIONAL INFORMATION

Calories 235	Sugars 31g
Protein 5g	Fat 1g
Carbohydrate . . .55g	Saturates 0.3g

35 mins   45 mins

SERVES 10

INGREDIENTS

butter, for greasing

generous 2 cups all-purpose flour

1 tsp salt

1½ tsp baking powder

scant 1 cup light brown sugar

1 tsp lime zest, grated

1 egg, lightly beaten

1 banana, mashed with 1 tbsp lime juice

⅔ cup low-fat unsweetened yogurt

⅔ cup golden raisins

TOPPING

generous 1 cup confectioners' sugar

1–2 tsp lime juice

½ tsp finely grated lime zest

to decorate

banana chips

finely grated lime zest

1 Grease a deep round 7-inch/18-cm cake pan with butter and line with baking parchment.

2 Sift the flour, salt, and baking powder into a mixing bowl and stir in the sugar and lime zest.

3 Make a well in the center of the dry ingredients and add the egg, banana, yogurt, and golden raisins. Mix well until thoroughly incorporated.

4 Spoon the mixture into the pan and smooth the surface. Bake in a preheated oven, 350°F/180°C, for 40–45 minutes until firm to the touch or until a skewer inserted in the center comes out clean. Let cool in the pan for 10 minutes, then turn out onto a wire rack.

5 To make the topping, strain the sugar into a small bowl and mix with the lime juice to form a soft, but not too runny frosting. Stir in the grated lime zest. Drizzle the lime frosting over the top of the cake, letting it run down the sides too.

6 Decorate the cake with banana chips and lime zest. Before serving, let the cake stand for 15 minutes so that the frosting sets.

VARIATION
For a delicious alternative, replace the lime zest and juice with orange, and the golden raisins with chopped apricots.

White Chocolate Florentines

These attractive jeweled cookies are coated with white chocolate to give them a delicious flavor.

NUTRITIONAL INFORMATION

Calories 235	Sugars 20g
Protein 3g	Fat 17g
Carbohydrate ...20g	Saturates 7g

 20 mins   15 mins

SERVES 4

INGREDIENTS

¾ cup plus 2 tbsp butter

1 cup superfine sugar

1 cup walnuts, chopped

1 cup almonds, chopped

½ cup golden raisins, chopped

¼ cup candied cherries, chopped

¼ cup mixed candied peel, chopped finely

2 tbsp light cream

8 oz/225 g white chocolate

1 Line 3–4 cookie sheets with nonstick baking parchment.

2 Melt the butter over low heat and then add the sugar, stirring until it has dissolved. Boil the mixture for exactly 1 minute. Remove from the heat.

3 Add the chopped walnuts, almonds, golden raisins, candied cherries and peel, and the light cream to the pan, stirring well to mix.

4 Drop heaped teaspoonfuls of the mixture on to the cookie sheets, allowing plenty of room for them to spread while cooking. Bake in a preheated oven, at 350°F/180°C, for 10 minutes or until golden brown.

5 Remove the cookies from the oven and neaten the edges with a knife while they are still warm. Let the cookies cool slightly, then transfer them to a wire rack to cool completely.

6 Melt the chocolate in a bowl placed over a pan of gently simmering water. Spread the underside of the cookies with chocolate and use a fork to make wavy lines across the surface.

7 Let the Florentines stand on the wire rack until the chocolate has cooled completely, then store them in an airtight container, kept in a cool place.

COOK'S TIP

A combination of white and dark chocolate Florentines looks very attractive, especially if you are making them as gifts. Pack them in pretty boxes, lined with tissue paper and tied with some ribbon.

Florentine Twists

These famous and delicious Florentine biscuits are twisted into curls or cones and then just the ends are dipped in chocolate.

NUTRITIONAL INFORMATION

Calories 28   Sugars 15g
Protein ....1g   Fat 7g
Carbohydrate ...15g   Saturates 4g

20 mins   20 mins

MAKES 20

INGREDIENTS

6 tbsp butter

½ cup superfine sugar

½ cup blanched or flaked almonds, chopped roughly

¼ cup raisins, chopped

⅓ cup chopped mixed peel

⅓ cup candied cherries, chopped

¼ cup dried apricots, chopped finely

finely grated zest of ½ lemon or ½ small orange

about 4½ oz/125 g dark or white chocolate

1 Line 2–3 cookie sheets with non-stick baking parchment; then grease 4–6 cream horn molds, or a fairly thin rolling pin, or wooden spoon handles.

2 Melt the butter and sugar together gently in a pan and then bring to a boil for 1 minute. Remove the pan from the heat and stir in all the remaining ingredients, except for the chocolate. Let the mixture cool.

3 Put heaped teaspoonfuls of the mixture on to the cookie sheets, keeping them well apart, only 3–4 per sheet, and flatten slightly.

4 Bake in a preheated oven, at 350°F 180°C, for 10–12 minutes, or until golden. Let the biscuits cool until they begin to firm up. As they cool, press the edges back to form a neat shape. Remove each one with a spatula and wrap quickly around a cream horn mold, or lay over the rolling pin or spoon handles. If they become too firm to bend, return to the oven briefly to soften.

5 Let get cold and crisp and then slip carefully off the horn molds or remove from the rolling pin or spoons.

6 Melt the chocolate in a heatproof bowl over a pan of hot water, or in a microwave oven set on Full Power for about 45 seconds, and stir until smooth.

7 Either dip the end of each Florentine twist into the chocolate or, using a pastry brush, paint chocolate to come about halfway up the twist. As the chocolate sets, it can be marked into wavy lines with a fork. Let set completely.

Chocolate Brownies

You really can have a low-fat chocolate treat. These moist bars contain a dried fruit paste, which enables you to bake without adding any fat.

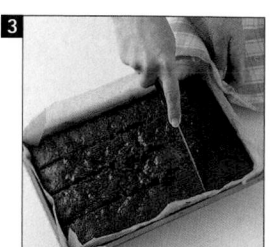

NUTRITIONAL INFORMATION

Calories	283	Sugars	........49g
Protein	.........5g	Fat	..........4g
Carbohydrate	...61g	Saturates	.......2g

 1¼ hrs   35–40 mins

MAKES 12

I N G R E D I E N T S

⅓ cup unsweetened pitted dates, chopped

⅓ cup no-soak dried prunes, chopped

6 tbsp unsweetened apple juice

4 medium eggs, beaten

2 cups dark brown sugar

1 tsp vanilla extract

4 tbsp low-fat drinking chocolate powder, plus extra for dusting

2 tbsp unsweetened cocoa

1½ cups all-purpose flour

⅓ cup dark chocolate chips

F R O S T I N G

¾ cup confectioners' sugar

1–2 tsp water

1 tsp vanilla extract

COOK'S TIP

Make double the amount, cut one of the cakes into bars and open freeze, then store in plastic bags. Take out pieces of cake as and when you need them—they'll take no time at all to thaw.

1 Preheat the oven to 350°F/180°C. Grease and line a 7 x 11 inch/18 x 28 cm cake pan with baking parchment. Place the chopped dates and prunes in a small pan and add the apple juice. Bring to a boil, cover, and simmer for 10 minutes until soft. Beat to form a smooth paste, then let cool.

2 Place the cooled fruit in a mixing bowl and stir in the eggs, sugar, and vanilla extract. Sift in 4 tablespoons of drinking chocolate, the cocoa, and the flour, and fold in along with the chocolate chips until well incorporated.

3 Spoon the mixture into the prepared pan and smooth over the top. Bake for 25–30 minutes until a skewer inserted into the center comes out clean. Cut into 12 bars and let cool in the pan for 10 minutes. Transfer to a wire rack to cool completely.

4 To make the frosting, strain the sugar into a bowl and mix with sufficient water and the vanilla extract to form a soft, but not too runny, frosting.

5 Drizzle the frosting over the chocolate brownies and allow to set. Dust with the extra chocolate powder before serving.

Rice Muffins

Italian rice gives these delicate muffins an interesting texture. They are delicious—and very indulgent—served with a swirl of Amaretto butter.

NUTRITIONAL INFORMATION

Calories	203	Sugars	.........6g
Protein	.........3g	Fat	..........12g
Carbohydrate	...20g	Saturates	.......7g

15 mins   15 mins

MAKES 12 MUFFINS

I N G R E D I E N T S

1 cup plus 2 tbsp all-purpose flour

1 tbsp baking powder

½ tsp baking soda

½ tsp salt

1 egg

2 tbsp honey

½ cup milk

2 tbsp sunflower oil

½ tsp almond extract

2¼ oz/60 g cooked arborio rice

2–3 amaretti biscuits, roughly crushed

A M A R E T T O   B U T T E R

½ cup sweet butter, at room temperature

1 tbsp honey

1–2 tbsp Amaretto liqueur

1–2 tbsp mascarpone

1 Sift the all-purpose flour, baking powder, baking soda, and salt into a large bowl and stir to combine. Make a well in the center.

2 In another bowl, beat the egg, honey, milk, oil, and almond extract with an electric mixer for about 2 minutes until light and foamy. Gradually beat in the rice.

Pour into the well and, using a fork, stir lightly until just combined. Do not over beat; the mixture can be slightly lumpy.

3 Spoon the batter into a lightly greased 12-cup muffin pan or two 6-cup pans. Sprinkle each muffin with some of the amaretti crumbs and bake in a preheated oven at 400°F/200°C for about 15 minutes until risen and golden; the tops of the muffins should spring back lightly when pressed.

4 Cool in the pans on a wire rack for about 1 minute. Carefully remove the muffins and cool slightly.

5 To make the Amaretto butter, put the butter and honey in a small bowl and beat until creamy. Add the Amaretto and mascarpone and beat together. Spoon into a small serving bowl and serve with the warm muffins.

COOK'S TIP
Use paper liners to line the muffin pan cups to avoid sticking.

Christmas Shortbread

Make this wonderful shortbread and then give it the Christmas touch by cutting it into shapes with seasonal cookie cutters.

NUTRITIONAL INFORMATION

Calories 162   Sugars 10g
Protein ....1g   Fat 9g
Carbohydrate ...21g   Saturates 6g

45 mins   15 mins

MAKES 24

INGREDIENTS

½ cup superfine sugar

1 cup butter

3 cups all-purpose flour, strained

pinch of salt

TO DECORATE

6 tbsp confectioners' sugar

silver balls

candied cherries

angelica

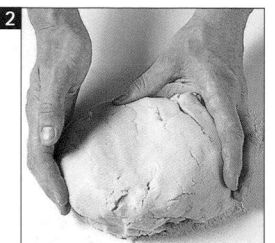
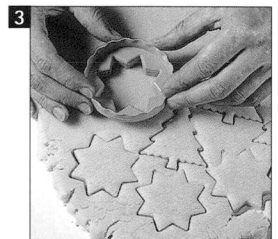

1 Beat the sugar and butter together in a large bowl until they are combined (thorough creaming is not necessary.)

2 Sift in the flour and salt and work together to form a stiff dough. Turn out on to a lightly floured surface. Knead lightly for a few moments until smooth, but avoid overhandling. Chill in the refrigerator for 10–15 minutes.

3 Roll out the shortbread dough on a lightly floured work surface and cut into shapes with small Christmas cutters, such as bells, stars, and angels. Place on greased cookie sheets.

4 Bake the cookies in a preheated oven, 350°F/180°C for 10–15 minutes, until pale golden brown. Let cool on the cookie sheets for 10 minutes, then transfer to wire racks to cool completely.

5 Sift the confectioners' sugar, mix it with a little water to make a glacé frosting, and use to frost the cookies.

6 Decorate the frosted cookies with silver balls and tiny pieces of candied cherries and angelica.

7 Store in an airtight container or wrap the cookies individually in cellophane, tie them with colored ribbon or string, and then hang them on the Christmas tree as edible decorations.

Christmas Tree Clusters

Popcorn is the perfect nibble to have around at Christmas. If wrapped in cellophane, these clusters make ideal decorations for the Christmas tree.

NUTRITIONAL INFORMATION

Calories	94	Sugars	.......14g
Protein	........1g	Fat	..........4g
Carbohydrate	...15g	Saturates	.....0.3g

10 mins   10 mins

MAKES 16

INGREDIENTS

1 tbsp vegetable oil

2 tbsp unpopped corn

2 tbsp butter

4 tbsp light brown sugar

4 tbsp light corn syrup

1 oz/25 g candied cherries, chopped

½ cup golden raisins or raisins

⅓ cup ground almonds

1 tbsp nibbed almonds

½ tsp ground apple spice

1 To pop the corn, heat the vegetable oil in a large pan or in a popcorn pan. The oil is hot enough when a kernel spins around in the pan. Add the unpopped corn, cover tightly, and pop the corn over medium-high heat, shaking the pan frequently.

2 Remove the pan from the heat but do not remove the lid until the popping sound subsides.

3 Put the butter, sugar, and syrup into a large pan and heat gently, stirring frequently, to dissolve the sugar. Do not let the mixture boil. Remove from the heat once the sugar is dissolved.

4 Add the popped corn, candied cherries, golden raisins or raisins, ground almonds and nibbed almonds, and apple spice to the syrup mixture, stirring well to coat the ingredients thoroughly. Let cool for a few minutes.

5 Shape the mixture into small balls. Let the balls cool completely, then wrap them in cellophane and tie with coloured ribbon or string and hang from the Christmas tree.

VARIATION
Omit the cherries, golden raisins, ground almonds, and apple spice and replace with ½ cup roughly chopped pecan nuts and ½ tsp ground cinnamon to make Pecan Nut Clusters.

Christmas Rice Crêpes

These delicious crêpes are almost like little rice desserts scented with Christmas mincemeat. Serve them with a rum-flavored custard.

NUTRITIONAL INFORMATION

Calories 121	Sugars 13g	
Protein 2g	Fat 5g	
Carbohydrate . . .18g	Saturates 2g	

15 mins, plus cooling

45 mins

MAKES ABOUT 24 PANCAKES

I N G R E D I E N T S

3 cups milk

salt

½ cup long-grain white rice

1 cinnamon stick

5 tbsp sugar

⅓ cup all-purpose flour

1 tsp baking powder

¾ tsp baking soda

2 eggs, beaten

½ cup sour cream

2 tbsp dark rum

1 tsp vanilla extract

½ tsp almond extract

2 tbsp butter, melted

12 oz/350 g homemade or bought mincemeat

melted butter, for cooking

ground cinnamon, for dusting

1 To make the crêpes, bring the milk to a boil in a pan. Add a pinch of salt and sprinkle in the rice. Add the cinnamon stick and simmer gently for 35 minutes or until the rice is tender and the milk is almost absorbed.

2 Remove from the heat, add the sugar, and stir until dissolved. Discard the cinnamon stick and pour into a large bowl. Cool, stirring occasionally, for about 30 minutes.

3 Combine the flour, baking powder, baking soda, and a pinch of salt and set aside. Beat the eggs with the sour cream, rum, vanilla and almond extracts, and the melted butter.

4 Whisk the egg mixture into the rice, then stir in the flour mixture until just blended; do not over-mix. Fold in the mincemeat.

5 Heat a large skillet or griddle, and brush with butter. Stir the batter and drop 2–3 tablespoons on to the skillet. Cook for about 2 minutes until the undersides are golden and the tops covered with bubbles that burst open. Gently turn and cook for another minute. Keep warm.

6 Dust the crêpes lightly with cinnamon and serve on a warmed serving plate.

Chocolate Fudge Dessert

This fabulous steamed sponge, served with a rich chocolate fudge sauce, is perfect for cold winter days.

10 mins   35–40 mins

SERVES 6

INGREDIENTS

generous ⅓ cup soft margarine

1¼ cups self-rising flour

½ cup light corn syrup

3 eggs

¼ cup unsweetened cocoa

CHOCOLATE FUDGE SAUCE

3½ oz/100 g dark chocolate

½ cup sweetened condensed milk

4 tbsp heavy cream

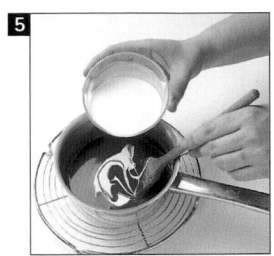

1 Lightly grease a 5 cup/1.2 liter heatproof bowl.

2 Place the ingredients for the sponge in a separate mixing bowl and beat until well combined and smooth.

3 Spoon into the prepared bowl and level the top. Cover with a disk of waxed paper and tie a pleated sheet of aluminum foil over the bowl. Steam for 1½-2 hours until the sponge is cooked and springy to the touch.

4 To make the sauce, break the chocolate into small pieces and place in a small pan with the sweetened condensed milk. Heat gently, stirring, until the chocolate has melted.

5 Remove the pan from the heat and stir in the heavy cream.

6 To serve the dessert, turn it out onto a warm serving plate and pour over a little of the chocolate fudge sauce. Serve immediately, handing round the remaining sauce separately.

Coconut Cream Molds

Smooth, creamy, and refreshing—these tempting little custards are made with an unusual combination of coconut milk, cream, and eggs.

NUTRITIONAL INFORMATION

Calories 288	Sugar 24g	
Protein 4g	Fat 20g	
Carbohydrate ...25g	Saturates 14g	

 10 mins   45 mins

SERVES 8

INGREDIENTS

CARAMEL

scant ¾ cup granulated sugar

¾ cup water

CUSTARD

1¼ cups water

3 oz/90g creamed coconut, chopped

2 eggs

2 egg yolks

1½ tbsp superfine sugar

1¼ cups light cream

sliced banana or slivers of fresh pineapple

1–2 tbsp freshly grated or shredded coconut

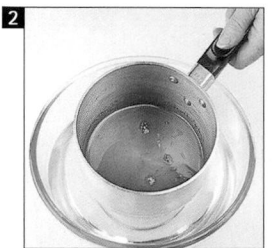

1 Have ready 8 small ovenproof dishes about ⅔ cup/150 ml capacity. To make the caramel, place the granulated sugar and water in a pan and heat gently to dissolve the sugar, then boil rapidly, without stirring, until the mixture turns a rich golden brown.

2 Immediately remove the pan from the heat and dip the base into a bowl of cold water to prevent the caramel cooking further. Quickly but carefully divide the caramel among the ovenproof dishes to coat the bases.

3 To make the custard, place the water in the same pan as you used for the caramel, add the coconut, and heat, stirring constantly, until the coconut dissolves. Place the eggs, egg yolks, and sugar in a bowl and beat well with a fork. Add the hot coconut milk and stir well to dissolve the sugar. Stir in the cream and strain the mixture into a pitcher.

4 Arrange the dishes in a roasting pan and fill with enough cold water to come halfway up the sides of the dishes.

Pour the custard mixture into the caramel-lined dishes, cover with waxed paper or foil, and cook in a preheated oven, 300°F/150°C, for about 40 minutes, or until set.

5 Remove the dishes, let cool, then chill overnight. To serve, run a knife around the edge of each dish and turn out onto a serving plate.

6 Serve with slices of banana or slivers of fresh pineapple sprinkled with freshly grated or shredded coconut.

Raspberry Fool

This dish is very easy to make and can be prepared in advance and stored in the refrigerator until required.

NUTRITIONAL INFORMATION

Calories 288	Sugars 19g	
Protein 4g	Fat 22g	
Carbohydrate ...19g	Saturates 14g	

1¼ hrs   0 mins

SERVES 4

INGREDIENTS

10 oz/300 g fresh raspberries

6 tbsp confectioners' sugar

½ pint/300 ml crème fraîche (see page 8), plus extra to decorate

½ tsp vanilla extract

2 egg whites

raspberries and lemon balm leaves, to decorate

1 Put the raspberries and confectioners' sugar in a food processor or blender and process until smooth, or press through a strainer with the back of a spoon.

2 Reserve 1 tablespoon per portion of crème fraîche for decorating.

3 Put the vanilla extract and remaining crème fraîche in a bowl and stir in the raspberry mixture.

4 Whisk the egg whites in a separate mixing bowl until stiff peaks form. Gently fold the egg whites into the raspberry mixture using a metal spoon, until fully incorporated.

5 Spoon the raspberry fool into individual serving dishes and chill for at least 1 hour. Decorate with the reserved crème fraîche, raspberries, and lemon balm leaves and serve.

COOK'S TIP
Although this dessert is best made with fresh raspberries in season, an acceptable result can be achieved with frozen raspberries, which are available from most food stores.

Cinnamon Pears

These spicy sweet pears are accompanied by a delicious melt-in-the-mouth cream, which is relatively low in fat.

NUTRITIONAL INFORMATION

Calories 190	Sugars 28g
Protein 6g	Fat 7g
Carbohydrate ...28g	Saturates 4g

🍮 🍮

🧊 10 mins   🕐 25 mins

SERVES 4

INGREDIENTS

1 lemon

4 firm ripe pears

1¼ cups hard cider or
  unsweetened apple juice

1 cinnamon stick, broken in half

mint leaves, to decorate

MAPLE RICOTTA CREAM

½ cup ricotta cheese

½ cup unsweetened yogurt

½ tsp ground cinnamon

½ tsp grated lemon zest

1 tbsp maple syrup

lemon zest, to decorate

3 Add the cider or apple juice and the cinnamon stick. Gently bring to a boil, then lower the heat and simmer for 10 minutes. Carefully remove the pears using a slotted spoon, and reserve the cooking juice. Put the pears in a warm heatproof serving dish, cover with foil, and keep warm in a low oven.

4 Return the pan to the heat, bring to a boil, then simmer for about 8–10 minutes, until reduced by half. Spoon over the pears.

5 To make the maple ricotta cream, mix together all the ingredients. Decorate with lemon zest and serve with the pears.

1 Using a swivel vegetable peeler, remove the lemon zest and put it in a nonstick skillet. Squeeze the lemon and pour the juice into a shallow bowl.

2 Peel, halve, and core the pears. Toss them in the lemon juice to prevent them from discoloring. Add them to the skillet and pour over the lemon juice remaining in the bowl.

Poached Allspice Pears

These pears are moist and delicious after poaching in a sugar and allspice mixture. They are wonderful served hot or cold.

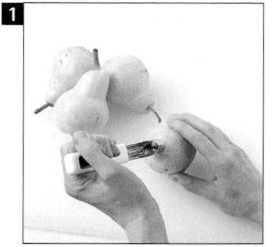

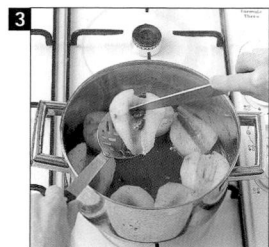

NUTRITIONAL INFORMATION

Calories 157	Sugars 17g
Protein 5g	Fat 19g
Carbohydrate ...17g	Saturates 12g

 5 mins   🕐 15 mins

SERVES 4

INGREDIENTS

4 large, ripe pears

1¼ cups orange juice

2 tsp ground allspice

⅓ cup raisins

2 tbsp light brown sugar

grated orange zest, to decorate

1 Using an apple corer, core the pears. Using a sharp knife, peel the pears and cut them in half.

2 Place the pear halves in a large pan. Add the orange juice, allspice, raisins, and sugar to the pan and heat gently, stirring, until the sugar has dissolved. Bring the mixture to a boil for 1 minute.

3 Reduce the heat to low and let simmer for 10 minutes, or until the pears are cooked, but still fairly firm—test them by inserting the tip of a sharp knife.

4 Remove the pears from the pan with a slotted spoon and transfer to serving plates.

5 Decorate the pears with orange zest and serve hot, with the syrup.

COOK'S TIP
The Chinese do not usually have desserts to finish off a meal, except at banquets and special occasions. Sweet dishes are usually served as snacks, but fruit is refreshing at the end of a big meal.

Panforte di Siena

This famous Tuscan honey and nut cake is a Christmas specialty.
In Italy it is sold in pretty boxes, and served in very thin slices.

NUTRITIONAL INFORMATION

Calories 257   Sugars 29g
Protein . . . . .5g   Fat 13g
Carbohydrate . . .33g   Saturates 1g

🐻 🐻 🐻

 10 mins   🕐 1¼ hrs

SERVES 12

I N G R E D I E N T S

1 cup split whole almonds

1 cup filberts

3 oz/90 g cut mixed peel

½ cup no-soak dried apricots

2 oz/60 g candied pineapple

grated zest of 1 large orange

scant ½ cup all-purpose flour

2 tbsp unsweetened cocoa

2 tsp ground cinnamon

½ cup superfine sugar

6 tbsp honey

confectioners' sugar, for dredging

1 Toast the almonds under the broiler until they are lightly browned, and place in a bowl.

2 Toast the filberts until the skins split. Place on a dry dish cloth and rub off the skins. Roughly chop the filberts and add them to the almonds along with the mixed peel.

3 Chop the apricots and pineapple fairly finely, add to the nuts with the orange zest, and mix well.

4 Sift the flour with the cocoa and cinnamon, add to the nut mixture; mix.

5 Line a round 8 inch/20 cm cake pan or deep loose-based quiche pan with nonstick baking parchment.

6 Put the sugar and honey into a pan and heat until the sugar dissolves, then boil gently for about 5 minutes or until the mixture thickens and begins to turn a deeper shade of brown. Quickly add to the nut mixture and stir well to mix evenly. Turn the mixture into the prepared pan and level the top using the back of a damp spoon.

7 Cook the cake in a preheated oven, at 300°F/150°C, for 1 hour. Remove from the oven and let get completely cold in the pan. Take out of the pan and carefully peel off the baking parchment. Before serving, dredge the panforte di Siena heavily with strained confectioners' sugar. Serve in very thin slices.

Steamed Coffee Sponge

This sponge dessert is very light and is delicious served with a coffee or chocolate sauce.

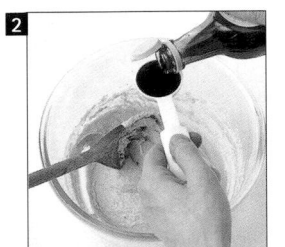
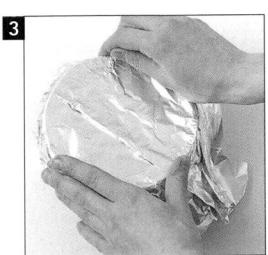

NUTRITIONAL INFORMATION

Calories 343   Sugars 21g
Protein . . . . .9g   Fat 12g
Carbohydrate . . .54g   Saturates 4g

10 mins   1–1¼ hrs

SERVES 4

INGREDIENTS

2 tbsp margarine

2 tbsp brown sugar

2 eggs

5½ tbsp all-purpose flour

¾ tsp baking powder

6 tbsp milk

1 tsp coffee extract

SAUCE

1¼ cups milk

1 tbsp brown sugar

1 tsp unsweetened cocoa

2 tbsp cornstarch

1 Lightly grease a 2½ cup heatproof bowl. Cream the margarine and sugar until the mixture is light and fluffy, then beat in the eggs.

2 Gradually stir in the flour and baking powder, then stir in the milk and coffee extract to make a smooth batter.

3 Spoon the mixture into the bowl and cover with a pleated piece of baking parchment and then a pleated piece of foil, securing around the bowl with tightly tied string.

4 Place the bowl in a steamer or large pan half full of boiling water. Cover and steam for 1–1¼ hours or until the sponge is cooked through.

5 To make the sauce, put the milk, sugar, and unsweetened cocoa in a pan and heat until the sugar dissolves.

Blend the cornstarch with 4 tablespoons of water to a paste and stir into the pan. Bring the sauce to a boil, stirring until thickened. Cook for 1 minute.

6 Turn the sponge out onto a warmed serving plate and spoon the sauce over the top. Serve immediately.

Rice & Banana Brûlée

Take a can of creamed rice, flavor it with orange zest, preserved ginger, raisins, and sliced bananas and top with a brown sugar glaze.

NUTRITIONAL INFORMATION

Calories	509	Sugars 98g
Protein	.........9g	Fat 6g
Carbohydrate	...112g	Saturates 4g

50 mins | 2–3 mins

SERVES 2

INGREDIENTS

14 oz/400 g can creamed rice

grated zest of ½ orange

2 pieces of preserved ginger, finely chopped

2 tsp ginger syrup from the jar

⅓ cup raisins

1–2 bananas

1–2 tsp lemon juice

4–5 tbsp raw sugar

1 Empty the can of creamed rice into a bowl and stir in the grated orange zest, ginger, ginger syrup, and raisins.

2 Cut the bananas diagonally into slices, toss in the lemon juice to prevent them discoloring, then drain, and divide them between 2 individual flameproof dishes.

3 Spoon the rice mixture in an even layer over the bananas so that the dishes are almost full.

4 Sprinkle an even layer of sugar over the rice in each dish.

5 Place the dishes under a preheated moderate broiler and heat until the sugar melts, taking care that the sugar does not burn.

6 Let cool until the caramel sets, then chill in the refrigerator until ready to serve. Tap the caramel with the back of a spoon to break it.

COOK'S TIP

Canned creamed rice is very versatile and is delicious heated with orange segments and grated apples added. Try it served cold with grated chocolate and mixed chopped nuts stirred through it.

Indian Bread Pudding

This, the Indian equivalent of the English bread and butter pudding, is rather a special dessert, usually cooked for special occasions.

NUTRITIONAL INFORMATION

Calories 445   Sugars 43g
Protein . . . . .10g   Fat 20g
Carbohydrate . . .60g   Saturates 11g

🍲 20 mins   🕐 25 mins

SERVES 6

INGREDIENTS

6 medium slices bread

5 tbsp ghee (preferably pure)

¾ cup sugar

1¼ cups water

3 green cardamoms, without husks

2½ cups milk

¾ cup evaporated milk or khoya
    (see Cook's Tip)

½ tsp saffron strands

heavy cream, to serve (optional)

TO DECORATE

8 pistachio nuts, soaked, peeled and chopped

chopped almonds

2 leaves varak (edible silver leaf, see
    page 912) (optional)

1 Cut the bread slices into quarters. Heat the ghee in a large, heavy skillet. Add the bread slices and cook, turning once, until a crisp golden brown color. Place the cooked bread in the base of a heatproof dish and set aside.

2 To make a syrup, place the sugar, water, and cardamom seeds in a pan and bring the mixture to a boil over medium heat, stirring constantly, until the sugar has dissolved. Boil until the syrup thickens, then pour the syrup over the cooked bread.

3 Put the milk, evaporated milk or khoya (see Cook's Tip,) and the saffron in a separate pan and bring to a boil over low heat. Simmer until it has halved in volume. Pour the mixture over the syrup-coated bread.

4 Decorate the dessert with the pistachios, chopped almonds, and varq (if using.) Serve the bread pudding with heavy cream, if liked.

COOK'S TIP
To make khoya, bring 3¾ cups milk to the boil in a large, heavy pan. Reduce the heat and boil, stirring occasionally, for 35–40 minutes, until reduced to a quarter of its volume and resembling a sticky dough.

Apple Fritters

These apple fritters are coated in a light, spiced batter and deep-fried until crisp and golden. Serve warm with an unusual almond sauce.

NUTRITIONAL INFORMATION

Calories	438	Sugars	........15g
Protein	.........6g	Fat	..........32g
Carbohydrate	...35g	Saturates	.......4g

15 mins   15 mins

SERVES 4

I N G R E D I E N T S

⅞ cup all-purpose flour

pinch of salt

½ tsp ground cinnamon

¾ cup warm water

4 tsp vegetable oil

2 egg whites

2 eating apples, peeled

vegetable or sunflower oil,
    for deep-frying

superfine sugar and cinnamon,
    to decorate

S A U C E

⅔ cup unsweetened yogurt

½ tsp almond extract

2 tsp clear honey

4 Using a sharp knife, cut the apples into chunks and dip the pieces of apple into the batter to coat.

5 Heat the oil for deep-frying to 350°F/180°C or until a cube of bread browns in 30 seconds. Fry the apple pieces, in batches if necessary, for about 3–4 minutes until they are light golden brown and puffy.

6 Remove the apple fritters from the oil with a slotted spoon and drain on absorbent paper towels.

7 Mix together the superfine sugar and the cinnamon and sprinkle over the warm fritters.

8 Mix the sauce ingredients in a serving bowl and serve with the fritters.

1 Sift the flour and salt together into a large mixing bowl.

2 Add the cinnamon and mix well. Stir in the warm water and vegetable oil to make a smooth batter.

3 Whisk the egg whites until stiff peaks form and fold into the batter.

Fruit Crumble

Any fruits in season can be used in this wholesome dessert.
It is suitable for vegans as it contains no dairy produce.

NUTRITIONAL INFORMATION

Calories 426   Sugars 37g
Protein . . . . .8g   Fat 16g
Carbohydrate . . .67g   Saturates 4g

 10 mins   30 mins

SERVES 6

I N G R E D I E N T S

vegan margarine, for greasing

6 dessert pears, peeled, cored, quartered, and sliced

1 tbsp chopped preserved ginger

1 tbsp molasses

2 tbsp orange juice

T O P P I N G

1½ cups all-purpose flour

6 tbsp vegan margarine, cut into small pieces

¼ cup slivered almonds

⅓ cup porridge oats

¼ cup molasses

soy custard, to serve

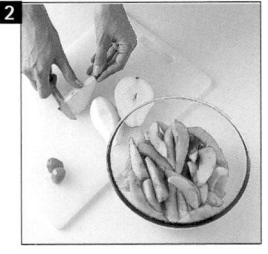  

1 Lightly grease a 4-cup/1-litre ovenproof dish with vegan margarine.

2 Prepare the pears. In a bowl, mix together the pears, ginger, molasses, and orange juice. Spoon the mixture into the prepared dish.

3 To make the crumble topping, strain the flour into a mixing bowl. Add the margarine and rub it in with your fingertips until the mixture resembles fine bread crumbs. Stir in the slivered almonds, porridge oats, and molasses. Mix well until thoroughly combined.

4 Sprinkle the crumble topping evenly over the pear and ginger mixture in the dish, pressing it down gently with the back of a spoon.

5 Bake in a preheated oven, 375°F/ 190°C, for about 30 minutes, or until the topping is crisp and golden and the fruit tender.

6 Serve the crumble immediately with soy custard, if using.

VARIATION
Stir 1 teaspoon ground allspice into the crumble mixture in step 3 for added flavor, if you prefer.

Baked Coconut Rice Dessert

A wonderful baked rice dessert cooked with flavorsome coconut milk and a little lime rind. Serve hot or chilled with fresh or stewed fruit.

NUTRITIONAL INFORMATION

Calories	211	Sugars	........27g
Protein	.........5g	Fat	..........2g
Carbohydrate	...46g	Saturates	.......1g

 5 mins   2½ hrs

SERVES 4–6

INGREDIENTS

½ cup short or round-grain pudding rice

2½ cups coconut milk

1¼ cups milk

1 large strip lime rind

⅓ cup superfine sugar

knob of butter

pinch of ground star anise (optional)

fresh or stewed fruit, to serve

1 Lightly grease a 2½ pint/1.5 litre shallow ovenproof dish.

2 Mix the pudding rice with the coconut milk, milk, lime rind, and superfine sugar until all the ingredients are well blended.

3 Pour the rice mixture into the greased ovenproof dish and dot the surface with a little butter. Bake in the oven for about 30 minutes.

4 Remove the dish from the oven. Remove and discard the strip of lime from the rice dessert.

5 Stir the mixture well, add the pinch of ground star anise, if using, return to the oven and cook for a further 1–2 hours or until almost all the milk has been absorbed and a golden brown skin has baked on the top of the pudding. Cover the top of the pudding with foil if it starts to brown too much toward the end of the cooking time.

6 Serve the baked coconut rice dessert warm, or chilled if you prefer, with fresh or stewed fruit.

Chocolate Mousse

This is a light and fluffy mousse with a subtle hint of orange.
It is wickedly delicious served with a fresh fruit sauce.

NUTRITIONAL INFORMATION

Calories 164   Sugars 24g
Protein ....5g   Fat 5g
Carbohydrate ...25g   Saturates 3g

 2¼ hrs   5 mins

SERVES 8

I N G R E D I E N T S

3½ oz/100 g semisweet chocolate, melted

1¼ cups unsweetened yogurt

⅔ cup Quark

4 tbsp superfine sugar

1 tbsp orange juice

1 tbsp brandy

1½ tsp gelozone (vegetarian gelatin)

9 tbsp cold water

2 large egg whites

TO DECORATE

roughly grated bittersweet and
white chocolate

orange zest

1 Put the melted chocolate, yogurt, Quark, sugar, orange juice, and brandy in a food processor or blender and process for 30 seconds. Transfer the mixture to a large bowl.

2 Sprinkle the gelozone over the water and stir until dissolved.

3 In a pan, bring the gelozone and water to a boil for 2 minutes. Cool slightly, then thoroughly stir into the chocolate mixture.

4 Whisk the egg whites until stiff peaks form and fold into the chocolate mixture using a metal spoon.

5 Line a 1 lb/450 g loaf pan with plastic wrap. Spoon in the mousse and let set in the refrigerator for 2 hours.

6 Turn the mousse out onto a serving plate, decorate with grated chocolate and orange zest, and serve.

COOK'S TIP
For a quick fruit sauce, process a can of mandarin segments in natural juice in a food processor and press through a strainer. Stir in 1 tablespoon honey and serve with the mousse.

Quick Syrup Sponge

You won't believe your eyes when you see just how quickly this light-as-air sponge cooks in the microwave oven!

NUTRITIONAL INFORMATION

Calories	650	Sugars	........60g
Protein	........10g	Fat	..........31g
Carbohydrate	...89g	Saturates	.......7g

15 mins   5 mins

SERVES 4

INGREDIENTS

9 tbsp butter or margarine

4 tbsp light corn syrup

6 tbsp superfine sugar

2 eggs

1 cup self-rising flour

1 tsp baking powder

about 2 tbsp warm water

custard, to serve

1 Grease a 2½ pint/1.5 litre heatproof bowl with a small amount of the butter or margarine. Spoon the syrup into the basin.

2 Cream the remaining butter or margarine with the sugar until light and fluffy. Gradually add the eggs, beating well between each addition.

3 Sift the flour and baking powder together, then fold into the creamed mixture using a large metal spoon. Add enough water to give a soft, dropping consistency. Spoon into the heatproof bowl and level the surface.

4 Cover with microwave-safe plastic wrap, leaving a small space to allow air to escape. Microwave on HIGH power for 4 minutes, then remove the sponge from the microwave and let stand for 5 minutes, while it continues to cook.

5 Turn the sponge out on to a warm serving plate. Serve with custard.

COOK'S TIP

If you don't have a microwave, the sponge can be steamed. Cover the bowl with a piece of pleated baking parchment and a piece of pleated foil. Place in a pan, add boiling water, and steam for 1½ hours.

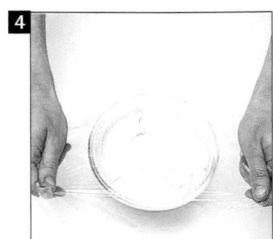

Mixed Fruit Crust

In this crusty dessert, tropical fruits are flavored with ginger and coconut, for something a little different and very tasty.

NUTRITIONAL INFORMATION

Calories	602	Sugars	........51g
Protein	.........6g	Fat	..........29g
Carbohydrate	...84g	Saturates	......11g

10 mins   50 mins

SERVES 4

INGREDIENTS

2 mangoes, sliced

1 papaya, seeded and sliced

8 oz fresh pineapple, cubed

1½ tsp ground ginger

7 tbsp margarine

scant ½ cup light brown sugar

1½ cups all-purpose flour

⅔ cup dry shredded coconut, plus extra to decorate

1 Place the fruit in a pan with ½ teaspoon of the ground ginger, 2 tablespoons of the margarine, and 4 tablespoons of the sugar. Cook over low heat for 10 minutes until the fruit softens. Spoon the fruit into the bottom of a shallow casserole.

2 Combine the flour and remaining ginger. Rub in the remaining margarine until the mixture resembles fine bread crumbs. Stir in the remaining sugar and the coconut and spoon over the fruit to cover completely.

3 Cook the crumble in a preheated oven, 350°F/180°C, for about 40 minutes or until the top is crisp. Decorate with a sprinkling of dry shredded coconut and serve immediately.

Saffron-Spiced Rice Dessert

This rich dessert is cooked in milk delicately flavored with saffron, then mixed with dried fruit, almonds, and cream before baking.

NUTRITIONAL INFORMATION

Calories	339	Sugars	........28g
Protein	.........9g	Fat	..........16g
Carbohydrate	...41g	Saturates	.......9g

5 mins   1 hour

SERVES 4

INGREDIENTS

2½ cups creamy milk

several pinches of saffron strands, finely crushed (see Cook's Tip)

⅓ cup pudding rice

1 cinnamon stick or piece of cassia bark

3½ tbsp sugar

¼ cup seedless raisins or golden raisins

¼ cup ready-to-eat dried apricots, chopped

1 egg, beaten

5 tbsp light cream

1 tbsp butter, diced

1 tbsp slivered almonds

freshly grated nutmeg, for sprinkling

cream, for serving (optional)

1 Place the milk and crushed saffron in a nonstick pan and bring to a boil. Stir in the rice and cinnamon stick, reduce the heat, and simmer very gently, uncovered, stirring frequently, for 25 minutes, until tender.

2 Remove the pan from the heat. Remove and discard the cinnamon stick from the rice mixture. Stir in the sugar, the raisins or golden raisins, and the dried apricots, then beat in the egg, cream, and diced butter.

3 Transfer the mixture to a greased ovenproof pie or quiche dish and sprinkle with the slivered almonds and freshly grated nutmeg to taste. Cook in a preheated oven, 350°F/180°C, for about 25–30 minutes, until the mixture is set and lightly golden. Serve the dessert hot with extra cream, if wished.

COOK'S TIP

For a slightly stronger flavor, place the saffron strands on a small piece of foil and toast them lightly under a hot broiler for a few moments and then crush between your fingers and thumb.

Passion Cake

Decorating this moist, rich carrot cake with sugared flowers lifts
it into the celebration class. It is a perfect choice for Easter.

NUTRITIONAL INFORMATION

Calories 506	Sugars 40g
Protein 10g	Fat 27g
Carbohydrate . . .60g	Saturates 4g

 15 mins   1½ hours

SERVES 10

I N G R E D I E N T S

⅔ cup corn oil

¾ cup golden superfine sugar

4 tbsp unsweetened yogurt

3 eggs, plus 1 extra yolk

1 tsp vanilla extract

1 cup walnut pieces, chopped

1 cup carrots, grated

1 banana, mashed

scant 1½ cups all-purpose flour

¾ cup fine oatmeal

1 tsp baking soda

1 tsp baking powder

1 tsp ground cinnamon

½ tsp salt

F R O S T I N G

¾ cup soft cheese

4 tbsp unsweetened yogurt

¾ cup confectioners' sugar

1 tsp grated lemon zest

2 tsp lemon juice

D E C O R A T I O N

primroses and violets

1 egg white, lightly beaten

2 tbsp superfine sugar

1 Grease and line a 9 inch/23 cm round cake pan. Beat together the oil, sugar, yogurt, eggs, egg yolk, and vanilla extract. Beat in the chopped walnuts, grated carrot, and banana.

2 Sift together the remaining cake ingredients and gradually beat into the mixture.

3 Pour the mixture into the pan and level the surface. Bake in a preheated oven, 350°F/180°C, for about 1½ hours, or until the cake is firm. Let cool in the pan for 15 minutes, then turn out onto a wire rack to cool completely.

4 To make the frosting, beat together the soft cheese and the yogurt. Strain in the confectioners' sugar and stir in the lemon zest and juice. Spread the frosting over the top and sides of the cake.

5 To prepare the decoration, dip the flowers quickly in the beaten egg white, then sprinkle with caster sugar to cover the surface completely. Place well apart on baking parchment.

6 Leave the flowers in a warm, dry place for several hours until they are dry and crisp, then arrange them in a pattern on top of the cake.

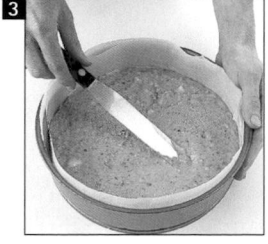

Indian Vermicelli Dessert

Indian vermicelli, which is very fine, is delicious cooked in milk and ghee. Muslims make this for a religious festival called Eid.

NUTRITIONAL INFORMATION

Calories	397	Sugars	........42g
Protein	........11g	Fat	..........17g
Carbohydrate	...54g	Saturates	.......8g

5 mins   20 mins

SERVES 6

I N G R E D I E N T S

2 tbsp pistachio nuts (optional)

2 tbsp slivered almonds

3 tbsp ghee

100 g/3½ oz seviyan (Indian vermicelli)

3½ cups milk

¾ cup evaporated milk

8 tbsp sugar

6 dried dates, pitted

1 Soak the pistachio nuts (if using) in a bowl of water for at least 3 hours. Peel the pistachios and mix them with the slivered almonds. Chop the nuts finely and set aside.

2 Melt the ghee in a large pan and lightly cook the seviyan. Reduce the heat immediately (the seviyan will turn golden very quickly so be careful not to burn it) and if necessary remove the pan from the heat (do not worry if some bits are a little darker than others).

3 Add the milk to the seviyan and bring to a boil over low heat, taking care that it does not boil over.

4 Add the evaporated milk, sugar, and dates to the mixture in the pan. Simmer over low heat, uncovered, stirring occasionally, for about 10 minutes. When the consistency starts to thicken, remove from the heat and pour the dessert into a warmed serving bowl.

5 Decorate the dessert with the chopped pistachio nuts (if using) and the slivered almonds.

COOK'S TIP

You will find seviyan (Indian vermicelli) in Indian foodstores. This dessert can be served warm or cold.

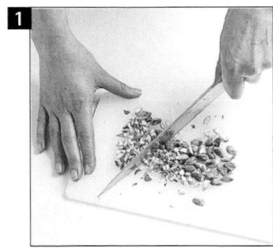  

Bread & Butter Pudding

Everyone has their own favorite recipe for this dish. This one has added marmalade and grated apples for a really rich and unique taste.

NUTRITIONAL INFORMATION

Calories 427   Sugars 63g
Protein ....9g   Fat 13g
Carbohydrate ...74g   Saturates 7g

45 mins   1 hr

SERVES 6

INGREDIENTS

4 tbsp butter, softened

4–5 slices white or whole-wheat bread

4 tbsp chunky orange marmalade

grated zest of 1 lemon

½–¾ cup golden raisins

¼ cup chopped candied peel

1 tsp ground cinnamon or allspice

1 cooking apple, peeled, cored, and coarsely grated

scant ½ cup brown sugar

3 eggs

generous 2 cups milk

2 tbsp raw brown sugar

1 Use the softened butter to grease an ovenproof dish and to spread on the slices of bread, then spread the bread with the marmalade.

2 Place a layer of bread in the bottom of the dish and sprinkle with the lemon zest, half the golden raisins, half the candied peel, half the spice, all of the apple, and half the brown sugar. Add another layer of bread, cutting it so that it fits the dish.

3 Sprinkle over most of the remaining golden raisins and all the remaining candied peel, spice, and brown sugar, scattering it evenly over the bread. Top with a final layer of bread, again cutting to fit the dish.

4 Lightly beat together the eggs and milk and then carefully strain the mixture over the bread in the dish. If time allows, let the pudding stand for 20–30 minutes.

5 Sprinkle the raw brown sugar over the top and scatter over the remaining golden raisins. Cook in a preheated oven, 400°F/200°C, for 50–60 minutes, until risen and golden brown. Serve immediately or let cool and serve cold.

Apricot Brûlée

Serve this melt-in-the-mouth dessert with crisp-baked meringues for an extra-special occasion.

NUTRITIONAL INFORMATION

Calories	307	Sugars	. . . . .38g
Protein	. . . . .5g	Fat	. . . . .16g
Carbohydrate	. . .38g	Saturates	. . . . . . .9g

 2¼ hrs   35 mins

SERVES 6

INGREDIENTS

3¼ cup unsulfured dried apricots

⅔ cup orange juice

4 egg yolks

2 tbsp superfine sugar

⅔ cup unsweetened yogurt

⅔ cup heavy cream

1 tsp vanilla extract

6 tbsp raw brown sugar

meringues, to serve (optional)

1 Place the apricots and orange juice in a bowl and let soak for at least 1 hour. Pour into a small pan, bring slowly to a boil, and simmer for 20 minutes. Process in a blender or food processor or chop very finely and push through a strainer with the back of a wooden spoon.

2 Beat together the egg yolks and sugar until the mixture is light and fluffy. Place the yogurt in a small pan, add the cream and vanilla, and bring to a boil over low heat.

3 Pour the yogurt mixture over the eggs, beating all the time, then transfer to the top of a double boiler or place the bowl over a pan of simmering water. Stir until the custard thickens. Divide the apricot mixture between 6 ramekins and carefully pour on the custard. Cool, then chill in the refrigerator at least 1 hour.

4 Sprinkle the raw brown sugar evenly over the custard and place under a preheated broiler until the sugar caramelizes. Let cool. To serve the brûlée, crack the hard caramel topping with the back of a tablespoon.

Spiced Steamed Pudding

Steamed puddings are irresistible on a winter day, but the texture of this pudding is so light it can be served throughout the year.

NUTRITIONAL INFORMATION

Calories	488	Sugars	........56g
Protein	.........5g	Fat	..........19g
Carbohydrate	...78g	Saturates	.......4g

15 mins   1½ hrs

SERVES 6

I N G R E D I E N T S

2 tbsp light corn syrup, plus extra to serve

9 tbsp butter or margarine

½ cup superfine or light brown sugar

2 eggs

scant 1½ cups self-rising flour

¾ tsp ground cinnamon or apple spice

grated zest of 1 orange

1 tbsp orange juice

¾ cup golden raisins

2 pieces preserved ginger, finely chopped

1 eating apple, peeled, cored, and coarsely grated

1 Thoroughly grease a 1½ pint/850 ml heatproof bowl. Put the light corn syrup into the bowl.

2 Cream the butter or margarine and sugar together until very light and fluffy and pale in color. Beat in the eggs, one at a time, following each with a spoonful of the flour.

3 Sift the remaining flour with the cinnamon or apple spice and fold into the mixture, followed by the orange zest and juice. Fold in the golden raisins, then the ginger and apple.

4 Turn the mixture into the heatproof bowl and level the top. Cover with a piece of pleated, greased baking parchment, tucking the edges under the rim of the bowl.

5 Cover with a sheet of pleated foil. Tie securely in place with string, with a piece of string tied over the top of the basin for a handle to make it easy to lift out of the pan.

6 Put the bowl into a pan half-filled with boiling water, cover, and steam for 1½ hours, adding more boiling water to the pan as necessary during cooking.

7 To serve the spiced steamed pudding, remove the foil and the baking parchment, turn the pudding out onto a warmed serving plate, and serve at once in slices with a little of the light corn syrup poured over the top.

Pistachio Dessert

Rather an attractive-looking dessert, especially when decorated with varak, this is a dish that can be prepared in advance.

NUTRITIONAL INFORMATION

Calories	676	Sugars	.......98g
Protein	........15g	Fat	..........27g
Carbohydrate	...98g	Saturates	.......9g

15 mins   10 mins

SERVES 6

INGREDIENTS

3½ cups water

½ lb pistachio nuts

½ lb powdered milk

2 generous cups sugar

2 cardamoms, with seeds crushed

2 tbsp rosewater

a few strands of saffron

TO DECORATE

2 tbsp slivered almonds

mint leaves

1 Put about 2½ cups water in a pan and bring to a boil. Remove the pan from the heat, add the pistachios to the water, and let soak for about 5 minutes. Drain the pistachios thoroughly and remove the skins.

COOK'S TIP

It is best to buy whole pistachio nuts and grind them yourself, rather than using packets of ready-ground nuts. Freshly ground nuts have the best flavor, as grinding releases their natural oils.

2 Process the pistachios in a food processor or grind them in a mortar with a pestle.

3 Add the dried milk powder to the ground pistachios and mix well.

4 To make the syrup, place the remaining water and the sugar in a pan and heat gently. When the liquid begins to thicken, add the cardamom seeds, rosewater, and saffron.

5 Add the syrup to the pistachio mixture and cook, stirring constantly, for about 5 minutes, until the mixture thickens. Let the mixture cool slightly.

6 Once the mixture is cool enough to handle, roll it into balls in the palms of your hands.

7 Decorate with the slivered almonds and fresh mint leaves and let set before serving.

Upside-Down Cake

This recipe shows how a classic favorite can be adapted for vegans by using vegetarian margarine and oil instead of butter and eggs.

NUTRITIONAL INFORMATION

Calories 354   Sugars 31g
Protein . . . . .3g   Fat 15g
Carbohydrate . . .56g   Saturates 2g

15 mins   50 mins

SERVES 4

I N G R E D I E N T S

¼ cup vegan margarine, cut into small pieces, plus extra for greasing

15 oz/425 g canned unsweetened pineapple pieces, drained, juice reserved

4 tsp cornstarch

¼ cup brown sugar

½ cup water

zest of 1 lemon

SPONGE CAKE

4 tbsp sunflower oil

⅓ cup brown sugar

⅔ cup water

1¼ cups all-purpose flour

2 tsp baking powder

1 tsp ground cinnamon

1 Grease a deep 7-inch/18-cm cake pan with a little vegan margarine.

2 Mix the reserved pineapple juice with the cornstarch to a smooth paste. Put the paste in a pan with the sugar, margarine, and water and stir over low heat until the sugar has dissolved. Bring to a boil and simmer for 2–3 minutes until thickened. Let cool slightly.

3 To make the sponge cake, heat the oil, sugar, and water in a pan until the sugar has dissolved, but do not let boil. Remove from the heat and let cool. Sift the flour, baking powder, and ground cinnamon into a bowl. Pour in the cooled sugar syrup and beat well to form a batter.

4 Place the pineapple pieces and lemon zest on the bottom of the prepared pan and pour over 4 tablespoons of the pineapple syrup. Spoon the sponge batter on top, leveling the surface.

5 Bake in a preheated oven, 350°F/ 180°C, for 35–40 minutes until set and a toothpick inserted into the center comes out clean. Invert onto a plate, let stand for 5 minutes, then remove the pan. Serve with the remaining syrup.

Caramelized Oranges

The secret of these oranges is to allow them to marinate
in the syrup for at least 24 hours, so the flavors amalgamate.

NUTRITIONAL INFORMATION

Calories 235   Sugars 59g
Protein ....2g   Fat 0.2g
Carbohydrate ...59g   Saturates 0g

3¼ hrs   20 mins

SERVES 6

INGREDIENTS

6 large oranges

1 generous cup sugar

1 cup water

6 whole cloves (optional)

2–4 tbsp orange-flavored liqueur
 or brandy

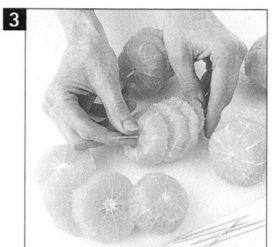

1 Using a citrus zester or potato peeler,
pare the zest from 2 of the oranges in
narrow strips without any white pith
attached. If using a potato peeler, cut the
peel into very thin strips.

2 Put the strips into a small pan and
barely cover with water. Bring to a
boil and simmer for 5 minutes. Drain the
strips and reserve the water.

3 Cut away all the white pith and peel
from the remaining oranges using a
very sharp knife, then cut horizontally into
4 slices. Reassemble the oranges and hold
in place with wooden toothpicks. Stand in
a heatproof dish.

4 Put the sugar and water into a heavy
pan with the cloves, if using. Bring to
a boil and simmer gently until the sugar
has dissolved, then boil hard without
stirring until the syrup thickens and begins
to color. Continue to cook until a light

golden brown, then remove from the heat
and carefully pour in the reserved orange
zest liquid.

5 Place over gentle heat until the
caramel has fully dissolved again,
then remove from the heat and add the
liqueur or brandy. Pour over the oranges.

6 Sprinkle the orange strips over the
oranges, cover with plastic wrap, and
let get cold. Chill for at least 3 hours and
preferably for 24–48 hours before serving.
If time allows, spoon the syrup over the
oranges several times while they are
marinating. Discard the toothpicks before
serving the oranges.

Cherry Clafoutis

This is a hot dessert that is simple and quick to put together. Try the batter with other fruits—apricots and plums are particularly delicious.

NUTRITIONAL INFORMATION

Calories 261	Sugars 24g	
Protein 10g	Fat 6g	
Carbohydrate . . .40g	Saturates 3g	

 10 mins 40 mins

SERVES 6

I N G R E D I E N T S

1 cup all-purpose flour

4 eggs, lightly beaten

2 tbsp superfine sugar

pinch of salt

2½ cups milk

butter, for greasing

1 lb/450 g black cherries, fresh or canned, pitted

3 tbsp brandy

1 tbsp sugar, to decorate

3 Thoroughly grease a 3 pint/1.75 liter ovenproof serving dish with butter and pour in about half of the batter.

4 Spoon over the cherries and pour the remaining batter over the top. Sprinkle the brandy over the batter.

5 Bake in a preheated oven, 350°F/180°C, for 40 minutes, or until risen and golden brown.

6 Remove from the oven and sprinkle over the sugar just before serving. Serve the clafoutis warm.

1 Sift the flour into a large mixing bowl. Make a well in the center and add the eggs, sugar, and salt. Gradually, draw in the flour from around the edges and whisk.

2 Pour in the milk and whisk the batter thoroughly until very smooth.

Sweet Saffron Rice

This is a traditional dessert, which is quick and easy to make and looks very impressive, especially decorated with pistachio nuts and varak.

NUTRITIONAL INFORMATION

Calories 460	Sugars 57g
Protein 4g	Fat 9g
Carbohydrate ...97g	Saturates 5g

5 mins

35 mins

SERVES 4

INGREDIENTS

1 cup basmati rice

1 cup sugar

1 pinch saffron strands

1¼ cups water

2 tbsp vegetable ghee

3 cloves

3 cardamoms

¼ cup golden raisins

TO DECORATE

a few pistachio nuts (optional)

varak (silver leaf) (optional)

1 Rinse the rice twice and bring to a boil in a pan of water, stirring constantly. Remove the pan from the heat when the rice is half-cooked, drain the rice thoroughly, and set aside.

2 In a separate pan, boil the sugar and saffron in the water, stirring constantly, until the syrup thickens. Set the syrup aside until required.

3 In another pan, heat the ghee with the cloves and cardamoms, stirring occasionally, then remove the pan from the heat.

4 Return the rice to low heat and stir in the golden raisins.

5 Pour the syrup over the rice mixture and stir to mix.

6 Pour the ghee mixture over the rice and simmer over low heat for about 10–15 minutes. Check to see whether the rice is cooked. If it is not, add a little boiling water, cover, and continue to simmer until tender.

7 Serve warm, decorated with pistachio nuts and varak (silver leaf), if desired.

COOK'S TIP
Basmati rice is the "prince of rices" and comes from the Himalayan foothills. Basmati means "fragrant" and this rice has a superb texture and flavor.

Traditional Apple Pie

This two-crust apple pie can be served either hot or cold. The apples can be flavored with other spices or grated citrus zest.

NUTRITIONAL INFORMATION

Calories ....577 Sugars 36g
Protein ....6g Fat 28g
Carbohydrate ...80g Saturates 9g

55 mins   50 mins

SERVES 6

INGREDIENTS

1¾–2¼ lb cooking apples, peeled, cored, and sliced

scant ¾ cup brown or white sugar, plus extra for sprinkling

½–1 tsp ground cinnamon, apple spice, or ground ginger

1–2 tbsp water

SHORTCRUST PIE DOUGH

3 cups all-purpose flour

pinch of salt

6 tbsp butter or margarine

6 tbsp white vegetable shortening

about 6 tbsp cold water

beaten egg or milk, for glazing

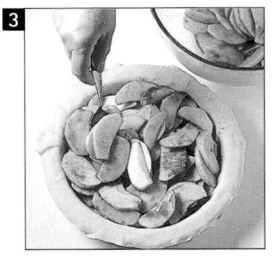

1 To make the pie dough, sift the flour and salt into a mixing bowl. Add the butter or margarine and shortening and rub in with the fingertips until the mixture resembles fine bread crumbs. Add the water and gather the mixture together into a dough. Wrap the dough in foil and chill for 30 minutes.

2 Roll out almost two-thirds of the pie dough thinly and use it to line an 8–9 inch/20–23 cm deep pie plate or shallow pie pan.

3 Mix the apples with the sugar and spice and pack into the pie shell; the filling can come up above the rim. Add the water if liked, particularly if the apples are a dry variety.

4 Roll out the remaining pie dough to form a lid. Dampen the edges of the pie rim with water and position the lid, pressing the edges firmly together. Trim the edges and crimp them decoratively.

5 Use the trimmings to cut out leaves or other shapes to decorate the top of the pie, dampen, and attach. Glaze the top of the pie with beaten egg or milk, make 1–2 slits in the top, and put the pie on a cookie sheet.

6 Bake the pie in a preheated oven, 425°F/220°C, for 20 minutes, then reduce the temperature to 350°F/180°C and cook for a further 30 minutes, or until the pastry is a light golden brown. Serve the pie hot or cold, sprinkled with brown or white sugar.

Lemon & Lime Syllabub

This dessert is rich but absolutely delicious. It is not, however, for the calorie conscious as it contains a high proportion of cream.

NUTRITIONAL INFORMATION

Calories 403	Sugars 16g	
Protein 2g	Fat 36g	
Carbohydrate ...16g	Saturates 22g	

4¼ hrs   0 mins

SERVES 4

INGREDIENTS

4 tbsp superfine sugar

grated zest and juice of 1 small lemon

grated zest and juice of 1 small lime

4 tbsp Marsala or medium sherry

1¼ cups heavy cream

lime and lemon zest, to decorate

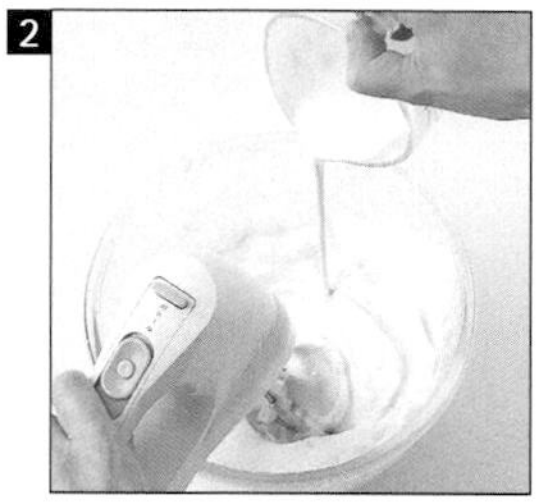

1 Put the superfine sugar, the lemon juice and zest, the lime juice and zest, and the Marsala or sherry in a bowl, mix well and let infuse for 2 hours.

2 Add the heavy cream to the fruit juice mixture and whisk until it just holds its shape.

3 Spoon the mixture into 4 tall serving glasses and chill in the refrigerator for at least 2 hours.

4 Decorate the syllabub with lime and lemon rind and serve.

Fruity Crêpe Bundles

This unusual crêpe is filled with a sweet cream flavored with ginger, nuts, and apricots and served with a raspberry and orange sauce.

NUTRITIONAL INFORMATION

Calories	610	Sugars	........60g
Protein	........19g	Fat	..........20g
Carbohydrate	...94g	Saturates	.......5g

 15 mins   35 mins

SERVES 2

I N G R E D I E N T S

BATTER

½ cup all-purpose flour

pinch of salt

¼ tsp ground cinnamon

1 egg

generous ½ cup milk

white vegetable shortening, for cooking

FILLING

1½ tsp all-purpose flour, strained

1½ tsp cornstarch

1 tbsp superfine sugar

1 egg

⅔ cup milk

4 tbsp chopped nuts

scant ¼ cup ready-to-eat dried apricots, chopped

1 piece of preserved or candied ginger, finely chopped

SAUCE

3 tbsp raspberry preserve

4½ tsp orange juice

finely grated zest of ¼ orange

1 To make the batter, sift the flour, salt, and cinnamon into a bowl and make a well in the center. Add the egg and milk and gradually beat in until smooth.

2 Melt a little shortening in a medium skillet. Pour in half the batter. Cook for 2 minutes until golden, then turn and cook the other side for about 1 minute until browned. Set aside and make a second crêpe.

3 For the filling, beat the flour with the cornstarch, sugar, and egg. Gently heat the milk in a pan, then beat 2 tablespoons into the flour mixture. Transfer to the pan and cook gently, stirring constantly until thick. Remove from the heat, cover with baking parchment to prevent a skin forming, and let cool.

4 Beat the chopped nuts and apricots, and the preserved ginger into the cooled mixture and put a heaping tablespoonful in the center of each crêpe. Gather and squeeze the edges together to make a bundle. Place in a casserole and bake in a preheated oven, 350°F/180°C, for 15–20 minutes until hot and golden, but not too brown.

5 To make the sauce, melt the preserve gently with the orange juice, then strain. Return to a clean pan with the orange zest and heat through. Serve with the crêpes.

Rice Dessert

Indian rice dessert is cooked in a pan over low heat, rather than in the oven like the British version.

NUTRITIONAL INFORMATION

Calories 152	Sugars 23g
Protein 5g	Fat 3g
Carbohydrate ...29g	Saturates 1g

10 mins   30 mins

SERVES 4

INGREDIENTS

scant ½ cup basmati rice

5 cups milk

8 tbsp sugar

varak (silver leaf) or chopped pistachio nuts, to decorate

1 Rinse the rice and place in a large pan. Add 2½ cups of the milk and bring to a boil over very low heat.

2 Cook, stirring occasionally, until the milk has been completely absorbed by the rice.

3 Remove the pan from the heat. Mash the rice, making swift, round movements in the pan, for at least 5 minutes, until all of the lumps have been removed.

4 Gradually add the remaining 2½ cups milk. Bring to a boil again over low heat, stirring occasionally.

5 Add the sugar and continue to cook, stirring constantly, for about 7–10 minutes, or until the mixture is quite thick in consistency.

6 Transfer the rice dessert to a heatproof serving bowl. Decorate with varq (silver leaf) or chopped pistachio nuts and serve on its own or with pooris.

COOK'S TIP

Varak is edible silver that is used to decorate elaborate dishes prepared for special occasions and celebrations in India. It is pure silver that has been beaten until it is wafer thin. It comes with a backing paper that is peeled off as the varak is laid on the cooked food.

Chocolate Cheesecake

This cheesecake takes a little time to prepare and cook, but is well worth the effort. It is quite rich and is good served with a little fresh fruit.

NUTRITIONAL INFORMATION

Calories 471	Sugars 20g
Protein 10g	Fat 33g
Carbohydrate . . .28g	Saturates 5g

1¼ hrs

1–1¼ hrs

SERVES 12

I N G R E D I E N T S

generous ¾ cup all-purpose flour

scant 1 cup ground almonds

scant 1 cup molasses sugar

scant ¾ cup margarine

1½ lb/675 g firm bean curd

¾ cup vegetable oil

½ cup orange juice

¾ cup brandy

6 tbsp unsweetened cocoa, plus extra
   to decorate

2 tsp almond extract

TO DECORATE

confectioners' sugar

cape gooseberries (golden berries)

1 Put the flour, ground almonds, and 1 tablespoon of the sugar in a bowl and mix well. Rub the margarine into the mixture to form a dough.

2 Lightly grease and line the bottom of a 9 inch/23 cm springform pan. Press the dough into the bottom of the pan to cover, pushing the dough right up to the edge of the pan.

3 Roughly chop the bean curd and put in a food processor with the vegetable oil, orange juice, brandy, unsweetened cocoa, almond extract, and remaining sugar and process until smooth and creamy. Pour over the base in the pan and cook in a preheated oven, 325°F/160°C, for about 1–1¼ hours or until set.

4 Let cool in the pan for 5 minutes, then remove from the pan, and chill in the refrigerator. Dust with confectioners' sugar and unsweetened cocoa. Decorate with cape gooseberries and serve.

COOK'S TIP
Cape gooseberries make an attractive decoration for many desserts.

Stuffed Pooris

This is a very old family recipe from India. The pooris freeze well, so it pays to make a large quantity and reheat them in the oven.

NUTRITIONAL INFORMATION

Calories ......429 Sugars 22g

Protein ....9g Fat 21g

Carbohydrate ...54g Saturates 7g

6½ hrs   1 hr

MAKES 10

INGREDIENTS

POORIS

1 cup coarse semolina

⅞ cup all-purpose flour

½ tsp salt

4½ tsp ghee, plus extra for frying

⅔ cup milk

FILLING

8 tbsp chana dhal

3¾ cups water

5 tbsp ghee

2 green cardamoms, peeled

4 cloves

8 tbsp sugar

2 tbsp ground almonds

½ tsp saffron strands

½ cup golden raisins

1 To make the pooris, place the semolina, flour, and salt in a bowl and mix. Add the ghee and rub in with your fingertips. Add the milk and mix to form a dough. Knead the dough for 5 minutes, cover, and let rise for about 3 hours. Knead the dough on a floured surface for 15 minutes.

2 Roll out the dough until it measures 10 inches/25 cm and divide into ten portions. Roll out each of these into 5 inch/12.5 cm rounds and set aside.

3 To make the filling, soak the chana dhal for at least 3 hours. Place the dhal in a pan and add 3 cups of the water. Bring to a boil over medium heat and cook until all of the water has evaporated and the dhal is soft enough to be mashed into a paste.

4 Meanwhile, heat the ghee. Add the cardamom seeds and cloves. Lower the heat, add the dhal paste, and stir for 5–7 minutes.

5 Fold in the sugar and almonds and cook, stirring constantly, for 10 minutes. Add the saffron and golden raisins and blend until thickened. Cook, stirring constantly, for 5 minutes.

6 Spoon the filling on to one half of each dough round. Dampen the edges with water and fold the other half over, pressing to seal.

7 Heat the ghee in a pan and cook the filled pooris, in batches, over low heat until golden. Drain on paper towels and serve immediately.

Summer Puddings

A wonderful mixture of summer fruits encased in slices of white bread which soak up all the deep red, flavorful juices.

NUTRITIONAL INFORMATION

Calories 250	Sugars 41g
Protein 4g	Fat 4g
Carbohydrate ...53g	Saturates 2g

 10 mins   10 mins

SERVES 6

I N G R E D I E N T S

vegetable oil or butter, for greasing

6–8 thin slices white bread, crusts removed

¾ cup superfine sugar

1¼ cups water

½ lb/225 g strawberries

1 lb/450 g raspberries

1¼ cups black-and/or red currants

1½ cups blackberries or loganberries

mint sprigs, to decorate

pouring cream, to serve

1 Grease 6 ⅔ cup molds with a little butter or oil.

2 Line the molds with the bread, cutting it so it fits snugly.

3 Place the sugar in a pan with the water and heat gently, stirring frequently until dissolved, then bring to a boil and boil for 2 minutes.

4 Reserve 6 large strawberries for decoration. Add half the raspberries and the rest of the fruits to the syrup, cutting the strawberries in half if large, and simmer gently for a few minutes, until they are beginning to soften but still retain their shape.

5 Spoon the fruits and some of the liquid into the molds. Cover with more slices of bread. Spoon a little juice around the sides of the molds so the bread is well soaked. Cover with a saucer and a heavy weight, let cool, then chill thoroughly, preferably overnight.

6 Process the remaining raspberries in a food processor or blender, or press through a nonmetallic strainer. Add enough of the liquid from the fruits to give a coating consistency.

7 Turn onto serving plates and spoon the raspberry sauce over. Decorate with the mint sprigs and reserved strawberries and serve with cream.

Meringue-Topped Rice

This dessert is really two in one—a rice dessert base with a melt-in-the-mouth meringue topping. Double heaven!

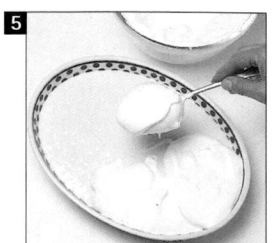

NUTRITIONAL INFORMATION

Calories	358	Sugars	........56g
Protein	........10g	Fat	...........5g
Carbohydrate	...72g	Saturates	.......2g

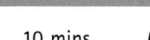   10 mins   1½ hrs

SERVES 6–8

I N G R E D I E N T S

½ cup water

5 cups milk

½ cup long-grain white rice

2–3 strips of lemon zest

1 cinnamon stick

1 vanilla pod, split

generous ½ cup sugar

3 tbsp cornstarch

4 egg yolks

M E R I N G U E

6 egg whites

¼ tsp cream of tartar

1 cup superfine sugar

1 Bring the water and 225 ml/8 fl oz of the milk to a boil in a large heavy pan. Add the rice, lemon zest, cinnamon stick and vanilla pod and reduce the heat to low. Cover and simmer for about 20 minutes until the rice is tender and all the liquid is absorbed. Remove the lemon zest, cinnamon stick, and vanilla pod from the pan and add the remaining milk; return to a boil.

2 Stir together the sugar and the cornstarch. Stir in a little of the hot rice-milk to make a paste, then stir into the pan of rice. Cook, stirring constantly, until the mixture boils and thickens. Boil for 1 minute, then remove from the heat to cool slightly.

3 Beat the egg yolks until smooth. Stir a large spoonful of the hot rice mixture into the yolks, beating until well blended, then stir into the rice mixture. Pour into a 5¼ pint/3 liter baking dish.

4 To make the meringue, beat the egg whites with the cream of tartar in a large bowl to form stiff peaks. Add the sugar, 2 tablespoons at a time, beating well after each addition, until the mixture is stiff and glossy.

5 Gently spoon the meringue over the top of the rice pudding, spreading evenly. Make decorative swirls with the back of a spoon.

6 Bake in a preheated oven at 300°F/ 150°C for about 1 hour until the top is golden and set. Turn off the oven, open the door, and let the pudding cool in the oven. Serve warm, at room temperature, or cold.

Crêpes with Apples

The sharpness of the apples contrasts with the sweetness of the butterscotch sauce in this mouthwatering crêpe recipe.

NUTRITIONAL INFORMATION

Calories 543   Sugars 55g
Protein . . . . .8g   Fat 24g
Carbohydrate . . .78g   Saturates 14g

15 mins   45 mins

SERVES 4

INGREDIENTS

generous 1 cup all-purpose flour

pinch of salt

1 tsp finely grated lemon zest

1 egg

1¼ cups milk

1–2 tbsp vegetable oil, plus extra
for greasing

pared lemon zest, to garnish

FILLING

½ lb cooking apples, peeled, cored and
sliced

2 tbsp golden raisins

SAUCE

6 tbsp butter

3 tbsp light corn syrup

⅓ cup molasses sugar

1 tbsp rum or brandy (optional)

1 tbsp lemon juice

1 Sift the flour and salt into a bowl. Add the lemon zest, egg, and milk and whisk to make a smooth batter.

2 Heat a little oil in a heavy skillet. Make 8 thin crêpes, using extra oil as required. Stack the cooked crêpes, layering them with paper towels or baking parchment, and keep warm.

3 To make the filling, cook the apples with the golden raisins in a little water over low heat until soft. Divide the mixture evenly among the crêpes and roll up or fold into triangles. Brush a casserole with a little oil and arrange the crêpes in it. Bake in a preheated oven, 325°F/160°C, for about 15 minutes until warmed through.

4 To make the sauce, melt the butter, syrup, and sugar together in a pan, stirring well. Add the rum or brandy, if using, and the lemon juice. Do not let the mixture boil.

5 Serve the crêpes on warm plates, with a little sauce poured over, and garnished with lemon zest.

Portuguese Rice Dessert

This buttery, spicy, egg-rich rice dessert is quite irresistible—
and even more so when served with a topping of thick cream.

NUTRITIONAL INFORMATION

Calories	356	Sugars	........22g
Protein	.........7g	Fat	..........19g
Carbohydrate	...43g	Saturates	......10g

10 mins

50 mins

SERVES 6–8

I N G R E D I E N T S

1 generous cup Spanish valencia, Italian arborio, or pudding rice

pinch salt

1 lemon

2 cups milk

⅔ cup light cream

1 cinnamon stick

6 tbsp butter

¾ cup sugar (or to taste)

8 egg yolks

ground cinnamon, for dusting

thick or heavy cream, to serve

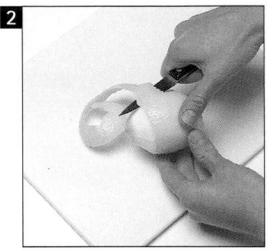

1 Bring a pan of water to a boil. Sprinkle in the rice and salt and return to a boil; reduce the heat and simmer until just tender. Drain, rinse under cold water, and drain again.

2 Using a small sharp knife or swivel-bladed vegetable peeler, and working in a circular motion, try to peel the zest off the lemon in one curly piece; this will make it easier to remove from the dessert later. Alternatively, peel off in strips.

3 Bring the milk and cream to a simmer over medium heat. Add the rice, cinnamon stick, butter, and the lemon zest "curl" or strips. Reduce the heat to low and simmer gently for about 20 minutes until thick and creamy. Remove from the heat; remove and discard the cinnamon stick and the lemon zest. Add the sugar, stirring until it has dissolved.

4 In a large bowl, beat the egg yolks until well blended. Gradually beat in the rice mixture until thick and smooth. Continue to stir frequently to prevent the eggs curdling, until slightly cooled, then pour into a bowl or 6–8 individual glasses. Dust with cinnamon and serve with cream.

Florentine Rice Dessert

This very sophisticated rice dessert from Florence is a cross between a mousse and a soufflé, and is best served warm.

NUTRITIONAL INFORMATION

Calories 836   Sugars 127g
Protein ....14g   Fat 25g
Carbohydrate ..148g   Saturates 14g

 15 mins   1 hr

SERVES 6

INGREDIENTS

⅞ cup long-grain white rice or Italian arborio rice

pinch of salt

4 cups milk

5 eggs

2 cups sugar or 1 lb/450 g honey, or a mixture

½ cup butter, melted and cooled

2 tbsp orange flower water or 4 tbsp orange-flavored liqueur

¾ cup diced candied orange peel

¾ cup orange marmalade

2–3 tablespoons water

confectioners' sugar, for dusting

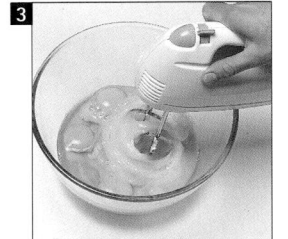

1 Put the rice and salt in a large, heavy pan. Add the milk and bring to a boil, stirring occasionally. Reduce the heat to low and simmer gently for about 25 minutes until the rice is tender and creamy. Remove from the heat.

2 Pass the cooked rice through a food mill into a large bowl, or process in a food processor for about 30 seconds until smooth. Set aside. Stir from time to time to prevent a skin forming.

3 Meanwhile, using an electric mixer, beat the eggs with the sugar in a large bowl for about 4 minutes until very light and creamy. Gently fold into the rice with the melted butter. Stir in half the orange flower water, then stir in the candied orange peel.

4 Turn into a well-buttered 3½ pint/ 2 liter soufflé dish or charlotte mold. Place the dish in a roasting pan and pour in enough boiling water to come 1½ inches/4 cm up the side of the dish.

5 Bake in a preheated oven, at 350°F/180°C, for about 25 minutes until the dessert is puffed and lightly set. Transfer the dish to a wire rack and let cool slightly.

6 Heat the marmalade with the water, stirring until it has dissolved and become smooth. Stir in the remaining orange-flower water and pour into a pitcher. Dust the top of the dessert with the confectioners' sugar and serve warm with the marmalade sauce.

Rhubarb & Orange Crumble

A mixture of rhubarb and apples flavored with orange zest, brown sugar, and spices and topped with a crunchy crumble topping.

NUTRITIONAL INFORMATION

Calories 516   Sugars 45g
Protein . . . . .6g   Fat 22g
Carbohydrate . . .77g   Saturates 4g

    15 mins   45 mins

SERVES 6

INGREDIENTS

1 lb/450 g rhubarb

1 lb/450 g cooking apples

grated zest and juice of 1 orange

½–1 tsp ground cinnamon

6 tbsp light soft brown sugar

TOPPING

2 cups all-purpose flour

9 tbsp butter or margarine

⅞ cup light soft brown sugar

⅔ cup toasted chopped hazelnuts

2 tbsp raw brown sugar (optional)

1   Cut the rhubarb into 1 inch/2.5 cm lengths and place in a large pan.

2   Peel, core, and slice the apples and add to the rhubarb, together with the grated orange zest and juice.

3   Bring to a boil, lower the heat, and simmer for 2–3 minutes, until the fruit begins to soften.

4   Add the cinnamon and sugar to taste and turn the mixture into an ovenproof dish. Make sure that the dish is not more than two-thirds full.

5   Sift the flour into a bowl and rub in the butter or margarine until the mixture resembles fine bread crumbs (this can be done by hand or in a food processor.) Stir in the sugar, followed by the nuts.

6   Spoon the crumble mixture evenly over the fruit in the dish and level the top. Sprinkle with the raw brown sugar, if liked.

7   Cook in a preheated oven, 400°F/200°C, for 30–40 minutes, until the topping is browned. Serve the crumble hot or cold.

VARIATION

Other flavorings, such as ⅓ cup chopped preserved ginger, can be added either to the fruit or the crumb mixture. Any fruit, or mixtures of fruit can be topped with crumble.

Traditional Tiramisu

A favourite Italian dessert flavored with coffee and Amaretto.
You could substitute the Amaretto with brandy or Marsala.

NUTRITIONAL INFORMATION

Calories	569	Sugars	........28g
Protein	........12g	Fat	..........43g
Carbohydrate	...34g	Saturates	......22g

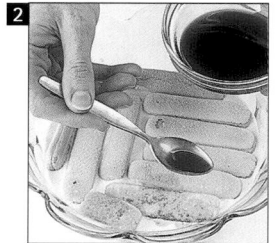

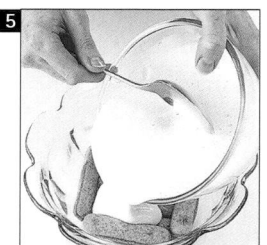

2¼ hrs   5 mins

SERVES 6

INGREDIENTS

20–24 ladyfingers

2 tbsp cold black coffee

2 tbsp coffee extract

2 tbsp Amaretto

4 egg yolks

6 tbsp superfine sugar

few drops of vanilla extract

grated zest of ½ lemon

12 oz /350 g mascarpone cheese

2 tsp lemon juice

1 cup heavy cream

1 tbsp milk

2 tbsp slivered almonds, lightly toasted

2 tbsp unsweetened cocoa

1 tbsp confectioners' sugar

1 Arrange almost half of the lady-fingers in the base of a glass bowl or serving dish.

2 Combine the black coffee, coffee extract and Amaretto together and sprinkle just over half of the mixture over the ladyfingers.

3 Put the egg yolks into a heatproof bowl with the sugar, vanilla extract, and lemon zest. Stand the bowl over a pan of gently simmering water and whisk the mixture until very thick and creamy and the whisk leaves a very heavy trail when lifted from the bowl.

4 Put the mascarpone in a separate bowl with the lemon juice and beat until smooth.

5 Combine the egg and mascarpone cheese mixtures and when evenly blended pour half over the ladyfingers and spread out evenly.

6 Add another layer of ladyfingers, sprinkle with the remaining coffee and Amaretto mixture, then cover with the rest of the cheese and egg mixture. Chill the tiramisu for at least 2 hours and preferably longer, or overnight.

7 To serve, whip the cream and milk together until fairly stiff and spread or pipe over the dessert. Sprinkle with the slivered almonds, then strain an even layer of unsweetened cocoa so the top is completely covered. Strain a light layer of confectioners' sugar over the cocoa.

Pink Syllabubs

The pretty pink color of this dessert is achieved by adding blackcurrant liqueur to the wine and cream before whipping.

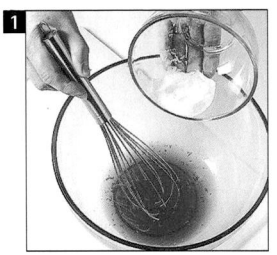

NUTRITIONAL INFORMATION

Calories 536	Sugars 17g
Protein 2g	Fat 48g
Carbohydrate ...17g	Saturates 30g

45 mins   0 mins

SERVES 2

INGREDIENTS

5 tbsp white wine

2–3 tsp blackcurrant liqueur (crème de cassis)

finely grated zest of ½ lemon or orange

1 tbsp superfine sugar

¾ cup heavy cream

4 lady-fingers (optional)

TO DECORATE

fresh fruit, such as strawberries, raspberries, or redcurrants, or pecan or walnut halves

mint sprigs

1 Mix together the white wine, blackcurrant liqueur, grated lemon or orange zest, and superfine sugar in a bowl and let stand for at least 30 minutes.

2 Add the cream to the wine mixture and whip until the mixture has thickened enough to stand in soft peaks.

3 If you are using the ladyfingers, break them up roughly and divide them between 2 glasses.

4 For a decorative effect, put the mixture into a pastry bag fitted with a large star or plain tip and pipe it over the ladyfingers. Alternatively, simply pour the syllabub over the ladyfingers. Chill until ready to serve.

5 Before serving, decorate each syllabub with slices or small pieces of fresh soft fruit or nuts, and sprigs of mint.

COOK'S TIP

These syllabubs will keep in the refrigerator for 48 hours, so it is worth making more than you need, and keeping the extra for another day.

Berry Cheesecake

Use a mixture of berries, such as blueberries, blackberries, raspberries, and strawberries, for a really fruity cheesecake.

NUTRITIONAL INFORMATION

Calories ....478 Sugars 28g
Protein ....10g Fat 32g
Carbohydrate ...40g Saturates 15g

2¼ hrs   5 mins

SERVES 8

I N G R E D I E N T S

BASE

6 tbsp margarine

6 oz/175 g oatmeal cookies

⅔ cup shredded coconut

TOPPING

1½ tsp gelozone

9 tbsp cold water

½ cup evaporated milk

1 egg

6 tbsp light brown sugar

2 cups soft cream cheese

3 cups mixed berries

2 tbsp clear honey

1 Put the margarine in a pan and heat until melted. Put the cookies in a food processor and process until thoroughly crushed or crush finely with a rolling pin. Stir the crumbs into the margarine, together with the coconut.

2 Press the mixture evenly into a base-lined 8 inch/ 20 cm springform pan and let chill in the refrigerator while you are preparing the filling.

3 To make the topping, sprinkle the gelozone over the water and stir to dissolve. Bring to a boil and boil for 2 minutes. Let cool slightly.

4 Put the milk, egg, sugar, and soft cream cheese in a bowl and beat until smooth. Stir in ½ cup of the berries. Add the gelozone in a stream, stirring constantly.

5 Spoon the mixture on to the cookie base and return to the refrigerator to chill for 2 hours, or until set.

6 Remove the cheesecake carefully from the pan and transfer to a serving plate.

7 Arrange the remaining berries on top of the cheesecake and drizzle the honey over the top. Serve.

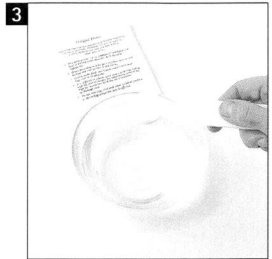

Sweet Fruit Wontons

These sweet wontons are very adaptable and may be filled with whole, small fruits or a spicy chopped mixture as here.

NUTRITIONAL INFORMATION

Calories 244   Sugars 25g
Protein . . . . .2g   Fat 12g
Carbohydrate . . .35g   Saturates 3g

10 mins   15 mins

SERVES 4

I N G R E D I E N T S

12 wonton wrappers

2 tsp cornstarch

6 tsp cold water

oil, for deep-frying

2 tbsp clear honey

selection of fresh fruit (such as kiwi fruit, limes, oranges, mango, and apples), sliced, to serve

F I L L I N G

1 cup chopped dried, pitted dates

2 tsp dark brown sugar

½ tsp ground cinnamon

1 To make the filling, mix together the dates, sugar, and cinnamon in a bowl.

2 Spread out the wonton wrappers on a cutting board and spoon a little of the filling into the center of each wrapper.

3 Blend the cornstarch and water and brush this mixture around the edges of the wrappers.

4 Fold the wrappers over the filling, bringing the edges together, then bring the two corners together, sealing with the cornstarch mixture.

5 Heat the oil for deep-frying in a wok to 350°F/180°C, or until a cube of bread browns in 30 seconds. Fry the wontons, in batches, for 2-3 minutes, until golden. Remove the wontons from the oil with a slotted spoon and leave to drain on absorbent paper towels.

6 Place the clear honey in a bowl and stand it in warm water, to soften it slightly. Drizzle the honey over the sweet fruit wontons and serve with a selection of fresh fruit.

COOK'S TIP

Wonton wrappers may be found in Chinese grocery stores. Alternatively, use half the quantity of the dough made for Wonton Soup (page 113).

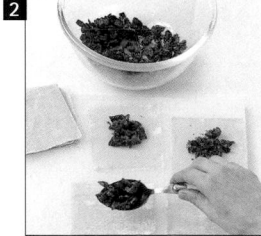

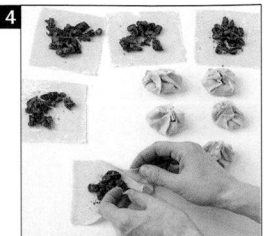

Boston Chocolate Pie

This lighter version of the popular chocolate cream pie is made with yogurt and crème fraîche (see page 8).

NUTRITIONAL INFORMATION

Calories 795   Sugars 73g
Protein ....13g   Fat 40g
Carbohydrate ...99g   Saturates 21g

 25 mins   35 mins

SERVES 6

INGREDIENTS

½ lb shortcrust pie dough

chocolate caraque

½ lb dark chocolate

FILLING

3 eggs

½ cup superfine sugar

scant ½ cup all-purpose flour, plus extra for dusting

1 tbsp confectioners' sugar

pinch of salt

1 tsp vanilla extract

1¾ cups milk

⅔ cup unsweetened yogurt

5½ oz/150 g dark chocolate, broken into pieces

2 tbsp kirsch

TOPPING

⅔ cup crème fraîche (see page 8)

1 Roll out the pie dough and use to line a 9 inch/23 cm loose-based quiche pan. Prick the base with a fork, line with baking parchment, and fill with dried beans. Bake blind for 20 minutes. Remove the beans and paper and return to the oven for 5 minutes. Remove from the oven and place the pan on a wire rack to cool.

2 To make the chocolate caraque, put pieces of chocolate on a plate over a pan of simmering water until melted. Spread on a cool surface with a spatula. When cool, scrape it into curls with a sharp knife.

3 To make the filling, beat the eggs and sugar until fluffy. Strain in the flour, confectioners' sugar, and salt. Stir in the vanilla extract. Bring the milk and yogurt to a boil in a small pan and strain on to the egg mixture. Pour into a double boiler or set over a pan of simmering water. Stir until it coats the back of a spoon.

4 Gently heat the chocolate and kirsch in a small pan until melted. Stir into the custard. Remove from the heat and stand the double boiler or bowl in cold water. Let cool, then pour the chocolate mixture into the pie shell. Spread the crème fraîche over the chocolate, and arrange the caraque rolls on top.

Fresh Fruit Compôte

Elderflower cordial is used in the syrup for this refreshing fruit compôte, giving it a delightfully summery flavor.

NUTRITIONAL INFORMATION

Calories 255	Sugars 61g
Protein 4g	Fat 1g
Carbohydrate ... 61g	Saturates 0.2g

20 mins   15 mins

SERVES 4

INGREDIENTS

1 lemon

¼ cup superfine sugar

4 tbsp elderflower cordial

1¼ cups water

4 eating apples

2 cups blackberries

2 fresh figs

TOPPING

⅔ cup thick unsweetened yogurt

2 tbsp clear honey

1 Thinly pare the zest from the lemon using a swivel vegetable peeler. Squeeze the juice. Put the lemon zest and juice into a pan, together with the sugar, elderflower cordial and water. Set over low heat and simmer, uncovered, for 10 minutes.

2 Peel, core, and slice the apples. Add the apples to the pan. Simmer gently for about 4–5 minutes, until just tender. Remove the pan from the heat and let cool.

3 When cold, transfer the apples and syrup to a serving bowl and add the blackberries. Slice and add the figs. Stir gently to mix. Cover and chill in the refrigerator until ready to serve.

4 Spoon the yogurt into a small serving bowl and drizzle the honey over the top. Cover and chill before serving.

COOK'S TIP

Greek-style yogurt may be made from cow's or ewe's milk. The former is often strained to make it more concentrated and has a high fat content, which perfectly counterbalances the sharpness and acidity of fruit.

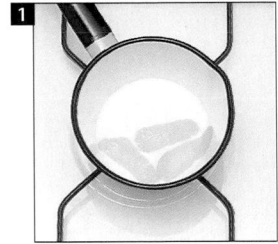

Fall Fruit Bread Pudding

This is like a summer pudding, but it uses fruits which appear later in the year. This dessert requires chilling overnight so prepare in advance.

NUTRITIONAL INFORMATION

Calories	177	Sugars	........29g
Protein	.........3g	Fat	...........1g
Carbohydrate	...42g	Saturates	.....0.1g

 10 mins   15 mins

SERVES 8

INGREDIENTS

2 lb/900 g mixed blackberries, chopped apples, chopped pears

1 cup soft light brown sugar

1 tsp cinnamon

8 oz/225 g white bread, thinly sliced, crusts removed (about 12 slices)

1 Place the fruit in a large pan with the soft light brown sugar, cinnamon, and 7 tablespoons of water, stir, and bring to a boil. Reduce the heat and simmer for 5–10 minutes so that the fruits soften but still hold their shape.

2 Meanwhile, line the base and sides of a 3¾ cup heatproof bowl with the bread slices, ensuring that there are no gaps between the pieces of bread.

3 Spoon the fruit into the center of the bread-lined bowl and cover the fruit with the remaining bread.

4 Place a saucer on top of the bread and place a heavy weight on it. Chill the pudding in the refrigerator overnight.

5 When ready to serve the pudding, turn it out on to a serving plate and serve immediately.

COOK'S TIP

This pudding would be delicious served with vanilla ice cream to counteract the tartness of the blackberries. Stand the pudding on a plate when chilling to catch any juices that run down the sides of the basin.

Semolina Dessert

This dish is eaten with pooris and potato curry for breakfast in northern India, but you can serve it with fresh cream for a delicious dessert.

NUTRITIONAL INFORMATION

Calories	676	Sugars	........66g
Protein	........10g	Fat	..........31g
Carbohydrate	...96g	Saturates	......19g

 5 mins   10 mins

SERVES 4

I N G R E D I E N T S

6 tbsp pure ghee

3 whole cloves

3 whole cardamoms

8 tbsp coarse semolina

½ tsp saffron

½ cup golden raisins

10 tbsp sugar

1¼ cups water

1¼ cups milk

cream, to serve

TO DECORATE

⅓ cup shredded coconut, toasted

¼ cup chopped almonds

⅓ cup pistachio nuts, soaked and chopped (optional)

1 Place the ghee in a pan and melt over medium heat.

2 Add the cloves and the whole cardamoms to the melted butter and reduce the heat, stirring to mix.

3 Add the semolina to the mixture in the pan and stir-fry until it turns a little darker.

4 Add the saffron, golden raisins, and sugar to the semolina mixture, stirring to combine thoroughly.

5 Pour in the water and milk and cook, stirring the mixture continuously until the semolina has softened. Add a little more water if required.

6 Remove the pan from the heat and transfer the semolina to a warmed serving dish.

7 Decorate the semolina dessert with the toasted coconut, chopped almonds, and pistachios. Serve with a little cream drizzled over the top.

Coconut Sweet

Quick and easy to make, this sweet is very similar to coconut ice.
Pink food coloring may be added towards the end if desired.

NUTRITIONAL INFORMATION

Calories 338   Sugars 5g
Protein ....4g   Fat 34g
Carbohydrate ....5g   Saturates 26g

1¼ hrs   15 mins

SERVES 6

INGREDIENTS

6 tbsp butter

2⅓ cups shredded coconut

¾ cup condensed milk

a few drops of pink food coloring (optional)

3 Stir in the condensed milk and the
pink food coloring (if using) and mix
continuously for 7–10 minutes.

1 Place the butter in a heavy pan and
melt over low heat, stirring constantly
so that the butter doesn't burn on the
base of the pan.

4 Remove the pan from the heat, set
aside, and let cool slightly.

5 Once cool enough to handle, shape
the coconut mixture into long blocks
and cut into equal-sized rectangles. Let set
for about 1 hour, then serve.

2 Add the shredded coconut to the
melted butter, stirring to mix.

VARIATION

If you prefer, you could divide the
coconut mixture in step 2, and add
the pink food coloring to only one
half of the mixture. This way, you
will have an attractive combination
of pink and white coconut sweets.

Sweet Carrot Halva

This nutritious dessert is flavored with spices, nuts, and raisins.
The nutritional information does not include serving with cream.

NUTRITIONAL INFORMATION

Calories	284	Sugars	.......33g
Protein	.........7g	Fat	..........14g
Carbohydrate	...34g	Saturates	.......3g

10 mins   55 mins

SERVES 6

INGREDIENTS

3½ cups grated carrots

3 cups milk

1 cinnamon stick or piece of cassia bark (optional)

4 tbsp vegetable ghee or oil

5 tbsp granulated sugar

⅓ cup unsalted pistachio nuts, chopped

4 tbsp blanched almonds, slivered or chopped

½ cup seedless raisins

8 cardamom pods, split and seeds removed and crushed

heavy cream, to serve

1 Put the grated carrots, milk and cinnamon or cassia, if using, into a large, heavy pan and bring to a boil.

Reduce the heat to very low and simmer, uncovered, for 35–40 minutes, or until the mixture is thick (with no milk remaining.) Stir the mixture frequently during cooking to prevent it from sticking.

2 Remove and discard the cinnamon or cassia. Heat the ghee or oil in a nonstick skillet, add the carrot mixture and stir-fry over medium heat for about 5 minutes, or until the carrots take on a glossy sheen.

3 Add the sugar, pistachios, almonds, raisins, and crushed cardamom seeds, mix thoroughly, and continue stir-frying for a further 3–4 minutes. Serve warm or cold with heavy cream.

COOK'S TIP

The quickest and easiest way to grate this quantity of carrots is by using a food processor fitted with the appropriate blade.

Satsuma & Pecan Pavlova

Make this spectacular dessert for the perfect way to round off a special occasion. You can make the meringue base well in advance.

NUTRITIONAL INFORMATION

Calories 339	Sugars 36g	
Protein 3g	Fat 21g	
Carbohydrate ...37g	Saturates 10g	

 2½ hrs   3 hrs

SERVES 8

I N G R E D I E N T S

4 egg whites

1 firmly packed cup light soft sugar

1¼ cups heavy or whipping cream

generous ½ cup pecan nuts

4 satsumas, peeled

1 passion fruit or pomegranate

1 Line 2 cookie sheets with nonstick baking parchment or waxed paper. Draw a 9 inch/23 cm circle on one of the sheets.

2 Whip the egg whites in a large, grease-free bowl until stiff. Add the sugar gradually, continuing to beat until the mixture is very glossy.

3 Pipe or spoon a layer of meringue mixture on to the circle marked on the baking parchment; then pipe large rosettes or place spoonfuls on top of the meringue's outer edge. Pipe any remaining meringue mixture in tiny rosettes on the second cookie sheet.

4 Bake in a preheated oven, 275°F/140°C for 2–3 hours, making sure that the oven is well-ventilated by using a folded dish cloth to keep the door slightly open. Remove from the oven and let cool completely. When cold, peel off the baking parchment carefully.

5 Whip the heavy or whipping cream in a large chilled bowl until thick. Spoon about one-third into a pastry bag, fitted with a star tip. Reserve a few pecan nuts and 1 satsuma for decoration. Chop the remaining nuts and fruit, and fold into the remaining cream.

6 Pile on top of the meringue base and decorate with the meringue rosettes, piped cream, satsuma segments, and pecan nuts. Scoop the seeds from the passion fruit or pomegranate with a teaspoon and sprinkle them on top.

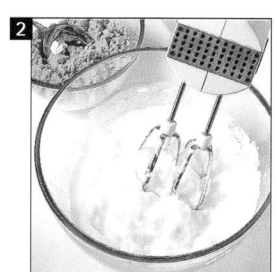

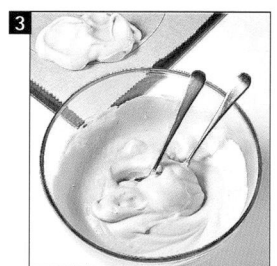

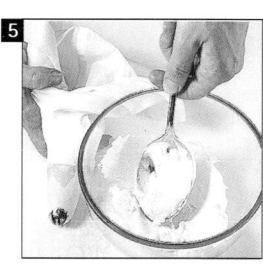

Baked Cheesecake

This cheesecake has a rich creamy texture, but contains no dairy produce at all, as it is made with bean curd.

NUTRITIONAL INFORMATION

Calories 282   Sugars 17g
Protein . . . . .9g   Fat 15g
Carbohydrate . . .29g   Saturates 4g

 2¼ hrs   45 mins

SERVES 6

INGREDIENTS

4 tbsp vegan margarine, melted, plus extra
 for greasing

2¼ cups graham cracker crumbs

⅓ cup chopped pitted dates

4 tbsp lemon juice

zest of 1 lemon

3 tbsp water

12 oz/350 g firm bean curd

⅔ cup apple juice

1 banana, mashed

1 tsp vanilla extract

1 mango, peeled, pitted, and chopped

1 Lightly grease a 7-inch/18-cm circular loose-bottomed cake pan with a little vegan margarine.

VARIATION
Silken bean curd may be substituted for the firm bean curd to give a softer texture; it will take 40–50 minutes to set.

2 Mix together the graham cracker crumbs and melted margarine in a bowl. Press the mixture into the base of the prepared pan.

3 Put the chopped dates, lemon juice, lemon zest, and water into a pan and bring to a boil. Simmer gently for 5 minutes until the dates are soft, then mash them roughly with a fork.

4 Place the mixture in a blender or food processor with the bean curd, apple juice, mashed banana, and vanilla extract

and process until the mixture forms a thick, smooth paste.

5 Pour the bean curd paste onto the prepared cracker crumb base.

6 Bake in a preheated oven, 350°F/ 180°C, for 30–40 minutes, until lightly golden. Let cool in the pan, then chill thoroughly before serving.

7 Place the chopped mango in a blender and process until smooth. Serve it as a sauce with the cheesecake.

Cherry Crêpes

This dish can be made with either fresh pitted cherries or, if time is short, with canned cherries for extra speed.

NUTRITIONAL INFORMATION

Calories	345	Sugars	........25g
Protein	.........8g	Fat	...........11g
Carbohydrate	...56g	Saturates	.......2g

🐚 🐚 🐚

🍲 10 mins   🕐 15 mins

SERVES 4

INGREDIENTS

FILLING

14 oz/400 g can pitted cherries

½ tsp almond extract

½ tsp apple spice

2 tbsp cornstarch

CRÊPES

100 g/3½ oz all-purpose flour

pinch of salt

2 tbsp chopped mint

1 egg

1¼ cups milk

vegetable oil, for frying

confectioners' sugar and toasted slivered almonds, to decorate

2 To make the crêpes, strain the flour into a bowl with the salt. Add the chopped mint and make a well in the center. Gradually beat in the egg and milk to make a smooth batter.

3 Heat 1 tablespoon of oil in an 7 inch/ 18 cm skillet; pour off the oil when hot. Add just enough batter to coat the base of the skillet and cook for 1–2 minutes, or until the underside is cooked. Flip the crêpe over and cook for 1 minute. Remove from the pan and keep warm. Repeat to use up all the batter.

4 Spoon a quarter of the cherry filling on to a quarter of each crêpe and fold the crêpe into a cone shape. Dust with confectioners' sugar and sprinkle over the slivered almonds. Serve immediately.

1 Put the cherries and 1¼ cups of the can juice in a pan with the almond extract and apple spice. Stir in the cornstarch and bring to a boil, stirring until thickened and clear. Set aside.

Almond & Pistachio Dessert

Rich and mouth-watering, this dessert can be prepared well in advance of the meal. It is best served cold.

NUTRITIONAL INFORMATION

Calories	565	Sugars	........37g
Protein	.........8g	Fat	..........43g
Carbohydrate	...38g	Saturates	......16g

 1¼ hrs   15 mins

SERVES 6

INGREDIENTS

6 tbsp sweet butter

2 cups ground almonds

1 cup sugar

⅔ cup light cream

8 almonds, chopped

10 pistachio nuts, chopped

1 Place the butter in a medium-size pan, preferably nonstick. Melt the butter, stirring well.

2 Add the ground almonds, sugar, and cream to the melted butter in the pan, stirring to combine. Reduce the heat and stir constantly for 10-12 minutes, scraping the base of the pan.

3 Increase the heat until the mixture turns a little darker in color.

4 Transfer the almond mixture to a shallow serving dish and smooth the top with the back of a spoon.

5 Decorate the top of the dessert with the chopped almonds and pistachios.

6 Leave the dessert to set for about 1 hour, then cut into diamond shapes and serve cold.

COOK'S TIP

This almond dessert can be made in advance and stored in an airtight container in the refrigerator for several days. You could use a variety of shaped dough cutters, to cut the dessert into different shapes, rather than diamonds, if you prefer.

Mocha Swirl Mousse

A combination of feather-light yet rich chocolate and coffee mousses, whipped and attractively presented in serving glasses.

NUTRITIONAL INFORMATION

Calories 542   Sugars 12g
Protein ....5g   Fat 6g
Carbohydrate ...13g   Saturates 4g

1¼ hrs   0 mins

SERVES 4

INGREDIENTS

1 tbsp coffee and chicory extract

2 tsp unsweetened cocoa, plus extra for dusting

1 tsp low-fat drinking chocolate powder

⅔ cup low-fat crème fraîche, plus 4 tsp to serve (see page 8)

2 tsp powdered gelozone

2 tbsp boiling water

2 large egg whites

2 tbsp superfine sugar

4 chocolate coffee beans, to serve

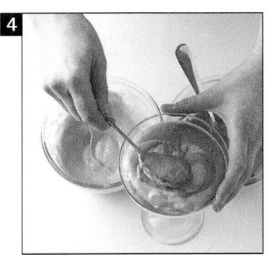

1 Place the coffee and chicory extract in one bowl, and 2 teaspoons of cocoa and the drinking chocolate in another bowl. Divide the crème fraîche between the 2 bowls and mix both well.

2 Dissolve the gelozone in the boiling water and set aside. In a grease-free bowl, whisk the egg whites and sugar until stiff and divide this evenly between the two mixtures.

3 Divide the gelozone between the 2 mixtures and, using a large metal spoon, gently fold until well mixed.

4 Spoon small amounts of the chocolate and coffee mousses alternately into 4 serving glasses and swirl together gently. Chill for 1 hour or until set.

5 To serve, top each mousse with a teaspoon of the crème fraîche, a chocolate coffee bean, and a light dusting of unsweetened cocoa and serve immediately.

COOK'S TIP
The vegetarian equivalent of gelatin, called gelozone, is available from health-food stores.

Brown Sugar Pavlovas

This simple combination of fudgey meringue topped with mascarpone and raspberries is the perfect finale to any meal.

NUTRITIONAL INFORMATION

Calories 155	Sugars 34g
Protein 5g	Fat 0.2g
Carbohydrate ...35g	Saturates 0g

🍰 🍰

🧊 1 hr   🕐 1 hr

SERVES 4

I N G R E D I E N T S

2 large egg whites

1 tsp cornstarch

1 tsp raspberry vinegar

½ cup light brown sugar, crushed free of lumps

2 tbsp red currant jelly

2 tbsp unsweetened orange juice

¾ cup low-fat mascarpone cheese

1 cup raspberries, thawed if frozen

rose-scented geranium leaves, to decorate (optional)

1 Line a large cookie sheet with baking parchment. Whisk the egg whites until very stiff and dry. Gently fold in the cornstarch and vinegar.

2 Gradually whisk in the sugar, a spoonful at a time, until the mixture is thick and glossy.

3 Divide the mixture into 4 and spoon onto the prepared cookie sheet, spaced well apart. Smooth each heap into a circle, about 4 inches/10 cm in diameter, and bake in a preheated oven, 300°F/150°C, for 40–45 minutes until crisp and a light golden brown color. Let the meringue cool on the cookie sheet.

4 Place the red currant jelly and orange juice in a small pan and heat, stirring, until melted. Let cool for 10 minutes.

5 Using a spatula, carefully remove each pavlova from the baking parchment and transfer to a serving plate. Top with the mascarpone and the raspberries. Glaze the fruit with the red currant jelly mixture, and decorate with the rose-scented geranium leaves, if using.

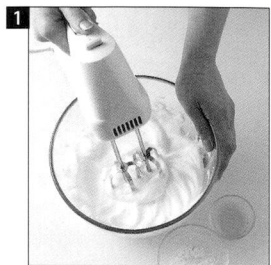

COOK'S TIP

Make a large pavlova by forming the meringue into a circle, measuring 7 inches/18 cm across, on a lined cookie sheet, and baking for 1 hour.

Almond Cheesecakes

These creamy cheese desserts are so delicious that it's hard to believe that they are low in fat—a healthy and tasty option.

1¼ hrs 10 mins

SERVES 4

INGREDIENTS

12 amaretti cookies

1 egg white, lightly beaten

1 cup skim-milk soft cheese

½ tsp almond extract

½ tsp finely grated lime zest

scant ¼ cup ground almonds

2 tbsp superfine sugar

⅓ cup golden raisins

2 tsp powdered gelozone

2 tbsp boiling water

2 tbsp lime juice

TO DECORATE

2 tbsp slivered toasted almonds

strips of lime zest

1 Place the cookies in a clean plastic bag, seal the bag, and using a rolling pin, crush them into small pieces.

2 Place the amaretti crumbs in a bowl and stir in the egg white to bind them together.

3 Arrange 4 non-stick dough rings or poached egg rings, 3½ inches/9 cm across, on a cookie sheet lined with baking parchment.

4 Divide the amaretti mixture into 4 equal portions and spoon it into the rings, pressing it down well. Bake in a preheated oven, 350°F/180°C, for about 10 minutes until crisp. Remove from the oven and let cool in the rings.

5 Put the soft cheese, almond extract, lime zest, ground almonds, sugar, and golden raisins in a bowl and beat thoroughly until well mixed.

6 Dissolve the gelozone in the boiling water and stir in the lime juice. Fold into the cheese mixture and spoon over the amaretti bases. Smooth over the tops and chill for 1 hour or until set.

7 Loosen the cheesecakes from the rings using a small spatula and transfer to serving plates. Decorate with slivered toasted almonds and strips of lime zest and serve.

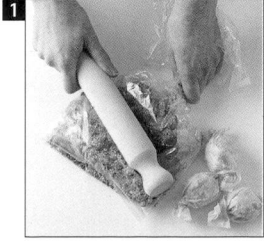

Pavlova

This delicious dessert originated in Australia. Serve it with sharp fruits, such as summer berries, to balance the sweetness of the meringue.

NUTRITIONAL INFORMATION

Calories 354	Sugars 34g
Protein 3g	Fat 24g
Carbohydrate ...34g	Saturates 15g

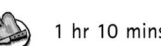

🍰 1 hr 10 mins 🕐 1¼ hrs

MAKES 6

INGREDIENTS

3 egg whites

¾ cup superfine sugar

1¼ cups heavy cream, lightly whipped

fresh fruit of your choice (raspberries, strawberries, peaches, passion fruit, ground cherries)

salt

1 Line a cookie sheet with a sheet of baking parchment.

2 Whisk the egg whites with a pinch of salt in a large bowl until they form soft peaks.

3 Whisk in the sugar, a little at a time, whisking well after each addition until all of the sugar has been incorporated and the meringue is smooth and glossy.

4 Spoon three-quarters of the meringue onto the cookie sheet, forming a circle 8 inches/20-cm in diameter.

5 Place spoonfuls of the remaining meringue all around the edge of the circle, joining the meringue up to make a nest shape.

6 Bake in a preheated oven, 275°F/ 140°C, for 1¼ hours.

7 Turn the heat off, but let the pavlova stand in the oven until it is completely cold.

8 To serve, place the pavlova on a serving dish. Spread with the lightly whipped cream, then arrange the fresh fruit on top.

COOK'S TIP

If you are worried about creating the right shape, draw a circle on the baking parchment, turn the paper over, then spoon the meringue inside the outline.

Baked Apples with Berries

This winter dessert is a classic dish. Large, fluffy apples are hollowed out and filled with spices, almonds, and blackberries.

NUTRITIONAL INFORMATION

Calories 228   Sugars 31g
Protein . . . . .1g   Fat 2g
Carbohydrate . . .31g   Saturates 0.2g

10 mins   45 mins

SERVES 4

I N G R E D I E N T S

4 medium-size cooking apples

1 tbsp lemon juice

1 cup prepared blackberries, thawed if frozen

1 tbsp slivered almonds

½ tsp ground allspice

½ tsp finely grated lemon zest

2 tbsp raw brown sugar

1¼ cups ruby port

1 cinnamon stick, broken

2 tsp cornstarch blended with 2 tbsp cold water

low-fat custard, to serve

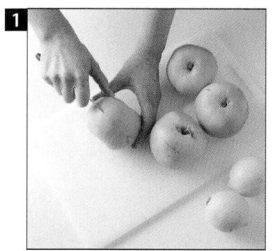
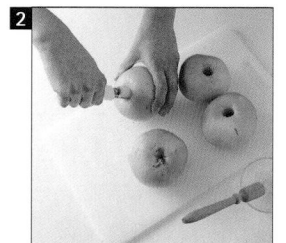

1 Wash and dry the apples. Using a small sharp knife, make a shallow cut through the skin around the middle of each apple—this will help the apples to cook through.

2 Core the apples, brush the centers with the lemon juice to prevent them from browning, and stand them in an ovenproof dish.

3 In a bowl, combine the blackberries, almonds, allspice, lemon zest, and sugar. Using a teaspoon, spoon the mixture into the center of each apple.

4 Pour the port into the dish, add the cinnamon stick, and bake the apples in a preheated oven, 400°F/200°C, for 35–40 minutes or until tender and soft.

5 Drain the cooking juices into a small pan and set over low heat. Keep the apples warm.

6 Discard the cinnamon from the cooking juices and add the cornstarch mixture to the pan. Heat, stirring constantly, until thickened.

7 Heat the custard until piping hot. Pour the sauce over the apples and serve with the custard.

Mixed Fruit Brûlées

Traditionally a rich mixture made with cream, this fruit-based version is just as tempting using low-fat smetana and yogurt as a topping.

NUTRITIONAL INFORMATION

Calories 165	Sugars 21g
Protein 5g	Fat 7g
Carbohydrate ...21g	Saturates 5g

5 mins

5 mins

SERVES 4

INGREDIENTS

1 lb/450 g prepared assorted summer fruits, such as strawberries, raspberries, black currants, red currants, and cherries, thawed if frozen

⅔ cup smetana

⅔ cup low-fat unsweetened yogurt

1 tsp vanilla extract

4 tbsp raw sugar

1 Divide the prepared strawberries, raspberries, black currants, red currants, and cherries evenly among 4 small heatproof ramekin dishes.

2 Combine the smetana, yogurt, and vanilla extract.

3 Spoon the mixture over the fruit, to cover it completely.

4 Top each serving with 1 tablespoon raw sugar and place the desserts under a preheated broiler for 2–3 minutes until the sugar melts and begins to caramelize. Let the brulées stand for a couple of minutes before serving, to set the topping a little.

COOK'S TIP

Look out for half-fat creams, in light and heavy varieties. They are good substitutes for occasional use. Alternatively, in this recipe, double the quantity of yogurt for a lower-fat version.

New Age Spotted Dick

This is a deliciously moist low-fat pudding. The sauce is in the center of the pudding, and will spill out when the pudding is cut.

NUTRITIONAL INFORMATION

Calories	529	Sugars	........41g
Protein	.........9g	Fat	..........31g
Carbohydrate	...58g	Saturates	......4g

25 mins   1¼ hrs

SERVES 6–8

INGREDIENTS

1 cup raisins

½ cup corn oil, plus a little for brushing

½ cup superfine sugar

⅓ cup ground almonds

2 eggs, lightly beaten

scant 1½ cups self-rising flour

SAUCE

½ cup walnuts, chopped

⅔ cup ground almonds

1¼ cups semi-skim milk

4 tbsp granulated sugar

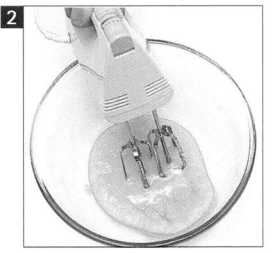  

1 Put the raisins in a pan with ¼ cup water. Bring to a boil, then remove from the heat. Let steep for 10 minutes, then drain.

2 Whisk together the oil, sugar, and ground almonds until thick and syrupy; this will need about 8 minutes of beating (on medium speed if using an electric whisk.)

3 Add the eggs, one at a time, beating well after each addition. Combine the flour and raisins. Stir into the mixture.

4 Brush a 4 cup/1 liter heatproof bowl with oil, or line with baking paper.

5 Put all the sauce ingredients into a pan. Bring to a boil, stir, and simmer for 10 minutes.

6 Transfer the sponge mixture to the greased bowl and pour on the hot sauce. Place on a cookie sheet.

7 Bake in a preheated oven at 340°F/ 170°C for about 1 hour or until well risen. Lay a piece of baking parchment across the top of the pudding if it starts to brown too quickly.

8 Let cool for 2–3 minutes in the bowl before turning out on to a warm serving plate.

COOK'S TIP
Always soak raisins before baking them, as they retain their moisture nicely and you taste the flavor of them instead of biting on a dried-out raisin.

Summer Fruit Clafoutis

Serve this mouthwatering French-style fruit-in-batter dessert hot or cold with low-fat yogurt.

NUTRITIONAL INFORMATION

Calories . . . . . . .228 Sugars 26g
Protein . . . . .9g Fat 2g
Carbohydrate . . .42g Saturates 1g

🦪 🦪 🦪

🧊 1¾ hrs   🕐 50 mins

SERVES 4

I N G R E D I E N T S

1 lb/450 g prepared fresh assorted soft fruits, such as blackberries, raspberries, strawberries, blueberries, cherries, gooseberries, red currants, black currants

4 tbsp soft fruit liqueur such as crème de cassis, kirsch, or framboise

4 tbsp nonfat dry milk

1 cup all-purpose flour

pinch of salt

¼ cup superfine sugar

2 eggs, beaten

1¼ cups skim milk

1 tsp vanilla extract

2 tsp superfine sugar, for dusting

TO SERVE

assorted soft fruits

low-fat unsweetened yogurt

1 Place the assorted fruits in a mixing bowl and spoon over the fruit liqueur. Cover and let chill for 1 hour for the fruit to macerate.

2 In a large bowl, combine the nonfat dry milk, flour, salt, and sugar. Make a well in the center and gradually whisk in the eggs, milk, and vanilla extract, using a balloon whisk, until smooth. Transfer to a pitcher and let stand for 30 minutes.

3 Line the base of a 9 inch/23 cm round ovenproof dish with baking parchment and spoon in all the fruits and their juices.

4 Whisk the batter again and pour it over the fruits, stand the dish on a cookie sheet, and bake in a preheated oven, 400°F/200°C, for 50 minutes until firm, risen, and golden brown.

5 Dust with superfine sugar. Serve immediately with extra fruits and low-fat unsweetened yogurt.

Orange Syllabub

A zesty, creamy whip made from yogurt and milk with a hint of orange, served with light and luscious sweet sponge cakes.

NUTRITIONAL INFORMATION

Calories	464	Sugars	........74g
Protein	........22g	Fat	...........5g
Carbohydrate	...89g	Saturates	......2g

1½ hrs   10 mins

SERVES 4

INGREDIENTS

4 oranges

2½ cups low-fat unsweetened yogurt

6 tbsp low-fat skim milk powder

4 tbsp superfine sugar

1 tbsp grated orange zest

4 tbsp orange juice

2 egg whites

fresh orange zest to decorate

SPONGE HEARTS

2 eggs, size 2

6 tbsp superfine sugar

⅓ cup all-purpose flour

⅓ cup whole-wheat flour

1 tbsp hot water

1 tsp confectioners' sugar

1 Slice off the tops and bottoms of the oranges and the skin. Then cut out the segments, removing the zest and membranes between each one. Divide the orange segments between 4 dessert glasses, then chill.

2 In a mixing bowl, combine the yogurt, milk powder, sugar, orange zest, and juice. Cover and chill for 1 hour. Whisk the egg whites until stiff, then fold into the yogurt mixture. Pile on to the orange slices and chill for an hour. Decorate with fresh orange zest.

3 To make the sponge hearts, line a 6 x 10 inch/15 x 25 cm baking pan with baking parchment. Whisk the eggs and superfine sugar together until thick and pale. Strain in the flours, then fold in using a large metal spoon, adding the hot water at the same time.

4 Pour into the pan and bake in a preheated oven at 425°F/220°C for 9–10 minutes until golden on top and firm to the touch.

5 Turn the sponge out on to a sheet of baking parchment. Using a 2 inch/ 5 cm heart-shaped cutter, stamp out hearts. Transfer to a wire rack to cool. Lightly dust with confectioners' sugar before serving with the syllabub.

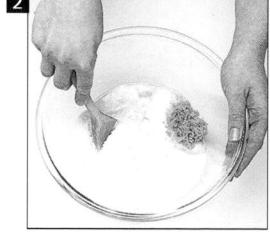

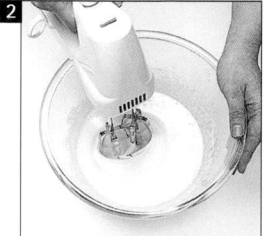

Chinese Fruit Salad

The syrup for this colorful and unusual fruit salad is filled with Chinese flavors for a refreshing dessert.

NUTRITIONAL INFORMATION

Calories 405	Sugars 81g	
Protein 3g	Fat 6g	
Carbohydrate ...83g	Saturates 1g	

1¾ hrs   10 mins

SERVES 4

INGREDIENTS

5 tbsp Chinese rice wine or
   dry sherry

zest and juice of 1 lemon

3½ cups water

1 cup superfine sugar

2 cloves

1 inch/2.5 cm piece cinnamon
   stick, bruised

1 vanilla bean

pinch of mixed spice·

1 star anise pod

1 inch/2.5 cm piece fresh ginger root, sliced

½ cup unsalted cashew nuts

2 kiwi fruits

1 star fruit

1 cup strawberries

14 oz/400 g can lychees in syrup, drained

1 piece preserved ginger, drained and sliced

chopped mint, to decorate

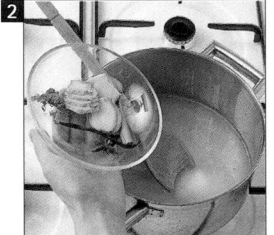  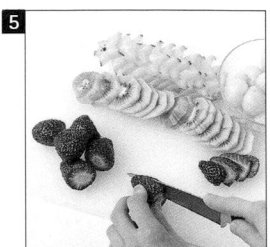

1 Put the Chinese rice wine or sherry in a pan, together with the lemon zest, water, and juice.

2 Add the superfine sugar, cloves, bruised cinnamon stick, vanilla bean, mixed spice, star anise, and fresh ginger root to the pan.

3 Heat the mixture in the pan gently over low heat, stirring constantly, until the sugar has dissolved, and then bring it to a boil. Reduce the heat and simmer the mixture for 5 minutes, then let cool completely.

4 Strain the syrup into a bowl or pitcher, discarding the flavorings. Stir in the cashew nuts, cover with plastic wrap, and chill in the refrigerator.

5 Meanwhile, prepare the fruits: halve and slice the kiwi fruit, slice the star fruit, and hull and slice the strawberries.

6 Spoon the prepared fruit into a dish with the lychees and ginger. Stir through gently to mix.

7 Pour the syrup over the fruit, decorate with chopped mint, and serve.

Exotic Fruit Salad

This is a sophisticated fruit salad that makes use of some of the exotic fruits that are now available everywhere.

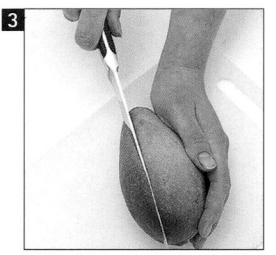
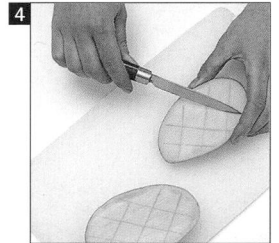
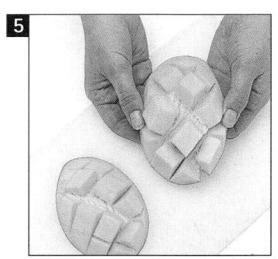

NUTRITIONAL INFORMATION

Calories 149	Sugars 39g
Protein 1g	Fat 0.1g
Carbohydrate . . .39g	Saturates 0g

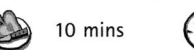 10 mins   (clock) 15 mins

SERVES 6

I N G R E D I E N T S

3 passion fruit

½ cup superfine sugar

⅔ cup water

1 mango

10 lychees, canned or fresh

1 star fruit

1 Halve the passion fruit and press the flesh through a strainer into a pan.

2 Add the sugar and water to the pan and bring to a gentle boil, stirring.

3 Put the mango on a cutting board and cut a thick slice from either side, cutting as near to the pit as possible. Cut away as much flesh as possible in large chunks from the pit section.

4 Take the 2 side slices and make 3 cuts through the flesh but not the skin, and 3 more at right angles to make a lattice pattern.

5 Push the mango skin inside out so that the cubed flesh is exposed and you can easily cut it off.

6 Peel and pit the lychees and cut the star fruit into 12 slices.

7 Add all the mango flesh, the lychees, and the star fruit to the passion fruit syrup and poach gently for 5 minutes. Remove the fruit with a perforated spoon.

8 Bring the syrup to a boil and cook for 5 minutes until it thickens slightly.

9 To serve, transfer all the fruit to individual serving glasses, pour over the sugar syrup, and serve warm.

COOK'S TIP
A delicious accompaniment to any exotic fruit dish is cardamom cream. Crush the seeds from 8 cardamom pods, add 1½ cups whipping cream, and whip until soft peaks form.

Tropical Fruit Salad

Papayas are ready to eat when they yield to gentle pressure.
Serve in the shells of baby pineapples for a stunning effect.

NUTRITIONAL INFORMATION

Calories	69	Sugars 13g
Protein	.........1g	Fat 0.3g
Carbohydrate	...14g	Saturates 0g

 10 mins   0 mins

SERVES 8

INGREDIENTS

1 papaya

2 tbsp fresh orange juice

3 tbsp rum

2 bananas

2 guavas

1 small pineapple or 2 baby pineapples

2 passion fruit

pineapple leaves to decorate

1 Cut the papaya in half and remove the seeds. Peel and slice the flesh into a bowl. Pour over the orange juice together with the rum.

2 Slice the bananas, peel and slice the guavas, and add both to the bowl.

COOK'S TIP

Guavas have a heavenly smell when ripe—their scent will fill a whole room. They should give to gentle pressure when ripe, and their skins should be yellow. The canned varieties are very good and have a pink tinge to the flesh.

3 Cut the top and base from the pineapple, then cut off the skin.

4 Slice the pineapple flesh, discard the core, then cut the flesh into pieces and add to the bowl.

5 Halve the passion fruit, scoop out the flesh with a teaspoon, add to the bowl, and stir well to mix.

6 Spoon the salad into glass bowls and decorate with pineapple leaves.

Mango & Passion Fruit Salad

The rich mascarpone cream that accompanies the exotic fruit salad gives this Chinese dessert an Italian twist.

NUTRITIONAL INFORMATION

Calories 211   Sugars 18g
Protein ....6g   Fat 10g
Carbohydrate ...18g   Saturates 6g

1¼ hrs   0 mins

SERVES 4

INGREDIENTS

1 large mango

2 oranges

4 passion fruit

2 tbsp orange-flavored liqueur such as Grand Marnier

mint or geranium leaves, to decorate

MASCARPONE CREAM

4½ oz/125 g mascarpone cheese

1 tbsp clear honey

4 tbsp thick unsweetened yogurt

few drops vanilla extract

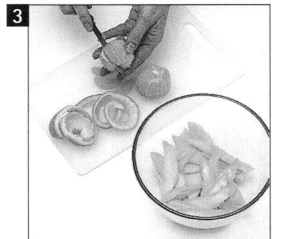

1 Using a sharp knife, cut the mango in half lengthwise as close to the pit as possible. Remove the pit, using a sharp knife.

2 Peel off the mango skin, cut the flesh into slices, and place in a large bowl.

3 Peel the oranges, removing all the pith, and cut into segments. Add to the bowl with any juices.

4 Halve the passion fruit, scoop out the flesh and add to the bowl with the orange-flavored liqueur. Mix together all the ingredients in the bowl.

5 Cover the bowl with plastic wrap and chill in the refrigerator for 1 hour. Turn into individual glass serving dishes.

6 To make the mascarpone cream, blend the mascarpone cheese and honey together. Add the unsweetened yogurt and the vanilla extract and stir until thoroughly blended.

7 Serve the fruit salad with the mascarpone cream, decorated with mint or geranium leaves.

COOK'S TIP

Passion fruit are ready to eat when their skins are well dimpled. Substitute guava or pineapple for the passion fruit, if you prefer.

Aromatic Fruit Salad

The fruits in this salad are arranged attractively on serving plates with a spicy syrup spooned over.

NUTRITIONAL INFORMATION

Calories ....125 Sugars 29g
Protein ....3g Fat 1g
Carbohydrate ...29g Saturates 0.2g

25 mins   5 mins

SERVES 6

I N G R E D I E N T S

3½ tbsp granulated sugar

⅔ cup water

1 cinnamon stick or large piece of cassia bark

4 cardamom pods, crushed

1 clove

juice of 1 orange

juice of 1 lime

½ honeydew melon

a good-sized wedge of watermelon

2 ripe guavas

3 ripe nectarines

about 18 strawberries

a little toasted shredded coconut, for sprinkling

sprigs of mint or rose petals, to decorate

strained low-fat unsweetened yogurt, for serving

1 First prepare the syrup. Put the sugar, water, cinnamon, cardamom pods, and clove into a pan and bring to a boil, stirring to dissolve the sugar. Simmer for 2 minutes, then remove from the heat.

2 Add the orange and lime juices to the syrup and let cool and infuse while preparing the fruits.

3 Peel and remove the seeds from the honeydew melon and watermelon and cut the flesh into neat slices.

4 Cut the guavas in half, scoop out the seeds, then peel carefully and slice the flesh neatly.

5 Cut the nectarines into slices and hull and slice the strawberries.

6 Arrange the slices of fruit attractively on 6 serving plates.

7 Strain the prepared cooled syrup and spoon over the sliced fruits.

8 Sprinkle the fruit salad with a little toasted coconut. Decorate each serving with sprigs of mint or rose petals and serve with yogurt.

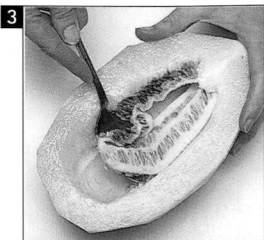

Tropical Fruit Fool

Fruit fools are always popular, and this light, tangy version will be no exception. You can use your favorite fruits in this recipe.

NUTRITIONAL INFORMATION

Calories	149	Sugars	........25g
Protein	.........6g	Fat	..........0.4g
Carbohydrate	...32g	Saturates	.....0.2g

35 mins

0 mins

SERVES 4

INGREDIENTS

1 medium ripe mango

2 kiwi fruit

1 medium banana

2 tbsp lime juice

½ tsp finely grated lime zest, plus extra to decorate

2 egg whites

15 oz/425 g can low-fat custard

½ tsp vanilla extract

2 passion fruit

 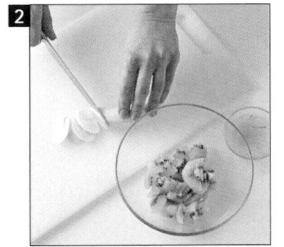 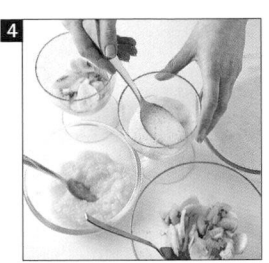

1 Peel the mango, then slice either side of the smooth, flat, central pit. Roughly chop the flesh and process the fruit in a food processor or blender until smooth. Alternatively, mash with a fork.

2 Peel the kiwi fruit, chop the flesh into small pieces, and place in a bowl. Peel and chop the banana, and add to the bowl. Toss all of the fruit in the lime juice and zest and mix well.

3 In a grease-free bowl, whisk the egg whites until stiff and then gently fold in the custard and vanilla extract until thoroughly mixed.

4 In 4 tall glasses, alternately layer the chopped fruit, mango purée, and custard mixture, finishing with the custard on top. Let chill in the refrigerator for 20 minutes.

5 When you are ready to serve the dessert, halve the passion fruits, scoop out the seeds, and spoon over the fruit fools. Decorate each serving with the extra lime zest, and serve.

VARIATION
Other tropical fruits to try include papaya purée, with chopped pineapple and dates or pomegranate seeds to decorate.

Melon & Kiwi Salad

A refreshing fruit salad, ideal to serve after a rich meal. This recipe uses galia melon, but Charentais or cantaloup melons are also good.

NUTRITIONAL INFORMATION

Calories 88   Sugars 17g
Protein ....1g   Fat 0.2g
Carbohydrate ...17g   Saturates 0g

1¼ hrs   0 mins

SERVES 4

INGREDIENTS

½ Galia melon

2 kiwi fruit

18–20 white seedless grapes

1 papaya, halved

3 tbsp orange-flavored liqueur such as Cointreau

1 tbsp chopped lemon verbena, lemon balm, or mint

sprigs of lemon verbena or cape gooseberries (golden berries), to decorate

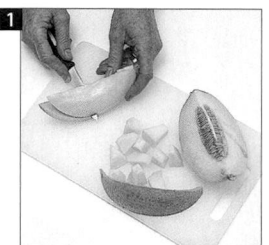 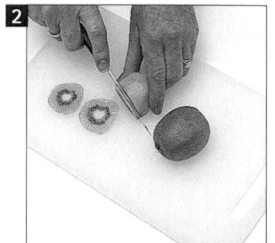 

1 Remove the seeds from the melon, cut it into 4 slices, and carefully cut away the skin. Cut the flesh into cubes and put into a bowl.

COOK'S TIP

Lemon balm or sweet balm is a fragrant lemon-scented plant with slightly hairy serrated leaves and a pronounced lemon flavor. Lemon verbena can also be used— this has an even stronger lemon flavor and smooth, elongated leaves.

2 Peel the kiwi fruit and cut across into slices. Add to the melon with the white grapes.

3 Remove the seeds from the papaya and cut off the skin. Slice the flesh thickly and cut into diagonal pieces. Add to the fruit bowl and mix well.

4 Mix together the liqueur and the chopped lemon verbena, pour over the fruit, and let macerate for 1 hour, stirring occasionally.

5 Spoon the fruit salad into glasses, pour over the juices, and decorate with lemon verbena sprigs or cape gooseberries.

Summer Fruit Salad

A mixture of soft summer fruits in an orange-flavored syrup with a dash of port. Serve with low-fat yogurt.

NUTRITIONAL INFORMATION

Calories 110	Sugars 26g	
Protein 1g	Fat 0.1g	
Carbohydrate ...26g	Saturates 0g	

5 mins   10 mins

SERVES 6

INGREDIENTS

6 tbsp superfine sugar

5 tbsp water

grated zest and juice of 1 small orange

2¼ cups red currants, stripped from their stalks

2 tsp arrowroot

2 tbsp port

1 cup blackberries

1 cup blueberries

1 cup strawberries

1⅓ cups raspberries

low-fat unsweetened yogurt, to serve

1 Put the sugar, water, and grated orange zest into a heavy pan and heat gently, stirring until the sugar has completely dissolved.

2 Add the red currants and orange juice, bring to a boil, and simmer gently for 2–3 minutes.

3 Strain the fruit, reserving the syrup, and put into a bowl.

4 Blend the arrowroot with a little water. Return the syrup to the pan, add the arrowroot, and bring to a boil, stirring constantly until thickened.

5 Add the port and mix together well, then pour the syrup over the red currants in the bowl.

6 Add the blackberries, blueberries, strawberries, and raspberries. Mix the fruit together and let cool until required.

7 Serve the fruit salad in individual glass dishes, topped with a spoonful of low-fat unsweetened yogurt.

COOK'S TIP
Although this salad is really best made with fresh fruits in season, you can achieve an acceptable result with frozen equivalents, with perhaps the exception of strawberries. You can buy frozen fruits of the forest, which would be ideal, in most food stores.

Chocolate Cheese Pots

These super-light desserts are just the thing if you have a craving for chocolate. Serve them on their own or with a selection of fruits.

NUTRITIONAL INFORMATION

Calories	117	Sugars	17g
Protein	9g	Fat	1g
Carbohydrate	18g	Saturates	1g

 40 mins   0 mins

SERVES 4

INGREDIENTS

1¼ cup ricotta cheese

⅔ cup low-fat unsweetened yogurt

2 tbsp confectioners' sugar

4 tsp low-fat drinking chocolate powder

4 tsp unsweetened cocoa

1 tsp vanilla extract

2 tbsp dark rum, optional

2 egg whites

4 chocolate cake decorations

TO SERVE

pieces of kiwi fruit, orange, and banana

strawberries and raspberries

1 Combine the ricotta cheese and low-fat yogurt in a bowl. Strain in the confectioners' sugar, drinking chocolate, and unsweetened cocoa and mix well. Add the vanilla extract and rum, if using.

2 In a clean bowl, whisk the egg whites until stiff. Using a metal spoon, gently fold the egg whites into the chocolate mixture.

3 Spoon the yogurt and chocolate mixture into 4 small china dessert pots and let chill in the refrigerator for about 30 minutes.

4 Decorate each chocolate cheese pot with a chocolate cake decoration and serve with an assortment of fresh fruit, such as pieces of kiwi fruit, orange, banana, strawberries, and raspberries.

COOK'S TIP

This chocolate mixture can also be used as a cheesecake filling. Make the base out of crushed amaretti cookies and egg white, and set the filling with 2 teaspoons of powdered gelozone dissolved in 2 tablespoons of boiling water.

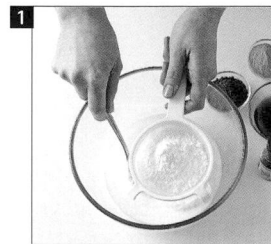

Tropical Fruit Rice Mold

A rice dessert with a twist—light flakes of rice with a tang of pineapple and lime. You can serve it with any selection of your favorite fruits.

NUTRITIONAL INFORMATION

Calories ....145 Sugars 18g
Protein ....7g Fat 1g
Carbohydrate ...30g Saturates 0.3g

4¼ hrs   25 mins

SERVES 8

INGREDIENTS

1⅓ cups short-grain or pudding rice, rinsed

3½ cups skim milk

1 tbsp superfine sugar

4 tbsp white rum with coconut or unsweetened pineapple juice

¾ cup low-fat unsweetened yogurt

14 oz/400 g can pineapple pieces in natural juice, drained and chopped

1 tsp grated lime zest

1 tbsp lime juice

1 package powdered gelozone, dissolved in 3 tbsp boiling water

lime wedges, to decorate

mixed tropical fruits, such as passion fruit, baby pineapple, papaya, mango, star fruit, to serve

1 Place the rice and milk in a pan. Bring to a boil, then simmer gently, uncovered, for 20 minutes until the rice is soft and the milk is absorbed. Stir the mixture occasionally and keep the heat low to prevent sticking.

2 Transfer the mixture to a mixing bowl and let cool.

3 Stir the sugar, white rum with coconut or pineapple juice, yogurt, pineapple pieces, lime zest, and juice into the rice. Fold in the gelozone mixture.

4 Rinse a 2½ pint/1.5 liter nonstick ring mold or ring cake pan with water and spoon in the rice mixture. Press down well, level the top with the back of a spoon, and chill for 2 hours until firm.

5 To serve, gently loosen the rice from the mold with a small spatula and invert it carefully onto a serving plate.

6 Decorate with lime wedges and fill the centre with assorted tropical fruits.

COOK'S TIP
Try serving this dessert with a light sauce made from 1¼ cups tropical fruit or pineapple juice thickened with 2 tsp arrowroot.

Blackberry Pudding

A delicious dessert to make when blackberries are in abundance!
If blackberries are unavailable, try using currants or gooseberries.

NUTRITIONAL INFORMATION

Calories 455   Sugars 47g
Protein ....7g   Fat 18g
Carbohydrate ...70g   Saturates 11g

15–20 mins   30 mins

SERVES 4

INGREDIENTS

butter, for greasing

1 lb/450 g blackberries

⅓ cup superfine sugar, plus extra for sprinkling

1 egg

⅓ cup brown sugar

6 tbsp butter, melted

½ cup milk

scant 1 cup self-rising flour

1 Lightly grease a large 3½-cup/900-ml ovenproof dish with a little butter.

2 In a large mixing bowl, gently mix together the blackberries and superfine sugar until well combined.

3 Transfer the blackberry and sugar mixture to the prepared ovenproof dish, spreading it out evenly.

4 Beat the egg and brown sugar in a separate mixing bowl. Stir in the melted butter and milk.

5 Sift the flour into the egg and butter mixture and fold together lightly to form a smooth batter.

6 Carefully spread the batter over the blackberry and sugar mixture in the ovenproof dish.

7 Bake the blackberry pudding in a preheated oven, 350°F/180°C, for about 25–30 minutes until the topping is firm and golden.

8 Sprinkle the pudding with a little sugar and serve hot.

VARIATION

You can add 2 tablespoons of unsweetened cocoa to the batter in step 5, if you prefer a chocolate flavor.

Sticky Sesame Bananas

These tasty morsels are a real treat. Pieces of banana are
dipped in caramel and then sprinkled with a few sesame seeds.

NUTRITIONAL INFORMATION

Calories 215	Sugars 38g	
Protein 6g	Fat 3g	
Carbohydrate . . .41g	Saturates 1g	

10 mins   20 mins

SERVES 4

INGREDIENTS

4 ripe medium bananas

3 tbsp lemon juice

generous 1 cup superfine sugar

4 tbsp cold water

2 tbsp sesame seeds

⅔ cup low-fat unsweetened yogurt

1 tbsp confectioners' sugar

1 tsp vanilla extract

TO DECORATE

shredded lemon zest

shredded lime zest

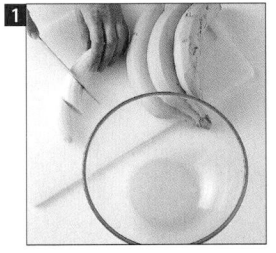

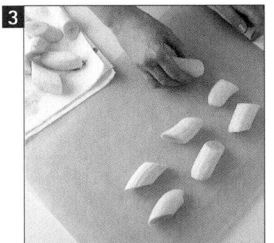

1 Peel the bananas and cut into 2 inch/ 5 cm pieces. Place the banana pieces in a bowl, spoon over the lemon juice, and stir well to coat—this will help prevent the bananas from discoloring.

2 Place the sugar and water in a small pan and heat gently, stirring constantly, until the sugar dissolves. Bring to a boil and cook for 5–6 minutes until the mixture turns golden brown.

3 Meanwhile, drain the bananas and blot with paper towels to dry. Line a cookie sheet or board with baking parchment and arrange the bananas, well spaced apart, on top.

4 When the caramel is ready, drizzle it over the bananas, working quickly because the caramel sets almost instantly. Sprinkle the sesame seeds over the caramelized bananas and let cool for 10 minutes.

5 Combine the yogurt, confectioners' sugar, and vanilla extract.

6 Peel the bananas away from the baking parchment and arrange on serving plates.

7 Serve the yogurt as a dip, decorated with shredded lemon and lime zest.

Apricot & Orange Jell-o

These bright, fruity little desserts are really easy to make. Serve them with low-fat ice cream and be transported back to childhood!

NUTRITIONAL INFORMATION

Calories	206	Sugars	........36g
Protein	.........8g	Fat	..........5g
Carbohydrate	...36g	Saturates	......3g

4¼ hrs   25 mins

SERVES 4

INGREDIENTS

1½ cups no-soak dried apricots

1¼ cups unsweetened orange juice

2 tbsp lemon juice

2–3 tsp clear honey

1 tbsp powdered gelozone

4 tbsp boiling water

TO DECORATE

orange segments

sprigs of mint

CINNAMON "CREAM"

½ cup medium-fat ricotta cheese

½ cup low-fat unsweetened yogurt

1 tsp ground cinnamon

1 tbsp clear honey

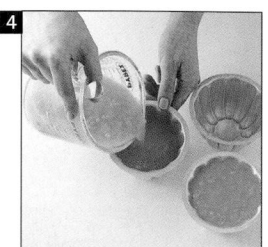

1 Place the apricots in a pan and pour in the orange juice. Bring to a boil, cover, and simmer for 15–20 minutes until the apricots are plump and soft. Let cool for 10 minutes.

2 Transfer the mixture to a blender or food processor and blend until smooth. Stir in the lemon juice and add the honey. Pour the mixture into a measuring pitcher and make up to 2½ cups with cold water.

3 Dissolve the gelozone in the boiling water and then stir it into the apricot mixture in the pitcher.

4 Pour the mixture into 4 individual molds, each ⅝ cup/150 ml, or into 1 large mold, 2½ cups/600 ml. Let chill until set.

5 Meanwhile, make the cinnamon "cream." Mix all the ingredients

together and place in a small bowl. Cover the mixture and let chill until needed.

6 To turn out the jell-o, dip the molds in hot water for a few seconds and invert onto serving plates.

7 Decorate the jell-o with the orange segments and sprigs of mint. Serve with the cinnamon "cream," dusted with a little extra cinnamon.

Lime Mousse with Mango

Lime-flavored cream molds, served with a fresh mango and lime sauce, make a stunning dessert.

NUTRITIONAL INFORMATION

Calories 254	Sugars 17g	
Protein 5g	Fat 19g	
Carbohydrate ...17g	Saturates 12g	

10 mins   0 mins

SERVES 4

INGREDIENTS

1 generous cup unsweetened yogurt

grated zest of 1 lime

1 tbsp superfine sugar

½ cup heavy cream

MANGO SAUCE

1 mango

juice of 1 lime

4 tsp superfine sugar

TO DECORATE

4 cape gooseberries (golden berries)

strips of lime zest

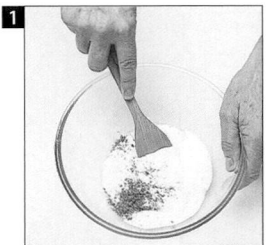
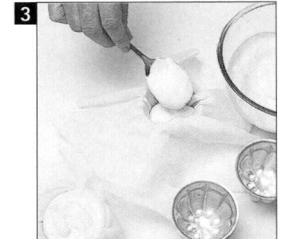
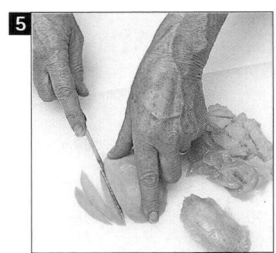

1 Put the yogurt, lime zest, and sugar in a bowl and mix together.

2 Whisk the double cream in a separate bowl and fold into the yogurt.

3 Line 4 decorative molds or ramekins with cheesecloth or plastic wrap and divide the mixture evenly between them. Fold the cheesecloth or plastic wrap over the top and press down firmly.

4 To make the sauce, slice through the mango on each side of the large flat pit, then cut the flesh from the pit. Remove the skin.

5 Cut off 12 thin slices and set aside. Chop the remaining mango and put in a food processor with the lime juice and sugar. Blend until smooth. Alternatively, push the mango through a strainer, then mix with the lime juice and sugar.

6 Turn out the molds on to serving plates. Arrange 3 slices of mango on each plate, pour some sauce around, decorate, and serve.

COOK'S TIP
Cape gooseberries (golden berries) have a tart and mildly scented flavor and make an excellent decoration for many desserts. Peel back the papery husks to expose the bright orange fruits.

Raspberry Risotto

Why shouldn't risotto be served as a dessert? If you think about it, most risottos are really savory rice desserts. This is really delicious—try it.

NUTRITIONAL INFORMATION

Calories	595	Sugars	........54g
Protein	.........8g	Fat	..........26g
Carbohydrate	...81g	Saturates	......16g

15 mins   30 mins

SERVES 4–6

INGREDIENTS

2 cups milk

16 fl oz/450 ml can unsweetened coconut milk

pinch of salt

1 vanilla bean, split

2–3 strips lemon zest

2 tbsp sweet butter

1¼ cups arborio rice

4 tbsp dry white vermouth

½ cup sugar

½ cup heavy or whipping cream

2–3 tbsp raspberry-flavored liqueur

¾ lb/350 g fresh raspberries

2 tbsp good-quality raspberry jelly or preserve

squeeze of lemon juice

toasted slivered almonds, to decorate (optional)

1 Heat the milk in a heavy pan with the coconut milk, salt, vanilla bean, and lemon zest until bubbles begin to form around the edge of the pan. Reduce the heat to low and keep the milk mixture hot, stirring occasionally.

2 Heat the butter in another large heavy pan over medium heat until foaming. Add the rice and cook, stirring, for 2 minutes to coat well.

3 Add the vermouth; it will bubble and steam rapidly. Cook, stirring, until the wine is completely absorbed. Gradually add the hot milk, about ½ cup at a time, allowing each addition of milk to be absorbed completely before adding the next.

4 When half the milk has been added, stir in the sugar until dissolved. Continue stirring and adding the milk until the rice is tender, but still firm to the bite: this should take about 25 minutes. Remove the pan from the heat and remove the vanilla bean and lemon strips. Stir in half the cream, the liqueur, and half the fresh raspberries; cover.

5 Heat the raspberry jelly with the lemon juice and 1–2 tablespoons water, stirring until smooth. Remove from the heat, add the remaining raspberries, and mix. Stir the remaining cream into the risotto and serve with the glazed raspberries. Decorate if wished.

Strawberry Roulade

Serve this moist, light sponge cake rolled up with a creamy almond and strawberry filling for a delicious dessert.

NUTRITIONAL INFORMATION

Calories	166	Sugars	........19g
Protein	.........6g	Fat	...........3g
Carbohydrate	...30g	Saturates	......1g

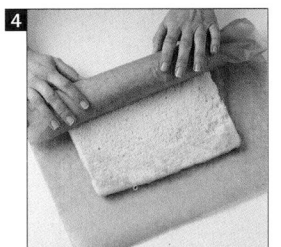

  30 mins   🕐 10 mins

SERVES 8

INGREDIENTS

3 large eggs

⅔ cup superfine sugar

scant 1 cup all-purpose flour

1 tbsp hot water

FILLING

¾ cup low-fat mascarpone

1 tsp almond extract

1½ cups small strawberries

TO DECORATE

1 tbsp slivered almonds, toasted

1 tsp confectioners' sugar

a few strawberries

1 Line a 14 x 10 inch/35 x 25 cm jelly roll pan with baking parchment.

2 Place the eggs in a heatproof bowl with the superfine sugar. Place the bowl over a pan of hot water and whisk until pale and thick.

3 Remove the bowl from the pan. Strain in the flour and fold into the eggs along with the hot water. Pour the mixture into the pan and bake in a preheated oven, 425°F/220°C, for 8–10 minutes until golden and set.

4 Turn out the cake onto a sheet of baking parchment. Peel off the lining paper and roll up the sponge cake tightly along with the baking parchment. Wrap in a dish cloth and let cool.

5 Mix together the mascarpone and the almond extract. Reserving a few strawberries for decoration, wash, hull, and slice the rest. Chill the mascarpone mixture and the strawberries in the refrigerator until required.

6 Unroll the cake, spread the mascarpone mixture over the surface, and sprinkle with sliced strawberries. Roll the cake up again and transfer to a serving plate. Sprinkle with almonds and lightly dust with confectioners' sugar. Decorate with the reserved strawberries.

Ricotta-Lemon Cheesecake

Italian bakers pride themselves on their baked ricotta cheesecakes, studded with fruit soaked in spirits.

NUTRITIONAL INFORMATION

Calories	188	Sugars	........21g
Protein	.........6g	Fat	...........8g
Carbohydrate	...23g	Saturates	.......4g

3¾ hrs   30–40 mins

SERVES 6–8

INGREDIENTS

generous ⅓ cup golden raisins

3 tbsp Marsala or grappa

butter, for greasing

2 tbsp semolina, plus extra for dusting

1½ cups ricotta cheese, drained

3 large egg yolks, beaten

½ cup superfine sugar

3 tbsp lemon juice

2 tbsp candied orange peel, finely chopped

finely grated zest of 2 large lemons

TO DECORATE

confectioners' sugar

fresh mint sprigs

red currants or berries (optional)

1 Soak the golden raisins in the Marsala or grappa in a small bowl for about 30 minutes or until the liquid has been absorbed and the fruit is swollen.

2 Cut out a circle of baking parchment to fit the bottom of a loose-based 8 inch/20 cm round cake pan that is about 2 inches/5 cm deep. Grease the side and base of the pan and line the base. Lightly dust with semolina and tip out the excess.

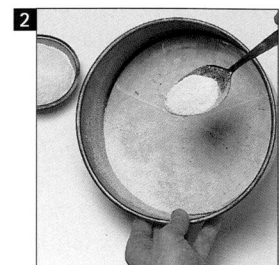

3 Using a wooden spoon, press the ricotta cheese though a nylon strainer into a bowl. Beat in the egg yolks, sugar, semolina, and lemon juice and continue beating until blended.

4 Fold in the golden raisins, orange peel, and lemon zest. Pour into the prepared pan and smooth the surface.

5 Bake the cheesecake in the center of a preheated oven, 350°F/180°C, for about 30–40 minutes or until firm when you press the top and coming away slightly from the side of the pan.

6 Turn off the oven and open the door. Let the cheesecake cool in the turned-off oven for 2–3 hours. To serve, remove from the pan and transfer to a plate. Strain over a layer of confectioners' sugar from at least 12 inches/30 cm above the cheesecake to dust the top and sides lightly. Decorate with mint and red currants, if wished.

Balsamic Strawberries

Generations of Italian cooks have known that the unlikely combination of freshly ground black pepper and ripe, juicy strawberries is fantastic.

NUTRITIONAL INFORMATION

Calories	132	Sugars 5g
Protein	.........1g	Fat 12g
Carbohydrate	....5g	Saturates 7g

4¼ hrs   0 mins

SERVES 4–6

INGREDIENTS

1 lb/450 g fresh strawberries

2–3 tbsp balsamic vinegar

fresh mint leaves, torn, plus extra to decorate (optional)

½–¾ cup mascarpone cheese

pepper

1 Wipe the strawberries with a damp cloth, rather than rinsing them, so they do not become soggy. Using a paring knife, cut off the green stalks at the top and use the tip of the knife to remove the core or hull.

2 Cut each strawberry in half lengthwise or into quarters if large. Transfer to a bowl.

3 Add the balsamic vinegar, allowing ½ tablespoon per person. Add several twists of ground black pepper, then gently stir together. Cover with plastic wrap and chill for up to 4 hours.

4 Just before serving, stir in torn mint leaves to taste. Spoon the mascarpone into bowls and spoon the berries on top. Decorate with a few mint leaves, if wished. Sprinkle with extra pepper to taste.

COOK'S TIP

This is most enjoyable when it is made with the best-quality balsamic vinegar, one that has aged slowly and has turned thick and syrupy. Unfortunately, the genuine mixture is always expensive. Less expensive versions are artificially sweetened and colored with caramel.

Piña Colada Pineapple

The flavors of pineapple and coconut blend as well together on the grill as they do in the well-known cocktail.

NUTRITIONAL INFORMATION

Calories 231   Sugars 22g
Protein . . . . .1g   Fat 15g
Carbohydrate . . .22g   Saturates 11g

  15 mins

25 mins

SERVES 4

INGREDIENTS

1 small pineapple

2 tbsp sweet butter

2 tbsp molasses sugar

½ cup grated fresh coconut

2 tbsp coconut-flavored liqueur or rum

  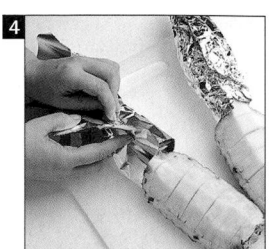

1 Using a very sharp knife, cut the pineapple into quarters and then remove the tough core from the center, leaving the leaves attached.

2 Carefully cut the pineapple flesh away from the skin. Remove any "eyes" with small sharp knife. Make horizontal cuts across the flesh of the pineapple quarters.

3 Place the butter in a pan and heat gently until melted, stirring constantly.

Brush the melted butter over the pineapple and sprinkle with the sugar.

4 Cover the pineapple leaves with kitchen foil to prevent them from burning and transfer the pineapple quarters to a rack set over hot coals.

5 Grill the pineapple for about 10 minutes.

6 Sprinkle the coconut over the pineapple and grill, cut side up, for a further 5–10 minutes or until the pineapple is piping hot.

7 Transfer the pineapple to serving plates and remove the foil from the leaves. Spoon a little coconut-flavored liqueur or rum over the pineapple and serve immediately.

COOK'S TIP

Fresh coconut has the best flavor for this dish. If you prefer, however, you can use dry shredded coconut.

Fruit Salad & Ginger Syrup

This is a very special fruit salad made from the most exotic and colorful fruits, soaked in a syrup made with fresh ginger and ginger wine.

NUTRITIONAL INFORMATION

Calories . . . . .225 Sugars 45g
Protein . . . . .2g Fat 4g
Carbohydrate . . .45g Saturates 3g

4½ hrs   5 mins

SERVES 4

INGREDIENTS

1 inch/2.5 cm piece ginger root, peeled and chopped

4 tbsp superfine sugar

⅔ cup water

grated zest and juice of 1 lime

4 tbsp ginger wine

1 fresh pineapple, peeled, cored, and cut into bite-sized pieces

2 ripe mangoes, peeled, pitted, and diced

4 kiwi fruit, peeled and sliced

1 papaya, peeled, seeded, and diced

2 passion fruit, halved and flesh removed

¾ lb/350 g lychees, peeled and pitted

¼ fresh coconut, grated

cape gooseberries (golden berries), to decorate (optional)

coconut ice cream, to serve (optional)

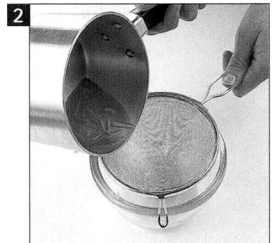

1 Place the ginger, sugar, water, and lime juice in a pan and bring slowly to a boil. Simmer for 1 minute, remove from the heat, and let cool slightly.

2 Strain the syrup, add the ginger wine, and mix well. Cool completely.

3 Place the prepared fruit in a serving bowl. Add the cold syrup and mix well. Cover and chill the fruit in the refrigerator for 2–4 hours.

4 Just before serving, add half of the grated coconut to the salad and mix well. Sprinkle the remainder on top.

5 If using cape gooseberries to decorate the salad, peel back each calyx to form a flower. Wipe the berries clean, then arrange them around the side of the fruit salad before serving.

COOK'S TIP

Cape gooseberries are golden in color and make a delightful decoration to many fruit-based desserts.

Thai Rice Dessert

This Thai-style version of rice dessert is mildly spiced and creamy, with a rich custard topping. It's excellent served warm or cold.

NUTRITIONAL INFORMATION

Calories 351	Sugars 16g
Protein 7g	Fat 21g
Carbohydrate . . .37g	Saturates 16g

🔥 🔥

🍲 10 mins   🕐 1–1¼ hrs

SERVES 4

INGREDIENTS

½ cup short grain rice

2 tbsp palm sugar

1 cardamom pod, split

1¼ cups coconut milk

⅔ cup water

3 eggs

scant 1 cup coconut cream

1½ tbsp superfine sugar

sweetened coconut flakes, to decorate

fresh fruit, to serve

1 Place the rice and palm sugar in a pan. Crush the seeds from the cardamom pod in a mortar with a pestle and add to the pan. Stir in the coconut milk and water.

2 Bring to a boil, stirring to dissolve the sugar. Lower the heat and simmer, uncovered, stirring occasionally, for about 20 minutes until the rice is tender and most of the liquid is absorbed.

3 Spoon the rice into 4 individual ovenproof dishes and spread evenly. Place the dishes in a wide roasting pan with hot water to come about halfway up the sides.

4 Beat the eggs with the coconut cream and superfine sugar and spoon over the rice.

5 Cover with foil and bake in a preheated oven, 350°F/180°C, for 45–50 minutes, or until the custard sets.

6 Serve the rice desserts warm or cold, with fresh fruit and decorated with coconut flakes.

COOK'S TIP

Cardamom is quite a powerful spice, so if you find it too strong, it can be left out altogether or replaced with a little ground cinnamon.

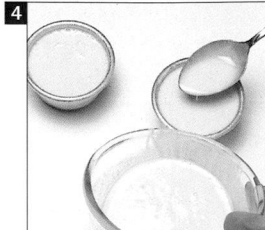

Kesari Kheer

This is a classic Indian milk dessert, full of exotic spices.
This version contains saffron, which gives it a lovely deep-yellow color.

NUTRITIONAL INFORMATION

Calories 470	Sugars 42g	
Protein 11g	Fat 25g	
Carbohydrate . . .53g	Saturates 13g	

5 mins,
plus chilling

1 hr

SERVES 4–6

INGREDIENTS

2 tbsp clarified butter or ghee

scant ½ cup basmati rice, washed and
well drained

6½ cups milk

½ cup sugar or to taste

10–12 green cardamom pods, crushed to
remove the black seeds (pods discarded)

½ cup golden raisins or raisins

large pinch saffron threads, about ½ tsp,
soaked in 2–3 tbsp milk

⅔ cup green pistachios, lightly toasted

⅔ cup heavy cream, whipped (optional)

ground cinnamon, for dusting

varak (edible silver foil, see page 912) to
decorate (optional)

1 Melt the butter in a large, heavy pan over medium heat. Pour in the rice and cook, stirring almost constantly, for about 6 minutes until the rice grains are translucent and a deep golden brown.

2 Pour in the milk and bring to a boil over high heat. Reduce the heat to medium-high and simmer for about 30 minutes, stirring occasionally, until the milk has reduced by about half.

3 Add the sugar, cardamom seeds, and golden raisins and cook for a further 20 minutes or until reduced and thick. Stir in the saffron-milk mixture and simmer over low heat until as thick as possible, stirring almost constantly. Remove from the heat and stir in half the pistachios.

4 Place the pan in a larger pan of iced water and stir until cool. If using, stir in the cream, then spoon into a serving bowl and chill.

5 To serve, dust the top of the dessert with ground cinnamon. Sprinkle with the remaining pistachios and, if using, decorate with pieces of varak.

COOK'S TIP
Using the whipped heavy cream in this recipe is not authentic, but it does make the pudding very light.

Aztec Oranges

Simplicity itself, this refreshing orange dessert is hard to beat and is the perfect follow-up to a hearty, spiced entrée dish.

NUTRITIONAL INFORMATION

Calories . . . . .98 Sugars 20g
Protein . . . . .2g Fat 0g
Carbohydrate . . .20g Saturates 0g

45 mins   0 mins

SERVES 4–6

INGREDIENTS

6 oranges

1 lime

2 tbsp tequila

2 tbsp orange-flavored liqueur

brown sugar, to taste

fine lime zest strips, to decorate (see Cook's Tip)

1 Using a sharp knife, cut a slice off the top and bottom of the oranges, then remove the peel and pith, cutting downward and taking care to retain the shape of the oranges.

2 Holding the oranges on their side, cut them horizontally into slices.

3 Place the oranges in a bowl. Cut the lime in half and squeeze over the oranges. Sprinkle with the tequila and liqueur, then sprinkle with sugar to taste.

4 Cover with plastic wrap and chill in the refrigerator until ready to serve, then transfer to a serving dish, and garnish with lime strips.

COOK'S TIP

To make the decoration, finely pare the zest from a lime using a vegetable peeler, then cut into thin strips. Blanch in boiling water for 2 minutes. Drain and rinse under cold running water. Drain again and pat dry with paper towels.

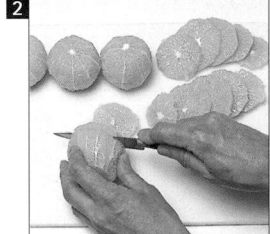

Italian Lemon Rice Cake

This lemony cake should have a crisp crust with a soft moist center. Soaking the currants in rum brings out their fruitiness.

NUTRITIONAL INFORMATION

Calories 283	Sugars 24g	
Protein 7g	Fat 10g	
Carbohydrate ...41g	Saturates 6g	

 1¼ hrs 1¼ hrs

SERVES 8–10

I N G R E D I E N T S

4 cups milk

pinch of salt

1¾ cups risotto or round grain rice

1 vanilla bean, split

¼ cup currants

¼ cup rum or water

2 tsp melted butter, for greasing

cornmeal or polenta, for dusting

¾ cup sugar

grated zest of 1 large lemon

4 tbsp butter, diced

3 eggs

2–3 tbsp lemon juice (optional)

confectioners' sugar

TO SERVE

¾ cup mascarpone cheese

2 tbsp rum

2 tbsp whipping cream

1 Bring the milk to a boil. Sprinkle in the salt and rice and bring back to a boil. Add the vanilla bean and seeds. Lower the heat and simmer, stirring occasionally, for 30 minutes.

2 Meanwhile, bring the currants and rum to a boil, then set aside.

3 Brush the base and side of a 10 inch/25 cm loose-bottomed cake pan with butter. Dust with about 2–3 tablespoons of cornmeal and shake out any excess.

4 Remove the rice from the heat and remove the vanilla bean. Stir in all but 1 tablespoon of sugar, with the lemon zest and butter, until the sugar is dissolved. Place in ice water to cool. Stir in the soaked currants and remaining rum.

5 Beat the eggs, with an electric mixer, for about 2 minutes until light and

foamy. Gradually beat in about half the rice mixture, then stir in the rest. If using, stir in the lemon juice.

6 Pour into the prepared pan and smooth the top. Sprinkle with the reserved sugar and bake in a preheated oven, 325°F/160°C, for about 40 minutes until risen and golden and slightly firm. Cool in the pan on a wire rack.

7 Turn out and dust with confectioners' sugar. Transfer the cake to a serving plate. Whisk the mascarpone with the rum and cream and serve with the cake.

Ginger & Apricot Alaskas

No ice cream in this Alaska but a mixture of apples and apricots poached in orange juice and enclosed in meringue.

NUTRITIONAL INFORMATION

Calories 442   Sugars 77g
Protein . . . . .7g   Fat 9g
Carbohydrate . . .83g   Saturates 3g

15 mins   10 mins

SERVES 2

INGREDIENTS

2 slices rich, dark ginger cake, about
   2 cm/¾ inch thick

1–2 tbsp ginger wine or rum

1 eating apple

6 ready-to-eat dried apricots, chopped

4 tbsp orange juice or water

15 g/½ oz slivered almonds

2 small egg whites

½ cup superfine sugar

1 Place each slice of ginger cake on an ovenproof plate and sprinkle with the ginger wine or rum.

2 Quarter, core, and slice the apple into a small pan. Add the chopped apricots and orange juice or water, and simmer the mixture over low heat for about 5 minutes, or until tender.

3 Stir the slivered almonds into the cooked fruit and spoon the mixture equally over the slices of soaked cake, piling it up in the center.

4 Whisk the egg whites until very stiff and dry, then whisk in the sugar, a little at a time, making sure the meringue has become stiff again before adding the next quantity of sugar.

5 Either pipe or spread the meringue over the fruit and cake, making sure that both are completely covered.

6 Place in a preheated oven, 400°F/ 200°C, for 4–5 minutes, until golden brown. Serve hot.

VARIATION

A slice of vanilla, coffee, or chocolate ice cream can be placed on the fruit before adding the meringue, but this must be done at the last minute and the dessert must be eaten immediately after it is removed from the oven.

Eve's Dessert

This is a popular family dessert with soft apples on the bottom and a light buttery sponge cake topping.

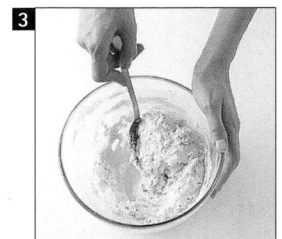

NUTRITIONAL INFORMATION

Calories	365	Sugars	........40g
Protein	.........5g	Fat	..........14g
Carbohydrate	...58g	Saturates	.......7g

 15 mins 45 mins

SERVES 4

INGREDIENTS

6 tbsp butter, plus extra for greasing

1lb/450 g cooking apples, peeled, cored, and sliced

½ cup granulated sugar

1 tbsp lemon juice

scant ½ cup golden raisins

scant ½ cup superfine sugar

1 egg, beaten

1⅓ cups self-rising flour

3 tbsp milk

¼ cup sliced almonds

custard or heavy cream, to serve

1 Grease a 3¾ cup casserole with a little butter.

2 Mix the apples with the granulated sugar, lemon juice, and golden raisins. Spoon the mixture into the casserole.

3 In a bowl, cream the butter and superfine sugar together until pale. Add the beaten egg, a little at a time.

4 Carefully fold in the self-rising flour and stir in the milk to give a soft, pourable consistency.

5 Spread the mixture over the apples and sprinkle with the sliced almonds.

6 Bake in a preheated oven, 350°F/ 180°C, for 40–45 minutes until the sponge cake topping is well risen and golden brown.

7 Serve the dessert piping hot, accompanied by homemade custard or heavy cream.

COOK'S TIP
To increase the almond flavor of this dessert, add ¼ cup ground almonds with the flour in step 4.

Raspberry Shortcake

For this lovely summery dessert, two crisp rounds of shortbread are sandwiched together with fresh raspberries and lightly whipped cream.

NUTRITIONAL INFORMATION

Calories 496	Sugars 14g
Protein 4g	Fat 41g
Carbohydrate ...30g	Saturates 26g

 40 mins   15 mins

SERVES 8

INGREDIENTS

7 tbsp butter, cut into cubes, plus extra for greasing

1½ cups self-rising flour

scant ½ cup superfine sugar

1 egg yolk

1 tbsp rose water

2½ cups whipping cream, lightly whipped

1⅓ cups raspberries, plus a few extra for decoration

TO DECORATE

confectioners' sugar

mint leaves

1 Lightly grease 2 cookie sheets with a little butter.

2 To make the shortcake, sift the self-rising flour into a bowl. Add the butter and rub it into the flour with your fingertips until the mixture resembles fine bread crumbs.

3 Stir the sugar, egg yolk, and rose water into the mixture and bring together with your fingers to form a soft dough. Divide the dough in half.

4 Roll out each piece of dough to an 8 inch/20 cm round on a lightly floured counter. Carefully lift each of them with the rolling pin onto the prepared cookie sheets. Gently crimp the edges of the dough with your finger.

5 Bake in a preheated oven, 375°F/ 190°C, for 15 minutes until lightly golden. Transfer the shortcakes to a wire rack and let cool completely.

6 Mix the whipped cream with the raspberries and spoon the mixture on top of 1 of the shortcakes, spreading it out evenly.

7 Top with the other shortcake round, dust with a little confectioners' sugar, and decorate with the extra raspberries and mint leaves.

COOK'S TIP

The shortcake can be made a few days in advance and stored in an airtight container until required.

Peaches & Mascarpone

If you prepare these in advance, all you have to do is pop the peaches on the barbecue grill when you are ready to serve them.

NUTRITIONAL INFORMATION

Calories	301	Sugars	........24g
Protein	.........6g	Fat	..........20g
Carbohydrate	...24g	Saturates	.......9g

 10 mins 10 mins

SERVES 4

INGREDIENTS

4 peaches

¾ cup mascarpone cheese

⅓ cup pecans or walnuts, chopped

1 tsp sunflower oil

4 tbsp maple syrup

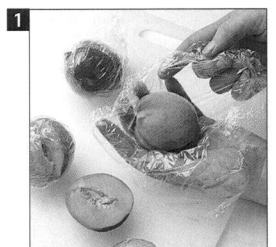

1 Cut the peaches in half and remove the pits. If you are preparing this recipe in advance, press the peach halves together again and wrap them in plastic wrap until required.

2 Combine the mascarpone and pecans or walnuts in a small bowl. Let chill in the refrigerator until required.

3 When ready to serve, brush the peaches with a little sunflower oil and place on a rack set over medium hot coals. Grill for 5–10 minutes, turning once, until hot.

4 Transfer the peaches to a serving dish and top with the mascarpone cheese mixture. Drizzle the maple syrup over the peaches and mascarpone filling and serve immediately.

VARIATION
You can use nectarines instead of peaches for this recipe. Remember to choose ripe but firm fruit which won't go soft and mushy when it is grilled. Prepare the nectarines in the same way as the peaches and grill or 5–10 minutes.

Green Fruit Salad

This delightfully refreshing fruit salad is the perfect finale for a Chinese meal. It has a lovely light syrup made with fresh mint and honey.

NUTRITIONAL INFORMATION

Calories	157	Sugars	........34g
Protein	.........1g	Fat	..........0.2g
Carbohydrate	...34g	Saturates	.......0g

30 mins   15 mins

SERVES 4

INGREDIENTS

1 small Charentais or honeydew melon

2 green apples

2 kiwi fruit

16 seedless white grapes

fresh mint sprigs, to decorate

SYRUP

1 orange

⅔ cup white wine

⅔ cup water

4 tbsp honey

fresh mint sprigs

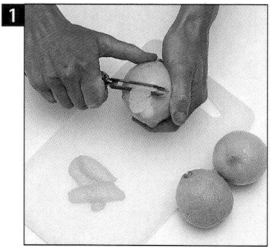

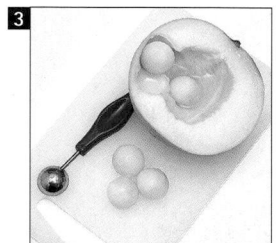

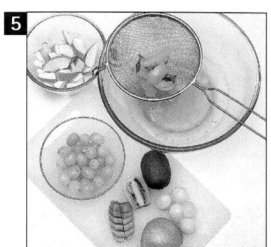

COOK'S TIP

Single-flower honey has a better, more individual flavor than blended honey. Acacia honey is typically Chinese, but you could also try clove, lemon blossom, lime flower, or orange blossom.

1 To make the syrup, pare the zest from the orange using a potato peeler. Put the orange zest in a pan with the white wine, water, and honey. Bring to a boil, then simmer gently for 10 minutes.

2 Remove the syrup from the heat. Add the mint sprigs and let cool.

3 To prepare the fruit, first slice the melon in half and scoop out the seeds. Use a melon baller or a teaspoon to make melon balls.

4 Core and chop the apples. Peel and slice the kiwi fruit.

5 Strain the cooled syrup into a serving bowl. Remove and reserve the orange zest, and discard the mint sprigs. Add the apple, grapes, kiwi fruit, and melon to the bowl. Stir through gently to mix.

6 Serve the fruit salad, decorated with sprigs of fresh mint and some of the reserved orange zest.

Chocolate Meringues

The Mexican name for these delicate meringues is suspiros, meaning "sighs"—supposedly the contented sighs of the nuns who created them.

NUTRITIONAL INFORMATION

Calories	550	Sugars	........11g
Protein	.........1g	Fat	...........1g
Carbohydrate	....11g	Saturates	.......1g

1¼ hrs   2 hrs

SERVES 4

INGREDIENTS

4–5 egg whites, at room temperature

a pinch of salt

¼ tsp cream of tartar

¼–½ tsp vanilla extract

¾–1 cup superfine sugar

⅛–¼ tsp ground cinnamon

4 oz/115 g dark or bitter chocolate, grated

TO SERVE

ground cinnamon

4 oz/115 g strawberries

chocolate-flavored cream (see Cook's Tip)

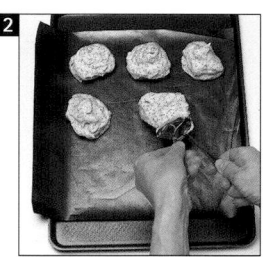

1 Whisk the egg whites until they are foamy, then add the salt and cream of tartar and beat until very stiff. Whisk in the vanilla, then slowly whisk in the sugar, a small amount at a time, until the meringue is shiny and stiff. This should take about 3 minutes by hand, and under a minute with an electric whisk.

2 Whisk in the cinnamon and grated chocolate. Spoon mounds of about 2 tablespoons, on to an ungreased, non-stick cookie sheet. Space the mounds well.

3 Place in a preheated oven, 300°F/ 150°C, and cook for 2 hours until set, then carefully remove from the cookie sheet. If the meringues are too moist and soft, return them to the oven to firm up and dry out more. Let cool completely.

4 Serve the meringues dusted with cinnamon and accompanied by strawberries and the chocolate-flavored cream (see Cook's Tip).

COOK'S TIP
To make the flavored cream, simply stir half-melted chocolate pieces into stiffly whipped cream, then chill until solid.

Toasted Tropical Fruit

Spear some chunks of exotic tropical fruits on to kabob sticks,
sear them over the grill, and serve with this amazing chocolate dip.

NUTRITIONAL INFORMATION

Calories	435	Sugars	........60g
Protein	.........6g	Fat	...........11g
Carbohydrate	...68g	Saturates	.......6g

🍲 45 mins   🕐 5 mins

SERVES 4

INGREDIENTS

DIP

4½ oz/125 g dark chocolate,
  broken into pieces

2 tbsp light corn syrup

1 tbsp unsweetened cocoa

1 tbsp cornstarch

¾ cup milk

KABOBS

1 mango

1 papaya

2 kiwi fruit

½ small pineapple

1 large banana

2 tbsp lemon juice

⅔ cup white rum

1 Put all the ingredients for the chocolate dip into a heavy pan. Heat over the grill or over low heat, stirring constantly, until thickened and smooth. Keep warm at the edge of the grill.

2 Slice the mango on each side of its large, flat pit. Cut the flesh into chunks, removing the peel. Halve the papaya, remove the seeds with a spoon, and cut it into chunks. Peel the kiwi fruit and slice it into chunks. Peel and cut the pineapple into chunks. Peel and slice the banana and dip the pieces in the lemon juice to prevent them from discoloring.

3 Thread the pieces of fruit alternately on to 4 wooden skewers. Place them in a shallow dish and pour over the rum. Let the fruit soak up the flavor of the rum for at least 30 minutes, until ready to grill.

4 Cook the kabobs over the hot coals, turning frequently, for about 2 minutes, until the fruit is seared. Serve immediately, accompanied by the hot chocolate dip.

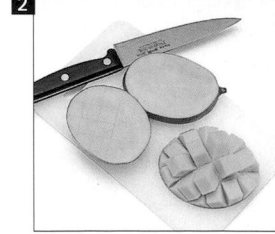

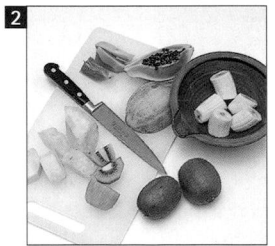

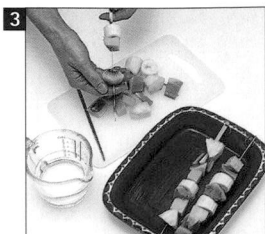

Bunuelo Stars

These delicious, crisp little stars, coated in cinnamon sugar, are a Mexican treat, and are very simple to make.

NUTRITIONAL INFORMATION

Calories ....299 Sugars 32g
Protein ....4g Fat 61g
Carbohydrate ...61g Saturates 1g

 5 mins   5 mins

SERVES 4

INGREDIENTS

4 flour tortillas

3 tbsp ground cinnamon

6-8 tbsp sugar

vegetable oil, for frying

chocolate ice cream, to serve

fine orange zest strips, to decorate

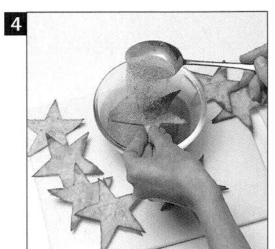

1 Using a sharp knife or kitchen scissors cut each tortilla into star shapes.

2 Mix the cinnamon and sugar together and set them aside.

3 Heat the oil in a shallow, wide skillet until it is hot enough to brown a cube of bread in 30 seconds. Working one at a time, fry the star-shaped tortillas until one side is golden, then turn and cook until golden on the other side. Remove from the hot oil with a slotted spoon and drain on paper towels.

4 Sprinkle generously with the cinnamon and sugar mixture. Serve with chocolate ice cream, sprinkled with orange zest strips.

COOK'S TIP

These star-shaped bunuelos make an attractive decoration for an ice cream sundae with Mexican flavors, caramel, cinnamon, coffee, chocolate.

Deep-Fried Sweetmeats

This is one of the most popular Indian sweetmeats. The flavor and beautiful aroma come from the rosewater in the syrup.

NUTRITIONAL INFORMATION

Calories	325	Sugars	........25g
Protein	.........3g	Fat	.........24g
Carbohydrate	...25g	Saturates	......12g

  20 mins   20 mins

SERVES 6-8

INGREDIENTS

5 tbsp dry milk powder

1½ tbsp all-purpose flour

1 tsp baking powder

1½ tbsp sweet butter

1 medium egg

1 tsp milk to mix (if required)

10 tbsp pure or vegetable ghee

SYRUP

3 cups water

8 tbsp sugar

2 green cardamoms, peeled, with seeds crushed

1 large pinch saffron strands

2 tbsp rosewater

1 Place the dry milk powder, flour, and baking powder in a bowl.

2 Place the sweet butter in a pan and heat, stirring, until melted.

3 Whisk the egg in a bowl. Add the melted butter and whisked egg to the dry ingredients and blend together with a fork (and add the 1 teaspoon extra milk at this stage if necessary) to form a soft dough.

4 Break the dough into about 12 small pieces and shape, in the palms of your hands, into small, smooth balls.

5 Heat the ghee in a deep skillet. Reduce the heat and start cooking the dough balls, about 3-4 at a time, tossing and turning gently with a perforated spoon until a dark golden brown color. Remove the sweetmeats from the pan and set aside in a deep serving bowl.

6 To make the syrup, boil the water and sugar in a pan for 7–10 minutes. Add the crushed cardamom seeds and saffron, and pour over the sweetmeats.

7 Pour the rosewater sparingly over the top. Let soak for about 10 minutes for the sweetmeats to soak up some of the syrup. Serve hot or cold.

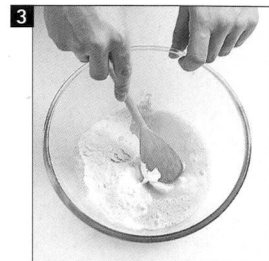

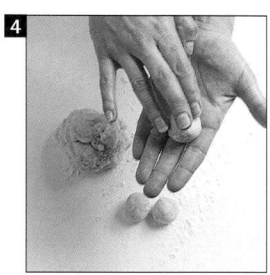

Oranges in Spiced Caramel

Unusually, some of the spice in this delicious and impressive orange dessert is provided by the addition of black pepper to the caramel!

NUTRITIONAL INFORMATION

Calories	257	Sugars	........56g
Protein	.........3g	Fat	..........4g
Carbohydrate	...56g	Saturates	.....0.5g

15 mins   10 mins

SERVES 4

I N G R E D I E N T S

4 large, juicy oranges

4–6 tbsp shelled pistachio nuts, chopped, to decorate

SPICED CARAMEL

1¼ cups superfine sugar

5 black peppercorns, lightly crushed

4 cloves

1 green cardamom pod, lightly crushed

1¼ cups water

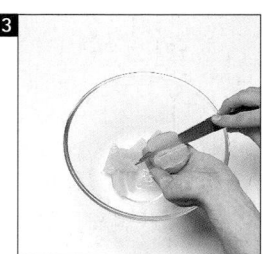

1 To make the spiced caramel, put the sugar, peppercorns, cloves, cardamom pod, and ⅔ cup of the water in a pan and stir to dissolve the sugar over medium heat. When the sugar has dissolved, turn up the heat and boil, without stirring, until the syrup thickens and turns a deep caramel color. Use a wet pastry brush to brush the syrup down from the side of the pan if necessary.

2 Very carefully, pour in another ⅔ cup water, standing back because it will splatter. Remove from the heat and, using a long-handled wooden spoon, stir until all the caramel has dissolved. Let cool.

3 Carefully pare off the orange zest and pith, so the oranges retain their shape. Leave the oranges whole, or, working over a bowl, cut into segments, cutting the flesh away from the membranes.

4 Pour over the caramel syrup with the spices and stir together. Cover and chill until ready to serve. Serve the dessert in individual bowls, sprinkled with chopped pistachio nuts.

VARIATION
Turn this Spanish dessert into a Sicilian-style one by using the blood-red oranges that grow in great profusion on the island.

Baked Sweet Ravioli

These unusual and scrumptious little parcels are the perfect dessert for anyone with a really sweet tooth.

NUTRITIONAL INFORMATION

Calories 765   Sugars 56g
Protein ....16g   Fat 30g
Carbohydrate ...114g   Saturates 15g

 1½ hrs   20 mins

SERVES 4

I N G R E D I E N T S

PASTA

3¾ cups all-purpose flour

⅔ cup butter, plus extra for greasing

¾ cup superfine sugar

4 eggs

1 oz/25 g yeast

½ cup lukewarm milk

FILLING

⅔ cup chestnut paste

½ cup unsweetened cocoa

generous ¼ cup superfine sugar

½ cup chopped almonds

1 cup crushed amaretti cookies

generous ½ cup orange marmalade

1 To make the sweet pasta dough, sift the flour into a mixing bowl, then add the butter, sugar, and 3 of the eggs and mix well to combine.

2 Mix together the yeast and warm milk in a small bowl and, when thoroughly combined, mix into the dough.

3 Knead the dough for 20 minutes, cover with a clean cloth, and set aside in a warm place for 1 hour to rise.

4 In a separate bowl, mix together the chestnut paste, unsweetened cocoa, sugar, almonds, crushed amaretti cookies, and orange marmalade.

5 Grease 1 or 2 cookie sheets with a little butter.

6 Lightly flour the counter. Roll out the pasta dough into a thin sheet and cut into 2-inch/5-cm circles with a plain dough cutter.

7 Put a spoonful of filling onto each circle and then fold in half, pressing the edges to seal.

8 Arrange on the prepared cookie sheet, spacing the ravioli out well to let them rise.

9 Beat the remaining egg and brush all over the ravioli to glaze. Bake in a preheated oven, 350°F/180°C, for 20 minutes. Serve hot.

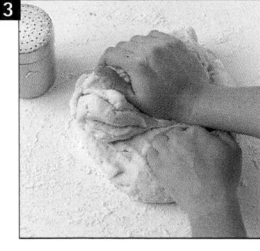

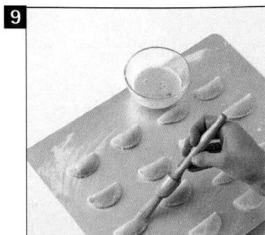

Honey & Nut Nests

Pistachio nuts and honey are combined with crisp cooked angel hair pasta in this unusual and charming dessert.

NUTRITIONAL INFORMATION

Calories	802	Sugars	........53g
Protein	........13g	Fat	..........48g
Carbohydrate	...85g	Saturates	......16g

🧂 10 mins   🕐 1 hr

SERVES 4

INGREDIENTS

8 oz/225 g dried angel hair pasta

½ cup butter

1½ cups chopped pistachio nuts

½ cup sugar

⅓ cup clear honey

⅔ cup water

2 tsp lemon juice

salt

Greek-style yogurt, to serve

1 Bring a large pan of lightly salted water to a boil. Add the angel hair pasta, bring back to a boil, and cook for 8–10 minutes or until tender, but still firm to the bite. Drain the pasta and return to the pan. Add the butter and toss to coat the pasta thoroughly. Let cool.

2 Arrange 4 small tart or poaching rings on a cookie sheet. Divide the angel hair pasta into 8 equal quantities and spoon 4 of them into the rings. Press down lightly. Top the pasta with half of the nuts, then add the remaining pasta.

3 Bake in a preheated oven, 350°F/180°C, for 45 minutes, or until golden brown.

4 Meanwhile, put the sugar, honey, and water in a pan and bring to a boil over low heat, stirring constantly until the sugar has dissolved completely. Simmer for 10 minutes, add the lemon juice, and simmer for a further 5 minutes.

5 Using a spatula, carefully transfer the nests to a serving dish. Pour over the honey syrup, sprinkle over the remaining nuts, and let cool completely before serving. Serve at room temperature and hand the Greek-style yogurt separately.

COOK'S TIP
Angel hair pasta is also known as capelli d'angelo. Long and very fine, it is usually sold in small bunches that already resemble nests.

Raspberry Almond Spirals

This is the ultimate in self-indulgence—a truly delicious dessert that tastes every bit as good as it looks.

NUTRITIONAL INFORMATION

Calories 235   Sugars 20g
Protein ....7g   Fat 7g
Carbohydrate ...36g   Saturates 1g

 5 mins   20 mins

SERVES 4

I N G R E D I E N T S

½ cup fusilli

4 cups raspberries

2 tbsp superfine sugar

1 tbsp lemon juice

4 tbsp slivered almonds

3 tbsp raspberry liqueur

1 Bring a large pan of lightly salted water to a boil. Add the fusilli and cook until tender, but still firm to the bite. Drain the fusilli thoroughly, then return to the pan and let cool.

2 Using a spoon, firmly press ⅓ cup of the raspberries through a strainer set over a large mixing bowl to form a smooth paste.

3 Put the raspberry paste and sugar in a small pan and simmer over low heat, stirring occasionally, for 5 minutes. Stir in the lemon juice and set the sauce aside until required.

4 Add the remaining raspberries to the fusilli in the pan and mix together well. Transfer the raspberry and fusilli mixture to a serving dish.

5 Spread the almonds out on a cookie sheet and toast under the broiler until golden brown. Remove and let cool slightly.

6 Stir the raspberry liqueur into the reserved raspberry sauce and mix together well until very smooth. Pour the raspberry sauce over the fusilli, then generously sprinkle over the toasted almonds, and serve.

COOK'S TIP

You could use almost any sweet, really ripe berry for making this dessert. Strawberries and blackberries are especially suitable, combined with the correspondingly flavored liqueur.

Egg Mousse with Marsala

Known as zabaglione in Italy, this warm mousse will not keep, so make it fresh and serve immediately.

NUTRITIONAL INFORMATION

Calories	158	Sugars	........29g
Protein	.........1g	Fat	...........1g
Carbohydrate	...29g	Saturates	.....0.2g

 15 mins 0 mins

SERVES 4

I N G R E D I E N T S

5 egg yolks

½ cup superfine sugar

⅔ cup Marsala wine or sweet sherry

amaretti cookies, to serve (optional)

1 Place the egg yolks in a mixing bowl. Add the sugar to the egg yolks and whisk until the mixture is thick and very pale and has doubled in volume.

2 Place the bowl containing the egg yolk and sugar mixture over a pan of simmering water.

3 Add the Marsala wine or sherry to the egg yolk and sugar mixture and continue whisking until the foam mixture becomes warm. This process may take as long as 10 minutes.

4 Pour the mixture, which should be foamy and light, into 4 wine glasses.

5 Serve the mousse warm with fresh fruit or amaretti cookies, if you wish.

COOK'S TIP
Any other type of liqueur may be used instead of the Marsala wine or sweet sherry, if you prefer. Serve soft fruits, such as strawberries or raspberries, with the zabaglione—it's a delicious combination!

Marinated Peaches

A very simple but incredibly pleasing dessert, which is especially good for a dinner party on a hot summer day.

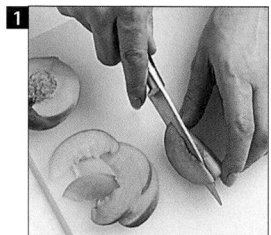
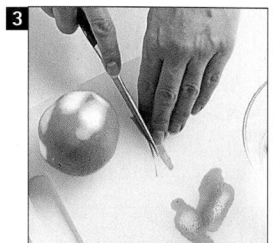

NUTRITIONAL INFORMATION

Calories 89   Sugars 14g
Protein ....1g   Fat 0g
Carbohydrate ...14g   Saturates 0g

10 mins, plus chilling   0 mins

SERVES 4

INGREDIENTS

4 large ripe peaches

2 tbsp confectioners' sugar, sifted

pared zest and juice of 1 orange

¾ cup medium or sweet white wine, chilled

1 Using a sharp knife, halve the peaches, then remove the pits and discard them. Peel the peaches, if you prefer. Slice the peaches into thin wedges.

2 Place the peach wedges in a glass serving bowl and sprinkle over the confectioners' sugar.

3 Using a sharp knife, pare the zest from the orange, cut it into short, thin sticks, then place them in a bowl of cold water and set aside.

4 Pour the wine and the juice from the orange over the peaches.

5 Let the peaches marinate and chill in the refrigerator for at least 1 hour.

6 Remove the orange peel from the cold water and pat dry with paper towels. Garnish the peaches with the strips of orange peel and serve at once.

COOK'S TIP

There is absolutely no need to use expensive wine in this recipe, so it can be quite economical to make.

Steamed Coconut Cake

This steamed coconut cake, steeped in a lime and ginger syrup, is typical of Thai desserts and sweets, and has a distinctly Chinese influence.

NUTRITIONAL INFORMATION

Calories	243	Sugars	........17g
Protein	.........4g	Fat	..........12g
Carbohydrate	...31g	Saturates	.......8g

15 mins   30 mins

SERVES 8

INGREDIENTS

2 extra large eggs, separated

pinch of salt

½ cup superfine sugar

5 tbsp butter, melted and cooled

5 tbsp coconut milk

1¼ cups self-rising flour

½ tsp baking powder

3 tbsp shredded coconut

4 tbsp preserved ginger syrup

3 tbsp lime juice

TO DECORATE

3 pieces preserved ginger, diced

curls of fresh grated coconut

strips of lime zest

1 Line a 7 inch/18 cm steamer basket with an 11 inch/28 cm circle of nonstick baking parchment.

2 Whisk the egg whites with the salt until stiff. Gradually whisk in the sugar, 1 tablespoon at a time, whisking hard after each addition until the mixture stands in stiff peaks.

3 Whisk in the yolks, then quickly stir in the butter and coconut milk. Strain the flour and baking powder over the mixture, then fold in lightly with a large metal spoon. Fold in the coconut.

4 Spoon the mixture into the steamer basket and tuck the spare paper over the top. Place the basket over boiling water, cover, and steam for 30 minutes.

5 Turn the cake onto a plate, remove the paper, and cool slightly. Mix the ginger syrup and lime juice together, and spoon over the cake. Cut into squares and top with ginger, coconut, and lime zest.

COOK'S TIP
Coconuts grow on tropical beaches all around the world, but probably originated in South East Asia, and it is here that coconut is most important in cooking.

Sticky Rice Balls

The gluten in the rice is sufficient to hold these attractive, delicately colored balls together—definitely a recipe for a sweet tooth!

NUTRITIONAL INFORMATION

Calories	762	Sugars	.......131g
Protein	.........6g	Fat	............1g
Carbohydrate	..187g	Saturates	.......0g

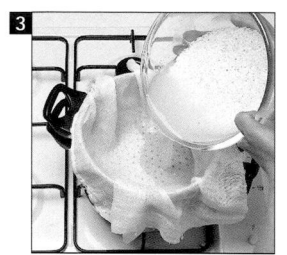

 15 mins, plus soaking   35 mins

SERVES 4

I N G R E D I E N T S

1½ cups glutinous (sticky) rice

pink and green food colorings

2½ cups granulated sugar

1¼ cups water

few drops of rose water or jasmine essence

1 Place the rice in a bowl and add enough cold water to cover. Let soak for 3 hours, or overnight.

2 Drain the rice and rinse thoroughly in cold water.

3 Line the top part of a steamer with cheesecloth and pour the rice into it. Place over boiling water, cover and steam

the rice for 30 minutes. Remove and let cool.

4 Heat the sugar, water, and essences gently until the sugar dissolves. Bring to a boil and boil for 4–5 minutes to reduce to a thin syrup. Remove the pan from the heat and set aside.

5 Divide the rice in half and color one half pale pink, the other half pale green. Shape into small balls.

6 Using 2 forks, dip the rice balls into the syrup, drain off the excess, and pile onto a dish. Scatter with rose petals or jasmine flowers.

COOK'S TIP

If you prefer, the rice balls can be shaped in small molds like dariole molds as seen in the photo at right.

Caramel Apple Wedges

Crisp apple slices are deep-fried in a sesame seed batter and given a delicious caramel coat—a wonderful Hallowe'en treat.

NUTRITIONAL INFORMATION

Calories 345	Sugars 12g	
Protein 4g	Fat 21g	
Carbohydrate ...35g	Saturates 2g	

15 mins   15 mins

SERVES 4

INGREDIENTS

1 cup rice flour

1 medium egg

½ cup cold water

4 crisp dessert apples

2½ tbsp sesame seeds

1¼ cups superfine sugar

2 tbsp vegetable oil

extra vegetable oil for deep frying

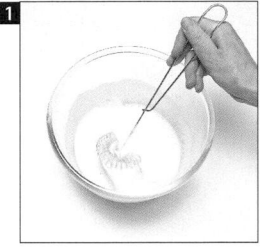 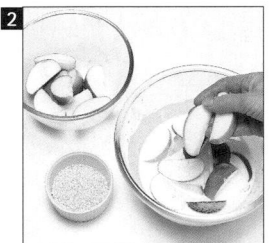 

1 Place the flour, egg, and water in a bowl and whisk well until a smooth, thick batter forms.

2 Core the apples and cut each into 8 wedges. Drop into the batter and stir in the sesame seeds.

3 Place the sugar and 2 tablespoons oil in a heavy pan and heat, stirring, until the sugar dissolves. Continue to stir until the syrup just begins to turn pale golden. Remove from the heat but keep warm.

4 Heat the oil for frying in a wok or deep pan to 350° F/180°C, or until a cube of bread turns golden brown in 30 seconds. Lift the apple pieces one by one from the batter, using chopsticks or tongs, lower into the hot oil, and cook for 2–3 minutes until golden brown and crisp.

5 Remove with a perforated spoon and dip very quickly into the sugar mixture. Dip briefly into iced water and drain on absorbent paper towels. Serve immediately.

COOK'S TIP
Take care not to overheat the sugar syrup or it will become difficult to handle and burn. If it begins to set before you have finished dipping the apple pieces, warm it slightly over the heat until it becomes liquid again.

Banana Fritters

These wonderful little fritters are fried in a coconut batter for a special flavor. Rice flour makes the batter especially crisp.

NUTRITIONAL INFORMATION

Calories	345	Sugars	........31g
Protein	.........6g	Fat	..........12g
Carbohydrate	...55g	Saturates	.......2g

10 mins   10 mins

SERVES 4

INGREDIENTS

9 tbsp all-purpose flour

2 tbsp rice flour

1 tbsp superfine sugar

1 egg, separated

⅔ cup coconut milk

4 large bananas

sunflower oil for deep frying

TO DECORATE

1 tsp confectioners' sugar

1 tsp ground cinnamon

1 Sift the all-purpose flour, rice flour, and sugar into a bowl and make a well in the center. Add the egg yolk and coconut milk and beat until a smooth, thick batter forms.

COOK'S TIP
If you can buy the baby finger bananas that are popular in this dish in the East, leave them whole for coating and frying.

2 Whisk the egg white in a clean, dry bowl until stiff enough to hold soft peaks. Fold it into the batter lightly and evenly.

3 Heat a 2½ inch depth of sunflower oil in a large pan to 350° F/180°C, or until a cube of bread browns in 30 seconds. Cut the bananas in half

crosswise, then dip them quickly into the batter to coat. Drop them carefully into the hot oil and cook in batches for 2–3 minutes until they are golden brown, turning once.

4 Drain well on paper towels. Sprinkle with confectioners' sugar and cinnamon, and serve immediately.

Coconut Custard Squares

A delicious variation of baked custard, these squares are made with coconut milk. The light brown sugar gives the squares a rich color.

NUTRITIONAL INFORMATION

Calories 324   Sugars 49g
Protein ....12g   Fat 11g
Carbohydrate ...49g   Saturates 4g

10 mins   40 mins

SERVES 4

I N G R E D I E N T S

1 tsp. butter, melted

6 large eggs

1¾ cups coconut milk

¾ cup soft light brown sugar

pinch of salt

shreds of coconut and lime zest, to decorate

1 Brush the butter over the inside of a 7½ inch square buttered ovenproof dish or pan, about 1½ inch deep.

2 Beat the eggs in a large bowl and beat in the coconut milk, sugar, and salt. Place the bowl over a pan of gently simmering water and stir the mixture with a wooden spoon for 15 minutes, or until it begins to thicken. Pour into the prepared dish or pan.

3 Bake the custard in a preheated oven at 350° F/180°C for 20–25 minutes until just set. Remove from the oven and let cool completely.

4 Cut the custard into squares and serve scattered with strips of coconut and lime zest.

COOK'S TIP
Keep and eye on the custard as it bakes, as if it overcooks the texture will be spoiled. When it comes out of the oven it should be barely set and still slightly wobbly in the center, then it will firm up slightly as it cools.

Summer Fruit Dessert

A sweet cream cheese dessert that complements the tartness of fresh summer fruits rather well.

NUTRITIONAL INFORMATION

Calories 725   Sugars 36g
Protein . . . . .10g   Fat 59g
Carbohydrate . . .36g   Saturates 36g

5 mins, plus chilling   0 mins

SERVES 4

INGREDIENTS

1 lb/450 g mascarpone cheese

½ cup superfine sugar

4 egg yolks

14 oz frozen summer fruits, such as raspberries and redcurrants

red currants, to garnish

amaretti cookies, to serve

1 Place the mascarpone cheese in a large mixing bowl and beat with a wooden spoon until smooth.

2 Stir the egg yolks and sugar into the mascarpone cheese, mixing well. Let the mixture chill in the refrigerator for about 1 hour.

3 Spoon a layer of the mascarpone mixture into the bottom of 4 individual serving dishes. Spoon a layer of the summer fruits on top. Repeat the layers in the same order, reserving some of the mascarpone mixture for the top.

4 Let the mousses chill in the refrigerator for about 20 minutes. The fruits should still be slightly frozen.

5 Serve the mascarpone mousses with amaretti cookies.

VARIATION

Try adding 3 tablespoons of your favorite liqueur to the mascarpone cheese mixture in step 1, if you prefer.

Mascarpone Cheesecake

The mascarpone gives this baked cheesecake a wonderfully tangy flavor. Ricotta cheese could be used as an alternative.

NUTRITIONAL INFORMATION

Calories	327	Sugars	........25g
Protein	.........9g	Fat	..........18g
Carbohydrate	...33g	Saturates	......11g

15 mins   50 mins

SERVES 4

INGREDIENTS

4 tbsp sweet butter, plus extra for greasing

3 cups ginger cookie crumbs

1 tablespoon chopped preserved ginger

2¼ cups mascarpone cheese

finely grated zest and juice of 2 lemons

½ cup superfine sugar

2 large eggs, separated

fruit coulis (see Cook's Tip), to serve

1 Grease and line the base of a 10-inch/25-cm spring-form cake pan or loose-bottomed pan.

2 Melt the butter in a pan and stir in the crushed cookies and chopped ginger. Use the mixture to line the pan, pressing the mixture about ¼ inch/5 mm up the sides.

3 Beat together the cheese, lemon zest and juice, sugar, and egg yolks until quite smooth.

4 Whisk the egg whites until they are stiff and fold into the cheese and lemon mixture.

5 Pour the mixture into the pan and bake in a preheated oven, 350°F/180°C, for about 35–45 minutes, or until just set. Don't worry if the cheesecake cracks or sinks—this is quite normal.

6 Let the cheesecake cool completely in the pan. Serve with fruit coulis (see Cook's Tip.)

COOK'S TIP
Fruit coulis can be made by cooking 14 oz/400 g fruit, such as blueberries, for 5 minutes with 2 tablespoons of water. Strain the mixture, then stir in 1 tablespoon (or more to taste) of strained confectioners' sugar. Let cool before serving.

Tiramisu Layers

This is a modern version of the well-known and very traditional chocolate dessert from Italy.

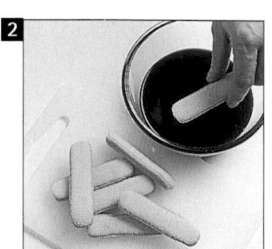

NUTRITIONAL INFORMATION

Calories	990	Sugars	........69g
Protein	........11g	Fat	..........75g
Carbohydrate	...84g	Saturates	......42g

1 hr 25 mins   5 mins

SERVES 4

INGREDIENTS

⅔ cup heavy cream

10½ oz/300 g dark chocolate

14 oz/400 g mascarpone cheese

1¾ cups black coffee with ¼ cup superfine sugar, cooled

6 tbsp dark rum or brandy

36 ladyfingers

unsweetened cocoa, to dust

1 Whip the cream until it just holds its shape. Melt the chocolate in a bowl set over a pan of simmering water, stirring occasionally. Let the chocolate cool slightly, then stir it into the mascarpone and cream.

2 Mix the coffee and rum together in a bowl. Dip the lady-fingers into the mixture briefly so that they absorb the coffee and rum mixture but do not become soggy.

3 Arrange 3 ladyfingers on 3 serving plates.

4 Spoon a layer of the chocolate, mascarpone, and cream mixture over the ladyfingers.

5 Place 3 more ladyfingers on top of the chocolate and mascarpone mixture. Spread another layer of chocolate and mascarpone and place 3 more lady-fingers on top.

6 Let the tiramisu chill for at least 1 hour in the refrigerator. Dust the top with a little unsweetened cocoa, just before serving.

VARIATION
Try adding ⅓ cup toasted, chopped hazelnuts to the chocolate and mascarpone mixture in Step 1, if you prefer.

Tuscan Pudding

These baked mini-ricotta puddings are delicious served warm or chilled and will keep in the refrigerator for 3–4 days.

NUTRITIONAL INFORMATION

Calories	293	Sugars	.......28g
Protein	.........9g	Fat	..........17g
Carbohydrate	...28g	Saturates	.......9g

 20 mins   15 mins

SERVES 4

INGREDIENTS

1 tbsp butter

⅔ cup mixed dried fruit

generous 1 cup ricotta cheese

3 egg yolks

¼ cup superfine sugar

1 tsp cinnamon

finely grated zest of 1 orange, plus extra to decorate

crème fraîche, to serve (see page 8)

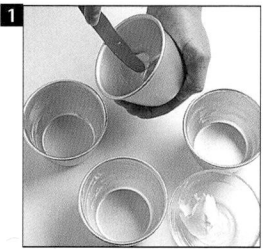

1 Lightly grease 4 mini ovenproof bowls or ramekin dishes with the butter.

2 Put the dried fruit in a bowl and cover with warm water. Let soak for 10 minutes.

3 Beat the ricotta cheese with the egg yolks in a bowl. Stir in the superfine sugar, cinnamon, and orange zest and mix to combine.

4 Drain the dried fruit in a strainer set over a bowl. Mix the drained fruit with the ricotta cheese mixture.

5 Spoon the mixture into the bowls or ramekin dishes.

6 Bake in a preheated oven, 350°F/ 180°C, for 15 minutes. The tops should just be firm to the touch, but they should not brown.

7 Decorate the puddings with grated orange zest. Serve warm or chilled with a spoon of crème fraîche, if liked.

COOK'S TIP
Crème fraîche has a slightly sour, nutty taste and is very thick. It is suitable for cooking, but has the same fat content as heavy cream.

Orange Crème à Catalanas

This delectable, orange-flavored custard is thoroughly chilled before being finished with a caramelized sugar topping.

NUTRITIONAL INFORMATION

Calories 265   Sugars 33g
Protein . . . . .8g   Fat 9g
Carbohydrate . . .41g   Saturates 3g

 25 mins, plus cooling   30 mins

SERVES 8

INGREDIENTS

4 cups milk

finely grated zest of 6 large oranges

9 large egg yolks

1 cup superfine sugar, plus extra for the topping

3 tbsp cornstarch

1 Put the milk and orange zest in a pan over medium-high heat. Bring to a boil, then remove from the heat, cover, and let cool for 2 hours.

2 Return the milk to the heat and simmer for 10 minutes. Put the egg yolks and sugar in a heatproof bowl over a pan of boiling water. Whisk until creamy and the sugar has dissolved.

3 Add 5 tablespoons of the flavored milk to the cornstarch, stirring until smooth. Stir into the milk. Strain the milk into the eggs, whisking until blended.

4 Rinse out the pan and put a layer of water in the bottom. Put the bowl on top of the pan, making sure the base does not touch the water. Simmer over medium heat, whisking, until the custard is thick enough to coat the back of a wooden spoon, which can take 20 minutes. Do not let boil.

5 Pour into eight ²/₃ cup ramekins and let cool. Cover each with a piece of plastic wrap and let chill in the refrigerator for at least 6 hours.

6 When ready to serve, sprinkle the top of each ramekin with a layer of sugar. Use a kitchen blowtorch to melt and caramelize the sugar. Let stand for a few minutes until the caramel hardens, then serve at once. Do not return to the refrigerator or the topping will become soft.

COOK'S TIP

A kitchen blowtorch is the best way to melt the sugar quickly and guarantee a crisp topping. These are sold at good kitchen-supply stores. Alternatively, you can melt the sugar under a preheated hot grill.

Spanish Flan

This gorgeous "flan" is a version of crème caramel. It needs to be served well chilled, so is a great dessert to make in advance for a dinner party.

 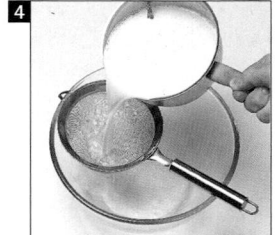 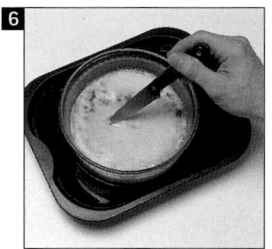

NUTRITIONAL INFORMATION

Calories 215	Sugars 35g	
Protein 7g	Fat 6g	
Carbohydrate . . .35g	Saturates 3g	

 10 mins, plus chilling   1¼–1½ hrs

SERVES 4–6

I N G R E D I E N T S

butter, for greasing

¾ cup plus 2 tbsp superfine sugar

4 tbsp water

juice of ½ lemon

2¼ cups milk

1 vanilla bean

2 large eggs

2 large egg yolks

1 Lightly grease the sides of a 5-cup souffle dish. To make the caramel, put a scant ⅓ cup sugar with the water in a pan over medium-high heat and cook, stirring, until the sugar dissolves. Boil until the syrup takes on a deep golden brown color.

2 Immediately remove from the heat and add a few drops of lemon juice. Pour into the souffle dish and swirl around. Set aside.

3 Pour the milk into a pan. Slit the vanilla bean lengthwise and add it to the milk. Bring to a boil, remove the pan from the heat, and stir in the remaining sugar, stirring until it dissolves. Set the pan aside.

4 Beat the eggs and egg yolks together in a bowl. Pour the milk mixture over them, whisking. Remove the vanilla bean. Strain the egg mixture into a bowl, then transfer to the souffle dish.

5 Place the dish in a roasting pan filled with enough boiling water to come two-thirds up the side.

6 Bake in a preheated oven at 325°F for 75–90 minutes until a knife inserted in the center comes out clean, and let cool.

7 Cover with plastic wrap and refrigerate for at least 24 hours.

8 To serve, run a round-bladed knife around the edge of the dish. Place an upturned serving plate with a rim on top, then invert the plate and dish, giving a sharp shake halfway over. Lift off the souffle dish.

COOK'S TIP
The lemon juice is added to the caramel in Step 2 to stop the cooking process, to prevent it from burning.

Pear Cake

This is a really moist cake, deliciously flavored with chopped pears and cinnamon and drizzled with honey.

NUTRITIONAL INFORMATION

Calories	119	Sugars	........16g
Protein	.........2g	Fat	..........0.3g
Carbohydrate	...29g	Saturates	.......0g

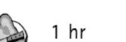

1 hr   1½ hrs

SERVES 12

INGREDIENTS

margarine, for greasing

4 pears, peeled and cored

2 tbsp water

1¾ cups all-purpose flour

2 tsp baking powder

scant ½ cup brown sugar

4 tbsp milk

2 tbsp honey, plus extra for drizzling

2 tsp ground cinnamon

2 egg whites

1 Grease and line the base of an 8 inch/20 cm cake pan.

2 Put 1 pear in a food processor with the water and process until almost smooth. Transfer to a mixing bowl.

3 Sift in the flour and baking powder. Beat in the sugar, milk, honey, and cinnamon and mix well.

4 Chop all but 1 of the remaining pears and add to the mixture.

5 Whisk the egg whites until peaks form and gently fold into the mixture until fully blended.

6 Slice the remaining pear and arrange it in a fan pattern on the bottom of the prepared pan.

7 Spoon the cake mixture into the pan and cook in a preheated oven, 300°F/150°C, for 1¼–1½ hours or until cooked through and golden.

8 Remove the cake from the oven and let cool in the pan for 10 minutes. Turn the cake out onto a wire cooling rack and drizzle with honey. Let cool completely, then cut into slices to serve.

COOK'S TIP

To test if the cake is cooked through, insert a toothpick into the center—if it comes out clean, the cake is cooked. If not, return the cake to the oven and test at frequent intervals.

Oat & Raisin Cookies

These oaty, fruity cookies couldn't be easier to make and are delicious served with a creamy rum-and-raisin ice cream.

NUTRITIONAL INFORMATION

Calories . . . . . . .227 Sugars 22g
Protein . . . . .4g Fat 7g
Carbohydrate . . .39g Saturates 3g

 50 mins   15 mins

SERVES 4

I N G R E D I E N T S

4 tbsp butter, plus extra for greasing

⅔ cup superfine sugar

1 egg, beaten

½ cup all-purpose flour

½ tsp salt

½ tsp baking powder

1¾ cups rolled oats

scant 1 cup raisins

2 tbsp sesame seeds

1 Lightly grease 2 cookie sheets with a little butter.

2 In a large mixing bowl, cream together the butter and sugar until light and fluffy.

3 Gradually add the beaten egg, beating well after each addition, until thoroughly combined.

4 Sift the flour, salt, and baking powder into the creamed mixture. Mix gently to combine. Add the rolled oats, raisins, and sesame seeds and mix together until thoroughly combined.

5 Place spoonfuls of the mixture, spaced well apart on the prepared cookie sheets to allow room to expand during cooking, and flatten them slightly with the back of a spoon.

6 Bake the cookies in a preheated oven, 350°F/180°C, for 15 minutes.

7 Let the cookies cool slightly on the cookie sheets.

8 Carefully transfer the cookies to a wire rack and let cool completely before serving.

COOK'S TIP

To enjoy these cookies at their best, store them in an airtight container.

Vanilla Tea Cake

This really is a gorgeous cake to serve with afternoon tea, light and delicious. Using vanilla sugar adds a very special taste and aroma.

NUTRITIONAL INFORMATION

Calories	260	Sugars	........23g
Protein	.........4g	Fat	..........14g
Carbohydrate	...31g	Saturates	.......7g

  15 mins   1½ hrs

MAKES 12–15 SLICES

INGREDIENTS

½ lb/225 g good quality candied fruit, such as cherries and orange, lemon, and lime peels, or Candied Citrus Peel

¾ cup ground almonds

finely grated zest of ½ lemon

generous ½ cup all-purpose flour

generous ½ cup self-rising flour

¾ cup butter, softened, plus extra for greasing

¾ cup plus 2 tbsp vanilla-flavored sugar (see Cook's Tip)

½ tsp vanilla extract

3 large eggs, lightly beaten

pinch of salt

candied fruit, to decorate

  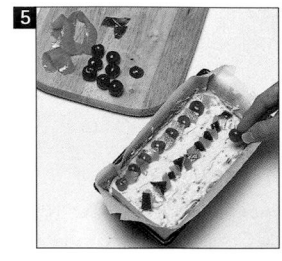

1 Grease an 8½ x 4½ x 2-inch bread pan, and line the base with a piece of waxed paper.

2 Chop the fruit into small pieces, reserving a few of the larger slices for the top. Combine with the ground almonds, lemon zest, and 2 tablespoons of the measured flour. Set aside.

3 Beat the butter and sugar together until creamy. Beat in the vanilla extract and eggs, a little at a time.

4 Sift both flours and the salt into the creamed mixture, then fold in. Fold in the fruit and ground almonds.

5 Spoon into the pan and smooth the surface. Arrange the reserved fruit slices on the top. Loosely cover the pan with foil, making sure it does not touch the cake. Bake in a preheated oven at 350°F/180°C for about 1½ hours until risen and a skewer inserted into the center comes out clean.

6 Let cool in the pan on a wire rack for 5 minutes, then turn out and remove lining. Cool completely.

7 Wrap in aluminum foil and store in an airtight container for up to 4 days. Decorated with the candied fruit when ready to serve.

COOK'S TIP

Make your own vanilla-flavored sugar by storing a sliced vanilla bean in a closed jar of superfine sugar.

Almond Cookies

These mouth-wateringly crisp Mediterranean cookies are lovely with coffee, and are also a perfect accompaniment for creamy desserts.

NUTRITIONAL INFORMATION

Calories	125	Sugars	.........4g
Protein	.........2g	Fat	...........8g
Carbohydrate	....11g	Saturates	.......4g

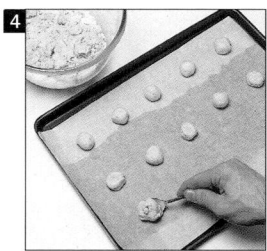

🍳 15 mins   🕐 25 mins

MAKES ABOUT 32 BISCUITS

INGREDIENTS

generous 1 cup unblanched almonds

1 cup butter, softened

6 tbsp confectioners' sugar, plus extra for sifting

scant 2 cups all-purpose flour

2 tsp vanilla extract

½ tsp almond extract

1 Line 2 cookie sheets with waxed paper. Using a cook's knife, finely chop the almonds, or process them in a small food processor, taking care not to overprocess them into a paste. Set aside.

2 Put the butter in a bowl and beat with an electric mixer until smooth. Strain in the confectioners' sugar and continue beating until creamed and smooth.

3 Sift in the flour from above the bowl and beat it in until blended. Add the vanilla and almond extracts and beat again to form a soft dough. Stir in the chopped almonds.

4 Using a teaspoon, shape the dough into 32 round balls about the size of walnuts. Place on the prepared cookie sheets, spacing them apart. Bake in a preheated oven at 350°F/180°C for 20–25 minutes until set and just starting to turn golden brown.

5 Let the cookies stand on the cookie sheets for 2 minutes to firm up. Strain a thick layer of confectioners' sugar over them. Transfer to a wire rack and let them cool completely.

6 Lightly dust with more confectioners' sugar, just before serving. Store the cookies in an airtight container for up to one week.

VARIATION
Although not a true Mediterranean ingredient, pecans can be used instead of the almonds. Alternatively, add 2 teaspoons finely grated orange zest to the dough in Step 3.

Rich Chocolate Loaf

Another rich chocolate dessert, this loaf is very simple to make and can be served as a coffee-time treat as well.

NUTRITIONAL INFORMATION

Calories . . . . .118 Sugars 16g
Protein . . . . .3g Fat 12g
Carbohydrate . . .18g Saturates 6g

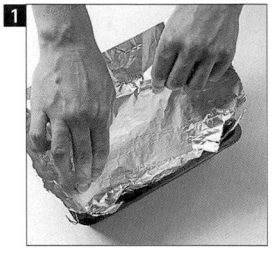
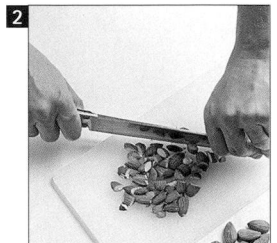

 1 hr 20 mins   5 mins

MAKES 16 SLICES

I N G R E D I E N T S

5½ oz/150 g dark chocolate

6 tbsp sweet butter

scant 1 cup sweetened condensed milk

2 tsp cinnamon

¾ cup almonds

1½ cups amaretti cookies, broken

8 dried no-soak apricots, coarsely chopped

1 Line a 1½ lb/675 g loaf pan with a sheet of foil.

2 Using a sharp knife, roughly chop the almonds.

3 Place the chocolate, butter, milk, and cinnamon in a heavy pan. Heat the chocolate mixture over low heat for 3–4 minutes, stirring with a wooden spoon, until the chocolate has melted. Beat the mixture well.

4 Stir the almonds, broken cookies, and chopped apricots into the chocolate mixture, stirring with a wooden spoon, until well mixed.

5 Pour the mixture into the prepared pan and chill in the refrigerator for about 1 hour or until set. Cut the loaf into slices to serve.

COOK'S TIP

To melt chocolate, first break it into manageable pieces. The smaller the pieces, the quicker it will melt.

Sweet Risotto Cake

Served with your favorite summer berries and a scented mascarpone cream, this baked sweet risotto makes an unusual dessert.

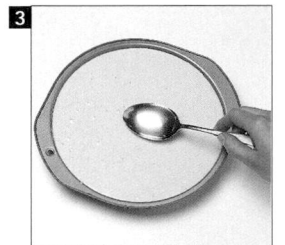

NUTRITIONAL INFORMATION

Calories 444	Sugars 21g	
Protein 9g	Fat 21g	
Carbohydrate . . .54g	Saturates 13g	

 20 mins   45 mins

SERVES 6–8

I N G R E D I E N T S

½ cup arborio rice

1½ cups milk

3–4 tbsp sugar

½ tsp freshly grated nutmeg

salt

1½ cups all-purpose flour

1½ tsp baking powder

1 tsp baking soda

1–2 tbsp superfine sugar

1 egg

¾ cup milk

½ cup sour cream or yogurt

1 tbsp butter, melted

2 tbsp honey

½ tsp almond extract

2 tbsp toasted slivered almonds

2 tbsp melted butter, for greasing

confectioners' sugar, for dusting (optional)

MUSCAT BERRIES

1 lb/450 g mixed summer berries, such as strawberries, raspberries, and blueberries

4 tbsp Muscat wine

1–2 tbsp sugar

MASCARPONE CREAM

2 tbsp Muscat wine

1 tbsp honey

½ tsp almond extract

1 x 8 oz tub mascarpone

1 Put the rice, milk, sugar, nutmeg, and ½ teaspoon of salt in a heavy pan. Bring to a boil, reduce the heat slightly, and cook, stirring constantly, until the rice is tender and the milk has almost been absorbed. Let cool.

2 Combine the flour, baking powder, baking soda, pinch of salt, and the sugar. In a bowl, beat the egg, milk, sour cream, butter, honey, and almond extract with an electric mixer until smooth. Gradually beat in the rice. Stir in the flour mixture and the almonds.

3 Gently spoon the mixture into a 9–10 inch/23–25 cm well-greased cake pan with removable base, smoothing the top evenly. Bake in a preheated oven at 325°F/160°C for about 20 minutes until golden. Cool in the pan on a wire rack.

4 Put the mixed berries in a bowl and add the wine and sugar. To make the mascarpone cream, stir all the ingredients together and chill.

5 Remove the sides of the cake pan and carefully slide the cake on to a serving plate. Dust with icing sugar and serve the cake warm with the Muscat berries and mascarpone cream (the cream can be piped on top of the cake for a decorative finish, if liked).

Torta de Cielo

"Cielo" is the Mexican word for "heaven," and this cake really is heavenly—and very easy to make for a teatime treat or dessert.

NUTRITIONAL INFORMATION

Calories	753	Sugars	........41g
Protein	........13g	Fat	..........51g
Carbohydrate	...64g	Saturates	......23g

 10 mins   40–50 mins

SERVES 4–6

INGREDIENTS

1 cup shelled almonds, in their skins

1 cup sweet butter, at room temperature

1 cup plus 2 tbsp sugar

3 eggs, lightly beaten

1 tsp almond extract

1 tsp vanilla extract

9 tbsp all-purpose flour

a pinch of salt

butter, for greasing

TO SERVE

confectioners' sugar, for dusting

slivered almonds, toasted

1 Lightly butter an 8 inch/20 cm round or square cake pan and line with baking parchment.

2 Put the almonds in a food processor to form a "crumbly" mixture. Set aside.

3 Beat together the butter and sugar in a bowl until smooth and fluffy. Beat in the eggs, almonds, and almond and vanilla extracts until well blended.

4 Stir in the flour and salt and mix briefly, until the flour is just incorporated.

5 Pour or spoon the batter into the greased pan and smooth the surface. Bake in a preheated oven at 350°F/180°C for 40–50 minutes or until the cake feels spongy when gently pressed.

6 Remove from the oven, and let cool on a wire rack. To serve, dust the cake with confectioners' sugar and decorate with toasted almonds.

Churros

Another Mexican treat, these are like crisp little doughnuts, but with a delicious lemon and spice flavor.

NUTRITIONAL INFORMATION

Calories 439	Sugars 0.5g	
Protein 9g	Fat 35g	
Carbohydrate ...24g	Saturates 15g	

15 mins   15 mins

SERVES 4

INGREDIENTS

1 cup water

zest of 1 lemon

6 tbsp butter

⅛ tsp salt

1 cup all-purpose flour

¼ tsp ground cinnamon, plus extra for dusting

½–1 tsp vanilla extract

3 eggs

oil, for frying

about 5 tbsp sugar

1 Place the water with the lemon zest in a heavy pan. Bring to a boil, add the butter and salt, and cook for a few moments until the butter melts.

2 Add the flour all at once, with the cinnamon and vanilla extract, then remove the pan from the heat and stir rapidly until it forms the consistency of mashed potatoes.

3 Beat in the eggs, one at a time, using a wooden spoon; if you have difficulty incorporating the eggs to a smooth mixture, use a potato masher, then when it is mixed, return to a wooden spoon and mix until smooth.

4 Heat 1 inch oil in a deep skillet until it is hot enough to brown a cube of bread in 30 seconds.

5 Place the batter in a pastry bag with a wide tip, then squeeze out 5 inch lengths directly into the hot oil, making sure that the churros are about 3-4 inches apart, as they will puff up as they cook. You may need cook them in 2 or 3 batches.

6 Cook the churros in the hot oil for about 2 minutes on each side, until they are golden brown. Remove from the pan with a slotted spoon and drain on paper towels.

7 Dust generously with sugar and sprinkle with cinnamon to taste. Serve either hot or at room temperature.

Banana & Cranberry Loaf

The addition of chopped nuts, candied peel, fresh orange juice, and dried cranberries makes this a rich, moist tea bread.

NUTRITIONAL INFORMATION

Calories	388	Sugars	........40g
Protein	.........5g	Fat	..........17g
Carbohydrate	...57g	Saturates	.......2g

 45 mins   1 hr

SERVES 8

I N G R E D I E N T S

butter, for greasing

1½ cups self-rising flour

½ tsp baking powder

⅔ cup soft brown sugar

2 bananas, mashed

⅓ cup chopped candied peel

¼ cup chopped mixed nuts

½ cup dried cranberries

5–6 tbsp orange juice

2 eggs, beaten

⅔ cup sunflower oil

¾ cup confectioners' sugar, sifted

grated zest of 1 orange

1 Grease a 2 lb/900 g loaf pan and line the base with baking parchment.

2 Sift the flour and baking powder into a mixing bowl.

3 Stir in the brown sugar, mashed bananas, chopped candied peel, nuts, and dried cranberries.

4 Stir together the orange juice, eggs, and sunflower oil until well combined.

5 Add the mixture to the dry ingredients and mix until thoroughly blended.

Spoon the mixture into the prepared loaf pan and smooth the top.

6 Bake in a preheated oven, 350°F/ 180°C, for about 1 hour until firm to the touch or until a toothpick inserted into the center of the loaf comes out clean.

7 Turn out the loaf and let cool on a wire rack.

8 Mix the confectioners' sugar with a little water and drizzle the frosting over the loaf. Sprinkle the orange zest over the top. Let the frosting set before slicing.

COOK'S TIP

This tea bread will keep for a couple of days. Wrap it carefully and store in a cool, dry place.

Tarte au Citron

Although this classic French lemon tart is quite rich, it is also very refreshing, making an ideal dessert to follow a hearty entrée.

NUTRITIONAL INFORMATION

Calories	369	Sugars	........14g
Protein	.........7g	Fat	..........25g
Carbohydrate	...31g	Saturates	......14g

15 mins, plus chilling   35 mins

SERVES 6–8

INGREDIENTS

grated zest of 2–3 large lemons

⅔ cup lemon juice

½ cup superfine sugar

½ cup heavy cream

3 large eggs

3 large egg yolks

confectioners' sugar, for dusting

CRUST

1¼ cups all-purpose flour

½ tsp salt

8 tbsp cold sweet butter, diced

1 egg yolk beaten with 2 tbsp ice-cold water

1 To make the crust, sift the flour and salt into a bowl. Using your fingertips, rub the butter into the flour until the mixture resembles fine crumbs. Add the egg yolk and water and stir together to make a dough.

2 Gather the dough into a ball, wrap in plastic wrap, and refrigerate for at least 1 hour. Roll out on a lightly floured counter and use to line a 10-9-inch fluted tart pan with a removable base. Prick the base all over with a fork and line with a sheet of waxed paper and baking beans.

3 Bake in a preheated oven at 400°F/ 200°C for 15 minutes or until the pastry looks set. Remove the paper and beans. Reduce the oven temperature to 375°F/190°C.

4 Beat the lemon zest, lemon juice, and sugar together until blended. Slowly beat in the heavy cream, and finally beat in the eggs and yolks, one by one.

5 Set the pie shell on a cookie sheet and pour in the filling. Transfer to the preheated oven and bake the dessert for 20 minutes until the filling is set.

6 Cool completely on a wire rack. Dust with confectioners' sugar, and serve.

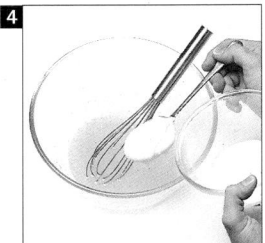

Pine Nut Tartlets

Pine nuts and orange zest are popular ingredients in Mediterranean dishes—here they add a twist of flavor to luscious chocolate tartlets.

NUTRITIONAL INFORMATION

Calories 654	Sugars 61g	
Protein 11g	Fat 33g	
Carbohydrate ...85g	Saturates 14g	

🕙 1 hr 40 mins 🕐 45 mins

SERVES 4

INGREDIENTS

2 oz/55 g dark chocolate with at least 70% cocoa solids

4 tbsp sweet butter

¾ cup plus 2 tbsp superfine sugar

5 tbsp light brown sugar

6 tbsp milk

3½ tbsp light corn syrup

finely grated zest of 2 large oranges and 2 tbsp freshly squeezed juice

1 tsp vanilla extract

3 large eggs, lightly beaten

generous ¾ cup pine nuts

TARTLET SHELLS

1¾ cups all-purpose flour

pinch of salt

generous ⅓ cup butter

1 cup confectioners' sugar

1 large egg and 2 large egg yolks

1 To make the pie dough, sift the flour and a pinch of salt into a bowl. Make a well in the center and add the butter, confectioners' sugar, whole egg, and egg yolks. Using your fingertips, mix the ingredients in the well into a paste.

2 Gradually incorporate the surrounding flour to make a soft dough. Quickly and lightly knead the dough. Shape into a

ball, wrap in plastic wrap, and chill for at least 1 hour.

3 Roll the pastry into 8 circles, 6 inches/15 cm across. Use to line 8 loose-bottomed 4 inch/10 cm tartlet pans. Line each with baking parchment to fit and top with baking beans. Chill for 10 minutes.

4 Bake in a preheated oven, 400°F/ 200°C, for 5 minutes. Remove the paper and beans and bake for a further 8 minutes. Let cool on a wire rack. Reduce the oven temperature to 350°F/180°C.

5 Meanwhile, break the chocolate into a pan over medium heat. Add the butter and stir until blended.

6 Stir in the remaining ingredients. Spoon the filling into the tartlet shells on a cookie sheet. Bake for 25–30 minutes, or until the tops puff up and crack and feel set. Cover with baking parchment for the final 5 minutes if the shells are browning too much.

7 Transfer to a wire rack and let cool for at least 15 minutes. Serve warm or at room temperature.

Lavender Hearts

If you've never thought of using lavender to flavor your baking, these beautiful little heart-shaped cookies will soon convert you!

NUTRITIONAL INFORMATION

Calories	....	.36
Protein	....	.1g
Carbohydrate	....	.5g

Sugars	....	..2g
Fat	....	..1g
Saturates	....	..1g

20 mins   10 mins

MAKES ABOUT 48 BISCUITS

INGREDIENTS

1⅔ cups all-purpose flour, plus extra for dusting

7 tbsp chilled butter, diced

6 tbsp Lavender Sugar (see page 1014), or ordinary superfine sugar

1 large egg

1 tbsp dried lavender flowers, very finely chopped

TO DECORATE

about 4 tbsp confectioners' sugar

about 1 tsp water

about 2 tbsp fresh lavender flowers

1 Line 2 cookie sheets with waxed paper. Put the flour in a bowl, add the butter, and lightly rub in with your fingertips until the mixture resembles fine crumbs. Stir in the sugar.

2 Lightly beat the egg, then add to the flour and butter mixture with the dried lavender flowers. Stir the mixture to form a stiff paste.

3 Turn out the dough onto a lightly floured counter and roll out until about ¼ inch thick.

4 Using a 2-inch heart-shaped cookie cutter, press out 48 cookies, occasionally dipping the cutter into extra flour, and re-rolling the trimmings as necessary. Transfer the pastry hearts to the cookie sheets.

5 Prick the surface of each heart with a fork. Bake in a preheated oven at 350°F/170°C and bake for approximately 10 minutes, or until the cookies are lightly browned. Transfer to a wire rack placed over a sheet of waxed paper to cool.

6 Strain the confectioners' sugar into a bowl. Add 1 teaspoon cold water and stir until a thin, smooth frosting forms, adding a little extra water if necessary.

7 Drizzle the frosting from the tip of the spoon over the cooled cookies in a random pattern. Immediately sprinkle with the fresh lavender flowers while the frosting is still soft so that they stick. Let stand for at least 15 minutes until the frosting has set. Store for up to 4 days in an airtight container.

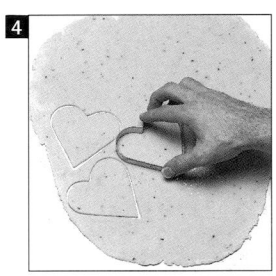

Cannoli

No Sicilian celebration is complete without cannoli. If you can't find the molds, use large dried pasta tubes covered with foil, shiny side out.

NUTRITIONAL INFORMATION

Calories	171	Sugars	.........8g
Protein	.........5g	Fat	...........9g
Carbohydrate	...18g	Saturates	.......4g

1¾ hrs   15–20 mins

MAKES 20

INGREDIENTS

3 tbsp lemon juice

3 tbsp water

1 large egg

1¾ cups all-purpose flour

1 tbsp superfine sugar

1 tsp ground allspice

pinch of salt

2 tbsp butter, softened

sunflower oil, for deep-frying

1 small egg white, lightly beaten

confectioners' sugar

FILLING

3¼ cups ricotta cheese, drained

4 tbsp confectioners' sugar

1 tsp vanilla extract

finely grated zest of 1 large orange

4 tbsp very finely chopped candied fruit

1¾ oz/50 g dark chocolate, grated

pinch of ground cinnamon

2 tbsp Marsala wine or orange juice

1 Combine the lemon juice, water, and egg. Quickly process the flour, sugar, spice, and salt in a food processor. Add the butter, then, with the motor running, pour the egg mixture through the feed tube. Process just until a dough is formed.

2 Turn the dough out onto a lightly floured counter and knead lightly. Wrap and chile in the refrigerator for at least 1 hour.

3 Meanwhile, make the filling. Beat the ricotta cheese until smooth. Strain in the confectioners' sugar, then beat in the remaining ingredients. Cover and let chile until required.

4 Roll out the dough on a floured counter until ¹⁄₁₆ inch/1.5 mm thick. Using a ruler, cut out 3½ x 3 inch/ 8.5 x 7.5 cm pieces, re-rolling and cutting the trimmings; the dough should make about 20 pieces.

5 Heat 2 inches/5 cm oil in a pan to 375°F/190°C. Roll a piece of dough around a greased cannoli mold, to just overlap the edge. Seal with egg white, pressing firmly. Repeat with all the molds you have. Fry 2 or 3 molds until the cannoli are golden, crisp, and bubbly.

6 Remove with a slotted spoon and drain on paper towels. Let cool, then carefully slide off the molds. Repeat with the remaining cannoli.

7 Pipe in the filling no more than 30 minutes before serving to prevent the cannoli becoming soggy. Decorate with strained confectioners' sugar.

 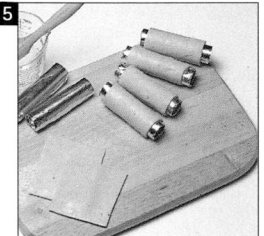 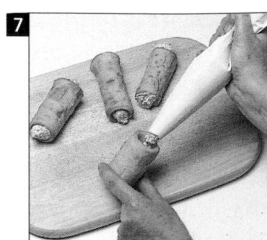

Baklava

This traditional Greek pastry is truly delectable. It is also very rich and highly calorific, so serve it in very small pieces.

🕐 20 mins

🕐 1¼ hrs

MAKES 25 PIECES

I N G R E D I E N T S

2 cups walnut halves

1¾ cups shelled pistachio nuts

¾ cup blanched almonds

4 tbsp pine nuts, finely chopped

finely grated zest of 2 large oranges

6 tbsp sesame seeds

1 tbsp sugar

½ tsp ground cinnamon

½ tsp ground allspice

about 1¼ cups butter, melted

23 sheets phyllo pastry, each 10 inches square, defrosted if frozen

S Y R U P

3 cups superfine sugar

2¼ cups water

5 tbsp honey

3 cloves

2 large strips lemon zest

1 To make the filling, put the walnuts, pistachio nuts, almonds, and pine nuts in a food processor and pulse until finely chopped but not ground. Transfer to a bowl and stir in the orange zest, sesame seeds, sugar, cinnamon, and allspice.

2 Butter a 10-inch square, 2-inch deep ovenproof dish. Cut the stacked sheets to size, using a ruler. Keep the sheets covered with a damp dish cloth.

3 Place a sheet of phyllo on the bottom of the dish and brush with melted butter. Top with 7 more sheets, brushing with butter between each layer.

4 Sprinkle with a generous 1 cup of the filling. Top with 3 more sheets of phyllo, brushing each one with butter. Continue layering until all the phyllo and filling are used, ending with a top layer of 3 sheets of phyllo. Brush the top with butter.

5 Using a very sharp knife and a ruler, cut into 25 x 2-inch squares. Brush again with butter. Bake in a preheated oven at 325°F/170°C for 1 hour.

6 Meanwhile, put all the syrup ingredients in a pan, stirring to dissolve the sugar. Bring to a boil, then simmer for 15 minutes, without stirring, until a thin syrup forms. Cool.

7 Remove the baklava from the oven and pour the syrup over the top. Let the baklava set in the dish, then remove the squares to serve.

Creamy Fruit Parfait

On the tiny Greek island of Kythera, this luscious combination of summer fruits and yogurt is served at tavernas as well as in homes.

15 mins   0 mins

SERVES 4–6

I N G R E D I E N T S

1⅓ cups cherries

2 large peaches

2 large apricots

3 cups thick unsweetened yogurt

½ cup walnut halves

2 tbsp flower-scented honey

fresh red currants or berries, to decorate (optional)

1 To prepare the fruit, use a cherry or olive pitter to remove the cherry pits. Cut each cherry in half. Cut the peaches and apricots in half lengthwise and remove the pits, then finely chop the flesh of all the fruit.

2 Place the finely chopped cherries, peaches, and apricots in a bowl and gently stir together.

3 Spoon one-third of the yogurt into an attractive glass serving bowl. Top with half the fruit mixture.

4 Repeat with another layer of yogurt and fruit and, finally, top with the remaining yogurt.

5 Place the walnuts in a small food processor and pulse until chopped, but not finely ground.

6 Sprinkle the walnuts over the top layer of the yogurt.

7 Drizzle the honey over the nuts and yogurt. Cover the bowl with plastic wrap and chill in the refrigerator for at least 1 hour. Decorate the bowl with a small bunch of red currants, if using, just before serving.

Espresso Granita

Enjoy this crunchy granita as a cooling mid-morning
snack or as a light dessert at the end of an al fresco supper.

NUTRITIONAL INFORMATION

Calories 133   Sugars 35g
Protein ....0g   Fat 0g
Carbohydrate ...35g   Saturates 0g

4 hrs   5 mins

SERVES 4–6

INGREDIENTS

1 cup superfine sugar

2½ cups water

½ tsp vanilla extract

2½ cups very strong espresso
    coffee, chilled

fresh mint, to decorate

1 Put the sugar in a pan with the water
and stir over low heat to dissolve the
sugar. Increase the heat and boil for
4 minutes, without stirring. Use a wet
pastry brush to brush down any spatters
on the side of the pan.

2 Remove the pan from the heat and
pour the syrup into a heatproof
nonmetallic bowl. Sit the bowl in the
kitchen sink filled with ice water to speed
up the cooling process. Stir in the vanilla
extract and coffee and let cool completely.

3 Transfer to a shallow metal container,
cover, and freeze for up to 3 months.

4 Before serving, chill individual serving
bowls in the refrigerator.

5 To serve, invert the container onto a
cutting board. Rinse a cloth in very
hot water, wring it out, then rub on the
bottom of the container for 15 seconds.
Give the container a sharp shake and the
mixture should fall out.

6 Break up the granita with a knife and
transfer to a food processor. Process
until it becomes grainy and crunchy. Serve
in the chilled bowls, decorated with mint.

COOK'S TIP
A very dark, fruit-flavored espresso
is the only choice for this Italian
specialty. Otherwise the flavor
will be marred by the freezing.

Vanilla Ice Cream

Italy is synonymous with ice cream. This home-made version of real vanilla ice cream is absolutely delicious and so easy to make.

NUTRITIONAL INFORMATION

Calories	652	Sugars	........33g
Protein	.........8g	Fat	..........55g
Carbohydrate	...33g	Saturates	......32g

 5 mins, plus cooling 🕐 10 mins

SERVES 4–6

I N G R E D I E N T S

2½ cups heavy cream

1 vanilla bean

pared zest of 1 lemon

4 eggs, beaten

2 egg yolks

6 oz superfine sugar

1 Place the cream in a heavy pan and heat gently, whisking. Add the vanilla bean, lemon zest, eggs, and egg yolks and heat until the mixture reaches just below boiling point.

2 Reduce the heat and cook for 8–10 minutes, whisking the mixture continuously, until thickened. Stir the sugar into the cream mixture, set aside and let cool, then strain the cream mixture through a strainer.

3 Slit open the vanilla bean, scoop out the seeds, and stir into the cream.

4 Pour the mixture into a shallow freezing container with a lid and freeze overnight until set.

COOK'S TIP

Ice cream is one of the traditional dishes of Italy. Everyone eats it and there are numerous gelato stalls selling a wide variety of flavors, usually in a cone.

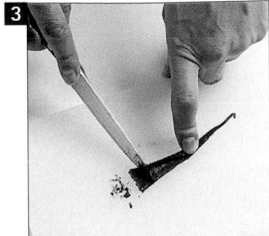

Lemon & Coffee Slushes

A delightful end to a meal, granitas are made from slushy ice rather than frozen solid, so they need to be served very quickly.

NUTRITIONAL INFORMATION

Calories 159	Sugars 38g	
Protein 1g	Fat 0g	
Carbohydrate ...38g	Saturates 0g	

  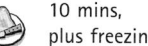

10 mins, plus freezing

6 mins

SERVES 4

INGREDIENTS

LEMON GRANITA

3 lemons

¾ cup lemon juice

½ cup superfine sugar

2¼ cups cold water

COFFEE GRANITA

2 tbsp instant coffee

2 tbsp sugar

2 tbsp hot water

2½ cups cold water

2 tbsp rum or brandy

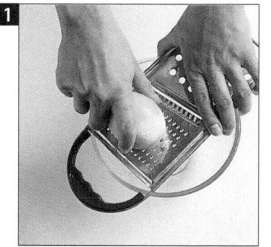  

1 To make lemon granita, finely grate the lemon zest. Place the lemon zest, juice, and superfine sugar in a pan. Bring the mixture to a boil and let simmer for 5–6 minutes, or until thick and syrupy. Let cool.

2 Once cooled, stir in the cold water and pour into a shallow freezer container with a lid. Freeze for 4–5 hours, stirring occasionally to break up the ice. Serve as a palate cleanser between dinner courses.

3 To make coffee granita, place the coffee and sugar in a bowl and pour over the hot water, stirring until dissolved.

4 Stir in the cold water together with the rum or brandy.

5 Pour the mixture into a shallow freezer container with a lid. Freeze for at least 6 hours, stirring every 1–2 hours in order to create a grainy texture. Serve with cream after dinner, if you wish.

VARIATION
If you would prefer a non-alcoholic version of the coffee granita, simply omit the rum or brandy and add extra instant coffee instead.

Frozen Citrus Soufflés

These delicious desserts are a refreshing way to end a meal.
They can be made in advance and kept in the freezer until required.

NUTRITIONAL INFORMATION

Calories 364   Sugars 27g
Protein ....11g   Fat 24g
Carbohydrate ...27g   Saturates 14g

 35 mins   🕐 0 mins

SERVES 4

INGREDIENTS

1 tbsp gelozone

6 tbsp very hot water

3 eggs, separated

6 tbsp superfine sugar

finely grated zest and juice of 1 lemon,
   ½ lime and ½ orange

⅔ cup heavy cream

½ cup unsweetened yogurt

thin lemon, lime, and orange slices,
   to decorate

1 Tie waxed paper collars around 4 individual soufflé or ramekin dishes or around 1 large (6 inch/15 cm diameter) soufflé dish.

2 Sprinkle the gelozone into the very hot (not boiling) water, stirring well to disperse. Let the mixture stand for 2–3 minutes, stirring occasionally, to give a completely clear liquid. Let cool for 10–15 minutes.

3 Meanwhile, whisk the egg yolks and sugar, using a hand-held electric mixer or wire whisk, until very pale and light in texture. Add the zest and juice from the fruits, mixing well. Stir in the cooled gelozone liquid, making sure that it is thoroughly incorporated.

4 Put the cream in a large chilled bowl and whip until it holds its shape. Stir the yogurt and then add it to the cream, mixing it in gently. Fold the cream mixture into the citrus mixture, using a large metal spoon.

5 Using a clean whisk, beat the egg whites in a clean bowl until stiff and then gently fold them into the citrus mixture, using a metal spoon.

6 Pour the mixture into the prepared dishes, almost to the top of their collars. Allow some room for the mixture to expand on freezing. Transfer the dishes to the freezer and open-freeze for about 2 hours, until frozen.

7 Remove from the freezer 10 minutes before serving. Peel away the paper collars carefully and decorate with the slices of lemon, lime, and orange.

Chocolate Chip Ice Cream

This marvelous frozen dessert offers the best of both worlds—delicious chocolate chip cookies and a rich dairy-flavored ice.

NUTRITIONAL INFORMATION

Calories 238   Sugars 23g
Protein . . . . .9g   Fat 10g
Carbohydrate . . .30g   Saturates 4g

6 hrs   5 mins

SERVES 6

INGREDIENTS

1¼ cups milk

1 vanilla bean

2 eggs

2 egg yolks

4 tbsp superfine sugar

1¼ cups unsweetened yogurt

¼ lb chocolate chip cookies, broken into small pieces

1 Pour the milk into a small pan, add the vanilla bean, and bring to a boil over low heat. Remove from the heat, cover the pan, and let cool.

2 Beat the eggs and egg yolks in a double boiler or in a bowl set over a pan of simmering water. Add the sugar and continue beating until the mixture is pale and creamy.

3 Reheat the milk to simmering point and strain it over the egg mixture. Stir continuously until the custard is thick enough to coat the back of a spoon. Remove the custard from the heat and stand the pan or bowl in cold water to prevent any further cooking. Wash and dry the vanilla bean for future use.

4 Stir the yogurt into the cooled custard and beat until it is well blended. When the mixture is thoroughly cold, stir in the broken cookies.

5 Transfer the mixture to a chilled metal cake pan or plastic container, cover, and freeze for 4 hours. Remove from the freezer every hour, transfer to a chilled bowl, and beat vigorously to prevent ice crystals forming, then return to the freezer. Alternatively, freeze the mixture in an ice-cream maker, following the manufacturer's instructions.

6 An hour before you are ready to serve the ice cream, transfer it to the main part of the refrigerator to soften slightly. Serve scoops of the ice cream in individual glass bowls.

Lavender Ice Cream

This delicious ice cream, flavored with lavender flowers, has the wonderful scent of a summer garden.

NUTRITIONAL INFORMATION

Calories 294	Sugars 24g
Protein 5g	Fat 21g
Carbohydrate ...24g	Saturates 11g

35 mins, plus freezing

0 mins

SERVES 6–8

INGREDIENTS

flowers from 10–12 large sprigs fresh lavender, plus extra to decorate

6 large egg yolks

¾ cup superfine sugar, or Lavender Sugar (see Cook's Tip)

2¼ cups milk

1 cup plus 2 tbsp heavy cream

1 tsp vanilla extract

1 Strip the small flowers from the stems, discarding any brown or green bits. Place them in a small strainer and rinse, then pat dry thoroughly with paper towels. Set aside.

2 Put the egg yolk and sugar in a heatproof bowl that will sit over a pan with plenty of room underneath. Using an electric mixer, beat the eggs and sugar together until they are thick.

3 Put the milk, cream, and vanilla in the pan over low heat and bring to a simmer, stirring. Pour the hot milk over the egg mixture, whisking constantly. Rinse the pan and place 1 inch water in the bottom. Place the bowl on top, making sure the base does not touch the water. Turn the heat to medium-high.

4 Cook the mixture, stirring, until it is just thick enough to coat the back of the spoon.

5 Remove the custard from the heat and stir in the flowers. Cool, then cover and let infuse for 2 hours, chilling for the last 30 minutes. Strain the mixture through a plastic strainer to remove the lavender flowers.

6 Churn in an ice-cream maker, following the manufacturer's instructions. Alternatively, freeze and whisk as in Step 5 of Vanilla Ice Cream (see page 000).

7 Transfer to a freezerproof bowl, smooth the top and cover with plastic wrap or aluminum foil. Store in the freezer for up to 3 months.

8 Let soften in the refrigerator for 20 minutes before serving. Decorate with fresh lavender flowers.

COOK'S TIP

To make Lavender Sugar, put 1lb. 2 oz. sugar in a food processor and add 4½ oz lavender flowers. Process until blended, then leave in a sealed container for 10 days. Strain out the flower bits and store the sugar in a sealed jar.

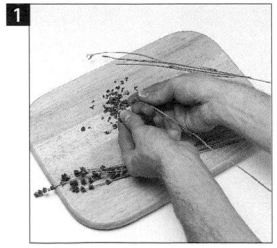

Mint-Chocolate Gelato

Rich, creamy gelati, or ice creams, are one of the great Italian culinary contributions to the world. This version is made with fresh mint.

NUTRITIONAL INFORMATION

Calories 575	Sugars 53g	
Protein 17g	Fat 34g	
Carbohydrate . . .54g	Saturates 18g	

5–6 hrs   20 mins

SERVES 4

I N G R E D I E N T S

6 large eggs

¾ cup superfine sugar

1¼ cups milk

⅔ cup heavy cream

large handful of fresh mint leaves, rinsed and dried

2 drops green food coloring, optional

2 oz/55 g dark chocolate, finely chopped

1 Put the eggs and sugar in a heatproof bowl that will sit over a pan with plenty of room underneath. Using an electric mixer, beat the eggs and sugar together until thick and creamy.

2 Put the milk and cream in the pan and bring to a simmer, where small bubbles appear all around the edge, stirring. Pour on to the eggs, whisking constantly. Rinse the pan and put 1 inch/2.5 cm water in the bottom. Place the bowl on top, making sure the bottom does not touch the water. Turn the heat to medium–high.

3 Transfer the mixture to a pan and cook the mixture, stirring constantly, until it is thick enough to coat the back of the spoon and leave a mark when you pull your finger across it.

4 Tear the mint leaves and stir them into the custard. Remove the custard from the heat. Let cool, then cover and let infuse for at least 2 hours, chilling for the last 30 minutes.

5 Strain the mixture through a small nylon strainer to remove the pieces of mint. Stir in the food coloring, if using. Transfer to a freezer container and freeze the mixture for 1–2 hours until frozen 1 inch/2.5 cm from the sides.

6 Scrape into a bowl and beat again until smooth. Stir in the chocolate pieces, smooth the top, and cover with plastic wrap or foil.

7 Freeze until set, for up to 3 months. Place in the refrigerator to soften for 20 minutes before serving.

Orange & Bitters Sherbet

Made from a distinctive Italian drink and freshly squeezed orange juice, this smooth, pale-pink sherbet is a cooling dessert with a refreshing tang.

NUTRITIONAL INFORMATION

Calories 212   Sugars 52g
Protein . . . . .2g   Fat 0g
Carbohydrate . . .52g   Saturates 0g

  3 hrs   3–5 mins

SERVES 4–6

INGREDIENTS

3–4 large oranges

generous 1 cup superfine sugar

2½ cups water

3 tbsp red Italian bitters, such
  as Campari

2 extra large egg whites

TO DECORATE

fresh mint leaves

candied citrus peel (optional)

4 Roll the 3 pared oranges back and forth on the counter, pressing them down firmly. Cut them in half and squeeze ½ cup juice. If you need more juice, squeeze the remaining orange.

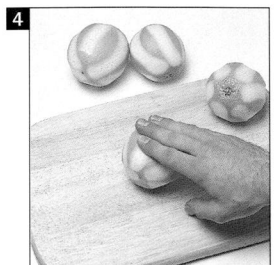

5 When the syrup is cool, stir in the orange juice and bitters. Strain into a container, cover, and chill for at least 30 minutes.

6 Put the mixture in an ice-cream maker and churn for about 15 minutes. Alternatively, follow the instructions on page 1011. Whisk the egg whites in a clean, grease-free bowl until stiff peaks form.

7 Add the egg whites to the ice-cream maker and continue churning for 5 minutes or according to the manufacturer's instructions. Transfer to a shallow, freezerproof container, cover, and freeze for up to 2 months.

8 About 15 minutes before serving, place the ice cream in the refrigerator to soften, then scoop into bowls and serve decorated with mint leaves and candied citrus peel, if wished.

1 Working over a bowl to catch any juice, pare the zest from 3 of the oranges, without removing the bitter white pith. If some of the pith does come off with the zest, use the knife to scrape it off.

2 Put the sugar and water in a pan and stir over low heat until dissolved. Increase the heat and boil for 2 minutes, without stirring. Using a wet pastry brush, brush any crystals down the side of the pan, if necessary.

3 Remove the pan from the heat and pour into a heatproof nonmetallic bowl. Add the orange zest and set aside to steep while the mixture cools to room temperature.

Italian Rice Ice Cream

It stands to reason that a nation which thinks of risotto as its national dish should produce a rice ice cream—and this one is excellent.

NUTRITIONAL INFORMATION

Calories 570	Sugars 51g
Protein 10g	Fat 31g
Carbohydrate . . .44g	Saturates 16g

 15 mins, plus chilling 25 mins

MAKES ABOUT 1.2 LITRES/2 PINTS

INGREDIENTS

½ cup short-grain pudding rice

500 ml/18 fl oz milk

7 tbsp sugar

3 tbsp good-quality honey

½ tsp lemon extract

1 tsp vanilla extract

6 oz/175 g good-quality lemon curd

2¼ cups heavy or whipping cream

grated zest and juice of 1 large lemon

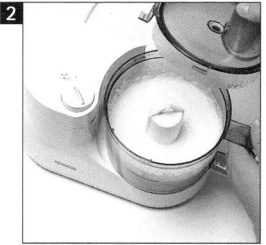

1 Put the rice and milk in a large, heavy pan and bring to a gentle simmer, stirring occasionally; do not let it boil. Reduce the heat to low, cover, and simmer very gently for about 10 minutes, stirring occasionally, until the rice is just tender and the liquid absorbed.

2 Remove from the heat and stir in the sugar, honey, and the lemon and vanilla extracts, stirring until the sugar is dissolved. Pour into a food processor and pulse 3 or 4 times. The mixture should be thick and creamy, but it should not be completely smooth.

3 Put the lemon curd in a bowl and gradually beat in about 1 cup of the cream. Stir in the rice mixture with the lemon zest and juice until blended. Lightly whip the remaining cream until it just begins to hold its shape, then fold into the lemon-rice mixture. Chill.

4 Stir the rice mixture and pour into an ice-cream maker. Churn according to the manufacturers' instructions for 15–20 minutes. Transfer to a freezerproof container and freeze for 6–8 hours or overnight. Transfer to the refrigerator about 1 hour before serving.

COOK'S TIP

If you do not have an ice-cream maker, transfer the chilled rice mixture to a freezerproof container. Freeze for 1 hour until slightly slushy, then whisk to break up any crystals and refreeze. Repeat twice more.

Italian Drowned Ice Cream

A classic vanilla ice cream is topped with steaming coffee to make a wonderful instant dessert. Remember to serve in heatproof bowls.

NUTRITIONAL INFORMATION

Calories 646   Sugars 48g
Protein . . . . .10g   Fat 47g
Carbohydrate . . .48g   Saturates 26g

7½ hrs   10 mins

SERVES 4

INGREDIENTS

2 cups freshly made espresso coffee

chocolate-covered coffee beans,
    to decorate

VANILLA ICE CREAM

1 vanilla bean

6 large egg yolks

⅔ cup superfine sugar, or vanilla-flavored sugar (sugar that has been stored with a vanilla bean)

2¼ cups milk

1 cup plus 2 tbsp heavy cream

1 To make the ice cream, slit the vanilla bean lengthwise and scrape out the tiny brown seeds. Set aside.

2 Put the yolks and sugar in a heatproof bowl that will sit over a pan with plenty of room underneath. Beat the eggs and sugar together until thick and creamy.

3 Put the milk, cream, and vanilla seeds in the pan over low heat and bring to a simmer. Pour the milk over the egg mixture, whisking. Pour 1 inch/2.5 cm of water in the bottom of a pan. Place the bowl on top, ensuring that the base does not touch the water. Turn the heat to medium–high.

4 Cook the mixture, stirring constantly, until it is thick enough to coat the back of the spoon. Remove from the heat, transfer to a bowl, and let cool.

5 Churn the mixture in an ice-cream maker, following the manufacturer's instructions. Alternatively, place it in a freezerproof container and freeze for 1 hour. Turn out into a bowl and whisk to break up the ice crystals, then return to the freezer. Repeat 4 times at 30-minute intervals.

6 Transfer the ice cream to a freezerproof bowl, smooth the top, and cover with plastic wrap or foil. Freeze for up to 3 months.

7 Soften in the refrigerator for 20 minutes before serving. Place scoops of ice cream in each bowl. Pour over coffee and sprinkle with coffee beans.

Mango & Lime Sherbet

A refreshing sherbet is the perfect way to round off a spicy Thai meal, and mangoes make a deliciously smooth-textured, velvety sherbet.

NUTRITIONAL INFORMATION

Calories	158	Sugars	........34g
Protein	.........1g	Fat	...........3g
Carbohydrate	...34g	Saturates	.......2g

4 hrs   4 mins

SERVES 4

INGREDIENTS

6 tbsp superfine sugar

scant ½ cup water

zest of 3 limes, finely grated

2 tbsp coconut cream

2 large, ripe mangoes

generous ½ cup lime juice

curls of fresh coconut, toasted, to decorate

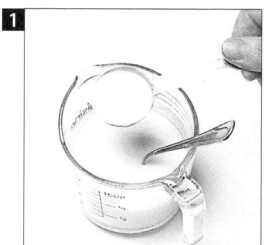

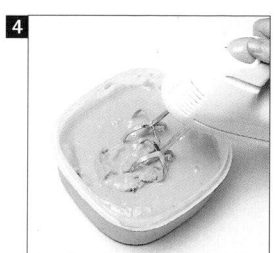

1 Place the sugar, water, and lime zest in a small pan and heat gently, stirring constantly, until the sugar dissolves. Boil rapidly for 2 minutes to reduce slightly, then remove from the heat and strain into a bowl or pitcher. Stir in the coconut cream and let cool.

2 Halve the mangoes, remove the pits, and peel thinly. Chop the flesh coarsely and place in a food processor with the lime juice. Process to a smooth purée and transfer to a small bowl.

3 Pour the cooled syrup into the mango purée, mixing evenly. Tip into a freezer container and freeze for 1 hour, or until slushy in texture. (Alternatively, use an electric ice-cream maker.)

4 Remove the container from the freezer and beat with an electric mixer to break up the ice crystals. Refreeze for a further hour, then remove from the freezer, and beat the contents again until smooth.

5 Cover the container, return to the freezer, and freeze until firm. To serve, remove from the freezer and let stand at room temperature for about 15 minutes to soften slightly before scooping. Sprinkle with toasted coconut to serve.

Citrus Meringue Crush

This is an excellent way to use up leftover meringue shells and is very simple to prepare. Serve with a spoonful of tangy fruit sauce.

NUTRITIONAL INFORMATION

Calories ....165 Sugars 32g
Protein ....5g Fat 1g
Carbohydrate ...37g Saturates 0.4g

2 hrs   10 mins

SERVES 4

I N G R E D I E N T S

8 ready-made meringue nests

1¼ cups low-fat unsweetened yogurt

½ tsp finely grated orange zest

½ tsp finely grated lemon zest

½ tsp finely grated lime zest

2 tbsp orange liqueur or unsweetened orange juice

TO DECORATE

sliced kumquat

grated lime zest

SAUCE

2 oz kumquats

½ cup unsweetened orange juice

2 tbsp lemon juice

2 tbsp lime juice

2 tbsp water

2–3 tsp superfine sugar

1 tsp cornstarch mixed with 1 tbsp water

1 Place the meringues in a plastic bag and using a rolling pin, crush into small pieces. Place in a mixing bowl. Stir in the yogurt, grated citrus zest, and the liqueur or juice. Spoon the mixture into 4 small molds and freeze for 1½–2 hours until firm.

2 Thinly slice the kumquats and place them in a small pan with the fruit juices and water. Bring gently to a boil and then simmer over low heat for 3–4 minutes until the kumquats soften.

3 Sweeten with sugar to taste, stir in the cornstarch mixture, and cook, stirring, until thickened. Pour into a small bowl, cover the surface with plastic wrap, and set aside to cool—the plastic wrap will help prevent a skin from forming. Chill in the refrigerator until required.

4 To serve, dip the meringue molds in hot water for 5 seconds or until they loosen and turn onto serving plates. Spoon over a little sauce, decorate with slices of kumquat and lime zest, and serve.

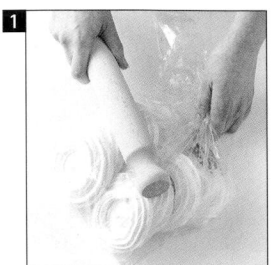

Brown Bread Ice Cream

Although it sounds unusual, this yogurt-based recipe is delicious.
It contains no cream and is ideal for a low-fat diet.

NUTRITIONAL INFORMATION

Calories 264	Sugars 25g
Protein 12g	Fat 6g
Carbohydrate ...43g	Saturates 1g

2¼ hrs   5 mins

SERVES 4

INGREDIENTS

2½ cups fresh whole-wheat bread crumbs

⅓ cup finely chopped walnuts

4 tbsp superfine sugar

½ tsp ground nutmeg

1 tsp finely grated orange zest

2 cups low-fat unsweetened yogurt

2 large egg whites

TO DECORATE

walnut halves

orange slices

fresh mint

1 Preheat the broiler to medium. Mix the bread crumbs, walnuts, and sugar and spread over a sheet of foil in the broiler pan.

2 Broil the bread crumb mixture, stirring frequently, for 5 minutes until crisp and evenly browned (take care that the sugar does not burn.) Remove from the heat and let cool.

3 When cool, transfer to a mixing bowl and mix in the nutmeg, orange zest, and yogurt. In another bowl, whisk the egg whites until stiff. Gently fold into the bread crumb mixture, using a metal spoon.

4 Spoon the mixture into 4 small molds, smooth over the tops, and freeze for 1½–2 hours until firm.

5 To serve, hold the bases of the molds in hot water for a few seconds, then immediately turn the ice cream out on to serving plates.

6 Serve at once, decorated with the walnuts, oranges, and fresh mint.

COOK'S TIP
If you don't have small molds, use ramekins or teacups or, if you prefer, use one large bowl. Alternatively, spoon the mixture into a large freezerproof container to freeze and serve the ice cream in scoops.

Index